OXFORD

Learner's
Spanish
Dictionary

Project management
Nicholas Rollin
Joanna Brough

Editors
Ximena Castillo
Jane Horwood
Amanda Leigh
Meic Haines
Stephanie Parker

Consultant
Isabel Sudea

OXFORD
UNIVERSITY PRESS

OXFORD
UNIVERSITY PRESS

Great Clarendon Street, Oxford OX2 6DP

Oxford University Press is a department of the University of Oxford.
It furthers the University's objective of excellence in research, scholarship,
and education by publishing worldwide in

Oxford   New York

Auckland   Cape Town   Dar es Salaam   Hong Kong   Karachi
Kuala Lumpur   Madrid   Melbourne   Mexico City   Nairobi
New Delhi   Shanghai   Taipei   Toronto

With offices in

Argentina   Austria   Brazil   Chile   Czech Republic   France   Greece
Guatemala   Hungary   Italy   Japan   Poland   Portugal   Singapore
South Korea   Switzerland   Thailand   Turkey   Ukraine   Vietnam

Oxford is a registered trade mark of Oxford University Press
in the UK and in certain other countries

© Oxford University Press 2006

Database right Oxford University Press (maker)

First published 2006

British Library Cataloguing in Publication Data

Data available

ISBN-13: 978-0-19-911370-5

ISBN-10: 0-19-911370-X

1 3 5 7 9 10 8 6 4 2

Printed in Italy by Legoprint

This dictionary contains some words which have or are asserted to have proprietary status
as trademarks or otherwise. Their inclusion does not imply that they have acquired for legal
purposes a non-proprietary or general significance, nor any other judgement concerning
their legal status. In cases where the editorial staff have some evidence that a word has
proprietary status this is indicated in the entry for that word by the label ™ or ® but no
judgement concerning the legal status of such words is made or implied thereby.

Contents

Introduction

This bilingual dictionary has been specifically written for students of Spanish – from those just starting out all the way up to those preparing for exams. It presents essential information in a format designed to be clear and easy to consult. There are two main sections: Spanish–English and English–Spanish. These sections are divided by a central section in full colour.

TIP To help you find words quickly, the first word on each page is printed top left and the last word on the page is printed top right.

Spanish–English

Look up Spanish words – listed alphabetically – to find their meaning in English. When a word has more than one meaning, make sure you choose the one that is most relevant.

TIP Look at the number after a verb you look up and find that number in the verb tables: it shows the endings for that verb.

English–Spanish

Look up English words – listed alphabetically – to find out how to say them in Spanish. When you find the Spanish word, the entry will tell you whether it is masculine (*masc*) or feminine (*fem*). To choose the right word and use it properly, make sure you read through the examples provided.

TIP To find out more about the Spanish translation that you are given, look it up on the Spanish-English side of the dictionary afterwards.

Colour section

In the colour section you will find reference material such as: verb tables for regular verbs and the most common irregular verbs, key vocabulary (grouped by theme to help you in your oral exam: Leisure and holiday, Career and future plans, etc.), classroom language, useful phrases (e.g. days, months, dates, time); sample letters with key opening and closing phrases; email and text messaging vocabulary; a sample CV and hints for job applications.

Get to know your dictionary

User-friendly layout

- **Two-colour layout**
  Headwords (words you are looking up) are in blue for easy identification.

- **Easy to navigate**
  The alphabet runs down the side of each page indicating what letter
  you are looking at, and whether you are on the Spanish–English or
  English–Spanish side of the dictionary:

- **The key symbol**
  The key symbol is explained along the bottom of every other page.

  ♪ indicates key words

Clear entries

- **Parts of speech written out in full**
  Noun, *verb*, *adjective*, *adverb*, *conjunction*, *preposition* or *determiner*
  are all written out clearly after the headword:

  to **baptize** *verb*
     bautizar [22]

- **Gender of nouns and adjectives**
  Both the definite (or if appropriate, the indefinite) article and the
  abbreviations *masc* and *fem* are used on both sides of the dictionary
  to make it clear whether a word is masculine or feminine.

  ♪ **balcony** *noun*　　　　　　　　　　**creased** *adjective*
    el **balcón** *masc*　　　　　　　**arrugado** *masc*, **arrugada** *fem*

Abbreviations used are:

masc	masculine	*fem*	feminine
pl	plural	*adj*	adjective
adv	adverb	*prep*	preposition
conj	conjunction	*excl*	exclamation

- **All variants shown**
  Normally the masculine and feminine singular forms of adjectives, nouns, and pronouns are given. Where relevant the plural forms are also given.

  ♪ el **cual** *masc pronoun*, la **cual** *fem pron*, los **cuales** *masc plural*, las **cuales** *fem plural*

- **Pointers to other parts of speech**
  Where a word can do more than one job (be a noun *and* a verb, for example), a helpful pointer reminds students to check other parts of speech:

  ♪ **back** *adjective* ▷ see **back** *adv, noun, verb*
    1 (*wheel, seat*) **trasero** *masc*, **trasera** *fem*
      the back seat of the car el asiento trasero del coche
    2 **the back garden** el jardín de atrás
      the back gate la verja de atrás

Extra help with verbs

- **Heavy-duty verbs**
  Common verbs are given special treatment in tinted panels:

  > ♪ **hacer** *verb* [7]
  > 1 **to make**
  >   **hacer un ruido** to make a noise
  >   **hacer un pastel** to make a cake
  >   **hacer la cama** to make the bed

- **Verb tables in centre section** (*see* **Introduction**)
  The centre section contains full conjugations for regular -*ar*, -*er* and -*ir* verbs plus the most common irregular verbs.

- **Links to verb tables**
  On both sides of the dictionary, each Spanish verb is followed by a number linking it to the central verb tables:

  to **baptize** *verb*   **cuchichear** *verb* [17]
    bautizar [22]   **to whisper**

- **Use of *to* before a verb**
  On the English–Spanish side of the dictionary, English verbs are preceded by *to* (see above).

- **Irregular forms of verbs**
  If you look up past participles and non-infinitive forms of a verb, you are cross-referenced to the relevant headword:

  cuelga, **cuelgo**, **etc** *verb* ▷ **colgar**

Extra help with difficult points of Spanish

· Extra help with grammar and spelling
'Word tips' give extra help with tricky grammatical points and
reminders on how Spanish spelling is different from English:

WORD TIP Adjectives and nouns for nationality,
regional origin and language do not have capital
letters in Spanish.

· Typical problem areas
Extra help is given with traditionally problem areas, such as talking
about jobs and professions:

ₛ **a** *determiner*

4 (*saying what you do*) **She's a doctor.** Es
médica.
I'm a student. Soy estudiante.

WORD TIP *a* is not translated into Spanish when
you say your profession.

· False friends
False friends are shown on the Spanish–English side of the dictionary:

WORD TIP *actual* in Spanish does not mean *actual*
in English; for the meaning of *actual* ▷ **verdadero**

Language in context – example sentences

· Thousands of example sentences
Thousands of examples of 'real language' are given at an appropriate
level for the age group, progressing from simpler to more complex
sentences:

el **cine** *masc noun*
> **cinema**
> **ir al cine** to go to the cinema
> **Vámonos al cine.** Let's go to the cinema.
> **¿Qué ponen en el cine?** What's on at the
> cinema?
> · **el cine de barrio** local cinema

· World Spanish
Both European and Latin American Spanish are represented on both
sides of the dictionary:

ₛ **car** *noun*
> el **coche** *masc*, (*Latin America*) el **carro** *masc*
> **a car crash** un accidente de coche
> **He parked the car.** Aparcó el coche.
> **We're going by car.** Vamos en coche.

· Correctly punctuated
All example sentences are correctly punctuated with capital letters and
full stops (see above).

Additional features

• Core vocabulary highlighted

The dictionary includes all the key curriculum words secondary school pupils need and a key symbol highlights the key words you must know to prepare for your exams.

♪ el **balcón** *masc noun*
balcony

• Colour section

The full colour central section will help you communicate in both written and spoken Spanish.

• Mini-infos

Boxed notes provide quirky and interesting cultural information throughout the A–Z text:

mini info *palabras*

Muchas palabras usadas en la vida diaria son de origen árabe . Se identifican porque comienzan con las letras al-, ar-, az-; por ejemplo alfombra, arroz, azúcar. También hay muchos nombres como el río *Guadalquivir* o la *Alhambra*.

• Language functions covered

Exam syllabus language functions, such as requests and demands, are covered within example sentences:

♪ el **café** *masc noun*
  1 **cafe** *(place)*
  2 **coffee**
    ¿Quieres un café? Do you want a cup of coffee?
  • el **café con leche** white coffee
  • el **café cortado** coffee with a dash of milk
  • el **café descafeinado** decaffeinated coffee
  • el **café solo** black coffee

A a

ℰ a *preposition*
1 (*showing movement*) **to**
Voy al mercado. I'm going to the market.
Iremos al cine. We'll go to cinema.
Gira a la derecha. Turn right.

WORD TIP *a + el* becomes *al*.

2 (*with words of giving, sending, talking, etc*) **to**
Se lo di a Laura. I gave it to Laura.
Le mandé un regalo a mi madre. I sent a present to my mother.
Le da clases de piano a mi hermana. She gives my sister piano lessons.
3 (*showing where something is*) **Está a la izquierda.** It's on the left.
Están sentados a la mesa. They are sitting at the table.
Siéntate al sol. Sit in the sun.
Estaban a mi lado. They were beside me.
Está a diez kilómetros de aquí. It's ten kilometres from here.
La vi a lo lejos. I saw her in the distance.
4 (*showing time*) **at**
a las diez at ten o'clock
a medianoche at midnight
Se casó a los veinte años. She married at twenty.
¿A qué hora termina? What time does it end?
5 (*with dates*) **Estamos a dos de febrero.** It's the second of February.
6 (*saying how often, how much, etc*) **dos veces al día** twice a day
a tres euros el kilo three euros a kilo
a ochenta kilómetros por hora at eighty kilometres an hour
7 (*showing method*) **ir a pie** to go on foot
hecho a mano handmade
escrito a mano handwritten
a lápiz in pencil
8 (*showing intention*) **Voy a hacer los deberes.** I'm going to do my homework.
Nos fuimos a dormir. We went to sleep.
Se han ido a nadar. They've gone swimming.
Salimos a pasear. We went out for a walk.
9 (*in commands*) **¡A dormir!** Go to sleep!
¡A comer! Come and eat!
10 (*with a person object*) **Vi a tu padre.** I saw your father.
Llamé a tu hermano. I rang your brother.

WORD TIP *padre* and *hermano* are the person objects. *a* is not translated in English.

la **abadía** *fem noun*
abbey

ℰ abajo *adverb*
1 **aquí abajo** down here
allí abajo down there
2 **downstairs**
Están abajo. They're downstairs.
Ven abajo. Come downstairs.
3 **de abajo** below, down below
el piso de abajo the flat below

abalanzarse *reflexive verb* [22]
abalanzarse sobre alguien to leap on somebody
Se abalanzaron a la ventana. They rushed to the window.

abandonado *masc adjective*, **abandonada** *fem*
1 **deserted**
una casa abandonada a deserted house
2 **abandoned**
un coche abandonado an abandoned car
3 **neglected**
sentirse abandonado to feel neglected

abandonar *verb* [17]
1 **to leave**
En verano la gente abandona la ciudad para irse a la playa. In summer people leave the city to go to the seaside.
2 **to abandon**
Abandonó a su familia. He left his family.

el **abanico** *masc noun*
fan

abarcar *verb* [31]
1 **to cover**
Abarca el periodo entre 2000 y 2005. It covers the period between 2000 and 2005.
2 **to see**
Desde aquí se puede abarcar toda la ciudad. From here you can see the whole city.

abarrotado *masc adjective*, **abarrotada** *fem*
packed
un bar abarrotado de gente a bar packed with people

el **abecedario** *masc noun*
alphabet

el **abedul** *masc noun*
birch

a
b
c
d
e
f
g
h
i
j
k
l
m
n
ñ
o
p
q
r
s
t
u
v
w
x
y
z

ℰ indicates key words
1

la **abeja** *fem noun*
  bee

el **abejorro** *masc noun*
  bumblebee

la **abertura** *fem noun*
1 opening
2 hole

el **abeto** *masc noun*
  fir tree

♂ **abierto** *masc adjective*, **abierta** *fem*
1 open
  abierto al público open to the public
  La puerta está abierta. The door's open.
  El grifo está abierto. The tap's running.
2 open-minded
  Mis padres son muy abiertos. My parents
  are very open-minded.

abochornado *masc adjective*,
  abochornada *fem*
  embarrassed

el **abogado** *masc noun*, la **abogada** *fem*
1 lawyer
2 solicitor

abolir *verb* [19]
  to abolish

la **abolladura** *fem noun*
  dent

abollar *verb* [17]
  to dent

abollarse *reflexive verb* [17]
  to get dented

abonar *verb* [17]
1 to pay (*a bill*)
2 to fertilize (*a field or plant*)

abonarse *reflexive verb* [17]
1 to subscribe
  abonarse a una revista to subscribe to a
  magazine
2 to buy a season ticket

el **abono** *masc noun*
1 fertilizer
2 season ticket
  sacar un abono para la piscina to buy a
  season ticket for the swimming pool

abordar *verb* [17]
1 to tackle (*a problem*)
2 to raise (*a subject*)

aborrecer *verb* [35]
  to detest
  Aborrezco los callos. I hate tripe.

el **aborto** *masc noun*
1 abortion
2 miscarriage

abotonarse *reflexive verb* [17]
  to do your buttons up
  Abotónate la chaqueta. Do your jacket up.

abrasado *masc adjective*, **abrasada** *fem*
1 burnt
  Murieron abrasados por las llamas. They
  burned to death.
2 boiling hot

abrasador *masc adjective*, **abrasadora**
  fem
  burning hot (*the weather*)
  Hacía un calor abrasador. It was burning
  hot.

abrasar *verb* [17]
  to burn
  El sol abrasaba. The sun was burning hot.

abrazar *verb* [22]
  to hug

abrazarse *reflexive verb* [22]
  to hug each other

♂ el **abrazo** *masc noun*
  hug
  un fuerte abrazo all the best (*at the end of a*
  letter)

el **abrebotellas** *masc noun, pl:* los
  abrebotellas
  bottle opener

el **abrelatas** *masc noun, pl:* los **abrelatas**
  tin opener

la **abreviatura** *fem noun*
  abbreviation

el **abridor** *masc noun*
1 bottle opener
2 tin opener

abrigar *verb* [28]
  to be warm (*jumper, coat*)

abrigarse *reflexive verb* [28]
  to wrap up warmly

♂ el **abrigo** *masc noun*
1 coat
  ropa de abrigo warm clothes
2 shelter
  al abrigo de los árboles in the shelter of the
  trees

♂ **abril** *masc noun*
April
en abril in April
el 5 de abril on 5 April

WORD TIP Names of months and days start with small letters in Spanish.

♂ **abrir** *verb* [46]
1 **to open**
Abre la ventana. Open the window.
Abrió la boca para hablar. He opened his mouth to speak.
abrir algo de par en par to open something wide
2 **to turn on** (*a tap*)
abrir el agua to turn the water on

abrirse *reflexive verb* [46]
to open
La puerta se abrió. The door opened.
¿Cómo se abre? How do you open it?

abrocharse *reflexive verb* [17]
1 **to do up your buttons**
Abróchate la chaqueta. Do your jacket up.
2 **to fasten** (*a seat belt*)
Abróchense los cinturones. Fasten your seat belts.

absoluto *masc adjective*, **absoluta** *fem*
1 **absolute**
2 **en absoluto** not at all
'¿Te importa?'—'En absoluto.' 'Do you mind?'—'Not at all.'

absorbente *masc & fem adjective*
absorbent

absorber *verb* [18]
to absorb

abstemio *masc adjective*, **abstemia** *fem*
teetotal
Es abstemio. He's teetotal.

abstracto *masc adjective*, **abstracta** *fem*
abstract

absurdo *masc adjective*, **absurda** *fem*
absurd

abuchear *verb* [17]
to boo
El público abucheó al árbitro. The crowd booed the referee.

♂ el **abuelo** *masc noun*, la **abuela** *fem*
1 **grandfather**
2 **grandmother**
3 **mis abuelos** my grandparents

♂ **aburrido** *masc adjective*, **aburrida** *fem*
1 **boring**
ser aburrido, *fem* aburrida to be boring

Sus clases son muy aburridas. His lessons are really boring.
2 **bored**
estar aburrido, *fem* aburrida to be bored
Siempre está aburrida. She is always bored.

♂ el **aburrimiento** *masc noun*
boredom
¡Qué aburrimiento! How boring!

♂ **aburrirse** *reflexive verb* [19]
to get bored

abusar *verb* [17]
1 **abusar (de)** to take too much (*alcohol, etc*), to take too many (*pills, etc*)
2 **abusar de** to take advantage of
Están abusando de tu amabilidad. They are taking advantage of your kindness.

abusivo *masc adjective*, **abusiva** *fem*
1 **excessive** (*price*)
2 **unfair** (*rule, law*)

el **abuso** *masc noun*
1 **abuse**
2 **outrage**
¡Esto es un verdadero abuso! This is really outrageous!
• el **abuso del alcohol** alcohol abuse

aC *abbreviation*
(= *antes de Cristo*) **BC, before Christ**

acá *adverb*
here
¡Ven acá! Come here!

acabado *masc adjective*, **acabada** *fem*
finished

♂ **acabar** *verb* [17]
1 **to finish**
La fiesta acabó muy tarde. The party finished very late.
¿Has acabado con el abrelatas? Have you finished with the tin opener?
2 **to end**
La palabra acaba en 'r'. The word ends in 'r'.
La historia acaba bien. The story has a happy ending.
3 **acabar de hacer algo** to have just done something
4 Acaba de salir. He's just gone out.
Acabo de hablar con él. I've just spoken to him.
Acabamos de llegar. We've just arrived.
Acabábamos de terminar. We had just finished.

WORD TIP *acabar de* in the present tense is translated by *have -ed* in English. In the imperfect tense, it is translated by *had -ed* in English.

acabarse *reflexive verb* [17]
1 **to be over** *(parties, films, etc)*
Cuando se acabó la película. When the film was over.
2 **to run out** *(money, food, drinks)*
Se ha acabado el pan. The bread's run out.
Se me acabó el dinero. I ran out of money.

♪ la **academia** *fem noun*
school
• la **academia de idiomas** language school

académico *masc adjective,* **académica** *fem*
academic

la **acampada** *fem noun*
camping
ir de acampada to go camping

acampar *verb* [17]
to camp

el **acantilado** *masc noun*
cliff

acariciar *verb* [17]
1 **to caress** *(a person)*
2 **to stroke** *(a cat, a dog)*

acaso *adverb*
por si acaso just in case

acatarrado *masc adjective,* **acatarrada** *fem*
estar acatarrado to have a cold

acatarrarse *reflexive verb* [17]
to catch a cold

acceder *verb* [18]
1 acceder a algo to agree to something
Accedió a verla. He agreed to see her.
2 **to access** *(information, computer files)*

accesible *masc & fem adjective*
1 **accessible** *(place)*
2 **affordable**
a precios accesibles at affordable prices

los **accesorios** *plural masc noun*
accessories

accidental *masc & fem adjective*
accidental

el **accidente** *masc noun*
accident
tener un accidente to have an accident
• el **accidente de circulación** road accident

la **acción** *fem noun*
1 **act**
una buena acción a good deed
2 **share** *(in a company)*

el **acebo** *masc noun*
holly

♪ el **aceite** *masc noun*
oil
• el **aceite de oliva** olive oil

aceitoso *masc adjective,* **aceitosa** *fem*
oily

la **aceituna** *fem noun*
olive

el **acelerador** *masc noun*
accelerator
pisar el acelerador to put your foot down *(to accelerate)*

acelerar *verb* [17]
to accelerate

el **acento** *masc noun*
1 **accent**
tener acento andaluz to have an Andalusian accent
Casi no tienes acento. You have hardly any accent.
2 **accent** *(on a letter in written Spanish)*
• el **acento agudo** acute accent

acentuarse *reflexive verb* [20]
to have an accent
Se acentúa en la última sílaba. It has an accent on the last syllable.

aceptable *masc & fem adjective*
acceptable

♪ **aceptar** *verb* [17]
1 **to accept** *(an invitation, an apology)*
2 aceptar hacer algo to agree to do something
Aceptaron dejármelo. They agreed to lend it to me.

♪ la **acera** *fem noun*
pavement

♪ **acerca de** *preposition*
about

♪ **acercar** *verb* [31]
1 **to move closer**
Acerqué la silla a la ventana. I moved the chair nearer the window.
Acércame un poco la lámpara. Bring the lamp closer to me.
2 **to pass**
Acércame ese libro. Pass me that book.
3 acercar a alguien a un lugar to give somebody a lift somewhere
Me acercó a la oficina. She gave me a lift to the office.

acercarse *reflexive verb* [31]
1 **to come close**
   Acércate más. Come closer., Get closer.
2 **to get close to**
   Se acercó a la ventana. She got close to the window.

ꝗ el **acero** *masc noun*
   steel

acertado *masc adjective*, **acertada** *fem*
   right (*decision or answer*)

ꝗ **acertar** *verb* [29]
1 **to be right**
   ¡Has acertado! You've got it right!
2 **acertar algo** to get something right
   Acertó todas las respuestas. She got all the answers right.
3 **acertar en el blanco** to hit the target

el **ácido** *masc noun*
   acid

el **acierto** *masc noun*
1 **correct answer**
2 **good decision**
   Ese regalo fue un acierto. That present was a good idea.

la **aclaración** *fem noun*
   explanation

aclarar *verb* [17]
   to make clear

aclararse *reflexive verb* [17]
   to understand
   Aún no me aclaro. I still don't understand.

el **acné** *masc noun*
   acne

acoger *verb* [3]
1 **to receive** (*some news, a proposal*)
2 **to take in** (*a refugee, an orphan*)
3 **to welcome** (*a visitor*)

ꝗ **acompañar** *verb* [17]
1 **to go with**
   La acompañé al dentista. I went with her to the dentist's.
   Te acompaño a tu casa. I'll see you home.
2 **to keep company**
   El perro me acompaña mucho. The dog keeps me company a lot.

aconsejar *verb* [17]
   to advise

el **acontecimiento** *masc noun*
   event

ꝗ **acordarse** *reflexive verb* [24]
   to remember
   No me acuerdo. I don't remember
   acordarse de algo to remember something
   Acuérdate de traer dinero. Remember to bring money.
   ¿Te acuerdas de él? Do you remember him?

el **acorde** *masc noun*
   chord

el **acordeón** *masc noun*
   accordion

acortar *verb* [17]
   to shorten

ꝗ **acostarse** *reflexive verb* [24]
1 **to go to bed**
   ¿A qué hora te acuestas? What time do you go to bed?
   Normalmente me acuesto a las diez y media. I usually go to bed at half past ten.
2 **acostarse con alguien** to sleep with somebody

acostumbrado *masc adjective*,
   acostumbrada *fem*
   estar acostumbrado, *fem* **acostumbrada a algo** to be used to something
   Está acostumbrada a levantarse temprano. She's used to getting up early.

acostumbrarse *reflexive verb* [17]
   acostumbrarse a algo to get used to something
   No se acostumbra al nuevo horario. She can't get used to the new timetable.

el & la **acróbata** *masc & fem noun*
   acrobat

la **actitud** *fem noun*
   attitude

ꝗ la **actividad** *fem noun*
   activity

activo *masc adjective*, **activa** *fem*
   active

el **acto** *masc noun*
1 **act**
2 **en el acto** immediately

el **actor** *masc noun*
   actor

la **actriz** *fem noun*
   actress

la **actuación** *fem noun*
   performance (*in a play or film*)

ꝗ indicates key words   5

ℰ **actual** *masc & fem adjective*
 present, **current**
 la situación actual the present situation
 el actual presidente the current president

> **WORD TIP** *actual* in Spanish does not mean *actual*
> in English; for the meaning of *actual* ▷ **verdadero**

la **actualidad** *fem noun*
 1 **en la actualidad** at present, at the moment
 En la actualidad viven en Madrid. At present they're living in Madrid.
 2 **nowadays**
 En la actualidad es más fácil viajar.
 Nowadays it's easier to travel.

actualmente *adverb*
 1 **at present**
 Actualmente trabaja en un banco. At present he's working in a bank.
 2 **nowadays**
 Actualmente se fabrica con máquinas.
 Nowadays it's made by machine.

> **WORD TIP** *actualmente* in Spanish does not mean
> *actually* in English; for the meaning of *actually* see
> *en realidad*. ▷ **realidad**

actuar *verb* [20]
 to act

la **acuarela** *fem noun*
 watercolour

el **acuario** *masc noun* ▷ **see acuario** *masc &
 fem noun*
 aquarium

acuario *masc & fem noun*
 ▷ **see acuario** *noun*
 Aquarius
 Soy acuario. I'm an Aquarius.

> **WORD TIP** Use a small letter in Spanish to say *I
> am Aquarius*, etc with star signs.

Acuario *masc noun*
 Aquarius

acudir *verb* [19]
 acudir a algo to attend something

ℰ el **acuerdo** *masc noun*
 1 **agreement**
 Llegaron a un acuerdo. They reached an agreement.
 2 **estar de acuerdo (en algo)** to agree (on something)
 Están de acuerdo en la fecha. They agree on the date.
 No estoy de acuerdo. I don't agree.
 ponerse de acuerdo to come to an agreement
 3 **¡De acuerdo!** Okay!

la **acusación** *fem noun*
 accusation

acusar *verb* [17]
 to accuse
 acusar a alguien de algo to accuse somebody of something
 Me acusó de mentir. He accused me of lying.

la **acústica** *fem noun*
 acoustics

el **adaptador** *masc noun*
 adaptor

adaptar *verb* [17]
 to adapt

adaptarse *reflexive verb* [17]
 adaptarse a algo to adapt to something

a. de C. *abbreviation*
 (= *antes de Cristo*) **BC** (*before Christ*)

adecuado *masc adjective*, **adecuada** *fem*
 1 **suitable**
 ser adecuado para algo to be suitable for something
 2 **appropriate**, **right**
 El momento no es adecuado. It's not the right moment.

adelantado *masc adjective*, **adelantada**
 fem
 1 **advanced**
 2 **fast** (*when talking about clocks, watches*)
 Tu reloj va adelantado. Your watch is fast.
 3 **pagar por adelantado** to pay in advance

el **adelantamiento** *masc noun*
 overtaking

adelantar *verb* [17]
 1 **to bring forward** (*a date or trip*)
 2 **to overtake** (*when driving*)
 3 **to put forward** (*a clock or watch*)

ℰ **adelante** *adverb*
 1 **forward**
 más adelante further on
 ir hacia adelante to go forward
 Hay que seguir adelante hasta llegar al semáforo. You must go on until you reach the lights.
 2 (*in expressions*)
 más adelante: Hablaremos sobre ello más adelante. We'll talk about it later on.
 ¡Adelante! Come in!

adelgazar *verb* [22]
 to lose weight
 He adelgazado tres kilos. I've lost three kilos.

⚡ además *adverb*
1 además de as well as
    Además de hacerlos los diseña. He designs
    as well as makes them.
    Son tres, además de la madre. There are
    three, not counting the mother.
2 **besides** (*when you add to what you've already
    said*)
    Además, no es mi problema. Besides, it's
    not my problem.
    No ayuda y además se queja. He doesn't
    help and he complains as well.

⚡ adentro *adverb*
    inside
    Ven adentro. Come inside.
    Todos pasaron adentro. They all went
    inside.

adicto *masc noun,* **adicta** *fem*
    addict

⚡ adiós *exclamation*
1 **bye!**
2 **hello!** (*when you meet somebody in the street*)

el **aditivo** *masc noun*
    additive

la **adivinanza** *fem noun*
    riddle

adivinar *verb* [17]
    to guess

el **adivino** *masc noun,* la **adivina** *fem*
    fortune-teller

el **adjetivo** *masc noun*
    adjective

adjuntar *verb* [17]
1 **to enclose** (*a document*)
2 **to attach** (*to an e-mail*)

adjunto *masc adjective,* **adjunta** *fem*
    enclosed

la **administración** *fem noun*
    administration
  • la **administración pública** civil service

admirable *masc & fem adjective*
    admirable

la **admiración** *fem noun*
1 **admiration**
    sentir admiración por alguien to admire
    someone
2 (*in punctuation*) **un signo de admiración** an
    exclamation mark

el **admirador** *masc noun,* la **admiradora**
    fem
    admirer

admirar *verb* [17]
    to admire

admitir *verb* [19]
1 **to admit**
    Admitió su responsabilidad. She admitted
    her responsibility.
2 **'No se admiten perros'** 'No dogs allowed'
    'No se admiten devoluciones' 'No
    Returns' (*sign in a shop*)

el & la **adolescente** *masc & fem noun*
    adolescent

⚡ adonde *adverb* ▷ see **adónde** *adv*
    where
    La ciudad adonde vamos. The city where
    we're going.

⚡ adónde *adverb* ▷ see **adonde** *adv*
    where
    ¿Adónde vas? Where are you going?
    'Me voy de viaje.'—'¿Adónde?' 'I'm going
    away.'—'Where?'

adoptar *verb* [17]
    to adopt

adoptivo *masc adjective,* **adoptiva** *fem*
1 **adoptive** (*parents*)
2 **adopted** (*child*)

adorar *verb* [17]
    to adore

adosado *masc adjective,* **adosada** *fem*
    attached (*housing*)

el **adorno** *masc noun*
    ornament
  • los **adornos de Navidad** Christmas
    decorations

adquirir *verb* [47]
    to acquire

adrede *adverb*
    on purpose

⚡ la aduana *fem noun*
    customs
    pasar por la aduana to go through customs
    libre de derechos de aduana duty-free

⚡ adulto *masc adjective,* **adulta** *fem*
    ▷ see **adulto** *noun*
    adult

⚡ el adulto *masc noun,* la **adulta** *fem*
    ▷ see **adulto** *adj*
    adult

el **adverbio** *masc noun*
    adverb

la **advertencia** *fem noun*
    warning

a
b
c
d
e
f
g
h
i
j
k
l
m
n
ñ
o
p
q
r
s
t
u
v
w
x
y
z

⚡ indicates key words   7

advertir *verb* [14]
  to warn
  Quedas advertido. You've been warned.
  Le advertí que no llegase tarde otra vez. I
  warned him not to be late again.

aéreo *masc adjective*, **aérea** *fem*
  air (*traffic*)

el **aerobic** *masc noun*
  aerobics

el **aeromozo** *masc noun*, la **aeromoza** *fem*
  (*Latin America*) **flight attendant**

ₛ el **aeropuerto** *masc noun*
  airport

el **aerosol** *masc noun*
  aerosol

el **afán** *masc noun*
  eagerness
  Tienen afán de aprender. They are eager to
  learn.

afectar *verb* [17]
  to affect

el **afecto** *masc noun*
  affection
  tenerle afecto a alguien to be fond of
  somebody

afectuoso *masc adjective*, **afectuosa** *fem*
  affectionate (*person*)
  Recibe un afectuoso saludo. With best
  wishes. (*friendly letter ending*)

ₛ **afeitarse** *reflexive verb* [17]
1 **to shave**
  Hoy no me he afeitado. I haven't shaved
  today.
2 **to shave off** (*a beard, moustache*)
  Se ha afeitado la barba. He's shaved his
  beard off.

ₛ la **afición** *fem noun*
  interest
  hobby
  ¿Qué aficiones tienes? What are your
  interests?
  Mi afición principal es la fotografía. My
  main interest is photography.
  Lo hago por afición. I do it as a hobby.

ₛ **aficionado** *masc adjective*, **aficionada** *fem*
  ▷ see **aficionado** *noun*
1 ser aficionado, aficionada a algo to be keen
  on something
  Soy muy aficionada al ski. I'm a very keen
  skier (*girl speaking*).
  Soy muy aficionado a los deportes. I'm very
  keen on sport (*boy speaking*).

2 **amateur**
  un equipo aficionado an amateur team

ₛ el **aficionado** *masc noun*, la **aficionada**
  fem ▷ see **aficionado** *adj*
1 **fan**
  un aficionado al jazz a jazz fan
  un aficionado al rugby a rugby fan
  para los aficionados a la cocina for those
  who like cooking
2 **amateur**
  un grupo de aficionados a group of
  amateurs

ₛ **aficionarse** *reflexive verb* [17]
  aficionarse a algo to get keen on
  something

afilar *verb* [17]
  to sharpen

afinar *verb* [17]
  to tune (*an instrument*)

la **afirmación** *fem noun*
  statement

afirmar *verb* [17]
1 **to state**
  Afirmó que era de su familia. He stated that
  it belonged to his family.
2 afirmar con la cabeza to nod one's
  agreement

afirmativo *masc adjective*, **afirmativa** *fem*
  affirmative

aflojar *verb* [17]
1 **to loosen**
2 aflojar la marcha to slow down

afónico *masc adjective*, **afónica** *fem*
  estar afónico to have lost your voice
  Está afónica. She's lost her voice.

afortunadamente *adverb*
  fortunately

afortunado *masc adjective*, **afortunada**
  fem
  fortunate

África *fem noun*
  Africa
  Soy de África. I'm from Africa.

africano *masc adjective & noun*, **africana**
  fem adjective & noun
1 **African**
2 un africano, una africana African

WORD TIP Adjectives and nouns for nationality
and regional origin do not have capital letters in
Spanish.

ɕ **afuera** *adverb*
   outside, **out**
   Salimos afuera. We went outside.

ɕ las **afueras** *plural fem noun*
   las afueras the outskirts
   las afueras de Valencia the outskirts of
   Valencia

agachar *verb* [17]
   agachar la cabeza to lower your head

agacharse *reflexive verb* [17]
1 to bend down
2 to duck

agarrar *verb* [17]
   to grab

agarrarse *reflexive verb* [17]
   to hold on
   Se agarró a la barandilla. She held on to the
   handrail.

ɕ la **agencia** *fem noun*
   agency
 • la **agencia de viajes** travel agency
 • la **agencia inmobiliaria** estate agent's

la **agenda** *fem noun*
1 diary
2 agenda

el & la **agente** *masc & fem noun*
   agent
 • el & la **agente de policía** police officer
 • el & la **agente inmobiliario** estate agent

agitar *verb* [17]
   to shake

agosto *masc noun*
   August
   en agosto in August
   el 12 de agosto on 12 August

> **WORD TIP** Names of months and days start with
> small letters in Spanish.

agotado *masc adjective*, **agotada** *fem*
1 worn out
   Estoy agotado. I'm worn out.
2 sold out (*goods in a shop*)
3 flat (*battery*)

agotador *masc adjective*, **agotadora** *fem*
   exhausting

agotarse *reflexive verb* [17]
1 to wear yourself out
2 to sell out (*goods*)
3 to go flat (*batteries*)
4 to run out (*reserves or supplies*)
5 Se me está agotando la paciencia. My
   patience is running out.

ɕ **agradable** *masc & fem adjective*
   pleasant

ɕ **agradecer** *verb* [35]
1 agradecerle algo a alguien to be grateful to
   somebody for something
   Te agradezco tu ayuda. I'm grateful to you
   for your help.
2 to thank
   Te lo agradezco. Thank you.
   Nos agradecieron el regalo. They thanked
   us for the present.
   ¡Y así nos lo agradeces! And that's the
   thanks we get from you!

ɕ **agradecido** *masc adjective*, **agradecida**
   fem
   grateful
   Le estoy muy agradecido. I'm very grateful
   to you. (*using the polite form*)

el **agradecimiento** *masc noun*
   gratitude

la **agresión** *fem noun*
   aggression

agresivo *masc adjective*, **agresiva** *fem*
   aggressive

agrícola *masc & fem adjective*
   agricultural
   productos agrícolas farm products

el **agricultor** *masc noun*, la **agricultora**
   fem
   farmer

la **agricultura** *fem noun*
1 agriculture
2 farming
 • la **agricultura biológica** organic farming

agridulce *masc & fem adjective*
   bittersweet

agringado *masc adjective*, **agringada** *fem*
   (*Latin America*) **having American ways**

agrio *masc adjective*, **agria** *fem*
   sour

ɕ el **agua** *fem noun*
   water
   un vaso de agua a glass of water
   El agua está fría. The water is cold.
   ¿Quieres agua? Would you like some
   water?

> **WORD TIP** agua takes el or un in the singular even
> though it is feminine.

 • el **agua corriente** running water
 • el **agua de colonia** eau de cologne
 • el **agua mineral con gas** sparkling mineral
   water ▸▸

a
b
c
d
e
f
g
h
i
j
k
l
m
n
ñ
o
p
q
r
s
t
u
v
w
x
y
z

- el **agua mineral sin gas** still mineral water
- el **agua potable** drinking water

el **aguacate** *masc noun*
avocado

el **aguacero** *masc noun*
downpour

el & la **aguafiestas** *masc & fem noun*, pl,
aguafiestas
spoilsport

la **aguanieve** *fem noun*
sleet

aguantar *verb* [17]
1 **to bear** (*pain or heat*)
No aguanto este calor. I can't bear this
heat.
2 **to take**
No aguanto más. I can't take any more.
3 **aguantar la respiración** to hold your
breath
aguantar la risa to stop yourself laughing
4 **to hold** (*an object*)
Aguanta esta caja un momento. Hold this
box for a minute.

aguantarse *reflexive verb* [17]
Tendrás que aguantarte. You'll have to put
up with it.

agudo *masc adjective*, **aguda** *fem*
1 **acute** (*pain*)
2 **acute** (*accent*)
3 **high-pitched** (*voice or sound*)
4 **stressed on the last syllable** (*word*)

el **aguijón** *masc noun*
sting

el **águila** *fem noun*
eagle
Vimos un águila. We saw an eagle.

WORD TIP *águila* takes *el* or *un* in the singular
even though it is feminine.

la **aguja** *fem noun*
1 **needle** (*for sewing or knitting*)
2 **hand** (*of a watch or clock*)

el **agujero** *masc noun*
hole

las **agujetas** *plural fem noun*
stiffness (*from exercise*)
Tengo muchas agujetas. I'm really stiff.

ℰ **ahí** *adverb*
1 **there**
Ahí están. There they are.
Ponlo ahí. Put it there.
2 Tenemos que ir por ahí. We have to go that
way.

Dejó las llaves por ahí. She left the keys
somewhere.
Había unas doscientas personas o por ahí.
There were about two hundred people
there.

el **ahijado** *masc noun*, la **ahijada** *fem*
1 **godson**
2 **goddaughter**
3 **mis ahijados** my godchildren

ahogado *masc adjective*, **ahogada** *fem*
1 **morir ahogado** to drown
2 **morir ahogado** to suffocate

ahogarse *reflexive verb* [28]
1 **to drown**
Se ahogó en el río. He drowned in the river.
2 **to suffocate**

ℰ **ahora** *adverb*
1 **now**
Ahora vamos a trabajar. Now we're going
to work.
¿Qué vas a hacer ahora? What are you
going to do now?
ahora mismo right now
Ahora mismo lo traigo. I'll bring it right
away.
2 **in a moment, shortly**
Ahora viene. She'll come shortly.
Ahora vuelvo. I'll be back in a moment.
Ahora lo hago. I'll do it in a moment.
3 (*in expressions*) **de ahora en adelante** from
now on
por ahora for the time being
¡Hasta ahora! See you soon!

ahorcar *verb* [31]
to hang (*in executions*)

ahorcarse *reflexive verb* [31]
to hang yourself

ahorita *adverb*
(*Latin America*)
1 **just now**
2 **right now**

ℰ **ahorrar** *verb* [17]
to save

los **ahorros** *plural masc noun*
savings
todos mis ahorros all my savings

ahumado *masc adjective*, **ahumada** *fem*
smoked

ℰ el **aire** *masc noun*
1 **air**
al aire libre in the open air
teatro al aire libre open-air theatre
salir a tomar el aire to go out for some fresh
air

En verano disfrutamos la vida al aire libre.
In summer we enjoy life in the open air.

2 wind
Hace mucho aire. It's very windy.

3 appearance
Tiene un aire interesante. It looks
interesting.
Llegó con aire preocupado. She arrived
looking worried.

- el **aire acondicionado** air conditioning

aislado *masc adjective*, **aislada** *fem*
isolated

♪ el **ajedrez** *masc noun*
chess
jugar al ajedrez to play chess

el **ajillo** *masc noun*
al ajillo with garlic
gambas al ajillo garlic prawns

♪ el **ajo** *masc noun*
garlic
un diente de ajo a clove of garlic
una cabeza de ajo a head of garlic

ajustar *verb* [17]
1 to adjust (*a seat, a safety belt*)
2 to fit

♪ **al** *preposition + determiner*
1 to the
Fuimos al colegio. We went to school.
Se lo di al camarero. I gave it to the waiter.
2 (*with verb infinitives*) **as, when**
Al salir nos encontramos con Marta. As we
were leaving we met Marta.
Tengan cuidado al bajar del autobús. Be
careful when leaving the bus.

WORD TIP al is formed by a + el; see a for more
examples.

el **ala** *fem noun*
1 wing
el ala del avión the plane's wing
El pájaro bate las alas. The bird beats its
wings.
El hospital tiene dos alas. The hospital has
two wings.
2 wing, winger (*in sports*)

WORD TIP ala takes el or un in the singular even
though it is feminine.

la **alabanza** *fem noun*
praise

alabar *verb* [17]
to praise

el **alambre** *masc noun*
wire
- el **alambre de púas** barbed wire

el **álamo** *masc noun*
poplar tree

el **alargador** *masc noun*
extension lead

alargar *verb* [28]
1 to lengthen
Voy a alargar esta falda un poco. I'm going
to lengthen this skirt a bit.
2 to extend (*a visit, a holiday*)
Queremos alargar la vacaciones. We want
to extend our holidays.
3 to stretch out (*an arm*)
Alargué el brazo para alcanzarlo. I
stretched out my arm to reach it.

alargarse *reflexive verb* [28]
1 to get longer
Los días se van alargando. The days are
getting longer.
2 to go on
La conferencia se alargó mucho. The
conference went on for a long time.

la **alarma** *fem noun*
alarm
- la **alarma contra incendios** fire alarm

alarmante *masc & fem adjective*
alarming

el **albañil** *masc noun*
1 builder
2 bricklayer

el **albaricoque** *masc noun*
apricot

♪ el **albergue** *masc noun*
1 hostel
2 refuge (*in the mountains*)
- el **albergue juvenil** youth hostel

la **albóndiga** *fem noun*
meatball

el **albornoz** *masc noun*
bathrobe

alborotar *verb* [17]
alborotar a los niños to get the children
excited

alborotarse *reflexive verb* [17]
to get excited

el **alboroto** *masc noun*
racket
¡Qué alboroto! What a racket!

a
b
c
d
e
f
g
h
i
j
k
l
m
n
ñ
o
p
q
r
s
t
u
v
w
x
y
z

el **álbum** *masc noun*
album
el mejor álbum del grupo the group's best
album
• el **álbum de fotografías** photograph
album

la **alcachofa** *fem noun*
artichoke

el **alcalde** *masc noun*, la **alcaldesa** *fem*
1 **mayor**
2 **mayoress**

el **alcázar** *masc noun*
1 **fortress**
2 **palace** (*especially a Moorish one*)

alcanzar *verb* [22]
1 **to reach**
No alcanzo a la ventana. I can't reach the
window.
La temperatura alcanzó los treinta grados.
The temperature reached thirty.
2 **to catch up with**
Nos alcanzó en el último momento. He
caught up with us at the last muinute.
No pude alcanzar al resto del grupo. I
couldn't catch up with the rest of the
group.
3 alcanzarle algo a alguien to pass somebody
something
¿Me alcanzas las tijeras? Can you pass me
the scissors?
4 **to be enough**
Veinte euros nos alcanzan. Twenty euros
will be enough.
No alcanzan los vasos. There aren't enough
glasses.

el **alcohol** *masc noun*
alcohol

alcohólico *masc adjective*, **alcohólica** *fem*
▷ see **alcohólico** *noun*
alcoholic

el **alcohólico** *masc noun*, la **alcohólica** *fem*
▷ see **alcohólico** *adj*
alcoholic

el **alcoholismo** *masc noun*
alcoholism

la **aldaba** *fem noun*
knocker

ℰ la **aldea** *fem noun*
village

ℰ el **aldeano** *masc noun*, la **aldeana** *fem*
villager

ℰ **alegrar** *verb* [17]
to cheer up
Verla les alegró mucho. Seeing her really
cheered them up.
Me alegra saberlo. I'm glad to hear it.

alegrarse *reflexive verb* [17]
1 **to be happy**, **to be glad**
Me alegro de verte. I'm glad to see you.
¡Cuánto me alegro! I'm so happy!
Se alegró de venir. He was glad to come.
Me alegro mucho por ellos. I'm very happy
for them.
Me alegro de haberte llamado. I'm glad I
phoned you.
2 (*as a reply*) Me alegro. That's good.

ℰ **alegre** *masc & fem adjective*
1 **happy**
una cara alegre a happy face
2 **cheerful**
Soy una persona muy alegre. I'm a cheerful
kind of person.
3 **bright** (*colour*)

ℰ la **alegría** *fem noun*
happiness
¡Qué alegría veros! It's great to see you!
¡Qué alegría me das! That makes me really
happy!
saltar de alegría to jump for joy

alejar *verb* [17]
alejar algo de alguien to move something
away from somebody

alejarse *reflexive verb* [17]
to move away
¡Aléjate del fuego! Move away from the
fire!

alemán *masc adjective & noun*, **alemana**
fem adjective & noun
1 **German**
2 (*person*) un alemán, una alemana German
el alemán German (*the language*)

WORD TIP Adjectives and nouns for nationality,
regional origin, and language do not have capital
letters in Spanish.

Alemania *fem noun*
Germany
Soy de Alemania. I'm from Germany.

la **alergia** *fem noun*
allergy
tener alergia a algo to be allergic to
something
• la **alergia al polen** hayfever

alerta *masc & fem adjective*
▷ see **alerta** *noun*
alert

la **alerta** *fem noun* ▷ see **alerta** *adj*
estar alerta por algo to be on the alert for
something
Hay que estar alerta por los carteristas. Be
on the alert for pickpockets.

alfabético *masc adjective*, **alfabética** *fem*
alphabetical
**por orden alfabético in alphabetical
order**

el **alfabeto** *masc noun*
alphabet

la **alfarería** *fem noun*
pottery

el **alféizar** *masc noun*
sill
el alféizar de la ventana the windowsill

el **alfiler** *masc noun*
pin

ꝺ la **alfombra** *fem noun*
1 **rug**
2 (*Latin America*) **carpet**

la **alfombrilla** *fem noun*
mat
• **la alfombrilla de baño** bath mat

el **alga** *fem noun*
seaweed

WORD TIP *alga* takes *el* or *un* in the singular even
though it is feminine.

ꝺ **algo** *pronoun* ▷ see **algo** *adv*
1 **something**
Tienes que beber algo. You must drink
something.
algo así something like that
Su padre es director be banco, o algo así.
Her father's a bank manager, or something
like that.
2 **anything**
¿Te pasa algo? Is there anything the matter
with you?
¿Has tomado algo de aquí? Have you taken
anything from here?
3 **some**, **any**
algo de ... some ..., any ...
Queda algo de pan. There's some bread
left.
¿Tienes algo de leche? Do you have any
milk?

ꝺ **algo** *adverb* ▷ see **algo** *pron*
(*with an adjective*) **a bit**
Estoy algo cansado. I'm a bit tired.

ꝺ el **algodón** *masc noun*
cotton
una camisa de algodón a cotton shirt

ꝺ **alguien** *pronoun*
1 **somebody**, **someone**
Hay alguien en la puerta. There's someone
at the door.
2 **anybody**, **anyone**
¿Has hablado con alguien? Have you
spoken to anybody?
Si pregunta alguien, di que sí. If anyone
asks, say yes.

ꝺ **algún** *adjective* ▷ **alguno, alguna**

ꝺ **alguno** *masc adjective*, **alguna** *fem*
▷ see **alguno** *pron*
1 **some**
Tiene que ser algún niño. It must be some
kid.
Compré algunas cosas. I bought some
things.
Nos hicieron algunas preguntas. They
asked us some questions.
Algunos participantes no sabían las reglas.
Some participants didn't know the rules.
2 (*in questions or with si*) **any**
¿Tienes alguna razón para no ir? Do you
have any reason for not going?
¿Tienes algún problema? Have you got any
problems?
**Si tiene alguna pregunta, no dude en
llamarnos.** If you have a question, don't
hesitate to call us. (*polite form*)
3 (*in expressions*) **en algún lugar** somewhere
en algún momento sometime
alguna vez sometimes, ever
Alguna vez lo he pensado. I've thought
about it sometimes.
¿Has estado alguna vez en España? Have
you ever been to Spain?

WORD TIP *alguno* becomes *algún* before a
masculine singular noun.

ꝺ **alguno** *masc pronoun*, **alguna** *fem pronoun*
▷ see **alguno** *adj*
1 (*singular*) **one**
alguno de vosotros one of you
para alguna de sus hijas for one of her
daughters
Tiene que haber alguno aquí. There must
be one here.
2 (*plural*) **some**
Algunos de ellos no fueron. Some of them
didn't go.
Faltan algunas. There are some missing.
3 (*in questions or with si*) **any**
Me sobran entradas, ¿quieres alguna? I've
got tickets to spare, do you want any?
Si alguno te interesa, cómpralo. If you're
interested in any of them, buy it.

a b c d e f g h i j k l m n ñ o p q r s t u v w x y z

aliado *masc adjective*, **aliada** *fem*
▷ see **aliado** *noun*
allied

el **aliado** *masc noun*, la **aliada** *fem*
▷ see **aliado** *adj*
ally

la **alianza** *fem noun*
1 **alliance**
2 **wedding ring**

los **alicates** *plural masc noun*
1 **pliers**
2 **nail clippers**

el **aliento** *masc noun*
breath
estar sin aliento to be out of breath
recuperar el aliento to get your breath
back
Tiene mal aliento She's got bad breath.

ʃ la **alimentación** *fem noun*
diet
una alimentación equilibrada a balanced
diet

ʃ **alimentar** *verb* [17]
1 **to feed**
2 **to be nutritious**
Las lentejas alimentan mucho. Lentils are
very nutritious.

alimentarse *reflexive verb* [17]
to feed
Se alimentan de insectos. They feed on
insects.

alimenticio *masc adjective*, **alimenticia**
fem
1 **food**
la industria alimenticia the food industry
productos alimenticios foodstuffs
2 **nutritious**
Ese plato es muy alimenticio. That dish is
very nutritious.

ʃ el **alimento** *masc noun*
food
El arroz es su alimento básico. Rice is their
staple food.
Las lentejas son un buen alimento. Lentils
are a good food.

la **alineación** *fem noun*
line-up *(in a team)*

aliñar *verb* [17]
1 **to dress** *(a salad)*
2 **to season**

el **aliño** *masc noun*
1 **salad dressing**

2 **seasoning**

el **alioli** *masc noun*
garlic mayonnaise

alistarse *reflexive verb* [17]
to join up
alistarse en el ejército to join the army

aliviar *verb* [17]
to relieve *(pain)*

ʃ **allá** *adverb*
1 **there**, **over there**
allá abajo down there
¡Allá voy! Here I come!, I'm on my way!
Ahora vamos para allá. We're on our way.
2 **más allá** further away
Está más allá de la estación. It's beyond the
station.
3 *(in time)* **back**
allá en los años noventa back in the
nineties

ʃ **allí** *adverb*
there
allí arriba up there
Lo puso por allí. She put it somewhere
around there.
Se fueron por allí. They went that way.

el **alma** *fem noun*
soul

WORD TIP *alma* takes *el* or *un* in the singular even
though it is feminine.

ʃ el **almacén** *masc noun*
warehouse

almacenar *verb* [17]
to store *(goods)*

los **almacenes** *plural masc noun*
department store
abrir unos almacenes to open a
department store

la **almeja** *fem noun*
clam *(the shellfish)*

la **almendra** *fem noun*
almond

el **almíbar** *masc noun*
syrup

el **almidón** *masc noun*
starch

la **almohada** *fem noun*
pillow
una funda de almohada a pillowcase
• la **almohada de plumas** feather pillow

el **almohadón** *masc noun*
cushion

ₛ **almorzar** *verb* [26]
1 **to have lunch**
   Almorzamos a las doce y media. We have lunch at 12.30.
2 **to have for lunch**
   Almorzamos sopa y tortilla. We had soup and omelette for lunch.
3 **to have a mid-morning snack** (*in some areas of Spain*)

ₛ el **almuerzo** *masc noun*
1 **lunch**
2 **mid-morning snack** (*in some areas of Spain*)

el **alojamiento** *masc noun*
   accommodation

alojarse *reflexive verb* [17]
   to stay
   Se alojaron en un hotel de cinco estrellas. They stayed in a five-star hotel.

la **alondra** *fem noun*
   lark (*the bird*)

los **Alpes** *plural masc noun*
   los Alpes the Alps

el **alpinismo** *masc noun*
   mountaineering

el & la **alpinista** *masc & fem noun*
   mountaineer

ₛ **alquilar** *verb* [17]
1 **to rent**
   Hemos alquilado un apartamento en la playa. We've rented an apartment at the seaside.
2 **to hire** (*cars, bicycles, etc*)
   alquilar una bicicleta to hire a bike
3 **to let** (*a house, flat, room*)
   Se aquila la casa. The house is to let.
4 **to hire out** (*equipment*)
   Allí alquilan botas de esquiar. They hire out ski boots there.

alquilarse *reflexive verb* [17]
   to let, to rent
   'Se alquila' 'To let' (*on a sign*)
   Se alquilan coches. Cars for hire.

ₛ el **alquiler** *masc noun*
1 **rent** (*for a flat, house, etc*)
   una casa de alquiler a rented house
   una casa en alquiler a house to let
2 **hire charge** (*for cars or equipment*)
   coches de alquiler hire cars

el **alquitrán** *masc noun*
   tar

ₛ **alrededor** *adverb*
1 **around**
   mirar alrededor to look around
   a nuestro alrededor around us
   un jardín con un muro alrededor a garden with a wall around it
2 **alrededor de algo** around something
   Se sentaron alrededor de la mesa. They sat around the table.
   Cuesta alrededor de veinte euros. It costs around twenty euros.
   Su padre tiene alrededor de cuarenta años. Her father is about forty (years old).

ₛ los **alrededores** *plural masc noun*
1 **outskirts** (*of a town or city*)
   en los alrededores de Valencia on the outskirts of Valencia
2 **surrounding area** (*of an airport or building*)
   en los alrededores del puerto in the port area

ₛ el **alta** *fem noun*
1 **darse de alta** to sign on, to join
   Me di de alta en el club de tenis. I joined the tennis club.
2 **dar de alta a alguien** to discharge someone (*from hospital*)
   Le dieron de alta después de dos días. She was discharged after two days.

> **WORD TIP** *alta* takes *el* or *un* in the singular even though it is feminine.

el **altavoz** *masc noun*, los *pl*: **altavoces**
1 **loudspeaker**
2 **megaphone**

alternar *verb* [17]
   to alternate

alternarse *reflexive verb* [17]
   to take turns
   Nos alternábamos para hacer la comida. We took turns to cook.

la **alternativa** *fem noun*
   ▷ see **alternativo** *adj*
   alternative
   No hay otra alternativa. There's no alternative.

alternativo *masc adjective*, **alternativa** *fem* ▷ see **alternativa** *noun*
   alternative

la **altitud** *fem noun*
   altitude

altivo *masc adjective*, **altiva** *fem*
   arrogant

a
b
c
d
e
f
g
h
i
j
k
l
m
n
ñ
o
p
q
r
s
t
u
v
w
x
y
z

♂ **alto** *masc adjective*, **alta** *fem*
▷ see **alto** *noun, adv*

1 high
una habitación de techo alto a room with a high ceiling
en lo alto de la torre at the top of the tower
La montaña más alta de España. The highest mountain in Spain.
Los precios están muy altos. Prices are very high.
en lo alto de la torre at the top of the tower
Sacó la nota más alta. He got the highest mark.

2 tall
Todos sus hijos son muy altos. All their children are very tall.
Ella es más alta que él. She's taller than he is.

3 loud
en voz alta in a loud voice
No pongas la radio tan alta. Don't put the radio on so loud.

♂ el **alto** *masc noun* ▷ see **alto** *adj, adv*
de alto high
un muro de dos metros de alto a two-metre high wall

♂ **alto** *adverb* ▷ see **alto** *adj, noun*

1 loud
Habla un poco más alto, por favor. Speak a little louder, please.

2 high
volar alto to fly high

la **altura** *fem noun*

1 height
a la misma altura at the same height
¿Qué altura tiene? How high is it?

2 altitude
Volábamos a una altura de 10.000 m. We were flying at an altitude of 10,000 metres.

3 a estas alturas at this stage
A estas alturas no importa. It doesn't matter at this stage.

la **alubia** *fem noun*
haricot bean

la **alucinación** *fem noun*
hallucination

alucinado *masc adjective*, **alucinada** *fem*
(*informal*) estar alucinado, *fem* alucinada to be stunned
Nos quedamos alucinados. We were stunned.

alucinante *masc & fem adjective*
(*informal*) **amazing**
Es un espectáculo alucinante. It's an amazing spectacle.

alucinar *verb* [17] (*informal*)

1 to amaze
Me alucina. It amazes me.

2 alucinar con algo to be amazed by something
Con esta grabación alucinas. You'll be amazed by this recording.

el **alud** *masc noun*

1 avalanche

2 landslide

el **aluminio** *masc noun*
aluminium

♂ el **alumno** *masc noun*, la **alumna** *fem*

1 pupil
¿Cuántos alumnos hay en tu colegio? How many pupils are there in your school?

la **alusión** *fem noun*
allusion

♂ el **ama de casa** *fem noun*
housewife
un ama de casa a housewife

WORD TIP *ama* takes *el* or *un* in the singular even though it is feminine.

la **amabilidad** *fem noun*
kindness
Tuvieron la amabilidad de ayudarme. They were kind enough to help me.

♂ **amable** *masc & fem adjective*
kind
¿Sería tan amable de sujetar esto? Would you be so kind as to hold this?

amaestrar *verb* [17]
to train (*a dog, a horse, etc*)

♂ el **amanecer** *masc noun*
▷ see **amanecer** *verb*
dawn
al amanecer at dawn

♂ **amanecer** *verb* [35]
▷ see **amanecer** *noun*

1 to get light
¿A qué hora amanece? What time does it get light?

2 to wake up
Amanece tarde. She gets up late.

amante *masc & fem adjective*
▷ see **amante** *noun*
ser amante de algo to be fond of something

Son grandes amantes del cine. They're great cinema fans.

el & la **amante** *masc & fem noun*
▷ see **amante** *adj*
lover

la **amapola** *fem noun*
poppy

amar *verb* [17]
to love

amargo *masc adjective*, **amarga** *fem*
bitter

ꝗ **amarillo** *masc adjective*, **amarilla** *fem*
▷ see **amarillo** *noun*
yellow
una cinta amarilla a yellow ribbon

ꝗ el **amarillo** *masc noun* ▷ see **amarillo** *adj*
yellow

amarrar *verb* [1]
(*Latin America*) **to tie**

amarrarse *reflexive verb*
(*Latin America*) **to tie up**
amarrarse los zapatos to tie up your shoe laces

amasar *verb* [17]
to knead (*dough*)

el **Amazonas** *masc noun*
the (River) Amazon

la **ambición** *fem noun*
ambition

ambicioso *masc adjective*, **ambiciosa** *fem*
ambitious

el **ambientador** *masc noun*
air freshener

ambiental *masc & fem adjective*
environmental

el **ambiente** *masc noun*
1 **environment**
la contaminación del ambiente the pollution of the environment
2 **atmosphere** (*at a party, a match*)
Había muy buen ambiente. There was a good atmosphere.

ambiguo *masc adjective*, **ambigua** *fem*
ambiguous

ꝗ **ambos** *plural masc adjective & pronoun*,
ambas *plural fem adj & pron*
both
ambas ciudades both cities
ambos hermanos both brothers
Ambas se quedaron. Both of them stayed

behind (*girls*).
Ambos vinieron. Both of them came (*boys*).

la **ambulancia** *fem noun*
ambulance

ambulante *masc & fem adjective*
travelling
un grupo de teatro ambulante a travelling theatre group
una biblioteca ambulante a mobile library

el **ambulatorio** *masc noun*
outpatients' department

el **amén** *masc noun*
amen

la **amenaza** *fem noun*
threat

amenazador *masc adjective*,
amenazadora *fem*
threatening

amenazar *verb* [22]
to threaten
Amenazó con despedirme. He threatened to fire me.
amenazar de muerte a alguien to threaten to kill somebody

ꝗ **América** *fem noun*
America
Soy de América. I'm from America.
• **América Central** Central America
• **América del Sur** South America
• **América Latina** Latin America

ꝗ la **americana** *fem noun*
jacket

ꝗ **americano** *masc adjective*, **americana**
fem ▷ see **americano** *noun*
1 **American** (*from the USA*)
2 **Latin American**

ꝗ un **americano** *masc noun*, una
americana *fem* ▷ see **americano** *adj*
1 **American** (*from the USA*)
2 **Latin American**

WORD TIP Adjectives and nouns for nationality and regional origin do not have capital letters in Spanish.

la **ametralladora** *fem noun*
machine gun

ꝗ **amigo** *masc adjective*, **amiga** *fem*
▷ see **amigo** *noun*
hacerse amigos to become friends
Son muy amigos. They are very good friends.

ᵹ el **amigo** *masc noun*, la **amiga** *fem*
▷ see **amigo** *adj*
friend
un amigo nuestro a friend of ours
un amigo de Carmen a friend of Carmen's
Son amigos íntimos. They are very close
friends.
mi amigo del alma my best friend
· el **amigo por correspondencia**, la **amiga
por correspondencia** *fem* penfriend

la **amistad** *fem noun*
1 **friendship**
2 las amistades **friends**
Tiene muchas amistades. She has a lot of
friends.

amistoso *masc adjective*, **amistosa** *fem*
friendly
un partido amistoso a friendly match

el **amo** *masc noun*, el **ama** *fem*
owner
el amo del perro the owner of the dog

amontonar *verb* [17]
to pile up

amontonarse *reflexive verb* [17]
to pile up

ᵹ el **amor** *masc noun*
love
amor mío my love
· el **amor a primera vista** love at first sight
· el **amor propio** self-esteem

amoroso *masc adjective*, **amorosa** *fem*
to do with love
las relaciones amorosas love relationships

ampliar *verb* [32]
1 **to enlarge** (*a photograph*)
2 **to extend** (*a road or building*)
3 **to increase** (*your vocabulary, knowledge*)

el **amplificador** *masc noun*
amplifier

amplio *masc adjective*, **amplia** *fem*
1 **wide** (*road*)
2 **spacious** (*room*)
3 **loose-fitting** (*clothes*)

la **amplitud** *fem noun*
1 **width** (*of a road*)
2 **spaciousness** (*of a room*)

la **ampolla** *fem noun*
blister
Me han salido ampollas en las manos. I've
got blisters on my hands.

ᵹ **amueblado** *masc adjective*, **amueblada**
fem
furnished
un piso amueblado a furnished flat

ᵹ **amueblar** *verb* [17]
to furnish (*a house or room*)

analfabeto *masc adjective*, **analfabeta**
fem
illiterate

el **analgésico** *masc noun*
painkiller

el **análisis** *masc noun*
analysis

analizar *verb* [22]
to analyse

la **anatomía** *fem noun*
anatomy

ᵹ **ancho** *masc adjective*, **ancha** *fem*
▷ see **ancho** *noun*
1 **wide**
una carretera muy ancha a very wide road
2 **broad**
ser ancho de espaldas to have broad
shoulders
3 **loose-fitting** (*clothes*)
Te está muy ancho. It's too loose for you.

ᵹ el **ancho** *masc noun* ▷ see **ancho** *adj*
width
¿Cuánto tiene de ancho? How wide is it?
Tiene dos metros de ancho. It's two metres
wide.

la **anchoa** *fem noun*
anchovy

la **anchura** *fem noun*
width
¿Qué anchura tiene? How wide is it?
Tiene una anchura de cinco metros. It's five
metres wide.

anciano *masc adjective*, **anciana** *fem*
▷ see **anciano** *noun*
elderly
un hombre muy anciano a very elderly man

ᵹ el **anciano** *masc noun*, la **anciana** *fem*
▷ see **anciano** *adj*
1 **old man**
2 **old woman**

el **ancla** *fem noun*
anchor
echar anclas to drop anchor

WORD TIP *ancla* takes *el* or *un* in the singular even
though it is feminine.

Andalucía *fem noun*
Andalusia (*the southernmost province of Spain*)

andaluz *masc adjective & noun*, **andaluza**
fem adjective & noun
1 **Andalusian**
2 (*person*) **un andaluz, una andaluza**
Andalusian

WORD TIP Adjectives and nouns for nationality
and regional origin do not have capital letters in
Spanish.

---

el **andamio** *masc noun*
scaffolding

ᔆ **andar** *verb* [21]
1 **to walk**
¿Has venido andando? Did you walk here?
Casi no podía andar. I could hardly walk.
2 (*saying how things are*) **andar bien** to go well
andar mal to go badly
¿Cómo andas? How are you?
¿Cómo andas de dinero? How are you
doing for money?
3 **to work**
Mi coche no anda. My car's not going well.
4 (*expressing surprise*) ¡Anda! si es Pedro. Well,
if it isn't Pedro!
5 (*telling somebody to do something*) **Anda, date
prisa.** Come on, hurry up.

ᔆ el **andén** *masc noun*
platform

los **Andes** *plural masc noun*
los Andes the Andes

mini-info **Andes**

Los Andes es la cordillera más larga del mundo,
extendiéndose desde Colombia hasta Tierra del
Fuego por 6.400 km.

el **andinismo** *masc noun*
(*Latin America*) **mountain climbing**

el & la **andinista** *masc & fem noun*
(*Latin America*) **mountain climber**

Andorra *fem noun*
Andorra

el **andrajo** *masc noun*
rag
Iba vestido de andrajos. He was dressed in
rags.

la **anécdota** *fem noun*
anecdote

la **anestesia** *fem noun*
1 **anaesthesia**
2 **anaesthetic**

el **anfitrión** *masc noun* la **anfitriona** *fem*
1 **host**
2 **hostess**

el **ángel** *masc noun*
angel
No es ningún angelito. He's no angel.

angelical *masc & fem adjective*
angelic

las **anginas** *plural fem noun*
throat infection
tener anginas to have a throat infection

el **anglicano** *masc noun*, la **anglicana** *fem*
Anglican

angosto *masc adjective*, **angosta** *fem*
(*Latin America*) **narrow**

la **anguila** *fem noun*
eel

angustiado *masc adjective*, **angustiada**
fem
worried
Están angustiados porque no saben nada
de él. They are really worried because they
haven't heard from him.

angustiarse *reflexive verb* [17]
to get worried
No hay por qué angustiarse. There's no
reason to get worried.

angustioso *masc adjective*, **angustiosa**
fem
worrying

el **anillo** *masc noun*
ring
el Señor de los Anillos the Lord of the
Rings
• el **anillo de boda** wedding ring

ᔆ **animado** *masc adjective*, **animada** *fem*
1 **lively** (*bar, party, etc*)
2 **in good spirits**
Estaba muy animada. She was in high
spirits.

animal *masc & fem adjective*
▷ see **animal** *noun*
stupid
¡Qué animal eres! You're so stupid!

ᔆ el **animal** *masc noun* ▷ see **animal** *adj*
1 **animal**
2 **brute**
Es un animal. He's a brute.

a
b
c
d
e
f
g
h
i
j
k
l
m
n
ñ
o
p
q
r
s
t
u
v
w
x
y
z

el **animal doméstico** *masc noun*
1 **domestic animal**
2 **pet**
   ¿Tienes algún animal doméstico? Do you have any pets?

ƒ **animar** *verb* [17]
1 **to liven up** (*a party, etc*)
2 **to cheer up** (*a person*)
3 **to cheer on**

animarse *reflexive verb* [17]
   to cheer up
   ¡Anímate! Cheer up!

el **ánimo** *masc noun*
1 No tengo ánimo para nada. I don't feel in the mood for anything.
   Se la ve con mucho ánimo. She's in high spirits.
2 ¡Ánimo! Cheer up!

el **aniversario** *masc noun*
   anniversary

ƒ **anoche** *adverb*
   last night
   Anoche no dormí bien. I didn't sleep well last night.
   antes de anoche the night before last

ƒ **anochecer** *verb* [35]
   ▷ see **anochecer** *noun*
   to get dark
   Está anocheciendo. It's getting dark.

ƒ el **anochecer** *masc noun*
   ▷ see **anochecer** *verb*
   nightfall
   al anochecer at nightfall

anónimo *masc adjective*, **anónima** *fem*
   ▷ see **anónimo** *noun*
   anonymous

el **anónimo** *masc noun* ▷ see **anónimo** *adj*
   anonymous letter

anormal *masc & fem adjective*
   abnormal

anotar *verb* [17]
   to write down

la **ansiedad** *fem noun*
   anxiety

ante *preposition* ▷ see **ante** *noun*
   before
   ante el juez before the judge

el **ante** *masc noun* ▷ see **ante** *prep*
   suede

ƒ **anteanoche** *adverb*
   ▷ see **antenoche** *adv*
   the night before last

ƒ **anteayer** *adverb* ▷ see **antier** *adv*
   the day before yesterday

antemano *adverb*
   de antemano in advance

la **antena** *fem noun*
1 **aerial**
2 **antenna**
• la **antena parabólica** satellite dish

antenoche *adverb*
   ▷ see **anteanoche** *adv*
   (*Latin America*) **the night before last**

los **anteojos** *plural masc noun*
   (*Latin America*) **glassess**

los **antepasados** *plural masc noun*
   ancestors

ƒ **anterior** *masc & fem adjective*
   previous
   la noche anterior the previous night
   anterior a algo prior to something

ƒ **antes** *adverb*
1 **before**
   la noche antes the night before
   Deberías haberlo dicho antes. You should have said it before.
2 antes de before
   antes del viernes before Friday
   Piénsalo antes de comprarlo. Think about it before you buy it.
3 **earlier**
   Este año la primavera ha llegado antes. This year spring has come earlier.
   A las cinco está bien, no hace falta que vengas antes. Five is fine, you don't need to come any earlier.
4 **first**
   Ésta va antes. This goes first.
5 lo antes posible as soon as possible

el **antibiótico** *masc noun*
   antibiotic

la **anticipación** *fem noun*
   con mucha anticipación well in advance
   con dos días de anticipación two days in advance

el **anticipo** *masc noun*
   advance

la **anticoncepción** *noun*
   contraception

el **anticonceptivo** *masc noun*
   contraceptive

anticuado *masc adjective*, **anticuada** *fem*
old-fashioned

el **antídoto** *masc noun*
antidote

antier *adverb* ▷ see **anteayer** *adv*
(*Latin America*) **the day before yesterday**

ᵹ la **antigüedad** *fem noun*
1 **en la antigüedad** in the old days
2 **antique**
una tienda de antigüedades an antique
shop
3 **seniority** (*at work*)

ᵹ **antiguamente** *adverb*
in the old days

ᵹ **antiguo** *masc adjective*, **antigua** *fem*
1 **old**
una costumbre muy antigua a very old
tradition
2 **ancient**
una civilización antigua an ancient
civilization
3 **former**
el antiguo presidente the former president

las **Antillas** *plural fem noun*
las Antillas the West Indies

ᵹ **antipático** *masc adjective*, **antipática** *fem*
unpleasant
Es muy antipático. He's very unpleasant.
¡Qué mujer más antipática! What a horrible
woman!

antojarse *reflexive verb* [17]
Se le antojó un helado. He fancied an ice-
cream.
Se me antojó comprar el jarrón. I felt like
buying the vase.

la **antropología** *fem noun*
anthropology

anual *masc & fem adjective*
annual

anualmente *adverb*
yearly

ᵹ **anunciar** *verb* [17]
1 **to announce** (*a piece of news, a decision*)
2 **to advertise** (*a product, a service*)

ᵹ el **anuncio** *masc noun*
1 **announcement**
2 **advertisement**

el **anzuelo** *masc noun*
hook

añadidura *in phrase*
por añadidura in addition

añadir *verb* [19]
to add

ᵹ el **año** *masc noun*
1 **year**
el año pasado last year
los años cincuenta the fifties
2 (*talking about age*) ¿Cuántos años tienes?
How old are you?
Mi madre tiene cincuenta años. My mother
is fifty.
• el **año bisiesto** leap year
• el **Año Nuevo** New Year

ᵹ **apagado** *masc adjective*, **apagada** *fem*
1 **off, turned off**
con la luz apagada with the light off
¿Está apagada la televisión? Is the
television off?
2 **out**
El fuego estaba casi apagado. The fire was
almost out.

ᵹ **apagar** *verb* [28]
1 **to switch off** (*the television, the light*)
2 **to put out** (*a fire, a cigarette*)

el **apagón** *masc noun*
power cut

el **aparato** *masc noun*
1 **appliance**
2 los aparatos de laboratorio laboratory
equipment
3 **piece of apparatus** (*in the gym*)
• los **aparatos eléctricos** electrical
appliances

ᵹ el **aparcamiento** *masc noun*
car park

ᵹ **aparcar** *verb* [31]
to park

aparecer *verb* [35]
1 **to appear** (*a person or symptom*)
2 **to turn up** (*things that got lost*)

aparente *masc & fem adjective*
apparent

la **apariencia** *fem noun*
1 **appearance**
A juzgar por las apariencias. Judging by
appearances.
En apariencia no estaba roto. It appeared
not to be broken.
Un niño de apariencia delicada. A delicate-
looking child.

apartado *masc adjective*, **apartada** *fem*
isolated

ᵹ indicates key words   21

ℰ el **apartamento** *masc noun*
(*Latin America*) **flat**, **apartment**

apartar *verb* [17]
1 **to move away**
Aparta la manta del fuego. Move the blanket away from the fire.
2 **to move out of the way**
Aparta la planta para que pueda ver. Move the plant out of the way so that I can see.

apartarse *reflexive verb* [17]
to move away
Se apartó de la ventana. She moved away from the window.

ℰ **aparte** *adverb*
1 **aside**
poner algo aparte to put something aside
llamar a alguien aparte to call somebody aside
2 **separately**
Esto lo pago aparte. I'll pay for this separately.
3 **aparte de eso** apart from that

apasionado *masc adjective*, **apasionada** *fem*
passionate

apasionar *verb* [17]
El deporte me apasiona. I have a passion for sports.
La ópera no me apasiona. I'm not wild about opera.

apearse de *reflexive verb* [17]
1 **to get off** (*a bus, a train*)
2 **to get out of** (*a car*)
3 **to dismount from** (*a horse*)

apellidarse *reflexive verb* [17]
Me apellido Alejos. My surname is Alejos.

ℰ el **apellido** *masc noun*
surname
¿Qué apellido tienes? What's your surname?
• el **apellido de soltera** maiden name

ℰ **apenas** *adverb*
1 **hardly**
Apenas hay suficiente. There's hardly enough.
2 **hardly ever**
Ahora apenas nos vemos. We hardly ever see each other now.
3 **scarcely**
Hace apenas tres horas que se fueron. It's scarcely three hours since they left.
Apenas lo veo. I can scarcely see it.

4 **just**
Apenas me había sentado, cuando sonó el teléfono. I had just sat down when the telephone rang.

el **apéndice** *masc noun*
appendix

la **apendicitis** *fem noun*
appendicitis

ℰ el **aperitivo** *masc noun*
1 **aperitif** (*before a meal*)
2 **nibbles** (*food*)

ℰ **apetecer** *verb* [35]
No me apetece. I don't feel like it.
¿Te apetece ir a cenar fuera? Do you fancy going out for dinner?
Me apetecen las sardinas. I fancy the sardines.
Haz lo que te apetezca. Do whatever you feel like.

> **WORD TIP** Use *apetece*, *apetecía*, etc if what you feel like, or don't feel like, is singular or an infinitive. Use *apetecen*, *apetecían*, etc if what you like, or don't like, is plural.

el **apetito** *masc noun*
appetite
No tengo apetito. I don't feel hungry.
Me ha abierto el apetito. It has given me an appetite.

el **apio** *masc noun*
celery

aplastar *verb* [17]
to squash

aplaudir *verb* [19]
to applaud

el **aplauso** *masc noun*
round of applause
los aplausos del público the applause of the audience

el **aplazamiento** *masc noun*
postponement

aplazar *verb* [22]
to postpone

aplicado *masc adjective*, **aplicada** *fem*
hard-working

aplicar *verb* [31]
to apply

el **apodo** *masc noun*
nickname

apostar *verb* [24]
1 **to bet**
Te apuesto cincuenta euros. I bet you fifty euros.

Te apuesto a que no viene. I bet she won't come.

apostar a las carreras to bet on the horses
Apostaron por el favorito. They bet on the favourite.

2 apostar por to back, to go for

el **apóstrofo** *masc noun*
(*Grammar*) **apostrophe**

apoyar *verb* [17]
1 to support (*a candidate, a plan, etc*)
2 to lean
Apoyé la bicicleta en la pared. I leaned the bicycle against the wall.
3 to rest
Apoya la cabeza en este cojín. Rest your head on this cushion.

apoyarse *reflexive verb* [17]
apoyarse en to lean on
Me apoyé en la puerta. I leaned against the door.

el **apoyo** *masc noun*
support

apreciar *verb* [17]
1 to appreciate
2 apreciar a alguien to be fond of somebody
La aprecio mucho. I'm very fond of her.

el **aprecio** *masc noun*
sentir aprecio por alguien to be fond of somebody

ƒ **aprender** *verb* [18]
to learn
aprender español to learn Spanish
aprender a conducir to learn to drive
aprender algo de memoria to learn something by heart
¿Qué has aprendido hoy?
What did you learn today?

el **aprendiz** *masc noun*, la **aprendiza** *fem*
apprentice

el **aprendizaje** *masc noun*
apprenticeship

apretado *masc adjective*, **apretada** *fem*
tight

apretar *verb* [29]
1 to press (*a button*)
2 to tighten (*a bolt or knot*)
3 apretar el acelerador to put your foot on the accelerator
4 to be too tight (*shoes*)
5 to squeeze
Me apretó el brazo. She squeezed my arm.

el **apretón** *masc noun*
un apretón de manos a handshake

el **aprieto** *masc noun*
predicament
meterse en un aprieto to get into a predicament
poner a alguien en un aprieto to put somebody in an awkward situation

aprisa *adverb*
quickly

ƒ **aprobar** *verb* [24]
1 to approve (*a plan, a decision, etc*)
2 to approve of (*behaviour, an idea*)
3 to pass
aprobar un examen to pass an exam

aprovechado *masc adjective*, **aprovechada** *fem*
Es un aprovechado. He takes advantage of people.

ƒ **aprovechar** *verb* [17]
1 to make the most of (*an opportunity, an offer, a skill*)
Quiero aprovechar esta oportunidad para ... I want to take this opportunity to ...
Aproveché para decírselo. I took the chance to tell him.
2 to make use of
Podemos aprovechar esta madera. We can use this wood.
3 (*a person*) **to take advantage of**
4 (*at meals*) ¡Que aproveche! Enjoy your meal!

ƒ **aproximadamente** *adverb*
approximately, **roughly**

aproximado *masc adjective*, **aproximada** *fem*
approximate, **rough**

aproximar *verb* [17]
to bring nearer

aproximarse *reflexive verb* [17]
1 aproximarse a algo to go up to something
Se aproximó a la ventana. She went up to the window.
Se aproximó a mí. He came up to me.
2 to approach
Se aproximaba el momento. The moment was approaching.

apto *masc adjective*, **apta** *fem*
apto para algo suitable for something

la **apuesta** *fem noun*
bet
hacerle una apuesta a alguien to make a bet with somebody ▸▸

a
b
c
d
e
f
g
h
i
j
k
l
m
n
ñ
o
p
q
r
s
t
u
v
w
x
y
z

Me hicieron una apuesta. They made a bet with me.

ℰ **apuntar** *verb* [17]

1 **to write down** (*a telephone number, an address, etc*)

2 **to point out**
Apuntó con el dedo hacia la torre. She pointed out the tower.

3 **to aim**
Me apuntó con la pistola. He aimed the gun at me.

apuntarse *reflexive verb* [17]
apuntarse a algo to put your name down for something
Se apuntó a clases de guitarra. She put her name down for guitar classes.
¡Yo me apunto! I'm up for that!

ℰ los **apuntes** *plural masc noun*
notes
tomar apuntes to take notes

apurado *masc adjective*, **apurada** *fem*
(*Latin America*) **in a hurry**

apurarse *reflexive verb* []
(*Latin America*) **to hurry**
¡Apúrate! Hurry up!

el **apuro** *masc noun*
estar en un apuro to be in a tight spot
pasar apuros to go through a bad patch

ℰ **aquel** *masc adjective*, **aquella** *fem*
▷ see **aquel** *pron*

1 **that**
en aquel momento at that moment
en aquella habitación in that room

2 aquellos, aquellas those
aquellos hombres those men
aquellas mujeres those women

ℰ **aquel** *masc pronoun*, **aquella** *fem*
▷ see **aquel** *adj*

1 **that one**
Quiero aquel. I want that one (*for a masc noun*).
Quiero aquella. I want that one (*for a fem noun*).

2 aquellos, aquellas those
Estas no, dame aquellos. Not these, give me those (*for a masc pl noun*).
Estas no, dame aquellas. Not these, give me those (*for a fem pl noun*).

ℰ **aquél**, **aquélla**, **aquéllos**, **aquéllas** *pronoun*

WORD TIP The pronouns *aquel, aquella, aquellos, and aquellas* take an accent when it is not clear whether a pronoun or an adjective is being used.
▷ **aquel, aquella**

ℰ **aquello** *pronoun*
that
¿Qué es aquello? What's that?
Aquello que vimos. What we saw.

WORD TIP *aquello* never changes.

ℰ **aquí** *adverb*
here
Lo puse aquí abajo. I put it down here.
Aquí llegan. Here they are.
Debe estar por aquí. It must be around here.
El vino es de aquí. The wine is from here.

árabe *masc & fem adjective* ▷ see **árabe** *noun*

1 **Arab** (*country*)

2 **Arabic** (*letter, number*)

un & una **árabe** *masc & fem noun*
▷ see **árabe** *adj*

1 **Arab** (*person*)

2 el árabe Arabic (*the language*)

WORD TIP Adjectives and nouns for nationality, regional origin, and language do not have capital letters in Spanish.

Aragón *masc noun*
Aragon (*a region of North-East Spain*)

aragonés *masc adjective & noun*, **aragonesa** *fem adjective & noun*

1 **Aragonese**

2 un aragonés, una aragonesa
Aragonese (*person*)

WORD TIP Adjectives and nouns for nationality and regional origin do not have capital letters in Spanish.

la **araña** *fem noun*
spider

arañar *verb* [17]
to scratch

el **arañazo** *masc noun*
scratch

el **árbitro** *masc noun*, la **árbitra** *fem*

1 **referee**

2 **umpire**

ℰ el **árbol** *masc noun*
tree
• el árbol de Navidad Christmas tree

el **arbusto** *masc noun*
bush

el **arcén** *masc noun*
hard shoulder (*on the motorway*)

el **archivador** *masc noun*

1 **filing cabinet**

2 **ring binder**

archivar *verb* [17]
 to file

el **archivo** *masc noun*
1 archive
2 file (*on a computer*)

la **arcilla** *fem noun*
 clay

el **arco** *masc noun*
1 arch
2 bow (*for arrows, for a violin*)
3 (*Latin America*) goal
• el **arco iris** rainbow

arder *verb* [18]
 to burn
 El bosque estaba ardiendo. The forest was
 burning.

ardiente *masc & fem adjective*
 burning

la **ardilla** *fem noun*
 squirrel

el **área** *fem noun*
 area
 las áreas más peligrosas the most
 dangerous areas
• el **área de penalty** penalty area

 WORD TIP *área* takes *el* or *un* in the singular even
 though it is feminine.

la **arena** *fem noun*
 sand

Argentina *fem noun*
 Argentina
 Soy de Argentina. **I'm from Argentina.**

argentino *masc adjective*, **argentina** *fem*
 ▷ see **argentino** *noun*
 Argentinian

un **argentino** *masc noun*, una **argentina**
 fem ▷ see **argentino** *adj*
 Argentinian

 WORD TIP Adjectives and nouns for nationality
 and regional origin do not have capital letters in
 Spanish.

el **argot** *masc noun*
 slang
• el **argot juvenil** youth slang

el **argumento** *masc noun*
1 argument
2 plot (*of a film, a play, etc*)

aries *masc & fem noun* ▷ see **Aries** *noun*
 Aries
 Soy aries. I'm Aries.

 WORD TIP Use a small letter in Spanish to say *I
 am Aries*, etc with star signs.

Aries *masc noun* ▷ see **aries** *noun*
 Aries

la **aritmética** *fem noun*
 arithmetic

el **arma** *fem noun*
 weapon
• el **arma blanca** knife (*as a weapon*)
• el **arma de fuego** firearm
• las **armas nucleares** nuclear weapons

 WORD TIP *arma* takes *el* or *un* in the singular
 even though it is feminine.

armado *masc adjective*, **armada** *fem*
 armed

armar *verb* [17]
1 to arm
2 to assemble (*a piece of furniture*)
3 to pitch (*a tent*)
4 (*informal*) armar ruido to make a noise
 armar jaleo to make a racket
 armar un escándalo to cause a scene

armarse *reflexive verb* [17]
1 armarse un lío to get confused
 Me armé un lío con las fechas. I got
 confused with the dates.
2 armarse de paciencia to be patient

ꝰ el **armario** *masc noun*
1 wardrobe
2 cupboard

la **armonía** *fem noun*
 harmony

la **armónica** *fem noun*
 harmonica

armonioso *masc adjective*, **armoniosa**
 fem
 harmonious

el **aro** *masc noun*
1 hoop
2 hoop earring

el **aroma** *masc noun*
1 scent
2 aroma

aromático *masc adjective*, **aromática** *fem*
 aromatic

el **arpa** *fem noun*
 harp

 WORD TIP *arpa* takes *el* or *un* in the singular even
 though it is feminine.

la **arqueología** *fem noun*
 archaeology

a
b
c
d
e
f
g
h
i
j
k
l
m
n
ñ
o
p
q
r
s
t
u
v
w
x
y
z

el **arqueólogo** *masc noun*, la **arqueóloga**
fem
archaeologist

el **arquero** *masc noun*, la **arquera** *fem*
(*Latin America*) **goalkeeper**

el **arquitecto** *masc noun*, la **arquitecta**
fem
architect

la **arquitectura** *fem noun*
architecture

⚥ **arrancar** *verb* [31]
1 **to tear out**
arrancar una hoja del cuaderno to tear out
a sheet from the notebook
2 **to tear off**
arrancar una etiqueta to tear off a label
3 **to pull up** (*a plant*)
4 **to pull off** (*a button*)
5 **to snatch**
Me arrancó el libro de las manos. She
snatched the book from my hands.
6 **to start** (*cars, engines*)
7 **to boot up** (*computers*)

arrastrar *verb* [17]
to drag (*an object*)

arrastrarse *reflexive verb* [17]
to crawl

arrebatar *verb* [17]
to snatch

⚥ **arreglado** *masc adjective*, **arreglada** *fem*
1 **tidy**
Deja tu habitación arreglada. Leave your
room tidy.
2 **well dressed**
Siempre va muy arreglado. He's always
very well dressed.

⚥ **arreglar** *verb* [17]
1 **to fix**
2 **to mend**
3 **to tidy** (*a room, a house*)
4 **to sort out** (*a problem*)
No te preocupes, yo lo arreglaré. Don't
worry, I'll sort it out.

arreglarse *reflexive verb* [17]
1 **to get ready**
Me arreglo enseguida y salimos. I'll get
ready straight away and we can go out.
2 **to dress up**
Mi hermana siempre se arregla mucho. My
sister always dresses up a lot.
3 arreglárselas to manage
Se las arregla muy bien sola. She manages
very well on her own.

arrepentirse *reflexive verb* [14]
arrepentirse de algo to regret something
No me arrepiento. I don't regret it.

arrestar *verb* [17]
to arrest
Queda usted arrestado. You're under
arrest.

el **arresto** *masc noun*
arrest

⚥ **arriba** *adverb*
1 **up**
aquí arriba up here
Lo puse más arriba. I put it a bit higher up.
2 **de arriba** above
el cajón de arriba the drawer above
3 **upstairs**
Ha ido arriba. He's gone upstairs.
Viven en el piso de arriba. They live
upstairs.
4 arriba de todo at the very top
de arriba abajo from top to bottom

arriesgado *masc adjective*, **arriesgada**
fem
risky

arriesgar *verb* [28]
to risk

arriesgarse *reflexive verb* [28]
to take a risk

la **arroba** *fem noun*
1 **@**, **at** (*in email addresses*)
juanrobledo@easycom.com
juanrobledo@easycom.com (*said as* **punto**,
com *for* **dot, com**)
2 **former measurement of weight**

arrodillarse *reflexive verb* [17]
to kneel down
Estaba arrodillado. He was on his knees.

arrogante *masc & fem adjective*
arrogant

arrojar *verb* [17]
to throw

arropar *verb* [17]
1 **to wrap up** (*a child, a sick person*)
2 **to tuck in** (*in bed*)

arroparse *reflexive verb* [17]
to wrap up
Arrópate bien. Wrap up well.

el **arroyo** *masc noun*
stream

⚥ el **arroz** *masc noun*
rice

la **arruga** *fem noun*
wrinkle

arrugar *verb* [28]
1 to wrinkle
2 to crease
3 to crumple up

arruinar *verb* [17]
to ruin

arruinarse *reflexive verb* [17]
to go bankrupt

ᵹ el **arte** *masc noun*
art
las artes the arts
• el **arte moderno** modern art
• las **artes gráficas** graphic arts

WORD TIP *arte* is *masc* in the singular, but *fem* in the plural.

la **artesanía** *fem noun*
1 crafts
artesanía tradicional traditional crafts
objetos de artesanía handicrafts
2 craftsmanship
3 craftwork
la artesanía de la zona the local craftwork

el **artesano** *masc noun*, la **artesana** *fem*
1 craftsman
2 craftswoman

ártico *masc adjective*, **ártica** *fem*
▷ see **Ártico** *noun*
Arctic

WORD TIP Adjectives and nouns for regional origin do not have capital letters in Spanish.

el **Ártico** *masc noun* ▷ see **ártico** *adj*
el Ártico the Arctic

la **articulación** *fem noun*
joint (*in your arm, leg, etc*)

ᵹ el **artículo** *masc noun*
article
• el **artículo definido** definite article
• los **artículos de papelería** stationery

artificial *masc & fem adjective*
artificial

ᵹ el & la **artista** *masc & fem noun*
artist

artístico *masc adjective*, **artística** *fem*
artistic

la **arveja** *fem noun*
(*Latin America*) pea

el **arzobispo** *masc noun*
archbishop

el **asa** *fem noun*
handle
Tómalo por el asa. Take it by the handle.

WORD TIP *asa* takes *el* or *un* in the singular even though it is feminine.

ᵹ el **asado** *masc noun*
roast

la **asamblea** *fem noun*
meeting

asar *verb* [17]
1 to roast (*meat*)
2 to bake (*vegetables*)

ascender *verb* [36]
1 to be promoted
Ha ascendido. He's been promoted.
2 to promote (*an employee*)
3 to rise (*temperature, prices or a balloon*)
ascender a to amount to
La cuenta asciende a quinientos euros. The bill amounts to five hundred euros.

el **ascenso** *masc noun*
promotion

ᵹ el **ascensor** *masc noun*
lift

el **asco** *masc noun*
¡Qué asco! How disgusting!
Esta sopa me da asco. This soup is disgusting.
La película es un asco. The film is disgusting.

asegurar *verb* [17]
1 to assure
Te aseguro que ... I can assure you that ...
2 to insure
3 to secure

asegurarse *reflexive verb* [17]
to make sure
Asegúrate de cerrar la llave. Make sure you turn the tap off.

asentir *verb* [14]
asentir con la cabeza to nod (*in agreement*)

ᵹ el **aseo** *masc noun*
toilet
• los **aseos de señoras** the Ladies

asesinar *verb* [17]
to murder

el **asesinato** *masc noun*
murder

el **asesino** *masc noun*, la **asesina** *fem*
murderer

el **asesor** *masc noun*, la **asesora** *fem*
  adviser

la **asfixia** *fem noun*
  1 asphyxia
  2 suffocation
  Tenía una sensación de asfixia. I felt I was
  suffocating.

asfixiante *masc & fem adjective*
  1 asphyxiating (*air, fumes*)
  2 suffocating (*heat*)

asfixiarse *reflexive verb* [17]
  1 to suffocate
  2 to choke to death

ℰ **así** *adverb*
  1 like this
  Hazlo así. Do it like this.
  2 like that
  El pueblo se llama Robellón, o algo así. The
  village is called Robellón, or something like
  that.
  3 that way
  Me llevaré el coche, así podremos volver
  pronto. I'll take the car, that way we can
  come back early.
  4 así que so
  Así que te vas de vacaciones. So you're
  going on holiday.
  5 así es that's right
  6 así, así so, so
  '¿Te gusta?'—'Así, así.' 'Do you like it?'—
  'So, so.'
  7 ¡Así me gusta! That's what I like to see!
  ¡Así se hace! Well done!

Asia *fem noun*
  Asia

asiático *masc adjective & noun*, **asiática** *fem
adjective & noun*
  1 Asian
  2 un asiático, una asiática Asian (*person*)

> **WORD TIP** Adjectives and nouns for nationality
> and regional origin do not have capital letters in
> Spanish.

ℰ el **asiento** *masc noun*
  seat
  • el **asiento delantero** front seat
  • el **asiento trasero** back seat

ℰ la **asignatura** *fem noun*
  subject

el **asilo** *masc noun*
  home (*for old people*)
  • el **asilo político** political asylum

la **asistenta** *fem noun*
  cleaning lady
  ¿Hay servicio de asistenta? Is there a maid
  service?

el & la **asistente** *masc & fem noun*
  assistant
  • el **asistente social** social worker

ℰ **asistir** *verb* [19]
  asistir a algo to attend something
  Asistió a la reunión. He attended the
  meeting.
  No ha asistido a clases hoy. She has not
  been to school today.

el **asma** *fem noun*
  asthma

> **WORD TIP** asma takes el or un in the singular even
> though it is feminine.

asmático *masc adjective*, **asmática** *fem*
  asthmatic

la **asociación** *fem noun*
  association

asociar *verb* [17]
  to associate (*ideas, words, etc*)

asociarse *reflexive verb* [17]
  to go into partnership (*in business*)

asolar *verb* [17]
  to devastate (*a region, coast, etc*)

asomar *verb* [17]
  asomar la cabeza to stick your head out
  Abrió la ventana y asomó la cabeza. She
  opened the window and stuck her head
  out.
  'No asomar la cabeza por la ventana' 'Do
  not lean out of the window'

asomarse *reflexive verb* [17]
  Se asomó a la ventana. He had a look out of
  the window.
  'Prohibido asomarse por la ventana' 'Do
  not lean out of the window'

asombrar *verb* [17]
  to amaze
  Me asombra su actitud. Her attitude
  amazes me.

asombrarse *reflexive verb* [17]
  to be amazed

el **asombro** *masc noun*
  surprise
  con cara de asombro with a look of surprise
  on her face

a b c d e f g h i j k l m n ñ o p q r s t u v w x y z

asombroso *masc adjective*, **asombrosa** *fem*
amazing

el **aspecto** *masc noun*
look
¿Qué aspecto tenían? What did they look like?
Una mujer de aspecto elegante. An elegant-looking woman.
Tienes muy buen aspecto. You look very well.
Tiene aspecto de policía. He looks like an policeman.

áspero *masc adjective*, **áspera** *fem*
rough

el **aspirador** *masc noun* ▷ **aspiradora**

la **aspiradora** *fem noun*
vacuum cleaner
pasar la aspiradora to vacuum
Tengo que pasar la aspiradora en el salón. I must vacuum the living room.

la **aspirina** *fem noun*
aspirin

el **asterisco** *masc noun*
asterisk

la **astilla** *fem noun*
splinter

la **astrología** *fem noun*
astrology

el **astrólogo** *masc noun*, la **astróloga** *fem*
astrologer

el & la **astronauta** *masc & fem noun*
astronaut

la **astronomía** *fem noun*
astronomy

el **astrónomo** *masc noun*, la **astrónoma** *fem*
astronomer

asturiano *masc adjective & noun*, **asturiana** *fem adjective & noun*
1 **Asturian, from Asturias** (*a region in north-west Spain*)
2 un asturiano, una asturiana Asturian

WORD TIP Adjectives and nouns for nationality and regional origin do not have capital letters in Spanish.

astuto *masc adjective*, **astuta** *fem*
1 **shrewd**
2 **crafty**
Eso fue muy astuto por su parte. That was very crafty of her.

el **asunto** *masc noun*
1 **matter**
asuntos de negocios business matters
un asunto complicado a complicated matter
2 **business**
No quiero saber nada de este asunto. I don't want to know anything about this business.
No es asunto tuyo. It's none of your business.

asustar *verb* [17]
to frighten

asustarse *reflexive verb* [17]
to get frightened
Me asusté al oír un ruido. I got frightened when I heard a noise.

atacar *verb* [31]
to attack

el **atajo** *masc noun*
short cut

el **ataque** *masc noun*
1 **attack**
2 **fit**
un ataque de celos a fit of jealousy
Me dio un ataque de risa. I got a fit of the giggles.
• el **ataque cardíaco** heart attack

atar *verb* [17]
to tie (up)

el **atardecer** *masc noun*
dusk
al atardecer at dusk

atardecer *verb* [35]
to get dark
Estaba atardeciendo. It was getting dark.

atascar *verb* [31]
to block (*a pipe*)

atascarse *reflexive verb* [31]
to get blocked

el **atasco** *masc noun*
1 **traffic jam**
2 **blockage**

el **ataúd** *masc noun*
coffin

ℰ la **atención** *fem noun*
attention
prestar atención to pay attention
No pones atención en lo que haces. You don't concentrate on what you are doing.
¡Atención, por favor! Your attention, please!

a
b
c
d
e
f
g
h
i
j
k
l
m
n
ñ
o
p
q
r
s
t
u
v
w
x
y
z

atender verb [36]
1 **to pay attention**
Atiende a la profesora. Pay attention to
your teacher.
2 ¿La atiende alguien? Are you being served?

el **atentado** masc noun
attack
Un atentado contra el presidente. An
assasination attempt on the president.
• el **atentado terrorista** terrorist attack

atentamente adverb
1 **attentively**
2 Le saluda atentamente. Yours faithfully,
Yours sincerely

atento masc adjective, **atenta** fem
attentive

el **ateo** masc noun la **atea** fem
atheist

♂ el **aterrizaje** masc noun
landing (of a plane)

♂ **aterrizar** verb [22]
to land (planes)

aterrorizar verb [22]
to terrify

el **ático** masc noun
1 **top-floor apartment**
2 **loft**

el **atizador** masc noun
poker

atlántico masc adjective, **atlántica** fem
▷ see **Atlántico** noun

el **Atlántico** masc noun
▷ see **atlántico** adj
el Atlántico the Atlantic

el **atlas** masc noun
atlas

el & la **atleta** masc & fem noun
athlete

atlético masc adjective, **atlética** fem
1 **athletic** (person)
2 una competición atlética an athletics
competition

el **atletismo** masc noun
athletics

atómico masc adjective, **atómica** fem
atomic

el **átomo** masc noun
atom

♂ el **atracador** masc noun, la **atracadora**
fem
1 **robber**
2 **mugger**

♂ **atracar** verb [31]
1 **to hold up** (a bank or a shop)
2 **to mug** (a person)

la **atracción** fem noun
attraction

♂ el **atraco** masc noun
1 **hold-up** (of a bank or a shop)
2 **mugging**

atractivo masc adjective, **atractiva** fem
attractive

atraer verb [42]
to attract

atragantarse reflexive verb [17]
atragantarse con algo to choke on
something

atrapar verb [17]
to catch

♂ **atrás** adverb
1 **back**
Nos sentamos demasiado atrás. We sat too
far back.
hacia atrás backwards
la parte de atrás the back
2 **at the back**
Esto va atrás. This goes at the back.
3 quedarse atrás to be left behind

atrasado masc adjective, **atrasada** fem
1 **slow** (watch or clock)
Llevo el reloj atrasado. My watch is slow.
2 **backward** (country)
3 **old-fashioned** (ideas, people)
4 **behind**
Voy atrasado en los estudios. I'm behind at
school.
Van muy atrasados con los ensayos.
They're very behind with the rehearsals.

atrasar verb [17]
1 **to put back** (a watch or clock)
Hay que atrasar los relojes una hora. We
have to put the clocks back an hour.
2 **to lose time** (a watch or clock)
Este reloj atrasa. This watch loses time.
3 **to postpone**

atrasarse reflexive verb [17]
to lose time (a watch or clock)

atravesar verb [29]
to cross

atrayente *masc & fem adjective*
 appealing

atreverse *reflexive verb* [18]
 to dare
 No me atrevo a preguntarle. I don't dare ask him.

atrevido *masc adjective*, **atrevida** *fem*
1 **daring**
2 **cheeky**
 ¡Qué niño más atrevido! What a cheeky child!

atropellar *verb* [17]
 to run over, **to knock down**
 Lo atropelló un coche. He was run over by a car.

el **atún** *masc noun*
 tuna

el **audífono** *masc noun*
 hearing aid

ſ el **aula** *fem noun*
1 **classroom**
2 **lecture theatre**

 WORD TIP *aula* takes *el* or *un* in the singular even though it is feminine.

el **aullido** *masc noun*
 howl

aumentar *verb* [17]
1 **to increase**
 Aumentó en un cinco por ciento. It increased by five per cent.
2 **to rise** (*temperature, pressure*)

el **aumento** *masc noun*
1 **increase**
2 **rise**

ſ **aun** *adverb* ▷ see **aún** *adv*
 even
 aun así even so
 ni aun con tu ayuda not even with your help

ſ **aún** *adverb* ▷ see **aun** *adv*
1 **still**
 Aún estoy esperando. I'm still waiting.
2 **yet**
 Aún no se lo he dicho a ellos. I haven't told them yet.
3 **even**
 Este es aún mejor. This one is even better.

ſ **aunque** *conjunction*
1 **although**
 Aunque estaba cansada, la ayudé. Although I was tired, I helped her.
2 **even if**, **even though**
 Aunque parezca mentira, ... Even if it

seems untrue, ...
 Aunque llegues tarde, llámame. Even if you arrive late, give me a ring.

 WORD TIP When *aunque* means *even if*, it is followed by a verb in the subjunctive.

el & la **au pair** *masc & fem noun, pl:* **au pairs**
 au pair

el **auricular** *masc noun*
1 **receiver** (*of a phone*)
2 los auriculares **headphones**

ſ **ausente** *masc & fem adjective*
 absent
 estar ausente to be absent, to be away

Australia *fem noun*
 Australia
 Soy de Australia. I'm from Australia.

australiano *masc adjective*, **australiana** *fem* ▷ see **australiano** *noun*
 Australian

un **australiano** *masc noun*, una **australiana** *fem* ▷ see **australiano** *adj*
 Australian

 WORD TIP Adjectives and nouns for nationality and regional origin do not have capital letters in Spanish.

Austria *fem noun*
 Austria
 Soy de Austria. I'm from Austria.

austriaco *masc adjective & noun*, **austriaca** *fem adjective & noun*
1 **Austrian**
2 un austriaco, una austriaca Austrian

 WORD TIP Adjectives and nouns for nationality and regional origin do not have capital letters in Spanish.

auténtico *masc adjective*, **auténtica** *fem*
 authentic

ſ el **auto** *masc noun*
 (*Latin America*) **car**

autoadhesivo *masc adjective*, **autoadhesiva** *fem*
 self-adhesive

la **autobiografía** *fem noun*
 autobiography

ſ el **autobús** *masc noun*
 bus
 coger el autobús to catch the bus
 perder el autobús **to miss the bus**

ſ el **autocar** *masc noun*
 coach

la **autoescuela** *fem noun*
  driving school

el **autógrafo** *masc noun*
  autograph

automático *masc adjective*, **automática** *fem*
  automatic

♂ el **automóvil** *masc noun*
  car

el **automovilismo** *masc noun*
  1 motoring
  2 motor racing

el & la **automovilista** *masc & fem noun*
  motorist

la **autonomía** *fem noun*
  1 autonomy
  2 autonomous region (one of the seventeen self-governing areas into which Spain is divided)

autonómico *masc adjective*, **autonómica** *fem*
  regional (relating to the seventeen autonomous regions into which Spain is divided)

♂ la **autopista** *fem noun*
  motorway

el **autor** *masc noun*, la **autora** *fem*
  author

la **autoridad** *fem noun*
  authority

autoritario *masc adjective*, **autoritaria** *fem*
  authoritarian

la **autorización** *fem noun*
  authorization

autorizar *verb* [22]
  to authorize

♂ el **autoservicio** *masc noun*
  1 self-service restaurant
  2 supermarket

♂ el **autostop**, **auto-stop** *masc noun*
  hitch-hiking
  hacer autostop to hitch-hike

♂ el & la **autostopista** *masc & fem noun*
  hitch-hiker

♂ la **autovía** *fem noun*
  dual carriageway

el & la **auxiliar** *masc & fem noun*
  assistant
  • el & la **auxiliar de vuelo** flight attendant

el **auxilio** *masc noun*
  aid
  acudir en auxilio de alguien to go to somebody's aid
  primeros auxilios first aid

la **avalancha** *fem noun*
  avalanche

avanzar *verb* [22]
  1 **to move forward** (traffic, people)
  2 **to make progress** (students, researchers)
  3 **to wind on** (a tape)

la **avaricia** *fem noun*
  greed

avaricioso *masc adjective*, **avariciosa** *fem*
  greedy

♂ **Avda.** *abbreviation*
  (= Avenida) **Ave.**, **Avenue** (in addresses)

♂ el **AVE** *masc noun*
  (= Alta Velocidad Española) **Spanish high-speed train**

♂ el **ave** *fem noun*
  bird
  un ave a bird
  las aves rapiñas birds of prey

> **WORD TIP** ave takes el or un in the singular even though it is feminine.

la **avellana** *fem noun*
  hazelnut

♂ la **avenida** *fem noun*
  avenue

la **aventura** *fem noun*
  adventure

aventurero *masc adjective*, **aventurera** *fem*
  adventurous

avergonzado *masc adjective*, **avergonzada** *fem*
  1 ashamed
  2 embarrassed

la **avería** *fem noun*
  breakdown (of a car, etc)
  sufrir una avería to break down

averiado *masc adjective*, **averiada** *fem*
  1 broken down
  2 out of order

el **avestruz** *masc noun*
  ostrich

♂ el **avión** *masc noun*
  aeroplane
  • el **avión a reacción** jet (plane)

avisar *verb* [17]
1 **avisar a alguien de algo** to let somebody
   know about something
   Le avisé del problema. I let him know about
   the problem.
   Me avisaron que llegarían tarde. They told
   me they would be late.
2 **to warn**
   Les avisé del peligro que corrían. I warned
   them about the danger they were in.
3 **to call**
   avisar al médico to call the doctor

el **aviso** *masc noun*
1 **warning**
   El profesor ya le ha dado tres avisos. The
   teacher has already given him three
   warnings.
   sin previo aviso without prior warning
2 **notice**
   hasta nuevo aviso until further notice
3 **Último aviso para los pasajeros del vuelo ...**
   Last call for passengers on flight ...

la **avispa** *fem noun*
   wasp

la **axila** *fem noun*
   armpit

♂ **ayer** *adverb*
   yesterday
   antes de ayer the day before yesterday

♂ la **ayuda** *fem noun*
1 **help**
   ir en ayuda de alguien to go to somebody's
   help
2 **aid** (to a country, etc)

el & la **ayudante** *masc & fem noun*
   helper, assistant

♂ **ayudar** *verb* [17]
   to help
   ¿En qué puedo ayudarle? How can I help
   you?

♂ el **ayuntamiento** *masc noun*
1 **town council**
2 **city council**
3 **town hall**

♂ la **azafata** *fem noun*
1 **flight attendant**
2 **trade fair attendant**

el **azar** *masc noun*
1 **chance**
   por azar by chance
2 **al azar** at random

el **azote** *masc noun*
   smack

la **azotea** *fem noun*
   (flat) roof

♂ el & la **azúcar** *masc or fem noun*
   sugar
   un terrón de azúcar a sugar lump
   • el **azúcar blanco** white sugar
   • el **azúcar de caña** cane sugar
   • el **azúcar glas**, el **azúcar glaseado** icing
     sugar
   • el **azúcar moreno** brown sugar

   WORD TIP The compounds with *azúcar* can also
   be feminine.

el **azucarero** *masc noun*
   sugar bowl

♂ **azul** *masc & fem adjective* ▷ see **azul** *noun*
   blue
   ojos azules blue eyes

♂ el **azul** *masc noun* ▷ see **azul** *adj*
   blue
   • el **azul celeste** sky blue
   • el **azul claro** light blue
   • el **azul marino** navy blue

el **azulejo** *masc noun*
   tile

a
b
c
d
e
f
g
h
i
j
k
l
m
n
ñ
o
p
q
r
s
t
u
v
w
x
y
z

B b

la **baca** *fem noun*
  luggage-rack

♂ el **bacalao** *masc noun*
  cod

♂ el **bachillerato** *masc noun*
  Bachillerato (*the two-year secondary education course leading to university entrance*)

la **baguette** *fem noun*
  baguette, **French stick**

Bahamas *plural fem noun*
  las Bahamas the Bahamas
  las islas Bahamas the Bahama Islands

bahameño *masc adjective & noun*,
bahameña *fem adjective & noun*
1 **Bahamian**
2 un bahameño, una bahameña
  Bahamian (*person*)

> **WORD TIP** Adjectives and nouns for nationality and regional origin do not have capital letters in Spanish.

la **bahía** *fem noun*
  bay

♂ **bailar** *verb* [17]
  to dance
  bailar flamenco to do flamenco dancing

el **bailarín** *masc noun*, la **bailarina** *fem*
  dancer

el **baile** *masc noun*
1 **dance**
2 **dancing**
  una clase de baile a dancing class

> **mini info** *baile*
>
> En España hay muchos bailes tradicionales pero el flamenco, una combinación de guitarra, canto y baile es el más famoso; hoy también la salsa y los ritmos latinos se bailan por todo el mundo.

♂ **bajar** *verb* [17]
1 **to bring down**
  ¿Puedes bajarme el abrigo? Could you bring down my coat?
2 (*Computers*) **to download** (*a program, a file*)
3 **to take down**
  Baja las maletas a recepción. Take the suitcases down to reception.
4 **to go down**
  El ascensor está bajando. The lift's going down.
  Bajamos por las escaleras. We went down the stairs.

Baje por esta calle hasta llegar a la plaza. Go down this street until you get to the square (*formal use*).
5 **to come down**
  ¡Ya bajo! I'm coming down!
6 **to fall** (*temperatures, prices*)
7 **to turn down** (*the volume*)
  Baja la tele. Turn the television down.
8 **to lower** (*a blind*)
9 **to reduce** (*prices*)

bajarse *reflexive verb* [17]
  bajarse de un coche to get out of a car
  Se bajó de la bicicleta. He got off the bike.

♂ **bajo** *masc adjective*, **baja** *fem*
  ▷ **see bajo** *adv, noun, prep*
1 **short**
  Soy bastante bajo I'm quite short (*boy speaking*).
  Soy bastante baja I'm quite short (*girl speaking*).
2 **low**
  Los precios están bajos. Prices are low.
  Pon la música baja. Put the music on low.

♂ **bajo** *adverb* ▷ **see bajo** *adj, noun, prep*
1 **low**
  volar bajo to fly low
2 **quietly**
  hablar bajo to speak quietly

♂ **bajo** *preposition* ▷ **see bajo** *adj, adv, noun*
1 **under**
  bajo los árboles under the trees
2 La temperatura está bajo cero. The temperature's below zero.

el **bajo** *masc noun* ▷ **see bajo** *adj, adv, prep*
  ground floor

la **bala** *fem noun*
  bullet

el **balancín** *masc noun*
1 **seesaw**
2 **swing seat**
3 **rocking chair**

la **balanza** *fem noun*
  scales

balbucear *verb* [17]
  to stammer

♂ el **balcón** *masc noun*
  balcony

la **baldosa** *fem noun*
  tile

las **Baleares** *plural fem noun*
  las islas Baleares the Balearic Islands

la **ballena** *fem noun*
  whale

el **ballet** *masc noun*
  ballet

el **balón** *masc noun*
  ball
  un balón de fútbol a football

♪ el **baloncesto** *masc noun*
  basketball

el **balonmano** *masc noun*
  handball

el **balonvolea** *masc noun*
  volleyball

la **balsa** *fem noun*
1 raft
2 pond

la **banca** *fem noun*
  banking

el **banco** *masc noun*
1 bench (*in a park*)
2 pew (*in church*)
3 bank (*for loans, savings*)
  Trabaja en un banco. She works in a bank.

la **banda** *fem noun*
1 band (*of musicians*)
2 gang (*of criminals*)
• la **banda sonora** soundtrack

la **bandeja** *fem noun*
  tray

la **bandera** *fem noun*
  flag

la **banderilla** *fem noun*
  banderilla (*a decorated dart used in
  bullfighting*)

el **bandido** *masc noun*, la **bandida** *fem*
  bandit

el **banquero** *masc noun*, la **banquera** *fem*
  banker

la **banqueta** *fem noun*
  stool

el **banquete** *masc noun*
  banquet
  un banquete de bodas a wedding banquet

♪ el **bañador** *masc noun*
1 swimming trunks

2 swimming costume

♪ **bañar** *verb* [17]
  bañar a un bebé to bath a baby

bañarse *reflexive verb* [17]
1 to have a bath
  Voy a bañarme esta noche. I'm going to
  have a bath tonight.
2 to have a swim
  ¿Te apetece bañarte? Do you fancy going
  for a swim?

♪ la **bañera** *fem noun*
  bath (*bathtub*)

♪ el **baño** *masc noun*
1 bathroom
  ¿Dónde está el baño? Where's the
  bathroom?
2 bath
  darse un baño to have a bath
  Voy a darme un baño. I'm going to have a
  bath.
3 swim
  darse un baño to go for a swim
  ¿Te apetece darte un baño? Do you fancy
  going for a swim?

♪ el **bar** *masc noun*
  bar

la **baraja** *fem noun*
  pack of cards

barajar *verb* [17]
  to shuffle (*a pack of cards*)

la **barandilla** *fem noun*
  rail

la **baratija** *fem noun*
  knick-knack

♪ **barato** *masc adjective*, **barata** *fem*
  cheap
  Es muy barato. It's very cheap.

la **barba** *fem noun*
  beard
  afeitarse la barba to shave off your beard
  dejarse barba to grow a beard
  Voy a dejarme barba. I'm going to grow a
  beard.

la **barbacoa** *fem noun*
  barbecue

barbadense *masc & fem adjective & noun*
1 Barbadian
2 un & una barbadense Barbadian (*person*)

WORD TIP Adjectives and nouns for nationality
and regional origin do not have capital letters in
Spanish.

a
b
c
d
e
f
g
h
i
j
k
l
m
n
ñ
o
p
q
r
s
t
u
v
w
x
y
z

Barbados *masc noun*
Barbados

♂ la **barbaridad** *fem noun*
1 atrocity
2 (*saying something is very bad*) **Nos cobraron una barbaridad.** They charged us a fortune.
3 **Eso es una barbaridad.** That's far too much.
4 **Deja de decir barbaridades.** Stop talking nonsense.
5 **¡Qué barbaridad!** That's terrible!

el **barbero** *masc noun*
barber

la **barbilla** *fem noun*
chin

la **barca** *fem noun*
boat
• la **barca de pesca** fishing boat
• la **barca de remos** rowing boat

el **Barça** *masc noun*
(*informal*) **Barcelona Football Club**

Barcelona *fem noun*
Barcelona

♂ el **barco** *masc noun*
1 boat
viajar en barco to travel by boat
2 ship
• el **barco de guerra** warship
• el **barco de pesca** fishing boat

el **barniz** *masc noun*
varnish
• el **barniz de uñas** nail varnish

el **barómetro** *masc noun*
barometer

♂ la **barra** *fem noun*
1 rail (*for clothes*)
2 bar
Nos sirvieron en la barra. They served us at the bar.
• la **barra de jabón** bar of soap
• la **barra de labios** lipstick
• la **barra de pan** baguette

barrer *verb* [18]
to sweep

la **barrera** *fem noun*
barrier

♂ la **barriga** *fem noun*
stomach, tummy
tener dolor de barriga to have stomachache
Tengo dolor de barriga. I have stomachache.

el **barril** *masc noun*
barrel

♂ el **barrio** *masc noun*
area (*of a town*)
• los **barrios bajos** the slums

el **barro** *masc noun*
1 mud
lleno de barro covered in mud
2 clay (*for making pots*)

los **bártulos** *plural masc noun*
(*informal*) **stuff**, **things**
Llévate todos tus bártulos. Take all your stuff away.

basar *verb* [17]
to base
basar algo en algo to base something on something
En eso baso mi opinión. I base my views on that.

basarse *reflexive verb* [17]
¿En qué te basas para decir eso? What basis do you have for saying that?

la **base** *fem noun*
1 base
2 **a base de** by
Lo aprendió a base de repetirlo. He learnt it by repeating it.
• la **base de datos** database
• la **base de maquillaje** foundation (*make-up*)

básico *masc adjective*, **básica** *fem*
basic

♂ **bastante** *masc & fem adjective*
▷ see **bastante** *adv, pron*
1 enough
Tenemos bastante pan. We've got enough bread.
No tenemos bastantes sillas. We don't have enough chairs.
2 quite a lot of
bastante gente quite a lot of people
Bebimos bastante café. We drank quite a lot of coffee.
Compramos bastantes regalos. We bought quite a lot of presents.

WORD TIP *bastante* takes *-s* in the plural when it is an adjective.

bastante *adverb, pronoun*
▷ see **bastante** *adj*
1 enough
Con esto tenemos bastante. We have enough with this.
Compramos bastante para toda la semana.

We bought enough for the whole week.
¿Has comido bastante? Have you eaten enough?

2 quite
Estaba bastante contenta. She was quite happy.
Ha mejorado bastante. He's improved quite a lot.

> **WORD TIP** *bastante* does not change when it is an adverb or pronoun.

bastar *verb* [17]
1 to be enough
Con eso basta. That's enough.
¡Ya basta! That's enough!
2 Basta con preguntarle. You just need to ask him.

el **bastón** *masc noun*
walking stick

el **bastoncillo** *masc noun*
cotton bud

♪ la **basura** *fem noun*
1 rubbish
Hay que sacar la basura. We must put the rubbish out.
2 dustbin, bin
tirar algo a la basura to put something in the dustbin
Tíralo a la basura. Throw it in the dustbin.

el **basurero** *masc noun*
▷ see **basurero** *noun*
rubbish tip

el **basurero** *masc noun*, la **basurera** *fem*
▷ see **basurero** *masc noun*
refuse collector

la **bata** *fem noun*
1 dressing gown
2 una bata de médico a white doctor's coat

la **batalla** *fem noun*
battle

el **bate** *masc noun*
bat

la **batería** *fem noun* ▷ see **batería** *masc & fem noun*
1 battery (*for a car*)
2 drum kit
tocar la batería to play the drums

el & la **batería** *masc & fem noun*
▷ see **batería** *fem noun*
drummer

el **batido** *masc noun*
milkshake
un batido de fresa a strawberry milkshake

la **batidora** *fem noun*
food mixer

batir *verb* [19]
1 to beat (*in recipes*)
batir los huevos beat the eggs
2 to whip (*cream*)
3 (*Sports*) **batir un récord** to break a record

el **baúl** *masc noun*
trunk (*for clothes*)

el **bautismo** *masc noun*
baptism

bautizar *verb* [22]
to christen

el **bautizo** *masc noun*
christening

la **baya** *fem noun*
berry

la **bayeta** *fem noun*
cloth (*for wiping*)

el **bebé** *masc noun*
baby (*el bebé can be a girl or boy*)

♪ la **beber** *verb* [18]
to drink
¿Quieres beber algo? Do you want something to drink?

♪ la **bebida** *fem noun*
drink
una bebida refrescante a refreshing drink

la **beca** *fem noun*
1 grant
2 scholarship

♪ el **béisbol** *masc noun*
baseball

el **belén** *masc noun*
nativity scene, crib

belga *masc & fem adjective & noun*
1 Belgian
2 un & una belga Belgian (*person*)

> **WORD TIP** Adjectives and nouns for nationality and regional origin do not have capital letters in Spanish.

Bélgica *fem noun*
Belgium

la **belleza** *fem noun*
beauty

bello *masc adjective*, **bella** *fem*
beautiful

bendito *masc adjective*, **bendita** *fem*
1 blessed
2 holy (*water, bread in church*)

a
b
c
d
e
f
g
h
i
j
k
l
m
n
ñ
o
p
q
r
s
t
u
v
w
x
y
z

beneficiar *verb* [17]
  to benefit

el **beneficio** *masc noun*
  1 benefit
  2 profit

benéfico *masc adjective*, **benéfica** *fem*
  charity
  una organización benéfica a charity

la **berenjena** *fem noun*
  aubergine

el **berro** *masc noun*
  watercress

la **besamel** *fem noun*
  white sauce

besar *verb* [17]
  to kiss

♪ el **beso** *masc noun*
  kiss
  darle un beso a alguien to give someone a kiss
  Dame un beso. Give me a kiss.
  Me dio un beso en la mejilla. He gave me a kiss on the cheek.

bestia *masc & fem adjective*
  ▷ see **bestia** *noun*
  1 (*informal*) **ignorant**
  2 No seas bestia y habla bien. Don't be so rude, mind your language.

la **bestia** *fem noun* ▷ see **bestia** *adj*
  1 beast (*animal*)
  2 (*informal*) **idiot**
  Es una bestia, no sabe nada. He's so thick, he doesn't know a thing.
  3 brute

el **betún** *masc noun*
  shoe polish

la **Biblia** *fem noun*
  Bible

♪ la **biblioteca** *fem noun*
  library

el **bibliotecario** *masc noun*, la **bibliotecaria** *fem*
  librarian

el **bicho** *masc noun*
  creepy-crawly

la **bici** *fem noun*
  bike
  montar en bici to ride a bike
  Vine en bici. I came by bike.

♪ la **bicicleta** *fem noun*
  bicycle
  montar en bicicleta to ride a bicycle
  ¿Sabes montar en bicicleta? Can you ride a bicycle?

♪ el **bien** *masc noun* ▷ see **bien** *adv, adj*
  good
  la diferencia entre el bien y el mal the difference between good and evil

♪ **bien** *adverb, adjective* ▷ see **bien** *noun*
  1 well
  Lo has hecho muy bien. You've done it very well.
  No me siento bien. I don't feel well.
  '¿Cómo están tus padres?'—'Muy bien, gracias.' 'How are your parents?'—'Very well, thank you!'
  Hablas muy bien español. You speak very good Spanish.
  2 all right
  ¿Estás bien en esa silla? Are you all right in that chair?
  Así está bien. It's all right like this.
  3 nice
  Huele bien. It smells nice.
  Sabe bien. It tastes nice.
  4 properly
  No funciona bien. It doesn't work properly.
  5 (*in exclamations*) ¡Bien! That's right!
  ¡Bien hecho! Well done!
  ¡Muy bien! All right!, Ok!

el **bienestar** *masc noun*
  welfare

la **bienvenida** *fem noun*
  ▷ see **bienvenido** *adj*
  welcome
  dar la bienvenida a alguien to welcome somebody
  Le dieron una cálida bienvenida. She was given a warm welcome.

♪ **bienvenido** *masc adjective*, **bienvenida** *fem* ▷ see **bienvenida** *noun*
  welcome
  ¡Bienvenido! Welcome! (*speaking to one person*)
  ¡Bienvenidos! Welcome! (*speaking to two or more people*)
  Aquí siempre sois bienvenidos. You're always welcome here (*familiar form*).

el **bigote** *masc noun*
  moustache

el **bikini** *masc noun*
  bikini

bilingüe *masc & fem adjective*
bilingual

el **billar** *masc noun*
1 **billiards**
2 **pool**
3 **snooker**

los **billares** *plural masc noun*
amusement arcade

♂ el **billete** *masc noun*
1 **note** (*money*)
un billete de cincuenta euros a fifty-euro note
2 **ticket**
un billete de tren a train ticket
• el **billete de banco** bank note
• el **billete de ida** single ticket
• el **billete de ida y vuelta** return ticket
• el **billete sencillo** single ticket

la **billetera** *fem noun*
wallet

el **billetero** *masc noun*
wallet

la **biografía** *fem noun*
biography

la **biología** *fem noun*
biology

el **biólogo** *masc noun*, la **bióloga** *fem*
biologist

el **biquini** *masc noun*
bikini

el **bisabuelo** *masc noun*, la **bisabuela** *fem*
1 **great-grandfather**
2 **great-grandmother**
3 mis bisabuelos my great-grandparents

el **bisnieto** *masc noun*, la **bisnieta** *fem*
1 **great-grandson**
2 **great-granddaughter**
3 mis bisnietos my great-grandchildren

♂ el **bistec** *masc noun*
steak

el **bizcocho** *masc noun*
sponge cake

♂ **blanco** *masc adjective*, **blanca** *fem*
▷ see **blanco** noun
white
una bandera blanca a white flag

el **blanco** *masc noun* ▷ see **blanco** adj
1 (*Colour*) **white**
2 un blanco a white man
una blanca a white woman

3 **target**
dar en el blanco to hit the target

blando *masc adjective*, **blanda** *fem*
1 **soft**
un colchón blando a soft mattress
La mantequilla se ha puesto blanda. The butter's gone soft.
2 **tender** (*meat*)
3 **soft** (*person*)

WORD TIP *blando* does not mean *bland* in English; for the meaning of *bland* see ▷ SOSO.

el **bloc** *masc noun*
writing pad

♂ el **bloque** *masc noun*
block
un bloque de pisos a block of flats

bloquear *verb* [17]
to block
Un camión bloqueaba la calle. A lorry was blocking the street.

♂ la **blusa** *fem noun*
blouse

♂ **bobo** *masc adjective*, **boba** *fem*
(*informal*) **silly**
Eres bobo. You are silly.

♂ la **boca** *fem noun*
1 **mouth**
No abrió la boca en toda la tarde. He didn't say a word all afternoon.
2 (*in expressions*) **boca abajo** face down (*cards, photographs*)
boca arriba face up (*cards, photographs*)
Pon el vaso boca arriba. Put the glass the right way up.
• la **boca de incendios** fire hydrant
• la **boca de metro** entrance to the underground (railway)
• la **boca de riego** irrigation hydrant

♂ la **bocacalle** *fem noun*
side street
Es la segunda bocacalle a la derecha. It's the second turning on the right.

♂ el **bocadillo** *masc noun*
1 **sandwich** (*made with French bread and no butter*)
un bocadillo de queso a cheese baguette
2 **speech bubble** (*in a cartoon*)

el **bocado** *masc noun*
1 **mouthful** (of food)
2 **bite to eat**

la **bocata** *fem noun*
sandwich

a b c d e f g h i j k l m n ñ o p q r s t u v w x y z

♂ indicates key words

la **bocatería** *fem noun*
  sandwich bar

el **bochorno** *masc noun*
1 Hoy hace bochorno. It's really muggy today.
2 **embarrassment**
  ¡Qué bochorno pasamos! We were so embarrassed!
  Fue un bochorno. It was really embarrassing.

la **bocina** *fem noun*
  horn (*of a car*)

♂ la **boda** *fem noun*
  wedding
  • las **bodas de oro** golden wedding
  • las **bodas de plata** silver wedding

♂ la **bodega** *fem noun*
1 **cellar**
2 **wine merchant's**
3 **wine bar**

la **bofetada** *fem noun*
  slap

el **bofetón** *masc noun*
  slap

la **boina** *fem noun*
  beret

la **bola** *fem noun*
1 **ball**
2 **scoop** (*of ice cream*)
3 (*informal*) **fib**
  contar bolas to tell fibs
  • la **bola de billar** billiard ball
  • la **bola de nieve** snowball

la **bolera** *fem noun*
  bowling alley

el **boletín** *masc noun*
1 **bulletin**
2 **school report**
  • el **boletín informativo** news bulletin
  • el **boletín meteorológico** weather report

el **boleto** *masc noun*
1 (*Latin America*) **ticket** (*in buses, cinemas, etc*)
2 **ticket** (*for raffles, lotteries, etc*)
3 **coupon** (*for the football pools*)

el **boli** *masc noun*
  (*informal*) **ballpoint pen**

♂ el **bolígrafo** *masc noun*
  ballpoint pen

Bolivia *fem noun*
  Bolivia

boliviano *masc adjective & noun*, **boliviana** *fem adjective & noun*
1 **Bolivian**
2 un boliviano, una boliviana Bolivian (*person*)

WORD TIP Adjectives and nouns for nationality and regional origin do not have capital letters in Spanish.

el **bollo** *masc noun*
  bun

♂ la **bolsa** *fem noun*
  bag
  una bolsa de palomitas a bag of popcorn
  mi bolsa de la compra my shopping bag
  • la **bolsa de la basura** bin liner
  • la **bolsa de plástico** plastic bag
  • la **bolsa (de valores)** the stock exchange
  • la **bolsa de viaje** travel bag

el **bolsillo** *masc noun*
  pocket
  un libro de bolsillo a paperback book
  un diccionario de bolsillo a pocket dictionary

♂ el **bolso** *masc noun*
  handbag
  Me robaron el bolso. My handbag was stolen.
  • el **bolso de mano**, el **bolso de viaje** overnight bag

la **bomba** *fem noun*
1 **bomb**
  Pusieron una bomba en un restaurante. They planted a bomb in a restaurant.
  lanzar una bomba to drop a bomb
2 (*informal*) pasarlo bomba to have a terrific time
  Lo pasamos bomba. We had a terrific time.
3 **pump**
  • la **bomba atómica** atomic bomb
  • la **bomba de agua** water pump
  • la **bomba de bicicleta** bicycle pump

el **bombardeo** *masc noun*
  bombing
  el bombardeo de Guernica the bombing of Guernica

el **bombero** *masc noun*, la **bombera** *fem*
  firefighter

la **bombilla** *fem noun*
  light bulb
  Se ha fundido la bombilla. The bulb's gone.

el **bombón** *masc noun*
  chocolate
  una caja de bombones a box of chocolates

bonachón *masc adj*, **bonachona** *fem*
(*informal*) **kind**

la **bondad** *fem noun*
kindness

♪ **bonito** *masc adjective*, **bonita** *fem*
pretty
un pueblo muy bonito a very pretty village
una falda muy bonita a nice skirt
Es una chica muy bonita. She's a very pretty girl.

el **bono** *masc noun*
voucher

boquiabierto *masc adjective*,
boquiabierta *fem*
astonished
Me quedé boquiabierto. I was astonished.

el **bordado** *masc noun*
embroidery

bordar *verb* [17]
to embroider

borde *masc & fem adjective*
▷ see **borde** *noun*
(*informal*) **stroppy**
Se puso muy borde conmigo. He got very stroppy with me.

el **borde** *masc noun* ▷ see **borde** *adj*
1 **edge**
Me di con el borde de la mesa. I bumped myself on the edge of the table.
Se acercó al borde del andén. He went up to the edge of the platform.
2 **rim** (*of a glass or cup*)
3 llenar algo hasta el borde to fill something to the brim
4 el borde del río the river bank
5 al borde de la guerra on the brink of war
al borde de las lágrimas on the verge of tears

bordear *verb* [17]
to go round (*the edge of something*)
Bordeamos el lago. We went round the lake.

el **bordillo** *masc noun*
kerb

bordo *masc noun*
a bordo on board (*a plane, boat*)
Subimos a bordo. We went on board.

la **borrachera** *fem noun*
cogerse una borrachera to get drunk

borracho *masc adjective*, **borracha** *fem*
▷ see **borracho** *noun*
drunk
Estaban borrachos. They were drunk.

el **borracho** *masc noun*, la **borracha** *fem*
▷ see **borracho** *adj*
drunk

el **borrador** *masc noun*
1 **rough draft**
Hacedlo primero en borrador. Do it in rough first.
Usa papel de borrador. Use rough paper.
2 **board rubber** (*eraser*)

borrar *verb* [17]
1 **to rub out** (*a pencil mark or word*)
2 **to erase** (*a track or tape*)
3 **to clean** (*the blackboard*)
4 **to delete** (*in wordprocessing*)

borrarse *reflexive verb* [17]
to fade
Se ha borrado el nombre. The name has faded.

la **borrasca** *fem noun*
1 **area of low pressure**
2 **storm**

el **borrón** *masc noun*
blot

borroso *masc adjective*, **borrosa** *fem*
1 **blurred** (*image, photograph*)
2 **vague** (*memory*)

♪ el **bosque** *masc noun*
1 **wood**
2 **forest**
el bosque ecuatorial the tropical rainforest

bostezar *verb* [22]
to yawn

♪ la **bota** *fem noun*
boot
• las **botas de agua** wellingtons
• las **botas de esquiar** ski boots

la **botadura** *fem noun*
launch (*of a ship*)

la **botánica** *fem noun* ▷ see **botánico** *adj*
botany

botánico *masc adjective*, **botánica** *fem*
▷ see **botánica** *noun*
botanic

botar *verb* [17]
to launch (*a ship*)

la **botavara** *fem noun*
boom (*of boat*)

a
b
c
d
e
f
g
h
i
j
k
l
m
n
ñ
o
p
q
r
s
t
u
v
w
x
y
z

a
b
c
d
e
f
g
h
i
j
k
l
m
n
ñ
o
p
q
r
s
t
u
v
w
x
y
z

el **bote** *masc noun*
1 **boat**
2 **jar**
  un bote de aceitunas a jar of olives
3 **can**
  un bote de barniz a can of varnish
4 **jump**
  pegar un bote to jump
  Pegué un bote de alegría. I jumped for joy.
- el **bote de pesca** fishing boat
- el **bote de remos** rowing boat
- el **bote salvavidas** lifeboat

la **botella** *fem noun*
  bottle

el **botijo** *masc noun*
  drinking jug (*with a spout: with practice you can drink the water as it spurts out in an arc*)

el **botiquín** *masc noun*
  medicine cabinet
- el **botiquín de primeros auxilios** first aid kit

el **botón** *masc noun*
  button (*on clothes, a machine*)
  coser un botón to sew on a button
  Se me ha caído un botón. I've lost a button.
  el botón de grabar the record button
  Aprieta este botón. Press this button.

el **boxeador** *masc noun*, la **boxeadora** *fem*
  boxer

boxear *verb* [17]
  to box

el **boxeo** *masc noun*
  boxing
  un combate de boxeo a boxing match

las **bragas** *plural fem noun*
  knickers, panties
  un par de bragas a pair of knickers

la **bragueta** *fem noun*
  flies (*in trousers*)

Brasil *masc noun*
  Brazil

brasileño *masc adjective & noun*, **brasileña** *fem adjective & noun*
1 **Brazilian**
2 un brasileño, una brasileña Brazilian (*person*)

WORD TIP Adjectives and nouns for nationality and regional origin do not have capital letters in Spanish.

bravo *masc adjective*, **brava** *fem*
▷ **see bravo** *excl*
fierce (*animal*)

bravo *exclamation* ▷ **see bravo** *adj*
  ¡Bravo! Well done!, Bravo!

el **brazo** *masc noun*
  arm
  cruzar los brazos to cross your arms
  Me cogió del brazo. He took me by the arm.
  Iban del brazo. They were walking along arm in arm.
  Cogió al niño en brazos. He picked the child up in his arms.
  Yo llevaba al bebé en brazos. I was carrying the baby in my arms.

el **brecol** *masc noun*
  broccoli

breve *masc & fem adjective*
  short
  una pausa breve a short pause

brevemente *adverb*
  briefly

el **brezo** *masc noun*
  heather

el **bribón** *masc noun*, la **bribona** *fem*
  rascal

el **bricolaje** *masc noun*
  DIY

el **brillante** *masc noun* ▷ **see brillante** *adj*
  diamond

brillante *masc & fem adjective*
  ▷ **see brillante** *noun*
1 **shiny**
2 **bright** (*light or colour*)

brillar *verb* [17]
1 **to shine**
2 **to sparkle**

brindar *verb* [17]
  to toast

el **brindis** *masc noun*
  toast
  hacer un brindis por alguien to drink a toast to somebody
  Hicieron un brindis por los novios. They drank a toast to the newly-weds.

la **brisa** *fem noun*
  breeze

el **británico** *masc adjective*, **británica** *fem*
  ▷ **see británico** *noun*
  British

♂ un **británico** *masc noun*, una **británica** *fem* ▷ see **británico** *adj*

1 **British man**
2 **British woman**
3 los británicos **the British**

> **WORD TIP** Adjectives and nouns for nationality and regional origin do not have capital letters in Spanish.

la **brocha** *fem noun*

1 **paintbrush**
2 brocha de afeitar **shaving brush**

el **broche** *masc noun*
> **brooch**

♂ la **broma** *fem noun*
> **joke**
> bromas aparte **joking apart**
> Lo he dicho en broma. **I was joking.**
> ¡Ni en broma! **No way!**
> hacerle una broma a alguien **to play a joke on somebody**
> Siempre le hacen bromas a su hermano. **They're always playing jokes on her brother.**

bromear *verb* [17]
> **to joke**

bromista *masc & fem adjective*
> ▷ see **bromista** *noun*
> Es muy bromista. **He's always joking.**

el & la **bromista** *masc & fem noun*
> ▷ see **bromista** *adj*
> Es un bromista. **He's always joking.**

la **bronca** *fem noun*

1 (*informal*) armar una bronca **to kick up a fuss**
> Si no me devuelven el dinero, voy a armar una bronca. **If they don't give me the money back I'm going to kick up a fuss.**
2 **telling-off**
> echar una bronca a alguien **to tell somebody off**
> La profe te va a echar una buena bronca. **Teacher's going to give you a real telling-off.**

bronceado *masc adjective*, **bronceada** *fem*
> **suntanned**

el **bronceador** *masc noun*
> **suntan lotion**

♂ **broncearse** *reflexive verb* [17]
> **to get a suntan**

la **bronquitis** *fem noun*
> **bronchitis**

el **brote** *masc noun*
> **bud**

el **brujo** *masc noun*, la **bruja** *fem*

1 **wizard**
2 **witch**

la **brújula** *fem noun*
> **compass**

la **bruma** *fem noun*
> **mist**

bruto *masc adjective*, **bruta** *fem*

1 **ignorant**
2 **rude**
> Es muy bruto, ¡dice unas cosas! **He's so rude, he says terrible things!**
3 ¡Qué bruto! ¡cómo trata a su hijo! **What a brute he is! What a way to treat his child!**

el **buceador** *masc noun*, la **buceadora** *fem*
> **diver**

bucear *verb* [17]
> **to dive**

el **budismo** *masc noun*
> (*Religion*) **Buddhism**

budista *masc & fem adjective & noun*

1 **Buddhist**
2 un & una budista **Buddhist**

> **WORD TIP** Adjectives and nouns for religion do not have capital letters in Spanish.

♂ **buen** *adjective* ▷ **bueno**

♂ **bueno** *adverb* ▷ see **bueno** *adj*
> **okay**, **well**, **right**
> '¿Quieres venir?'—'Bueno.' **'Do you want to come?'—'Okay.'**
> Bueno, no importa. **Well, it doesn't matter.**
> Bueno, no estoy segura. **Well, I'm not sure.**
> Bueno, ya basta. **Right, that's enough.**

♂ **bueno** *masc adjective*, **buena** *fem*
> ▷ see **bueno** *adv*

1 **good**
> de buena calidad **good quality**
> Es muy buena persona. **She's a very good person.**
> Es muy buen amigo mío. **He's a very good friend of mine.**
> ser bueno para algo **to be good at something** (*a skill*)
> Es muy buena para las matemáticas. **She's very good at maths.**
> ¡Buen viaje! **Have a good journey!**
2 **nice**
> ¡Qué buen tiempo hace! **Isn't the weather nice!** ▸▸

a
b
c
d
e
f
g
h
i
j
k
l
m
n
ñ
o
p
q
r
s
t
u
v
w
x
y
z

El pastel estaba muy bueno. The cake was very nice.
¡Está buenísimo! It's delicious!

WORD TIP *bueno* becomes **buen** before a masculine singular noun.

- **buenos días** good morning
- **buenas noches** good evening, goodnight
- **buenas tardes** good afternoon, good evening

la **bufanda** *fem noun*
scarf

bufar *verb* [17]
to snort

el **bufet** *masc noun*
buffet

el **bufón** *masc noun*
clown (*silly person*)

la **buhardilla** *fem noun*
attic

el **búho** *masc noun*
owl

la **bujía** *fem noun*
spark plug

el **bulto** *masc noun*
1 **piece of luggage**
¿Cuántos bultos llevas? How many pieces of luggage do you have?
2 **bag**
¿Te llevo los bultos? Shall I carry your bags?
Iba cargada de bultos. She was carrying lots of bags.
3 **shape**
Vi un bulto en la oscuridad. I saw a shape in the darkness.
4 **bulkiness**
5 **lump** (*in your body*)

el **bungalow** *masc noun*
cabin, chalet (*in holiday resorts*)

el **buñuelo** *masc noun*
fritter

el **buque** *masc noun*
ship
- el **buque de guerra** warship

la **burbuja** *fem noun*
1 **bubble**
2 una bebida sin burbujas a still drink
una bebida con burbujas a fizzy drink

burdo *masc adjective*, **burda** *fem*
coarse

burlarse *reflexive verb* [17]
burlarse de alguien to make fun of somebody
¡Deja de burlarte de mí! Stop making fun of me!

la **burocracia** *fem noun*
bureaucracy

la **burrada** *fem noun*
(*informal*) ¡Vaya burrada has dicho! What a stupid thing to say.
¡No hagas esa burrada! Don't do such a stupid thing.
Sólo dijo burradas. He just talked rubbish.

♫ **burro** *masc adjective*, **burra** *fem*
▷ see **burro** *noun*
stupid
¡Qué burra soy! How stupid of me! (*girl speaking*)

♫ el **burro** *masc noun*, la **burra** *fem*
▷ see **burro** *adj*
1 **donkey**
2 (*informal*) **idiot**
Es un burro. He's really stupid.

el **bus** *masc noun*
bus

la **busca** *fem noun*
search
ir en busca de algo to go in search of something
Fueron en busca del niño perdido. They went to search for the child.

el **buscador** *masc noun*
(*Computers*) **search engine**

♫ **buscar** *verb* [31]
1 **to look for**
¿Qué buscas? What are you looking for?
Mi hermana está buscando trabajo. My sister's looking for a job.
Estoy buscando un ayudante. I'm looking for an assistant
2 **to look**
Si no lo encuentras aquí, busca en la oficina. If you don't find it here, look in the office.
3 ir a buscar algo to go to pick up something
Mañana iré a buscar mis cosas. I'll go and pick up my things tomorrow.
4 ir a buscar a alguien to pick somebody up
Yo te iré a buscar al aeropuerto. I'll pick you up at the airport.

5 **ir a buscar a alguien** to go to get someone
Fueron a buscar a un médico. They went to
get a doctor.

la **búsqueda** *fem noun*
   search

ᵟ la **butaca** *fem noun*
1 **armchair**
2 **seat**
   una butaca de patio a seat in the stalls (*in a cinema or theatre*)

el **butano** *masc noun*
   butane gas
   una bombona de butano a bottle of butane gas

el **buzo** *masc noun*
   diver

ᵟ el **buzón** *masc noun*
1 **letterbox**
2 **postbox**
   • el **buzón de voz** voice mail

a
b
c
d
e
f
g
h
i
j
k
l
m
n
ñ
o
p
q
r
s
t
u
v
w
x
y
z

C c

la **caballa** *fem noun*
mackerel

♂ el , **caballero** *masc noun*
1 **gentleman**
Es un verdadero caballero. He's a real gentleman.
2 **sir**
Caballero, ¿me deja pasar? Could you let me through, sir?
3 **Caballeros** Gents (*toilets*), men's clothing department (*in a store*)

♂ el **caballo** *masc noun*
1 **horse**
montar a caballo to ride a horse
2 **knight** (*in chess*)
3 **horse** (*in Spanish cards: equivalent to the queen*)
• el **caballo de carreras** racehorse

la **cabaña** *fem noun*
cabin

cabecear *verb* [17]
to head (*a ball in football*)

la **cabecera** *fem noun*
1 **headboard** (*of a bed*)
2 **head** (*of table*)
Se sentó a la cabecera de la mesa. He sat at the head of the table.

el **cabello** *masc noun*
hair
Tiene el cabello rubio. She has blonde hair.
• el **cabello liso** straight hair
• el **cabello rizado** curly hair

caber *verb* [33]
1 **caber en** to fit into
El monitor no cabe en la caja. The monitor doesn't fit into the box.
No cabemos en el coche. We won't fit into the car.
2 **No cabe nada más.** There's no room for anything else.
¿Caben estos libros en la maleta? Is there room for these books in the suitcase?
3 **caber por algo** to fit through something
No cabe por la puerta. It wouldn't fit through the door.

♂ la **cabeza** *fem noun*
1 **head**
Me duele la cabeza. I've got a headache.
lavarse la cabeza to wash your hair

Tengo que lavarme la cabeza. I've got to wash my hair.
2 **de cabeza** head first
tirarse al agua de cabeza to dive into the water head first
3 **cabeza abajo** upside down
El cuadro está cabeza abajo. The picture's upside down.
4 **a la cabeza de** at the head of
Iban a la cabeza de la manifestación. They were at the head of the demonstration.
• la **cabeza de ajo** bulb of garlic
• el & la **cabeza rapada** skinhead

♂ la **cabina** *fem noun*
1 **cab** (*of a lorry*)
2 **cockpit** (*of a plane*)
3 **cabin** (*on a plane, a boat*)
4 **booth** (*in a language lab*)
• la **cabina de teléfonos**, la **cabina telefónica** telephone box

el **cabo** *masc noun*
1 **end**
al cabo de after, at the end of
al cabo de una semana after one week
2 **end** (*of a piece of string*)
3 **cape** (*in geography*)
el **Cabo de Hornos** Cape Horn
4 **corporal**

la **cabra** *fem noun*
goat

cabré, **cabría**, **etc** *verb* ▷ caber

♂ el **cacahuete** *masc noun*
peanut

el **cacao** *masc noun*
1 **cocoa** (*hot drink*)
2 **lipsalve**

la **cacerola** *fem noun*
saucepan, **pan**

el **cachete** *masc noun*
1 **slap**
2 **cheek**

el **cachorro** *masc noun*, la **cachorra** *fem*
puppy

♂ **cada** *invariable adjective*
1 **each**
un alumno de cada clase a pupil from each class

Hay diez para cada uno. There are ten for each one.

2 every
cada día every day
Me llama cada tres días. She phones me every three days.

3 cada vez más ... more and more
Viene cada vez más. She comes more and more.
Se ponía cada vez más rojo. He was going redder and redder.
Juega cada vez mejor. She's playing better and better.
Canta cada vez peor. He sings worse and worse.
Se parecen cada vez más. They look more and more alike.

4 cada vez menos ... less and less
Nos visita cada vez menos. She visits us less and less.
Es cada vez menos gordo. He's getting less and less fat.
Se parecen cada vez menos. They look less and less alike.

WORD TIP *cada* never changes.

ᔔla **cadena** *fem noun*
1 chain
una cadena de hierro an iron chain
tirar de la cadena to flush the toilet
2 channel (*on the TV*)
Lo ponen en la segunda cadena. They're showing it on Channel Two.
3 station (*on the radio*)
4 cadenas *plural* snow chains
• la **cadena antirrobo** bicycle chain
• la **cadena de supermercados** supermarket chain
• la **cadena musical** hi-fi system
• la **cadena perpetua** life imprisonment

ᔔla **cadera** *fem noun*
hip

caducar *verb* [31]
to expire (*credit cards, cheques, etc*)
Caduca a los tres años. It expires in three years.

ᔔ**caer** *verb* [34]
1 to fall (*accidentally*)
El jarrón cayó al suelo. The vase fell to the ground.
2 dejar caer algo to drop something (*on purpose*)
Dejé caer la pelota. I dropped the ball.
3 caerle bien a alguien to like someone
Tu hermano me cae bien. I like your brother.

4 caerle mal a alguien to dislike someone
Ana me cae mal. I don't like Ana.

caerse *reflexive verb* [34]
1 to fall
Me caí por las escaleras. I fell down the stairs.
Se cayó de la bici. He fell off his bike.
Tropecé y me caí. I tripped and fell down.
2 caérsele algo a alguien to drop something (*by accident*)
Se me cayó el plato. I dropped the plate.

ᔔel **café** *masc noun*
1 cafe (*place*)
2 coffee
¿Quieres un café? Do you want a cup of coffee?
• el **café con leche** white coffee
• el **café cortado** coffee with a dash of milk
• el **café descafeinado** decaffeinated coffee
• el **café solo** black coffee

ᔔla **cafetera** *fem noun*
coffee maker

ᔔla **cafetería** *fem noun*
cafe

caído *masc adjective*, **caída** *fem*
fallen

caiga, **caigo**, **etc** *verb* ▷ **caer**

el **caimán** *masc noun*
alligator

ᔔla **caja** *fem noun*
1 box
2 crate
una caja de naranjas a crate of oranges
3 checkout (*in a supermarket*)
Pague en caja. Pay at the checkout.
4 till (*in a shop*)
• la **caja de ahorros** savings bank
• la **caja de cambios** gearbox
• la **caja de cartón** cardboard box
• la **caja de las herramientas** toolbox
• la **caja fuerte** safe (*in a bank*)

ᔔel **cajero** *masc noun*, la **cajera** *fem*
1 cashier
2 checkout operator
• el **cajero automático** cash dispenser

el **cajón** *masc noun*
drawer

ᔔel **calabacín** *masc noun*
courgette

_ð_ el **calamar** _masc noun_
squid
calamares a la romana squid rings fried in batter

el **calambre** _masc noun_
1 **cramp**
Me dio un calambre. I got cramp.
2 **electric shock**
La lámpara me ha dado calambre. The lamp gave me an electric shock.

la **calamidad** _fem noun_
disaster

la **calavera** _fem noun_
skull

_ð_ el **calcetín** _masc noun_
sock
unos calcetines a pair of socks

la **calcomanía** _fem noun_
transfer (_sticker_)

_ð_ la **calculadora** _fem noun_
calculator

calcular _verb_ [17]
1 **to calculate**
1 **to work out**

el **caldo** _masc noun_
1 **stock**
2 **broth**
• el **caldo de verdura** vegetable soup

_ð_ la **calefacción** _fem noun_
heating
• la **calefacción central** central heating
• la **calefacción de gas** gas heating

el **calendario** _masc noun_
calendar

el **calentador** _masc noun_
1 **boiler**
2 **water heater**

calentar _verb_ [29]
1 **to heat (up)**
Voy a calentar la sopa. I'm going to heat the soup.
2 **to give off heat**
Esta estufa calienta mucho. This heater gives off a lot of heat.
3 **calentar los músculos** to warm up (_in sports_)

calentarse _reflexive verb_ [29]
to heat up

la **calidad** _fem noun_
quality
materiales de calidad high quality materials

productos de mala calidad poor quality products

calienta, **caliento**, **etc** _verb_ ▷ **calentar**

_ð_ **caliente** _masc & fem adjective_
1 **hot**
un baño caliente a hot bath
Los platos están muy calientes. The plates are very hot.
2 **warm**
En el salón se está más caliente. It's warmer in the living-room.

la **calificación** _fem noun_
mark
Obtuvo buenas calificaciónes. He got good marks.

callado _masc adjective_, **callada** _fem_
quiet
¡Estate callado! Be quiet!

_ð_ **callar** _verb_ [17]
to be quiet
Calla, no oigo. Be quiet, I can't hear.
¡Calla ya! Shut up!

callarse _reflexive verb_ [17]
to go quiet
Al verla todos se callaron. When they saw her everybody went quiet.
¡Cállate! Shut up!

_ð_ la **calle** _fem noun_
street (_in addresses, the word **calle** is shortened to 'C/'_)
una calle cortada a cul-de-sac
Calle Santa Isabel, C/ Santa Isabel Santa Isabel Street
• la **calle de sentido doble** two-way street
• la **calle de sentido único** one-way street

el **callejón** _masc noun_
alley
• el **callejón sin salida** dead end

la **calma** _fem noun_
calm
Hazlo con calma. Do it calmly.
mantener la calma to keep calm
La ciudad está en calma. The city is calm.

calmar _verb_ [17]
to calm down

calmarse _reflexive verb_ [17]
to calm down
Después de un rato me calmé. After a while I calmed down .

ᔔ el **calor** *masc noun*
1 heat
el calor de la estufa the heat of the stove
2 hacer calor to be hot (*weather, etc*)
Hace mucho calor. It's very hot.
¡Qué calor hace! It's so hot!
3 tener calor to be hot (*people, etc*)
Tengo mucho calor. I'm very hot.
▷ **frío**

ᔔ **caluroso** *masc adjective*, **calurosa** *fem*
hot (*day, place*)

ᔔ **calvo** *masc adjective*, **calva** *fem*
bald
quedarse calvo to go bald

ᔔ el **calzado** *masc noun*
footwear

ᔔ **calzar** *verb* [22]
¿Qué número calzas? What shoe size do you take?

ᔔ los **calzoncillos** *plural masc noun*
underpants
unos calzoncillos a pair of underpants

ᔔ la **cama** *fem noun*
bed
¡A la cama! Off to bed!
hacer la cama to make the bed
Tienes que hacer la cama. You must make your bed.
• la **cama de matrimonio** double bed
• la **cama elástica** trampoline
• la **cama individual** single bed
• las **camas gemelas** twin beds

la **cámara** *fem noun* ▷ see **cámara** *masc noun*
1 camera
2 camera woman
• la **cámara de vídeo** video camera
• la **cámara digital** digital camera
• la **cámara fotográfica** camera

el **cámara** *masc noun* ▷ see **cámara** *fem noun*
camera man

ᔔ el **camarero** *masc noun*, la **camarera** *fem*
1 waiter
2 waitress
• la **camarera de habitación** chambermaid

ᔔ el **camarón** *masc noun*
shrimp

ᔔ **cambiar** *verb* [17]
1 to change
Tengo que cambiar libras a euros. I must change pounds into euros.

El tiempo está cambiando. The weather is changing.
2 cambiar de to change
cambiar de idea to change your mind
cambiar de canal to change channels
Ha cambiado de trabajo. He's changed his job.
3 to exchange (*in a shop*)
Quiero cambiar estos zapatos. I want to exchange these shoes.
4 cambiar de casa to move house
5 cambiar algo a alguien to swap
Te cambio mi pluma por esa cinta. I'll swap my pen for that tape.

cambiarse *reflexive verb* [17]
1 to get changed
Voy a cambiarme. I'm going to get changed.
2 cambiarse de algo to change
Voy a cambiarme de ropa. I'm going to change my clothes.
Han cambiado de idea. They've changed their minds.
Nos cambiamos de casa el año pasado. We moved house last year.

ᔔ el **cambio** *masc noun*
1 change
un cambio a mejor a change for the better
Ha habido un cambio de planes. There's been a change of plan.
2 exchange (*in a shop*)
No se admiten cambios. Goods will not be exchanged.
3 change (*coins*)
¿Tienes cambio? Do you have any change?
Se ha equivocado al darme el cambio. You've given me the wrong change.
'Cambio' 'Bureau de change' (*for buying euros, etc*)
4 a cambio de in exchange for
Le di la mochila a cambio de su riñonera. I gave him the rucksack in exchange for the money belt.
• el **cambio de sentido** U-turn (*in driving*)

el **camello** *masc noun*
camel

la **camilla** *fem noun*
stretcher

ᔔ **caminar** *verb* [17]
to walk
Me gusta caminar. I like walking.

la **caminata** *fem noun*
long walk, **trek**

a
b
c
d
e
f
g
h
i
j
k
l
m
n
ñ
o
p
q
r
s
t
u
v
w
x
y
z

ᔔ indicates key words

el camino *masc noun*
1 **road**
Todos los caminos están cortados. All the roads are closed.
2 **path**
un camino por el bosque a path through the forest
3 **way**
¿Puede indicarme el camino a la estación? Could you tell me the way to the station? (*formal form*)
Yo sé el camino. I know the way.

el camión *masc noun*
1 **lorry**, **truck**
2 (*Mexico*) **bus**
• el **camión cisterna** petrol tanker
• el **camión de la mudanza** removal van

el camionero *masc noun*, la **camionera** *fem*
lorry driver, **truck driver**

la camioneta *fem noun*
van

la camisa *fem noun*
shirt

la camiseta *fem noun*
1 **T-shirt**
2 **vest**

el camisón *masc noun*
nightdress

el campamento *masc noun*
camp
Se han ido de campamento. They've gone camping.

la campana *fem noun*
bell
tocar la campana to ring the bell

la campaña *fem noun*
campaign
• la **campaña electoral** election campaign

el campeón *masc noun*, la **campeona** *fem*
champion
los campeones mundiales the world champions

el campeonato *masc noun*
championship

el campesino *masc noun*, la **campesina** *fem*
1 **country person**
2 **peasant**

el camping *masc noun*
campsite
ir de camping to go camping

el & la campista *masc & fem noun*
camper (*person*)

el campo *masc noun*
1 **country** (*not the city*)
una casa en el campo a house in the country
vivir en el campo to live in the country
2 **countryside**
El campo está muy bonito. The countryside is looking very pretty.
3 **field**
un campo de trigo a field of wheat
• el **campo de fútbol** football pitch

la cana *fem noun*
white hair
Le están saliendo canas. He's going grey.

Canadá *masc noun*
Canada

canadiense *masc & fem adjective*
▷ see **canadiense** *noun*
Canadian

un & una **canadiense** *masc & fem noun*
▷ see **canadiense** *adj*
Canadian

WORD TIP Adjectives and nouns for nationality and regional origin do not have capital letters in Spanish.

el canal *masc noun*
1 **channel** (*on the TV*)
No cambies de canal. Don't change channels.
2 **channel** (*for water*)
3 **canal**
• el **Canal de la Mancha** English Channel
• el **Canal de Panamá** Panama Canal

el canario *masc noun*
canary

canario *masc adjective & noun*, **canaria** *fem adjective & noun*
1 **of or from the Canary Islands**
2 un canario, una canaria Canary Islander

WORD TIP Adjectives and nouns for nationality and regional origin do not have capital letters in Spanish.

la canasta *fem noun*
(*Latin America*) **basket**

el canasto *masc noun*
basket (*usually with a lid*)

cancelar *verb* [17]
to cancel

el cáncer *masc noun*
cancer
Tiene cáncer. He's got cancer.

- el **cáncer de mama** breast cancer
- el **cáncer de piel** skin cancer

cáncer *masc & fem noun* ▷ see **cáncer, Cáncer** *noun*
Cancer (*sign of the zodiac*)
Soy cáncer. I'm Cancer.

WORD TIP Use a small letter in Spanish to say *I am Cancer*, etc with star signs.

Cáncer *masc noun* ▷ see **cáncer** *noun*
Cancer (*sign of the zodiac*)

ᔫ la **cancha** *fem noun*
1 **court** (*for tennis, basketball, etc*)
2 **ground** (*for football, hockey, etc*)

ᔫ la **canción** *fem noun*
song
- la **canción de cuna** lullaby

el **candado** *masc noun*
padlock

el **candelabro** *masc noun*
candlestick
un candelabro dorado a brass candlestick

el **candidato** *masc noun*, la **candidata** *fem*
candidate
el candidato a la presidencia the candidate for the presidency

la **canela** *fem noun*
cinnamon
- la **canela en polvo** ground cinnamon
- la **canela en rama** stick cinnamon

ᔫ el **cangrejo** *masc noun*
1 **crab**
2 **crayfish**

el **canguro** *masc noun* ▷ see **canguro** *masc & fem noun*
kangaroo

el & la **canguro** *masc & fem noun*
▷ see **canguro** *masc noun*
babysitter

la **canica** *fem noun*
marble
jugar a las canicas to play marbles

ᔫ la **canoa** *fem noun*
canoe

ᔫ **cansado** *masc adjective*, **cansada** *fem*
1 **tired**
Estoy muy cansado. I'm very tired.
2 **tiring**
Esperar es muy cansado. Waiting is very tiring.

ᔫ **cansar** *verb* [17]
1 **to make tired**
Le cansa andar. Walking makes him tired.
2 **to be tiring**
Es un trabajo que cansa mucho. It's a very tiring job.
3 **to be boring**
Esta música cansa un poco. This music's a bit boring.

cansarse *reflexive verb* [17]
1 **to get tired**
Se cansa muy fácilmente. He gets tired very easily.
2 **to get bored**
Me canso de repetir siempre lo mismo. I get bored always repeating the same thing.

el **Cantábrico** *masc noun*
el mar Cantábrico the Bay of Biscay (*on the north coast of Spain*)

ᔫ el & la **cantante** *masc & fem noun*
singer

ᔫ **cantar** *verb* [17]
to sing

el **canto** *masc noun*
singing

la **cantera** *fem noun*
quarry

ᔫ la **cantidad** *fem noun*
1 **amount**
una enorme cantidad de nieve a huge amount of snow
2 ¿Qué cantidad de vasos necesitamos? How many glasses do we need?
Mira la cantidad de comida que nos queda. See how much food is left over.
3 **tanta cantidad** so much
No pongas tanta cantidad de leche. Don't put so much milk in.
4 **cantidad de, cantidades de** lots of
Había cantidad de gente. There were lots of people.
'¿Hay flores?'—'Cantidades.' 'Are there flowers?'—'Loads.'
5 **sum**
una cantidad importante de dinero a large sum of money

ᔫ la **cantina** *fem noun*
1 **cafeteria**
2 **canteen**

la **caña** *fem noun*
1 **cane**
- la **caña de azúcar** sugar cane
- la **caña de pescar** fishing rod

♂ la **cañería** *fem noun*
1 **pipe**
2 **plumbing**

el **cañón** *noun*
cannon

la **capa** *fem noun*
1 **layer**
2 **cape**
3 **cloak**
• la **capa de ozono** ozone layer

la **capacidad** *fem noun*
capacity

capaz *masc & fem adjective*, **capaces** *plural*
capable
ser capaz de hacer algo to be capable of
doing something
Es capaz de hacerlo. He's capable of doing
it.
No fueron capaces de darme una
respuesta. They weren't able to give me an
answer.

♂ la **capital** *fem noun*
1 **capital**
la capital de España the capital of Spain
2 **Valencia capital** the city of Valencia (*in
contrast to the province*)

el **capitán** *masc noun*, la **capitana** *fem*
captain (*of a team, ship, etc*)

el **capítulo** *masc noun*
1 **chapter**
2 **episode** (*of a TV series*)

el **capó** *masc noun*
bonnet (*of a car*)

el **capricho** *masc noun*
whim

la **capucha** *fem noun*
hood (*of an anorak, etc*)

capricornio *masc & fem noun*
▷ see **Capricornio** *masc noun*
Capricorn
Es capricornio. He's Capricorn.

WORD TIP Use a small letter in Spanish to say *I
am Capricorn*, etc, with star signs.

Capricornio *masc noun*
▷ see **capricornio** *masc & fem noun*
Capricorn (*sign of the zodiac*)

♂ la **cara** *fem noun*
1 **face**
Tiene una cara bonita. She has a pretty
face.
Tienes cara de cansada. You look tired.
tener mala cara to look ill

Tu hermana tiene mala cara. Your sister
looks ill.
2 **side**
la otra cara del disco the other side of the
record
3 **¿Cara o cruz?** Heads or tails?

el **caracol** *masc noun*
1 **snail**
2 **winkle**

♂ el **carácter** *masc noun, pl:* los **caracteres**
character
No tiene mucho carácter. He doesn't have
much character.
Es una persona de buen carácter. She's a
good-natured person.

la **característica** *fem noun*
characteristic

♂ **caramba** *exclamation*
1 **Good heavens!**
2 **Damn it!**

♂ el **caramelo** *masc noun*
1 **sweet**
un caramelo de menta a mint
2 **caramel**

la **caravana** *fem noun*
1 **tailback**
una caravana de diez kilómetros a ten-
kilometre tailback
Hay caravana para entrar en Sevilla.
There's a tailback into Seville.
2 **caravan**

el **carbón** *masc noun*
coal
• el **carbón vegetal** charcoal

la **cárcel** *fem noun*
jail
meter a alguien en la cárcel to put
somebody in jail
Lo metieron en la cárcel por robo. He was
sent to jail for robbery.

el **cardenal** *masc noun*
1 **bruise**
2 (*Religion*) **cardinal**

cardíaco *masc adjective*, **cardíaca** *fem*
heart
un ataque cardíaco a heart attack

la **carga** *fem noun*
1 **load**
2 **cargo**
3 **refill** (*for a pen*)
4 **burden**
Es una carga para la familia. It's a burden on
the family.

5 charge (*by police, soldiers*)
¡A la carga! Charge!
• la **carga máxima** maximum load

cargado *masc adjective*, **cargada** *fem*
1 loaded
La pistola estaba cargada. The gun was loaded.
2 ir cargado, *fem* cargada de algo to be loaded with something
Iba cargado de paquetes. He was loaded with parcels.
3 stuffy
un ambiente cargado a stuffy atmosphere

cargar *verb* [28]
1 to load (*a lorry, a weapon*)
2 to fill

el **cargo** *masc noun*
1 position
un cargo de responsabilidad a position of responsibility
2 a cargo de in charge of
Estoy a cargo del departamento. I'm in charge of the department.
Dejó los niños a mi cargo. She left the children in my care.

el **Caribe** *masc noun*
el Caribe the Caribbean
el mar Caribe the Caribbean Sea

caribeño *masc adjective & noun*, **caribeña** *fem adjective & noun*
1 Caribbean
2 un caribeño, una caribeña Caribbean

WORD TIP Adjectives and nouns for nationality and regional origin do not have capital letters in Spanish.

ᵟ el **cariño** *masc noun*
1 affection
tenerle cariño a to be fond of
Les tengo cariño. I'm fond of them.
tomarle cariño a to become fond of
Les tomó cariño. He became fond of them.
2 Con cariño, Maya. Love, Maya (*as a letter ending*)
3 dear
Ven, cariño. Come here, dear.

ᵟ **cariñoso** *masc adjective*, **cariñosa** *fem*
1 affectionate, **loving** (*a person*)
2 warm
un cariñoso saludo best wishes (*as a letter ending*)

el **carmín** *masc noun*
lipstick

el **carnaval** *masc noun*
carnival

ᵟ el **carné**, **carnet** *masc noun*
card
• el **carné de conducir** driving licence
• el **carné de estudiante** student card
• el **carné de identidad** identity card

ᵟ la **carne** *fem noun*
1 meat
2 flesh
• la **carne de cerdo** pork
• la **carne de cordero** lamb
• la **carne de ternera** veal
• la **carne de vaca** beef

ᵟ la **carnicería** *fem noun*
butcher's (shop)

ᵟ el **carnicero** *masc noun*, la **carnicera** *fem*
butcher

carnívoro *masc adjective*, **carnívora** *fem*
carnivorous

ᵟ **caro** *masc adjective*, **cara** *fem*
expensive
un restaurante caro an expensive restaurant
Es demasiado caro. It's too expensive.

la **carpa** *fem noun*
(*Latin America*) **tent**

ᵟ la **carpeta** *fem noun*
folder
• la **carpeta de anillas** ring binder

el **carpintero** *masc noun*, la **carpintera** *fem*
carpenter

la **carrera** *fem noun*
1 race
la carrera de los cien metros the one hundred metres race
echar una carrera to have a race (*against somebody*)
Echamos una carrera. Let's have a race.
Eché una carrera y alcancé el autobús. I ran and caught the bus.
2 degree course
hacer una carrera to study for a degree
Quiero hacer una carrera. I want to go to university.
hacer la carrera de algo to study for a degree in something
Quiero hacer la carrera de medicina. I want to study medicine.
• la **carrera automovilística** car race
• la **carrera de obstáculos** steeple chase
• la **carrera de relevos** relay race
• las **carreras de caballos** the races (*with horses*)

a
b
c
d
e
f
g
h
i
j
k
l
m
n
ñ
o
p
q
r
s
t
u
v
w
x
y
z

la **carreta** *fem noun*
  cart

la **carretera** *fem noun*
  road
  la carretera de Málaga the road to Málaga
  Vinimos por carretera. We came by road.
  • la **carretera comarcal** B-road
  • la **carretera de circunvalación** ring road
  • la **carretera nacional** A-road

la **carretilla** *fem noun*
  wheelbarrow

♂ el **carril** *masc noun*
  lane
  • el **carril bus** bus lane

el **carrito** *masc noun*
  trolley

el **carro** *masc noun*
  1 cart
  2 (*Latin America*) car
  • el **carro de combate** tank

♀ la **carta** *fem noun*
  1 letter
  mandar una carta to send a letter
  echar una carta al correo to post a letter
  2 menu
  ¿Nos trae la carta, por favor? Could you
  bring us the menu, please?
  3 card (*in a pack*)
  jugar a las cartas to play cards
  ¿Te gusta jugar a las cartas? Do you like
  playing cards?
  • la **carta certificada** registered letter

el **cartel** *masc noun*
  1 poster (*for advertising*)
  2 sign
  ¿Qué dice el cartel? What does the sign
  say?

♀ la **cartelera** *fem noun*
  la cartelera de cine 'what's on' at the
  cinema
  La obra lleva tres años en cartelera. The
  play has been running for three years.
  La película sigue en cartelera. The film is
  still showing.

♀ la **cartera** *fem noun*
  1 wallet
  2 briefcase
  3 school bag

el & la **carterista** *masc & fem noun*
  pickpocket

♂ el **cartero** *masc noun*, la **cartera** *fem*
  1 postman
  2 postwoman

el **cartón** *masc noun*
  cardboard

♀ la **casa** *fem noun*
  1 house
  Mi casa tiene tres dormitorios. My house
  has three bedrooms.
  2 home
  No están en casa. They're not at home.
  Estoy pasando unos días en casa de Juan.
  I'm staying at Juan's for a few days.
  El Valencia juega en casa Valencia is playing
  at home.
  • la **casa adosada** semi-detached house
  • la **casa de huéspedes** guesthouse
  • la **casa rural** house in the country (*for
    holiday rental*)

♂ **casado** *masc adjective*, **casada** *fem*
  married
  estar casado to be married
  ¿Está casada? Is she married?
  Están casados desde hace tres meses. They
  have been married for three months.

♂ **casarse** *reflexive verb* [17]
  to get married
  casarse con alguien to marry someone
  Se casó con mi primo. She married my
  cousin.

cascar *verb* [31]
  to crack (*a nut*)

♀ la **cáscara** *fem noun*
  1 peel
  2 shell

el **casco** *masc noun*
  1 helmet
  2 hoof (*of a horse*)
  3 empty bottle
  4 cascos *plural* headphones
  • el **casco protector** safety helmet, crash
    helmet
  • el **casco urbano** the town centre

el **caserío** *masc noun*
  1 farmhouse
  2 hamlet

casero *masc adjective*, **casera** *fem*
  ▷ see **casero** *noun*
  homemade
  productos caseros homemade products

el **casero** *masc noun*, la **casera** *fem*
  ▷ see **casero** *adj*
  1 landlord
  2 landlady

la **caseta** *fem noun*
  1 kennel
  2 hut (*for a watchman, a guard*)
  3 stand (*in a fair*)

54

ᶜ el **casete** *masc noun* ▷ see **casete, cassette** *noun*
  cassette recorder

ᶜ el & la **casete** *masc & fem noun* ▷ see **casete, cassette** *noun*
  cassette

ᶜ **casi** *adverb*
1 **almost**, **nearly**
  Son casi las cuatro. It's almost four o'clock.
  Casi me caigo. I nearly fell over.
  Casi todos son turistas. Almost all of them are tourists.
2 **hardly**
  Casi no había gente. There was hardly anybody there.
  casi nadie hardly anyone
  No había casi nadie. There was hardly anyone there.
  casi nunca hardly ever
  No viene casi nunca. She hardly ever comes.

la **casilla** *fem noun*
1 **square** (*in a crossword*)
2 **box** (*on a form*)
3 (*Latin America*) **post office box**

ᶜ el **caso** *masc noun*
1 **case**
  en ese caso in that case
  en caso de accidente in case of accident
  en todo caso, en cualquier caso in any case
  en el peor de los casos if the worst comes to the worst
2 El caso es que ... The thing is that ...
3 hacer caso de algo to pay attention to something
  Haz caso de las señales. Pay attention to the signs.
4 hacerle caso a alguien to do as one is told
  No me hace caso. He doesn't do as I tell him to.

la **caspa** *fem noun*
  dandruff

ᶜ el & la **cassette** *masc & fem noun*
  cassette

la **castaña** *fem noun* ▷ see **castaño** *adj*
  chestnut

castaño *masc adjective*, **castaña** *fem* ▷ see **castaña** *fem noun*
  chestnut brown

el **castaño** *masc noun* ▷ see **castaño** *adj*
  chestnut tree

las **castañuelas** *plural fem noun*
  castanets (*the hand-held pair of clackers used in flamenco dancing*)

ᶜ **castellano** *masc adjective*, **castellana** *fem* ▷ see **castellano** *noun*
  Castilian

ᶜ un **castellano** *masc noun*, una **castellana** *fem* ▷ see **castellano** *adj*
1 **Castilian** (*person from Castile*)
2 el castellano **Castilian Spanish** (*the Spanish spoken in the central part of Spain*)

WORD TIP Adjectives and nouns for nationality, regional origin and language, do not have capital letters in Spanish.

ᶜ **castigar** *verb* [28]
1 **to punish**
2 castigar a alguien por algo to punish someone for something
  Le castigaron por llegar tarde. She was punished for coming in late.
3 **to give a detention to** (*at school*)
  La profesora me dejó castigado. The teacher gave me a detention.

el **castigo** *masc noun*
  punishment

Castilla *fem noun*
  Castile (*name of the central part of Spain*)

ᶜ el **castillo** *masc noun*
  castle
• el castillo de arena sandcastle

la **casualidad** *fem noun*
1 **chance**
  por casualidad by chance
  Lo vi por casualidad. I saw it by chance.
2 Da la casualidad de que ... It so happens that ...
3 **coincidence**
  ¡Qué casualidad! What a coincidence!

ᶜ **catalán** *masc adjective & noun*, **catalana** *fem adjective & noun*
1 **Catalan**
2 un catalán, una catalana Catalan (*person from Catalonia*)
  el catalán Catalan (*the language spoken in Cataluña*)

WORD TIP Adjectives and nouns for nationality, regional origin, and language do not have capital letters in Spanish.

ᶜ **Cataluña**, **Catalunya** *fem noun*
  Catalonia (*a region of north-east Spain*)

la **catarata** *fem noun*
1 **waterfall**
2 **cataract** (*of the eye*)

a
b
c
d
e
f
g
h
i
j
k
l
m
n
ñ
o
p
q
r
s
t
u
v
w
x
y
z

a
b
c
d
e
f
g
h
i
j
k
l
m
n
ñ
o
p
q
r
s
t
u
v
w
x
y
z

♂ el **catarro** *masc noun*
cold
coger un catarro to catch a cold
Vas a coger un catarro! You're going to
catch a cold!

♂ **catear** *verb* [17]
(*informal*) **to fail**
He cateado las mates. I've failed maths.
Me han cateado en inglés. I've been failed
in English.

♂ la **catedral** *fem noun*
cathedral

la **categoría** *fem noun*
1 **category**
2 de primera categoría first class
un hotel de mucha categoría a top-of-the-
range hotel
un restaurante de poca categoría a third-
rate restaurant

♂ **católico** *masc adjective & noun*, **católica** *fem*
adjective & noun
1 **Catholic**
2 un católico, una católica Catholic

WORD TIP Adjectives and nouns for religion do
not have capital letters in Spanish.

♂ **catorce** *number*
1 **fourteen**
Tiene catorce años. He's fourteen (years
old).
2 (*in dates*) **fourteenth**
el catorce de mayo the fourteenth of May

el **caucho** *masc noun*
rubber

♂ la **causa** *fem noun*
1 **cause**
la causa del accidente the cause of the
accident
2 a causa de because of
A causa de eso se marcharon pronto.
Because of that they left early.

♂ **causar** *verb* [17]
to cause
Ha causado muchos problemas. He's
caused a lot of problems.

el **cautiverio** *masc noun*
captivity
mantener a alguien en cautiverio to keep
someone in captivity

el **cautivo** *masc noun*, la **cautiva** *fem*
prisoner

♂ el **cava** *masc noun*
cava (*sparkling wine from Cataluña*)

cavar *verb* [17]
to dig

la **caverna** *fem noun*
cave

cayendo *verb* ▷ caer

la **caza** *fem noun*
hunting
ir de caza to go hunting

la **cazadora** *fem noun*
jacket
la cazadora de piel leather jacket

cazar *verb* [22]
to hunt

♂ la **cazuela** *fem noun*
casserole

♂ el **CD** *masc noun*
CD

♂ la **cebada** *fem noun*
barley

♂ la **cebolla** *fem noun*
onion

♂ la **cebolleta** *fem noun*
spring onion

♂ el **cebollino** *masc noun*
chives

ceder *verb* [18]
1 **to give in**
Finalmente cedí. I finally gave in.
2 ceder algo a alguien to give up
Le cedí mi asiento a un anciano. I gave up
my seat to an elderly man.
3 ceder el paso to give way

♂ el **cederom** *masc noun*
CDROM

la **ceguera** *fem noun*
blindness

♂ la **ceja** *fem noun*
eyebrow

la **celda** *fem noun*
cell (*in a prison*)

la **celebración** *fem noun*
celebration

celebrar *verb* [17]
1 **to celebrate**
Tenemos que celebrarlo. We must
celebrate it.
2 **to hold** (*a meeting*)

celebrarse *reflexive verb* [17]
to be held
La recepción se celebró en el Hotel Victoria. The reception was held in the Victoria Hotel.

célebre *masc & fem adjective*
famous

ᴶ el **celo** *masc noun*
Sellotape

los **celos** *plural masc noun*
1 **jealousy**
2 **tener celos de alguien** to be jealous of somebody
Tiene celos de su hermana pequeña. She's jealous of her little sister.
3 **darle celos a alguien** to make somebody feel jealous
Lo hace para darte celos. He does it to make you feel jealous.

celoso *masc adjective*, **celosa** *fem*
jealous

el **celular** *masc noun*
(*Latin America*) **mobile phone**

el **cementerio** *masc noun*
cemetery

el **cemento** *masc noun*
cement

ᴶ la **cena** *fem noun*
1 **supper**
¿Qué hay de cena? What's for supper?
2 **dinner** (*in the evening*)

ᴶ **cenar** *verb* [17]
to have dinner (*in the evening*)
Normalmente cenamos a las nueve. We normally have dinner at nine.
Cenamos fuera. We went out for dinner.

ᴶ el **cenicero** *masc noun*
ashtray

ceñido *masc adjective*, **ceñida** *fem*
tight
una camiseta muy ceñida a very tight T-shirt

la **ceniza** *fem noun*
ash

ᴶ el **ceño** *masc noun*
fruncir el ceño to frown

ᴶ el **centavo** *masc noun*
1 **one hundredth**
2 **cent** (*in the dollar system*)

el **centenar** *masc noun*
hundred
un centenar de libros (about) a hundred books
centenares de cartas hundreds of letters

ᴶ el **centenario** *masc noun*
centenary

ᴶ el **centeno** *masc noun*
rye

la **centésima** *fem noun*
▷ see **centésimo** *adj*
hundredth
una centésima de segundo a hundredth of a second

centésimo *masc adjective*, **centésima** *fem*
▷ see **centésima** *noun*
hundredth

centígrado *masc adjective*, **centígrada** *fem*
centigrade

ᴶ el **centímetro** *masc noun*
centimetre

ᴶ **céntimo** *masc noun*
1 **cent** (*in the euro system*)
El euro se divide en cien céntimos. The euro is divided into a hundred cents.
2 **penny**
No tengo ni un céntimo. I don't have a penny.

ᴶ **central** *masc & fem adjective*
▷ see **central** *noun*
central

ᴶ la **central** *fem noun* ▷ see **central** *adj*
1 **head office**
2 **power station**
• la **central de correos** general post office
• la **central nuclear** nuclear power
• la **central telefónica** telephone exchange

ᴶ **céntrico** *masc adjective*, **céntrica** *fem*
central
un barrio céntrico a central part of town

centrifugar *verb* [28]
to spin-dry

ᴶ el **centro** *masc noun*
centre
el centro de la ciudad the town centre, the city centre
Estaba justo en el centro. It was right in the middle.
• el **centro comercial** shopping mall
• el **centro cultural** cultural centre ▸▸

Spanish-English

- el **centro polideportivo** sports complex

 centro

> Madrid está en el centro de España y de la plaza de Puerta del Sol se miden todas las distancias por carretera a otros puntos del país.

cepillar *verb* [17]
to brush

cepillarse *reflexive verb* [17]
to brush
cepillarse los dientes to brush your teeth
cepillarse el pelo to brush your hair

el **cepillo** *masc noun*
brush
- el **cepillo de dientes** toothbrush
- el **cepillo del pelo** hairbrush

la **cera** *fem noun*
wax

la **cerámica** *fem noun*
pottery

cerca *adverb*
1 **near**, **close**
Viven aquí cerca. They live near here.
Ponlos cerca el uno del otro. Put them close to each other.
2 **nearby**
Mi casa está cerca. My house is nearby.
3 **cerca de** near
Se sentó cerca de mí. He sat near me.
Vivo cerca del colegio. I live near the school.
Vive muy cerca de mí. She lives very near me.
4 **cerca de** almost, about (*with amounts*)
cerca de diez mil personas almost ten thousand people

la **cercanía** *fem noun*
closeness
las cercanías the surrounding area
Barcelona y sus cercanías Barcelona and its surrounding area
en las cercanías del aeropuerto in the area near the airport

cercano *masc adjective*, **cercana** *fem*
nearby, **near**
las casas cercanas the nearby houses
en un futuro cercano in the near future
estar cercano a algo to be near something
los pueblos que están cercanos al aeropuerto the villages near the airport

el **cerdo** *masc noun*, la **cerda** *fem*
1 **pig**

2 el **cerdo** pork
No como cerdo. I don't eat pork.

los **cereales** *plural masc noun*
cereals

la **ceremonia** *fem noun*
ceremony

la **cereza** *fem noun*
cherry

la **cerilla** *fem noun*
match

el **cero** *masc noun*
1 **zero**
tres grados bajo cero three degrees below zero
El prefijo de Birmingham es cero, uno, dos, uno. The Birmingham dialling code is 0121.
2 **love** (*in tennis*)
3 **nil** (*in sport*)
Empatamos cero a cero. We drew nil-nil.

cerrado *masc adjective*, **cerrada** *fem*
1 **closed**
La ventana está cerrada. The window's closed.
2 El grifo está cerrado. The tap's turned off.
3 cerrado con llave locked
'Cerrado por obras' 'Closed for Repairs'

la **cerradura** *fem noun*
1 **lock**
2 el ojo de la cerradura the keyhole

cerrar *verb* [29]
1 **to close**
Cierra la puerta. Close the door.
Cerramos a las ocho. We close at eight.
2 Han cerrado la fábrica. The factory has been closed.
3 cerrar con llave to lock up
No te olvides de cerrar con llave. Don't forget to lock up.
4 **to turn off** (*a tap*)
cerrar el grifo to turn off the tap
5 **to put the top on** (*a bottle*)
Cierra la botella. Put the top on the bottle.
¿Has cerrado el frasco? Have you put the lid on the jar?

cerrarse *reflexive verb* [29]
to close
La puerta se cerró. The door closed.

certificado *masc adjective*, **certificada** *fem* ▷ see **certificado** *noun*
registered (*letters, parcels*)

el **certificado** *masc noun*
▷ see **certificado** *adj*
certificate

certificar *verb* [31]
  to certify

ᶘ la **cervecería** *fem noun*
1 brewery
2 bar (*selling different kinds of beer*)

ᶘ la **cerveza** *fem noun*
  beer
  ¿Quieres una cerveza? Do you want a beer?
- la **cerveza de barril** draught beer
- la **cerveza negra** stout
- la **cerveza rubia** lager

ᶘ el **césped** *masc noun*
  lawn
  'Prohibido pisar el césped' 'Keep off the grass'

la **cesta** *fem noun*
  basket
- la **cesta de mimbre** wicker basket
- la **cesta de Navidad** Christmas hamper

el **cesto** *masc noun*
  basket

chalado *masc adjective*, **chalada** *fem* (*informal*) **wacky**

el **chalé**, **chalet** *masc noun*
1 villa
2 detached house (*on an estate*)
- el **chalé adosado** semi-detached house (*on an estate*)

ᶘ el **chaleco** *masc noun*
  waistcoast
  un chaleco de punto a sleeveless sweater
- el **chaleco antibalas** bullet-proof vest
- el **chaleco salvavidas** life jacket

ᶘ el & la **champán**, el & la **champaña** *masc & fem noun*
  champagne

ᶘ el **champiñón** *masc noun*
  mushroom

ᶘ el **champú** *masc noun*
  shampoo

ᶘ las **chanclas** *plural fem noun*
  flip-flops

ᶘ el **chándal** *masc noun*
  tracksuit

chao *exclamation*
  (*Latin America*) **bye**, **bye-bye**

la **chapa** *fem noun*
1 top (*of a bottle*)
2 badge
  una chapa de policía a police badge

el **chapapote** *masc noun*
  oil (*polluting a beach*)

ᶘ el **chaparrón** *masc noun*
  downpour

ᶘ la **chaqueta** *fem noun*
  jacket
- la **chaqueta de punto** cardigan

la **charca** *fem noun*
  pond

el **charco** *masc noun*
  puddle
  No pises los charcos. Don't walk in the puddles.

ᶘ la **charcutería** *fem noun*
  delicatessen (*specializing in pork products*)

ᶘ **charlar** *verb* [17]
  to chat

el **chasco** *masc noun*
  disappointment
  Me llevé un chasco. I felt really disappointed.

ᶘ el **chat** *masc noun*
  chatroom

ᶘ el **cheque** *masc noun*
  cheque
  un cheque a nombre de Alberto López a cheque payable to Alberto López
  cobrar un cheque to cash a cheque
- el **cheque de viaje**, el **cheque de viajero** traveller's cheque

ᶘ el **chequeo** *masc noun*
  checkup
  hacerse un chequeo to have a checkup

chévere *adjective*
  (*Latin America*) **great**, **fantastic**

ᶘ la **chica** *fem* ▷ see **chico** *noun, adj*
1 girl
2 girlfriend
    ▷ **chico** *noun*

el **chichón** *masc noun*
  bump
  Me di un golpe en la cabeza y me ha salido un chichón. I banged my head and now I've got a bump.

ᶘ el **chicle** *masc noun*
  chewing gum
  ¿Quieres un chicle? Do you want some chewing gum?
- el **chicle de globos** bubblegum

a
b
c
d
e
f
g
h
i
j
k
l
m
n
ñ
o
p
q
r
s
t
u
v
w
x
y
z

a
b
c
d
e
f
g
h
i
j
k
l
m
n
ñ
o
p
q
r
s
t
u
v
w
x
y
z

♂ **chico** *masc adjective*, **chica** *fem*
▷ see **chico** *noun*
small
Estos zapatos son muy chicos. These shoes are very small.

♂ el **chico** *masc noun*, la **chica** *fem*
▷ see **chico** *adj*
1 **boy**
un chico y dos chicas a boy and two girls
unos chicos some children (*all boys, or boys and girls*)
Había unos chicos jugando en la calle. There were some children playing in the street.
2 **guy**
Sale con un chico. She's going out with a guy.

♂ **chico** *masc adjective*, **chica** *fem*
▷ see **chico** *noun*
small
Estos zapatos son muy chicos. These shoes are very small.

chiflado *masc adjective*, **chiflada** *fem*
(*informal*) **wacky**

♂ **Chile** *masc noun* ▷ see **chile** *noun*
Chile

el **chile** *masc noun* ▷ see **Chile** *noun*
chilli (*hot pepper*)

chileno *masc adjective & noun*, **chilena** *fem*
adjective & noun
1 **Chilean**
2 un chileno, una chilena Chilean (*person*)

WORD TIP Adjectives and nouns for nationality and regional origin do not have capital letters in Spanish.

♂ **chillar** *verb* [17]
1 **to shout**
2 **to scream**

♂ la **chimenea** *fem noun*
1 **chimney**
2 **fireplace**

♂ **China** *fem noun*
(la) China China

la **chincheta** *fem noun*
drawing pin

chino *masc adjective & noun*, **china** *fem*
adjective & noun
1 **Chinese**
2 un chino, una china Chinese man, Chinese woman

3 el **chino** Chinese (*the language*)

WORD TIP Adjectives and nouns for nationality, regional origin, and language do not have capital letters in Spanish.

Chipre *fem noun*
Cyprus

chirriar *verb* [32]
to squeak (*doors, hinges, etc*)

chis *exclamation*
1 **Shush!**
2 ¡Chis, chis! Hey! (*calling somebody in the street*)

♂ el **chisme** *masc noun*
1 **piece of gossip**
Siempre está contando chismes. He's always gossiping
2 **thing**
¿Para qué sirve este chisme? What's this thing for?

la **chispa** *fem noun*
1 **spark**
2 una chispa de algo (*informal*) a small amount of something
una chispa de ginebra a dash of gin
Ponle una chispa de sal. Add a pinch of salt to it.

chispa *invariable adjective*
(*informal*) **tipsy**
Estaba un poco chispa. She was a bit tipsy.

♂ el **chiste** *masc noun*
joke
contar un chiste to tell a joke
• el **chiste verde** dirty joke

chocar *verb* [31]
1 **to crash**
Dos coches chocaron en la autopista. Two cars crashed on the motorway.
2 chocar con algo to crash into something
Chocaron con una farola. They crashed into a lamp-post.
Me choqué con ella. I bumped into her.

♂ el **chocolate** *masc noun*
chocolate
una barra de chocolate a bar of chocolate
• el **chocolate con leche** milk chocolate
• el **chocolate negro** dark chocolate

♂ la **chocolatina** *fem noun*
chocolate bar

el **chófer** *masc noun*
driver (*of car, taxi, etc*)

el **chollo** *masc noun* (*informal*)
1 **cushy job**
2 **bargain**

ₛ el **choque** *masc noun*
1 **crash**
   un choque frontal a head-on collision
2 **clash**
   choques entre manifestantes y la policía
   clashes between demonstrators and police

ₛ el **chorizo** *masc noun*
   chorizo (*a spicy dark red, salami-shaped sausage*)

chorizo

El chorizo es una salchicha parecida al salami. Es muy apreciado y en su primer viaje espacial en 1998, el astronauta Pedro Duque se llevó en su equipaje un chorizo de León.

la **chorrada** *fem noun*
   (*informal*)
1 **nonsense**
   decir chorradas to talk nonsense
   Eso es una chorrada. That's nonsense.
2 **tiny thing**
   Se enfada por cualquier chorrada. He gets upset over the tiniest thing.

la **choza** *fem noun*
   hut

ₛ el **chubasco** *masc noun*
   (heavy) shower
   Habrá chubascos en el noroeste. There will be heavy showers in the north-west.

la **chuchería** *fem noun*
   trinket

ₛ la **chuleta** *fem noun*
   chop
   · la **chuleta de cerdo** pork chop

chupar *verb* [17]
   to suck

chuparse *reflexive verb* [17]
   to suck
   chuparse el dedo to suck your thumb

ₛ el **churro** *masc noun*
1 **twists of batter deep-fried in olive oil**
   (*eaten hot with coffee or drinking chocolate*)
2 (*informal*) **botched job**
3 (*informal*) **piece of luck**

ₛ **chutar** *verb* [17]
   to shoot (*at goal*)

ₛ el **cibercafé** *masc noun*
   Internet cafe
   ¿Dónde hay un cibercafé? Where is there an Internet cafe?

ₛ el & la **cibernauta** *masc & fem noun*
   surfer (*on the Internet*)

la **cicatriz** *fem noun*
   scar

ₛ el **ciclismo** *masc noun*
   cycling

el & la **ciclista** *masc & fem noun*
   cyclist

ciego *masc adjective*, **ciega** *fem*
   ▷ see **ciego** *noun*
   blind
   quedarse ciego to go blind

el **ciego** *masc noun*, la **ciega** *fem*
   ▷ see **ciego** *adj*
   blind person
   los ciegos the blind

ₛ el **cielo** *masc noun*
1 **sky**
2 **heaven**
   ir al cielo to go to heaven
   ¡Cielos! Good heavens!

ₛ **cien** *number*
   hundred
   cien personas a hundred people
   el cien por cien a hundred per cent
   cien mil euros a hundred thousand euros ▷ **ciento**

ₛ la **ciencia** *fem noun*
1 **science**
2 ciencias science (*as a subject at school*)
   · la **ciencia ficción** science fiction
   · las **Ciencias de la Información** Media Studies
   · las **Ciencias Empresariales** Business Studies
   · las **ciencias naturales** natural science

el **cieno** *masc noun*
   silt

científico *masc adjective*, **científica** *fem*
   ▷ see **científico** *noun*
   scientific

el **científico** *masc noun*, la **científica** *fem*
   ▷ see **científico** *adj*
   scientist

ₛ **ciento** *number* ▷ see **cien** *number*
1 **hundred**
   ciento cinco one hundred and five
   cientos de cartas hundreds of letters
   doscientos diez two hundred and ten ▷ **cien**
2 por ciento per cent
   Suspendieron el ocho por ciento. Eight per cent failed. ▸▸

a
b
c
d
e
f
g
h
i
j
k
l
m
n
ñ
o
p
q
r
s
t
u
v
w
x
y
z

Aprobaron un noventa por ciento. Ninety per cent passed.

WORD TIP Spanish uses *el* or *un* with percentages.

cierra, **cierro**, **etc** *verb* ▷ **cerrar**

ℰ **cierto** *masc adjective*, **cierta** *fem*
1 **true**
Sí, es cierto. Yes, it's true.
2 **certain**
cierta clase de negocios certain types of business
en cierta ocasión on a certain occasion
3 (*in expressions*) **en cierto modo** in a way
En cierto modo, lo entiendo. In a way, I understand.
hasta cierto punto up to a point
por cierto by the way
Por cierto, ¿has llamado a Ana? By the way, have you phoned Ana?

ℰ el **ciervo** *masc noun*
1 **deer**
2 **stag**

la **cifra** *fem noun*
figure
una cifra muy alta a very high figure

ℰ el **cigarrillo** *masc noun*
cigarrette

la **cigüeña** *fem noun*
stork

el **cilindro** *masc noun*
cylinder

la **cima** *fem noun*
top (*of a mountain*)

ℰ **cinco** *number*
1 **five**
Julia tiene cinco años. Julia's five (years old).
2 (*saying the date*) **fifth**
Hoy es día cinco. Today is the fifth.
3 (*telling the time*) **five**
Son las cinco. It's five o'clock.
a las dos y cinco at five past two

ℰ **cincuenta** *number*
fifty
Mi madre tiene cincuenta años. My mum's fifty (years old).
cincuenta y ocho fifty-eight
los años cincuenta the fifties

ℰ el **cine** *masc noun*
cinema
ir al cine to go to the cinema
Vámonos al cine. Let's go to the cinema.

¿Qué ponen en el cine? What's on at the cinema?
• el **cine de barrio** local cinema

el & la **cineasta** *masc & fem noun*
film-maker

la **cinta** *fem noun*
1 **ribbon**
una cinta para el pelo a hair ribbon
2 **tape**
grabar una cinta to record a tape
• la **cinta adhesiva** adhesive tape
• la **cinta de vídeo** video tape
• la **cinta magnetofónica** magnetic tape
• la **cinta métrica** tape measure
• la **cinta virgen** blank tape

ℰ la **cintura** *fem noun*
waist
¿Cuánto tienes de cintura? What's your waist measurement?

ℰ el **cinturón** *masc noun*
belt
Es cinturón negro de karate. He's a karate black belt.
• el **cinturón de seguridad** seatbelt

el **circo** *masc noun*
circus

la **circulación** *fem noun*
1 **circulation**
2 **traffic**

ℰ **circular** *verb* ▷ see **circular** *adj, noun* [17]
1 **to flow** (*liquids, blood, water*)
2 **to drive**
Circulen por la derecha. Drive on the right.
El coche circulaba a mucha velocidad. The car was travelling very fast.

circular *masc & fem adjective*
▷ see **circular** *verb, noun*
circular

la **circular** *fem noun* ▷ see **circular** *verb, adj*
circular (*letter, note*)

el **círculo** *masc noun*
circle

ℰ la **circunferencia** *fem noun*
circumference

la **circunstancia** *fem noun*
1 **reason**
Por alguna circunstancia no pudo hacerlo. He couldn't do it for some reason.
2 **circumstances**
bajo ninguna circunstancia under no circumstances

en estas circunstancias in these
circumstances
dadas las circunstancias given the
circumstances

el **cirio** *masc noun*
candle

♪ la **ciruela** *fem noun*
plum
- la **ciruela pasa** prune

la **cirugía** *fem noun*
surgery
- la **cirugía estética** cosmetic surgery
- la **cirugía láser** laser surgery

el **cirujano** *masc noun*, la **cirujana** *fem*
surgeon

el **cisne** *masc noun*
swan

♪ la **cita** *fem noun*
1 **appointment**
Tengo cita con el médico. I've got an
appointment to see the doctor.
El dentista me ha dado cita para el jueves.
The dentist has given me an appointment
for Thursday.
darse cita to arrange to meet
Se dieron cita en el bar. They arranged to
meet in the bar.
2 **date**
Esta noche tengo una cita con mi novio.
I've got a date with my boyfriend tonight.
3 **quotation**

citar *verb* [17]
1 **to quote** (*a writer or book*)
2 **to mention**
Citó algunos casos. He mentioned a few
cases.
3 **to give an appointment**
El médico me ha citado para esta tarde. The
doctor's given me an appointment for this
afternoon.

citarse *reflexive verb* [17]
to arrange to meet
Se citaron para las cinco. They arranged to
meet at five.

♪ la **ciudad** *fem noun*
1 **town**
2 **city**
- la **ciudad dormitorio** dormitory town
- la **ciudad universitaria** university campus

el **ciudadano** *masc noun*, la **ciudadana**
fem
citizen

civil *masc & fem adjective* ▷ see **civil** *noun*
1 **civil**
un matrimonio civil a civil marriage
casarse por lo civil to have civil wedding
2 **civilian**
la población civil the civilian population

el & la **civil** *masc & fem noun* ▷ see **civil** *adj*
civilian

el **clarinete** *masc noun*
clarinet

♪ **claro** *masc adjective*, **clara** *fem*
▷ see **claro** *adv*
1 **clear**
Está muy claro. It's very clear.
Su explicación fue muy clara. His
explanation was very clear.
2 **light**
un verde claro a light green
un chico de ojos claros a boy with light-
coloured eyes
3 **bright**
un día claro a bright day, sunny day

♪ **claro** *adverb* ▷ see **claro** *adj*
1 **clearly**
Habla más claro. Speak more clearly.
Lo veo claro. I can see it clearly.
2 **¡Claro!** Of course!
¡Claro que sí! Yes, of course!
¡Claro que no! No, of course not!

♪ la **clase** *fem noun*
1 **class** (*in school, in society*)
la clase de matemáticas the maths class
una familia de clase media a middle-class
family
Tenemos clase de español tres veces por
semana. We have Spanish classes three
times a week.
Toda la clase se va de excursión. The whole
class is going on an excursion.
2 **dar clase de algo** to teach something
Mi padre da clase de física en un colegio.
My father teaches physics in a school.
dar clase de algo to have lessons in
something
Da clases de música por las tardes. She has
music lessons in the evenings.
dar clase a alguien to teach somebody
Me da clases de inglés. He teaches me
English.
3 **classroom**
¿En qué clase están? What classroom are
they in?
4 **kind**, **type**
de primera clase top-quality   ▸▸

a
b
c
d
e
f
g
h
i
j
k
l
m
n
ñ
o
p
q
r
s
t
u
v
w
x
y
z

¿Qué clase de material? What kind of material?

5 **class** (*in travel*)
viajar en segunda clase to travel second class

6 **class** (*elegance*)
Tiene mucha clase. She has a lot of class.

• la **clase ejecutiva**, la **clase preferente** business class
• la **clase social** social class
• la **clase turista** economy class

clásico *masc adjective*, **clásica** *fem*

1 **classic**
la clásica broma the classic joke

2 **classical** (*music, decorations*)

3 **traditional** (*methods*)

la **clasificación** *fem noun*

1 **classification**

2 **qualifying** (*in sports*)
sin posibilidades de clasificación with no chance of qualifying

3 **table** (*in sports*)
La clasificación final es la siguiente ... The final table is as follows ...

clasificar *verb* [31]
to put in order (*papers, cards, etc*)

clasificarse *reflexive verb* [17]
to qualify
clasificarse para algo to qualify for something
Se clasificaron para la final. They qualified for the final.

clavar *verb* [17]
to hammer
Clavó un clavo en la pared. He hammered a nail into the wall.

clave *invariable adjective* ▷ see **clave** *noun*
key
un factor clave a key factor

la **clave** *fem noun* ▷ see **clave** *adj*

1 **key** (*to a mystery, a problem*)
La clave es ... The key to it is ...

2 **code**
un mensaje en clave a coded message

3 (*in music*) **clef**
• la **clave de sol** treble clef

la **clavija** *fem noun*

1 **peg**

2 **plug** (*for electrical appliances*)

el **clavo** *masc noun*

1 **nail**

2 **clove** (*of spice*)

el **claxon** *masc noun*
horn (*of a car*)

♫ el **clic** *masc noun*
click
un doble clic a double click
hacer clic en algo to click on something
Haz clic en el icono. Click on the icon.

♫ el **cliente** *masc noun*, la **clienta** *fem*

1 **customer**

2 **client** (*of a company, a lawyer*)

3 **guest** (*in a hotel*)

♫ el **clima** *masc noun*
climate

climatizado *masc adjective*, **climatizada** *fem*
air-conditioned

la **clínica** *fem noun*
private hospital

el **clip** *masc noun*
paper clip
• el **clip para el pelo** hairgrip

el **club** *masc noun*
club
un club de jóvenes a youth club

la **coartada** *fem noun*
alibi

♫ **cobarde** *masc & fem adjective*
▷ see **cobarde** *noun*
cowardly

♫ el & la **cobarde** *masc & fem noun*
▷ see **cobarde** *adj*
coward

♫ el **cobrador** *masc noun*, la **cobradora** *fem*
conductor

♫ **cobrar** *verb* [17]

1 **to get paid**
Cobro mil cuatrocientos euros al mes. I get paid one thousand four hundred euros a month.
Cobramos a fin de mes. We get paid at the end of the month.
Cobra el paro. He's paid unemployment benefit.
Cobra bastante de pensión. He gets a good pension.

2 **to charge**
Me cobraron sesenta euros por todo. They charged me sixty euros for everything.
cobrar de más to overcharge
cobrar de menos to undercharge

3 to collect (*a debt, the rent, dues*)
Han venido a cobrar el alquiler. They've come to collect the rent.

4 to cash
cobrar un cheque de viajero to cash a traveller's cheque

ʃ **el cobre** *masc noun*
copper

ʃ **la cocaína** *fem noun*
cocaine

ʃ **cocer** *verb* [41]

1 to boil (*eggs, vegetables*)
cocer algo a fuego lento to simmer something over a low heat

2 to bake

ʃ **el coche** *masc noun*

1 car
ir en coche to go by car

2 carriage (*of train*)
- **el coche bomba** car bomb
- **el coche de alquiler** hire car
- **el coche de bomberos** fire engine
- **el coche de carreras** racing car
- **el coche restaurante** restaurant car

ʃ **el cochecito de bebé** *masc noun*
pram

ʃ **la cochera** *fem noun*
bus depot

el cocido *masc noun*
stew (*containing meat and chickpeas*)

ʃ **la cocina** *fem noun*

1 kitchen
¿Dónde está la cocina? Where's the kitchen?

2 cooker

3 cooking
la cocina española Spanish cooking
un libro de cocina a cookery book
- **la cocina de gas**, **la cocina de butano** gas cooker
- **la cocina eléctrica** electric cooker

ʃ **cocinar** *verb* [17]
to cook
Cocina muy bien. He cooks very well.
cocinar algo a fuego lento to cook something on a low heat

ʃ **el cocinero** *masc noun*, **la cocinera** *fem*
cook

ʃ **el coco** *masc noun*

1 coconut

2 (*informal*) **head**
Me duele el coco. I've got a headache

ʃ **el cocotero** *masc noun*
coconut tree

ʃ **el cocodrilo** *masc noun*
crocodile

ʃ **el cóctel** *masc noun*

1 cocktail

2 cocktail party

el código *masc noun*
code
- **el código de barras** bar code
- **el código postal** postcode

ʃ **el codo** *masc noun*
elbow

la codorniz *fem noun*
quail

ʃ **coger** *verb* [3]

1 to take
coger el autobús to take the bus
La cogí del brazo. I took her by the arm.
No quería coger el dinero. He didn't want to take the money.

2 to get
coger el teléfono to answer the phone
Voy a coger entradas para el concierto. I'm going to get some concert tickets.
Coge por la Calle Díaz. Go down Díaz Street.

3 to catch
coger un resfriado to catch a cold
coger una insolación to get sunstroke
No pudo coger la pelota. He couldn't catch the ball.
Cogieron al asesino. They caught the murderer.
Coge el metro en Sol. Catch the metro at Sol (station).

4 to pick
coger fresas to pick strawberries
coger algo del suelo to pick something up from the floor

cogerse *reflexive verb* [3]

1 cogerse de algo to hold on to something
Cógete de la barra. Hold on to the rail.

2 Se cogieron de la mano. They took each other by the hand.

WORD TIP In Spain *coger* is the usual word for *to take, catch* etc., but in parts of Latin America it is the four-letter word. In Latin America always use *tomar* instead.

cogido *masc adjective*, **cogida** *fem*

1 taken
Esta silla ya está cogida. This chair is already taken.

2 ir cogidos de la mano to walk hand in hand
ir cogidos del brazo to walk arm in arm

ʃ indicates key words   65

cohibido *masc adjective*, **cohibida** *fem*
1 awkward
2 inhibited

la **coincidencia** *fem noun*
coincidence
¡Qué coincidencia! What a coincidence!

coincidir *verb* [19]
1 to coincide
2 coincidir en algo **to agree about something**

coja, **cojas**, **etc** *verb* ▷ coger

el **cojín** *masc noun*
cushion

cojo *masc adjective*, **coja** *fem*
1 lame
Es cojo. He's lame (*ser because it's permanent*).
2 Está coja. She has a limp (*estar because it's temporary*).

ℰ la **col** *fem noun*
cabbage
• las **coles de Bruselas** Brussels sprouts

ℰ la **cola** *fem noun*
1 tail
2 queue
hacer cola to queue up
saltarse la cola to jump the queue
Me puse a la cola. I joined the queue.
3 glue
Lo pegué con cola. I glued it.
• la **cola de carpintero** wood glue

la **colada** *fem noun*
laundry
hacer la colada to do the washing

el **colador** *masc noun*
strainer

colar *verb* [24]
to strain (*vegetables*)

colarse *reflexive verb* [24]
1 to jump the queue
Esa señora se ha colado. That lady has jumped the queue.
2 colarse en un sitio to get in somewhere without paying
Se coló en el cine. He got into the cinema without paying.

la **colcha** *fem noun*
bedspread

ℰ el **colchón** *masc noun*
mattress
• el **colchón de aire** air bed

ℰ la **colección** *fem noun*
collection

ℰ **coleccionar** *verb* [17]
to collect

el & la **coleccionista** *masc & fem noun*
collector

el & la **colega** *masc & fem noun*
colleague

el **cole** *masc noun*
(*informal*) **school**

ℰ el **colegial** *masc noun*, la **colegiala** *fem*
1 schoolboy
2 schoolgirl

ℰ el **colegio** *masc noun*
school
Mi hermano ya va al colegio. My brother's going to school now.
• el **colegio mayor** hall of residence
• el **colegio privado** private school
• el **colegio público** state school

ℰ la **coleta** *fem noun*
ponytail

colgar *verb* [23]
1 to hang
2 colgar la ropa to hang out the washing
3 colgar un cuadro to hang up a picture
4 **to hang up** (*when telephoning*)
Cuelga el teléfono. Hang up.
Me ha colgado. She's hung up on me.
No cuelgue. Hold the line (*polite form*).

colgarse *reflexive verb* [23]
(*Computers*) **to crash**

ℰ la **coliflor** *fem noun*
cauliflower

ℰ la **colilla** *fem noun*
cigarette end

ℰ la **colina** *fem noun*
hill

la **colisión** *fem noun*
collision

ℰ el **collar** *masc noun*
1 necklace
un collar de perlas a string of pearls
2 collar (*for a dog*)

el **colmo** *masc noun*
¡Esto es el colmo! This is the last straw!
¡Y para colmo … ! And to cap it all … !
el colmo de la incompetencia the height of incompetence

la **colocación** *fem noun*
job
Está buscando colocación. He's looking for a job.

ꟛ **colocar** *verb* [31]
1 **to put**
Colócalo ahí. Put it there.
¿Dónde coloco esta silla? Where should I put this chair?
2 Aún tenemos que colocar los muebles. We still have to arrange the furniture.
3 colocar a alguien to get somebody a job
Su tío lo ha colocado. His uncle's got him a job.

colocarse *reflexive verb* [31]
to find a job
Se ha colocado muy bien. She's found a very good job.

Colombia *fem noun*
Colombia

colombiano *masc adjective & noun,*
colombiana *fem adjective & noun*
1 **Colombian**
2 un colombiano, una colombiana Colombian

WORD TIP Adjectives and nouns for nationality and regional origin do not have capital letters in Spanish.

ꟛ la **colonia** *fem noun*
1 **(eau de) cologne**
2 **colony**
3 una colonia de vacaciones a summer camp

coloquial *masc & fem adjective*
colloquial

el **coloquio** *masc noun*
discussion

ꟛ el **color** *masc noun*
colour
¿De qué color es? What colour is it?
Es de color azul. It's blue.
colores claros light colours
telas de colores coloured fabrics

colorado *masc adjective,* **colorada** *fem*
red
ponerse colorado to go red
¡Te has puesto colorado! You've gone red!

el **colorante** *masc noun*
colouring

ꟛ **colorear** *verb* [17]
to colour
Coloréalo de rojo. Colour it red.

ꟛ el **colorete** *masc noun*
blusher

ꟛ la **columna** *fem noun*
1 **column**

2 **spine**
la columna vertebral the spine

columpiar *verb* [17]
to push (*on a swing*)

columpiarse *reflexive verb* [17]
to play on a swing

el **columpio** *masc noun*
swing (*in a park*)

la **coma** *fem noun* ▷ see **coma** *masc noun*
1 **comma**
2 **decimal point** (*In Spain a comma is used in decimals.*)
dos coma cinco two point five

el **coma** *masc noun* ▷ see **coma** *fem noun*
(*Medicine*) **coma**
entrar en coma to go into a coma

la **comadrona** *fem noun*
midwife

el & la **comandante** *masc & fem noun*
major

la **comba** *fem noun*
skipping rope
saltar a la comba to skip
jugar a la comba to skip

el **combate** *masc noun*
1 **combat** (*between soldiers*)
2 **fight** (*in boxing*)

la **combinación** *fem noun*
1 **combination**
2 **slip** (*girl's clothing*)

combinar *verb* [17]
to combine

la **comedia** *fem noun*
comedy
• la **comedia musical** musical

ꟛ el **comedor** *masc noun*
1 **dining-room**
2 **dining hall**
3 **canteen**

ꟛ **comentar** *verb* [17]
1 **to talk about**
Comentamos la noticia. We talked about the news.
2 **to mention**
Me lo comentó de pasada. He mentioned it to me in passing.
3 **to remark**
Comentó que ... He remarked that ...

ꟛ el **comentario** *masc noun*
comment
sin comentarios no comment

ꟛ indicates key words   67

ʃ **comenzar** *verb* [25]

to begin, **to start**
¿Cuándo comienzan las clases? When do lessons start?
Hemos comenzado los preparativos. We've begun the preparations.
Comenzó explicando que ... He began by explaining that ...
comenzar a hacer algo to begin to do something
Ha comenzado a llover. It's begun to rain.
Comencé a estudiar español hace dos años. I began learning Spanish two years ago.

WORD TIP To say, to begin by, use *comenzar* + -*ando*, or -*iendo*; to say, to begin to, use *comenzar a* + *infinitive*.

ʃ **comer** *verb* [18]

1 **to eat**
¿Te gusta comer pescado? Do you like eating fish?

2 (*Spain*) **to have lunch**
En casa comemos a la una. At home we have lunch at one.
¿Qué había de comer? What was for lunch?

3 (*Latin America*) **to have dinner**

4 **to take** (*a piece in chess, draughts*)
Te como el caballo. I take your knight.

---

comercial *masc & fem adjective*
commercial
un centro comercial a shopping centre
el centro comercial de la ciudad the commercial centre of the town

ʃ el & la **comerciante** *masc & fem noun*
shopkeeper

ʃ el **comercio** *masc noun*

1 **trade**
el comercio de animales exóticos the trade in exotic animals

2 **shop**
un comercio pequeño a small shop

los **comestibles** *plural masc noun*
food

la **cometa** *fem noun*

1 **kite**
hacer volar una cometa to fly a kite

2 **comet**

cometer *verb* [18]

1 **to commit** (*a crime*)

2 **to make** (*a mistake*)
He cometido un error. I've made a mistake.

ʃ el **cómic** *masc noun*
comic

cómico *masc adjective*, **cómica** *fem*
▷ see **cómico** *noun*

1 **funny** (*situation, face*)

2 **comic** (*actor*)

el & la **cómico** *masc & fem noun*
▷ see **cómico** *adj*
comedian

ʃ la **comida** *fem noun*

1 **food**
Tenemos suficiente comida. We have enough food.

2 **meal**
tres comidas al día three meals a day
Mi comida fuerte es a mediodía. I have my main meal at midday.

3 (*Spain*) **lunch**
a la hora de la comida at lunch time

4 (*Latin America*) **dinner** (*at night*)

• la **comida rápida** fast food

comienza, **comienzo**, **etc** *verb* ▷ comenzar

ʃ el **comienzo** *masc noun*
beginning
al comienzo in the beginning
el comienzo del año escolar the beginning of the school year

las **comillas** *plural fem noun*
inverted commas
poner algo entre comillas to put something in inverted commas

ʃ el **comino** *masc noun*
cumin

ʃ la **comisaría** *fem noun*
police station

la **comisión** *fem noun*
commission

como *conjunction* ▷ see **cómo**, **como** *adv*

1 **as**, **in the way that**
Lo hice como me dijeron. I did it as I was told to.
Como tú quieras. Just as you like.
Hazlo como quieras. Do it however you want to.

2 **since**, **because**
Como no llamaste, no te esperé. Since you didn't call, I didn't wait for you.

3 **if**
Como no tengas cuidado te vas a caer. If you're not careful you'll fall.

ℰ **como** *adverb* ▷ see **cómo** *adv*, **como** *conj*

1 **like** (*in comparisons*)
uno como éste one like this one
ser como ... to be like ...
Eres como tu padre. You're like your father.
tan ... como ... as ... as ...
Es tan negro como el carbón It's as black as coal.
como si as if
Es como si fuéramos niños. It's as if we were children.

2 **such as** (*giving examples*)
metales como el oro y la plata metals such as gold and silver

3 **around**
Eran como cincuenta personas. There were around fifty people.
como a las dos y media around half past two

4 **como mucho** at the most
como poco at least
Serán como mucho quince niños. There will be at most fifteen children.

ℰ **cómo** *adverb* ▷ see **como** *adv, conj*

1 (*in questions*) **how**
¿Cómo estás? How are you?
¿Cómo se escribe tu nombre? How do you write your name?
No sé cómo se enteraron. I don't know how they found out.

2 (*in questions*) **what**
¿Cómo es? What's she like?
¿Cómo es tu casa? What's your house like?

3 (*when you don't hear*) ¿Cómo? Pardon?

4 (*in exclamations*) ¡Cómo quema! It's so hot!
¡Cómo se parecen! They are so like each other!
¡Cómo no! Of course!, Please do!
¡Cómo! ¿no lo has hecho? What! you haven't done it?

WORD TIP *cómo*, with an accent, is used for questions (¿...?) and exclamations (¡...!).

ℰ la **cómoda** *fem noun*
chest of drawers

el **comodín** *masc noun*
joker (*in a pack of cards*)

cómodo *masc adjective*, **cómoda** *fem*
comfortable
¿Estás cómodo? Are you comfortable?
un sillón muy cómodo a very comfortable armchair
ponerse cómodo to make yourself comfortable
Ponte cómoda. Make yourself comfortable (*speaking to a girl*).

ℰ el **compact disc**, el **compacto** *masc noun*
1 **CD**
2 **CD player**

ℰ el **compañero** *masc noun*, la **compañera** *fem*
1 **colleague**
mis compañeros de trabajo my workmates
2 un compañero de clase a school mate
su compañera de piso her flatmate
3 **partner** (*in a relationship*)

la **compañía** *fem noun*
company
el director de la compañía the manager of the company
hacerle compañía a alguien to keep somebody company
Yo le hacía compañía. I kept her company.

la **comparación** *fem noun*
comparison
hacer una comparación entre dos cosas to make a comparison between two thing
Haz una comparación entre los dos dibujos. Make a comparison between the two pictures.
en comparación con in comparison with
Es alto en comparación con su hermano. He's tall in comparison with his brother.

comparar *verb* [17]
to compare

ℰ **compartir** *verb* [19]
to share
compartir algo con alguien to share something with somebody
Compartieron su comida conmigo. They shared their food with me.

el **compás** *masc noun*
1 **time, rhythm**
llevar el compás to keep time
2 **pair of compasses**

compensar *verb* [29]
to compensate

la **competencia** *fem noun*
competition (*in business, etc*)
Nos hacen la competencia. They're in competition with us.

la **competición** *fem noun*
competition (*in sports*)

competir *verb* [57]
to compete

compita, **compito**, **etc** *verb* ▷ **competir**

ℰ **completamente** *adverb*
completely

a
b
c
d
e
f
g
h
i
j
k
l
m
n
ñ
o
p
q
r
s
t
u
v
w
x
y
z

completar verb [17]
to complete

completo masc adjective, **completa** fem
1 complete
2 full
El hotel está completo. The hotel is full.
'Completo' 'No vacancies'

ℰ **complicado** masc adjective, **complicada** fem
complicated

ℰ **complicar** verb [31]
to complicate

complicarse reflexive verb [31]
to become complicated
La situación se ha complicado. The situation has become complicated.

componer verb [11]
1 to make up
El equipo está compuesto de once jugadores. The team is made up of eleven players.
2 to compose (music, a poem)
3 (Latin America) to repair
Hay que componer el radio.

componerse reflexive verb [11]
componerse de to be made up of
Su dieta se compone sólo de verduras. His diet is made up only of vegetables.

ℰ el **comportamiento** masc noun
behaviour
mal comportamiento bad behaviour

comportarse reflexive verb [17]
to behave
comportarse mal to behave badly

la **composición** fem noun
composition

el **compositor** masc noun, la **compositora** fem
composer

ℰ la **compra** fem noun
purchase
Fue una buena compra. It was a good buy.
ir de compras to go shopping
Mañana nos vamos de compras. We're going shopping tomorrow.
hacer la compra to do the shopping
Su padre siempre hace la compra. Her father always does the shopping.

el **comprador** masc noun, la **compradora** fem
buyer

ℰ **comprar** verb [17]
1 to buy
2 comprarle algo a alguien to buy something for somebody (as a present)
Le compré a Juan un videojuego para su cumpleaños. I bought Juan a videogame for his birthday.
3 comprarle algo a alguien to buy something from somebody
Voy a comprarle su bicicleta. I'm going to buy his bike from him.

ℰ **comprender** verb [18]
to understand
No comprendo la pregunta. I don't understand the question.
No me comprenden. They don't understand me.

la **comprensión** fem noun
comprehension
un ejercicio de comprensión a comprehension test

la **compresa** fem noun
sanitary towel

el **comprimido** masc noun
pill

comprobar verb [24]
to check
Hay que comprobar la factura. We must check the bill.

el **compromiso** masc noun
1 appointment, commitment
Mañana no puedo, tengo un compromiso. Tomorrow is out, I've got an appointment.
Tiene muchos compromisos. She has a lot of commitments.
2 commitment
3 obligation
sin compromiso without obligation
4 poner a alguien en un compromiso to put somebody in an awkward situation
Ahora me has puesto en un compromiso. Now you've put me in an awkward situation.
• el **compromiso político** political commitment

ℰ el **computador** masc noun
(Latin America) computer
▷ ordenador

ℰ la **computadora** fem noun
(Latin America) computer
▷ ordenador

♯ **común** *masc & fem adjective*
>**common**
>en común in common
>**No tenemos nada en común.** We have nothing in common.
>**trabajar en común** to work together

la **comunicación** *fem noun*
1 **communication**
2 **ponerse en comunicación con alguien** to get in touch with someone
>**Se puso en comunicación conmigo en cuanto llegó.** He got in touch with me as soon as he arrived.
3 **cortarse la comunicación** to be cut off (*on the phone*)
>**Se ha cortado la comunicación.** I've been cut off.
4 (*in transport*) **Las comunicaciones son buenas.** The communications are good.
>**un barrio con buenas comunicaciones** an area with good public transport services

♯ **comunicar** *verb* [31]
1 **to be busy** (*when telephoning*)
>**Está comunicando.** The line is busy.
2 **to inform**
>**Debo comunicarles que ...** I must inform you that ...

comunicarse *reflexive verb* [31]
1 **to communicate**
>**comunicarse por carta** to communicate by letter
2 **to be in touch**
>**No puedo comunicarme con él.** I can't get in touch with him.

la **comunidad** *fem noun*
>**community**
• la **Comunidad Europea** the European Community

la **comunión** *fem noun*
>**communion**
>(*Religion*) **hacer la primera comunión** to take first communion

♯ **con** *preposition*
1 **with**
>**Vine con mi primo.** I came with my cousin.
>**Divídelo con un cuchillo.** Divide it up with a knife.
2 **to**
>**hablar con alguien** to speak to somebody
>**estar casado con alguien** to be married to somebody
3 **and**
>**bistec con patatas** steak and chips
>**pan con mantequilla** bread and butter

4 **con tal de que** as long as
>**Te lo dejo, con tal de que lo cuides.** I'll lend it to you as long as you look after it.

el **concejal** *masc noun*, la **concejala** *fem*
>**councillor**
>**Su tía es concejala.** Her aunt is a councillor.

la **concentración** *fem noun*
>**concentration**

concentrar *verb* [17]
>**to concentrate**

concentrarse *reflexive verb* [17]
>**to concentrate**
>**Me concentré en mi trabajo.** I concentrated on my work.

♯ la **concha** *fem noun*
>**shell**

concienzudo *masc adjective*, **concienzuda** *fem*
>**conscientious**

♯ el **concierto** *masc noun*
>**concert**
>**un concierto de música rock** a rock concert

la **conclusión** *fem noun*
>**conclusion**
>**llegar a una conclusión** to reach a conclusion

♯ **concurrido** *masc adjective*, **concurrida** *fem*
1 **busy** (*bar, street, market*)
2 **well-attended** (*concert, exhibition*)

el **concurso** *masc noun*
>**competition**
>**un programa concurso** a quiz show
• el **concurso hípico** show-jumping competition

el **conde** *masc noun*, la **condesa** *fem noun*
1 **count**
2 **countess**

la **condición** *fem noun*
>**condition**
>**a condición de que, con la condición de que** on condition that
>**Te lo presto con la condición de que me lo devuelvas mañana.** I'll lend it to you on condition that you give it back tomorrow.

♯ el **condón** *masc noun*
>**condom**

♯ **conducir** *verb* [60]
1 **to drive**
>**Yo conduzco.** I'll drive.
2 **to lead**
>**el camino que conduce al pueblo** the road that leads to the village

a
b
c
d
e
f
g
h
i
j
k
l
m
n
ñ
o
p
q
r
s
t
u
v
w
x
y
z

♂ el **conductor** *masc noun*, la **conductora**
  fem
  driver

conduje, **condujo** *verb* ▷ **conducir**

conduzca, **conduzco**, **etc** *verb* ▷
  conducir

conectar *verb*[17]
  to connect
  conectar la impresora al ordenador to
  connect the printer to the computer

el **conejillo de Indias** *masc noun*
  guinea pig

el **conejo** *masc noun*, la **coneja** *fem*
  rabbit

la **conexión** *fem noun*
  connection

♂ la **conferencia** *fem noun*
1 **lecture**
2 **long-distance call**
  una conferencia interurbana a long-
  distance telephone call
  • la **conferencia de prensa** press
    conference

confesar *verb*[29]
  to confess

la **confianza** *fem noun*
1 **trust**
  una persona de confianza a person you can
  trust
2 **tener confianza en alguien** to have
  confidence in somebody
  Tiene mucha confianza en sí mismo. He's
  very self-confident.
3 **tener confianza con alguien** to know
  somebody very well
  Tenemos mucha confianza. We know each
  other very well.

confiar *verb*[32]
  to trust
  Confío en ti. I trust you.

la **confidencia** *fem noun*
  confidence
  hacerle una confidencia a alguien to tell
  somebody something in confidence

confirmar *verb*[17]
  to confirm

♂ la **confitería** *fem noun*
  patisserie, pastry shop

la **confitura** *fem noun*
  fruit preserve

♂ **conforme** *masc & fem adjective*
1 **estar conforme** to agree
  No estoy conforme. I don't agree.
  ¿Conformes? Do you agree? (*speaking to
  more than one person*)
2 **¡Conforme!** Ok! (*one person replying*)
  estar conforme con algo to be happy with
  something
  Estoy conforme con tu decisión. **I'm
  happy with your decision.**
  No estoy conforme con el precio. **I'm not
  happy witht he price.**

confortable *masc & fem adjective*
  comfortable

confortar *verb*[17]
  to comfort

♂ **confundir** *verb*[19]
1 **to confuse**
  No me confundas. Don't confuse me.
2 **to get mixed up**
  He confundido las fechas. I've got the
  dates mixed up.
3 **confundir a alguien con alguien** to mistake
  somebody for somebody else
  La confundí con Cristina. I mistook her for
  Cristina.

confundirse *reflexive verb*[19]
1 **to make a mistake**
  Creo que se ha confundido con la cuenta. I
  think you've made a mistake with the
  bill. (*speaking formally*)
2 Se confundió de número. He got the wrong
  number.

♂ la **confusión** *fem noun*
  confusion

♂ **confuso** *masc adjective*, **confusa** *fem*
1 **confusing**
  Esto es muy confuso. This is very confusing.
2 **confused**
  Estaba confusa. She was confused.

♂ **congelado** *masc adjective*, **congelada** *fem*
1 **frozen**
  alimentos congelados frozen food
  ¡Estoy congelada! I'm freezing!
2 Murió congelado. He died from exposure.
3 Tenía un dedo congelado. He had frostbite
  in one finger.

♂ el **congelador** *masc noun*
1 **freezer compartment**
2 **deep freezer**

♂ **congelar** *verb*[17]
  to freeze

congelarse *reflexive verb* [17]
to freeze
¡Me estoy congelando! I'm freezing!

♂ **conjugar** *verb* [28]
to conjugate

conjunto *masc adjective*, **conjunta** *fem*
▷ see **conjunto** *noun*
joint
un esfuerzo conjunto a joint effort

el **conjunto** *masc noun* ▷ see **conjunto** *adj*
1 **group**
un conjunto de personas a group of people
un conjunto de música pop a pop group
2 **collection**
un conjunto de cosas a collection of things
3 **outfit**
un conjunto de falda y chaleco a matching
skirt and waistcoat
4 **en conjunto** as a whole
En conjunto el trabajo está bien. As a whole
the work is all right.

♂ **conmigo** *pronoun*
1 **with me**
Ven conmigo. Come with me.
2 **to me**
No habló conmigo. He didn't talk to me.
3 **conmigo mismo** *masc*, **conmigo misma** *fem*
with myself
No estoy contento conmigo mismo. I'm
not happy with myself.

WORD TIP *con* + *mí* becomes *conmigo*, which does
not change.

♂ **conocer** *verb* [35]
1 **to know** (*people, places, stories, etc*)
Los conozco de vista. I know them by
sight.
¿Conoces España? Do you know Spain?
Conozco la historia. I know the story.
2 **to meet**, **to get to know**
Conocí a su hermana en Santander. I met
her sister in Santander.
3 **to recognize**
Te conocí por la forma de andar. I
recognized you by the way you walk.

conocerse *reflexive verb* [35]
1 **to know each other**
Se conocen bien. They know each other
well.
2 **to get to know each other**
Nos conocimos en Jaca. We got to know
each other in Jaca.

WORD TIP For the other Spanish verb for *to
know* ▷ **saber**.

conocido *masc adjective*, **conocida** *fem*
▷ see **conocido** *noun*
1 **well-known** (*actor, song*)
una canción conocida a well-known song
2 **familiar**
una cara conocida a familiar face

el **conocido** *masc noun*, la **conocida** *fem*
▷ see **conocido** *adj*
acquaintance

♂ el **conocimiento** *masc noun*
knowledge

conozca, **conozco**, **etc** *verb* ▷ **conocer**

♂ **conque** *conjunction*
so
Conque esta es tu novia. So, this is your
girlfriend.

la **consecuencia** *fem noun*
consequence

♂ **conseguir** *verb* [64]
1 **to achieve**
Han conseguido su objetivo. They've
achieved their objective.
2 **to get**
He conseguido un trabajo. I've got a job.
3 **conseguir hacer algo** to manage to do
something
Conseguimos persuadirle que se quedara.
We managed to persuade him to stay.

el **consejero** *masc noun*, la **consejera** *fem*
1 **adviser**
2 **board member** (*of a company*)
3 **minister** (*in some autonomous Spanish
parliaments*)
• el **consejero delegado** la **consejera
delegada** managing director

♂ el **consejo** *masc noun*
1 **piece of advice**
Te doy un consejo. I'll give you a piece of
advice.
2 **consejos** advice
No hacen caso de mis consejos. They don't
follow my advice.
3 **board** (*of a company, school, etc*)
4 **council** (*in local government*)
• el **consejo de administración** board of
directors
• el **Consejo de Europa** the Council of
Europe
• el **consejo de ministros** cabinet meeting
• el **consejo escolar** board of governors (*of a
school*)

♂ el & la **conserje** *masc & fem noun*
1 **caretaker** (*in a school, a public building*)
2 **receptionist** (*in a hotel*)

a b c d e f g h i j k l m n ñ o p q r s t u v w x y z

conservador *masc adjective,*
conservadora *fem*
▷ see **concervador** *noun*
conservative

el **conservador** *masc noun,* la
conservadora *fem*
▷ see **concervador** *adj*
conservative

conservar *verb* [17]
1 **to preserve** *(food)*
2 **to keep up** *(traditions)*
3 **to keep**
Conservo todas sus cartas. I keep all her letters.
Intenta conservar la calma. Try to keep calm.

conservarse *reflexive verb* [17]
to keep *(foods)*
Las manzanas se conservan bien. Apples keep well.

las **conservas** *plural fem noun*
tinned food

ℰ **considerable** *masc & fem adjective*
considerable
un número considerable de estudiantes a considerable number of students

la **consideración** *fem noun*
consideración
tomar algo en consideración to take something into consideration
Tienes que tomar en consideración el tiempo que tardarás en llegar. You must take into consideration the time it will take you get here.

considerar *verb* [17]
to consider

consiga, **consigo**, **consiguiendo**, **etc** *verb* ▷ **conseguir**

la **consigna** *fem noun*
left-luggage office

ℰ **consigo** *pronoun*
1 **with him, with her**
Lo trae consigo. He's bringing it with him., She's bringing it with her.
2 consigo mismo **with himself**
consigo misma **with herself**
No está contento consigo mismo. He is not happy with himself.
Está enfadada consigo misma. She is angry with herself.
3 **with them**
El dinero que tenían consigo. The money they had with them.

4 **with you** *(when talking politely)*
Si usted quiere lo puede traer consigo. If you wish, you can bring it with you.

WORD TIP con + sí becomes consigo, which does not change.

ℰ **consistir** *verb* [19]
consistir en algo to consist of something
Consiste en tres sillas y una mesa. It consists of three chairs and a table.
El trabajo consiste en … The job involves …

ℰ la **consonante** *fem noun*
consonant *(all the letters except a, e, i, o, u)*

constante *masc & fem adjective*
constant

ℰ **constipado** *masc adjective,* **constipada** *fem* ▷ see **constipado** *noun*
estar constipado to have a cold
No fui a la piscina porque estaba constipada. I didn't go to the pool because I had a cold.

WORD TIP constipado does not mean constipated in English; for the meaning of constipated ▷ **estreñido**.

el **constipado** *masc noun*
▷ see **constipado** *adj*
cold
coger un constipado to catch a cold

constiparse *reflexive verb* [17]
to catch a cold
Me he constipado. I've caught a cold.

el **constructor** *masc noun,* la
constructora *fem*
builder

ℰ **construir** *verb* [54]
to build

construya, **construyendo**, **construyo**, **etc** *verb* ▷ **construir**

el & la **cónsul** *masc & fem noun*
consul

el **consulado** *masc noun*
consulate

ℰ la **consulta** *fem noun*
1 **surgery**
horas de consulta surgery hours
Pasa consulta de cuatro a siete. His surgery hours are from four to seven.
2 **hacer una consulta a aguien** to ask something
¿Te puedo hacer una consulta? **Can I ask you a question?**
un libro de consulta a reference book

✗ **consultar** *verb* [17]
1 **to consult**
consultarle algo a alguien to consult somebody about something
Se lo voy a consultar al médico. I'm going to consult the doctor about it.
2 **to look up**
Tengo que consultarlo en el diccionario. I have to look it up in the dictionary.

✗ el **consultorio** *masc noun*
surgery

la **consumición** *fem noun*
drink (*in a bar, cafe*)
consumición mínima cuatro euros minimum charge four euros

el **consumo** *masc noun*
consumption

el & la **contable** *masc & fem noun*
accountant

el **contacto** *masc noun*
1 **contact**
estar en contacto to be in contact
2 **ignition** (*in a car*)

el **contado** *masc noun*
al contado cash
pagar al contado to pay cash
Lo compré al contado. I paid for it in cash.

el **contador** *masc noun*
meter (*for electricity, water, in a taxi*)

✗ **contagiar** *verb* [17]
to pass on (*an illness*)
No quiero contagiarte el resfriado. I don't want to give you my cold.

contagiarse *reflexive verb* [17]
to become infected
Se ha contagiado de su hermana. She's got it from her sister.

✗ la **contaminación** *fem noun*
1 **pollution** (*of the environment*)
2 **contamination** (*by radioactivity*)

✗ **contaminar** *verb* [17]
1 **to pollute** (*the air, water, sea*)
2 **to contaminate** (*with radioactivity*)

✗ **contar** *verb* [24]
1 **to count**
Cuenta el dinero. Count the money.
2 **contar con alguien** to count on somebody
Puedes contar conmigo. You can count on me.
3 **to tell**
Cuéntamelo. Tell me about it.
Le conté el secreto. I told him the secret.

4 **to count**
Eso no cuenta. That doesn't count.
El trabajo cuenta para mi nota final. The essay counts towards my final mark.

el **contenedor** *masc noun*
1 **container**
2 **skip**
3 un contenedor de vidrio a bottle bank

✗ **contener** *verb* [9]
1 **to contain**
No contiene conservantes. It does not contain preservatives.
2 **to hold back** (*tears, laughter, breath*)
contener la respiración to hold your breath
No pudo contener la risa. She couldn't stop herself laughing.

✗ el **contenido** *masc noun*
1 **contents**
el contenido de la botella the contents of the bottle
2 **content**
el contenido del libro the content of the book

✗ **contento** *masc adjective*, **contenta** *fem*
1 **happy**
Mis padres están muy contentos. My parents are very happy.
2 **pleased**
Estoy contento de verte. I'm pleased to see you.

la **contestación** *fem noun*
1 **answer**
No nos dio una contestación. He didn't give us an answer.
2 **reply**
Quedo a la espera de su contestación. Looking forward to your reply.

✗ el **contestador**, el **contestador automático** *masc noun*
answering machine

✗ **contestar** *verb* [17]
1 **to answer**
No contestó. He didn't answer.
contestar el teléfono to answer the phone
2 **contestar a** to reply to (*a letter, a question*)
No ha contestado a mi carta. He hasn't replied to my letter.

el **contexto** *masc noun*
context

✗ **contigo** *pronoun*
1 **with you**
Yo voy contigo. I'm going with you. ▸▸

✗ indicates key words   75

2 to you
No hablo contigo. I'm not talking to you.

3 contigo mismo *masc*, **contigo misma** *fem*
with yourself
¿Estás contento contigo mismo? Are you
pleased with yourself?

WORD TIP *con* + *ti* becomes *contigo*, which does
not change.

ʃ el **continente** *masc noun*
continent

la **continuación** *fem noun*
continuation
A continuación ... Next ...

ʃ **continuamente** *adverb*
continuously

ʃ **continuar** *verb* [20]
to continue
Continuaron viviendo allí. They went living
there.
Continúe todo recto. Keep going straight
on. (*street directions, polite form*)
Continuará. To be continued.

continuo *masc adjective*, **continua** *fem*
constant

ʃ **contra** *preposition*
against
Son dos contra uno. It's two against one.
Lo apoyó contra la pared. He leant it
against the wall.
El coche chocó contra el árbol. The car
crashed into the tree.
estar en contra de algo to be against
something
Estoy en contra de la decisión. I'm against
the decision.

el & la **contrabandista** *masc & fem noun*
smuggler

el **contrabando** *masc noun*
1 smuggling
2 smuggled goods

contrario *masc adjective*, **contraria** *fem*
▷ see **contrario** *noun*
1 opposite
la dirección contraria the opposite
direction
Soy contrario a las reformas. I'm opposed
to the reforms.
pasarse al bando contrario to go over to
the opposing side
todo lo contrario quite the opposite
2 de lo contrario otherwise

el **contrario** *masc noun*
▷ see **contrario** *adj*
1 opposite
al contrario on the contrary
Al contrario, me gusta mucho. On the
contrary, I like it a lot.
Es al contrario. It's the opposite way round.
2 por el contrario on the other hand

contrarreloj *adjective*
a contrarreloj against the clock
una carrera a contrarreloj a race against
the clock

la **contraseña** *fem noun*
password

el **contrato** *masc noun*
contract

la **contribución** *fem noun*
1 contribution
2 tax

ʃ el **control** *masc noun*
1 control
estar bajo control to be under control
2 llevar el control de algo to keep a check on
something
Ella lleva el control de los gastos en casa.
She keeps a check on the household
expenses.
3 checkpoint
• el **control de la natalidad** birth control
• el **control de pasaportes** passport control
• el **control remoto** remote control

controlar *verb* [17]
1 to control
2 to keep a check on
controlar el peso to keep a check on your
weight
controlar las entradas y salidas to keep an
eye on the comings and goings

controvertido *masc adjective*,
controvertida *fem*
controversial
una decisión controvertida a controversial
decision

convencer *verb* [44]
1 to convince
2 to persuade
Le convencimos para que fuera. We
persuaded him to go.
3 No me convence mucho la idea. I'm not
sure about the idea.

conveniente *masc & fem adjective*
1 convenient
2 advisable

76

♪ **convenir** *verb* [15]
1 **to be advisable**
Conviene informarse antes. It's advisable to find out in advance.
Te conviene descansar. It would be advisable to rest.
Te conviene preguntar. You should ask.
2 **convenirle a alguien** to suit someone
Me conviene el sábado. Saturday suits me.
Lo hace porque le conviene. He does it because it suits him.
3 **convenir en algo** to agree on something
Convinieron en reunirse en la oficina del director. They agreed to meet in the headmaster's office.
4 Sueldo a convenir. Salary negotiable.

el **convento** *masc noun*
convent

convenza, **convenzo**, **etc** *verb* ▷ **convencer**

♪ la **conversación** *fem noun*
conversation

conversar *verb* [17]
(*Latin America*) **to chat**

♪ **convertir** *verb* [14]
1 **convertir algo en algo** to turn something into something
Convirtió las libras en euros. He converted the pounds into euros.
2 **to convert** (*to a religion*)

convertirse *reflexive verb* [14]
1 **convertirse en algo** to turn into something
Se convirtió en una estrella. She turned into a star.
2 **to convert**
Se convirtió al budismo. She converted to Buddhism.

convierta, **convierto**, **etc** *verb* ▷ **convertir**

el **coñac** *masc noun*
brandy

el & la **cooperante** *masc & fem noun*
voluteer aid worker

cooperar *verb* [17]
to cooperate

♪ la **copa** *fem noun*
1 **wine glass**
una copa de vino a glass of wine
2 **drink**
tomar una copa to have a drink
Te invito a una copa. I'll buy you a drink.
3 **cup** (*prize in sports, etc*)
la Copa de Europa the European Cup

la **copia** *fem noun*
copy
· la **copia de seguridad** back-up copy

♪ **copiar** *verb* [17]
1 **to copy** (*cheat in exams, etc*)
2 **to make a copy of** (*a document*)
3 **to copy down** (*notes, etc*)

el **coraje** *masc noun*
courage

♪ el **corazón** *masc noun*
1 **heart**
una persona de gran corazón a kind-hearted person
Sufre del corazón. He has heart trouble.
2 **sweetheart**
Vamos, corazón. Let's go sweetheart.

♪ la **corbata** *fem noun*
tie

el **corcho** *masc noun*
cork

♪ el **cordero** *masc noun*
lamb
una pierna de cordero a leg of lamb
una chuleta de cordero a lamb chop

la **cordillera** *masc noun*
mountain range

♪ el **cordón** *masc noun*
1 **string**
2 **flex** (*of electrical appliance*)
· el **cordón de zapato** shoelace

♪ el **coro** *masc noun*
choir
a coro in chorus

la **corona** *fem noun*
1 **crown**
2 **wreath**
una corona de flores a wreath of flowers

el & la **coronel** *masc noun*
colonel

el **corral** *masc noun*
farmyard

♪ la **correa** *fem noun*
1 **strap**
2 **lead** (*for a dog*)
· la **correa de reloj** watchstrap

♪ la **corrección** *fem noun*
correction

correctamente *adverb*
1 **politely**
2 **correctly**
¿Has rellenado el formulario correctamente? Have you filled in the form correctly?

♪ indicates key words   77

correcto *masc adjective*, **correcta** *fem*

1 **correct**, **right**
la respuesta correcta the right answer

2 **polite**
Siempre es muy correcto. He's always very polite.

ℰ el **corrector ortográfico** *masc noun*
spelling checker

el **corredor** *masc noun*, la **corredora** *fem*
runner
• el **corredor de coches** racing driver
• el **corredor de fondo** long-distance runner

ℰ **corregir** *verb* [48]
to correct

ℰ el **correo** *masc noun*

1 **post**
mandar algo por correo to send something by post
Mándalo por correo aéreo. Send it by air mail.
echar algo al correo to post something

2 **Correos** the post office
Voy a Correos. I'm going to the post office.

WORD TIP *Correos is spelt with a capita C; it is never used with* el *when it means post office.*

• el **correo aéreo** airmail
• el **correo electrónico** electronic mail; email
• el **correo urgente** special delivery

ℰ **correr** *verb* [18]

1 **to run**
¡Corre, que vas a perder el bus! Run, you're going to miss the bus!
Salió corriendo de la habitación. She ran out of the room.
echar a correr to start running
En seguida echaron a correr. They started running straight away.

2 **to go fast** (*cars, bikes, drivers*)
Este coche corre mucho. This car goes very fast

3 (*expressing speed*) Hice la comida corriendo. I made dinner quickly.
Vino corriendo a verme. She rushed to see me.

4 **to draw**
Por favor, corre las cortinas. Please draw the curtains.

correrse *reflexive verb* [17]
to move up
Córrete a un lado. Move up to make room.

ℰ **correspondiente** *masc & fem adjective*
corresponding

el & la **corresponsal** *masc & fem noun*
correspondent (*in journalism*)

ℰ la **corrida** *fem noun* ▷ see **corrido** *adj*
bullfight
Corrida de toros en Almería Bullfights in Almería (*title of poster*)

corrido *masc adjective*, **corrida** *fem*
▷ see **corrida** *noun*
embarrassed

ℰ **corriente** *masc & fem adjective*
▷ see **corriente** *noun*

1 **common**
un error muy corriente a very common mistake
una chica normal y corriente an ordinary kind of girl
Lo más corriente es ... The most usual thing is ...

2 **running**
agua corriente en todas las habitaciones running water in all rooms

3 estar al corriente de algo to be aware of something
Siempre está al corriente de lo que pasa. She's always up to date with what's going on.

ℰ la **corriente** *fem noun* ▷ see **corriente** *adj*

1 **current** (*in the sea*)
La corriente es muy fuerte. The current's very strong.

2 **current** (*electricity*)
No hay corriente. There's no electricity.

3 **draught**
Hace corriente. There's a draught.

corrija, **corrijo**, **etc** *verb* ▷ **corregir**

corrompido *masc adjective*, **corrompida** *fem*
corrupt

corrupto *masc adjective*, **corrupta** *fem*
corrupt

ℰ el **cortacésped** *masc noun*
lawnmower

cortado *masc adjective*, **cortada** *fem*
▷ see **cortado** *noun*

1 **closed** (*road, street, mountain pass*)

2 **off**
La leche está cortada. The milk is off.

3 ser muy cortado (*informal*) to be very shy
Su novio es un poco cortado. Her boyfriend's a bit shy.

4 **embarrassed**
estar cortado (*informal*) to be embarrassed

el **cortado** *masc noun* ▷ see **cortado** *adj*
small cup of coffee (*with a dash of milk*)

ℰ **cortar** *verb* [17]

1 **to cut**
cortar un pastel to cut a cake
cortar algo por la mitad to cut something
in two
Corta la tarta por la mitad. Cut the cake in
two.

2 cortar el césped to mow the lawn

3 **to chop**
cortar leña to chop wood
cortar un árbol to chop down a tree

4 **to cut off**
Nos han cortado la luz. Our electricity has
been cut off.

cortarse *reflexive verb* [17]

1 **to cut oneself**
Me he cortado la mano. I've cut my hand.

2 cortarse el pelo to have your hair cut
Mañana me voy a cortar el pelo. I'm going
to have my hair cut tomorrow.

3 **to be cut off**
Se ha cortado el agua. The water's been cut
off.

4 **to go off**
Se ha cortado la leche. The milk's gone off.

el **cortaúñas** *masc noun*
nail clippers

el **corte** *masc noun* ▷ see **corte** *noun*

1 **cut**
hacerse un corte to cut yourself
Se hizo un corte en el dedo. He cut his
finger.
un corte de pelo a haircut
Ha habido un corte de agua. The water's
been cut off.

2 corte y confección dressmaking

3 (*informal*) **embarrassment**
¡Qué corte! How embarrassing!

la **corte** *fem noun* ▷ see **corte** *noun*
court
la Corte Suprema the Supreme Court
las Cortes the Spanish Parliament (*in Madrid*)

cortés *masc & fem adjective*
polite

ℰ la **corteza** *fem noun*

1 **bark** (*of a tree*)

2 **rind** (*of cheese*)

3 **crust** (*of bread*)

4 **peel** (*of an orange or a lemon*)

ℰ la **cortina** *fem noun*
curtain

ℰ **corto** *masc adjective*, **corta** *fem*
short

ℰ la **cosa** *fem noun*

1 **thing**
Se llevó todas sus cosas. He took all his
things.
Te he comprado una cosa. I've bought
something for you.
¿Qué tal van las cosas? How are things?

2 alguna cosa something
Por si pasa alguna cosa. In case something
happens.

3 alguna cosa anything (*in questions*)
¿Buscas alguna cosa en especial? Are you
looking for anything in particular?
¿Quiere alguna otra cosa? Do you want
anything else?

4 cualquier cosa anything
Si necesitas alguna cosa, dímelo. If you
need anything, tell me.

la **cosecha** *fem noun*

1 **harvest**

2 **crop**

3 **vintage** (*of wine*)

cosechar *verb* [17]
to harvest

ℰ **coser** *verb* [18]
to sew

cosmético *masc adjective*, **cosmética** *fem*
▷ see **cosmético** *noun*
cosmetic

el **cosmético** *masc noun*
▷ see **cosmético** *adj*
cosmetic

las **cosquillas** *plural fem noun*
hacerle cosquillas a alguien to tickle
somebody
tener cosquillas to be ticklish

la **costa** *fem noun*
coast

el **costado** *masc noun*
side

ℰ **costar** *verb* [24]

1 **to cost**
¿Cuánto cuesta? How much does it
cost?
Cuesta muy caro. It's very expensive.
La comida cuesta poco. Food is cheap.
Me costó barato. It didn't cost me very
much.

2 **to be hard**
Cuesta mucho entenderlo. It's very hard to
understand. ▸▸

a
b
c
d
e
f
g
h
i
j
k
l
m
n
ñ
o
p
q
r
s
t
u
v
w
x
y
z

Cuesta un poco acostumbrarse. It takes a bit of getting used to.
Me costó hacerlo. I found it difficult to do.

Costa Rica *fem noun*
Costa Rica

costarricense *masc & fem adjective & noun*
1 **Costa Rican**
2 **un & una costarricense** Costa Rican

WORD TIP Adjectives and nouns for nationality and regional origin do not have capital letters in Spanish.

♪ el **coste** *masc noun*
cost

la **costilla** *fem noun*
rib

costoso *masc adjective*, **costosa** *fem*
expensive

la **costra** *fem noun*
scab

♪ la **costumbre** *fem noun*
1 **habit**
Viene los martes por costumbre. He comes on Tuesdays out of habit.
Tengo la costumbre de hacerlo así. I'm in the habit of doing it this way.
2 **de costumbre** as usual
el lugar de costumbre the usual place
3 **custom**

la **costura** *fem noun*
1 **needlework**
2 **seam**

cotidiano *masc adjective*, **cotidiana** *fem*
daily

cotilla *masc & fem noun*
gossip
Es muy cotilla. He's such a gossip.

cotillear *verb* [17]
to gossip

♪ el **cráneo** *fem noun*
skull

la **creación** *fem noun*
creation

creador *masc adjective*, **creadora** *fem*
▷ see **creador** noun
creative

el **creador** *masc noun*, la **creadora** *fem*
▷ see **creador** adj
creator

crear *verb* [17]
to create

crecer *verb* [35]
1 **to grow**
Su hermana ha crecido mucho. His sister's grown a lot.
2 **to grow up**
Creció en Escocia. She grew up in Scotalnd.

el **crédito** *masc noun*
1 **credit** (*in a shop*)
2 **loan** (*from a bank*)
• el **crédito hipotecario** mortgage

♪ **creer** *verb* [37]
1 **to think**
Creo que se llama Nekane. I think she's called Nekane.
¿Crees que me llamará? Do you think he'll phone me?
Creo que sí. I think so.
Creo que no. I don't think so.
2 **to believe**
No lo creo. I don't believe it.
¿Crees en Dios? Do you believe in God?

creíble *masc & fem adjective*
believable

♪ la **crema** *fem noun*
cream
• la **crema bronceadora** suntan lotion
• la **crema hidratante** moisturizer

♪ la **cremallera** *fem noun*
zip
subirse la cremallera to do up your zip

el **crepúsculo** *masc noun*
twilight

creyendo, **creyó**, etc *verb* ▷ **creer**

crezca, **crezco**, etc *verb* ▷ **crecer**

el **crío** *masc noun*, la **cría** *fem*
1 **child**
2 **la cría** baby animal
una cría de leopardo a baby leopard

el **criado** *masc noun*, la **criada** *fem*
servant

criar *verb* [17]
1 **to bring up**
Lo crió su tía. He was brought up by his aunt.
2 **to breed**
criar ganado to breed cattle

criarse *reflexive verb* [17]
to grow up
Se crió en un pueblo. He grew up in a village.

♂ el **crimen** *masc noun*
1 **crime**
cometer un crimen to commit a crime
2 **murder**
cometer un crimen to commit murder

el & la **criminal** *masc & fem noun*
criminal

la **crisis** *fem noun*
1 **crisis**
2 (*Medicine*) **attack**

♂ el **cristal** *masc noun*
1 **glass**
Es de cristal. It's made of glass.
2 **window pane**
limpiar los cristales to clean the windows.
La pelota rompió un cristal. The ball broke a
window pane.
3 **piece of broken glass**
El suelo estaba lleno de cristales. The floor
was covered with broken glass.

el **cristianismo** *masc noun*
Christianity

cristiano *masc adjective & noun*, **cristiana**
fem adjective & noun
1 **Christian**
2 un cristiano, una cristiana Christian

> **WORD TIP** Adjectives and nouns for religion do
> not have capital letters in Spanish.

Cristo *masc noun*
(*Religion*) **Christ**

el **criterio** *masc noun*
1 **judgement**
2 **guideline**

la **crítica** *fem noun*
1 **criticism**
Recibió duras críticas. He came in for a lot
of harsh criticism.
2 **review**
La película ha recibido muy buenas críticas.
The film has had very good reviews.

criticar *verb* [31]
1 **to criticize** (*a person, a plan*)
2 **to review** (*a film, an album*)

el **cromo** *masc noun*
sticker

♂ el **cruce** *masc noun*
1 **crossroads**
2 'Cruce peligroso' 'Dangerous Junction'
3 **crossing**
• el **cruce de peatones** pedestrian crossing

el **crucero** *masc noun*
cruise (*on a ship*)

♂ el **crucigrama** *masc noun*
crossword

crudo *masc adjective*, **cruda** *fem*
1 **raw**
una zanahoria cruda a raw carrot
2 La carne está cruda. The meat is raw.
3 **harsh**
la cruda realidad the harsh reality

cruel *masc & fem adjective*
cruel

la **crueldad** *fem noun*
cruelty
Trataron a los prisioneros con gran
crueldad. **The prisoners were treated
with great cruelty.**

la **cruz** *fem noun*, **cruces** *plural*
1 **cross**
2 ¿Cara o cruz? Heads or tails?
• la **Cruz Roja** the Red Cross

♂ **cruzar** *verb* [22]
1 **to cross** (*a street, road*)
cruzar la calle to cross the road.
Crucé la calle corriendo. I ran across the
road.
2 **to cross** (*your arms, legs*)
cruzar los brazos to cross your arms

cruzarse *reflexive verb* [22]
1 **to cross** (*roads, paths, letters*)
2 **to pass each other**
Me crucé con ella en la calle. I met her in the
street.
Los dos coches se cruzaron. The two cars
passed each other.

♂ el **cuaderno** *masc noun*
1 **exercise book**
2 **notebook**

la **cuadra** *fem noun*
stable

♂ **cuadrado** *masc adjective*, **cuadrada** *fem*
▷ see **cuadrado** *noun*
square
de forma cuadrada square-shaped

♂ el **cuadrado** *masc noun*
▷ see **cuadrado** *adj*
square (*shape*)

♂ el **cuadro** *masc noun*
1 **painting**
2 **picture**
3 (*in designs*) a cuadros, de cuadros checked
una tela a cuadros a checked cloth

a
b
c
d
e
f
g
h
i
j
k
l
m
n
ñ
o
p
q
r
s
t
u
v
w
x
y
z

ᔍ el **cual** *masc pronoun*, la **cual** *fem pron*, los **cuales** *masc plural*, las **cuales** *fem plural*
▷ see **cuál** *pron*

1 (*talking about people*) **Pregunté a mi hermano, el cual me dio las señas.** I asked my brother, who gave me the address. (*el cual* for *hermano*)
Las chicas a las cuales invité. The girls whom I invited (*las cuales* for *chicas*).

2 (*talking about things*) **La casa en la cual se encontraron drogas.** The house in which drugs were found (*la cual* for *casa*).
Los ingredientes con los cuales se prepara este plato. The ingredients with which this dish is made (*los cuales* for *ingredientes*).

3 (*talking about something mentioned before*) **lo cual** which
No ha llamado, lo cual es extraño. He hasn't rung, which is strange.

4 **por lo cual** therefore

ᔍ **cuál** *masc & fem pronoun*, **cuáles** *plural masc & fem* ▷ see **cual** *pron*

1 **what**
¿Cuál es su profesión? What's your profession?
¿Cuáles son tus preferencias? What are your preferences?

2 **which, which one**
¿Cuál te gusta más? Which one do you like best?

WORD TIP *cuál* with an accent is used for questions (*¿...?*).

cualesquiera *adjective, pronoun* ▷ **cualquiera**

la **cualidad** *fem noun*
quality

ᔍ **cualquier** *adjective* ▷ **cualquiera**

ᔍ **cualquiera**, **cualesquiera** *adjective* ▷ see **cualquiera** *pron*
any
Tráeme cualquier vaso., **Tráeme un vaso cualquiera.** Bring me any glass.
Cualquier alumna sabe eso., **Una alumna cualquiera sabe eso.** Any schoolgirl knows that.

WORD TIP *cualquiera* becomes *cualquier* before a singular noun.

ᔍ **cualquiera** *pronoun*
▷ see **cualquiera** *adj*

1 **anybody, anyone**
Cualquiera lo sabe. Anybody knows that.

2 **any one (of them)**
Cualquiera servirá. Any one of them will do.

3 **either** (*of two people or things*)
'¿Cuál de los dos quieres?'—'Cualquiera.' 'Which of the two do you want?'—'Either of them.'

4 **whichever one** (*of more than two people or things*)
Coge cualquiera que quieras. Pick whichever one you want.
Toma cualesquiera que quieras. Take whichever ones you want.

WORD TIP *cualquiera* is singular; *cualesquiera* is plural.

ᔍ **cuando** *conjunction* ▷ see **cuándo** *adv*
when
Cuando estuve en Barcelona. When I was in Barcelona.
Cuando la vea la próxima semana. When I see her next week.

ᔍ **cuándo** *adverb* ▷ see **cuando** *conj*
when?
¿Cuándo la conociste? When did you meet her?
¿Desde cuándo? Since when?
No sé cuándo llegará. I don't know when he'll arrive.

WORD TIP *cuándo* with an accent, is used for questions (*¿...?*).

ᔍ **cuanto** *adverb, adjective & pronoun*, **cuanta** *fem* ▷ see **cuánto** *adv, adj, pron*

1 **as much, as much as**
Corta cuanta tela necesites. Cut as much fabric as you need.
Tengo cuanto necesito. I've got as much as I need.
Llama cuanto quieras. Phone as much as you want.

2 **cuantos, cuantas** as many as
Compra cuantos libros necesites. Buy as many books as you need.
Tengo cuantos necesito. I have as many as I need.

3 **unos cuantos, unas cuantas** a few
unos cuantos empleados a few employees
unas cuantas señoras a few ladies

4 **cuanto más ...** the more ...
Cuanto más pides, más te darán. The more you ask, the more you'll be given.

5 **cuanto menos ...** the less ...
Cuanto menos ruido hagas mejor. The less noise you make, the better.

ᔍ **cuánto** *adverb, adjective & pronoun*, **cuánta** *adjective & pronoun*

1 **cuánto, cuánta** how much
¿Cuánto café quieres? How much coffee do you want?

¿Cuánto cuesta? How much does it cost?
'Pon agua'—'¿Cuánta?' 'Add some water'—'How much?'
¿Cuanto tiempo has tardado en hacerlo? How long did you take to do it?

2 **cuántos, cuántas** how many
¿Cuántas tazas saco? How many cups should I put out?
Dime cuántos necesitas. Tell me how many you need.

3 (in exclamations) **¡Cuántas personas hay!** What a lot of people there are!
¡Cuántas hay! What a lot there are!
¡Cuánta comida has hecho! What a lot of food you've prepared!
¡Cuánto ha quedado! What a lot is left over!
¡Cuánto te quiero! How I love you!

WORD TIP *cuánto*, with an accent, is used for questions (¿...?) and exclamations (¡...!).

ƒ **cuarenta** *number*
forty
cuarenta y siete forty-seven
Mi madre tiene cuarenta años. My mum's forty.

la **cuaresma** *fem noun*
Lent

la **cuarta** *fem noun*
fourth gear
meter la cuarta to change into fourth

cuartel *noun*
barracks
· el **cuartel general** headquarters

ƒ el **cuarto** *masc noun* ▷ see **cuarto** *adj*
1 **quarter** (when telling the time)
a las doce menos cuarto at quarter to twelve
Son las dos y cuarto. It's quarter past two.
2 **quarter**
un cuarto de kilo a quarter of a kilo
Corté la tarta en cuatro cuartos. I cut the cake into four quarters.
3 **room**
el cuarto de los niños the children's bedroom
· el **cuarto de baño** bathroom
· el **cuarto de estar** living room
· los **cuartos de final** quarter finals

ƒ **cuarto** *masc adjective*, **cuarta** *fem*
▷ see **cuarto** *noun*
fourth
en el cuarto piso on the fourth floor
llegar en cuarto lugar to finish in fourth position

ƒ **cuatro** *number*
1 **four**
Juan tiene cuatro años. Juan's four (years old).
Son las cuatro. It's four o'clock.
2 **fourth** (in dates)
el cuatro de mayo the fourth of May

ƒ **cuatrocientos**, **cuatrocientas** *number*
four hundred
cuatrocientos quince four hundred and fifteen

Cuba *fem noun*
Cuba

cubano *masc adjective & noun*, **cubana** *fem adjective & noun*
1 **Cuban**
2 **un cubano, una cubana** Cuban

WORD TIP Adjectives and nouns for nationality and regional origin do not have capital letters in Spanish.

ƒ **cubierto** *masc adjective*, **cubierta** *fem*
▷ see **cubierto** *noun*
covered
estar cubierto de algo to be covered with something
El suelo estaba cubierto de papeles. The ground was covered with paper.

el **cubierto** *masc noun* ▷ see **cubierto** *adj*
1 **los cubiertos** the cutlery
Pon los cubiertos en la mesa. Put the knives and forks on the table.
2 **poner otro cubierto en la mesa** to lay another place at the table
· los **cubiertos de plata** silver cutlery

ƒ el **cubo** *masc noun*
1 **cube**
2 **bucket**
un cubo de agua a bucket of water
· el **cubo de la basura** bin

el **cubrecama** *masc noun*
bedspread

ƒ **cubrir** *verb* [46]
to cover

cubrirse *reflexive verb* [46]
1 **to cover yourself**
Me cubrí las rodillas. I covered my legs.
2 **to cloud over**
El cielo se ha cubierto. The sky has clouded over.

ƒ la **cucaracha** *fem noun*
cockroach

a b c d e f g h i j k l m n ñ o p q r s t u v w x y z

ℰ la **cuchara** *fem noun*
spoon
- la **cuchara de postre** dessert spoon
- la **cuchara sopera** soup spoon

ℰ la **cucharada** *fem noun*
spoonful

ℰ la **cucharadita** *fem noun*
teaspoonful

ℰ la **cucharilla**, la **cucharita** *fem noun*
teaspoon
una cucharilla de café, una cucharita de café a coffee spoon

cuchichear *verb* [17]
to whisper

ℰ la **cuchilla** *fem noun*
blade
- la **cuchilla de afeitar** razor blade

ℰ el **cuchillo** *masc noun*
knife

cuelga, cuelgo, etc *verb* ▷ **colgar**

ℰ el **cuello** *masc noun*
1 **neck**
2 **collar**
el cuello de la camisa the shirt collar
un jersey de cuello alto a polo-neck jumper

el **cuenco** *masc noun*
bowl

cuenta, cuento, etc *verb* ▷ **contar**

ℰ la **cuenta** *fem noun* ▷ see **cuento** *noun*
1 **bill**
¿Nos trae la cuenta, por favor? Could you bring us the bill, please?
2 **account** (*in a bank*)
hacer cuentas to do the accounts
Haz las cuentas de lo que te debo. Work out how much I owe you.
trabajar por su cuenta to be self-employed
Mi padre trabaja por su propia cuenta. My father's self-employed.
3 **darse cuenta de algo** to realize something
Me di cuenta de que había perdido la cartera. I realized I'd lost my wallet.
4 **sum**
hacer una cuenta to do a sum
llevar la cuenta de algo to keep count of something
Lleva la cuenta de lo que está gastando. Keep count of what he's spending.
5 **más de la cuenta** too much
Bebió más de la cuenta. He drank too much.
6 **bead** (*of a necklace*)
- la **cuenta atrás** countdown

- la **cuenta corriente** current account
- la **cuenta de ahorros** savings account

ℰ el **cuento** *masc noun*
1 **short story**
2 **tale**
3 No me vengas con tus cuentos. Don't come to me with your stories.
- el **cuento de hadas** fairy tale

la **cuerda** *fem noun*
1 **rope**
2 saltar a la cuerda to skip
3 darle cuerda a algo to wind something up
darle cuerda a un reloj to wind a clock

el **cuerno** *masc noun*
1 **horn**
2 **antler**

el **cuero** *masc noun*
leather
un bolso de cuero a leather bag
- el **cuero cabelludo** scalp

ℰ el **cuerpo** *masc noun*
body

el **cuervo** *masc noun*
crow

cuesta, cueste, etc *verb* ▷ **costar**

la **cuesta** *fem noun*
1 **slope**
subir una cuesta to go up a slope
ir cuesta arriba to go uphill
ir cuesta abajo to go downhill

ℰ la **cuestión** *fem noun*
matter
Hablaremos de esta cuestión más tarde. We'll talk about this later.
La cuestión es ... The thing is ...

ℰ la **cueva** *fem noun*
cave

cueza, cuezo, etc *verb* ▷ **cocer**

ℰ el **cuidado** *masc noun* ▷ see **cuidado** *excl*
1 **tener cuidado con algo** to be careful with something
Ten cuidado con los vasos. Be careful with the glasses.
¡Cuidado con el escalón! Mind the step!
2 **hacer algo con cuidado** to do something carefully
Lo cogí con cuidado. I picked it up carefully.
3 **care**
el cuidado de la salud health care
- los **cuidados intensivos** intensive care

cuidado *exclamation* ▷ see **cuidado** *noun*
   ¡Cuidado! Watch out!
   ¡Cuidado con el perro! Beware of the dog!

cuidadoso *masc adjective*, **cuidadosa** *fem*
   careful

ᵍ **cuidar** *verb* [17]
   1 cuidar a alguien
      cuidar de alguien to look after someone
      Yo cuido a los niños. I look after the
      children.
      Cuidan de su padre enfermo. They look
      after their sick father.

   cuidarse *reflexive verb*
      to take care of yourself
      ¡Cuídate! Take care!, Take care of yourself!

ᵍ la **culebra** *fem noun*
   snake

el **culebrón** *masc noun*
   soap opera (*TV entertainment*)

ᵍ el **culo** *masc noun* (*informal*)
   bum

ᵍ la **culpa** *fem noun*
   1 **fault**
      Es su culpa. It's his fault.
      No es mi culpa. It's not my fault.
      Luis tiene la culpa. It's Luis's fault.
   2 echarle la culpa a alguien to blame
      someone
      Me echan la culpa de lo que pasó. They
      blame me for what happened.
   3 **guilt**
      Ella tiene la culpa. She's the guilty one.

culpable *masc & fem adjective*
   ▷ see **culpable** *noun*
   1 **guilty**
      sentirse culpable de algo to feel guilty
      about something
   2 ser culpable de un crimen to be guilty of a
      crime

el & la **culpable** *masc & fem noun*
   ▷ see **culpable** *adj*
   guilty one
   Él es el culpable. He's the guilty one.

ᵍ **culpar** *verb* [17]
   to blame
   culpar a alguien de algo to blame
   somebody for something
   Le culparon del incendio. He was blamed
   for the fire.

cultivar *verb* [17]
   1 **to grow** (*fruit, vegetables*)
   2 **to cultivate** (*land*)

el **culto** *masc noun*
   1 **cult**
   2 **worship**
      la libertad de culto the freedom of worship

ᵍ la **cultura** *fem noun*
   1 **culture**
   2 **knowledge**
      preguntas de cultura general general
      knowledge questions

el **culturismo** *masc noun*
   bodybuilding

ᵍ el **cumpleaños** *masc noun*
   birthday
   fiesta de cumpleaños birthday party
   ¿Cuándo es tu cumpleaños? When's your
   birthday?
   ¡Feliz cumpleaños! Happy Birthday!

ᵍ **cumplir** *verb* [19]
   1 (*talking about age*) ¿Cuándo cumples años?
      When's your birthday?
      Mañana cumplo quince años. I'll be fifteen
      tomorrow.
      ¡Que cumplas muchos más! Many happy
      returns!
   2 **to keep** (*a promise*)
      cumplir una promesa to keep a promise
      No has cumplido con tus obligaciones. You
      haven't done your duty.
   3 **to fulfil** (*conditions*)
   4 **to carry out** (*a task, an order*)
   5 **to serve**
      cumplir una condena to serve a sentence

la **cuna** *fem noun*
   1 **cradle**
   2 **cot**

el **cuñado** *masc noun*, la **cuñada** *fem*
   1 **brother-in-law**
   2 **sister-in-law**

cupe, cupiera, cupo, etc *verb* ▷ **caber**

ᵍ el **cura** *masc noun* ▷ see **cura** *noun*
   priest

la **cura** *fem noun* ▷ see **cura** *noun*
   cure

curar *verb* [17]
   1 **to cure** (*an illness, a sick person*)
   2 **to dress** (*a wound*)

curarse *reflexive verb* [17]
   to get better

a
b
c
d
e
f
g
h
i
j
k
l
m
n
ñ
o
p
q
r
s
t
u
v
w
x
y
z

ᵍ indicates key words   85

curioso *masc adjective*, **curiosa** *fem*
  curious
  ¡Qué curiosa eres! You're so curious!
  Lo curioso es que ... The funny thing is ...
  Es curioso que ... It's strange that ...

cursar *verb* [17]
1 **to study** (*physics, maths, etc*)
2 **to be in** (*a year at school, etc*)
  Estoy cursando cuarto de ESO. I'm in year
  four of ESO.

el **curioso** *masc noun*, la **curiosa** *fem*
  busybody

♪ el **cursillo** *masc noun*
  (short) course

♪ el **currículum** *masc noun*
  CV, curriculum vitae

la **cursiva** *fem noun*
  italics
  en cursiva in italics

♪ el **curso** *masc noun*
1 **year** (*in school*)
  ¿En qué curso estás? What year are you in?

Mi hermana está en el primer curso. My
sister's in first year.
2 **course** (*programme of study*)
• el **curso escolar** academic year
• el **curso intensivo** intensive course

♪ el **cursor** *masc noun*
  cursor

la **curva** *fem noun* ▷ see **curvo** *adj*
  bend
  una curva peligrosa a sharp bend
  tomar una curva to take a bend

curvo *masc adjective*, **curva** *fem*
  ▷ see **curva** *noun*
  curved

♪ **cuyo** *masc adjective*, **cuya** *fem*
  whose
  El amigo cuyo ordenador utilicé. The friend
  whose computer I used.
  Las chicas cuya familia llegó ayer. The girls
  whose family arrived yesterday.

WORD TIP *cuyo, cuya* agrees with the thing
owned; *ordenador* and *familia* above.

D d

el **dado** *masc noun*
  dice
  tirar los dados to throw the dice

la **dama** *fem noun*
  lady
  damas y caballeros ladies and gentlemen
• la **dama de honor** bridesmaid

dan *verb* ▷ **dar**

danés *masc adjective & noun*, **danesa** *fem adjective & noun*
1 Danish
2 **un danés, una danesa** Dane (*person*)
  el danés Danish (*the language*)

> **WORD TIP** Adjectives and nouns for nationality, regional origin, and language do not have capital letters in Spanish.

la **danza** *fem noun*
  dance
  estudiar danza to study dance

♫**dañar** *verb* [17]
  to damage

dañino *masc adjective*, **dañina** *fem*
  harmful

el **daño** *masc noun*
1 **hacerle daño a alguien** to hurt someone
  No quiero hacerte daño. I don't want to hurt you.
  hacerse daño to hurt yourself
  Te vas a hacer daño. You are going to hurt yourself.
  ¿Se hizo daño al caer? Did she hurt herself when she fell?
  Me hice daño en la pierna. I hurt my leg.
2 damage
  Diez casas sufrieron daños. Ten houses suffered damage.

♫**dar** *verb* [4]
1 **to give**
  Dale esta carta a María. Give this letter to María.
  Me dio su número de teléfono. He gave me his telephone number.
  Dame un beso. Give me a kiss.
  Dale recuerdos. Give him my regards.
  ¿Me da un kilo de tomates? Can I have a kilo of tomatoes?
  Me dieron un premio. I got a prize.
  dar las gracias to say thank you
  darle de comer a alguien to feed somebody

  Les dio de comer a los niños. He fed the children.
2 **to turn on**
  dar la luz to turn on the light
  darle a un botón to press a button
  darle a un interruptor to flick a switch
3 **to strike** (*the hour*)
  El reloj dio las doce. The clock struck twelve.
4 **to give** (*a party*)
  Va a dar una fiesta mañana. He's having a party tomorrow.
  ¿Qué dan en el cine? What's on at the cinema?
5 **to say**
  dar los buenos días to say good morning
6 **to go for** (*a stroll, a walk, a drive, etc*)
  dar un paseo to go for a walk
  Vamos a dar una vuelta en el coche. We're going for a drive.
7 (*saying something has an effect*) **Me dio miedo.** It scared me.
  Este jersey da mucho calor. This jumper is very warm.
  Las patatas fritas le dieron sed. The crisps made him thirsty.
8 (*with rooms, buildings, etc*) **dar a un lugar** to open onto a place
  La puerta da al salón. The door opens into the living room.
  La habitación da al mar. The room looks onto the sea.

darse *reflexive verb* [4]
1 **to have**
  darse un baño to have a bath
  darse una ducha to have a shower
2 **darse un golpe** to bump yourself
  Me di con el pie en el bordillo. I hit my foot on the kerb.
3 (*with skills*) **Se le dan bien las matemáticas.** She's good at maths.
  No se me da bien pintar. I'm not good at painting.

el **dardo** *masc noun*
  dart
  jugar a los dardos to play darts

la **dársena** *fem noun*
1 **bay** (*in a bus station*)
2 **dry dock** (*for ships*)

a
b
c
d
e
f
g
h
i
j
k
l
m
n
ñ
o
p
q
r
s
t
u
v
w
x
y
z

♫ indicates key words   87

♪ el **dato** *masc noun*

1 piece of information
No tengo todos los datos. I don't have all the information.

2 los datos **data**
• los **datos informativos** information
• los **datos personales** personal details

♪ **dC** *abbreviation*
(= *después de Cristo*) **AD**

d. de J.C. *abbreviation*
(= *después de Jesucristo*) **AD**

♪ **de** *preposition* ▷ see **dé** *verb*

1 of
el nombre del libro the name of the book
un vaso de leche a glass of milk
una caja de naranjas a box of oranges
un tercio del total a third of the total
el mes de marzo the month of March

2 (*to show belonging*) el coche de mis padres
my parents' car
Esto es de Juan. This is Juan's.
Fuimos a casa de Isa. We went to Isa's house.

3 from
Soy de Sevilla. I'm from Sevilla.
de Madrid a Bilbao from Madrid to Bilbao
de la cabeza a los pies from head to toe
No hemos tenido noticias de María. We haven't heard from María.

4 made of
flores de plástico plastic flowers
una silla de madera a wooden chair
Es de hierro. It's made of iron.

5 (*describing people, things*) un hombre de veinte años a twenty-year-old man
una moneda de dos euros a two-euro coin
una clase de español a Spanish lesson
una película de miedo a horror film
una niña de pelo corto a girl with short hair
Es la chica del jersey a rayas. It's the girl with the striped jumper.

6 (*showing use*) los vasos del vino the wine glasses
el cubo de la basura the rubbish bin

7 (*to say something is best, biggest, etc*) el mejor de todos the best of all
la ciudad más grande del mundo the biggest city in the world
el más inteligente de la clase the cleverest in the class
el más bonito de los tres the prettiest of the three

8 than (*in comparisons*)
más de quince more than fifteen
El doble de lo que yo gano. Twice what I earn.

9 (*in names*) la estación de Victoria Victoria Station
la ciudad de Barcelona Barcelona

10 (*in time expressions*) a las dos de la tarde at two in the afternoon
de día by day
Viajaron de día. They travelled by day.
Trabajan de noche. They work at night.

11 trabajar de algo to work as something
Trabajo de enfermera. I work as a nurse.

WORD TIP *de* + *el* becomes *del*.

dé *verb* ▷ **dar**

♪ **debajo** *adverb, preposition*

1 underneath
Pon un plato debajo. Put a plate underneath.

2 El que está debajo. The one that's underneath.

3 debajo de under, underneath
Está debajo del sofá. It's under the sofa.

4 por debajo de under, below
a temperaturas por debajo de los cinco grados at temperatures below ten degrees
El agua entró por debajo de la puerta. The water came in under the door.

WORD TIP *debajo* is used by itself; *debajo de* is followed by a noun or pronoun.

♪ el **deber** *masc noun* ▷ see **deber** *verb*

1 duty
cumplir con tu deber to do your duty

2 los deberes **homework**
hacer los deberes to do your homework
Aún no he hecho los deberes. I haven't done my homework yet.

♪ **deber** *verb* [18] ▷ see **deber** *noun*

1 to owe
Te debo veinte euros. I owe you twenty euros.

2 must
Debes intentarlo. You must try.
Deberás estudiar mucho. You will have to study hard.

3 should
Deberías descansar. You should have a rest.
Deberías haber seguido mis consejos. You should have followed my advice.

debido *masc adjective*, **debida** *fem*

1 due
a su debido tiempo in due course
con el debido respeto with due respect
con el debido cuidado with the necessary care

2 como es debido properly
Pórtate como es debido. Behave properly.

3 debido a due to
No podía trabajar debido al accidente. She was unable to work due to the accident.

♪ **débil** *masc & fem adjective*
weak

♪ la **década** *fem noun*
decade
la década de los sesenta the sixties

♪ la **decena** *fem noun*
una decena de libros about ten books
Divídelos por decenas. Divide them into tens.

decente *masc & fem adjective*
decent

la **decepción** *fem noun*
disappointment

WORD TIP *decepción* does not mean *deception* in English; for the meaning of *deception* ▷ **engaño**.

♪ **decepcionar** *verb* [17]
to disappoint
La película nos decepcionó. The film disappointed us.

♪ **decidir** *verb* [19]
to decide
Decidí quedarme. I decided to stay.

decidirse *reflexive verb* [19]
1 to make up your mind
Aún no se ha decidido. She hasn't made up her mind.
2 decidirse a hacer algo to decide to do something
Se decidió a ir de vacaciones. She decided to go on holiday.
Se decidió a aprender a conducir. He decided to learn to drive.

♪ **décimo** *masc adjective*, **décima** *fem*
tenth
el décimo piso the tenth floor
una décima parte a tenth

♪ **decir** *verb* [5]
1 to say
Dice que sí viene. He says he is coming.
¿Qué dijiste? What did you say?
Aquí dice que ... It says here that ...
¡No me digas! You don't say!
2 to tell
Me ha dicho que no viene. He's told me he's not coming.
Dime lo que quieres. Tell me what you want.
No digas mentiras. Don't tell lies.
3 (*on the phone*) ¿Diga?, ¿Dígame? Hello?
4 (*when someone speaks to you*) Dime. Yes?
'¡Alicia!'—'¿Dime?' 'Alicia!'—'Yes?'

♪ la **decisión** *fem noun*
decision
tomar una decisión to make a decision

declarar *verb* [17]
1 to declare
declarar la guerra to declare war
¿Algo que declarar? Anything to declare? (*at customs*)
2 to give evidence
Se ha negado a declarar. He's refused to give evidence.

declararse *reflexive verb* [17]
declararse culpable to plead guilty
declararse inocente to plead not guilty

el **decorador** *masc noun*, la **decoradora** *fem*
interior designer

decorar *verb* [17]
to decorate

♪ el **dedo** *masc noun*
1 finger
hacer dedo to hitch-hike
2 el dedo del pie toe
el dedo gordo del pie the big toe
• el **dedo anular** ring finger
• el **dedo corazón** middle finger
• el **dedo índice** index finger
• el **dedo meñique** little finger
• el **dedo pulgar** thumb

♪ el **defecto** *masc noun*
flaw, defect

♪ **defectuoso** *masc adjective*, **defectuosa** *fem*
faulty

♪ **defender** *verb* [36]
to defend

defenderse *reflexive verb* [36]
1 to defend yourself
2 to get by
Me defiendo en inglés. I get by in English.

♪ la **defensa** *fem noun*
1 defence
2 defender (*in sport*)
• la **defensa personal** self-defence

el **defensor** *masc noun*, la **defensora** *fem*
defender
• el **defensor del pueblo** ombudsman

♪ **deficiente** *masc & fem adjective*
deficient
una alimentación deficiente en vitaminas a diet deficient in vitamins

a
b
c
d
e
f
g
h
i
j
k
l
m
n
ñ
o
p
q
r
s
t
u
v
w
x
y
z

♪ la **definición** *fem noun*
  definition

definitivo *masc adjective*, **definitiva** *fem*
  definitive

♪ **dejar** *verb* [17]
  1 to leave
    Quiere dejar el colegio. She wants to leave school.
    Ha dejado a su novia. He's left his girlfriend.
    ¡Déjala en paz! Leave her alone!

  2 to let
    ¡Déjame entrar! Let me in!
    No la dejan salir los domingos. They don't let her go out on Sundays.

  3 to lend
    ¿Me dejas un boli? Can you lend me a pen?
    Le he dejado mis apuntes. I've lent him my notes.

  4 dejar caer algo to drop something
    Dejó caer los libros en el escritorio. She dropped the books on the desk.

  5 dejar de hacer algo to stop doing something
    ¡Deja de molestar! Stop being a nuisance!
    dejar de fumar to give up smoking
    No dejes de llamarme cuando llegues. Make sure you phone me when you get there.

dejarse *reflexive verb* [17]
  1 to leave
    Me he dejado las gafas en el coche. I left my glasses in the car.

  2 dejarse barba to grow a beard
    dejarse el pelo largo to grow your hair long

♪ **del** *preposition*
  of the
    el respaldo del asiento the back of the chair

  WORD TIP *de* + *el* becomes *del*. ▷ **de**

♪ el **delantal** *masc noun*
  apron

♪ **delante** *adverb, preposition*
  1 ir delante to go on ahead
  2 de delante front
    el asiento de delante the front seat
    la parte de delante the front part
  3 por delante: Entraron por delante. They came in through the front.
    Lleva un bolsillo por delante. It has a pocket at the front.
  4 delante de in front of
    delante de mí in front of me

Está delante de la iglesia. It's in front of the church.

WORD TIP *delante* is used by itself; *delante de* is followed by a noun or pronoun.

♪ **delantero** *masc adjective*, **delantera** *fem*
  ▷ see **delantero** *noun*
  front
    la rueda delantera the front wheel

♪ el **delantero** *masc noun*, la **delantera** *fem*
  ▷ see **delantero** *adj*
  forward (*in sport*)

♪ **deletrear** *verb* [17]
  to spell
    ¿Me lo deletreas? Could you spell it for me?

♪ el **delfín** *masc noun*
  dolphin

♪ **delgado** *masc adjective*, **delgada** *fem*
  thin

delicado *masc adjective*, **delicada** *fem*
  1 delicate
    una situación delicada a delicate situation
  2 fragile (*a piece of china, etc*)
  3 sensitive (*skin*)

♪ **delicioso** *masc adjective*, **deliciosa** *fem*
  delicious

♪ el & la **delincuente** *masc & fem noun*
  criminal

el **delito** *masc noun*
  crime
    cometer un delito to commit a crime

♪ **demás** *invariable adjective*
  ▷ see **demás** *pron*
    los demás alumnos the rest of the pupils
    las demás cartas the rest of the letters

  WORD TIP *demás* never changes.

♪ **demás** *pronoun* ▷ see **demás** *adj*
  1 lo demás the rest
    Lo demás lo traigo mañana. I'll bring the rest tomorrow.
    Aquí está todo lo demás. Here's everything else.
  2 los demás, las demás the rest, the others
    los problemas de los demás other people's problems
    Los demás se quedan aquí. The rest can stay here.

♪ **demasiado** *masc adjective & pronoun*,
  demasiada *fem adj & pron*
  ▷ see **demasiado** *adv*
  1 too much
    Gasta demasiado. He spends too much.

Gasta demasiado dinero. He spends too much money.
Hay demasiada comida. There is too much food.
Preparó demasiados. She got too much ready.
Hacía demasiado calor. It was too hot.

2 too many
demasiadas veces too many times, too often
Eran demasiados. There were too many of them.
Hay demasiadas personas aquí. There are too many people here.

ℰ **demasiado** *adverb*
▷ see **demasiado** *adj, pron*

1 too much
No trabajes demasiado. Don't work too hard.

2 too
Los billetes eran demasiado caros. The tickets were too expensive.

ℰ la **democracia** *fem noun*
democracy

demoler *verb* [38]
to demolish

la **demolición** *fem noun*
demolition

ℰ el **demonio** *masc noun*
devil

ℰ la **demora** *fem noun*
delay
sin demora without delay

demos, **den** *verb* ▷ **dar**

la **densidad** *fem noun*
1 thickness (*of vegetation*)
2 density

dentado *masc adjective*, **dentada** *fem*
jagged

ℰ el **dentífrico** *masc noun*
toothpaste

ℰ el & la **dentista** *masc & fem noun*
dentist

ℰ **dentro** *adverb, preposition*
1 inside
desde dentro from inside
aquí dentro in here
allí dentro in there
Ponlo aquí dentro. Put it in here.

2 inside, **indoors**
Está dentro. She's inside.
pasar dentro to go inside, to go indoors

3 dentro de inside, in
dentro del edificio inside the building
dentro de la caja in the box
dentro de dos semanas in two weeks' time
dentro de poco shortly

4 por dentro on the inside
Por dentro es verde. It's green on the inside.
Lo limpié por dentro. I've cleaned the inside.

WORD TIP *dentro* is used by itself; *dentro de* is followed by a noun or pronoun.

la **denuncia** *fem noun*
1 report (*to the police*)
2 statement

denunciar *verb* [17]
to report (*a person, crime*)
Hay que denunciarlo en la comisaría. You must report it at the police station.

ℰ el **departamento** *masc noun*
1 department
2 (*Latin America*) **apartment**, **flat**

ℰ **depender** *verb* [18]
to depend
depender de algo to depend on something
Depende del resultado. It depends on the result.
'¿Se lo vas a decir?'—'Depende.' 'Are you going to tell him?'—'It depends.'

ℰ el **dependiente** *masc noun*, la **dependienta** *fem*
shop assistant

ℰ el **deporte** *masc noun*
sport
hacer deporte to play sports
Me gusta hacer deporte. I like playing sports.
• los **deportes acuáticos** water sports
• los **deportes de invierno** winter sports

mini info **deporte**

La pelota vasca es el deporte más rápido del mundo; la pelota alcanza una velocidad de unas 260 kilómetros por hora.

ℰ **deportista** *masc & fem adjective*
▷ see **deportista** *noun*
sporty
Soy muy deportista. I do a lot of sport.
Jack es muy buen deportista. Jack's very good at games.

ℰ el & la **deportista** *masc & fem noun*
▷ see **deportista** *adj*
1 sportsman
2 sportswoman

ℰ indicates key words

a
b
c
d
e
f
g
h
i
j
k
l
m
n
ñ
o
p
q
r
s
t
u
v
w
x
y
z

Ⓢ **deportivo** *masc adjective,* **deportiva** *fem*
  ▷ **see deportivo** *noun*
  sports
  ropa deportiva sports clothes, casual
  clothes
  un club deportivo a sports club

Ⓢ el **deportivo** *masc noun*
  ▷ **see deportivo** *adj*
  sports car

Ⓢ **depositar** *verb* [17]
  1 to place
  Deposite su solicitud en esta caja. Place
  your application in this box.
  2 to deposit *(money in an account)*

Ⓢ el **depósito** *masc noun*
  deposit

  deprimente *masc & fem adjective*
  depressing

Ⓢ **deprimido** *masc adjective,* **deprimida** *fem*
  depressed
  Ha estado muy deprimida. She has been
  very depressed.

Ⓢ **deprimirse** *reflexive verb* [19]
  to get depressed

Ⓢ **deprisa** *adverb*
  fast, quickly
  No lo hagas tan deprisa. Don't do it so
  quickly.
  Andaba muy deprisa. He was walking very
  fast.
  ¡Deprisa, vístete! Hurry up and get
  dressed!

Ⓢ la **derecha** *fem noun* ▷ **see derecho** *adj*
  1 right *(when talking of right and left)*
  girar a la derecha to turn right
  Está a la derecha. It's on the right., It's on
  the right-hand side.
  la segunda calle a la derecha the second
  street on the right
  Se sentaron a mi derecha. They sat on my
  right.
  En Europa se conduce por la derecha. In
  Europe you drive on the right.
  2 right hand
  Escribo con la derecha. I write with my right
  hand.
  3 *(in politics)* **la derecha** the right
  ser de derechas to be right-wing

Ⓢ **derecho** *masc adjective,* **derecha** *fem*
  ▷ **see derecha** *noun,* **derecho** *adv, noun*
  1 right *(talking about left and right)*
  la mano derecha your right hand
  el guante derecho the right glove

  en el cuadro superior derecho in the top
  right-hand square
  2 straight *(when talking about pictures)*
  No está derecho. It's not straight.
  Ponlo derecho. Put it straight.
  Siéntate derecho. Sit up straight.

Ⓢ **derecho** *adverb* ▷ **see derecho** *adj, noun*
  straight
  Siga todo derecho. Go straight on.
  Me fui derecho al director. I went straight
  to the headmaster.

Ⓢ el **derecho** *masc noun* ▷ **see derecho** *adj,*
  adv
  1 right
  tener derecho a algo to have the right to
  something
  Tienes derecho a reclamar. You have the
  right to complain.
  2 law
  estudiar derecho to study law
  • **el derecho penal** criminal law
  • **los derechos humanos** human rights

Ⓢ **derramar** *verb* [17]
  to spill
  He derramado el café en la alfombra. I've
  spilt the coffee on the carpet.

  derramarse *reflexive verb* [7]
  to spill
  Se derramó la leche. The milk has spilt.

Ⓢ **derribar** *verb* [17]
  1 to demolish *(a building or wall)*
  2 to break down *(a door)*
  3 to shoot down *(a plane)*

Ⓢ **derrotar** *verb* [17]
  to defeat

  des *verb* ▷ **dar**

Ⓢ **desabrochar** *verb* [17]
  to undo *(a jacket or shirt)*

  desabrocharse *reflexive verb* [17]
  to undo
  Se desabrochó la chaqueta. He undid his
  jacket.

  desafilado *masc adjective,* **desafilada** *fem*
  blunt

Ⓢ **desafortunadamente** *adverb*
  unfortunately

Ⓢ **desafortunado** *masc adjective,*
  desafortunada *fem*
  1 unlucky *(person)*
  2 unfortunate *(event)*

Ⓢ **desagradable** *masc & fem adjective*
  unpleasant

$\mathcal{S}$ **desanimado** *masc adjective*, **desanimada** *fem*
  discouraged

$\mathcal{S}$ **desaparecer** *verb* [35]
  1 to disappear
  La tradición está desapareciendo. The tradition is dying out.
  2 to go missing (*talking about a person or an object*)

la **desaparición** *fem noun*
  disappearance

$\mathcal{S}$ **desaprovechar** *verb* [17]
  to waste (*paper, time, an opportunity*)

$\mathcal{S}$ el **desarrollo** *masc noun*
  development

$\mathcal{S}$ el **desastre** *masc noun*
  disaster

$\mathcal{S}$ **desatar** *verb* [17]
  to untie

desatarse *reflexive verb* [17]
  to come undone (*knots, laces*)

desatornillar *verb* [17]
  to unscrew

$\mathcal{S}$ **desayunar** *verb* [17]
  1 to have breakfast
  Desayuné muy temprano. I had breakfast very early.
  2 to have for breakfast
  Desayuno café y tostadas. I have coffee and toast for breakfast.

$\mathcal{S}$ el **desayuno** *masc noun*
  breakfast
  tomar el desayuno to have breakfast

desbordar *verb* [17]
  to exceed

desbordarse *reflexive verb* [17]
  to overflow
  El río se desbordó. The river overflowed its banks.

$\mathcal{S}$ **descafeinado** *masc adjective*, **descafeinada** *fem*
  decaffeinated

$\mathcal{S}$ **descalificar** *verb* [31]
  to disqualify

descalzarse *reflexive verb* [22]
  to take your shoes off

$\mathcal{S}$ **descalzo** *masc adjective*, **descalza** *fem*
  barefoot

$\mathcal{S}$ **descansado** *masc adjective*, **descansada** *fem*
  rested

$\mathcal{S}$ **descansar** *verb* [17]
  to rest
  descansar la vista to rest your eyes
  Necesitas descansar. You need to rest.

$\mathcal{S}$ el **descansillo** *masc noun*
  landing (*on stairs*)

$\mathcal{S}$ el **descanso** *masc noun*
  1 rest
  2 half-time

el **descapotable** *masc noun*
  convertible (*car*)

descargar *verb* [28]
  1 to unload (*goods*)
  2 to download (*data, images*)

$\mathcal{S}$ **descender** *verb* [36]
  1 to descend (*a plane*)
  2 to go down (*a mountaineer*)
  3 to fall (*prices, temperature*)

el **descenso** *masc noun*
  1 fall (*in temperature, etc*)
  2 descent

$\mathcal{S}$ **descolgar** *verb* [23]
  1 to pick up (*the phone*)
  2 dejar el teléfono descolgado to leave the phone off the hook
  3 to take down (*a picture, curtains*)

descomponerse *reflexive verb* [11]
  (*Latin America*) **to break down**

descompuesto *masc adjective*, **descompuesta** *fem*
  (*Latin America*) **broken**
  El radio está descompuesto. The radio's not working.

$\mathcal{S}$ **desconectar** *verb* [17]
  to disconnect
  ¿Has desconectado el ordenador? Have you disconnected the computer?

$\mathcal{S}$ **desconfiar** *verb* [32]
  desconfiar de alguien to mistrust someone
  Desconfía de toda la gente. He mistrusts everybody., He doesn't trust anybody.

$\mathcal{S}$ **descongelar** *verb* [17]
  to defrost

decongelarse *reflexive verb* [17]
  to defrost

a
b
c
d
e
f
g
h
i
j
k
l
m
n
ñ
o
p
q
r
s
t
u
v
w
x
y
z

ℰ **desconocido** *masc adjective*,
　　desconocida *fem*
　　▷ see **desconocido** *noun*
　unknown

ℰ el **desconocido** *masc noun*, la
　　desconocida *fem*
　　▷ see **desconocido** *adj*
　stranger

descontento *masc adjective*,
　　descontenta *fem*
　　▷ see **descontento** *noun*
　dissatisfied
　quedar descontento con algo to be
　dissatisfied with something

　el **descontento** *masc noun*
　　▷ see **descontento** *adj*
　dissatisfaction

ℰ **describir** *verb* [52]
　to describe

ℰ la **descripción** *fem noun*
　description

descrito *verb* ▷ **describir**

ℰ **descubrir** *verb* [53]
　1 to discover
　2 to unveil (*a statue*)

ℰ el **descuento** *masc noun*
　discount

ℰ **descuidado** *masc adjective*, **descuidada**
　fem
　1 careless (*person*)
　2 neglected
　El jardín está muy descuidado. The garden
　is very neglected.

ℰ **desde** *preposition*
　1 from
　Se ve desde la ventana. You can see it from
　the window.
　Puedes mandarlo desde Madrid. You can
　send it from Madrid.
　Mídelo desde este extremo hasta el otro.
　Measure it from this end to the other.
　2 (*with exact times*) **from**
　desde el primer momento from the start
　desde las tres hasta las cinco from three to
　five o'clock
　3 desde luego of course
　Desde luego les conozco. Of course I know
　them.
　4 (*with an exact time as the start*) **since**
　Vivo aquí desde 2002. I have been living
　here since 2002.
　5 (*saying how long*) **desde hace** for
　No les veo desde hace años. I haven't seen
　them for years.

Trabajo allí desde hace tres meses. I've
been working there for three months.
6 (*asking how long?*) **desde cuándo** for
　¿Desde cuándo vives en Coventry? How
　long have you lived in Coventry?
　¿Desde cuándo son novios? How long have
　they been going out?

WORD TIP In phrases with *desde* Spanish uses the
present tense when the activity or state is still
going on.

ℰ **desear** *verb* [17]
　1 to wish
　Te deseo lo mejor. I wish you all the best.
　Te deseo un feliz cumpleaños. Wishing you
　a happy birthday (*in a card*)
　2 to want
　Deseaba ir a la fiesta. She wanted to go to
　the party.
　¿Qué desea? Can I help you? (*in a shop*)
　Estoy deseando verte. I'm looking forward
　to seeing you.
　Están deseando que llegue el verano. They
　can't wait for the summer to come.

desembarcar *verb* [31]
　1 to unload
　2 to disembark

ℰ **desempleado** *masc adjective*,
　　desempleada *fem*
　　▷ see **desempleado** *noun*
　unemployed

ℰ el **desempleado** *masc noun*, la
　　desempleada *fem*
　　▷ see **desempleado** *adj*
　unemployed person

ℰ el **desempleo** *masc noun*
　unemployment
　cobrar subsidio de desempleo to get
　unemployment benefit

ℰ **desenchufar** *verb* [17]
　to unplug

desenroscar *verb* [31]
　to unscrew (*a lid, a screw*)

ℰ **desenvolver** *verb* [45]
　to unwrap

ℰ el **deseo** *masc noun*
　1 wish
　pedir un deseo to make a wish
　Se cumplió mi deseo. My wish came true.
　con mis mejores deseos best wishes
　2 desire

ℰ **desfavorable** *masc & fem adjective*
　unfavourable

ℰ el **desfile** *masc noun*
   parade
   • el **desfile de modelos** fashion show

ℰ la **desgracia** *fem noun*
   misfortune
   por desgracia unfortunately

   WORD TIP *desgracia* does not mean *disgrace* in
   English; for the meaning of *disgrace* ▷ **vergüenza**.

desgraciadamente *adverb*
   unfortunately

ℰ **desgraciado** *masc adjective*,
   desgraciada *fem*
  1 **unhappy**
    Soy muy desgraciado. I'm very unhappy.
  2 **ill-fated**
    aquel desgraciado día that ill-fated day

ℰ **deshacer** *verb* [7]
  1 **to undo** (*a knot*)
  2 **to unwrap** (*a parcel*)
    deshacer las maletas to unpack
  3 **to take apart** (*a clock, etc*)
  4 **to crumble** (*a biscuit, etc*)

deshacerse *reflexive verb* [7]
  1 **to come undone** (*a knot or seam*)
  2 **to melt** (*ice*)
  3 to come apart
    Se deshizo en mis manos. It came apart in
    my hands.
  4 **deshacerse de algo** to get rid of something
    Voy a deshacerme de este sofá. I'm going
    to get rid of this sofa.

el **deshielo** *masc noun*
   thaw

ℰ **desierto** *masc adjective*, **desierta** *fem*
   ▷ see **desierto** *noun*
   deserted

ℰ el **desierto** *masc noun* ▷ see **desierto** *adj*
   desert

ℰ **designar** *verb* [17]
   to appoint

ℰ **desigual** *masc & fem adjective*
  1 **uneven** (*a surface or road*)
  2 **unequal** (*a fight*)

desmaquillarse *reflexive verb* [17]
   to take off your make-up

ℰ **desmayarse** *reflexive verb* [17]
   to faint

ℰ **desmontar** *verb* [17]
  1 **to take apart** (*a machine, etc*)
  2 **to take down** (*a tent*)

ℰ **desnudar** *verb* [17]
   to undress

desnudarse *reflexive verb* [17]
   to take your clothes off, **to get
   undressed**

ℰ **desnudo** *masc adjective*, **desnuda** *fem*
  1 **naked** (*person, body*)
  2 **bare** (*arms, shoulders*)
    con los hombros desnudos with bare
    shoulders

ℰ **desobedecer** *verb* [35]
   to disobey
   Desobedeció el reglamento. She
   disobeyed the rules.

desobedezca, **desobedezco**, **etc** *verb* ▷
   desobedecer

ℰ **desobediente** *masc & fem adjective*
   disobedient
   Eres muy desobediente. You are very
   disobedient.

ℰ el **desodorante** *masc noun*
   deodorant

ℰ el **desorden** *masc noun*
   mess

desorganizado *masc adjective*,
   desorganizada *fem*
   disorganized

el **despacho** *masc noun*
  1 **office**
  2 **study** (*at home*)
  • el **despacho de billetes** ticket office
  • el **despacho de lotería** lottery agency

ℰ **despacio** *adverb*
   slowly
   Hazlo despacio. Do it slowly.
   ¡Más despacio! Slower!

ℰ la **despedida** *fem noun*
   farewell
   una cena de despedida a farewell dinner

ℰ **despedir** *verb* [57]
  1 **to say goodbye to**
    Fuimos todos a despedirla. We all went to
    say goodbye to her.
    ¿Vendrás a despedirme a la estación? Will
    you come to see me off at the station?
  2 **to sack**, **to fire** (*an employee*)
    Lo despidieron. He was sacked.
  3 **to lay off** (*the workforce*)
    Han despedido a la mitad de la plantilla.
    They've laid off half the employees.

a
b
c
d
e
f
g
h
i
j
k
l
m
n
ñ
o
p
q
r
s
t
u
v
w
x
y
z

despedirse *reflexive verb* [57]
to say goodbye
Se fue sin depedirse. He went without
saying goodbye.
despedirse de alguien to say goodbye to
someone
Nos despedimos del director el último día.
We said goodbye to the headmaster on the
last day.

ᔕ **despegar** *verb* [28]
1 **to take off** (*a plane*)
2 **to peel off** (*a label or a sticker*)

despegarse *reflexive verb* [28]
to come unstuck

ᔕ el **despegue** *masc noun*
takeoff (*of a plane*)

ᔕ **despejado** *masc adjective*, **despejada** *fem*
clear (*sky, day*)

ᔕ **despejar** *verb* [17]
to clear (*a room of people*)

ᔕ **desperdiciar** *verb* [17]
to waste (*food, paper, an opportunity, etc*)

ᔕ el **desperdicio** *masc noun*
1 **waste**
Es un desperdicio tirar esta comida. It's a
waste to throw this food away.
2 **los desperdicios** scraps

ᔕ el **despertador** *masc noun*
alarm (clock)
poner el despertador to set the alarm
Puse el despertador para las siete de la
mañana. I set the alarm for seven a.m.

ᔕ **despertar** *verb* [29]
to wake up
¿Puedes despertarme a las siete? Can you
wake me up at seven?

despertarse *reflexive verb* [29]
to wake up
Me desperté a las diez. I woke up at ten.

despida, despido, etc *verb* ▷ **despedir**

despierta, despierto, etc *verb*
▷ see **despierto** *adj* ▷ **despertar**

ᔕ **despierto** *masc adjective*, **despierta** *fem*
▷ see **despierto** *verb*
awake

ᔕ **despistado** *masc adjective*, **despistada**
fem ▷ see **despistado** *noun*
absent-minded

ᔕ el **despistado** *masc noun*, la **despistada**
fem ▷ see **despistado** *adj*
scatterbrain

desplegar *verb* [30]
to unfold

despliega, despliego, etc *verb* ▷
desplegar

ᔕ **después** *adverb, preposition*
1 **afterwards**
poco después shortly afterwards
Después me fui. Afterwards I went away .
2 **later**
Lo haré después. I'll do it later.
Se vieron mucho después. They saw each
other much later.
3 **después de** after
después de todo after all
después de las clases after school
Después de verte me sentí mejor. After
seeing you I felt better.

WORD TIP *después* is used by itself; *después de* is
followed by a noun or pronoun.

ᔕ el **destino** *masc noun*
1 **destination**
¿Qué destino tiene? What's its
destination?
el vuelo con destino a Milán the plane to
Milan
2 **fate**

ᔕ el **destornillador** *masc noun*
screwdriver

ᔕ la **destrucción** *fem noun*
destruction

ᔕ **destruir** *verb* [54]
to destroy

ᔕ el **desván** *masc noun*
attic

ᔕ la **desventaja** *fem noun*
disadvantage
estar en desventaja to be at a disadvantage

ᔕ **desvestirse** *reflexive verb* [57]
to undress, **to get undressed**

ᔕ **desviar** *verb* [32]
to divert (*a plane or traffic*)

ᔕ el **desvío** *masc noun*
diversion
tomar un desvío to make a detour

ᔕ el **detalle** *masc noun*
detail
Me describió el lugar con todo detalle. He
described the place to me in great detail.

ᔕ el & la **detective** *masc & fem noun*
detective
• el **detective privado** private detective

ꝭ detener *verb* [9]
1 **to stop** (*traffic*)
2 **to arrest**
   ¡Queda detenido! You're under arrest!

detenerse *reflexive verb* [9]
   to stop
   detenerse a hacer algo to stop to do something
   Me detuve a descansar. I stopped to rest.

ꝭ el detergente *masc noun*
1 **washing powder**
2 **washing-up liquid**

ꝭ el determinante *masc noun*
   (*Grammar*) **determiner**

ꝭ detestar *verb* [17]
   to detest

ꝭ detrás *adverb*
1 **behind**
   Creo que están detrás. I think they're behind.
2 **detrás de** behind
   detrás de la estación behind the station
   Ponte detrás de mí. Go behind me.
3 **por detrás** at the back
   Se abrocha por detrás. It buttons up at the back.
   Entraron por detrás. They got in at the back.

WORD TIP *detrás* is used by itself; *detrás de* is followed by a noun or pronoun.

ꝭ la deuda *fem noun*
   debt
   Tiene muchas deudas. He has a lot of debts.

ꝭ devolver *verb* [45]
1 **to return**, **to give back** (*something that you have borrowed*)
   Lo devolví a su dueño. I returned it to its owner.
   Te devolveré el libro mañana. I'll give you the book back tomorrow.
2 **to take back** (*something you've bought*)
   He devuelto la camisa. I've taken the shirt back.
3 **to refund**
   Me devolvieron el coste de las entradas. I was refunded the cost of the tickets.
4 **to be sick** (*vomit*)
   Creo que voy a devolver. I think I'm going to be sick.

devuelto, **devuelvo**, etc *verb* ▷ **devolver**

di *verb* ▷ **dar**

ꝭ el día *masc noun*
1 **day**
   todos los días every day
   ¿Qué día es hoy? What day is it today?
   cada día every day
   buenos días good morning
2 (*talking about dates*) **el día tres de mayo** the third of May
3 **hacerse de día** to get light (*at dawn*)
   Aún no se ha hecho de día. It's not light yet.
   en pleno día in broad daylight
4 **estar al día** to be up to date
   poner a alguien al día to bring someone up to date
   Me puso al día de todo lo sucedido. He brought me up to date on everything that had happened.
 • el **día de fiesta** holiday
 • el **día de los enamorados** St Valentine's Day
 • el **día de los Inocentes** the 28th of December (*equivalent to April Fool's Day in Spain*)
 • el **día del padre** Father's Day
 • el **día de Reyes** Twelfth Night (*6 January*)
 • el **día festivo** public holiday
 • el **día laborable** working day
 • el **día libre** day off

diabético *masc adjective & noun*, **diabética** *fem adjective & noun*
1 **diabetic**
2 un diabético, una diabética diabetic

ꝭ el diablo *masc noun*
   devil

el diagnóstico *masc noun*
   diagnosis
   emitir un diagnóstico to make a diagnosis

diagonal *masc & fem adjective*
   ▷ see **diagonal** *noun*
   diagonal

la diagonal *fem noun* ▷ see **diagonal** *adj*
   diagonal

el diagrama *masc noun*
   diagram

el dial *masc noun*
   dial

ꝭ el diálogo *masc noun*
1 **conversation**
2 **dialogue**

ꝭ el diamante *masc noun*
   diamond

ꝭ el diámetro *masc noun*
   diameter

ぢ la **diapositiva** *fem noun*
　slide (*for a projector*)

diario *masc adjective*, **diaria** *fem*
　▷ see **diario** *noun*

1 ▷ **daily**
　la rutina diaria the daily routine
　a diario every day
　Se escriben a diario. They write to each
　other every day.

2 ▷ **a day**
　Ensayan dos horas diarias. They practise
　two hours a day.

3 ▷ **de diario** everyday
　ropa de diario everyday clothes

ぢ el **diario** *masc noun* ▷ see **diario** *adj*

1 ▷ **diary**
　llevar un diario to keep a diary

2 ▷ **newspaper**

ぢ la **diarrea** *fem noun*
　diarrhoea

ぢ **dibujar** *verb* [17]
　to draw

ぢ el **dibujo** *masc noun*
　drawing
　hacer un dibujo to do a drawing
　• el **dibujo técnico** technical drawing
　• los **dibujos animados** cartoons

ぢ el **diccionario** *masc noun*
　dictionary

dice, **dicho**, etc *verb* ▷ **decir**

ぢ **diciembre** *masc noun*
　December
　en diciembre in December
　el 25 de diciembre on 25 December

> **WORD TIP** Months of the year start with small
> letters in Spanish.

ぢ el **dictado** *masc noun*
　dictation

ぢ **diecinueve** *number*

1 ▷ **nineteen**
　Tiene diecinueve años. She's nineteen
　(years old).

2 (*saying the date*) **nineteenth**
　el diecinueve de agosto the nineteenth of
　August

ぢ **dieciocho** *number*

1 ▷ **eighteen**
　Tiene dieciocho años. She's eighteen
　(years old).

2 (*saying the date*) **eighteenth**
　el dieciocho de agosto the eighteenth of
　August

ぢ **dieciséis** *number*

1 ▷ **sixteen**
　Tiene dieciséis años. She's sixteen (years
　old).

2 (*saying the date*) **sixteenth**
　el dieciséis de agosto the sixteenth of
　August

ぢ **diecisiete** *number*

1 ▷ **seventeen**
　Tiene diecisiete años. She's seventeen
　(years old).

2 (*saying the date*) **seventeenth**
　el diecisiete de agosto the seventeenth of
　August

ぢ el **diente** *masc noun*
　tooth
　Se le ha caído un diente. She's lost a tooth.
　Ya le están saliendo los dientes. He's
　already teething.
　• el **diente de ajo** clove of garlic

diera, **dieras**, etc *verb* ▷ **dar**

ぢ el **diesel** *masc noun*
　diesel

ぢ la **dieta** *fem noun*
　diet
　estar a dieta to be on a diet
　ponerse a dieta to go on a diet

ぢ **diez** *number*

1 ▷ **ten**
　Tiene diez años. She's ten (years old).

2 (*saying the date*) **tenth**
　el diez de agosto the tenth of August

3 (*telling the time*) **ten**
　Son las diez. It's ten o'clock.
　a las diez y cinco at five past ten

ぢ la **diferencia** *fem noun*

1 ▷ **difference**
　Hay poca diferencia de precio. There's not
　much difference in price.

2 ▷ **a diferencia de** unlike
　a diferencia de su padre unlike his father

ぢ **diferente** *masc & fem adjective*
　different
　ser diferente a, ser diferente de to be
　different from
　Es diferente a su hermana. She is different
　from her sister.
　Son diferentes de los demás. They are
　different from the others.

ぢ **difícil** *masc & fem adjective*
　difficult

a
b
c
d
e
f
g
h
i
j
k
l
m
n
ñ
o
p
q
r
s
t
u
v
w
x
y
z

ᶘ la **dificultad** *fem noun*
> **difficulty**
> con muchas dificultades with great
> difficulty

diga, **digo**, **etc** *verb* ▷ **decir**

diluir *verb* [54]
1 **to dilute**
2 **to thin** (*paint*)

la **dimensión** *fem noun*
> **dimension**

la **dimisión** *fem noun*
> **resignation**
> presentar la dimisión to hand in your
> resignation

dimitir *verb* [19]
> **to resign**

dimos *verb* ▷ **dar**

Dinamarca *fem noun*
> **Denmark**

ᶘ el **dinero** *masc noun*
> **money**
> ¿Cuánto dinero tienes? How much money
> have you got?
> No tengo dinero. I haven't got any money.
> Es gente de dinero. They are wealthy
> people.
> • el **dinero de bolsillo** pocket money
> • el **dinero en efectivo** cash
> • el **dinero suelto** change

ᶘ el **dinosaurio** *masc noun*
> **dinosaur**

dio *verb* ▷ **dar**

ᶘ el **dios** *masc noun*, la **diosa** *fem*
> ▷ see **Dios** *noun*
1 **god**
2 **goddess**

ᶘ el **Dios** *masc noun* ▷ see **dios** *noun*
> **God**
> gracias a Dios thank heavens
> ¡Por Dios! For heaven's sake!
> ¡Dios mío! Oh, my God!
> ¡Sabe Dios! God knows!

el **diploma** *masc noun*
> **diploma**

diplomático *masc adjective*,
diplomática *fem*
> ▷ see **diplomático** *noun*
> **diplomatic**

el **diplomático** *masc noun*, la
diplomática *fem*
> ▷ see **diplomático** *adj*
> **diplomat**

el **diputado** *masc noun*, la **diputada** *fem*
> **member of parliament**

dirá, **diré**, **etc** *verb* ▷ **decir**

ᶘ la **dirección** *fem noun*
1 **address**
> Mi dirección es … My address is …
2 **direction**
> ¿En qué dirección se fueron? What
> direction did they go in?
> Venían en dirección contraria. They were
> coming the other way.
3 (*on signs*)
> 'Dirección prohibida' 'No entry'
> 'Dirección obligatoria' 'One way'
4 **management** (*of a company*)

ᶘ **directo** *masc adjective*, **directa** *fem*
> ▷ see **directo** *adv*
1 **direct**
> ¿Hay un vuelo directo a Santiago? Is there a
> direct flight to Santiago?
2 **un tren directo** a through train
3 (*in television and radio*) **en directo** live
> una retransmisión en directo a live
> broadcast

ᶘ **directo** *adverb* ▷ see **directo** *adj*
> **direct**
> El autobús va directo al aeropuerto. The
> bus goes direct to the airport.

ᶘ el **director** *masc noun*, la **directora** *fem*
1 **headmaster**
2 **headmistress**
3 **manager** (*of a company*)
4 **director** (*of a film or play*)
5 **editor** (*of a newspaper*)
> • el **director de orquesta** conductor

ᶘ **dirigir** *verb* [49]
1 **to manage** (*a company*)
2 **to direct** (*a film or play*)
3 **to conduct** (*an orchestra*)
4 **dirigir algo a alguien** to address something
> to somebody (*a message or a letter*)
> La carta venía dirigida a mí. The letter was
> addressed to me.
> No me dirigió la palabra en toda la tarde.
> He didn't say a word to me all afternoon.

dirigirse *reflexive verb* [49]
> **dirigirse a algo, dirigirse hacia algo** to head
> towards something
> Se dirigió hacia la puerta. He headed
> towards the door.

a
b
c
d
e
f
g
h
i
j
k
l
m
n
ñ
o
p
q
r
s
t
u
v
w
x
y
z

la **discapacidad** *fem noun*
disability
¿Tiene alguna discapacidad? Does she have a disability?

♂ la **disciplina** *fem noun*
discipline

la **disco** *fem noun* ▷ see **disco** *masc*
disco (*for dancing*)

♂ el **disco** *masc noun* ▷ see **disco** *fem*
1 **record**
grabar un disco to make a record
2 **disk** (*for a computer*)
3 **traffic light**
El disco se ha puesto rojo. The lights are red.
• el **disco compacto** compact disc
• el **disco compacto interactivo** interactive compact disc
• el **disco duro** hard disk
• el **disco flexible** floppy disk
• el **disco sencillo** single

♂ la **discoteca** *fem noun*
disco

♂ la **disculpa** *fem noun*
apology
pedir disculpas a alguien por algo to apologize to someone for something
Le pidió disculpas por su comportamiento. He apologized to her for his behaviour.

♂ **disculparse** *reflexive verb* [17]
to apologize
Se disculpó por llegar tarde. She apologized for arriving late.

la **discusión** *fem noun*
1 **argument**
2 **discussion**

discutir *verb* [19]
1 **to argue**
Ha discutido con su novio. She's had an argument with her boyfriend
2 **to discuss**

el **diseñador** *masc noun*, la **diseñadora** *fem*
designer
• el **diseñador gráfico**, la **diseñadora gráfica** graphic designer

diseñar *verb* [17]
to design

el **diseño** *masc noun*
design

el **disfraz** *masc noun*
1 **disguise**

2 **costume**, **fancy dress outfit**
un disfraz de pirata a pirate outfit
una fiesta de disfraces a fancy dress party

disfrazarse *reflexive verb* [22]
to dress up
disfrazarse de algo to dress up as something
Me disfracé de bruja. I dressed up as a witch.

♂ **disfrutar** *verb* [17]
to enjoy yourself
disfrutar de algo to enjoy something
Disfruté mucho de las vacaciones. I really enjoyed my holiday.

disgustar *verb* [17]
to upset

disgustarse *reflexive verb* [17]
to get upset

el **disgusto** *masc noun*
1 **argument**
2 llevarse un disgusto to get upset

WORD TIP *disgusto* does not mean *disgust* in English; for the meaning of *disgust* ▷ **asco**.

♂ el **diskette** *masc noun*
diskette, **floppy disk**

la **disminución** *fem noun*
decrease

disminuir *verb* [54]
1 **to decrease**
El número de visitantes ha diminuido. The number of visitors has decreased.
2 **to reduce** (*speed, costs*)

el **disolvente** *masc noun*
solvent

disolver *verb* [45]
to dissolve

disolverse *reflexive verb* [45]
to dissolve

disparar *verb* [17]
1 **to fire**, **to shoot** (*with a gun*)
2 **to shoot** (*in football, etc*)

el **disparo** *masc noun*
shot

disponible *masc & fem adjective*
available

la **disposición** *fem noun*
1 **aptitude**
2 estar a la disposición de alguien to be at somebody's disposal

dispuesto *masc adjective*, **dispuesta** *fem*
1 **ready**
Todo está dispuesto. Everything's ready.
2 **estar dispuesto a hacer algo** to be prepared to do something
No estoy dispuesto a esperar. I'm not prepared to wait.

la **disputa** *fem noun*
1 **argument**
2 **dispute**

disputarse *reflexive verb* [17]
1 **to compete for** (*a title, a cup*)
2 **to fight over** (*an inheritance, a bill*)

el **disquete** *masc noun*
diskette, **floppy disk**

la **disquetera** *fem noun*
disk drive

la **distancia** *fem noun*
distance
Está a poca distancia. It's not far.
¿A qué distancia está el colegio de tu casa? How far is the school from your house?
Los dos postes están a una distancia de dos metros. The two posts are two metres apart.

diste *verb* ▷ **dar**

distinguir *verb* [50]
to distinguish

distinguirse *reflexive verb* [50]
1 **distinguirse por algo** to distinguish yourself by something
2 **distinguirse de algo** to differ from something

distintivo *masc adjective*, **distintiva** *fem*
distinctive

ℰ **distinto** *masc adjective*, **distinta** *fem*
different
ser distinto a algo to be different from something
Son muy distintos. They are very different.
Es distinto al resto. It's different from the rest.

WORD TIP *distinto* does not mean *distinct* in English; for the meaning of *distinct* ▷ **claro**.

la **distracción** *fem noun*
1 **entertainment**
Es su distracción favorita. It's his favourite entertainment.
La tele le sirve de distracción. Television is a way of passing the time for him.
2 (*lack of attention*) Se lo quitaron en un momento de distracción. They stole it

from her when she wasn't paying attention.

ℰ **distraer** *verb* [42]
1 **to distract**
distraer a alguien de algo to distract somebody from something
El ruido la distrajo de la película. The noise distracted her from the film.
2 **to keep busy**
La costura me distrae. Sewing keeps me busy.

distraerse *reflexive verb* [42]
1 **to let your attention wander**
Se distrajo un momento y se lo robaron. His attention wandered for a moment and he got robbed.
2 **to keep busy**
Se distrae con la jardinería. Gardening keeps him busy.

el **distribuidor** *masc noun*, la **distribuidora** *fem*
distributor

distribuir *verb* [54]
to distribute

el **distrito** *masc noun*
district
• el **distrito postal** postal area

ℰ la **diversión** *fem noun*
1 **fun**
por diversión for fun
2 (*leisure activity*) un lugar lleno de diversiones a place with plenty of things to do

WORD TIP *diversión* does not mean *diversion* in English; for the meaning of *diversion* ▷ **desvío**.

ℰ **divertido** *masc adjective*, **divertida** *fem*
1 **funny**
Es un chico muy divertido. He's really funny.
2 **enjoyable**
La fiesta fue muy divertida. The party was really enjoyable.

ℰ **divertir** *verb* [14]
to amuse

divertirse *reflexive verb* [14]
to enjoy yourself, **to have fun**
¡Que te diviertas! Enjoy yourself!, Have fun!

dividir *verb* [19]
to divide

la **divisa** *fem noun*
currency
• las **divisas extranjeras** foreign currency

la **división** *fem noun*
  division

◊ **divorciado** *masc adjective*, **divorciada**
  fem ▷ see **divorciado** *noun*
  divorced
  Mis padres están divorciados. My parents
  are divorced.

◊ el **divorciado** *masc noun*, la **divorciada**
  fem ▷ see **divorciado** *adj*
  divorcee

◊ **divorciarse** *reflexive verb* [17]
  to get divorced
  Se divorciaron en México. They got
  divorced in Mexico.

el **divorcio** *masc noun*
  divorce

el **DNI** *masc noun*
  (=Documento Nacional de Identidad) **identity**
  card

◊ **doblar** *verb* [17]
  1 to fold (*a piece of paper or clothes*)
  2 to bend (*a piece of metal or your leg*)
  3 to double (*an offer or amount*)
  4 doblar la esquina to turn the corner

◊ **doble** *masc & fem adjective* ▷ see **doble** *noun*
  double

◊ el **doble** *masc noun* ▷ see **doble** *adj*
  el doble de: el doble de personas twice as
  many people
  el doble de harina que de azúcar twice as
  much flour as sugar
  el doble de peso twice the weight
  el doble de largo twice the length

los **dobles** *plural masc noun* ▷ see **doble** *adj*,
noun
  doubles (*in tennis*)
  la final de los dobles femeninos the final of
  the women's doubles

doce *number*
  1 twelve
  Tiene doce años. She's twelve (years old).
  2 (*saying the date*) **twelfth**
  el doce de enero the twelfth of January
  3 (*telling the time*) **twelve**
  a las doce at twelve o'clock
  Son las doce del mediodía. It's twelve
  noon.
  a las doce de la noche at midnight

doceavo *masc adjective*, **doceava** *fem*
  twelfth

◊ la **docena** *fem noun*
  dozen
  una docena de huevos a dozen eggs

◊ el **doctor** *masc noun*, la **doctora** *fem*
  doctor

◊ la **documentación** *fem noun*
  1 papers
  No llevaba mi documentación. I didn't
  have my papers on me.
  2 documents (*for a car*)

documental *masc & fem adjective*
  ▷ see **documental** *noun*
  un programa documental a documentary

el **documental** *masc noun*
  ▷ see **documental** *adj*
  documentary

◊ el **documento** *masc noun*
  document
  • el **documento de identidad** identity card

el **dólar** *masc noun*
  dollar

◊ **doler** *verb* [38]
  to hurt
  Me duele el tobillo. My ankle hurts.
  No duele nada. It doesn't hurt at all.
  ¿Te duele mucho? Does it hurt a lot?
  Me duele la cabeza. I've got a headache.
  Le dolía el estómago. He had
  stomachache.

◊ el **dolor** *masc noun*
  pain
  Tengo dolor de garganta. I have a sore
  throat.
  Tengo dolor de muelas. I have toothache.

doméstico *masc adjective*, **doméstica** *fem*
  domestic

◊ el **domicilio** *masc noun*
  address
  en su domicilio particular in his own home

el **domingo** *masc noun*
  Sunday
  el domingo on Sunday
  el domingo pasado last Sunday
  los domingos on Sundays
  cada domingo every Sunday
  Los domingos nos vamos a la piscina. We
  go to the pool on Sundays.
  el domingo por la mañana on Sunday
  morning
  • el **domingo de Resurrección** Easter
  Sunday

WORD TIP Names of months and days start with
small letters in Spanish.

a b c d e f g h i j k l m n ñ o p q r s t u v w x y z

el **dominical** *masc noun*
1 **Sunday newspaper**
2 **Sunday supplement**

el **dominó** *masc noun*
dominoes
jugar al dominó to play dominoes

ᵭ **don** *masc noun*
Mr
Don Juan Pozo Mr Juan Pozo (*don is used to show respect. It goes before the person's first name.*)

la **donación** *fem noun*
donation

ᵭ **donde** *adverb* ▷ see **dónde** *adv*
where
El sitio donde nací. The place where I was born.
El lugar a donde nos dirigimos. The place we're going to.
Iré a donde quiera. I'll go wherever I want.
Ponlo donde sea. Put it down anywhere.

ᵭ **dónde** *adverb* ▷ see **donde** *adv*
where
¿De dónde eres? Where are you from?
¿Dónde está mi abrigo? Where's my coat?
No sé dónde lo guarda. I don't know where he keeps it.
¿Por dónde se va a la oficina de correos? What's the way to the post office?

WORD TIP *dónde*, with an accent, is used for questions (¿...?).

el **donut** *masc noun*
doughnut

ᵭ **doña** *fem noun*
Mrs, Ms
Doña María del Valle Mrs María del Valle (*doña is used to show respect. It goes before the person's first name.*)

ᵭ **dorado** *masc adjective*, **dorada** *fem*
gold, golden (*in colour*)

dormido *masc adjective*, **dormida** *fem*
asleep
estar dormido to be asleep
quedarse dormido to fall asleep

ᵭ **dormir** *verb* [51]
1 **to sleep**
¿Has dormido bien? Did you sleep well?
¡A dormir! Time for bed!
Ya es hora de irse a dormir. It's time to go to bed.
2 **to get to sleep**
No puedo dormir. I can't get to sleep.
No he dormido nada. I couldn't sleep at all.

3 estar durmiendo to be asleep
Juan está todavía durmiendo. Juan is still asleep.
4 dormir la siesta to have a nap

dormirse *reflexive verb* [51]
1 **to fall asleep**
No puedo dormirme. I can't get to sleep.
2 **to oversleep**
Me dormí y llegué tarde al trabajo. I overslept and was late for work.

ᵭ el **dormitorio** *masc noun*
1 **bedroom**
2 **dormitory**

ᵭ el **dorso** *masc noun*
back (*of a piece of paper, a hand, an animal*)

dos *number*
1 **two**
Tiene dos años. She's two (years old).
2 (*saying the date*) **second**
el dos de enero the second of January
3 (*telling the time*) **two**
Son las dos. It's two o'clock.
a las dos y media at half past two

doscientos, **doscientas** *number*
two hundred
doscientos veinte two hundred and twenty

doy *verb* ▷ **dar**

el **dragón** *masc noun*
dragon

el **drama** *masc noun*
1 **drama**
2 **play**

dramático *masc adjective*, **dramática** *fem*
dramatic

ᵭ la **droga** *fem noun*
drug

el **drogadicto** *masc noun*, la **drogadicta** *fem*
drug addict

la **droguería** *fem noun*
1 **hardware shop** (*specializing in household items*)
2 **chemist's**

ᵭ la **ducha** *fem noun*
shower
darse una ducha to have a shower

ᵭ **ducharse** *reflexive verb* [17]
to have a shower

a
b
c
d
e
f
g
h
i
j
k
l
m
n
ñ
o
p
q
r
s
t
u
v
w
x
y
z

la **duda** *fem noun*
1 **doubt**
   Sin duda es el mejor. It's undoubtedly the best.
   No me queda la menor duda. I have no doubts whatsoever.
2 **query**
   ¿Tienes alguna duda? Do you have any queries?
   Tengo algunas dudas. I have a few queries.

dudar *verb* [17]
   to doubt
   Lo dudo. I doubt it.
   No dudes en preguntar. Don't hesitate to ask.
   Dudo que sepa hacerlo. I doubt he knows how to do it.

WORD TIP *dudar que* is followed by a verb in the subjunctive.

duela, **duelo**, etc *verb* ▷ **doler**

el **dueño** *masc noun*, la **dueña** *fem*
1 **owner**
   Se lo devolví a la dueña. I returned it to its owner.
   ¿Quién es el dueño de este coche? Who's the owner of this car?
2 **landlord** (*of a pub or a guesthouse*)
3 **landlady** (*of a pub or a guesthouse*)

duerma, **duermo**, etc *verb* ▷ **dormir**

♪ **dulce** *masc & fem adjective* ▷ **see dulce** *noun*
   sweet

♪ el **dulce** *masc noun* ▷ **see dulce** *adj*
   los dulces sweet things

la **duna** *fem noun*
   dune

duodécimo *masc adjective*, **duodécima** *fem*
   twelfth

el **duque** *masc noun*, la **duquesa** *fem*
1 **duke**
2 **duchess**

la **duración** *fem noun*
   length
   la duración de la película the length of the film
   un disco de larga duración an LP

♪ **durante** *preposition*
1 **during**
   durante aquel tiempo during that time
   Lo haré durante las vacaciones. I'll do it during the holidays.
   durante todo el partido throughout the match
2 (*for a specific period of time*) **for**
   No se vieron durante tres semanas. They didn't see each other for three weeks.

♪ **durar** *verb* [17]
   to last
   ¿Cuánto dura? How long is it?
   No dura mucho. It's not very long.
   La guerra duró tres años. The war lasted three years.

el **durazno** *masc noun*
   (*Latin America*) **peach**

la **dureza** *fem noun*
   hardness

♪ **duro** *masc adjective*, **dura** *fem*
   ▷ **see duro** *adv, noun*
1 **hard**
   Al secarse se pone duro. It goes hard when it dries.
   Fue un golpe muy duro para todos. It was a hard blow for all of us.
2 **strict** (*teacher*)
   un profesor muy duro a very strict teacher
3 **tough** (*meat*)
4 **stale** (*bread*)
5 ser duro de oído to be hard of hearing

♪ **duro** *adverb* ▷ **see duro** *adj, noun*
   hard
   estudiar duro to study hard

el **duro** *masc noun* ▷ **see duro** *adj, adv*
   five-peseta coin (*no longer used*)
   No tengo ni un duro. I'm broke.

el **DVD** *masc noun*
   DVD (*player, disk*)

E e

e *conjunction*

and

español e inglés Spanish and English
padres e hijos parents and children

WORD TIP And is normally *y* in Spanish, but *e* before words beginning with *i-* or *hi-*.

⚡ **echar** *verb* [17]

1 **to throw, to throw out**
Échale agua al fuego. Throw water on the fire.
Eché la botella a la basura. I threw the bottle out.
Los eché de mi casa. I threw them out of my house.
echar una carta (al correo) to post a letter
echar a alguien del trabajo to sack someone
Lo han echado del trabajo. He's been sacked.

2 **to put**
Échale más leche al café. Put more milk in the coffee.
Tengo que echar gasolina al coche. I must put some petrol in the car.

3 **to show**
Echan una película en la tele. They're showing a film on the television.
¿Qué echan en el cine? What's on at the cinema?

4 **echar de menos a alguien** to miss somebody
Echamos de menos a mi hermana. We miss my sister.
Te hecho mucho de menos. I miss you a lot.

⚡ **echarse** *verb reflexive* [17]

1 **echarse al suelo** to throw yourself on the ground

2 **to move**
echarse para atrás to move backwards
Se echó a la derecha. He moved to the right.
Me eché a un lado. I moved to one side.

3 **echarse una siesta** to have a nap

el eclipse *masc noun*
eclipse

el eco *masc noun*
echo

ecológico *masc adjective*, **ecológica** *fem*
ecological
un desastre ecológoco an environmental disaster

ecologista *masc & fem adjective*
ecologist

la economía *fem noun*

1 **economy**
la economía europea the European economy

2 **economics**
estudiar economía to study economics

económico *masc adjective*, **económica** *fem*

1 **economic**
una crisis económica an economic crisis

2 **financial**
los problemas económicos de la zona the financial problems of the area

3 **cheap**
un vuelo económico a cheap flight

4 **thrifty** (*person*)

⚡ **la ecuación** *fem noun*
equation

el ecuador *masc noun* ▷ see **Ecuador** *noun*
the equator (*in geography*)

Ecuador *masc noun* ▷ see **ecuador** *noun*
Ecuador (*the Latin American country on the equator*)

ecuatoriano *masc adjective & noun*, **ecuatoriana** *fem adjective & noun*

1 **Ecuadorian**

2 **un ecuatoriano, una ecuatoriana** Ecuadorian

WORD TIP Adjectives and nouns for nationality and regional origin do not have capital letters in Spanish.

⚡ **la edad** *fem noun*

age
¿Qué edad tienes? How old are you?
Carmen y yo tenemos la misma edad. Carmen and I are the same age.
Una mujer de unos treinta años de edad. A woman of about thirty.
Está en la edad del pavo. She's at the awkward age.

• **la edad de piedra** the Stone Age
• **la edad media** the Middle Ages

⚡ indicates key words   **105**

a
b
c
d
e
f
g
h
i
j
k
l
m
n
ñ
o
p
q
r
s
t
u
v
w
x
y
z

Spanish-English

a
b
c
d
e
f
g
h
i
j
k
l
m
n
ñ
o
p
q
r
s
t
u
v
w
x
y
z

la **edición** *fem noun*
1 **edition**
2 **one of a series**
la sexta **edición del festival** the sixth in the series of festivals
• la **edición de bolsillo** pocket edition

el **edificio** *masc noun*
building

editar *verb* [17]
1 **to publish**
2 **to edit** (*a text, in IT*)

la **editorial** *fem noun*
publishing company

el **edredón** *masc noun*
quilt
• el **edredón nórdico** duvet

♪ la **educación** *fem noun*
1 **education**
el ministerio de educación the ministry of education
2 **manners**
¡Qué mala educación! What bad manners!
Eso es de mala educación. That's bad manners.
• la **educación a distancia** distance learning
• la **educación física** physical education
• la **educación secundaria** secondary education

educado *masc adjective*, **educada** *fem*
polite
una persona bien educada a polite person
una persona mal educada a rude person

♪ **educar** *verb* [31]
1 **to educate**
Me eduqué en un colegio público. I was educated in a state school.
2 **to bring up**
La educó su tía. Her aunt brought her up.

EE.UU. *abbreviation*
(= *los Estados Unidos*) **USA**

WORD TIP *Estados Unidos is often used without los.*

efectivo *masc adjective*, **efectiva** *fem*
▷ see **efectivo** *noun*
effective (*remedy, method*)

el **efectivo** *masc noun* ▷ see **efectivo** *adj*
cash
pagar en efectivo to pay cash
mil euros en efectivo a thousand euros in cash

el **efecto** *masc noun*
1 **effect**
La pastilla no me hizo efecto. The pill didn't have any effect on me.
2 **en efecto that's right**
En efecto llegaron a las diez. That's right, they arrived at ten.
• el **efecto invernadero** greenhouse effect
• los **efectos especiales** special effects
• los **efectos secundarios** side effects

♪ **efectuar** *verb* [20]
to carry out
efectuar una búsqueda to carry out a search
El tren efectuará su salida a las nueve y treinta. The train will depart at 9:30.

eficaz *masc & fem adjective*, pl: **eficaces**
effective
un remedio eficaz an effective treatment

egoísta *masc & fem adjective & noun*
1 **selfish**
2 Eres un egoísta., Eres una egoísta. You're very selfish.

ejecutar *verb* [17]
to execute

ejecutivo *masc adjective*, **ejecutiva** *fem*
▷ see **ejecutivo** *noun*
executive

el **ejecutivo** *masc noun*, la **ejecutiva** *fem*
▷ see **ejecutivo** *adj*
executive

el **ejemplar** *masc noun*
1 **copy** (*of a book*)
2 **issue** (*of a magazine*)
3 **specimen** (*of an animal, a plant*)

el **ejemplo** *masc noun*
example
por ejemplo for example
Ese caso es un mal ejemplo. That case is a bad example.
dar buen ejemplo to set a good example
El capitán de equipo tiene que dar buen ejemplo. The captain of the team has to set a good example.

♪ el **ejercicio** *masc noun*
exercise
hacer ejercicio to take exercise
Hago ejercicio todos los días. I take exercise every day.

♪ el **ejército** *masc noun*
army
alistarse en el ejército to join the army
• el **ejército de aire** air force
• el **ejército de tierra** army

♪ **el** *masc determiner* ▷ see **él** *masc pron*

1 (*before masc sing nouns*) **the**
el sol the sun
el libro blanco the white book

2 (*for la with fem nouns with stressed 'a' or 'ha'*) **el agua** the water
el hada the fairy

3 (*when el is not translated*)
el señor Martínez Mr Martínez
el coche de Juan Juan's car
El caviar es muy caro. Caviar is very dear.

4 (*with parts of the body, clothes*) **Se rompió el brazo.** She broke her arm.
Se cortó el dedo. He cut his finger.
Me quité el abrigo. I took my coat off.

5 (*with dates, days of the week*) **el dos de mayo** the second of May
Iré el próximo lunes. I'll go next Monday.
El miércoles abren a las diez. They open at ten on Wednesdays.

6 (*for a masc noun, which is known about, e.g. el coche below*) **Me gusta el rojo.** I like the red one.
El mío es mejor. Mine is better.
El suyo es más caro. His is more expensive.
el mío y el de usted mine and yours
Éste es el de María. This one is María's.
Me gusta más el de Toni. I like Toni's better.
El que yo compré. The one (that) I bought.
El que quieras. Whichever you want.

7 (*with a*) **to the**
La llevaron al hospital. They took her to the hospital.

WORD TIP *a + el* becomes *al*. See also *la, los and las.*

♪ **él** *masc pronoun*

1 (*as the subject*) **he**
Él no lo sabe. He doesn't know.
él mismo he himself

2 (*with a preposition before él*) **him**
Estaba hablando con él. I was talking to him.
Pregúntale a él. Ask him.
Iba detrás de él. I was behind him.

3 (*with de showing ownership*) **Es de él.** It's his.

elástico *masc adjective*, **elástica** *fem*
elastic

la **elección** *fem noun*
1 **choice**
no tener elección to have no choice
2 **las elecciones** the election
convocar elecciones to call an election

el **electorado** *masc noun*
electorate

electoral *masc & fem adjective*
electoral
una campaña electoral an election campaign

la **electricidad** *fem noun*
electricity

el & la **electricista** *masc & fem noun*
electrician

eléctrico *masc adjective*, **eléctrica** *fem*
1 **electric**
2 **electrical**

electrocutar *verb* [17]
to electrocute

el **electrodoméstico** *masc noun*
electrical appliance

electrónico *masc adjective*, **electrónica** *fem*
electronic

♪ el **electrotrén** *masc noun*
electric express train

el **elefante** *masc noun*
elephant

elegante *masc & fem adjective*
1 **elegant**
2 **smart**
Siempre va muy elegante. He's always very smartly dressed.

♪ **elegir** *verb* [48]
to choose

el **elemento** *masc noun*
element

el **elepé** *masc noun*
LP

elija, elijo *verb* ▷ **elegir**

eliminar *verb* [17]
1 **to eliminate**
Nuestro equipo fue eliminado. Our team was eliminated.
2 **to remove**
Elimina manchas. It removes stains.

la **eliminatoria** *fem noun*
qualifying round

eliminatorio *masc adjective*,
eliminatoria *fem*
qualifying (*round or match*)

ella *fem pronoun* ▷ see **ellas** *pron*

1 (*as the subject*) **she**
Ella no lo sabe. She doesn't know.
ella misma she herself

2 (*with a preposition before ella*) **her**
Estaba hablando con ella. I was talking to her.
Pregúntale a ella. Ask her.
Yo iba detrás de ella. I was behind her.

3 (*with de showing ownership*) Es de ella. It's hers.

ellas *fem plural pronoun* ▷ see **ella** *pron*

1 (*as the subject*) **they**
Ellas no lo saben. They don't know.
ellas mismas they themselves

2 (*with a preposition before ella*) **them**
Estaba hablando con ellas. I was talking to them.
Pregúntales a ellas. Ask them.
Iba detrás de ellas. I was behind them.

3 (*with de showing ownership*) Es de ellas. It's theirs.

WORD TIP *ellas* is the fem plural form of the pronoun; it refers to two or more females.

ello *pronoun* ▷ see **ellos** *pron*

1 **it**
No sé mucho de ello. I don't know much about it.

2 **this**
Para ello es necesario ... For this, you must ...

WORD TIP When *ello* stands alone, it never changes.

ellos *masc plural pronoun* ▷ see **ello** *pron*

1 (*as the subject*) **they**
Ellos no lo saben. They don't know.
ellos mismos they themselves

2 (*with a preposition before ellos*) **them**
Estaba hablando con ellos. I was talking to them.
Pregúntales a ellos. Ask them.
Iba detrás de ellos. I was behind them.

3 (*with de showing ownership*) Es de ellos. It's theirs.

WORD TIP *ellos* is the masc plural form of the pronoun; it refers to two or more males, a male and female, or males and females

la **embajada** *fem noun*
embassy

el **embajador** *masc noun*, la **embajadora** *fem*
ambassador

el **embalse** *masc noun*
reservoir

embarazada *fem adjective*
pregnant
quedarse embarazada to get pregnant
Estoy embarazada de tres meses. I'm three months pregnant.

la **embarazada** *fem noun*
pregnant woman

el **embarazo** *masc noun*
1 **pregnancy**
2 **embarrassment**

la **embarcación** *fem noun*
vessel (*boat*)

el **embarcadero** *masc noun*
wharf

embarcar *verb* [31]
1 **to board** (*a plane*)
2 **to go on board** (*on a boat*)
3 **to load** (*goods, luggage*)

embarcarse *reflexive verb* [31]
1 **to board** (*a plane*)
2 **to go on board** (*a ship*)
3 embarcarse en algo to get involved in something

emborracharse *reflexive verb* [17]
to get drunk

el **embargo** *masc noun*
embargo
• sin embargo nevertheless
▷ **sin**

la **emboscada** *fem noun*
ambush

el **embotellamiento** *masc noun*
traffic jam

el **embrague** *masc noun*
clutch

embrujado *masc adjective*, **embrujada** *fem*
1 **haunted**
2 **bewitched**

la **emergencia** *fem noun*
emergency
salida de emergencia emergency exit

el & la **emigrante** *masc & fem noun*
emigrant

emigrar *verb* [17]
to emigrate

la **emisión** *fem noun*
1 **emission** (*of gas, pollutants, etc*)
2 **broadcast** (*in radio, tv*)

la **emisora** *fem noun*
radio station

la **emoción** *fem noun*
1 **emotion**
2 **excitement**
una película llena de emoción a really exciting film
¡Qué emoción! How exciting!

emocionado *masc adjective*,
emocionada *fem*
1 **moved**
2 **excited**

emocional *masc & fem adjective*
emotional

emocionante *masc & fem adjective*
1 **moving**
Hubo emocionantes escenas en el aeropuerto. There were moving scenes at the airport.
2 **exciting**
una película emocionante an exciting film
¡Qué emocionante! How exciting!

el **emoticón** *masc noun*
smiley, **emoticon**

el **empacho** *masc noun*
(*informal*) tener empacho to have a stomach-ache (*from over-eating*)
Se cogió un empacho de pasteles. He ate so many cakes he had a stomachache.

el **empalme** *masc noun*
junction (*on a railway*)

la **empanada** *fem noun*
pastie
una empanada de atún a tuna pie

empapado *masc adjective*, **empapada** *fem*
soaking wet
Venían empapados. They were soaking wet.

empaparse *verb* [17]
to get soaking wet

empastar *verb* [17]
to fill (*a tooth*)

el **empaste** *masc noun*
filling (*for a tooth*)

empatar *verb* [17]
to draw
Empataron dos a dos. They drew two all

el **empate** *masc noun*
1 **draw** (*in sport*)
2 **tie** (*in voting, etc*)

empecé *verb* ▷ **empezar**

empeorar *verb* [17]
1 **to get worse**
La situación ha empeorado. The situation has got worse.
2 **to make worse**
Va a empeorar las cosas. It's going to make things worse.

el **emperador** *masc noun*
emperor

la **emperatriz** *fem noun*, **emperatrices** *plural*
empress

♪ **empezar** *verb* [25]
to begin, **to start**
El colegio empieza el quince de septiembre. School begins on the fifteenth of September.
Empiezo el colegio en enero. I start school in January.
Empezaré otra vez. I'll start again.
Empezó diciendo que … He began by saying that …
empezar a hacer algo to begin to do something
Empezó a llover. It started to rain.

> **WORD TIP** To say, to begin by, use *empezar* + -*ando*, or -*iendo*; to say, to begin to, use *empezar a* + *infinitive*.

empiece, **empieza**, **empiezo**, **etc** *verb*
▷ **empezar**

empinado *masc adjective*, **empinada** *fem*
steep (*slopes, streets*)

el **emplazamiento** *masc noun*
situation, **location**

♪ el **empleado** *masc noun*, la **empleada** *fem*
employee
los empleados the staff (*in a company*)
Todos los empleados se beneficiarán. All the staff will benefit.

emplear *verb* [17]
1 **to employ**
Emplean 300 trabajadores en la fábrica. They employ 300 workers at the factory.
2 **to use**
Emplearon materiales viejos. They used old materials.

♪ el **empleo** *masc noun*
1 **employment**
2 **job**
buscar empleo to look for a job
3 **estar sin empleo** to be unemployed

a
b
c
d
e
f
g
h
i
j
k
l
m
n
ñ
o
p
q
r
s
t
u
v
w
x
y
z

empollar *verb* [17]

1 (*informal*) **to swot** (*for exams*)

2 **to incubate** (*eggs*)

el **empollón** *masc noun,* la **empollona** *fem*
(*informal*) **swot**

emprendedor *masc adjective,*
  emprendedora *fem*
enterprising

la **empresa** *fem noun*
  company

♂ **empujar** *verb* [17]
  to push

♂ **en** *preposition*

1 **in**
en español in Spanish
en invierno in winter
Ponlo en el cajón. Put it in the drawer.
Vivo en Londres. I live in London.

2 **into**
Entró en la casa. He went into the house.

3 **on**
Está en la mesa. It's on the table.
Viven en el segundo piso. They live on the
second floor.

4 **at**
Estaré en casa toda la tarde. I'll be at home
all afternoon.
Es muy buena en inglés. She's very good at
English.

5 **by**
ir en coche to go by car

la **enagua** *fem noun,* pl: las **enaguas**
  petticoat

enamorado *masc adjective,* **enamorada**
fem
in love
estar enamorado de alguien to be in love
with someone
Está enamorado de ella. He is in love with
her.
Está enamorada de él. She is in love with
him.

enamorarse *reflexive verb* [17]
to fall in love
Se enamoraron. They fell in love.
enamorase de alguien to fall in love with
someone
Se enamoró de ella. He fell in love with her.

el **enano** *masc noun,* la **enana** *fem*
dwarf

♂ **encantado** *masc adjective,* **encantada**
fem

1 ¡Encantado de conocerle! Pleased to meet
you! (*boy speaking; formal style*)
¡Encantada de conocerle! Pleased to meet
you! (*girl speaking; formal style*)

2 **delighted**
Están encantados con la casa. They're
delighted with the house.

3 **enchanted** (*castle, life*)

encantador *masc adjective,*
  encantadora *fem*
  ▷ **see encantador** *noun*

1 **lovely** (*thing*)

2 **charming** (*person*)

el **encantador** *masc noun,* la
  encantadora *fem*
  ▷ **see encantador** *adj*
  magician

• el **encantador de serpientes** snake-
charmer

encantar *verb* [17]
Me encanta el regalo. I love the present.
Nos encanta el hotel. We love the hotel.
Le encantan las joyas. She loves the jewels.
Nos encantaría venir a verte. We'd love to
come and see you.

> **WORD TIP** Use *encanta, encantó, encantaba,*
> *encantaría, etc* if what you love is singular or an
> infinitive. Use *encantan, encantaron, encantaban,*
> *encantarían, etc* if what you love is plural.

encargado *masc adjective,* **encargada**
fem ▷ **see encargado** *noun*
encargado de algo responsible for
something
La persona encargada del reparto. The
person responsible for the delivery.

el **encargado** *masc noun,* la **encargada**
fem ▷ **see encargado** *adj*
manager

el **encendedor** *masc noun*
  lighter

♂ **encender** *verb* [36]

1 **to light** (*a cigarette, match*)

2 **to turn on** (*the lights, tv*)

♂ **encendido** *masc adjective,* **encendida** *fem*

1 **on** (*radio, cooker*)

2 **burning** (*match, hay*)

el **encerado** *masc noun*
  blackboard

encerrar *verb* [36]

1 **to lock up** (*a person*)

2 **to lock away** (*papers, money*)

enchufar *verb* [17]
1 **to plug in** (*to the socket*)
2 **to turn on** (*the tv, the kettle*)

el **enchufe** *masc noun*
plug (*for a socket*)

la **enciclopedia** *fem noun*
encyclopedia

encienda, **enciendo**, **etc** *verb* ▷ **encender**

♪ **encima** *adverb*
1 **on, on top**
Ponlo ahí encima. Put it on there.
Había un plástico encima. There was a
piece of plastic on top.
No llevaba el carnet de identidad encima.
He didn't have his identity card on him.
2 **el de encima, la de encima** the top one
el piso de encima the flat above
3 **encima de** on, on top of (*someting*)
encima del armario on top of the wardrobe
Está encima de la cama. It's on the bed.
Llevaba una gabardina encima de la
chaqueta. I was wearing a raincoat over my
jacket.
4 **por encima de** above, over (*something*)
Las temperaturas están por encima de lo
normal. Temperatures are above normal.
5 **encima de** as well, too
Encima de llegar tarde se queja. He arrives
late and he complains as well.
¡Y encima no me lo devolvió! And on top of
that he didn't give it back to me!

WORD TIP *encima* is used by itself; *encima de* is
followed by a noun or pronoun.

♪ **encontrar** *verb* [24]
to find
No encuentro mis gafas en ninguna parte. I
can't find my glasses anywhere.
Las encontré en la cocina. I found them in
the kitchen.

encontrarse *reflexive verb* [24]
1 **encontrarse con** to meet
Me encontré con ella en la calle. I met her in
the street.
2 **to feel**
No me encuentro bien. I don't feel well.
3 **to find**
Me encontré un billete de diez euros. I
found a ten-euro note.

encuentra, **encuentras**, **encuentro**,
etc *verb* ▷ **encontrar**

la **encuesta** *fem noun*
survey
• la **encuesta de opinión** opinion poll

el **enemigo** *masc noun*, la **enemiga** *fem*
enemy

la **energía** *fem noun*
energy
• la **energía nuclear** nuclear energy
• la **energía solar** solar energy

enérgico *masc adjective*, **enérgica** *fem*
energetic

enero *masc noun*
January
en enero in January
el 14 de enero on 14 January

WORD TIP Names of months and days start with
small letters in Spanish.

♪ **enfadado** *masc adjective*, **enfadada** *fem*
1 **angry**
2 **annoyed**

♪ **enfadar** *verb* [17]
1 **to make angry**
2 **to annoy**

enfadarse *reflexive verb* [17]
1 **to get annoyed**
Se enfadó conmigo. He got annoyed with
me.
No te enfades. Don't get annoyed.
2 **to get angry**
Se enfadó muchísimo. He got really angry.
3 **to get cross**
Mamá se va a enfadar. Mum's going to get
cross.

el **énfasis** *masc noun*
emphasis

♪ **enfermar** *verb* [17]
to get ill

♪ la **enfermedad** *fem noun*
illness, **disease**

la **enfermería** *fem noun*
1 **nursing**
2 **infirmary**

♪ el **enfermero** *masc noun*, la **enfermera**
fem
nurse

♪ **enfermo** *masc adjective*, **enferma** *fem*
▷ see **enfermo** *noun*
ill
Está gravemente enferma. She's seriously
ill.
caer enfermo to fall ill

♪ el **enfermo** *masc noun*, la **enferma** *fem*
▷ see **enfermo** *adj*
1 **sick person**
los enfermos sick people
2 **patient**

a
b
c
d
e
f
g
h
i
j
k
l
m
n
ñ
o
p
q
r
s
t
u
v
w
x
y
z

♂ enfrente *adverb*
opposite
La estación está enfrente de la catedral.
The station is opposite the cathedral.
de enfrente: la casa de enfrente the house
opposite

engañar *verb* [17]
1 **to deceive**
2 **to cheat, to swindle**
3 **to be unfaithful to**

engañarse *reflexive verb* [17]
to fool yourself

el **engaño** *masc noun*
1 **deception**
2 **swindle**

engordar *verb* [17]
1 **to put on weight**
Ha engordado mucho. He's put on a lot of
weight.
2 **to be fattening**
La mantequilla engorda. Butter is
fattening.

♂ la enhorabuena *fem noun*
¡Enhorabuena por ganar el premio!
Congratulations on winning the prize!
darle la enhorabuena a alguien to
congratulate someone

enjuagar *verb* [28]
to rinse
enjuagar los platos to rinse the plates

enjuagarse *reflexive verb* [28]
enjuagarse el pelo to rinse your hair

enmohecerse *reflexive verb* [35]
to go mouldy

enojado *masc adjective*, **enojada** *fem*
(*Latin America*) **angry**

enojar *verb* [17]
(*Latin America*) **to annoy**

enojarse *reflexive verb* [17]
to get annoyed
Se enojó conmigo. He got annoyed with
me.
No te enojes. Don't get annoyed.

enorme *masc & fem adjective*
huge

enormemente *adverb*
extremely, very
Estaba enormemente preocupado. He was
extremely worried.

enrollar *verb* [17]
to roll up

enroscar *verb* [31]
1 **to wind**
2 **to screw on**

la **ensaimada** *fem noun*
pastry (*shaped like a spiral and dusted with icing
sugar*)

♂ la ensalada *fem noun*
salad
• la **ensalada de frutas** fruit salad
• la **ensalada mixta** mixed salad

la **ensaladera** *fem noun*
salad bowl

la **ensaladilla**, la **ensaladilla rusa** *fem
noun*
potato salad

el **ensayo** *masc noun*
1 **rehearsal**
2 **essay**
3 **try** (*in rugby*)
• el **ensayo general** dress rehearsal

enseguida *adverb*
right away
Enseguida lo traigo. I'll bring right away.

la **enseñanza** *fem noun*
1 **teaching**
la enseñanza de música the teaching of
music
2 **education**
• la **enseñanza primaria** primary education
• la **enseñanza secundaria** secondary
education
• la **enseñanza superior** higher education

enseñar *verb* [17]
1 **to teach**
Enseña matemáticas. She teaches maths.
enseñarle a alguien a hacer algo to teach
somebody something
Mi padre me enseñó a nadar. My father
taught me to swim.
2 **to show**
Enséñame tus fotos. Show me your photos.
Nos enseñó la casa. He showed us the house.

ensuciar *verb* [17]
to make dirty
No ensucies la mesa. Don't make the table
dirty.
Ensucié el mantel de aceite de oliva. I got
olive oil on the tablecloth.

ensuciarse *reflexive verb* [17]
to get dirty
Te vas a ensuciar las manos. You're going
to get your hands dirty.
Me he ensuciado las botas de barro. I've
got mud on my boots.

♂ **entender** *verb* [36]

1 **to understand**
Entiendo lo que dicen. I can understand what they're saying.
¿Entiendes la pregunta? Do you understand the question?
No le entiendo. I can't understand you. (*formal use*)

2 **entender algo mal** to misunderstand something
La entendí mal. I misunderstood her.

3 **entender de algo** to know about something
Entiendo un poco de fontanería. I know a bit about plumbing.
Entiendo un poco de español. I can understand a little bit of Spanish.

entenderse *reflexive verb* [36]

entenderse con alguien to get along with someone
Se entiende muy bien con su hermana. She gets along very well with her sister.
Nos entendemos muy bien. We get along very well.

♂ **entendido** *masc adjective*, **entendida** *fem*

1 **understood**
Queda bien entendido. It's clearly understood.
¿Entendido? Is that clear?

2 **ser entendido en algo** to know about something
Es muy entendido en informática. He knows a lot about computers.

enterarse *reflexive verb* [17]

1 **enterarse de algo** to find out about something

2 **enterarse de lo que pasa** to realize what is happening

entero *masc adjective*, **entera** *fem*

whole
un día entero a whole day
Estuve esperando tres horas enteras. I was waiting for three whole hours.

enterrar *verb* [29]

to bury

entienda, **entiendes**, **entiendo**, etc
verb ▷ entender

♂ **entonces** *adverb*

1 **then**
Entonces llegó Carlos. Then Carlos arrived.
Desde entonces vivimos en Marbella. Since then we've lived in Marbella.

2 **so**, **ok**
Entonces nos vemos mañana. So we'll see each other tomorrow.

♂ la **entrada** *fem noun*

1 **entrance**, **way in**
¿Dónde está la entrada? Where is the entrance?

2 **ticket** (*for the cinema, a match, bull fight, etc*)
¿Cuánto cuesta la entrada? How much is a ticket?
Tenemos que sacar las entradas. We must buy the tickets.
Los niños pagan media entrada. It's half-price for children.
'Entrada libre' 'Admission free'

3 **entry**
la entrada de nuevos miembros en la Unión Europea the entry of new members into the European Union

4 **tackle** (*in football*)

5 **starter** (*on menus*)

6 **deposit** (*for a purchase*)

♂ **entrar** *verb* [17]

1 **to enter**, **to get in**
Entraron por una ventana They got in through a window.

2 **to come in**
¡Entra! Come in!

3 **to go in**
Llama antes de entrar. Knock before you go in.
Entraron en la clase corriendo. They ran into the classroom.

4 **entrar en** to go into
Entramos en la sala de espera. We went into the waiting rom.

5 **dejar entrar a alguien** to let someone in
No le dejes entrar. Don't let him in.

6 **hacer entrar a alguien** to show someone in
Le hizo entrar a su oficina. He showed him in.

7 **to fit**
No entra por la puerta. It doesn't fit through the door.
El desayuno no entra en el precio. Breakfast is not included in the price.

8 **to join**
Entraron en la UE. They joined the EU.

9 (*with feelings of cold, hunger, etc*) **Me entró hambre.** I got hungry.
Te va a entrar frío si te sientas fuera. You'll get cold if you sit outside.

10 (*informal*) (*about understanding something*) **No me entra.** I don't get it.
No le entran las matemáticas. He just doesn't get maths.

a
b
c
d
e
f
g
h
i
j
k
l
m
n
ñ
o
p
q
r
s
t
u
v
w
x
y
z

a
b
c
d
e
f
g
h
i
j
k
l
m
n
ñ
o
p
q
r
s
t
u
v
w
x
y
z

♂ **entre** *preposition*

1 between
Estaba sentado entre Jaime y Margarita. I was sitting between Jaime and Margarita.
Lo hicimos entre todos. We did it between us.

2 among
Lo encontré entre mis papeles. I found it among my papers.

3 by (*in maths*)
Nueve dividido entre tres. Nine divided by three.

entreabierto *masc adjective*,
entreabierta *fem*
half-open

el **entreacto** *masc noun*
interval

la **entrega** *fem noun*
1 delivery (*of goods*)
2 presentation (*of a prize, award*)
3 la fecha límite para la entrega de solicitudes the deadline for handing in applications

♂ **entregar** *verb* [28]
1 to deliver, **to hand in**
Vino a entregar una carta. He came to deliver a letter.
Tenemos que entregar el trabajo el próximo lunes. We have to hand in the essay next Monday.
Me entregó los documentos. He handed me the documents.
2 to present (*a prize, an award*)
El alcalde entregó los premios. The mayor presented the prizes.
3 to surrender (*a town, weapons*)
4 to hand over (*a criminal, a prisoner*)

entregarse *reflexive verb* [28]
to give yourself up
Se entregó a la policía. He gave himself up to the police.

♂ el **entremés** *masc noun*, **entremeses** *plural*
starter (*in a meal*)

el **entrenador** *masc noun*, la **entrenadora** *fem*
1 manager (*of a professional sports team*)
2 trainer (*of a team, horse, dog, etc*)

el **entrenamiento** *masc noun*
training

♂ **entrenar** *verb* [17]
to train
Entrenamos los martes y jueves. We train on Tuesdays and Thursdays.

entrenarse *reflexive verb* [17]
to train

entretanto *adverb*
in the meantime

entretenido *masc adjective*, **entretenida** *fem*
entertaining

la **entrevista** *fem noun*
interview
• la **entrevista de trabajo** job interview

entrevistar *verb* [17]
to interview

entumecido *masc adjective*, **entumecida** *fem*
numb

entusiasmar *verb* [17]
Me entusiasma la idea. I really like the idea.
Le entusiasma el deporte. She's really keen on sports.
A mi padre no le entusiasma viajar. My father's not keen on travel.

entusiasmarse *reflexive verb* [17]
entusiasmarse con algo to get keen about something
Se entusiasmaron con la idea. They got keen on the idea.

el **entusiasmo** *masc noun*
enthusiasm

♂ **enviar** *verb* [32]
to send
Te enviaré un mensaje de texto. I'll send you a text message.

la **envidia** *fem noun*
1 envy
Se muere de envidia. He's green with envy.
2 jealousy
tenerle envidia a alguien to be jealous of someone
Me tienen envidia. They're jealous of me.
Le tiene envidia a su hermana. She's envious of her sister.

envidiar *verb* [17]
to be envious of
Me envidia que saqué mejores notas que ella. She's envious that I got better marks than she did.

envidioso *masc adjective*, **envidiosa** *fem*
envious

ᵹ **envolver** verb [45]
to wrap up
envolver un regalo to wrap up a present

ᵹ **envuelto** masc adjective, **envuelta** fem
1 **wrapped**
envuelto para regalo gift-wrapped
2 **estar envuelto en algo** to be involved in something
Está envuelto en un asunto de drogas. He's involved in something to do with drugs.

envuelto verb ▷ envolver

la **epidemia** fem noun
epidemic

el **episodio** masc noun
episode

la **época** fem noun
1 **time**
En aquella época vivíamos en Málaga. At that time we were living in Málaga.
Es de la época de los romanos. It's from the time of the Romans.
2 **season**
en la época de la cosecha at harvest time

el **equilibrio** masc noun
balance
estar en equilibrio to be in balance
perder el equilibrio to lose your balance

ᵹ el **equipaje** masc noun
luggage
• el **equipaje de mano** hand luggage

ᵹ el **equipo** masc noun
1 **team**
el equipo visitante the away team
formar un buen equipo to make a good team
El trabajo en equipo es muy importante. Team work is very important.
2 **equipment**
• el **equipo de alta fidelidad** hi-fi system
• el **equipo de música** sound system

la **equis** fem noun
(the Spanish name for) **letter X**

la **equitación** fem noun
horse riding

equivaler verb [43]
equivaler a algo to be equivalent to something
Veinte euros equivalen a quice libras. Twenty euros are equivalent to fifteen pounds.

ᵹ **equivocado** masc adjective, **equivocada** fem
wrong
Estás equivocada. You're wrong. (talking to a girl)

ᵹ **equivocarse** reflexive verb [31]
1 **to make a mistake**
Me he equivocado. I've made a mistake.
equivocarse de algo to make a mistake about something
Me equivoqué de carpeta. I took the wrong folder.
Se equivocó de calle. He took the wrong street.
2 **to be wrong**
Te equivocas si piensas eso. You're wrong if you think like that.

era, érais, eras, eres, etc verb ▷ ser

el **error** masc noun
mistake
cometer un error to make a mistake
un error de cálculo a miscalculation
• el **error tipográfico** typing error

eructar verb [17]
to burp

el **eructo** masc noun
burp

es verb ▷ ser

ᵹ **esa, ésa** fem adjective & pronoun
that, that one
▷ ese adj, pron

ᵹ **esas, ésas** fem plural adjective & pronoun
those, those ones
▷ ese adj, pron

la **escala** fem noun
1 **stopover**
Hicieron escala en Florida. They stopped over in Florida.
2 **scale** (of a map, measurements)
a gran escala on a large scale
3 **scale** (in music)

la **escalada** fem noun
1 **(rock) climbing**
2 **climb**

el **escalador** masc noun, la **escaladora** fem
climber

escalar verb [17]
1 **to climb** (a mountain)
2 **to move up** (a league table)

a
b
c
d
e
f
g
h
i
j
k
l
m
n
ñ
o
p
q
r
s
t
u
v
w
x
y
z

♂ la **escalera** *fem noun*
staircase
bajar la escalera to go down the stairs
subir la escalera to go up the stairs
una escalera de mano a ladder
- la **escalera de caracol** spiral staircase
- la **escalera de incendios** fire escape
- la **escalera mecánica** escalator

el **escalofrío** *masc noun*
1 **shiver** (*from cold*)
tener escalofríos to be shivering
2 **shudder** (*with horror*)
darle escalofríos a alguien to make
someone shudder

el **escalón** *masc noun*
step

el **escalope** *masc noun*
escalope

el **escándalo** *masc noun*
1 **scandal**
¡Su comportamiento fue un escándalo! His
behaviour was really outrageous!
2 **racket**
armar un escándalo to make a racket
¡Qué escándalo están armando! what a
racket they are making!
- el **escándalo político** political scandal

escandaloso *masc adjective*,
escandalosa *fem*
1 **shocking** (*behaviour or clothes*)
2 **noisy** (*people*)

Escandinavia *fem noun*
Scandinavia

escandinavo *masc adjective & noun*,
escandinava *fem adjective & noun*
1 **Scandinavian**
2 **un escandinavo, una escandinava**
Scandinavian

WORD TIP Adjectives and nouns for nationality
and regional origin do not have capital letters in
Spanish.

el **escáner** *masc noun*
1 **scanner**
2 **scan**

escapar *verb* [17]
to escape
escapar de algo to escape from something

escaparse *reflexive verb* [17]
1 **to escape**
Se ha escapado de la cárcel. He's escaped
from prison.
2 **to run away**
escaparse de casa to run away from home
3 **to leak** (*gas, water, etc*)

el **escaparate** *masc noun*
shop window

el **escarabajo** *masc noun*
beetle

la **escarcha** *fem noun*
frost

la **escasez** *fem noun, pl:* las **escaseces**
shortage
Hay escasez de agua. There's a water
shortage.

la **escayola** *fem noun*
plaster (*for broken bones*)

la **escena** *fem noun*
scene

el **escenario** *masc noun*
stage

el **esclavo** *masc noun,* la **esclava** *fem*
slave

la **esclusa** *fem noun*
lock (*on a canal*)

la **escoba** *fem noun*
broom

♂ **escocés** *masc adjective,* **escocesa** *fem*
▷ see **escocés** *noun*
Scottish

♂ un **escocés** *masc noun,* una **escocesa** *fem*
▷ see **escocés** *adj*
Scot
los escoceses the Scots

WORD TIP Adjectives and nouns for nationality
and regional origin do not have capital letters in
Spanish.

♂ **Escocia** *fem noun*
Scotland
Soy de Escocia. I'm from Scotland.

♂ **escoger** *verb* [3]
to choose
Escoge el que te guste más. Choose the
one you like best. (*familiar form*)
Escoged el que os guste más. Choose the
one you like best. (*familiar plural form*)

escoja, escojo, etc *verb* ▷ **escoger**

escolar *masc & fem adjective*
▷ see **escolar** *noun*
school
la vida escolar school life

el & la **escolar** *masc & fem noun*
▷ see **escolar** *adj*
1 **schoolboy**
2 **schoolgirl**

esconder *verb* [18]
  to hide

esconderse *reflexive verb* [18]
  to hide
  esconderse de alguien to hide from
  someone
  Se escondió del profesor. She hid from the
  teacher.

escondido *masc adjective*, **escondida** *fem*
  hidden

escorpio, **escorpión** *masc & fem noun*
  ▷ see **escorpión** *noun*
  Scorpio (*star sign*)
  Soy escorpio. I'm Scorpio.

> **WORD TIP** Use a small letter in Spanish to say *I am Scorpio*, etc with star signs.

el **escorpión** *masc noun*
  ▷ see **escorpio** *noun*
  scorpion

♪ **escribir** *verb* [52]
  1 to write
  escribir una novela to write a novel
  Le escribí una postal. I wrote him a
  postcard.
  2 escribir a máquina to type

escribirse *reflexive verb*
  to spell
  ¿Cómo se escribe tu nombre? How do you
  spell your name?
  Se escribe así. You spell it like this.

escrito *verb* ▷ **escribir**

el **escritor** *masc noun*, la **escritora** *fem*
  writer

el **escritorio** *masc noun*
  1 desk
  2 (*Latin America*) **office**

♪ **escuchar** *verb* [17]
  1 to listen
  Escuchamos atentamente. We listened
  carefully.
  2 to listen to
  Escúchame. Listen to me.
  Escucha bien lo que digo. Listen carefully to
  what I say.

♪ la **escuela** *fem noun*
  school (*usually primary*)
  • la **escuela nocturna** night school
  • la **escuela primaria** primary school

el **escultor** *masc noun*, la **escultora** *fem*
  sculptor

la **escultura** *fem noun*
  sculpture

escupir *verb* [19]
  1 to spit
  escupirle a alguien to spit at someone
  Le escupió en la cara. She spat in his face.
  2 to spit out
  Escupió la comida. He spat out the food.

el **escúter** *masc noun*
  motor scooter

♪ **ese** *masc adjective*, **esa** *fem* ▷ see **ese** *pron*
  1 that
  ese libro that book
  esa chica that girl
  Ese chico es mi primo. That boy is my
  cousin.
  ¿Quién es esa chica? Who is that girl?
  2 esos, esas those
  esos zapatos those shoes
  esas camisas those shirts
  Esos chicos son de mi clase. Those boys are
  in my class.
  ¿Quienes son esos chicos? Who are those
  boys?

♪ **ese**, **esa**, **ése**, **ésa** *pronoun* ▷ see **ese** *adj*
  1 that one
  Ese es más bonito. That one is nicer (*for a
  masc noun*).
  Me gusta más esa. I like that one better (*for
  a fem noun*).
  ¿Quién es esa? Who is that? (*girl*)
  ¿Quién es ese? Who is that? (*boy*)
  2 esos, esas those ones
  Esos son más bonitos. Those ones are
  prettier (*for a masc pl noun*).
  Me gustan más esas. I like those ones
  better (*for a fem pl noun*).

el **esfuerzo** *masc noun*
  effort
  hacer un esfuerzo to make an effort

el **esguince** *masc noun*
  sprain

el **eslogan** *masc noun*
  slogan

eslovaco *masc adjective & noun*, **eslovaca**
fem adjective & noun
  1 Slovak
  2 un eslovaco, una eslovaca Slovak

> **WORD TIP** Adjectives and nouns for nationality and regional origin do not have capital letters in Spanish.

Eslovaquia *fem noun*
  Slovakia

Eslovenia *fem noun*
  Slovenia

a
b
c
d
e
f
g
h
i
j
k
l
m
n
ñ
o
p
q
r
s
t
u
v
w
x
y
z

esloveno *masc adjective & noun*, **eslovena** *fem adjective & noun*

1 **Slovene**

2 **un esloveno, una eslovena** Slovene

> **WORD TIP** Adjectives and nouns for nationality and regional origin do not have capital letters in Spanish.

⚐ **eso** *pronoun*

1 **that**
Eso no importa. That doesn't matter.
¿Qué es eso? What's that?
Por eso no vinimos. That's why we didn't come.

2 **a eso de ... about ...**
a eso de las ocho about eight o'clock

> **WORD TIP** *eso* never changes.

la **ESO** *fem*
(= *Educación Secundaria Obligatoria*) **secondary education programme** *(for the 12-16 age group in Spain)*

⚐ **esos** *masc plural adjective*, **esas** *fem plural adjective*
those
▷ **ese** *adj, pron*

⚐ **esos, ésos, esas/ésas** *pronoun*
those ones
▷ **ese** *adj, pron*

la **espada** *fem noun*
sword

espabilado *masc adjective*, **espabilada** *fem*
alert, on-the-ball

el **espacio** *masc noun*

1 **space, room**
dejar un espacio leave a space
No tenemos suficiente espacio. We don't have enough room.

2 **el espacio** space
la exploración del espacio the exploration of space

los **espaguetis** *plural masc noun*
spaghetti

⚐ la **espalda** *fem noun*

1 **back**
Me duele la espalda. My back hurts.
nadar a espalda to swim backstroke
¿Sabes nadar a espalda? Can you do the backstoke?

⚐ **España** *fem noun*
Spain

⚐ **español** *masc adjective*, **española** *fem*
▷ see **español** *noun*
Spanish

⚐ un **español** *masc noun*, una **española** *fem*
▷ see **español** *adj*

1 **Spaniard**
los españoles the Spaniards, the Spanish

2 **el español** Spanish *(the language)*

> **WORD TIP** Adjectives and nouns for nationality, regional origin, and language do not have capital letters in Spanish.

el **espantapájaros** *masc noun, pl:* los **espantapájaros**
scarecrow

espantoso *masc adjective*, **espantosa** *fem*

1 **horrific** *(crime)*

2 **horrible**
un vestido espantoso a horrible dress
Tiene un gusto espantoso. He has a horrible sense of taste.

3 **Hacía un frío espantoso.** It was terribly cold.
Tengo un sueño espantoso. I'm terribly sleepy.

el **esparadrapo** *masc noun*
sticking plaster

el **esparcimiento** *masc noun*
relaxation

el **espárrago** *masc noun*
asparagus

la **especia** *fem noun*
spice

⚐ **especial** *masc & fem adjective*
special

la **especialidad** *fem noun*
speciality

especializarse *reflexive verb* [22]
to specialize
Voy a especializarme en ciencias. I'm going to specialize in science.

⚐ el **espectáculo** *masc noun*

1 **sight**
Era un espectáculo espantoso. It was a terrible sight.

2 **show**
el mundo del espectáculo show business

el **espectador** *masc noun*, la **espectadora** *fem*
spectator

el **espejo** *masc noun*
mirror

• el **espejo retrovisor** rear-view mirror

espera *fem noun*
wait
una corta espera a short wait
estar a la espera de algo to be waiting for something
Estabamos a la espera de su llamada. We were waiting for her call.

la **esperanza** *fem noun*
hope
Hay pocas esperanzas de encontrarlos. There's little hope of finding them.
darle esperanzas a alguien to raise somebody's hopes
No quiero darle esperanzas de que vendrá. I don't want to raise his hopes that she'll come.

esperar *verb* [17]
1 **to wait**
Espera aquí. Wait here. (*informal use*)
Espere un momento. Wait a minute. (*formal use*)
2 **to wait for**
Te he estado esperando más de una hora. I've been waiting for you for more than an hour.
3 **to hope**
Espero que vengas. I hope you'll come.
Espero que sí., Eso espero. I hope so.
4 **to expect**
No esperaba esa respuesta. I didn't expect that answer.

espeso *masc adjective*, **espesa** *fem*
thick

el **espesor** *masc noun*
thickness

la **espesura** *fem noun*
thickness
Tiene diez centímetros de espesura. It's ten centimetres thick.

el & la **espía** *masc & fem noun*
spy

espiar *verb* [32]
to spy on

la **espina** *fem noun*
thorn

las **espinacas** *fem plural noun*
spinach

el **espionaje** *masc noun*
spying, espionage

espléndido *masc adjective*, **espléndida** *fem*
1 **splendid** (*occasion, weather, house*)
2 **generous** (*a person*)

el **espliego** *masc noun*
lavender

la **esponja** *fem noun*
sponge

el **esposo** *masc noun*, la **esposa** *fem noun*
1 **husband**
el esposo de mi hermana my sister's husband
2 **wife**
la esposa de Juan Juan's wife
3 **las esposas** handcuffs
Le pusieron esposas. He was handcuffed.

la **espuma** *fem noun*
1 **foam**
2 **lather** (*of soap*)
3 **froth** (*of beer*)
· la **espuma de afeitar** shaving foam
· la **espuma para el pelo** styling mousse

espumoso *masc adjective*, **espumosa** *fem*
1 **foaming**
2 **frothy** (*beer*)
3 un vino espumoso a sparkling wine

el **esqueleto** *masc noun*
skeleton

el **esquí** *masc noun*
1 **ski**
2 **skiing**
practicar el esquí to go skiing
· el **esquí acuático** waterskiing
· el **esquí nórdico**, el **esquí de fondo** cross-country skiing

el **esquiador** *masc noun*, la **esquiadora** *fem*
skier

esquiar *verb* [32]
to ski

esquimal *masc & fem adjective & noun*
1 **Eskimo**
2 un & una esquimal Eskimo

WORD TIP Adjectives and nouns for nationality and regional origin do not have capital letters in Spanish.

la **esquina** *fem noun*
corner (*of a street*)
doblar la esquina to turn the corner
Vivo en la esquina de la calle León con la calle Viriato. I live on the corner of León Street and Viriato Street.

esta *fem adjective*
this
▷ **este, esta** *adjective*

a b c d e f g h i j k l m n ñ o p q r s t u v w x y z

esta, **ésta** *fem pronoun*
this one
▷ **este** *pronoun*

está *verb* ▷ **estar**

la estación *fem noun*
1 **station** (*for trains, buses*)
2 **season** (*of the year*)
la estación de las lluvias the rainy season
El otoño es mi estación preferida. Autumn is my favourite season.
- la **estación de autobuses** bus station
- la **estación de esquí** ski resort
- la **estación de servicio** petrol station

el estacionamiento *masc noun*
(*Latin America*) **car park**

estacionar *verb* [17]
to park
estacionar en doble fila to double-park

estacionario *masc adjective*,
estacionaria *fem*
stationary

el estadio *masc noun*
stadium
- el **estadio de fútbol** football stadium

el estado *masc noun*
1 **state**
2 **en buen estado** in good condition (*a picture, table, etc*)
3 **estar en estado** to be pregnant
- el **estado civil** marital status
- el **estado de bienestar** welfare state
- el **estado de cuenta** bank statement

los Estados Unidos *plural masc noun*
United States

> **WORD TIP** *Estados Unidos* is often used without *los*

estadounidense *masc & fem adjective*
American, US

> **WORD TIP** Adjectives and nouns for nationality and regional origin do not have capital letters in Spanish.

la estafa *fem noun*
swindle
¡Qué estafa! What rip-off!

estáis *verb* ▷ **estar**

la estampilla *fem noun*
(*Latin America*) **stamp**

estallar *verb* [17]
1 **to explode** (*a bomb*)
2 **to burst** (*a balloon*)
3 **to blow out** (*a tyre*)

la estancia *fem noun*
stay
Su estancia en Madrid durará tres días. His stay in Madrid will last three days.

el estanco *masc noun*
tobacconist's (*also selling stamps, post cards, stationery, etc*)

el estanque *masc noun*
pond

el estante *masc noun*
shelf

la estantería *fem noun*
1 **shelves**
2 **bookcase**

estar *verb* [2]
1 (*saying where someone or something is*) **to be**
¿Dónde está mi abrigo? Where's my coat?
¿Has estado en Buenos Aires? Have you been to Buenos Aires?
Estaré en Leeds un mes. I'll be in Leeds for a month.
2 (*asking, saying how someone is feeling*)
¿Cómo estás? How are you? (*about a boy or girl*)
Estoy muy bien, gracias. I'm very well, thank you (*boy or girl speaking.*)
Estoy mal. I'm not well (*boy or girl speaking*)
¿Cómo está? How is he?, How is she?
Está mal. He's not well., She's not well.
Estoy contento. I'm happy (*boy speaking*).
Estoy contenta. I'm happy (*girl speaking*).
3 (*saying how someone or something is*)
Esta paella está muy buena. This paella is very good.
La sopa está fría. The soup is cold.
Con ese vestido estás muy guapa. You look very nice in that dress.
Todavía no está terminado. It's not finished yet.
Esa falda te está corta. This skirt is too short for you.
Está casada. She's married.
4 (*saying what's happening*) **to be + -ing**
Está nevando. It's snowing.
Están viajando por África. They're travelling around Africa.
Estaban sentados allí. They were sitting over there.
5 **estar de + noun** to be (*doing something*)
Está de viaje. She's away on a trip.
Están de vacaciones. They're on holiday.
6 (*with dates*)
Estamos a tres de julio. It's the third of July.

7 (asking, saying if something's ready)
¿Están ya las fotocopias? Are the photocopies ready?
Sí, ya están. Yes, they're ready.
Pulsas el botón y ya está. You press the button and that's it.

WORD TIP For the other Spanish verb for to be
▷ **ser**.

estarse reflexive verb [2]
to stay
Se está horas mirando la tele. He watches TV for hours.
Se estuvo sentado toda la tarde. He was sitting down all afternoon.
¡Estate quieto! Keep still!

la **estatua** fem noun
statue

el **estatus** masc noun
status

♂ **este** masc adjective, **esta** fem
▷ see **este** pron, noun
1 this
en este momento at this moment
en esta caja in this box
2 estos, estas those
estos chicos these boys
estas chicas these girls

♂ **este, esta, éste, ésta** pronoun
▷ see **este** adj, noun
1 this one
Quiero este. I want this one (for a masc noun).
Quiero esta. I want that one (for a fem noun).
2 estos, estas those
Estas no, dame aquellos. Not these, give me those (for a masc pl noun).
Estas no, dame aquellas. Not these, give me those (for a fem pl noun).

♂ **este** masc noun, invariable adjective
▷ see **este** adj, pron
east
ir hacia el este to go east
la costa este de Escocia the east coast of Scotland
al este de Granada to the east of Granada
en el este de España in the east of Spain

esté, estén verb ▷ **estar**

la **estera** fem noun
1 rush matting
2 rush mat
3 beach mat

el **estéreo** masc noun
stereo

estés verb ▷ **estar**

el & la **esteticista** masc & fem noun
beautician

el **estilo** masc noun
1 style
2 ni nada por el estilo or anything like that
o algo por el estilo or something of the kind

la **estilográfica** fem noun
fountain pen

♂ **estimado** masc adjective, **estimada** fem
dear (in formal letters)
Estimado Señor Pérez Dear Mr Pérez
Estimada Señora Dear Madam

estirar verb [17]
to stretch

♂ **esto** pronoun
this
¿Qué es esto? What is this?
Esto es lo más importante. This is the most important thing.

WORD TIP esto never changes.

el **estofado** masc noun
stew

♂ el **estómago** masc noun
stomach
Me duele el estómago. I've got stomachache.

Estonia fem noun
Estonia

estonio masc adjective & noun, **estonia** fem adjective & noun
1 Estonian
2 un estonio, una estonia Estonian

WORD TIP Adjectives and nouns for nationality and regional origin do not have capital letters in Spanish.

♂ **estornudar** verb [17]
to sneeze

el **estornudo** masc noun
sneeze

estoy verb ▷ **estar**

♂ **estrecho** masc adjective, **estrecha** fem
1 narrow
una calle estrecha a narrow street
2 tight
Me queda muy estrecho. It's too tight for me.

♂ la **estrella** fem noun
star
• la **estrella de cine** film star
• la **estrella fugaz** shooting star

a b c d e f g h i j k l m n ñ o p q r s t u v w x y z

♂ indicates key words   121

estrellarse *reflexive verb* [17]
to crash
estrellarse contra algo to crash into
something
Se estrelló contra un árbol. He crashed into
a tree.

estrenar *verb* [17]
to show for the first time out (*films, plays*)
La película se estrena el próximo lunes. The
film comes out next Monday.
El domingo estrenaré los zapatos. I'll wear
my new shoes on Sunday.
Aún no he estrenado la bici. I haven't used
the new bike yet.

el **estreno** *masc noun*
première, **first showing** (*of a film*)

estreñido *masc adjective*, **estreñida** *fem*
constipated

estresado *masc adjective*, **estresada** *fem*
stressed

estricto *masc adjective*, **estricta** *fem*
strict

ℰ **estropear** *verb* [17]
1 **to break**
Vas a estropear la tele si sigues haciendo
eso. You'll wreck the TV if you carry on
doing that.
2 **to spoil**
El tiempo nos estropeó las vacaciones. The
weather spoiled our holidays.
3 **to damage**
Me estropeó el coche. He damaged my car.
4 **to ruin** (*a carpet or dress, for example*)

estropearse *reflexive verb* [17]
1 **to break down**
Se ha estropeado el coche otra vez. The
car's broken down again.
2 **to go off** (*fruit*)
3 **to go bad** (*milk or fish*)
4 **to get ruined** (*a carpet or dress, for example*)

la **estructura** *fem noun*
structure

el **estuche** *masc noun*
case (*for glasses, pencils, etc*)

ℰ el & la **estudiante** *masc & fem noun*
student

ℰ **estudiar** *verb* [17]
1 **to study**
estudiar medicina to study medicine
2 **to learn**
Tenemos que estudiar dos temas para
mañana. We have to study two topics for
tomorrow.

ℰ el **estudio** *masc noun*
1 **studio** (*in a house*)
2 **studio flat**
3 **study**
el estudio de la naturaleza the study of
nature

ℰ los **estudios** *plural masc noun*
studies
• los **estudios de mercado** market research
• los **estudios superiores** higher education

la **estufa** *fem noun*
1 **heater**
2 **fire**

ℰ **estupendo** *masc adjective*, **estupenda**
fem
great
¿Ganaste? ¡Estupendo! Did you win? Great!

estúpido *masc adjective*, **estúpida** *fem*
▷ see **estúpido** *noun*
stupid

el **estúpido** *masc noun*, la **estúpida** *fem*
▷ see **estúpido** *adj*
stupid person
Es un estúpido. He's really stupid.

estuve, **estuviste**, **estuvo**, **etc** *verb* ▷
estar

la **etapa** *fem noun*
stage
por etapas in stages

el **etcétera** *masc noun*
etcetera

la **eternidad** *fem noun*
eternity

la **ética** *fem noun*
ethics

la **etiqueta** *masc noun*
1 **label**
2 **price tag**

el **euro** *masc noun*
euro
El euro se divide en cien céntimos. The euro
is divided into a hundred cents.

el **eurodiputado** *masc noun*, la
eurodiputada *fem*
**MEP, Member of the European
Parliament**

Europa *fem noun*
Europe

europeo *masc adjective & noun,* **europea** *fem adjective & noun*

1 European

2 un europeo, una europea European

> **WORD TIP** Adjectives and nouns for nationality and regional origin do not have capital letters in Spanish.

la **eurozona** *fem noun*
eurozone

Euskadi *fem noun*
the Basque Country (*Euskadi is the Basque language name for the area of Spain bordering South-West France*)

euskera *masc & fem adjective, masc noun*

1 Basque

2 el euskera Basque (*the language*)

> **WORD TIP** Adjectives and nouns for nationality, regional origin, and language do not have capital letters in Spanish.

la **evaluación** *fem noun*
assessment

evaporarse *reflexive verb* [17]
to evaporate

la **evidencia** *fem noun*
evidence

evidente *masc & fem adjective*
obvious

evidentemente *adverb*
obviously

evitar *verb* [17]

1 to avoid
Evitan tomar la responsabilidad. They avoid taking responsibility.

2 to prevent
evitar un accidente to prevent an accident

la **evolución** *fem noun*
evolution

exactamente *adverb*
exactly

exacto *masc adjective,* **exacta** *fem*

1 exact

2 accurate

exagerar *verb* [17]
to exaggerate

ᵹ el **examen** *masc noun*
exam
hacer un examen to take an exam
presentarse a un examen to sit an exam
aprobar un examen to pass an exam
• el **examen oral** oral exam

examinar *verb* [17]
to examine

examinarse *reflexive verb* [17]
to take an exam

excelente *masc & fem adjective*
excellent

la **excepción** *fem noun*
exception
hacer una excepción to make an exception
a excepción de with the exception of

excepcional *masc & fem adjective*
exceptional

excepcionalmente *adverb*
exceptionally

ᵹ **excepto** *preposition*
except for

exclusivo *masc adjective,* **exclusiva** *fem*
exclusive

la **excursión** *fem noun*
trip
irse de excursión to go away on a trip
Nos vamos de excursión al campo. We're going on a trip into the countryside.

la **excusa** *fem noun*
excuse
poner excusas to make excuses

exigente *masc & fem adjective*
demanding

exigir *verb* [49]
to demand

exiliado *masc adjective,* **exiliada** *fem*
exiled

existir *verb* [19]

1 to exist

2 Existen motivos para pensarlo. There are reasons to think that.

el **éxito** *masc noun*
success
tener éxito to be successful

> **WORD TIP** *éxito* does not mean *exit* in English; for the meaning of *exit* ▷ **salida**.

ᵹ la **experiencia** *fem noun*
experience
• la **experiencia laboral** work experience

a
b
c
d
e
f
g
h
i
j
k
l
m
n
ñ
o
p
q
r
s
t
u
v
w
x
y
z

experimentado *masc adjective*,
  experimentada *fem*
  experienced

el **experimento** *masc noun*
  experiment

el **experto** *masc noun*, la **experta** *fem*
  expert

la **explicación** *fem noun*
  explanation

ᔒ **explicar** *verb* [31]
  to explain

explorar *verb* [17]
  to explore

explotar *verb* [17]
  to explode

la **exportación** *fem noun*
  export
  La lana es la exportación más importante.
  Wool is the most important export.

exportar *verb* [17]
  to export
  Rusia exporta mucha madera y petróleo.
  Russia exports a lot of oil and timber.

la **exposición** *fem noun*
  exhibition

expresar *verb* [17]
  to express

la **expresión** *fem noun*
  expression

expreso *masc adjective*, **expresa** *fem*
  ▷ see **expreso** *noun*
  express

el **expreso** *masc noun* ▷ see **expreso** *adj*
  1 express train
  2 espresso (*coffee*)

extenderse *reflexive verb* [36]
  to stretch out
  Se extiende hasta Tierra del Fuego. It
  stretches as far as Tierra del Fuego.

exterior *masc & fem adjective*
  ▷ see **exterior** *noun*
  1 outer (*layer*)
  2 outside (*temperature*)
  3 la parte exterior de la casa the outside of
  the house
  4 foreign
  • la **política exterior** foreign policy

ᔒ el **exterior** *masc noun* ▷ see **exterior** *adj*
  1 exterior, outside
  el exterior de la casa the outside of the
  house
  2 outward appearance
  En su exterior estaba tranquilo. His
  outward appearance was calm.

externo *masc adjective*, **externa** *fem*
  external, outward

la **extinción** *fem noun*
  extinction
  una especie en peligro de extinción an
  endangered species

extincto *masc adjective*, **extincta** *fem*
  extinct

el **extintor** *masc noun*
  extinguisher
  • el **extintor (de incendios)** fire
  extinguisher

ᔒ **extraescolar** *masc & fem adjective*
  out-of-school
  las actividades extraescolares out-of-
  school activities

extrañar *verb* [17]
  Le extrañó verla allí. He was surprised to
  see her there.
  Me extraña que no hayan llamado. I'm
  surprised they haven't phoned.

ᔒ **extranjero** *masc adjective*, **extranjera**
  fem ▷ see **extranjero** *noun*
  foreign

ᔒ el **extranjero** *masc noun*, la **extranjera**
  fem ▷ see **extranjero** *adj, noun*
  foreigner

 extranjeros

Más de 50 millones de extranjeros visitan España
cada año de los cuales 14 millones son del Reino
Unido. Actualmente casi un millón viven allí
permanentemente y otros dos millones tienen
una residencia secundaria (casa) en el país.

ᔒ el **extranjero** *masc noun*
  ▷ see **extranjero** *adj, noun*
  vivir en el extranjero to live abroad
  Viaja mucho al extranjero. He travels
  abroad a lot.

ᔒ **extraño** *masc adjective*, **extraña** *fem*
  ▷ see **extraño** *noun*
  strange

♂ el **extraño** *masc noun*, la **extraña** *fem*
▷ see **extraño** *adj*
stranger

extraordinario *masc adjective*,
extraordinaria *fem*
extraordinary

el & la **extraterrestre** *masc & fem noun*
alien (*from outer space*)

extremo *masc adjective*, **extrema** *fem*
▷ see **extremo** *noun*
extreme

el **extremo** *masc noun* ▷ see **extremo** *adj*,
noun
extreme
con extremo **cuidado** extremely
carefully

el **extremo** *masc noun*, la **extrema** *fem*
▷ see **extremo** *adj, noun*
winger (*in sports*)

extrovertido *masc adjective*,
extrovertida *fem*
extrovert

F f

♂ la **fábrica** *fem noun*
factory

fabricar *verb* [31]
to manufacture

♂ **fácil** *masc & fem adjective*
easy
Es un trabajo fácil. It's an easy job.
ser fácil de hacer to be easy to do
Es fácil de entender. It's easy to
understand.

la **facilidad** *fem noun*
ease
Lo hice con facilidad. I did it with ease.
tener facilidad de palabra to have a way
with words

♂ **fácilmente** *adverb*
easily

la **factura** *fem noun*
bill, **invoice**
la factura del gas the gas bill

♂ la **facultad** *fem noun*
1 (*part of a university*) **faculty**
la Facultad de Medicina the Faculty of
Medicine
un compañero de facultad a fellow student
2 (*ability*) **faculty**
perder facultades to lose your faculties

facultativo *masc adjective*, **facultativa**
fem
1 **optional**
2 **medical**

♂ la **faena** *fem noun*
chore
• las **faenas de la casa** housework

♂ el **faisán** *masc noun*, los **faisanes** *plural*
pheasant

♂ la **falda** *fem noun*
skirt
• la **falda de tubo** straight skirt

la **falda escocesa** *fem noun*
1 **tartan skirt** (*for a woman*)
2 **kilt** (*for a man*)

la **falla** *fem noun*
flaw

♂ **fallar** *verb* [17]
1 **to fail** (*equipment, brakes*)
Fallaron los frenos. The brakes failed.

2 **to go wrong** (*a plan*)
Algo ha fallado. Something's gone wrong.
Me falló la puntería. I missed. (*the target*)

♂ el **fallo** *masc noun*
1 **fault**
El motor tiene un fallo. There's something
wrong with the engine.
2 **failure**
un fallo en el sistema a failure in the system
3 **verdict** (*in a court*)
• el **fallo humano** human error

la **falsificación** *fem noun*
forgery
El cuadro es una falsificación. The picture is
a forgery.

♂ **falso** *masc adjective*, **falsa** *fem*
1 **false** (*document, name*)
2 **fake** (*diamond, picture*)

♂ la **falta** *fem noun*
1 **lack**
una falta de algo a lack of something
la falta de personal staff shortage
por falta de dinero due to lack of money
2 poner una falta a alguien to mark someone
absent
Ya tiene tres faltas. He's been absent three
times already.
3 **foul** (*in sport*)
sacar la falta to take the free kick
4 **infringement**, **fault**
una falta grave a serious infringement
5 hacer falta hacer algo to need to do
something
Hace falta comprar pan. We need to buy
bread.
No hace falta cambiarlo. We don't need to
change it.
No hace falta que me esperes. You don't
need to wait for me.
6 hacerle falta algo a alguien to need
something
Me hace falta un bolígrafo. I need a pen.
No me hace falta nada más, gracias. I don't
need any more, thank you.

WORD TIP What you need is always the subject of
hacer falta.

• la **falta de asistencia** absence (*from school*)
• la **falta de educación** bad manners
• la **falta de ortografía** spelling mistake

♂ **faltar** *verb* [17]
1 **to be missing**
¿Quién falta? Who's missing?
2 (*not to turn up*) **faltar a algo** to be absent
from something
faltar al colegio to be absent from school
3 (*saying you need, lack something*) **Nos falta
práctica.** We need practice.
Le falta interés. He lacks interest.
Nos faltan mil euros para poder comprarlo.
We need a thousand euros to buy it.
Nos faltó tiempo. We didn't have enough
time.
4 (*in time expressions*) **Sólo faltan tres horas.**
There are only three hours to go.
Faltan diez días para mi cumpleaños. It's
ten days to my birthday.
Falta poco para el verano. It's not long
before it's summer.

WORD TIP What you need, who is missing, etc is
always the subject of *faltar*.

♂ **la fama** *fem noun*
1 **fame**
2 **reputation**
tener buena fama to have a good
reputation
tener fama de mentiroso to have a
reputation for being a liar

♂ **la familia** *fem noun*
family
pasar las fiestas en familia to spend the
holiday with the family

♂ **familiar** *masc & fem adjective*
▷ see **familiar** *noun*
1 **family**
Tiene problemas familiares. She has family
problems.
2 **familiar**
Su cara me resulta familiar. Her face is
familiar.

♂ **el & la familiar** *masc & fem noun*
▷ see **familiar** *adj*
relative

♂ **famoso** *masc adjective*, **famosa** *fem*
famous
ser famoso, *fem* **famosa por algo** to be
famous for something
Es famosa por su poesía. She is famous for
her poetry.

♂ **la fantasía** *fem noun*
1 **fantasy**
un mundo de fantasía a fantasy world
2 **imagination**
tener mucha fantasía to have a lot of
imagination

♂ **el fantasma** *masc noun*
ghost

♂ **fantástico** *masc adjective*, **fantástica** *fem*
fantastic

♂ **farmacéutico** *masc adjective*,
farmacéutica *fem*
▷ see **farmacéutico** *noun*
pharmaceutical

♂ **el farmacéutico** *masc noun*, la
farmacéutica *fem*
▷ see **farmacéutico** *adj*
chemist, **pharmacist**

♂ **la farmacia** *fem noun*
chemist's, **pharmacy**
• **la farmacia de guardia** duty chemist

el faro *masc noun*
1 **lighthouse**
2 **headlamp**

♂ **la farola** *fem noun*
1 **streetlight**
2 **lamp post**

fascinar *verb* [17]
to fascinate

♂ **fastidiar** *verb* [17]
1 **to bother**
¡Deja de fastidiarme! Stop bothering me!
2 **to be annoying**
Sólo lo hacen para fastidiar. They only do it
to annoy.
¡Deja de fastidiar! Stop being a pain!

fastidiarse *reflexive verb* [17]
(*showing irritation*) **¡Que se fastidie!** He'll
have to put up with it!
¡Te fastidias! Tough!

♂ **el fastidio** *masc noun*
annoyance
¡Qué fastidio! How annoying!

♂ **fatal** *masc & fem adjective* ▷ see **fatal** *adv*
1 (*informal*) **awful**
Me siento fatal. I feel awful.
El tiempo fue fatal. The weather was awful.
2 **fatal** (*accident, illness*)

♂ **fatal** *adverb* ▷ see **fatal** *adj*
(*informal*) **really badly**
hacer algo fatal to do something really
badly
Canto fatal. I am hopeless at singing.

♂ **el favor** *masc noun*
1 **favour**
Me pidió un favor. She asked me a favour.
hacerle un favor a alguien to do someone a
favour ▸▸

a
b
c
d
e
f
g
h
i
j
k
l
m
n
ñ
o
p
q
r
s
t
u
v
w
x
y
z

¿Me haces un favor? Can you do me a favour

estar a favor de algo to be in favour of something

Estoy a favor de la propuesta. I'm in favour of the proposal.

2 por favor please

Pase, por favor. Please come in. (*formal use*)

♂ **favorito** *masc adjective*, **favorita** *fem*
favourite

♂ el **fax** *masc noun*
fax

♂ la **fe** *fem noun*
faith

♂ **febrero** *masc noun*
February
en febrero in February
el 14 de febrero on 14 February

WORD TIP Names of months and days start with small letters in Spanish.

♂ la **fecha** *fem noun*
date
¿A qué fecha estamos hoy? What's the date today?
• la **fecha de caducidad** use-by date
• la **fecha de nacimiento** date of birth

♂ la **felicidad** *fem noun*
1 happiness
2 (*in general*) ¡Felicidades! Congratulations!
3 (*for birthdays*) ¡Felicidades! Happy birthday!

♂ **felicitar** *verb* [17]
1 (*in general*) felicitar a alguien to congratulate someone
¡Te felicito! Congratulations!
2 (*for birthdays*) felicitar a alguien to wish someone happy birthday
¡Te felicito! Happy birthday!

♂ **feliz** *masc & fem adjective*, **felices** *plural*
happy
¡Feliz Año Nuevo! Happy New Year!
¡Feliz Navidad! Merry Christmas!
¡Feliz cumpleaños! Happy birthday!
¡Felices Pascuas! Happy Easter!

el **felpudo** *masc noun*
doormat

♂ **femenino** *masc adjective*, **femenina** *fem*
1 women's (*team, fashion*)
el equipo femenino the women's team
2 feminine (*style, manners, noun*)
3 female
el sexo femenino the female sex

el **femenino** *masc noun*
▷ see **femenino** *adj*
(*Grammar*) **feminine**

♂ **fenomenal** *masc & fem adjective*
▷ see **fenomenal** *adv*
(*informal*) **great**
una fiesta fenomenal a great party

♂ **fenomenal** *adverb* ▷ see **fenomenal** *adj*
pasarlo fenomenal to have a great time
¡Lo pasamos fenomenal! We had a great time!

♂ **feo** *masc adjective*, **fea** *fem*
ugly

♂ la **feria** *fem noun*
fair

♂ **feroz** *masc & fem adjective*, *pl:* **feroces**
fierce

♂ la **ferretería** *fem noun*
ironmonger's, **hardware store**

♂ el **ferrocarril** *masc noun*
railway

♂ el **ferry** *masc noun*, *pl:* **ferrys**, **ferries**
ferry

♂ **festivo** *masc adjective*, **festiva** *fem*
1 festive (*atmosphere*)
2 un día festivo a public holiday

fiable *masc & fem adjective*
reliable

♂ el **fiambre** *masc noun*
cold cut of meat

♂ **fiarse** *reflexive verb* [32]
1 fiarse de algo to believe something
No te fíes de los periódicos. Don't believe what you read in the newspapers.
2 fiarse de alguien to trust someone
No te fíes de él. Don't trust him.

la **fibra** *fem noun*
fibre

♂ la **ficción** *fem noun*
fiction

♂ la **ficha** *fem noun*
1 counter (*in board games*)
2 index card
3 token (*for a public telephone in a bar, etc*)
• la **ficha médica** medical card
• la **ficha policial** police record
• la **ficha técnica** (technical) specifications, product description

♂ el **fideo** *masc noun*
noodle

♂ la **fiebre** *fem noun*
1 **temperature**
tener fiebre to have a temperature
Le ha subido la fiebre. His temperature has gone up.
Le ha bajado la fiebre. Her temperature has gone down.
2 **fever**
• la **fiebre del heno** hay fever

♂ **fiel** *masc & fem adjective*
1 **faithful**
No le es fiel a su mujer. He's not faithful to his wife.
2 **loyal** (*friend*)
3 **accurate** (*translation, copy*)

♂ la **fiesta** *fem noun*
1 **party**
Dan una fiesta mañana. They are having a party tomorrow.
2 **public holiday**
Mañana es fiesta. Tomorrow's a holiday.

la **figura** *fem noun*
figure

figurar *verb* [17]
to appear (*on a list, document*)
Su nombre no figura en la lista. Your name is not on the list. (*formal use*)

figurarse *reflexive verb* [17]
to imagine
Me figuro que sí. I imagine so.

♂ **fijar** *verb* [17]
1 **to fix**
fijar una fecha to fix a date
2 **to stick** (*bills, posters*)
No fijar carteles. Stick no bills.

fijarse *reflexive verb* [17]
1 **fijarse en algo** to take note of something
Fíjate en el nombre de la calle. Look carefully at the name of the street.
2 **fijarse en algo** to notice something
Se fija en todo. She notices everything.

♂ **fijo** *masc adjective*, **fija** *fem*
1 **fixed**
precios fijos fixed prices
Está fijo a la pared. It's fixed to the wall.
¿Está la escalera bien fija? Is the ladder steady?
2 **permanent** (*jobs*)

♂ la **fila** *fem noun*
1 **line**
en fila india in single file
ponerse en fila to stand in a line
Tuvimos que ponernos en fila. We had to line up.
2 **row** (*of seats in theatre, cinema*)

♂ el **filete** *masc noun*
1 **fillet** (*of meat or fish*)
filetes de lenguado fillets of sole
un filete de cerdo a pork fillet, a pork steak

♂ **filmar** *verb* [17]
1 **to shoot** (*a film*)
2 **to film** (*a person, an event*)

♂ la **filosofía** *fem noun*
philosophy

♂ el **fin** *masc noun*
1 **end**
el fin de mes the end of the month
a fines de junio at the end of June
llegar al fin de algo to get to the end of something
2 **por fin, al fin** at last
Por fin llegaste. At last you've arrived.
3 **en fin** well
En fin, ¿qué le vamos a hacer? Well, what's to be done about it?
• el **fin de año** New Year's Eve
• el **fin de semana** weekend

♂ **final** *masc & fem adjective* ▷ see **final** *noun*
final

♂ el **final** *masc noun* ▷ see **final** *adj, noun*
1 **end**
el final del partido the end of the match
al final de la calle at the end of the street
el final de las vacaciones the end of the holidays
2 **ending**
una película con final feliz a film with a happy ending
3 **al final** in the end
Al final lo conseguí. In the end I got it.

♂ la **final** *fem noun* ▷ see **final** *adj, noun*
final (*of a competition*)

♂ la **finca** *fem noun*
1 **plot of land**
2 **farm**

finlandés *masc adjective & noun*,
finlandesa *fem adjective & noun*
1 **Finnish**
2 (*person*) **un finlandés, una finlandesa** Finn
el finlandés Finnish (*the language*)

WORD TIP Adjectives and nouns for nationality, regional origin, and language do not have capital letters in Spanish.

♂ **Finlandia** *fem noun*
Finland

♂ indicates key words   129

♂ **fino** *masc adjective*, **fina** *fem*
▷ see **fino** *noun*
1 **fine** (*hair, sand, line*)
2 **thin** (*layer, slice*)
3 **slender** (*waist or finger*)
4 **subtle** (*sense of humour*)
5 **refined** (*manners, person*)
6 **acute** (*senses*)
tener el oído muy fino to have a very acute sense of hearing
tener el olfato muy fino to have a very acute sense of smell

el **fino** *masc noun* ▷ see **fino** *adj*
dry sherry

♂ la **firma** *fem noun*
1 **signature**
2 **company**

♂ **firmar** *verb* [17]
to sign

♂ **firme** *masc & fem adjective*
1 **steady** (*ladders, chairs*)
con pulso firme with a steady hand
2 **firm** (*beliefs, physique, attitude*)
mostrarse firme con alguien to be firm with somebody

♂ la **fisica** *fem noun* ▷ see **fisico** *adj, noun*
physics

♂ **fisico** *masc adjective*, **fisica** *fem*
▷ see **fisica, fisico** *noun*
physical

el **fisico** *masc noun*, la **fisica** *fem*
▷ see **fisico** *adj, noun*
physicist

el **fisico** *masc noun* ▷ see **fisico** *adj, noun*
1 **physique**
2 **appearance**

la **fisioterapia** *fem noun*
physiotherapy

♂ **flaco** *masc adjective*, **flaca** *fem*
thin

♂ **flamenco** *masc adjective*, **flamenca** *fem*
▷ see **flamenco** *noun*
flamenco
el baile flamenco flamenco dancing

♂ el **flamenco** *masc noun*
▷ see **flamenco** *adj*
1 **flamenco dancing**
2 **flamingo** (*bird*)

♂ el **flan** *masc noun*
crème caramel

♂ la **flauta** *fem noun*
flute
• la **flauta dulce** recorder

♂ la **flecha** *fem noun*
arrow

♂ el **flequillo** *masc noun*
fringe

♂ **flexible** *masc & fem adjective*
flexible

♂ **flojo** *masc adjective*, **floja** *fem*
1 **loose** (*knot, screw*)
2 **slack** (*rope*)
3 **weak** (*coffee or tea*)
4 **poor** (*a piece of work*)
5 **lazy** (*pupil, student*)

♂ la **flor** *fem noun*
flower
de flores flower-patterned
una falda de flores a flower-patterned skirt
estar en flor to be in flower

el **florero** *masc noun*
vase

el & la **florista** *masc & fem noun*
florist

la **floristería** *fem noun*
florist's

la **flota** *fem noun*
fleet

♂ **flotar** *verb* [17]
to float

♂ **fluido** *masc adjective*, **fluida** *fem*
▷ see **fluido** *noun*
1 **fluid** (*substance*)
2 **free-flowing** (*traffic*)
La circulación está fluida. The traffic is flowing freely.

el **fluido** *masc noun* ▷ see **fluido** *adj*
fluid

♂ **fluir** *verb* [54]
to flow

♂ el **flujo** *masc noun*
flow

♂ la **foca** *fem noun*
seal (*animal*)

♂ el **foco** *masc noun*
1 **focus**
el foco de atención the focus of attention
2 **spotlight**

♂ **folclórico** _masc adjective_, **folclórica** _fem_
 folk
 la musica folclórica folk music

♂ el **folleto** _masc noun_
 1 **leaflet**
 2 **brochure**

♂ el **fondo** _masc noun_
 1 **bottom**
 el fondo del lago the bottom of the lake
 al fondo del baúl at the bottom of the trunk
 sin fondo bottomless
 llegar al fondo de algo to get to the bottom
 of something
 Llegaron al fondo de la cuestión. They got
 to the bottom of the matter.
 2 **back**
 Está al fondo de la sala. It's at the back of
 the room.
 3 **end**
 al fondo del pasillo at the end of the
 corridor
 4 **kitty**
 Tenemos un fondo común para estas
 cosas. We have a kitty for these things.
 5 los fondos **funds**
 recaudar fondos to raise funds
 6 a fondo **in depth**
 estudiar algo a fondo to study something
 in depth
 prepararse a fondo to prepare thoroughly
 7 de fondo **background**
 el ruido de fondo background noise
 la música de fondo background music

♂ el **fontanero** _masc noun_, la **fontanera** _fem_
 plumber

♂ el **footing** _masc noun_
 jogging
 hacer footing to go jogging

el **forastero** _masc noun_, la **forastera** _fem_
 stranger

♂ la **forma** _fem noun_
 1 **shape**
 en forma de cruz in the shape of a cross
 con la forma de una hoja leaf-shaped
 Tiene forma cuadrada. It's square.
 2 **way**
 Es mi forma de ser. It's the way I am.
 3 en forma **fit**
 mantenerse en forma to keep fit
 4 de todas formas **anyway**
 De todas formas, estamos en contacto.
 Anyway, we're in touch.

la **formación** _fem noun_
 1 **education**
 un chico con una buena formación a well-
 educated boy
 2 **training**
 • la **formación profesional** vocational
 training

formal _masc & fem adjective_
 1 **reliable** (_person_)
 2 **formal** (_dinner, or invitation_)
 3 **firm** (_offer_)

formar _verb_ [17]
 1 **to form**
 formar parejas to get into pairs (_in a class, for
 games, etc_)
 formar un grupo de música to form a band
 2 **to make up**
 El equipo está formado por doce
 miembros. The team is made up of twelve
 members.
 3 **to train** (_teachers, engineers, etc_)

formarse _reflexive verb_ [17]
 to form
 Se formó un atasco. A traffic jam formed.
 Se está formando hielo en la carretera. Ice
 is forming on the road.

formidable _masc & fem adjective_
 fantastic (_informal_)

la **fórmula** _fem noun_
 formula

el **formulario** _masc noun_
 form

la **fortuna** _fem noun_
 1 **fortune** (_riches_)
 ganar una fortuna to earn a fortune
 2 **luck** (_good fortune_)
 Tuve la buena fortuna de conocerlos. I was
 lucky enough to meet them.
 por fortuna fortunately

forzar _verb_ [26]
 1 **to force**
 Me forzaron a aceptar. They forced me to
 accept.
 2 forzar la vista to strain your eyes

forzarse _reflexive verb_ [26]
 forzarse a hacer algo to force yourself to do
 something
 Me fuerzo a ir al gimnasio tres veces por
 semana. I force myself to go to the gym
 three times a week.

la **fosa** _fem noun_
 pit
 • las **fosas nasales** nostrils

a
b
c
d
e
f
g
h
i
j
k
l
m
n
ñ
o
p
q
r
s
t
u
v
w
x
y
z

♂ el **fósforo** *masc noun*
match (*to make fire*)

♀ la **foto** *fem noun*
photo
sacar una foto to take a photo
Sacamos muchas fotos durante las
vacaciones. We took many pictures during
the holiday.

la **fotocopia** *fem noun*
photocopy

la **fotocopiadora** *fem noun*
photocopier

fotocopiar *verb* [17]
to photocopy

♀ la **fotografía** *fem noun*
1 **photography**
2 **photograph**
sacar una fotografía to take a photograph

el **fotógrafo** *masc noun*, la **fotógrafa** *fem*
photographer

fracasar *verb* [17]
to fail

el **fracaso** *masc noun*
failure

la **fractura** *fem noun*
fracture

frágil *masc & fem adjective*
fragile

♀ la **frambuesa** *fem noun*
raspberry
la mermelada de frambuesas raspberry
jam

francés *masc adjective & noun*, **francesa** *fem*
adjective & noun
1 **French**
un coche francés a French car
2 (*person*) un francés **Frenchman**
3 (*person*) una francesa **Frenchwoman**
4 los franceses **the French** (*people*)
5 el francés **French** (*the language*)

WORD TIP Adjectives and nouns for nationality,
regional origin, and language do not have capital
letters in Spanish.

♀ **Francia** *fem noun*
France

♂ el **frasco** *masc noun*
1 **bottle**
2 **jar**
un frasco de mermelada a jar of jam

♀ la **frase** *fem noun*
1 **sentence**

2 **phrase**
• la **frase hecha** set phrase

el **fraude** *masc noun*
fraud

♀ la **frecuencia** *fem noun*
frequency
con frecuencia often

♂ **frecuente** *masc & fem adjective*
frequent

♂ **frecuentemente** *adverb*
often, **frequently**

♂ el **fregadero** *masc noun*
sink (*in the kitchen*)

♂ **fregar** *verb* [30]
1 **to wash**
fregar los platos to wash the dishes
fregar el suelo to mop the floor
2 **to scrub**

freír *verb* [53]
to fry

frenar *verb* [17]
1 **to brake** (*when driving*)
2 **to slow down** (*a process*)

el **freno** *masc noun*
brake

♂ el **frente** *masc noun* ▷ see **frente** *fem*
1 **front** (*in a war, in weather reports*)
2 al frente **forwards**
dar un paso al frente to step forwards
3 al frente de at the head of
estar al frente del desfile to be at the head
of the procession
4 de frente **head on**
Los camiones chocaron de frente. The
lorries collided head on.
5 frente a **opposite**
Está frente a la iglesia. It's opposite the
church.
6 hacer frente a algo to face something (*a
problem, an attacker*)

♀ la **frente** *fem noun* ▷ see **frente** *masc*
forehead

♀ la **fresa** *fem noun*
strawberry
la mermelada de fresas strawberry jam

♂ **fresco** *masc adjective*, **fresca** *fem*
▷ see **fresco** *noun*
1 **cool**
una bebida fresca a cool drink
una brisa fresca a cool breeze
2 Hoy hace fresco. It's chilly today.

3 **fresh** (*vegetables, fish, milk*)
pescado fresco fresh fish

4 pintura fresca wet paint

5 (*informal*) ser muy fresco to have a nerve
Es muy fresca. She's got a nerve.
¡Qué fresco! What a nerve!

ᵹ el **fresco** *masc noun* ▷ see **fresco** *adj*
fresh air
tomar el fresco to get some fresh air
estar al fresco to be out in the fresh air
Hace fresco. It's chilly.

fría, frío, etc *verb* ▷ **freír**

friega, friego, friegue, etc *verb* ▷ **fregar**

ᵹ el **frigorífico** *masc noun*
fridge

ᵹ el **frijol** *masc noun*
bean

ᵹ **frío** *masc adjective*, **fría** *fem* ▷ see **frío** *noun*
cold
un día frío a cold day

ᵹ el **frío** *masc noun* ▷ see **frío** *adj*
1 **cold**
2 hacer frío to be cold (*weather, etc*)
Hace frío. It's cold.
¡Qué frío hace! It's so cold!
3 tener frío to be cold (*people, etc*)
Tengo mucho frío. I'm very cold.
▷ **calor**

ᵹ **frito** *masc adjective*, **frita** *fem*
fried
huevos fritos fried eggs

ᵹ la **frontera** *fem noun*
border
Cruzamos la frontera en Irún. We crossed
the border at Irún.

ᵹ el **frontón** *masc noun*
1 (*Sport*) **pelota court**
2 (*Sport*) **the game of pelota** (*a traditional
Basque game*)

frotar *verb* [17]
to rub

frotarse *reflexive verb* [17]
to rub

fruncir *verb* [66]
fruncir el ceño to frown

frustrante *masc & fem adjective*
frustrating

frustrar *verb* [17]
1 **to frustrate** (*a person*)
2 **to spoil** (*plans*)

ᵹ la **fruta** *fem noun*
fruit
fruta de la temporada fruit in season

ᵹ la **frutería** *fem noun*
fruit shop

el **frutero** *masc noun*
fruit bowl

el **fruto** *masc noun*
fruit
• los **frutos secos** nuts and dried fruits

fue *verb* ▷ **ser, ir**

ᵹ el **fuego** *masc noun*
1 **fire**
encender el fuego to light the fire
¿Tienes fuego? Have you got a light?
prenderle fuego a algo to set fire to
something
Prendió fuego al bosque. She set fire to the
woods.
2 (*in cooking*) cocinar algo a fuego lento to
cook something on a low heat
• los **fuegos artificiales** fireworks

la **fuente** *fem noun*
1 **spring** (*water source*)
2 **fountain**
3 **large dish**
una fuente de servir a serving dish
una fuente de horno an oven-proof dish

fuera, fuéramos, etc *verb*
▷ see **fuera** *adv* ▷ **ser, ir**

ᵹ **fuera** *adverb* ▷ see **fuera** *verb*
1 **out**
¡Sal fuera! Go out!
ahí fuera out there
Salimos a cenar fuera. We went out for
dinner.
El jefe está fuera. The boss is away.
2 **outside**
Están esperando fuera. They're waiting
outside.
Deja las cajas fuera. Leave the boxes
outside.
Por fuera es plateado. It's silver on the
outside.
la parte de fuera de la maleta the outside of
the suitcase
3 fuera de out of, outside of
fuera de peligro out of danger
estar fuera de lugar to be out of place
estar fuera de juego to be offside
Están fuera del país. They're abroad.

a
b
c
d
e
f
g
h
i
j
k
l
m
n
ñ
o
p
q
r
s
t
u
v
w
x
y
z

fueron verb ▷ **ser, ir**

ℰ **fuerte** masc & fem adjective ▷ see **fuerte** adv

1 **strong**
   ser fuerte to be strong
   un olor fuerte a strong smell
   una escena fuerte a violent scene

2 **loud**
   No pongas la música tan fuerte. Don't play the music so loud.

3 **big**
   un beso fuerte a big kiss
   Tomamos una comida fuerte al mediodía. We have a big meal at lunchtime.

4 **hard** (blow, punch)

5 **severe**
   un dolor fuerte a severe pain

ℰ **fuerte** adverb ▷ see **fuerte** adj

1 **hard**
   Pégale fuerte. Hit it hard.

2 **tight**
   Agárralo fuerte. Hold it tight.

3 **a lot**
   Comimos fuerte. We ate a lot.

ℰ la **fuerza** fem noun

1 **strength**
   tener fuerza to be strong
   No tuvo fuerza para levantarlo. He wasn't strong enough to lift it.
   Empuja con todas tus fuerzas. Push as hard as you can.

2 **force**
   por la fuerza by force
   Lo obligaron a salir por la fuerza. They forced him to go outside.

3 **a fuerza de** by
   Aprobó a fuerza de estudiar mucho. He passed by studying hard.
   • la **fuerza aérea** air force
   • la **fuerza de voluntad** willpower
   • las **fuerzas armadas** armed forces

la **fuga** fem noun

1 **leak** (of gas, water)
   una fuga de gas a gas leak

2 **escape**
   un intento de fuga an attempted escape
   darse a la fuga to run away

fui, fuimos, fuiste, etc verb ▷ **ser, ir**

el **fumador** masc noun, la **fumadora** fem
   smoker
   'No fumadores' 'No-smoking section'

ℰ **fumar** verb [17]
   to smoke
   ¿Fumas? Do you smoke?
   No fumo. I don't smoke.

la **función** fem noun

1 **function**

2 **performance**
   • la **función de noche** late-night performance

ℰ **funcionar** verb [17]

1 **to work**
   ¿Cómo funciona? How does it work?
   'No funciona' 'Out of order'

2 **to run**
   Funciona con electricidad. It runs on electricity.

el **funcionario** masc noun, la **funcionaria** fem
   civil servant
   Mi padre es funcionario. My father's a civil servant.

la **funda** fem noun

1 **cover** (for a cushion, pillow, etc)

2 **sleeve** (of a record)

3 **pillowcase**

fundamental masc & fem adjective
   fundamental

fundir verb [19]
   to melt

fundirse reflexive verb [19]

1 **to melt**

2 **to be founded** (companies)

el **funeral** masc noun
   funeral

la **funeraria** fem noun
   undertaker's

ℰ la **furgoneta** fem noun
   van

la **furia** fem noun
   fury
   estar hecho una furia (informal) to be furious

ℰ **furioso** masc adjective, **furiosa** fem
   furious
   ponerse furioso to get furious

el **fusible** masc noun
   fuse
   Saltaron los fusibles. The fuses blew.

el **fusil** *masc noun*
  rifle

fusionar *verb* [17]
  to merge

♂ el **futbito** *masc noun*
  five-a-side football

♂ el **fútbol** *masc noun*
  football
  jugar al fútbol to play football

---

mini info | *fútbol*

Uruguay ganó la primera Copa Mundial de fútbol que se celebró en su país en julio de 1930.

♂ el **futbolín** *masc noun*
  1 table football
  2 los futbolines amusement arcade

♂ el & la **futbolista** *masc & fem noun*
  footballer

♂ el **fútbol sala** *masc noun*
  indoor football

♂ **futuro** *masc adjective*, **futura** *fem*
  ▷ see **futuro** *noun*
  future

♂ el **futuro** *masc noun* ▷ see **futuro** *adj*
  future
  en el futuro in future

a
b
c
d
e
f
g
h
i
j
k
l
m
n
ñ
o
p
q
r
s
t
u
v
w
x
y
z

G g

las **gafas** *plural fem noun*
   glasses
   llevar gafas to wear glasses
- las **gafas de sol** sunglasses

el **galápago** *masc noun*
1 **giant turtle**
2 **terrapin**

la **galaxia** *fem noun*
   galaxy

la **galería** *fem noun*
   gallery
- la **galería comercial** shopping mall
- la **galería de arte** art gallery

ℰ **galés** *masc adjective*, **galesa** *fem*
   ▷ see **galés** *noun*
   Welsh

ℰ un **galés** *masc noun*, una **galesa** *fem*
   ▷ see **galés** *adj*
1 **Welshman**
   los galeses the Welsh (*people*)
2 **Welshwoman**
3 **el galés** Welsh (*the language*)

> **WORD TIP** Adjectives and nouns for nationality, regional origin, and language do not have capital letters in Spanish.

ℰ **Gales** *masc noun*
   el país de Gales Wales
   Soy de Gales. I'm from Wales.

Galicia *fem noun*
   Galicia (*the province in North-West Spain*)

gallego *masc adjective & noun*, **gallega** *fem adjective & noun*
1 **Galician**
2 **un gallego, una gallega** Galician
3 **el gallego** Galician (*the language of Galicia*)

> **WORD TIP** Adjectives and nouns for nationality, regional origin, and language do not have capital letters in Spanish.

ℰ la **galleta** *fem noun*
   biscuit

la **gallina** *fem noun*
   hen

el **gallo** *masc noun*
   cockerel

galopar *verb* [17]
   to gallop

la **gama** *fem noun*
   range (*of products, etc*)
   una amplia gama de colores a wide range of colours

la **gamba** *fem noun*
   prawn
   gambas a la plancha grilled prawns

el **gamberro** *masc noun*, la **gamberra** *fem*
   rowdy, hooligan
   Es muy gamberro. He's a real rowdy.

ℰ la **gana** *fem noun*
1 **darle la gana a alguien** to feel like it
   Lo hago, porque me da la gana. I do it just because I feel like it.
   No quiero hacerlo, porque no me da la gana. I don't want to do it, because I don't feel like it.
   Siempre hace lo que le da la gana. She always does just as she pleases.
2 **tener ganas de hacer algo** to feel like doing something
   Tengo ganas de verlos. I want to see them.
   No tengo ganas de ir al cine. I don't feel like going to the cinema.
3 (*in expressions*) **hacer algo sin ganas** to do something half-heartedly
   hacer algo de buena gana to do something willingly
   hacer algo de mala gana to do something reluctantly

el **ganado** *masc noun*
   cattle
   el ganado lanar sheep
   el ganado vacuno cattle (*cows*)

el **ganador** *masc noun*, la **ganadora** *fem*
   winner

ganador *masc adjective*, **ganadora** *fem*
   winning
   el equipo ganador the winning team

la **ganancia** *fem noun*
   profit

ℰ **ganar** *verb* [17]
1 **to win**
   ganar una carrera to win a race
   ganar una medalla to win a medal
   Ganaron el primer premio. They won first prize.

2 to earn
Gano bastante dinero. I earn a lot of money.

3 ganarle a alguien en algo to beat someone at something
Le gané. I beat her.
Les ganamos en natación, pero ellos nos ganaron en fútbol. We beat them at swimming, but they beat us at football.

ganarse *reflexive verb* [17]
to earn
Se ganó veinte libras repartiendo folletos. She earned twenty pounds handing out leaflets.
ganarse la vida to earn your living
Se gana la vida pintando. He earns his living by painting.

el **gancho** *masc noun*
hook

ᔓ la **ganga** *fem noun*
bargain
¡Qué ganga! What a bargain!

el **ganso** *masc noun*, la **gansa** *fem*
1 goose
2 (*informal*) ser un ganso to be a clown
hacer el ganso to clown around

el **garaje** *masc noun*
garage

la **garantía** *fem noun*
guarantee
estar bajo garantía to be under guarantee

garantizar *verb* [22]
to guarantee

el **garbanzo** *masc noun*
chickpea

la **garganta** *fem noun*
throat
Me duele la garganta. I have a sore throat.

el **gas** *masc noun*
gas
una cocina a gas a gas cooker
• los **gases tóxicos** toxic fumes

la **gaseosa** *fem noun*
lemonade

el **gasoil**, **gasóleo** *masc noun*
1 diesel
2 heating oil

ᔓ la **gasolina** *fem noun*
petrol
Voy a echar gasolina al coche. I'm going to put some petrol in the car.
• la **gasolina sin plomo** unleaded petrol

la **gasolinera** *fem noun*
petrol station

ᔓ **gastar** *verb* [17]
1 to spend
Gasta todo lo que gana. He spends everything he earns.
2 to use
Me gastó todo el champú. She used up all my shampoo.
Mi coche gasta mucha gasolina. My car uses a lot of petrol.
3 to take (*in shoe sizes, etc*)
¿Qué número de pie gastas? What shoe size do you take?
4 to waste
Gasta mucho en caramelos. He wastes a lot of money on sweets.

gastarse *reflexive verb* [17]
to run out
Se han gastado las pilas. The batteries have run out.

el **gasto** *masc noun*
expense
Tenemos muchos gastos. We have a lot of expenses.
• los **gastos de envío** postage and packing
• los **gastos de desplazamiento** travel expenses

la **gastronomía** *fem noun*
gastronomy

gatear *verb* [17]
to crawl

ᔓ el **gato** *masc noun*, la **gata** *fem*
cat

la **gaviota** *fem noun*
seagull

el **gazpacho** *masc noun*
gazpacho (*a cold soup made with tomatoes, cucumber, and other vegetables*)

el **gel** *masc noun*
gel

la **gelatina** *fem noun*
jelly

el **gemelo** *masc noun*, la **gemela** *fem*
twin

los **gemelos** *plural masc noun*
1 binoculars
2 twins

a
b
c
d
e
f
g
h
i
j
k
l
m
n
ñ
o
p
q
r
s
t
u
v
w
x
y
z

géminis *masc & fem noun*
▷ see **Géminis** *noun*
Gemini (*person born under Gemini*)
Soy géminis. I'm Gemini.

WORD TIP Use a small letter in Spanish to say *I am Gemini*, etc with star signs.

Géminis *masc noun* ▷ see **géminis** *noun*
Gemini (*the constellation*)

gemir *verb* [57]
to groan
gemir de dolor to groan with pain

la **generación** *fem noun*
generation

general *masc & fem adjective*
▷ see **general** *noun*
general
en general in general
por lo general generally
en términos generales in general terms

el & la **general** *masc & fem noun*
▷ see **general** *adj*
general
el general Serrano General Serrano

generalmente *adverb*
generally

generoso *masc adjective*, **generosa** *fem*
generous

la **genética** *fem noun*
genetics

♂ **genial** *masc & fem adjective*
1 **brilliant**
una idea genial a brilliant idea
2 (*informal*) **great**, **brilliant**
¡Es genial! It's great!

el **genio** *masc noun*
1 **genius**
Ana es un genio. Ana is a genius.
2 **temper**
tener mal genio to be bad-tempered
¡Vaya genio! What a temper!

♂ la **gente** *fem noun*
people
Vino mucha gente. Lots of people came.
La gente dice que ... People say that ...
La gente de por aquí es muy simpática. The people round here are very nice.

WORD TIP *gente* takes a singular verb in Spanish.

la **geografía** *fem noun*
geography

la **geometría** *fem noun*
geometry

el **geranio** *masc noun*
geranium

el & la **gerente** *masc & fem noun*
manager
el gerente de la fábrica the factory manager

la **gestión** *fem noun*
1 **management**
la gestión de la empresa the management of the company
2 Papá tiene que hacer una gestión en el banco. Dad has some business to do at the bank.

el **gesto** *masc noun*
gesture
Me hizo un gesto para que me acercara. He gestured to me to come over.
Hice un gesto de asentimiento. I nodded to say yes.

Gibraltar *masc noun*
Gibraltar
el Estrecho de Gibraltar the Straits of Gibraltar

el **gigabyte** *masc noun*
gigabyte
un disco duro de treinta gigabytes a thirty gigabyte hard disk

el **gigante** *masc noun*, la **giganta** *fem*
giant

la **gimnasia** *fem noun*
gymnastics
hacer gimnasia to do PE
Es bueno hacer gimnasia. It's good to do PE.
una clase de gimnasia a PE class
• la **gimnasia de mantenimiento** keep-fit exercises

el **gimnasio** *masc noun*
gym

el **gin tonic** *masc noun*
gin and tonic

la **ginebra** *fem noun*
gin

♂ **girar** *verb* [17]
1 **to turn**
Gira a la derecha en el semáforo. Turn right at the traffic lights.
girar la cabeza to turn your head
2 **to go round**
La tierra gira alrededor del sol. The earth goes round the sun.
3 **to spin**
4 girar un cheque to write out a cheque
5 girar dinero to send money

el **girasol** *masc noun*
  sunflower

el **gitano** *masc noun*, la **gitana** *fem*
  gypsy

el **glaciar** *masc noun*
  glacier

el **globo** *masc noun*
  balloon

la **gloria** *fem noun*
  glory

la **glorieta** *fem noun*
1 **square** (*in a town*)
2 **roundabout** (*on the road*)

glotón *masc adjective*, **glotona** *fem*
  greedy

gobernar *verb* [17]
1 **to rule**
2 **to govern**

el **gobierno** *masc noun*
  government

ƒ el **gol** *masc noun*
  goal
  marcar un gol to score a goal
  ganar por tres goles a dos to win by three goals to two
  perder por un gol a cero to lose by one goal to nil

el **golf** *masc noun*
  golf
  jugar al golf to play golf

el & la **golfista** *masc & fem noun*
  golfer

el **golfo** *masc noun*
1 **gulf** (*in geography*)
2 **scoundrel**
  ¡Qué golfo eres! What a scoundrel you are!
3 **little rascal** (*to a child*)

la **golondrina** *fem noun*
  swallow

la **golosina** *fem noun*
  sweet
  No comas tantas golosinas. Don't eat so many sweets.

ƒ el **golpe** *masc noun*
1 **blow**
  Fue un duro golpe. It was a hard blow.
2 **knock**
  darse un golpe to knock yourself
  Se dió un golpe en la cabeza. He knocked his head.

3 **darle un golpe a alguien** to hit someone
  Le dio un golpe en la cara. She hit him in the face.
4 **tap**
  dar unos golpes en la mesa to tap the table
5 **de golpe** with a bang
  La ventana se cerró de golpe. The window slammed shut.
  Cerré el baúl de golpe. I slammed the trunk shut.

ƒ **golpear** *verb* [17]
1 **to hit**
  Le golpeé la cabeza con la revista. I hit him on the head with the magazine.
2 **to bang**
  La ventana golpeaba por el viento. The window was banging in the wind.
3 **to beat**
  golpear un tambor to beat a drum

golpearse *reflexive verb* [17]
  to bang
  Se golpeó la pierna con la mesa. She banged her leg on the table.

la **goma** *fem noun*
1 **rubber**
  botas de goma rubber boots
2 **una goma elástica** a rubber band
  • la **goma de borrar** rubber (*for pencil writing*)
  • la **goma espuma** foam rubber

ƒ **gordo** *masc adjective*, **gorda** *fem*
  ▷ see **gordo** *noun*
1 **fat**
  ponerse gordo to get fat
  ¡Qué gordo te has puesto! You've got so fat.
2 **thick** (*book, sweater*)
3 **serious** (*problem or mistake*)

el **gordo** *masc noun*, la **gorda** *fem*
  ▷ see **gordo** *adj*
1 **fat man** (*or boy*)
2 **fat woman** (*or girl*)
3 **el gordo jackpot** (*in the state lottery*)
  Le tocó el gordo. He won the jackpot.

el **gorila** *masc noun*
  gorilla

la **gorra** *fem noun*
  cap

el **gorro** *masc noun*
  cap

la **gota** *fem noun*
1 **drop**
2 **una gota de** (*informal*) a drop of
  Tomaré una gota de café. I'll have a drop of coffee.

gotear *verb* [17]
  to drip

gozar *verb* [22]
  to enjoy
  Gozo mucho oyendo música. I enjoy
  listening to music a lot.
  gozar de algo to enjoy something
  Todos gozamos del espectáculo. We all
  enjoyed the show.

la **grabación** *fem noun*
  recording

el **grabador** *masc noun*
  tape recorder

la **grabadora** *fem noun*
  tape recorder
  • la **grabadora de DVD** DVD recorder

grabar *verb* [17]
  to record
  grabar música de Internet to record music
  on the Internet

♂ la **gracia** *fem noun*
  1 **joke**
  2 **tener gracia** to be funny
     Esa broma no tiene gracia. That joke isn't
     funny.
     Tiene mucha gracia contando cosas. She's
     very good at telling funny stories.
     Me hace gracia verlo. Seeing it makes me
     laugh.
  3 **no hacerle gracia alguien**
     No me hace ninguna gracia ir. I don't like
     the idea of going at all.

♂ las **gracias** *plural fem noun*
  thank you
  muchas gracias thank you very much
  'Muchas gracias.'—'A Usted.' 'Thank you
  very much.'—'Thank you' (*polite form*).
  darle las gracias a alguien to thank
  someone
  Antes de irme, les di las gracias. Before
  leaving, I thanked them.

♂ **gracioso** *masc adjective*, **graciosa** *fem*
  funny

el **grado** *masc noun*
  degree
  veinte grados centígrados twenty degrees
  centigrade
  cinco grados bajo cero five degrees below
  zero

gradual *masc & fem adjective*
  gradual

graduarse *reflexive verb* [20]
  to graduate

el **gráfico** *masc noun*
  graph
  • los **gráficos** graphics (*in computing*)

la **gramática** *fem noun*
  grammar

el **gramo** *masc noun*
  gram

gran *adjective* ▷ **grande**

♂ **Gran Bretaña** *fem noun*
  Great Britain

♂ **grande**, **gran** *adjective*
  1 **big**, **large**
     una casa grande a big house
     La chaqueta me queda muy grande. The
     jacket's very big for me.
     un gran número de personas a large
     number of people
     Deme una más grande. Give me a larger
     size.
  2 **great**
     una gran oportunidad a great opportunity
     Es una gran actora. She's a great actor.
     Soy un gran aficionado del Atlético. I'm a
     great Atlético fan.
  3 **grown-up**
     Cuando sea grande … When I'm grown up
     …
     Ya eres muy grande para hacer eso. You're
     too old to do that.

WORD TIP *grande* becomes *gran* before a singular
noun. *grande* shows size; *gran* shows greatness.

los **grandes almacenes** *plural masc noun*
  department store
  Los venden en los grandes almacenes.
  They're sold in department stores.

el **Gran Hermano** *masc noun*
  Big Brother

el **granizado** *masc noun*
  crushed ice drink
  granizado de limón iced lemon drink

granizar *verb* [22]
  to hail

el **granizo** *masc noun*
  hail

la **granja** *fem noun*
  farm

el **granjero** *masc noun*, la **granjera** *fem*
  farmer
  Es granjero. He's a farmer.

el **grano** *masc noun*
1 **grain**
 un grano de arena a grain of sand
2 **(coffee) bean**
3 **spot**, **pimple**
 Me ha salido un grano. I've got a spot.

la **grapa** *fem noun*
 staple

la **grapadora** *fem noun*
 stapler

grapar *verb* [17]
 to staple

la **grasa** *fem noun*
1 **fat**
 el contenido de grasa the fat content
 La comida tiene mucha grasa. The food is
 very fatty.
2 **grease**
 El horno estaba lleno de grasa. The oven
 was covered in grease.

grasiento *masc adjective*, **grasienta** *fem*
 greasy

ℰ **gratis** *adjective, adverb*
 free
 entrada gratis free entry
 Entramos gratis. We got in free.
 WORD TIP *gratis* never changes.

gratuito *masc adjective*, **gratuita** *fem*
 free
 La entrada es gratuita. Entry is free.

la **grava** *fem noun*
 gravel

ℰ **grave** *masc & fem adjective*
 serious
 una enfermedad grave serious illness
 Está muy grave. He's seriously ill.

la **gravedad** *fem noun*
1 **gravity** (*in physics*)
2 **seriousness** (*of a problem*)

Grecia *fem noun*
 Greece
 Ancient Greece la Grecia antigua

griego *masc adjective & noun*, **griega** *fem*
adjective & noun
1 **Greek**
2 un griego, una griega Greek
3 el griego Greek (*the language*)
 WORD TIP Adjectives and nouns for nationality,
 regional origin, and language do not have capital
 letters in Spanish.

ℰ el **grifo** *masc noun*
 tap
 abrir el grifo to turn on the tap
 cerrar el grifo to turn off the tap

el **grillo** *masc noun*
 cricket (*insect*)

la **gripe** *fem noun*
 flu
 tener gripe to have flu
 Hoy no viene, tiene gripe. She's not
 coming today, she's got flu.
• la **gripe aviar** bird flu
 WORD TIP *gripe* does not mean *gripe* in English;
 for the meaning of *gripe* ▷ **queja**

ℰ **gris** *masc & fem adjective* ▷ see **gris** *noun*
 grey
 No me gustan los grises. I don't like the
 grey ones.

ℰ el **gris** *masc noun* ▷ see **gris** *adj*
 grey

ℰ **gritar** *verb* [17]
 to shout
 ¡No grites! Don't shout!
 gritar de alegría to shout for joy
 gritar de dolor to scream with pain

el **grito** *masc noun*
1 **shout**
 dar un grito to shout
2 **cry**, **scream**
 un grito de protesta a cry of protest
 un grito de dolor a cry of pain
 un grito de horror a scream of horror

la **grosella** *fem noun*
 redcurrant

la **grosería** *fem noun*
 rude remark
 No digas groserías. Don't be so rude.
 ¡Qué grosería! How rude!

grosero *masc adjective*, **grosera** *fem*
 rude

la **grúa** *fem noun*
1 **crane**
2 **break-down truck**
 No aparcar, llamamos grúa. Parked cars
 will be towed away. (*street sign*)

grueso *masc adjective*, **gruesa** *fem*
1 **thick**
2 **fat**

gruñón *masc adjective*, **gruñona** *fem*
 grumpy

ℰ indicates key words　　　　　　　　　141

♂ el **grupo** *masc noun*
group
salir en grupo to go out in a group
un grupo musical a group (*playing music*)

la **gruta** *fem noun*
grotto

el **guante** *masc noun*
glove

♂ **guapo** *masc adjective*, **guapa** *fem*
good-looking
¡Qué guapa es! Isn't she good-looking!
¡Qué guapo es! Isn't he handsome!
¡Qué guapo estás! How smart you're
looking!

el & la **guarda** *masc & fem noun*
1 **guard**
2 **keeper** (*in a park, museum*)

el **guardabarros** *masc noun*
mudguard

el & la **guardaespaldas** *masc & fem noun*,
pl: **guardaespaldas**
bodyguard

♂ **guardar** *verb* [17]
1 **to keep**
Guardo todas sus cartas. I keep all his
letters.
2 **to put away**
Guarda tus cosas. Put your things away.
3 (*Computers*) **to save**
Hay que guardar tu trabajo. You must save
your work.

el **guardarropa** *masc noun*
cloakroom (*in restaurant, theatre, etc*)

la **guardería infantil** *fem noun*
nursery

el & la **guardia** *masc & fem noun*
1 **policeman**
2 **policewoman**
3 la Guardia Civil the Civil Guard (*Spanish
national police force with dark green uniforms*)
• el **guardia jurado** security guard
• el **guardia urbano** policeman

el **guardián** *masc noun*, la **guardiana** *fem*
1 **guard**
2 **guardian**

la **guarnición** *fem noun*
1 **side dish**
2 **topping**

guarro *masc adjective*, **guarra** *fem*
▷ see **guarro** *noun*
1 (*informal*) **filthy**
2 **disgusting** (*person*)

el **guarro** *masc noun*, la **guarra** *fem*
▷ see **guarro** *adj*
(*informal*) **filthy pig**

guatemalteco *masc adjective & noun*,
guatemalteca *fem adjective & noun*
1 **Guatemalan**
2 un guatemalteco, una guatemalteca
Guatemalan

WORD TIP Adjectives and nouns for nationality
and regional origin do not have capital letters in
Spanish.

guau *exclamation*
wow!

guay *invariable adjective, adverb*
(*informal*) **fantastic**, **cool**
¡Qué música más guay! What cool music!
Lo pasé guay. I had a cool time.

la **guayaba** *fem noun*
guava

la **guerra** *fem noun*
war
la guerra del Golfo the Gulf War

la **guerrilla** *fem noun*
guerrilla unit

el **guerrillero** *masc noun*, la **guerrillera**
fem
guerrilla, **guerrilla fighter**

♂ la **guía** *fem noun*
1 **guide** (*a book, map, etc*)
una guía de restaurantes a restaurant
guide
2 **map** (*of a city or town*)
una guía urbana de Sevilla a town map of
Sevilla
• la **guía del ocio** entertainment guide
• la **guía telefónica** telephone directory

el & la **guía** *masc & fem noun*
guide (*person*)
Es guía turístico. He's a tourist guide.

guiar *verb* [32]
to guide

guiarse *reflexive verb* [32]
guiarse por un mapa to follow a map

el **guijarro** *masc noun*
pebble

guiñar *verb* [17]
to wink

el **guiño** *masc noun*
wink

el **guión** *masc noun*
1 **dash**
2 **hyphen**
   una palabra con guión a hyphenated word
3 **script** *(of a film)*

el & la **guionista** *masc & fem noun*
   scriptwriter

el **guisante** *masc noun*
   pea

guisar *verb* [17]
   to cook
   Guisa muy bien. He's a very good cook.

la **guitarra** *fem noun* ▷ see **guitarra** *masc & fem noun*
   guitar
   la guitarra española the Spanish guitar

el & la **guitarra** *masc & fem noun*
   ▷ see **guitarra** *fem*
   guitarist

el & la **guitarrista** *masc & fem noun*
   guitarist

el **gusano** *masc noun*
   worm

♪ **gustar** *verb* [17]
1 *(to say what you like, don't like)* Me gusta el café. I like coffee. (*café is singular, so gusta*)
   Me gusta nadar. I like swimming. (*nadar is an infinitive, so gusta*)
   No me gustan las matemáticas. I don't like maths. (*matemáticas is plural, so gustan*)
   A mi padre le gustan las fresas. My dad likes strawberries. (*fresas is plural, so gustan*)
   ¿Te gustó la película? Did you like the

---

film? (*película is singular, so gustó*)
   No me gustaron los amigos de Paco. I didn't like Paco's friends. (*amigos is plural, so gustaron*)
   Antes no me gustaban las fiestas. I didn't use to like parties. (*fiestas is plural, so gustaban*)
   ¿Te gustaría visitar Bilbao? Would you like to visit Bilbao? (*visitar is an infinitive, so gustaría*)
   A nosotros nos gustaría ir a Guatemala. We would like to go to Guatemala. (*ir is an infinitive, so gustaría*)
2 **me gusta más ... que ...** I prefer ... to ...
   Me gusta más jugar al tenis que nadar. I like playing tennis better than swimming. (*jugar is an infinitive, so gusta*)
   A Belén le gustan más los gatos que los perros. Belén prefers cats to dogs. (*gatos is plural, so gustan*)

WORD TIP Use *gusta, gustó, gustaba, gustaría, etc* if what you like, or don't like, is *singular* or an infinitive. Use *gustan, gustaron, gustaban, gustarían, etc* if what you like, or don't like is *plural*.

---

el **gusto** *masc noun*
1 **taste**
   Tiene buen gusto. It tastes nice.
   Tengo mal gusto en la boca. I have a nasty taste in my mouth.
   tener gusto a algo to taste of something
   Tiene gusto a menta. It tastes of mint.
2 **taste** *(likes and dislikes)*
   Tiene muy buen gusto. She has very good taste.
3 *(in introductions)* **Mucho gusto.** Pleased to meet you.

H h

ₛ **ha** *verb* ▷ **haber**

el **haba** *fem noun*
1 **bean**
2 **broad bean**

WORD TIP *haba* takes *el* or *un* in the singular even though it is feminine.

ₛ **habéis** *verb* ▷ **haber**

ₛ **haber** *verb* [6]
1 (*forming past tenses using* **have** *and* **had**) **to have**
Ha venido Laura. Laura has come.
He comprado el pan. I have bought the bread.
No habían llegado. They hadn't arrived.
No había comido cuando llegamos. She had not eaten when we arrived.
2 **haber de** to have to, must
He de ir a la oficina. I have to go to the office.
Ha de ser tarde. It must be late.
3 (*with the singular forms:* hay, había, *etc*) **hay** there is, there are
había there was, there were
habrá there will be
Hay una carta para ti. There's a letter for you.
No hay sopa. There isn't any soup.
Hay muchos errores. There are many mistakes.
Ha habido varios cambios. There have been several changes.
Había un señor en la puerta. There was a man at the door.
Había más de treinta personas. There were more than thirty people.
Hubo un accidente ayer. There was an accident yesterday.
Hubo cinco muertos. There were five dead.
Habrá bocadillos y bebidas. There will be sandwiches and drinks.
'¿Qué van a tomar de postre?'—'¿Hay helado?' 'What would you like for pudding?'—'Have you got ice cream?'
4 (*in expressions*) 'Gracias.'—'No hay de qué.' 'Thank you.'—'Don't mention it.'
Hola ¿qué hay? Hello, how are things?
5 (*to say* must *with the forms:* hay que, había que, *etc*) Hay que comprar leche. We must buy milk.
Habrá que hacerlo. It'll have to be done.
Hay que leer las instrucciones. We must read the instructions.
¿Qué hay que hacer? What needs to be done?

WORD TIP The choice of I, must, you must, we need, etc depends on who you are speaking to.

ₛ **hábil** *masc & fem adjective*
1 **skilful**
un político muy hábil a very clever politician
Es una jugadora hábil. She is a skilful player.
2 **working**
un día hábil a working day

ₛ la **habilidad** *fem noun*
skill

ₛ la **habitación** *fem noun*
room
• la **habitación doble** double room
• la **habitación individual** single room
• la **habitación sencilla** single room

ₛ el & la **habitante** *masc & fem noun*
inhabitant
¿Cuántos habitantes tiene Granada? How many people live in Granada?

el **habla** *fem noun*
1 (*answering the phone*) **al habla** speaking
'¿Está el Señor López?'—'Al habla.' 'Is Sr López there?'—'Speaking.'
2 **speech**
Se quedó sin habla. He was speechless.
3 (*with languages*) un país de habla hispana a Spanish-speaking country

WORD TIP *habla* takes *el* or *un* in the singular even though it is feminine.

ₛ **hablador** *masc adjective*, **habladora** *fem*
▷ see **hablador** *noun*
1 **talkative**
2 **gossipy**

ₛ el **hablador** *masc noun*, la **habladora** *fem*
▷ see **hablador** *adj*
1 **chatterbox**
2 **gossip**

ₛ **hablar** *verb* [17]
1 **to speak**
hablar en voz baja to speak in a low voice
Habla con acento inglés. She speaks with an English accent.
Sabe hablar inglés. He speaks English.
¿Hablas algún idioma? Do you speak any

foreign languages?
'Se habla inglés' 'English spoken' (*shop notice*)

2 to speak (*on the phone*)
¿Quién habla? Who's speaking, please?
Está hablando por teléfono. He's on the phone.

3 to talk
No habla mucho. She doesn't talk very much.
hablar con alguien to talk to somebody
Está hablando con mi madre. He's talking to my mother.
hablar de algo to talk about something
Habla mucho de ti. She talks about you a lot.
Habló de sus proyectos. He talked about his plans.

habrán, habré, etc *verb* ▷ **haber**

🎵 **hacer** *verb* [7]

1 to make
hacer un ruido to make a noise
hacer un pastel to make a cake
hacer la cama to make the bed

2 to do
hacer los deberes to do your homework
No sé qué hacer. I don't know what to do.
¿Qué haces? What are you doing?
¿Qué hace tu padre? What does your father do? (*for a living*)

3 to cook
hacer la comida to cook lunch
hacer la cena to cook dinner

4 to build (*a house, road*)

5 (*for heat, cold, weather conditions*) **Hace frío.** It's cold.
Hace calor. It's hot.
Hacía mucho viento. It was very windy.
Este verano ha hecho muy buen tiempo. The weather's been very good this summer.

6 hacer a alguien hacer algo to make someone do something
Le hice repetirlo. I made him do it again.
Eso me hizo pensar. That made me think.

7 (*for time*) **Hace tres días.** Three days ago.
Hace tres días que se fueron. They left three days ago.
Eso pasó hace mucho tiempo. That happened a long time ago.
La vi hace poco. I saw her a little while ago.
¿Cuánto tiempo hace que vives aquí? How long have you been living here?
Hacía dos meses que no iba a verlos.

I hadn't been to see them for two months.
Trabaja aquí desde hace tres meses. She's been working here for three months.

> **WORD TIP** In phrases where *desde hace* means *for* in time expressions, Spanish uses the present tense and English the present perfect (have been + ing).

hacerse *reflexive verb* [7]

1 to become
hacerse famoso to become famous
Se hicieron amigos. They became friends.
Se están haciendo viejos. They're getting old.

2 hacerse algo to do something to yourself
Me he hecho un corte en el dedo. I've cut my finger.

3 hacerse algo to make something for yourself
Me he hecho un vestido. I've made myself a dress.
Se ha hecho una mesa para la cocina. She's made a table for her kitchen.

4 (*used impersonally*) **¿Cómo se hace?** How do you do it?

🎵 el **hacha** *fem noun*
axe

> **WORD TIP** *hacha* takes *el* or *un* in the singular even though it is feminine.

🎵 **hacia** *preposition*

1 towards
hacia el norte northwards
Vinieron hacia mí. They came towards me.
Muévelo hacia abajo. Move it down.

2 (*with time*) **about**
Llamaré hacia las dos de la tarde. I'll call at about two o'clock.
Te pagaré hacia final de mes. I'll pay you towards the end of the month.

🎵 la **hacienda** *fem noun*
ranch (*especially in Latin America*)

🎵 el **hada** *fem noun*
fairy

> **WORD TIP** *hada* takes *el* or *un* in the singular even though it is feminine.

🎵 **haga, hago, etc** *verb* ▷ **hacer**

🎵 **Haití** *masc noun*
Haiti

haitiano *masc adjective & noun*, **haitiana** *fem adjective & noun*

1 Haitian ▶▶

a
b
c
d
e
f
g
h
i
j
k
l
m
n
ñ
o
p
q
r
s
t
u
v
w
x
y
z

2 un **haitiano**, una **haitiana** Haitian

> **WORD TIP** Adjectives and nouns for nationality, regional origin, and language do not have capital letters in Spanish.

halagar *verb* [28]
 to flatter

♂ el **halcón** *masc noun*
 falcon

♂ **hallar** *verb* [17]
 to find
 No hallaron una solución. They couldn't find a solution.

hallarse *reflexive verb* [17]
 (*formal*)
 1 to be
 El pueblo se halla cerca del mar. The village is near the sea.
 2 to feel
 Me hallaba tranquilo. I was feeling calm.

♂ la **hamaca** *fem noun*
 hammock

♂ el **hambre** *fem noun*
 hunger
 tener hambre to be hungry
 ¿Tienes hambre? Are you hungry?
 No, no tengo hambre. No, I'm not hungry.
 Sí, me muero de hambre. Yes, I'm starving.
 El ejercicio da hambre. Exercise makes you hungry.

> **WORD TIP** *hambre* takes *el* or *un* in the singular even though it is feminine. Use *tener* to say you're feeling hungry, hot, etc

♂ la **hamburguesa** *fem noun*
 hamburger

♂ la **hamburguesería** *fem noun*
 hamburger bar

♂ el **hámster** *masc noun*
 hamster

♂ **han** *verb* ▷ **haber**

♂ **harán**, **haré**, **etc** *verb* ▷ **hacer**

♂ la **harina** *fem noun*
 flour
 • la **harina con levadura** self-raising flour
 • la **harina integral** wholemeal flour

♂ **hartarse** *reflexive verb* [17]
 to get fed up
 hartarse de algo to get fed up with something
 Me harté de esperar. I got fed up with waiting.
 Me estoy hartando de este estilo. I'm getting fed up with this style.

♂ **harto** *masc adjective*, **harta** *fem*
 estar harto de algo to be fed up with something
 Estoy harta de tus excusas. I'm fed up with your excuses.
 Están hartos de comer siempre lo mismo. They're fed up with always eating the same thing.

♂ **has** *verb* ▷ **haber**

♂ **hasta** *preposition*
 1 until
 Me quedo hasta la semana que viene. I'm staying until next week.
 hasta que until
 Esperamos hasta que paró de llover. We waited until it stopped raining.
 No lo mandes hasta que yo lo diga. Don't send it until I tell you.
 2 (*in greetings*) ¡Hasta mañana! See you tomorrow!
 ¡Hasta luego! See you later!
 ¡Hasta pronto! See you soon!
 ¡Hasta el sábado! See you on Saturday!
 3 up to
 Hasta hace tres meses. Up to three months ago.
 hasta ahora up to now
 Hasta ahora no lo hemos visto. We haven't seen him up to now.
 4 even
 Hasta un niño sabe eso. Even a child knows that.

♂ **hay** *verb* ▷ **haber**

♂ **haz** *verb* ▷ **hacer**

♂ **he** *verb* ▷ **haber**

 el **hechizo** *masc noun*
 1 spell
 2 fascination

♂ **hecho** *masc adjective*, **hecha** *fem*
 ▷ see **hecho** *noun*
 1 made
 hecho a mano hand-made
 zapatos hechos a mano hand-made shoes
 2 done
 un trabajo bien hecho a job well done
 ¡Bien hecho! Well done!

♂ el **hecho** *masc noun* ▷ see **hecho** *adj*
 1 fact
 El hecho es que ... The fact is ...
 ¿Cuáles son los hechos? What are the facts?
 de hecho in fact
 2 action
 Tenemos que pasar de las palabras a los hechos. We must stop talking and take action.

la **helada** *fem noun*
  frost

ᔕ la **heladería** *fem noun*
  ice cream parlour

ᔕ el **heladero** *masc noun*, la **heladera** *fem*
  ice cream seller

ᔕ **helado** *masc adjective*, **helada** *fem*
  ▷ see **helado** *noun*
  1 **frozen**
    El río estaba helado. The river was frozen.
    La pobre chica estaba helada. The poor girl
    was frozen.
  2 **freezing**
    Estoy helado. I'm freezing.
    La casa está helada. The house is freezing.
    Tienes las manos heladas. Your hands are
    freezing.

ᔕ el **helado** *masc noun* ▷ see **helado** *adj*
  ice cream
    un helado de fresa a strawberry ice cream
    helados de todos sabores ice creams of all
    flavours

ᔕ **helar** *verb* [29]
  to freeze
    Esta noche va a helar. There's going to be a
    frost tonight.

  helarse *reflexive verb* [29]
    to freeze
    El río se ha helado. The river has frozen
    over.

la **hélice** *fem noun*
  propeller

ᔕ el **helicóptero** *masc noun*
  helicopter

ᔕ **hemos** *verb* ▷ **haber**

el **heno** *masc noun*
  hay

ᔕ **heredar** *verb* [17]
  to inherit
    heredar el trono to succeed to the throne

ᔕ el **heredero** *masc noun*, la **heredera** *fem*
  heir
    Es la heredera de una fortuna. She is the
    heir to a fortune.

ᔕ la **herida** *fem noun* ▷ see **herido** *adj*
  injury

ᔕ **herido** *masc adjective*, **herida** *fem*
  ▷ see **herida** *noun*
  1 **injured**
    estar gravemente herido to be seriously
    injured

  2 **wounded**
    Resultó herido en la pelea. He was
    wounded in the fight.

ᔕ **herir** *verb* [14]
  1 **to wound**
    Fue herido de muerte. He was fatally
    wounded.
  2 **to hurt**
    Hirieron mis sentimientos. They hurt my
    feelings.

ᔕ la **hermana** *fem noun*
  ▷ see **hermano** *noun*
  sister
    Tengo una hermana. I have one sister.
  • la **hermana gemela** twin sister
  • la **hermana política** sister-in-law

ᔕ el **hermanastro** *masc noun*, la
  hermanastra *fem*
  1 **stepbrother**
  2 **stepsister**
  3 **half-brother**
  4 **half-sister**

ᔕ el **hermano** *masc noun*
  ▷ see **hermana** *noun*
  1 **brother**
    Tengo dos hermanos. I have two brothers.
  2 **hermanos** brothers and sisters
    ¿Tienes hermanos? Do you have any
    brothers and sisters?
  • el **hermano gemelo** twin brother
  • el **hermano político** brother-in-law

ᔕ **hermoso** *masc adjective*, **hermosa** *fem*
  beautiful

ᔕ el **héroe** *masc noun*
  hero

ᔕ la **heroína** *fem noun*
  1 **heroine**
  2 **heroin** (*the drug*)

ᔕ la **herramienta** *fem noun*
  tool

ᔕ **hervir** *verb* [14]
  to boil
    hervir las patatas to boil the potatoes
    El agua está hirviendo. The water is boiling.

ᔕ **hice** *verb* ▷ **hacer**

  hidratante *masc & fem adjective*
    moisturizing

ᔕ la **hiedra** *fem noun*
  ivy

ᔕ el **hielo** *masc noun*
  ice
    un cubito de hielo an ice cube

a
b
c
d
e
f
g
h
i
j
k
l
m
n
ñ
o
p
q
r
s
t
u
v
w
x
y
z

⚥ la **hierba** *fem noun*
1 grass
  'No pisar la hierba' 'Do not walk on the grass'
2 herb
  hierbas aromáticas aromatic herbs
3 una hierba mala a weed
 • las **hierbas de cocina** herbs (*for cooking*)

⚥ el **hierro** *masc noun*
  iron

⚥ el **hígado** *masc noun*
  liver

⚥ **higiénico** *masc adjective*, **higiénica** *fem*
  hygienic

⚥ el **higo** *masc noun*
  fig

⚥ la **hija** *fem noun* ▷ see **hijo** *noun*
  daughter
 • la **hija política** daughter-in-law

⚥ el **hijo** *masc noun* ▷ see **hija** *noun*
1 son
  Su hijo se llama Carlos. Their son is called Carlos.
2 hijos children
  Tienen tres hijos. They have three children.
 • el **hijo político** son-in-law

⚥ el **hilo** *masc noun*
  thread

⚥ el **himno** *masc noun*
  hymn

⚥ el & la **hincha** *masc & fem noun*
  supporter
  Es hincha del Sevilla. He's a Seville supporter.

⚥ **hinchado** *masc adjective*, **hinchada** *fem*
  swollen

⚥ **hinchar** *verb* [17]
1 to blow up (*a balloon*)
2 to pump up (*a tyre*)

hincharse *reflexive verb* [17]
  to swell up
  Se me ha hinchado el tobillo. My ankle has swollen up.

la **hinchazón** *fem noun*
  swelling

⚥ **hindú** *masc & fem adjective & noun*
1 Hindu
2 un & una Hindu Hindu
  los hindúes the Hindus

WORD TIP Adjectives and nouns for religion do not have capital letters in Spanish.

el **hinduismo** *masc noun*
  (*Religion*) el hinduismo Hinduism

WORD TIP Religions are spelt with a small letter in Spanish.

⚥ el **hipermercado** *masc noun*
  hypermarket

hipnotizar *verb* [25]
  to hypnotize

⚥ el **hipo** *masc noun*
  hiccups
  tener hipo to have hiccups

⚥ la **hipoteca** *fem noun*
  mortgage

⚥ **hispano** *masc adjective*, **hispana** *fem*
  ▷ see **hispano** *noun*
1 Hispanic (*to do with Spanish*)
  países de habla hispana Spanish-speaking countries
2 Hispanic, Spanish American (*in the United States*)

⚥ un **hispano** *masc noun*, una **hispana** *fem*
  ▷ see **hispano** *adj*
  Hispanic
  En Estados Unidos hay cada vez más hispanos. There are more and more Hispanics in the United States.

WORD TIP Adjectives and nouns for nationality, regional origin, and language do not have capital letters in Spanish.

⚥ **Hispanoamérica** *fem noun*
  Latin America

hispanoamericano *masc adjective & noun*,
hispanoamericana *fem adjective & noun*
1 Latin American
2 un hispanoamericano, una hispanoamericano Latin American

⚥ **hispanohablante** *masc & fem adjective*
  ▷ see **hispanohablante** *noun*
  Spanish-speaking
  una comunidad hispanohablante a Spanish-speaking community

⚥ el & la **hispanohablante** *masc & fem noun*
  ▷ see **hispanohablante** *adj*
  Spanish speaker

WORD TIP Adjectives and nouns for nationality and regional origin do not have capital letters in Spanish.

 hispanohablantes

Más de 350 millones de personas hablan español como primera lengua.

ℰ la **historia** *fem noun*
1 **history**
la historia de Chile the history of Chile
2 **story**
una apasionante historia de aventuras an exciting adventure story
una historia de miedo a horror story

ℰ **histórico** *masc adjective*, **histórica** *fem*
1 **historical**
documentos históricos historical documents
2 **historic**
un acontecimiento histórico a historic event

ℰ la **historieta** *fem noun*
cartoon

ℰ **hizo** *verb* ▷ **hacer**

ℰ el **hogar** *masc noun*
home
una persona sin hogar a homeless person
las labores del hogar the housework
Éste es mi hogar. This is my home.

ℰ la **hoguera** *fem noun*
bonfire

ℰ la **hoja** *fem noun*
1 **leaf** (*of a tree, plant*)
2 **sheet** (*of paper, metal*)
3 **page** (*of a book*)

ℰ **hola** *exclamation*
hello

Holanda *fem noun*
Holland

holandés *masc adjective & noun*,
holandesa *fem adjective & noun*
1 **Dutch**
2 un holandés Dutchman
una holandesa Dutchwoman
3 el holandés Dutch (*the language*)

WORD TIP Adjectives and nouns for nationality, regional origin, and language do not have capital letters in Spanish.

holgazán *masc adjective*, **holgazana** *fem*
lazy

ℰ el **hombre** *masc noun*
1 **man** (*the human race*)
El hombre moderno es más numeroso. Modern man is more numerous.
2 (*in exclamations*) ¡Hombre, por supuesto! Of course!
¡Hombre! ¡Tú por aquí! Hey! Look who's here!
• el **hombre del tiempo** weatherman
• el **hombre de negocios** businessman
• el **hombre rana** frogman

ℰ el **hombro** *masc noun*
shoulder

el **homenaje** *masc noun*
tribute
rendir homenaje a alguien to pay tribute to someone

ℰ **homosexual** *masc & fem adjective*
▷ see **homosexual** *noun*
homosexual

ℰ el & la **homosexual** *masc & fem noun*
▷ see **homosexual** *adj*
homosexual

ℰ **hondo** *masc adjective*, **honda** *fem*
▷ see **hondo** *adv*
deep
un pozo hondo a deep well
en lo más hondo del lago in the deepest part of the lake

ℰ **hondo** *adverb* ▷ see **hondo** *adj*
deeply
respirar hondo to breathe deeply

Honduras *fem noun*
Honduras

hondureño *masc adjective & noun*,
hondureña *fem adjective & noun*
1 **Honduran**
2 un hondureño, una hondureña Honduran

WORD TIP Adjectives and nouns for nationality, regional origin, and language do not have capital letters in Spanish.

ℰ **honesto** *masc adjective*, **honesta** *fem*
honest

ℰ el **hongo** *masc noun*
1 **fungus**
2 tener hongos to have athlete's foot
3 (*Latin America*) **mushroom**

ℰ el **honor** *masc noun*
honour
en honor de in honour of
una recepción en honor del equipo visitante a reception in honour of the visiting team

la **honra** *fem noun*
honour

la **honradez** *fem noun*
honesty

honrado *masc adjective*, **honrada** *fem*
honest

ℰ la **hora** *fem noun*
1 **hour**
media hora half an hour
hora y media an hour and a half

a
b
c
d
e
f
g
h
i
j
k
l
m
n
ñ
o
p
q
r
s
t
u
v
w
x
y
z

a las quince horas at three p.m.
La película dura dos horas. The film lasts two hours.
El bus sale cada hora. The bus leaves every hour.
Hablamos horas y horas. We talked for hours.

2 **time**
¿Qué hora es? What's the time?
¿Tiene hora? Have you got the time?
¿Me puede dar la hora? Could you tell me what time it is?
¿A qué hora empieza? What time does it start?
Ya es hora de entrar. It's time to go in.
a la hora de comer at lunchtime
llegar a la hora to arrive on time

3 (in expressions) a todas horas all the time
a última hora at the last minute
a primera hora de la mañana first thing in the morning
una noticia de última hora some news just in

4 (at the doctor's, dentist's) pedir hora to make an appointment
He pedido hora con el dentista. I've made an appointment to see the dentist.
• la **hora punta** rush hour
• las **horas de trabajo** working hours
• las **horas de visita** visiting hours
• las **horas extra** overtime

las **horas libres** plural fem noun
free time
¿Qué haces en tus horas libres? What do you do in your free time?

ℰ el **horario** masc noun
1 timetable
• el **horario de clase** school timetable
• el **horario de visitas** visiting hours

ℰ la **horchata** fem noun
tiger nut milk (thick, white, cold drink made from tiger nuts)

ℰ la **horchatería** fem noun
refreshment stall (selling horchata)

ℰ **horizontal** masc & fem adjective
horizontal

ℰ el **horizonte** masc noun
horizon

ℰ la **hormiga** fem noun
ant

el **hormigón** masc noun
concrete

ℰ el **horno** masc noun
1 oven
verduras al horno oven-cooked vegetables
En verano la ciudad es como un horno. In summer the town is like an oven.

2 kiln
• el **horno microondas** microwave oven

ℰ el **horóscopo** masc noun
horoscope

ℰ la **horquilla** fem noun
hairpin

ℰ **horrible** masc & fem adjective
horrible

ℰ el **horror** masc noun
horror
¡Qué horror! (informal) How awful!

horrorizar verb [22]
to horrify

ℰ **horroroso** masc adjective, **horrorosa** fem
1 horrific (crime)
2 (informal) awful (dress, book, picture)

la **hortaliza** fem noun
vegetable

hospedarse reflexive verb [17]
to stay, to put up at
Nos hospedamos en una pensión. We stayed in a guesthouse.

ℰ el **hospital** masc noun
hospital

la **hospitalidad** fem noun
hospitality

ℰ el **hostal** masc noun
(small, inexpensive) hotel

la **hostelería** fem noun
hotel industry

ℰ el **hotel** masc noun
hotel
un hotel de cuatro estrellas a four-star hotel

el **hotelero** masc noun, la **hotelera** fem
hotel manager

ℰ **hoy** adverb
1 today
Hoy es mi cumpleaños. It's my birthday today.
el periódico de hoy today's paper
¿A qué estamos hoy? What day is it today?

2 hoy día, hoy en día nowadays
Hoy en día el cuarenta por ciento de los alumnos van a la universidad. Nowadays forty per cent of pupils go to university.

ℰ el **hoyo** masc noun
hole (in the ground, for golf)

ℰ **hube, hubo, etc** verb ▷ haber

la **hucha** fem noun
moneybox

hueco *masc adjective,* **hueca** *fem*
▷ see **hueco** *noun*
 hollow

ℰ el **hueco** *masc noun*
1 **hollow** *(in a surface)*
2 **hole**
3 **gap** *(in your timetable, schedule)*
4 **space**
 un hueco para aparcar a parking space
 Hazme un hueco. Make some room for me.
 • el **hueco de la escalera** stairwell

ℰ **huela**, **huelo**, etc *verb* ▷ **oler**

ℰ la **huelga** *fem noun*
 strike
 hacer huelga to strike
 estar en huelga to be on strike
 • la **huelga de celo** work-to-rule
 • la **huelga de hambre** hunger strike

ℰ la **huella** *fem noun*
1 **footprint**
2 **track** *(of an animal, a tyre)*
 las **huellas dactilares** fingerprints

ℰ el **huérfano** *masc noun,* la **huérfana** *fem*
 orphan

ℰ la **huerta** *fem noun* ▷ **huerto**

ℰ el **huerto** *masc noun*
1 **vegetable garden**
2 **orchard**

ℰ el **hueso** *masc noun*
1 **bone**
 romperse un hueso to break a bone
2 **stone** *(in fruit)*

ℰ el & la **huésped** *masc & fem noun*
 guest

 huesudo *masc adjective,* **huesuda** *fem*
 bony

ℰ el **huevo** *masc noun*
 egg
 • el **huevo de Pascua** Easter egg
 • el **huevo duro** hard-boiled egg
 • el **huevo escalfado** poached egg
 • el **huevo frito** fried egg
 • el **huevo pasado por agua** boiled egg
 • los **huevos revueltos** scrambled eggs

ℰ **huir** *verb* [54]
 to flee, to run away
 huir de la policía to flee from the police

ℰ **humano** *masc adjective,* **humana** *fem*
 ▷ see **humano** *noun*
1 **human**
 la especie humana race
 Es humano cometer errores. It's human to
 make mistakes.

2 **humane**
 una política humana hacia los animales a
 humane policy to animals

ℰ el **humano** *masc noun,* la **humana** *fem*
 ▷ see **humano** *adj*
 human being

ℰ la **humedad** *fem noun*
1 **dampness**
 La casa tiene humedad. The house is damp.
2 **humidity**
3 **moisture**

ℰ **húmedo** *masc adjective,* **húmeda** *fem*
1 **damp** *(house, weather, clothes)*
2 **humid** *(climate)*
3 **moist** *(lips, eyes)*

 humillar *verb* [17]
 to humiliate

ℰ el **humo** *masc noun*
 smoke

ℰ el **humor** *masc noun*
1 **humour**
 tener sentido del humor to have a sense of
 humour
2 **mood**
 estar de buen humor to be in a good mood
 estar de mal humor to be in a bad mood
 No estoy de humor para verlos. I'm not in
 the mood to see them.

ℰ **hundir** *verb* [19]
 to sink

 hundirse *reflexive verb* [19]
1 **to sink** *(ships, coins)*
2 **to collapse** *(buildings, mines)*

 húngaro *masc adjective & noun,* **húngara**
 fem adjective & noun
1 **Hungarian**
2 *(person)* un húngaro, una húngara
 Hungarian
3 el **húngaro** Hungarian *(the language)*

 WORD TIP Adjectives and nouns for nationality,
 regional origin, and language do not have capital
 letters in Spanish.

ℰ **Hungría** *fem noun*
 Hungary

ℰ el **huracán** *masc noun*
 hurricane
 un huracán de categoría cuatro a
 category four hurricane

ℰ **hurra** *exclamation*
 hurrah!

ℰ **huyas**, **huyo**, etc *verb* ▷ **huir**

a
b
c
d
e
f
g
h
i
j
k
l
m
n
ñ
o
p
q
r
s
t
u
v
w
x
y
z

I i

ſ **iba, iban, etc** *verb* ▷ **ir**

ſ **ibérico** *masc adjective*, **ibérica** *fem*
Iberian (*to do with Spain & Portugal*)

ſ el **iceberg** *masc noun*, **icebergs** *plural*
iceberg

ſ el **icono** *masc noun*
icon

ſ la **ida** *fem noun*
departure
un billete de ida a single ticket
un billete de ida y vuelta a return ticket

ſ la **idea** *fem noun*
idea
Tengo una idea. I've got an idea.
No tienen ni idea de cómo hacerlo. They
have no idea how to do it.
'¿A qué hora llegan?'—'No tengo ni idea.'
'What time will they arrive?'—'I have no
idea.'

ſ **ideal** *masc & fem adjective*
ideal

ſ **idéntico** *masc adjective*, **idéntica** *fem*
identical
Es idéntico a su padre. He's just like his
father.

la **identidad** *fem noun*
identity
un carné de identidad an identity card

ſ la **identificación** *fem noun*
identification

ſ **identificar** *verb* [31]
to identify

identificarse *reflexive verb* [31]
1 **to identify yourself**
2 **identificarse con alguien** to identify with
somebody
Me identifico con sus ideales sociales. I
identify with her social ideals.

ſ el **idioma** *masc noun*
language
Hablo tres idiomas. I speak three
languages.

ſ **idiota** *masc & fem adjective*
▷ see **idiota** *noun*
stupid

ſ el & la **idiota** *masc & fem noun*
▷ see **idiota** *adj*
idiot

ſ **ido** *verb* ▷ **ir**

ſ la **iglesia** *fem noun*
church
ir a la iglesia to go to church
casarse por la iglesia to have a church
wedding

ſ **ignorante** *masc & fem adjective*
ignorant

ſ **ignorar** *verb* [17]
1 **to ignore**
No me gusta que me ignoren. I don't like
being ignored.
2 **not to know**
Ignoro las razones. I don't know the
reasons.

ſ **igual** *masc & fem adjective* ▷ see **igual** *adv*
1 **same**
uno de igual tamaño one of the same size
Son iguales. They are the same.
Parecen todos iguales. They all look the
same.
ser igual a algo to be the same as
something
Era igual a éste. It was the same as this one.
ser igual que algo to be the same as
something
No es igual que los demás. It's not the same
as the others.
2 **equal**
dos equipos iguales two equal teams
ser [1] igual a algo to be equal to something
Cien centímetros son iguales a un metro. A
hundred centimetres are equal to one
metre.
3 **dar igual a alguien: Todo le da igual.** He
doesn't care about anything.
Les da igual lo uno que lo otro. Either way it
makes no difference to them.
**'¿Quieres salir o quedar en casa?'—'Me da
igual.'** 'Do you want to go out or stay at
home?'—'I don't mind.'

ſ **igual** *adverb* ▷ see **igual** *adj*
1 **the same**
Suenan igual. They sound the same.
2 **equally**
Los quiero a todos igual. I like them all
equally.

Los dos sistemas son igual de buenos. Both systems are equally good.
3 (*in comparisons*) **igual que** just like
Es géminis, igual que yo. She's a Gemini, just like me.
Es igual de alto que su padre. He's as tall as his father.
Es igual de ancho que la mesa. It's as wide as the table.
4 **maybe**
Igual la vemos en la fiesta. Maybe we'll see her at the party.
Igual no viene. He may not even come.
5 **al igual que** just like
6 **anyway**
¿Tú no quieres venir? Yo voy igual. Don't you want to come? Well, I'm going anyway.

♪ la **igualdad** *fem noun*
equality
en igualdad de condiciones on equal terms
· la **igualdad de oportunidades** equal opportunities

♪ **igualmente** *adverb*
1 **equally**
Son todos igualmente buenos. They are all equally good.
2 (*to return good wishes*)
'Que pases un buen fin de semana.'— 'Igualmente.' 'Have a good week end.'— 'You too.'

♪ **ilegal** *masc & fem adjective*
illegal

♪ **ilegalmente** *adverb*
illegally

♪ **ileso** *masc adjective*, **ilesa** *fem*
unhurt, uninjured

ilimitado *masc adjective*, **ilimitada** *fem*
unlimited

♪ la **iluminación** *fem noun*
1 **lighting** (*in a room, hall*)
2 **illumination** (*of a building, statue*)

♪ la **iluminar** *verb* [17]
1 **to light** (*a room, hall*)
2 **to illuminate** (*a building, statue*)

♪ la **ilusión** *fem noun*
1 **illusion**
2 **hope**
Su ilusión es ir a América. She hopes to go to America.
3 **hacerle ilusión hacer algo** to really want to do something
Me hace ilusión ir al circo. I really want to go to the circus.

la **ilustración** *fem noun*
illustration

ilustrar *verb* [17]
to illustrate

♪ la **imagen** *fem noun, pl:* las **imágenes**
1 **image**
Es la viva imagen de su madre. She's the image of her mother.
El presidente trata de mejorar su imagen. The president is trying to improve his image.
2 **picture** (*on a TV screen*)
3 **reflection** (*in a mirror*)

♪ la **imaginación** *fem noun*
imagination
No tienes imaginación. You have no imagination.
Son imaginaciones suyas. He's just imagining things.

♪ **imaginar** *verb* [17]
to imagine

♪ **imaginarse** *reflexive verb* [17]
to imagine
Me imagino que vendrá mañana. I imagine he'll come tomorrow.
Me imagino que sí. I imagine so.
Me imagino que no. I suppose not

♪ el **imán** *masc noun*, **imanes** *plural*
magnet

♪ **imbécil** *masc & fem adjective*
▷ see **imbécil** *noun*
stupid

♪ el & la **imbécil** *masc & fem noun*
▷ see **imbécil** *adj*
idiot

♪ **imitar** *verb* [17]
to imitate

la **impaciencia** *fem noun*
impatience

♪ **impaciente** *masc & fem adjective*
impatient

impactante *masc & fem adjective*
1 **shocking** (*piece of news*)
2 **powerful** (*advertising*)

el **impacto** *masc noun*
impact

♪ **impar** *masc & fem adjective*
odd (*number*)

impecable *masc & fem adjective*
impeccable

a
b
c
d
e
f
g
h
i
j
k
l
m
n
ñ
o
p
q
r
s
t
u
v
w
x
y
z

Spanish-English

ℰ **impedir** *verb* [57]
1 **to prevent**
impedirle a alguien hacer algo to prevent someone from doing something
El dolor le impedía caminar. The pain prevented her from walking.
impedirle a alguien que haga algo to prevent someone from doing something
Tienes que impedirle que se vaya. You have to prevent him from going.
2 **impedir el paso a alguien** to block someone's way

ℰ el **imperativo** *masc noun*
(*Grammar*) **imperative**

el **imperdible** *masc noun*
safety pin

imperfecto *masc adjective*, **imperfecta**
fem ▷ see **imperfecto** *noun*
imperfect

ℰ el **imperfecto** *masc noun*
▷ see **imperfecto** *adj*
(*Grammar*) **imperfect**

ℰ el **impermeable** *masc noun*
raincoat

impersonal *masc & fem adjective*
impersonal

implicar *verb* [31]
to involve

imponer *verb* [11]
to impose (*a condition, a punishment*)

ℰ la **importación** *fem noun*
import
artículos de importación imported goods

ℰ la **importancia** *fem noun*
importance
darle importancia a algo to attach importance to something
No le di importancia a lo que dijo. I didn't attach any importance to what he said.

ℰ **importante** *masc & fem adjective*
1 **important**
Lo importante es ... The important thing is ...
2 **significant** (*quantities, sums, amounts*)
una importante suma de dinero a significant sum of money

ℰ **importar** *verb* [17]
1 **to import** (*goods*)
2 **to matter**
Importa mucho el color. The colour matters a lot.
No importa. It doesn't matter.

Me importa mucho. It matters a lot to me.
Me importa ayudarles. I want to help them.
¿Y a ti que te importa? What's it to do with you?
3 (*making polite requests*) **¿Le importaría comprobarlo?** Would you mind checking it?
¿Le importa que abra la ventanilla? Do you mind if I open the window?

el **importe** *masc noun*
amount

ℰ **imposible** *masc & fem adjective*
impossible
misión imposible mission impossible

ℰ la **impresión** *fem noun*
impression
causar una buena impresión to make a good impression
Me da la impresión de que ... I have the feeling that ...

ℰ **impresionante** *masc & fem adjective*
1 **incredible** (*success, amount*)
2 **shocking** (*scene, pictures*)

ℰ **impresionar** *verb* [17]
1 **to impress**
Quiere impresionarte. She wants to impress you.
2 **to shock**
La violencia de la película me impresionó mucho. The film's violence shocked me.
Me impresionó mucho verlos discutir. Seeing them argue really shook me.

ℰ **impreso** *masc adjective*, **impresa** *fem*
▷ see **impreso** *noun*
printed

ℰ el **impreso** *masc noun* ▷ see **impreso** *adj*
form
• el **impreso de solicitud** application form

ℰ la **impresora** *fem noun*
printer
• la **impresora láser** laser printer

imprevisible *masc & fem adjective*
1 **unpredictable**
2 **unforeseeable**

ℰ **imprevisto** *masc adjective*, **imprevista**
fem ▷ see **imprevisto** *noun*
unforeseen, unexpected

ℰ el **imprevisto** *masc noun*
▷ see **imprevisto** *adj*
unforeseen event

ℰ **improviso** *in phrase*
    de improviso unexpectedly, out of the blue

imprudente *masc & fem adjective*
    ▷ see **imprudente** *noun*
    careless
    un conductor imprudente a careless driver

el & la **imprudente** *masc & fem noun*
    ▷ see **imprudente** *adj*
    careless person
    Es un imprudente conduciendo. He's a
    careless driver.

ℰ el **impuesto** *masc noun*
    tax
   • el **impuesto sobre la renta** income tax

impulsivo *masc adjective*, **impulsiva** *fem*
    impulsive

inaccesible *masc & fem adjective*
1   **inaccessible** (*place*)
2   **unapproachable** (*person*)

ℰ **inaceptable** *masc & fem adjective*
    unacceptable

inadecuado *masc adjective*, **inadecuada**
fem
1   **inappropriate**
2   **inadequate**

inadmisible *masc & fem adjective*
    unacceptable

ℰ **inadvertido** *masc adjective*, **inadvertida**
fem
    pasar inadvertido to go unnoticed

ℰ **inalámbrico** *masc adjective*, **inalámbrica**
fem
1   **wireless** (*technology*)
2   **cordless** (*phone*)

ℰ **incapaz** *masc & fem adjective, pl:* **incapaces**
    incapable
    ser incapaz de hacer algo to be incapable of
    doing something
    Fui incapaz de entenderlo. I was unable to
    understand it.
    Son incapaces de hacerlo. They are
    incapable of doing it.

ℰ el **incendio** *masc noun*
    fire
   • el **incendio forestal** forest fire
   • el **incendio provocado** arson attack

la **incertidumbre** *fem noun*
    uncertainty

incierto *masc adjective*, **incierta** *fem*
    uncertain

incitar *verb* [17]
    incitar a alguien a hacer algo to incite
    someone to do something

ℰ **incluido** *masc adjective*, **incluida** *fem*
    included
    Dos mil euros, todo incluido. Two
    thousand euros, everything included.
    Seremos diez personas, nosotros
    incluidos. There will be ten people
    including us.

ℰ **incluir** *verb* [54]
1   **to include**
2   **to enclose** (*something in a letter*)

inclusive *adverb*
    inclusive
    las páginas veinte a treinta inclusive pages
    twenty to thirty inclusive

ℰ **incluso** *adverb*
    even
    Es incluso difícil para los profesores. It's
    even difficult for the teachers.

ℰ **incluya, incluyo, etc** *verb* ▷ **incluir**

ℰ **incoloro** *masc adjective*, **incolora** *fem*
    colourless

ℰ **incómodo** *masc adjective*, **incómoda** *fem*
    uncomfortable

incompetente *masc & fem adjective*
    incompetent

ℰ **incompleto** *masc adjective*, **incompleta**
fem
    incomplete

ℰ **incomprensible** *masc & fem adjective*
    incomprehensible

incondicional *masc & fem adjective*
    unconditional

ℰ **inconsciente** *masc & fem adjective*
    unconscious

ℰ **inconveniente** *masc & fem adjective*
    ▷ see **inconveniente** *noun*
    inconvenient

el **inconveniente** *masc noun*
    ▷ see **inconveniente** *adj*
1   **disadvantage, drawback**
    El plan tiene varios inconvenientes. The
    plan has several drawbacks.
2   **objection**
    No tenemos ningún inconveniente salir
    más temprano. We have no objection to
    leaving earlier.

incorporar *verb* [17]
    to incorporate

a
b
c
d
e
f
g
h
i
j
k
l
m
n
ñ
o
p
q
r
s
t
u
v
w
x
y
z

a
b
c
d
e
f
g
h
i
j
k
l
m
n
ñ
o
p
q
r
s
t
u
v
w
x
y
z

incorporarse *reflexive verb* [17]
1 **to sit up**
2 **incorporarse a algo** to join something (*a club, a group*)

ℰ **incorrecto** *masc adjective*, **incorrecta** *fem*
   incorrect

ℰ **increíble** *masc & fem adjective*
   incredible

indecente *masc & fem adjective*
   indecent

indeciso *masc adjective*, **indecisa** *fem*
1 **indecisive**
2 **undecided**
   Están indecisos sobre la cantidad. They're undecided about the quantity.

indefenso *masc adjective*, **indefensa** *fem*
   defenceless

ℰ **indefinidamente** *adverb*
   indefinitely, for good

ℰ **indefinido** *masc adjective*, **indefinida** *fem*
1 **indefinite**
2 **vague** (*outline, smell*)

indemnizar *verb* [22]
   to compensate
   Los indemnizaron con veinte mil euros. They received twenty thousand euros in compensation.
   indemnizar a alguien por algo to compensate someone for something

la indemnización *fem noun*
   compensation
   Le pagaron una indemnización. They paid her compensation.

ℰ **la independencia** *fem noun*
   independence

ℰ **independiente** *masc & fem adjective*
   independent

ℰ **la India** *fem noun*
   (la) India India

ℰ **la indicación** *fem noun*
1 **indication**
2 **sign**
   Hay una indicación en el camino. There's a sign on the road.
   Me hizo una indicación para que lo siguiese. He signalled to me to follow him.

ℰ **indicar** *verb* [31]
1 **to indicate**
   Hay una flecha que indica el camino. There's an arrow indicating the way.

2 **to point out**
   Me indicó el lugar en el mapa. He pointed out the place on the map.

ℰ **el índice** *masc noun*
   index

ℰ **indiferente** *masc & fem adjective*
   indifferent
   Es indiferente al peligro. He is indifferent to danger.
   El precio me es indiferente. The price doesn't matter to me.

ℰ **indígena** *masc & fem adjective*
   native

indígenas

Mucho antes de llegar Cristóbal Colón a las Américas en 1492 varias poblaciones indígenas, unas bastante avanzadas, vivían allí. En México había los Aztecas; en Guatemala, los Maya y en el Perú, los Incas.

ℰ **la indigestión** *fem noun*
   indigestion

indigesto *masc adjective*, **indigesta** *fem*
   indigestible

la indignación *fem noun*
1 **indignation**
2 **outrage**

indignar *verb* [17]
1 **indignar a alguien** to make someone angry
2 **to outrage**

indignarse *reflexive verb* [17]
   to get very angry

indio *masc adjective & noun*, **india** *fem adjective & noun*
1 **Indian**
2 **un indio, una india** Indian

WORD TIP Adjectives and nouns for nationality, regional origin, and language do not have capital letters in Spanish. In Latin America *indio* refers to the native peoples of Latin America, not the Indian subcontinent.

la indirecta *fem noun* ▷ see **indirecto** *adj*
   hint
   soltar una indirecta to drop a hint

ℰ **indirecto** *masc adjective*, **indirecta** *fem* ▷ see **indirecta** *noun*
   indirect

ℰ **indiscreto** *masc adjective*, **indiscreta** *fem*
   indiscreet

ℰ **indispensable** *masc & fem adjective*
   essential

indispuesto *masc adjective*, **indispuesta** *fem*
   estar indispuesto to be unwell

ᵈ **individual** *masc & fem adjective*
1 **individual**
2 **single**
   una cama individual a single bed

los **individuales** *plural masc noun*
   singles (*in tennis*)
   la final de los individuales masculinos the final of the men's singles

ᵈ el **individuo** *masc noun*
1 **person**
   un individuo con pelo largo a person with long hair
2 (*pejorative*) **character**
   un individuo con muy mal aspecto a nasty-looking character

ᵈ la **industria** *fem noun*
   industry

ᵈ **industrial** *masc & fem adjective*
   industrial

ineficaz *masc & fem adjective*, **ineficaces** *plural*
1 **ineffective** (*remedy, measure*)
2 **inefficient** (*person*)

ᵈ **inepto** *masc adjective*, **inepta** *fem*
   incompetent

ᵈ **inesperado** *masc adjective*, **inesperada** *fem*
   unexpected

ᵈ **inevitable** *masc & fem adjective*
   unavoidable
   Era inevitable que pasase. It was bound to happen.

ᵈ **inexperto** *masc adjective*, **inexperta** *fem*
   inexperienced

ᵈ la **infancia** *fem noun*
   childhood

ᵈ **infantil** *masc & fem adjective*
1 **for children**
   un programa infantil a children's programme
2 **childish**
   Eres muy infantil. You're very childish.
3 **childlike**

ᵈ el **infarto** *masc noun*
   heart attack
   Le dio un infarto. He had a heart attack.

ᵈ la **infección** *fem noun*
   infection

ᵈ **infectar** *verb* [17]
   to infect

infectarse *reflexive verb* [17]
   to become infected
   La herida se infectó. The wound became infected.

ᵈ **infeliz** *masc & fem adjective*, **infelices** *plural*
   unhappy
   ser infeliz to be unhappy

inferior *masc & fem adjective*
1 **lower** (*shelf, part, etc*)
2 **inferior** (*quality*)

infiel *masc & fem adjective*
   unfaithful
   serle infiel a alguien to be unfaithful to someone

ᵈ el **infierno** *masc noun*
   hell

ᵈ el **infinitivo** *masc noun*
   infinitive

ᵈ **infinito** *masc adjective*, **infinita** *fem*
   ▷ see **infinito** *noun*
   infinite

ᵈ el **infinito** *masc noun* ▷ see **infinito** *adj*
   infinity

ᵈ **inflable** *masc & fem adjective*
   inflatable

la **inflación** *fem noun*
   inflation

ᵈ **inflamable** *masc & fem adjective*
   inflammable

ᵈ **inflar** *verb* [17]
1 **to inflate** (*a tyre*)
2 **to blow up** (*a balloon*)

la **influencia** *fem noun*
   influence

influir *verb* [54]
   to influence

ᵈ la **información** *fem noun*
1 **information**
   Busco información sobre el servicio de autobuses. I'm looking for information about the bus service.
   Es una información muy práctica. It's a very useful piece of information.
2 (*in newspaper or TV news*) **news**
   la información internacional the foreign news
3 '**Información**' 'Information Desk' (*in an airport, station, etc*) ▸▸

ᵈ indicates key words   157

4 (*in telephoning*) **directory enquiries**
llamar a información to call directory
enquiries

♪ **informal** *masc & fem adjective*
1 **informal** (*chat, meal*)
2 **casual** (*clothes*)
3 **unreliable** (*person*)

♪ **informar** *verb* [17]
to inform
Me informaron mal. I was misinformed.
¿Podría informarme sobre ... ? Could you
give me information about ... ?

informarse *reflexive verb* [17]
to find out information
Me informaré sobre el horario. I'll find out
about the timetable.

♪ la **informática** *fem noun*
computing, information technology

♪ el **informe** *masc noun*
report

♪ la **infracción** *fem noun*
offence
cometer una infracción to commit an
offence
• la **infracción de tráfico** traffic offence

la **infusión** *fem noun*
herbal tea
la infusión de menta peppermint tea

♪ el **ingeniero** *masc noun*, la **ingeniera** *fem*
engineer
• el **ingeniero agrónomo**, la **ingeniera
agrónoma** agonomist
• el **ingeniero de caminos**, la **ingeniera de
caminos** civil engineer

♪ **ingenuo** *masc adjective*, **ingenua** *fem*
▷ see **ingenuo** *noun*
naive

♪ el **ingenuo** *masc noun*, la **ingenua** *fem*
▷ see **ingenuo** *adj*
Eres un ingenuo. You're so naive.

♪ **Inglaterra** *fem noun*
England
Soy de Inglaterra. I'm from England.

♪ **inglés** *masc adjective*, **inglesa** *fem*
▷ see **inglés** *noun*
English

♪ un **inglés** *masc noun*, una **inglesa** *fem*
▷ see **inglés** *adj*
1 **Englishman**
2 **Englishwoman**
3 los ingleses the English, English people

4 el inglés English (*the language*)
¿Hablas inglés? Do you speak English.

WORD TIP Adjectives and nouns for nationality,
regional origin, and language do not have capital
letters in Spanish.

ingrato *masc adjective*, **ingrata** *fem*
ungrateful

♪ el **ingrediente** *masc noun*
ingredient

el **ingreso** *masc noun*
1 **admission** (*to hospital, university*)
2 **deposit** (*in a bank account*)
3 los ingresos income

♪ **inicial** *masc & fem adjective*
▷ see **inicial** *noun*
initial

♪ la **inicial** *fem noun* ▷ see **inicial** *adj*
initial
Estas son mis iniciales. These are my
initials.

la **iniciativa** *fem noun*
initiative
por iniciativa propia on her own initiative

♪ **injusto** *masc adjective*, **injusta** *fem*
unfair

inmaduro *masc adjective*, **inmadura** *fem*
immature

las **inmediaciones** *plural fem noun*
surrounding area
en las inmediaciones de Bilbao in the area
surrounding Bilbao

♪ **inmediatamente** *adverb*
immediately

♪ **inmediato** *masc adjective*, **inmediata** *fem*
immediate
de inmediato immediately
Volvieron de inmediato. They came back
immediately.

♪ **inmenso** *masc adjective*, **inmensa** *fem*
1 **immense** (*happiness, quantity*)
2 **huge** (*house, room*)

♪ la **inmigración** *fem noun*
immigration

♪ el & la **inmigrante** *masc & fem noun*
immigrant

la **inmobiliaria** *fem noun*
1 **estate agent's**
2 **building company** (*developing housing,
tourist resorts, etc*)

♪ **inmoral** *masc & fem adjective*
immoral

inmunizar *verb* [22]
  to immunize

ꝗ **innecesario** *masc adjective*, **innecesaria** *fem*
  unnecessary

la **innovación** *fem noun*
  innovation

innumerable *masc & fem adjective*
  countless

la **inocentada** *fem noun*
  practical joke
  gastarle una inocentada a alguien to play a practical joke on someone (*Often one played on 28 December, which is similar to April Fool's Day.*)

ꝗ **inocente** *masc & fem adjective*
  1 innocent
  2 naive▷ **día**

ꝗ **inofensivo** *masc adjective*, **inofensiva** *fem*
  harmless

ꝗ **inolvidable** *masc & fem adjective*
  unforgettable
  unas vacaciones inolvidables an unforgetable holiday

ꝗ **inoxidable** *masc & fem adjective*
  rust-proof
  el acero inoxidable stainless steel

ꝗ **inquieto** *masc adjective*, **inquieta** *fem*
  1 worried
  2 restless

la **inquietud** *fem noun*
  1 worry
  2 interest
  Es una persona con inquietudes. She's a person with many interests.
  3 restlessness

ꝗ el **inquilino** *masc noun*, la **inquilina** *fem*
  tenant

ꝗ **inscribir** *verb* [52]
  1 to register (*on a course*)
  2 to engrave

inscribirse *reflexive verb* [52]
  to register

ꝗ la **inscripción** *fem noun*
  1 registration (*on a course*)
  La inscripción es el martes. Registration is on Tuesday.
  2 inscription

ꝗ el **insecto** *masc noun*
  insect

insertar *verb* [17]
  to insert

insignificante *masc & fem adjective*
  insignificant

ꝗ **insistir** *verb* [19]
  to insist
  insistir en algo to insist on something
  Insiste en que es verdad. She insists that it's true.

ꝗ la **insolación** *fem noun*
  sunstroke
  coger una insolación to get sunstroke

ꝗ **insolente** *masc & fem adjective*
  rude

insólito *masc adjective*, **insólita** *fem*
  unheard of
  un acontecimiento insólito an unheard of event

insonorizado *masc adjective*, **insonorizada** *fem*
  soundproofed

ꝗ **insoportable** *masc & fem adjective*
  unbearable

la **inspección** *fem noun*
  inspection

inspeccionar *verb* [17]
  to inspect

ꝗ el **inspector** *masc noun*, la **inspectora** *fem*
  inspector

la **inspiración** *fem noun*
  inspiration

inspirar *verb* [17]
  to inspire

inspirarse *reflexive verb* [17]
  inspirarse en algo to be inspired by something
  Se inspiró en la naturaleza. He was inspired by nature.

la **instalación** *fem noun*
  installation

ꝗ **instalar** *verb* [17]
  to install (*a washing machine, a computer*)

instalarse *reflexive verb* [17]
  to install yourself
  Se instaló en el sillón. He installed himself in the armchair.

instantáneo *masc adjective*, **instantánea** *fem*
  1 instant (*coffee, soup*)
  2 immediate (*reaction, result*)

♂ el **instante** *masc noun*
  moment
  Vuelvo en un instante. I'll be back in a moment.
  Un instante, por favor. One moment, please.
  Hacían preguntas a cada instante. They asked questions constantly.

♂ el **instinto** *masc noun*
  instinct
  por instinto instinctively
  • el **instinto de conservación** survival instinct

♂ el **instituto** *masc noun*
  1 **institute**
  2 **(secondary) school**

♂ la **instrucción** *fem noun*
  1 **education**
  2 las instrucciones **instructions** (*for a computer, TV, etc*)

♂ el **instructor** *masc noun*, la **instructora** *fem*
  instructor
  • el **instructor de autoescuela** driving instructor
  • el **instructor de esquí** ski instructor

instruir *verb* [54]
  1 **to instruct**
  2 **to educate**

♂ el **instrumento** *masc noun*
  instrument
  tocar un instrumento to play an instrument

insuficiente *masc & fem adjective*
  ▷ see **insuficiente** *noun*
  inadequate

♂ el **insuficiente** *masc noun*
  ▷ see **insuficiente** *adj*
  fail (*in exams*)

♂ **insultar** *verb* [17]
  to insult

♂ el **insulto** *masc noun*
  insult

♂ **intacto** *masc adjective*, **intacta** *fem*
  undamaged, **in one piece**
  El envío llegó intacto. The consignment arrived undamaged.

♂ **integral** *masc & fem adjective*
  1 **comprehensive** (*plan, education*)
  2 **wholemeal** (*flour, bread*)

íntegro *masc adjective*, **íntegra** *fem*
  complete (*text*)
  la versión íntegra de la película the full-length version of the film

el **integrismo** *masc noun*
  (*Religion*) **fundamentalism**

♂ **intelectual** *masc & fem adjective*
  ▷ see **intelectual** *noun*
  intellectual

♂ el & la **intelectual** *masc & fem noun*
  ▷ see **intelectual** *adj*
  intellectual

♂ la **inteligencia** *fem noun*
  intelligence

♂ **inteligente** *masc & fem adjective*
  1 **intelligent**
  2 **smart** (*bomb, terminal*)

♂ la **intención** *fem noun*
  intention
  Esa fue mi intención. That was my intention.
  No era mi intención ofenderla. I didn't mean to offend her.
  Tiene buenas intenciones. She means well.
  Lo hizo con la intención de ayudar. He did it with the intention of helping.

♂ **intensivo** *masc adjective*, **intensiva** *fem*
  intensive

♂ **intenso** *masc adjective*, **intensa** *fem*
  intense

♂ **intentar** *verb* [17]
  to try
  ¡Inténtalo otra vez! Try again!
  intentar hacer algo to try to do something
  Intenté cerrarlo. I tried to shut it.
  Intenta llegar temprano. Try to arrive early.

el **intento** *masc noun*
  attempt
  Lo consiguió al tercer intento. She succeeded at the third attempt.

♂ **intercambiar** *verb* [17]
  1 **to exchange** (*ideas*)
  2 **to swap** (*stamps, magazines, toys*)

intercambiarse *reflexive verb* [17]
  to swap
  Se intercambiaron los números de teléfono. They swapped telephone numbers.

♂ el **intercambio** *masc noun*
  1 **exchange** (*of ideas*)
  2 **swap** (*of stamps, magazines*)

3 **exchange** (*visit*)
Fui a Málaga de intercambio. I went to
Málaga on an exchange.

♂ el **interés** *masc noun*
interest
su interés por la historia her interest in
history
Es de gran interés para mí. It's of great
interest to me.

♂ **interesante** *masc & fem adjective*
interesting
una película interesante an interesting
film
Resultó poco interesante. It wasn't very
interesting.

♂ **interesar** *verb* [17]
1 interesarle algo a alguien to be interested
in something
Me interesa el deporte. I'm interested in
sport.
¿Te interesa la historia? Are you interested
in history?

2 **to have to do with**
Eso no le interesa. That doesn't have
anything to do with her.

interesarse *reflexive verb* [17]
interesarse por algo to take an interest in
something
Se interesa por todo lo que hago. He takes
an interest in everything I do.

♂ el **interfono** *masc noun*
1 **entryphone**
2 **intercom**

♂ **interior** *masc & fem adjective*
▷ see **interior** *noun*
1 **interior**
una escalera interior an interior staircase
un piso interior a flat with windows facing
into an inner courtyard
2 **inside**
en la parte interior on the inside

♂ el **interior** *masc noun* ▷ see **interior** *adj*
1 **inside**
el interior de la caja the inside of the box
En mi interior, tenía miedo. Deep down
inside, I was afraid.
2 **interior** (*of a country*)

♂ **intermedio** *masc adjective*, **intermedia**
fem ▷ see **intermedio** *noun*
1 **intermediate** (*level, stage*)
2 **medium**
de tamaño intermedio medium-sized

♂ el **intermedio** *masc noun*
▷ see **intermedio** *adj*
interval

♂ **intermitente** *masc & fem adjective*
flashing (*light*)

♂ **internacional** *masc & fem adjective*
international
un vuelo internacional an international
flight

♂ el **internado** *masc noun*
boarding school

♂ el & la **internauta** *masc & fem noun*
surfer (*on the Internet*)

♂ **Internet** *masc noun*
Internet
la era de Internet the age of the Internet
en Internet on the Internet
estar conectado a Internet to be on the
Internet

WORD TIP *Internet in Spanish is normally used
without el.*

♂ **interno** *masc adjective*, **interna** *fem*
▷ see **interno** *noun*
internal

♂ el **interno** *masc noun*, la **interna** *fem*
▷ see **interno** *adj*
boarder (*in a boarding school*)

♂ **interpretar** *verb* [17]
1 **to interpret** (*a comment, a text*)
2 interpretar un papel to play a part (*in a play,
a film, etc*)
interpretar una canción to sing a song
interpretar una pieza de música to perform
a piece of music

♂ el & la **intérprete** *masc & fem noun*
1 **interpreter**
2 **performer** (*of a piece of music*)
3 **singer** (*of a song*)

la **interrogación** *fem noun*
interrogation

♂ el & la **interrogante** *masc & fem noun*
1 **question**
Quedan muchos interrogantes sin
responder. There are many questions left
unanswered.
2 **question mark**
Pon un interrogante. Write a question
mark.

♂ **interrogar** *verb* [28]
1 **to question** (*a suspect*)
2 **to interrogate** (*a prisoner*)

a
b
c
d
e
f
g
h
i
j
k
l
m
n
ñ
o
p
q
r
s
t
u
v
w
x
y
z

ℰ **interrumpir** *verb* [19]
1 to interrupt
Perdone que interrumpa. Excuse my interrupting.
¡No me interrumpas! Don't interrupt.
2 to stop
Las lluvias interrumpieron las obras. The rain stopped the building works.

ℰ la **interrupción** *fem noun*
interruption

ℰ el **interruptor** *masc noun*
switch

ℰ **interurbano** *masc adjective*,
interurbana *fem*
long-distance
una llamada interurbana a long-distance call
un tren interurbano an intercity train

ℰ el **intervalo** *masc noun*
interval

la **intervención** *fem noun*
intervention

intervenir *verb* [15]
1 to take part
intervenir en las discusiones to take part in the discussions
2 to intervene
No quiero intervenir. I don't want to intervene.
3 intervenir a alguien to operate on somebody

ℰ la **interviú** *fem noun*
interview

intimidar *verb* [17]
to intimidate

íntimo *masc adjective*, **íntima** *fem*
1 private
su vida íntima her private life
una cena íntima a very private dinner
2 intimate
un ambiente íntimo an intimate atmosphere
3 close (*friend, friendship*)

intolerante *masc & fem adjective*
intolerant

ℰ la **intoxicación** *fem noun*
poisoning
• la **intoxicación alimenticia** food poisoning

ℰ **intransitivo** *masc adjective*, **intransitiva** *fem*
intransitive

la **intriga** *fem noun*
intrigue

ℰ **introducir** *verb* [60]
1 to introduce
introducir cambios to introduce changes
2 to insert
Introduzca la moneda en la ranura. Insert the coin in the slot.

introducirse *reflexive verb* [60]
to get in
El ladrón se introdujo por la ventana. The burglar got in through the window.
El agua se introducía por las ranuras. The water was coming in through the cracks.

ℰ el **intruso** *masc noun*, la **intrusa** *fem*
intruder

intuitivo *masc adjective*, **intuitiva** *fem*
intuitive

ℰ la **inundación** *fem noun*
flood
Ha habido inundaciones en Cataluña. There have been floods in Catalonia.

ℰ **inútil** *masc & fem adjective*
useless
Es inútil intentarlo. It's useless trying.

ℰ **invadir** *verb* [19]
to invade

ℰ el **inválido** *masc noun*, la **inválida** *fem*
disabled person
los inválidos disabled people

ℰ la **invasión** *fem noun*
invasion

ℰ **inventar** *verb* [17]
1 to invent
2 to make up (*a story, a game*)

inventarse *reflexive verb* [17]
to invent, **to make up**
Se inventó una excusa. He made up an excuse.

ℰ el **invento** *masc noun*
invention
el invento del teléfono
the invention of the telephone

ℰ el **invernadero** *masc noun*
greenhouse

la **inversión** *fem noun*
investment

ℰ **inverso** *masc adjective*, **inversa** *fem*
reverse (*order*)
hacer algo a la inversa to do something the other way round

♂ la **investigación** *fem noun*
1 **investigation** (*of a crime, an accident*)
2 **research**
• la **investigación de mercado** market research

♂ el **invierno** *masc noun*
winter
en invierno in winter
el invierno pasado last winter

invisible *masc & fem adjective*
invisible

♂ la **invitación** *fem noun*
invitation
una invitación para la boda an invitation to the wedding

♂ el **invitado** *masc noun*, la **invitada** *fem*
guest

♂ **invitar** *verb* [17]
1 **to invite**
invitar a alguien a una fiesta to invite someone to a party
Me han invitado a su casa. They've invited me to their house.
2 (*offering to pay*) ¡Yo invito! It's on me!
Te invito a cenar. I'll take you out for dinner.
Nos invitó a una copa. He bought us a drink.

involuntario *masc adjective*, **involuntaria** *fem*
involuntary

♂ la **inyección** *fem noun*
injection

♂ **ir** *verb* [8]
1 **to go** (*to a place*)
¿Adónde vas? Where are you going?
Voy a casa de Alicia. I'm going to Alicia's house.
Iremos al museo. We'll go to the museum.
Aún no va al colegio. She doesn't go to school yet.
El camino va a la playa. The road goes to the beach.
¿Cómo se va a la estación? How do you get to the station?
2 **to go** (*belong in a particular place*)
¿Dónde van los platos? Where do the plates go?
3 **to come**
¡Ya voy! I'm coming!
'¡Fernando!'—'¡Voy!' '¡Fernando!'— 'Coming!'

4 (*talking about progress*) ¿Cómo van las cosas? How are things going?
¿Cómo te va? How are you?
¿Cómo va el enfermo? How's the patient doing?
Todo va muy bien. Everything is going well.
Le va muy bien en el trabajo. Things are going well for him at work.
Me fue muy mal en la entrevista. Things went very badly at the interview.
5 (*for how something works*) La lavadora no va bien. The washing machine is not working properly.
6 (*for how clothes, etc look*) El negro te va bien. Black suits you.
Iba con un abrigo marrón. He was wearing a brown coat.
Iban bien vestidos. They were well dressed.
ir con algo to go with something
Esos zapatos no van con esa falda. Those shoes don't go with that skirt.
7 (*talking about activities*) ir de vacaciones to go on holiday
ir de compras to go shopping
ir a la compra to do the shopping
Siempre voy yo a la compra. I'm always the one who does the shopping.
8 (*saying how you go*) ir a pie to go on foot
ir de pie to stand (all the way)
ir a caballo to go on horseback
ir en coche to go by car
ir en avión to go by plane
ir en bicicleta to go by bike
Fueron en coche. They drove here.
¿Vamos en taxi? Shall we go by taxi?
Va en bicicleta a todas partes. She goes everywhere by bike.
9 ir a hacer algo to be going to do something
Voy a comprar leche. I'm going to buy some milk.
Voy a ser médico. I'm going to be a doctor.
Iré a recogerla. I'll go to pick her up.
¡Te vas a caer! You're going to fall!
Iba a mandártelo hoy. I was going to send it to you today.
Dijo que lo iba a pensar. She said she was going to think it over.
Se lo voy a decir. I'm going to tell him.
10 ir a por algo to go to get something, to fetch something
Voy a por pan. I'm going to get some bread.
ir a por alguien to go to get someone, to fetch somebody ▸▸

Ha ido a por su madre. He's gone to get his mother.
Fuimos a por ella. We went to fetch her.

11 **ir a hacer algo** to go to do something
¿Has ido a verla? ¿Have you been to see her?
Fuimos a ver su casa nueva. We went to see their new house.

12 (*talking about a process*) **ir haciendo algo Su salud va mejorando.** Her health is getting better.
Poco a poco va aprendiendo. She's learning little by little.
La situación ha ido empeorando. The situation has been getting worse and worse.
Iban acercándose. They were getting closer.

13 (*in suggestions and orders*) **¡Vamos!** Come on!
¡Vamos, date prisa! Come on, hurry up!
Vamos a trabajar. Let's get to work.
Vamos a discutir el asunto. Let's discuss the matter.

14 (*expressing surprise, annoyance*) **¡Vaya, si es Carlos!** Hey, it's Carlos!
¡Vaya, se ha fundido la luz! Oh dear, the light has gone!
¡Vaya, no lo encuentro! Bother, I can't find it!
¡Vaya hombre, un billete de cincuenta euros! Hey look, a fifty-euro note!

15 (*saying you don't agree*) '**¿Te molesta?**'— '**¡Qué va!**' 'Do you mind?'—'Not at all!'
'**¿Lo ha hecho él solo?**'—'**¡Qué va!**' 'Did he do it on his own?'—'Not likely!'

irse *reflexive verb* [8]
1 **to leave**
Nos fuimos pronto. We left early.
Bueno, me voy. Well, I'm off.
Vámonos, que se hace tarde. Let's go, it's getting late.
2 **to go away**
Se fueron a casa. They went off home.
3 **to go** (*pain*)
¿Se te ha ido el dolor de cabeza? Has your headache gone?

ᶠ la **ira** *fem noun*
rage
en un arrebato de ira in a fit of rage

Irak *masc noun*
Iraq

Irán *masc noun*
Iran

iraní *masc & fem adjective & noun*, *pl*: **iraníes**
1 **Iranian**
2 **un & una iraní** Iranian

> **WORD TIP** Adjectives and nouns for nationality, regional origin, and language do not have capital letters in Spanish.

iraquí *masc & fem adjective & noun*, *pl*: **iraquíes**
1 **Iraqi**
2 **un & una iraquí** Iraqi

> **WORD TIP** Adjectives and nouns for nationality, regional origin, and language do not have capital letters in Spanish.

ᶠ **Irlanda** *fem noun*
Ireland
Soy de Irlanda. I'm from Ireland.

ᶠ **irlandés** *masc adjective*, **irlandesa** *fem*
▷ see **irlandés** *noun*
Irish

ᶠ un **irlandés** *masc noun*, una **irlandesa** *fem*
▷ see **irlandés** *adj*
1 **Irishman**
2 **Irishwoman**
3 **los irlandeses** the Irish, Irish people
4 **el irlandés** Irish (*the language*)

> **WORD TIP** Adjectives and nouns for nationality, regional origin, and language do not have capital letters in Spanish.

la **ironía** *fem noun*
irony

ᶠ **irónico** *masc adjective*, **irónica** *fem*
ironic

irreal *masc & fem adjective*
unreal

ᶠ **irresponsable** *masc & fem adjective*
irresponsible

la **irritación** *fem noun*
irritation

irritar *verb* [17]
1 **to irritate** (*eyes, throat, skin*)
2 **to irritate**, **to annoy**

irritarse *reflexive verb* [17]
1 **to become irritated** (*eyes, throat, skin*)
2 **to get annoyed**, **to get irritated**

ᶠ la **isla** *fem noun*
island

el **islam**, el **Islam** *masc noun*
(*Religion*) **Islam**

> **WORD TIP** Islam is always used with *el* and may be written with a capital I.

islámico *masc adjective*, **islámica** *fem adjective*
Islamic

> **WORD TIP** Adjectives and nouns for religion do not have capital letters in Spanish.

islandés *masc adjective & noun*, **islandesa** *fem adjective & noun*
1 **Icelander**
2 un islandés, una islandesa Icelander

> **WORD TIP** Adjectives and nouns for nationality and regional origin do not have capital letters in Spanish.

⚜ **Islandia** *fem noun*
Iceland

⚜ **Israel** *masc noun*
Israel

israelí *masc & fem adjective & noun*, *pl:* **israelíes**
1 **Israeli**
2 un & una israelí Israeli

> **WORD TIP** Adjectives and nouns for nationality and regional origin do not have capital letters in Spanish.

⚜ **Italia** *fem noun*
Italy

italiano *masc adjective & noun*, **italiana** *fem adjective & noun*
1 **Italian**
2 un italiano, una italiana Italian
3 el italiano Italian (*the language*)

> **WORD TIP** Adjectives and nouns for nationality, regional origin, and language do not have capital letters in Spanish.

⚜ el **itinerario** *masc noun*
itinerary, **route**

⚜ el **IVA** *masc noun*
(= *Impuesto al Valor Añadido*) **VAT** (*Value Added Tax*)

⚜ la **izquierda** *fem noun* ▷ see **izquierdo** *adj*
1 **left** (*when talking of left and right*)
girar a la izquierda to turn left
Está a la izquierda. It's on the left., It's on the left-hand side.
la segunda calle a la izquierda the second street on the left
Se sentaron a mi izquierda. They sat on my left.
En Gran Bretaña se conduce por la izquierda. In Great Britain you drive on the left.
2 **left hand**
Escribo con la izquierda. I write with my left hand.
3 (*in politics*) la izquierda the left
ser de izquierdas to be left-wing

⚜ **izquierdo** *masc adjective*, **izquierda** *fem* ▷ see **izquierda** *noun*
left (*when talking of left and right*)
la mano izquierda your left hand
el guante izquierdo the left glove
en el cuadro superior izquierdo in the top left-hand square

a
b
c
d
e
f
g
h
i
j
k
l
m
n
ñ
o
p
q
r
s
t
u
v
w
x
y
z

J j

el **jabalí** *masc noun*, jabalíes *plural*
wild boar

ʃ el **jabón** *masc noun*
soap
una pastilla de jabón a bar of soap

la **jabonera** *fem noun*
soapdish

jalar *verb* [ ]
(*Latin America*) **to pull**

el **jalón** *masc noun*
(*Latin America*) **pull**

Jamaica *fem noun*
Jamaica

jamaicano *masc adjective & noun*,
jamaicana *fem adjective & noun*
1 Jamaican
2 un jamaicano, una jamaicana Jamaican

WORD TIP Adjectives and nouns for nationality
and regional origin do not have capital letters in
Spanish.

ʃ **jamás** *adverb*
never
No lo he visto jamás. I've never seen it.
Nunca jamás volveré. I'll never ever go
back again.

ʃ el **jamón** *masc noun*
ham
• el **jamón de York** cooked ham
• el **jamón serrano** cured raw ham

Japón *masc noun*
(el) Japón Japan

japonés *masc adjective & noun*, **japonesa**
fem adjective & noun
1 Japanese
2 un japonés, una japonesa Japanese
3 el japonés Japanese (*the language*)

WORD TIP Adjectives and nouns for nationality,
regional origin, and language do not have capital
letters in Spanish.

el **jaque mate** *masc noun*
(*Chess*) **checkmate**
dar jaque mate a alguien to checkmate
somebody

el **jarabe** *masc noun*
syrup
jarabe para la tos cough mixture

ʃ el **jardín** *masc noun*
1 garden
Nuestra casa tiene un jardín. Our house has
a garden.
• el **jardín de infancia** nursery school

el **jardinero** *masc noun*, la **jardinera** *fem*
gardener

ʃ la **jarra** *fem noun*
jug

el **jarro** *masc noun*
jug

el **jarrón** *masc noun*
vase

la **jaula** *fem noun*
cage

ʃ el **jefe** *masc noun*, la **jefa** *fem*
1 boss (*at work*)
2 manager (*of a company*)
3 chief
el jefe de policía the chief of police
el jefe de bomberos the chief fire officer
4 leader (*of a group*)

el **jengibre** *masc noun*
ginger

ʃ el **jerez** *masc noun*
sherry

ʃ el **jersey** *masc noun*, jerseys *plural*
sweater

Jesucristo *masc noun*
Jesus Christ

el **jinete** *masc noun*
1 rider
2 jockey

los **JJ.OO.** *plural masc abbreviation*
(= *los Juegos Olímpicos*) **Olympic Games**

la **jornada** *fem noun*
day
una jornada de trabajo a working day
trabajar media jornada to work half days
trabajar jornada completa to work full time

ʃ **joven** *masc & fem adjective, pl:* **jóvenes**
▷ see **joven** noun
young
la moda joven young fashion
las personas jóvenes young people

joven

joven

joven **jugar**

el & la joven *masc & fem noun*, pl: **jóvenes**
▷ see **joven** *adj*
1 **young man**
2 **young woman**
3 los jóvenes **young people**

el **jovencito** *masc noun*, la **jovencita** *fem*
1 **young man**
2 **young woman**

la **joya** *fem noun*
1 **piece of jewellery**
No me gustan las joyas. I don't like jewellery.
2 **gem** (*stone, person*)
Esa chica es una joya. That girl's a real gem.

la **joyería** *fem noun*
jeweller's shop

la **jubilación** *fem noun*
retirement

jubilado *masc adjective*, **jubilada** *fem*
▷ see **jubilado** *noun*
retired

el **jubilado** *masc noun*, la **jubilada** *fem*
▷ see **jubilado** *adj*
pensioner
los jubilados **retired people**

jubilarse *reflexive verb* [17]
to retire

el **judaísmo** *masc noun*
Judaism

WORD TIP Adjectives and nouns for religion do not have capital letters in Spanish.

la judía *fem noun* ▷ see **judío** *adj, noun*
bean
• las **judías blancas** haricot beans
• las **judías pintas** kidney beans
• las **judías verdes** green beans

judío *masc adjective*, **judía** *fem*
▷ see **judío** *noun*
Jewish

el **judío** *masc noun*, la **judía** *fem*
▷ see **judío** *adj*
Jew

WORD TIP Adjectives and nouns for religions and peoples do not have capital letters in Spanish.

el **judo** *masc noun*
judo
hacer judo to do judo

juega, juego, etc *verb* ▷ see **juego** *noun*
▷ **jugar**

el juego *masc noun* ▷ see **juega, juego, etc** *verb*
1 **game**
Sólo es un juego. It's only a game.
2 **gambling**
Es aficionado al juego. He likes gambling.
3 **play**
juego limpio fair play
fuera de juego offside
después de diez minutos de juego after ten minutes of play
4 **set**
un juego de llaves a set of keys
5 hacer juego con algo to match something
No hace juego con los pantalones. It doesn't match the trousers.
• el **juego de azar** game of chance
• el **juego de manos** conjuring trick
• el **juego de palabras** play on words
• los **juegos de mesa** board games
• los **Juegos Olímpicos** the Olympic Games
• los **Juegos Paralímpicos** the Paralympic Games

juegue, etc *verb* ▷ **jugar**

la **juerga** *fem noun*
(*informal*) **irse de juerga** to go out partying
Nos fuimos de juerga. We went out partying.

el & la **juerguista** *masc & fem noun*
(*informal*) **party animal**

el jueves *masc noun*
Thursday
el jueves on Thursday
el jueves pasado last Thursday
los jueves on Thursdays
cada jueves every Thursday
Reparten los jueves. They deliver on Thursdays.

WORD TIP Names of months and days start with small letters in Spanish.

el & la **juez** *masc & fem noun*, la **jueza** *fem*, **jueces, juezas** *plural*
1 **judge**
2 **referee**

WORD TIP *juez* and *jueces* can be men and women judges; *jueza* and *juezas* are for women.

el **jugador** *masc noun*, la **jugadora** *fem*
1 **player**
2 **gambler**

jugar *verb* [27]
1 **to play**
jugar al fútbol to play football
jugar a la pelota to play ball ▸▸

Spanish-English

¿A qué quieres jugar? What do you want to play?

2 to gamble
Ahora ya no juega. He doesn't gamble any more.

3 to move (in board games)
Te toca jugar a ti. It's your turn to move.

el **jugo** masc noun
juice
• el **jugo de fruta** fruit juice

jugoso masc adjective, **jugosa** fem
juicy

el **juguete** masc noun
toy
un coche de juguete a toy car

la **juguetería** fem noun
toyshop

el **juicio** masc noun
1 trial (in court)
2 sense
No tiene ningún juicio. He has no sense.
perder el juicio to lose one's mind

ƒ **julio** masc noun
July
en julio in July
el 28 de julio on 28 July

WORD TIP Names of months and days start with small letters in Spanish.

la **jungla** fem noun
jungle

ƒ **junio** masc noun
June
en junio in June
el primero de junio on 1 June

WORD TIP Names of months and days start with small letters in Spanish.

júnior adjective
junior
los jugadores júniors the junior players

la **junta** fem noun
1 committee
2 board (of a company)
3 meeting
4 regional government
una junta autonómica a regional government (in Spain's devolved government system)
la Junta de Andalucía the Andalusian Regional Government

ƒ **juntar** verb [17]
1 to put together
Juntad las mesas. Put the tables together.
2 to join

juntarse reflexive verb [17]
1 to join
Los cables se juntan así. You join the wires like this.
2 to get together
Me junté con unos amigos. I met some friends.
Se han juntado otra vez. They've got together again.
3 to get closer
Juntaos más. Get closer together.

ƒ **junto** masc adjective, **junta** fem
1 together
Ahora todos juntos. All together now.
No los pongas tan juntos. Don't put them so close together.
2 junto a next to
Ponlo junto a la ventana. Put it next to the window.
3 junto con together with
Bátelo junto con los huevos. Beat it up together with the eggs.

el **jurado** masc noun
jury

jurar verb [17]
to swear
Es verdad. Te lo juro. It's true. I swear.

jurídico masc adjective, **jurídica** fem
legal

justamente adverb
1 fairly
No lo han tratado justamente. He hasn't been fairly treated.
2 exactly
¡Justamente! Exactly!
Justamente eso es lo que yo quería decir. That's exactly what I meant.

la **justicia** fem noun
justice

justificar verb [31]
to justify

ƒ **justo** masc adjective, **justa** fem
▷ see **justo** adv
1 fair
una sociedad justa a fair society
No has sido justo con él. You haven't been fair to him.
2 exact
la cantidad justa the exact amount
Son ciento cincuenta euros justos. That's exactly one hundred and fifty euros.
3 lo justo just enough
Viven con lo justo. They have just enough to live on.

Tengo lo justo para el autobús. I have just enough for the bus fare.

4 **tight** (*clothes, shoes*)
Te está un poco justo. It's a bit tight on you.
Los zapatos me quedan muy justos. The shoes are too tight on me.

justo *adverb* ▷ see **justo** *adj*
just
justo a tiempo just in time
justo en frente del cine just opposite the cinema
justo en el centro right in the middle

juvenil *masc & fem adjective*
1 **youthful** (*appearance*)
2 **young** (*fashion*)
3 **junior** (*team or competition*)

la **juventud** *fem noun*
youth
la juventud de hoy the youth of today

el **juzgado** *masc noun*
court

juzgar *verb* [28]
1 **to judge**
Te he juzgado mal. I've misjudged you.
2 **to try** (*a case, a person in court*)

K k

kaki *invariable adjective*
khaki

WORD TIP *kaki* never changes.

el **kárate** *masc noun*
karate
hacer kárate to do karate

el **karting** *masc noun*
go-karting
to go go-karting hacer karting

♂ el **ketchup** *masc noun*
ketchup

Kg. *abbreviation*
(= *kilogramo*) **kg, kilogram**

♂ el **kilo** *masc noun*
kilo

♂ el **kilogramo** *masc noun*
kilogram

♂ el **kilómetro** *masc noun*
kilometre
Está a cinco kilómetros de la costa. It's five kilometres from the sea.

♂ el **kiosco** *masc noun*
1 **kiosk** (*selling sweets, cigarettes, etc*)
2 **newspaper kiosk**
3 **stand**
un kiosko de helados an ice cream stand
el kiosko de la orquesta the bandstand

el **kiwi** *masc noun*
1 **kiwi fruit**
2 **kiwi** (*New Zealand bird*)

Km. *abbreviation*
(= *Kilómetro*) **km, kilometre**

el **koala** *masc noun*
koala bear

a
b
c
d
e
f
g
h
i
j
k
l
m
n
ñ
o
p
q
r
s
t
u
v
w
x
y
z

L l

ſ **la** *fem determiner* ▷ **see la** *pron*
 1 (*before fem sing nouns*) **the**
   la moto the motor bike
   la casa grande the big house
 2 (*with parts of the body, clothes*) **Se rompió la pierna.** She broke her leg.
   Se afeitó la barba. He shaved off his beard.
   Me quité la chaqueta. I took my jacket off.
 3 (*talking about time*) **a las diez de la mañana** at ten in the morning
   Iré la próxima semana. I'll go next week.
 4 (*when la is not translated*)
   irse a la cama to go to bed
   la maleta de Isabel Isabel's suitcase
   la señora Martínez Mrs Martínez
   No me gusta la sandía. I don't like watermelon.
 5 (*for a fem noun, which is known about, e.g. la camisa below.*) **Me gustó la verde.** I liked the green one.
   La mía es roja. Mine is red.
   Esa es la tuya. That one is yours.
   Esta es la de Ana. This one is Ana's.

   WORD TIP See also **el**, **los** and **las**.

ſ **la** *fem pronoun* ▷ **see la** *determiner*
 1 (*as direct object*) **her** (*person*)
   La acompañé a casa. I took her home.
   Voy a verla mañana. I am going to see her tomorrow.
 2 (*as direct object*) **it** (*thing*)
   Compré una camiseta, pero la voy a devolver. I bought a T-shirt, but I'm going to take it back.
   ¡Dámela ahora! Give it to me now!
 3 (*as direct object*) **you** (*polite form*)
   A usted la llamaron hace un momento. They called you a moment ago.

ſ **el labio** *masc noun*
   lip

laborable *masc & fem adjective*
   un día laborable a working day

ſ **el laboratorio** *masc noun*
   laboratory

la laca *fem noun*
 1 **lacquer**
 2 **hairspray**
 • **la laca de uñas** nail varnish

la ladera *fem noun*
   slope

ſ **el lado** *masc noun*
 1 **side**
   el otro lado the other side
   al otro lado de la carretera on the other side of the road
   hacerse a un lado to move aside
   Hazte a un lado. Move aside.
 2 **al lado de** next to
   al lado de Miguel next to Miguel
   Se sentó a mi lado. He sat next to me.
   Viven en la casa de al lado. They live next door.
 3 **de lado**
   Ponlo de lado. Put it on its side.
   tumbarse de lado to lie on your side
 4 **por todos lados** everywhere
   Lo he buscado por todos lados. I've looked for it everywhere.
 5 **en ningún lado**, **por ningún lado** nowhere, not anywhere
   No está por ningún lado. It's nowhere.
   No lo encuentro en ningún lado. I can't find it anywhere.
 6 **en algún lado** somewhere
   Debe estar en algún lado. It must be somewhere.
 7 **por otro lado ...** on the other hand ...
   Por otro lado, hay el problema de ... On the other hand, there's the problem of ...

ſ **ladrar** *verb* [17]
   to bark

ſ **el ladrillo** *masc noun*
   brick

ſ **el ladrón** *masc noun*, **la ladrona** *fem*
 1 **thief**
 2 **burglar**
 3 **robber** (*of banks*)

ſ **el lagarto** *masc noun*
   lizard

ſ **el lago** *masc noun*
   lake

ſ **la lágrima** *fem noun*
   tear

ſ **la laguna** *fem noun*
 1 **lake**
 2 **lagoon**

lamentar *verb* [17]
   to regret
   Lo lamento mucho. I'm very sorry. ▸▸

a
b
c
d
e
f
g
h
i
j
k
l
m
n
ñ
o
p
q
r
s
t
u
v
w
x
y
z

Lamento no poder ayudarle. I'm sorry I can't help you.

Lamento tener que informarle de ... I regret to have to inform you that ...

lamer *verb* [18]
  to lick

♂ la **lámpara** *fem noun*
  lamp
  • la **lámpara de pie** standard lamp

♂ la **lana** *fem noun*
  wool
  una chaqueta de lana a wool jacket
  pura lana virgen pure new wool

♂ la **langosta** *fem noun*
  lobster

♂ el **langostino** *masc noun*
  king prawn

♂ la **lanza** *fem noun*
  spear

el **lanzamiento** *masc noun*
  launch (*of rocket, product*)

♂ **lanzar** *verb* [22]
  1 to throw (*a ball or stone*)
  2 to launch (*a product or an attack*)

lanzarse *reflexive verb* [22]
  1 to throw yourself
    Se lanzó al agua. He threw himself into the water.
    lanzarse en paracaídas to parachute
  2 lanzarse sobre alguien to pounce on someone
    Se lanzó sobre el ladrón. He pounced on the burglar.

♂ el **lápiz** *masc noun*, **lápices** *plural*
  pencil
  • los **lápices de colores** crayons
  • el **lápiz de labios** lipstick
  • el **lápiz de ojos** eyeliner

♂ **largo** *masc adjective*, **larga** *fem*
    ▷ see **largo** *noun*
  1 long
    una falda larga a long skirt
    un largo recorrido a long journey
    Te está muy largo. It's too long for you.
  2 a lo largo de along
    a lo largo de la costa along the coast
  3 a lo largo de throughout
    a lo largo del día throughout the day

♂ el **largo** *masc noun* ▷ see **largo** *adj*
  length
  ¿Cuánto mide de largo? How long is it?

Mide cinco metros de largo. It is five metres long.

♂ **las** *plural fem determiner* ▷ see **las** *pron*
  1 (*before fem plural nouns*) the
    Deja las cajas ahí. Leave the boxes there.
  2 (*with parts of the body, clothes*) Se lavó las manos. She washed her hands.
    Me quité las botas. I took my boots off.
  3 (*talking about time*) a las ocho de la mañana at eight in the morning
    Son las siete y cinco. It's five past seven.
  4 (*when las is not translated*) las maletas de Isabel Isabel's suitcases
    Me gustan las naranjas. I like oranges.
  5 (*for a fem plural noun, which is known about, e.g. las camisetas below*) Las mías son rojas. Mine are red.
    Esas son las tuyas. Those are yours.
    Me gustaron las verdes. I liked the green ones.
  6 Éstas son las de Ana. These ones are Ana's.
    las mías y las de usted mine and yours
    Me gustan más las de Toni. I like Toni's better.
    las que yo compré the ones I bought
    las que quieras whichever you want

  WORD TIP See also *el*, *la* and *los*.

♂ **las** *plural fem pronoun* ▷ see **las** *determiner*
  1 (*as direct object*) them (*people, things*)
    Las vi ayer. I saw them yesterday.
    Te las puedes llevar. You can take them with you.
    Quiero verlas. I want to see them.
    ¡Dámelas ahora! Give them to me now!
  2 (*as direct object*) you (*plural polite form*)
    ¿Las atienden, señoras? Are you being served, ladies?

♂ el **láser** *masc noun*
  laser
  un rayo láser a laser beam

♂ la **lástima** *fem noun*
  ¡Qué lástima! What a shame!
  Su madre me da lástima. I feel sorry for her mother.
  Es una lástima que no puedas venir. How sad that you can't come.

  WORD TIP *ser una lástima que* is followed by a verb in the subjunctive.

♂ la **lata** *fem noun*
  1 tin
    una lata de tomates a tin of tomatoes
    en lata tinned
    unas sardinas en lata tinned sardines
  2 (*informal*) nuisance
    ¡Qué lata! What a nuisance!

Es una lata tener que esperar. It's a nuisance having to wait.
dar la lata (*informal*) to be a nuisance
Siempre están dando la lata. They're always such a nuisance.

ℰ **el latín** *masc noun*
Latin

> **WORD TIP** Use a small letter for languages in Spanish.

ℰ **Latinoamérica** *fem noun*
Latin America

latinoamericano *masc adjective & noun,*
latinoamericana *fem adjective & noun*
1 **Latin American**
2 **un latinoamericano, una latinoamericana** Latin American

> **WORD TIP** Adjectives and nouns for nationality and regional origin do not have capital letters in Spanish.

el latón *masc noun*
brass

ℰ **el laurel** *masc noun*
1 **laurel**
2 **bay tree**
una hoja de laurel a bayleaf

ℰ **el lavabo** *masc noun*
1 **washbasin**
2 **toilet**
¿Dónde están los lavabos? Where are the toilets?

ℰ **el lavado** *masc noun*
wash
- **el lavado a mano** handwashing
- **el lavado en seco** dry cleaning

ℰ **la lavadora** *fem noun*
washing machine
- **la lavadora automática** automatic washing machine

la lavanda *fem noun*
lavender

ℰ **la lavandería** *fem noun*
1 **laundry**
2 **laundrette**

ℰ **el lavaplatos** *masc noun*, lavaplatos *plural*
dishwasher

ℰ **lavar** *verb* [17]
1 **to wash**
lavar los platos to wash the dishes
Lavé la ropa. I washed the clothes.
Lavó el coche. He washed the car.
2 **lavar un abrigo en seco** to dry-clean a coat

lavarse *reflexive verb* [17]
to wash
lavarse las manos to wash your hands
lavarse los dientes to clean your teeth
lavarse el pelo to wash your hair
Me lavo la cabeza todos los días. I wash my hair everyday.

ℰ **el lavavajillas** *masc noun,*
pl: los **lavavajillas**
dishwasher

ℰ **el lazo** *masc noun*
ribbon

ℰ **la** *fem pronoun* ▷ see **la** *determiner*
1 (*as direct object*) **her** (*person*)
La acompañé a casa. I took her home.
Voy a verla mañana. I am going to see her tomorrow.
2 (*as direct object*) **it** (*thing*)
Compré una camiseta, pero la voy a devolver. I bought a T-shirt, but I'm going to take it back.
¡Dámela ahora! Give it to me now!
3 (*as direct object*) **you** (*polite form*)
A usted la llamaron hace un momento. They called you a moment ago.

ℰ **le** *masc & fem pronoun*
1 (*as indirect object*) **him**
Le di las llaves. I gave him the keys.
Le mandé el paquete el lunes. I sent him the parcel on Monday.
¿Qué le quitaron? What did they take from him?
Tengo algo que decirle. I've got something to tell him.
Dale las llaves. Give him the keys.
2 (*as indirect object*) **her**
Le mandé el paquete el lunes. I sent her the parcel on Monday.
Me encontré con Inés y le di las llaves. I met Inés and gave her the keys.
¿Qué le quitaron? What did they take from her?
Tengo algo que decirle. I've got something to tell her.
Dale las llaves. Give her the keys.
3 (*as indirect object*) **you** (*polite form*)
Tengo algo que decirle. I've got something to tell you.
Le mandé el paquete el lunes. I sent you the parcel on Monday.
¿Le llevo las maletas a su habitación? Shall I carry your suitcases to your room?
4 (*as indirect object*) **it**
Le puse la tapa. I put the lid on it.
Le puse otra estantería. I added another shelf to it.

a
b
c
d
e
f
g
h
i
j
k
l
m
n
ñ
o
p
q
r
s
t
u
v
w
x
y
z

♂ la **lección** *fem noun*
lesson

♂ la **leche** *fem noun*
milk
- la **leche descremada**, la **leche desnatada**
skimmed milk
- la **leche en polvo** powdered milk
- la **leche entera** full-cream milk

♂ la **lechuga** *fem noun*
lettuce

el **lector** *masc noun*, la **lectora** *fem*
reader
- el **lector de DVD** DVD player

♂ la **lectura** *fem noun*
reading

WORD TIP *lectura* does not mean *lecture* in
English; for the meaning of *lecture* ▷ **conferencia**.

♂ **leer** *verb* [37]
to read
Estoy leyendo una novela I'm reading a
novel.
¿Has leído a Lorca? Have you read Lorca?

legal *masc & fem adjective*
legal

legendario *masc adjective*, **legendaria**
fem
legendary

♂ las **legumbres** *plural fem noun*
1 **pulses** (beans, lentils, etc)
2 **vegetables**

♂ **lejano** *masc adjective*, **lejana** *fem*
distant
Son parientes lejanos. They are distant
relatives.

el **Lejano Oriente** *masc noun*
the Far East

♂ la **lejía** *fem noun*
bleach

♂ **lejos** *adverb*
1 **far**
No está muy lejos. It's not very far.
¿Está lejos de aquí? Is it far from here?
Está demasiado lejos para ir andando. It's
too far to walk.
2 **a long way**
Está muy lejos. It's a long way (away).
Está lejos del centro. It's a long way from
the centre.
Viven lejos de aquí. They live a long way
from here.

3 desde lejos from a long way off
Desde lejos se ve la catedral. You can see
the cathedral from a long way off.

♂ la **lengua** *fem noun*
1 **tongue**
morderse la lengua to bite your tongue
2 **language**
una lengua muy difícil a very difficult
language
- la **lengua materna** mother tongue

♂ el **lenguado** *masc noun*
sole (*the fish*)

♂ el **lenguaje** *masc noun*
language
- el **lenguaje corporal** body language

♂ **lentamente** *adverb*
slowly

♂ la **lente** *fem noun*
lens
- las **lentes de contacto** contact lenses

♂ la **lenteja** *fem noun*
lentil

los **lentes** *plural masc noun*
(*Latin America*) **glasses**

la **lentilla** *fem noun*
contact lens

♂ **lento** *masc adjective*, **lenta** *fem*
▷ see **lento** *adv*
slow
Son muy lentos. They're very slow.

♂ **lento** *adverb* ▷ see **lento** *adj*
slowly
Caminan muy lento. They're walking very
slowly.

♂ la **leña** *fem noun*
firewood

♂ el **leño** *masc noun*
log

♂ **leo** *masc & fem noun* ▷ see **Leo** *noun*
Leo
Es leo. She's Leo.

WORD TIP Use a small letter in Spanish to say *I
am Leo*, etc with star signs.

♂ el **Leo** *masc noun* ▷ see **leo** *noun*
Leo (*star sign*)

♂ el **león** *masc noun*, la **leona** *fem*
1 **lion**
2 **lioness**

♂ el **leopardo** *masc noun*
leopard

a
b
c
d
e
f
g
h
i
j
k
l
m
n
ñ
o
p
q
r
s
t
u
v
w
x
y
z

los **leotardos** *plural masc noun*
  woollen tights

ƒ **les** *plural masc & fem pronoun*
1 (*as indirect object*) **them**
  Les di las llaves. I gave them the keys.
  Les mandé el paquete el martes. I sent
  them the parcel on Tuesday.
  Tengo algo que decirles. I've got
  something to tell them.
  Dales las llaves. Give them the keys.
  ¿Qué les quitaron? What did they take
  from them?
  Les puse la tapa. I put the lids on them.
2 (*as indirect object*) **you** (*plural polite form*)
  Les mandé el paquete el martes. I sent you
  the parcel on Tuesday.
  Tengo algo que darles. I've got something
  to give you.

ƒ la **lesión** *fem noun*
  injury

letón *masc adjective & noun*, **letona** *fem
adjective & noun*
1 **Latvian**
2 un letón, una letona Latvian

> **WORD TIP** Adjectives and nouns for nationality
> and regional origin do not have capital letters in
> Spanish.

ƒ **Letonia** *fem noun*
  Latvia

ƒ la **letra** *fem noun*
1 **letter** (*of the alphabet*)
2 **handwriting**
  Tiene muy buena letra. Her handwriting is
  very good.
  Casi no se le entiende la letra. You can
  hardly read his handwriting.
3 **lyrics** (*of a song*)
  • la **letra mayúscula** capital letter
  • la **letra minúscula** lower-case letter

ƒ el **letrero** *masc noun*
  notice, sign

la **levadura** *fem noun*
  yeast

leve *masc & fem adjective*
  minor (*injury*)

ƒ **levantar** *verb* [17]
1 **to lift**
  levantar un peso to lift a weight
  Levanta la tapa. Lift the lid.
2 **to raise**
  levantar la mano to raise your hand
  levantar la voz to raise your voice

3 **to pick up**
  Levantamos a la niña del suelo. We picked
  the girl up from the floor.
4 levantar la mesa to clear the table

levantarse *reflexive verb* [17]
1 **to get up** (*out of bed*)
  Me levanto a las siete. I get up at seven
  o'clock.
  Los domingos nos levantamos tarde. On
  Sundays we get up late.
2 **to get up, to stand up**
  Todos se levantaron. Everyone stood up.
  levantarse de la mesa to get up from the
  table

ƒ la **ley** *fem noun*
  law
  violar la ley to break the law

ƒ la **leyenda** *fem noun*
1 **legend**
2 **key** (*to a map*)

ƒ **leyó** *verb* ▷ **leer**

libanés *masc adjective & noun*, **libanesa** *fem
adjective & noun*
1 **Lebanese**
2 un libanés, una libanesa Lebanese

> **WORD TIP** Adjectives and nouns for nationality
> and regional origin do not have capital letters in
> Spanish.

Líbano *masc noun*
  (el) Líbano Lebanon

ƒ **liberar** *verb* [17]
1 **to free**
2 **to liberate**

ƒ la **libertad** *fem noun*
  freedom
  • la **libertad condicional** parole
  • la **libertad de expresión** freedom of
  speech

ƒ la **libra** *fem noun* ▷ see **libra, Libra** *noun*
  pound
  diez libras esterlinas ten pounds sterling

ƒ **libra** *masc & fem noun* ▷ see **libra,
  Libra** *noun*
  Libra
  Susana es libra. Susana's Libra.

> **WORD TIP** Use a small letter in Spanish to say *I
> am Libra*, etc with star signs.

ƒ el **Libra** *masc noun* ▷ see **libra** *noun*
  Libra (*star sign*)

librar *verb* [17]
  librar a alguien de algo to save someone
  from something ▸▸

a
b
c
d
e
f
g
h
i
j
k
l
m
n
ñ
o
p
q
r
s
t
u
v
w
x
y
z

Los libraron de morir ahogados. He saved them from drowning.

librarse *reflexive verb* [17]

1 **librarse de algo** to save yourself from something
Se libró de morir ahogado. He saved himself from drowning.
Me libré del castigo. I escaped punishment.

2 **librarse de una obligación** to get out of an obligation
Se libró de lavar los platos. He got out of doing the dishes.

ℰ **libre** *masc & fem adjective*

1 **free**
un país libre a free country
en mis ratos libres in my free time
Tengo el día libre. I'm free all day.
¿Está libre este asiento? Is this seat free?
los quinientos metros libres the five hundred metres freestyle

2 **trabajar por libre** to work freelance
Trabaja por libre como traductora. She works as a freelance translator.

ℰ la **librería** *fem noun*

1 **bookshop**
2 **bookcase**

WORD TIP *librería* does not mean *library* in English; for the meaning of *library* ▷ **biblioteca**.

ℰ la **libreta** *fem noun*
notebook

ℰ el **libro** *masc noun*
book
• el **libro de bolsillo** paperback
• el **libro de reclamaciones** complaints book (*in hotels etc*)
• el **libro de texto** text book

🛈 *mini-info* **libro de familia**

Cada familia en España recibe un Libro de Familia del gobierno como registro oficial. Hay que presentar este libro cuando los hijos tienen 14 años por ejemplo, para obtener su Documento Nacional de Identidad (DNI).

ℰ la **licencia** *fem noun*
licence, **permit**

el **licenciado** *masc noun*, la **licenciada** *fem*
graduate

la **licenciatura** *fem noun*
university degree

ℰ el **licor** *masc noun*
liqueur

ℰ la **licuadora** *fem noun*
liquidizer

ℰ el & la **líder** *masc & fem noun*
leader (*of a political party, union, etc*)

ℰ la **liebre** *fem noun*
hare

ℰ la **liga** *fem noun*
league
la liga de fútbol the football league

ligeramente *adverb*
slightly

ℰ **ligero** *masc adjective*, **ligera** *fem*

1 **light** (*not heavy*)
un paquete ligero a light parcel
tener el sueño ligero to be a light sleeper

2 **slight**
un ligero sabor a almendras a slight taste of almonds
Hay un ligero problema. There's a slight problem.

3 **thin** (*fabric*)

4 **fast**
un caballo muy ligero a very fast horse

ℰ la **lima** *fem noun*

1 **file** (*tool*)
2 **lime** (*fruit*)
• la **lima de uñas** nail file

ℰ **limitar** *verb* [17]

1 **to limit**
Tuvieron que limitar el número de estudiantes. They had to limit the number of students.

2 **limitar con un país** to border on a country
España limita con Francia. Spain borders on France.

limitarse *reflexive verb* [17]
limitarse a algo: Me limité a hacer sólo una pregunta. I limited myself to asking one question.
Me limité a ayudarlos con el ordenador. I just helped them with the computer.

ℰ el **límite** *masc noun*

1 **limit**
Hay un tiempo límite. There's a time limit.
2 **la fecha límite** the deadline
3 **border** (*of a country*)
• el **límite de velocidad** speed limit

ℰ el **limón** *masc noun*
lemon

ℰ la **limonada** *fem noun*
lemonade

♂ el **limonero** *masc noun*
  lemon tree

la **limosna** *fem noun*
  pedir limosna to beg
  Nunca doy limosna. I never give money to
  beggars.

♂ el **limpiaparabrisas** *masc noun, pl:* los
  limpiaparabrisas
  windscreen wiper

♂ **limpiar** *verb* [17]
  1 **to clean**
    limpiar la casa to clean the house
    Limpié los zapatos. I cleaned my shoes.
  2 **to clean off**
    Limpió la mancha que había en la mesa.
    She cleaned the dirty mark off the table.
  3 **to wipe**
  4 **Limpió la mesa con un trapo.** He wiped the
    table.
  5 **limpiar algo en seco** to dry-clean
    something
    Hay que limpiarlo en seco. It must be dry-
    cleaned.

♂ la **limpieza** *fem noun*
  1 **cleanliness**
  2 **cleaning**
    hacer la limpieza to do the cleaning
    la señora de la limpieza the cleaning lady
  • la **limpieza de cutis** facial
  • la **limpieza en seco** dry-cleaning

la **limpieza general** *fem noun*
  spring-clean
  Voy a hacer una limpieza general. I'm
  going to have a spring-clean.

♂ **limpio** *masc adjective,* **limpia** *fem*
  1 **clean**
    ¿Tienes las manos limpias? Are your hands
    clean?
  2 **clear** *(sky)*
    un cielo limpio, sin nubes a clear, cloudless
    sky
  3 **fair** *(game, business deal)*
  4 **pasar algo a limpio** to make a fair copy of
    something
    Tuve que pasar a limpio la redacción. I had
    to make a fair copy of the essay.

♂ el **lince**
  lynx *(the animal)*

♂ **lindo** *masc adjective,* **linda** *fem*
  lovely

♂ la **línea** *fem noun*
  1 **line** *(mark)*
    una línea recta a straight line

2 **line** *(of a poem, letter, etc)*
  escribirle unas líneas a alguien to drop
  someone a line
  leer entre líneas to read between the lines
3 **line** *(in telecommunications)*
  Se ha cortado la línea. The line has gone
  dead.
4 **line** *(of products)*
  una nueva línea de juegos a new line of
  games
5 **de primera línea** top-quality
  productos de primera línea top-quality
  products
  un jugador de primera línea a top player
6 **line** *(of the railway, metro)*
  el final de la línea the end of the line
  No hay servicio en la línea 5. There is no
  service on Line 5.
7 **route** *(of a bus service)*
  No hay servicio en la línea 5. There is no
  service on route number 5.
  No hay línea directa. There is no direct
  service.
8 **figure**
  cuidar la línea to watch your figure
  • la **línea aérea** airline
  • la **línea de llegada** finishing line
  • la **línea de meta** goal line
  • la **línea regular** airline *(operating scheduled
    flights)*
  • la **línea telefónica** telephone line

♂ el **lino** *masc noun*
  linen

♂ la **linterna** *fem noun*
  torch

♂ el **lío** *masc noun (informal)*
  1 **mess**
    hacerse un lío to get muddled up
    ¡Vaya lío! What a mess!
    Me hice un lío con las fechas. I got the dates
    all muddled up.
  2 **trouble**
    ¡No te metas en líos! Keep out of trouble!
    armar un lío to kick up a fuss
    Armó un lío tremendo. He kicked up a real
    fuss.

♂ la **liquidación** *fem noun*
  1 **sale**
  2 **liquidation** *(of a business)*
    entrar en liquidación to go into liquidation
  3 **settlement** *(of a debt, an account)*
    • la **liquidación por cierre** closing-down
      sale
    • la **liquidación total** clearance sale

a
b
c
d
e
f
g
h
i
j
k
l
m
n
ñ
o
p
q
r
s
t
u
v
w
x
y
z

♂ **líquido** *masc adjective*, **líquida** *fem*
▷ see **líquido** *noun*
liquid

♂ el **líquido** *masc noun* ▷ see **líquido** *adj*
liquid

♂ **liso** *masc adjective*, **lisa** *fem*
1 **smooth** (*skin, surface*)
2 **straight** (*hair*)
3 **flat** (*ground*)

♂ la **lista** *fem noun* ▷ see **listo** *adj*
1 **list**
hacer una lista to make a list
No estás en la lista. You're not on the list.
2 **register** (*at school*)
pasar lista to take the register
• la **lista de bodas** wedding list
• la **lista de espera** waiting list
• la **lista de la compra** shopping list
• la **lista de precios** price list
• la **lista de vinos** wine list

♂ el **listín** *masc noun*
telephone directory, **phone book**

♂ **listo** *masc adjective*, **lista** *adjective*
▷ see **lista** *noun*
1 **clever**
Se cree muy lista. She thinks she's very
clever.
2 **ready**
estar listo to be ready
Ya estamos listos para salir. We're ready to
go now.

♂ la **litera** *fem noun*
1 **bunk bed** (*piece of furniture*)
2 **berth** (*in a ship*)
3 **couchette** (*on a train*)

♂ la **literatura** *fem noun*
literature

♂ el **litro** *masc noun*
litre

♂ **Lituania** *fem noun*
Lithuania

lituano *masc adjective & noun*, **lituana** *fem
adjective & noun*
1 **Lithuanian**
2 **un lituano, una lituana** Lithuanian

WORD TIP Adjectives and nouns for nationality
and regional origin do not have capital letters in
Spanish.

♂ la **llama** *fem noun*
1 **flame**
2 **llama**

♂ la **llamada** *fem noun*
call
• la **llamada a cobro revertido** reverse-
charge call
• la **llamada interurbana** long-distance call
• la **llamada telefónica** telephone call
• la **llamada urbana** local call

♂ **llamar** *verb* [17]
1 **to call**
Te llama tu madre. Your mother is calling
you.
llamar al médico to call the doctor
Llamamos a un taxi. We called a taxi.
La llamamos Tintina. We call her Tintina.
2 **to phone**
¿Cuándo llamarás? When will you phone?
llamar a alguien por teléfono to phone
someone
Lo llamé por teléfono. I phoned him.

llamarse *reflexive verb* [17]
to be called
Se llama Ángeles. She's called Ángeles.
¿Cómo te llamas? What's your name?

llano *masc adjective*, **llana** *fem*
flat, **level** (*ground*)

♂ la **llave** *fem noun*
1 **key**
cerrar algo con llave to lock something
Cerró la puerta con llave. He locked the
door.
2 **switch** (*for a light*)
3 (*Latin America*) **tap**
4 **spanner**
• la **llave de contacto** ignition key
• la **llave de judo** judo hold
• la **llave inglesa** adjustable spanner
• la **llave maestra** master key

♂ el **llavero** *masc noun*
keyring

♂ la **llegada** *fem noun*
arrival
A su llegada al hotel ... On his arrival at the
hotel ...

♂ **llegar** *verb* [28]
1 **to arrive**
¿Cuándo llegan tus primos? When are your
cousins arriving?
Llegan a las siete. They arrive at seven.
Siempre llega tarde. He's always late.
Llegó justo a tiempo. He was just in time.
llegar a un lugar to arrive somewhere
Llegó a Madrid. He arrived in Madrid
Llegó al aeropuerto a las dos. She arrived at
the airport at two o'clock.
Cenaremos cuando lleguemos a casa.

We'll have dinner when we get home.
llegar de un lugar to arrive from somewhere
Acaba de llegar de Caracas. He's just arrived from Caracas.

2 to come
Ya llega el invierno. Winter is coming.
Pensé que nunca llegaría este momento. I thought this moment would never come.

3 to reach
Las cortinas llegan hasta el suelo. The curtains go down to the floor.
No llego a la lámpara. I can't reach the lamp.
Esa cuerda no llega al otro lado. That rope won't reach the other side.
Llegué a la conclusión de que mentía. I reached the conclusion that he was lying.
Llegamos a un acuerdo. We reached an agreement.

4 to be enough
Con tres litros de leche llega para todos. Three litres of milk will be enough for everybody.
No me llega el dinero. I have'nt got enough money.

5 llegar a hacer algo to get to do something
Llegué a conocerlo. I got to meet him.
No llegué a verlo. I didn't get to see it.

6 llegar a ser to become
Llegó a ser famoso. He became famous.
Nunca llegó a director. He never became director.

ℰ **llenar** verb [17]

1 to fill
llenar la bañera to fill the bath
Llene el depósito, por favor. Fill up the tank, please.
llenar algo de algo to fill something up with something
Llené la bañera de agua. I filled the bath up with water.
Le llenaron la cabeza de ideas. They filled his head with ideas.

2 fill in (a form)
Llenó la solicitud. She filled in the application form.

llenarse reflexive verb [17]
to fill up
El tren siempre se llena aquí. The train always fills up here.
llenarse de algo to fill with something
El cubo se llenó de agua. The bucket filled with water.
Se le llenaron los ojos de lágrimas. Her eyes filled with tears.

ℰ **lleno** masc adjective, **llena** fem

1 full
estar lleno de algo to be full of something
La botella está llena de agua. The bottle is full of water.

2 covered
estar lleno de algo to be covered with something
El suelo estaba lleno de papeles. The floor was covered with papers.

3 full (of food)
No gracias, estoy lleno. No thanks, I'm full.

ℰ **llevar** verb [17]

1 to take (from one place to another)
Te lo puedes llevar. You can take it with you.
Le llevé unas flores. I took her some flowers.
Llevaré una botella de vino a la fiesta. I'll take a bottle of wine to the party.
Te lo llevaré el sábado. I'll bring it on Saturday.
Yo te puedo llevar a la estación. I can take you to the station.
La llevé a comer a un restaurante. I took her for lunch to a restaurant.
La llevé en coche a su casa. I drove her home.

2 to carry
Yo llevaba al niño en brazos. I was carrying the baby in my arms.
Los atracadores llevaban pistolas. The robbers carried guns.

3 to have
¿Qué llevas en el bolso? What have you got in your bag?
No llevo las llaves encima. I don't have the keys on me.

4 to wear
No llevo reloj. I'm not wearing a watch.
Llevaba un vestido verde. She was wearing a green dress.

5 to take (time)
Lleva tiempo. It takes time.
Me llevó dos semanas terminarlo. It took me two weeks to finish it.

6 to be (talking about time)
¿Cuánto tiempo llevas trabajando aquí? How long have you been working here?
Llevamos dos semanas en Londres. We've been in London for two weeks.
Lleva media hora hablando por teléfono. He's been on the phone for half an hour.
El tren lleva una hora de retraso. The train's an hour late.

7 (to be taller than, ahead of, etc) **Le llevo cuatro años.** I'm four years older than him. ▸▸

a
b
c
d
e
f
g
h
i
j
k
l
m
n
ñ
o
p
q
r
s
t
u
v
w
x
y
z

a
b
c
d
e
f
g
h
i
j
k
l
m
n
ñ
o
p
q
r
s
t
u
v
w
x
y
z

Mi hijo te lleva unos centímetros. My son is a few centimetres taller than you.
Nos llevan tres días de ventaja. They have a three-day lead over us.

8 to lead
El camino que lleva al río. The road that leads to the river.
¿Adónde lleva este camino? ¿Where does this road go?

9 to run (to be in charge of)
Su padre lleva la tienda. Her father runs the shop.
Lleva la contabilidad de la empresa. He does the company accounts.

llevarse reflexive verb [17]

1 to take (away)
Se llevó los discos. He took the records.
Ya puedes llevarte esto. You can take this away now.
Nos lo llevamos a la playa. We took him off to the beach.
Los ladrones se llevaron las joyas. The thieves went off with the jewels.

2 llevarse bien con alguien to get on with someone
Se llevan bien. They get on well.
Nos llevamos mal. We don't get on.

♂ **llorar** verb [17]
to cry
Lo hizo llorar. She made him cry.

♂ **llover** verb [38]
to rain
Está lloviendo. It's raining.

♂ la **llovizna** fem noun
drizzle

♂ **llueva, llueve, etc** verb ▷ **llover**

♂ la **lluvia** fem noun
rain
un día de lluvia a rainy day
• la **lluvia ácida** acid rain

♂ **lluvioso** masc adjective, **lluviosa** fem
rainy

♂ **lo** determiner ▷ see **lo** pron
1 (lo + adjective) **the ... thing**
Lo mejor es ... The best thing is ...
Lo curioso es ... The funny thing is ...
Prefiero lo salado a lo dulce. I prefer savoury things to sweet things.

2 (for someone's belongings) **lo mío** mine
Esto es lo tuyo. That's yours.
Esto es lo de mi madre. This is my mother's.
Lo vuestro está en la habitación. Your things are in the bedroom.

Lo de Marta lo he puesto en la mesa. I've put Marta's things on the table.

3 (talking about an event) **¿Sabes lo de Eva?** Have you heard about Eva?
Le conté lo tuyo. I told her about you.
Lo de Pablo es muy raro. It's really strange this thing with Pablo.
Lo del accidente fue horrible. That thing about the accident was horrible.

4 lo que what
Eso es lo que yo compré. That's what I bought.
Toma lo que quieras. Take whatever you want.
Dime todo lo que sepas. Tell me everything you know.

♂ **lo** masc pronoun ▷ see **lo** determiner
1 (as direct object) **him**
Lo vi ayer. I saw him yesterday.
Voy a verlo mañana. I am going to see him tomorrow.

2 (as direct object) **it** (thing)
Lo metí en tu bolso. I put it in your bag.
Léelo en voz alta. Read it aloud.
Ya lo sé. I know.

3 (as direct object) **you** (polite form)
A usted no lo llamaron. They didn't call you.

♂ el **lobo** masc noun
wolf

local masc & fem adjective ▷ see **local** masc noun
local

♂ el **local** masc noun ▷ see **local** masc & fem adj
premises

♂ la **localidad** fem noun
1 town
una pequeña localidad a small town
2 seat (in a cinema, concert hall, etc)
'No hay localidades' 'Sold out'

♂ la **loción** fem noun
lotion
• la **loción bronceadora** suntan lotion
• la **loción para después del afeitado** aftershave lotion

♂ **loco** masc adjective, **loca** fem
▷ see **loco** noun
mad
¡Estás loco! You're mad!
estar loco por alguien to be crazy about somebody
Estaba loco por ella. He was crazy about her.
(informal) **volver loco a alguien** to drive someone mad

¡Este niño me va a volver loco! That child's going to drive me mad!
Las fresas la vuelven loca. She loves strawberries.

∫ el **loco** *masc noun*, la **loca** *fem*
▷ see **loco** *adj*
1 **madman**
2 **madwoman**

∫ la **locomotora** *fem noun*
engine (*of a train*)

∫ la **locura** *fem noun*
1 **madness**
2 (*mad thing, idea*) Eso es una locura. That's crazy.
Es otra de sus locuras. It's another of his crazy ideas.

∫ el **locutor** *masc noun*, la **locutora** *fem*
1 **announcer**
2 **newsreader**
• el **locutor deportivo** sports commentator

lógico *masc adjective*, **lógica** *fem*
logical

∫ **lograr** *verb* [17]
1 **to achieve**
lograr la victoria to achieve victory
2 **lograr hacer algo** to manage to do something
Logré terminar el ejercicio. I managed to finish the exercise.
No lograron terminarlo. They didn't manage to finish it.
lograr que alguien haga algo to get someone to do something
Lograron que lo hiciera a tiempo. They got him to finish it in time.

WORD TIP *lograr que* is followed by a verb in the subjunctive.

∫ la **lombriz** *fem noun*
earthworm

∫ el **lomo** *masc noun*
1 **back** (*of an animal*)
2 **spine** (*of a book*)
3 (*Latin America*) **steak**
• el **lomo de cerdo** loin of pork

∫ la **loncha** *fem noun*
slice
una loncha de bacon a rasher of bacon
una loncha de jamón a slice of ham

londinense *masc & fem adjective & noun*
1 **London**
2 un & una londinense Londoner

WORD TIP Adjectives and nouns for regional origin do not have capital letters in Spanish.

∫ **Londres** *masc noun*
London

∫ la **longaniza** *fem noun*
spicy pork sausage

∫ la **longitud** *fem noun*
length
Tiene doce metros de longitud. It's twelve metres long.
• la **longitud de onda** wavelength

∫ el **loro** *masc noun*, la **lora** *fem*
parrot

∫ **los** *plural masc determiner* ▷ see **los** *pron*
1 (*before masc plural nouns*) **the**
Deja los libros ahí. Leave the books there.
2 (*when los is not translated*) los discos de Isabel Isabel's records
No me gustan los tomates. I don't like tomatoes.
3 (*for parts of the body, clothes*) Se frotó los ojos. She rubbed her eyes.
Me puse los zapatos. I put my shoes on.
4 (*for a masc plural noun, which is known about, e.g. los pañuelos below*)
Los míos son rojos. Mine are red.
Ésos son los tuyos. Those are yours.
Me gustaron los verdes. I liked the green ones.
5 Estos son los de Ana. These ones are Ana's.
los míos y los de usted mine and yours
Me gustan más los de Toni. I like Toni's better.
los que yo compré the ones I bought
los que quieras whichever ones you want

WORD TIP See also *el*, *la* and *las*.

∫ **los** *plural masc pronoun* ▷ see **los** *determiner*
1 (*as direct object*) **them**
Los vi ayer. I saw them yesterday.
Te los puedes llevar. You can take them with you.
Quiero verlos. I want to see them.
¡Dámelos ahora! Give them to me now!
2 (*as direct object*) **you** (*plural polite form*)
Los oí, caballeros. I heard you, gentlemen.

el **lote** *masc noun*
batch
un lote de pedidos a batch of orders

∫ la **lotería** *fem noun*
lottery
Les tocó la lotería. They won the lottery.

las **luces** *masc noun* ▷ **luz**
• las **luces cortas**, **luces de cruce** dipped headlights
• las **luces de freno** brake lights
• las **luces largas** full beam

ſ la lucha *fem noun*
 1 fight, struggle
  la lucha contra el cáncer the fight against
  cancer
  la lucha por la supervivencia the struggle
  for survival
 2 wrestling

ſ luchar *verb* [17]
 1 to fight (*in combat*)
  Luchó en la guerra del Golfo. He fought in
  the Gulf War.
 2 to fight, to struggle
  luchar por algo to fight for something
  Lucharon por la paz. They fought for peace.
 3 to wrestle (*in sport*)

ſ luego *adverb*
 1 then
  Luego vino su madre. Then her mother came.
 2 later
  Luego te veo. I'll see you later.
  ¡Hasta luego! See you later!
 3 afterwards
  Luego te arrepentirás. You'll be sorry
  afterwards.
  Luego podemos cenar. We can have dinner
  afterwards.
 4 then
  Primero está su casa y luego la mía. First
  comes her house and then mine.
  Primero iré al banco y luego a tu casa. I'll go
  to the bank first and then to your house.

ſ el lugar *masc noun*
 1 place
  un lugar precioso a beautiful place
  en cualquier lugar anywhere
  en otro lugar somewhere else
  por cualquier otro lugar anywhere else
  Tiene que estar en algún lugar. It must be
  somewhere.
 2 tener lugar to take place
  El concierto tendrá lugar en la plaza. The
  concert will take place in the square.
 3 (*saying the order of things*) **en primer lugar**
  first of all
  En primer lugar, hay que recordar ... First of
  all, we must remember ...
  en segundo lugar ... secondly ...
  en último lugar last of all
  Llegó en último lugar. He finished last (*in a
  race*).
 4 room
  No hay lugar para nada más. There's no
  room for anything else.
 5 en lugar de instead of
  En lugar de ir de compras, fuimos a la
  piscina. Instead of going shopping, we
  went to the pool.

 • **el lugar de nacimiento** place of birth

lúgubre *masc & fem adjective*
 gloomy

ſ el lujo *masc noun*
 luxury
 un apartamento de lujo a luxury apartment

ſ lujoso *masc adjective*, **lujosa** *fem*
 luxurious

ſ luminoso *masc adjective*, **luminosa** *fem*
 1 bright (*room, idea*)
 2 luminous

ſ la luna *fem noun*
 1 moon
  Esta noche hay luna. The moon is out
  tonight.
 2 mirror
 3 shop window
 • la **luna creciente** waxing moon
 • la **luna de miel** honeymoon
 • la **luna llena** full moon
 • la **luna menguante** waning moon

ſ el lunar *masc noun*
 1 mole (*on your skin*)
 2 polka dot
  una camisa de lunares a polka-dot shirt

ſ el lunes *masc noun*
 Monday
  el lunes on Monday
  el lunes pasado last Monday
  los lunes on Mondays
  cada lunes every Monday
  La tienda está cerrada los lunes. The shop is
  closed on Mondays.
  Te llamaré el lunes por la tarde. I'll phone
  you on Monday evening.

 WORD TIP Names of months and days start with
 small letters in Spanish.

ſ la lupa *fem noun*
 magnifying glass

 el luto *masc noun*
 mourning
 ir de luto to be in mourning
 ponerse de luto to go into mourning

ſ Luxemburgo *masc noun*
 Luxembourg

ſ la luz *fem noun, pl: las* **luces**
 1 light
  dar la luz to switch on the light
  apagar la luz to switch off the light
 2 electricity
  Se ha ido la luz. The electricity's gone off.
 3 dar a luz to give birth
  Dio a luz a un niño. She gave birth to a boy.
 • la **luz del sol** sunlight

M m

los **macarrones** *plural masc noun*
  macaroni

la **macedonia** *fem noun*
  fruit salad

la **maceta** *fem noun*
  flowerpot

ʃ **machista** *masc & fem adjective*
  ▷ see **machista** *noun*
  sexist
  un comportamiento machista sexist
  behaviour

ʃ el & la **machista** *masc & fem noun*
  ▷ see **machista** *adj*
  male chauvinist
  Mi jefe es un machista asqueroso. My boss
  is a disgusting male chauvinist.

ʃ **macho** *masc adjective*
  male
  un ratón macho a male mouse
  una ballena macho a bull whale

ʃ la **madera** *fem noun*
  1 **wood**
    Son de madera. They're made of wood.
    una silla de madera a wooden chair
  2 **timber**
    madera canadiense importada imported
    Canadian timber

ʃ la **madrastra** *fem noun*
  stepmother
  Se lleva muy bien con su madrastra. He
  gets on very well with his stepmother.

ʃ la **madre** *fem noun*
  1 **mother**
    Es huérfano de madre. He doesn't have a
    mother.
  2 *(exclamation)* ¡Madre mía! My goodness!
  • la **madre soltera** single mother
  • la **madre política** mother-in-law

ʃ **Madrid** *fem noun*
  Madrid

ʃ **madrileño** *masc adjective*, **madrileña** *fem*
  ▷ see **madrileño** *noun*
  of Madrid, from Madrid
  las iglesias madrileñas the churches of
  Madrid
  los inviernos madrileños the Madrid
  winters

ʃ un **madrileño** *masc noun*, una **madrileña**
  fem noun ▷ see **madrileño** *adj*
  person from Madrid
  Se casó con un madrileño. She married a
  man from Madrid.

  WORD TIP Adjectives and nouns for nationality
  and regional origin do not have capital letters in
  Spanish.

ʃ la **madrina** *fem noun*
  godmother

ʃ la **madrugada** *fem noun*
  dawn
  de madrugada at dawn
  Nos levantamos de madrugada. We got up
  at dawn.
  Llegamos de madrugada. We arrived in the
  early hours of the morning.
  a las cuatro de la madrugada at four in the
  morning

  madrugar *verb* [28]
  to get up early

ʃ **madurar** *verb* [17]
  1 **to ripen** *(fruit, etc)*
  2 **to mature** *(people, ideas)*

ʃ **maduro** *masc adjective*, **madura** *fem*
  1 **ripe** *(fruit, etc)*
  2 **mature** *(person)*
    Es muy poco maduro. He's quite
    immature.

ʃ el **maestro** *masc noun*, la **maestra** *fem noun*
  1 **teacher** *(in primary school)*
  2 **master** *(of a trade)*
    un maestro carpintero a master carpenter
    Su mamá es maestra panadera. Her mum's
    a master baker.

ʃ la **magdalena** *fem noun*
  fairycake

ʃ la **magia** *fem noun*
  magic
  como por arte de magia as if by magic

mágico *masc adjective*, **mágica** *fem*
  magical

magnético *masc adjective*, **magnética**
  fem
  magnetic

a
b
c
d
e
f
g
h
i
j
k
l
m
n
ñ
o
p
q
r
s
t
u
v
w
x
y
z

♂ el **magnetofón**, **magnetófono** *masc noun*
tape recorder

♂ **magnífico** *masc adjective*, **magnífica** *fem*
1 **wonderful**
2 **magnificent**

♂ el **mago** *masc noun*, la **maga** *fem*
1 **magician**
2 **wizard**

♀ la **mahonesa** *fem noun*
mayonnaise

el **mail** *masc noun*
email (*the message*)

♂ el **maíz** *masc noun*
1 **sweetcorn**
una mazorca de maíz a corn on the cob
2 **maize**
el maíz transgénico genetically modified maize

♂ **mal** *masc & fem adjective* ▷ **see mal** *adv, noun*
1 **bad**
Es un mal amigo. He's a bad friend.
Vinieron en mal momento. They came at a bad time.
No está mal. It's not bad.
2 **wrong**
Está mal criticar. It's wrong to criticize.
La respuesta está mal. The answer's wrong.
3 **ill**
¿Te sientes mal? Do you feel ill?
Su padre está muy mal. His father's very ill.

WORD TIP *mal* is used before a masc singular noun instead of *malo*. In other situations use *malo, mala*. ▷ **malo**

♂ **mal** *adverb* ▷ **see mal** *adj, noun*
1 **badly**
Está muy mal pintado. It's really badly painted.
Lo leyó muy mal. She read it very badly.
El país marcha mal. The country's not doing well.
Le va muy mal en el trabajo. He's doing very badly at work.
2 **wrong**
Lo hizo mal. He did it wrong.
Hace mal en no pedir perdón. He's wrong not to apologize.
3 **contestarle mal a alguien** to answer someone back
Le contestó mal a la profesora. He answered the teacher back.
4 **Te oigo mal.** I can't hear you very well.

5 Olía muy mal. There was a nasty smell.
La comida sabe mal. The food tastes horrible.
6 **portarse mal** to misbehave
entender mal algo to misunderstand something
Entendió mal lo que le dije. She misunderstood what I said to her.
7 **¡Menos mal!** Thank goodness!

♂ el **mal** *masc noun* ▷ **see mal** *adj, adv*
evil
el bien y el mal good and evil

los **malabarismos** *plural masc noun*
hacer malabarismos to juggle
Hace malabarismos con plátanos. She juggles bananas.

el & la **malabarista** *masc & fem noun*
juggler

la **malanga** *fem noun*
eddo

♂ **malcriado** *masc adjective*, **malcriada** *fem*
▷ **see malcriado** *noun*
1 **spoilt**
una niña malcriada a spoilt little girl
2 **naughty**

♂ el **malcriado** *masc noun*, la **malcriada** *fem*
▷ **see malcriado** *adj*
Es un malcriado. He's really spoilt.

♀ la **maldición** *fem noun*
1 **curse**
La bruja les echó una maldición. The witch put a curse on them.
2 **soltar una maldición** to swear
3 **¡Maldición!** Damn!

maleducado *masc adjective*,
maleducada *fem*
▷ **see maleducado** *noun*
rude
¡Qué niños tan maleducados! What rude children!

♂ el **maleducado** *masc noun*, la
maleducada *fem*
▷ **see maleducado** *adj*
Es una maleducada. She's really rude.

♂ el **malentendido** *masc noun*
misunderstanding
Desgraciadamente, hubo un malentendido. Unfortunately there was a misunderstanding.

♀ la **maleta** *fem noun*
suitcase
hacer la maleta to pack a suitcase

a b c d e f g h i j k l m n ñ o p q r s t u v w x y z

Ya he hecho la maleta. I've already packed my suitcase.

♂ el **maletero** *masc noun*
boot (*of a car*)
No cabe nada más en el maletero. There's no room for anything else in the boot.

♂ el **maletín** *masc noun*
1 **briefcase**
2 **overnight case**
3 el maletín del médico the doctor's bag

♂ el **malhumor** *masc noun*
bad temper
estar de malhumor to be in a bad mood

el **mall** *masc noun*
(*Latin America*) **shopping centre**

la **malla** *fem noun*
1 **mesh** (*of net*)
una bolsa de malla a string bag
2 **leotard** (*for gymnastics*)
3 mallas leggings
• la **malla de alambre** wire mesh

♂ **Mallorca** *fem noun*
Majorca

mallorquín *masc adjective & noun,*
mallorquina *fem adjective & noun*
1 **Majorcan**
2 un mallorquín, una mallorquina Majorcan

WORD TIP Adjectives and nouns for nationality and regional origin do not have capital letters in Spanish.

♂ **malo** *masc adjective,* **mala** *fem*
1 **bad**
de mala calidad bad quality
una mala costumbre a bad habit
Es malo para la salud. It's bad for your health.
2 **naughty, nasty**
¡Qué niño más malo! What a naughty child!
No seas mala y devuélveselo. Don't be nasty, give it back to her.
3 Ayer hizo malo. The weather was bad yesterday.
Nos hizo muy malo durante las vacaciones. We had horrible weather during the holidays.
4 estar malo to be ill
El pobre está muy malo. The poor thing is in a really bad way.
No puede venir porque está mala. She can't come because she's ill.
5 estar malo to be off (*food*)
La leche está mala. The milk's gone off.

6 estar malo to taste horrible
La sopa estaba muy mala. The soup was horrible.
7 ser malo para algo to be bad at something (*a skill*)
Soy malo para las matemáticas. I'm bad at maths. ▷ **mal**

♂ la **mamá** *fem noun*
(*informal*) **mum**
Dile a tu mamá que la espero abajo. Tell your mum I'll wait for her downstairs.
La maestra quiere hablar con todas las mamás. The teacher wants to talk to all our mums.

♂ el **mamífero** *masc noun*
mammal
¿Los canguros son mamíferos? Are kangaroos mammals?

♂ la **manada** *fem noun*
1 **herd** (*of cattle*)
2 **pack** (*of dogs*)
3 **gang** (*of young people*)

♂ la **mancha** *fem noun*
1 **stain**
una mancha de chocolate a chocolate stain
quitar una mancha to remove a stain
2 **mark**
• la **mancha de petróleo** oil slick

♂ **manchar** *verb* [17]
1 **to get (something) dirty**
Me has manchado la camiseta. You've got my tee-shirt all dirty.
Mancharon la alfombra de barro. They got mud all over the carpet.
2 **to stain**
Manché el mantel de café. I got coffee stains on the tablecloth.

mancharse *reflexive verb* [17]
to get yourself dirty
Cuidado, no te manches. Careful, don't get yourself dirty.
Se manchó los pantalones de barro. He got mud all over his trousers.

manchego *masc adjective & noun,*
manchega *fem adjective & noun*
1 **Manchegan, from La Mancha** (*a region in central Spain*)
2 un manchego, una manchega person from La Mancha

WORD TIP Adjectives and nouns for nationality and regional origin do not have capital letters in Spanish.

el **manchón** *masc noun*
stain

a
b
c
d
e
f
g
h
i
j
k
l
m
n
ñ
o
p
q
r
s
t
u
v
w
x
y
z

a
b
c
d
e
f
g
h
i
j
k
l

m

n
ñ
o
p
q
r
s
t
u
v
w
x
y
z

ℰ **mandar** *verb* [17]

1 to order

2 Le gusta mandar. She likes to give the orders.

3 mandar a alguien hacer algo to tell somebody to do something
Me mandó recoger la habitación. She told me to tidy my bedroom.
Haz lo que te mandan. Do as you're told.

4 to send
mandarle una carta a alguien to send somebody a letter
Le mandó una postal a su novia. He sent his girfriend a postcard.
Los mandé a comprar fruta. I sent them to buy some fruit.

5 mandar llamar a alguien to send for someone
Mandó llamar al doctor. She sent for the doctor.

ℰ la **mandarina** *fem noun*
mandarin, **tangerine**

el **mando** *masc noun*

1 command
estar al mando de algo to be in charge of something
Estaba al mando del pelotón. She was in charge of the platoon.

2 controls *(of a machine, TV set)*

• el **mando a distancia** remote control

ℰ **manejar** *verb* [17]

1 to use *(a computer, dictionary)*
2 to operate *(a machine)*
3 to manage *(a business)*
4 *(Latin America)* **to drive** *(a vehicle)*
¿Sabes manejar? Can you drive?

ℰ la **manera** *fem noun*

1 way
Busca la manera más fácil de hacerlo. Find the easiest way to do it.
Lo hice a mi manera. I did it my way.
Es su manera de ser. It's the way he is.
No hubo manera de arreglarlo. There was no way of fixing it.

2 de alguna manera somehow
Me las arreglaré de alguna manera. I'll manage it somehow.

3 de cualquier manera
any old how
Puedes decorarlo de cualquier manera. You can decorate it any way you want.

4 de una manera u otra one way or another

5 ¡De ninguna manera! No way!
'¿Me dejas el coche?'—'¡De ninguna

manera!' 'Can I borrow your car?'—'No way!'

6 de todas maneras anyway
De todas maneras no pensaba comprarlo. I wasn't thinking of buying it anyway.

7 de manera que so
De manera que al final no la vi. So I didn't see her after all.

ℰ la **manga** *fem noun*

1 sleeve
una camisa de manga corta a short-sleeved shirt
sin mangas sleeveless

2 hose *(for watering)*

ℰ el **mango** *masc noun*

1 handle *(of a knife, tool)*
2 mango *(fruit)*

ℰ la **manguera** *fem noun*
hosepipe

ℰ la **manía** *fem noun*

1 Tiene la manía del orden. He's obsessed with tidiness.
Es maja pero tiene sus manías. She's nice but she has her funny little ways.

2 tenerle manía a alguien to have it in for somebody
Tu hermano me tiene manía. Your brother has it in for me.

ℰ **maniático** *masc adjective*, **maniática** *fem*
▷ see **maniático** *noun*
fussy
Es un poco maniática con la comida. She's a bit fussy about her food.

ℰ el **maniático** *masc noun*, la **maniática** *fem*
▷ see **maniático** *adj*
Es un maniático de la limpieza. He's obsessed with cleanliness.

la **manifestación** *fem noun*

1 demonstration
una manifestación en contra de la guerra a demonstration against the war

2 sign *(of emotion, disapproval)*
3 manifestaciones statements

manifestar *verb* [29]

1 to express *(disapproval, an opinion)*
Quiero manifestar mi agradecimiento. I would like to express my gratitude.

2 to show *(emotions)*

manifestarse *reflexive verb* [29]

1 to demonstrate
manifestarse en contra de algo to demonstrate against something

186

2 manifestarse en contra de algo to speak out against something
Se manifestó en contra del racismo. She spoke out against racism.

3 to become evident

el **manillar** masc noun
handlebars
Tengo el manillar flojo. My handlebars are loose.

ᔒ **manipular** verb [17]
1 to operate (a machine)
2 to manipulate (data, information)
3 to handle (goods)
Hay que tener las manos limpias para manipular alimentos. You have to have clean hands to handle food.

el **maniquí** masc noun
mannequin

la **manivela** fem noun
handle

ᔒ la **mano** fem noun ▷ see **mano** masc
1 hand
levantar la mano to put your hand up
ir de la mano to go hand in hand
Dame la mano. Hold my hand.
Lo tiene en la mano izquierda. He has it in his left hand.
coger a alguien de la mano to take somebody's hand
Cogió al niño de la mano. She took the child's hand.
Iban cogidos de la mano. They were walking hand in hand.
2 darle la mano a alguien to shake somebody's hand
Se dieron la mano. They shook hands.
3 decir adiós con la mano to wave goodbye
4 coat (of paint)
una mano de pintura a coat of paint
5 (in expressions) hecho a mano handmade
6 a mano izquierda on the left
a mano derecha on the right

el **mano** masc noun, la **mana** fem
▷ see **mano** fem
(Latin America) **buddy**, **mate**

el **manómetro** masc noun
pressure gauge

ᔒ la **mansión** fem noun
mansion
una mansión restaurada de la época victoriana a restored Victorian mansion

manso masc adjective, **mansa** fem
1 tame (an animal)
2 gentle (a person)

ᔒ la **manta** fem noun
blanket
una manta de lana a woollen blanket
• la **manta eléctrica** electric blanket

la **manteca** fem noun
lard

ᔒ el **mantecado** masc noun
almond delicacy (eaten at Christmas)

ᔒ el **mantel** masc noun
tablecloth

ᔒ **mantendrá**, **mantendría**, etc verb ▷ **mantener**

ᔒ **mantener** verb [9]
1 to keep
mantener la calma to keep calm
mantener el equilibrio to keep your balance
2 to support (a family)
Tiene que mantener a sus seis hermanos. He has to support his six brothers and sisters.

mantenerse reflexive verb [9]
to keep
mantenerse en equilibrio to keep your balance
mantenerse en contacto con alguien to keep in touch with somebody
Se mantuvo en contacto con sus compañeros de colegio. She kept in touch with her school friends.

ᔒ **mantengo**, **mantenga**, etc verb ▷ **mantener**

el **mantenimiento** masc noun
1 maintenance
2 Hace ejercicios de mantenimiento. She does keep-fit exercises.

ᔒ la **mantequilla** fem noun
butter
mantequilla sin sal unsalted butter
pan con mantequilla bread and butter

ᔒ la **mantilla** fem noun
mantilla (traditional lace headscarf)

ᔒ **mantuve**, **mantuvo**, etc verb ▷ **mantener**

manual masc & fem adjective
manual

a
b
c
d
e
f
g
h
i
j
k
l
m
n
ñ
o
p
q
r
s
t
u
v
w
x
y
z

♂ la manzana *fem noun*
1 **apple**
zumo de manzana apple juice
2 **block** (*in a town*)
dar una vuelta a la manzana to go round
the block

♂ la manzanilla *fem noun*
1 **camomile tea**
Tomé una manzanilla para calmarme los
nervios. I had a camomile tea to settle my
nerves.
2 **dry sherry**

♂ el manzano *masc noun*
apple tree
Los manzanos están en flor. The apple
trees are in bloom.

♂ mañana *adverb* ▷ see **mañana** *noun*
tomorrow
pasado mañana the day after tomorrow
¡Hasta mañana! See you tomorrow!
mañana por la tarde tomorrow afternoon

♂ la mañana *fem noun* ▷ see **mañana** *adv*
morning
por la mañana in the morning
mañana por la mañana tomorrow morning
a la mañana siguiente the next morning
a las once de la mañana at eleven o'clock in
the morning

♂ el mapa *masc noun*
map
• el **mapa de carreteras** road map
• el **mapa de sitio** site map (*on website*)

♂ el maquillaje *masc noun*
make-up

♂ maquillar *verb* [17]
to make up
La vestí y maquillé para la foto. I dressed
her and made her up for the photo.

maquillarse *reflexive verb* [17]
to put your make-up on
Apenas se maquilla. She hardly wears any
make-up.

♂ la máquina *fem noun*
machine
escribir a máquina to type
• la **máquina de afeitar** electric shaver
• la **máquina de coser** sewing machine
• la **máquina de escribir** typewriter
• la **máquina expendedora** vending
machine
• la **máquina fotográfica** camera
• la **máquina tragamonedas** slot machine

♂ la maquinaria *fem noun*
machinery

♂ la maquinilla *fem noun*
safety razor
una maquinilla desechable a disposable
razor

♂ el mar *masc noun*
sea
viajar por mar to travel by sea
• el **mar Cantábrico** Bay of Biscay
• el **mar de Irlanda** Irish Sea
• el **mar del Norte** North Sea
• el **mar Mediterráneo** Mediterranean Sea

♂ el & la maratón *masc & fem noun*
marathon
participar en el maratón de Nueva York to
take part in the New York marathon

♂ la maravilla *fem noun*
wonder
Es una maravilla de casa. It's a wonderful
house
Baila de maravilla. He's a fantastic dancer.

♂ maravilloso *masc adjective*, **maravillosa**
fem
wonderful
Hace un tiempo maravilloso aquí. The
weather's fantastic here.

♂ la marca *fem noun*
1 **mark**
El cuadro ha dejado una marca en la pared.
The picture has left a mark on the wall.
2 **brand**
artículos de marca brand products
ropa de marca designer clothes
3 **record** (*in sports*)
batir una marca to break a record
establecer una nueva marca to establish a
new record
• la **marca registrada** registered trademark

♂ el marcador *masc noun*
scoreboard
¿Cómo va el marcador? What's the score?

♂ marcar *verb* [31]
1 **to mark**
La experiencia me marcó mucho. The
experience really marked me.
2 Mi reloj marca las nueve. My watch says
nine o'clock.
El termómetro marcaba cinco grados. The
thermometer was registering five degrees.
3 marcar un número to dial a number
Marca oo 44 para Gran Bretaña. Dial oo 44
for Britain.

4 **marcar un gol** to score a goal

5 **marcar el ritmo, marcar el compás** to beat time

𝓢 la **marcha** *fem noun*

1 **hike**
ir de marcha to go hiking
Fuimos de marcha a la montaña. We went hiking in the mountains.
¡En marcha! Let's go!

2 **march** (*demonstration*)

3 **gear** (*in a car*)
cambiar de marcha to change gear
meter la marcha atrás to go into reverse
un coche de cinco marchas a car with five gears

4 **speed**
disminuir la marcha to reduce speed

5 **estar en marcha** to be running (*engines, machines*)

6 **poner en marcha** to start (*a car, machine*)

7 (*in expressions*) **ir de marcha** to go out partying
una discoteca con mucha marcha a really fun disco
¡Qué marcha tiene ese grupo! This group's really wild!

𝓢 **marchar** *verb* [17]

1 **to go, to work**
¿Cómo marcha el negocio? How's the business going?
Esto no marcha. This isn't working.

2 **to march**

3 (*in bars, cafes*) **¡Marchando dos cafés!** Two coffees coming up!

marcharse *reflexive verb* [17]

to leave
Nos marchamos mañana. We're leaving tomorrow.

𝓢 el **marco** *masc noun*

1 **frame** (*of picture, etc*)
el marco de la puerta the doorframe

2 **setting** (*for events*)

3 **goalposts**

𝓢 la **marea** *fem noun*

tide
Está subiendo la marea. The tide's coming in.
Cuando baje la marea. When the tide goes out.

· la **marea alta** high tide

· la **marea baja** low tide

· la **marea negra** oil slick

𝓢 **mareado** *masc adjective*, **mareada** *fem*

1 **sick**
Estoy mareado. I feel sick.

2 **dizzy**
Se siente mareada. She feels dizzy.

3 **estar mareado** to be muddled up
Estoy mareada con tantos números. I'm muddled up with all these numbers.

𝓢 **marear** *verb* [17]

1 **to make you feel sick**
El movimiento del bote la mareaba. The motion of the boat made her feel sick.

2 **to make you dizzy**
¿Te ha mareado el tiovivo? Has the roundabout made you dizzy?

3 **to confuse**
Me marearon a preguntas. They asked me so many questions my head was spinning.

marearse *reflexive verb* [17]

1 **to get dizzy**

2 **to feel faint**

3 **to get tipsy**

𝓢 el **mareo** *masc noun*

1 **sick feeling**
Me dan mareos si viajo en coche. I get carsick.

2 **seasickness**
tabletas para el mareo seasick tablets

3 **dizziness**

𝓢 el **marfil** *masc noun*

ivory
Está prohibida la importación de marfil. Importation of ivory is forbidden.

𝓢 la **margarina** *fem noun*

margarine
una margarina baja en grasas a low-fat margarine

𝓢 la **margarita** *fem noun*

1 **daisy**

2 **marguerite** (*larger flower*)

𝓢 el **margen** *masc noun*

margin
escribir algo en el margen to write something in the margin

𝓢 el **marido** *masc noun*

husband

𝓢 la **marina** *fem noun*

navy
la marina mercante the merchant navy

a
b
c
d
e
f
g
h
i
j
k
l
m
n
ñ
o
p
q
r
s
t
u
v
w
x
y
z

marinero   **más**

♂ el **marinero** *masc noun*
sailor
Mi abuelo fue marinero. My grandfather was a sailor.

la **marioneta** *fem noun*
puppet

♀ la **mariposa** *fem noun*
1 **butterfly**
2 nadar mariposa to swim butterfly
¿Sabes nadar mariposa? Can you swim butterfly?
• la **mariposa nocturna** moth

♀ la **mariquita** *fem noun*
ladybird

♂ el **marisco** *masc noun*
shellfish, **seafood**
Pedimos marisco y cerveza. We ordered seafood and beer.

♂ el **mármol** *masc noun*
marble
una escalera de mármol a marble staircase

♂ **marrón** *masc & fem adjective*
▷ see **marrón** *noun*
brown
una falda marrón a brown skirt
unos zapatos marrones a pair of brown shoes
unos pantalones marrón claro a pair of light brown trousers

♂ el **marrón** *masc noun* ▷ see **marrón** *adj*
brown
Prefiero el marrón al verde. I prefer brown to green.

♂ el **martes** *masc noun*
Tuesday
el martes on Tuesday
el martes pasado last Tuesday
los martes on Tuesdays
cada martes every Tuesday
El bar está cerrado los martes. The bar is closed on Tuesdays.

WORD TIP Names of months and days start with small letters in Spanish.

♂ el **martillo** *masc noun*
hammer
Esto se arregla pronto con un martillo y unos clavos. This can soon be fixed with a hammer and some nails.
• el **martillo neumático** pneumatic drill

♂ **marzo** *masc noun*
March
en marzo in March
el 17 de marzo on 17 March

WORD TIP Names of months and days start with small letters in Spanish.

♂ **más** *adjective, adverb, pronoun*
▷ see **más** *prep*
1 **more**
tres más three more
Pon más azúcar. Add more sugar.
¿Necesitas más? Do you need any more?
No comas más. Don't eat any more.
Éste me gusta más. I like this one more.
2 Hay que hacerlo más rápido. We must do it faster.
3 (*to say 'most'*) el de más peso the heaviest one
los más altos the tallest ones
los de más prestigio the most prestigious ones
el libro con más páginas the book with the most pages
El que más me gusta. The one I like the most.
4 (*in comparisons*) más blanco que la nieve whiter than snow
Es un poco más grande. It's a bit bigger.
Es mucho más grande. It's much bigger.
Ayer vino más gente que hoy. More people came yesterday than today.
Es más interesante que su primer libro. It's more interesting than his first book.
Me gusta más el de piel que el de tela. I like the leather one more than the cloth one.
5 (*in comparisons: with numbers*) más de … more than …
más de veinte kilos more than twenty kilos
Vinieron más de veinte personas. More than twenty people came.
6 de más to spare, to be left over
Hay tres pasteles de más. There are three cakes left over.
Tengo un billete de más. I have a spare ticket.
Hay tres sillas de más. There are three chairs too many.
7 (*in time expressions*) No me quedo más. I won't stay any longer.
No lo hagas más. Don't do it again.
No les he visto más. I've never seen them again.
8 no … más only
No tardo más de diez minutos. I'll only take ten minutes.
No es más que un resfriado. It's only a cold.

9 (*in expressions*) **alguien más** anybody else
¿Esperas a alguien más? Are you expecting anybody else?
nadie más nobody else
No quiero nada más. I don't want anything else.
algo más anything else
¿Querías algo más? Did you want anything else?
más que nunca more than ever
más o menos more or less

10 (*in exclamations*) **¡Qué niña más bonita!** What a beautiful little girl!
¡Qué libros más pesados! What heavy books!

ᵇ **más** *preposition* ▷ see **más** *adv, adj, pron*
plus
cinco más siete five plus seven

la **masa** *fem noun*
1 dough
Espera que suba la masa. Wait for the dough to rise.

2 pastry
• la **masa de hojaldre** puff pastry

el **masaje** *masc noun*
massage

la **máscara** *fem noun*
mask

la **mascarilla** *fem noun*
mask

ᵇ **masculino** *masc adjective*, **masculina** *fem*
▷ see **masculino** *noun*
1 men's (*team, fashion*)
el equipo masculino the men's team
2 masculine (*style, manners, noun*)
3 male
el sexo masculino the male sex

el **masculino** *masc noun*
▷ see **masculino** *adj*
(*Grammar*) **masculine**

ᵇ **masticar** *verb* [31]
to chew

el **mástil** *masc noun*
1 mast
2 flagpole

ᵇ el **matador** *masc noun*
matador (*bull fighter who kills one of the six bulls at a corrida de toros*)

la **matanza** *fem noun*
1 massacre (*of people*)
2 slaughter (*of animals*)

ᵇ **matar** *verb* [17]
to kill
¡Han matado al Presidente! The President's been killed!
Lo mató a cuchilladas. She stabbed him to death.
Estas botas me matan. These boots are killing me.

matarse *reflexive verb* [17]
1 to kill yourself
Si te vas me mato. If you leave I'll kill myself.
Su primo se mató de un tiro. His cousin shot himself.

2 to get killed
Si sigues conduciendo así, te vas a matar. If you carry on driving like that you're going to get killed.

mate *masc & fem adjective* ▷ see **mate** *noun*
matt

el **mate** *masc noun* ▷ see **mate** *adj*
jaque mate checkmate

ᵇ las **matemáticas** *plural fem noun*
maths
Soy un negado para las matemáticas. I'm hopeless at maths.

ᵇ la **materia** *fem noun*
1 matter
materia orgánica organic matter
materia grasa fat
2 subject (*of study, of a book*)
• la **materia prima** raw material

material *masc & fem adjective*
▷ see **material** *noun*
material

el **material** *masc noun* ▷ see **material** *adj*
material
materiales para la construcción building materials

maternal *masc & fem adjective*
maternal

ᵇ **materno** *masc adjective*, **materna** *fem*
1 motherly
2 Su lengua materna es el bengalí. Bengali is her mother tongue.
3 sus abuelos maternos his maternal grandparents

el **matiz** *masc noun*
shade (*of a colour*)

a
b
c
d
e
f
g
h
i
j
k
l
m
n
ñ
o
p
q
r
s
t
u
v
w
x
y
z

ℰ la **matrícula** *fem noun*

1 **registration**
hacer la matrícula to register
¿Has hecho la matrícula de la clase de ténis? Have you registered for the tennis lessons?

2 **registration number** (*of a car*)
un coche con matrícula de Sevilla a car with a Seville number plate
Tiene un BMW con matrícula personalizada. She has a BMW with a personalized number plate.

• la **matrícula de honor** distinction (*for school work*)

ℰ el **matrimonio** *masc noun*

1 **marriage**

2 **married couple**
Son un matrimonio muy unido. They're a very close couple.

• el **matrimonio civil** civil wedding

máximo *masc adjective*, **máxima** *fem*

1 **maximum**
el precio máximo the maximum price

2 **top** (*speed*)

3 **highest**
el punto máximo the highest point

ℰ **mayo** *masc noun*

May
en mayo in May
el dos de mayo the second of May
Nos conocimos el cuatro de mayo. We met on the fourth of May.

WORD TIP Names of months and days start with small letters in Spanish.

ℰ la **mayonesa** *fem noun*

mayonnaise
No se puede preparar mayonesa sin aceite de oliva. You can't make mayonnaise without olive oil.

ℰ **mayor** *masc & fem adjective*
▷ see **mayor** *noun*

1 **greater**
una cantidad tres veces mayor a quantity three times greater
la mayor parte de los estudiantes most of the students

2 **greatest**
el mayor desastre the greatest disaster

3 **higher**
un número mayor que cien a number higher than one hundred

4 **highest**
el mayor número de casos the highest number of cases

5 **bigger**
¿Tienes una talla mayor? Do you have a bigger size?

6 **biggest**
el de mayor tamaño the biggest one

7 **older**
su hermano mayor his older brother
Es tres años mayor que su hermana. He's three years older than his sister.

8 **oldest**
mi hermana mayor my oldest sister
Soy el mayor de todos mis hermanos. I'm the oldest of all my brothers and sisters.

9 **adult, grown-up**
una persona mayor an adult
ser mayor de edad to be of age (*over 18*)
Cuando seas mayor … When you're grown up …

10 **elderly**
una señora mayor an elderly lady
Ya son muy mayores. They're quite old now.

ℰ el & la **mayor** *masc & fem noun*
▷ see **mayor** *adj*

1 **adult**

2 **los mayores** grown-ups, adults
Había más niños que mayores en la fiesta. There were more children than grown-ups at the party.
No hables así con tus mayores. Don't speak like that to your elders.

3 **los mayores** the elderly

ℰ la **mayoría** *fem noun*

majority
la mayoría de … most of …
Se ha vendido la mayoría de los artículos. Most of the items have been sold.

ℰ la **mayúscula** *fem noun*

capital letter
Se escribe con mayúscula. It's spelt with a capital letter.

ℰ **mayúsculo** *masc adjective*, **mayúscula** *fem* ▷ see **mayúscula** *noun*

1 **capital** (*letter*)
Cardiff se escribe con c mayúscula. Cardiff is spelled with a capital c.

2 (*informal*) **terrible** (*mistake, fright*)
Cometió un error mayúsculo. He committed a terrible mistake.

el **mazapán** *masc noun*

marzipan

ℰ **me** *pronoun*

1 (*as direct object*) **me**
Me invitó a su fiesta. She invited me to her party.
No me han visto. They haven't seen me.

2 (*as indirect object*) **to me**
Me mintió. He lied to me.
Me lo dieron mis primas My cousins gave it to me.
Me lo ha comprado mi madre. My mother bought it for me.
¿Puedes enviármelos? Can you send them to me?
No me dijo nada. She didn't say anything to me.

3 (*in reflexive verbs*) **myself**
Me corté. I cut myself.
Me reí mucho. I laughed a lot.
Voy a bañarme. I'm going for a swim.
Me senté a la mesa. I sat at the table.

4 (*with parts of the body, clothes*) **Me quité el abrigo.** I took my coat off.
Me limpié los pies al entrar. I wiped my feet at the door.

5 (*to have something done*) **El sábado iré a cortarme el pelo.** I'll go and have my hair cut on Saturday.
¿Me abres esto? Will you open this for me?

mecánico *masc adjective*, **mecánica** *fem*
▷ see **mecánico** *noun*
mechanical

ℰ **el mecánico** *masc noun*, la **mecánica** *fem*
▷ see **mecánico** *adj*
mechanic
Mi hermana es mecánica. My sister's a mechanic.

ℰ la **mecanografía** *fem noun*
typing
Soy una negada para la mecanografía. I'm hopeless at typing.

la **mecedora** *fem noun*
rocking chair

ℰ el **mechero** *masc noun*
lighter
un mechero desechable a disposable lighter

la **medalla** *fem noun*
medal
la medalla de oro the gold medal

la **media** *fem noun* ▷ see **media** *fem noun*
average
la media de altura the average height
una media de cien euros diarios an average

of a hundred euro per day
la media europea the European average

ℰ la **media** *fem noun* ▷ see **media** *noun*

1 **stocking**

2 unas medias **tights**

3 (*Latin America*) **sock**

4 (*telling the time*) **a las dos y media** at half past two
tres horas y media three and a half hours

5 (*in expressions*) **hacer algo a medias** to do things by halves
Siempre hace las cosas a medias He always leaves things half-done.
Lo dejó a medias. He didn't finish it.
pagar a medias to pay half each
Lo hicimos a medias. We did it between the two of us.

ℰ **mediados** *plural masc noun*
a mediados de año halfway through the year
hacia mediados de abril around mid-April
Se fue a mediados de semana. He left midweek.

ℰ **mediano** *masc adjective*, **mediana** *fem*

1 **medium**
Es de peso mediano. He's of medium weight.
¿Lo tienen en talla mediana? Do you have it in medium size?

2 **average**
un hombre de mediana inteligencia a man of average intelligence
una canción de mediana calidad a mediocre song

ℰ la **medianoche** *fem noun*
midnight
a medianoche at midnight

ℰ el **medicamento** *masc noun*
medicine
recetar un medicamento to prescrib a medicine

ℰ la **medicina** *fem noun*
medicine
estudiar medicina to study medicine
tomarse la medicina to take your medicine

ℰ **médico** *masc adjective*, **médica** *fem*
▷ see **médico** *noun*
medical
un reconocimiento médico a medical examination

a
b
c
d
e
f
g
h
i
j
k
l
m
n
ñ
o
p
q
r
s
t
u
v
w
x
y
z

δ el **médico** *masc noun*, la **médica** *fem*
  ▷ see **médico** *adj*
  doctor
  • el **médico de cabecera** family doctor

la **medida** *fem noun*
1 **tomar medidas a algo** to measure
  something
2 **measurement**
  ¿Qué medidas tiene la mesa? What are the
  measurements of the table?
3 **un traje a medida** a made-to-measure suit
4 **a medida que ...** as ...
  A medida que pase el tiempo lo
  entenderás. As time goes by you'll
  understand.
5 **en gran medida** to a large extent
  en cierta medida to a certain extent
  en la medida de lo posible as far as possible

δ **medieval** *masc & fem adjective*
  medieval

δ el **medio ambiente** *masc noun*
  environment
  el Ministerio de Medio Ambiente the
  Ministry of the Environment

δ **medio** *masc adjective*, **media** *fem*
  ▷ see **medio** *adv, noun*
1 **half**
  medio kilo half a kilo
  media docena half a dozen
2 **average**
  de estatura media of average height
  el ciudadano medio the average citizen
3 **half** (*in time expressions*)
  • la **media hora** half an hour
  • la **media pensión** half board (*in a hotel*)

δ **medio** *adverb* ▷ see **medio** *adj, noun*
  half
  Ya está medio convencido. He's half
  convinced now.
  Estaba medio borracha. She was half
  drunk.

δ el **medio** *masc noun* ▷ see **medio** *adj, adv*
1 **middle**
  Ponlo en el medio. Put it in the middle.
  la casa de en medio the house in the middle
  No pudimos conversar en medio de todo
  aquel jaleo. We couldn't talk amid all that
  racket.
2 **quitarse de en medio** to get out of the way
3 **way**
  Es el mejor medio de hacerlo. It's the best
  way to do it.
  No hubo medio de localizarlo. There was
  no way of finding him.

  Lo intenté por todos los medios. I tried
  every possible way.
  Trata por todos los medios de convencerlo.
  Try any way you can to persuade him.
4 **means**
  por cualquier medio by any means
  por medio de un interruptor by means of a
  switch
  Lo conseguí por medio de un amigo. I
  obtained it through a friend.
  • los **medios de comunicación** the media
  • los **medios de transporte** means of
  transport

δ el **mediodía** *masc noun*
  midday
  al mediodía at midday

δ **medir** *verb* [57]
1 **to measure**
  Midió la mesa. She measured the table.
2 **to be** (*in width, length, height*)
  ¿Cuánto mide de ancho? How wide is it?
  Mide sesenta centímetros de largo. It's
  sixty centimetres long.
  ¿Cuánto mides? How tall are you?
  Mido un metro sesenta. I'm one metre
  sixty.

δ **mediterráneo** *masc adjective*,
  mediterránea *fem*
  ▷ see **Mediterráneo** *noun*
  Mediterranean
  el clima mediterráneo the Mediterranean
  climate

  WORD TIP Adjectives for regional origin do not
  have capital letters in Spanish.

δ el **Mediterráneo** *masc noun*
  ▷ see **mediterráneo** *adj*
  el Mediterráneo the Mediterranean

mejicano *masc adjective & noun*, **mejicana**
  fem adjective & noun ▷ **mexicano,**
  mexicana

Méjico *masc noun* ▷ **México**

δ la **mejilla** *fem noun*
  cheek
  Me arden las mejillas. My cheeks are
  stinging.

δ el **mejillón** *masc noun*
  mussel

δ **mejor** *masc & fem adjective* ▷ see **mejor** *adv,*
  noun
1 **better**
  Éste es de mejor calidad. This one is better
  quality.
  los mejores aguacates the best avocados

cuanto antes mejor the earlier the better
Tu bici es mejor que la mía. Your bike is better than mine.
Es mejor que no vayamos. It's better if we don't go.

2 best
el mejor alumno de la clase the best pupil in the class
Lo mejor sería esperar aquí. The best thing would be to wait here.

ᵟ **mejor** *adverb* ▷ see **mejor** *adj, noun*
1 better
Isabel toca la guitarra mejor. Isabel plays the guitar better.
mejor que better than
mejor que el otro better than the other one
Canta mejor que nadie. He sings better than anybody.
cada vez mejor better and better

2 best
Es la que mejor dibuja. She's the one that draws the best.
Hazlo lo mejor que puedas. Do your best.

3 a lo mejor maybe
A lo mejor es de Sara. Maybe it's Sara's.
A lo mejor no voy. I might not go.

4 Mejor no preguntes. It's better if you don't ask.
Mejor déjalo así. It's better if you leave it like this.
Mejor venid en tren. You'd be better coming by train.

ᵟ **el & la mejor** *masc & fem noun*
▷ see **mejor** *adj, noun*
el mejor, la mejor the best one
Escoge el mejor. Pick the best one.
Estas naranjas son las mejores que he visto. These oranges are the best I've seen.

la mejora *fem noun*
improvement

ᵟ **mejorar** *verb* [17]
1 to improve
Tiene que mejorar la letra. Hee must improve his handwriting.

2 to get better
Ha mejorado del estómago. He's got over his stomach problems.

mejorarse *reflexive verb* [17]
to get better
¡Que te mejores! Get well soon!
¿Se mejoró del resfriado? Is her cold better?

ᵟ **mellizo** *masc adjective*, **melliza** *fem*
▷ see **mellizo** *noun*
twin
hermanas mellizas twin sisters

ᵟ **el mellizo** *masc noun*, **la melliza** *fem*
▷ see **mellizo** *adj*
twin

ᵟ **el melocotón** *masc noun*
peach

la melodía *fem noun*
melody

ᵟ **el melón** *masc noun*
melon

ᵟ **la memoria** *fem noun*
1 memory
aprenderse algo de memoria to learn something by heart
Se ha aprendido el poema de memoria. He's learnt the poem by heart.

2 memorias memoirs

mencionar *verb* [17]
to mention

mendigar *verb* [17]
to beg

el mendigo *masc noun*, **la mendiga** *fem*
beggar

la menestra *fem noun*
menestra de verduras vegetable stew

ᵟ **el meñique** *masc noun*
little finger

ᵟ **menor** *masc & fem adjective*
▷ see **menor** *noun*
1 younger
mi hermana menor my younger sister
Soy menor que tú. I'm younger than you.

2 youngest
el menor de la familia the youngest of the family

3 less
Su importancia es cada vez menor. It gets less and less important all the time.
en menor grado to a lesser extent

4 least
con el menor esfuerzo posible with as little effort as possible

5 minor
de menor importancia of minor importance

6 smaller
un número menor de alumnos a smaller number of pupils ▸▸

ᵟ indicates key words   **195**

7 smallest
hasta el menor detalle even the smallest
detail

8 No tengo la menor idea. I haven't got the
slightest idea.

♂ el & la **menor** masc & fem noun
▷ **see menor** adj
minor (under 18)
no apto para menores not suitable for
under-18s

♂ **menos** invariable adjective
▷ **see menos** adv, pron, prep

1 less
de menos peso of less weight

2 fewer
Hay menos gente que ayer. There are
fewer people than yesterday.

♂ **menos** adverb ▷ **see menos** adj, pron, prep

1 less
Ahora sale menos. He goes out less now.
Ahora los veo menos. I see less of them.
cada vez menos less and less

2 least
el menos alto the shortest one
las menos informadas the least well-
informed
Es lo menos que esperaba. It's the least I
expected.
Compro siempre los menos caros. I always
buy the least expensive ones.
el que corre menos the slowest runner of all

3 (in comparisons) menos que ... less than ...
Habla menos que yo. He speaks less than I
do.
Cuesta menos que el otro. It costs less than
the other one.

4 (in comparisons with numbers) menos de ...
less than ...
adultos de menos de treinta años adults
aged under thirty
Cuesta menos de cien euros. It costs less
than a hundred euros.
Vinieron menos de veinte. Fewer than
twenty came.

♂ **menos** pronoun ▷ **see menos** adj, adv, prep

1 less
Ahora compramos menos. We buy less
now.

2 (in expressions) al menos, por lo menos at
least
de menos under
cobrar de menos cobrar de menos
Hay diez tarjetas de menos. There are ten
cards too few.
¡Menos mal! Thank goodness!

♂ **menos** preposition ▷ **see menos** adj, adv,
pron

1 except
todos menos su madre everybody except
her mother

2 (telling the time) a las dos menos veinte at
twenty minutes to two
Son las ocho menos diez. It's ten to eight.

♂ el **mensaje** masc noun
message
Te dejó un mensaje. She left you a
message.
¿Hay algún mensaje para mí? Are there any
messages for me.
• el **mensaje de texto** text message

♂ el **mensajero** masc noun, la **mensajera**
fem

1 messenger

2 courier
un servicio de mensajeros a courier service

menso masc adjective, **mensa** fem
(Latin America) **stupid**

♂ **mensual** masc & fem adjective
monthly
un boletín mensual a monthly bulletin
dos cientos euros mensuales two hundred
euros a month

♂ **mensualmente** adverb
monthly
Se cobrará mensualmente. It will be
charged monthly.

♂ la **menta** fem noun
mint
un caramelo de menta a mint
¿Por qué no tomas un té de menta? Why
don't you have a peppermint tea?

♂ **mental** masc & fem adjective
mental
Hizo un esfuerzo mental para recordarlo.
He made a mental effort to remember it.

♂ la **mente** fem noun
mind
Perdón, tenía la mente en otra cosa. Sorry,
my mind was on something else.
Se le quedó la mente en blanco. Her mind
went blank.

♂ **mentir** verb [14]
to lie
Nos está mintiendo. He's lying to us.
No me mientas más. Stop lying to me.

a
b
c
d
e
f
g
h
i
j
k
l
m
n
ñ
o
p
q
r
s
t
u
v
w
x
y
z

♂ la **mentira** *fem noun*
lie
decir mentiras to tell lies
¡Mentira! No fui yo. That's a lie! It wasn't me.

♂ el **mentiroso** *masc noun*, la **mentirosa** *fem*
liar

♂ el **mentón** *masc noun*
chin
Me di en el mentón contra la mesa. I bumped my chin on the table.

♂ el **menú** *masc noun*
menu
el menú del día the set menu
• el **menú desplegable** (*Computing*) pull-down menu

♂ **menudo** *masc adjective*, **menuda** *fem*
1 **small**
Es muy menuda. She's quite small.
2 **a menudo** often
Nos vemos a menudo. We see each other often.
3 **¡Menudo problema!** What a problem!
¡Menuda moto! What an incredible motorbike!

♂ el **mercado** *masc noun*
market
ir al mercado to go to the market
• el **Mercado Común** the Common Market
• el **mercado negro** black market

♂ las **mercancías** *plural fem noun*
goods
mercancías importadas imported goods
un tren de mercancías a goods train

♂ la **mercería** *fem noun*
haberdashery (*selling sewing materials, buttons, etc*)

♂ **merecer** *verb* [35]
1 **to deserve**
Mereces un castigo. You deserve to be punished.
2 **merecer la pena** to be worthwhile
La película merece la pena. The film is worth seeing.
No merece la pena volver. It's not worth going back.

merecerse *reflexive verb* [35]
to deserve
No me merezco que me traten así. I don't deserve to be treated like this.
Se lo tiene bien merecido. It serves him right.

♂ **merendar** *verb* [29]
to have a teatime snack
Siempre merienda pan y chocolate. He always has bread and chocolate in the afternoon.
¿Quieres merendar algo? Do you want something to eat for tea?
¡A merendar! Teatime!

♂ **merezca, merezco, etc** *verb* ▷ merecer

meridional *masc & fem adjective*
southern

♂ la **merienda** *fem noun*
▷ see **merienda** *verb*
1 **afternoon snack**
2 **ir de merienda** to go for a picnic
• la **merienda campestre** picnic

♂ **merienda, meriendo, etc** *verb*
▷ see **merienda** *noun* ▷ merendar

el **mérito** *masc noun*
merit

♂ la **merluza** *fem noun*
hake

♂ la **mermelada** *fem noun*
jam
mermelada de fresas strawberry jam
mermelada de naranjas marmalade

WORD TIP *mermelada* does not mean *marmalade* in English, but *jam* in general.

♂ el **mes** *masc noun*
month
el mes que viene next month
mil euros al mes a thousand euros a month
hace dos meses two months ago
un bebé de siete meses a seven-month-old baby

♂ la **mesa** *fem noun*
table
poner la mesa to set the table
quitar la mesa, recoger la mesa to clear the table
sentarse a la mesa to sit at the table
¡A la mesa! Food's ready!

el **mesero** *masc noun*, la **mesera** *fem*
(*Latin America*)
1 **waiter**
2 **waitress**

♂ la **mesita** *fem noun*
una mesita de noche a bedside table

el **mesón** *masc noun*
1 **restaurant** (*traditional kind*)
2 **inn**

a
b
c
d
e
f
g
h
i
j
k
l
m
n
ñ
o
p
q
r
s
t
u
v
w
x
y
z

♂ indicates key words　　　　　　　　**197**

ƒ la meta *fem noun*
1 **aim**
Tiene como meta ser actriz. Her aim is to become an actress.
2 **finishing line** (*in race*)

ƒ el metal *masc noun*
metal
metales pesados heavy metals

ƒ metálico *masc adjective*, **metálica** *fem*
metallic

ƒ meteorológico *masc adjective*,
meteorológica *fem*
meteorological
un parte meteorológico a weather forecast

ƒ meter *verb* [18]
1 **to put (something) in**
Metió la mano. He put his hand in.
Mételo en la carpeta. Put it in the folder.
2 **to fit**
¿Puedes meter algo más en la maleta? Can you fit anything else in the suitcase?
3 **meter un gol** to score a goal
4 **meter la primera** to put the car in first gear
meter la marcha atrás to put the car into reverse

meterse *reflexive verb* [18]
1 **meterse en** to get in(to)
meterse en la cama to get into bed
2 **meterse en algo** to get involved in something
Se metió en un asunto turbio. He got mixed up in some shady business.
No te metas en mis asuntos. Mind your own business.

el método *masc noun*
method

ƒ métrico *masc adjective*, **métrica** *fem*
metric

ƒ el metro *masc noun*
1 **underground railway**
el Metro de Londres the London Underground
2 **metre**
los cien metros libres the hundred metres freestyle

ƒ mexicano *masc adjective & noun*,
mexicana *fem adjective & noun*
1 **Mexican**
2 un mexicano, una mexicana Mexican

> **WORD TIP** Adjectives and nouns for nationality and regional origin do not have capital letters in Spanish.

ƒ México *masc noun*
Mexico

ƒ la mezcla *fem noun*
1 **mixture**
Añadí una pizca de sal a la mezcla. I added a pinch of salt to the mixture.
2 **mix**
una mezcla de culturas a mix of cultures

ƒ mezclar *verb* [17]
1 **to mix**
Hay que mezclarlo con agua. It has to be mixed with water.
2 **to mix up**
Has mezclado todos los papeles. You've mixed up all the papers.

mezclarse *reflexive verb* [17]
mezclarse en algo to get mixed up in something
Evitó mezclarse en el asunto. She avoided getting mixed up in the matter.

ƒ la mezquita *fem noun*
mosque

ƒ mi *masc & fem adjective*
my
mi madre my mother
mis amigos my friends

ƒ mí *pronoun*
1 (*after prepositions*) **me**
detrás de mí behind me
Se olvidaron de mí. They forgot about me.
¿Es para mí? Is it for me?
Me lo dio a mí. He gave it to me.
2 A mí me gusta. I like it.
A mí me parece que … I think that …
3 mí mismo, mí misma myself
Voy a guardar el último para mí mismo. I'm going to keep the last one for myself.
Sé cuidar de mí misma. I can look after myself.
4 por mí … as far as I'm concerned …

ƒ el micrófono *masc noun*
microphone

el microondas *masc noun, pl:* los **microondas**
microwave oven

ƒ el microscopio *masc noun*
microscope
Lo miré en el microscopio. I looked at it under the microscope.

mida, midiendo, midió, mido, etc *verb*
▷ **medir**

ℰ el **miedo** *masc noun*
fear
¡Qué miedo! How frightening!
tener miedo to be scared
Tengo mucho miedo. I'm really scared.
¿Tienes miedo de intentarlo? Are you afraid of trying?
Le tengo miedo a la ocuridad. I'm afraid of the dark.
Le da miedo la altura. She's afraid of heights.
Les da miedo ir solos. They're afraid of going on their own.

ℰ **miedoso** *masc adjective*, **miedosa** *fem*
¡No seas miedoso! Don't be so scared!
Es muy miedoso. He's afraid of everything.

ℰ la **miel** *fem noun*
honey

ℰ el & la **miembro** *masc & fem noun*
▷ see **miembro** *masc noun*
member
Se hizo miembro del partido. She became a member of the party.

el **miembro** *masc noun*
▷ see **miembro** *masc & fem noun*
limb (*of the body*)

ℰ **mienta**, **miento**, **etc** *verb* ▷ **mentir**

ℰ **mientras** *adverb* ▷ see **mientras** *conj*
meanwhile
mientras tanto in the meantime
Mientras tanto él estaba esperando en la estación. In the meantime he was waiting at the station.

ℰ **mientras** *conjunction* ▷ see **mientras** *adv*
1 **while**
Pon la mesa mientras yo hago la comida.
Lay the table while I cook the meal.
2 **as long as**
Mientras yo viva ... As long as I'm alive ...

ℰ el **miércoles** *masc noun*
Wednesday
el miércoles on Wednesday
el miércoles pasado last Wednesday
los miércoles on Wednesdays
cada miércoles every Wednesday
Abren los miércoles. They're open on Wednesdays.

WORD TIP Names of months and days start with small letters in Spanish.

ℰ la **miga** *fem noun*
crumb

ℰ **mil** *number*
thousand
mil cien one thousand one hundred
mil doscientos cincuenta one thousand two hundred and fifty
cinco mil euros five thousand euros
Acudieron miles de personas. Thousands of people attended.

el **milagro** *masc noun*
miracle

ℰ el **milenio** *masc noun*
millennium

ℰ **milésimo** *masc adjective*, **milésima** *fem*
thousandth

ℰ la **mili** *fem noun*
(*informal*) **military service**
Hizo la mili en Ceuta. He did his military service in Ceuta.

ℰ el **milímetro** *masc noun*
milimetre
Tiene diez milímetros de espesor. It's ten millimetres thick.

ℰ **militar** *masc & fem adjective*
▷ see **militar** *noun*
military

ℰ el & la **militar** *masc & fem noun*
▷ see **militar** *adj*
soldier
Su tía es militar. His aunt's a soldier.

ℰ **millón** *number*
million
un millón de euros a million euros
un millón dos cientos mil one million two hundred thousand
tres millones de habitantes three million inhabitants
un millón de gracias thank you ever so much

ℰ el **millonario** *masc noun*, la **millonaria** *fem*
millionaire

mimado *masc adjective*, **mimada** *fem*
spoilt (*child*)

ℰ la **mina** *fem noun*
mine
una mina de carbón a coalmine

ℰ **mineral** *masc & fem adjective*
▷ see **mineral** *noun*
mineral

ℰ el **mineral** *masc noun* ▷ see **mineral** *adj*
mineral

a
b
c
d
e
f
g
h
i
j
k
l
m
n
ñ
o
p
q
r
s
t
u
v
w
x
y
z

a
b
c
d
e
f
g
h
i
j
k
l
m
n
ñ
o
p
q
r
s
t
u
v
w
x
y
z

minero *masc adjective,* **minera** *fem*
▷ see **minero** *noun*
mining
una zona minera a mining area

♪ el **minero** *masc noun,* la **minera** *fem*
▷ see **minero** *adj*
miner

♪ la **mini** *fem noun*
(*informal*) **mini**

♪ la **minifalda** *fem noun*
miniskirt

♪ **mínimo** *masc adjective,* **mínima** *fem*
▷ see **mínimo** *noun*
minimum
la cantidad mínima the minimum quantity
No me importa lo más mínimo. I couldn't
care less.

♪ el **mínimo** *masc noun* ▷ see **mínimo** *adj*
minimum
un mínimo de cien euros a minimum of one
hundred euros
cinco años como mínimo at least five years

♪ el **ministerio** *masc noun*
ministry
el Ministerio del Interior the Interior
Ministry (*the Home Office in the UK*)

♪ el **ministro** *masc noun,* la **ministra** *fem*
minister
la Ministra de Salud Pública the Public
Health Minister

♪ la **minoría** *fem noun*
minority

♪ **mintamos, mintió, etc** *verb* ▷ **mentir**

♪ la **minúscula** *fem noun*
▷ see **minúsculo** *adj*
small letter
¿Se escribe con mayúscula o minúscula? Is
it spelt with a capital or a small letter?

minúsculo *masc adjective,* **minúscula** *fem*
▷ see **minúscula** *noun*
tiny

♪ **minusválido** *masc adjective,*
minusválida *fem*
▷ see **minusválido** *noun*
disabled

♪ el **minusválido** *masc noun,* la
minusválida *fem*
▷ see **minusválido** *adj*
disabled person
coches para minusválidos cars for the
disabled

♪ el **minuto** *masc noun*
minute

♪ **mío** *masc adjective,* **mía** *fem* ▷ see **mío** *pron*
mine
una amiga mía a friend of mine
unos dibujos míos some of my drawings

♪ el **mío** *pronoun,* la **mía** *fem* ▷ see **mío** *adj*
mine
El mío es verde. Mine is green.
¿Dónde están las mías? Where are mine?

miope *masc & fem adjective*
shortsighted

♪ la **mirada** *fem noun*
look
una mirada alegre a happy look
bajar la mirada to look down
dirigirle una mirada a alguien to look at
somebody
Me dirigió una mirada. She looked at me.
echarle una mirada a algo to have a look at
something
Voy a echarle una mirada al periódico. I'm
going to have a look at the newspaper.

♪ **mirar** *verb* [17]
1 to look
Miré afuera. I looked outside.
Mira en el cajón Look in the drawer.
2 mirar algo to look at something
Me miró. He looked at me.
¡No me mires así! Don't look at me like that!
Miró la foto con interés. He looked at the
photo with interest.
3 to watch
mirar la tele to watch TV
4 mirar fijamente to stare at
Miraba fijamente la pantalla. He was
staring at the screen.

mirarse *reflexive verb* [17]
mirarse en el espejo to look at yourself in
the mirror
mirarse las manos to look at your hands

el **mirlo** *masc noun*
blackbird

♪ la **misa** *fem noun*
mass
ir a misa to go to mass

♪ **miserable** *masc & fem adjective*
1 wretched (*conditions*)
2 mean (*person*)

ᵟ la **miseria** *fem noun*
1 **misery**
2 **poverty**
Viven en la miseria. They live in poverty.
3 **pittance**
Gana una miseria. He earns a pittance.

ᵟ el **misil** *masc noun*
missile

ᵟ **mismo** *masc adjective*, **misma** *fem*
▷ see **mismo** *adv, pron*
1 **same**
al mismo tiempo at the same time
Iba en la misma dirección que yo. She was going in the same direction as me.
Llevan los mismos zapatos. They have the same shoes.
2 **very**
en este mismo lugar in this very spot
en ese mismo momento right at that moment
3 yo mismo I myself
Lo vi yo mismo. I saw it myself.
Lo dijo ella misma. She said it herself.
Eso mismo dije yo. That's just what I said.

ᵟ **mismo** *adverb* ▷ see **mismo** *adj, pron*
right
ahora mismo right now
Está ahí mismo. It's right there.
al lado mismo de casa right next to the house

ᵟ **mismo** *masc pronoun*, **misma** *fem pronoun*
▷ see **mismo** *adj, adv*
1 el mismo the same one
He usado la misma. I've used the same one.
Sara tiene los mismos que tú. Sara has the same ones as you.
2 lo mismo the same thing
Siempre dice lo mismo. He always says the same thing.
Tiene lo mismo que yo. She has the same as me.
dar lo mismo to not matter
Da lo mismo el color. The colour doesn't matter.

ᵟ el **misterio** *masc noun*
mystery

ᵟ **misterioso** *masc adjective*, **misteriosa** *fem*
mysterious

ᵟ la **mitad** *fem noun*
1 **half**
la mitad del pastel half the cake
a mitad de precio at half-price

2 **halfway**
llenar algo hasta la mitad to half-fill something
Llenó la botella hasta la mitad. She half-filled the bottle.
A mitad de camino paramos a comer. We stopped halfway to eat.
Lo he leído hasta la mitad. I'm halfway through reading it.
3 cortar algo por la mitad to cut something in two
Cortó la manzana por la mitad. He cut the apple in two.

ᵟ el **mito** *masc noun*
myth
mitos griegos Greek myths

ᵟ **mixto** *masc adjective*, **mixta** *fem*
mixed

el **mobiliario** *masc noun*
furniture
· el **mobiliario de cocina** kitchen fittings

ᵟ la **mochila** *fem noun*
1 **backpack**
2 **school bag**

ᵟ los **mocos** *plural masc noun*
tener mocos to have a runny nose
limpiarse los mocos to wipe your nose

ᵟ la **moda** *fem noun*
fashion
la moda juvenil young fashion
estar de moda to be in fashion
pasarse de moda to go out of fashion
Están muy de moda. They are very fashionable.
Siempre va a la última moda. He's always wearing the latest fashion.

ᵟ los **modales** *plural masc noun*
manners
tener buenos modales to have good manners

ᵟ el **modelo** *masc noun* ▷ see **modelo** *masc & fem noun*
model
el último modelo the latest model
utilizar algo como modelo to use something as a model

ᵟ el & la **modelo** *masc & fem noun*
▷ see **modelo** *masc noun*
model (*in fashion*)
Sale con una modelo brasileña. He's going out with a Brazilian model.

a
b
c
d
e
f
g
h
i
j
k
l
m
n
ñ
o
p
q
r
s
t
u
v
w
x
y
z

♂ **moderno** *masc adjective*, **moderna** *fem*
1 **modern**
2 **trendy**

♂ **modesto** *masc adjective*, **modesta** *fem*
1 **modest** (*person, attitude*)
2 **humble** (*status, lifestyle*)

modificar *verb* [31]
  to change

♂ el **modisto** *masc noun*, la **modista** *fem*
1 **dressmaker**
2 **(fashion) designer**

♂ el **modo** *masc noun*
1 **way**
  Lo haré a mi modo. I'll do it my way.
  A mi modo de ver ... To my way of thinking
  ...
  No hubo modo. There was no way (of doing
  it).
  Lo hizo de cualquier modo. He did it any old
  way.
  ¡De ningún modo! No way!
  De cualquier modo, te llamaré antes. In any
  case, I'll phone you first.
2 de modo que ... so ...
3 ¿De modo que te vas? So you're off, are
  you?
4 de modo que ... so that ...
  Déjalo aquí de modo que la vea cuando
  vuelva. Leave it here so that he sees it when
  he comes back.
5 (*in expressions*) de todos modos anyway
  De todos modos, no iba a comprarlo.
  Anyway I wasn't going to buy it.
  en cierto modo somehow
• el **modo de empleo** instructions for use

♂ **mohoso** *masc adjective*, **mohosa** *fem*
  mouldy

♂ **mojado** *masc adjective*, **mojada** *fem*
  wet
  calcetines mojados wet socks

♂ **mojar** *verb* [17]
  to wet
  Me has mojado la camisa. You've wet my
  shirt.

mojarse *reflexive verb* [17]
  to get wet
  Me mojé volviendo a casa. I got wet
  coming home.
  Se me mojó el pelo. My hair got wet.

♂ **moler** *verb* [38]
  to grind

♂ **molestar** *verb* [17]
1 **to disturb**
  'No molestar' 'Do not disturb'
  No molestes a tu madre, que está
  trabajando. Don't disturb your mother,
  she's working.
2 **to bother**
  ¿Te molesta que ponga la tele? Do you
  mind if I put the TV on?
  Perdone que le moleste. Sorry to bother
  you. (*polite form*)
3 **to annoy**
  Me molesta que no me hayan invitado. I'm
  annoyed that they haven't invited me.

molestarse *reflexive verb* [17]
1 **to get upset**
  Se molestó porque fuimos sin ella. She got
  upset because we went without her.
2 molestarse en hacer algo to bother to do
  something
  No se molestó en preguntar. She didn't
  bother to find out.

♂ la **molestia** *fem noun*
1 **trouble**
  No es ninguna molestia. It's no trouble at
  all.
  causar molestias a alguien to be a nuisance
  to someone
  Los niños no me causaron ninguna
  molestia. The children were no nuisance at
  all.
2 tomarse la molestia de hacer algo to take
  the trouble to do something
  Ni se tomó la molestia de avisarme. He
  didn't even bother to let me know.
3 Perdone la molestia. Sorry to bother you.
4 Si no es molestia ... If you don't mind ...
  ¿Me llevas, si no es molestia? Would you
  mind giving me a lift?

molesto *masc adjective*, **molesta** *fem*
1 **annoying**
  un ruido molesto an annoying noise
2 **uncomfortable**
3 estar molesto to be upset
  Sé que está molesta conmigo. I know she's
  upset with me.

♂ el **momento** *masc noun*
  moment
  dentro de un momento in a moment
  de momento at the moment
  justo en ese momento right at that
  moment
  ¡Un momento! Just a moment!
  en cualquier momento any moment
  en este momento right now

ℰ la **monarquía** *fem noun*
monarchy

ℰ el **monasterio** *masc noun*
monastery

ℰ la **moneda** *fem noun*
1 coin
una moneda de dos euros a two euro coin
2 currency
Quería pagar en moneda suiza. He wanted to pay in Swiss currency.

ℰ el **monedero** *masc noun*
purse

ℰ la **monja** *fem noun*
nun

ℰ el **monje** *masc noun*
monk

ℰ **mono** *masc adjective*, **mona** *fem*
▷ see **mono** *noun*
1 cute (baby, puppy)
2 pretty (person, garment)

ℰ el **mono** *masc noun*, la **mona** *fem*
▷ see **mono** *adj*
monkey

ℰ el **monopatín** *masc noun*
skateboard

ℰ el **monstruo** *masc noun*
monster

ℰ la **montaña** *fem noun*
mountain
en la montaña in the mountains
• la **montaña rusa** roller coaster

el **montañismo** *masc noun*
mountain climbing

montañoso *masc adjective*, **montañosa** *fem*
mountainous

ℰ **montar** *verb* [17]
1 to get in
montar en el coche to get in the car
2 to get on
montar en el avión to get on the plane
3 to ride
montar a caballo to ride a horse
montar en la moto to get on the motorbike
montar en bicicleta to ride a bike
4 to get on (a horse)
Montó su caballo y se fue. He got on his horse and left.
5 to put on (a play)
6 to set up (a business, exhibition)
7 to put up (a tent)

8 montar un escándalo (informal) to cause a scene

montarse *reflexive verb* [17]
1 to get on
Se montó en el tren. He got on the train.
2 to get in
montarse en un coche to get into a car

ℰ el **monte** *masc noun*
1 mountain
2 woodland
• el **monte de piedad** pawnbroker's shop

ℰ el **montón** *masc noun*
1 pile
Puse todas las revistas en un montón. I put all the magazines in a pile.
2 un montón de algo, montones de algo
loads of something
Había un montón de niños. There were loads of children.
Tiene montones de dinero. She has loads of money.
Me gusta un montón. (informal) I like it a lot.
3 del montón (informal) run-of-the mill
un cantante del montón an run-of-the mill singer

ℰ el **monumento** *masc noun*
monument
un monumento a los caídos a war memorial

ℰ la **moqueta** *fem noun*
fitted carpet

ℰ la **mora** *fem noun* ▷ see **moro** *adj*
blackberry
recoger moras to pick blackberries

ℰ **morado** *masc adjective*, **morada** *fem*
▷ see **morado** *noun*
purple

ℰ el **morado** *masc noun* ▷ see **morado** *adj*
purple

moral *masc & fem adjective*
▷ see **moral** *noun*
moral
el apoyo moral moral support

ℰ la **moral** *fem noun* ▷ see **moral** *adj*
1 morals
No tienen ninguna moral. They have no morals.
2 morale
estar bajo de moral to feel low

ℰ la **morcilla** *fem noun*
black pudding

ℰ indicates key words   203

♂ **morder** *verb* [38]
to bite
No te preocupes, no muerde. Don't worry, he doesn't bite.

♂ el **mordisco** *masc noun*
bite
darle un mordisco a algo to bite (on) something
Le dio un mordisco a la manzana. He took a bite out of the apple.

♂ **moreno** *masc adjective*, **morena** *fem*
1 **dark** (*hair*)
2 Es morena. She's dark-haired.
3 estar moreno to be tanned
ponerse moreno to get tanned

♂ **morir** *verb* [55]
to die
morir ahogado to drown
morir en un accidente to be killed in an accident

morirse *reflexive verb* [55]
1 **to die**
Se murió de un infarto. He died of a heart attack.
Me muero de hambre. I'm starving.
Me muero de ganas de verla. I'm dying to see her.
¡Me muero de frío! I'm freezing!
2 morirse por hacer algo to be dying to do something
Se muere por ir a la playa. He's dying to go to the beach.

♂ **moro** *masc adjective*, **mora** *fem*
▷ see **moro** *noun*
Moorish

♂ un **moro** *masc noun*, una **mora** *fem*
▷ see **moro** *adj*
1 **Moor** (*the Muslim occupiers of parts of Spain between 711 and 1492*)
2 **North African**

WORD TIP Adjectives and nouns for nationality and regional origin do not have capital letters in Spanish.

♂ **mortal** *masc & fem adjective*
1 **fatal** (*illness, accident*)
2 **lethal** (*blow, dose*)

♂ la **mosca** *fem noun*
fly

♂ el **mosquito** *masc noun*
mosquito

♂ la **mostaza** *fem noun*
mustard

♂ el **mostrador** *masc noun*
1 **counter** (*in a shop*)
2 **bar** (*in a pub*)
3 **check-in desk** (*at an airport*)

♂ **mostrar** *verb* [24]
to show
Muéstrame cómo se hace. Show me how to do it.

mostrarse *reflexive verb* [24]
mostrarse interesado en algo to show interest in something
mostrarse amable to be kind
mostrarse contento to be happy

♂ el **motivo** *masc noun*
1 **cause**
el motivo del accidente the cause of the accident
2 **reason**
por motivos personales for personal reasons

♂ la **moto** *fem noun*
motorbike
montar en moto to ride a motorbike
montar en la moto to get on the motorbike
• la **moto acuática** jetski

♂ la **motocicleta** *fem noun*
motorbike

♂ el & la **motociclista** *masc & fem noun*
motorcyclist

♂ el **motor** *masc noun*
engine
• el **motor a reacción** jet engine

la **motora** *fem noun*
motorboat

♂ el & la **motorista** *masc & fem noun*
motorcyclist

WORD TIP motorista does not mean motorist in English; for the meaning of motorist ▷ **automovilista**

♂ **mover** *verb* [38]
to move
Ayúdame a mover estas cajas. Help me to move these boxes.

moverse *reflexive verb* [38]
to move
No me atreví a moverme. I didn't dare move.
No te muevas. Don't move.
Deja de moverte. Stop fidgeting.

el **móvil** *masc noun*
mobile phone
Llámame al móvil. Call me on my mobile.

♂ el **movimiento** *masc noun*
movement
ponerse en movimiento to start moving

♂ el **mozo** *masc noun*, la **moza** *fem*
1 **young boy**
2 **young girl**
· el **mozo de estación** porter

el **MP3** *masc noun*
MP3 player

♂ el **muchacho** *masc noun*, la **muchacha** *fem*
1 **boy**
2 **girl**

♂ la **muchedumbre** *fem noun*
crowd

♂ **mucho** *masc adjective*, **mucha** *fem*
  ▷ see **mucho** *adv, pron*
1 **a lot of**
mucha lluvia a lot of rain
mucho lodo a lot of mud
Sucedió hace mucho tiempo. It happened
a long time ago.
2 **much**
No queda mucho tiempo. There's not
much time left.
¿Queda mucha cerveza? Is there much
beer left?
3 **many**
¿Había muchos niños? Were there many
children?
muchas veces many times
4 (*in expressions*) Hacía mucho frío. It was very
cold.
Tengo mucho sueño. I'm very sleepy.
5 Tengo mucha prisa. I'm in a real hurry.
6 muchas gracias thanks a lot
mucho gusto nice to meet you
Lo haré con mucho gusto. I'd be very
pleased to do it.

♂ **mucho** *adverb* ▷ see **mucho** *adj, pron*
1 **a lot**
Lo usan mucho. They use it a lot.
Eso es mucho mejor. That's a lot better.
Salen mucho. They go out a lot.
trabajar mucho to work very hard
Voy a estudiar mucho. I'm going to study
very hard.
2 **very**
Lo siento mucho. I'm very sorry.
'¿Te interesa?'—'Mucho.' 'Are you
interested?'—'Very.'
3 mucho más much more
Es mucho más grande. It's much bigger.

4 (*in expressions*) mucho antes long before
mucho después long after
5 como mucho at the most
quince kilómetros como mucho fifteen
kilometres at the most
6 ni mucho menos far from it

♂ **mucho** *masc pronoun*, **mucha** *fem*
  ▷ see **mucho** *adj, adv*
1 **a lot**
Tienes mucho que aprender. You have a lot
to learn.
Traté de sacar el agua, pero aún quedaba
mucha. I tried to get the water out, but
there was still a lot left.
2 **much**
No tengo mucho. I haven't got much.
3 **many**
No quedan muchas. There aren't many
left.
Muchos se sorprendieron. Many were
surprised.
4 (*in time expressions*) Tardan mucho. They are
taking a long time.
¿Hace mucho que ha llamado? Is it a long
time since she called?
Hace mucho que no sé nada de ella. It's a
long time since I last heard from her.
No falta mucho para mi cumpleaños. It's
not long to my birthday now.

♂ la **mudanza** *fem noun*
removal
un camión de mudanzas a removal van
estar de mudanza to be in the process of
moving

♂ **mudar** *verb* [17]
1 **to move** (*from one house to another*)
2 mudar a un bebé to change a baby

mudarse *reflexive verb* [17]
1 **to change your clothes**
2 **to move**
mudarse de casa to move house

mudo *masc adjective*, **muda** *fem*
dumb

♂ el **mueble** *masc noun*
piece of furniture
muebles de oficina office furniture
muebles de época antique furniture

♂ la **muela** *fem noun*
back tooth
tener dolor de muelas to have toothache
· la **muela del juicio** wisdom tooth

♪ **muera, muero, etc** *verb* ▷ **morir**

♪ **muerda, muerdo, etc** *verb* ▷ **morder**

♪ la **muerte** *fem noun*
 death
 una muerte repentina a sudden death
 amenazas de muerte death threats
 estar condenado a muerte to be sentenced
 to death

♪ **muerto** *masc adjective*, **muerta** *fem*
 ▷ see **muerto** *noun*
 dead
 Están muertos. They're dead.
 muerto de sed dying of thirst
 Estoy muerto de frío. I'm freezing to death.
 Estamos muertos de hambre. We're
 starving.
 Las niñas estaban muertas de cansancio.
 The girls were dead tired.

 WORD TIP Always use *estar* for 'to be' with
 muerto, ta.

♪ el **muerto** *masc noun*, la **muerta** *fem*
 ▷ see **muerto** *adj*
 dead person
 Hubo un muerto en la explosión. One
 person died in the explosion.
 No ha habido muertos. There were no
 casualties.

♪ **muestra, muestro, etc** *verb* ▷ **mostrar**

♪ **mueva, muevo, etc** *verb* ▷ **mover**

♪ la **mujer** *fem noun*
 1 woman
 mujeres diputadas women members of
 parliament
 2 wife
 mi mujer my wife

♪ la **muleta** *fem noun*
 crutch

 el **mulo** *masc noun*, la **mula** *fem*
 mule

♪ la **multa** *fem noun*
 fine
 Me pusieron una multa. I was fined.

 multicolor *masc & fem adjective*
 multicoloured

♪ la **multiplicación** *fem noun*
 multiplication

♪ **multiplicar** *verb* [31]
 to multiply
 Multiplica trece por siete. Multiply thirteen
 by seven.

♪ **mundial** *masc & fem adjective*
 ▷ see **mundial** *noun*
 world
 un récord mundial a world record
 la economía mundial the world
 economy
 de fama mundial world-famous

♪ el **mundial** *masc noun* ▷ see **mundial** *adj*
 el mundial de fútbol the World Cup

♪ el **mundo** *masc noun*
 1 world
 2 todo el mundo everybody, everyone

 las **municiones** *plural fem noun*
 ammunition

♪ **municipal** *masc & fem adjective*
 1 **municipal** (*library, elections*)
 2 **local** (*taxes*)

♪ la **muñeca** *fem noun*
 1 doll
 jugar a las muñecas to play dolls
 2 wrist
 • la muñeca de trapo rag doll

♪ el **muñeco** *masc noun*
 1 dummy
 2 doll
 • el muñeco de peluche soft toy

♪ la **muralla** *fem noun*
 wall (*of a city, as defence, etc*)
 la Gran Muralla de China the Great Wall of
 China

♪ el **murciélago** *masc noun*
 bat

♪ **muriendo, murió, etc** *verb* ▷ **morir**

 el **murmullo** *masc noun*
 1 whispering
 hablar en un murmullo to whisper
 2 murmur

♪ **murmurar** *verb* [17]
 1 to whisper
 2 to murmur
 3 murmurar sobre alguien to gossip about
 someone
 Se murmura que … The rumour is that …

♪ el **muro** *masc noun*
 wall

♪ el **músculo** *masc noun*
 muscle

♪ el **museo** *masc noun*
 1 museum
 2 gallery
 un museo de pintura an art gallery

a
b
c
d
e
f
g
h
i
j
k
l
m
n
ñ
o
p
q
r
s
t
u
v
w
x
y
z

- el **museo de arte moderno** modern art museum
- el **museo de cera** waxworks

♪ la **música** *fem noun*
  music
- la **música clásica** classical music
- la **música en directo, música en vivo** live music
- la **música pop** pop music

musical *masc & fem adjective*
  musical

♪ el & la **músico** *masc & fem noun*
1 **musician**
2 **composer**

♪ el **muslo** *masc noun*
1 **thigh**
2 **leg** (*of chicken*)

musulmán *masc adjective & noun*,
musulmana *fem adjective & noun*
1 **Muslim**
2 un musulmán, una musulmana Muslim

WORD TIP Adjectives and nouns for religion do not have capital letters in Spanish.

mutuo *masc adjective*, **mutua** *fem*
  mutual

♪ **muy** *adverb*
1 **very**
  Es muy fácil. It's very easy.
  Está muy bien. It's very good.
  Muy bien, sigamos. Ok, let's go on.
2 **too**
  Era muy pequeño para entenderlo. He was too small to understand it.
3 (*in letters*) Muy señor mío: Dear Sir,

a
b
c
d
e
f
g
h
i
j
k
l
m
n
ñ
o
p
q
r
s
t
u
v
w
x
y
z

Spanish-English

N n

el **nabo** *masc noun*
turnip

el **nácar** *masc noun*
mother-of-pearl

♪ **nacer** *verb* [35]
to be born
¿Dónde naciste? Where were you born?
Nací en Nottingham. I was born in Nottingham.

♪ **nacido** *masc adjective*, **nacida** *fem*
born
nacido en Sevilla born in Seville
un niño recién nacido a new-born baby

♪ el **nacimiento** *masc noun*
1 **birth**
Es madrileño de nacimiento. He was born in Madrid.
2 **crib** (*nativity scene*)

♪ la **nación** *fem noun*
nation

♪ **nacional** *masc & fem adjective*
national

♪ la **nacionalidad** *fem noun*
nationality
¿De qué nacionalidad eres? What nationality are you?
Es de nacionalidad británica. He's British.

♪ **nada** *adverb* ▷ see **nada** *pron*
at all
No me gusta nada. I don't like it at all.
No me ayudan nada. They don't help me at all.

♪ **nada** *pronoun* ▷ see **nada** *adv*
1 **nothing, not ... anything**
No queda nada. There's nothing left.
No hay nada nuevo. There's nothing new.
No me dijeron nada. They didn't say anything to me.
Yo no sé nada de eso. I don't know anything about that.
Es mejor que nada. It's better than nothing.
2 (*in expressions*) nada de: No tengo nada de dinero. I have no money at all.
nada más nothing else
No quiero nada más. I don't want anything else.
Sólo quiero hablar con ella, nada más. I only want to speak to her, nothing else.

Nada más, gracias. That's all thank you.
nada más que only
No quiero nada más que un kilo. I only want one kilo.
De nada. You're welcome.
'Gracias.'—'De nada.' 'Thank you.'—'You're welcome.'
3 **love** (*in tennis*)
treinta nada thirty love

♪ **nadar** *verb* [17]
to swim
nadar a braza to swim breaststroke

♪ **nadie** *pronoun*
nobody, not ... anybody
Nadie llamó., No llamó nadie. Nobody phoned.
Nadie sabrá. No one will know.
No se lo dije a nadie. I didn't tell anybody.

♪ el **nailon** *masc noun*
nylon

♪ el **naipe** *masc noun*
card, playing card
juegos de naipes card games

la **nana** *fem noun*
lullaby

♪ **naranja** *invariable adjective*
▷ see **naranja** *noun*, **naranjo** *noun*
orange
unos pantalones naranja a pair of orange trousers

WORD TIP *naranja* never changes.

♪ la **naranja** *fem noun* ▷ see **naranja** *adj*, *noun*, **naranjo** *noun*
orange (*the fruit*)
un zumo de naranja an orange juice

♪ el **naranja** *masc noun* ▷ see **naranja** *adj*, *noun*, **naranjo** *masc noun*
orange (*the colour*)

♪ la **naranjada** *fem noun*
orangeade

el **naranjo** *masc noun* ▷ see **naranja** *adj*, *noun*
orange tree

el & la **narcotraficante** *masc & fem noun*
drugs trafficker

el **narcotráfico** *masc noun*
drugs trade

ᵹ la **nariz** *fem noun*
nose
sonarse la nariz to blow your nose
Me sale sangre de la nariz. I've got a nosebleed.

ᵹ la **nata** *fem noun*
cream
- la **nata líquida** single cream
- la **nata montada** whipped cream
- la **nata para montar** double cream

ᵹ la **natación** *fem noun*
swimming

ᵹ las **natillas** *plural fem noun*
cold custard *(eaten as a pudding)*

ᵹ **natural** *masc & fem adjective*
natural *(state, ingredients, ability, etc)*
historia natural natural history
Es natural que lo hagan. It's natural that they should do it.

WORD TIP *ser natural que* is followed by a verb in the subjunctive.

ᵹ la **naturaleza** *fem noun*
nature
respetar la naturaleza to respect nature
- la **naturaleza humana** human nature
- la **naturaleza muerta** still life

naturalmente *adverb*
naturally

las **náuseas** *plural fem noun*
nausea
tener náuseas to feel sick
El olor me daba náuseas. The smell made me feel sick.

nauseabundo *masc adjective*,
nauseabunda *fem*
nauseating

ᵹ la **navaja** *fem noun*
penknife
- la **navaja de afeitar** cut-throat razor

ᵹ la **nave** *fem noun*
ship
- la **nave espacial** spaceship
- la **nave industrial** industrial premises

ᵹ **navegar** *verb* [28]
1 **to navigate**
2 **to sail**
3 *(Computers)* **navegar en Internet** to surf the Internet
navegar por la red to surf the Net

ᵹ la **Navidad** *fem noun*
1 **Christmas**
el día de Navidad Christmas Day
feliz Navidad Merry Christmas
2 **Navidades** the Christmas season
Pasaré las Navidades con mi familia. I'll spend Christmas with my family.

ᵹ **nazca, nazco, etc** *verb* ▷ **nacer**

ᵹ la **neblina** *fem noun*
mist
Hay neblina. It's misty.

ᵹ **necesario** *masc adjective*, **necesaria** *fem*
necessary
No es necesario hacer todos los ejercicios. It's not necessary to do all the exercises.
No es necesario que lo hagas. There's no need for you to do it.

WORD TIP *ser necesario que* is followed by a verb in the subjunctive.

ᵹ la **necesidad** *fem noun*
need
No hay necesidad de llamarlos. There's no need to call them.
En caso de necesidad me lo prestará. She'll lend it to me if necessary.

ᵹ **necesitar** *verb* [17]
to need
No necesitas llevar el pasaporte. You don't need to take your passport.
'Se necesita camarero con experiencia' 'Experienced waiter required' *(on sign)*

ᵹ la **nectarina** *fem noun*
nectarine

neerlandés *masc adjective & noun*,
neerlandesa *fem adjective & noun*
1 **Dutch**
2 **un neerlandés, una neerlandesa** Dutchman, Dutchwoman
3 **el neerlandés** Dutch *(the language)*

WORD TIP Adjectives and nouns for nationality, regional origin, and language do not have capital letters in Spanish.

nefasto *masc adjective*, **nefasta** *fem*
1 **disastrous** *(consequences)*
2 **awful** *(weather, taste in clothes)*

ᵹ **negar** *verb* [30]
1 **to deny**
Lo niega todo. He denies everything.
2 **to refuse**
Nos negaron su ayuda. They refused to help us.

a
b
c
d
e
f
g
h
i
j
k
l
m
n
ñ
o
p
q
r
s
t
u
v
w
x
y
z

negarse *reflexive verb* [30]
to refuse
negarse a hacer **algo** to refuse to do something
Se niega a ayudarme. He refuses to help me.

ƒ **negativo** *masc adjective*, **negativa** *fem*
negative

la **negociación** *fem noun*
negotiation

ƒ **negociar** *verb* [17]
to negotiate

ƒ el **negocio** *masc noun*
1 **business** (*firm*)
montar un **negocio** to set up a business
un viaje de negocios a business trip
2 los negocios business (*commercial dealings*)
Se dedica a los negocios. She's in business.
3 **deal**
hacer un buen negocio to make a good deal

ƒ **negro** *masc adjective*, **negra** *fem*
▷ see **negro** *noun*
black
Llevaba un traje negro. He was wearing a black suit.

el **negro** *masc noun* ▷ see **negro** *adj*
1 (*Colour*) **black**
2 un negro a black man
una negra a black woman

ƒ **neozelandés** *masc adjective*,
neozelandesa *fem*
▷ see **neozelandés** *noun*
1 **(of) New Zealand**
el gobierno neocelandés the New Zealand government
2 **from New Zealand**
Es neocelandesa. She is from New Zealand.

ƒ un **neozelandés** *masc noun*, una
neozelandesa *fem*
▷ see **neozelandés** *adj*
New Zealander

WORD TIP Adjectives and nouns for nationality and regional origin do not have capital letters in Spanish.

ƒ el **nervio** *masc noun*
nerve
Tengo muchos nervios. I'm very nervous.

ƒ **nervioso** *masc adjective*, **nerviosa** *fem*
nervous
ponerse nervioso to get nervous

ƒ el **neumático** *masc noun*
tyre

la **neumonía** *fem noun*
pneumonia

ƒ **neutro** *masc adjective*, **neutra** *fem*
1 **neutral**
2 **neuter** (*in grammar*)

ƒ la **nevada** *fem noun*
snowfall

ƒ **nevar** *verb* [29]
to snow
Está nevando. It's snowing.

ƒ la **nevasca** *fem noun*
snow storm

ƒ la **nevera** *fem noun*
fridge

ƒ **ni** *conjunction*
1 ni ... ni ... neither ... nor ...
ni uno ni otro neither one nor the other
No es ni grande ni pequeño. It's neither big nor small.
2 no ... ni ... neither ... nor ...
No vino él ni su hermana. Neither he nor his sister came.
No es mío ni suyo. It's not mine and it's not hers either.
una casa sin luz ni agua corriente a house with neither electricity nor running water
'Yo no pienso ir.'—'Ni yo tampoco.' 'I don't intend going.'—'Neither do I.'
3 **not one, not a single one**
Ni uno de ellos llamó. Not one of them called.
No vendieron ni un libro. They didn't sell a single book.
4 ¡Ni hablar! No way!
'¿Puedes hacerlo ahora?'—'¡Ni hablar!' 'Can you do it now?'—'No way!'

Nicaragua *fem noun*
Nicaragua

nicaragüense *masc & fem adjective & noun*
1 **Nicaraguan**
2 un & una nicaragüense Nicaraguan

WORD TIP Adjectives and nouns for nationality and regional origin do not have capital letters in Spanish.

ƒ el **nido** *masc noun*
nest

ꝸ la **niebla** *fem noun*
  fog
  Hay mucha niebla. It's very foggy.

ꝸ el **nieto** *masc noun*, la **nieta** *fem*
1 grandson
2 granddaughter
3 **mis nietos** my grandchildren

ꝸ **nieva**, **nieve**, etc *verb* ▷ **nevar**

ꝸ la **nieve** *fem noun*
1 snow

ꝸ **ningún** *adjective* ▷ **ninguno**

ꝸ **ninguno** *masc adjective*, **ninguna** *fem*
  ▷ see **ninguno** *pron*
  not ... any, **no**
  No trajeron ninguna caja. They didn't bring any boxes.
  No he comprado ningún libro. I didn't buy any books.
  No hay ninguna necesidad. There's no need.

  WORD TIP *ninguno becomes ningún before a masc singular noun.*

ꝸ **ninguno** *pronoun* ▷ see **ninguno** *adj*
1 **neither**, **not ... either**
  Ninguno de los dos vale. Neither of them is suitable.
  Ninguno de los dos me gusta. I don't like either of them.
2 **none**, **not ... any**
  ninguno de los que estaban allí none of those who were there.
  No compró ninguno. He didn't buy any of them.
3 **nobody**
  Ninguno lo vio. Nobody saw him.
  Toca mejor que ninguno. He plays better than anybody.

ꝸ la **niña** *fem noun*
1 girl
2 child
  La conozco desde niña. I've known her since I was a child.

ꝸ la **niñera** *fem noun*
  nanny

la **niñez** *fem noun*
  childhood

ꝸ el **niño** *masc noun*
1 boy
2 child
  De niño era muy tímido. He was very shy as a child.
  Van a tener un niño. They're going to have a baby.

3 **niños** children
  ropa de niños children's clothes

 niños refugiados
> En abril de 1937, tras el bombardeo de Guernica, unos 4000 niños vascos llegaron a Inglaterra refugiados de la Guerra Civil en España.

ꝸ el **nitrógeno** *masc noun*
  nitrogen

ꝸ el **nivel** *masc noun*
1 **level**
  el nivel del agua the level of the water
2 **standard**
  • **el nivel de vida** standard of living

ꝸ **no** *adverb*
1 *(in replies)* **no**
  '¿Es tuyo?'—'No.' 'Is it yours?'—'No.'
  No, no quiero. No, I don't want to.
  '¿Es nuevo?'—'Creo que no.' 'Is it new?'—'I don't think so.'
  Ellos lo saben, pero yo no. They know, but I don't.
2 **not**
  no mucho not much
  ahí no not there
  No es mi amigo. He's not my friend.
  No sabe nadar. He can't swim.
  No se sabe. It's not known.
3 *(with other negatives)* **No comió nada.** He didn't eat anything.
  No vi a nadie. I didn't see anybody.
  No voy nunca al cine. I never go to the cinema.
  No se parecen en nada. They are not similar at all.
4 *(asking for confirmation)* **Somos siete ¿no?** There are seven of us, aren't there?
  Tú hablaste con ella, ¿no? You spoke to her, didn't you?
5 *(before a noun)* **non-**
  la no violencia non-violence
  los no fumadores non smokers

ꝸ la **noche** *fem noun*
1 **night**
  a las once de la noche at eleven o'clock at night
  esta noche tonight
  por la noche at night
  el lunes por la noche Monday night
  la noche anterior the night before
  de noche at night
  buenas noches goodnight
  hacerse de noche to get dark
2 **evening**
  a las ocho de la noche at eight o'clock ▸▸

a
b
c
d
e
f
g
h
i
j
k
l
m
n
ñ
o
p
q
r
s
t
u
v
w
x
y
z

in the evening
esta noche this evening
por la noche in the evening
el lunes por la noche Monday evening
la noche anterior the previous evening
de noche in the evening
buenas noches good evening

♂ la **Nochebuena** *fem noun*
  Christmas Eve

♂ la **Nochevieja** *fem noun*
  New Year's Eve

nocturno *masc adjective*, **nocturna** *fem*
1 **nocturnal**
2 **evening**
  clases nocturnas evening classes

nomás *adverb*
  (*Latin America*) **Démelo así nomás.** Just give it
  to me like that.

nombrar *verb* [17]
1 **to mention**
2 **to appoint**

♂ el **nombre** *masc noun*
1 **name**
  ¿Qué nombre tiene el grupo? What's the
  name of the group?
  ¿Qué nombre le van a poner al niño? What
  are they going to call the baby?
2 (*on forms*) **'Nombre'** 'First name'
  'Nombre y apellidos' 'Full name'
3 **noun**
  • el **nombre de pila** first name

no obstante *in phrase*
  no obstante nevertheless
  **No obstante nos fuimos y disfrutamos
  mucho.** Nevertheless we went and had a
  good time.

♂ el **nordeste**, el **noreste** *masc noun*
  northeast

♂ la **norma** *fem noun*
  rule

♂ el **normal** *masc & fem adjective*
  normal
  Eso es normal. That's normal.
  un jugador normal y corriente a run-of-the-
  mil player

♂ el **normalmente** *adverb*
  normally
  Normalmente no salgo de noche. I don't
  normally go out at night.

♂ el **noroeste** *masc noun*
  northwest

♂ **norte** *masc noun, invariable adjective*
  north
  ir hacia el norte to go north
  la costa norte de España the north coast of
  Spain
  al norte del Sevilla to the north of Seville
  en el norte de Francia in the north of France

Norteamérica *fem noun*
  North America

norteamericano *masc adjective & noun*,
  norteamericana *fem adjective & noun*
1 **North American**
2 **un norteamericano, una norteamericana**
  North American

WORD TIP Adjectives and nouns for nationality
and regional origin do not have capital letters in
Spanish.

♂ **Noruega** *fem noun*
  Norway

noruego *masc adjective & noun*, **noruega**
  fem adjective & noun
1 **Norwegian**
2 **un noruego, una noruega** Norwegian
3 **el noruego** Norwegian (*the language*)

WORD TIP Adjectives and nouns of nationality,
regional origin, and language do not have capital
letters in Spanish.

♂ **nos** *pronoun*
1 (*as direct object*) **us**
  Nos invitaron a la fiesta. They invited us to
  the party.
  Viene a vernos mañana. He is coming to
  see us tomorrow.
2 (*as indirect object*) **to us**, **us**
  Nos mintió. He lied to us.
  Danos las llaves. Give us the keys.
3 (*with reflexive verbs*) **ourselves**
  Nos divertimos. We enjoyed ourselves.
  Nos reímos mucho. We laughed a lot.
  Vamos a bañarnos. Let's go for a swim.
  Nos sentamos a la mesa. We sat down at
  the table.
  (*with parts of the body, clothes*) **Nos quitamos
  los abrigos.** We took our coats off.
4 (*showing interaction*) **each other**
  Siempre nos ayudamos. We always help
  each other.

♂ **nosotros** *plural masc pronoun*, **nosotras**
  plural fem pronoun
1 (*as subject*) **we**
  Lo hicimos nosotras. We did it.
  nosostros mismos we ourselves
2 (*after prepositions*) **us**
  Estaban hablando con nosotros. They were
  talking to us.

Iban detrás de nosotros. They were behind us.
Es de nosotros. It's ours.

WORD TIP *nosotros* is used to refer to two or more males, or males and females.

♂ la **nota** *fem noun*
1 **note**
tomar nota de algo to write something down
Toma nota de eso. Write that down.
tomar notas to take notes
2 **mark** (*in school*)
¿Qué nota has sacado en física? What did you get in physics?
sacar buenas notas to get good marks
· la **nota musical** note

notable *masc & fem adjective*
▷ see **notable** *noun*
distinct
una notable mejora a distinct improvement

el **notable** *masc noun* ▷ see **notable** *adj*
pass mark (*between 70% and 85%*)

♂ **notar** *verb* [17]
to notice
Notó que la puerta estaba abierta. She noticed that the door was open.
Te noto preocupado. You look worried.
Se nota que ... You can tell that ...

el **notario** *masc noun*, la **notaria** *fem*
notary public (*a kind of lawyer*)

♂ la **noticia** *fem noun*
1 (*noticia: singular*) una noticia interesante an interesting piece of news
La noticia me sorprendió. The news surprised me.
Nos dio la buena noticia. He gave us the good news.
2 (*noticias: plural*) **news**
las noticias de las nueve the nine o'clock news
Tengo buenas noticias. I've got good news.

♂ **novecientos** *masc number*, **novecientas** *fem number*
nine hundred
novecientos veinte nine hundred and twenty

♂ la **novela** *fem noun*
novel

♂ **noveno** *masc adjective*, **novena** *fem*
ninth
el noveno piso the ninth floor

♂ **noventa** *number*
ninety
noventa y siete ninety-seven
los años noventa the nineties
Tiene noventa años. She's ninety (years old).

♂ la **novia** *fem noun*
1 **bride**
2 **fiancée**
3 **girlfriend**

♂ **noviembre** *masc noun*
November
en noviembre in November
el 11 de noviembre on 11 November

WORD TIP Names of months and days start with small letters in Spanish.

♂ la **novillada** *fem noun*
bullfight for young bulls

♂ los **novillos** *plural masc noun*
hacer novillos to play truant

♂ el **novio** *masc noun*
1 **groom** (*at a wedding*)
los novios the bride and groom
2 **fiancé**
3 **boyfriend**
Llevan tres meses de novios. They've been going out for three months.

♂ la **nube** *fem noun*
cloud
un cielo cubierto de nubes a cloudy sky

♂ **nublado** *masc adjective*, **nublada** *fem*
cloudy
Estaba nublado. It was cloudy.

♂ **nublarse** *reflexive verb* [17]
to cloud over
Se nubló por la tarde. It clouded over in the afternoon.

la **nubosidad** *fem noun*
cloud cover

nuclear *masc & fem adjective*
▷ see **nuclear** *noun*
nuclear

la **nuclear** *fem noun* ▷ see **nuclear** *adj*
nuclear power station

♂ el **nudillo** *masc noun*
knuckle

♂ el **nudo** *masc noun*
knot
hacer un nudo to tie a knot

a b c d e f g h i j k l m n ñ o p q r s t u v w x y z

la **nuera** *fem noun*
daughter-in-law

♪ **nuestro** *masc adjective*, **nuestra** *fem*
▷ see **nuestro** *pron*
our
nuestra casa our house
nuestros padres our parents
un familiar nuestro a relative of ours

♪ el **nuestro** *masc pronoun*, la **nuestra** *fem*
ours
La nuestra es verde. Ours is green.
Los nuestros están en el salón. Ours are in the living room.
Aquel es el nuestro. That one is ours.

♪ **nueve** *number*
1 **nine**
Jaime tiene nueve años. Jaime's nine (years old).
2 (*saying the date*) **ninth**
el nueve de marzo the ninth of March
3 (*when telling the time*) **nine**
a las nueve y diez at ten past nine
Son las nueve. It's nine o'clock.

♪ **nuevo** *masc adjective*, **nueva** *fem*
1 **new**
mis zapatos nuevos my new shoes
No dijo nada nuevo. She didn't say anything new.
¿Qué hay de nuevo? What's new?

Ha surgido un nuevo problema. A new problem has cropped up.
2 **de nuevo** again
Tenemos que empezar de nuevo. We have to start again.

♪ la **nuez** *fem noun*
1 **walnut**
2 **Adam's apple**
· la **nuez moscada** nutmeg

♪ el **número** *masc noun*
1 **number**
Dame tu número. Give me your telephone number.
2 **issue** (*of a magazine, newspaper*)
3 **size** (*for shoes, clothes*)
¿Qué número de zapatos calzas? What size shoes do you take?
· el **número de teléfono** telephone number
· el **número primo** prime number
· el **número romano** Roman numeral

♪ **nunca** *adverb*
never
nunca más never again
casi nunca hardly ever
más que nunca more than ever
Nunca he estado en Valencia. I've never been to Valencia.

nutritivo *masc adjective*, **nutritiva** *fem*
nourishing

Ñ ñ

ñoño *masc adjective,* **ñoña** *fem*
 pathetic (*feeble*)
 No seas ñoño. Don't be so pathetic.

a
b
c
d
e
f
g
h
i
j
k
l
m
n
ñ
o
p
q
r
s
t
u
v
w
x
y
z

O o

o *conjunction*

1 **or**
antes **o** después sooner or later
plata **u** oro silver or gold
11 **ó** 12 11 or 12

2 **o ... o ...** either ... or ...
O me acompañas **o** te quedas aquí. Either you come with me or you stay here.

3 **o sea** so
¿**O sea** que no te importa? So you don't mind?

4 **o sea ...** in other words ...
las niñas, **o sea** Juana y Maite the girls, in other words Juana and Maite

> **WORD TIP** *o* is the usual word for English *or*, but it becomes *u* before another word starting with *o*. When *o* is between numbers, it becomes *ó*.

el **oasis** *masc noun, pl:* los **oasis**
oasis

obedecer *verb* [35]
to obey
Se niega a obedecerme. He refuses to obey me.

obedezca, **obedezco**, **etc** *verb* ▷ **obedecer**

la **obediencia** *fem noun*
obedience

obediente *masc & fem adjective*
obedient

♂ el **obispo** *masc noun*
bishop

objetivo *masc adjective*, **objetiva** *fem*
▷ see **objetivo** *noun*
objective

♂ el **objetivo** *masc noun* ▷ see **objetivo** *adj*
objective

♂ el **objeto** *masc noun*
object
• los **objetos de valor** valuables
• **objetos perdidos** lost property office (*no article*)

♂ **obligar** *verb* [28]
obligar a alguien a hacer algo to make somebody do something
Lo obligaron a salir. They made him leave.
Nos obligó a hacerlo de nuevo. She made us do it again.

obligarse *reflexive verb* [28]
obligarse a hacer algo to make yourself do something
Se obliga a hacer ejercicio todos los días. He makes himself take exercise every day.

♂ **obligatorio** *masc adjective*, **obligatoria** *fem*
compulsory

♂ la **obra** *fem noun*

1 **deed**
una buena obra a good deed

2 **play**
una obra de Shakespeare a Shakespeare play

3 obras building work
estar en obras to be having some building work done
Estamos en obras. We're having some building work done.
'Obras' 'Roadworks'
• la **obra de arte** work of art
• la **obra maestra** masterpiece

♂ el **obrero** *masc noun*, la **obrera** *fem*
worker

obsceno *masc adjective*, **obscena** *fem*
obscene

♂ la **obscuridad** *fem noun* ▷ **oscuridad**

♂ **obscuro** *masc adjective*, **obscura** *fem* ▷ **oscuro**

♂ la **observación** *fem noun*

1 **observation**
La tienen en observación. She's under observation.

2 **remark**
Hizo varias observaciones al respecto. She made several remarks about it.

observador *adjective masc*, **observadora** *fem*
▷ see **observador** *noun*
observant

el **observador** *masc noun*, la **observadora** *fem*
▷ see **observador** *adj*
observer

ꞇ **observar** *verb* [17]
1 **to watch**
observar un eclipse to watch an eclipse
2 **to comment**
Observó que todavía quedaba mucho que hacer. He commented that there was still a lot to be done.

ꞇ el **observatorio** *masc noun*
observatory

la **obsesión** *fem noun*
obsession
Tiene una obsesión con la limpieza. He has an obsession with cleanliness.
Tiene la obsesión de que la siguen. She's obsessed with the idea that she's being followed.

ꞇ el **obstáculo** *masc noun*
obstacle
superar un obstáculo to overcome an obstacle

obstinado *masc adjective*, **obstinada** *fem*
obstinate

obstinarse *reflexive verb* [17]
obstinarse en hacer algo to insist on doing something
Se obstinó en abrir la puerta. He insisted on opening the window.

ꞇ **obtendré**, **obtendría**, etc *verb* ▷ **obtener**

ꞇ **obtener** *verb* [9]
1 **to obtain**, **to get**
Obtuvo las mejores notas. She got the best marks.
2 **to win**
obtener el premio to win the prize

ꞇ **obtenga**, **obtengo**, **obtuve**, etc *verb* ▷ **obtener**

ꞇ **obvio** *masc adjective*, **obvia** *fem*
obvious
Es obvio que la quiere. It's obvious that he loves her.

la **oca** *fem noun*
goose

ꞇ la **ocasión** *fem noun*
1 **occasion**
2 **opportunity**
Si hay ocasión. If there's an opportunity.
3 (*in advertising*) **precios de ocasión** bargain prices
coches de ocasión second-hand cars

ꞇ **ocasionar** *verb* [17]
to cause
La tormenta ocasionó muchos daños. The storm caused a lot of damage.

ꞇ **occidental** *masc & fem adjective*
western
la costa occidental the western coast

ꞇ el **Occidente** *masc noun*
the West (*Europe and America*)

ꞇ el **océano** *masc noun*
ocean
el océano Atlántico the Atlantic Ocean
el océano Pacífico the Pacific Ocean

ꞇ **ochenta** *number*
eighty
Tiene ochenta años. She's eighty (years old).
ochenta y cinco eighty-five
los años ochenta the eighties

ꞇ **ocho** *number*
1 **eight**
Tiene ocho años. She's eight (years old).
2 **eighth** (*in dates*)
Estamos a ocho. It's the eighth today.
3 **eight** (*in clock time*)
Son las ocho. It's eight o'clock.

ꞇ **ochocientos**, **ochocientas** *number*
eight hundred
ochocientos siete eight hundred and seven

el **ocio** *masc noun*
spare time
en mis ratos de ocio in my spare time

ocioso *masc adjective*, **ociosa** *fem*
idle

el **ócorro** *masc noun*
okra

octavo *masc adjective*, **octava** *fem*
eighth
el octavo piso the eighth floor

ꞇ **octubre** *masc noun*
October
en octubre in October
el 31 de octubre on 31 October

WORD TIP Names of months and days start with small letters in Spanish.

 12 de octubre

El 12 de octubre es el Día de la Hispanidad, fiesta nacional de España y los 23 países hispanohablantes cuando se celebra el descubrimiento de América por Cristóbal Colón en 1492.

a
b
c
d
e
f
g
h
i
j
k
l
m
n
ñ
o
p
q
r
s
t
u
v
w
x
y
z

la **ocupación** *fem noun*
   occupation

♪ **ocupado** *masc adjective*, **ocupada** *fem*
1 **busy**
   Está muy ocupado. He's very busy.
2 **engaged**, **busy**
   La línea está ocupada. The line is engaged.
3 **taken**
   ¿Está ocupado este asiento? Is this seat
   taken?

♪ **ocupar** *verb* [17]
1 ocupar un asiento to have a seat
   Ocupa el asiento 11b. He's in seat 11b.
   ¿Quién ocupa esa habitación? Who's in
   that room?
2 **to occupy** (*land, a building*)
3 **to spend** (*time*)
   ¿En qué ocupas tu tiempo libre? How do
   you spend your free time?
   Ocupo mi tiempo libre jugando al tenis. I
   spend my free time playing tennis.

ocuparse *reflexive verb* [17]
   ocuparse de algo, de alguien to take care of
   something, someone
   Yo me ocupo de ello. I'll look after that.
   ¿Quién se ocupa de los niños? Who takes
   care of the children?

♪ **ocurrir** *verb* [19]
   to happen
   ¿Qué le ocurre? What's the matter with
   him?
   Me ocurrió una cosa muy graciosa.
   Something really funny happened to me.

ocurrirse *reflexive verb* [19]
   Se me ocurre que podemos ... I think we
   can ...
   ¿Se te ocurre alguna idea? Can you think of
   anything?
   No se me ocurre nada. I just can't think of
   anything.

♪ **odiar** *verb* [17]
   to hate
   Odio el invierno. I hate the winter.

♪ el **odio** *masc noun*
   hate, **hatred**
   Le tiene odio. She hates him.

♪ **oeste** *masc noun, invariable adjective*
   west
   ir hacia el oeste to go west
   la costa oeste de Irlanda the west coast of
   Ireland
   al oeste de Madrid to the west of Madrid
   en el oeste de España in the west of Spain

ofender *verb* [18]
   to offend

ofenderse *reflexive verb* [18]
   to take offence

♪ la **oferta** *fem noun*
   offer
   una oferta de trabajo a job offer
   estar de oferta to be on offer
   Esos zapatos están de oferta. Those shoes
   are on offer.

oficial *masc & fem adjective*
   ▷ see **oficial** *noun*
   official

el & la **oficial** *masc & fem noun*
   ▷ see **oficial** *adj*
   officer

♪ la **oficina** *fem noun*
   office
   • la **oficina de cambio** bureau de change
   • la **oficina de correos** post office
   • la **oficina de (información y) turismo**
     tourist (information) office
   • la **oficina de objetos perdidos** lost
     property (office)

♪ el & la **oficinista** *masc & fem noun*
   office worker
   Es oficinista. He's an office worker.

el **oficio** *masc noun*
1 **trade**
2 **service** (*in church*)

♪ **ofrecer** *verb* [35]
   to offer
   Ofreció ir a buscarla a la estación. He
   offered to collect her from the station.

ofrecerse *reflexive verb* [35]
   to volunteer
   ofrecerse para hacer algo to offer to do
   something
   Se ofreció para llevarnos en el coche. She
   offered to take us in the car.

♪ el **ofrezca**, **ofrezco**, etc *verb* ▷ ofrecer

♪ el **oído** *masc noun*
1 **ear**
   tener dolor de oídos to have earache
2 tener buen oído to have a good ear (*for
   music*)

♪ **oiga**, **oigo**, etc *verb* ▷ oir

♪ **oír** *verb* [56]
1 **to hear**
   No oigo nada. I can't hear anything.

2　to listen to
oír las noticias to listen to the news
Me gusta oír música. I like listening to music.

3　(*calling to someone*) **¡Oye! No olvides la carta.** Hey! Don't forget the letter.
¡Oiga! ¿Cuánto le debemos? Excuse me! How much do we owe you? (*to a waiter, barman, etc*)

ℰ **ojalá** *exclamation*

1　(*as a reply*) **I hope so**
'Seguro que te van a invitar.'—'¡Ojalá!' 'Of course you'll be invited.'—'I hope so!'

2　(*with wishes*) **¡Ojalá me llame!** I hope he rings me!
¡Ojalá que venga! I hope she comes!

WORD TIP A verb following *ojalá* goes in the *subjunctive*.

ℰ el **ojo** *masc noun*

1　**eye**
con los ojos cerrados with your eyes closed
Tiene los ojos azules. He has blue eyes.
Tiene los ojos claros. He has pale eyes. (*blue, green, or grey rather than brown*)

2　(*on signs, etc*) **¡Ojo!** Careful!
¡Ojo! Pinta Wet Paint

· el **ojo de la cerradura** keyhole

ℰ la **ola** *fem noun*

wave

· la **ola de calor** heatwave
· la **ola de frío** cold spell

ℰ **ole, olé** *exclamation*
olé (*at bullfights, flamenco dancing, etc*)

ℰ **oler** *verb* [39]
to smell
oler una flor to smell a flower
oler a algo to smell of something
Huele a ajo. It smells of garlic.

ℰ las **olimpiadas** *plural fem noun*
Olympic Games
las Olimpiadas del 2012 the 2012 Olympic Games

ℰ **olímpico** *masc adjective*, **olímpica** *fem adjective*
Olympic
los Juegos olímpicos the Olympic Games

ℰ la **oliva** *fem noun*
olive
el aceite de oliva olive oil

ℰ el **olivo** *masc noun*
olive tree

ℰ la **olla** *fem noun*
pan
· la **olla a presión** pressure cooker

ℰ el **olor** *masc noun*
smell
Tiene un olor raro. It has a funny smell.
Tiene olor a almendras. It smells of almonds.

ℰ **olvidar** *verb* [17]
to forget
¡Olvídalo! Forget it!
Olvidé el paraguas. I forgot my umbrella.

olvidarse *reflexive verb* [17]
to forget
Se me olvidó llamarte. I forgot to ring you.
Se me olvidó la cartera. I forgot my wallet.
olvidarse de to forget
Me olvidé de traerlo. I forgot to bring it.

ℰ el **ombligo** *masc noun*
navel

omitir *verb* [19]
to omit

ℰ **once** *number*

1　**eleven**
Tiene once años. She's eleven (years old).

2　**eleventh** (*in dates*)
Hoy estamos a once. It's the eleventh today.

3　**eleven** (*in clock time*)
Son las once. It's eleven o'clock.

onceavo *masc adjective*, **onceava** *fem*
eleventh

ℰ la **onda** *fem noun*
wave
estar en la onda (*informal*) to be trendy
¡No estás en la onda! You're not with it!
· la **onda corta** short wave
· la **onda larga** long wave
· la **onda media** medium wave

ondulado *masc adjective*, **ondulada** *fem*
wavy

la **ONG** *fem noun*
(= *Organización No-Gubernamental*) **NGO** (*Non-Governmental Organization*)

la **ONU** *fem noun*
(= *Organización de las Naciones Unidas*) **UN** (*United Nations*)
un país miembro de la ONU a UN member country

opcional *masc & fem adjective*
optional

a
b
c
d
e
f
g
h
i
j
k
l
m
n
ñ
o
p
q
r
s
t
u
v
w
x
y
z

ə la **ópera** *fem noun*
opera

ə la **operación** *fem noun*
operation
Ha sufrido una operación. He's had an operation.
- **operación retorno** the rush to get back to the cities at the end of major holidays
- **operación salida** the rush to get out of the cities when major holidays begin

el **operador** *masc noun*, la **operadora** *fem*
operator

ə **operar** *verb* [17]
1 **to operate on** (*a person*)
¿Tendrán que operarlo? Will they have to operate on him?
La operaron de la pierna. She had an operation on her leg.
2 **to produce** (*a change*)

operarse *reflexive verb* [17]
to have an operation
Se va a operar del corazón. She's going to have a heart operation.

ə **opinar** *verb* [17]
1 **to think**
Opino que ... I think that ...
¿Qué opinas del diseño? What do you think of the design?
2 **to express an opinion**
Prefiero no opinar. I prefer not to give an opinion.

ə la **opinión** *fem noun*
opinion
en mi opinión in my opinion
cambiar de opinión to change your mind
He cambiado de opinión. I've changed my mind.
¿Cuál es tu opinión? What do you think?
- la **opinión pública** public opinion

ə **oponer** *verb* [11]
1 **to raise** (*an objection*)
2 **oponer resistencia** to put up a fight

oponerse *reflexive verb* [11]
oponerse a algo to be against something
Me opongo a la idea. I'm against the idea.
Se oponen a los cambios de las reglas. They are against the changes in the rules.

ə la **oportunidad** *fem noun*
chance, **opportunity**
aprovechar una oportunidad to make the most of an opportunity
Tuve la oportunidad de visitar el castillo. I had the chance to visit the castle.

ə **oportuno** *masc adjective*, **oportuna** *fem*
right, **good**
Es un momento oportuno. It's the right moment.

la **oposición** *fem noun*
1 **opposition**
2 **oposiciones** competitive public exams for a government job

ə **optativo** *masc adjective*, **optativa** *fem*
optional

el **óptico** *masc noun*, la **óptica** *fem*
optician

el **optimismo** *masc noun*
optimism

optimista *masc & fem adjective*
▷ see **optimista** *noun*
optimistic

el & la **optimista** *masc & fem noun*
▷ see **optimista** *adj*
optimist

ə **opuesto** *masc adjective*, **opuesta** *fem*
1 **conflicting** (*views, opinions*)
2 **opposite**
Venían en dirección opuesta. They were coming from the opposite direction.

ə la **oración** *fem noun*
1 (*Gramar*) **sentence**
2 **prayer**

ə **oral** *masc & fem adjective* ▷ see **oral** *noun*
oral

ə el **oral** *masc noun* ▷ see **oral** *adj*
oral exam

ə el **orden** *masc noun* ▷ see **orden** *fem noun*
1 (*arranging*) **order**
en orden alfabético in alphabetical order
en orden de importancia in order of importance
arreglados en orden de tamaño arranged according to size
Ponlos en orden. Put them in order.
2 mantener el orden to keep order
poner la habitación en orden to tidy up the room
¡Orden! Order!

ə la **orden** *fem noun* ▷ see **orden** *fem noun*
1 **order**
dar una orden to give an order
2 **warrant**
una orden de detención an arrest warrant
3 (*Religion*) **order**
una orden religiosa a religious order

ᵩ **ordenado** *masc adjective*, **ordenada** *fem*
tidy
Es muy ordenado. He's very tidy.

ᵩ el **ordenador** *masc noun*
computer

ᵩ **ordenar** *verb* [17]
1 **to tidy up** (*a room, house*)
2 **to put in order**
ordenar algo alfabéticamente to put
something in alphabetical order
3 **to order**
Nos ordenó seguir. He ordered us to carry
on.

ordinario *masc adjective*, **ordinaria** *fem*
1 **vulgar**
Su novio es muy ordinario. Her boyfriend's
very vulgar.
2 **usual**
3 **run-of-the-mill**
un vino ordinario a run-of-the-mill wine

WORD TIP *ordinario* does not mean *ordinary* in
English; for the meaning of *ordinary* ▷ **corriente**.

ᵩ la **oreja** *fem noun*
ear

ᵩ **orgánico** *masc adjective*, **orgánica** *fem*
adjective
organic

la **organización** *fem noun*
organization

organizar *verb* [22]
1 **to organize**
2 **to arrange**
Organicé una visita a las cuevas. I arranged
a visit to the caves.

ᵩ el **órgano** *masc noun*
organ

ᵩ el **orgullo** *masc noun*
pride
Tiene mucho orgullo. He's very proud.

ᵩ **orgulloso** *masc adjective*, **orgullosa** *fem*
proud
estar orgulloso de algo to be proud of
something
Está muy orgulloso de su bici He's very
proud of his bike.

la **orientación** *fem noun*
1 (*aspect*) ¿Qué orientación tiene la casa?
Which way does the house face?
2 **bearings** (*in navigation*)
3 **orientation** (*tendency*)
• la **orientación profesional** careers
guidance

ᵩ **oriental** *masc & fem adjective*
eastern
la costa oriental the eastern coast

orientar *verb* [17]
1 **to give directions to**
Me orientó para ir a Correos. She gave me
directions to get to the Post Office.
2 **to give guidance to** (*a young person, student*)
3 **to place**
La orienté hacia el este. I placed it facing
east.

orientarse *reflexive verb* [17]
to get your bearings

ᵩ el **Oriente** *masc noun*
the East (*the countries east of Europe*)
el Lejano Oriente the Far East
el Oriente Medio the Middle East

ᵩ **original** *masc & fem adjective*
▷ see **original** *noun*
original

ᵩ el **original** *masc noun* ▷ see **original** *adj*
original

ᵩ la **orilla** *fem noun*
1 **bank**
sentados a la orilla del río sitting on the
river bank
a orillas del Duero on the banks of the
Duero
2 **shore**
una casa a orillas del mar a house by the sea

ornamental *masc & fem adjective*
ornamental

ᵩ el **oro** *masc noun*
gold
una medalla de oro a gold medal

ᵩ la **orquesta** *fem noun*
orchestra
una orquesta de jazz a jazz band

ᵩ la **ortiga** *fem noun*
nettle

ᵩ la **ortografía** *fem noun*
spelling

ᵩ la **oruga** *fem noun*
caterpillar

ᵩ **os** *pronoun*
1 **you**
Os vimos desde la ventana. We saw you
from the window.
¿Os dieron suficiente información? Did
they give you enough information? ▸▸

2 **to you**
Os mintió. He lied to you.

3 **yourselves**
Os tenéis que portar bien. You must
behave yourselves.

4 **each other**
¿Os conocéis? Do you know each other?

5 (*with reflexive verbs*) ¿Os divertisteis? Did you
have a good time?
Iros a bañar. Go for a swim.

6 (*with parts of the body, clothes*) **Os podéis
quitar los abrigos.** You can take your coats
off.
¿Os habéis lavado las manos? Have you
washed your hands?

7 (*to have something done*) **Os tenéis que cortar
el pelo.** You must get your hair cut.

WORD TIP Use *os* to talk to more than one person
who you know them well. See also *tú* and *vosotros*.

osado *masc adjective*, **osada** *fem*
bold

♪ la **oscuridad** *fem noun*
darkness

♪ **oscuro** *masc adjective*, **oscura** *fem*
dark
a oscuras in the dark

el **osito** *masc noun*
un osito de peluche a teddy bear

♪ el **oso** *masc noun*, la **osa** *fem*
bear
• el **oso polar** polar bear

♪ la **ostra** *fem noun*
1 **oyster**
2 ¡Ostras! Good grief!

♪ la **OTAN** *fem noun*
(= *Organización del Tratado del Atlántico
Norte*) **NATO**
un miembro de la OTAN a member of
NATO

♪ el **otoño** *masc noun*
autumn
en otoño in the autumn
el otoño pasado last autumn

♪ **otro** *masc adjective*, **otra** *fem*
▷ see **otro** *pron*
1 **another**
¿Te has comprado otro CD? Have you
bought another CD?
Añade otros dos. Add another two.

2 **other**
en otros colores in other colours
La otra tarde le vi. I saw him the other
evening.
¿No tienes ningún otro color? Don't you
have any other colours?

3 **otra cosa** something else
¿Quieres alguna otra cosa? Do you want
something else?
Me gustaría comprarle otra cosa. I would
like to buy her something else.
Eso es otra cosa diferente. That's
something different.
No me gusta ninguna otra cosa. I don't like
anything else.

4 **otra vez** again
Hazlo otra vez. Do it again.

♪ **otro**, **otra** *pronoun* ▷ see **otro** *adj*
1 **another one**
Este no, dame otro. Not this one, give me
another one.

2 **el otro, la otra** the other one
El otro te queda mejor. The other one suits
you better.
Las otras están en el cajón. The other ones
are in the drawer.
Los otros vendrán en coche. The others will
come by car.
A otros les gustaría. Other people would
like it.

3 (*in time expressions*) **un mes sí y otro no** every
other month
de un día para otro from one day to the
next

♪ la **oveja** *fem noun*
sheep

♪ el **OVNI** *masc noun*
(= *Objeto Volante No Identificado*) **UFO**

oxidado *masc adjective*, **oxidada** *fem*
rusty

♪ el **oxígeno** *masc noun*
oxygen

♪ **oye**, **oyendo**, **oyó** *verb* ▷ **oír**

♪ el **ozono** *masc noun*
ozone
el agujero en la capa de ozono the hole in
the ozone layer

P p

el **pabellón** *masc noun*
1 **block** (*part of a building, etc*)
2 **pavilion** (*in a trade fair, etc*)
3 **summerhouse**
- el **pabellón deportivo** sports hall

ᵹ la **paciencia** *fem noun*
patience
tener **paciencia** to be patient
Ten paciencia, ya vendrá. Be patient, she'll
soon be here.

paciente *masc & fem adjective*
▷ see **paciente** *noun*
patient

el & la **paciente** *masc & fem noun*
▷ see **paciente** *adj*
patient

el **Pacífico** *masc noun* ▷ see **pacífico** *adj*
el **Pacífico** the Pacific, the Pacific Ocean

padecer *verb* [35]
to suffer
padecer de algo to suffer from something
Padece del corazón. He has heart trouble.

ᵹ el **padrastro** *masc noun*
stepfather

ᵹ el **padre** *masc noun*
1 **father**
2 mis padres my parents
3 (*Religion*) el padre Antonio Father Anthony

ᵹ el **padrino** *masc noun*
1 **godfather**
2 mis padrinos my godparents
- el **padrino de boda** man, giving away the
bride (*usually her father, who also acts as best
man*)

ᵹ la **paella** *fem noun*
paella (*rice dish, containing chicken and seafood*)

la **paga** *fem noun*
1 **pocket money**
¡Me ha suspendido la paga! She's stopped
my pocket money!
2 **pay**
Recibimos la paga el día treinta. We get our
pay on the thirtieth.
- la **paga extra** bonus pay (*a month's salary,
usually paid at Christmas and in July*)

ᵹ **pagar** *verb* [28]
1 **to pay**
¿Cuánto pagaste por la bici? How much did
you pay for the bike?
2 **to pay for** (*tickets, drinks, etc*)
Tengo que pagar el café. I have to pay for
the coffee.
3 **to pay off** (*a debt*)
4 **to repay** (*a favour*)

ᵹ la **página** *fem noun*
page
en la página ocho on page eight
- la **página web** web page

ᵹ el **pago** *masc noun*
payment
efectuar un pago to make a payment
- el **pago al contado** cash payment
- el **pago anticipado** payment in advance
- el **pago inicial** down payment

ᵹ el **país** *masc noun*
country
los países de habla hispana Spanish-
speaking countries

ᵹ el **paisaje** *masc noun*
landscape

los **Países Bajos** *plural masc noun*
los Países Bajos the Netherlands

ᵹ el **País de Gales** *masc noun*
el País de Gales Wales

ᵹ el **País Vasco** *masc noun*
el País Vasco the Basque Country (*a region in
northern Spain with its own language and culture*)

ᵹ la **paja** *fem noun*
1 **straw**
un sombrero de paja a straw hat
un tejado de paja a thatched roof
2 una pajita a drinking straw

la **pajarita** *fem noun*
bow tie

ᵹ el **pájaro** *masc noun*
bird

ᵹ la **pala** *fem noun*
1 **spade**
2 **shovel**
3 **bat** (*for table tennis*)
4 **slice** (*for serving cake, fish, etc*)

♂ la **palabra** *fem noun*

1 word
una redacción de quinientas palabras a five hundred word essay
No entendí ni una palabra. I didn't understand a word.

2 word, promise
Cumplió con su palabra. He kept his word.
Faltó a su palabra. She broke her word.

3 speech
el don de la palabra the gift of speech

4 pedir la palabra to ask permission to speak

• la **palabra compuesta** compound word

palabras

> Muchas palabras usadas en la vida diaria son de origen árabe. Se identifican porque comienzan con las letras al-, ar-, az-; por ejemplo alfombra, arroz, azúcar. También hay muchos nombres como el río *Guadalquivir* o la *Alhambra*.

la **palabrota** *fem noun*
swearword
decir palabrotas to swear
No digas palabrotas. Don't swear.

♂ el **palacio** *masc noun*
palace

• el **palacio de congresos** conference centre
• el **palacio de deportes** sports centre

la **palanca** *fem noun*

1 lever
abrir algo haciendo palanca to lever something open

2 crowbar

• la **palanca de cambios** gearstick
• la **palanca de mando** joystick

la **paleta** *fem noun*

1 palette (*for paints*)
2 spatula (*for cooking*)
3 trowel (*for cementing*)
4 bat (*for table tennis*)

palidecer *verb* [35]
to go pale

♂ **pálido** *masc adjective*, **pálida** *fem*
pale
Tiene la tez pálida. She has a pale complexion.
Estás muy pálido. You're looking very pale.

el **palillo** *masc noun*

1 chopstick
2 (*Music*) drumstick

• el **palillo de dientes** toothpick

♂ la **palma** *fem noun*

1 palm tree
2 palm (*of hand*)
dar palmas to clap your hands

♂ el **palmera** *fem noun*
palm tree

♂ el **palmero** *fem noun*
palm grower

♂ el **palo** *masc noun*

1 stick
2 pole (*for tents*)
3 club (*for golf*)
4 mast (*of a ship*)

• el **palo de escoba** broomstick

♂ la **paloma** *fem noun*

1 pigeon
2 dove

• la **paloma de la paz** dove of peace

♂ las **palomitas** *plural fem noun*
popcorn

la **palta** *fem noun*
(*South America*) avocado (pear)

♂ el **pan** *masc noun*

1 bread
una rebanada de pan a slice of bread
una barra de pan a French loaf
¿Quieres pan con mantequilla? Do you want bread and butter?

2 loaf
Cómprame dos panes. Buy me two loaves.

• el **pan blanco** white bread
• el **pan de molde** tin loaf
• el **pan integral** wholemeal bread
• el **pan rallado** breadcrumbs
• el **pan tostado** toast

> **WORD TIP** pan does not mean pan in English; for the meaning of pan ▷ **cacerola**.

la **pana** *fem noun*
corduroy
unos pantalones de pana a pair of corduroy trousers

♂ la **panadería** *fem noun*
bakery

♂ el **panadero** *masc noun*, la **panadera** *fem*
baker

♂ **Panamá** *masc noun*
Panama
el Canal de Panamá the Panama Canal

panameño *masc adjective & noun,*
  panameña *fem adjective & noun*
1 **Panamanian**
2 **un panameño, una panameña**
  Panamanian

> **WORD TIP** Adjectives and nouns for nationality
> and regional origin do not have capital letters in
> Spanish.

la **pancarta** *fem noun*
  banner

la **panceta** *fem noun*
  belly pork

♪ la **pandereta** *fem noun*
  tambourine
  tocar la pandereta to play the tambourine

♪ el **panecillo** *masc noun*
  bread roll

el **pánico** *masc noun*
  panic
  tenerle pánico a algo to be terrified of
  something
  Les tiene pánico a los perros. He's terrified
  of dogs.

el **panorama** *masc noun*
1 **view, panorama**
  Tiene un bello panorama de la sierra. It has
  a beautiful view of the mountains.
2 **outlook**
  El panorama es deprimente. The outlook is
  depressing.

♪ la **pantalla** *fem noun*
1 **screen** (*of a TV, computer*)
2 **shade** (*of a lamp*)
  • la **pantalla grande** big screen

♪ el **pantalón** *masc noun*
  trousers
  un pantalón a pair of trousers

♪ los **pantalones** *plural masc noun*
  trousers
  un par de pantalones, unos pantalones a
  pair of trousers
  • los **pantalones cortos** shorts
  • los **pantalones de peto** dungarees
  • los **pantalones vaqueros** jeans

el **pantano** *masc noun*
1 **marsh, swamp**
2 **reservoir**

pantanoso *masc adjective*, **pantanosa**
  fem
  marshy, swampy

♪ la **pantorrilla** *fem noun*
  calf (*of your leg*)

♪ el **panty, panti** *masc noun*
  tights
  comprar unos pantys to buy a pair of of
  tights

el **pañal** *masc noun*
  nappy
  • el **pañal desechable** disposable nappy

el **paño** *masc noun*
  cloth
  un paño a piece of cloth
  • el **paño de cocina** dishcloth

♪ el **pañuelo** *masc noun*
1 **handkerchief**
2 **headscarf**
3 **neckerchief**

la **papa** *fem noun*
  (*Latin America*) **potato**
  • las **papas fritas**
1 **chips**
2 **crisps**

♪ el **Papa** *masc noun*
  (*Religion*) **Pope**

♪ el **papá** *masc noun*
1 **daddy**
2 (*informal*) **mis papás** my mum and dad

el **papagayo** *masc noun*
  parrot

la **papaya** *masc noun*
  pawpaw

♪ el **papel** *masc noun*
  paper
  un trozo de papel a piece of paper
  Hay un papel en la mesa. There is piece of
  paper on the table.
  • el **papel aluminio** aluminium foil
  • el **papel de envolver** wrapping paper
  • el **papel de lija** sandpaper
  • el **papel higiénico** toilet paper
  • el **papel pintado** wallpaper

♪ la **papelera** *fem noun*
1 **wastepaper basket**
2 **litter bin** (*in the street*)

la **papelería** *fem noun*
  stationer's

las **paperas** *plural fem noun*
  mumps

ℰ el **paquete** *masc noun*

1 **parcel**
mandar un paquete to send a parcel

2 **packet**
un paquete de cigarrillos a packet of
cigarettes

ℰ **Paquistán** *masc noun*
Pakistan

paquistaní *masc & fem adjective & noun*

1 **Pakistani**

2 un & una paquistaní Pakistani

> **WORD TIP** Adjectives and nouns for nationality
> and regional origin do not have capital letters in
> Spanish.

ℰ **par** *masc & fem adjective* ▷ see **par** *noun*
even
un número par an even number

ℰ el **par** *masc noun* ▷ see **par** *adj*

1 **pair**
un par de zapatos a pair of shoes

2 **couple**
un par de veces a couple of times

3 de par en par wide open
La puerta estaba abierta de par en par. The
door was wide open.

ℰ **para** *preposition*

1 **for**
Es para ti. It's for you.
Sirve para limpiar compactos. It's for
cleaning CDs.
¿Para qué lo quieres? What do you want it
for?
Hay suficiente para todos. There's enough
for everybody.

2 (*with times, dates*) **by**
Tiene que estar listo para las tres. It has to
be ready by three o'clock.
Estará terminado para el doce. It'll be
finished by the twelfth.
Tráeme la falda para mañana. Bring me the
skirt by tomorrow.

3 **to**
Se lo dijo para sí. He said it to himself.
Me quedé en casa para ver la película. I
stayed at home to watch the film.
Es demasiado largo para recordarlo. It's
too long to remember.

4 (*showing direction*) Vamos para la estación.
We're going to the station.
Me voy para casa. I'm going home.

5 para que so that
Déjalo ahí para que lo vea. Leave it there so
that he'll see it.

> **WORD TIP** *para que* is followed by a verb in the
> subjunctive.

ℰ el **parabrisas** *masc noun, pl:* los
parabrisas
windscreen

el **paracaídas** *masc noun, pl:* los
paracaídas
parachute
lanzarse en paracaídas to parachute
Se lanzaron en paracaídas desde el avión.
They parachuted out of the plane.

ℰ el **parachoques** *masc noun, pl:* los
parachoques
bumper

ℰ la **parada** *fem noun* ▷ see **parado** *adj, noun*
stop (*for buses, etc*)

- la **parada del autobús** bus stop
- la **parada de taxis** taxi rank

el **paradero** *masc noun*
(*Latin America*) **bus stop**

ℰ **parado** *masc adjective,* **parada** *fem*
▷ see **parada** *noun,* **parado** *noun*

1 **unemployed**

2 (*Latin America*) estar parado to stand

el **parado** *masc noun,* la **parada** *fem*
▷ see **parada** *noun,* **parado** *adj*
unemployed person
Hay un millón de parados. There are one
million unemployed.

ℰ el **parador** *masc noun*
Spanish state-owned hotel (*in a restored
historic building, e.g. a castle, monastery, etc*)

ℰ el **paraguas** *masc noun, pl:* los **paraguas**
umbrella

ℰ el **Paraguay** *masc noun*
Paraguay

paraguayo *masc adjective & noun,*
paraguaya *fem adjective & noun*

1 **Paraguayan**

2 un paraguayo, una paraguaya Paraguayan

> **WORD TIP** Adjectives and nouns for nationality
> and regional origin do not have capital letters in
> Spanish.

ℰ el **paraíso** *masc noun*
paradise

paralelo *masc adjective,* **paralela** *fem*
▷ see **paralelo** *noun*
parallel
ser paralelo a algo to be parallel to
something

el **paralelo** *masc noun* ▷ see **paralelo** *adj*
parallel

ℰ el **parapente** *masc noun*
paragliding
practicar parapente to go paragliding

ꝑ **parar** *verb* [17]

1 **to stop**
Para el coche. Stop the car.
Paramos un momento. We stopped for moment.
parar de hacer algo to stop doing something
No paró de hablar durante toda la tarde. He didn't stop talking all afternoon.
Bailamos sin parar. We didn't stop dancing.

2 **to save** (*in football, hockey*)
parar un gol to make a save

3 ir a parar to end up
Fueron a parar al hospital. They ended up in hospital.
¡No sé adónde vamos a ir a parar! I don't know what the world is coming to!

4 Para un momento. Hang on a minute.

pararse *reflexive verb* [17]

1 **to stop**
Se paró a pensar. He stopped to think.
No te pares ahí. Don't stop there.
Mi reloj se ha parado. My watch has stopped.

2 (*Latin America*) **to stand up**

el **pararrayos** *masc noun*,
pl: los **pararrayos**
lightning conductor

el **parasol** *masc noun*

1 **visor** (*in car*)

2 **parasol**

la **parcela** *fem noun*
plot of land

> **WORD TIP** parcela does not mean *parcel* in English; for the meaning of *parcel* ▷ **paquete**.

ꝑ el **parche** *masc noun*
patch

ꝑ el **parchís** *masc noun*
ludo
jugar al parchís to play ludo

ꝑ **parecer** *verb* [35]

1 **to seem, to look**
El coche parece nuevo. The car seems new.
Parece que no vienen. It seems they're not coming
Parece de madera. It looks as if it's made of wood.
Parece que está roto. It seems to be broken.
Parece que va a llover. It looks like rain.

2 (*when giving your opinion*) Me parece demasiado complicado. It seems too complicated to me.

¿Qué te pareció la película? What did you think of the film?
Me parece que llegan hoy. I think they arrive today.
Me parece que no. I don't think so.
Me parece que sí. It looks that way.
Le pareció muy mal que no llamasen. He thought it was really bad of them not to call.

3 según parece, al parecer apparently
Según parece, hay un retraso de tres horas. Apparently there's a three hour delay.

parecerse *reflexive verb* [35]
to look like, to be like
Se parece mucho a su padre. She looks very like her father.
Se parece mucho a su hermano. He's very like his brother.
Me parezco mucho a mi padre. I look very like my father.

ꝑ **parecido** *masc adjective*, **parecida** *fem*
▷ see **parecido** *noun*

1 **similar**
Es muy parecida a su tía. She's very similar to her aunt.

2 ser bien parecido to be good-looking

ꝑ el **parecido** *masc noun* ▷ see **parecido** *adj*
similarity
El parecido es increíble. The similarity is incredible.
Tiene un gran parecido con su prima. She's a lot like her cousin.

ꝑ la **pared** *fem noun*
wall

ꝑ la **pareja** *fem noun*

1 **couple**

2 **partner**
mi pareja my partner (*man or woman*)

3 **pair**
trabajar en pareja to work in pairs

4 (*one of a pair*) He perdido la pareja de este guante. I've lost my other glove.

ꝑ el **paréntesis** *masc noun*, pl: los **paréntesis**
brackets
entre paréntesis in brackets

ꝑ **parezca, parezco,** etc *verb* ▷ **parecer**

ꝑ el & la **pariente** *masc & fem noun*
relative
una pariente lejana a distant relative

ꝑ el **parking** *masc noun*
car park

ꝑ el **parlamento** *masc noun*
parliament

a
b
c
d
e
f
g
h
i
j
k
l
m
n
ñ
o
p
q
r
s
t
u
v
w
x
y
z

♂ el **paro** *masc noun*
 1 **unemployment**
   estar en paro to be unemployed
   cobrar el paro to get unemployment
   benefit
 2 **strike**
   un paro de 24 horas a 24-hour strike
 • el **paro cardíaco** heart failure

♂ **parpadear** *verb* [17]
   to blink

♂ el **párpado** *masc noun*
   eyelid

♂ el **parque** *masc noun*
   park
 • el **parque de atracciones** amusement
   park
 • el **parque de bomberos** fire station
 • el **parque eólico** wind farm
 • el **parque infantil** play park
 • el **parque móvil** fleet (*of cars, lorries, etc*)
 • el **parque nacional** national park
 • el **parque natural** nature reserve
 • el **parque temático** theme park
 • el **parque zoológico** zoo

🛈 mini info **parque nacional**

El primer parque nacional se estableció en 1918
en España y hoy hay once, con más de 200
parques regionales.

parquear *verb* []
   (*Latin America*) **to park**

el **parqueo** *masc noun*
   (*Latin America*) **parking**

♂ el **parquímetro** *masc noun*
   parking meter

♂ el **párrafo** *masc noun*
   paragraph

la **parrilla** *fem noun*
   grill
   trucha a la parrilla grilled trout
   chuletas a la parrilla barbecued chops

la **parroquia** *fem noun*
 1 **parish**
 2 **parish church**

♂ la **parte** *fem noun* ▷ see **parte** *masc noun*
 1 **part**
   la parte antigua de la ciudad the old part of
   town
   Es parte de Asia. It's part of Asia.
   Forma parte del programa. It's part of the
   syllabus.

 2 **share**
   mi parte del trabajo my share of the work
   una tercera parte de la herencia a third of
   the inheritance
 3 **la mayor parte de** most of
   la mayor parte de los profesores most of
   the teachers
 4 **en parte** partly
   En parte tienen razón. They're partly right.
 5 **de parte de** on behalf of
   ¿De parte de quién? Who's calling? (*on the
   phone*)
   saludos de parte de Juan Juan says hello
   Felicítalos de mi parte. Give them my
   congratulations.
 6 (*to give your point of view*) **(yo) por mi parte** ...
   as far as I'm concerned ...
   (ellos) por su parte ... as far as they're
   concerned ...
 7 (*in expressions meaning 'where'*) **en alguna
   parte, por alguna parte** somewhere
   en cualquier parte, por cualquier parte
   anywhere
   en todas partes, por todas partes
   everywhere
   No vamos a ninguna parte. We're not
   going anywhere.
 • la **parte de la oración** part of speech

♂ el **parte** *masc noun* ▷ see **parte** *fem noun*
   report
 • el **parte meteorológico** weather report

la **partera** *fem noun*
   midwife

la **participación** *fem noun*
 1 **participation**
 2 **share in lottery ticket**

♂ **participar** *verb* [17]
   to participate, to take part
   participar en algo to take part in something

el **participio** *masc noun*
   participle
 • el **participio pasado** past participle

♂ **particular** *masc & fem adjective*
 1 **private** (*lessons, teacher, etc*)
   un colegio particular a private school
 2 **mi teléfono particular** my home telephone
   number
   nuestro domicilio particular our home
   address
 3 **special**
   Tiene un olor particular. It has a very special
   smell.
   Y eso ¿qué tiene de particular? What's so

strange about that?
Es muy particular. He's very peculiar.

la **partida** *fem noun*
game
una partida de ajedrez a game of chess

ℰ el **partido** *masc noun*
1 **party** (*political*)
un partido de izquierdas a left-wing party
2 **game**, **match**
un partido de rugby a rugby match

ℰ **partir** *verb* [19]
1 **to cut** (*a loaf, melon, etc*)
partir algo por la mitad to cut something in half
Partió la manzana por la mitad. He cut the apple in half.
2 **to break** (*a branch, twig*)
Lo partió en dos. She broke it in two.
3 **to crack** (*a nut*)
4 **to leave** (*trains, people*)
El tren parte a medianoche. The train leaves at midnight.
5 **a partir de** from
a partir de ese momento from that moment on
a partir de ahora from now on

partirse *reflexive verb* [19]
to break
Me partí un diente. I broke a tooth.
La rama se partió. The branch broke.

la **partitura** *fem noun*
score (*in music*)

el **parto** *masc noun*
labour (*in pregnancy*)
estar de parto to be in labour

ℰ la **pasa** *fem noun*
raisin

ℰ **pasado** *masc adjective*, **pasada** *fem*
▷ see **pasado** *noun*
1 **last** (*with days, months, seasons*)
el verano pasado last summer
el domingo pasado last Sunday
2 **after**
pasado mañana the day after tomorrow
Son las diez pasadas. It's past ten o'clock.
Pasados los exámenes, nos vamos de vacaciones. After the exams, we're going on holiday.
3 **off** (*milk, fruit*)
La leche está pasada. The milk is off.
4 **overcooked** (*meat*)
El filete está muy pasado. The steak is overcooked.

el **pasado** *masc noun* ▷ see **pasado** *adj*
1 **past**
en el pasado in the past.
2 **past tense**

ℰ el **pasaje** *masc noun*
ticket
sacar un pasaje para ... to buy a ticket to ...

ℰ el **pasajero** *masc noun*, la **pasajera**, *fem*
passenger

el **pasamanos** *masc noun*,
pl: los **pasamanos**
1 **banister**
2 **handrail**

ℰ el **pasaporte** *masc noun*
passport
sacar el pasaporte to get a passport
Tengo que renovar el pasaporte. I must renew my passport.

ℰ **pasar** *verb* [17]
1 **to pass**
¿Me pasas las tijeras? Could you pass me the scissors?
Me pasó el balón. He passed the ball to me.
Nos pasó el resfriado. She gave us her cold.
2 **to go past**
Pasó un bus hace cinco minutos. A bus went past five minutes ago.
3 **to come past**, **to call in**
Pasaron por aquí. They came past this way.
El cartero pasa a las diez. The postman comes at ten.
Pasaré por tu casa. I'll call in at your house.
4 **to get past**
No podíamos pasar. We couldn't get past.
5 **to go in**
Pasaron todos al salón. They all went into the living room.
6 **to come in**
Pase, por favor. Please come in. (*polite form*)
7 **to sift**
Pasó la harina por el cedazo. He sifted the flour.
8 **pasar la aspiradora** to vacuum
Pasé la aspiradora por la habitación. I vacuumed the bedroom.
9 **to happen**
¿Qué pasa? What's happening?
No le ha pasado nada. Nothing has happened to him.
¿Qué te pasa? What's the matter?
No pasa nada. Nohing's the matter.
10 **to spend** (*time*)
Siempre pasamos las vacaciones en Canarias. We always spend our holidays in the Canary Islands.

a
b
c
d
e
f
g
h
i
j
k
l
m
n
ñ
o
p
q
r
s
t
u
v
w
x
y
z

Pasé la noche en casa de Candela. I spent the night at Candela's house.

11 **pasarlo bien, mal** to have a good, bad time
Lo pasamos muy bien. We had a very good time.
Lo pasé muy mal en las vacaciones. I had a terrible time on my holidays.

12 (when telephoning) **Le paso con el Señor Muñoz.** I'll put you through to Mr Muñoz.

pasarse reflexive verb [17]

1 **to go off** (milk, fish)
2 **to go bad** (vegetables, fruit)
3 **to spend** (time)
Nos pasamos las vacaciones en Murcia. We spent our hoildays in Murcia.
Se pasa todo el tiempo leyendo. She spends all her time reading.

4 **to call by**
Pásate por mi casa a las siete. Call by at my house at seven.

5 **to go past** (too far)
Nos pasamos de parada. We missed our stop.

♂ el **pasatiempo** masc noun
hobby
Mi pasatiempo favorito es tocar la guitarra. My favourite hobby is playing the guitar.

♂ la **Pascua** fem noun
1 **Easter**
¡Felices Pascuas! Happy Easter!
2 **Christmas**
¡Felices Pascuas! Merry Christmas!

♂ **pasear** verb [17]
1 **to go for a walk**
Me gusta pasear por la playa. I like walking on the beach.
sacar al perro a pasear to take the dog for a walk
2 **to go out** (in the car, on bike, etc)
pasear en coche to go for a drive
Fuimos a pasear en bici. We went for a bike ride.

pasearse reflexive verb [17]
to go for a walk

♂ el **paseo** masc noun
1 **walk**
2 **stroll**
3 **dar un paseo** to go out
Vamos a dar un paseo. Let's go for a walk.
dar un paseo en coche to go for a drive
dar un paseo en bicicleta to go for a bike ride

♂ el **pasillo** masc noun
corridor
al fondo del pasillo at the end of the corridor

la **pasión** fem noun
passion

pasivo masc adjective, **pasiva** fem
passive
un fumador pasivo a passive smoker

♂ el **paso** masc noun
1 **step**
paso a paso step by step
un paso importante an important step
dar un paso adelante to take a step forward
2 **footsteps**
oír pasos to hear footsteps
3 **passing**
el paso del tiempo the passing of time
4 **float** (in a procession)
5 (on signs) **'Ceda el paso'** 'Give way'
6 **'Prohibido el paso'** 'No entry'
7 Te viene de paso., Te pilla de paso. It's on your way.
• el **paso a nivel** level crossing
• el **paso de cebra** zebra crossing
• el **paso de peatones** pedestrian crossing
• el **paso elevado** flyover
• el **paso subterráneo**
1 **subway** (for pedestrians)
2 **underpass** (for cars)

♂ la **pasta** fem noun
1 **paste**
pasta de tomates tomato paste
2 **biscuit**
3 **pastry**
4 **pasta**
• la **pasta de dientes** toothpaste

♂ el **pastel** masc noun
cake
un pastel de chocolate a chocolate cake

♂ la **pastelería** fem noun
cake shop

♂ la **pastilla** fem noun
tablet, pill
pastillas para dormir sleeping pills
• la **pastilla de jabón** bar of soap

el **pasto** masc noun
(Latin America) **grass**

el **pastor** masc noun, la **pastora** fem
1 **shepherd**
2 **shepherdess**
3 **minister** (of religion)
• el **pastor alemán** Alsatian, German shepherd

♂ la **pata** *fem noun* ▷ see **pato** *noun*
1 **leg**
2 **paw**
Se ha lastimado la pata. She's hurt her paw.
3 (*informal*) meter la pata to put your foot in it
He metido la pata de nuevo. I've put my foot in it again.

♂ la **patada** *fem noun*
kick
darle una patada a alguien to kick someone
Le dio una patada al árbitro. He kicked the referee.
darle una patada a algo to kick something
Le dio una patada a la puerta. He kicked the door.

la **patata** *fem noun*
potato
• las **patatas bravas** spicy sautéed potatoes

las **patatas fritas** *plural fem noun*
1 **chips, french fried potatoes**
2 **crisps**

paternal *masc & fem adjective*
paternal

la **patera** *fem noun*
small boat (*used by illegal immigrants*)

♂ el **patín** *masc noun*
1 **roller skate**
2 **ice skate**
3 **skateboard**
4 **pedalo**
• los **patines de hielo** ice skates
• los **patines en línea** Rollerblades®

el **patinador** *masc noun*, la **patinadora** *fem*
skater

♂ el **patinaje** *masc noun*
1 **roller skating**
2 **ice skating**
• el **patinaje artístico** figure skating
• el **patinaje en línea** rollerblading

♂ **patinar** *verb* [1]
1 **to roller-skate**
2 **to ice-skate**
3 **to rollerblade**
4 **to slip**
Patiné en una mancha de aceite. I slipped on a patch of oil.
5 **to skid** (*cars, bikes*)

♂ el **patio** *masc noun*
1 **courtyard**
2 **patio**
3 **playground** (*of school*)

♂ el **pato** *masc noun*, la **pata** *fem noun*
duck

♂ la **patria** *fem noun*
homeland

patrocinar *verb* [17]
to sponsor

♂ el **patrón** *masc noun*
1 **boss**
2 **skipper** (*of a boat*)
3 **landlord** (*of a guesthouse, a bar*)

la **patrona** *fem noun*
1 **boss**
2 **landlady** (*of a guesthouse, a bar*)

la **patrulla** *fem noun*
patrol
una patrulla de rescate a rescue party

la **patrullera** *fem noun*
patrol boat

el **patrullero** *masc noun*
1 **patrol boat**
2 **patrol plane**
3 **patrol car**

♂ la **pausa** *fem noun*
pause
hacer una pausa to have a break
Haremos una pausa a mediodía. We'll have a break at midday.

♂ el **pavo** *masc noun*, la **pava** *fem*
turkey
• el **pavo real** peacock

♂ el **payaso** *masc noun*, la **payasa** *fem*
clown

♂ la **paz** *fem noun*, pl: las **paces**
1 **peace**
2 hacer las paces to make up
Nos peleamos pero al final hicimos las paces. We had a fight, but we made up in the end.
3 dejar a alguien en paz to leave somebody alone
¡Deja a tu hermano en paz! Leave your brother alone!
¡Estos niños nunca me dejan en paz! These children never give me a moment's peace!

PD *abbreviation*
P.S. (*at the end of a letter*)

el **peaje** *masc noun*
toll (*on a bridge, motorway*)
una carretera de peaje a toll road

♂ el **peatón** *masc & fem noun*
pedestrian

peatonal *masc & fem adjective*
pedestrian, for pedestrians

♀ la **peca** *fem noun*
freckle

el **pecado** *masc noun*
sin

♂ el **pecho** *masc noun*
1 **chest**
2 **bust** (*woman's*)
3 **breast**
dar el pecho a un bebé to breastfeed a baby

♀ la **pechuga** *fem noun*
breast (*of chicken, turkey, etc*)
una pechuga de pollo a chicken breast

♂ el **pedal** *masc noun*
pedal
• el **pedal de arranque** kickstart

♂ el **pedazo** *masc noun*
piece
un pedazo de queso a piece of cheese
hacer pedazos algo to smash something to
pieces
Hizo pedazos el vaso. He smashed the glass
to pieces.
El jarrón se cayó y se hizo pedazos. The vase
fell and smashed to pieces.

el **pedido** *masc noun*
order (*in buying, selling*)
hacer un pedido to place an order

♂ **pedir** *verb* [57]
1 **to ask for**
pedir ayuda to ask for help
pedir un favor to ask a favour
pedir consejo to ask for advice
Piden medio millón por el cuadro. They're
asking half a million for the picture.
Me pidió que le comprara el libro. He asked
me to buy him the book.
2 **pedir perdón** to apologize
3 **pedir prestado algo** to ask to borrow
something
pedir dinero prestado to ask to borrow
some money
Me pidió prestada la moto. He asked to
borrow my motorbike.
4 **pedir hora** to make an appointment (*at the
doctor's, dentist's*)
5 **to order** (*in a restaurant, cafe*)
¿Qué vas a pedir? What are you going to
order?

Pedí pollo, no pescado. I ordered chicken,
not fish.

WORD TIP For the other Spanish verb for *to ask* ▷
preguntar.

♂ **pegajoso** *masc adjective*, **pegajosa** *fem*
sticky
Tienes las manos pegajosas. Your hands
are sticky.

♂ el **pegamento** *masc noun*
glue

♂ **pegar** *verb* [28]
1 **to stick**
He pegado una foto suya en la pared. I've
stuck a picture of him on the wall.
2 **to glue**
Pegué los pedazos del plato. I glued the
pieces of the plate together.
copiar y pegar to copy and paste (*in word
processing*)
3 **to hit**
Me pegó. He hit me.
(*informal*) **pegarle una patada a alguien** to
kick somebody
Le pegó una patada a su hermano. He
kicked his brother.
(*informal*) **pegarle una paliza a alguien** to
give somebody a beating
(*informal*) **pegarle un susto a alguien** to give
somebody a fright
¡Me pegaste un susto tremendo! You gave
me a terrible fright!
Le pegaron una buena paliza. They gave
him a real beating.
4 (*in expressions*) **pegar un grito** to yell
pegar un salto to jump
pegar saltos de alegría to jump for joy
Me vas a pegar el resfriado. You're going to
give me your cold.

pegarse *reflexive verb* [28]
1 **to hit each other**
Empezaron a pegarse. They started hitting
each other.
2 **to stick**
Este sello no se pega. This stamp won't
stick.

♀ la **pegatina** *fem noun*
sticker

♂ el **peinado** *masc noun*
hairstyle
Ese peinado no te sienta. That hairstyle
doesn't suit you.

♂ **peinar** *verb* [17]
1 **to comb**
2 **to brush**

peinarse *reflexive verb* [17]
1 **to comb your hair**
2 **to brush your hair**

♂ el **peine** *masc noun*
comb

la **pela** *fem noun*
(*informal*) **penny**
No me quedan pelas. I haven't got a penny.

♂ **pelar** *verb* [17]
1 **to peel** (*potatoes, apples*)
2 (*informal*) **pelar a alguien** to cut somebody's hair

pelarse *reflexive verb* [17]
1 **to peel** (*from sunburn*)
Se me está pelando la nariz. My nose is peeling.
2 (*informal*) **to have your hair cut**
¡Te pelaste! You've had your hair cut!

♂ el **peldaño** *masc noun*
1 **step**
Cuidado con el útimo peldaño. Be careful of the bottom step.
2 **rung**
una escala de diez peldaños a ladder with ten rungs

♂ la **pelea** *fem noun*
1 **fight**
2 **row**
Tuvo una pelea con su novio. She had a row with her boyfriend.

♂ **pelear** *verb* [17]
1 **to fight**
2 **to quarrel**
Pelean por cualquier cosa. They fight over anything.

pelearse *reflexive verb* [17]
1 **to fight**
Había dos chicos peleándose. There were two boys fighting.
2 **to quarrel**
Se pelearon por dinero. They quarrelled over money.
Siempre se pelea con su novio. She's always quarrelling with her boyfriend.

♂ la **película** *fem noun*
1 **film**
¿Qué película ponen hoy? What film are they showing today?
una película de terror a horror film
una película de risa a comedy film
una película de suspense a thriller
2 **film** (*for a camera*)
un rollo de película a roll of film

♂ el **peligro** *masc noun*
danger
estar en peligro, correr peligro to be in danger
fuera de peligro out of danger
un peligro para la salud a health risk
un peligro de incendio a fire hazard
poner a alguien en peligro to put somebody at risk
Puso en peligro a su familia. She put her family at risk.

 peligro

El lince ibérico está en peligro de extinción; sólo quedan entre 100 y 120 ejemplares.

♂ **peligroso** *masc adjective*, **peligrosa** *fem*
dangerous
una curva peligrosa a dangerous bend

♂ **pelirrojo** *masc adjective*, **pelirroja** *fem*
1 **red-haired**
2 pelo pelirrojo red hair

pellizcar *verb* [31]
to pinch
¡No me pellizques! Stop pinching me!

el **pellizco** *masc noun*
pinch
Le di un pellizco en el brazo. I pinched her arm.

♂ el **pelo** *masc noun*
1 **hair**
pelo liso, pelo lacio straight hair
pelo rizado curly hair
Tengo el pelo negro. I've got black hair.
2 un pelo de la barba a whisker
3 **fur** (*of an animal*)
4 **tomarle el pelo a alguien** to pull somebody's leg
Te están tomando el pelo. They're pulling your leg.
Creí que era verdad, pero me estaba tomando el pelo. I thought it was true, but she was pulling my leg.

♂ la **pelota** *fem noun*
ball (*for football, tennis etc*)
una pelota de fútbol a football
• la **pelota vasca** pelota (*Basque game played in a walled court*)

la **peluca** *fem noun*
wig

el **peluche** *masc noun*
un juguete de peluche a cuddly toy
un osito de peluche a teddy bear

a
b
c
d
e
f
g
h
i
j
k
l
m
n
ñ
o
p
q
r
s
t
u
v
w
x
y
z

♂ indicates key words   233

♂ **peludo** *masc adjective*, **peluda** *fem*
  hairy

♀ la **peluquería** *fem noun*
  hairdresser's

♂ el **peluquero** *masc noun*, la **peluquera** *fem*
  hairdresser

♀ la **pena** *fem noun*
  1 shame
    ¡Qué pena! What a shame!
    Es una pena que no puedas venir. It's a shame you can't come.
  2 sadness
    Me da pena verla así. It makes me sad to see her like that.
  3 Sara me da mucha pena. I'm really sorry for Sara.
  4 sentence
    la pena de muerte the death sentence
  5 valer la pena to be worth it
    No vale la pena. It's not worth it.
    Vale la pena ver la película. The film's worth seeing.
  6 penas problems
    Cuéntame tus penas. Tell me all your problems.

♂ el **penalti** *masc noun*
  penalty

pendiente *masc & fem adjective*
  ▷ **see pendiente** *noun*
  unresolved
  una cuenta pendiente an unpaid bill
  un asunto pendiente an unresolved problem

♂ el **pendiente** *masc noun*
  ▷ **see pendiente** *adj, fem noun*
  earring
  He perdido la pareja de este pendiente. I've lost my other earring.

♀ la **pendiente** *fem noun*
  ▷ **see pendiente** *adj, masc noun*
  slope
  una pendiente muy pronunciada a very steep slope
  un camino en pendiente an uphill path

♂ el **pene** *masc noun*
  penis

penetrar *verb* [17]
  to penetrate

♀ la **península** *fem noun*
  peninsula
  la Península Ibérica the Iberian Peninsula

♂ el **penique** *masc noun*
  penny
  Vale ochenta peniques. It's only worth eighty pence.

♂ el **pensamiento** *masc noun*
  thought
  Creo que me adivina el pensamiento. I think she can read my thoughts.

♂ **pensar** *verb* [29]
  1 to think
    Pienso que está bien. I think it's all right.
    Piénsalo bien antes de decidir. Think about it carefully before deciding anything.
    Pensándolo bien ... On second thoughts ...
  2 pensar en alguien to think about somebody
    Estaba pensando en ti. I was thinking about you.
  3 pensar en algo to think of something
    ¿En qué piensas? What are you thinking about?
    Pienso en las vacaciones. I'm thinking about the holidays.
  4 pensar de alguien to think of someone
    ¿Qué piensas del nuevo entrenador? What do you think of the new coach?
  5 pensar hacer algo to intend to do something
    Pensamos volver mañana. We're intending to come back tomorrow.
    ¿Piensas llamarlo? Are you thinking of calling him?

♀ la **pensión** *fem noun*
  1 pension
    cobrar la pensión to draw your pension
  2 guesthouse
  3 media pensión half board
  • la **pensión completa** full board
  • la **pensión de viudedad** widow's pension

el & la **pensionista** *masc & fem noun*
  pensioner

♂ **peor** *masc & fem adjective* ▷ **see peor** *adv, noun*
  1 worse
    No hay nada peor. There's nothing worse.
    Éstas son peores que las de la otra tienda. These are worse than the ones in the other shop.
    mucho peor much worse
  2 worst
    mi peor enemigo my worst enemy
    en el peor de los casos in the worst case scenario
  3 peor para ti it's your loss

peor *adverb* ▷ see **peor** *adj, noun*
worse
cada vez peor worse and worse
de mal en peor from bad to worse
Yo juego peor que tú. I play worse than you do.
Ella canta aún peor. She sings even worse.
Tu hermano juega aún peor que Iñaki. Your brother plays even worse than Iñaki.

♂ **el & la peor** *masc & fem noun*
▷ see **peor** *adjective, adverb*
el peor, la peor the worst one
Es el peor del equipo. He's the worst one in the team.
los peores, las peores the worst ones
Estas uvas son las peores que he probado. These grapes are the worst ones I've tasted.

♂ **el pepinillo** *masc noun*
gherkin

♂ **el pepino** *masc noun*
cucumber
Corta el pepino en rodajas. Slice the cucumber.

♂ **pequeño** *masc adjective*, **pequeña** *fem*
▷ see **pequeño** *noun*
1 **small**
un coche pequeño a small car
Dame otro más pequeño. Give me a smaller one.
La chaqueta me está pequeña. The jacket's too small for me.
2 **little**
un pequeño esfuerzo a little effort
3 **young**
mi hermana pequeña my little sister
Vivimos allí de pequeños. We lived there when we were young.

♂ **el pequeño** *masc noun*, **la pequeña** *fem*
▷ see **pequeño** *adj*
small child
Hay dos pequeños en el jardín. There are two little boys in the garden.
¿Cómo se llama la pequeña? What's the little girl's name?
¿Han comido los pequeños? Have the little ones eaten?

♂ **la pera** *fem noun*
pear
Déme un kilo de peras. Give me a kilo of pears.

el peral *masc noun*
pear tree

♂ **la percha** *fem noun*
1 **hanger**
2 **coat hook**

♂ **perder** *verb* [36]
1 **to lose**
perder la paciencia to lose patience
perder el conocimiento to lose consciousness
He perdido la cartera. I've lost my wallet.
Perdimos tres partidos seguidos. We lost three games in a row.
2 **to miss**
perder el tren to miss the train
Perdimos el vuelo. We missed the flight.
Has perdido una gran oportunidad. You've missed a great opportunity.
3 **perder el tiempo** to waste time
No pierdas el tiempo. Don't waste your time.
Pierde horas enteras mirando por la ventana. He wastes hours on end staring out of the window.
4 **perder la costumbre** to get out of the habit

perderse *reflexive verb* [36]
1 **to get lost**
Me he perdido. I'm lost.
¿Se ha perdido? Are you lost? (*polite form*)
No os perdáis en el bosque. Don't get lost in the woods.
2 **perderse algo** to lose something (*glasses, money, etc*)
Se me ha perdido la llave. I've lost my key.
3 **perderse algo** to miss something (*a programme, a chance*)
No quiero perderme el último episodio. I don't want to miss the final episode.
No te la pierdas esta oportunidad. Don't miss ithis opportunity.

♂ **la pérdida** *fem noun*
1 **loss**
2 **Es una pérdida de tiempo.** It's a waste of time.
3 **Está enfrente del supermercado, no tiene pérdida.** It's opposite the supermarket, you can't miss it.

la perdiz *fem noun*
partridge

♂ **el perdón** *masc noun*
▷ see **perdón** *exclamation*
pardon
pedir perdón to apologize, to say sorry
Le pedí perdón por lo que había dicho. I apologized to her for what I'd said.

♂ indicates key words   235

♂ **perdón** *exclamation* ▷ see **perdón** *noun*
  1 excuse me
    Perdón, ¿usted es el gerente? Excuse me, are you the manager?
  2 sorry
    Perdón, no te vi. Sorry, I didn't see you.

♂ **perdonar** *verb* [17]
  1 to forgive
    No la he perdonado. I haven't forgiven her.
  2 to let off (*without a punishment*)
    Te perdono el castigo. I'll let you off.
  3 (*when interrupting, apologizing, etc*) ¡Perdona! Sorry!
    ¡Perdone! Excuse me! (*polite form*)
    Perdone la molestia. Sorry to bother you.

la **peregrinación** *fem noun*
  pilgrimage
    irse de peregrinación to go on a pilgrimage

♂ el **perejil** *masc noun*
  parsley
    perejil picado chopped parsley

♂ la **pereza** *fem noun*
  laziness

♂ **perezoso** *masc adjective*, **perezosa** *fem*
  lazy
    No seas tan perezoso. Don't be so lazy.

perfeccionar *verb* [17]
  1 to improve (*a skill*)
    Quiero perfeccionar mi español. I want to improve my Spanish.
  2 to perfect

♂ **perfectamente** *adverb*
  perfectly
    Te entiendo perfectamente. I understand you perfectly.

♂ **perfecto** *masc adjective*, **perfecta** *fem*
  perfect
    Tiene un dominio perfecto del inglés. She has a perfect command of English.

el **perfil** *masc noun*
  profile
    Me parece mejor visto de perfil. It looks better to me from the side.

♂ el **perfume** *masc noun*
  perfume
    un frasco de perfume a bottle of perfume

la **perfumería** *fem noun*
  perfume shop

♂ el **periódico** *masc noun*
  newspaper
    un periódico semanal a weekly newspaper

el & la **periodista** *masc & fem noun*
  journalist

♂ el **período, periodo** *masc noun*
  period (*of time*)
    un período bastante largo quite a long period

el **periquito** *masc noun*
  budgie

la **perla** *fem noun*
  pearl

♂ **permanecer** *verb* [35]
  1 to stay (*in a place*)
    Permanecí un año en Sevilla. I stayed for a year in Seville.
  2 to remain
    permanecer callado to remain silent
    permanecer a la escucha to stay tuned

♂ **permanente** *masc & adjective*
    ▷ see **permanente** *noun*
  permanent
    'Servicio permanente' '24 hour service'

la **permanente** *fem noun*
    ▷ see **permanente** *adj*
  perm
    hacerse la permanente to have your hair permed

♂ **permanezca, permanezco, etc** *verb*
    ▷ **permanecer**

♂ el **permiso** *masc noun*
  1 permission
    darle permiso a alguien para hacer algo to give somebody permission to do something, to allow somebody to do something
    Nos dio permiso para copiar las cartas. He gave us permission to copy the letters.
    No le dieron permiso para ir a la fiesta. He wasn't allowed to go the party.
  2 con permiso may I come in? (*when you knock on a door*), excuse me (*to get past someone*)
  3 leave
    estar de permiso to be on leave
    un permiso de una semana a week's leave
  4 permit
    • el **permiso de conducir** driving licence
    • el **permiso de trabajo** work permit

♂ **permitir** *verb* [19]
  1 to allow
    Me permitió llevarlo. She allowed me to take it away.
    No nos permitieron entrar. They didn't allow us in.
  2 No te permito que me contestes. I won't have you answering me back.

3 (*asking permission*) ¿**Me permite?** May I?
¿**Me permite una sugerencia?** May I make a
suggestion?
4 to make possible
Este proceso **permite** ahorrar más
combustible. This process makes it
possible to save more fuel.

♂ **pero** *conjunction*
1 but
Es ligero, **pero** muy fuerte. It's light, but
very strong.
2 (*showing surprise, impatience*) **Pero** ¿qué
haces ahí arriba? Just what are you doing
up there?
¡**Pero** ya te dije que no viene! How many
times do I have to tell you he's not coming!

el **perrito** *masc noun*
puppy
- el **perrito caliente** hot dog

♂ el **perro** *masc noun*, la **perra** *fem*
dog
- el **perro callejero** stray dog
- el **perro guardián** guard dog
- el **perro guía** guide dog

la **persecución** *fem noun*
1 pursuit
Salieron en persecución de los ladrones.
They set off in pursuit of the thieves.
2 persecution

perseguir *verb* [64]
to pursue

♂ la **persiana** *fem noun*
blind

♂ **persiga**, **persigo**, **persiguió**, **etc** *verb*
▷ **perseguir**

persistir *verb* [19]
to persist

♂ la **persona** *fem noun*
1 person
Él es una persona importante. He is an
important person.
Vino en persona para agradecernos. She
came in person to thank us.
Nos dio cuatro por persona. He gave us
four each.
2 las personas people
Había diez personas. There were ten
people.

el **personaje** *masc noun*
1 character (*in a book, play*)
2 important figure, **celebrity**
un personaje del mundo del cine an
important figure in the film world

personal *masc & fem adjective*
▷ see **personal** *noun*
personal

el **personal** *masc noun*
▷ see **personal** *adjective*
staff

la **personalidad** *fem noun*
personality

la **perspectiva** *fem noun*
1 perspective
2 prospect
Las perspectivas son buenas. The
prospects are good.

persuadir *verb* [19]
to persuade
persuadir a alguien de que haga algo to
persuade somebody to do something
Trata de persuadirla de que se quede. Try
to persuade her to stay.

♂ **pertenecer** *verb* [35]
to belong
pertenecer a alguien to belong to
somebody
Pertenece a mi tía. It belongs to my aunt.
¿A quién pertenece? Who does it belong
to?

♂ **pertenezca**, **pertenezco**, **etc** *verb* ▷
pertenecer

♂ **Perú**, **el Perú** *masc noun*
Peru

peruano *masc adjective & noun*, **peruana**
fem adjective & noun
1 Peruvian
2 un peruano, una peruana Peruvian

WORD TIP Adjectives and nouns for nationality
and regional origin do not have capital letters in
Spanish.

la **pesa** *fem noun*
weight
hacer pesas to do weightlifting

♂ la **pesadilla** *fem noun*
nightmare
Tuve otra pesadilla anoche. I had another
nightmare last night.

♂ **pesado** *masc adjective*, **pesada** *fem*
▷ see **pesado** *noun*
1 heavy (*box, suitcase*)
2 ser muy pesado to be boring (*a job, book,
film*)
3 ser muy pesado to be a pain
Tu hermanito es muy pesado. Your little
brother's a real pain.

a
b
c
d
e
f
g
h
i
j
k
l
m
n
ñ
o
p
q
r
s
t
u
v
w
x
y
z

a
b
c
d
e
f
g
h
i
j
k
l
m
n
ñ
o
p
q
r
s
t
u
v
w
x
y
z

el pesado *masc noun*, **la pesada** *fem*
  ▷ see **pesado** *adj*
  (*informal*) **bore**, **pain**
  ¡Eres un pesado! You're such a pain!

pesar *verb* [17]
1 **to weigh**
  Peso sesenta kilos. I weigh sixty kilos.
  Hay que pesar el equipaje. The luggage has
  to be weighed.
2 **pesar mucho** to be very heavy
  Puedo llevarlo, no pesa mucho. I can carry
  it, it's not very heavy.
  ¿Te pesan mucho las bolsas? Are the bags
  too heavy for you?

la pesca *fem noun*
  fishing
  ir de pesca to go fishing

la pescadería *fem noun*
  fishmonger's

el pescado *masc noun*
  fish (*as food*)
  El pescado alimenta mucho. Fish is very
  nourishing. ▷ **pez**

el pescador *masc noun*, **la pescadora** *fem*
1 **fisherman**
2 **fisherwoman**

pescar *verb* [31]
1 **to fish**
  ir a pescar to go fishing
  Salieron a pescar tiburón. They went out
  shark-fishing
2 **to catch**
  No pescamos nada. We didn't catch
  anything.

la peseta *fem noun*
  peseta (*Spanish currency before the euro; 500
  pesetas = 3.00 euros*)

pesimista *masc & fem adjective*
  ▷ see **pesimista** *noun*
  pessimistic

el & la pesimista *masc & fem noun*
  ▷ see **pesimista** *adj*
  pessimist

el peso *masc noun*
  weight
  perder peso to lose weight
  ganar peso to put on weight
  vender al peso to sell by weight
  • el **peso bruto** gross weight

pesquero *masc adjective*, **pesquera** *fem*
  fishing
  la industria pesquera the fishing industry

la pestaña *fem noun*
  eyelash

el pétalo *masc noun*
  petal

el petardo *masc noun*
  banger (*firework*)

el petróleo *masc noun*
  oil
  una refinería de petróleo an oil refinery

el petrolero *masc noun*
  oil tanker (*ship*)

el pez *masc noun*, *pl:* los **peces**
  fish (*as a living creature*)
  Vimos cientos de peces. We saw hundreds
  of fish. ▷ **pescado**
  • el **pez de colores** goldfish
  • el **pez espada** swordfish

el piano *masc noun*
  piano
  tocar el piano to play the piano
  • el **piano de cola** grand piano

picado *masc adjective*, **picada** *fem*
1 **decayed** (*tooth*)
  Tengo una muela picada. I have a cavity in
  one of my back teeth.
2 **minced** (*meat*)
3 **choppy** (*choppy*)
  El mar estaba picado. The sea was choppy.
4 (*informal*) **estar picado** to be miffed
  Está picada porque no la llamaste. She's
  miffed that you didn't call her.

la picadura *fem noun*
  bite, **sting**
  una picadura de mosquito a mosquito bite
  Tenía picaduras de abeja por todo el
  cuerpo. He was covered in bee stings.

picante *masc & fem adjective*
  hot (*spicy*)
  una salsa picante a hot sauce

el picaporte *masc noun*
  door handle

picar *verb* [31]
1 **to sting** (*insects*)
2 **to mince** (*meat*)
3 **to chop** (*vegetables*)
4 **to rot** (*teeth*)
5 **to be hot** (*spicy foods*)
  Esta salsa pica mucho. This sauce is very
  hot.
6 **to itch**
  Me pica la nariz. My nose is itching.
7 **Me pican los ojos.** My eyes are stinging.

8   **to nibble** (*bar snacks*)
Nos trajo algo para picar. He brought us
something to nibble.

el **pico** *masc noun*
1   **beak**
2   **pick** (*for digging*)
3   **peak** (*of a mountain*)
4   **corner** (*of a table*)
5   un cuello de pico a V-neck
6   ... y pico ... and something
Le costó tres mil y pico. It cost him three
thousand and something.
Llegaron a las cinco y pico. They arrived just
after five.

ʃ **pida**, **pido**, **pidió**, etc *verb* ▷ **pedir**

ʃ el **pie** *masc noun*
1   **foot**
ir a pie to walk, to go on foot
Si no viene el taxi iremos a pie. If the taxi
doesn't come we'll walk.
Tuvo que volver a pie. He had to walk back.
2   de pie standing
estar de pie to be standing.
ponerse de pie to stand up
3   **base** (*of a lamp, glass*)

ʃ la **piedra** *fem noun*
1   **stone**
un banco de piedra a stone bench
tener piedras en el riñón to have kidney
stones
2   **flint** (*of a lighter*)
• la **piedra filosofal** philosopher's stone
• la **piedra preciosa** precious stone

ʃ la **piel** *fem noun*
1   **skin**
tener la piel seca to have dry skin
2   **peel** (*of fruit*)
3   **fur**
un abrigo de pieles a fur coat
4   **leather**
un bolso de piel a leather bag

ʃ **piensa**, **pienso**, etc *verb* ▷ **pensar**

ʃ la **pierna** *fem noun*
leg
cruzar las piernas to cross your legs

ʃ la **pieza** *fem noun*
1   **piece**
2   (*Latin America*) **bedroom**
• la **pieza de recambio**, la **pieza de repuesto**
spare part

ʃ el **pijama** *masc noun*
pyjamas
un pijama de algodón a pair of cotton
pyjamas

ʃ la **pila** *fem noun*
1   **pile**
una pila de libros a pile of books
2   **battery**
Funciona con pilas. It runs on batteries.
3   **sink** (*in a kitchen*)
4   **basin** (*in a bathroom*)

la **píldora** *fem noun*
pill

el & la **piloto** *masc & fem noun*
pilot

ʃ el **pimentón** *masc noun*
1   **paprika**
2   **cayenne pepper**

ʃ la **pimienta** *fem noun*
pepper
• la **pimienta blanca** white pepper
• la **pimienta negra** black pepper

ʃ el **pimiento** *masc noun*
pepper
• el **pimiento rojo** red pepper
• el **pimiento verde** green pepper

ʃ el **pimpón** *masc noun*
table tennis

ʃ el **pincel** *masc noun*
1   **paintbrush**
2   **make-up brush**

el & la **pinchadiscos** *masc & fem noun,*
pl: **pinchadiscos**
disc jockey, DJ

ʃ **pinchar** *verb* [17]
1   **to prick**
Las espinas le pinchaban la cara. The thorns
pricked his face.
2   **to be prickly**
3   **to burst** (*a balloon*)
Me ha pinchado el globo. He's burst my
balloon.
4   **to have a puncture**
Creo que hemos pinchado. I think we've
got a puncture.
5   (*Computers*) **to click on**
6   (*informal*) **to give an injection to**

pincharse *reflexive verb* [17]
1   **to burst** (*balloons*)
Se le pincharon todos los globos. All his
balloons burst.   ▸▸

a
b
c
d
e
f
g
h
i
j
k
l
m
n
ñ
o
p
q
r
s
t
u
v
w
x
y
z

2 to puncture
Se me ha pinchado una rueda. I've got a puncture.

el pinchazo *masc noun*
puncture
Tuvimos un pinchazo. We had a puncture.

el pincho *masc noun*
1 bar snack
2 prickle *(on bush)*

el pingüino *masc noun*
penguin

el pino *masc noun*
pine tree
muebles de pino pine furniture

la pinta *fem noun*
1 Tiene pinta de oficinista. He looks like an office worker.
¡Qué pinta más rara! That looks really odd!
La comida tiene muy buena pinta. The food looks delicious.
2 pint *(of beer, etc)*

las pintadas *plural fem noun*
graffiti

pintado *masc adjective*, **pintada** *fem*
painted
pintado a mano hand-painted
La casa estaba pintada de blanco. The house was painted white.

pintar *verb* [17]
to paint
Lo pinté de negro. I painted it black.

el pintor *masc noun*, **la pintora** *fem*
painter

pintoresco *masc adjective*, **pintoresca** *fem*
picturesque

la pintura *fem noun*
1 paint
pintura amarilla yellow paint
una mano de pintura a coat of paint
2 painting
una pintura abstracta an abstract painting
3 pinturas crayons
• la **pintura al óleo** oil painting

la pinza *fem noun*
1 clothes peg
2 hairgrip
3 pincer
4 dart *(in clothing)*

las pinzas *plural fem noun*
tweezers

la piña *fem noun*
1 pineapple
jugo de piña pineapple juice
2 pine cone

la pipa *fem noun*
1 pipe
fumar en pipa to smoke a pipe
2 pipas sunflower seeds

la piragua *fem noun*
canoe

el piragüismo *masc noun*
canoeing

la pirámide *fem noun*
pyramid

los Pirineos *plural masc noun*
los Pirineos the Pyrenees

el piropo *masc noun*
compliment

el piruli *masc noun*
lollipop

pisar *verb* [17]
1 to step
pisar a alguien to step on somebody's foot
pisar algo to tread on something
2 'Prohibido pisar el césped'. 'Keep off the grass'.

piscina *noun*
swimming pool
una piscina al aire libre an open-air swimming pool
la parte honda de la piscina the deep end of the pool
la parte poco profunda de la piscina the shallow end of the pool

piscis *masc & fem noun* ▷ see **Piscis** *noun*
Pisces
Soy piscis. I'm Pisces.

WORD TIP Use a small letter in Spanish to say *I am Pisces*, etc with star signs.

Piscis *masc noun* ▷ see **piscis** *noun*
Pisces

el piso *masc noun*
1 floor, storey
Vivo en el tercer piso. I live on the third floor.
un edificio de cinco pisos a five-storey building
un autobús de dos pisos a double-decker bus

2 **flat**
un piso de dos cientos metros cuadrados. a four-hundred square metre flat

3 (*Latin America*) **floor** (*of a room*)

ᵟ la **pista** *fem noun*
1 **track**
seguirle la pista a alguien to be on somebody's trail
La policía les está siguiendo la pista. The police are on their trail.
2 **racecourse**
- la **pista de aterrizaje** runway
- la **pista de atletismo** athletics track
- la **pista de esquí** ski slope
- la **pista de hielo** ice rink
- la **pista de patinaje** skating rink
- la **pista de tenis** tennis court

el **pistacho** *masc noun*
pistachio

ᵟ la **pistola** *fem noun*
gun

pitar *verb* [17]
1 **to blow a whistle**
2 **to toot the horn** (*in a car*)

el **pito** *masc noun*
1 **whistle**
tocar el pito to blow the whistle
2 **horn**
tocar el pito to toot the horn

ᵟ la **pizarra** *fem noun*
1 **blackboard**
2 **slate**
techos de pizarra slate roofs

la **placa** *fem noun*
1 **plate**, **sheet** (*of metal*)
2 **badge**
- la **placa de matrícula** number plate

el **placer** *masc noun*
pleasure

ᵟ el **plan** *masc noun*
1 **plan**
hacer planes to make plans
¿Qué planes tienes para las vacaciones? What are your plans for the holidays?
2 (*informal*) en plan ...: viajar en plan económico to travel on the cheap
Lo dije en plan de broma. I was only kidding.
- el **plan de capacitación** training scheme
- el **plan de estudios** syllabus

ᵟ la **plancha** *fem noun*
1 **iron** (*for clothes*)
pasarle la plancha a una camisa to iron a shirt
No necesita plancha. It doesn't need ironing.
2 (*in cooking*) **a la plancha** grilled
pescado a la plancha grilled fish
3 **sheet**
una plancha de plástico a sheet of plastic
- la **plancha de vela** sailboard

ᵟ **planchar** *verb* [17]
to iron
Te planché el pantalón. I ironed your trousers.

planear *verb* [17]
1 **to plan**
2 **to glide**

ᵟ el **planeta** *masc noun*
planet
descubrir un planeta nuevo to discover a new planet

ᵟ **plano** *masc adjective*, **plana** *fem*
▷ see **plano** *noun*
flat (*land*, *field*)
un terreno plano a flat plot of land

ᵟ el **plano** *masc noun* ▷ see **plano** *adj*
1 **street map**
un plano de Madrid a street map of Madrid
2 **plan** (*of a building*)

ᵟ la **planta** *fem noun*
1 **plant**
regar las plantas to water the plants
2 **floor**
en la sexta planta on the sixth floor
- la **planta baja** ground floor

plantar *verb* [17]
to plant

ᵟ el **plástico** *masc noun*
plastic
bolsas de plástico plastic bags

ᵟ la **plata** *fem noun*
1 **silver**
cubiertos de plata silver cutlery
la medalla de plata the silver medal.
2 (*Latin America*) **money**
Perdió un montón de plata. He lost loads of money.

la **plataforma** *fem noun*
platform
- la **plataforma de lanzamiento** launching pad
- la **plataforma petrolera** oil rig

a
b
c
d
e
f
g
h
i
j
k
l
m
n
ñ
o
p
q
r
s
t
u
v
w
x
y
z

ƃ el **plátano** *masc noun*
banana
un rácimo de plátanos a bunch of bananas

la **plática** *fem noun*
(*Latin America*) **talk**

platicar *verb* [31]
(*Latin America*) **to talk, to chat**

el **platillo** *masc noun*
saucer
• el **platillo volante** flying saucer

ƃ el **plato** *masc noun*
1 **plate**
lavar los platos to wash the dishes
2 **dish**
un plato típico de Cataluña a typical
Catalan dish
3 **course**
Tomaré pescado de primer plato. I'll have
fish for the first course.
¿Y de segundo plato? And for your second
course?
• el **plato combinado** complete meal served
on one plate
• el **plato de postre** dessert plate
• el **plato del día** dish of the day
• el **plato fuerte** main course
• el **plato llano** dinner plate

ƃ la **playa** *fem noun*
1 **beach**
pasar el día en la playa to spend the day on
the beach
2 **seaside**
veranear en la playa to spend your summer
holidays at the seaside

la **playera** *fem noun*
canvas shoe

ƃ la **plaza** *fem noun*
1 **square** (*in a town, city*)
la Plaza Mayor the Main Square
2 **market**
Los martes hay plaza. Tuesday is market
day.
3 **seat** (*on bus, train*)
¿Quedan plazas? Are there any seats left?
4 **position** (*at work*)
Hay plazas vacantes. There are vacancies.
• la **plaza de aparcamiento** parking space
• la **plaza de toros** bullring

ƃ el **plazo** *masc noun*
1 **period**
un plazo de dos meses a two-months
period

El plazo de entrega acaba el día once. The
deadline is on the eleventh.
2 (*in expressions*) **a corto plazo** in the short
term
a largo plazo in the long term
planes a largo plazo long-term plans
pagar algo a plazos to pay for something in
instalments
• el **plazo de vencimiento** expiry date (*of
passport, licence, etc*)

plegar *verb* [30]
to fold

pleno *masc adjective*, **plena** *fem*
1 **full**
2 **en pleno verano** in the middle of summer
en pleno centro right in the centre of town

pliega, pliego, pliegue, etc *verb* ▷
plegar

el **plomo** *masc noun*
1 **lead**
sin plomo lead-free
2 **fuse**
Se han fundido los plomos. The fuses have
blown.
3 **ser un plomo** to be a real drag
¡Esa película es un plomo! That film's a real
drag!

ƃ la **pluma** *fem noun*
1 **feather**
2 **pen**

el **plumier** *masc noun*
pencil case

plural *masc & fem adjective*
▷ see **plural** *noun*
plural

el **plural** *masc noun*
(*Grammar*) **plural**
en plural in the plural

la **población** *fem noun*
population

ƃ **pobre** *masc & fem adjective*
▷ see **pobre** *noun*
poor
Su familia es muy pobre. His family is very
poor.
¡Pobre Jaime! Poor Jaime!
Esta pobre chica está enferma. This poor
girl is ill.

ƃ el & la **pobre** *masc & fem noun*
▷ see **pobre** *adj*
poor person
los pobres the poor

¡La pobre! Ha perdido el billete. Poor thing! She's lost her ticket.

♪ la **pobreza** *fem noun*
poverty
Vimos tanta pobreza. We saw so much poverty.

la **pocilga** *fem noun*
pigsty
Tu habitación está hecha una pocilga. Your room is a pigsty.

♪ **poco** *masc adjective*, **poca** *fem*
▷ see **poco** *pron, adv*
1 **little**
con poco esfuerzo with little effort
Hay poco pan. There isn't much bread.
Es poca cosa. It's not much.
2 **few**
pocos días más tarde a few days later
pocas veces not often
Había pocas personas. There were only a few people.
Pocas veces la he tenido que esperar. It's not often I've had to wait for her.
Ha venido pocas veces aquí. She's only been here a few times.
Cuesta unos pocos euros. It costs just a few euros.

♪ **poco**, **poca** *pronoun* ▷ see **poco** *adj, adv*
1 **little**
Basta con poco. A little is enough.
Queda poco. There's not much left.
poco a poco little by little
2 **few**
Vinieron pocos. Only a few came.
Quedan pocas de las viejas costumbres. Few of the old customs remain.
Pon unos pocos aquí. Put a few here.
3 **un poco** a bit
Espera un poco. Wait a bit.
un poco de sal a bit of salt
Me fastidia un poco. It's a bit irritating.
4 (*in time expressions*) **hace poco** not long ago
Hace poco que me llamó. He called me not long ago.
Aún voy a tardar un poco. I'm going to take a little more time.
Falta poco para las cinco. It's almost five o'clock.
dentro de poco soon
poco antes de comer shortly before eating
poco después de su llegada not long after he arrived

♪ **poco** *adverb* ▷ see **poco** *adj, pron*
not very much
Habla poco. He doesn't talk very much.

un cantante poco conocido a little-known singer
Soy muy poco paciente. I'm very impatient.
Están poco interesados. They aren't very interested.
Nos vemos muy poco. We hardly ever see each other.

♪ **poder** *verb* [10] ▷ see **poder** *noun*
1 (*expressing ability*) **can**, **to be able to**
Puedo hacerlo para mañana. I can do it by tomorrow.
¿Puedes venir hoy? Can you come today?
No puede levantarlo. He can't lift it.
No pude ir. I couldn't go.
Pueden hacerlo solos. They can do it on their own.
Hazlo lo mejor que puedas. Do it as best you can.
¿Podrás ayudarme? Will you be able to help me?
¿Pudiste encontrarlo? Were you able to find it?
2 (*asking permission politely*) **may**
¿Se puede? May I come in?
¿Puedo abrir la ventana? May I open the window?
¿Podría usar tu ordenador? May I use your computer?
3 (*expressing possibility*) Podría suceder. It could happen.
Puede que se haya roto. It may have got broken.
Has podido romperlo. You could have broken it.
Puede que llegue más tarde. He might come later.
'¿Se habrán olvidado?'—'Puede ser.'
'Could they have forgotten?'—'They might have.'
Puede ser que no lo sepa. It might be that she doesn't know.
Puede ser que se haya perdido. He might have got lost.
4 (*making suggestions*) Podrías preguntar. You could ask.
Podríamos comer fuera. We could eat out.
5 (*in difficult situations*) **to cope**
¡Ya no puedo más! I can't cope any more!
No puede con tanto trabajo. She can't cope with so much work.
6 (*when telling someone off*) ¡Podrías haberlo dicho! You might have said so!
7 **Si puede ser.** If possible.

♪ indicates key words   243

♂ el **poder** *masc noun* ▷ see **poder** *verb*
  power
  Llegaron al poder en 1997. They came to
  power in 1997.

poderoso *masc adjective*, **poderosa** *fem*
  powerful

♂ **podrá, podré, podría, etc** *verb* ▷
  poder

podrido *masc adjective*, **podrida** *fem*
  rotten

el **poema** *masc noun*
  poem

la **poesía** *fem noun*
  poetry

el & la **poeta** *masc & fem noun*
  poet

el **póker** *masc noun*
  poker (*card game*)
  ¿Sabes jugar al póker? Do you know how to
  play poker?

polaco *masc adjective & noun*, **polaca** *fem*
  adjective & noun
  1 **Polish**
  2 un polaco, una polaca Pole
  3 **Polish** (*the language*)

WORD TIP Adjectives and nouns for nationality,
regional origin and language, do not have capital
letters in Spanish.

polémico *masc adjective*, **polémica** *fem*
  controversial
  una decisión polémica a controversial
  decision

♂ el & la **policía** *masc & fem noun*
  ▷ see **policía** *fem noun*
  police officer
  Mi hermana es policía. My sister's a
  policewoman.
  Pregunta al policía. Ask the policeman.

♂ la **policía** *fem noun* ▷ see **policía** *noun*
  police (*the force*)
  • la **policía antidisturbios** riot police

policíaco *masc adjective*, **policíaca** *fem*
  una novela policíaca a detective novel

♂ el **polideportivo** *masc noun*
  sports centre

el **polígono industrial** *masc noun*
  industrial estate

la **polilla** *fem noun*
  moth

♂ la **política** *fem noun* ▷ see **político** *adj*,
  noun
  1 **politics**
  2 **policy** (*of a government, an organization, etc*)
  la política exterior foreign policy

♂ **político** *masc adjective*, **política** *fem*
  ▷ see **política** *noun*, **político** *noun*
  political

el **político** *masc noun*, la **política** *fem*
  ▷ see **política** *fem noun*, **político** *adj*
  politician

la **póliza** *fem noun*
  policy (*insurance document*)

el **pollito** *masc noun*, la **pollita** *fem*
  chick

♂ el **pollo** *masc noun*
  chicken
  • el **pollo asado** roast chicken

♂ el **polo** *masc noun*
  1 **pole** (*in physics, geography*)
  los polos positivo y negativo the positive
  and negative poles
  2 **ice-lolly**
  3 (*Sports*) **polo**
  • el **Polo Norte** North Pole

♂ **Polonia** *fem noun*
  Poland

la **polución** *fem noun*
  pollution

♂ el **polvo** *masc noun*
  1 **dust**
  quitar el polvo a los muebles to dust the
  furniture
  2 (*informal*) **estar hecho polvo** to be worn out
  Después de la excursión nos quedamos
  hechos polvo. We were worn out after the
  trip.
  Este sofá está hecho polvo. This sofa's a
  wreck.
  3 **polvos** face powder
  • los **polvos de talco** talcum powder

el **polvorón** *masc noun*
  pastry (*made with almonds; eaten at Christmas
  time*)

la **pomada** *fem noun*
  ointment

♂ el **pomelo** *masc noun*
  grapefruit

♂ **pondría, pondrías, etc** *verb* ▷ **poner**

ᵟ **poner** verb [11]

1 to put
Ponlo en la mesa. Put it on the table.
Lo puse en el armario. I put it in the wardrobe.
Pusimos diez euros cada uno. We put in ten euros each.
Le puso la silla al caballo. She put the saddle on the horse.

2 (in cafés, etc) ¿Qué les pongo? What can I get you?
¿Me pone un café? Can I have a coffee please?
¿Le pongo más sopa? Would you like some more soup?

3 to turn on (the radio, a CD, etc)
poner la tele to put on the telly
poner música to put on some music
Pon el volumen más alto. Turn the volume up.

4 to set (a clock, timer, etc)
poner el despertador to set the alarm clock
Puse el despertador a las ocho. I set the alarm clock for eight.

5 to install (heating, an alarm system, etc)
Van a poner calefacción central. They're going to install central heating.

6 to fit (a carpet)

7 (with names) ¿Qué nombre le vais a poner al niño? What are you going to call the baby?
Le pusieron el apodo de 'el Rubio'. They nicknamed him 'Blondy'.

8 (with films, plays, etc) poner una película to show a film
poner una obra de teatro to put on a play
¿Qué ponen en el 'Roxy'? What's on at the 'Roxy'?

9 to start up
poner un negocio to start up a business
poner una tienda to open a shop

10 (on the phone) ¿Me pone con el señor Muñoz? Could you put me through to Mr Muñoz?

11 poner a alguien + adjective to make somebody + adjective
poner a alguien triste to make somebody sad
No me pongas nerviosa. Don't make me nervous.
poner a alguien de mal humor to put somebody in a bad mood
Me pone siempre de mal humor. He always puts me in a bad mood.

12 poner la mesa to lay the table

13 poner atención to pay attention

14 ponerle una inyección a alguien to give somebody an injection

ᵟ **ponga, pongo, etc** verb ▷ **poner**

el **poni** masc noun
pony

popular masc & fem adjective
popular

ᵟ **por** preposition

1 for
por ejemplo for example
por esa razón for that reason
Lo hago por tu bien. I'm doing it for your benefit.
Me ofrecieron dos mil euros por el coche viejo. They offered me two thousand euros for the old car.

2 through
No entra por la ventana. It won't go in through the window.
Me enteré por mi hermana. I heard through my sister.
Pasamos por Toledo. We went through Toledo.

3 by (by means of)
mandar algo por correo to send something by post
viajar por carretera to travel by road
¿Cuánto cuesta enviarlos por avión? How much does it cost to send them by air?
Nos mantenemos en contacto por correo electrónico. We keep in touch by email.
Lo dijeron por la tele. They said so on TV.

4 by (someone)
diseño por Santiago Calatrava design by Santiago Calatrava
Fue criado por su tía. He was brought up by his aunt.

5 because of
Suspendieron el partido por la lluvia. The game was cancelled because of the rain.
Lo expulsaron por mala conducta. He was thrown out for bad behaviour.
Por eso no lo hice. That's why I didn't do it.

6 ¿Por qué? Why?
'¿Por qué lo hiciste?'—'Porque me dio la gana.' 'Why did you do it?'—'Because I felt like it.' (See also: porque)

7 (in calculations) Cinco por tres son quince. Five times three is fifteen.
Mide tres metros por cuatro. It measures three metres by four.

8 (in time expressions) por la mañana in the morning

9 por la noche at night

10 (saying where) por todos lados everywhere
andar por la calle to walk along the road
Lo dejé por aquí. I left it around here somewhere. ▸▸

a
b
c
d
e
f
g
h
i
j
k
l
m
n
ñ
o
p
q
r
s
t
u
v
w
x
y
z

Viven por la Avenida de Sitges. They live somewhere around Sitges Avenue.
¿Por dónde queda la estación? Whereabouts is the station?

11 (*saying the rate*) **per**, **each**
treinta euros por persona thirty euros per person
a cien kilómetros por hora at a hundred kilometres an hour
por ciento per cent
un descuento del diez por ciento a ten per cent discount
un diez por ciento de los estudiantes ten per cent of the students

> **WORD TIP** Spanish always has *el* or *un* before percentages.

12 (*in expressions*) **por adelantado** in advance
por escrito in writing
por fin at last
Me levanto por lo general a las ocho. I usually get up at eight.
por lo tanto therefore
por supuesto of course

el **porcentaje** *masc noun*
percentage

el **porche** *masc noun*
porch

la **porción** *fem noun*
1 portion
una porción de tarta a slice of cake
2 share

ꝼ **porque** *conjunction*
because
Está enfadado porque no le saludaste. He's annoyed because you didn't say hello.
'¿Por qué hiciste eso?'—'Porque sí.' 'Why did you do that?'—'Just because I felt like it.'
'¿Por qué no viniste ayer?'—'Porque no.' 'Why didn't you come yesterday?'—'I didn't feel like it.'

> **WORD TIP** *¿por qué?*, two words and accented, is *why?*; *porque*, one word, is *because*.

el **porrón** *masc noun*
wine bottle (*from which you drink, holding it away from your mouth*)

ꝼ la **portada** *fem noun*
1 title page (*of a book*)
2 cover (*of a magazine*)
3 front page (*of a newspaper*)

el **portaequipajes** *masc noun*, *pl:* los **portaequipajes**
1 roof rack
2 luggage rack (*on a train*)

ꝼ **portarse** *reflexive verb* [17]
to behave
portarse mal to behave badly
¡Pórtate bien! Behave yourself!

portátil *masc & fem adjective*
▷ see **portátil** *noun*
portable

el **portátil** *masc noun* ▷ see **portátil** *adj*
laptop (computer)

el **portazo** *masc noun*
dar un portazo to slam the door
Oí un portazo. I heard a door slamming.

ꝼ la **portería** *fem noun*
goal

ꝼ el **portero** *masc noun*, la **portera** *fem*
1 goalkeeper
2 caretaker
3 porter
· el **portero automático** entry-phone

portorriqueño *masc adjective & noun*, **portorriqueña** *fem adjective & noun*
1 Puerto Rican
2 un portorriqueño, una portorriqueña Puerto Rican

> **WORD TIP** Adjectives and nouns for nationality and regional origin do not have capital letters in Spanish.

ꝼ **Portugal** *masc noun*
Portugal

portugués *masc adjective & noun*, **portuguesa** *fem adjective & noun*
1 Portuguese
2 un portugués, una portuguesa Portuguese man, Portuguese woman
3 Portuguese (*the language*)

> **WORD TIP** Adjectives and nouns for nationality, regional origin, and language do not have capital letters in Spanish.

el **porvenir** *masc noun*
future

posar *verb* [17]
1 to pose
2 to put down

posarse *reflexive verb* [17]
to land (*birds*)

poseer *verb* [37]
1 to own
2 to hold (*a title, record*)

ꝼ la **posibilidad** *fem noun*
1 possibility
Es una posibilidad. It's a possibility.

2 tener posibilidades de hacer algo to have a good chance of doing something
Tienen muchas posibilidades de ganar. They have a good chance of winning.
¿Qué posibilidades tienen? What are their chances?

ᔒ **posible** *masc & fem adjective*
▷ see **posible** *adv*
possible
a ser posible if possible
No fue posible impedirlo. It was impossible to avoid it.
Es posible que venga hoy. She may come today.
Hice todo lo posible para ayudarla. I did all I could to help her.

ᔒ **posible** *adverb* ▷ see **posible** *adj*
lo más tarde posible as late as possible
Hazlo lo mejor posible. Do the best you can.

la **posición** *fem noun*
position
en quinta posición in fifth place
mantener algo en posición vertical to keep something upright
• la **posición social** social status

positivo *masc adjective*, **positiva** *fem*
positive

ᔒ **postal** *masc & fem adjective*
▷ see **postal** *noun*
postal

ᔒ la **postal** *fem noun* ▷ see **postal** *adj*
postcard

el **poste** *masc noun*
1 post
2 pole

el **póster** *masc noun*
poster

posterior *masc & fem adjective*
1 back
el asiento posterior the back seat
la parte posterior de la casa the back of the house
2 subsequent, later
en años posteriores in later years

la **postilla** *fem noun*
scab

postizo *masc adjective*, **postiza** *fem*
false
una dentadura postiza a set of false teeth

ᔒ el **postre** *masc noun*
pudding, dessert
¿Qué hay de postre? What's for pudding?
De postre tenemos ... For dessert, we have ...

potable *masc & fem adjective*
agua potable drinking water

potencial *masc & fem adjective*
potential

ᔒ la **práctica** *fem noun*
1 practice
He perdido la práctica. I'm out of practice.
Lo aprenderás con la práctica. You'll learn with practice.
2 **prácticas** *plural* practical work (*in school subjects*), teaching practice (*for trainee teachers*)

ᔒ **practicar** *verb* [31]
1 to practise
practicar el violín to practise the violin
2 **practicar deportes** to do sports

ᔒ **práctico** *masc adjective*, **práctica** *fem*
practical
una solución muy práctica a very practical solution
Tiene gran sentido práctico. He's a very practical person.

la **pradera** *fem noun*
grassland, prairie

el **prado** *masc noun*
meadow

la **precaución** *fem noun*
1 precaution
tomar precauciones to take precautions
2 caution
actuar con precaución to act with caution

precedente *masc & fem adjective*
previous

ᔒ el **precio** *masc noun*
price
precios de saldo bargain prices
¿Qué precio tiene? How much is it?
Los precios han subido mucho. Prices have gone up a lot.
• el **precio al por mayor** wholesale price
• el **precio al por menor** retail price
• el **precio fijo** fixed price

ᔒ **precioso** *masc adjective*, **preciosa** *fem*
1 beautiful
¡Qué vestido más precioso! What a beautiful dress! ▸▸

a
b
c
d
e
f
g
h
i
j
k
l
m
n
ñ
o
p
q
r
s
t
u
v
w
x
y
z

2 precious
piedras preciosas precious stones

el **precipicio** *masc noun*
precipice

la **precipitación** *fem noun*
1 rush
hacer algo con mucha precipitación to do
something in a rush
Salió con mucha precipitación. He rushed
out.
2 precipitaciones (*plural*) rainfall
Habrá precipitaciones moderadas. There
will be moderate rainfall.

precipitarse *reflexive verb* [17]
to rush
No te precipites. Don't rush into anything.
precipitarse hacia algo to rush towards
something
Todos se precipitaron hacia la salida de
emergencia. Everyone rushed for the
emergency exit.

precisamente *adverb*
precisely

la **precisión** *fem noun*
precision

preciso *masc adjective*, **precisa** *fem*
1 precise
Necesito datos más precisos. I need more
precise information.
Llegaron en el momento preciso. They
arrived just in time.
En este preciso momento no puedo. Right
now I can't.
2 ser preciso to be necessary
si es preciso if necessary
No es preciso pagar por adelantado. It's
not necessary to pay in advance.
Es preciso que vayas hoy. You must go
today.

predilecto *masc adjective*, **predilecta** *fem*
favourite

preescolar *masc & fem adjective*
preschool
un programa de educación preescolar a
preschool educational programme

la **preferencia** *fem noun*
1 preference
tener preferencia por algo to have a
preference for something
2 right of way
Yo tenía preferencia. I had right of way.
3 priority
tener preferencia to have priority

Tendremos preferencia sobre los que
llegan después. We'll have priority over
those who arrive after us.

preferible *masc & fem adjective*
preferable
ser preferible a algo to be preferable to
something
Es preferible que no venga. It's better if he
doesn't come.

♪ **preferido** *masc adjective*, **preferida** *fem*
favourite
Mi comida preferida es la china. My
favourite food is Chinese.

♪ **preferir** *verb* [14]
to prefer
¿Cuál prefieres? Which do you prefer?
preferir algo a algo to prefer something to
something
Prefiero el campo a la playa. I prefer the
country to the seaside.
Preferiría no tener que ir. I'd rather not
have to go.

♪ **prefiera**, **prefiero**, etc *verb* ▷ **preferir**

el **prefijo** *masc noun*
1 prefix
2 dialling code
el prefijo de España the dialling code for
Spain

♪ la **pregunta** *fem noun*
question
hacer una pregunta to ask a question

♪ **preguntar** *verb* [17]
to ask
Pregúntale si quiere venir. Ask him if he
wants to come.
Le pregunté sobre los vuelos. I asked her
about the flights.
preguntar por alguien to ask about
someone
Me preguntó por tus padres. He asked me
about your parents.

preguntarse *reflexive verb* [17]
to wonder
Me pregunto si dice la verdad. I wonder if
he's telling the truth.

WORD TIP For the other Spanish verb for *to ask* ▷
pedir.

el **prejuicio** *masc noun*
prejudice
tener prejuicios contra algo to be
prejudiced against something

prematuro *masc adjective,* **prematura** *fem*
  premature

premiar *verb* [17]
  premiar a alguien to give somebody a prize

♂ el **premio** *masc noun*
  prize
  el premio al mejor ensayo the prize for the best essay
  ganar un premio to win a prize
  ¿Qué dan de premio? What's the prize?
  Me tocó el premio gordo. I won the jackpot.
  darle un premio a alguien to give someone a prize
  • el **premio gordo** jackpot (*in the lottery*)

prender *verb* [18]
1 **to catch** (*a criminal*)
2 **to light** (*cigarette, match*)
  La leña no prende. The wood won't light.
3 **prenderle fuego a algo** to set fire to something
  Le prendió fuego a la casa. She set fire to the house.
4 (*Latin America*) **to turn on** (*the radio, the lights*)

♂ la **prensa** *fem noun*
  la prensa the press
  leer la prensa to read the newspapers

♂ **preocupado** *masc adjective,* **preocupada** *fem*
  worried
  estar preocupado por algo to be worried about something
  Estoy preocupada por Carmen. I'm worried about Carmen.

♂ **preocupar** *verb* [17]
  to worry
  Me preocupan los exámenes. I'm worried about the exams.
  ¿Qué te preocupa? What's worrying you?

preocuparse *reflexive verb* [17]
  to get worried
  Se preocupó porque no la llamé. She got worried because I didn't phone her.
  No se preocupe. Don't worry about it. (*polite form*)
  No te preocupes. Don't worry about it. (*informal form*)

la **preparación** *fem noun*
1 **preparation**
2 **training** (*in sport*)
3 **un trabajador con muy buena preparación** a highly trained worker

♂ **preparar** *verb* [17]
1 **to prepare**
  preparar la cena to prepare dinner
  preparar un examen to prepare for an exam
2 **to train** (*a player, athlete*)
3 **to coach** (*a student*)
4 **preparar la cuenta** to draw up the bill

prepararse *reflexive verb* [17]
  to get ready
  Es hora de prepararnos para salir. It's time we got ready to go.

los **preparativos** *plural masc noun*
  preparations

la **preposición** *fem noun*
  preposition

la **presa** *fem noun*
1 **dam**
2 **reservoir**
3 **prey**
4 **ser presa del terror** to be seized with panic

la **presencia** *fem noun*
  presence
  en presencia de sus padres in front of his parents

la **presentación** *fem noun*
1 **introduction**
  hacer las presentaciones to do the introductions
2 **presentation**

el **presentador** *masc noun,* la **presentadora** *fem*
  presenter

♂ **presentar** *verb* [17]
1 **to introduce**
  Te presento a mi novio. This is my boyfriend.
  Nos presentó a su jefe. He introduced us to his boss.
2 **to present** (*a programme*)
3 **to submit** (*an application*)
4 **to launch** (*a product*)
5 **to show** (*a permit, passport*)

presentarse *reflexive verb* [17]
1 **to introduce yourself**
2 **to arrive**
  Se presentaron sin avisar a nadie. They arrived without letting anybody know.
3 **presentarse voluntario** to volunteer
4 **presentarse a un examen** to sit an exam
5 **presentarse a un concurso** to enter a competition ▸▸

a
b
c
d
e
f
g
h
i
j
k
l
m
n
ñ
o
p
q
r
s
t
u
v
w
x
y
z

6 presentarse para un cargo to apply for a post

7 presentarse a la presidencia to run for the presidency

presente *masc & fem adjective*
▷ see **presente** *noun*
present, **here** (*when calling the register*)

el **presente** *masc noun* ▷ see **presente** *adj*
present

el **preservativo** *masc noun*
condom

la **presidencia** *fem noun*
presidency

el **presidente** *masc noun*, la **presidenta** *fem*
president
el presidente del gobierno the prime minister

la **presión** *fem noun*
1 **pressure**
2 la presión atmosférica atmospheric pressure

♂ **preso** *masc adjective*, **presa** *fem*
▷ see **preso** *noun*
estar preso to be in prison
meter preso a alguien to send somebody to prison
Metieron presos a los delincuentes. The criminals were sent to prison.

♂ el **preso** *masc noun*, la **presa** *fem*
▷ see **preso** *adj*
prisoner
• el preso político political prisoner

el **préstamo** *masc noun*
loan
• el préstamo hipotecario mortgage

♂ **prestar** *verb* [17]
1 **to lend**
Le presté dinero para el coche. I lent him money for the car.
¿Me prestas tu abrigo? Could you lend me your coat?
2 prestar atención to pay attention

el **prestidigitador** *masc noun*, la **prestidigitadora** *fem*
conjurer

presumido *masc adjective*, **presumida** *fem* ▷ see **presumido** *noun*
conceited

el **presumido** *masc noun*, la **presumida** *fem* ▷ see **presumido** *adj*
Es un presumido. He's so conceited.

presumir *verb* [19]
to show off
Presumen de casa grande. They like to boast about how big their house is.
Presume de guapa. She thinks she's so good-looking.

el **presupuesto** *masc noun*
1 **budget** (*in business, government*)
2 **estimate** (*for repairs, etc*)

pretender *verb* [18]
1 **to try**
¿Qué pretende conseguir? What is he trying to achieve?
¿Qué pretendes decir con eso? What are you getting at?
Pretendía que pagase yo. She was trying to get me to pay for it.
2 pretender que alguien haga algo to expect somebody to do something
Pretende que yo le ayude. He expects me to help him.

WORD TIP *pretender* in Spanish, does not mean *to pretend*; for the meaning of *pretend* ▷ **fingir**

el **pretexto** *masc noun*
pretext, **excuse**
Siempre tiene algún pretexto para no hacerlo. He always has some excuse or other for not doing it.

prevenir *verb* [15]
1 **to prevent**
Previene la malaria. It prevents malaria.
2 **to warn**
Hay que prevenirles de las inundaciones. We must warn them about the floods.

prever *verb* [16]
to foresee

previsto *masc adjective*, **prevista** *fem*
a la hora prevista at the scheduled time
Está previsto que vengan mañana. They're due to come tomorrow.

♂ la **primavera** *fem noun*
spring
en primavera in spring
la primavera pasada last spring

♂ **primer** *adjective*
first

▷ **primero, primera** *adjective*
el primer ministro the prime minister
en el primer piso on the first floor

WORD TIP *primero* is used instead of *primero* before a masc singular noun.

♂ **primero** *masc adjective, pronoun,* **primera**
fem ▷ see **primero** *adv*
first
primera clase first class
Sólo leí las veinte primeras páginas. I only read the first twenty pages.
el primero de mayo the first of May
Soy el primero. I'm first.
Llegó en primer lugar. He finished in first position.

♂ **primero** *adverb* ▷ see **primero** *adj, pron*
first
Yo estaba primero. I was here first.
Primero vamos a informarnos. First of all, let's find out.

la **primicia** *fem noun*
1 **scoop** (*news story*)
2 **first showing** (*of film*)

♂ el **primo** *masc noun,* la **prima** *fem*
cousin
Hoy vienen mis primos Julio y Sara My cousins Julio and Sara are coming today.

♂ la **princesa** *fem noun*
princess

♂ **principal** *masc & fem adjective*
main
la calle principal del pueblo the village's main street

♂ el **príncipe** *masc noun*
prince
un príncipe ruso a Russian prince
los Príncipes de Asturias the Prince and Princess of Asturias (*Príncipe de Asturias is the title of Spain's crown prince*)

el **principiante** *masc noun,* la
principianta *fem*
beginner

♂ el **principio** *masc noun*
1 **beginning**
a principios de mes at the beginning of the month
a principios de siglo at the turn of the century
al principio de la temporada at the beginning of the season
un buen principio a good start

2 **principle**
Se niega por principio a hacerlo. He refuses to do it on principle.

♂ la **prisa** *fem noun*
1 **hurry**
tener prisa to be in a hurry
Tengo mucha prisa. I'm in a real hurry.
darse prisa to hurry up
Date prisa, que llegamos tarde. Hurry up or we'll be late.
2 **de prisa** fast
hacer algo de prisa to do something fast
Hizo los deberes de prisa. He rushed through his homework.
a toda prisa in a hurry
3 **correr prisa** to be urgent
Este trabajo corre prisa. This job is urgent.

la **prisión** *fem noun*
prison

el **prisionero** *masc noun,* la **prisionera**
fem
prisoner

los **prismáticos** *plural masc noun*
binoculars

privado *masc adjective,* **privada** *fem*
private
la vida privada private life
en privado in private

privar *verb* [17]
privar a alguien de algo to deprive somebody of something
Lo privaron de su libertad. He was deprived of his freedom.

privarse *reflexive verb* [17]
privarse de algo to deprive yourself of something
Se priva de todo lujo. She deprives herself of all luxuries.

privilegiado *masc adjective,*
privilegiada *fem*
privileged

el **privilegio** *masc noun*
privilege

probable *masc & fem adjective*
probable
Es probable que lo traiga hoy. He'll probably bring it today.

el **probador** *masc noun*
changing room

♂ probar *verb* [24]
1 to try
Prueba a abrirlo con esta llave. Try opening it with this key.
Es la primera vez que lo pruebo. It's the first time I've tried it.
Probar no cuesta nada. There's no harm in trying.
2 to taste
Pruébalo. Taste it.
¿Has probado la sopa? Have you tasted the soup?
3 to test (*the brakes*)
4 to prove
Esta carta prueba que mintió. This letter proves she lied.
No pudo probar su inocencia. He could not prove his innocence.

probarse *reflexive verb* [24]
to try on
Quisiera probarme este vestido. I'd like to try on this dress.
¿Quiere probárselo? Would you like to try it on?

la probeta *fem noun*
test tube
un niño probeta a test-tube baby

♂ el problema *masc noun*
problem
un problema muy importante a major problem
resolver un problema to solve a problem

♂ procedente *masc & fem adjective*
from
el vuelo procedente de Londres the flight from London

proceder *verb* [18]
1 proceder de algo to come from something
Su familia procede de Italia. His family comes from Italy.
2 to proceed
Hay que proceder con cautela. We must proceed with caution.

el procesador *masc noun*
un procesador de textos a word processor

la procesión *fem noun*
procession

el proceso *masc noun*
1 process
un proceso químico a chemical process
2 processing
• **el proceso de datos** data processing

♂ procurar *verb* [17]
procurar hacer algo to try to do something
Procura terminarlo para el viernes. Try to finish it by Friday.

la producción *fem noun*
production

♂ producir *verb* [60]
1 to produce
producir coches to produce cars
2 to cause
La tormenta produjo daños importantes. The storm caused extensive damage.

♂ el producto *masc noun*
product
un producto químico a chemical product
productos alimenticios foodstuffs
• **el producto lácteo** dairy product

productor *masc adjective*, **productora** *fem* ▷ see **productor** *noun*
producing
países productores de petróleo oil-producing countries

el productor *masc noun*, la **productora** *fem* ▷ see **productor** *adj*
producer

♂ produje, produzca, etc *verb* ▷ **producir**

♂ el & la profe *masc & fem noun*
teacher (*informal*)

♂ la profesión *fem noun*
profession, trade
Es arquitecta de profesión. She's an architect by profession.
Era fontanero de profesión. He was a plumber by trade.
Profesión: guardia jurado Occupation: Security guard

♂ profesional *masc & fem adjective*
professional
Es fotógrafa profesional. She's a professional photographer.

♂ el profesor *masc noun*, la **profesora** *fem*
1 teacher (*in a secondary school*)
Soy profesor de francés. I'm a teacher of French.
2 lecturer (*in a university*)

la profundidad *fem noun*
depth

♂ profundo *masc adjective*, **profunda** *fem*
deep
un río muy profundo a very deep river
una laguna poco profunda a shallow lake

♂ el **programa** *masc noun*

1 **programme** (*on TV, radio*)
un programa sobre la pobreza a programme about poverty

2 (*Computers*) **program**
Puedes bajar el programa gratis. You can download the program free.

• el **programa informático** computer program

el **programador** *masc noun*, la **programadora** *fem*
programmer

programar *verb* [17]
to program (*a computer*)

progresar *verb* [17]
to progress

el **progreso** *masc noun*
progress
hacer progresos to make progress

♂ **prohibido** *masc adjective*, **prohibida** *fem*
forbidden
Está terminantemente prohibido. It's strictly forbidden.
'Prohibido fumar' 'No smoking'
'Prohibido el paso', 'Prohibida la entrada' 'No entry'
'Prohibido pisar el césped' 'Keep off the grass'

♂ **prohibir** *verb* [58]
to prohibit
Se prohíbe la entrada a menores de dieciséis años. No admission to persons under 16.
Nos han prohibido escribirnos. They've forbidden us to write to each other.

prolongar *verb* [28]
to prolong

prolongarse *reflexive verb* [28]
to go on (*matches, parties*)

el **promedio** *masc noun*
average
un promedio de quince libras por semana an average of fifteen pounds a week
una vez a la semana como promedio once a week on average

la **promesa** *fem noun*
promise
cumplir con una promesa to keep a promise
faltar a una promesa to break a promise

♂ **prometer** *verb* [18]
to promise
Prometió llamarme. She promised to call me.
Vendrá pronto, te lo prometo. He'll come soon, I promise.

el **prometido** *masc noun*, la **prometida** *fem*
1 **fiancé** (*man*)
2 **fiancée** (*woman*)

la **promoción** *fem noun*
promotion

♂ el **pronombre** *masc noun*
pronoun

♂ el **pronóstico** *masc noun*
1 **forecast** (*for weather, events*)
2 **prognosis** (*for illness*)
• el **pronóstico del tiempo** weather forecast

♂ **pronto** *masc adjective*, **pronta** *fem*
▷ see **pronto** *adv*
prompt
una pronta respuesta a prompt reply
Le deseo una pronta mejoría. I wish her a speedy recovery.

♂ **pronto** *adverb* ▷ see **pronto** *adj*
1 **soon**
Vengan tan pronto como sea posible. Come as soon as possible.
¡Hasta pronto! See you soon!
2 **quickly**
Respondieron muy pronto. They answered very quickly.
3 **early**
Se marcharon pronto. They left early.
4 **de pronto** all of a sudden

la **pronunciación** *fem noun*
pronunciation

pronunciar *verb* [17]
to pronounce
¿Cómo se pronuncia este nombre? How do you pronounce this name?

la **propaganda** *fem noun*
1 **advertising**
hacer propaganda de un producto to advertise a product
2 **propaganda** (*in politics*)

la **propiedad** *fem noun*
property
ser propiedad de alguien to belong to somebody
Es propiedad del estado. It's state property.
• la **propiedad privada** private property

♂ el **propietario** *masc noun*, la **propietaria** *fem*
owner
El propietario vive en el sótano. The owner lives in the basement.
Es propietaria de cinco hoteles. She owns five hotels.

♀ la **propina** *fem noun*
tip
Le dejé dos euros de propina. I left him a two euro tip.

♂ **propio** *masc adjective*, **propia** *fem*
1 **own**
mi propio hermano my own brother
Tiene coche propio. She has her own car.
2 (*for emphasis*) La propia Elena lo admitió. Elena herself admitted it.
El propio director se equivocó. The headmaster himself made a mistake.

♂ **proponer** *verb* [11]
1 **to suggest**
Nos propuso ir a cenar fuera. He suggested we went out for dinner.
Propongo que vayas en tren. I suggest you go by train.
2 **to propose**
proponer una idea to propose an idea
proponer un trato to make a proposition
3 **to put forward** (*a candidate*)

proponerse *reflexive verb* [11]
1 **to set yourself a goal**
Me propuse encontrar un trabajo. I set myself the goal of finding a job.
Siempre consigue lo que se propone. He always achieves what he sets out to do.
¿Qué se proponen? What have they got in mind?
2 **to decide**
Se propuso ir a verlos. He decided to go and see them.

la **proporción** *fem noun*
proportion
en proporción in proportion
las proporciones del edificio the dimensions of the building

la **proposición** *fem noun*
proposal

el **propósito** *masc noun*
intention

la **prórroga** *fem noun*
1 **extension** (*of time limit*)
2 **extra time** (*in sports*)

el **prospecto** *masc noun*
1 **patient information leaflet** (*supplied with medicine*)
2 **advertising leaflet**

próspero *masc adjective*, **próspera** *fem*
1 **prosperous**
2 ¡Próspero Año Nuevo! A prosperous New Year to you!

la **prostituta** *fem noun*
prostitute

♂ el & la **protagonista** *masc & fem noun*
1 **leading player** (*in a play*)
2 **main character** (*in a film, a story*)
3 **leading figure**
los protagonistas de la guerra civil the leading figures in the civil war

la **protección** *fem noun*
protection

protector *masc adjective*, **protectora** *fem*
▷ see **protector** *noun*
1 **protective**
2 Sociedad Protectora de Animales Society for the Prevention of Cruelty to Animals

el **protector** *masc noun*, la **protectora** *fem*
▷ see **protector** *adj*
protector

♂ **proteger** *verb* [3]
to protect
Te protegerá del frío. It will protect you from the cold.

protegerse *reflexive verb* [3]
to protect yourself

protegido *masc adjective*, **protegida** *fem*
protected

la **protesta** *fem noun*
protest
en señal de protesta in protest

protestante *masc & fem adjective & noun*
1 **Protestant**
2 un & una protestante Protestant

WORD TIP Adjectives and nouns for religion do not have capital letters in Spanish.

protestar *verb* [17]
to protest

♂ el **provecho** *masc noun*
1 **benefit**
Siempre piensa en su propio provecho. He always thinks of his own interests.
sacar provecho de algo to benefit from something

Sacó mucho provecho de su viaje a Paris.
He greatly benefited from his trip to Paris.

2 ¡Buen provecho! Enjoy your meal!

proveniente *masc & fem adjective*
personas provenientes de otros países
people from other countries

el **proverbio** *masc noun*
proverb

♪ la **provincia** *fem noun*
province
una ciudad de provincias a provincial town

provisional *masc & fem adjective*
provisional

provocador *masc adjective,*
provocadora *fem*
▷ see **provocador** *noun*
provocative

el **provocador** *masc noun,* la
provocadora *fem*
▷ see **provocador** *adj*
political agitator

♪ **provocar** *verb* [31]
1 to provoke (*a person*)
2 to cause (*an explosion, fire*)
Provocaron el incendio forestal. They
caused the forest fire.

la **proximidad** *fem noun*
proximity

♪ **próximo** *masc adjective,* **próxima** *fem*
1 next
la próxima semana next week
la próxima parada the next stop
2 (*in time*) en fecha próxima in the near future
Ya está próximo su aniversario. It will soon
be their anniversary.

♪ el **proyecto** *masc noun*
1 project
2 plan
¿Qué proyectos tienes para el verano?
What are your plans for the summer?
3 Tengo varios trabajos en proyecto. I've got
several jobs lined up.

el **proyector** *masc noun*
projector

prudente *masc & fem adjective*
sensible
Sé prudente conduciendo. Drive carefully.

♪ la **prueba** *fem noun* ▷ see **prueba** *verb*
1 proof
No tienen pruebas. They have no proof.
2 test

3 hacer la prueba to try
Hice la prueba y funcionó. I tried and it
worked.
Haz la prueba de limpiarlo con lejía. Try
cleaning it with bleach.

4 a prueba on trial
unos trabajadores a prueba workers on
probation

5 a prueba de ... ...-proof
a prueba de balas bullet-proof
a prueba de agua waterproof

♪ , **prueba**, etc *verb* ▷ see **prueba** *noun* ▷
probar

♪ el **psicólogo** *masc noun,* la **psicóloga** *fem*
psychologist

♪ el & la **psiquiatra** *masc & fem noun*
psychiatrist

publicar *verb* [31]
to publish

la **publicidad** *fem noun*
1 publicity
2 advertising

♪ **público** *masc adjective,* **pública** *fem*
▷ see **público** *noun*
public
el transporte público public transport

♪ el **público** *masc noun* ▷ see **público** *adj*
1 public
Prefiere no cantar en público. She prefers
not to sing in public.
2 audience

♪ **pude**, **pudo**, etc *verb* ▷ **poder**

pudrir *verb* [59]
to rot

pudrirse *reflexive verb* [59]
to rot

♪ el **pueblo** *masc noun*
1 village
2 small town
3 people
el pueblo español the Spanish people

♪ el **puente** *masc noun*
1 bridge
2 hacer puente to take a long weekend
• el **puente aéreo** shuttle service
• el **puente colgante** suspension bridge
• el **puente levadizo** drawbridge
• el **puente peatonal** footbridge

♪ la **puerca** *fem noun*
pig, sow

♂ el **puerco** *masc noun*
pig, **boar**

♂ el **puerro** *masc noun*
leek

♀ la **puerta** *fem noun*
1 **door**
Llaman a la puerta. Someone's knocking at the door.
Quedamos en la puerta del cine. We arranged to meet outside the cinema.
2 **gate**
la puerta del jardín the garden gate
• la **puerta de embarque** gate (in an airport)
• la **puerta giratoria** revolving door
• la **puerta principal** main door
• la **puerta trasera** back door

♂ el **puerto** *masc noun*
1 **port**
2 **harbour**
• el **puerto de montaña** mountain pass
• el **puerto deportivo** marina
• el **puerto marítimo** seaport
• el **puerto pesquero** fishing port

♂ **Puerto Rico** *masc noun*
Puerto Rico

puertorriqueño *masc adjective & noun*,
puertorriqueña *fem adjective & noun*
1 **Puerto Rican**
2 un puertorriqueño, una puertorriqueña
Puerto Rican

WORD TIP Adjectives and nouns for nationality and regional origin do not have capital letters in Spanish.

♀ **pues** *conjunction*
1 **well**
Pues bien, como te iba diciendo ... Well, as I was telling you ...
Pues no estoy seguro. Well, I'm really sure.
Pues mira, ahora no me acuerdo. Well, look, I can't remember now.
2 (for emphasis) ¡Pues no vayas! Well, don't go then!
Pues si no te gusta el libro, no lo leas. If you don't like the book, don't read it then.
¡Pues claro! Of course!
¡Pues claro que no! Of course not!
'¿Lo querías tú?'—'¡Pues sí!' 'Did you want it?'—'Yes, of course I did!'

♀ **puesto** *masc adjective*, **puesta** *fem*
▷ see **puesto** *noun, conj*
1 **set** (tables, cutlery)
La mesa estaba puesta. The table was laid.
2 **on** (clothes)
Llevaba el abrigo puesto. I had my coat on.

♂ el **puesto** *masc noun* ▷ see **puesto** *adj, conj*
1 **position**
llegar en primer puesto to finish in first position
Sacó el primer puesto en el examen. She came top in the exam.
2 **job**
un puesto fijo a permanent job
puestos vacantes vacancies
Perdió su puesto de trabajo. He lost his job.
3 **stall** (in a market)
• el **puesto de socorro** first-aid post
• el **puesto de trabajo** job

♀ **puesto** *conjunction* ▷ see **puesto** *adj, noun*
puesto que ... since ...
Puesto que no ha venido, me voy. Since he hasn't come, I'm leaving.

♀ la **pulga** *fem noun*
flea

♀ la **pulgada** *fem noun*
inch
una pantalla de diecisiete pulgadas a seventeen inch screen

♂ el **pulgar** *masc noun*
thumb

pulir *verb* [19]
to polish

♂ el **pulmón** *masc noun*
lung
Padece de los pulmones. He has lung problems.

♂ el **pulpo** *masc noun*
octopus

pulsar *verb* [17]
1 **to press** (a key, a button)
2 **to pluck** (a string)

♀ la **pulsera** *fem noun*
1 **bracelet**
2 **watchstrap**

el **pulso** *masc noun*
1 **pulse**
Le tomó el pulso. He took her pulse.
2 tener buen pulso to have a steady hand
Me temblaba el pulso. My hand was shaking.
3 a pulso
dibujar algo a pulso to draw something freehand
Lo levantó a pulso. He lifted it with his hands.
4 echar un pulso to arm-wrestle

la **punta** *fem noun*
1 **point** (*of a knife, a needle*)
   Acaba en punta. It's pointed.
2 **tip** (*of pencil, tongue, finger, etc*)
3 **end**
   a la otra punta del pasillo at the other end
   of the corridor
4 **las puntas** ends (*of hair*)
   cortarse las puntas to have your hair
   trimmed
   tener las puntas abiertas to have split ends
5 **sacar punta a un lápiz** to sharpen a pencil

la **puntada** *fem noun*
   stitch

el **puntapié** *masc noun*
   kick
   darle un puntapié a alguien to kick
   someone

la **puntería** *fem noun*
   aim (*in shooting*)
   Tiene buena puntería. He's a good shot.

la **puntilla** *fem noun*
1 **ponerse de puntillas** to stand on tiptoe
   andar de puntillas to walk on tiptoe
2 **lace edging**

♂ el **punto** *masc noun*
1 **point**
   punto por punto point by point
   hasta cierto punto up to a point
   Llevan tres puntos de ventaja. They're
   three points ahead.
   Es mi punto débil. It's my weak point.
2 **estar a punto de hacer algo** to be about to
   do something
   Estaba a punto de salir cuando me llamó. I
   was about to leave when he called me.
3 **dot**
   el punto sobre la 'i' the dot on the 'i'
   rosa.ramirez@easycom.com (*said as rosa
   punto ramirez **arroba** easycom **punto** com*)
4 (*in time expressions*) **en punto** on the dot
   a las dos en punto at two on the dot
   llegar en punto to arrive exactly on time
5 **stitch**
   de punto knitted
   una falda de punto a knitted skirt
   hacer punto to knit
6 (*talking about food*) **estar algo en su punto** to
   be just right
   La carne está en su punto. The meat is just
   right.
• el **punto de vista** point of view
• el **punto final** full stop (*in punctuation*)
• el **punto muerto** neutral (*gear*)
• el **punto y coma** semicolon

♂ la **puntocom** *fem noun*
   una puntocom a dot-com company

el **punto negro** *masc noun*
1 **black spot** (*for accidents*)
2 **blackhead** (*on skin*)

♂ la **puntuación** *fem noun*
1 **punctuation**
2 **score** (*in sports*)
   Nuestro equipo obtuvo la máxima
   puntuación. Our team got the highest
   score.
3 **marks** (*in an exam*)

puntual *masc & fem adjective*
   punctual
   ser puntual to be always on time
   Llegaron puntuales. They arrived on time.

♂ el **puñetazo** *masc noun*
   punch
   Me dio un puñetazo. He punched me.
   Di un puñetazo en la mesa. I thumped on
   the table with my fist.

♂ el **puño** *masc noun*
1 **fist**
   Cerró el puño. He clenched his fist.
2 **cuff** (*of a shirt*)
3 **handle** (*of a tool*)

♂ la **pupila** *fem noun*
   pupil (*of your eye*)

♂ el **pupitre** *masc noun*
   desk (*in school*)

el **puré** *masc noun*
   purée
• el **puré de guisantes** pea soup
• el **puré de patatas** mashed potatoes

♂ **puro** *masc adjective*, **pura** *fem*
   ▷ see **puro** *noun*
   pure
   el aire puro del campo the pure country air
   Es de pura lana. It's made of pure wool.
   la pura verdad the simple truth
   de puro aburrimiento out of sheer
   boredom

♂ el **puro** *masc noun* ▷ see **puro** *adj*
   cigar

♂ **púrpura** *masc & fem adjective*
   purple

♂ **puse, puso, etc** *verb* ▷ **poner**

♂ el **puzzle** *masc noun*
   jigsaw puzzle

♂ indicates key words   257

Q q

que *pronoun* ▷ see **que** *conj*

1 **who**
el hombre que me lo dijo the man who told me
los que están interesados those who are interested

2 **which, that**
el libro que recomendé the book which I recommended
la marca que me gusta the brand (that) I like

3 el que prefiero the one (that) I prefer
las que vimos ayer the ones (that) we saw yesterday

que *conjunction* ▷ see **que** *pron*

1 **that**
Sé que le gusta. I know (that) he likes it.
Confirmó que viene. She confirmed that she's coming.
Dijo que no lo necesitaba. She said (that) she didn't need it.
Nos pidió que le ayudásemos. He asked us to help him.

2 (*in comparisons*) **than**
Es más alto que yo. He's taller than me.

3 (*in wishes*) Que te mejores pronto. Get well soon.
Que pases unas buenas vacaciones. Have a nice holiday.

4 (*in orders*) Que pasen. Show them in.
¡Que te calles! Shut up!

5 (*for emphasis*) ¡Que es mío! I'm telling you it's mine!
'¿Te importa?'—'¡Que no!' 'Do you mind?'—'I've already told you that I don't!'
¡Que te he dicho que sí me gusta! I've already told you I like it!

6 (*expressing surprise*) ¿Que tiene veinte años? She's twenty?

7 yo que tú ... if I were you ...

qué *adjective* ▷ see **qué** *adv, pron*

1 **which**
¿Qué abrigo es el tuyo? Which coat is yours?
¿Qué países visitaste? What countries did you visit?

2 **what** (*in exclamations*)
¡Qué casa tan bonita! What a pretty house!
¡Qué ojos tan grandes tienes! What big eyes you have!

qué *adverb* ▷ see **qué** *adj, pron*
¡Qué bonito! How nice!
¡Qué bien! Great!
¡Qué bien toca! Doesn't he play well!
¡Qué egoísta eres! You're so selfish!

qué *pronoun* ▷ see **qué** *adj, adv*

1 **what**
¿Qué es eso? What's that?
¿A qué te refieres? What are you referring to?

2 ¿Qué? What?

3 ¿Qué tal? How are you doing?
¿Qué tal va? How's it going?
¿Qué hay? How are things?
¿Qué hay de nuevo? What's new?

4 ¡Qué va! No way!

WORD TIP *qué*, with an accent, is used in questions and for emphasis.

el **quebradero** *masc noun*
worry

el **quebrado** *masc noun*
fraction

quebrar *verb* [29]
to break
Me ha quebrado el lápiz. He's broken my pencil.
¡No lo quiebres! Don't break it!

quedar *verb* [17]

1 **to be left**
Quedan tres paquetes. There are three packets left.
¿Te queda dinero? Do you have any money left?
No queda leche. There's no milk left.
Quedaban quince kilómetros. There were still fiteen kilometres to go.

2 (*in time expressions*) Aún queda tiempo. There's still time.
Aún quedan dos días. There are still two days to go.
¿Cuánto tiempo me queda? How much time do I have left?
Quedaban quince minutos para el final de la clase. It was still fifteen minutes till the end of the class.

3 (*saying what happened*) Quedó viudo. He was widowed.
Quedaron solos. They were left alone.
Quedó ciego tras el accidente. He was left

blind after the accident.
quedar en último lugar to end up last

4 (*about how something looks*) **Así queda mejor.**
It's better like this.
Queda muy feo con esa tela. It's horrible
with that material.

5 (*arranging to meet*) **Quedamos en la plaza.**
We arranged to meet in the square.
¿Te apetece quedar? Would you like to
meet?
¿Quedamos para el sábado? Shall we meet
on Saturday?

6 (*about clothes, hairstyles, etc*) **Me queda
apretado.** It's too tight on me.
¿Te queda bien? Does it fit you?
Ese color te queda muy bien. That colour
really suits you.
Esos vaqueros te quedan fenomenal.
Those jeans look great on you.

7 (*impressions*) **Quiere quedar bien con mi
familia.** She wants to make a good
impression on my family.

8 **Va a quedar mal si no lo hacemos.** It will
look bad if we don't do it.
Quedamos muy mal con sus padres. We
made a bad impression on her parents.

9 **quedar en algo** to agree on something
Quedamos en vernos hoy. We agreed to
see each other today.

10 **to be** (*talking about where something is*)
Queda bastante lejos. It's quite a long way
away.
Queda cerca de mi casa. It's near my house.
¿Dónde queda la estación? Where is the
station?

quedarse *reflexive verb* [17]

1 **to stay**
Se quedó en la cama. He stayed in bed.
Prefiero quedarme en casa. I'd rather stay
at home.
quedarse con algo to keep something
Se quedó con mi revista. He kept my
magazine.
Quédese con la vuelta. Keep the change.

2 (*saying what happened*) **quedarse ciego** to go
blind
quedarse calvo to lose your hair
quedarse asombrado to be amazed
Se quedó dormido. He fell asleep.
quedarse callado to remain silent
quedarse sin trabajo to lose your job

WORD TIP If the person is female, the adjective is
ciega, calva, asombrada, etc.

⚶ la **queja** *fem noun*
complaint, **gripe**
presentar una queja to make a complaint

**Presentó una queja al gerente por el mal
servicio.** She made a complaint to the
manager about the bad service.
Estamos hartos de sus quejas. We're sick of
his complaining.

los **quehaceres** *plural masc noun*
chores

⚶ **quejarse** *reflexive verb* [17]
to complain
Se quejan de la comida. They complain
about the food.
Se quejó de que tardé mucho. She
complained about how long I took.

quemado *masc adjective*, **quemada** *fem*
burnt

la **quemadura** *fem noun*
burn

⚶ **quemar** *verb* [17]

1 **to burn**

2 **to scald**
El vapor me ha quemado la mano. The
steam has scalded my hand.

3 **to be very hot**
La sopa quema mucho. The soup's really
hot.

4 **quemar un motor** to burn out an engine

5 **quemar calorías** to burn up calories

6 **¡Cómo quema el sol!** The sun's really
scorching!

quemarse *reflexive verb* [17]

1 **to burn yourself**
Me quemé la mano. I burnt my hand.

2 **to scald yourself**

3 **to get burnt**
¡Cómo te has quemado! You've really got
burnt! (*in the sun*)
El mantel se quemó un poco. The
tablecloth got a bit burnt.

4 **to burn down**
La casa se quemó toda. The house burned
down.

quepo, **quepa**, **quepamos**, **etc** *verb* ▷
caber

⚶ **querer** *verb* [12]

1 **to want**
Queremos volver a casa. We want to go
home.
No quiero ir al cine. I don't want to go to
the cinema.
¿Qué quieres para tu cumpleaños? What
do you want for your birthday?
¿Quieres apagar la tele, por favor? Would
you mind switching off the television,
please? ▸▸

⚶ indicates key words   259

querer que alguien haga algo to want somebody to do something
Quiero que me lo compres. I want you to buy it for me.

WORD TIP *querer que* is followed by a verb in the subjunctive.

2 **to love**
Te quiero. I love you.
3 *(making offers)* **¿Quieres beber algo?** Would you like something to drink?
Si quieres voy más tarde. If you like I'll go later.
4 *(in shops, cafés, etc)* **Yo quiero un café.** I'll have a coffee.
Quisiera ver vestidos largos. I would like to see some long dresses.
Quisiera reservar una mesa para cuatro. I'd like to book a table for four.
5 **querer decir algo** to mean something
¿Qué quieres decir? What do you mean?
¿Qué quiere decir esto? What does this mean?

quererse *reflexive verb* [17]
to love each other
Si os queréis tanto ¿por qué no os casáis? If you love each other so much, why don't you get married?

♂ **querido** *masc adjective*, **querida** *fem*
dear
Querido Pablo: Dear Pablo, *(starting a letter)*

♂ **querrá**, **querré**, **querría**, **etc** *verb* ▷ **querer**

♂ **el queso** *masc noun*
cheese
• **el queso para untar** cheese spread
• **el queso rallado** grated cheese

la quiebra *fem noun*
bankruptcy

♂ **quien** *pronoun* ▷ **see quién** *pron*
1 **who**
Creo que fue Iñaki quien lo sugirió. I think it was Iñaki who suggested it.
No fui yo quien lo dijo. It wasn't me who said it.
Ellos son quienes no quisieron ir. They're the ones who didn't want to go.
(when quien may not be translated) **la chica con quien bailé anoche** the girl I danced with last night
las personas con quienes habló the people he spoke to
2 **whom**, **who**
Isabel, a quien vi ayer ... Isabel, whom I saw yesterday ...

♂ **quién** *pronoun* ▷ **see quien** *pron*
1 **who**
¿Quién es? Who is it?
¿Quiénes son esos chavales? Who are those lads?
¡Quién lo hubiese dicho! Who would have said!
2 **which**
¿Quién de vosotros es Carlos? Which of you is Carlos?
3 **¿De quién?** Whose?
¿De quién es esta cartera? Whose is this wallet?
¿De quiénes son estas motos? Who do these motorbikes belong to?

WORD TIP *quién* with an accent is used for questions (¿...?).

quienquiera *pronoun*
whoever

♂ **quiera**, **quiere**, **etc** *verb* ▷ **querer**

♂ **quieto** *masc adjective*, **quieta** *fem*
still
¡Estate quieto! Keep still!

WORD TIP *quieto* does not mean *quiet* in English; for the meaning of *quiet* ▷ **silencioso**.

♂ **la química** *fem noun* ▷ **see químico** *adj*, **químico** *noun*
chemistry
Estudié química y física. I studied chemistry and physics.

químico *masc adjective*, **química** *fem* ▷ **see química** *noun*, **químico** *noun*
chemical

el químico *masc noun*, **la química** *fem* ▷ **see química** *noun*, **químico** *adj*
chemist

♂ **quince** *number*
1 **fifteen**
Tiene quince años. He's fifteen (years old).
2 **fifteenth** *(in dates)*
Hoy estamos a quince. It's the fifteenth today.
Llegará el día quince. She'll arrive on the fifteenth.
3 **quince días** a fortnight

el quinceañero *masc noun*, **la quinceañera** *fem*
teenager

♂ **la quincena** *fem noun*
una quincena a fortnight
la primera quincena de mayo the first two weeks in May

la **quiniela** *fem noun*
pools coupon
rellenar una quiniela to fill in a pools coupon
jugar a las quinielas to do the pools

ƒ **quinientos**, **quinientas** *number*
five hundred
quinientos cinco five hundred and five

quinto *masc adjective*, **quinta** *fem*
fifth
el quinto piso the fifth floor
llegar en quinto lugar to finish in fifth position

ƒ el **quiosco** *masc noun*
1 **news-stand**
2 el quiosco de los helados the ice cream stand
Está frente al quiosco de bebidas. It's opposite the drinks stand.
3 **kiosk**

ƒ el **quiosquero** *masc noun*, la **quiosquera** *fem*
1 **newspaper vendor**
2 **kiosk attendant**

quirúrgico *masc adjective*, **quirúrgica** *fem*
surgical
una intervención quirúrgica a surgical operation

ƒ **quise**, **quisiera**, **quiso**, **etc** *verb* ▷ **querer**

el **quitaesmalte** *masc noun*
nail varnish remover

el **quitanieves** *masc noun*, *pl:* los **quitanieves**
snowplough

ƒ **quitar** *verb* [17]
1 **to take off**
Quita los pies de la mesa. Take your feet off the table.
No puedo quitar la tapa. I can't get the lid off.
2 Le quité los zapatos al niño. I took the child's shoes off.
3 quitarle algo a alguien to take something from someone
Le quitaron la cartera. They took his wallet.
4 **to take away**
Quita esa silla de ahí. Take that chair away from there.
Le han quitado el carnet de conducir. They've taken his driving licence away.
5 **to remove**
quitar la suciedad to remove the dirtiness
quitar el polvo to dust

quitarse *reflexive verb* [17]
1 **to come out** (*a stain, mark*)
2 **to go away** (*a pain*)
3 quitarse algo to take something off
Se quitó el abrigo. He took his coat off.

ƒ **quizá**, **quizás** *adverb*
perhaps

a
b
c
d
e
f
g
h
i
j
k
l
m
n
ñ
o
p
q
r
s
t
u
v
w
x
y
z

R r

el **rábano** *masc noun*
   radish

la **rabia** *fem noun*
1 dar rabia a alguien to annoy somebody
   Eso me da mucha rabia. That makes me
   very annoyed.
   Le dio mucha rabia que no se lo dijeran. It
   really annoyed him that they didn't tell
   him.
2 tenerle rabia a alguien to hate somebody
   Le tengo rabia. I hate him.
3 rabies

el **rabo** *masc noun*
   tail

la **racha** *fem noun*
1 gust (*of wind*)
2 una racha de mala suerte a spell of bad luck
   pasar una mala racha to go through a bad
   patch
   tener una buena racha to be on a winning
   streak

el **racimo** *masc noun*
   bunch
   un racimo de uvas a bunch of grapes

ᵹ la **ración** *fem noun*
   portion
   una ración de gambas a portion of
   prawns (*in a tapas bar*)

racionar *verb* [17]
   to ration

el **racismo** *masc noun*
   racism

racista *masc & fem adjective & noun*
1 racist
2 el & la racista racist

el **radar** *masc noun*
1 radar
2 speed camera

la **radiación** *fem noun*
   radiation

radiactivo *masc adjective*, **radiactiva** *fem*
   radioactive

el **radiador** *masc noun*
   radiator

ᵹ la **radio** *fem noun* ▷ see **radio** *masc noun*
   radio
   escuchar la radio to listen to the radio
   oír algo por la radio to hear something on
   the radio
   poner la radio to switch on the radio

el **radio** *masc noun* ▷ see **radio** *fem noun*
1 radius
2 (*Latin America*) radio

el **radiocassette** *masc noun*
   radio cassette player

la **radiografía** *fem noun*
   X-ray
   hacerse una radiografía to have an X-ray
   taken

la **ráfaga** *fem noun*
1 gust
   una ráfaga de viento a gust of wind
2 burst (*of gunfire*)
   una ráfaga de ametralladora a burst of
   machine-gun fire

la **raíz** *fem noun, pl:* las **raíces**
   root
   echar raíces to take root
   a raíz de as a result of
 • la raíz cuadrada square root

rallado *masc adjective*, **rallada** *fem*
1 grated
2 pan rallado breadcrumbs

el **rallador** *masc noun*
   grater

rallar *verb* [17]
   to grate

la **rama** *fem noun*
   branch

el **ramo** *masc noun*
1 bunch (*of flowers*)
2 bouquet

la **rampa** *fem noun*
   ramp
 • la rampa de lanzamiento launch pad

la **rana** *fem noun*
   frog

ſ la **ranura** *fem noun*
  coin slot
  introducir la moneda en la ranura to put
  the coin in the slot

el **rape** *masc noun*
  1 **monkfish**
  2 llevar el pelo cortado al rape to have your
    hair closely cropped

ſ rápidamente *adverb*
  quickly

ſ rápido *masc adjective*, **rápida** *fem*
  ▷ see **rápido** *adverb, noun*
  1 **quick**, **fast**
    la comida rápida fast food
  2 **rapid**

ſ rápido *adverb* ▷ see **rápido** *adjective &*
    noun
  fast, **quickly**
  Lo más rápido que podía. As fast as I could.

ſ el **rápido** *masc noun* ▷ see **rápido** *adjective,*
    adverb
  express train

la **raqueta** *fem noun*
  1 **racket**
  2 **snowshoe**

raramente *adverb*
  rarely

ſ raro *masc adjective*, **rara** *fem*
  1 **strange**
    ¡Qué raro que no venga! How strange that
    he hasn't come!
  2 **rare**
    Es raro que vengan turistas a esta zona. It's
    rare for tourists to come to this area.

el **rascacielos** *invarable masc noun*
  skyscraper

rascar *verb* [31]
  to scratch

rascarse *reflexive verb* [31]
  to scratch yourself
  Se rascó la nariz. He scratched his nose.

rasgar *verb* [28]
  to tear

el **rasguño** *masc noun*
  scratch

el **rastrillo** *masc noun*
  rake

el **rastro** *masc noun*
  1 **trail**
    sin dejar rastro without a trace
  2 **flea market**

la **rata** *fem noun*
  rat

ſ el **ratero** *masc noun*, la **ratera** *fem*
  1 **pickpocket**
  2 **petty thief**

ſ el **rato** *masc noun*
  1 **while**
    dentro de un rato in a while
    después de un rato after a while
    al poco rato soon afterwards
    al rato after a while
    Tardaré un rato en hacerlo. It will take me a
    while to do it.
    Ya hace rato que se han ido. They went a
    while ago.
  2 **time**
    pasar el rato to kill time
    Pasamos unos buenos ratos allí. We had
    good times there.
    ¿Qué haces en tus ratos libres? What do
    you do in your spare time?

ſ el **ratón** *masc noun*
  mouse

la **raya** *fem noun*
  1 **line**
  2 **dash** (*in punctuation*)
  3 **parting** (*in your hair*)
    hacerse la raya to part your hair
  4 **a rayas** striped (*dress, cloth*)
    una falda a rayas a striped skirt
  5 **skate** (*kind of fish*)

rayar *verb* [17]
  1 **to scratch**
  2 **rayar en** to border on
    Raya en lo ridículo. It's bordering on the
    ridiculous.

el **rayo** *masc noun*
  1 **ray**
    un rayo de luz a ray of light
  2 **bolt of lightning**
  • el **rayo láser** laser beam
  • los **rayos X** X-rays

la **raza** *fem noun*
  1 **race**
  2 **breed**
    un perro de raza a pedigree dog

a
b
c
d
e
f
g
h
i
j
k
l
m
n
ñ
o
p
q
r
s
t
u
v
w
x
y
z

♂ la **razón** *fem noun*

1 **reason**
  por alguna razón for some reason
  con razón with good reason
  por razones de salud for health reasons
  ¿Por qué razón se marchó? Why did he go
  away?

2 tener razón to be right
  Tienes razón. You're right.
  No tienes razón en eso. You're wrong
  about that.
  darle la razón a alguien to agree that
  somebody is right
  Nos dieron la razón. They agreed with us.

3 **reason**, **sanity**
  perder la razón to lose your mind

4 *(on notices)* Razón: 279452 Call 279452 for
  information.

razonable *masc & fem adjective*
  reasonable

la **reacción** *fem noun*
  reaction

reacio *masc adjective*, **reacia** *fem*
  reluctant

el **reactor** *masc noun*
1 **reactor**
2 **jet**

real *masc & fem adjective*
1 **real**
2 **true**
  una historia real a true story
3 **royal**
  el palacio real the royal palace

la **realidad** *fem noun*
  reality
  hacerse realidad to become true
  en realidad in fact

realista *masc & fem adjective*
1 **realistic**
  Es muy realista. He's very realistic.
2 **royalist**

el **realizador** *masc noun*, la **realizadora**
  fem
  producer

realizar *verb* [22]
1 **to carry out** *(a task)*
2 **to make** *(a visit, a trip)*
3 **to fulfil** *(a dream)*

realizarse *reflexive verb* [22]
1 **to come true** *(dreams)*
2 **to fulfil yourself**

♂ la **rebaja** *fem noun*

1 **reduction**
  Lo rebajó a cuarenta euros. He reduced it
  to forty euros.
  hacer una rebaja to give a reduction
  Me hizo una rebaja de diez euros. He gave
  me a ten euro reduction.

2 las rebajas the sales
  Esa tienda está de rebajas. This shop has a
  sale on.

rebajar *verb* [17]
1 **to bring down** *(prices)*
2 **to reduce the price of** *(an item)*
  Todas las faldas están rebajadas. All the
  skirts are reduced.

la **rebanada** *fem noun*
  slice

el **rebaño** *masc noun*
1 **flock** *(of sheep)*
2 **herd** *(of goats)*

la **rebeca** *fem noun*
  cardigan

rebelarse *reflexive verb* [17]
  to rebel

rebelde *masc & fem adjective*
  ▷ see **rebelde** *noun*
1 **rebel**
2 **unruly** *(child)*
3 una tos rebelde a persistent cough

el & la **rebelde** *masc & fem noun*
  ▷ see **rebelde** *adjective*
  rebel

la **rebelión** *fem noun*
  rebellion

rebobinar *verb* [17]
  to rewind *(tapes)*

rebotar *verb* [17]
1 **to bounce**
  La pelota rebotó en el poste. The ball
  bounced off the post.
2 **to ricochet**

rebuznar *verb* [17]
  to bray *(donkeys)*

el **recado** *masc noun*
1 **message**
  Me han dejado un recado. They left a
  message for me.
2 **errand**
  hacer un recado to go on an errand

recalentar verb [29]
1 **to reheat** (food)
2 **to overheat** (engines)

el **recambio** masc noun
1 **spare part**
2 **refill** (for a pen)

recargar verb [28]
1 **to recharge** (batteries, etc)
2 **to top up** (mobile phones)

la **recepción** fem noun
reception

el & la **recepcionista** masc & fem noun
receptionist

la **receta** fem noun
1 **recipe**
2 **prescription**

rechazar verb [22]
to turn down, **to reject**

recetar verb [17]
to prescribe

el **recibidor** masc noun
entrance hall

♪ **recibir** verb [19]
1 **to receive**
He recibido un menaje de texto de Lola.
I've received a text from Lola.
2 **to get**
Recibí una llamada de Maricarmen. I got a
phone call from Maricarmen.
3 Lo recibieron con los brazos abiertos. He
was welcomed with open arms.
4 ir a recibir a alguien to go to meet
somebody
Fuimos a recibirlos a la estación. We went
to meet them at the station.
5 (letter endings) Recibe un fuerte abrazo. Best
wishes
Reciba un cordial saludo. Yours sincerely

♪ el **recibo** masc noun
1 **receipt**
2 **bill** (for water, electricity)

el **reciclaje** masc noun
recycling (of waste)

reciclar verb [17]
to recycle

♪ **recién** adverb
1 Pasteles recién hechos. Freshly baked
cakes.
'Recién pintado' 'Wet paint'
2 (Latin America) **just**, **only just**
• los **recién casados** newly-weds

• los **recién llegados** newcomers
• el **recién nacido** newborn baby

♪ **reciente** masc & fem adjective
recent

♪ **recientemente** adverb
recently

el **recipiente** masc noun
container

recitar verb [17]
to recite

la **reclamación** fem noun
1 **complaint**
hacer una reclamación to make a
complaint
2 **claim**
hacer una reclamación al seguro to make a
claim on insurance

♪ **reclamar** verb [17]
1 **to complain**
2 **to demand** (rights, money, better conditions)

♪ **recoger** verb [3]
1 **to pick up**
Recoge ese papel del suelo. Pick up that
piece of paper off the floor.
Fui a recogerlos a la estación. I went to pick
them up from the station.
2 **to tidy up**
Tienes que recoger tu habitación. You
must tidy up your room.
recoger la mesa to clear the table
3 **to collect** (money, signatures)
4 **to pick** (fruit, flowers)

recogerse reflexive verb [3]
recogerse el pelo to tie your hair back

la **recogida** fem noun
collection (of rubbish, mail)

la **recomendación** fem noun
1 **recommendation**
2 **reference** (for a job)

♪ **recomendar** verb [29]
to recommend

la **recompensa** fem noun
reward

recompensar verb [17]
to reward

reconciliarse reflexive verb [17]
reconciliarse con alguien to make it up
with somebody
Se ha reconciliado con su novia. He's made
it up with his girlfriend.

a
b
c
d
e
f
g
h
i
j
k
l
m
n
ñ
o
p
q
r
s
t
u
v
w
x
y
z

♪ indicates key words   265

reconocer *verb* [35]
1 **to recognize**
No la reconocí. I didn't recognize her.
2 **to admit** (*a mistake*)
3 **to examine** (*a patient*)

el **reconocimiento** *masc noun*
1 **recognition** (*of a voice, facts*)
2 **examination** (*of a patient*)
• el **reconocimiento médico** medical examination

reconozca, reconozcas, etc *verb* ▷ reconocer

el **récord** *masc noun, pl:* los **récords** record

♂ **recordar** *verb* [24]
1 **to remember**
Lo recuerdo muy bien. I remember it very well.
Recuerdo que terminamos pronto. I remember that we finished early.
2 **to remind**
Me recuerda a su madre. He reminds me of his mother.
3 **recordarle a alguien que haga algo** to remind somebody to do something
Recuérdale que compre pan. Remind him to buy bread.

recorrer *verb* [18]
1 **to cover** (*a distance*)
2 **to travel around** (*a country*)
3 **to go round** (*an exhibition, museum, etc*)

el **recorrido** *masc noun*
1 **distance**
2 **journey**
3 **route**

♂ el **recreo** *masc noun*
break (*at school*)

la **recta** *fem noun*
straight line

el **rectángulo** *masc noun*
rectangle

♂ **recto** *masc adjective,* **recta** *fem*
▷ see **recto** *adv*
1 **straight** (*lines*)
2 **honest**

♂ **recto** *adverb* ▷ see **recto** *adj*
seguir todo recto to carry straight on
Siga todo recto hasta el semáforo. Carry straight on until the traffic lights.

♂ **recuerda, recuerdo, etc** *verb* ▷ recordar

♂ el **recuerdo** *masc noun*
1 **memory**
Tengo buenos recuerdos de Valencia. I've got happy memories of Valencia.
2 **souvenir**
'Recuerdo de España' 'Souvenir from Spain'
3 **recuerdos** *plural* regards, greetings
Dale recuerdos a tu hermana de mi parte. Say hello to your sister from me.

recuperar *verb* [17]
1 **to get back** (*money, strength*)
2 **recuperar tiempo** to make up for lost time

recuperarse *reflexive verb* [17]
recuperarse de una enfermedad to get well after an illness

♂ la **red** *fem noun*
1 **net**
2 **network**
3 **la Red** the Net (*Internet*)

la **redacción** *fem noun*
1 **essay**
2 **editorial team** (*in a newspaper*)

el **redactor** *masc noun,* la **redactora** *fem*
editor

♂ **redondo** *masc adjective,* **redonda** *fem*
round
en números redondos in round figures

la **reducción** *fem noun*
reduction

♂ **reducido** *masc adjective,* **reducida** *fem*
1 **small** (*amount, size*)
2 **reduced** (*prices*)

reducir *verb* [60]
to reduce

reduje, reduzca, reduzco, etc *verb* ▷ reducir

reembolsar *verb* [17]
to refund

el **reembolso** *masc noun*
refund

reemplazar *verb* [22]
to replace
reemplazar a alguien to stand in for somebody
Me reemplazó durante las vacaciones. She stood in for me over the holidays.

el **reemplazo** *masc noun*
replacement

la **referencia** *fem noun*
  reference
  referencias references (*for a job*)
  hacer referencia a to refer to
  No hizo referencia al tema. He didn't refer
  to the subject.

referirse *reflexive verb* [14]
  referirise a to refer to
  Se refiere a ti. She's referring to you.
  ¿A qué te refieres? What are you referring
  to?

la **refinería** *fem noun*
  refinery

reflejar *verb* [17]
  to reflect

reflejarse *reflexive verb* [17]
  to be reflected

el **reflejo** *masc noun*
  1 **reflection**
  2 **reflex**
  3 **los reflejos** highlights (*in hair*)

la **reflexión** *fem noun*
  reflection

reflexionar *verb* [17]
  to think it over
  **Hay que reflexionar antes de tomar una
  decisión.** We must think it over before we
  take a decision.

la **reforestación** *fem noun*
  reforestation

la **reforma** *fem noun*
  1 **reform** (*of laws, system, etc*)
  2 **alteration** (*to a house, etc*)
  'cerrado por reformas' 'closed for repairs'

reformar *verb* [1]
  1 **to reform** (*a law, system, etc*)
  2 **to alter** (*a house, etc*)
  reformar la casa to do up the house

el **refrán** *masc noun*
  saying

refrescante *masc & fem adjective*
  refreshing

refrescar *verb* [31]
  1 **to get cooler** (*weather*)
  2 **to air** (*room*)
  3 **to refresh** (*your memory*)

ꕔ el **refresco** *masc noun*
  soft drink
  tomar un referesco to have a soft drink

el **refrigerio** *masc noun*
  light refreshments

el **refugiado** *masc noun*, la **refugiada** *fem*
  refugee
  un refugiado económico an economic
  refugee

refugiarse *reflexive verb* [17]
  to take shelter
  refugiarse de algo to take shelter from
  something
  Nos refugiamos de la lluvia. We took
  shelter from the rain.

el **refugio** *masc noun*
  shelter
  dar refugio a alguien to give somebody
  shelter
  un refugio de montaña a mountain refuge

la **regadera** *fem noun*
  watering can

ꕔ **regalar** *verb* [17]
  1 **to give** (*as a present*)
  Mi tío me ha regalado un reloj. My uncle
  has given me a watch.
  ¿Qué vas a regalarle por Navidad? What
  are you going to give her for Christmas?
  2 **to give away**
  Están regalando bolígrafos. They're giving
  away ball-point pens.
  ¿Te gusta? Te lo regalo. Do you like it? You
  can have it.

ꕔ el **regalo** *masc noun*
  1 **present**
  un regalo de cumpleaños a birthday
  present
  2 (*in promotions*) **de regalo: Compre dos y
  llévese uno de regalo.** Buy two and get one
  free.

regañar *verb* [17]
  1 **to tell off**
  Mi madre me regañó por llegar tarde. My
  mother told me off because I got home
  late.
  2 **regañar con alguien** to quarrel with
  somebody
  Ha regañado con su hermano. He's had an
  argument with his brother.

regar *verb* [30]
  to water

ꕔ el **régimen** *masc noun*
  diet
  ponerse a régimen to go on a diet
  Tengo que ponerme a régimen. I must go
  on a diet.

a
b
c
d
e
f
g
h
i
j
k
l
m
n
ñ
o
p
q
r
s
t
u
v
w
x
y
z

♂ la **región** *fem noun*
region

regional *masc & fem adjective*
regional

registrar *verb* [17]
1 **to search**
Nos registraron. We were searched.
La policía registró la casa. The police
searched the house.
2 **to go through**
Me registraron todos los papeles. They
went through all my papers.
3 **to register** (*a birth, car*)
4 **to record** (*temperature*)

registrarse *reflexive verb* [17]
1 **to register**
2 **to check in** (*at a hotel*)
Se registró a las cinco. She checked in at
five o'clock.

el **registro** *masc noun*
1 **search** (*by police, etc*)
2 **register**
• el **registro civil** registry office

♂ la **regla** *fem noun*
1 **ruler** (*for measuring*)
2 **rule**
por regla general as a general rule
3 estar con la regla to have your period

el **reglamento** *masc noun*
regulations

regresar *verb* [17]
to return, **to come back**
Siempre regresan tarde. They always come
back late.

el **regreso** *masc noun*
return

regular *adverb, masc & fem adjective*
1 **regular**
de tamaño regular regular-sized
'¿Qué tal está tu padre?'—'Regular.'
'How's your father?'—'So-so.'
2 **poor** (*mark*)
3 por lo regular as a general rule

la **regularidad** *fem noun*
regularity
con regularidad regularly

rehacer *verb* [7]
1 rehacer algo to do something again
2 Rehizo su vida. She rebuilt her life.

el & la **rehén** *masc & fem noun, pl:* **rehenes**
hostage

la **reina** *fem noun*
queen
la reina Sofía Queen Sofía
la reina de España the queen of Spain

el **reinado** *masc noun*
reign
durante el reinado del rey Juan Carlos in the
reign of King Juan Carlos

reinar *verb* [17]
to reign

el **reino** *masc noun*
kingdom
el Reino Unido the United Kingdom

♂ **reír** *verb* [61]
to laugh
echarse a reír to start laughing

reírse *reflexive verb* [61]
reírse de algo to laugh about something
Se están riendo de ti. They're laughing at
you.
reírse a carcajadas to roar with laughter

la **reja** *fem noun*
1 **railing**
2 **grille**
estar entre rejas to be behind bars

la **relación** *fem noun*
1 **relationship**
Se ha roto su relación. Their relationshp has
broken down.
2 **connection**
con relación a, en relación con compared
to
con relación al año pasado compared to
last year
• las **relaciones públicas** public relations

relacionado *masc adjective*, **relacionada**
fem
related

relacionar *verb* [17]
to relate
relacionar algo con algo to relate
something to something

relacionarse *reflexive verb* [17]
1 **to be related** (*facts, figures*)
2 relacionarse con alguien to get to know
someone
Se relacionó con muchos deportistas. He
got to know many sports people.

relajar *verb* [17]
to relax

relajarse *reflexive verb* [17]
to relax

el **relámpago** *masc noun*
flash of lightning

♪ la **religión** *fem noun*
religion

religioso *masc adjective*, **religiosa** *fem*
religious

♪ **rellenar** *verb* [17]
1 rellenar un impreso to fill in a form
2 **to stuff** (*a chicken, peppers*)
3 **to fill again**

relleno *masc adjective*, **rellena** *fem*
▷ see **relleno** *noun*
relleno de algo filled with something
stuffed (*chicken, peppers*)

el **relleno** *masc noun* ▷ see **relleno** *adjective*
1 **filling** (*for a pie*)
2 **stuffing** (*for a chicken*)

♪ el **reloj** *masc noun*
1 **clock**
2 **watch**
Mi reloj va atrasado. My watch is slow.
- el **reloj de pulsera** wristwatch
- el **reloj despertador** alarm clock
- el **reloj digital** digital clock

la **relojería** *fem noun*
shop selling watches and clocks

remar *verb* [17]
to row

el **remate** *masc noun*
1 **shot** (*in football*)
un remate de cabeza a header
2 **smash** (*in tennis*)

remediar *verb* [17]
1 **to help doing something**
No lo puede remediar. He can't help it.
2 **to put something right**
No pudimos remediarlo. We couldn't put it
right.

el **remedio** *masc noun*
1 **remedy**
remedios naturales natural remedies
No hay más remedio. There's no other
alternative.
2 (*Latin America*) **medicine**

remendar *verb* [29]
to mend (*clothes, etc*)

el **remite** *masc noun*
name and address (*of sender, for returning a
letter*)

♪ el & la **remitente** *masc & fem noun*
sender (*of a letter*)

el **remo** *masc noun*
oar

remojar *verb* [17]
to soak

el **remojo** *masc noun*
poner algo en remojo to soak something
poner los garbanzos en remojo to put the
chickpeas to soak

la **remolacha** *fem noun*
beetroot

remolcar *verb* [31]
to tow

el **remolino** *masc noun*
1 **whirlpool**
2 **whirlwind**

el **remolque** *masc noun*
1 **trailer**
2 llevar algo a remolque to tow something

el **remordimiento** *masc noun*
feeling of guilt
tener remordimientos de conciencia to
feel guilty

remoto *masc adjective*, **remota** *fem*
remote

remover *verb* [38]
1 **to stir** (*a sauce, the soup*)
2 **to toss** (*a salad*)
3 **to turn over** (*soil*)

remueva, remuevo, etc *verb* ▷ **remover**

el **renacuajo** *masc noun*
tadpole

el **rencor** *masc noun*
guardarle rencor a alguien to bear
someone a grudge

la **rendición** *fem noun*
surrender

rendir *verb* [57]
1 **to tire out**
2 **to be profitable** (*businesses*)
3 **to be productive** (*worker*)

rendirse *reflexive verb* [57]
to surrender
¿Te rindes? Do you give up?

♪ la **RENFE** *fem noun*
(= Red Nacional de Ferrocarriles Españoles) **the
Spanish national rail network**

el **renglón** *masc noun*
line (*of print, text*)

la **renta** *fem noun*
1 rent
2 income

rentable *masc & fem adjective*
  profitable

renovar *verb* [1]
1 **to renew** (*a passport, licence*)
2 **to renovate** (*a house, a room*)
3 **to update** (*your clothes*)

renunciar *verb* [17]
  renunciar a to give up (*a right, an idea*)
  renunciar a un puesto to resign from a job

la **reparación** *fem noun*
  repair
  un taller de reparaciones a repair shop

♂ **reparar** *verb* [17]
1 **to repair**
2 **to mend** (*clothes*)
3 **reparar en algo** to notice something

repartir *verb* [19]
1 **to deliver**
  Repartimos a domicilio. We make home deliveries.
2 **to hand out** (*leaflets, exam papers*)
3 **to share**
  Lo repartiremos entre todos nosotros. We'll share it between us.

el **reparto** *masc noun*
1 **delivery**
2 **share-out**
  hacer el reparto del dinero to share out the money
  • **el reparto a domicilio** home delivery service

repasar *verb* [17]
1 **to revise**
  repasar los apuntes to revise your notes
2 **to check** (*figures*)
3 **to clean** (*a room*)

el **repaso** *masc noun*
1 **revision**
  darles un repaso a los apuntes to revise your notes
2 **check** (*for mistakes*)
3 **clean-up** (*of a room*)

repente *in phrase*
  de repente all of a sudden

repentino *masc adjective*, **repentina** *fem*
  sudden

la **repetición** *fem noun*
  repetition
  • **la repetición de la jugada** action replay

♂ **repetir** *verb* [57]
1 **to repeat**
  ¿Puede repetirlo? Would you say that again?
2 **to have a second helping**
  ¿Quieres repetir? Would you like a second helping?

la **repisa** *fem noun*
1 **shelf**
2 **ledge** (*of a window*)
3 **mantlepiece** (*of chimney*)

♂ **repita, repitió, repito, etc** *verb* ▷
  repetir

repleto *masc adjective*, **repleta** *fem*
  full up
  estar repleto de algo to be packed with something
  una sala repleta de gente a room packed with people

el **repollo** *masc noun*
  cabbage

reponer *verb* [11]
1 **to replace** (*stores, stocks*)
2 **to repeat** (*a series, programme*)

reponerse *reflexive verb* [11]
  to recover
  reponerse de una enfermedad to recover from an illness

el **reportaje** *masc noun*
1 **article** (*in a newspaper*)
2 **report** (*on TV*)

el **reportero** *masc noun*, la **reportera** *fem*
  reporter

reposar *verb* [17]
1 **to rest**
2 **dejar reposar** to leave to stand

el **reposo** *masc noun*
  rest

la **repostería** *fem noun*
  confectionery

el & la **representante** *masc & fem noun*
  representative

representar *verb* [17]
1 **to represent** (*your school, a person*)
  Representa el concepto de libertad. It represents the idea of liberty.
2 **to put on** (*a play*)
  representar una obra to perform a play
3 **to play** (*a part*)

la **reproducción** *fem noun*
  reproduction

el **reproductor** *masc noun*
  player
- el **reproductor de discos compactos** CD player
- el **reproductor de MP3** MP3 player

reproducir *verb* [60]
  to reproduce

reproducirse *reflexive verb* [60]
  to reproduce

el **reptil** *masc noun*
  reptile

la **república** *fem noun*
  republic

♂ la **República Dominicana** *fem noun*
  the Dominican Republic

repugnante *masc & fem adjective*
  disgusting

repuesto *masc noun*
  spare part
  de repuesto, una rueda de repuesto a spare wheel

la **reputación** *fem noun*
  reputation

el **requesón** *masc noun*
  cottage cheese

el **requisito** *masc noun*
  requirement

la **resaca** *fem noun*
  hangover

resbaladizo *masc adjective*, **resbaladiza** *fem*
  slippery

resaltar *verb* [17]
1 to stand out (*colours*)
2 to stress (*the strong points*)

resbalar *verb* [17]
  to slip

resbalarse *reflexive verb* [17]
  to slip
  resbalarse con una piel de plátano to slip on a banana skin

rescatar *verb* [17]
  to rescue

el **rescate** *masc noun*
  rescue
  una operación de rescate a rescue operation

la **reserva** *fem noun*
1 reservation (*in a hotel, etc*)
  hacer una reserva to make a reservation
2 reserve
  los jugadores de reserva the reserve players
3 supply (*of fuel*)
4 reservation, doubt
  Tengo mis reservas. I have my doubts.
- la **reserva natural** nature reserve

la **reservación** *fem noun*
  (*Latin America*) reservation

reservado *masc adjective*, **reservada** *fem*
  reserved

♂ **reservar** *verb* [17]
1 to put by (*savings, food*)
2 to book (*a room, a table*)

♂ el **resfriado** *masc noun*
  cold
  tener un resfriado to have a cold

resfriarse *reflexive verb* [32]
  to catch a cold
  Me he resfriado. I've caught a cold.

♂ la **residencia** *fem noun*
1 residence
  un permiso de residencia a residence permit
2 hall of residence (*for students*)
- la **residencia de ancianos** old people's home

residir *verb* [19]
  residir en to live in
  Reside en Londres. She lives in London.

♂ los **residuos** *plural masc noun*
  waste
- los **residuos nucleares** nuclear waste
- los **residuos tóxicos** toxic waste

la **resistencia** *fem noun*
1 resistance
2 stamina
  tener mucha resistencia to have a lot of stamina

resistir *verb* [19]
1 to resist
2 to stand (*pain, cold, heat*)
  ¡No lo resisto! I can't stand it!

resistirse *reflexive verb* [19]
  to resist

resolver *verb* [45]
1 to solve (*a crime, a mystery*)
2 to sort out (*problems*)
3 to decide (*a match, etc*)

a
b
c
d
e
f
g
h
i
j
k
l
m
n
ñ
o
p
q
r
s
t
u
v
w
x
y
z

el **resorte** *masc noun*
  spring (*in a mechanism*)

♂ el **respaldo** *masc noun*
1 **back** (*of a chair*)
2 **support** (*for a person*)

♂ el **respecto** *masc noun*
1 al respecto: No hay más información al respecto. There is no more informaton about it.
2 con respecto a: Con respecto a lo que me contaste, ... Regarding what you told me, ...

respetable *masc & fem adjective*
  respectable

respetar *verb* [17]
1 **to respect** (*a person*)
2 **to obey** (*rules, the law, etc*)

el **respeto** *masc noun*
  respect
  tenerle mucho respeto a alguien to have a lot of respect for someone

la **respiración** *fem noun*
  breathing
  contener la respiración to hold your breath

respirar *verb* [17]
  to breathe

responder *verb* [18]
1 **to answer**
  responder a un mail to answer an email
  No me respondió. He didn't answer me.
2 **to respond** (*to treatment*)
3 responder por algo, alguien to be reponsible for something, someone

la **responsabilidad** *fem noun*
  responsibility

responsable *masc & fem adjective*
  ▷ see **responsable** *noun*
  responsible

el & la **responsable** *masc & fem noun*
  ▷ see **responsable** *adjective*
1 **person responsible**
2 **person in charge**
  ¿Quién es el responsable? Who's the person in charge?

la **respuesta** *fem noun*
1 **answer**, **reply** (*to a message, enquiry etc*)
2 **response** (*from the public*)

restante *masc & fem adjective*
  remaining
  lo restante the remainder

restar *verb* [17]
  to take away (*in maths*)

♂ el **restaurante** *masc noun*
  restaurant

restaurar *verb* [17]
  to restore

el **resto** *masc noun*
1 **rest**
  el resto de la clase the rest of the clase
2 los restos **leftovers** (*from a meal*)
3 los restos **remains** (*of a body*)

la **restricción** *fem noun*
  restriction

restringir *verb* [49]
  to restrict

restringirse *reflexive verb* [49]
  to restrict yourself

el **resultado** *masc noun*
  result
  un resultado muy positivo a very positive result
  unos resultados inesperados some unexpected results

resultar *verb* [17]
1 **to come of**
  ¿Qué resultará de esto? What's going to come of this?
2 **to be**
  Así resulta más fácil. It's easier this way.
  Varios manifestantes reultaron heridos. Several demonstrators were injured.

el **resumen** *masc noun*
  summary

resumir *verb* [19]
1 **to summarize**
2 **to sum up**
  Resumiendo, ... To cut a long story short, ...

retener *verb* [9]
1 **to keep** (*a person from doing something, etc*)
2 **to remember**

retirar *verb* [17]
1 **to take away** (*a passport, a licence*)
2 **to move back**
  Retira esa silla. Move that chair back.

retirarse *reflexive verb* [17]
1 **to move back**
2 **to retire**

retrasado *masc adjective*, **retrasada** *fem*
▷ see **retrasado** *noun*
1 **mentally handicapped**
2 **behind** (*in schedule, etc*)
Vamos muy retrasados con el trabajo.
We're very late with the job.
3 Mi reloj va retrasado. My watch is slow.

el **retrasado** *masc noun*, la **retrasada** *fem*
▷ see **retrasado** *adj*
mentally handicapped person
los retrasados mentales the menatlly
handicapped

retrasar *verb* [17]
1 **to delay** (*a trip*)
2 **to put back** (*a watch*)

retrasarse *reflexive verb* [17]
1 **to be late**
Me retrasé unos minutos. I was a few
minutes late.
2 **to fall behind** (*in studies*)

♂ el **retraso** *masc noun*
1 **delay**
una media hora de retraso a half-hour
delay
Llevan retraso. They're late.
2 **con retraso** late
Llegaron con retraso. They arrived late.

el **retrato** *masc noun*
portrait

♂ el **retrete** *masc noun*
toilet

el **retrovisor** *masc noun*
1 **rear-view mirror**
2 **wing mirror**

el **reuma** *masc noun*
rheumatism

♂ la **reunión** *fem noun*
1 **meeting**
asistir a una reunión to attend a meeting
2 **reunion**
una reunión de antiguos alumnos a
reunion of former pupils

reunir *verb* [62]
1 **to gather** (*information*)
2 **to call together** (*members, students, etc*)
3 **to have**
Reúne los elementos que busco. It has
everything I'm looking for.
4 **reunir dinero** to raise money

reunirse *reflexive verb* [62]
to meet, **to get together**

la **revancha** *fem noun*
1 **revenge**
tomarse la revancha to get your own back
2 **return game**
jugar la revancha to play a rematch

revelar *verb* [17]
1 **to reveal**
2 **to develop** (*a film*)

la **reverencia** *fem noun*
bow, **curtsey**
hacer una reverencia to bow, to curtsey

reventar *verb* [17]
1 **to burst** (*balloons, tyres, etc*)
2 **to explode**

el **reverso** *masc noun*
back

el **revés** *masc noun*
1 **al revés** inside out
Tu jersey está al revés. Your jumper is
inside out.
2 **al revés** upside down
Ese cuadro está al revés. That picture's
upside down.
3 **inside**
el revés del abrigo the inside of the coat
4 **backhander** (*in tennis*)
el revés de la página the back of the page

revisar *verb* [17]
1 **to check** (*a bill, a machine, writing*)
2 **to revise**
3 **to service** (*a car*)

la **revisión** *fem noun*
1 **revision**
2 **(medical) checkup**
3 **service** (*for a car, etc*)

♂ el **revisor** *masc noun*, la **revisora** *fem*
ticket inspector

♂ la **revista** *fem noun*
magazine

la **revolución** *fem noun*
revolution

revolver *verb* [45]
1 **to stir** (*soup, sauce*)
2 **to turn upside down**
Me revolvieron todos los cajones. They
went through all my drawers.
Le habían revuelto todos sus papeles.
They'd left all his papers in a mess.

el **revólver** *masc noun*
pistol

a
b
c
d
e
f
g
h
i
j
k
l
m
n
ñ
o
p
q
r
s
t
u
v
w
x
y
z

revuelto *masc adjective*, **revuelta** *fem*

1 **in a mess**
Los papeles estaban todos revueltos. All the papers were in a mess.

2 **rough** (*sea*)

3 **unsettled** (*weather*)

el **rey** *masc noun*

1 **king**

2 los reyes de España the King and Queen of Spain

 rey

> España tiene una familia real. El actual rey se llama Don Juan Carlos de Borbón y Borbón y la reina Doña Sofía. Felipe, Príncipe de Asturias, es el heredero al trono español.

rezar *verb* [22]
to pray

ría, rían, etc *verb* ▷ **reír**

la **riada** *fem noun*
flood

la **ribera** *fem noun*
riverbank
la ribera del Tajo the bank of the Tagus

♂ **rico** *masc adjective*, **rica** *fem* ▷ see **rico** *noun*

1 **rich** (*people*)

2 **good** (*food*)
La sopa está muy rica. The soup is very good.

♂ el **rico** *masc noun*, la **rica** *fem* ▷ see **rico** *adj*
rich person
los ricos the rich

ridículo *masc adjective*, **ridícula** *fem*
▷ see **ridículo** *noun*
ridiculous

el **ridículo** *masc noun*
▷ see **ridículo** *adjective*
hacer el ridículo to make a fool of yourself
dejar a alguien en ridículo to make a fool of somebody
Lo dejó en ridículo. She made a fool of him.

ríe, ríen, etc *verb* ▷ **reír**

riega, riego, riegue, etc *verb* ▷ **regar**

la **rienda** *fem noun*
rein

♂ el **riesgo** *masc noun*
risk
un riesgo para la salud a health hazard
correr un riesgo to run a risk
Corres el riesgo de que te suspendan. You're running the risk of being failed.

la **rifa** *fem noun*
raffle

el **rímel** *masc noun*
mascara

el **rincón** *masc noun*

1 **corner** (*of a room*)

2 en el rincón de mi habitación in the corner of my bedroom
Lo buscamos en todos los rincones. We looked everywhere for it.

el **rinoceronte** *masc noun*
rhinoceros

la **riña** *fem noun*

1 **fight**
una riña callejera a street fight

2 **quarrel**
Tuvo una riña con su novia. He had a quarrel with his girlfriend.

el **riñón** *masc noun*

1 **kidney**

2 los riñones lower back
tener dolor de riñones to have backache

♂ el **río** ▷ see **río** *verb masc noun*
river
ir río abajo to go downstream
ir río arriba to go upstream

rió ▷ see **río** *noun verb* ▷ **reír**

la **riqueza** *fem noun*
wealth

la **risa** *fem noun*

1 **laugh**
una risa histérica an hysterical laugh
¡Qué risa! What a laugh!
(*informal*) morirse de risa to die of laughter
Nos moríamos de risa. We were dying of laughter.

2 risas *plural* laughter
Se oían risas. You could hear laughter.

el **ritmo** *masc noun*
rhythm
llevar el ritmo to keep time
marcar el ritmo to beat time

el & la **rival** *masc & fem noun*
rival

rizado *masc adjective*, **rizada** *fem*
curly

el **rizo** *masc noun*
curl

♂ **robar** *verb* [17]

1 **to steal**
robarle algo a alguien to steal something from somebody

Les robó dinero a sus padres. He stole money from his parents.

2 to rob
robar un banco to rob a bank
robar en una casa to rob a house

3 to rip (somebody) off
¡Me han robado! I've been ripped off!

el **roble** *masc noun*
oak

el **robo** *masc noun*
1 robbery
¡Esto es un robo! This is a rip-off!
2 burglary
3 break-in

la **roca** *fem noun*
rock

el **rocío** *masc noun*
dew

la **rodaja** *fem noun*
slice (*of chorizo, fruit, etc*)
cortar en rodajas to slice

rodar *verb* [24]
1 to roll (*stones, logs, etc*)
2 to turn (*a wheel*)
3 to shoot (*a film*)

rodeado *masc adjective*, **rodeada** *fem*
surrounded
rodeado de espectadores surrounded by on-lookers

rodear *verb* [17]
to surround

la **rodilla** *fem noun*
knee
ponerse de rodillas to kneel down

ſ **rogar** *verb* [24]
to beg
Te ruego que me perdones. I beg you to forgive me.
Le rogué que volviera. I begged her to come back.
'Se ruega no fumar' 'No smoking'

ſ **rojo** *masc adjective*, **roja** *fem*
▷ see **rojo** noun
red
ponerse rojo to go red

ſ el **rojo** *masc noun* ▷ see **rojo** adj
red

el **rollo** *masc noun*
1 roll (*of paper, film*)
un rollo de tela a roll of fabric
un rollo de papel higiénico a toilet roll
2 coil (*of rope, wire*)
3 (*informal*) **bore**
¡Vaya rollo de película! What a boring film!
4 (*informal*) **business**
Es mal rollo. It's a bad business.

romántico *masc adjective*, **romántica** *fem*
romantic

el **rompecabezas** *masc noun*,
pl: los **rompecabezas**
puzzle

ſ **romper** *verb* [40]
1 to break
Vas a romper la silla. You're going to break the chair.
romper algo en mil pedazos to smash something to pieces
2 to tear
Rompió la carta en pedazos. He tore up the letter.
3 to break down
Los bomberos rompieron la puerta. The firemen broke down the door.

romperse *reflexive verb* [40]
1 to break (*by itself*)
La lámpara se ha roto. The lamp has broken.
2 to break (*a leg, arm, rib, etc*)
Se rompió el brazo. She broke her leg.

el **rompiente** *masc noun*
breaker (*wave*)

el **ron** *masc noun*
rum

roncar *verb* [31]
to snore

ronco *masc adjective*, **ronca** *fem*
hoarse
quedarse ronco to go hoarse

la **ronda** *fem noun*
1 round
Esta ronda la pago yo. It's my round.
2 patrol
hacer la ronda to be on patrol

ronronear *verb* [31]
to purr

ſ la **ropa** *fem noun*
clothes
la ropa sucia dirty clothes ▶▶

a b c d e f g h i j k l m n ñ o p q **r** s t u v w x y z

cambiarse de ropa to change your clothes
quitarse la ropa to take your clothes off

• la **ropa interior** underwear

el **ropero** *masc noun*
wardrobe

♂ **rosa** *invariable adjective* ▷ see **rosa** *noun*
pink

WORD TIP *rosa, adjective, never changes.*

♂ la **rosa** *fem noun* ▷ see **rosa** *adj*
rose *(flower and plant)*

rosado *masc adjective*, **rosada** *fem*
▷ see **rosado** *noun*
pink

el **rosado** *masc noun* ▷ see **rosado** *adj*
1 **pink** *(colour)*
2 **rosé** *(wine)*

el **rosario** *masc noun*
(Religion) **rosary**

el **rosbif** *masc noun*
roast beef

el **rostro** *masc noun*
1 **face**
2 *(informal)* ¡Qué rostro! What a nerve!

♂ **roto** *masc adjective*, **rota** *fem*
1 **broken**
2 **torn**
3 **worn out** *(shoes)*

la **rotonda** *fem noun*
roundabout

el **rotulador** *masc noun*
felt-tip pen

♂ **rubio** *masc adjective*, **rubia** *fem*
blond, blonde
un chico rubio a blond boy
una actriz rubia a blonde actress
una cerveza rubia a lager
Soy rubia, pero mi novio es moreno. I'm
blonde, but my boyfriend has dark hair.

ruborizarse *reflexive verb* [22]
to blush

♂ la **rueda** *fem noun*
1 **wheel**
2 **tyre**
• la **rueda delantera** front wheel
• la **rueda de prensa** press conference
• la **rueda de repuesto** spare wheel

rugir *verb* [49]
to roar *(lions, wind, waves)*

♂ el **ruido** *masc noun*
noise
hacer ruido to make a noise
Estaban haciendo mucho ruido. They were
making a lot of noise.

♂ **ruidoso** *masc adjective*, **ruidosa** *fem*
noisy

la **ruina** *fem noun*
1 **ruin**
La empresa está en la ruina. The company
is in a terrible state.
La casa está en ruinas. The house is in
ruins.
2 las ruinas ruins
unas ruinas romanas some roman ruins
las ruinas del castillo the ruins of the
castle

el **ruiseñor** *masc noun*
nightingale

el **rulo** *masc noun*
roller *(curler)*

la **rulot** *fem noun*
caravan

Rumania, **Rumanía** *fem noun*
Romania

rumano *masc adjective & noun*, **rumana** *fem*
adjective & noun
1 **Romanian**
2 un rumano, una rumana Romanian
el rumano Romanian *(the language)*

WORD TIP Adjectives and nouns for nationality,
regional origin, and language do not have capital
letters in Spanish.

el **rumbo** *masc noun*
course
el rumbo que han tomado los
acontecimientos the course which events
have taken
Colón salió con rumbo al Nuevo Mundo.
Columbus set sail for the New World.
La nave espacial va rumbo a Marte. The
spaceship is on course to Mars.

el **rumor** *masc noun*
1 **rumour**
2 **murmur**

Rusia *fem noun*
Russia

ruso *masc adjective & noun*, **rusa** *fem adjective
& noun*

1 **Russian**

2 un ruso, una rusa Russian
el ruso Russian (*the language*)

WORD TIP Adjectives and nouns for nationality,
regional origin, and language do not have capital
letters in Spanish.

---

la **ruta** *fem noun*
   route

la **rutina** *fem noun*
   routine
   por rutina out of habit

a
b
c
d
e
f
g
h
i
j
k
l
m
n
ñ
o
p
q
r
s
t
u
v
w
x
y
z

S s

♂ el **sábado** *masc noun*
Saturday
el sábado on Saturday
el sábado pasado last Saturday
los sábados on Saturdays
cada sábado every Saturday
Jugamos los sábados. We play on
Saturdays.

WORD TIP Names of months and days start with
small letters in Spanish.

♂ la **sábana** *fem noun*
sheet (*for a bed*)

el **saber** *masc noun* ▷ see **saber** *verb*
knowledge

♂ **saber** *verb* [13] ▷ see **saber** *noun*
1 **to know** (*facts*)
Ya lo sé. I know.
No lo sabe. He doesn't know.
Sabe mucho del tema. He knows a lot
about it.
Sabía que no le gustaría hacerlo. I knew he
wouldn't want to do it.
saber algo de memoria to know something
by heart
2 (*know how to do something*) **can**
¿Sabes hablar francés? Can you speak
French?
Sabe montar en bicicleta. She can ride a
bike.
No sé tocar la guitarra. I can't play the
guitar.
3 **to find out**
Lo supe por su hermana. I found out
through her sister.
4 **to taste**
¡Qué bien sabe! It tastes really good!
La comida sabe muy rica. The food tastes
very nice.
saber a algo to taste of something
Sabe a fresa. It tastes of strawberry.

WORD TIP For the other Spanish verb for *to
know* ▷ **conocer**.

---

la **sabiduría** *fem noun*
wisdom

sabio *masc adjective*, **sabia** *fem*
wise

♂ el **sabor** *masc noun*
taste
Tiene un sabor a fresa. It tastes like
strawberry.

♂ **sabrá**, **sabré**, **sabría**, **etc** *verb* ▷ **saber**

sabroso *masc adjective*, **sabrosa** *fem*
tasty

el **sacacorchos** *masc noun*, pl: los
sacacorchos
corkscrew

♂ el **sacapuntas** *masc noun*,
pl: los **sacapuntas**
pencil sharpener

♂ **sacar** *verb* [31]
1 **to take out**
sacar al perro a pasear to take the dog for a
walk
sacar la basura to take the rubbish out
Saqué diez libras de la caja. I took ten
pounds from the till.
Sacó su monedero del bolso. She took her
purse out of her bag.
sacar a alguien a bailar to ask somebody to
dance
Lo sacó a bailar. She asked him to dance.
2 **to bring out** (*a books, a DVD*)
sacar un libro to publish a book
sacar un disco to release a record
3 **to get**, **to buy**
sacar entradas to buy tickets
Todavía no he sacado los billetes. I haven't
bought the tickets yet.
4 **to pull out** (*a pistol, a knife*)
Sacó su pistola He pulled out his gun.
5 **to get** (*marks*)
sacar buenas notas to get good marks
sacar malas notas to get bad marks
He sacado un siete en matemáticas. I got
seven (out of ten) in maths.
6 **to take** (*a picture*)
sacar una foto to take a photo
sacar una fotocopia to make a photocopy
7 **to serve** (*in tennis*)
Te toca a ti sacar. It's your service.
8 **to kick off** (*in football*)
Va a sacar Gómez. Gómez is going to kick
off.

sacarse *reflexive verb* [31]
1 **sacarse una muela** to have a tooth out
2 **sacarse una foto** to have one's photograph taken
   Me saqué una foto frente al palacio. I had my photograph taken in front of the palace.

el **sacerdote** *masc noun*
   priest

ᵍ el **saco** *masc noun*
1 **sack**
2 (*Latin America*) **coat**
• el **saco de dormir** sleeping bag

sacrificar *verb* [31]
1 **to sacrifice**
2 **to put down** (*an animal*)

el **sacrificio** *masc noun*
   sacrifice

la **sacudida** *fem noun*
1 **shake**
   Le di una sacudida. I gave it a shake.
2 El coche iba dando sacudidas. The car went shaking and jerking along.

sacudir *verb* [19]
1 **to shake** (*a bottle, cloth*)
2 **to shake off**
   Sacudió las migas del mantel. She shook the crumbs off the tablecloth.

sacudirse *reflexive verb* [19]
   to shake off
   Se sacudió el polvo de la chaqueta. He shook the dust off his jacket.

sagaz *masc & fem adjective*
   shrewd

sagitario *masc & fem noun*
   ▷ see **Sagitario** *noun*
   Sagittarius
   Es sagitario. She's Sagittarius.

   WORD TIP Use a small letter in Spanish to say *I am Sagitario*, etc with star signs.

Sagitario *masc noun* ▷ see **sagitario** *noun*
   Sagittarius

sagrado *masc adjective*, **sagrada** *fem*
1 **sacred**
2 **holy**

ᵍ la **sal** *fem noun*
   salt
• las **sales de baño** bath salts

ᵍ la **sala** *fem noun*
1 **room**
2 **hall**

3 **ward** (*in a hospital*)
• la **sala de espera** waiting room
• la **sala de estar** living room
• la **sala de exposiciones** exhibition hall
• la **sala de fiestas** night club
• la **sala de juegos** games room
• la **sala de profesores** staff room

salado *masc adjective*, **salada** *fem*
   salty
   agua salada salt water
   Está muy salado. It's very salty.

ᵍ el **salario** *masc noun*
1 **wages** (*weekly*)
2 **salary** (*monthly*)

ᵍ la **salchicha** *fem noun*
   sausage

el **salchichón** *masc noun*
   salami sausage

saldar *verb* [17]
1 **to settle** (*a debt*)
2 **to sell off**

el **saldo** *masc noun*
1 **balance** (*of an account*)
2 **settlement**
3 los saldos the sales (*in shopping*)
   precios de saldo sale prices
• el **saldo negativo** debit balance
• el **saldo positivo** credit balance

ᵍ **saldrá, saldré, saldría, salga, salgo, etc** *verb* ▷ **salir**

el **salero** *masc noun*
   salt cellar

ᵍ la **salida** *fem noun*
1 **exit**
2 **departure** (*of flight, etc*)

ᵍ **salir** *verb* [63]
1 **to go out**
   Salen mucho por la noche. They go out a lot in the evenings.
   Está saliendo con Ana. He's going out with Ana.
2 **to come out**
   Salieron uno a uno. They came out one by one.
   Salimos del cole a las tres y media. We come out of school at half past three.
   La noticia salió en el periódico. The news came out in the paper.
3 **to get out**
   No pude salir. I couldn't get out.
4 **to leave**
   El vuelo sale a las cinco. The flight leaves at five. ▸▸

salir de un sitio to leave a place
Salgo de casa a las ocho. I leave home at eight.
Salió de la casa corriendo. He ran out of the house.

5 **salir en la televisión** to appear on television

6 **to turn out**
Las cosas salieron bien. Things turned out well.
Todo salió como esperábamos. Everything turned out as we expected.

7 **Las vacaciones nos salieron muy caras.** Our holidays cost us a lot.
Si compras tres, sale más barato. It works out cheaper if you buy three.
El retrato te ha salido perfecto. Your picture has turned out just right.
El examen me salió fatal. The exam was really bad.

8 (about spots, hair) **Me ha salido un grano.** I've got a spot.
Le están saliendo canas. His hair's starting to go grey.
Le salía sangre de la nariz. His nose was bleeding.

salirse reflexive verb [63]

1 **to leave**
salirse del colegio to leave school
Jaime se ha salido del grupo. Jaime has left the group.
El coche se salió de la carretera. The car left the road.

2 (with liquids) **El agua se salió del fregadero.** The sink overflowed.
Se ha salido la leche. The milk has boiled over.

la **saliva** fem noun
saliva

salmón invariable adjective
▷ see **salmón** noun
salmon-pink

♂ el **salmón** masc noun
▷ see **salmón** adjective
salmon
• el **salmón ahumado** smoked salmon

♂ el **salón** masc noun

1 **living room**
2 **function room**
• el **salón de actos** assembly hall
• el **salón de belleza** beauty salon
• el **salón de fiestas** reception room

salpicar verb [31]
to splash

la **salsa** fem noun

1 **sauce**
2 **gravy**
3 **salsa** (music)
• la **salsa besamel** white sauce

el **saltamontes** masc noun,
pl: los **saltamontes**
grasshopper

saltar verb [17]

to jump
saltar al suelo to jump to the ground
saltar de la cama to jump out of bed
saltar un muro to jump over a wall
saltar por encima de la verja to jump over the fence

saltarse reflexive verb [17]

1 **to skip** (a page, a meeting)
2 (in driving) **Nos saltamos un semáforo en rojo.** We jumped a red light.

el **salto** masc noun

jump
dar un salto to jump
• el **salto con pértiga** pole vault
• el **salto de altura** high jump
• el **salto de longitud** long jump

♂ la **salud** fem noun ▷ see **salud** exclamation
health
estar bien de salud to be in good health

♂ **salud** exclamation ▷ see **salud** noun

1 **Cheers!**
¡A tu salud! Cheers!
2 (Latin America) **Bless you!**

saludable masc & fem adjective
healthy

♂ **saludar** verb [17]

1 **to say hello**
Nos saludó con la mano. She waved hello to us.
2 (formal letter endings) **Le saluda atentamente, Jaime Rodríguez** Yours sincerely, Jaime Rodríguez, Yours faithfully, Jaime Rodríguez

♂ el **saludo** masc noun

1 **greeting**
Te envían sus saludos. They send their regards.
Dale saludos de mi parte. Give him my regards.
2 (informal letter endings) **Un afectuoso saludo, Bea** Best wishes, Bea

salvadoreño *masc adjective & noun,*
salvadoreña *fem adjective & noun*
1 **Salvadorean**
2 un salvadoreño, una salvadoreña
Salvadorean

> **WORD TIP** Adjectives and nouns for nationality and regional origin do not have capital letters in Spanish.

salvaje *masc & fem adjective*
▷ see **salvaje** *noun*
1 **savage**
2 **wild**

el & la **salvaje** *masc & fem noun*
▷ see **salvaje** *adj*
savage

el **salvamanteles** *masc noun,*
pl: los **salvamanteles**
table mat

el **salvamento** *masc noun*
rescue
una operación de salvamento a rescue
operation

salvar *verb* [17]
to save *(lives)*

salvarse *reflexive verb* [17]
to survive

el **salvavidas** *masc noun,*
pl: los **salvavidas**
life jacket

salvo *preposition, conjunction*
except
salvo que unless

San *masc adjective*
Saint *(San is used for most male saints)*
San Andrés Saint Andrew ▷ **santo**

♪ **San Salvador** *masc noun*
San Salvador *(the country in Central America)*

sanar *verb* [17]
1 **to recover** *(patients)*
2 **to heal** *(injuries)*

♪ la **sandalia** *fem noun*
sandal

♪ la **sandía** *fem noun*
watermelon

♪ el **sándwich** *masc noun*
(toasted) sandwich

sangrar *verb* [17]
to bleed

♪ la **sangre** *fem noun*
blood

♪ la **sangría** *fem noun*
sangria *(a cold punch made with red wine and lemonade)*

sano *masc adjective,* **sana** *fem*
healthy

la **sanidad** *fem noun*
1 **health**
2 **public health**
la sanidad pública the health service

> **WORD TIP** *sanidad* does not mean *sanity* in English; for the meaning of *sanity* ▷ **razón**.

sanitario *masc adjective,* **sanitaria** *fem*
1 **health**
un control sanitario a health inspection
2 **sanitary**
las condiciones sanitarias the sanitary
conditions

♪ **santo** *masc adjective,* **santa** *fem*
▷ see **santo** *noun*
holy

♪ el **santo** *masc noun,* la **santa** *fem noun*
▷ see **santo** *adjective & noun*
1 **saint**
Santo Tomás Saint Thomas
Santa María Saint Mary
2 **name day** *(The day of the saint many people are named after.)*

 santo

Cada día del año tiene el nombre de un santo y los
españoles y latinoamericanos con ese nombre,
celebran ese día igual que su cumpleaños.

el **santuario** *noun*
shrine

♪ el **sapo** *masc noun*
toad

el **saque** *masc noun*
1 **serve** *(in tennis)*
2 **kick-off** *(in football)*
• el **saque de banda** throw in
• el **saque de esquina** corner kick

el **sarampión** *masc noun*
measles

el **sarcasmo** *masc noun*
sarcasm

♪ la **sardina** *fem noun*
sardine

el & la **sargento** *masc & fem noun*
sergeant

a
b
c
d
e
f
g
h
i
j
k
l
m
n
ñ
o
p
q
r
s
t
u
v
w
x
y
z

el **sarpullido** *masc noun*
rash
Me ha salido un sarpullido. I've come out in a rash.

♂ la **sartén** *fem noun*
frying pan

el & la **sastre** *masc & fem noun*
tailor

el **satélite** *masc noun*
satellite

el **satén** *masc noun*
satin

la **satisfacción** *fem noun*
satisfaction

satisfacer *verb* [7]
to satisfy
Sólo para satisfacer mi curiosidad. Just to satisfy my curiosity.
Satisface todos nuestros requisitos. It satisfies all our requirements.

satisfacerse *reflexive verb* [7]
to be satisfied

♂ **satisfecho** *masc adjective*, **satisfecha** *fem*
satisfied
Estamos muy satisfechos con los resultados. We are very happy with the results.

el **sauce** *masc noun*
willow

el **saxofón** *masc noun*
saxophone

sazonado *masc adjective*, **sazonada** *fem*
seasoned

sazonar *verb* [17]
to season

♂ **se** *pronoun*
1 (*with reflexive verbs*) **himself**, **herself**
Se cortó. He cut himself., She cut herself.
2 **itself**
Se desconecta solo. It disconnects itself.
3 **themselves**
¿Se han portado bien? Did they behave themselves?
4 **yourself** (*polite form*)
Espero que no se haya hecho daño. I hope you haven't hurt yourself.
5 **yourselves** (*polite form*)
¿Se han divertido ustedes? Did you enjoy yourselves?
6 (*showing interaction*) **each other**
Se quieren. They love each other.

Se miraron. They looked at each other.
Se lavó las manos. He washed his hands., She washed her hands.
Se pusieron la ropa. They put their clothes on.
7 **him**, **to him**, **her**, **to her**, etc
Se lo pregunté. I asked him., I asked her.
Se lo mandaré. I'll send it to him., I'll send it to her.
Cuando les vea se lo preguntaré. I'll ask them when I see them.
Cuando les vea se la daré. I'll give it to them when I see them.
Se lo dije a usted ayer. I told you yesterday (*polite form*).

WORD TIP To avoid *le* + *lo*, *les* + *los*, etc *se* is used instead of *le*, *les*.

8 (*in impersonal phrases*) **Se hace así.** It's done like this.
'Se vende piso' 'Flat for sale'
'Se habla inglés' 'English spoken'
9 (*with certain verbs*) **reírse: Me reí mucho.** I laughed a lot.
caerse: Se cayó. He fell down., She fell down.
pelearse: Se han peleado. They've had a fight.
levantarse: Se levantaron. They got up.

WORD TIP Many verbs in Spanish are used with the pronoun *-se* but are not translated with *himself*, *herself*, etc in English.

♂ **sé** *verb* ▷ see **se** *pronoun* ▷ **saber**

la **secadora** *fem noun*
dryer

el **secador de pelo** *masc noun*
hairdryer

secar *verb* [31]
to dry

secarse *reflexive verb* [31]
1 **to dry**, **to dry up**
¿Cuánto tarda en secarse la pintura? How long does the paint take to dry?
El río se seca completamente en el verano. The river dries up completely in summer.
2 **to dry yourself**
secarse el pelo to dry your hair
Sécate las manos con este trapo. Dry your hands with this cloth.

♂ la **sección** *fem noun*
1 **section**
2 **department**

♂ **seco** *masc adjective*, **seca** *fem*
dry
limpieza en seco dry-cleaning

la **secretaría** *fem noun*
  secretary's office

♂ el **secretario** *masc noun*, la **secretaria** *fem noun*
  secretary

secreto *masc adjective*, **secreta** *fem*
  ▷ see **secreto** *noun*
  secret

el **secreto** *masc noun*
  ▷ see **secreto** *adjective*
  secret

el **secuestrador** *masc noun*, la **secuestradora** *fem noun*
1 **hijacker**
2 **kidnapper**

secuestrar *verb* [17]
1 **to kidnap**
2 **to hijack**

el **secuestro** *masc noun*
1 **kidnapping**
2 **hijacking**

secundario *masc adjective*, **secundaria** *fem*
  secondary

♂ la **sed** *fem noun*
  thirst
  tener sed to be thirsty
  ¿Tienes sed? Are you thirsty?
  Sí, tengo sed. Yes, I'm thirsty.

WORD TIP Use *tener* to say you're thirsty, hot, etc.

la **seda** *fem noun*
  silk

el **sedal** *masc noun*
  fishing line

la **sede** *fem noun*
  la sede de las Olimpiadas the venue for the Olympics
  la sede de la empresa the company's head office
  la sede del gobierno the seat of government

♂ **seguida** *in phrase* ▷ see **seguido** *adjective, adverb*
  en seguida right away
  Voy en seguida. I'll be there right away.

seguido *masc adjective*, **seguida** *fem*
  ▷ see **seguida** *in phrase*, **seguido** *adverb*
1 **tres días seguidos** three days in a row
  Dan las dos películas seguidas. Two films are shown one after the other.

Los tres autobuses vinieron seguidos. The three buses came one after the other.
2 **seguido de alguien** followed by somebody
  Entró seguido de su ayudante. He came in followed by his assistant.

seguido *adverb* ▷ see **seguida** *in phrase*, **seguido** *adjective*
  todo seguido straight on
  Vaya todo seguido. Go straight on.

♂ **seguir** *verb* [64]
1 **to follow**
  seguir a alguien to follow somebody
  seguir una pista to follow up a clue
  seguir un consejo to follow a piece of advice
2 **to go on**, **to continue**
  Sigamos. Let's go on.
  El camino sigue hasta el pueblo. The road goes on to the village.
3 **seguir haciendo algo** to carry on doing something
  Seguí leyendo. I carried on reading.
  Siguen viviendo en Sevilla. They're still living in Seville.
4 **to go on** (*in a car, walking*)
  Siga todo recto. Go straight on. (*polite form, singular*)
  Sigan por esta calle. Carry on down this street. (*polite form, plural*)

♂ **según** *preposition, conjunction*
  ▷ see **según** *adverb*
1 **according to**
  según las normas according to the rules
  Según dijo él. From what he said.
2 **as**
  Según los vayas acabando. As you finish them.

según *adverb* ▷ see **según** *preposition, conjunction*
  '¿Te interesa apuntarte?'—'Según.'
  'Would you be interested in enrolling?'—'It depends.'

la **segunda** *fem noun*
  ▷ see **segundo** *adjective & noun*
  la segunda second gear

♂ **segundo** *masc adjective*, **segunda** *fem*
  ▷ see **segunda** *noun*, **segundo** *noun*
  second
  llegar en segundo lugar to finish in second place
  Viven en el segundo piso. They live on the second floor.
  Viajan en segunda clase. They travel second class.

a
b
c
d
e
f
g
h
i
j
k
l
m
n
ñ
o
p
q
r
s
t
u
v
w
x
y
z

♂ el **segundo** *masc noun*
> see **segunda** *noun*, **segundo** *adjective*
1 **second**
Espera un segundo. Wait a moment.
2 **el segundo** the main course
De segundo, tenemos ... For the main course, we have ...

la **seguridad** *fem noun*
1 **security**
2 **safety**
por razones de seguridad for safety reasons
3 **certainty**
Lo sé con seguridad. I know for certain.
• la **seguridad nacional** national security
• la **seguridad social** social security

seguramente *adverb*
probably
Seguramente irán . They'll probably go.
Seguramente no están. I expect they're not there.

♂ **seguro** *masc adjective*, **segura** *fem*
> see **seguro** *adv, noun*
1 **safe**
Aquí me siento seguro. I feel safe here.
La escalera no es muy segura. The ladder isn't very safe.
2 **seguro de sí mismo, segura de sí misma**
self-confident
Es muy segura de sí misma. She's very self-confident.
3 **sure**
Estoy completamente seguro. I'm absolutely certain.
¿Estás seguro de que se pone así? Are you sure this is the way to put it on?
4 **definite**
No es seguro todavía. It's not definite yet.
5 **reliable**
Es un método muy seguro. It's a very reliable method.

♂ **seguro** *adverb* > see **seguro** *adj, noun*
definitely
Irán seguro. They'll definitely go.
Seguro que no están. I bet they're not there.

el **seguro** *masc noun* > see **seguro** *adj, adv*
1 **insurance**
hacerse un seguro to take out insurance
¿Tienes seguro médico? Have you got medical insurance?
2 **clasp** (*of a bracelet*)
3 **safety catch** (*on a gun*)
4 **el Seguro** Social Security
• el **seguro a todo riesgo** comprehensive insurance
• el **seguro contra incendios** fire insurance

seis *number*
1 **six**
Tiene seis años. He's six (years old).
2 **sixth** (*in dates*)
el seis de junio the sixth of June
3 **six** (*in telling the time*)
Son las seis. It's six o'clock.

seiscientos, seiscientas *number*
six hundred
seiscientos dos six hundred and two

♂ la **selección** *fem noun*
1 **selection**
2 **team**
la selección española the Spanish team

seleccionar *verb* [17]
to select

la **selectividad** *fem noun*
university entrance exam

el **self-service** *masc noun*
self-service restaurant

♂ el **sello** *masc noun*
stamp
un sello para Gran Bretaña a stamp for Britain
un sello de setenta céntimos a seventy cent stamp
• el **sello discográfico** record label

♂ la **selva** *fem noun*
forest
• la **selva amazónica** Amazon rainforest
• la **selva tropical** tropical rainforest

♂ el **semáforo** *masc noun*
traffic lights
saltarse un semáforo en rojo to go through a red light
Cuando llegue al semáforo, gire a la derecha. When you get to the traffic lights, turn right.

♂ la **semana** *fem noun*
week
la próxima semana next week
entre semana during the week
Hace una semana. It's a week now.
• la **Semana Santa** Holy Week
en Semana Santa during Holy Week (*a time of great religious celebrations in many Spanish-speaking countries*)

♂ **semanal** *masc & fem adjective*
weekly

semanalmente *adverb*
weekly

sembrar *verb* [29]
1 **to sow**
2 **to plant**

semejante *masc & fem adjective*
similar
Es muy semejante al antiguo. It's very similar to the old one.

la semifinal *fem noun*
semifinal

la semilla *fem noun*
seed

la sémola *fem noun*
semolina

sencillo *masc adjective*, **sencilla** *fem*
▷ see **sencillo** *masc*
1 **simple**
2 **modest**
3 **straightforward** (*person*)

ℰ **el sencillo** *masc noun* ▷ see **sencillo** *adj*
1 **single** (*record*)
2 **single** (*ticket*)
3 (*Latin America*) **change**

la senda *fem noun*
path

el senderismo *masc noun*
hiking
hacer senderismo to go hiking

el & la senderista *masc & fem noun*
hiker

el sendero *masc noun*
path

el seno *masc noun*
1 **breast**
2 **bosom**

la sensación *fem noun*
1 **feeling**
una sensación de tristeza a feeling of sadness
Tengo la sensación de que ... I have the feeling that ...
2 **sense**
una sensación de pérdida a sense of loss
3 **sensation, stir**
causar sensación to cause a sensation
Su llegada causó sensación. Her arrival caused a sensation.

sensacional *masc & fem adjective*
sensational
una noticia sensacional a sensational piece of news

la sensatez *fem noun*
sense
tener sensatez to be sensible
actuar con sensatez to act sensibly

sensato *masc adjective*, **sensata** *fem*
sensible
un chico muy sensato a very sensible boy

la sensibilidad *fem noun*
sensitivity

sensible *masc & fem adjective*
1 **sensitive**
2 **noticeable**
un cambio sensible a noticeable change

WORD TIP *sensible* does not mean *sensible* in English; for the meaning of *sensible* ▷ **sensato**.

sensiblemente *adverb*
considerably

ℰ **sentado** *masc adjective*, **sentada** *fem*
estar sentado to be sitting
Están sentados en la terraza. They are sitting on the terrace.
Estábamos sentados a la mesa. We were sitting at the table.
Permanezcan sentados, por favor. Please remain seated.

ℰ **sentar** *verb* [29]
1 **to sit**
Sienta al niño en su silla. Sit the baby in his chair.
2 **to suit**
El rojo me sienta fatal. Red doesn't suit me at all.
Ese vestido te sienta muy bien. That dress really suits you.
3 sentarle bien a alguien to agree with somebody (*food*)
sentarle mal a alguien to not agree with somebody (*food*)
Los pimientos me sientan mal. Peppers don't agree with me.

sentarse *reflexive verb* [29]
to sit down
Siéntate. Sit down.
Siéntese. Do sit down (*polite form*).

el sentido *masc noun*
1 **meaning**
el sentido de la palabra the meaning of the word
No tiene sentido. It doesn't make sense.
2 **consciousness**
perder el sentido to lose consciousness
3 **direction**
Venían en sentido contrario. They were

coming from the opposite direction.
una calle de sentido único a one-way street
en sentido de las agujas del reloj clockwise
en el sentido contrario a las agujas del reloj anticlockwise
- **el sentido común** common sense
- **el sentido del humor** sense of humour

sentimental *masc & fem adjective*
sentimental
¿Qué tal tu vida sentimental? How's your love life?

el sentimiento *masc noun*
1 **feeling**
2 **Te acompaño en el sentimiento.** My condolences.

ʃ **sentir** *verb* [14]
1 **to feel**
   sentir dolor to feel pain
   sentir sed to feel thirsty
   sentir alegría to feel happy
2 **to hear**
   sentir pasos to hear footsteps
3 (*saying you're sorry*) **Lo siento mucho.** I'm very sorry.
   Siento llegar tarde. Sorry I'm late.
   Sentimos tener que comunicarle que ... We regret to inform you that ...

WORD TIP If you only say you are sorry, use *lo siento, lo sentimos*, etc. If you mention the reason, use *sentir* + the reason, without *lo*.

sentirse *reflexive verb* [14]
   to feel
   ¿Cómo te sientes? How do you feel?
   Me siento cansado. I feel tired.
   No se sentía bien y se fue a casa. He wasn't feeling well and he went home.

---

la seña *fem noun*
1 **sign**
   hacer una seña to make a sign
   Me hizo señas para que entrase. He made signs to me to come in.
2 **señas** address
   ¿Quieres darme tus señas? Would you like to give me your address?

ʃ **la señal** *fem noun*
1 **sign**
   las señales de carretera the road signs
   Es una buena señal. It's a good sign.
   hacer una señal to make a sign
   Nos está haciendo señales. She's signalling to us.
2 **tone** (*in an answering machine message*)
   Deje su mensaje después de la señal. Leave your message after the tone.

3 **deposit** (*when you buy something*)
- **la señal de marcar** dial tone
- **la señal de tráfico** traffic sign

señalar *verb* [17]
1 **to point**
   Señaló hacia la casa. He pointed to the house.
2 **to point out**
   Señaló que ... She pointed out that ...
3 **to fix** (*a date, time*)

señalarse *reflexive verb* [17]
   Se señaló la pierna. He pointed at his leg.

ʃ **el señor** *masc noun*
1 **Mr**
   el señor Muñoz Mr Muñoz
   los señores López Mr and Mrs López
2 (*referring to a man politely*) **gentleman, man**
   Hay un señor esperando. There's a gentleman waiting.
   Perdone señor, ¿me deja pasar? Excuse me, sir, could I get past?
3 (*in letters*) **Muy señor mío: ...** Dear Sir, ...
4 (*for emphasis*) **No señor, eso no se hace.** You just don't do that.
   Sí señor, es verdad. Yes, that's quite right.

ʃ **la señora** *fem noun*
1 **Mrs, Ms**
   la señora Gómez Mrs Gómez, Ms Gómez (*Spanish women keep their surnames after marrying.*)
2 (*referring to a woman politely*) **lady**
   Una señora nos ayudó. A lady helped us.
   Perdone señora, ¿me deja pasar? Excuse me, madam, could I get past?
   señoras y señores ladies and gentlemen
3 **wife**
   Le llamó su señora. Your wife rang you.
4 (*for emphasis*) **No señora, no fui yo.** It definitely wasn't me.
   Sí señora, es mío. It certainly is mine.

ʃ **la señorita** *fem noun*
1 **Miss, Ms**
   la señorita García Miss García, Ms García
   Aquí están mis deberes, señorita. Here's my homework, Miss. (*speaking to your teacher*)
2 **young lady**
   Le llama una señorita. A young lady is on the line for you.
3 (*for emphasis*) **No señorita, no se lo dejo.** I am certainly not lending it to you.

ʃ **sepa, sepan, etc** *verb* ▷ **saber**

la **separación** *fem noun*
1 **gap**
2 **separation**

separado *masc adjective*, **separada** *fem*
1 **separated**
2 **por separado** separately

separar *verb* [17]
1 **to separate**
2 **to move (something) away**
Separa la silla de la chimenea. Move the chair away from the fire.

separarse *reflexive verb* [17]
1 **to separate** (*couples*)
2 Se separaron hace dos años. They separated two years ago.

ℰ **septiembre** *masc noun*
September
en septiembre in September
el 11 de septiembre on 11 September

WORD TIP Names of months and days start with small letters in Spanish.

séptimo *masc adjective*, **séptima** *fem*
seventh
el séptimo piso the seventh floor

ℰ la **sequía** *fem noun*
drought

ℰ **ser** *verb* [1] ▷ see **ser** *noun*
1 (*describing people, things*) **to be**
Es alta y morena. She's tall and dark.
Es muy simpática. She's very nice.
Es muy bonito. It's very pretty.
Estas naranjas son buenísimas. These oranges are really nice
2 (*asking and saying who's there*) ¿Quién es? Who is it? (*when someone's at the door*) Hola, soy yo. Hello, it's me (*on the phone*).
3 (*when paying*) ¿Cuánto es? How much is that?
Son veinte euros. That's twenty euros.
4 (*in dates, times*) Hoy es once. Today's the eleventh.
Eran las seis y media. It was half past six.
5 (*saying what you do*) Soy estudiante. I'm a student.
Mi madre es abogada. My mother's a lawyer.
6 (*saying where, when things happen*) Eso fue el año pasado. That was last year.
La fiesta es en el gimnasio. The party's in the gym.
7 (*saying where you come from*) ser de to be from
Soy de Chester. I'm from Chester.

Es irlandés. He's Irish.
Ella es de Argentina. She's from Argentina.
8 (*showing ownership*) Era de mi hermana. It was my sister's.
El coche es de Juan. The car belongs to Juan.
9 (*saying how many you are*) Somos cuatro. There are four of us.
Eran tres. There were three of them.
10 (*saying what something is made of*) ser de to be made of
Es de madera. It's made of wood.
La silla es de metal. The chair's made of metal.
11 (*saying if someone is married, single*) Es soltero. He's single.
Es casada. She's married.
12 (*To form the passive with* -**ado** *and* -**ido** *forms of verbs*) **to be + -ed**
El puente fue derribado el año pasado. The bridge was demolished last year.
La casa fue construida en 1998. The house was built in 1998.
13 (*in expressions*)
ya sea ... o ... either ... or ...
ya sea por carta o por teléfono either by post or by telephone
14 o sea, ... so ..., that is ...
O sea, que no lo has terminado. So, you haven't finished.
Dentro de una semana, o sea el próximo jueves. In a week, that is next Thursday.
a no ser que + *subjunctive* unless
A no ser que le interese. Unless he's interested.

WORD TIP For the other Spanish verb for *to be* ▷ **estar**.

el **ser** *masc noun* ▷ see **ser** *verb*
being
• un **ser humano** human being
• un **ser vivo** living being

ℰ **será**, **seré**, **sería**, etc *verb* ▷ **ser**

la **serie** *fem noun*
1 **series**
fabricación en serie mass production
2 fuera de serie exceptional

ℰ **serio** *masc adjective*, **seria** *fem*
1 **serious**
ponerse serio to have a serious expression
un problema serio a serious problem
2 **reliable** (*person*)
3 **reputable** (*company*)
4 Lo digo en serio. I mean it.

♂ la **serpiente** *fem noun*
  snake

serrano *masc adjective*, **serrana** *fem*
  mountain, from the mountains
  un pueblo serrano a mountain village

♂ el **servicio** *masc noun*
  1 service
  servicio incluido service included
  servicio a domicilio home delivery service
  estar fuera de servicio to be out of service
  2 estar de servicio to be on duty
  3 'Servicios' 'Toilets'
  • el **servicio de atención al cliente**
    customer services
  • el **servicio militar** military service
  • los **servicios públicos** public services

♂ la **servilleta** *fem noun*
  serviette

♂ **servir** *verb* [57]
  1 to serve
  servir la sopa to serve the soup
  ¿Te sirvo más vino? Would you like some
  more wine?
  2 to be of use
  Estas herramientas ya no sirven. These
  tools are no use any more.
  No sirve para nada. It's useless.
  Yo no sirvo para camarera. I'm no good as a
  waitress.
  3 servir para algo to be used for something
  ¿Para qué sirve este interruptor? What's
  this switch for?
  Esto no nos sirve para abrirlo. This is no use
  for opening it.

servirse *reflexive verb* [57]
  to help yourself to
  Sírvete más. Help yourself to some more.
  Se sirvió ensalada. She helped herself to
  some salad.

sesenta *number*
  sixty
  Tiene sesenta años. He's sixty (years old).
  sesenta y dos sixty-two
  los años sesenta the sixties

♂ la **sesión** *fem noun*
  1 session
  2 performance
  la sesión de noche the evening
  performance
  • la **sesión continua** continuous
    performance

♂ la **seta** *fem noun*
  mushroom
  • la **seta venenosa** toadstool

setecientos, **setecientas** *number*
  seven hundred
  setecientos ochenta seven hundred and
  eighty

setenta *number*
  seventy
  Tiene setenta años. He's seventy (years
  old).
  setenta y dos seventy-two
  los años setenta the seventies

el **seto** *masc noun*
  hedge

severo *masc adjective*, **severa** *fem*
  1 severe (*person, punishment*)
  2 harsh (*climate*)

♂ el **sexo** *masc noun*
  sex

sexto *masc adjective*, **sexta** *fem*
  sixth
  el sexto piso the sixth floor

sexual *masc & fem adjective*
  sexual
  tener relaciones sexuales con alguien to
  have sex with someone

♂ **si** *conjunction* ▷ see **sí** *adv, pron*
  if
  Si nos invitan, iremos. If they invite us, we'll
  go.
  No sé si podré. I don't know if I'll be able to.
  Si lo hubiese sabido ... If I'd known ...
  Si tuviese dinero, lo compraría. If I had the
  money I'd buy it.

♂ **sí** *adverb* ▷ see **si** *conj*, **sí** *pron*
  yes
  Sí, es cierto. Yes, it's true.
  '¿Lo vas a comprar?'—'Sí.' 'Are you going
  to buy it?'—'Yes I am.'
  '¿Es suyo?'—'Creo que sí.' 'Is it hers?'—'I
  think so.'
  Ellos no lo saben, pero yo sí. They don't
  know, but I do.

♂ **sí** *pronoun* ▷ see **sí** *adv*, **si** *conj*
  1 himself, herself
  Lo dijo para sí. He said it to himself., She
  said it to herself.
  2 (*polite form*) **yourself, yourselves**
  Lo pensaron para sí. You thought of it
  yourselves.

3 itself
Este problema es, en sí mismo ... This problem is, in itself ...

4 themselves
Los dos hermanos lo quieren todo para sí. Both brothers want everything for themselves.

5 (emphasizing a particular person) **sí mismo, sí misma** himself, herself
Se ríe de sí misma. She laughs at herself.
Lo hizo por sí mismo. He did it by himself.
Quiere hacerlo por sí misma. She wants to do it by herself.
Lo dividieron entre sí. They divided it between themselves

Sicilia fem noun
Sicily

♪ el **sida** masc noun
(= Síndrome de inmunodeficiencia adquirida) **Aids** (= Aquired Immune Deficiency Syndrome)

♪ la **sidra** fem noun
cider

♪ **siempre** adverb
1 always
casi siempre almost always
Siempre van al mismo club. They always go to the same club.

2 para siempre for ever
Se quedaron allí para siempre. They stayed there for ever after.

3 como siempre as usual
la historia de siempre the usual story

4 siempre que whenever
Siempre que puedo. Whenever I can.

♪ **sienta**, **siento**, etc verb ▷ sentar, sentir

♪ la **sierra** fem noun
1 saw
2 mountain range
Veranean en la sierra. They spend their summer holidays in the mountains.

♪ la **siesta** fem noun
afternoon nap
echarse una siesta to have a nap
Está durmiendo la siesta. He's having a nap.

siete number
1 seven
Tiene siete años. She's seven (years old).

2 seventh (in dates)
Hoy es siete de abril. It's the seventh of April today.

3 seven (in clock time)
Son las siete. It's seven o'clock.

♪ **siga**, **sigan**, etc verb ▷ seguir

♪ la **sigla** fem noun
abbreviation
S.A. son las siglas de sociedad anónima. S.A. is the abbreviation for 'sociedad anónima.'

♪ el **siglo** masc noun
century
el siglo XX the 20th century (Use roman numbers for centuries in Spanish)
Hace un siglo que no nos vemos. (informal) We haven't seen each other for ages.

el **significado** masc noun
meaning

♪ **significar** verb [31]
to mean
¿Qué significa esto? What does this mean?
Eso no significa nada para él. That doesn't mean anything to him.

el **signo** masc noun
1 sign
¿De qué signo eres? What sign are you?
2 mark
• el **signo de exclamación** exclamation mark
• el **signo de interrogación** question mark
• el **signo del zodiaco** star sign

♪ **sigo**, **sigue**, etc verb ▷ seguir

♪ **siguiente** masc & fem adjective
▷ see **siguiente** noun
next, following
al día siguiente ... the next day ...

♪ el & la **siguiente** masc & fem noun
▷ see **siguiente** adjective
El siguiente, por favor. Next, please.

♪ **siguió** verb ▷ seguir

la **sílaba** fem noun
syllable

♪ **silbar** verb [17]
to whistle

el **silbato** masc noun
whistle (the instrument)

el **silbido** masc noun
whistle (the noise)

♪ el **silencio** masc noun
silence

♪ **silenciosamente** adverb
quietly

silencioso masc adjective, **silenciosa** fem
quiet

a
b
c
d
e
f
g
h
i
j
k
l
m
n
ñ
o
p
q
r
s
t
u
v
w
x
y
z

♂ la **silla** *fem noun*
  chair
  • la **silla eléctrica** electric chair
  • la **silla de ruedas** wheelchair

el **sillín** *masc noun*
  saddle (*on a bicycle*)

♂ el **sillón** *masc noun*
  armchair

el **símbolo** *masc noun*
  symbol

similar *masc & fem adjective*
  similar
  similar a algo similar to something

la **similitud** *fem noun*
  similarity

el **simio** *masc noun*
  ape

♂ **simpático** *masc adjective*, **simpática** *fem*
  nice
  Es muy simpático. He's very nice.

  WORD TIP *simpático* does not mean *sympathetic* in Spanish; for the meaning of *sympathetic* ▷ **comprensivo**.

simple *masc & fem adjective*
  1 **simple**
  2 **mere**
  una simple formalidad a mere formality

simplemente *adverb*
  simply

simplificar *verb* [31]
  to simplify

simular *verb* [17]
  1 **to pretend**
  2 **to fake**

simultáneo *masc adjective*, **simultánea** *fem*
  simultaneous

♂ **sin** *preposition*
  1 **without**
  sin esfuerzo without effort
  sin duda without a doubt
  Lo hice sin pensar. I did it without thinking.
  un agua mineral sin gas a still mineral water
  una cerveza sin alcohol a non-alcoholic beer
  Estamos sin azúcar. We're out of sugar.
  Nos quedamos sin dinero. We ran out of money.
  2 (*in expressions*) **sin querer** unintentionally
  sin hogar homeless
  sin sentido senseless

sin embargo nevertheless
  Sin embargo nos quedamos. Nevertheless we stayed.

la **sinagoga** *fem noun*
  synagogue

sinceramente *adverb*
  1 **sincerely**
  2 **quite honestly**

la **sinceridad** *fem noun*
  sincerity

sincero *masc adjective*, **sincera** *fem*
  sincere

el & la **sindicalista** *masc & fem noun*
  trade unionist

el **sindicato** *masc noun*
  trade union

el **singular** *masc noun*
  (*Grammar*) **singular**
  en singular in the singular

siniestro *masc adjective*, **siniestra** *fem*
  ▷ see **siniestro** *noun*
  sinister

el **siniestro** *masc noun*
  ▷ see **siniestro** *adjective*
  1 **accident**
  2 **disaster**

♂ **sino** *conjunction*
  but
  No es verde, sino amarillo. It's not green but yellow.

  WORD TIP *sino* is used after *no* to correct what has just been said.

sinónimo *masc adjective*, **sinónima** *fem*
  ▷ see **sinónimo** *noun*
  synonymous

♂ el **sinónimo** *masc noun*
  ▷ see **sinónimo** *adjective*
  synonym (*word meaning the same as another*)
  'Empezar' y 'comenzar' son sinónimos.
  'Empezar' and 'comenzar' are synonyms.

sintético *masc adjective*, **sintética** *fem*
  synthetic

♂ **sintieron**, **sintió**, etc *verb* ▷ **sentir**

el **síntoma** *masc noun*
  symptom

sintonizar *verb* [22]
  to tune in

♂ el & la **sinvergüenza** *masc & fem noun*
1 **swine**
2 **crook**
3 **rascal**

♂ **siquiera** *adverb*
1 **at least**
   Dales siquiera un poco de dinero. Give
   them at least a bit of money.
2 **ni siquiera** not even
   Ni siquiera me reconoció. She didn't even
   recognise me.

la **sirena** *fem noun*
1 **mermaid**
2 **siren** (*in a factory*)

el **sistema** *masc noun*
   system

♂ el **sitio** *masc noun*
1 **place**
   Ponlo otra vez en su sitio. Put it back in its
   place.
2 **room**
   hacer sitio to make room
   No tengo sitio en la maleta. I haven't got
   any room in my suitcase.
   Hay sitio para uno más. There's room for
   one more.
3 **seat**
   Hay un sitio al lado de la ventana. There's a
   seat by the window.
4 (*in expressions*) **en algún sitio** somewhere
   en cualquier sitio anywhere
   en ningún sitio nowhere
   en otro sitio somewhere else
5 **siege**
 • el **sitio web** web site

la **situación** *fem noun*
1 **situation**
2 **position**
   La situación de la casa es buena. The house
   is in a good position.

♂ **situado** *masc adjective*, **situada** *fem*
   situated

situar *verb* [20]
1 **to site** (*a building*)
2 **to set** (*a plot in a novel*)

situarse *reflexive verb* [20]
1 **to be situated**
2 **situarse en primer puesto** to be in first
   position
3 **situarse bien en la vida** to do very well for
   yourself in life

el **smoking** *masc noun*
   dinner jacket

> **WORD TIP** *smoking* does not mean *smoking* in
> English; for the meaning of *smoking* ▷ **fumar**.

el **SMS** *masc noun*
   text message
   enviar un SMS to send a text message

el **sobaco** *masc noun*
   armpit

♂ **sobra** *fem noun*
1 **de sobra** to spare
   Tenemos pan de sobra. We have bread to
   spare.
   Hay una silla de sobra. There's a spare
   chair.
   Como estaba de sobra me fui. I wasn't
   needed, so I left.
2 **las sobras** leftovers (*of food*)

♂ **sobrar** *verb* [17]
1 (*saying something is left over*) **Va a sobrar
   dinero.** There will be money left over.
   Nos ha sobrado vino. We have wine left
   over.
2 (*saying there is too much*) **Sobran tres sillas.**
   There are three chairs too many.
   Nos sobra tiempo. We have plenty of time.
   Le sobraba una entrada. He had a spare
   ticket.

♂ **sobre** *preposition* ▷ see **sobre** *noun*
1 **on**
   Está sobre la cama. It's on the bed.
2 **above**
   la lámpara que está sobre el sofá the lamp
   above the sofa
   sobre el nivel del mar above sea level
3 **over**
   el puente sobre el río the bridge over the
   river
4 **about**
   un artículo sobre el cambio climatológico
   an article about climate change
5 **sobre todo** especially

♂ el **sobre** *masc noun* ▷ see **sobre** *preposition*
   envelope

la **sobredosis** *fem noun*, pl: las **sobredosis**
   overdose

sobrenatural *masc & fem adjective*
   supernatural

sobrepasar *verb* [17]
   to exceed

a
b
c
d
e
f
g
h
i
j
k
l
m
n
ñ
o
p
q
r
s
t
u
v
w
x
y
z

a
b
c
d
e
f
g
h
i
j
k
l
m
n
ñ
o
p
q
r
s
t
u
v
w
x
y
z

♂ **sobresaliente** *masc & fem adjective*
▷ see **sobresaliente** *noun*
outstanding, **excellent**

♂ el **sobresaliente** *masc noun*
▷ see **sobresaliente** *adj*
mark between 8.5 and 10 (out of 10)

sobresalir *verb* [63]
1 **sobresalir en algo** to do very well in
something
Sobresale en los idiomas. She does very
well in languages.
2 **to overhang**

el **sobresalto** *masc noun*
fright
llevarse un sobresalto to get a fright

el & la **sobreviviente** *masc & fem noun*
survivor

sobrevivir *verb* [19]
to survive
sobrevivir a algo to survive something
No sobrevivió a la operación. He didn't
survive the operation.

♂ el **sobrino** *masc noun*, la **sobrina** *fem*
1 **nephew**
2 **niece**
mis sobrinos my nephews and nieces, my
nephews

sociable *masc & fem adjective*
sociable

social *masc & fem adjective*
social

socialista *masc & fem adjective & noun*
1 **socialist**
2 **el & la socialista** socialist

la **sociedad** *fem noun*
society
• la **sociedad anónima** public limited
company
• la **sociedad de consumo** consumer society

♂ el **socio** *masc noun*, la **socia** *fem*
member
hacerse socio de algo to join something
Se hizo socia del club de tenis. She joined
the tennis club

socorrer *verb* [18]
to help

el & la **socorrista** *masc & fem noun*
lifeguard
¿Hay un socorrista en la playa? Is there a
lifeguard at the beach?

el **socorro** *masc noun*
1 **help**
pedir socorro to ask for help
2 **¡Socorro!** Help!

♂ el **sofá** *masc noun*
sofa

sofocar *verb* [31]
to put out (*a fire*)

sofocarse *reflexive verb* [31]
to get worked up

♂ **sois** *verb* ▷ ser

la **soja** *fem noun*
soya

♂ el **sol** *masc noun*
sun
un día de sol a sunny day
sentarse al sol to lie in the sun
al ponerse el sol at sunset
Hacía sol. It was sunny.
El sol estaba saliendo. The sun was rising.

♂ **solamente** *adverb*
only

♂ el & la **soldado** *masc & fem noun*
soldier

♂ **soleado** *masc adjective*, **soleada** *fem*
sunny
un piso soleado a sunny flat

la **soledad** *fem noun*
loneliness

♂ **soler** *verb* [38]
1 **soler hacer algo** to usually do something
Suelen verse. They usually see each other.
Suele salir por las noches. He usually goes
out in the evenings.
2 **used to**
Solía venir los lunes. She used to come on
Mondays.

solicitar *verb* [17]
1 **to ask for** (*permission, an interview*)
2 **to apply for** (*a job*)

la **solicitud** *masc noun*
application

sólido *masc adjective*, **sólida** *fem*
1 **solid**
2 **sound**

solitario *masc adjective*, **solitaria** *fem*
lonely

ʃ **solo** *masc adjective*, **sola** *fem* ▷ see **sólo** *adv*
1 alone
Vive solo. He lives alone.
Cuando me quedé solo. When I was left alone.
2 lonely
sentirse solo to feel lonely
Está muy sola. She's very lonely.
3 on your own
Desde que murió su madre está sola. Since her mother died, she's been on her own.
4 by yourself
Lo hice sola. I did it by myself.
5 (*by itself*) un café solo a black coffee
un coñac solo a neat brandy
6 (*just one*) con una sola mano with one hand
sin una sola queja without a single complaint

ʃ **sólo** *adverb* ▷ see **solo** *adj*
only

el **solomillo** *masc noun*
fillet steak

soltar *verb* [24]
1 to let go of
¡Suéltame! Let go of me!
Le solté la mano. I let go of his hand.
2 to release (*a prisoner*)
3 to untie
soltar un nudo to untie a knot
4 soltar al perro to let the dog off the lead
5 (*with shouts, laughs*) soltar un grito to let out a cry
soltar una carcajada to let out a laugh
soltar una palabrota to come out with a swearword

soltarse *reflexive verb* [24]
1 to come undone (*a knot, bow*)
2 soltarse de algo to let go of something
Se soltó de mi mano. He let go of my hand.
No te sueltes de la barandilla. Don't let go of the banister.
3 soltarse el pelo to let your hair down

ʃ **soltero** *masc adjective*, **soltera** *fem*
▷ see **soltero** *noun*
single

ʃ el **soltero** *masc noun*, la **soltera** *fem noun*
▷ see **soltero** *adjective*
1 bachelor (*male*)
2 single woman

la **soltura** *fem noun*
con soltura with ease, without difficulty
hablar español con soltura to speak Spanish fluently

soluble *masc & fem adjective*
soluble

la **solución** *fem noun*
solution

solucionar *verb* [17]
1 to solve
2 to settle (*a conflict*)

ʃ la **sombra** *fem noun*
1 shadow
2 shade
dar sombra to give shade
sentarse en la sombra to sit in the shade
• la sombra de ojos eye shadow

ʃ el **sombrero** *masc noun*
hat

la **sombrilla** *fem noun*
1 sunshade
2 parasol

sombrío *masc adjective*, **sombría** *fem*
1 dark (*street, room*)
2 gloomy (*face, look*)

ʃ **somos**, **son** *verb* ▷ **ser**

ʃ **sonar** *verb* [24]
1 to ring (*a doorbell, telephone*)
Está sonando el teléfono. The telephone's ringing.
2 to sound
Suena raro. It sounds strange.
Suena a hueco. It sounds hollow.
3 to be familiar
Me suena mucho su cara. Her face is very familiar to me.
¿Carlos Ramírez? No me suena. Carlos Ramírez? The name doesn't ring a bell.

sonarse *reflexive verb* [24]
sonarse la nariz to blow one's nose

ʃ **soñar** *verb* [24]
to dream
Anoche soñé contigo. I dreamt about you last night.

el **sondeo** *masc noun*
survey

el **sonido** *masc noun*
sound

ʃ **sonreír** *verb* [61]
to smile
Me sonrió. He smiled at me.

sonreírse *reflexive verb* [61]
to smile

a
b
c
d
e
f
g
h
i
j
k
l
m
n
ñ
o
p
q
r
s
t
u
v
w
x
y
z

ſsonría, sonríe, sonrío, etc *verb*
  ▷ **sonreír**

ſla sonrisa *fem noun*
  smile

sonrojarse *verb* [17]
  to blush

ſla sopa *fem noun*
  soup
  sopa de pescado fish soup

ſsoplar *verb* [17]
  1 to blow
  soplar el polvo de la mesa to blow the dust off the table
  El viento sopla del oeste. The wind blows from the west.
  2 to blow out
  soplar las velas to blow out the candles
  3 (*with secrets, answers*) **soplarle la respuesta a alguien** to pass on the answer to someone (*in an exam*)

soportar *verb* [17]
  1 to stand (*a person, situation*)
  No soporto a Rafael. I can't stand Rafael.
  2 to bear (*pain*)
  3 to withstand (*heat*)

el soporte *masc noun*
  support

el sorbete *masc noun*
  sorbet

el sorbo *masc noun*
  1 sip
  beber a sorbos to sip
  2 gulp
  beberse algo de un sorbo to drink something in one gulp
  Se lo bebió de un sorbo. He drank it in one gulp.

sordo *masc adjective*, **sorda** *fem*
  ▷ see **sordo** *noun*
  deaf

el sordo *masc noun*, **la sorda** *fem noun*
  ▷ see **sordo** *adj*
  deaf person

sordomudo *masc adjective*, **sordomuda** *fem* ▷ see **sordomudo** *noun*
  deaf and dumb

el sordomudo *masc noun*, **la sordomuda** *fem noun* ▷ see **sordomudo** *adj*
  deaf mute

sorprendente *masc & fem adjective*
  surprising

sorprender *verb* [18]
  to surprise
  Me sorprende que se retrase. I'm surprised he's late.

sorprenderse *reflexive verb* [18]
  to be surprised

sorprendido *masc adjective*, **sorprendida** *fem*
  surprised

ſla sorpresa *fem noun*
  surprise

la sortija *fem noun*
  ring

soso *masc adjective*, **sosa** *fem*
  1 dull
  2 bland

el soso *masc noun*, **la sosa** *fem noun*
  ▷ see **soso** *adj*
  bore

la sospecha *fem noun*
  suspicion
  Tengo la sospecha de que ... I have a suspicion that ...

sospechar *verb* [17]
  to suspect

sospechoso *masc adjective*, **sospechosa** *fem*
  suspicious
  Me parece sospechoso. I find it suspicious.

el sostén *masc noun*
  1 support
  2 bra

sostener *verb* [9]
  1 to support (*an arch, ceiling, family*)
  2 to bear (*a weight, load*)

ſel sótano *masc noun*
  1 basement
  2 cellar

ſsoy *verb* ▷ **ser**

Sr. *abbreviation*
  (*short for: Señor*) **Mr**

Sra. *abbreviation*
  (*short for: Señora*) **Mrs**, **Ms**

Sres. *abbreviation*
  (*short for: Señores*) **Mr & Mrs**

Srta. *abbreviation*
  (*short for: Señorita*) **Miss**, **Ms**

⚿ **su** *masc & fem adjective*

1 his, **her**
su casa her house, his house
Ahí está con sus padres. There she is with her parents., There he is with his parents.

2 its
El perro duerme en su caseta. The dog sleeps in its kennel.

3 their
Es su coche. It's their car.

4 your *(polite form, singular & plural)*
Aquí tiene su sombrero. Here's your hat.
¿Son éstos sus zapatos? Are these your shoes?

suave *masc & fem adjective*

1 soft

2 smooth

3 gentle *(voice, climate)*

4 mild *(weather)*

el **suavizante** *masc noun*

1 fabric softener

2 hair conditioner

subdesarrollado *masc adjective*,
subdesarrollada *fem*
underdeveloped *(country)*

subestimar *verb* [17]
underestimate

la **subida** *fem noun*

1 rise *(in temperature, prices)*

2 climb *(up a hill, mountain)*

⚿ **subir** *verb* [19]

1 to go up
subir al tercer piso to go up to the third floor
El ascensor está subiendo. The lift is going up.
La temperatura ha subido tres grados. The temperature has gone up three degrees.

2 to come up
¡Sube! Come up!

3 to bring up
Súbeme un vaso de agua. Bring me up a glass of water.
Suba el equipaje, por favor. Bring the luggage up, please. *(polite form)*

4 to take up
¿Le subo las maletas a su habitación? Shall I take the luggage up to your room?

5 to put up
Han subido el precio de la gasolina. They've put up the price of petrol again.

6 *(with vehicles)* subir al tren to get on the train
subir a un coche to get into a car
subir a bordo to go on board

7 to turn up *(the volume)*
Subió un poco la música. He turned up the music a bit.

8 to raise
subir una persiana to raise a blind

9 to rise *(water, rivers)*
El agua está subiendo. The water is rising.

10 to come in *(tides)*

subirse *reflexive verb* [19]

1 subirse al tren to get on the train
subirse a un coche to get into a car

2 subirse a un árbol to climb up a tree

3 to pull up *(trousers, socks)*
subirse los calcetines to pull up your socks

súbitamente *adverb*
suddenly

súbito *masc adjective*, **súbita** *fem*
sudden

el **subjuntivo** *masc noun*
subjunctive

el **submarinismo** *masc noun*
scuba diving

el & la **submarinista** *masc & fem noun*

1 scuba diver

2 submariner

el **submarino** *masc noun*
submarine

subrayar *verb* [17]
to underline

el **subsidio** *masc noun*
subsidy
• el **subsidio de desempleo** unemployment benefit
• el **subsidio de invalidez** disability allowance

subterráneo *masc adjective*,
subterránea *fem*
▷ see **subterráneo** *noun*
underground

⚿ el **subterráneo** *masc noun*
▷ see **subterráneo** *adjective*
subway, **underpass**

los **subtítulos** *plural masc noun*
subtitles *(in films)*

el **suburbio** *masc noun*

1 slum area *(on the outskirts of a town)*

2 suburb

la **subvención** *fem noun*
subsidy

subvencionar *verb* [17]
  to subsidize

ᔥ **suceder** *verb* [18]
 1 **to happen**
   ¿Qué sucede? What's happening?
   Le ha sucedido algo. Something's
   happened to him.
   Lo que sucede es que ... The thing is that ...
 2 **to succeed** (*to the throne*)

el **suceso** *masc noun*
 1 **event**
 2 **incident**
   la página de sucesos accidents and crimes
   report (*in a newspaper*)

la **suciedad** *fem noun*
 1 **grime**
 2 **dirtiness**

ᔥ **sucio** *masc adjective*, **sucia** *fem*
 1 **dirty**
   Tienes la camisa sucia. Your shirt is dirty.
 2 **en sucio** in rough
   El trabajo sólo está en sucio. The essay is
   only in rough.

la **sucursal** *fem noun*
 1 **branch** (*of a bank, a business*)
 2 **office** (*of a company*)

ᔥ la **sudadera** *fem noun*
   sweatshirt

ᔥ **Sudamérica** *fem noun*
   South America

sudamericano *masc adjective & noun*,
   sudamericana *fem adjective & noun*
 1 **South American**
 2 **un sudamericano, una sudamericana**
   South American

WORD TIP Adjectives and nouns for nationality
and regional origin do not have capital letters in
Spanish.

sudar *verb* [17]
   to sweat

el **sudeste** *masc noun*
   southeast

el **sudoeste** *masc noun*
   southwest

el **sudor** *masc noun*
   sweat

Suecia *fem noun*
   Sweden

sueco *masc adjective & noun*, **sueca** *fem
   adjective & noun*
 1 **Swedish**

 2 **un sueco, una sueca** Swede
   el sueco Swedish (*the language*)

WORD TIP Adjectives and nouns for nationality,
regional origin, and language do not have capital
letters in Spanish.

el **suegro** *masc noun*, la **suegra** *fem*
 1 **father-in-law**
 2 **mother-in-law**
 3 **mis suegros** my parents in law

la **suela** *fem noun* ▷ see **suela** *verb*
   sole

suela, suelas, etc *verb* ▷ see **suela** *noun* ▷
   soler

el **sueldo** *masc noun*
 1 **salary**
 2 **pay**
   un aumento de sueldo a pay rise

ᔥ el **suelo** *masc noun* ▷ see **suelo** *verb*
 1 **floor**
 2 **ground**
   tirarse al suelo to throw yourself to the
   ground

ᔥ **suelo** *verb* ▷ see **suelo** *noun* ▷ soler

suelta, suelte, suelto, etc *verb* ▷ soltar

suelto *masc adjective*, **suelta** *fem*
   ▷ see **suelto** *noun*
 1 **loose**
   El perro está suelto. The dog is loose.
 2 **separately**
   Los venden sueltos. They are sold
   separately.

el **suelto** *masc noun* ▷ see **suelto** *adjective*
   change (*coins*)
   ¿Tienes suelto? Have you got any change?

ᔥ **suena, suene, sueno, etc** *verb* ▷ sonar

ᔥ **sueña, sueñe, sueño, etc** *verb* ▷ soñar

ᔥ el **sueño** *masc noun*
 1 **dream**
   Mi sueño es vivir en Los Ángeles. My dream
   is to live in Los Angeles.
 2 **tener sueño** to be sleepy

ᔥ la **suerte** *fem noun*
   luck
   tener suerte to be lucky
   traer mala suerte to bring bad luck
   ¡Qué mala suerte! What bad luck!
   ¡Suerte! Good luck!

ᔥ el **suéter** *masc noun*
   sweater

suficiente *masc & fem adjective & pronoun*
▷ see **suficiente** *noun*
enough
Tenemos suficiente dinero. We have
enough money.
No traigas más, tenemos suficientes.
Don't bring any more, we've got enough.

el **suficiente** *masc noun*
▷ see **suficiente** *adj, pron*
(in school) **pass** (equivalent to 50%)

sufrir *verb*[19]
1 **to suffer**
Sufre mucho. He's suffering a lot.
2 **to have**
sufrir un accidente to have an accident
Sufre una grave enfermedad. He has a
serious illness.

la **sugerencia** *fem noun*
suggestion

sugerir *verb*[14]
to suggest

sugiera, **sugiero**, **sugirieron**, **etc** *verb*
▷ **sugerir**

suicidarse *reflexive verb*[17]
to commit suicide

el **suicidio** *masc noun*
suicide

Suiza *fem noun*
Switzerland

suizo *masc adjective & noun*, **suiza** *fem*
adjective & noun
1 **Swiss**
2 un suizo, una suiza Swiss

WORD TIP Adjectives and nouns for nationality
and regional origin do not have capital letters in
Spanish.

♪ el **sujetador** *masc noun*
bra

sujeto *masc adjective*, **sujeta** *fem*
▷ see **sujeto** *noun*
1 **secure**
Está bien sujeto. It's really secure.
2 estar sujeto a algo to be liable to
something
Está sujeto a modificaciones. It's liable to
change.

♪ el **sujeto** *masc noun* ▷ see **sujeto** *adj*
subject

la **suma** *fem noun*
1 **addition**
2 en suma in short

sumar *verb*[17]
to add

♪ **supe**, **supiste**, **etc** *verb* ▷ **saber**

♪ **super**, **súper** *invariable adjective, adverb*
(*informal*) **super**
Cantan super bien. They sing really well.
Me lo pasé super bien. I had a great time.

WORD TIP super, súper never changes.

superar *verb*[17]
1 **to overcome** (*fear, problems*)
2 **to get over** (*a shock*)
3 **to exceed** (*expectations, temperatures*)

la **superficie** *fem noun*
surface

superior *masc & fem adjective*
1 **superior**
Es superior a los demás.. It's superior to the
rest.
2 **upper** (*lip, floor, storey*)
3 **higher** (*number, level, class*)

♪ el **supermercado** *masc noun*
supermarket

la **superstición** *fem noun*
superstition

supersticioso *masc adjective*,
supersticiosa *fem*
superstitious

supervisar *verb*[17]
supervise

el **supervisor** *masc noun*, la **supervisora**
fem noun
supervisor

el & la **superviviente** *masc & fem noun*
survivor

suplementario *masc adjective*,
suplementaria *fem*
additional

♪ el **suplemento** *masc noun*
supplement
Hay que pagar un suplemento. You have to
pay an additional charge.

supondrá, **supondré**, **supondría**, **etc**
verb ▷ **suponer**

suponer *verb*[11]
1 **to suppose**
Supongo que sí. I suppose so.
2 **to involve**
Supone volver a hacerlo. It involves doing it
again.

♪ indicates key words   297

suponga, supongo, etc *verb* ▷ **suponer**

el **supositorio** *masc noun*
   suppository

suprimir *verb* [19]
1 **to suppress** (*news*)
2 **to abolish**
3 **to delete**

ᶠ **supuesto** *in phrase*
   por supuesto of course
   Por supuesto que te acompañamos. Of
   course we'll go with you.

supuse, supuso *verb* ▷ **suponer**

ᶠ **sur** *masc noun, invariable adjective*
   south
   ir hacia el sur to go south
   la costa sur de Inglaterra the south coast of
   England
   al sur de Murcia south of Murcia
   en el sur de España in the south of Spain

ᶠ **Suramérica** *fem noun*
   South America

ᶠ **suramericano** *masc adjective & noun,*
   suramericana *fem adjective & noun*
1 **South American**
2 **un suramericano, una suramericana** South
   American

   WORD TIP Adjectives and nouns for nationality
   and regional origin do not have capital letters in
   Spanish.

el **sureste** *masc noun*
   southest

ᶠ el **surf** *masc noun*
   surfing
   practicar el surf to go surfing

ᶠ el & la **surfista** *masc & fem noun*
   surfer (*in the sea*)

el **suroeste** *masc noun*
   southwest

surtido *masc adjective,* **surtida** *fem*
   ▷ see **surtido** *noun*
1 **assorted**
2 **una tienda bien surtida** a well-stocked
   shop

el **surtido** *masc noun* ▷ see **surtido** *adj*
1 **assortment**
2 **selection**

el **surtidor** *masc noun*
   petrol pump

ᶠ **suspender** *verb* [18]
1 **to fail** (*in exams*)
   Hemos suspendido. We've failed.
   He suspendido la física. I've failed physics.
2 **to suspend** (*a payment, service*)
3 **to cancel**
   suspender un partido to cancel a match

el **suspense** *masc noun*
   suspense
   una película de suspense a thriller (*film*)

el **suspenso** *masc noun*
1 **fail** (*in an exam*)
2 **estar en suspenso** to be in suspense

suspirar *verb* [17]
   to sigh

el **suspiro** *masc noun*
   sigh

la **sustancia** *fem noun*
   substance

ᶠ el **sustantivo** *masc noun*
   noun

sustituir *verb* [54]
1 **to replace**
   sustituir algo por algo to replace
   something with something
   Sustituimos el azucar por la miel. We
   replaced the honey with sugar.
2 **sustituir a alguien** to stand in for
   someone (*at work*), to substitute for
   someone (*in sports*)
   Lo sustituyó en su ausencia. She stood in
   for him in his absence.
   **Zamorano sustituyó a Salas en el minuto
   20.** Zamorano came on for Salas in the
   twentieth minute.

el **sustituto** *masc noun,* la **sustituta** *fem*
   noun
1 **replacement**
2 **substitute**
3 **locum**

el **susto** *masc noun*
   fright
   darle un susto a alguien to give someone a
   fright
   ¡Qué susto me has dado! What a fright you
   gave me!
   ¡Qué susto me llevé! I got such a fright!

sustraer *verb* [42]
   to subtract

susurrar *verb* [17]
  to whisper

sutil *masc & fem adjective*
  subtle

ᔒ **suyo** *masc adjective*, **suya** *fem*
  ▷ see **suyo** *pron*

1 **his**, **hers**
  Esto es suyo. This is his., This is hers.
  un conocido suyo a friend of his, a friend of
  hers
  una vecina suya a neighbour of his, a
  neighbour of hers

2 **theirs**
  Estos son suyos. These are theirs.
  Venían con un amigo suyo. They came with
  a friend of theirs.
  Venían con unos amigos suyos. They came
  with some friends of theirs.

3 **yours** (*polite* *usted* form)
  un colega suyo a colleague of yours

WORD TIP *suyo, suya* agrees with the thing you
have or own: *conocido, vecina,* etc above. *suyo, suya*
goes after the noun.

ᔒ **suyo** *pronoun* ▷ see **suyo** *adj*

1 **his**, **hers**
  El suyo es gris. His is grey., Hers is grey.
  Las suyas son mejores. His are better., Hers
  are better.

2 **yours** (*polite* '*usted*' form)
  Aquí tiene el suyo. Here is yours.

3 **theirs**
  Este es mi coche. El suyo es más grande.
  This is my car. Theirs is bigger.
  Estos son los nuestros. Los suyos son más
  grandes. These are ours. Theirs are bigger.

WORD TIP *el suyo, la suya* agrees with the thing
you have or own.

T t

♂ el **tabaco** *masc noun*
1 **tobacco**
2 **cigarettes**
Tengo que comprar tabaco. I must buy some cigarettes.

♂ el **tabaquismo** *masc noun*
tobacco addiction

♂ la **taberna** *fem noun*
bar (*selling wine*)

♂ la **tabla** *fem noun*
1 **plank**
2 **board**
3 **pleat**
4 **table** (*of figures*)
• la **tabla de gimnasia** circuit training
• la **tabla de multiplicar** multiplication table
• la **tabla de planchar** ironing board
• la **tabla de vela** sailboard

el **tablao** *masc noun*
• el **tablao flamenco** flamenco dance bar

el **tablero** *masc noun*
1 **board** (*for chess, draughts*)
2 **noticeboard**
• el **tablero chino** Chinese checkers
• el **tablero de damas** draughtboard

el **tablón** *masc noun*
plank
• el **tablón de anuncios** noticeboard

♂ el **taburete** *masc noun*
stool

tacaño *masc adjective*, **tacaña** *fem*
▷ see **tacaño** *noun*
stingy

el **tacaño** *masc noun*, la **tacaña** *fem noun*
▷ see **tacaño** *adj*
miser

tachar *verb* [17]
to cross out

el **taco** *masc noun*
1 **cue** (*in billards*)
2 **stud** (*on a sports boot*)
3 (*informal*) **swearword**
decir tacos to swear

♂ el **tacón** *masc noun*
heel
zapatos de tacón alto high-heeled shoes
• el **tacón de aguja** stiletto heel

la **táctica** *fem noun*
1 **tactic**
2 **tactics**

el **tacto** *masc noun*
1 **sense of touch**
2 **feel**
3 **tact**
Fue una falta de tacto. It was very tactless.

♂ **TAF** *abbreviation* (= *Transferencia Automática de Fondos*) **automatic funds transfer**

la **tajada** *fem noun*
slice (*of melon, etc*)

♂ **tal** *masc & fem adjective* ▷ see **tal** *adv*
1 **such**
Tal cosa es imposible. Such a thing is impossible.
Lo hizo de tal manera que ... She did it in such a way that ...
Tales eran sus problemas que ... Such were his problems that ...
2 (*for emphasis*) **Nunca había visto tal cantidad de lluvia.** I had never seen such a lot of rain.
3 (*when you don't know someone*) **Una tal Señora González pregunta por ti.** Someone called Mrs González is asking for you.

♂ **tal** *adverb* ▷ see **tal** *adj*
1 (*informal*) (*asking questions*) **¿Qué tal?** How are things?
¿Qué tal estás? How are you doing?
¿Qué tal es su novia? What's his girlfriend like?
¿Qué tal estuvo la película? How was the film?
2 **tal vez** maybe
Tal vez iré el viernes. Maybe I'll go on Friday.
3 **tal cual** just the way it was
Lo dejaron tal cual. They left it just as it was.

el **talco** *masc noun*
talc
polvos de talco talcum powder

el **talento** *masc noun*
talent

♪ el **TALGO** *masc noun*
(= *Tren Articulado Ligero Goicoechea Oriol*) **express train** (*in Spain*)

♪ la **talla** *fem noun*
size (*for clothes, hats*)
unos pantalones de la talla 40 a pair of size 40 trousers
¿Qué talla de pantalones usa? What size of trousers do you take? (*polite form*)

♪ el **taller** *masc noun*
1 **workshop**
2 **garage**
llevar el coche al taller to take the car to the garage

♪ el **talón** *masc noun*
heel

el **talonario** *masc noun*
chequebook

♪ el **tamaño** *masc noun*
size
un tamaño más grande a larger size
de tamaño familiar family-sized
¿De qué tamaño es? What size is it?
¿Tiene un tamaño más pequeño? Do you have a smaller size?

♪ **también** *adverb*
too, **as well**
Ella también vive allí. She lives there too.
'Tengo quince años.'—'Yo también.' 'I'm fifteen.'—'Me too.'
'Yo quiero tarta.'—'Nosotros también.' 'I want some cake.'—'We do too.'
También estudia griego. He also studies Greek.

el **tambor** *masc noun*
drum

♪ **tampoco** *adverb*
1 **not ... either**
Él tampoco irá. He won't go either.
Ella no irá tampoco. She won't go either.
Ellos tampoco quieren jugar. They don't want to play either.
Ellas no pueden jugar tampoco. They can't play either.

WORD TIP *Tampoco* can be used with or without *no*, but its position in the sentence changes accordingly.

2 (*in short replies*) **neither do I** (*you, he, she, etc*)
'A mí no me gusta.'—'A mí tampoco.' 'I don't like it.'—'Neither do I.'
'A mí no me apetece ir.'—'A nosotros

tampoco.' 'I don't feel like going.'— 'Neither do we.'

el **tampón** *masc noun*
tampon

♪ **tan** *adverb*
1 **so** (+ *adverb or adjective*)
No es tan fácil. It's not so easy.
No corras tan rápido. Don't run so fast.
¡Qué casa tan grande! What a big house!
2 **such a** (+ *noun*)
Es una persona tan egoísta. He's such a selfish person.
Es una chica tan guapa. She's such a good-looking girl.
3 (*in comparisons*) **tan ... como ...** as ... as ...
Es tan alta como su padre. She's as tall as her father.
No era tan caro como el otro. It wasn't as expensive as the other one.
4 (*saying the result*) **tan ... que ...** so ... that ...
Era tan grande que no cabía por la puerta. It was so big that it would not fit through the door.

el **tanque** *masc noun*
tank

♪ **tanto** *masc adjective*, **tanta** *fem*
▷ see **tanto** *adv, noun, pron*
1 **so much**
tanto dinero so much money
tanta sal so much salt
Puso tanto azúcar al café, que no se podía beber. He put so much sugar in the coffee that it was undrinkable.
2 **so many**
tantos libros so many books
tantas cajas so many boxes
Había tanta gente que no cabíamos. There were so many people that there wasn't room for us.
3 **tanto ... como ...**, **tanta ... como ...** as much ... as ...
No gasta tanta gasolina como el coche viejo. It doesn't use as much petrol as the old car.
4 **tantos ... como ...**, **tantas ... como ...** as many ... as ...
Hay tantos alumnos como el año pasado. There are as many students as last year.
No hay tantas golondrinas como antes. There aren't as many swallows as before.

♪ **tanto** *adverb* ▷ see **tanto** *adj, pron, noun*
1 **so**
No corras tanto. Don't go so fast.
Se enfadó tanto. He got so upset. ▸▸

2 so much
No deberías gastar tanto. You shouldn't spend so much.

3 so often
Yo no los visito tanto. I don't visit them all that often.

4 so long
Lleva tanto hacerlo. It takes so long to do.

5 Pesa tanto como éste. It's as heavy as this one.

6 (with *mejor* and *peor*) tanto mejor so much the better
Si le gusta, tanto mejor. If she likes it, so much the better.
tanto peor so much the worse
Si no le gusta, tanto peor. If she doesn't like it, so much the worse.

el **tanto** *masc noun* ▷ see **tanto** *adj, adv, pron*

1 point, **goal**
marcar un tanto to score a point, to score a goal

2 an amount
Gana un tanto de cada venta. She gets an amount on each sale.

• el **tanto por ciento** percentage

ƒ **tanto** *masc pronoun*, **tanta** *fem*
▷ see **tanto** *adj, adv, noun*

1 tanto so much (for a masc noun)
tanta so much (for a fem noun)
No hace falta tanto., No hace falta tanta. We don't need so much.

2 tantos so many (for a masc plural noun)
tantas so many (for a fem plural noun)
Vinieron tantos que no había sillas libres. So many came that there weren't any chairs left.
Vendieron tantas que no quedan más. They sold so many that there are none left.

3 (talking about time) tanto so long
No tardes tanto como ayer. Don't take as long as yesterday.
'Me llevará dos días hacerlo.'—'¿Tanto?.' 'It'll take me two days to do it.'—'As long as that?.'

4 (in expressions) por lo tanto therefore
mientras tanto in the meantime
entre tanto in the meantime

ƒ la **tapa** *fem noun*

1 lid

2 top
tapa de rosca screw top

3 cover (of a book)

4 tapa (snack eaten in a 'tapas' bar)
un bar de tapas a tapas bar

comer de tapas to eat tapas for lunch (or supper, etc)

 tapas

Comenzaron como un pedazo de pan para cubrir el vaso para protegerlo de las moscas. Hoy en día se trata de una variedad enorme de pinchos o raciones para acompañar una bebida.

tapar *verb* [17]

1 to cover

2 to put the top on

3 to fill in
tapar un agujero to fill in a hole

4 to block up (a window, a door)

5 to blot out (sunlight, the view)

el **tapón** *masc noun*

1 cork

2 top (of a bottle)

3 plug (of a basin, bath, sink)

ƒ la **taquigrafía**
shorthand

ƒ la **taquilla** *fem noun*

1 box office
un éxito de taquilla a box office hit

2 ticket office

ƒ **tardar** *verb* [17]

1 to take (time)
¿Cuánto se tarda de Sevilla a Córdoba? How long does it take from Seville to Cordoba?
Tarda un par de horas. It takes a couple of hours.

2 to take a long time
Tardó mucho en contestarme. She took a long time to answer.
¡No tardes! Don't be long!
No tardes en volver. Come back soon.

3 a más tardar at the latest
a las cuatro a más tardar at four o'clock at the latest

ƒ **tarde** *adverb* ▷ see **tarde** *noun*
late
llegar tarde to be late
Se acuesta tarde. He goes to bed late.
Más vale tarde que nunca. better late than never.

ƒ la **tarde** *fem noun* ▷ see **tarde** *adv*
afternoon, evening
a las tres de la tarde at three in the afternoon
por la tarde in the afternoon, in the evening
Buenas tardes. Good afternoon., Good evening.

♂ la **tarea** *fem noun*
1 **task**
2 **las tareas de la casa** the housework
3 **homework**

♂ la **tarifa** *fem noun*
1 **price list**
2 **fare** (*for buses, taxis*)
3 **charge** (*for electricity, gas, postage*)

♂ la **tarjeta** *fem noun*
   card
   sacarle a alguien la tarjeta amarilla to show somebody the yellow card
   sacarle a alguien la tarjeta roja to show somebody the red card
 • la **tarjeta de crédito** credit card
 • la **tarjeta de cumpleaños** birthday card
 • la **tarjeta de embarque** boarding card
 • la **tarjeta de fidelidad** loyalty card
 • la **tarjeta de Navidad** Christmas card
 • la **tarjeta postal** postcard
 • la **tarjeta de prepago** top-up card
 • la **tarjeta SIM** SIM card

   la **tarrina** *fem noun*
   tub (*for food*)

♂ el **tarro** *masc noun*
   jar

♂ la **tarta** *fem noun*
1 **cake**
2 **tart**
 • la **tarta de cumpleaños** birthday cake
 • la **tarta helada** ice-cream cake

   la **tartera** *fem noun*
   sandwich box

♂ la **tasa** *fem noun*
1 **rate**
2 **valuation**
3 **tax**
 • la **tasa de desempleo** rate of unemployment
 • la **tasa de interés** interest rate

♂ el **tatuaje** *masc noun*
   tatoo

♂ **tauro** *masc & fem noun*
   Taurus
   Es tauro. He's Taurus.

WORD TIP Use a small letter in Spanish to say *I am Taurus*, etc with star signs.

♂ **Tauro** *masc noun*
   Taurus

♂ el **taxi** *masc noun*
   taxi

♂ el & la **taxista** *masc & fem noun*
   taxi driver

♂ la **taza** *fem noun*
1 **cup**
   una taza de café a cup of coffee
2 **(toilet) bowl**

♂ el **tazón** *masc noun*
   bowl

♂ **te** *pronoun*
1 **you**
   Te quiero. I love you.
   Te vi ayer. I saw you yesterday.
2 **to you**
   Te lo mandaré por correo. I'll post it to you.
3 (*with parts of the body, personal belongings*) **¿Te has cortado el dedo?** Have you cut your finger?
   ¿Quieres quitarte los zapatos? Do you want to take your shoes off?
4 (*about having things done*) **¿Te has cortado el pelo?** Have you had your hair cut?
5 **yourself**
   Cuídate mucho. Look after yourself.
6 **Siéntate.** Sit down.

WORD TIP *te* is used to refer to a person you know well. ▷ **usted, vosotros**

♂ el **té** *masc noun*
   tea
   a la hora del té at tea time
   Queremos té para dos. We'd like tea for two.

♂ el **teatro** *masc noun*
   theatre

♂ el **tebeo** *masc noun*
   comic (*for children*)

♂ el **techo** *masc noun*
1 **ceiling**
2 (*Latin America*) **roof**
3 **los sin techo** the homeless

♂ la **tecla** *fem noun*
   key

♂ el **teclado** *masc noun*
   keyboard

   la **técnica** *fem noun* ▷ see **técnico** *adj, noun*
   technique

técnico *masc adjective*, **técnica** *fem*
   ▷ see **técnica** *noun*, **técnico** *noun*
   technical

el **técnico** *masc noun*, la **técnica** *fem noun*
   ▷ see **técnica** *noun*, **técnico** *adj*
   technician

a b c d e f g h i j k l m n ñ o p q r s t u v w x y z

la **tecnología** *fem noun*
technology

la **teja** *fem noun*
tile

ℰ el **tejado** *masc noun*
roof

ℰ los **tejanos** *plural masc noun*
jeans

tejer *verb* [18]
1 to weave
2 to knit

la **tela** *fem noun*
1 fabric
una tela de algodón a cotton fabric
2 canvas (*for painting*)

ℰ la **telaraña** *fem noun*
1 spider's web
2 cobweb
3 spider diagram

ℰ la **tele** *fem noun*
(*informal*) **telly, TV**
ver la tele to watch telly
ver algo en la tele to see something on TV
poner la tele to switch on the telly

ℰ el **telediario** *masc noun*
television news

el **teleférico** *masc noun*
cablecar

ℰ **telefonear** *verb* [17]
to telephone

telefónico *masc adjective*, **telefónica** *fem*
telephone
una conversación telefónica a telephone
conversation
el listín telefónico telephone book

ℰ el **teléfono** *masc noun*
telephone
contestar el teléfono to answer the phone
colgar el teléfono to hang up
No tenemos teléfono. We don't have a
phone.
llamar por teléfono a alguien to phone
somebody
Al llegar, me llamó por teléfono. When she
arrived, she phoned me.
• el **teléfono celular** (*Latin America*) mobile
phone
• el **teléfono inalámbrico** cordless phone
• el **teléfono móvil** mobile phone

el **telegrama** *masc noun*
telegram

ℰ la **telenovela** *fem noun*
TV serial

el **telescopio** *masc noun*
telescope

ℰ la **televisión** *fem noun*
television
ver la televisión to watch television
poner la televisión to switch on the
television
El rey habló por televisión. The king spoke
on television.
Hoy ponen una película en la televisión.
There's a film on the television today.

ℰ el **televisor** *masc noun*
television set
• el **televisor de pantalla grande** wide-
screen television

ℰ el **tema** *masc noun*
1 subject
2 issue
un tema polémico a contentious issue

temblar *verb* [29]
1 to shiver
2 to shake
Le temblaban las manos. His hands were
shaking.

ℰ **temer** *verb* [18]
to fear (*danger, punishment*)
Tememos lo peor. We fear the worst.
temer a alguien to be afraid of somebody
Sus alumnos le temen. His pupils are afraid
of him.

temerse *reflexive verb* [18]
1 to fear
2 Me temo que no podré venir. I'm afraid I
won't be able to come.

ℰ la **temperatura** *fem noun*
temperature
Hace una temperatura de quince grados.
The temperature is fifteen degrees.
Ha subido la temperatura. The
temperature has risen.

la **tempestad** *fem noun*
storm

templado *masc adjective*, **templada** *fem*
1 mild (*climate*)
2 warm
3 lukewarm

a
b
c
d
e
f
g
h
i
j
k
l
m
n
ñ
o
p
q
r
s
t
u
v
w
x
y
z

ᔓla temporada *fem noun*
season
fuera de temporada out of season
la temporada alta the high season
la temporada baja the low season

ᔓtemprano *masc adjective,* **temprana** *fem*
▷ see **temprano** *adv*
early

ᔓtemprano *adverb* ▷ see **temprano** *adj*
early
tarde o temprano sooner or later
llegar temprano to arrive early

la tendencia *fem noun*
tendency

tender *verb* [36]
1 **tender a** to tend to
Tienden a visitarnos más en invierno. They tend to visit us more often in winter.
2 **tender la ropa** to hang out the washing

tenderse *reflexive verb* [36]
to lie down
tenderse al sol to lie down in the sun

el tendero *masc noun,* **la tendera** *fem noun*
shopkeeper

ᔓtendrá, tendré, tendría, etc *verb* ▷
tener

ᔓel tenedor *masc noun*
fork

ᔓtener *verb* [9]
1 **to have**
Tengo un hermano. I have a brother.
Tiene los ojos marrones. He has brown eyes.
tener dolor de cabeza to have a headache
No tengo tiempo. I haven't got the time.
¿Tienes hora? Have you got the time?
Ha tenido un niño. She has had a baby.
2 *(saying your age)* **to be**
¿Cuántos años tienes? How old are you?
Tengo catorce años. I'm fourteen (years old).
Ella tiene quince años. She's fifteen (years old).
3 **to be** *(hot, cold, hungry, thirsty, etc)*
tener calor to be hot
tener frío to be cold
tener hambre to be hungry
tener sed to be thirsty
Tengo calor. I'm hot.
4 **to be** *(careful, afraid, right, in a hurry, etc)*
tener cuidado to be careful
tener miedo to be afraid
tener razón to be right

tener prisa to be in a hurry
tener sueño to feel sleepy
No tengo miedo del perro. I'm not afraid of the dog.
Tenemos prisa. We're in a hurry.
5 **tener que hacer algo** to have to do something, must
Tengo que estudiar. I have to study.
Tengo que ir al dentista. I must go to the dentist's.
Tendría que ir al banco. I should go to the bank.
Tienes que hacer lo que diga el médico. You must do as the doctor says.
6 **tener que ver con alguien** to have to do with someone
No tiene nada que ver contigo. It has nothing to do with you.
7 *(saying something is done)* **tener + -ado, -ido form of the verb**
Lo tienen controlado. They've got it under control.
Lo tengo hecho. I've done it.
8 **tenerle envidia de alguien** to be jealous of somebody
Le tiene envidia. He's jealous of her.

ᔓtenga, tengo, etc *verb* ▷ **tener**

el & la teniente *masc & fem noun*
lieutenant

ᔓel tenis *masc noun*
tennis
• **el tenis de mesa** table tennis

ᔓel & la tenista *masc & fem noun*
tennis player

la tensión *fem noun*
1 **tension**
2 **stress**
3 **blood pressure**
tomarse la tensión to have your blood pressure taken

la tentación *fem noun*
temptation

tentar *verb* [29]
to tempt

teñir *verb* [65]
to dye

teñirse *reflexive verb* [65]
to dye
teñirse el pelo to have your hair dyed

ᔓ indicates key words   305

♂ **tercer** *masc adjective*
  third *adjective*
  el tercer piso the third floor

> **WORD TIP** *tercer* is used instead of *tercero* before a masc singular noun. ▷ **tercero**

♂ **tercero** *masc adjective*, **tercera** *fem*
  third
  el tercer piso the third floor
  la tercera puerta a la derecha the third door on the right
  llegar en tercer lugar to finish in third position
- **el Tercer Mundo** the Third World

> **WORD TIP** *tercero* becomes *tercer* before a masculine singular noun.

el terciopelo *masc noun*
  velvet

terminado *masc adjective*, **terminada** *fem*
  finished

terminal *masc & fem adjective*
  ▷ **see terminal** *noun*
  terminal

♂ **la terminal** *fem noun* ▷ **see terminal** *adj*
1 **terminal**
2 **bus station**

♂ **terminar** *verb* [17]
1 **to finish**
  Ya he terminado. I've finished now.
  ¿Cuándo termina el trimestre? When does term end?
  Terminó la novela en tres horas. He finished the novel in three hours.
  terminar de + infinitive to finish +ing
  He terminado de revisarlo. I've finished checking it.
2 **terminar con algo** to finish with something
  ¿Has terminado con el libro? Have you finished with the book?
  terminar con alguien to finish with someone
  Ha terminado con su novio. She's broken up with her boyfriend.
3 **to end up**
  Terminamos en una discoteca. We ended up in a disco.
  Terminó harta. In the end she got fed up.
  Terminaron por pelearse. They ended up having a fight.
4 **to end in**
  terminar en algo to end in something
  Su nombre termina en 't'. Her name ends in 't'.
  Termina en punta. It's pointed.

terminarse *reflexive verb* [17]
1 **to be over**
  La clase se termina a las doce. The lesson will be over at twelve.
2 **Se ha terminado la leche.** We've run out of milk.
  Se me terminó la tinta del boli. My pen ran out (of ink).

el termo® *masc noun*
  Thermos®

el termómetro *masc noun*
  thermometer

♂ **la ternera** *fem noun* ▷ **see ternero** *masc noun*
1 **veal**
2 **beef**

el ternero *masc noun*, **la ternera** *fem*
  ▷ **see ternera** *noun*
  calf

♂ **la terraza** *fem noun*
1 **balcony**
2 **terrace** (*of a cafe, bar*)
  Desayunamos en la terraza. We had breakfast on the terrace.

el terremoto *masc noun*
  earthquake

el terreno *masc noun*
1 **plot of land**
2 **field**
3 **land**
  La casa tiene mucho terreno. The house has a lot of land.
4 **el terreno de juego** football pitch

♂ **terrible** *masc & fem adjective*
  terrible

el territorio *masc noun*
  territory

el terrón *masc noun*
  lump (*of sugar, earth*)

el terror *masc noun*
  terror

el terrorismo *masc noun*
  terrorism

terrorista *masc & fem adjective & noun*
1 **terrorist**
2 **un & una terrorista** terrorist

el tesoro *masc noun*
  treasure

ᶘ el **test** *masc noun*

1 test

2 un examen tipo test a multiple-choice exam

el **testamento** *masc noun*
  will
  hacer testamento to make your will

el & la **testigo** *masc & fem noun*
  witness

el **tétano** *masc noun*
  tetanus

ᶘ la **tetera** *fem noun*
  1 teapot
  2 kettle

ᶘ el **texto** *masc noun*
  text

ᶘ **ti** *pronoun*
  1 you
    detrás de ti behind you
    Se olvidaron de ti. They forgot about you.
    A mí no me dijo nada. ¿Y a ti? He hasn't told me anything. - Has he told you?
  2 to you
    Te lo dio a ti. He gave it to you.
  3 ¿A ti te gusta? Do you like it?
    ¿A ti qué te parece? What do you think?
  4 ti mismo, ti misma yourself
    Sabes cuidar de ti misma. You can look after yourself.

  > **WORD TIP** ti is never written with an accent.

ᶘ la **tía** *fem noun*
  aunt

tibio *masc adjective*, **tibia** *fem*
  lukewarm

ᶘ el **tiburón** *masc noun*
  shark

tiembla, **tiemblo**, etc *verb* ▷ **temblar**

ᶘ el **tiempo** *masc noun*
  1 time
    al mismo tiempo at the same time
    por un tiempo for a time
    la mayor parte del tiempo most of the time
    Tenemos bastante tiempo. We've got plenty of time.
    Ha pasado mucho tiempo desde entonces. It's been a long time since then.
    Hace mucho tiempo que no la veo. I haven't seen her for a long time.
    ¿Cuánto tiempo hace que se fueron? How long ago did they go?
  2 (in expressions) a tiempo on time
    llegar a tiempo to be on time

¿Cada cuánto tiempo? How often?
cada cierto tiempo every so often
a su debido tiempo in due course
en aquellos tiempos in those days
trabajar a tiempo completo to work full time
trabajar a tiempo parcial to work part time

  3 weather
    el pronóstico del tiempo the weather forecast
    Nos hizo buen tiempo. We had nice weather.
    El tiempo fue espantoso. The weather was dreadful.

  4 half (in matches)
    el primer tiempo the first half
    el segundo tiempo the second half

  5 (Grammar) tense
  • el **tiempo libre** spare time

ᶘ la **tienda** *fem noun*
  1 shop
    una tienda de discos a record shop
    una tienda de recuerdos a souvenir shop
  • la **tienda de comestibles** grocer's
  • la **tienda de campaña** tent

tiendo, **tiendes**, etc *verb* ▷ **tender**

tierno *masc adjective*, **tierna** *fem*
  1 tender
  2 affectionate

ᶘ la **tierra** *fem noun*
  1 land
    viajar por tierra to travel overland
    tomar tierra to land (aeroplanes)
  2 earth, soil
  3 ground
  4 la Tierra the Earth (the planet)
    volver a la Tierra to return to Earth
  5 homeland
    volver a su tierra to go back to your homeland
  • la **tierra adentro** inland
  • la **tierra firme** solid ground

el **tiesto** *masc noun*
  flowerpot

ᶘ el **tigre** *masc noun*
  tiger

ᶘ las **tijeras** *plural fem noun*
  scissors
  un par de tijeras, unas tijeras a pair of scissors

a
b
c
d
e
f
g
h
i
j
k
l
m
n
ñ
o
p
q
r
s
t
u
v
w
x
y
z

♂ el **timbre** *masc noun*
   bell, **doorbell**
   tocar el timbre to ring the bell

♂ **tímido** *masc adjective*, **tímida** *fem*
  1 **shy**
  2 **timid**

la **tina** *fem noun*
  (*Latin America*) **bathtub**

la **tinta** *fem noun*
  ink

♂ **tinto** *masc adjective & masc noun*
  un vino tinto a red wine
  Es un tinto de la Rioja. It's a red wine from
  the Rioja.

la **tintorería** *fem noun*
  dry cleaner's

tiña, **tiñeron**, **tiño**, **tiñó**, **etc** *verb* ▷ **teñir**

♂ el **tío** *masc noun*
  1 **uncle**
  2 mis tíos my uncles, my aunt and uncle
  3 (*informal*) **guy**, **bloke**
  ¡Qué tío más pesado! What a bore that guy
  is!

♂ el **tiovivo** *masc noun*
  merry-go-round

típico *masc adjective*, **típica** *fem*
  1 **typical**
  2 **traditional**
  un plato típico de la región a traditional
  regional dish

♂ el **tipo** *masc noun*
  1 **type**
  coches de todo tipo cars of all types
  Me gusta este tipo de trabajo. I like this
  type of work.
  2 **figure**, **physique**
  Tiene buen tipo. She's got a good figure.
  3 (*informal*) **guy**, **bloke**
  • el **tipo de cambio** exchange rate
  • el **tipo de interés** interest rate

los **tirantes** *plural masc noun*
  braces

♂ **tirar** *verb* [17]
  1 **to throw**
  tirar algo al suelo to throw something on
  the floor
  2 tirarle algo a alguien to throw something
  to somebody, to throw something at
  somebody
  Tírame ese boli. Throw me that pen.
  Me tiró una piedra. He threw a stone at me.

  3 **to throw away**, **to throw out** (*as rubbish*)
  tirar algo a la basura to through something
  out
  Hay que tirar esos papeles. We need to
  throw those papers away.
  4 **to pull**
  'Tirar' 'Pull' (*on a door*)
  Tira un poco más. Pull a bit harder.
  5 tirar de algo to pull something
  Tira de la cuerda cuando yo te diga. Pull the
  rope when I tell you.
  6 **to shoot**
  tirar a puerta to shoot at goal
  tirar una flecha to shoot an arrow
  tirar una bomba to drop a bomb
  7 **to knock over**
  Tiré la taza sin querer. I knocked the cup
  over by accident.
  8 tirar abajo to knock down
  tirar la puerta abajo. to knock the door
  down.
  Tiraron el cine abajo. They knocked the
  cinema.
  9 **to get by**
  Vamos tirando. We're getting by.

tirarse *reflexive verb* [17]
  tirarse al suelo to throw yourself to the
  ground
  tirarse al río to jump into the river
  tirarse al agua del trampolín to dive into
  the water from the diving board
  tirarse en paracaídas to parachute, to bale
  out

♂ la **tirita** *fem noun*
  sticking plaster

tiritar *verb* [17]
  to shiver
  tiritar de frío to shiver with cold

el **tiro** *masc noun*
  1 **shot**
  disparar un tiro to fire a shot
  Se oyeron tiros. Shots were heard.
  Lo mataron de un tiro. They shot him dead.
  2 **shot** (*in sport*)
  • el **tiro al blanco** target shooting
  • el **tiro a portería** shot at goal
  • el **tiro libre** free kick

el **tirón** *masc noun*
  1 **pull**
  darle un tirón a algo to pull something
  Le dio un tirón de pelo. She pulled her hair.
  2 (*informal*) de un tirón in one go
  Se leyó el libro de un tirón. She read the
  book in one go.

a
b
c
d
e
f
g
h
i
j
k
l
m
n
ñ
o
p
q
r
s
t
u
v
w
x
y
z

títere

el **títere** *masc noun*
1 **puppet**
2 **títeres** puppet show

el **titular** *masc noun*
1 **headline** (*in newspaper*)
2 **account holder** (*in bank, etc*)

ʃ el **título** *masc noun*
1 **title** (*of a book*)
2 **heading** (*of a document*)
• el **título universitario** university degree

ʃ la **tiza** *fem noun*
chalk
una tiza a piece of chalk

ʃ la **toalla** *fem noun*
towel

ʃ el **tobillo** *masc noun*
ankle

el **tobogán** *masc noun*
1 **slide** (*in a park*)
2 **emergency chute** (*from a plane*)
3 **toboggan**

ʃ el **tocadiscos** *masc noun,*
pl: los **tocadiscos**
record player

ʃ el **tocador** *masc noun*
dressing table

ʃ **tocar** *verb* [31]
1 **to touch**
'No tocar' 'Do not touch' (*in a shop*)
Me tocó el hombro. He touched me on the shoulder.
2 **to play** (*an instrument*)
tocar el piano to play the piano
3 **to ring**
Tienes que tocar el timbre. You must ring the bell.
4 **tocarle a alguien hacer algo** to be somebody's turn to do something
Te toca jugar. It's your turn to play.
5 **tocarle a alguien algo** to win something
Les ha tocado la lotería. They've won the lottery.
Me ha tocado el primer premio. I've won the first prize.

tocarse *reflexive verb* [31]
to touch
Se tocó la cabeza. He touched his head.
Los dos cables se están tocando. The two cables are touching.

ʃ el **tocino** *masc noun*
bacon

todo

ʃ **todavía** *adverb*
1 **still**
Todavía queda suficiente pan. There's still enough bread.
Todavía nos vemos. We still see each other.
2 **yet**
Todavía no han llegado. They haven't arrived yet.
No salgas todavía. Don't go out yet.
3 **even**
todavía más temprano even earlier
Quieren todavía más. They want even more.

ʃ **todo** *masc adjective,* **toda** *fem*
▷ see **todo** *noun, pron*
1 **all**
todos mis amigos all my friends
todas las canciones all the songs
viajar por todo el mundo to travel all over the world
2 **whole**
toda la mañana the whole morning
toda la semana the whole week
Se comió toda la tarta. She ate the whole cake.
3 **every**
Vienen todos los días. They come every day.
Revisamos todos los cajones. We checked all the drawers.
4 (*for emphasis*) Estaba toda nerviosa. She was all nervous.
Está todo roto. It's completely broken.
Siga todo recto. Carry straight on.
5 (*in expressions*) a toda velocidad at top speed
Fue toda una aventura. It was quite an adventure.

el **todo** *masc noun* ▷ see **todo** *adj, pron*
el todo the whole

ʃ **todo**, **toda** *pronoun* ▷ see **todo** *adj, noun*
1 **everything**
a pesar de todo despite everything
Se lo conté todo. I told him everything.
2 **all**
todo o nada all or nothing
3 **todos, todas** everybody
Vinieron todos. Everybody came.
Todos estábamos de acuerdo. We were all in agreement.
4 (*in expressions*) ante todo, la seguridad ante todo security above all else
de todo, Tienen de todo. They've got all sorts of things.
sobre todo, Sobre todo no te olvides de los billetes. Above all, don't forget the tickets.

Spanish-English

a b c d e f g h i j k l m n ñ o p q r s t u v w x y z

ʃ indicates key words   309

♂ tomar verb [17]
1 **to take**
  tomar el autobús to take the bus
  Tomamos la primera calle a la izquierda.
  We took the first street on the left.
  Toma, tu billete. Here, here's your ticket.
  La tomó de la mano. She took her hand.
  Hay que tomar las pastillas después de
  comer. You must take the tablets after
  eating.
  tomar algo en serio to take something
  seriously
  No toma nada en serio. He doesn't
  anything seriously.
2 **to have** (something to drink, to eat)
  tomar el desayuno to have breakfast
  Voy a tomar postre. I'm going to have a
  dessert.
  ¿Te apetece tomar algo? Would you like
  something to drink?
  ¿Quieres tomar un café? Would you like a
  coffee?
3 tomar el sol to sunbathe
4 tomar el aire to get some fresh air

tomarse reflexive verb [17]
  to take
  tomarse unos días libres to take some
  days off
  Nos tomamos un día para visitar
  Granada. We took a day out to visit
  Granada.
  Se tomó la medicina. She took the
  medicine.

♂ el tomate masc noun
  tomato
  una salsa de tomate a tomato sauce

♀ la tonelada fem noun
  ton

♀ la tónica fem noun
  tonic water

el tono masc noun
1 **tone**
  en tono serio in a serious tone
2 **shade**
  telas de tonos suaves materials in soft
  shades
  • el **tono de llamada** ring tone
  • el **tono de marcar** dial tone
  • el **tono de ocupado** engaged tone

♀ la tontería fem noun
  decir tonterías to talk nonsense
  ¡Qué tonterías dices! What nonsense you
  talk!

Se pelearon por una tontería. They fell out
over something very silly.

♂ tonto masc adjective, **tonta** fem
  ▷ see **tonto** noun
  silly
  una pregunta tonta a silly question

♂ el tonto masc noun, la **tonta** fem
  ▷ see **tonto** adj
  idiot

el topo masc noun
  mole (the animal)

el torbellino masc noun
  whirlwind

♂ torcer verb [41]
1 **to turn**
  torcer la cabeza to turn your head
  torcer la esquina to turn the corner
  Tuerce a la derecha al final de la calle. Turn
  right at the end of the road.
2 **to wring out** (clothes)

torcerse reflexive verb [41]
  to twist
  torcerse el tobillo to twist your ankle

torcido masc adjective, **torcida** fem
1 **crooked**
  una línea torcida a crooked line
  El cuadro está torcido. The picture's
  crooked.
2 **twisted**
3 **bent**

♂ el torero masc noun, la **torera** fem noun
  bullfighter

♀ la tormenta fem noun
  storm
  • la **tormenta de nieve** snowstorm

♂ el tornado masc noun
  tornado

el torneo masc noun
  tournament

el tornillo masc noun
  screw

♂ el toro masc noun
1 **bull**
2 los toros bullfighting
  ir a los toros to go to a bullfight
  ¿Te gustan los toros? Do you like
  bullfighting?

la toronja fem noun
  (Latin America) **grapefruit**

torpe *masc & fem adjective*
1 **clumsy**
2 **awkward**

ᵹ la **torre** *fem noun*
1 **tower**
2 **rook**, **castle** (*in chess*)
• la **torre de alta tensión** pylon
• la **torre de control** control tower

ᵹ la **torta** *fem noun*
1 **cake**
2 (*informal*) **slap**
Le dio una torta. She slapped him.

ᵹ la **tortilla** *fem noun*
1 **omelette**
2 (*Mexico*) **tortilla** (*made of corn flour*)
• la **tortilla española** Spanish omelette (*with potatoes*)
• la **tortilla francesa** French omelette (*with eggs only*)

la **tortuga** *fem noun*
1 **tortoise**
2 **turtle**

torturar *verb* [17]
to torture

la **tos** *fem noun*
cough
Tengo tos. I've got a cough.

toser *verb* [18]
to cough

ᵹ la **tostada** *fem noun*
una tostada a piece of toast
Tomo tostadas para desayunar. I have toast for breakfast.

el **tostador** *masc noun*
toaster

la **tostadora** *fem noun*
toaster

ᵹ **tostar** *verb* [24]
1 **to toast** (*bread*)
2 **to roast** (*coffee*)

tostarse *reflexive verb* [24]
to tan, **to go brown**

ᵹ **total** *masc & fem adjective* ▷ see **total** noun
1 **total**
el precio total the total price
2 (*when summing up*) **so**
Total, no lo sabemos aún. So, we still don't know.

el **total** *masc noun* ▷ see **total** *adj*
total
¿Cuánto es el total? What's the total?

Son mil quinientas en total. It's one thousand five hundred in total.

la **totalidad** *fem noun*
la totalidad del colegio the whole school
la totalidad de los alumnos all the pupils

tóxico *masc adjective*, **tóxica** *fem*
toxic
residuos tóxicos toxic waste

el **toxicómano** *masc noun*, la **toxicómana** *fem*
drug addict

ᵹ **trabajador** *masc adjective*, **trabajadora** *fem* ▷ see **trabajador** noun
hard-working
Son muy trabajadores. They are very hard-working.

ᵹ el **trabajador** *masc noun*, la **trabajadora** *fem* ▷ see **trabajador** adj
worker

ᵹ **trabajar** *verb* [17]
to work
trabajar a tiempo completo to work full time
trabajar a tiempo parcial to work part time
Mi padre trabaja en un banco. My father works in a bank.
Elena trabaja de camarera. Elena works as a waitress.
Trabaja para una empresa americana. She works for an American company.

ᵹ el **trabajo** *masc noun*
1 **work**
estar sin trabajo to be out of work
vivir cerca del trabajo to live close to where you work
Costó mucho trabajo encontrarlo. It was hard work finding it.
2 **job**
buscar trabajo to look for a job
quedarse sin trabajo to lose your job
3 **essay**
un trabajo sobre el cambio climatológico an essay on climate change
• el **trabajo a tiempo completo** full-time work
• el **trabajo a tiempo parcial** part-time work
• el **trabajo fijo** steady job
• los **trabajos manuales** handicrafts

el **trabalenguas** *masc noun*, *pl*: los **trabalenguas**
tongue twister

el **tractor** *masc noun*
tractor

ᵹ indicates key words   311

la **tradición** *fem noun*
tradition

tradicional *masc & fem adjective*
traditional

la **traducción** *fem noun*
translation

traducir *verb* [60]
to translate
Tradúzcalo al inglés. Translate it into
English.

el **traductor** *masc noun*, la **traductora**
fem
translator

traduje, **traduzca**, **traduzco**, etc *verb* ▷
traducir

ƒ **traer** *verb* [42]
1 to bring
Trae a Enrique. You bring Enrique.
He traído la comida. I've brought the food.
La trajo a la estación. He brought her to the
station.
Me trae un café con leche, por favor. I'd like
a white coffee, please.
2 to have
El periódico trae un artículo sobre Ávila.
The newspaper has an article on Ávila in it.

el & la **traficante** *masc & fem noun*
dealer
• el **traficante de armas** arms dealer
• el **traficante de drogas** drugs dealer

ƒ el **tráfico** *masc noun*
1 traffic
2 trade
• el **tráfico de armas** arms trade
• el **tráfico de drogas** drug dealing

ƒ el & la **tragaperras** *masc & fem noun, pl:*
tragaperras
(*informal*) **slot machine**

tragar *verb* [28]
to swallow

tragarse *reflexive verb* [28]
to swallow
Se tragó el chicle. He swallowed his
chewing gum.

la **tragedia** *fem noun*
tragedy

trágico *masc adjective*, **trágica** *fem*
tragic

la **traición** *fem noun*
1 betrayal
2 una **traición** an act of treachery

el **traidor** *masc noun*, la **traidora** *fem*
traitor

ƒ **traiga**, **traigo**, **trajo**, etc *verb* ▷ traer

ƒ el **traje** *masc noun* ▷ see **traer** *verb*
1 suit
2 costume (*national, regional*)
• el **traje de baño** swimsuit, swimming
trunks
• el **traje de luces** bullfighter's costume
• el **traje típico** traditional dress

la **trampa** *fem noun*
trap
caer en la trampa to fall into the trap

ƒ el **tramposo** *masc noun*, la **tramposa** *fem*
cheat

el **trampolín** *masc noun*
1 springboard, diving board
2 trampoline
3 ski jump

el **tranquillo** *masc noun*
knack
cogerle el tranquillo a algo to get the knack
of something
Pronto le cogerás el tranquillo. You'll soon
get the knack of it.

ƒ **tranquilo** *masc adjective*, **tranquila** *fem*
1 quiet
un barrio tranquilo a quiet neighbourhood
2 calm
un ambiente tranquilo a calm environment
Es muy tranquilo. He's very calm.
Está bastante tranquila ante el examen.
She's quite calm about the exam.
¡Tranquilo! Keep calm!

el **transbordador** *masc noun*
ferry
• el **transbordador espacial** space shuttle

transbordar *verb* [17]
1 to transfer (*luggage, goods*)
2 to change (*trains*)

el **transbordo** *masc noun*
change
hacer transbordo to change (*trains, buses*)
Haz transbordo en Sol. Change at Sol.

el & la **transeúnte** *masc & fem noun*
passer-by

ƒ el **tránsito** *masc noun*
traffic
Hay mucho tránsito a esa hora. There's a
lot of traffic at that time.

la **transferencia** *fem noun*
  transfer
- la **transferencia bancaria** bank transfer

transformar *verb* [17]
1 to transform
2 to turn into
   Transformaron el garaje en una oficina.
   They turned the garage into an office.

transformarse *reflexive verb* [17]
   to be turned into

la **transfusión** *fem noun*
   transfusion

la **transmisión** *fem noun*
   broadcast
- la **transmisión en diferido** pre-recorded broadcast
- la **transmisión en directo** live broadcast

la **transparencia** *fem noun*
1 transparency
2 slide (*in photography, for OHP*)

transparente *masc & fem adjective*
   transparent

transportar *verb* [17]
   to transport, to carry (*people, goods*)

ℰ el **transporte** *masc noun*
   transport

ℰ el **tranvía** *masc noun*
   tram

el **trapo** *masc noun*
   cloth
- el **trapo de cocina** tea towel
- el **trapo del polvo** duster

ℰ **tras** *preposition*
1 after
   uno tras otra one after another
   hora tras hora hour after hour
   Tras despedirme, subí al autocar. After saying goodbye, I got into the coach.
2 behind
   La puerta se cerró tras ella. The door closed behind her.

ℰ **trasero** *masc adjective*, **trasera** *fem*
1 back
   la puerta trasera the back door
2 rear
   la rueda trasera the rear wheel

el **traslado** *masc noun*
   transfer (*of an employee*)

trasnochar *verb* [17]
   to stay up late

el **trasplante** *masc noun*
   transplant
   un trasplante de hígado a liver transplant

el **tratado** *masc noun*
   treaty

el **tratamiento** *masc noun*
1 treatment
2 processing

ℰ **tratar** *verb* [17]
1 to treat
   Me tratan muy bien. They treat me very well.
   Trátalo con cuidado. Treat it carefully.
   Hay que tratar el agua. The water must be treated.
2 (*speaking to somebody*) **tratar a alguien de usted** to speak to somebody using the 'usted' form
   tratar a alguien de tú to speak to somebody using the 'tú' form
3 **tratar de hacer algo** to try to do something
   Tratamos de ayudarla. We tried to help her.
   Trata de llamarme antes de las cinco. Try to call me before five.
4 **tratar de algo** to be about something
   ¿De qué trata la película? What's the film about?

tratarse *reflexive verb* [17]
   tratarse de algo to be about something
   Se trata de Javier. It's about Javier.
   Se trata de la vida en Hollywod. It's about life in Hollywood.

ℰ **través** *in phrases*
   a través de algo through something, across something
   a través del cristal through the window
   a través de los campos across the fields
   Lo encontré a través de Internet. I found it on the Internet.

travieso *masc adjective*, **traviesa** *fem*
   naughty

el **trayecto** *masc noun*
   journey, route
   final de trayecto end of the journey (*on public transport*)
   Hace el trayecto Málaga-Granada. It does the Málaga-Granada route.

trazar *verb* [22]
1 to trace
2 to draw (*a map*)
3 to draw up (*a plan*)

a
b
c
d
e
f
g
h
i
j
k
l
m
n
ñ
o
p
q
r
s
t
u
v
w
x
y
z

ℰ indicates key words

♂ **trece** *number*
1 **thirteen**
Tiene trece años. She's thirteen (years old).
2 **thirteenth** (*in dates*)
el trece de mayo the thirteenth of May

♂ **treinta** *number*
1 **thirty**
Tiene treinta años. She's thirty (years old).
treinta y siete thirty-seven
2 **thirtieth** (*in dates*)
el treinta de mayo the thirtieth of May

tremendo *masc adjective*, **tremenda** *fem*
1 **tremendous**
una tremenda victoria a tremendous victory
una tremenda derrota a tremendous defeat
2 **naughty**
un niño tremendo a naughty boy

♂ el **tren** *masc noun*
train
el tren a Barcelona the train to Barcelona
coger el tren to catch the train
viajar en tren to travel by train
• el **tren de aterrizaje** landing gear
• el **tren de alta velocidad** high-speed train
• el **tren de cercanías** local train
• el **tren directo** through train
• el **tren de largo recorrido** long-distance train
• el **tren de montaje** assembly line

 tren

El AVE (tren de alta velocidad) viaja a 350 kilómetros por hora y si llega con más de 5 minutos de retraso se le devuelve el importe del billete al viajero.

trepar *verb* [17]
to climb
trepar a un árbol to climb a tree

♂ **tres** *number*
1 **three**
Tiene tres años. She's three (years old).
2 **third** (*in dates*)
el tres de mayo the third of May
3 **three** (*in clock time*)
Son las tres. It's three o'clock.

♂ el **trescientos**, **trescientas** *number*
three hundred
trescientos veinte three hundred and twenty

♂ el **triángulo** *masc noun*
triangle

la **tribu** *fem noun*
tribe

el **tribunal** *masc noun*
1 **court**
2 **the judges** (*in a competition*)

el **trigo** *masc noun*
wheat

los **trillizos** *plural masc noun*, las **trillizas** *plural fem noun*
triplets

♂ el **trimestre** *masc noun*
1 **term** (*in school*)
2 **quarter** (*three months*)

el **trineo** *masc noun*
sledge

Trinidad *fem noun*
Trinidad

trinitense *masc & fem adjective & noun*
1 **Trinidadian**
2 un & una trinitense Trinidadian

WORD TIP Adjectives and nouns for nationality and regional origin do not have capital letters in Spanish.

triniteño *masc adjective & noun*, **triniteña** *fem adjective & noun*
1 **Trinidadian**
2 un triniteño, una triniteña Trinidadian

WORD TIP Adjectives and nouns for nationality and regional origin do not have capital letters in Spanish.

♂ la **tripa** *fem noun*
1 (*informal*) **tummy**
2 (*informal*) **belly**
3 **tripas** guts

triple *masc & fem adjective* ▷ see **triple** *noun*
triple

el **triple** *masc noun* ▷ see **triple** *adj*
el triple del precio original three times the original price
Es el triple de ancho. It's three times as wide.

triplicarse *reflexive verb* [31]
to triple
El precio se ha triplicado. The price has tripled.

la **tripulación** *fem noun*
crew

el & la **tripulante** *masc & fem noun*
crew member

ꝶ **triste** *masc & fem adjective*
1 sad
2 gloomy

ꝶ la **tristeza** *fem noun*
sadness

triunfar *verb* [17]
to triumph

el **triunfo** *masc noun*
1 victory
2 triumph

trivial *masc & fem adjective*
trivial

el **trofeo** *masc noun*
trophy

el **trombón** *masc noun*
trombone

la **trompeta** *fem noun*
trumpet

tronar *verb* [24]
to thunder

el **tronco** *masc noun*
1 trunk
2 log

el **trono** *masc noun*
throne

tropezar *verb* [25]
to trip
tropezar con algo to trip over something
Tropezó con una piedra. He tripped over a stone.

tropezarse *reflexive verb* [25]
tropezarse con alguien to bump into someone
Nos tropezamos con Paco en la calle. We bumped into Paco in the street.

el **trópico** *masc noun*
tropic

tropiece, tropiezo, etc *verb* ▷ **tropezar**

ꝶ **trotar** *verb* [17]
to trot

ꝶ el **trozo** *masc noun*
piece
un trozo de tela a piece of cloth
un trozo de queso a piece of cheese

ꝶ la **trucha** *fem noun*
trout

el **truco** *masc noun*
trick
un truco de cartas a card trick

ꝶ el **trueno** *masc noun*
thunder clap
Hubo truenos. There was thunder.

ꝶ **tu** *adjective*
your
tu casa your house
tus amigos your friends

ꝶ **tú** *pronoun* ▷ see **tu** *adj*
1 you
Tú sí lo sabes. You do know it.
2 tú mismo, tú misma yourself
Hazlo tú mismo. Do it yourself.
3 tratar a alguien de tú to speak to somebody using the 'tú' form

> **WORD TIP** tú is used to refer to a person you know well. ▷ **usted, vosotros**

ꝶ el **tubo** *masc noun*
tube
• el tubo de escape exhaust pipe

ꝶ la **tuerca** *fem noun*
nut

ꝶ **tuerza, tuerzo, etc** *verb* ▷ **torcer**

tuesta, tueste, tuesto, etc *verb* ▷ **tostar**

el **tulipán** *masc noun*
tulip

ꝶ la **tumba** *fem noun*
1 grave
2 tomb

ꝶ **tumbar** *verb* [17]
1 to knock down
tumbar a alguien de un puñetazo to floor somebody (with a punch)
2 to lay down

tumbarse *reflexive verb* [17]
to lie down
Se tumbó en el sofá. He lay down on the sofa.

ꝶ la **tumbona** *fem noun*
deckchair

tunecino *masc adjective & noun*, **tunecina** *fem adjective & noun*
1 Tunisian
2 un tunecino, una tunecina Tunisian

> **WORD TIP** Adjectives and nouns for nationality and regional origin do not have capital letters in Spanish.

ꝶ el **túnel** *masc noun*
tunnel

Túnez *masc noun*
Tunisia

a
b
c
d
e
f
g
h
i
j
k
l
m
n
ñ
o
p
q
r
s
t
u
v
w
x
y
z

el **turbante** *masc noun*
　turban

turco *masc adjective & noun*, **turca** *fem adjective & noun*
1 Turkish
2 un turco, una turca Turk
　el turco Turkish (*the language*)

> **WORD TIP** Adjectives and nouns for nationality, regional origin, and language do not have capital letters in Spanish.

ℰ el **turismo** *masc noun*
1 tourism
　la oficina de turismo the tourist office
　hacer turismo to go sightseeing
2 saloon car

ℰ **turístico** *masc adjective*, **turística** *fem*
　tourist
　una ruta turística a tourist route

ℰ el & la **turista** *masc & fem noun*
　tourist

turnarse *reflexive verb* [17]
　to take turns

ℰ el **turno** *masc noun*
1 turn
　tocarle el turno a alguien to be somebody's turn
　Te toca el turno a ti. It's your turn.
2 shift
　hacer turnos de siete horas to work seven-hour shifts
　・ el **turno de noche** night shift

Turquía *fem noun*
　Turkey

ℰ el **turrón** *masc noun*
　nougat (*traditionally eaten at Christmas*)

tutear *verb* [17]
　tutear a alguien to speak to somebody using the 'tú' form

tutearse *reflexive verb* [17]
　to use the 'tú' form to each other

ℰ el **tutor** *masc noun*, la **tutora** *fem*
1 class teacher
2 guardian

ℰ **tuvo, tuvieron, tuviste, etc** *verb* ▷ tener

ℰ **tuyo** *masc adjective*, **tuya** *fem*
　▷ see **tuyo** *pron*
　yours
　Esto es tuyo. This is yours.
　Estos son tuyos. These are yours.
　un amigo tuyo a friend of yours
　unos amigos tuyos some friends of yours
　una vecina tuya a neighbour of yours
　unos vecinos tuyos some neighbours of yours

> **WORD TIP** tuyo, tuya agrees with the thing you have or own: amigos, vecina, etc above. tuyo, tuya goes after the noun.

ℰ **tuyo, tuya** *pronoun* ▷ see **tuyo** *adj*
　yours
　El tuyo es verde., La tuya es verde. Yours is green.
　Los tuyos son mejores., Las tuyas son mejores. Yours are better.

> **WORD TIP** el tuyo, la tuya agrees with the thing you have or own.

U u

u *conjunction*
or
plata u oro silver or the gold
WORD TIP The usual word for *or*, *o*, becomes *u* before words beginning with *o-* or *ho-*.

ubicado *masc adjective*, **ubicada** *fem*
situated

Ucrania *fem noun*
Ukraine

ucraniano *masc adjective, noun*,
ucraniana *fem adjective, noun*
1 **Ukrainian**
2 **un ucraniano, una ucraniana** Ukrainian
el ucraniano Ukrainian (*the language*)
WORD TIP Adjectives and nouns for nationality, regional origin, and language do not have capital letters in Spanish.

Ud. *abbreviation*
you
WORD TIP singular polite form; short for *usted*

Uds. *abbreviation*
you
WORD TIP plural polite form; short for *ustedes*

la **UE** *fem noun*
(= *Unión Europea*) **EU** (*European Union*)

la **úlcera** *fem noun*
ulcer

últimamente *adverb*
lately

ᵟ **último** *masc adjective*, **última** *fem*
▷ see **último** *noun*
1 **last**
Llegó último. He came in last.
El último día fuimos a la playa. On the last day we went to the beach.
2 **latest**
su última película her latest film
lo último en equipo audio the latest in audio equipment
3 **bottom**
el último alumno de la clase the bottom student in the class
WORD TIP *último*, *última* goes before the noun.

ᵟ el **último** *masc noun*, la **última** *fem*
▷ see **último** *adj*
el último the last one
el último de la serie the last in the series

Ésta es la última que queda. This is the last one left.

el **ultramarinos** *masc noun*,
pl: los **ultramarinos**
grocer's shop

ᵟ **un** *masc determiner*, **una** *fem determiner*
a, an
un hombre a man
una manzana an apple
Tiene un gato. She has a cat.
un ala a wing
un hacha an axe
WORD TIP *un* is used instead of *una*, with fem nouns starting with stressed *a* or *ha*. ▷ **unos**

ᵟ **un** *number* ▷ see **un** *determiner*
one, a, an
un año one year, a year
Lleva un año abierto. It's been open for one year.
WORD TIP *un* means *one* before masc singular nouns. ▷ **uno** *number*

ᵟ **único** *masc adjective*, **única** *fem*
▷ see **único** *noun*
1 **unique**
una oportunidad única a unique opportunity
2 **only**
su único hijo her only child
Es hija única. She's an only child.
3 **talla única** one size

ᵟ el **único** *masc noun*, la **única** *fem*
▷ see **único** *adjective*
el único, la única the only one
El único que funciona. The only one that works.

la **unidad** *fem noun*
1 **unit**
2 **unity**
• la **unidad de cuidados intensivos**, la **unidad de vigilancia intensiva** intensive care unit

unido *masc adjective*, **unida** *fem*
1 **united**
2 **close** (*family, community*)
Las dos familias están muy unidas. The two families are very close.

a
b
c
d
e
f
g
h
i
j
k
l
m
n
ñ
o
p
q
r
s
t
u
v
w
x
y
z

♂ **uniforme** *masc & fem adjective*
▷ see **uniforme** *noun*
1 **uniform** (*size, speed*)
2 **even** (*surface*)

♂ el **uniforme** *masc noun*
▷ see **uniforme** *adj*
uniform

la **Unión Europea** *fem noun*
European Union

unir *verb* [19]
1 **to unite** (*groups of people*)
2 **to join** (*buildings*)
3 **to combine** (*qualities*)
El diseño une la elegancia con la eficacia.
The design combines elegance and
efficiency.

unirse *reflexive verb* [19]
1 **to unite** (*workers, employees*)
2 **to merge** (*organizations*)

♂ la **universidad** *fem noun*
university
ir a la universidad to go to university
estar en la universidad to be at university
• la **universidad a distancia** open university
• la **universidad laboral** technical college

universitario *masc adjective*,
universitaria *fem*
▷ see **universitario** *noun*
university
profesores universitarios university
teachers

el **universitario** *masc noun*, la
universitaria *fem*
▷ see **universitario** *adj*
university student

el **universo** *masc noun*
universe

uno, una *number* ▷ see **uno** *pronoun*
1 **one**
un hombre one man
una chica one girl
Compré sólo uno. I bought only one.
Hay una razón. There is one reason.
2 **first** (*in dates*)
el uno de enero the first of January
3 la una one o'clock
Es la una. It's one o'clock.
Llegaron a la una. They arrived at one
o'clock.

WORD TIP uno becomes un before a masculine
singular noun. ▷ **un**

uno, una *pronoun* ▷ see **uno** *number*
1 **one**
una para ti one for you
de uno en uno one by one

unos, unas *adjective*
unos, unas some, a few
Unos lo saben y otros no. Some know and
some don't.
Compré unos sobres. I bought some
envelopes.
Se quedarán unas horas. They will stay for a
few hours. ▷ **un, una, uno, una**

la **uña** *fem noun*
nail (*of fingers, toes*)
una uña del dedo del pie a toe nail

la **urbanización** *fem noun*
housing estate

urbano *masc adjective*, **urbana** *fem*
urban

la **urgencia** *fem noun*
1 **urgency**
2 (*in hospitals*) la sala de urgencias the
accident and emergency ward
'Urgencias' 'Accident and Emergency'

♂ **urgente** *masc & fem adjective*
1 **urgent**
2 **express** (*letters*)

urgentemente *adverb*
urgently
Quiere verte urgentemente. She wants to
see you urgently.

Uruguay *masc noun*
Uruguay

uruguayo *masc adjective & noun*,
uruguaya *fem adjective & noun*
1 **Uruguayan**
2 un uruguayo, una uruguaya Uruguayan

WORD TIP Adjectives and nouns for nationality
and regional origin do not have capital letters in
Spanish.

usado *masc adjective*, **usada** *fem*
1 **used**
2 **second-hand**
ropa usada second-hand clothes

♂ **usar** *verb* [17]
1 **to use**
Hay que usar aceite. You have to use oil.
2 **to wear** (*clothes, perfume*)
¿Qué perfume usas? What perfume do you
use?

el **uso** *masc noun*
  use
  instrucciones de uso instructions for use

ⓖ **usted** *pronoun*
  1 you
  Usted sí lo sabe. You do know it.
  2 usted mismo, usted misma yourselves
  Hágalo usted mismo., Hágalo usted misma. Do it yourself.
  3 tratar a alguien de usted to speak to somebody using the 'usted' form

  WORD TIP *usted, ustedes* are the polite forms for *you.* ▷ **tú, vosotros**

ⓖ **ustedes** *pronoun*
  you (*polite form: to more than one person*)
  ustedes mismos, ustedes mismas yourselves

usual *masc & fem adjective*
  usual

el **usuario** *masc noun*, la **usuaria** *fem*
  user

el **utensilio** *masc noun*
  1 tool
  2 utensil

ⓖ **útil** *masc & fem adjective*
  useful

ⓖ **utilizar** *verb* [22]
  to use
  Lo utilizan para mantenerse en contacto They use it to keep in touch.
  Se utiliza para limpiar ... It's used for cleaning ...

ⓖ la **uva** *fem noun*
  grape
  las uvas de la suerte the twelve grapes (*one for each month of the year*) eaten traditionally in Spain at midnight on New Year's Eve
  tomar las uvas to eat grapes (*at midnight on New Year's Eve*)

a
b
c
d
e
f
g
h
i
j
k
l
m
n
ñ
o
p
q
r
s
t
u
v
w
x
y
z

V v

ƒ la vaca *fem noun*
cow

ƒ las vacaciones *plural fem noun*
holiday, holidays
irse de vacaciones to go on holiday
tomarse unas vacaciones to take a holiday
estar de vacaciones to be on holiday
las vacaciones de Navidad the Christmas
holidays
Pasamos las vacaciones en la Costa Brava.
We spent the holidays on the Costa Brava.

 vacaciones

En España cada trabajador tiene derecho a 20 días
laborales pagados. Además hay 14 días festivos
anuales. Hay 7 nacionales, 5 que se celebran a
nivel regional y 2 días para las fiestas locales.

vaciar *verb* [32]
to empty

vacilar *verb* [17]
1 **to hesitate**
Lo hizo sin vacilar. He did it without
hesitating.
Vacilaba entre quedarse o no. She was
hesitating whether to stay or not.
2 (*informal*) **to fool around**
¡Deja de vacilar! Stop fooling about!
3 (*Latin America*) **to enjoy yourself**

ƒ vacío *masc adjective*, **vacía** *fem*
▷ see **vacío** *noun*
empty
una botella vacía an empty bottle
las calles vacías the empty streets

el vacío *masc noun* ▷ see **vacío** *adj*
vacuum

la vacuna *fem noun*
vaccine

vacunar *verb* [17]
to vaccinate

ƒ el vado *masc noun*
1 **dropped kerb**
2 'Vado Permanente' 'Keep clear'

vagabundo *masc adjective*, **vagabunda**
fem ▷ see **vagabundo** *noun*
un perro vagabundo a stray dog

el vagabundo *masc noun*, **la vagabunda**
fem ▷ see **vagabundo** *adj*
vagrant

vago *masc adjective*, **vaga** *fem*
▷ see **vago** *noun*
1 **vague**
2 **lazy**

el vago *masc noun*, **la vaga** *fem*
▷ see **vago** *adj*
layabout

el vagón *masc noun*
1 **carriage** (*of train*)
2 **wagon**

la vainilla *fem noun*
vanilla

ƒ valdrá, valdré, valdría,
etc *verb* ▷ **valer**

el vale *masc noun* ▷ see **valer** *verb*, **vale** *excl*
1 **voucher**
2 **credit slip**

ƒ vale *exclamation* ▷ see **vale** *noun*,
valer *verb*
okay
'Tú te encargas de las bebidas.'—'¡Vale!.'
'You look after the drinks.'—'Okay!'

valenciano *masc adjective & noun*,
valenciana *fem adjective & noun*
1 **Valencian**
2 un valenciano, una valenciana
Valencian (*person from Valencia*)
el valenciano Valencian (*the language spoken
in Valencia*)

WORD TIP Adjectives and nouns for nationality,
regional origin, and language do not have capital
letters in Spanish.

ƒ valer *verb* [43]
1 **to cost**
¿Cuánto vale? How much is it?
Vale cincuenta euros. It's fifty euros.
2 **to be worth**
Vale bastante dinero. It's worth quite a lot
of money.
3 valer la pena to be worth the trouble
Vale la pena el esfuerzo. It's worth the
effort.
No vale la pena. It's not worth the trouble.
4 **to be valid** (*tickets, coupons, etc*)
5 **to be allowed**
No vale preguntar. You're not allowed to
ask.
Eso no vale. That's not fair.

a
b
c
d
e
f
g
h
i
j
k
l
m
n
ñ
o
p
q
r
s
t
u
v
w
x
y
z

♂ **valga**, **valgo**, etc *verb* ▷ **valer**

válido *masc adjective*, **válida** *fem*
valid

valiente *masc & fem adjective*
brave

valioso *masc adjective*, **valiosa** *fem*
valuable

♂ el **valle** *masc noun*
valley

el **valor** *masc noun*
1 value
2 courage

valorar *verb* [17]
1 **to value** (*goods, advice, etc*)
2 **to assess** (*a situation*)

el **vals** *masc noun*
waltz

vamos *exclamation*
1 ¡Vamos! Come on!!
2 Vamos, ... Well, ...
    ▷ **ir**

el **vandalismo** *masc noun*
vandalism

vanidoso *masc adjective*, **vanidosa** *fem*
vain

vano *masc adjective*, **vana** *fem*
1 futile
Todo fue en vano. It was futile.
2 vain (*person*)

el **vapor** *masc noun*
steam
verduras al vapor steamed vegetables

♂ el **vaquero** *masc noun*
1 cowboy
2 unos vaqueros a pair of jeans

variado *masc adjective*, **variada** *fem*
varied

variar *verb* [32]
to vary (*prices, temperatures*)

la **varicela** *fem noun*
chicken pox

la **variedad** *fem noun*
variety

♂ **varios** *plural masc adjective & pronoun*,
varias *plural fem adjective & pronoun*
several
La vimos varias veces. We saw her several
times.

Hay varios similares. There are several
similar ones.

varón *masc adjective & noun*
male
un hijo varón a male child

varonil *masc & fem adjective*
manly

vasco *masc adjective & noun*, **vasca** *fem*
adjective & noun
1 Basque
2 un vasco, una vasca Basque
el vasco Basque (*the language*)

WORD TIP Adjectives and nouns for nationality,
regional origin, and language do not have capital
letters in Spanish.

la **vasija** *fem noun*
vessel

♂ el **vaso** *masc noun*
glass
un vaso de agua a glass of water
un vaso de papel a paper cup

♂ **vaya** *exclamation*
¡Vaya moto que se ha comprado! Hey, look
a that motorbike he's bought himself!

Vd. *abbreviation*
you

WORD TIP singular polite form; short for *usted*

Vds. *abbreviation*
you

WORD TIP plural polite form; short for *ustedes*

la **vecindad** *fem noun*
neighbourhood

♂ **vecino** *masc adjective*, **vecina** *fem*
    ▷ see **vecino** *noun*
neighbouring
los países vecinos the neighbouring
countries

♂ el **vecino** *masc noun*, la **vecina** *fem*
    ▷ see **vecino** *adj*
1 neighbour
2 local resident

♂ **vegetariano** *masc adjective*,
vegetariana *fem adj*
    ▷ see **vegetariano** *noun*
vegetarian

♂ el **vegetariano** *masc noun*, la
vegetariana *fem*
    ▷ see **vegetariano** *adj*
vegetarian

♂ indicates key words   321

el **vehículo** *masc noun*
  vehicle
- el **vehículo espacial** spacecraft

♂ **veía**, **veían**, etc *verb* ▷ **ver**

veinte *number*
1 **twenty**
  Tiene veinte años. She's twenty (years old).
  los años veinte the twenties (1920-1929)
2 **twentieth** (*in dates*)
  el veinte de diciembre the twentieth of
  December
3 (*in the 24-hour time system*) **a las veinte horas**
  at twenty hundred hours (8 p.m.)

la **vejez** *fem noun*
  old age

♂ la **vela** *fem noun*
1 **candle**
2 **sail**
3 **sailing**
4 **pasar la noche en vela** to be awake all night
  He pasado toda la noche en vela. I've been
  awake all night.

el **velero** *masc noun*
1 **sailing ship**
2 **sailing boat**

♂ la **velocidad** *fem noun*
1 **speed**
  a toda velocidad at top speed
  la velocidad máxima the maximum speed
  disminuir la velocidad to slow down
2 **gear** (*in a car, bicycle*)
  una bici de cinco velocidades a bike with
  five gears

la **vena** *fem noun*
  vein

vencedor *masc noun*, **vencedora** *fem*
noun
  winner

vencer *verb* [44]
1 **vencer a alguien** to defeat somebody
  Vencieron al equipo visitante. They
  defeated the visiting team.
2 **to win**
  Venció dos a uno. He won two to one.
3 **to expire** (*passports, contracts*)

vencido *masc adjective*, **vencida** *fem*
  defeated

la **venda** *fem noun*
  bandage

vendar *verb* [17]
1 **to bandage** (*a wound*)
2 **vendarle los ojos a alguien** to blindfold
  somebody

el **vendaval** *masc noun*
  gale

el **vendedor** *masc noun*, la **vendedora**
fem
1 **seller**
2 **salesman**, **saleswoman**
3 **shop assistant**
- el **vendedor ambulante** street seller

♂ **vender** *verb* [18]
  to sell
  Venden de todo. They sell everything.
  Los venden a cinco euros el kilo. They're
  selling them for five euros a kilo.
  Le he vendido la bicicleta. I've sold him the
  bicycle.
  'Se vende' 'For sale'
  Se venden muy bien. They sell very well.

la **vendimia** *fem noun*
  wine harvest

♂ **vendrá**, **vendré**, **vendría**, etc *verb*
  ▷ **venir**

el **veneno** *masc noun*
  poison

venenoso *masc adjective*, **venenosa** *fem*
  poisonous

venezolano *masc adjective & noun*,
venezolana *fem adjective & noun*
1 **Venezuelan**
2 **un venezolano, una venezolana**
  Venezuelan

WORD TIP Adjectives and nouns for nationality
and regional origin do not have capital letters in
Spanish.

Venezuela *fem noun*
  Venezuela

venga *exclamation* ▷ see **venga** *verb*
  ¡Venga! Come on!

♂ **venga**, **vengo**, etc *verb*
  ▷ see **venga** *excl* ▷ **venir**

la **venganza** *fem noun*
  revenge

vengarse *reflexive verb* [28]
  vengarse de alguien to get one's revenge
  on someone
  Se vengó de él. She got her revenge on
  him.

ᵟ **venir** *verb* [15]

1 to come
Ven a las siete. Come at seven.
Ya vienen. They're coming now..
Vino a verte. He came to see you.
Viene de Italia. It comes from Italy.

2 venir a por algo to come to fetch something
Vengo a por el paquete. I've come to fetch the parcel.
venir por alguien to come to collect somebody
Vengo por ti a las cinco. I'll come for you at five.

3 to be
La noticia viene en la primera página. The news is on the front page.

4 venirle bien a alguien to suit someone
Mañana me viene bien. Tomorrow suits me.
Esa camisa te viene bien. That shirt suits you.
¿Te viene bien quedar en la entrada? Is it okay for you if we meet at the entrance?
Esta parada de metro me viene muy bien. This tube station's very convenient for me.

5 (*in time expressions*) La semana que viene. Next week.
El domingo que viene. Next Sunday.

ᵟ la **venta** *fem noun*
sale
estar en venta to be for sale
Salió a la venta. It went on sale.

la **ventaja** *fem noun*
advantage
las ventajas y desventajas the advantages and disadvantages

ᵟ la **ventana** *fem noun*
window (*of a house*)

ᵟ la **ventanilla** *fem noun*
1 window (*in a train, car*)
2 till (*in a bank*)
3 ticket counter (*for train tickets, cinema tickets*)

la **ventilación** *fem noun*
ventilation

el **ventilador** *masc noun*
fan

la **ventisca** *fem noun*
blizzard

ᵟ **ver** *verb* [16]

1 to see
Los vi ayer. I saw them yesterday.
No lo veo. I can't see it.
No veo nada desde aquí. I can't see anything from here.
No veo bien de lejos. I'm shortsighted.
Ya veo cuál es el problema. I can see the problem now.
Ya veremos lo que hacemos. We'll see what we do.

2 to watch
ver la tele to watch TV
Anoche vimos una película muy buena. We watched a very good film last night.

3 to think
Lo que ha hecho no lo veo bien. I don't think what he's done is right.

4 tener que ver con algo to have something to do with something
Eso no tiene nada que ver. That has nothing to do with it.

5 (*in exclamations*) 'Mira lo que me compré.' —'¿A ver?' 'Look what I've bought.'— 'Let's see?'
A ver. ¿Qué te pasa? Right, what's the matter with you?

verse *reflexive verb* [16]

1 to see yourself
verse en el espejo to see yourself in the mirror

2 to see each other
Nos vemos todos los días. We see each other every day.

3 to meet
Nos vimos ayer. We met yesterday.

el & la **veraneante** *masc & fem noun*
holidaymaker

veranear *verb* [17]
veranear en to spend your summer holidays in
Veranean en la montaña. They spend their summer holidays in the mountains.

ᵟ el **verano** *masc noun*
summer
en verano in summer
el verano pasado last summer
Pasamos las vacaciones de verano en Mallorca. We spend the summer holidays in Mallorca.

veras *in phrase*
de veras
Lo siento de veras. I really am sorry.
¡De veras! Really!

la **verbena** *fem noun*
1 open-air dance
2 festival (*for a town or village's patron saint*)

el **verbo** *masc noun*
(*Grammar*) verb

♂ la **verdad** *fem noun*
1 truth
la pura verdad the absolute truth
Dime la verdad. Tell me the truth.
La verdad es que ... The truth is that ... ▸▸
La verdad, no me acuerdo. I don't remember, honestly.
2 ser verdad to be true
Eso es verdad. That's true.
3 (*in questions*) ¿No te gusta, verdad? You don't like it, do you?
¿Sabes hacerlo, verdad? You know how to do it, don't you?
Sí vienen, ¿verdad? They are coming, aren't they?
4 (*in expressions*) de verdad
un amigo de verdad a real friend
De verdad que no lo quiero. Really, I don't want it.

♂ **verdadero** *masc adjective*, **verdadera** *fem*
1 true
una historia verdadera a true story
su verdadero nombre his true name
2 (*for emphasis*) Es un verdadero idiota. He's a real idiot.

♂ **verde** *masc & fem adjective* ▷ see **verde** *noun*
1 green
una blusa verde oscuro a dark green blouse
Tiene los ojos verdes. She has green eyes.
2 dirty (*story, etc*)
un chiste verde a dirty joke

♂ el **verde** *masc noun* ▷ see **verde** *adj*
1 green
2 los Verdes the Greens (*in politics*)
• el **verde botella** bottle-green

la **verdulería** *fem noun*
greengrocer's

♂ la **verdura** *fem noun*
vegetable
un puesto de verduras a vegetable stall
Las verduras son muy saludables. Vegetables are very healthy.

vergonzoso *masc adjective*, **vergonzosa** *fem*
1 timid (*person*)
2 shameful (*act, behaviour*)

la **vergüenza** *fem noun*
1 shame
Me da vergüenza pensarlo. I'm ashamed to think about it.
¡Qué poca vergüenza tienes! Have you no shame at all?
2 embarrassment
No quiero, me da vergüenza. I don't want to, I'm too embarrassed.
Me da vergüenza hablar en público. I feel embarrassed when I have to speak in public.
¡Qué vergüenza! How embarrassing!
3 disgrace
Es una vergüenza. It's a disgrace.
¡Qué vergüenza! That's terrible.

la **verruga** *fem noun*
1 wart
2 verruca

la **versión** *fem noun*
version
una película en versión original a film which has not been dubbed (*a subtitled foreign film*)

el **vertedero** *masc noun*
rubbish tip

vertical *masc & fem adjective*
vertical
en posición vertical in a vertical position

el **vertido** *masc noun*
1 spillage (*of pollutants, etc*)
2 los vertidos effluent

el **vértigo** *masc noun*
vertigo
Me da vértigo mirar abajo. Looking down makes me dizzy.

♂ el **vestíbulo** *masc noun*
1 hall
2 foyer

♂ **vestido** *masc adjective*, **vestida** *fem*
▷ see **vestido** *noun*
dressed
ir bien, mal vestido to be well, badly dressed
Iba vestida de azul. She dressed in blue.
Tenemos que ir vestidos de uniforme. We have to wear uniform.

♂ el **vestido** *masc noun* ▷ see **vestido** *adj*
dress
• el **vestido de noche** evening dress
• el **vestido de novia** wedding dress

ᔣ **vestir** *verb* [57]
  to dress
  vestir bien, mal to dress well, badly

vestirse *reflexive verb* [57]
1 to get dressed
  Ya es hora de vestirnos. It's time to get
  dressed.
2 to dress
  Se viste a la última moda. She wears the
  latest fashions.
  Me gusta vestirme de azul. I like wearing
  blue.

el **vestuario** *masc noun*
1 wardrobe
2 changing room

el **veterinario** *masc noun*, la **veterinaria**
fem
  veterinary surgeon

ᔣ **vez** *fem noun, pl:* las **veces**
1 time
  una vez once
  dos veces twice
  tres veces al año three times a year
  La primera vez que fui al extranjero. The
  first time I went to abroad.
  ¿Has estado alguna vez en Italia? Have you
  ever been to Italy?
2 (*in expressions*) a la vez at the same time, at
  once
  algunas veces sometimes
  a veces sometimes
  cada vez each time
  de vez en cuando from time to time
  De vez en cuando nos manda una carta.
  Occasionally he sends us a letter.
  en vez de instead of
  otra vez again
  por última vez for the last time
  rara vez seldom
  tal vez perhaps, maybe
3 cada vez más more and more
  Hay cada vez más turistas. There are more
  and more tourists.
4 cada vez menos less and less, fewer and
  fewer
  Hay cada vez menos peces en el río. There
  are fewer and fewer fish in the river.
5 (*telling stories*) Érase una vez … Once upon a
  time …

ᔣ la **vía** *fem noun*
1 way, path
2 en vías de, un país en vías de desarrollo a
  developing country
3 (*in sending things*) por vía aérea by air
  por vía marítima by sea
  • la **vía de acceso** slip road

• la **vía férrea** railway track
• la **Vía Láctea** Milky Way

ᔣ **viajar** *verb* [17]
  to travel
  viajar en avión to travel by plane
  viajar a México to travel to Mexico

ᔣ el **viaje** *masc noun*
  journey, trip
  un viaje de quince días a two-week trip
  estar de viaje to be away
  hacer un viaje to go on a journey, to go on a
  trip
  salir de viaje to go on a journey, to go on a
  trip
  ¡Buen viaje! Have a good journey!
  • el **viaje de negocios** business trip
  • el **viaje de novios** honeymoon
  • el **viaje organizado** package tour

ᔣ el **viajero** *masc noun*, la **viajera** *fem*
1 traveller
2 passenger

la **víbora** *fem noun*
  viper

vibrar *verb* [17]
  to vibrate

el **vicio** *masc noun*
1 vice
2 bad habit
  Tengo el vicio de morderme las uñas. I have
  the bad habit of biting my nails.

la **víctima** *fem noun*
  victim
  El número de víctimas mortales asciende a
  25. The death toll has risen to 25.

la **victoria** *fem noun*
  victory

la **vid** *fem noun*
  vine (*grapes*)

ᔣ la **vida** *fem noun*
  life
  estar con vida to be alive
  llevar una vida muy activa to lead a very
  busy life
  Se gana la vida como mecánico. He earns
  his living as amechanic.
  La vida está muy cara. The cost of living is
  very high.

el **vídeo** *masc noun*
  video
  en vídeo on video

la **videocámara** *fem noun*
  video camera

el **videoclub** *masc noun*
　video shop

el **videojuego** *masc noun*
　video game

♂ el **vidrio** *masc noun*
　glass

♂ **viejo** *masc adjective*, **vieja** *fem*
　▷ see **viejo** *noun*
　old (*car, house, custom*)

♂ el **viejo** *masc noun*, la **vieja** *fem*
　▷ see **viejo** *adj*
　1 **old man**
　2 **old woman**

♂ el **viento** *masc noun*
　1 **wind**
　　Hace viento. It's windy.
　　El viento sopla del este. The wind is blowing
　　from the east.
　2 **guy rope** (*of tent*)

el **vientre** *masc noun*
　1 **belly**
　2 **womb**

♂ el **viernes** *masc noun*
　Friday
　　el viernes on Friday
　　el viernes pasado last Friday
　　los viernes on Fridays
　　cada viernes every Friday
　　Hay mercado los viernes. There's a market
　　on Fridays.

WORD TIP Names of months and days start with
small letters in Spanish.

vigésimo *masc adjective*, **vigésima** *fem*
　twentieth

el **villancico** *masc noun*
　Christmas carol

♂ el **vinagre** *masc noun*
　vinegar

♂ **vine**, **viniste**, **vino**, etc *verb* ▷ **venir**

♂ el **vino** *masc noun*
　wine
　• el **vino blanco** white wine
　• el **vino de mesa** table wine
　• el **vino tinto** red wine

el **viñedo** *masc noun*
　vineyard

violar *verb* [17]
　1 **to break** (*rules, regulations*)
　2 **to rape** (*a person*)

la **violencia** *fem noun*
　violence

violento *masc adjective*, **violenta** *fem*
　1 **violent**
　2 **embarrassing** (*situation*)

violeta *invariable adjective & fem noun*
　1 **violet** (*colour*)
　2 la **violeta** violet (*the flower*)

el **violín** *masc noun*
　violin
　　tocar el violín to play the violin

el **violoncelo**, **violonchelo** *masc noun*
　cello

virar *verb* [17]
　to swerve
　　El coche viró para esquivar al perro. The car
　　swerved to avoid the dog.

la **virgen** *fem noun*
　virgin
　　la Virgen María the Virgin Mary

virgo *masc & fem noun* ▷ see **Virgo** *noun*
　Virgo
　　Es virgo. He's Virgo.

WORD TIP Use a small letter in Spanish to say *I
am Virgo*, etc with star signs.

Virgo *masc noun* ▷ see **virgo** *noun*
　Virgo

la **virtud** *fem noun*
　virtue

el **virus** *masc noun*, pl: los **virus**
　(*Computers, Medicine*) **virus**
　　un software anti virus a piece of anti-virus
　　software

el **visado** *masc noun*
　visa

la **visibilidad** *fem noun*
　visibility

visible *masc & fem adjective*
　visible

la **visión** *fem noun*
　1 **vision**
　2 **sight**
　　perder la visión to lose your sight

♂ la **visita** *fem noun*
　1 **visit**
　　una visita a la feria a visit to the fair
　　horario de visita visiting times
　　hacerle una visita a alguien to visit
　　somebody
　　Les hizo una visita. She visited them.

2 visitor
Tienes una visita. You have a visitor.
Tienen visita. They have visitors.
3 hit (on a web site)

ᛤ **visitar** verb [17]
   to visit
   visitar el casco urbano to visit the old part
   of town
   visitar a mis abuelos to visit my
   grandparents

la **víspera** fem noun
   la víspera the day before
   la víspera del partido the day before the
   match

ᛤ la **vista** fem noun
1 view
   una vista preciosa a beautifu view
   El hotel tiene vistas al mar. The hotel has
   views over the sea.
2 eyesight
   tener buena, mala vista to have good, bad
   eyesight
   perder la vista to lose your sight
   El sol me hace daño a la vista. The sun's
   hurting my eyes.
   La conocemos de vista. We know her by
   sight.
3 (the direction you look) **bajar la vista** to look
   down
   levantar la vista to look up
4 estar a la vista to be within sight
   no estar a la vista to be out of sight
5 ¡Hasta la vista! See you!

ᛤ **vistieron**, **vistió**, etc verb ▷ vestir

ᛤ **visto** verb ▷ see **visto** adj ▷ ver

visto masc adjective, **vista** fem
   ▷ see **ver** verb
1 clear
   Está visto que … It's clear that …
2 por lo visto apparently
   Por lo visto se perdieron.. Apparently hey
   got lost.
3 estar bien, mal visto to be acceptable,
   unacceptable
   Está muy mal visto. It's just not acceptable.

la **vitamina** fem noun
   vitamin

la **vitrina** fem noun
   shop window

el **viudo** masc noun, la **viuda** fem
1 widower
2 widow

viva exclamation
   ¡Viva! Hurray!
   ¡Viva la novia! Three cheers for the bride!

la **vivienda** fem noun
1 housing
   el problema de la vivienda the housing
   problem
2 dwelling (could be a flat, huse etc)
   un bloque de viviendas a block of flats

ᛤ **vivir** verb [19]
1 to live
   Vivo en la calle Altamira. I live in Altamira
   Street.
   Vive en casa de su hermana. She lives
   with her sister.
   Vivimos un año en Alicante. We lived
   inAlicante for a year.
2 to live through, to have
   Vivimos unos momentos muy felices. We
   lived through some happy times.

---

vivo masc adjective, **viva** fem
   alive
   en vivo live (broadcast, concert, etc)
   Totavía están vivos. They're still alive.

WORD TIP Always use estar for 'to be' with vivo.

el **vocabulario** masc noun
   vocabulary

la **vocal** fem noun
   vowel (the letters a, e, i, o, u)

volante masc & fem adjective
   ▷ see **volante** noun
   flying

el **volante** masc noun ▷ see **volante** adj
   steering wheel

ᛤ **volar** verb [24]
1 to fly (planes, birds, people)
   Fue la primera vez que volé. It was the first
   time I flew.
2 to blow up
   volar un edificio to blow up a building

el **volcán** masc noun
   volcano

volcar verb [24]
1 to knock over
2 to turn over
   El camión volcó. The lorry turned over.
3 to empty (a box, a drawer)

volcarse reflexive verb [24]
1 to turn over (vehicles)
2 volcarse en algo to do all you can for
   something ▸▸

Se vuelca en su familia. She does all she can for her family.

el **vóleibol, voleibol** *masc noun*
volleyball
jugar al vóleibol to play volleyball

la **voltereta** *fem noun*
somersault

el **volumen** *masc noun*
volume
subir el volumen to turn up the volume
¡Baja el volumen! Turn the volume down!

la **voluntad** *fem noun*
1 **will**
Lo hicieron de buena voluntad. They did it willingly.
Lo hice por mi propia voluntad. I did it of my own free will.
2 **wish**
la voluntad de los padres the parents' wishes

voluntario *masc adjective*, **voluntaria**
fem ▷ see **voluntario** *noun*
voluntary

el **voluntario** *masc noun*, la **voluntaria**
fem ▷ see **voluntario** *adj*
volunteer

♂ **volver** *verb* [45]
1 **to come back**
Ya ha vuelto. He's already come back.
¿Cuándo volverás? When will you come back?
Volveré a eso de las siete. I'll be back by about seven.
¿Cuándo volviste de tu viaje? When did you get back from your trip?
2 **to go back**
volver al colegio to go back to school
¿Quieres que volvamos a casa? Do you want us to go back home?
Ha vuelto con su novia. He's gone back to his girlfriend.
No había vuelto a Sevilla desde el verano pasado. I hadn't been back to Seville since last summer.
3 **to turn**
volver la página to turn the page
Volvió la cabeza. She turned her head.
Al volver la esquina ... When I turned the corner ...
4 **volver a hacer algo** to do something again
Volví a revisarlo. I checked it again.
¡No lo vuelvas a hacer! Don't do it again!
Tenemos que volver a empezar. We have to start again.

5 **volver loco a alguien** to drive someone mad
Me vuelve loca con tantas preguntas. She's driving me mad with all her questions.
6 **volver en sí** to come round (*after fainting*)

volverse *reflexive verb* [45]
1 **to turn around**
Me volví para ver mejor. I turned around to see better.
2 **volverse de espaldas** to turn your back
¡No te vuelvas de espaldas cuando te estoy hablando! Don't turn your back on me when I'm talking to you!
3 **to come back**
volverse a casa to come back home
Se volvieron a las doce. They came back at twelve o'clock.
4 **to become**
volverse loco to go crazy
Se ha vuelto muy vanidosa. She's become very vain.
La situación se ha vuelto grave. The situation has become serious.

vomitar *verb* [17]
to be sick
tener ganas de vomitar to feel sick

vosotros, vosotras *pronoun*
you
¿Vosotras queréis ir? Do you want to go?
vosotros mismos *masc*, **vosotras mismas**
fem yourselves

WORD TIP *vosotros* is used to refer to two or more males, or males and females, who you know well.

votar *verb* [17]
1 **to vote on** (*a measure*)
2 **to vote for** (*a party, a candidate*)
¿Por quién votaste? Who did you vote for?
Siempre vota a los verdes. She always votes for the Greens.

el **voto** *masc noun*
1 **vote**
un voto a favor a vote for
un voto en contra a vote against
un voto secreto a secret ballot
2 **vow**
• el **voto de censura** vote of no confidence
• el **voto en blanco** blank ballot paper

♂ **voy** *verb* ▷ **ir**

♂ la **voz** *fem noun, pl:* las **voces**
voice
oír voces to hear voices
tener la voz tomada to be hoarse
hablar en voz baja quietly
hablar en voz alta to speak loudly
leer algo en voz alta to read something out loud

a
b
c
d
e
f
g
h
i
j
k
l
m
n
ñ
o
p
q
r
s
t
u
v
w
x
y
z

♂ el **vuelo** *masc noun*
flight
el vuelo 453 con destino Cardiff flight 453
to Cardiff
• el **vuelo regular** scheduled flight

♂ la **vuelta** *fem noun*
1 **change** (*coins*)
2 **turn**
una vuelta a la derecha a turn to the right
3 **return**
la vuelta al colegio the return to
school (*after the summer holidays*)
A la vuelta iremos al cine. We'll go to the
cinema when we come back.
4 **stage** (*in a competition*)
5 **round** (*in elections*)
6 **dar una vuelta** to go out (*for a walk, a drive,
etc*)
dar una vuelta en coche to go for a drive
¿Quieres dar una vuelta? Do you want to go
out for a walk?
7 **dar la vuelta a algo**
dar la vuelta a la página to turn over the
page
dar la vuelta a la esquina to turn the corner
dar una vuelta a la manzana to go round
the block
dar la vuelta al mundo to go round the
world

Dale la vuelta al cuadro. Turn the picture
round the other way.
dar la vuelta a un disco to turn a record over
8 **dar una vuelta alrededor de algo** to go out
for a tour around something
Dieron una vuelta alrededor de la ciudad.
They went out for a tour round the city.

el **vuelto** *masc noun*
(*Latin America*) **change** (*coins*)

♂ **vuelva**, **vuelvo**, **etc** *verb* ▷ **volver**

vuestro *masc adjective*, **vuestra** *fem*
▷ see **vuestro** *pron*
your (*talking to more than one person*)
vuestra casa your house
un familiar vuestro a relative of yours

vuestro, **vuestra** *pronoun*
▷ see **vuestro** *adj*
yours
La vuestra es verde. Yours is green.
Los vuestros están en el salón. Yours are in
the living room.
Aquel es el vuestro. That one is yours.

vulgar *masc & fem adjective*
1 **vulgar**
2 **common**

a
b
c
d
e
f
g
h
i
j
k
l
m
n
ñ
o
p
q
r
s
t
u
v
w
x
y
z

W w

el **walkman**® *masc noun*
personal stereo

ⵯ el **wáter** *masc noun*
toilet

el **whisky** *masc noun*
whisky

ⵯ el **windsurf** *masc noun*
windsurfing
hacer **windsurf** to go windsurfing

a
b
c
d
e
f
g
h
i
j
k
l
m
n
ñ
o
p
q
r
s
t
u
v
w
x
y
z

X x

el **xilófono** *masc noun*
  xylophone

Y y

ℰ y *conjunction*
1 **and**
   Amanda y yo Amanda and I
2 (*with numbers*) **treinta y siete** thirty-seven
3 (*in clock time*) **la una y media** half past one
   a las diez y veinte at twenty past ten
4 (*for emphasis*) **¿Y a mí qué?** So, what's it to me?

WORD TIP *y* becomes *e* before words beginning with *i-* or *hi-*.

ℰ ya *adverb*
1 **already**
   Ya está hecho. It's already done.
   ¿Has comido ya? Have you already eaten?
2 **yet**
   ¿Han llegado ya? Have they arrived yet?
3 **any more**
   Ya no importa. It doesn't matter any more.
4 **now**
   Tenemos que decidirnos ya. We must decide now.
   Ya es hora de irnos. We must go now.
5 (*in the future*) **Ya veremos.** We'll see about that.
   Ya te contaré. I'll tell you about it.
6 (*for emphasis*) **Ya lo sé.** I know.
   Ya entiendo. I understand.
   Ya era hora. About time too.
   ¡Ya está! That's it!
   ¡Ya voy! I'm just coming!
   ¡Ya lo creo! You bet!
7 (*in expressions*) **'Esto es de Juan'—'Ya.'** 'This is Juan's'—'I know.'

Preparados, listos, ¡Ya! Ready, steady, go!
'Yo no he sido'—'Ya, ya.' 'It wasn't me'—'Yeah, yeah!'
8 **ya que** since
   Ya que vas a estar aquí. Since you're going to be here.

el yate *masc noun*
   yacht

la yedra *fem noun*
   ivy

la yegua *fem noun*
   mare

la yema *fem noun*
1 **yolk**
2 **la yema del dedo** the fingertip

el yerno *masc noun*
   son-in-law

ℰ yo *pronoun*
1 **I**
   Yo no lo sé. I don't know.
2 **me**
   Soy yo. It's me.
3 **yo mismo, yo misma** myself
   Lo haré yo mismo. I'll do it myself.

el yoga *masc noun*
   yoga

ℰ el yogur *masc noun*
   yoghurt

el yudo *masc noun*
   judo

Z z

ᵹ la **zanahoria** *fem noun*
carrot

el **zancudo** *masc noun*
(*Latin America*) **mosquito**

la **zapatería** *fem noun*
shoe shop

el **zapatero** *masc noun*, la **zapatera** *fem*
1 **shoemaker**
2 **shoe repairer's**

la **zapatilla** *fem noun*
1 **slipper**
2 **canvas shoe**
• la **zapatilla de ballet** ballet shoe
• la **zapatilla de deporte** trainer
• la **zapatilla de esparto** espadrille

ᵹ el **zapato** *masc noun*
shoe
• el **zapato bajo** flat shoe
• el **zapato de tacón** high heeled shoe

> **Zara**
>
> España tiene muchos diseñadores de moda famosos pero es la marca de ropa Zara la que se conoce por todo el mundo. Se fundó en 1963 y hoy tiene más de 15.000 sucursales en 44 países.

la **zarzamora** *fem noun*
blackberry

la **zarzuela** *fem noun*
Spanish light opera

el **zodíaco**, **zodiaco** *masc noun*
zodiac

ᵹ la **zona** *fem noun*
area
Viven en la zona. **They live locally.**
• la **zona (azul)** short-term parking area (*requiring a parking disk*)
• la **zona comercial** commercial district
• la **zona peatonal** pedestrian precinct

zonzo *masc adjective*, **zonza** *fem*
(*Latin America: informal*) **silly**, **daft**

el **zoo** *masc noun*
zoo

el **zoológico** *masc noun*
zoo

el **zorro** *masc noun*, la **zorra** *fem*
1 **fox**
2 **vixen**

el **zueco** *masc noun*
clog

zumbar *verb* [17]
to buzz

ᵹ el **zumo** *masc noun*
juice
• el **zumo de fruta** fruit juice
• el **zumo de naranja** orange juice

zurdo *masc adjective*, **zurda** *fem*
left-handed

a
b
c
d
e
f
g
h
i
j
k
l
m
n
ñ
o
p
q
r
s
t
u
v
w
x
y
z

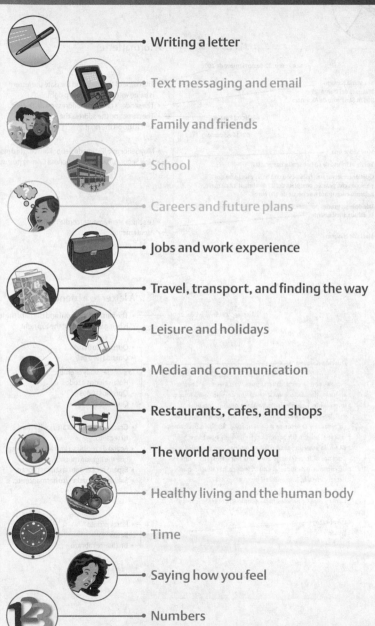

- Writing a letter
- Text messaging and email
- Family and friends
- School
- Careers and future plans
- **Jobs and work experience**
- **Travel, transport, and finding the way**
- Leisure and holidays
- Media and communication
- **Restaurants, cafes, and shops**
- **The world around you**
- Healthy living and the human body
- Time
- Saying how you feel
- Numbers

Writing a letter

A formal letter

San Pedro, 22 de noviembre de 2006

Sra María Navarro
Marqués del Duero, 25
29670 San Pedro de Alcántara

Hotel Paraíso
Calle Elche
03110 Alicante

Muy Señor mío

Recibí el folleto de su hotel; muchas gracias.

Quisiera reservar una habitacíon con baño y wc, para dos personas con pensión completa del 27 de abril al 12 de mayo. Adjunto encontrará un cheque de 100 euros.

Dándole las gracias por anticipado.
Le saluda atentamente

María de Navarro

- The name of the town and the date the letter is being written go at the top right.
- The sender's name and address go on the left.
- The name and the address the letter is being sent to go on the right.

- Muy Señor mío/Estimado Señor Ramírez (*to a man*)
- Muy Señora mía/Estimada Señora Gómez (*to a wom*

- Le saluda atentamente/cordialmente.
- Atentamente.

A letter to a friend

Chester, 23 de abril de 2006

Querida Catalina

Gracias por tu carta. Bueno pues, vas a venir a Chester en junio, ¡fantástico! Vas a visitar mi colegio. Será muy interesante. Es un colegio bastante grande con buenas instalaciones. Podrás ayudarme con mi español. Voy bien en español y el profe es muy simpático. También podremos visitar el pueblo un poco. Chester es muy bonito.
El fin de semana pasado, fui a Londres con mi amiga. Cogimos el tren (el viaje dura una hora en tren). Fuimos de compras y después al cine. Siempre hay mucho que hacer y ver allí. Vámonos en junio si quieres.

Espero recibir noticias tuyas pronto ... contesta ¡rápido!

Un abrazo
Susan

- The name of the town and the date the lett… is being written go at the top right.

- Querido (*to a boy*)
- Querida (*to a girl*)

To a whole family or group:
- Hola/saludos a todos
- Queridos todos
- Queridos amigos

- Gracias por tun carta/tu invitacíon/ tu regalito.
- Acabo de recibir su invitacíon/su carta que me agradó mucho (*formal*).
- Espero recibir noticias tuyas pronto.
- Saluda a tus padres/tu hermano, etc.

- Hasta pronto
- Besos
- Un (fuerte) abrazo

Text messaging

hl cm tva? vi a t hna atyer. s m simpatik
Hola, ¿cómo te va ? Vi a tu hermana anteayer. Es muy simpática

bbtt. stas bn ? vams al cin o 1kf mñn ?
Buenas tardes. ¿Estás bien? ¿Vamos al cine o a un café mañana?

- Certain words or syllables can be represented by letters or numbers that sound the same but take up less space, e.g. mñn, mñna = mañana.
- Accents are often left out. The syllables '-pe', '-te' and '-ca' can be replaced by the letters P, T and K etc.
- Another way of shortening words is leave out certain letters, especially vowels. For example, 'adiós' becomes 'a2' and 'cuando' becomes 'q&d'.
- 'Emoticons' are very popular, e.g. :-) = sonrisa, :-(= cara feliz, :-D = sonrisa de oreja a oreja

Abbreviation	Full Word	Abbreviation	Full Word	Abbreviation	Full Word
sn	sin	fsta	fiesta	msj	mensaje
simpatik	simpática	hna	hermana	pbrlm	problema
cin	cine	gf	jefe	xq	porque
fin d smn	fin de semana	ayr	ayer	x	por
atamñn	hasta mañana	j+	jamás	q&d	cuando
d+sia2	demasiados	dbres	deberes	na-	nada menos
taptecıkf?	te apetece un café ?	t&q	te quiero	resp s t gsta	responde si te gusta
lgo	luego	q	que	hno	hermano
bdias	buenos días	kf	café	hl cm tva?	¿hola cómo te va ?
bbtt	buenas tardes	qn	quién	s3ad	estresado
s	es	qay d nvo?	¿qué hay de nuevo	xfa	por favor
s dcir	es decir	l100to	lo siento	sp	siempre
dacurd	de acuerdo	eia	ella	stas bn?	estás bien?
npn	no pasa nada	mñn, mñna	mañana	stas ocu ?	¿estás ocupado ?
trist	triste	mdr	muerto de risa	vstrs	vosotros

Email

un correo electrónico, un email = an email
una dirección de correo electrónico = an email address
enviar un correo electrónico, un email = to send an email
recibir un correo electrónico, un email = to receive an email
un archivo = a file
un archivo adjunto = an attachment
una arroba = an *at* sign
una bandeja de entrada = an inbox
borrar un mensaje = to delete a message
un sitio web = a website
hacer click (en) = to click (on)
responder = reply
reenviar = forward
asunto = subject
copiar y pegar = to cut and paste
correo basura = spam

Hola Ana:

Llevo como tres horas en este cibercafé navegando en la Red y he encontrado muchísimos sitios interesantes. Aquí te mando uno que me gustó mucho. La dirección es http://www.zmag.org/Spanish/index.htm.

Te aconsejo que lo agregues a tus favoritos. ¿Se lo podrías pasar a Manuel? No tengo su dirección, ya que perdí mi agenda cuando se colgó mi disco duro. Como no he podido contestar mi correo electrónico, se ha llenado mi casilla, así es que tengo para varias horas más aquí.

Espero que todo esté bien en tu nuevo trabajo en México. Ojalá pueda visitarte pronto de nuevo.

Tengo excelentes recuerdos de Teotihuacán.
Un beso,
Pedro

Family and friends

Relationships

En mi familia, somos cinco.
There are five of us in my family.
Hay mis padres.
There are my parents.
mi padre/mi madre
my father/my mother
mi padrastro/mi madrastra
my stepfather/my stepmother
Tiene hijos.
He has children/She has children.
un hijo/una hija
a son/a daughter
Tengo un hermano/una hermana.
I have a brother/a sister.
un hermanastro/una hermanastra
a half-brother/a half-sister
un mellizo/una melliza
a twin brother/a twin sister
Soy hijo único.
I'm an only child (*boy speaking*).
Soy hija única.
I'm an only child (*girl speaking*).
Me llevo bien/No me llevo bien con …
I get on well/I don't get on well with …
· **mis abuelos.**
· my grandparents.
· **mi abuela/mi abuelo.**
· my grandmother/my grandfather.
· **mi tío/mi tía.**
· my uncle/my aunt.
· **mi primo** (*boy*)/**mi prima** (*girl*).
· my cousin.

Status

Es …   She/He is …
· **soltero / soltera.**   single.
· **casado** (man) / **casada** (woman).   married.
· **viudo** (man) / **viuda** (woman).   widower / widow

Está …   She/He is …
· **muerto** (man) / **muerta** (woman).   dead.
· **prometido / prometida.**   engaged.
· **separado** (man) / **separada** (woman).   separated.
· **divorciado** (man) / **divorciada** (woman).   divorce

Mi mejor amiga (girl) **se llama …**
Mi mejor amigo (boy) **se llama …**
My best friend is called …

Descriptions

Es …   He/she is …
alto/alta.   tall.
bajo/baja.   short.
rubio/rubia.   blond.
moreno/morena.   dark-haired.
simpático/simpática.   really nice.
pesado/pesada.   a pain.
Tengo un amigo/una amiga que tiene quince años …
I have a friend who is fifteen years old …
… a quien le encanta el deporte.
… and who loves sport.
… a quien le encantan los juegos vídeo.
… and who loves video games.

Mi asignatura preferida es …
My favourite subject is …

el francés
French

las ciencias
science

el diseño
art

el inglés
English

la química
chemistry

la música
music

el alemán
German

la física
physics

**la educacíon
física** PE

el español
Spanish

la biología
biology

la informática
computing

la tecnología
technology

la geografía
geography

Voy al colegioa pie. I walk to school.
Mi colegio se llama … My school is called …
Estoy en el terecero de ESO. I'm in Year 10.
Hay 25 alumnos en mi curso.
There are 25 pupils in my class.
Los cursos comienzan a las ocho y media.
Lessons start at half past eight.
Una clase dura 45 minutos.
A lesson lasts 45 minutes.
Los lunes, a las nueve, tengo matemáticas.
On Mondays at nine o'clock I have maths.
Hago inglés y español.
I do English and Spanish.
Soy fuerte en/voy bien en … (boy or girl)
I'm good at …
Soy débil en …
I'm not very good at …
Estoy estudiando para el examen de …
I'm studying for an exam called …
Tenemos muchos deberes.
We have a lot of homework.
Al mediodía, como en la cantina.
At midday, I have lunch in the canteen.

Classroom instructions

¡Pasa!/¡Entrad! (to two or more pupils)
Come in!
Sacad vuestros cuadernos.
Take out your exercise books.
Abrid vuestros libros a la página 23.
Open your books at page 23.
En silencio, por favor.
In silence, please.
Escuchad bien. Listen carefully.
Escuchad y repetid. Listen and repeat.
Trabaja con una pareja. (to one pupil)
Work with a partner.
Leed el primer párrafo.
Read the first paragraph.
Escribid una descripción.
Write a description.
Buscad las palabras en un diccionario.
Look up the words in a dictionary.

Classroom objects

un libro de texto a textbook
un cuaderno an exercise book
un lápiz a pencil
un bolígrafo a ballpoint pen
un rotulador a felt-tip pen
una regla a ruler
una goma a rubber
un sacapuntas a pencil sharpener
unas tijeras scissors
una calculadora a calculator

Careers and future plans

Este año estoy cursando el GCSE.
This year, I'm studying for the GCSE.
El año que viene, voy a hacer 8 exámenes.
Next year, I'll sit 8 exams.
Depués, me gustaría ...
Then, I'd like to ...
Más tarde, quisiera ...
Later on, I'd like to ...
Tengo la intención de ... I plan to ...
Quiero ... I want to ...

Mi ambición es ...
My ambition is to ...
• **estudiar.** study.
• **ir a la universidad.** go to university.
• **hacer un diploma.** do a diploma.
• **hacer un aprendizaje.** do an apprenticeship.
• **hacer la práctica laboral.** go on a work placement.
• **encontrar un empleo.** find a job.
• **viajar al extranjero.** go abroad.
Me gustaría ser ...
I'd like to be ...
• **profesor/profesora.** a teacher.
• **médico/médica.** a doctor.
Me gustaría trabajar ...
I'd like to work ...
• **con niños.** with children.
• **al aire libre.** outdoors.
• **en turismo.** in tourism.

Para mí, un empleo es ideal si ...
For me, a job is ideal if ...
• **es interesante.** it's interesting.
• **paga bien.** it's well paid.
• **me gusta.** I like it.

Cuando tenga treinta años ...
When I'm thirty ...
estaré casado/casada. I'll be married.
Tendré una familia. I'll have a family.
Iré de vacaciones. I'll go on holiday.

Mi ambición es ...
My ambition is to ...

estudiar
study

viajar al extranjero
go abroad

trabajar con niños
work with children

**trabajar
al aire libre**
work outdoors

ser médico/médica
be a doctor

**ser peluquero/
peluquera**
be a hairdresser

ser secretaria
be a secretary

ser contable
be an accountant

**ser mecánico/
mecánica**
be a car mechanic

abc
**ser profesor/
profesora**
be a teacher

Jobs and work experience

Writing a CV

- Remember the order of the information:
  —personal details
  —education
  —work experience
  —language skills (whether spoken or written), computer skills, interests and membership of any clubs or voluntary organizations.
- Check your spelling and grammar—if possible, get a Spanish speaker to help you with this.
- In Spain and Latin America, it is quite usual to include a passport-sized photo with your job application.
- Always handwrite a covering letter.

Spanish companies often use a graphologist (handwriting expert).

Sally Roberts

Dirección
27 Park Road
London N8 6PJ
tél: 0208 340 6549

sallyroberts@hotmail.com

Fecha de nacimiento: el dos de mayo 1990
Lugar de nacimiento: Londres
Nacionalidad: británica

Datos académicos
Preparación de los A levels (equivalente al bachillerato)
Asignaturas: inglés, español, historia y música

Desde 2006	Alexandra Park Sixth Form Centre (instituto)
2006	8 GCSE's (equivalente al Certificado: Graduada en Educación Secundaria)
	Optativas: matemáticas, ciencias, inglés, español, geografía, arte y diseño, música, tecnología
2001–2006	Park View Secondary School (colegio)

Experiencia profesional

2006	mes de agosto trabajando en una oficina local
2005	seis meses los sábados, vendedora en una zapatería local
2004	de canguro para una familia vecina

Otro
Lenguas extranjeras: español (nivel avanzado oral y escrito), francés/alemán (nivel básico)

Informática: formación a nivel medio en Microsoft Word

Cualidades personales: organizada, responsable, extrovertida

Aficiones: Deporte natación y surf, cine, lectura
Miembro del grupo local de arte dramático y de la orquesta de colegio

---

Me gustaría ...
I'd like to ...
- **trabajar en una tienda.**
  work in a shop.
- **hacer de canguro.**
  do babysitting.
- **hacer jardinería.**
  do gardening.
- **lavar coches.**
  wash cars.

Ye he trabajado en ...
I've already worked in ...
- **una oficina.** an office.
- **una fábrica.** a factory.
- **una gasolinera.** a petrol station.
- **un supermercado.** a supermarket.

Tengo experiencia. I have experience.
No he trabajado nunca. I've never worked.
He repartido periódicos.
I did a paper round.

durante un mes/un año for a month/a year

Encontré el empleo ... I found the job ...
- **fascinante.** fascinating.
- **pesado.** boring.
- **bien remunerado.** well paid.
- **mal pagado.** badly paid.

Gané ... I earned ...
- **7 euros la hora.** 7 euros an hour.
- **150 euros al mes.** 150 euros a month.

Tengo ...
I have ...
- **un empleo para el verano.** a summer job.
- **un empleo a tiempo completo.** a full-time job.
- **un empleo a tiempo parcial.** a part-time job.

El año pasado, hice las prácticas laborales.
Last year I did work experience.
Fue interesante.
It was interesting.

---

un empleado an employee (*man*)
una empleada an employee (*woman*)
un empleador an employer
el salario the salary/wages
los horas the hours
los títulos the qualifications
una carta de solicitud
letter of application/supporting statement
el currículo CV

Travel, transport, and finding the way

Voy ...
I'm going...

en avión
by plane

en tren
by train

en coche
by car

en autobús
by bus

en barco
by ship

en bici
by bike

en autocar
by coach

en taxi
by taxi

en moto
on a motorbike

---

salir/la salida to leave/departure
llegar/la llegada to arrive/arrival
viajar/un viaje to travel/a journey
el equipaje luggage

¿Nos encontramos ... ? Shall we meet ... ?
• **en el aeropuerto.** at the airport.
• **en el puerto.** at the port.
• **en la estación.** at the station.
• **en la estación de buses.** at the bus station.

Quisiera comprar ...
I'd like to buy ...

• **un billete de ida solo/de ida y vuelta a Madr**
• a single/a return to Madrid.
• **comprar un billete.**
• to buy a ticket.
• **reservar un asiento.**
• to reserve a seat.
• **consultar el horario.**
• to check the timetable.

¿De qué vía/andén sale el tren?
What platform does the train leave from?

¿Dónde está la parada de autobuses?
Where is the bus stop?

La estación de metro está aquí cerca.
The underground station is close by.

El año pasado fui a Francia.
Last year, I went to France.

Fuimos en coche.
We travelled by car.

No he ido nunca al extranjero.
I have never been abroad.

Mi pasatiempo preferido es …
My favourite pastime is …

la natación
going swimming

hacer turismo
going sight-seeing

hacer vela
going sailing

Mi pasatiempo preferido es …
My favourite pastime is …
• **salir con amigos.** going out with friends.
• **ir al centro (de la ciudad).** going into town.
• **ir de compras.** going shopping.
• **ir a un concierto.** going to concerts.
• **la lectura.** reading.
• **escuchar la música.** listening to music.
• **ver la tele.** watching TV.
• **jugar a la consola.** playing on a games console.

¿Vamos al parque?
Shall we go to the park?
Nos encontramos en el gimnasio.
We'll meet up at the gym.
Prefiero ir al estadio.
I'd rather go to the stadium.
¡Nos vemos en el cine!
See you at the cinema!
¡Nos vemos en la disco!
See you at the disco!

Durante la vacaciones, me alojaré …
During the holidays, I am going to stay …
• **en un hotel.** in a hotel.
• **en un albergue juvenil.**
  in a youth hostel.
• **en una casa de campo.**
  in a holiday home in the country.
• **en un camping.** at a campsite.
• **en la costa.** by the sea.
• **en las montañas.** in the mountains.
• **en el campo.** in the country.
• **en la playa.** at the beach.

montar a caballo
going horse-riding

hacer el esquí
going skiing

hacer el senderismo
going hiking

El verano pasado, fui a España.
Last summer, I went to Spain.
Este año, voy a quedarme en casa.
This year, I'll stay at home.
Cada verano, voy a Marruecos.
Every summer, I go to Morocco.
El próximo verano, voy a ir a Bilbao.
Next summer, I'll be going to Bilbao.

Top 10 media gadgets
un televisor (pantalla grande)
a (wide screen) TV
una antena parabólica a satellite dish
un MP3 an MP3 player
un DVD a DVD player
una consola de juegos a games console
un ordenador portátil laptop computer
una cámara digital a digital camera
una cámara vídeo a video camera
una cadena hifi a music system
un teléfono móvil a mobile phone

Television and cinema
ver la tele to watch TV
¿Qué programas hay en la tele?
What's on the telly?
Hay … There's …
• **un programa de deporte.**
a sports programme.
• **un documental.** a documentary.
• **un culebrón.** a soap.
• **un concurso.** a game show.
• **las noticias/el noticiero.** the news.
¿En qué cadena está?
What channel is it on?
Mi serie preferida es …
My favourite series is …
ir al cine. to go to the cinema.
Ponen … They're showing …
• **una película policíaca.** a detective film.
• **dibujos animados.** cartoons.
• **una comedia.** a comedy.
• **una película de terror.**
a horror film.
Vi Star Wars hace poco.
I saw Star Wars recently.

On the telephone
¡Diga! Hallo!
¿Puedo hablar con … ?
Can I speak to … ?
¿Quién llama? Who's calling?
No cuelgues. Hold on.
¿Puedo dejar un mensaje?
Can I leave a message?
Volveré a llamar más tarde.
I'll call back later.

Radio, newspapers and magazines

escuchar la radio to listen to the radio
Leo el periódico todos los días.
I read the newspaper every day.
Mi revista favorita/mi periódico preferido es …
My favourite magazine/newspaper is …

At the restaurant/cafe

Quisiera reservar ... I'd like to reserve ...
una mesa para cuatro personas.
a table for four people.
¿Qué desea? What would you like?
Me gustaría tomar ... I'd like ...
• **un café.** a coffee.
• **una taza de té.** a cup of tea.
• **un zumo de naranja.** an orange juice.
¿Tiene usted helado de vainilla?
Have you got vanilla ice-cream?
Para comenzar/como entrada deme ...
For a starter, I'll have ...
• **una sopa de cebolla.** onion soup.
• **una ensalada de tomate.** tomato salad.

hacer las compras ...
to go shopping (for food) ...

en la pastelería
at the cake shop

en farmacia
at the chemist's

en la carnicería
at the butcher's

en la charcutería
at the delicatessen

en el mercado
at the market

en la panadería
at the baker's

en el supermercado
at the supermarket

Como plato fuerte/principal ...
For my main course ...
• **el pollo asado.** roast chicken.
• **el filete de ternera.** fillet steak.
con ... with ...
• **guisantes.** peas.
• **patatas fritas.** chips.
De postre, me gustaría ...
For dessert, I'd like ...
• **la tarta de pera.** pear tart.
• **el mousse de chocolate.** chocolate mousse.
Para beber ...
To drink, I'll have ...
• **agua mineral.** mineral water.
• **un vino (blanco/tinto).** (white/red) wine.
La cuenta, por favor. The bill, please.
¿Cuánto es? How much is it?

The world around you

Hay ...
There is ...

una cocina
a kitchen

¿Vives ...? Do you live...?
• **en el centro.** in the city centre.
• **en las afueras.** in the suburbs.
• **en el campo.** in the country.
• **a orillas del mar.** at the sea-side.
• **en la montaña.** in the mountains.
Vivo en el norte/sur/este/oeste/centro de ...
I live in the north/south/east/west/centre of ...
Es una ciudad industrial/moderna/animada.
It's an industrial/a modern/a lively town.
Es un pueblo agrícola/tranquilo/turístico.
It's a farming/quiet/touristy village.

una sala de estar
a living room

a dining room

En mi ciudad, hay ...
In my town there is/are ...

• **unas tiendas.** shops.
• **unos restaurantes.** restaurants.
• **unas cafeterías.** cafes.
• **unos hoteles.** hotels.
• **un museo.** a museum.
• **una iglesia.** a church.
• **una piscina.** a swimming pool.
• **un cine.** a cinema.
• **un teatro.** a theatre.

un WC
a toilet

un dormitorio
a bedroom

un cuarto de baño
a bathroom

un estudio
an office/a study

un garaje
a garage

En la planta baja
On the ground floor
En la primera planta
On the first floor

un jardín
a garden

Vivo en ...
I live in ...
• **una casa.** a house.
• **un apartamento en el segundo piso.** a flat on the second floor.
Mi casa es pequeña/grande/moderna/vieja.
My home is small/big/modern/old.

Me gusta ... I like ...
Me gustan ... I like ... + plural
No me gusta ... I don't like ...
No me gustan ... I don't like ... + plural
- **la gaseosa.** fizzy drinks.
- **el alcohol.** alcohol.
- **el agua.** water.
- **el zumo de fruta.** fruit juice.
- **la leche.** milk.
- **el café.** coffee.
- **la fruta.** fruit.
- **los dulces/caramelos.** sweets.
- **la verdura.** vegetables.
- **la carne.** meat.

la frente — forehead
la nariz — nose
la boca — mouth
la barbilla — chin

los ojos — eyes
las orejas — ears
los dientes — teeth

Hay que evitar beber ...
You must avoid drinking ...
No debes fumar.
You mustn't smoke.

Es saludable/sano.
It's healthy.
No es saludable/sano.
It's unhealthy.

Para mantenerse en forma, hay que ...
To keep healthy, you have to ...
- **levantarse temprano.** to get up early.
- **acostarse temprano.** to go to bed early.
- **hacer deporte.** to take exercise.
- **ir a pie/caminar.** to walk.

la cabeza — head
el cuello — neck
el brazo — arm
la rodilla — knee

el pelo — hair
la garganta — throat
el hombro — shoulder
la mano — hand
el dedo — finger
la pierna — leg
el pie — foot

todos los días
every day
una vez a la/por semana
once a week
de vez en cuando
now and then
nunca
never
siempre
always

el desayuno breakfast
el almuerzo/la comida lunch
la cena dinner
Como fruta una vez al día.
I eat fruit once a day.
Tengo hambre. I'm hungry.
Tengo sed. I'm thirsty.
Tengo ganas de dormir. I'm sleepy.
Me duele la cabeza. I have a headache.

Time

The seasons

la primavera spring
el verano summer
el otoño autumn
el invierno winter

Days of the Week

lunes Monday
martes Tuesday
miércoles Wednesday
jueves Thursday
viernes Friday
sábado Saturday
domingo Sunday

Months

enero January
febrero February
marzo March
abril April
mayo May
junio June
julio July
agosto August
septiembre September
octubre October
noviembre November
diciembre December

Mi cumpleaños es en febrero.
My birthday is in February.
Se fue en marzo.
She left in March.
Llegamos el 11 de noviembre.
We're arriving on 11th November.
Ricardo nació el 2 de agosto.
Richard was born on 2nd August.
en el año 2006 (dos mil seis) in 20
en el año 1999 in 1999

 la una
one o' clock

 las cuatro y media
half past four

 las seis y cuarto
quarter past six

 las seis menos cuarto
quarter to six

 las nueve y diez
ten past nine

 las nueve menos diez
ten to nine

 las 19 horas
7pm (19.00)

 las trece horas y quince minutos
1.15pm (13.15)

 el mediodía
midday

 la media noche
midnight

The Time

¿Qué hora es? What time is it?
Es la una. It's one o'clock.
Son las cuatro y media.
It's half past four.
Son las seis y cuarto.
It's quarter past six.
Son las seis menos cuarto.
It's quarter to six.
Son las nueve y diez.
It's ten past nine.
Son las nueve menos diez .
It's ten to nine.
Es el mediodía. It's midday.
Es la media noche. It's midnight.
Son las diecinueve horas. It's 7pm (19.00).
Son las trece horas y quince minutos.
It's 1.15pm (13.15).

estar triste
to be sad

estar contento/contenta
to be happy

estar enfadado/enfadada
to be angry

estar enamorado/enamorada
to be in love

tener sueño
to be tired

tener miedo
to be afraid

tener frío
to be cold

tener calor
to be hot

tener hambre
to be hungry

Numbers

One is *uno* in Spanish, but it is *un* before a masculine noun and *una* before a feminine noun, so *un lápiz* but *una mesa*, *veintiún hombres*, *veintiuna mesas*, etc.

0	cero			
1	uno, un; *fem* una	1st	1°	primero, primer; *fem* primera
2	dos	2nd	2°	segundo, *fem* segunda
3	tres	3rd	3°	tercero, tercer; *fem* tercera
4	cuatro	4th	4°	cuarto, *fem* cuarta
5	cinco	5th	5°	quinto, *fem* quinto
6	seis	6th	6°	sexto, *fem* sexta
7	siete	7th	7°	séptimo, *fem* séptima
8	ocho	8th	8°	octavo, *fem* octava
9	nueve	9th	9°	noveno, *fem* novena
10	diez	10th	10°	décimo, *fem* décima
11	once	11th	11°	undécimo, *fem* decimoprimera
12	doce	12th	12°	duodécimo, *fem* decimosegunda
13	trece	13th	13°	decimotercero, *fem* decimotercera
14	catorce	14th	14°	decimocuarto, *fem* decimocuarta
15	quince	15th	15°	decimoquinto, *fem* decimoquinta
16	dieciséis	16th	16°	decimosexto, *fem* decimosexta
17	diecisiete	17th	17°	decimoséptimo, *fem* decimoséptima
18	dieciocho	18th	18°	decimoctavo, *fem* decimoctava
19	diecinueve	19th	19°	decimonoveno, *fem* decimonoveno
20	veinte	20th	20°	vigésimo, *fem* vigésima
21	veintiuno	21st	21°	vigesimoprimero, *fem* -a
22	veintidós	22nd	22°	veintidós or vigesimosegundo, *fem* -a
23	veintitrés	23rd	23°	veintitrés or vigesimotercero, *fem* -a
24	veinticuatro	24th	24°	veinticuatro or vigesimocuarto, *fem* -a
25	veinticinco	25th	25°	veinticinco or vigesimoquinto, *fem* -a
26	veintiséis	26th	26°	veintiséis or vigésimosexto, *fem* -a
27	veintisiete	27th	27°	veintisiete or vigésimoséptimo, *fem* -a
28	veintiocho	28th	28°	veintiocho or vigesimoctavo, *fem* -a
29	veintinueve	29th	29°	veintinueve or vigesimonoveno, *fem* -a
30	treinta	30th	30°	treinta or trigésimo, *fem* -a
31	treinta y uno	31st	31°	treinta y uno, *fem* treinta y una
32	treinta y dos	32nd	32°	treinta y dos
40	cuarenta	40th	40°	cuarenta or cuadragésimo, *fem* -a
50	cincuenta	50th	50°	cincuenta or quincuagésimo, *fem* -a
60	sesenta	60th	60°	sesenta or sexagésimo, *fem* -a
70	setenta	70th	70°	setenta or septuagésimo, *fem* -a
80	ochenta	80th	80°	ochenta or octogésimo, *fem* -a
90	noventa	90th	90°	noventa or nonagésimo, *fem* -a
100	cien	100th	100°	centésimo, *fem* centésima
101	ciento uno	101st	101°	ciento uno, *fem* ciento una
200	doscientos	200th	200°	doscientos, *fem* doscientas
201	doscientos uno	201st	201°	doscientos uno, *fem* doscientas una
500	quinientos	500th	500°	quinientos, *fem* quinientas
700	setecientos	700th	700°	setecientos, *fem* setecientas
900	novecientos	900th	900°	novecientos, *fem* novecientas

When writing longer numbers Spanish uses a space or a full stop instead of a comma—for example, 1 000 or 1.000 rather than 1,000. With ordinals write a raised ° after the number.

1.000	mil	1000th	1.000°	milésimo, *fem* -a
1.001	mil uno	1001st	1.001°	mil uno
2.000	dos mil	2000th	2.000°	dos mil
2.007	dos mil siete	2007th	2.007°	dos mil siete
1.000.000	un millón	1000000th	1.000.000°	millonésimo, *fem* -a

Major Spanish verbs

Regular –ar verbs

Regular –er verbs

Regular –ir verbs

Irregular –ar verbs

Irregular –er verbs

Irregular –ir verbs

[1] ser
to be

Present indicative
soy
eres
es
somos
sois
son

Conditional (present)
sería
serías
sería
seríamos
seríais
serían

Past simple indicative
fui
fuiste
fue
fuimos
fuisteis
fueron

Present subjunctive
sea
seas
sea
seamos
seáis
sean

Future indicative
seré
serás
será
seremos
seréis
serán

Imperfect subjunctive
fuera
fueras
fuera
fuéramos
fuerais
fueran

Imperfect indicative
era
eras
era
éramos
erais
eran

Imperative
sé (*tú*)
sea (*usted*)
seamos (*nosotros*)
sed (*vosotros*)
sean (*ustedes*)

Gerund
siendo

Past participle
sido

[2] **estar**
to be

Present indicative
estoy
estás
está
estamos
estáis
están

Conditional (present)
estaría
estarías
estaría
estaríamos
estaríais
estarían

Past simple indicative
estuve
estuviste
estuvo
estuvimos
estuvisteis
estuvieron

Present subjunctive
esté
estés
esté
estemos
estéis
estén

Future indicative
estaré
estarás
estará
estaremos
estaréis
estarán

Imperfect subjunctive
estuviera
estuvieras
estuviera
estuviéramos
estuvieras
estuvieran

Imperfect indicative
estaba
estabas
estaba
estábamos
estabais
estaban

Imperative
está (*tú*)
esté (*usted*)
estemos (*nosotros*)
estad (*vosotros*)
estén (*ustedes*)

Gerund
estando

Past participle
estado

[3] **coger**
to take

Present indicative
cojo
coges
coge
cogemos
cogéis
cogen

Conditional (present)
cogería
cogerías
cogería
cogeríamos
cogeríais
cogerían

Past simple indicative
cogí
cogiste
cogió
cogimos
cogisteis
cogieron

Present subjunctive
coja
cojas
coja
cojamos
cojáis
cojan

Future indicative
cogeré
cogerás
cogerá
cogeremos
cogeréis
cogerán

Imperfect subjunctive
cogiera
cogieras
cogiera
cogiéramos
cogierais
cogieran

Imperfect indicative
cogía
cogías
cogía
cogíamos
cogíais
cogían

Imperative
coge (*tú*)
coja (*usted*)
cojamos (*nosotros*)
coged (*vosotros*)
cojan (*ustedes*)

Gerund
cogiendo

Past participle
cogido

[4] **dar**
to give

Present indicative
doy
das
da
damos
dais
dan

Conditional (present)
daría
darías
daría
daríamos
daríais
darían

Past simple indicative
di
diste
dio
dimos
disteis
dieron

Present subjunctive
dé
des
dé
demos
deis
den

Future indicative
daré
darás
dará
daremos
daréis
darán

Imperfect subjunctive
diera
dieras
diera
diéramos
dierais
dieran

Imperfect indicative
daba
dabas
daba
dábamos
dabais
daban

Imperative
da (*tú*)
de (*usted*)
demos (*nosotros*)
dad (*vosotros*)
den (*ustedes*)

Gerund
dando

Past participle
dado

Verb tables

[5] decir
to say, to tell

Present indicative
digo
dices
dice
decimos
decís
dicen

Conditional (present)
diría
dirías
diría
diríamos
diríais
dirían

Past simple indicative
dije
dijiste
dijo
dijimos
dijisteis
dijeron

Present subjunctive
diga
digas
diga
digamos
digáis
digan

Future indicative
diré
dirás
dirá
diremos
diréis
dirán

Imperfect subjunctive
dijera
dijeras
dijera
dijéramos
dijerais
dijeran

Imperfect indicative
decía
decías
decía
decíamos
decíais
decían

Imperative
di (*tú*)
diga (*usted*)
digamos (*nosotros*)
decid (*vosotros*)
digan (*ustedes*)

Gerund
diciendo

Past participle
dicho

[6] **haber**
to have

Present indicative	Conditional
he	habría
has	habrías
ha	habría
hemos	habríamos
habéis	habríais
han	habrían

Past simple indicative	Present subjunctive
hube	haya
hubiste	hayas
hubo	haya
hubimos	hayamos
hubisteis	hayáis
hubieron	hayan

Future indicative	Imperfect subjunctive
habré	hubiera
habrás	hubieras
habrá	hubiera
habremos	hubiéramos
habréis	hubieras
habrán	hubieran

Imperfect indicative	Imperative
había	he (*tú*)
habías	haya (*usted*)
había	hayamos (*nosotros*)
habíamos	habed (*vosotros*)
habíais	hayan (*ustedes*)
habían	

Gerund	Past participle
habiendo	habido

[7] **hacer**
to make, to do

Present indicative	**Conditional (present)**
hago	haría
haces	harías
hace	haría
hacemos	haríamos
hacéis	haríais
hacen	harían

Past simple indicative	**Present subjunctive**
hice	haga
hiciste	hagas
hizo	haga
hicimos	hagamos
hicisteis	hagáis
hicieron	hagan

Future indicative	**Imperfect subjunctive**
haré	hiciera
harás	hicieras
hará	hiciera
haremos	hiciéramos
haréis	hicierais
harán	hicieran

Imperfect indicative	**Imperative**
hacía	haz (*tú*)
hacías	haga (*usted*)
hacía	hagamos (*nosotros*)
hacíamos	haced (*vosotros*)
hacíais	hagan (*ustedes*)
hacían	

Gerund	**Past participle**
haciendo	hecho

[8] ir
to have

Present indicative	Conditional
voy	iría
vas	irías
va	iría
vamos	iríamos
vais	iríais
van	irían

Past simple indicative	Present subjunctive
fui	vaya
fuiste	vayas
fue	vaya
fuimos	vayamos
fuisteis	vayáis
fueron	vayan

Future indicative	Imperfect subjunctive
iré	fuera
irás	fueras
irá	fuera
iremos	fuéramos
iréis	fuerais
irán	fueran

Imperfect indicative	Imperative
iba	ve (*tú*)
ibas	vaya (*usted*)
iba	vayamos (*nosotros*)
íabmos	id (*vosotros*)
ibais	vayan (*ustedes*)
iban	

Gerund	Past participle
yendo	ido

[9] **tener**
to have

Present indicative

tengo
tienes
tiene
tenemos
tenéis
tienen

Conditional (present)

tendría
tendrías
tendría
tendríamos
tendríais
tendrían

Past simple indicative

tuve
tuviste
tuvo
tuvimos
tuvisteis
tuvieron

Present subjunctive

tenga
tengas
tenga
tengamos
tengáis
tengan

Future indicative

tendré
tendrás
tendrá
tendremos
tendréis
tendrán

Imperfect subjunctive

tuviera
tuvieras
tuviera
tuviéramos
tuvierais
tuvieran

Imperfect indicative

tenía
tenías
tenía
teníamos
teníais
tenían

Imperative

ten (*tú*)
tenga (*usted*)
tengamos (*nosotros*)
tened (*vosotros*)
tengan (*ustedes*)

Gerund

teniendo

Past participle

tenido

[10] **poder**
to be able

Present indicative
puedo
puedes
puede
podemos
podéis
pueden

Conditional
podría
podrías
podría
podríamos
podríais
podrían

Past simple indicative
pude
pudiste
pudo
pudimos
pudisteis
pudieron

Present subjunctive
pueda
puedas
pueda
podamos
podáis
puedan

Future indicative
podré
podrás
podrá
podremos
podréis
podrán

Imperfect subjunctive
pudiera
pudieras
pudiera
pudiéramos
pudierais
pudieran

Imperfect indicative
podía
podías
podía
podíamos
podíais
podían

Imperative
puede (*tú*)
pueda (*usted*)
podamos (*nosotros*)
poded (*vosotros*)
puedan (*ustedes*)

Gerund
pudiendo

Past participle
podido

[11] poner
to put

Present indicative
pongo
pones
pone
ponemos
ponéis
ponen

Conditional (present)
pondría
pondrías
pondría
pondríamos
pondríais
pondrían

Past simple indicative
puse
pusiste
puso
pusimos
pusisteis
pusieron

Present subjunctive
ponga
pongas
ponga
pongamos
pongáis
pongan

Future indicative
pondré
pondrás
pondrá
pondremos
pondréis
pondrán

Imperfect subjunctive
pusiera
pusieras
pusiera
pusiéramos
pusierais
pusieran

Imperfect indicative
ponía
ponías
ponía
poníamos
poníais
ponían

Imperative
pon (*tú*)
ponga (*usted*)
pongamos (*nosotros*)
poned (*vosotros*)
pongan (*ustedes*)

Gerund
poniendo

Past participle
puesto

[12] querer
to want, to love

Present indicative
quiero
quieres
quiere
queremos
queréis
quieren

Conditional
querría
querrías
querría
querríamos
querríais
querrían

Past simple indicative
quise
quisiste
quiso
quisimos
quisisteis
quisieron

Present subjunctive
quiera
quieras
quiera
queramos
queráis
quieran

Future indicative
querré
querrás
querrá
querremos
querréis
querrán

Imperfect subjunctive
quisiera
quisieras
quisiera
quisiéramos
quisierais
quisieran

Imperfect indicative
quería
querías
quería
queríamos
queríais
querían

Imperative
quiere (*tú*)
quiera (*usted*)
queramos (*nosotros*)
quered (*vosotros*)
quieran (*ustedes*)

Gerund
queriendo

Past participle
querido

[13] saber
to know

Present indicative
sé
sabes
sabe
sabemos
sabéis
saben

Conditional (present)
sabría
sabrías
sabría
sabríamos
sabríais
sabrían

Past simple indicative
supe
supiste
supo
supimos
supisteis
supieron

Present subjunctive
sepa
sepas
sepa
sepamos
sepáis
sepan

Future indicative
sabré
sabrás
sabrá
sabremos
sabréis
sabrán

Imperfect subjunctive
supiera
supieras
supiera
supiera
supiéramos
supierais
supieran

Imperfect indicative
sabía
sabías
sabía
sabíamos
sabíais
sabían

Imperative
sabe (*tú*)
sepa (*usted*)
sepamos (*nosotros*)
sabed (*vosotros*)
sepan (*ustedes*)

Gerund
sabiendo

Past participle
sabido

[14] **sentir**
to feel

Present indicative
siento
sientes
siente
sentimos
sentís
sienten

Conditional
sentiría
sentirías
sentiría
sentiríamos
sentiríais
sentirían

Past simple indicative
sentí
sentiste
sintió
sentimos
sentisteis
sintieron

Present subjunctive
sienta
sientas
sienta
sintamos
sintáis
sientan

Future indicative
sentiré
sentirás
sentirá
sentiremos
sentiréis
sentirán

Imperfect subjunctive
sintiera
sientieras
sintiéramos
sintierais
sintieran

Imperfect indicative
sentía
sentías
sentía
sentíamos
sentíais
sentían

Imperative
siente (*tú*)
sienta (*usted*)
sintamos (*nosotros*)
sentid (*vosotros*)
sientan (*ustedes*)

Gerund
sintiendo

Past participle
sentido

[15] **venir**
to come

Present indicative
vengo
vienes
viene
venimos
venís
vienen

Conditional (present)
vendría
vendrías
vendría
vendríamos
vendríais
vendrían

Past simple indicative
vine
viniste
vino
vinimos
vinisteis
vinieron

Present subjunctive
venga
vengas
venga
vengamos
vengáis
vengan

Future indicative
vendré
vendrás
vendrá
vendremos
vendréis
vendrán

Imperfect subjunctive
viniera
vinieras
viniera
viniéramos
vinierais
vinieran

Imperfect indicative
venía
venías
venía
veníamos
veníais
venían

Imperative
ven (*tú*)
venga (*usted*)
vengamos (*nosotros*)
venid (*vosotros*)
vengan (*ustedes*)

Gerund
viniendo

Past participle
venido

[16] **ver**
to see

Present indicative
veo
ves
ve
vemos
veis
ven

Conditional
vería
verías
vería
veríamos
veríais
verían

Past simple indicative
vi
viste
vio
vimos
visteis
vieron

Present subjunctive
vea
veas
vea
veamos
veáis
vean

Future indicative
veré
verás
verá
veremos
veréis
verán

Imperfect subjunctive
viera
vieras
viera
viéramos
veáis
vieran

Imperfect indicative
veía
veías
veía
veíamos
veíais
veían

Imperative
ve (*tú*)
vea (*usted*)
veamos (*nosotros*)
ved (*vosotros*)
vean (*ustedes*)

Gerund
viendo

Past participle
visto

Regular verbs

[17] **hablar**
to talk, to speak

Present indicative
hablo
hablas
habla
hablamos
habláis
hablan

Conditional (present)
hablaría
hablarías
hablaría
hablaríamos
hablaríais
hablarían

Past simple indicative
hablé
hablaste
habló
hablamos
hablasteis
hablaron

Present subjunctive
hable
hables
hable
hablemos
habléis
hablen

Future indicative
hablaré
hablarás
hablará
hablaremos
hablaréis
hablarán

Imperfect subjunctive
hablara
hablaras
hablara
habláramos
hablarais
hablaran

Imperfect indicative
hablaba
hablabas
hablaba
hablábamos
hablabais
hablaban

Imperative
habla (*tú*)
hable (*usted*)
hablemos (*nosotros*)
hablad (*vosotros*)
hablen (*ustedes*)

Gerund
hablando

Past participle
hablado

[18] comer
to eat

Present indicative
como
comes
come
comemos
coméis
comen

Conditional
comería
comerías
comería
comeríamos
comeríais
comerían

Past simple indicative
comí
comiste
comió
comimos
comisteis
comieron

Present subjunctive
coma
comas
coma
comamos
comáis
coman

Future indicative
comeré
comerás
comerá
comeremos
comeréis
comerán

Imperfect subjunctive
comiera
comieras
comiera
comiéramos
comierais
comieran

Imperfect indicative
comía
comías
comía
comíamos
comíais
comían

Imperative
come (*tú*)
coma (*usted*)
comamos (*nosotros*)
comed (*vosotros*)
coman (*ustedes*)

Gerund
comiendo

Past participle
comido

[19] **vivir**
to live

Present indicative
vivo
vives
vive
vivimos
vivís
viven

Conditional (present)
viviría
vivirías
viviría
viviríamos
viviríais
vivirían

Past simple indicative
viví
viviste
vivió
vivimos
vivisteis
vivieron

Present subjunctive
viva
vivas
viva
vivamos
viváis
vivan

Future indicative
viviré
vivirás
vivirá
viviremos
viviréis
vivirán

Imperfect subjunctive
viviera
vivieras
viviera
viviéramos
vivierais
vivieran

Imperfect indicative
vivía
vivías
vivía
vivíamos
vivíais
vivían

Imperative
vive (*tú*)
viva (*usted*)
vivamos (*nosotros*)
vivid (*vosotros*)
vivan (*ustedes*)

Gerund
viviendo

Past participle
vivido

Irregular –ar verbs

[20] actuar like [17] **hablar** except:

Present indicative	Present subjunctive
actúo	actúe
actúas	actúes
actúa	actúe
actuamos	actuemos
actuáis	actuéis
actúan	actúen

Imperative
actúa (tú)
actúe (usted)
actuemos (nosotros)
actuad (vosotros)
actúen (ustedes)

[21] andar like [17] **hablar** except:

Past simple indicative	Imperfect subjunctive
anduve	anduviera
anduviste	anduvieras
anduvo	anduviera
anduvimos	anduviéramos
andivisteis	anduvierais
anduvieron	anduvieran

[22] cazar like [17] **hablar** except:

Past simple indicative	Present subjunctive
cacé	cace
cazaste	caces
cazó	cace
cazamos	cacemos
cazasteis	cacéis
cazaron	cacen

Imperative
caza (tú)
cace (usted)
cacemos (nosotros)
cazad (vosotros)
cacen (ustedes)

[23] colgar like [17] **hablar** except:

Present indicative	Present subjunctive
cuelgo	cuelgue
cuelgas	cuelgues
cuelga	cuelgue
colgamos	colguemos
colgáis	colguéis
cuelgan	cuelguen

Past simple indicative	Imperative
colgué	cuelga (tú)
colgaste	cuelgue (usted)
colgó	colguemos
colgamos	(nosotros)
colgasteis	colgad (vosotros)
colgaron	cuelguen (ustedes)

[24] contar like [17] **hablar** except:

Present indicative	Present subjunctive
cuento	cuente
cuentas	cuentes
cuenta	cuente
contamos	contemos
contáis	contéis
cuentan	cuenten

Imperative
cuenta (tú)
cuente (usted)
contemos
(nosotros)
contad (vosotros)
cuenten (ustedes)

Irregular –ar verbs

[25] empezar like [17] hablar except:

Present indicative	Present subjunctive
empiezo	empiece
empiezas	empieces
empieza	empiece
empezamos	empecemos
empezáis	empecéis
empiezan	empiecen

Past simple indicative	Imperative
empecé	empieza (tú)
empezaste	empiece (usted)
empezó	empecemos
empezamos	(nosotros)
empezasteis	empezad (vosotros)
empezaron	empiecen (ustedes)

[27] jugar like [17] hablar except:

Present indicative	Present subjunctive
juego	juegue
juegas	juegues
juega	juegue
jugamos	juguemos
jugáis	juguéis
juegan	jueguen

Past simple indicative	Imperative
jugué	juega (tú)
jugaste	juegue (usted)
jugó	juguemos
jugamos	(nosotros)
jugasteis	jugad (vosotros)
jugaron	jueguen (ustedes)

[26] forzar like [17] hablar except:

Present indicative	Present subjunctive
fuerzo	fuerce
fuerzas	fuerces
fuerza	fuerce
forzamos	forcemos
forzáis	forcéis
fuerzan	fuercen

Past simple indicative	Imperative
forcé	fuerza (tú)
forzaste	fuerce (usted)
forzó	forcemos
forzamos	(nosotros)
forzasteis	forzad (vosotros)
forzaron	fuercen (ustedes)

[28] pagar like [17] hablar except:

Past simple indicative	Present subjunctive
pagué	pague
pagaste	pagues
pagó	pague
pagamos	paguemos
pagasteis	paguéis
pagaron	paguen

	Imperative
	paga (tú)
	pague (usted)
	paguemos
	(nosotros)
	pagad (vosotros)
	paguen (ustedes)

Irregular –ar verbs

[29] pensar like [17] **hablar** except:

Present indicative	Present subjunctive
pienso	piense
piensas	pienses
piensa	piense
pensamos	pensemos
pensáis	penséis
piensan	piensen

Imperative
piensa (tú)
piense (usted)
pensemos (nosotros)
pensad (vosotros)
piensen (ustedes)

[31] sacar like [17] **hablar** except:

Past simple indicative	Present subjunctive
saqué	saque
sacaste	saques
sacó	saque
sacamos	saquemos
sacasteis	saquéis
sacaron	saquen

Imperative
saca (tú)
saque (usted)
saquemos (nosotros)
sacad (vosotros)
saquen (ustedes)

[30] regar like [17] **hablar** except:

Present indicative	Present subjunctive
riego	riegue
riegas	riegues
riega	riegue
regamos	reguemos
regáis	reguéis
riegan	rieguen

Past simple indicative	Imperative
regué	riega (tú)
regaste	riegue (usted)
regó	reguemos (nosotros)
regamos	regad (vosotros)
regasteis	rieguen (ustedes)
regaron	

[32] vaciar like [17] **hablar** except:

Present indicative	Present subjunctive
vacío	vacíe
vacías	vacíes
vacía	vacíe
vaciamos	vaciemos
vaciáis	vaciéis
vacían	vacíen

Imperative
vacía (tú)
vacíe (usted)
vaciemos (nosotros)
vaciad (vosotros)
vacíen (ustedes)

Irregular –er verbs

[33] caber like [18] comer except:

Present indicative	Conditional (present)
quepo	cabría
cabes	cabrías
cabe	cabría
cabemos	cabríamos
cabéis	cabríais
caben	cabrían

Past simple indicative	Present subjunctive
cupe	quepa
cupiste	quepas
cupo	quepa
cupimos	quepamos
cupisteis	quepáis
cupieron	quepan

Future indicative	Imperfect subjunctive
cabré	cupiera
cabrás	cupieras
cabrá	cupiera
cabremos	cupiéramos
cabréis	cupierais
cabrán	cupieran

Imperative
cabe (tú)
quepa (usted)
quepamos
(nosotros)
cabed (vosotros)
quepan (ustedes)

[34] caer like [18] comer except:

Present indicative	Imperfect subjunctive
caigo	cayera
caes	cayeras
cae	cayera
caemos	cayéramos
caéis	cayerais
caen	cayeran

Past simple indicative	Imperative
caí	cae (tú)
caíste	caiga (usted)
cayó	caigamos
caímos	(nosotros)
caísteis	caed (vosotros)
cayeron	caigan (ustedes)

Present subjunctive	Gerund
caiga	cayendo
caigas	
caiga	Past participle
caigamos	caido
caigáis	
caigan	

[35] conocer like [18] comer except:

Present indicative	Present subjunctive
conozco	conozca
conoces	conozcas
conoce	conozca
conocemos	conozcamos
conocéis	conozcáis
conocen	conozcan

Imperative
conoce (tú)
conozca (usted)
conozcamos
 (nosotros)
conoced (vosotros)
conozcan (ustedes)

Irregular –er verbs

[36] entender like [18] **comer** except:

Present indicative	Present subjunctive
entiendo	entienda
entiendes	entiendas
entiende	entienda
entendemos	entendamos
entendéis	entendáis
entienden	entiendan

Imperative
entiende (tú)
entienda (usted)
entendamos (nosotros)
entended (vosotros)
entiendan (ustedes)

[39] oler like [18] **comer** except:

Present indicative	Present subjunctive
huelo	huela
hueles	huelas
huele	huela
olemos	olamos
oléis	oláis
huelen	huelan

Imperative
huele (tú)
huela (usted)
olamos (nosotros)
oled (vosotros)
huelan (ustedes)

[37] leer like [18] **comer** except:

Past simple indicative	Imperfect subjunctive
leí	leyera
leíste	leyeras
leyó	leyera
leímos	layéramos
leísteis	leyerais
leyeron	leyeran

Gerund	Past participle
leyendo	leído

[40] romper like [18] **comer** except:

Past participle
roto

[38] mover like [18] **comer** except:

Present indicative	Present subjunctive
muevo	mueva
mueves	muevas
mueve	mueva
movemos	movamos
movéis	mováis
mueven	muevan

Imperative
mueve (tu)
mueva (usted)
movamos (nosotros)
moved (vosotros)
muevan (ustedes)

[41] torcer like [18] **comer** except:

Present indicative	Present subjunctive
tuerzo	tuerza
tuerces	tuerzas
tuerce	torzamos
torcemos	torzáis
torcéis	tuerzan
tuercen	

Imperative
tuerce (tú)
tuerza (usted)
torzamos (nosotros)
torced (vosotros)
tuerzan (ustedes)

Irregular –er verbs

[42] **traer**   like [18] **comer** except:

Present indicative	Past simple indicative
traigo	traje
traes	trajiste
trae	trajo
traemos	trajimos
traéis	trajisteis
traen	trajeron

Present subjunctive	Imperative
traiga	trae (tú)
traigas	traiga (usted)
traiga	traigamos
traigamos	(nosotros)
traigáis	traed (vosotros)
traigan	traigan (ustedes)

Imperfect subjunctive	Gerund
trajera	trayendo
trajeras	
trajera	
trajéramos	Past participle
trajerais	traído
trajeran	

[44] **vencer**   like [18] **comer** except:

Present indicative	Present subjunctive
venzo	venza
vences	venzas
vence	venza
vencemos	venzamos
vencéis	venzáis
vencen	venzan

	Imperative
	vence (tú)
	venza (usted)
	venzamos
	(nosotros)
	venced (vosotros)
	venzan (ustedes)

[43] **valer**   like [18] **comer** except:

Present indicative	Present subjunctive
valgo	valga
vales	valgas
vale	valga
valemos	valgamos
valéis	valgáis
valen	valgan

Future indicative	Imperfect subjunctive
valdré	valiera
valdrás	valieras
valdrá	valiera
valdremos	valiéramos
valdréis	valierais
valdrán	valieran

Conditional (present)	Imperative
valdría	vale (tú)
valdrías	valga (usted)
valdría	valgamos
valdríamos	(nosotros)
valdríais	valed (vosotros)
valdrían	valgan (ustedes)

[45] **volver**   like [18] **comer** except:

Present indicative	Imperative
vuelvo	vuelve (tú)
vuelves	vuelva (usted)
vuelve	volvamos
volvemos	(nosotros)
volvéis	volved (vosotros)
vuelven	vuelvan (ustedes)

Present subjunctive	Past participle
vuelva	vuelto
vuelvas	
vuelva	
volvamos	
volváis	
vuelvan	

Irregular –ir verbs

[46] **abrir** like [19] **vivir** except:

Past participle
abierto

[47] **adquirir** like [19] **vivir** except:

Present indicative	Imperative
adquiero	adquiere (tú)
adquieres	adquiera (usted)
adquiere	adquiramos
adquirimos	(nosotros)
adquirís	adquirid (vosotros)
adquieren	adquieran (ustedes)

Present subjunctive
adquiera
adquieras
adquiera
adquiramos
adquiráis
adquieran

[48] **corregir** like [19] **vivir** except:

Present indicative	Present subjunctive
corrijo	corrija
corriges	corrijas
corrige	corrija
corregimos	corrijamos
corregís	corrijáis
corrigen	corrijan

Past simple indicative	Imperative
corregí	corrige (tú)
corregiste	corrija (usted)
corrigió	corrijamos
corrigieron	(nosotros)
corregisteis	corregid (vosotros)
corrigieron	corrijan (ustedes)

[49] **dirigir** like [19] **vivir** except:

Present indicative	Present subjunctive
dirijo	dirija
diriges	dirijas
dirige	dirija
dirigimos	dirijamos
dirigís	dirijáis
dirigen	dirijan

Imperative
dirige (tú)
dirija (usted)
dirijamos (nosotros)
dirigid (vosotros)
dirijan (ustedes)

[50] **distinguir** like [19] **vivir** except:

Present indicative	Present subjunctive
distingo	distinga
distingues	distingas
distingue	distinga
distinguimos	distingamos
distinguís	distingáis
distinguen	distingan

Imperative
distingue (tú)
distinga (usted)
distingamos
(nosotros)
distinguid
(vosotros)
distingan (ustedes)

[51] **dormir** like [19] **vivir** except:

Present indicative	Imperfect subjunctive
duermo	durmiera
duermes	durmieras
duerme	durmiera
dormimos	durmiéramos
dormís	durmierais
duermen	durmieran

Past simple indicative	Imperative
dormí	duerme (tú)
dormiste	duerma (usted)
durmió	durmamos
dormimos	(nosotros)
dormisteis	dormid (vosotros)
durmieron	duerman (ustedes)

Present subjunctive	Gerund
duerma	durmiendo
duermas	
duerma	Past participle
durmamos	dormido
durmáis	
duerman	

Irregular verbs

Irregular –ir verbs

[52] escribir like [19] **vivir** except:

Past participle
escrito

[53] freír like [19] **vivir** except:

Present indicative	Imperfect subjunctive
frío	friera
fríes	frieras
fríe	friera
freímos	friéramos
freís	frierais
fríen	frieran

Past simple indicative	Imperative
freí	fríe (tú)
freíste	fría (usted)
frió	friamos (nosotros)
freímos	freíd (vosotros)
freísteis	frían (ustedes)
frieron	

Present subjunctive	Gerund
fría	friendo
frías	
fría	Past participle
friamos	frito
friáis	
frían	

[54] huir like [19] **vivir** except:

Present indicative	Imperfect subjunctive
huyo	huyera
huyes	huyeras
huye	huyera
huimos	huyéramos
huís	huyerais
huyen	huyeran

Past simple indicative	Imperative
huí	huye (tú)
huiste	huya (usted)
huyó	huyamos (nosotros)
huimos	huid (vosotros)
huisteis	huyan (ustedes)
huyeron	

Present subjunctive	Gerund
huya	huyendo
huyas	
huya	Past participle
huyamos	huido
huyáis	
huyan	

[55] morir like [19] **vivir** except:

Present indicative	Present subjunctive
muero	muera
mueres	mueras
muere	muera
morimos	muramos
morís	muráis
mueren	mueran

Past simple indicative	Imperfect subjunctive
morí	muriera
moriste	murieras
murió	muriera
morimos	muriéramos
moristeis	murierais
murieron	murieran

Gerund	Past participle
muriendo	muerto

Irregular –ir verbs

[56] oír   like [19] vivir except:

Present indicative	Present subjunctive
oigo	oiga
oyes	oigas
oye	oiga
oímos	oigamos
oís	oigáis
oyen	oigan

Past simple indicative	Imperfect subjunctive
oí	oyera
oíste	oyeras
oyó	oyera
oímos	oyéramos
oísteis	oyerais
oyeron	oyeran

Future indicative	Imperative
oiré	oye (tú)
oirás	oiga (usted)
oirá	oigamos (nosotros)
oiremos	oíd (vosotros)
oiréis	oigan (ustedes)
oirán	

Conditional (present)	Gerund
oiría	oyendo
oirías	
oiría	
oiríamos	Past participle
oiríais	oído
oirían	

Imperfect indicative	
oía	
oías	
oía	
oíamos	
oíais	
oían	

[57] pedir   like [19] vivir except:

Present indicative	Present subjunctive
pido	pida
pides	pidas
pide	pida
pedimos	pidamos
pedís	pidáis
piden	pidan

Past simple indicative	Imperfect subjunctive
pedí	pidiera
pediste	pidieras
pidió	pidiera
pedimos	pidiéramos
pedisteis	pidierais
pidieron	pidieran

Imperative
pide (tú)
pida (usted)
pidamos (nosotros)
pedid (vosotros)
pidan (ustedes)

[58] prohibir   like [19] vivir except:

Present indicative	Present subjunctive
prohíbo	prohíba
prohíbes	prohíbas
prohíbe	prohíba
prohibimos	prohíbamos
prohibís	prohibáis
prohíben	prohíban

Imperative
prohíbe (tú)
prohíba (usted)
prohibamos (nosotros)
prohibid (vosotros)
prohíban (ustedes)

Irregular verbs

Irregular –ir verbs

[59] pudrir like [19] **vivir** except:

Past participle
podrido

[60] reducir like [19] **vivir** except:

Present indicative	Present subjunctive
reduzco	reduzca
reduces	reduzcas
reduce	reduzca
reducimos	reduzcamos
reducís	reduzcáis
reducen	reduzcan

Past simple indicative	Imperfect subjunctive
reduje	redujera
redujiste	redujeras
redujo	redujera
redujimos	redujéramos
redujisteis	redujerais
redujeron	redujeran

Imperative
reduce (tú)
reduzca (usted)
reduzcamos (nosotros)
reducid (vosotros)
reduzcan (ustedes)

[61] reír like [19] **vivir** except:

Present indicative	Conditional (present)
río	reiriá
ríes	reirías
ríe	reiría
reímos	reiríamos
reís	reiríais
ríen	reirían

Imperfect indicative	Present subjunctive
reía	ría
reías	rías
reía	ría
reíamos	riamos
reiais	riáis
reían	rían

Past simple indicative	Imperfect subjunctive
reí	riera
reiste	rieras
rió	riera
reímos	riéramos
reisteis	rierais
rieron	rieran

Future indicative	Imperative
reiré	ríe (tú)
reirás	ría (usted)
reirá	riamos (nosotros)
reiremos	reíd (vosotros)
reiréis	rían (ustedes)
reirán	

[62] reunir like [19] **vivir** except:

Present indicative	Present subjunctive
reúno	reúna
réunes	reúnas
reúne	reúna
reunimos	reunamos
reunís	reunáis
reúnen	reúnan

Imperative
reúne (tú)
reúna (usted)
reunamos (nosotros)
reunid (vosotros)
reúnan (ustedes)

Irregular –ir verbs

[63] salir like [19] **vivir** except:

Present indicative	Present subjunctive
salgo	salga
sales	salgas
sale	salgamos
salimos	salgáis
salís	salgan
salen	

Future indicative	Imperfect subjunctive
saldré	saliera
saldrás	salieras
saldrá	saliera
saldremos	saliéramos
saldréis	salierais
saldrán	salieran

Conditional (present)	Imperative
saldría	sal (tú)
saldrías	salga (usted)
saldría	salgamos
saldríamos	(nosotros)
saldríais	salid (vosotros)
saldrían	salgan (ustedes)

[65] tenir like [19] **vivir** except:

Present indicative	Present subjunctive
tiño	tiña
tiñes	tiñas
tiñe	tiña
teñimos	tiñamos
teñís	tiñáis
tiñen	tiñan

Past simple indicative	Imperfect subjunctive
teñí	tiñera
teñiste	tiñeras
tiñó	tiñera
teñiesteis	tiñéramos
tiñeron	tiñerais
	tiñeran

	Imperative
	tiñe (tú)
	tiña (usted)
	tiñamos (nosotros)
	teñid (vosotros)
	tiñan (ustedes)

[64] seguir like [19] **vivir** except:

Present indicative	Present subjunctive
sigo	siga
sigues	sigas
sigue	siga
seguimos	sigamos
seguís	sigáis
siguen	sigan

Past simple indicative	Imperfect subjunctive
seguí	siguiera
seguiste	siguieras
siguió	siguiera
seguimos	siguiéramos
seguisteis	siguierais
siguieron	siguieran

	Imperative
	sigue (tú)
	siga (usted)
	sigamos (nosotros)
	seguid (vosotros)
	sigan (ustedes)

A a

ɕ a *determiner*

1 (*before a masc noun*) **un**
   a tree un árbol
   a boy un chico

2 (*before a fem noun*) **una**
   a table una mesa
   a girl una chica

3 (*saying how much, how fast, etc*) **five euros a
   kilo** cinco euros el kilo
   fifty kilometres an hour cincuenta
   kilómetros por hora
   three times a day tres veces al día

4 (*saying what you do*) **She's a doctor.** Es
   médica.
   I'm a student. Soy estudiante.

WORD TIP *a* is not translated into Spanish when
you say your profession.

to **abandon** *verb*
   abandonar [17]

abbey *noun*
   la **abadía** *fem*
   Westminster Abbey la abadía de
   Westminster

abbreviation *noun*
   la **abreviatura** *fem*

to **abide** *verb*
   I can't abide … No soporto …

ability *noun*
   la **capacidad** *fem*
   the ability to do something la capacidad de
   hacer algo
   Do it to the best of your ability. Hazlo lo
   mejor que puedas.
   I did it to the best of my ability. Lo hice lo
   mejor que pude.

able *adjective*
   to be able to do something poder [10]
   hacer algo
   Will you be able to come? ¿Podrás venir?
   She wasn't able to come. No pudo venir.

abnormal *adjective*
   anormal *masc & fem*

to **abolish** *verb*
   abolir [19]

abortion *noun*
   el **aborto** *masc*

ɕ about *adverb* ▷ see **about** *prep*

1 (*to give an idea of something*) **There are about
   sixty people.** Hay unas sesenta personas.
   at about three o'clock a eso de las tres,
   como a las tres
   about a month ago hace
   aproximadamente un mes

2 (*almost ready*) **to be about to do something**
   estar [2] a punto de hacer algo
   I'm about to leave the house. Estoy a punto
   de salir de la casa.

ɕ about *preposition* ▷ see **about** *adv*

1 (*on the subject of*) **sobre**
   a film about Picasso una película sobre
   Picasso
   What's it about? ¿De qué trata?

2 (*to talk, think on the subject of*) **acerca de**
   He wants to talk to you about your exam.
   Quiere hablarte acerca de tu examen.
   to talk about something hablar [17] de algo
   What is she talking about? ¿De qué está
   hablando?
   to think about somebody, something
   pensar [29] en alguien, algo
   I'm thinking about you. Estoy pensando en
   ti.
   She's thinking about her holidays. Está
   pensando en las vacaciones.

ɕ above *adverb* ▷ see **above** *prep*
   arriba
   See above. Ver arriba.
   the flat above el piso de arriba

ɕ above *preposition* ▷ see **above** *adv*

1 (*about where something is*) **encima de**
   above the sink encima del fregadero
   the flat above ours el piso que está encima
   del nuestro

2 (*about numbers*) **por encima de**
   temperatures above 20 degrees
   temperaturas por encima de los veinte
   grados

3 (*about age*) **mayor**
   pupils above 15 years old alumnos mayores
   de 15 años

ɕ abroad *adverb*
   to go abroad irse [8] al extranjero
   to live abroad vivir [19] en el extranjero
   My family lived abroad for three years. Mi
   familia vivió en el extranjero durante tres
   años.

a
b
c
d
e
f
g
h
i
j
k
l
m
n
o
p
q
r
s
t
u
v
w
x
y
z

abscess *noun*
  el **flemón** *masc*

abseiling *noun*
  el **rappel** *masc*

ℰ **absent** *adjective*
  ausente *masc & fem*
  He's absent from school today. Está ausente hoy.
  to be absent from faltar [17] a
  He was absent from the lesson. Faltó a clase.
  She's often absent from school. Falta a menudo al colegio.
  • **absent-minded** distraído *masc*, distraída *fem*

absolute *adjective*
  absoluto *masc*, **absoluta** *fem*
  an absolute disaster un desastre absoluto

ℰ **absolutely** *adverb*
  1 *(completely)* **totalmente**
    I'm absolutely certain. Estoy totalmente segura.
    It's absolutely dreadful. Es realmente terrible.
    You're absolutely right. Tienes toda la razón.
  2 *(saying you agree)* **Absolutely!** ¡Por supuesto!

to absorb *verb*
  absorber [18]

abuse *noun* ▷ see **abuse** *verb*
  1 *(violence to a child, a woman)* los **malos tratos** *masc plural*
  2 *(insults)* los **insultos** *masc plural*
  3 *(of alcohol, drugs)* alcohol abuse el alcoholismo *masc*
    drug abuse la drogadicción *fem*

to abuse *verb* ▷ see **abuse** *noun*
  to abuse somebody maltratar [17] a alguien

academic *adjective*
  académico *masc*, **académica** *fem*
  • **academic year** el año académico

to accelerate *verb*
  acelerar [17]

accelerator *noun*
  el **acelerador** *masc*

ℰ **accent** *noun*
  el **acento** *masc*
  She has a Spanish accent. Tiene acento español.

to accept *verb*
  aceptar [17]

acceptable *adjective*
  aceptable *masc & fem*

access *noun* ▷ see **access** *verb*
  el **acceso** *masc*

to access *verb* ▷ see **access** *noun*
  to access something obtener [9] acceso a algo

accessory *noun*
  el **accesorio** *masc*

ℰ **accident** *noun*
  1 *(when something goes wrong)* el **accidente** *masc*
    a road accident un accidente de carretera
    a car accident un accidente de coche
    to have an accident tener [9] un accidente
  2 *(chance)* la **casualidad** *fem*
    It's no accident. No es casualidad.
  3 *(by chance)* **by accident** por casualidad
    She broke it by accident. Lo rompió sin querer.
  4 *(without meaning to)* **by accident** sin querer
    I found it by accident. Lo encontré por casualidad.

accidental *adjective*
  fortuito *masc*, **fortuita** *fem*
  an accidental discovery un descubrimiento fortuito

accident & emergency *noun*
  las **urgencias** *fem pl*

accidentally *adverb*
  1 *(without meaning to)* **sin querer**
    I accidentally knocked over his glass. Le tiré el vaso sin querer.
  2 *(by chance)* **por casualidad**
    I accidentally discovered that ... Descubrí por casualidad que ...

ℰ **accommodation** *noun*
  el **alojamiento** *masc*
  I'm looking for accommodation. Busco alojamiento.
  What's the hotel accommodation like? ¿Cómo es el alojamiento en hotel?

ℰ **to accompany** *verb*
  to accompany somebody acompañar [17] a alguien
  Two teachers accompanied our party. Dos profesores acompañaron nuestro grupo.

according *in phrase*
  according to según
  according to Sophie según Sophie
  according to the guide book según la guía

accordion *noun*
  el **acordeón** *masc*

account noun

1 (in a bank, shop, post office) la **cuenta** fem
a bank account una cuenta bancaria
to open an account abrir [46] una cuenta
I have fifty pounds in my account. Tengo
cincuenta libras en mi cuenta.

2 (description of what happened) el **relato** masc

3 (in expressions) on account of debido a
The station is closed on account of the
strike. La estación está cerrada debido a la
huelga.
to take something into account tener [9]
algo en cuenta
We will take his illness into account.
Tendremos en cuenta su enfermedad.

ƌ **accountant** noun
el & la **contable** masc & fem
She's an accountant. Es contable.

accuracy noun
la **precisión** fem

accurate adjective
preciso masc, **precisa** fem

accurately adverb
con precisión

to **accuse** verb
acusar [17]
to accuse somebody of something acusar a
alguien de algo
He was accused of murder. Le acusaron de
asesinato.
to accuse somebody of doing something
acusar a alguien de hacer algo
She accused me of stealing her pen. Me
acusó de haber robado su pluma.

accustomed to adjective
to be accustomed to something estar [2]
acostumbrado, acostumbrada a algo
She's accustomed to having lots of
homework. Está acostumbrada a tener
muchos deberes.

ace adjective ▷ see **ace** noun
(informal) **de primera**
He's an ace drummer. Es un baterista de
primera.

ace noun ▷ see **ace** adj
el **as** masc
the ace of hearts el as de corazones

ƌ to **ache** verb
doler [38]
My arm aches. Me duele el brazo.
My muscles ache. Me duelen los músculos.

to **achieve** verb

1 **conseguir** [64]
She's achieved a great deal. Consiguió
mucho.
to achieve an ambition hacer [7] realidad
una ambición
to achieve an aim lograr [17] un objetivo
to achieve success tener [9] éxito

achievement noun
el **logro** masc
It's been a great achievement. Ha sido
todo un logro.

acid noun
el **ácido** masc
· acid rain la lluvia ácida

acne noun
el **acné** masc

acorn noun
la **bellota** fem

acrobat noun
el & la **acróbata** masc & fem

ƌ **across** preposition

1 (from one side to the other) **a través de**
a barrier across the street una barrera a
través de la calle
We walked across the park. Caminamos a
través del parque.
They ran across the road. Cruzaron la
carretera corriendo.

2 (on the other side of) **al otro lado de**
It's across the lake. Está al otro lado del
lago.
She lives in the house across the street.
Vive en la casa de enfrente.
She was sitting across from me. Estaba
sentada en frente de mí.

acrylic adjective
acrílico masc, **acrílica** fem

act noun ▷ see **act** verb
el **acto** masc

to **act** verb ▷ see **act** noun
actuar [20]

acting noun
la **actuación** fem
She wants to go into acting. Quiere ser
actriz.

action noun
la **acción** fem
· action replay la repetición de la jugada

active adjective
activo masc, **activa** fem

ƌ indicates key words   **385**

a
b
c
d
e
f
g
h
i
j
k
l
m
n
o
p
q
r
s
t
u
v
w
x
y
z

♂ **activity** *noun*
   actividad *fem*
   • **activity holiday** las vacaciones con
     actividades programadas

♂ **actor** *noun*
   el **actor** *masc*
   Who's your favourite actor? ¿Quién es tu
   actor favorito?

♂ **actress** *noun*
   la **actriz** *fem, fem pl:* las **actrices**
   Who's your favourite actress? ¿Quién es tu
   actriz favorita?

actual *adjective*
   real *masc & fem*
   actual cases casos reales
   his actual words sus palabras textuales
   in actual fact de hecho
   In actual fact, he didn't pay. De hecho, no
   pagó.

actually *adverb*
   (*in fact, as it happens*) **la verdad es que ...**
   Actually, I've changed my mind. La verdad
   es que he cambiado de idea.
   He's not actually here at the moment. La
   verdad es que no está aquí en este
   momento.
   Did she actually say that? ¿Dijo eso de
   verdad?

acupuncture *noun*
   la **acupuntura** *fem*

acute *adjective*
   agudo *masc*, **aguda** *fem*
   the acute accent as in café: é el acento
   agudo como en café: é

ad *noun*
   el **anuncio** *masc*
   to put an ad in the paper poner [11] un
   anuncio en el periódico
   the small ads los anuncios por palabras

AD *abbreviation of Anno Domini*
   d. de C. (*después de Cristo*)
   in 400 AD en el año 400 d. de C.

to **adapt** *verb*
   to adapt something adaptar [17] algo
   to adapt to something adaptarse [17] a
   algo
   She's adapted to her new school. Se ha
   adaptado a su nuevo colegio.

adaptor *noun*
   el **adaptador** *masc*

to **add** *verb*
   añadir [19]
   Add three eggs. Añade tres huevos.

   • **to add something up** sumar [17] **algo**

addict *noun*
   1 (*to drugs*) el **drogadicto** *masc*, la
     drogadicta *fem*
   2 (*of television, chocolate*) el **adicto** *masc*, la
     adicta *fem*
     She's a telly addict. Es una adicta a la
     televisión.
     He's a football addict. Es un fanático del
     fútbol.

addicted *adjective*
   1 (*to drugs, television, computer games*) **adicto**
     masc, **adicta** *fem*
     She's addicted to heroin. Es adicta a la
     heroína.
     He's addicted to the Net. Es un adicto a
     Internet.
   2 (*to food*) **I'm addicted to chocolate.** El
     chocolate es mi vicio (*informal*) .

♂ **addition** *noun*
   1 (*adding up*) la **suma** *fem*
   2 **in addition** además
     in addition to además de

♂ **additional** *adjective*
   adicional *masc & fem*
   the additional costs los costes adicionales

additive *noun*
   el **aditivo** *masc*

address *noun*
   1 (*where you live*) la **dirección** *fem*
     What's your address? ¿Cuál es tu
     dirección?
     to change your address cambiar [17] de
     domicilio
   2 (*on a form*) el **domicilio** *masc*
   • **address book** la libreta de direcciones

adequate *adjective*
   suficiente *masc & fem*

adhesive *adjective* ▷ see **adhesive** *noun*
   adhesivo *masc*, **adhesiva** *fem*

adhesive *noun* ▷ see **adhesive** *adj*
   el **pegamento** *masc*
   • **adhesive tape** la cinta adhesiva

adjective *noun*
   el **adjetivo** *masc*

to **adjust** *verb*
   1 (*the volume, the temperature*) **regular** [17]
   2 (*the height, the width*) **ajustar** [17]
   3 **to adjust to something** adaptarse [17] a
     algo
     She has adjusted to the changes. Se ha
     adaptado a los cambios.

adjustable *adjective*
regulable *masc & fem*

administration *noun*
la **administración** *fem*

admiral *noun*
el **almirante** *masc*

admiration *noun*
la **admiración** *fem*

to **admire** *verb*
admirar [17]

admission *noun*
la **entrada** *fem*
'No admission' 'Prohibida la entrada'
'Admission free' 'Entrada gratuita'

to **admit** *verb*
1 (*to confess*) **reconocer** [35]
I must admit that … debo reconocer que …
She admits she lied. Admite que mintió.
2 (*to allow in*) **dejar** [1] **entrar**
3 (*a patient*) **ingresar** [1]
She was admitted to hospital. La ingresaron en el hospital.

adolescence *noun*
la **adolescencia** *fem*

ꝺ **adolescent** *noun*
el & la **adolescente** *masc & fem*

to **adopt** *verb*
adoptar [17]

adopted *adjective*
adoptado *masc*, **adoptada** *fem*

adoption *noun*
la **adopción** *fem*

to **adore** *verb*
adorar [17]

Adriatic Sea *noun*
the Adriatic Sea el mar Adriático

ꝺ **adult** *adjective* ▷ see **adult** *noun*
adulto *masc*, **adulta** *fem*
the adult population la población adulta

ꝺ **adult** *noun* ▷ see **adult** *adj*
el **adulto** *masc*, la **adulta** *fem*
· **adult education** la educación para adultos

advance *noun* ▷ see **advance** *verb*
el **avance** *masc*
scientific advances los avances científicos

to **advance** *verb* ▷ see **advance** *noun*
avanzar [22]

advanced *adjective*
avanzado *masc*, **avanzada** *fem*

advantage *noun*
la **ventaja** *fem*
there are several advantages hay varias ventajas
to take advantage of something aprovechar [17] algo
I took advantage of the sales to buy myself some shoes. Aproveché las rebajas para comprarme unos zapatos.
to take advantage of somebody aprovecharse [17] de alguien
They take advantage of the tourists. Se aprovechan de los turistas.

adventure *noun*
la **aventura** *fem*

adventurous *adjective*
1 (*person*) **aventurero** *masc*, **aventurera** *fem*
2 (*design, designer, composer*) **innovador** *masc*, **innovadora** *fem*

adverb *noun*
el **adverbio** *masc*

ꝺ **advertisement**, **advert** *noun*
1 (*on television, radio, in a newspaper*) el **anuncio** *masc*
2 (*small ad in a newspaper*) el **anuncio por palabras**

to **advertise** *verb*
to advertise a product anunciar [17] un producto
to advertise something in the newspaper anunciar [17] algo en el periódico
I saw it advertised on telly. Lo vi anunciado en la tele.
I saw a bike advertised in the paper. Vi un anuncio de una bicicleta en el periódico.

ꝺ **advertising** *noun*
la **publicidad** *fem*
I'd like to work in advertising. Me gustaría trabajar en publicidad.

advice *noun* ▷ see **advise** *verb*
los **consejos** *masc plural*
a piece of advice un consejo
His advice is good. Sus consejos son buenos.
to give somebody advice aconsejar [17] a alguien
They gave me good advice. Me aconsejaron bien.
to ask for advice about something pedir [57] consejo sobre algo
Ask for advice about the exam. Pide consejo sobre el examen.

♂ to **advise** *verb* ▷ see **advice** *noun*
aconsejar [17]
to advise somebody to … aconsejar a
alguien que …
I advised him to study more. Le aconsejé
que estudiara más.
I advised her not to wait. Le aconsejé que
no esperara.

> **WORD TIP** The verb following *aconsejar* is in the
> subjunctive.

adviser *noun*
el **asesor** *masc*, la **asesora** *fem*

aerial *noun*
la **antena** *fem*

aerobics *noun*
el **aerobic** *masc*
to do aerobics hacer [7] aerobic

♂ **aeroplane** *noun*
el **avión** *masc*
We came by aeroplane. Vinimos en avión.

aerosol *noun*
el **aerosol** *masc*, el **spray** *masc*

affair *noun*
1 (*event*) el **asunto** *masc*
international affairs asuntos
internacionales
2 (*between lovers*) la **aventura** *fem*
a love affair una aventura amorosa

to **affect** *verb*
afectar [17]

affectionate *adjective*
cariñoso *masc*, **cariñosa** *fem*

to **afford** *verb*
to afford something poder [10] permitirse
algo
I can't afford a new DVD. No puedo
permitirme un nuevo DVD.
She can afford to fly in first class. Puede
permitirse el lujo de viajar en primera.

♂ **afraid** *adjective*
1 (*frightened*) **to be afraid of something** tener
[9] miedo de algo
I'm afraid. Tengo miedo.
I'm afraid of dogs. Tengo miedo de los
perros.
2 (*when giving bad news*) **temerse**
I'm afraid so. Me temo que sí.
I'm afraid not. Me temo que no.
I'm afraid there are not tickets left. Me
temo que no quedan entradas.

Africa *noun*
África *fem*

African *adjective & noun*
1 **africano** *masc*, **africana** *fem*
2 (*person*) un **africano** *masc*, una **africana** *fem*
the Africans los africanos *masc pl*

> **WORD TIP** Adjectives and nouns for nationality
> and regional origin do not have capital letters in
> Spanish.

♂ **after** *adverb, conjunction, preposition*
(*later in time*) **después**, **después de**
soon after poco después
after 10 o'clock después de las diez en
punto
after lunch después de comer
after school después del colegio
the day after tomorrow pasado mañana
after I've finished my homework después
de terminar mis deberes
after all después de todo
After all, she's only six. Después de todo,
sólo tiene seis años.

♂ **afternoon** *noun*
la **tarde** *fem*
this afternoon esta tarde
tomorrow afternoon mañana por la tarde
yesterday afternoon ayer por la tarde
on Saturday afternoon el sábado por la
tarde
on Saturday afternoons los sábados por la
tarde
at four o'clock in the afternoon a las cuatro
de la tarde
every afternoon todas las tardes
Good afternoon! ¡Buenas tardes!

afters *noun*
el **postre** *masc*

aftershave *noun*
la **loción para después del afeitado**

afterwards *adverb*
después
shortly afterwards poco después

♂ **again** *adverb*
1 (*one more time*) **otra vez**, **de nuevo**
Try again. Inténtalo otra vez.
I've forgotten it again. Se me ha olvidado
otra vez.
You should ask again. Deberías preguntar
de nuevo.
I want to see her again. Quiero volver a
verla.
Don't do it again. No lo vuelvas a hacer.

> **WORD TIP** Using *volver a* + infinitive is a very
> common way of expressing *again* in Spanish.

2 (*in expressions*) **again and again** una y otra
vez
Never again! ¡Nunca más!

ℰ **against** *preposition*
> **contra**
> **against the wall** contra la pared
> **to fight against terrorism** luchar [17] contra el terrorismo
> **I'm against the idea.** Estoy en contra de la idea.
> **They are playing against Scotland.** Juegan contra Escocia.

ℰ **age** *noun*
> 1 (*saying how old someone is*) **la edad** *fem*
> **at the age of fifteen** a la edad de quince años
> **What age is she?** ¿Cuántos años tiene?
> **She's the same age as me.** Tiene mi misma edad.
> **to be under age** ser [1] menor de edad
> 2 (*a long time*) **for ages**
> **I haven't seen Johnny for ages.** Hace siglos que no he visto a Johnny.
> **I haven't been to London for ages.** Hace un montón de tiempo que no voy a Londres.

ℰ **aged** *adjective*
> **a girl aged fourteen** una chica de catorce años
> **a man aged fifty** un hombre de cincuenta años

agenda *noun*
> **la agenda** *fem*

agent *noun*
> **el & la agente** *masc & fem*

aggressive *adjective*
> **agresivo** *masc*, **agresiva** *fem*

ℰ **ago** *adverb*
> **an hour ago** hace una hora
> **three days ago** hace tres días
> **five years ago** hace cinco años
> **a long time ago** hace mucho tiempo
> **not long ago** no hace mucho tiempo
> **How long ago was it?** ¿Cuánto tiempo hace de eso?

> **WORD TIP** Spanish uses *hace* and the amount of time to say *ago*.

ℰ to **agree** *verb*
> 1 **to agree with somebody** estar [2] de acuerdo con alguien
> **I agree with Laura.** Estoy de acuerdo con Laura.
> **I don't agree.** No estoy de acuerdo.
> **I agree that ...** estoy de acuerdo en que ...
> **I agree that it's too late now.** Estoy de acuerdo en que ya es demasiado tarde.
> 2 **to agree to do something** aceptar [18] hacer algo

> **Steve has agreed to help me.** Steve ha aceptado ayudarme.
> 3 (*food, drink*) **Coffee doesn't agree with me.** El café no me sienta bien.

ℰ **agreement** *noun*
> **el acuerdo** *masc*

agricultural *adjective*
> **agrícola** *masc & fem*
> **productos agrícolas** farm products

agriculture *noun*
> **la agricultura** *fem*

ahead *adverb*
> 1 (*in directions*) **straight ahead** todo recto
> **Go straight ahead until you get to the crossroads.** Siga todo recto hasta que llegues al cruce (*polite form of seguir*).
> 2 (*saying 'yes'*) **Go ahead!** ¡Adelante!
> 3 (*in competitions*) **to be ahead** llevar [17] la ventaja
> **Our team was ten points ahead.** Nuestro equipo llevaba diez puntos de ventaja.

aid *noun*
> **la ayuda** *fem*
> **aid to developing countries** la ayuda a los países en vías de desarrollo
> **in aid of** en beneficio de
> **a collection in aid of the homeless** una colecta en beneficio de la gente sin hogar

ℰ **Aids, AIDS** *noun*
> (= *Aquired Immune Deficiency Syndrome*) **el sida** *masc* (= *Síndrome de inmunodeficiencia adquirida*)
> **to have Aids** tener [9] sida

aim *noun* ▷ *see* **aim** *verb*
> **el objetivo** *masc*
> **We want to achieve all our aims.** Queremos conseguir todos nuestros objetivos.
> **Their aim is to control pollution.** Su objetivo es controlar la contaminación.

to **aim** *verb* ▷ *see* **aim** *noun*
> 1 (*a weapon*) **to aim a pistol at somebody** apuntar [17] una pistola a alguien
> 2 (*to intend*) **a campaign aimed at young people** una campaña dirigida a los jóvenes
> **to aim to do something** proponerse [11] hacer algo
> **We're aiming to finish it today.** Nos proponemos terminarlo hoy.

ℰ **air** *noun*
> 1 (*that you breathe*) **el aire** *masc*
> **in the open air** al aire libre
> **to go out for a breath of air** salir [63] a tomar el aire ▶▶

a b c d e f g h i j k l m n o p q r s t u v w x y z

2 (about travel by plane) **We came by air.**
Vinimos en avión.
- **airbag** el airbag
- **air-conditioned** con aire acondicionado
- **air conditioning** el aire acondicionado
- **air force** la fuerza aérea
- **air hostess** la azafata
- **airline** la línea aérea
- **airmail** el correo aéreo
  by airmail por correo aéreo
- **airport** el aeropuerto

aisle noun
el **pasillo** masc

alarm noun
la **alarma** fem
a burglar alarm una alarma antirrobo
The alarm has gone off. Ha sonado la
alarma.
- **alarm clock** el despertador

album noun
el **álbum** masc

alcohol noun
el **alcohol** masc

alcoholic adjective ▷ see **alcoholic** noun
alcohólico masc, alcohólica fem
alcoholic drinks bebidas alcohólicas

alcoholic noun ▷ see **alcoholic** adj
el **alcohólico** masc, la **alcohólica** fem
She's an alcoholic. Es alcohólica.

alert adjective ▷ see **alert** noun
espabilado masc, espabilada fem

alert noun ▷ see **alert** adj
la **alerta** fem
to be on the alert estar [2] alerta

A levels noun
la **selectividad** (Students take 'la selectividad'
at the same age as A levels are taken in Britain.) You
can explain A levels as follows: Son exámenes que
se realizan a dos niveles, AS y A2. Los exámenes AS
se hacen después de un año de preparación,
generalmente en cuatro o cinco asignaturas; los A2
abarcan un número menor de asignaturas que ya
se hayan estudiado para el nivel AS. Ambos
exámenes se califican desde A (nota máxima), a N
(sin calificar). La calificación de los A levels se toma
en cuenta para ingresar a la universidad)
▷ **selectividad**

alibi noun
la **coartada** fem

alien noun
1 (foreigner) el **extranjero** masc, la **extranjera**
fem

2 (from outer space) el & la **extraterrestre** masc
& fem

alike adjective
parecido masc, parecida fem
They're all alike. Son todos parecidos.
to look alike parecerse [35]
The two brothers look alike. Los dos
hermanos se parecen.

alive adjective
vivo masc, viva fem
to be alive estar [2] vivo

♂ **all** adjective, adverb ▷ see **all** pron
1 (with objects, periods of time) **todo** masc, **toda**
fem
all the knives todos los cuchillos
all the cups todas las tazas
all the time todo el tiempo
all day todo el día
all along desde el primer momento
I knew it all along. Lo supe desde el primer
momento.
2 (entirely) **completamente**
all alone completamente solo
She's all alone. Está completamente sola.
3 (in scores) **three all** tres iguales

♂ **all** pronoun ▷ see **all** adj, adv
1 (every one, the whole) **todo** masc pronoun,
toda fem pronoun
It's all I have. Es todo lo que tengo.
They're all there. Están todos allí.
They've eaten it all. Se lo han comido todo.
2 (in expressions) **first of all** en primer lugar
after all después de todo
not at all de nada (the answer to **gracias** or
'thank you')

allergic adjective
alérgico masc, alérgica fem
to be allergic to something ser [1] alérgico
a algo
I'm allergic to cats. Soy alérgica a los gatos.

allergy noun
la **alergia** fem

alligator noun
el **caimán** masc

♂ to **allow** verb
1 **to allow somebody to do something** dejar
[17] a alguien hacer algo
We are allowed to go out in the evenings.
Nos dejan salir por las noches.
I'm not allowed to go out during the week.
No me dejan salir durante la semana.
The teacher allowed them to go out. El
maestro les dejó salir.

⚘ all right *adverb*

1 (*when you agree*) **de acuerdo**, **vale** (*informal*)
'Come round to my house around six.' - 'All right.' 'Ven a mi casa a eso de las seis.' - 'De acuerdo.'
It's all right by me. Vale.

2 (*the way you want things*) Is everything all right? ¿Va todo bien?
Is it all right to leave the door open? ¿Está bien dejar la puerta abierta?

3 (*to talk about how you are*) **bien**
Are you all right? ¿Estás bien?
She's all right now. Ya está bien.

4 (*not bad*) The meal was all right. La comida no estuvo mal.

ally *noun*
el **aliado** *masc*, la **aliada** *fem*

almond *noun*
la **almendra** *fem*

almost *adverb*
casi
almost every day casi cada día
almost everybody casi todo el mundo
She's almost five. Tiene casi cinco años.

⚘ alone *adjective*
solo *masc*, **sola** *fem*
He lives alone. Vive solo.
Leave me alone! ¡Déjame en paz!
Leave that alone! ¡Deja eso!

⚘ along *preposition*

1 **por**
We go for walks along the beach. Nos paseamos por la playa.

2 **a lo largo de**
There are trees all along our road. Hay árboles a lo largo de la calle donde vivimos.

3 (*further away*) a bit further along un poco más adelante
She lives along the street from me. Vive más abajo en la misma calle.

aloud *adverb*
en voz alta
to read something aloud leer [37] algo en voz alta

⚘ alphabet *noun*
el **alfabeto** *masc*

alphabetical *adjective*
alfabético *masc*, **alfabética** *fem*
in alphabetical order por orden alfabético

Alps *plural noun*
the Alps los Alpes

⚘ already *adverb*
ya
They've already left. Ya se han ido.
It's six o'clock already! ¡Ya son las seis!

Alsatian *noun*
el **pastor alemán**

⚘ also *adverb*
también
I've also invited Karen. He invitado también a Karen.

to **alter** *verb*
cambiar [17]

alternate *adjective*
on alternate days un día sí y otro no

alternative *adjective*
▷ see **alternative** *noun*
otro *masc*, **otra** *fem*
to look for an alternative solution buscar [31] otra solución

alternative *noun* ▷ see **alternative** *adj*
la **alternativa** *fem*
We have no alternative. No tenemos alternativa.

alternatively *adverb*
o bien
Alternatively, we could go on Saturday. O bien podríamos ir el sábado.

alternative medicine *noun*
la **medicina alternativa**

although *conjunction*
aunque
Although she's ill, she wants to come. Aunque está enferma, quiere venir.

altitude *noun*
la **altitud** *fem*

altogether *adverb*

1 (*all in all*) **en total**
I've spent thirty pounds altogether. He gastado treinta libras en total.

2 (*completely*) **totalmente**
I'm not altogether convinced. No estoy totalmente convencido.

aluminium *noun*
el **aluminio** *masc*

⚘ always *adverb*
siempre
I always leave at five. Siempre salgo a las cinco.
I have always lived in Milton. Siempre he vivido en Milton.

am *verb* ▷ **be**

a
b
c
d
e
f
g
h
i
j
k
l
m
n
o
p
q
r
s
t
u
v
w
x
y
z

a.m. *abbreviation*
de la mañana
at 8 a.m. a las ocho de la mañana

amateur *noun*
el & la **amateur** *masc & fem*, **amateurs**
masc & fem pl
• **amateur dramatics** el teatro de amateurs

to **amaze** *verb*
asombrar [17]
What amazes me is ... Lo que me asombra
es ...

amazed *adjective*
asombrado *masc*, **asombrada** *fem*
I was amazed to see her. Me quedé
asombrado al verla.
She'll be amazed to find out. Se quedará
asombrada al enterarse.

amazement *noun*
el **asombro** *masc*
To my amazement she agreed. Para mi
gran sorpresa acepté.

amazing *adjective*
increíble *masc & fem*
They've got an amazing house. Tienen una
casa increíble.
She has an amazing number of friends.
Tiene un número increíble de amigos.

ambassador *noun*
el **embajador** *masc*, la **embajadora** *fem*

ᔎ **ambition** *noun*
la **ambición** *fem*

ambitious *adjective*
ambicioso *masc*, **ambiciosa** *fem*

ᔎ **ambulance** *noun*
la **ambulancia** *fem*
• **ambulance driver** el conductor de
ambulancia, la conductora de ambulancia

amenities *plural noun*
los **servicios públicos**

America *noun*
América *fem*
in America en América, en Estados Unidos
(*In Spanish, América often means the Latin
American countries.*)

American *adjective* ▷ see **American** *noun*
americano *masc*, **americana** *fem*

American *noun* ▷ see **American** *adj*
(*person*) un **americano** *masc*, una
americana *fem*
the Americans los americanos *masc pl*

WORD TIP Adjectives and nouns for nationality
and regional origin do not have capital letters in
Spanish.

ammunition *noun*
las **municiones** *fem pl*

ᔎ **among, amongst** *preposition*
entre
I found it among my books. Lo encontré
entre mis libros.
You can decide amongst yourselves.
Podéis decidirlo entre vosotros.

amount *noun*
la **cantidad** *fem*
an enormous amount of bread una enorme
cantidad de pan
a huge amount of work una enorme
cantidad de trabajo
a large amount of money una gran
cantidad de dinero
• to **amount to something**
ascender [36] a
The bill amounts to five hundred euros. La
cuenta asciende a quinientos euros.

amp *noun*
1 (*in electricity*) el **amperio** *masc*
2 (*amplifier*) el **amplificador** *masc*

amplifier *noun*
el **amplificador** *masc*

to **amuse** *verb*
divertir [14]

amusement arcade *noun*
el **salón de juegos recreativos**

amusement park *noun*
el **parque de atracciones**

ᔎ **amusing** *adjective*
divertido *masc*, **divertida** *fem*

an *determiner*
1 **un** (*masculine*)
2 **una** (*feminine*)
▷ **a**

anaesthetic *noun*
la **anestesia** *fem*

to **analyse** *verb*
analizar [22]

analysis *noun*
el **análisis** *masc*

ancestor *noun*
el **antepasado** *masc*, la **antepasada** *fem*

anchor noun
el **ancla** fem

> **WORD TIP** ancla takes el or un in the singular even though it is fem.

anchovy noun
el **anchoa** fem

> **WORD TIP** anchoa takes el or un in the singular even though it is fem.

ancient adjective
1 (historic) **antiguo** masc, **antigua** fem
an ancient castle un castillo antiguo
2 (very old) **viejísimo** masc, **viejísima** fem
an ancient pair of jeans unos vaqueros viejísimos

ꝸ **and** conjunction
1 **y**
Sean and Anna Sean y Anna
boys and girls chicos y chicas
2 (before words beginning with i or hi) **e**
Spain and Italy España e Italia
father and son padre e hijo
3 (in English numbers above 100) a hundred and one ciento uno
two hundred and thirty-one doscientos treinta y uno
4 (in expressions with -er and -er) **cada vez más**
...
bigger and bigger cada vez más grande
better and better cada vez mejor

Andalusia noun
Andalucía fem (the region in southern Spain)

Andalusian adjective & noun
1 **andaluz** masc, **andaluza** fem
2 (person) un **andaluz** masc, una **andaluza** fem
the Andalusians los andaluces

> **WORD TIP** Adjectives and nouns for nationality and regional origin do not have capital letters in Spanish.

angel noun
el **ángel** masc

anger noun
la **ira** fem

angle noun
el **ángulo** masc

angrily adverb
con enfado

ꝸ **angry** adjective
to be angry estar [2] enfadado, fem enfadada
She was angry with me. Estaba enfadada conmigo.
to get angry (about something) enfadarse [17] (por algo)

She got angry with us for being late. Se enfadó con nosotros por llegar tarde.

ꝸ **animal** noun
el **animal** masc

ankle noun
el **tobillo** masc
to break your ankle romperse [40] el tobillo

ꝸ **anniversary** noun
el **aniversario** masc
a wedding anniversary un aniversario de boda
the fortieth anniversary of ... el cuarenta aniversario de ...

to **announce** verb
anunciar [17]

announcement noun
el **anuncio** masc

to **annoy** verb
1 (to pester) **fastidiar** [17]
Don't annoy me! ¡No fastidies!
2 (to become angry) to be annoyed estar [2] enfadado, fem enfadada
to get annoyed (about something) enfadarse [17] (por algo)
He got annoyed about the radio. Se enfadó por la radio.

ꝸ **annoying** adjective
1 (person) **pesado** masc, **pesada** fem
2 (noise, habit) **irritante** masc & fem
3 (situation) How annoying! ¡Qué fastidio!
The whole thing's really annoying. Todo es un verdadero fastidio.

annual adjective
anual masc & fem

anorak noun
el **anorak** masc, pl: los **anoraks**

anorexia noun
la **anorexia** fem

ꝸ **another** adjective, pron
otro masc, **otra** fem
Would you like another Coke®? ¿Quieres otra Coca Cola®?
Yes, I'll have another. Sí, me bebo otra. (otra refers to Coca Cola®)
We need another three chairs.
Necesitamos otras tres sillas.
another two years otros dos años
I'll come another time. Vendré en otro momento.
another one otro, otra
I want to buy another one. Quiero comprar otro.

ⓢ **answer** *noun* ▷ see **answer** *verb*
1 (*to a question*) la **respuesta** *fem*
the right answer la respuesta correcta
the wrong answer la respuesta equivocada
2 (*to a problem*) the answer to a problem la solución a un problema

ⓢ to **answer** *verb* ▷ see **answer** *noun*
1 (*a person, the phone*) **contestar** [17]
to answer your mobile contestar el móvil
He has answered my text message. Ha contestado mi mensaje de texto.
Nobody's answering. Nadie contesta.
2 (*the door*) **abrir** [46] la puerta

answering machine *noun*
el **contestador automático**, el **contestador** *masc*
to leave a message on the answering machine dejar [17] un mensaje en el contestador

ant *noun*
la **hormiga** *fem*

Antarctic *noun*
the Antarctic la Antártida

anthem *noun*
el **himno** *masc*
the national anthem el himno nacional

antibiotic *noun*
el **antibiótico** *masc*

anticlockwise *adverb*
en el sentido contrario al de las agujas del reloj
It turns anticlockwise. Gira en el sentido contrario al de las agujas del reloj.

antique *adjective* ▷ see **antique** *noun*
antiguo *masc*, **antigua** *fem*
an antique table una mesa antigua

antique *noun* ▷ see **antique** *adj*
antiques las antigüedades
• **antique shop** la tienda de antigüedades

antiseptic *noun*
el **antiséptico** *masc*

ⓢ **anxious** *adjective*
preocupado *masc*, **preocupada** *fem*

anxiously *adverb*
con preocupación

ⓢ **any** *adjective* ▷ see **any** *adv, pron*
1 (*asking questions, saying no*) Is there any butter? ¿Hay mantequilla?
There isn't any flour. No hay harina.
Have you got any glasses? ¿Tienes vasos?
I haven't got any glasses. No tengo vasos.

She's gone without any money. Ha ido sin dinero.

> **WORD TIP** *any* is not translated in these examples.

2 (*stating facts*) **cualquier** (+ noun)
Any pupil knows that. Cualquier alumno lo sabe.
She could come any day. Podría venir cualquier día.
3 any one **cualquiera**
Any one will tell you. Cualquiera se lo dirá.
4 to be any more **quedar** [17] más
Is there any more? ¿Queda más?
Are there any more? ¿Quedan más?
There isn't any more butter. No queda más mantequilla.
There's hardly any more left. No queda casi nada.

ⓢ **any** *adverb* ▷ see **any** *adj, pron*
1 (*with -er adjectives*) Are you any better? ¿Te sientes mejor?
2 any more **ya no**
We don't go there any more. Ya no vamos allí.

ⓢ **any** *pronoun* ▷ see **any** *adj, adv*
1 (*in negative statements*) **ninguno** *masc pronoun*, **ninguna** *fem pronoun*
I don't want any. No quiero ninguno, *fem* ninguna.
2 (*in questions*) alguno *masc pronoun*, alguna *fem pronoun*
Do you want any? ¿Quieres alguno, *fem* alguna?

ⓢ **anybody**, **anyone** *pronoun*
1 (*in questions and after 'if'*) **alguien**
Does anybody need water? ¿Alguien necesita agua?
Is anybody at home? ¿Hay alguien en casa?
If anybody calls, tell them ... Si alguien llama, dile que ...
2 (*in negative statements*) not ... anybody no ... nadie
There isn't anybody at home. No hay nadie en casa.
I don't know anybody there. No conozco a nadie allí.
3 (*anybody at all*) **cualquiera**
Anybody can go. Puede ir cualquiera.
Any one will tell you. Cualquiera se lo dirá.

anyhow *adverb* ▷ **anyway**

anyone *pronoun* ▷ **anybody**

ⓢ **anything** *pronoun*
1 (*in questions*) **algo** (*invariable*)
Do you need anything? ¿Necesitas algo?

2 (*in negative statements*) **not … anything** no … nada
There isn't anything to eat. No hay nada para comer.

3 (*anything at all*) **cualquier cosa**
Anything could happen. Podría pasar cualquier cosa.

anyway, anyhow *adverb*
de todos modos
Anyway, I'll ring you before I leave. De todos modos te llamaré antes de salir.

♪ **anywhere** *adverb*

1 (*in questions*) **Have you seen my keys anywhere?** ¿Has visto mis llaves en algún sitio?
Are you going anywhere tomorrow? ¿Vas a algún sitio mañana?

2 (*in negative statements*) **not … anywhere** en ningún sitio
I can't find my keys anywhere. No encuentro mis llaves en ningún sitio.
I'm not going anywhere tonight. Esta noche no voy a ningún sitio.

3 (*to any place*) **a cualquier sitio**
You can take it anywhere. Puedes llevarlo a cualquier sitio.

4 (*in any place*) **en cualquier sitio**
Put your cases down anywhere. Pon las maletas en cualquier sitio.

apart *adjective, adverb*

1 (*separated*) **separado** *masc*, **separada** *fem*
They're too far apart. Están demasiado separados.
His parents live apart. Sus padres viven separados.

2 (*in measurements*) **to be two metres apart** estar [2] a dos metros de distancia

3 (*except*) **apart from** aparte de
Everybody came apart from Judy . Todo el mundo vino aparte de Judy.

apartment *noun*
el **apartamento** *masc*

ape *noun*
el **simio** *masc*

♪ to **apologize** *verb*

1 **disculparse** [17]
to apologize for something disculparse por algo
He apologized for his behaviour. Se disculpó por su comportamiento

2 **to apologize to somebody** pedirle [57] perdón a alguien
He apologized to Tanya. Le pidió perdón a Tanya.

apology *noun*
la **disculpa** *fem*

apostrophe *noun*
el **apóstrofe** *masc*

apparent *adjective*
aparente *masc & fem*

apparently *adverb*
al parecer, por lo visto

appeal *noun* ▷ see **appeal** *verb*
(*call*) **an appeal for calm** un llamamiento a la calma
an appeal for help una solicitud de ayuda

to **appeal** *verb* ▷ see **appeal** *noun*
to appeal to somebody atraer [42] a alguien
Horror films don't appeal to me. Las películas de miedo no me atraen.

to **appear** *verb*

1 (*to come into view*) **aparecer** [35]
Mick appeared at the door. Mick apareció en la puerta.

2 (*on TV*) **to appear on television** salir [63] en televisión

3 (*to seem*) **parecer** [35]
It appears that somebody has taken the key. Parece que alguien se ha llevado la llave.

appendicitis *noun*
la **apendicitis** *fem*

appendix *noun*
el **apéndice** *masc*

appetite *noun*
el **apetito** *masc*

♪ **appetizing** *adjective*
apetitoso *masc*, **apetitosa** *fem*

to **applaud** *verb*
aplaudir [19]

applause *noun*
los **aplausos** *masc plural*

♪ **apple** *noun*
la **manzana** *fem*
· **apple tree** el manzano

applicant *noun*
candidato *masc*, **candidata** *fem*

application *noun*
la **solicitud** *fem*
a job application una solicitud de trabajo
· **application form** el impreso de solicitud

to **apply** *verb*

1 *(for a job, a place, etc)* **to apply for something** solicitar [17] algo
I'm going to apply for the job. Voy a solicitar el trabajo.
I've applied for the course. He solicitado que me admitan en el curso.

2 *(to be relevant to)* **to apply to somebody** aplicarse [31] a alguien
It applies to everyone. Se aplica a todos.

♂ **appointment** *noun*
la **cita** *fem*
to make an appointment at the dentist's pedir [57] cita en el dentista
I've got a hair appointment at 4 o'clock. Tengo cita en la peluquería para las cuatro.

♂ to **appreciate** *verb*
agradecer [35]
I appreciate your help. Te agradezco tu ayuda.

apprentice *noun*
el **aprendiz** *masc*, la **aprendiza** *fem*

apprenticeship *noun*
el **aprendizaje** *masc*

to **approach** *verb*

1 **acercarse** [31] **a**
We are approaching Madrid. Nos acercamos a Madrid.

appropriate *adjective*
apropiado *masc*, **apropiada** *fem*

approval *noun*
la **aprobación** *fem*

to **approve** *verb*
I don't approve of her friends. No me gustan sus amigos.
I don't approve of his methods. No estoy de acuerdo con sus métodos.
Does he approve of the idea? ¿Le parece bien la idea?

approximate *adjective*
aproximado *masc*, **aproximada** *fem*

approximately *adverb*
aproximadamente
approximately fifty people aproximadamente cincuenta personas

♂ **apricot** *noun*
el **albaricoque** *masc*
• **apricot tree** el albaricoquero *masc*

♂ **April** *noun*
abril *masc*
in April en abril

> **WORD TIP** Names of months and days start with small letters in Spanish.

• **April Fool** el & la inocente
• **April Fool's Day** el día de los Santos Inocentes *(similar to April Fool's Day, but on the 28 December)*

apron *noun*
el **delantal** *masc*

aquarium *noun*
el **acuario** *masc*

Aquarius *noun*

1 *(the star sign)* el **Acuario** *masc*

2 *(person)* un & una **acuario** *masc & fem*
Sharon's Aquarius. Sharon es acuario.

> **WORD TIP** Use a small letter in Spanish to say *I am … etc* with star signs. Star signs in Spanish are used without *el, un, la, una.*

Arab *adjective & noun*

1 **árabe** *masc & fem*
the Arab countries los países árabes

2 *(person)* un & una **árabe** *masc & fem*
the Arabs los árabes *masc pl*

> **WORD TIP** Adjectives and nouns for nationality and regional origin do not have capital letters in Spanish.

arch *noun*
el **arco** *masc*

archaelogist *noun*
el **arqueólogo** *masc*, la **arqueóloga** *fem*
She's an archaeologist. Es arqueóloga.

archaeology *noun*
la **arqueología** *fem*

archbishop *noun*
el **arzobispo** *masc*

architect *noun*
el **arquitecto** *masc*, la **arquitecta** *fem*
He's an architect. Es arquitecto.

architecture *noun*
la **arquitectura** *fem*

Arctic *noun*
the Arctic el Ártico

are *verb* ▷ **be**

♂ **area** *noun*

1 *(region)* la **zona** *fem*
a poor area una zona pobre
in the Leeds area en la zona de Leeds

2 *(of a square, a circle)* el **área** *fem*

> **WORD TIP** *área* takes *el* or *un* in the singular even though it is fem.

aren't *short for* **are not** (*See:* **to be**)

Argentina *noun*
Argentina *fem*

Argentinian *adjective*
▷ see **Argentinian** *noun*
argentino *masc*, **argentina** *fem*

Argentinian *noun*
▷ see **Argentinian** *adj*
(*person*) un **argentino** *masc*, una **argentina** *fem*
the Argentinians los argentinos *masc pl*

> **WORD TIP** Adjectives and nouns for nationality and regional origin do not have capital letters in Spanish.

ᵟ to **argue** *verb*
discutir [19]
Jack and Jane are always arguing. Jack y Jane siempre están discutiendo.
to argue about something discutir sobre algo
They're arguing about the result. Están discutiendo sobre el resultado.

argument *noun*
la **discusión** *fem*
to have an argument discutir [19]

Aries *noun*
1 (*the star sign*) el **Aries** *masc*
2 (*person*) un & una **aries** *masc & fem*
Davina's Aries. Davina es aries.

> **WORD TIP** Use a small letter in Spanish to say *I am ...* etc with star signs. Star signs in Spanish are used without *el, un, la, una.*

arithmetic *noun*
la **aritmética** *fem*

ᵟ **arm** *noun*
el **brazo** *masc*
to go arm in arm ir [8] del brazo
to break your arm romperse [40] el brazo
She's broken her arm. Se ha roto el brazo.
• **armchair** el sillón

armed *adjective*
armado *masc*, **armada** *fem*
armed terrorists terroristas armados

armpit *noun*
la **axila** *fem*

arms *plural noun*
las **armas** *fem pl*

army *noun*
el **ejército** *masc*
to join the army alistarse [17] en el ejército

ᵟ **around** *adverb, preposition*
1 (*with places, times*) **alrededor de**
the countryside around Edinburgh el campo de alrededor de Edinburgo
We'll be there around ten. Estaremos allí alrededor de las diez.
We sat around the table. Nos sentamos alrededor de la mesa.
She has a scarf around her neck. Tiene una bufanda alrededor del cuello.
to travel around the world viajar [17] por el mundo
2 (*with amounts, ages*) We need around six kilos. Necesitamos unos seis quilos.
She's around fifteen. Tiene unos quince años.
3 (*nearby*) Is Phil around? ¿Está Phil por aquí?
Is there a post office around here? ¿Hay una oficina de correos por aquí?
It's around the corner. Está a la vuelta de la esquina.

ᵟ to **arrange** *verb*
to arrange to do something quedar [17] en hacer algo
We've arranged to go to the beach on Saturday. Quedamos en ir a la playa el domingo.

arrangement *noun*
1 (*agreement*) el **acuerdo** *masc*
2 (*of things*) la **disposición** *fem*

arrest *noun* ▷ see **arrest** *verb*
He's under arrest. Está detenido.
You're under arrest. Queda detenido.

to **arrest** *verb* ▷ see **arrest** *noun*
arrestar [17]

arrival *noun*
la **llegada** *fem*
Arrivals Llegadas

ᵟ to **arrive** *verb*
llegar [17]
They arrived at three. Llegaron a las tres.
We arrive in Barcelaona at one. Llegamos a Barcelona a la una.

arrow *noun*
la **flecha** *fem*

art *noun*
1 (*painting, sculpture, design*) el **arte** *masc*, las **artes** *fem pl*
modern art el arte moderno
the arts las artes
2 (*school subject*) el **dibujo** *masc*
the art class la clase de dibujo

> **WORD TIP** *arte* singular is masc, but *artes* plural is fem.

artery *noun*
la **arteria** *fem*

art gallery *noun*
el **museo de arte**

article *noun*
1 (*in a newspaper, magazine*) el **artículo** *masc*
a magazine article un artículo de revista
2 (*Grammar*) el **artículo** *masc*
the definite article el artículo definido (*in Spanish: el, la, los*)
the indefinite article el artículo indefinido (*in Spanish: un, una*)

artichoke *noun*
la **alcachofa** *fem*

artificial *adjective*
artificial *masc & fem*

artist *noun*
el & la **artista** *masc & fem*
He's an artist. Es artista.

artistic *adjective*
artístico *masc*, **artística** *fem*

art school *noun*
la **escuela de Bellas Artes**

♪ **as** *adverb, preposition* ▷ see **as** *conj*
1 (*in comparisons*) as ... as ... tan ... como ...
He's as tall as his brother. Es tan alto como su hermano.
You must be as tired as I am. Debes estar tan cansado como yo.
Do it as quickly as you can. Hazlo tan rápido como puedas.
as much ... as ... tanto *masc*, tanta *fem* como
You have as much time as I do. Tienes tanto tiempo como yo.
as many ... as ... tantos *masc pl*, tantas *fem pl* como
We have as many points as they do. Tenemos tantos puntos como ellos.
She has as many apples as I do. Tiene tantas manzanas como yo.
2 (*saying what you do*) to work as trabajar [17] de
He works as a taxi driver. Trabaja de taxista.

♪ **as** *conjunction* ▷ see **as** *adv, prep*
1 (*like*) **como**
as you know como sabes
as usual como siempre
as I told you como te dije
2 (*giving a reason*) **como**
As there were no trains, we took the bus. Como no había trenes, tomamos el autobús.

3 (*in expressions*) as soon as possible lo más pronto posible
as long as siempre que
Buy it, as long as it's good quality. Cómpralo, siempre que sea de buena calidad.

> **WORD TIP** *siempre que* is followed by a verb in the subjunctive.

asbestos *noun*
el **asbestos** *masc*

ash *noun*
la **ceniza** *fem*

ashamed *adjective*
to be ashamed estar [2] avergonzado, *fem* avergonzada
I was very ashamed of myself. Estaba muy avergonzado.
You should be ashamed of yourself! ¡Debería darte vergüenza!

ashtray *noun*
el **cenicero** *masc*

Asia *noun*
Asia *fem*

Asian *adjective* ▷ see **Asian** *noun*
1 (*from the continent of Asia*) **asiático** *masc*, **asiática** *fem*
2 (*from India*) **indio** *masc*, **india** *fem*
3 (*from Pakistan*) **paquistaní** *masc & fem*

Asian *noun* ▷ see **Asian** *adjective*
1 (*from Asia*) un **asiático** *masc*, una **asiática** *fem*
2 (*from India*) un **indio** *masc*, una **india** *fem*
3 (*from Pakistan*) un & una **paquistaní** *masc & fem*

> **WORD TIP** Adjectives and nouns for nationality and regional origin do not have capital letters in Spanish.

♪ to **ask** *verb*
1 (*to find out*) **preguntar** [17]
You can ask at reception. Puede preguntar en recepción. (*formal form*)
to ask somebody something preguntarle algo a alguien
I asked him where he lived. Le pregunté dónde vivía.
2 to ask for something pedir [57] algo
Ask for three coffees. Pide tres cafés.
to ask somebody to do something pedirle [57] a alguien que haga algo
Ask Danny to go with you. Pídele a Danny que vaya contigo.
3 to ask somebody a question hacerle [7] una pregunta a alguien

I asked you a question! ¡Te he hecho una pregunta!

4 (*to invite*) **invitar** [17]
They've asked us to a party at their house. Nos han invitado a una fiesta en su casa.
Paul's asked Janie out on Friday. Paul ha invitado a Janie a salir el viernes.

asleep *adjective*
dormido *masc*, **dormida** *fem*
to be asleep estar [2] dormido
Jason's asleep. Jason está dormido.
to fall asleep quedarse [17] dormido

asparagus *noun*
el **espárrago** *masc*

ᶠ **aspirin** *noun*
la **aspirina** *fem*

assignment *noun*
la **tarea** *fem*
to hand in an assignment entregar [28] una tarea

to **assist** *verb*
ayudar [17]

assistance *noun*
la **ayuda** *fem*

assistant *noun*
el & la **ayudante** *masc & fem*

association *noun*
la **asociación** *fem*

assorted *adjective*
variado *masc*, **variada** *fem*

assortment *noun*
el **surtido** *masc*
an assortment of sweets un surtido de caramelos

to **assume** *verb*
suponer [11]

to **assure** *verb*
asegurar [17]
You'll like it, I assure you. Te gustará, te lo aseguro.

asterisk *noun*
el **asterisco** *masc*

asthma *noun*
el **asma** *fem*
I have asthma. Sufro de asma.

WORD TIP *asma* takes *el* or *un* in the singular even though it is fem.

ᶠ **astonishing** *adjective*
asombroso *masc*, **asombrosa** *fem*
Her Spanish is astonishing. Su español es asombroso.

astrologer *noun*
el **astrólogo** *masc*, la **astróloga** *fem*

astrology *noun*
la **astrología** *fem*

astronaut *noun*
el & la **astronauta** *masc & fem*

astronomer *noun*
el **astrónomo** *masc*, la **astrónoma** *fem*

astronomy *noun*
la **astronomía** *fem*

ᶠ **at** *preposition*

1 (*talking about places*) **en**
at home en casa
at school en el colegio
There's someone at the door. Hay alguien en la puerta.
Dad's at work all day. Papá está en el trabajo todo el día.

2 (*talking about where people live, work*) **en**
at Emma's house en casa de Emma
at the hairdresser's en la peluquería
She's at her brother's this evening. Esta noche está en casa de su hermano.

3 (*talking about the time, periods of time*) **a**
at eight o'clock a las ocho
at night por la noche
We go there at weekends. Nos vamos allí los fines de semana.
at last por fin
He's found a job at last. Por fin ha encontrado un trabajo.

4 (*in email addresses*) la **arroba**
jason.foster@easylink.com jason-punto-foster-arroba-easylink-punto-com

athlete *noun*
el & la **atleta** *masc & fem*

athletic *adjective* ▷ see **athletics** *noun*
atlético *masc*, **atlética** *fem*

ᶠ **athletics** *noun* ▷ see **athletic** *adj*
el **atletismo** *masc*

Atlantic *noun*
the Atlantic el Atlántico

atlas *noun*
el **atlas** *masc*

atmosphere *noun*
la **atmósfera** *fem*

atom *noun*
el **átomo** *masc*

atomic *adjective*
atómico *masc*, **atómica** *fem*

a b c d e f g h i j k l m n o p q r s t u v w x y z

ℰ to **attach** *verb*
1 (*to fasten*) **sujetar** [17]
2 (*to tie*) **atar** [17]

attachment *noun*
1 (*in an email*) el **adjunto** *masc*
2 (*in a letter*) el **documento adjunto**

attack *noun* ▷ see **attack** *verb*
el **ataque** *masc*

to **attack** *verb* ▷ see **attack** *noun*
atacar [31]

attacker *noun*
el **agresor** *masc*, la **agresora** *fem*

attempt *noun* ▷ see **attempt** *verb*
el **intento** *masc*
at the second attempt al segundo intento

to **attempt** *verb* ▷ see **attempt** *noun*
to attempt to do something intentar [17]
hacer algo
I attempted to contact them. Intenté
ponerme en contacto con ellos.

to **attend** *verb*
asistir [19] a
to attend a class asistir a clase

ℰ **attention** *noun*
la **atención** *fem*
to pay attention to somebody prestar [17]
atención a alguien
I wasn't paying atttention to the teacher.
No estaba prestando atención al profesor.

attic *noun*
el **desván** *masc*, la **buhardilla** *fem*

attitude *noun*
la **actitud** *fem*

to **attract** *verb*
atraer [42]

attraction *noun*
la **atracción** *fem*

attractive *adjective*
atractivo *masc*, **atractiva** *fem*

aubergine *noun*
la **berenjena** *fem*

auction *noun*
la **subasta** *fem*

ℰ **audience** *noun*
el **público** *masc*
a member of the audience un espectador

ℰ **August** *noun*
agosto *masc*
in August en agosto

> **WORD TIP** Names of months and days start with small letters in Spanish.

ℰ **aunt**, **auntie** *noun*
la **tía** *fem*

au pair *noun*
el & la **au pair** *masc & fem*
I'm looking for a job as an au pair. Busco un
trabajo de au pair.

Australia *noun*
Australia *fem*

Australian *adjective & noun*
1 **australiano** *masc*, **australiana** *fem*
2 (*person*) un **australiano** *masc*, una
australiana *fem*
the Australians los australianos *masc pl*

> **WORD TIP** Adjectives and nouns for nationality and regional origin do not have capital letters in Spanish.

Austria *noun*
Austria *fem*

Austrian *adjective & noun*
1 **austriaco** *masc*, **austriaca** *fem*
2 (*person*) un **austriaco** *masc*, una **austriaca**
fem
the Austrians los austriacos *masc pl*

> **WORD TIP** Adjectives and nouns for nationality and regional origin do not have capital letters in Spanish.

ℰ **author** *noun*
el **autor** *masc*, la **autora** *fem*

autobiography *noun*
la **autobiografía** *fem*

autograph *noun*
el **autógrafo** *masc*

automatic *adjective*
automático *masc*, **automática** *fem*

automatically *adverb*
automáticamente

autumn *noun*
el **otoño** *masc*
in the autumn en otoño

availability *noun*
la **disponibilidad** *fem*

available *adjective*
disponible *masc & fem*

avalanche *noun*
la **avalancha** *fem*

ᵟ **avenue** noun
la **avenida** fem

ᵟ **average** adjective ▷ see **average** noun
1 (talking about age, height, weight) **medio** masc, **media** fem
his average speed su velocidad media
The average height of the pupils is ... La estatura media de los alumnos es ...
2 (neither good nor bad) **regular** masc & fem
The food is average. La comida es regular.

ᵟ **average** noun ▷ see **average** adj
la **media** fem
above average por encima de la media
below average por debajo de la media
on average como promedio
My marks are above average. Mis notas están por encima de la media.

avocado noun
el **aguacate** masc

to **avoid** verb
evitar[17]
She avoided me. Me evitó.
to avoid doing something evitar hacer algo
I avoid speaking to him. Evito hablar con él.

awake adjective
to be awake estar[2] despierto, fem despierta
Is Lola awake? ¿Está despierta Lola?

award noun
el **premio** masc
the award for the best CD el premio al mejor CD
to win an award ganar[17] un premio

aware adjective
to be aware of something ser[1] consciente de algo
I am aware of the problem. Soy consciente del problema.
We are more aware of environmental problems than before. Somos más conscientes de los problemas ecológicos que antes.

ᵟ **away** adverb
1 (with distances) **a long way away** muy lejos
not far away no muy lejos
Go away! ¡vete!
The thieves ran away. Los ladrones se escaparon.
How far away is it? ¿A qué distancia está?
It's two kilometres away. Está a dos kilómetros.
2 (not at home) to be away estar[2] fuera
I'll be away next week. Estaré fuera la próxima semana.
Laura's gone away for a week. Laura se ha ido por una semana.
We're playing away today. Hoy jugamos fuera de casa.

WORD TIP For expressions like to give away, to put away, etc, see to give, to put.

• **away match** el partido fuera de casa

ᵟ **awful** adjective
1 (very bad) **espantoso** masc, **espantosa** fem, **fatal** masc & fem
The film was awful! La película era espantosa.
How awful! ¡Qué horror!
I think he's awful. Me cae fatal.
There's an awful lot to do. Hay muchísimo que hacer.
2 (ill) **fatal**
I feel awful. Me siento fatal.
3 (guilty) I feel awful about it. Me siento muy culpable.

awkward adjective
1 (person, question) **difícil** masc & fem
an awkward child un niño difícil
an awkward question una pregunta difícil
2 (situation, silence) **incómodo** masc, **incómoda** fem
It's an awkward situation. Es una situación incómoda.
It's a bit awkward. Es un poco delicado.

axe noun
hacha fem

WORD TIP hacha takes el or un in the singular even though it is fem.

B b

♂ **baby** *noun*
  el **bebé** *masc*

to **babysit** *verb*
  hacer [7] **de canguro**

babysitter *noun*
  el & la **canguro** *masc & fem*

babysitting *noun*
  to go babysitting hacer [7] de canguro

♂ **bachelor** *noun*
  el **soltero** *masc*

♂ **back** *adjective* ▷ see **back** *adv, noun, verb*
  1 (*wheel, seat*) **trasero** *masc,* **trasera** *fem*
    the back seat of the car el asiento trasero
    del coche
  2 the back garden el jardín de atrás
    the back gate la verja de atrás

♂ **back** *adverb* ▷ see **back** *adj, noun, verb*
  1 to go back volver [45]
    to go back to school volver al colegio
    Lisa's gone back to London. Lisa ha vuelto a
    Londres.
  2 to come back volver [45]
    They've come back from Chile. Han vuelto
    de Chile.
    She's back at work. Ha vuelto al trabajo.
    Sue's not back yet. Sue no ha vuelto aún.
    She went by bus and walked back. Fue en
    autobús y volvió andando.
  3 to phone back volver [45] a llamar
    I'll ring back later. Te volveré a llamar más
    tarde.
  4 to give something back to somebody
    devolverle [45] algo a alguien
    I gave him back his cassettes. Le devolví sus
    cintas.
    Give it back! ¡Devuélvemelo!

♂ **back** *noun* ▷ see **back** *adj, adv, verb*
  1 (*of a person, a coat, etc*) la **espalda** *fem*
    to do something behind somebody's back
    hacer [7] algo a espaldas de alguien
  2 (*of an animal*) el **lomo** *masc*
  3 (*of a piece of paper, your hand*) el **dorso** *masc*
    on the back of the envelope en el dorso del
    sobre
  4 (*of a car, plane, hall*) el **fondo** *masc*
    We have seats at the back. Tenemos
    asientos al fondo.
    The children are at the back of the room.
    Los niños están al fondo de la habitación.

  5 (*of a building*) **la parte de atrás**
    a garden at the back of the house un jardín
    en la parte de atrás de la casa
  6 (*of a chair, sofa*) el **respaldo** *masc*
  7 (*in football, hockey, etc*) el & la **defensa** *masc &
    fem*

♂ to **back** *verb* ▷ see **back** *adj, adv, noun*
  1 (*a candidate*) **apoyar** [17]
  2 (*a horse*) **apostar** [24] **por**
  • to **back up a file**
    (*on a computer*) **hacer** [7] **una copia de
    seguridad de un archivo**
  • to **back somebody up**
    apoyar [17] **a alguien**

backache *noun*
  el **dolor de espalda**

backbone *noun*
  la **columna vertebral**

back door *noun*
  1 (*of a building*) la **puerta de atrás**
  2 (*of a car*) la **puerta trasera**

to **backfire** *verb*
  (*to turn out badly*) **salir** [63] **mal**

background *noun*
  1 (*of a person*) el **origen** *masc*
  2 (*of events, a situation*) el **contexto** *masc*
  3 (*in a picture, view*) el **fondo** *masc*
    the trees in the background los árboles del
    fondo
  • **background music** la música de fondo
  • **background noise** el ruido de fondo

backhand *noun*
  el **revés** *masc*

backing *noun*
  (*moral support*) el **apoyo** *masc*

backpack *noun* ▷ see **backpack** *verb*
  la **mochila** *fem*

to **backpack** *verb* ▷ see **backpack** *noun*
  to go backpacking viajar [17] con mochila

back seat *noun*
  el **asiento trasero**

♂ **backside** *noun*
  el **trasero** *masc*

backstroke *noun*
  el **estilo espalda**
  to swim backstroke nadar [17] a espalda

back to front *adverb*
al revés
Your jumper's on back to front. Te has puesto el jersey al revés.

backup *noun*
(*support*) el **apoyo** *masc*
- **backup disk** (*Computers*) el disco de seguridad

backwards *adverb*
(*to lean, to fall*) **hacia atrás**

bacon *noun*
el **bacon** *masc*
bacon and eggs huevos con bacon

ℰ **bad** *adjective*
1 (*not good*) **malo** *masc*, **mala** *fem*
a bad moment un mal momento
a bad experience una experiencia mala
It's bad for your health. Es malo para la salud.
2 (*accident, mistake*) **grave** *masc & fem*
a bad accident un accidente grave
3 (*headache, cold*) **fuerte** *masc & fem*
a bad cold un resfriado fuerte
4 (*food*) **podrido** *masc*, **podrida** *fem*
a bad apple una manzana podrida
to go bad estropearse [17]
5 (*rude*) bad language lenguaje grosero
6 (*naughty*) **malo** *masc*, **mala** *fem*
Bad dog! ¡(Perro) malo!
7 to be bad at something dársele [4] algo mal a alguien
I'm bad at physics. Se me da mal la física.
8 It's not bad. No está mal.
His new film's not bad. Su nueva película no está mal.

WORD TIP *malo* becomes *mal* before a masc singular noun.

badge *noun*
1 (*pin-on*) la **chapa** *fem*
2 (*policeman's*) **a police badge** una placa de policía

ℰ **badly** *adverb*
1 **mal**
He writes badly. Escribe mal.
I slept badly. Dormí mal.
My exam went badly. El examen me fue mal.
2 badly hurt gravemente herido
3 The car was badly damaged. El coche quedó muy estropeado.

bad-mannered *adjective*
maleducado *masc*, **maleducada** *fem*

badminton *noun*
el **bádminton** *masc*
to play badminton jugar [27] al bádminton

bad-tempered *adjective*
(*answer, look*) **malhumorado** *masc*,
malhumorada *fem*
to be bad-tempered (*for a while*) estar [2] de mal humor, (*always*) tener [9] mal genio

ℰ **bag** *noun*
1 (*made of plastic, paper*) la **bolsa** *fem*
2 (*handbag*) el **bolso** *masc*

baggage *noun*
el **equipaje** *masc*
- **baggage allowance** la franquicia de equipaje
- **baggage reclaim** la recogida de equipaje

bagpipes *plural noun*
la **gaita** *fem*
to play the bagpipes tocar [31] la gaita

bags *plural noun*
las **maletas** *fem pl*
to pack your bags hacer [7] las maletas

Bahamas *plural noun*
the Bahamas las Bahamas

Bahamian *adjective & noun*
1 **bahameño** *masc*, **bahameña** *fem*
2 (*person*) un **bahameño** *masc*, una **bahameña** *fem*
the Bahamians los bahameños *masc pl*

WORD TIP Adjectives and nouns for nationality and regional origin do not have capital letters in Spanish.

to **bake** *verb*
to bake a cake hornear [17] un pastel
to bake potatoes asar [17] patatas

baked *adjective*
1 (*fruit, vegetables*) **asado** *masc*, **asada** *fem*
baked apples manzanas asadas
a baked potato una patata asada
2 (*fish*) **al horno**
- **baked beans** las judías en salsa de tomate

ℰ **baker** *noun*
el **panadero** *masc*, la **panadera** *fem*
to go to the baker's ir [8] a la panadería

bakery *noun*
la **panadería** *fem*

balance *noun*
1 (*steadiness*) el **equilibrio** *masc*
to lose your balance perder [36] el equilibrio
2 (*of your bank account*) el **saldo** *masc*

a
b
c
d
e
f
g
h
i
j
k
l
m
n
o
p
q
r
s
t
u
v
w
x
y
z

balanced *adjective*
equilibrado *masc*, **equilibrada** *fem*

ℰ **balcony** *noun*
el **balcón** *masc*

bald *adjective*
calvo *masc*, **calva** *fem*

Balearic Islands *plural noun*
the Balearic Islands las Islas Baleares

ℰ **ball** *noun*
1 (*for tennis, golf*) la **pelota** *fem*
2 (*for football, volleyball*) el **balón** *masc*
3 (*of string, wool*) el **ovillo** *masc*

ballet *noun*
el **ballet** *masc*
· **ballet dancer** el bailarín de ballet, la bailarina de ballet

ℰ **balloon** *noun*
el **globo** *masc*

ballot *noun*
la **votación** *fem*

ballpoint pen *noun*
el **boli** *masc*, el **bolígrafo** *masc*

ban *noun* ▷ see **ban** *verb*
la **prohibición** *fem*
to put a ban on smoking prohibir[58] fumar

to **ban** *verb* ▷ see **ban** *noun*
prohibir[58]

ℰ **banana** *noun*
el **plátano** *masc*
a banana yoghurt **un yogur de plátano**

band *noun*
1 (*playing music*) el **grupo** *masc*
a rock band un grupo de rock
a jazz band (*big*) una orquesta de jazz, (*small*) un conjunto de jazz
a brass band una banda de música
2 a rubber band una goma elástica

bandage *noun* ▷ see **bandage** *verb*
la **venda** *fem*

to **bandage** *verb* ▷ see **bandage** *noun*
vendar[17]

bang *exclamation* ▷ see **bang** *noun, verb*
(*like a gun*) **¡pum!**

bang *noun* ▷ see **bang** *excl, verb*
1 (*noise*) el **estallido** *masc*
2 (*of a window*) el **golpe** *masc*
3 (*of a door*) el **portazo** *masc*

to **bang** *verb* ▷ see **bang** *excl, noun*
1 (*a table, a drum*) **golpear**[17]
He banged his fist on the table. Golpeó la mesa con el puño.
2 (*to knock*) **dar**[4] golpes a
to bang on the door dar golpes a la puerta
I banged my head on the door. Me di un golpe en la cabeza con la puerta.
I banged into the table. Me choqué con la mesa.
3 to bang the door aporrear[17] la puerta

bangle *noun*
la **pulsera** *fem*

banister *noun*, , **banisters** *plural noun*
la **barandilla** *noun*

ℰ **bank** *noun*
(*for money*) el **banco** *masc*
I'm going to the bank. Voy al banco.
· **bank account** la cuenta bancaria
· **bank balance** el saldo
· **bank card** la tarjeta bancaria
· **bank holiday** el día festivo
· **banknote** el billete de banco
· **bank statement** el extracto de cuenta

to **baptize** *verb*
bautizar[22]

ℰ **bar** *noun* ▷ see **bar** *verb*
1 (*where you have drinks*) el **bar** *masc*
Janet works in a bar. Janet trabaja en un bar.
2 (*the counter in a bar*) la **barra** *fem*
3 a bar of chocolate una tableta de chocolate
4 a bar of soap una pastilla de jabón
5 (*of wood, metal*) la **barra** *fem*
a metal bar una barra de metal
6 (*Music*) el **compás** *masc*

ℰ to **bar** *verb* ▷ see **bar** *noun*
(*to block physically*) **bloquear**[17]
to bar someone's way bloquear el paso a alguien

Barbadian *adjective & noun*
1 **barbadense** *masc & fem*
2 (*person*) un & una **barbadense**
the Barbadians los barbadenses

WORD TIP Adjectives and nouns for nationality and regional origin do not have capital letters in Spanish.

---

barbecue *noun* ▷ see **barbecue** *verb*
la **barbacoa** *fem*
There's a barbecue tonight. Hay una barbacoa esta noche.

to **barbecue** *verb* ▷ see **barbecue** *noun*
to barbecue a chicken asar[17] un pollo a la parrilla
barbecued chicken el pollo a la parrilla

barbed wire *noun*
el **alambre de púas**

bare *adjective*
desnudo *masc*, **desnuda** *fem*

barely *adverb*
a penas
She's barely twelve. A penas tiene doce años.

barefoot *adjective*
descalzo *masc*, **descalza** *fem*
to be barefoot estar[2] descalzo, *fem* descalza

bargain *noun*
la **ganga** *fem*
I got a bargain. Conseguí una ganga
It's a bargain! ¡Es una ganga!

barge *noun*
la **barcaza** *fem*

bark *noun* ▷ see **bark** *verb*
1 (*of a tree*) la **corteza** *fem*
2 (*of a dog*) el **ladrido** *masc*

to **bark** *verb* ▷ see **bark** *noun*
ladrar[17]

barley *noun*
la **cebada** *fem*

barmaid *noun*
la **camarera** *fem*

barman *noun*
el **camarero** *masc*

barn *noun*
el **granero** *masc*

barometer *noun*
el **barómetro** *masc*

barrel *noun*
el **tonel** *masc*

barrier *noun*
la **barrera** *fem*

base *noun*
la **base** *fem*

baseball *noun*
el **béisbol** *masc*
to play baseball jugar[27] al béisbol

based *adjective*
1 to be based on something basarse[17] en algo

The film is based on a true story. La película se basa en una historia real.
2 to be based in (*companies*) tener[9] su base en
3 to be based in (*people*) vivir[19] en
He's based in Bristol. Vive en Bristol.

♂ **basement** *noun*
el **sótano** *masc*
in the basement en el sótano

bash *noun*
1 el **golpe** *masc*
It's got a bash on the bumper. Tiene un golpe en el guardabarros.
2 (*informal*) I'll have a bash. Voy a probar.

basic *adjective*
1 (*elementary*) **básico** *masc*, **básica** *fem*
basic knowledge conocimientos básicos
2 the basic facts los hechos fundamentales
the basic salary el sueldo base
3 (*without frills*) sencillo *masc*, **sencilla** *fem*
The flat's a bit basic. El piso es bastante sencillo.

basically *adverb*
básicamente

basics *noun*
los **rudimentos** *masc plural*

basin *noun*
(*washbasin*) el **lavabo** *masc*

basis *noun*
1 la **base** *fem*
on the basis of something en base a algo
2 on a regular basis regularmente

♂ **basket** *noun*
1 la **cesta** *fem*
a shopping basket una cesta de la compra
a linen basket una cesta de ropa sucia
2 a waste-paper basket una papelera

basketball *noun*
el **baloncesto** *masc*
to play basketball jugar[27] al baloncesto

Basque *adjective & noun*
1 **vasco** *masc*, **vasca** *fem*
the Basque Country el País vasco, Euskadi (*the region's Basque name*)
2 (*person*) un **vasco** *masc*, una **vasca** *fem*
the Basques los vascos
3 (*the language*) el **vasco** *masc*, el **euskera** *masc* (*the language's Basque name*)

WORD TIP Adjectives and nouns for nationality, regional origin, and language do not have capital letters in Spanish.

bass noun
1 el **bajo** masc
   to play bass tocar [31] el bajo
2 a **double bass** un contrabajo
· **bass drum** el bombo
· **bass guitar** el bajo

bassoon noun
   el **fagot** masc
   to play the bassoon tocar [31] el fagot

bat noun
1 (for cricket, baseball) el **bate** masc
2 (for table tennis) la **paleta** fem
3 (the animal) el **murciélago** masc

batch noun
   el **lote** masc
   a batch of letters un lote de cartas

♪ **bath** noun
1 el **baño** masc
   I was in the bath. Estaba en el baño.
   to have a bath bañarse [17]
2 (bathtub) la **bañera** fem
   The bath's pink. La bañera es rosa.

to **bathe** verb
1 (a wound) **lavar** [17]
2 (to go swimming) **bañarse** [17]

♪ **bathroom** noun
   el **cuarto de baño**

bath towel noun
   la **toalla de baño**

batter noun
1 (for frying) el **rebozado** masc
   fish in batter pescado rebozado
2 (for pancakes) la **masa** fem

battery noun
1 (for a torch, a radio) la **pila** fem
2 (for a car) la **batería** fem

battle noun
   la **batalla** fem

bay noun
1 (on a coast) la **bahía** fem
   the Bay of Biscay el Golfo de Vizcaya
2 (in a bus station) la **dársena** fem

B.C. abbreviation
   (= before Christ) **a. de C.** (antes de Cristo)

♪ to **be** verb
   (Spanish has two verbs for to be, **ser** and **estar**)
1 (saying how someone or something always is) **ser** [1]
   She's blond. Es rubia.
   He's tall. Es alto.
   It's beautiful. Es precioso.
   Honey is sweet. La miel es dulce.

2 (saying alive or dead) **estar** [1]
   She's dead. Está muerta.
   He's still alive. Todavía está vivo.

3 (saying how someone or something is now) **estar** [2]
   She's angry. Está enfadada.
   I'm tired. Estoy cansado (boy speaking)., Estoy cansada (girl speaking).
   The soup is cold. La sopa está fría.
   These strawberries are delicious. Estas fresas están deliciosas.

4 (saying where someone or something is) **estar** [2]
   Dad's in the garden. Papá está en el jardín.
   Where's the butter? ¿Dónde está la mantequilla?
   It's on the table. Está en la mesa.
   When we were in Granada. Cuando estábamos en Granada.

5 there is, there are hay
   There is one mistake. Hay un error.
   There are two children outside. Hay dos niños fuera.
   There's more. Hay más.
   Is there a problem? ¿Hay algún problema?

   WORD TIP hay is the same for the singular and plural.

6 (saying what people do) **ser** [1]
   She's a teacher. Es profesora.
   He's a footballer. Es futbolista.

   WORD TIP a is not translated.

7 (with married) **estar** [2]
   She's married to Carl. Está casada con Carl.
   He's married to my sister. Está casado con mi hermana.

8 (telling the time) **ser** [1]
   It's exactly one o'clock. Es la una en punto. (es for one o'clock)
   It's half past five. Son las cinco y media. (son for the times after one o'clock)

9 (with days of the week, dates) **ser** [1]
   What day is it today? ¿Qué día es hoy?
   Today's Tuesday. Hoy es martes.
   It's the twentieth of May., It's May the twentieth. Es veinte de mayo.

10 (saying your age) **tener** [9]
   to be x years old tener x años
   He's fifteen years old. Tiene quince años.
   She's fourteen. Tiene catorce años.
   How old are you? ¿Cuántos años tienes?
   Sam's two. Sam tiene dos años.

11 (saying you're hot, cold, hungry, thirsty) **tener** [9]
   I'm hot. Tengo calor.
   I'm cold. Tengo frío.
   We're hungry. Tenemos hambre.
   Are you thirsty? ¿Tienes sed?

12 (talking about the weather) **hacer** [7]
   It's cold today. Hoy hace frío.

It's hot! ¡Qué calor hace!
It's a nice day. Hace buen día.

13 (*saying where you've been*) **estar** [2]
I've been to Alicante twice. He estado en Alicante dos veces.
Have you been to Spain before? ¿Has estado en España alguna vez?

14 (*for passive verb forms: to be -ed. Spanish often uses the third person plural in these cases*)
to be loved ser [1] amado
She is liked by everyone. Es apreciada por todos., Todos la aprecian (*third person pl form*).
The house was built in 2003. Construyeron la casa en 2003 (*third person pl form*).
He has been killed. Lo han matado (*third person pl form*).

ᔍ **beach** *noun*
la **playa** *fem*
on the beach en la playa
Let's go to the beach. Vamos a la playa.

bead *noun*
la **cuenta** *fem*

beak *noun*
el **pico** *masc*

beam *noun*
1 (*of light*) el **rayo** *masc*
2 (*for a roof*) la **viga** *fem*

bean *noun*
la **alubia** *fem*, la **judía** *fem*
baked beans alubias en salsa de tomate
green beans judías verdes

bear *noun* ▷ see **bear** *verb*
el **oso** *masc*

to **bear** *verb* ▷ see **bear** *noun*
1 **soportar** [17]
I can't bear him. No lo soporto.
I can't bear the idea. No soporto la idea.
2 to bear something in mind tener [9] algo en cuenta
I'll bear it in mind. Lo tendré en cuenta.

beard *noun*
la **barba** *fem*

bearded *adjective*
barbudo *masc*, **barbuda** *fem*

bearings *plural noun*
to get your bearings orientarse [17]

beast *noun*
(*animal*) la **bestia** *fem*
You beast! ¡Bruto!

beat *noun* ▷ see **beat** *verb*
el **ritmo** *masc*

to **beat** *verb* ▷ see **beat** *noun*
1 (*to defeat*) **ganarle a** [17]
We beat them! ¡Les hemos ganado!
He beat me at chess. Me ganó al ajedrez.
You can't beat a good meal. No hay nada mejor que una buena comida.
2 (*to hit repeatedly*) **golpear** [17]
3 (*eggs, a cake mixture*) **batir** [19]
• to beat somebody up
darle [4] **una paliza a alguien** (*informal*)

beautician *noun*
el & la **esteticista** *masc & fem*

ᔍ **beautiful** *adjective*
precioso *masc*, **preciosa** *fem*
a beautiful day un día precioso
How beautiful! ¡Qué precioso!

beautifully *adverb*
maravillosamente

beauty *noun*
la **belleza** *fem*
• beauty spot (*for tourists*) el lugar pintoresco

ᔍ **because** *conjunction*
porque
Because it's you. Porque eres tú.
Because it's cold. Porque hace frío.
because of a causa de
because of the accident a causa del accidente

to **become** *verb*
1 **hacerse** [7]
I want to become a lawyer. Quiero hacerme abogado.
She became famous. Se hizo famosa.
We became friends. Nos hicimos amigos.
2 (*become + adjective*) to become bored aburrirse [19]
to become tired cansarse [17]

WORD TIP *become* with an adjective is often translated by a reflexive verb, with *se*, in Spanish.

ᔍ **bed** *noun*
1 (*for sleeping in*) la **cama** *fem*
a double bed una cama de matrimonio
a single bed una cama individual
in bed en la cama
to go to bed ir [8] a la cama
She went to bed at nine o'clock. Se fue a la cama a las nueve., Se acostó a las nueve.
2 (*flower bed*) el **macizo** *masc*
• bedclothes la ropa de cama

bedding *noun*
la **ropa de cama**

a
b
c
d
e
f
g
h
i
j
k
l
m
n
o
p
q
r
s
t
u
v
w
x
y
z

♂ **bedroom** *noun*
la **habitación** *fem*
my bedroom window la ventana de mi habitación

bedside table *noun*
la **mesilla de noche**

bedsit *noun*
la **habitación amueblada de aquiler**

bedspread *noun*
la **colcha** *fem*

bedtime *noun*
It's bedtime. Es hora de acostarse.

bee *noun*
la **abeja** *fem*

beech *noun*
el **haya** *fem*

WORD TIP *haya* takes *el* or *un* in the singular even though it is fem.

♂ **beef** *noun*
la **carne de vaca**

beefburger *noun*
la **hamburguesa** *fem*

♂ **beer** *noun*
la **cerveza** *fem*
Two beers please. Dos cervezas, por favor.
• **beer can** la lata de cerveza

beetle *noun*
el **escarabajo** *masc*

beetroot *noun*
la **remolacha** *fem*

♂ **before** *adverb, preposition*
▷ see **before** *conj*
1 (*ahead of*) **antes de**
before Monday antes del lunes
before somebody antes que alguien
He left before me. Se fue antes que yo.
the day before el día anterior
the day before the wedding el día anterior a la boda
the day before yesterday anteayer
the week before la semana anterior
2 (*already*) **ya**
I've seen him before somewhere. Ya le he visto en algún sitio.
I had seen the film before. Ya había visto la película.
She'd never tried before. Nunca lo había intentado antes.

♂ **before** *conjunction* ▷ see **before** *adv, prep*
1 **antes de**
before doing something antes de hacer algo

I closed the windows before leaving. Cerré las ventanas antes de salir.
Phone before you leave. Llámame antes de salir.
2 **antes de que**
Phone me before they leave. Llámame antes de que salgan.
Oh, before I forget ... Ah, antes de que se me olvide ...

WORD TIP *antes de que* is followed by a verb in the subjunctive.

beforehand *adverb*
antes
Phone beforehand. Llama antes.

to **beg** *verb*
1 (*to ask for money*) **mendigar** [28]
2 (*to ask someone to do something*) **suplicarle a** [31]
She begged me not to leave. Me suplicó que no me marchase.

♂ to **begin** *verb*
1 **empezar** [25]
the words beginning with P las palabras que empiezan con P
The meeting begins at ten. La reunión empieza a las diez.
2 to begin to do something empezar a hacer algo
I'm beginning to understand. Empiezo a comprender.

beginner *noun*
el & la **principiante** *masc & fem*

beginning *noun*
1 (*start*) el **principio** *masc*
at the beginning al principio
at the beginning of the holidays al principio de las vacaciones
2 (*with a 'day', 'week', 'month', 'year'*) at the beginning of a principios de
at the beginning of the month a principios de mes

♂ **behalf** *noun*
on behalf of en nombre de

to **behave** *verb*
portarse [17]
He behaved badly. Se portó mal.
to behave yourself portarse bien
Behave yourselves! ¡Portaos bien!

behaviour *noun*
el **comportamiento** *masc*

♪**behind** *adverb* ▷ see **behind** *noun, prep*

1 (*to the back*) **detrás**
the car behind el coche de detrás
You go behind. Tú vas detrás.

2 (*where you were*) to leave something behind
olvidarse algo
I've left my keys behind. Me he olvidado las
llaves.
to stay behind quedarse [17]

3 (*not making progress*) He's behind in class. Va
retrasado en clase.

♪**behind** *noun* ▷ see **behind** *adv, prep*
el **trasero** *masc*

♪**behind** *preposition* ▷ see **behind** *adv, noun*
detrás de
behind the sofa detrás del sofá
behind them detrás de ellos

beige *adjective*
beige *invariable adj*
beige socks calcetines beige

Belgian *adjective & noun*

1 **belga** *masc & fem*

2 (*person*) un & una **belga** *masc & fem*
the Belgians los belgas

WORD TIP Adjectives and nouns for nationality
and regional origin do not have capital letters in
Spanish.

Belgium *noun*
Bélgica *fem*

belief *noun*
la **creencia** *fem*
his political beliefs sus creencias políticas

♪to **believe** *verb*

1 **creer** [37]
I believe you. Te creo.
They believed what I said. Se creyeron lo
que dije.
I don't believe you! ¡No te creo!

2 to believe in something creer en algo
Do you believe in ghosts. ¿Crees en
fantasmas?
I believe in God. Creo en Dios.

bell *noun*

1 (*in a church*) la **campana** *fem*

2 (*on a door*) el **timbre** *masc*
Ring the bell! ¡Toca el timbre!

3 (*for a cat, a toy*) el **cascabel** *masc*

to **belong** *verb*

1 (*showing ownership*) to belong to someone
ser [1] de alguien
That belongs to Lucy. Eso es de Lucy.

2 to belong to a club pertenecer [35] a un
club

3 (*in a particular place*) **ir** [8]
That chair belongs in the study. Esa silla va
en el estudio.
Where does this vase belong? ¿Adónde va
este jarrón?

belongings *plural noun*
las **pertenencias** *fem pl*
All my belongings are in London. Todas mis
pertenencias están en Londres.

♪**below** *adverb* ▷ see **below** *prep*
abajo
the flat below el piso de abajo
Shouts came from below. Se oyeron gritos
abajo.

♪**below** *preposition* ▷ see **below** *adv*
debajo de
below the window debajo de la ventana
the flat below yours el piso de debajo del
tuyo

♪**belt** *noun*
el **cinturón** *masc*

bench *noun*
el **banco** *masc*

bend *noun* ▷ see **bend** *verb*
(*in a road, river*) la **curva** *fem*

to **bend** *verb* ▷ see **bend** *noun*

1 (*your arm, your leg, a wire*) **doblar** [17]

2 (*roads, paths, rivers*) **torcer** [41]
The road bends to the right. La carretera
tuerce a la derecha.

3 (*people*) to bend down agacharse [17]
She bent down to look. Se agachó para
mirar.

beneath *preposition*
bajo

benefit *noun*
el **beneficio** *masc*
unemployment benefit el subsidio de
desempleo

bent *adjective*
doblado *masc*, **doblada** *fem*

beret *noun*
la **boina** *fem*

berry *noun*
la **baya** *fem*

♪**berth** *noun*
la **litera** *fem*

a
b
c
d
e
f
g
h
i
j
k
l
m
n
o
p
q
r
s
t
u
v
w
x
y
z

beside

beside *preposition*
> (*next to*) **al lado de**
> It's beside the table. Está al lado de la mesa.
> She was sitting beside me. Estaba sentada a mi lado.

besides *adverb*
> **además**
> Besides, it's too late. Además, es demasiado tarde.
> four dogs, and six cats besides cuatro perros y además seis gatos

best *adjective* ▷ see **best** *adv*
> **mejor** *masc & fem*
> the best song on the album la mejor canción del álbum
> It's the best. Es el mejor.
> That's the best car. Ese coche es el mejor.
> She's my best friend. Es mi mejor amiga.
> She's the best at tennis. Es la mejor jugando al tenis.
> He's the best at English. Es el mejor en inglés.
> The best thing to do is to phone them. Lo mejor es llamarlos por teléfono.
> It's the best I can do. Es lo más que puedo hacer.
> I did my best to help her. Hice todo lo posible para ayudarla.
> • **best man** el padrino de boda

best *adverb* ▷ see **best** *adj*
> **mejor**
> best of all lo mejor de todo
> He plays best. Es el que mejor juega.
> I like Barcelona best. Barcelona es la ciudad que más me gusta.

bet *noun* ▷ see **bet** *verb*
> la **apuesta** *fem*

to **bet** *verb* ▷ see **bet** *noun*
> **apostar** [24]
> to bet on a horse apostar por un caballo
> I bet you he'll forget! ¡Te apuesto algo a que se le olvida!

better *adjective* ▷ see **better** *adv*
> 1 (*in comparisons*) **mejor** *masc & fem*
>   She's found a better flat. Ha encontrado un piso mejor.
>   This road's better than the other one. Esta calle es mejor que la otra.
>   This pen writes better. Esta pluma escribe mejor.
>   even better todavía mejor
>   better still todavía mejor, aún mejor
>   It's even better than before. Es todavía mejor que antes.

> 2 (*less bad*) **to get better** mejorar [17]
>   My Spanish is getting better. Mi español está mejorando.
>   so much the better mucho mejor
>   the sooner the better cuanto antes mejor
> 3 (*less ill*) **to be better** estar [2] mejor
>   to feel better sentirse [14] mejor
>   I feel better today. Hoy me siento mejor.
>   I hope you get better soon. Espero que te mejores pronto.

better *adverb* ▷ see **better** *adj*
> I, you, she, etc had better **más vale que +** *subjunctive*
> You'd better phone at once. Más vale que llames ahora mismo.
> He'd better not go. Más vale que no vaya.
> I'd better go now. Más vale que me vaya ahora.

better off *adjective*
> 1 (*richer*) They're better off than us. Tienen más dinero que nosotros.
> 2 (*more comfortable*) **mejor** *masc & fem*
>   You'd be better off in bed. Estarás mejor en la cama.

between *preposition*
> **entre**
> between London and Dover entre Londres y Dover
> between you and me entre tú y yo
> I'll go sometime between Monday and Friday. Iré entre el lunes y el viernes.
> It's closed between 2 and 5. Está cerrado de dos a cinco.

to **beware** *verb*
> Beware of the dog! ¡Cuidado con el perro!

beyond *preposition*
> 1 (*in space and time*) **beyond the border** más allá de la frontera
> 2 (*too complicated for*) It's beyond me! ¡No lo entiendo!

Bible *noun*
> (*Religion*) the Bible la Biblia

bicycle *noun,*
> la **bicicleta** *fem*
> by bicycle en bicicleta
> • **bicycle lane** el carril de bicicletas
> • **bicycle pump** la bomba de bicicleta

big *adjective*
> 1 (*large*) **grande** *masc & fem*
>   a big house una casa grande
>   big cities ciudades grandes
>   It's too big for me. Es demasiado grande para mí.
>   a big disappointment una gran desilusión

2 (older) **mayor** masc & fem
  my big sister mi hermana mayor
  Big Brother el Gran Hermano

WORD TIP grande becomes gran when it comes
before a singular noun.

bigheaded adjective
  creído masc, **creída** fem
  to be bigheaded ser [1] un creído, fem una
  creída

big screen noun
  la **pantalla grande**

big toe noun
  el **dedo gordo del pie**

ᶘ **bike** noun
1 (with pedals) la **bici** fem
  I go to school by bike. Voy en bici al colegio.
  We went for a bike ride. Fuimos a dar una
  vuelta en bici.
2 (with a motor) la **moto** fem
  We went to the cinema by bike. Fuimos al
  cine en moto.
  She took me into town on her bike. Me
  llevó al centro en su moto.

bikini noun
  el **bikini** masc

bilingual adjective
  bilingüe masc & fem

ᶘ **bill** noun
1 (in a restaurant) la **cuenta** fem
  Can I have the bill, please? ¿Me trae la
  cuenta por favor?
2 (for gas, electricity, in a hotel) la **factura** fem

billiards noun
  el **billar** masc
  to play billiards jugar [27] al billar

billion noun
  los **mil millones** masc plural

bin noun
1 (dustbin) el **cubo de la basura**
2 (wastepaper bin) la **papelera** fem

ᶘ **binoculars** plural noun
  los **prismáticos** masc plural

biochemistry noun
  la **bioquímica** fem

biography noun
  la **biografía** fem

biologist noun
  el **biólogo** masc, la **bióloga** fem

ᶘ **biology** noun
  la **biología** fem

ᶘ **bird** noun
1 (small) el **pájaro** masc
2 (large) el **ave** fem

WORD TIP ave takes el and un in the singular even
though it is fem.

· **bird flu** la gripe aviar

birdwatching noun
  to go birdwatching ir [8] a observar pájaros

Biro® noun
  el **boli** masc

ᶘ **birth** noun
  el **nacimiento** masc
· **birth certificate** el certificado de
  nacimiento
· **birth control** el control de la natalidad

ᶘ **birthday** noun
  el **cumpleaños** masc, pl: los **cumpleaños**
  a birthday present un regalo de
  cumpleaños
  Happy birthday! ¡Feliz cumpleaños!

WORD TIP cumpleaños does not change in the
plural.

· **birthday cake** la tarta de cumpleaños
· **birthday card** la tarjeta de cumpleaños
· **birthday party** la fiesta de cumpleaños

ᶘ **biscuit** noun
  la **galleta** fem

bishop noun
  el **obispo** masc

ᶘ **bit** noun
1 (small piece) el **trozo** masc
  a bit of string un trozo de cordón
  a bit of chocolate un trozo de chocolate
  a bit of news una noticia
  a bit of advice un consejo
  to fall to bits hacerse [7] pedazos
2 (in a book, film) la **parte** fem
  This bit's brilliant! ¡Esta parte es genial!
3 (small quantity) **a bit** un poco
  a bit of something un poco de algo
  a bit of sugar un poco de azúcar
  with a bit of luck con un poco de suerte
  Wait a bit! ¡Espera un poco!
  bit by bit poco a poco
4 (rather) **a bit hot** un poco caliente
  a bit early un poco pronto
5 (for a horse) el **bocado** masc

bite noun ▷ see **bite** verb
1 (snack) el **bocado** masc
  I'll just have a bite before I go. Voy a tomar
  un bocado antes de irme. ▸▸

a
b
c
d
e
f
g
h
i
j
k
l
m
n
o
p
q
r
s
t
u
v
w
x
y
z

2 (*insect's*) la **picadura** *fem*
a mosquito bite una picadura de mosquito

3 (*dog's*) el **mordisco** *masc*
It gave me a bite. Me dio un mordisco.

to **bite** *verb* ▷ see **bite** *noun*

1 (*people, dogs*) **morder** [38]
to bite your nails morderse las uñas

2 (*insects*) **picar** [31]

bitter *adjective*
(*taste*) **amargo** *masc*, **amarga** *fem*

ℰ **black** *adjective*

1 (*in colour*) **negro** *masc*, **negra** *fem*
my black jacket mi chaqueta negra
a black coffee un café solo
to turn black volverse [45] negro

2 (*person*) a Black man un negro
a Black woman una negra

• **blackberry** la mora *fem*
• **blackbird** el mirlo *masc*
• **blackboard** la pizarra *fem*
• **blackcurrant** la grosella negra
• **black eye** el ojo morado

blackmail *noun* ▷ see **blackmail** *verb*
el **chantaje** *masc*

to **blackmail** *verb* ▷ see **blackmail** *noun*
chantajear [1]

black pudding *noun*
la **morcilla** *fem*

blade *noun*
la **hoja** *fem*

blame *noun* ▷ see **blame** *verb*
la **culpa** *fem*
to put the blame on somebody echarle [17] la culpa a alguien
to take the blame for something asumir [19] la responsabilidad de algo

to **blame** *verb* ▷ see **blame** *noun*
culpar [17]
to blame somebody for something culpar a alguien de algo
They blamed him for the accident. Lo culparon por el accidente.
She is to blame for it. Ella tiene la culpa.
I blame the parents! ¡Yo culpo a los padres!
I don't blame you! ¡No me extraña!

blank *noun* ▷ see **blank** *adj*
(*on forms*) el **espacio en blanco**

blank *adjective* ▷ see **blank** *noun*

1 (*page, cheque, screen*) **en blanco**

2 (*tape, disk*) **virgen**

3 My mind went blank. Me quedé en blanco.

ℰ **blanket** *noun*
la **manta** *fem*

blast *noun*

1 (*explosion*) la **explosión** *fem*

2 (*of air*) la **ráfaga** *fem*

3 at full blast: to play music at full blast poner [11] la música a todo volumen

blaze *noun* ▷ see **blaze** *verb*
el **incendio** *masc*

to **blaze** *verb* ▷ see **blaze** *noun*
arder [18]

blazer *noun*
el **blázer** *masc*

bleach *noun*
la **lejía** *fem*

to **bleed** *verb*
sangrar [17]
My nose is bleeding. Me está sangrando la nariz.

blend *noun* ▷ see **blend** *verb*
la **mezcla** *fem*

to **blend** *verb* ▷ see **blend** *noun*
mezclar [17]

blender *noun*
la **licuadora** *fem*

to **bless** *verb*
bendecir [5]
(*after a sneeze*) Bless you! ¡Jesús!

blind *adjective* ▷ see **blind** *noun*
ciego *masc*, **ciega** *fem*
to go blind quedarse [17] ciego (*of a boy*), quedarse [17] ciega (*of a girl*)

blind *noun* ▷ see **blind** *adj*
(*in a window*) la **persiana** *fem*

blindness *noun*
la **ceguera** *fem*

to **blink** *verb*
pestañear [17]

blister *noun*
la **ampolla** *fem*

blizzard *noun*
la **tormenta de nieve**

ℰ **block** *noun* ▷ see **block** *verb*

1 (*of flats, offices*) el **bloque** *masc*
a block of flats un bloque de pisos
an office block un bloque de oficinas

2 (*group of buildings*) la **manzana** *fem*
to take a walk round the block dar [4] la vuelta a la manzana

to **block** verb ▷ see **block** noun
1 (an exit, a road) **bloquear** [17]
2 (a drain, a hole) **atascar** [31]
The sink's blocked. El fregadero está atascado.

ᔔ **blond** adjective
rubio masc, **rubia** fem

ᔔ **blood** noun
la **sangre** fem
• blood test el análisis de sangre

blossom noun
la **flor** fem
to be in blossom estar [2] en flor

blot noun
el **borrón** masc

ᔔ **blouse** noun
la **blusa** fem

blow noun ▷ see **blow** verb
el **golpe** masc

ᔔ to **blow** verb ▷ see **blow** noun
1 (winds, people) **soplar** [17]
2 to blow off salir [63] volando
My hat blew off. Mi sombrero salió volando.
to blow away salir [63] volando
The tickets blew away. Los billetes salieron volando.
3 (in explosions) The bomb blew a hole in the wall. La bomba hizo un agujero en la pared.
4 to blow your nose sonarse [24] la nariz
• to blow something out
(a candle, flames) **apagar** [28] algo
• to blow up
(to explode) **explotar** [17]
• to blow something up
1 (a balloon, a tyre) **inflar** [17] algo
2 (a building, a car) **hacer** [7] volar algo
They blew up the president's residence. Hicieron volar la residencia del presidente.

blow-dry noun
el **brushing** masc
to have a blow-dry hacerse [7] el brushing

ᔔ **blue** adjective ▷ see **blue** noun
azul masc & fem
blue eyes ojos azules

blue noun ▷ see **blue** adj
el **azul**
• bluebell el jacinto silvestre

blunder noun
la **metedura de pata**

blunt adjective
1 (knife, scissors) **desafilado** masc, **desafilada** fem
2 (pencil) **sin punta**
3 (person) **directo** masc, **directa** fem

blurred adjective
1 (vision, image) **borroso** masc, **borrosa** fem
2 (photo) **movido** masc, **movida** fem

to **blush** verb
ponerse [11] colorado, fem colorada

board noun ▷ see **board** verb
1 (plank) la **tabla** fem
2 (blackboard) la **pizarra** fem
3 (notice board) el **tablón de anuncios**
4 (for a board game) el **tablero** masc
a chess board un tablero de ajedrez
5 (accommodation) full board pensión completa
half board media pensión
board and lodging comida y alojamiento
6 (on a boat, ship, plane) on board a bordo
on board the ferry a bordo del ferry

to **board** verb ▷ see **board** noun
embarcarse [31]

boarder noun
(at a school) el **interno** masc, la **interna** fem

board game noun
el **juego de mesa**

boarding card noun
la **tarjeta de embarque**

boarding school noun
el **internado** masc

to **boast** verb
presumir [19]
He was boasting about his new bike. Estaba presumiendo de su nueva bici.

ᔔ **boat** noun
1 (in general) el **barco** masc
2 (rowing boat) la **barca** fem

ᔔ **body** noun
1 (of a living person) el **cuerpo** masc
2 (of a dead person) el **cadáver** masc
• bodybuilding el culturismo masc
• bodyguard el & la guardaespaldas masc & fem

boil noun ▷ see **boil** verb
(swelling) el **furúnculo** masc

a
b
c
d
e
f
g
h
i
j
k
l
m
n
o
p
q
r
s
t
u
v
w
x
y
z

to **boil** *verb* ▷ see **boil** *noun*

1 (*liquids*) **hervir** [14]
The water's boiling. El agua está hirviendo.
I'm going to boil some water. Voy a hervir un poco de agua.

2 (*vegetables, pasta, an egg*) **to boil the vegetables** cocer [41] las verduras
to boil an egg cocer un huevo

• to **boil over**
salirse [63]

boiled egg *noun*
el **huevo pasado por agua**

boiler *noun*

1 (*for central heating*) el **calentador** *masc*
2 (*industrial*) la **caldera** *fem*

boiling *adjective*

1 (*water*) **que hierve**
2 (*weather*) **It's boiling hot today!** ¡Hoy hace un calor espantoso!

Bolivia *noun*
Bolivia *fem*

Bolivian *adjective* ▷ see **Bolivian** *noun*
boliviano *masc*, **boliviana** *fem*

Bolivian *noun* ▷ see **Bolivian** *adj*
(*person*) un **boliviano** *masc*, una **boliviana** *fem*
the Bolivians los bolivianos

WORD TIP Adjectives and nouns for nationality and regional origin do not have capital letters in Spanish.

bolt *noun* ▷ see **bolt** *verb*

1 (*large*) el **cerrojo** *masc*
2 (*small*) el **pestillo** *masc*

to **bolt** *verb* ▷ see **bolt** *noun*
(*a door*) **cerrar** [29] **con cerrojo**

bomb *noun* ▷ see **bomb** *verb*
la **bomba** *fem*

to **bomb** *verb* ▷ see **bomb** *noun*

1 (*from the air*) **bombardear** [17]
2 (*in a terrorist attack*) **lanzar** [31] **una bomba a**

bombing *noun*

1 (*in a war*) el **bombardeo** *masc*
2 (*a terrorist attack*) el **atentado terrorista**

bone *noun*

1 (*of a person, an animal*) el **hueso** *masc*
2 (*of a fish*) la **espina** *fem*

bonfire *noun*
la **hoguera** *fem*

bonnet *noun*
(*of a car*) el **capó** *masc*

bony *adjective*

1 (*fish*) **lleno de espinas** *masc*, **llena de espinas** *fem*
2 (*body*) **huesudo** *masc*, **huesuda** *fem*

to **boo** *verb*
abuchear [17]
The crowd booed the referee. El público abucheó al árbitro.

⚘ **book** *noun* ▷ see **book** *verb*

1 (*that you read*) el **libro** *masc*
a book about dinosaurs un libro sobre los dinosaurios
a biology book un libro de biología

2 (*that you write in*) **an exercise book** un cuaderno

3 (*of tickets, stamps, etc*) **a book of tickets** un taco de billetes
a book of stamps un librito de sellos

• **bookcase** la estantería *fem*

⚘ to **book** *verb* ▷ see **book** *noun*
reservar [17]
I booked a table for 8 o'clock. Reservé una mesa para las ocho.

⚘ **booking** *noun*
la **reserva** *fem*

• **booking office** la taquilla

⚘ **booklet** *noun*
el **folleto** *masc*

bookshelf *noun*
el **estante** *masc*

⚘ **bookshop** *noun*
la **librería** *fem*

⚘ **boot** *noun*

1 (*item of clothing*) la **bota** *fem*
walking boots botas de montaña
wellington boots botas de agua

2 (*short fashion boot*) el **botín** *masc*
3 (*of a car*) el **maletero** *masc*

border *noun*
(*between countries*) la **frontera** *fem*
We crossed the border at Irún. Cruzamos la frontera en Irún.

bore *noun*

1 (*informal: boring person*) el **pesado** *masc*, la **pesada** *fem*
2 (*informal: nuisance*) **What a bore!** ¡Qué rollo!

bored *adjective*
aburrido *masc*, **aburrida** *fem*
to be bored estar [2] aburrido
I'm bored. Estoy aburrido (*boy speaking*)., Estoy aburrida (*girl speaking*).
to get bored aburrirse [19]

ɗ **boring** *adjective*
aburrido *masc*, **aburrida** *fem*

ɗ to **born** *verb*
to be born nacer [35]
She was born on 1 June. Nació el primero de junio.
I was born in Manchester. Nací en Manchester.

to **borrow** *verb*
Can I borrow your bike? ¿Me prestas tu bici?
to borrow something from someone pedirle [57] algo prestado a alguien
I'll borrow some money from Dad. Le pediré dinero prestado a papá.

ɗ **boss** *noun*
el **jefe** *masc*, la **jefa** *fem*

bossy *adjective*
(*informal*) **mandón** *masc*, **mandona** *fem*

both *pronoun, adjective* ▷ see **both** *conj*
los dos *masc*, **las dos** *fem*
both my feet mis dos pies
They both came. Vinieron los dos.
They've both been sold. Los dos están vendidos.
Both sisters were there. Las dos hermanas estaban allí.

both *conjunction* ▷ see **both** *adj, pron*
both ... and tanto ... como
both at home and at school tanto en casa como en colegio
both in summer and in winter tanto en verano como en el invierno

ɗ **bother** *noun* ▷ see **bother** *verb*
los problemas *masc plural*
without any bother sin ningún problema
I've had a lot of bother with the car. He tenido muchos problemas con el coche.
It's no bother. No es ningún problema.
It's too much bother. No merece la pena molestarse.

ɗ to **bother** *verb* ▷ see **bother** *noun*
1 (*to disturb*) **molestar** [17]
I'm sorry to bother you. Siento molestarte.
2 (*to worry*) **preocuparse** [17]
That doesn't bother me at all. No me preocupa en absoluto.
Don't bother about dinner. No te preocupes de la cena.
3 (*to take the trouble*) **to bother to do something** molestarse [17]
She didn't even bother to come. Ni siquiera se molestó en venir.
Don't bother! ¡No te molestes!

ɗ **bottle** *noun*
la **botella** *fem*
· **bottle bank** el contenedor de botellas

bottle opener *noun*
el **abrebotellas**, *pl*: los **abrebotellas**

ɗ **bottom** *adjective* ▷ see **bottom** *noun*
1 (*lowest*) **de abajo**
the bottom shelf el estante de abajo
the bottom flat el piso bajo
the bottom sheet la sábana bajera
2 (*team, place*) **último** *masc*, **última** *fem*

ɗ **bottom** *noun* ▷ see **bottom** *adj*
1 (*of a page, a hill, a wall, steps*) el **pie** *masc*
at the bottom of the ladder al pie de la escalera
at the bottom of the page al pie de la página
2 (*of a bag, a hole, a street, etc*) el **fondo** *masc*
at the bottom of the lake en el fondo del lago
3 (*of a list*) el **final** *masc*
4 (*of a bottle*) el **culo** *masc*
5 (*buttocks*) el **trasero** *masc*

to **bounce** *verb*
rebotar [17]

bouncer *noun*
el **gorila** *masc* (*informal*)

bound *adjective*
He's bound to be late. Seguro que llega tarde.
That was bound to happen. Eso tenía que pasar.

boundary *noun*
la **línea divisoria**

bow *noun*
1 (*in a shoelace, ribbon*) el **lazo** *masc*
2 (*for playing the violin, shooting arrows*) el **arco** *masc*

ɗ **bowl** *noun* ▷ see **bowl** *verb*
1 (*for cereal*) el **bol** *masc*
2 (*for mixing food in*) el **cuenco** *masc*
3 (*for washing up*) el **barreño** *masc*
4 (*for salad, fruit*) **a salad bowl** una ensaladera
a fruit bowl un frutero

ɗ to **bowl** *verb* ▷ see **bowl** *noun*
(*a ball*) **lanzar** [22]

bowling *noun*
(*tenpins*) los **bolos** *masc plural*
to go bowling ir [8] a jugar a los bolos

bow tie *noun*
la **pajarita** *fem*, el **corbatín** *masc*

a
b
c
d
e
f
g
h
i
j
k
l
m
n
o
p
q
r
s
t
u
v
w
x
y
z

ℰ **box** *noun*
1 (*container*) la **caja** *fem*
a box of chocolates una caja de bombones
a cardboard box una caja de cartón
2 (*of matches*) la **cajetilla** *fem*
3 (*on a form*) el **recuadro** *masc*

boxer *noun*
1 (*fighter*) el **boxeador** *masc*
2 (*dog*) el **bóxer** *masc*
• **boxer shorts** los calzoncillos *masc plural*

boxing *noun*
el **boxeo** *masc*
a boxing match un combate de boxeo

Boxing Day *noun*
la **fiesta del 26 de diciembre**

box office *noun*
la **taquilla** *fem*

ℰ **boy** *noun*
el **niño** *masc*
a little boy un niño pequeño
• **boyfriend** el novio *masc*

bra *noun*
el **sujetador** *masc*

brace *noun*
el **aparato de los dientes**

bracelet *noun*
la **pulsera** *fem*

braces *plural noun*
los **tirantes** *masc plural*

bracket *noun*
in brackets entre paréntesis

brain *noun*
el **cerebro** *masc*
• **brainwave** la idea genial

ℰ **brake** *noun* ▷ see **brake** *verb*
el **freno** *masc*

ℰ to **brake** *verb* ▷ see **brake** *noun*
frenar [17]

bramble *noun*
la **zarzamora** *fem*

branch *noun*
1 (*of a tree*) la **rama** *fem*
2 (*of a shop, a company, a bank*) la **sucursal** *fem*
our Glasgow branch nuestra sucursal de Glasgow

ℰ **brand** *noun*
la **marca** *fem*

brand-new *adjective*
nuevo *masc*, **nueva** *fem*

brandy *noun*
el **coñac** *masc*

brass *noun*
1 (*the metal*) el **latón** *masc*
a brass candlestick un candelabro dorado
2 (*in an orchestra*) the brass los metales
• **brass band** la banda de música

Brazil *noun*
Brasil *masc*

Brazilian *adjective & noun*
1 **brasileño** *masc*, **brasileña** *fem*
2 (*person*) un **brasileño** *masc*, una **brasileña** *fem*
the Brazilians los brasileños *masc pl*

> **WORD TIP** Adjectives and nouns for nationality and regional origin do not have capital letters in Spanish.

brave *adjective*
valiente *masc & fem*

ℰ **bread** *noun*
el **pan** *masc*
a slice of bread una rebanada de pan

ℰ **break** *noun* ▷ see **break** *verb*
1 (*short rest*) el **descanso** *masc*
a fifteen-minute break un descanso de quince minutos
to take a break descansar [17] un rato
the Christmas break las vacaciones de Navidad
2 (*in school*) el **recreo** *masc*

ℰ to **break** *verb* ▷ see **break** *noun*
romper [40]
He broke a glass. Rompió un vaso.
to break your leg romperse una pierna
I broke my arm. Me rompí un brazo.
to break your promise romper una promesa
to break the rules infringir [49] las reglas
You mustn't break the rules. No debes infringir las reglas.
to break a record batir [19] un récord
to break the news dar [4] la noticia
• to **break down** averiarse [17]
The car broke down. El coche se estropeó
• to **break in** The thief broke in through the window. El ladrón entró a robar por la ventana.
The house was broken into. Entraron ladrones en la casa.
• to **break out**
1 (*fires*) declararse [17]
2 (*wars, storms*) estallar [17]
3 (*prisoners*) escaparse [17]
• to **break up**
1 (*family*) separarse [17]

2 (*couples*) **romper** [40]

3 (*crowds, clouds*) **dispersarse** [17]

4 (*for the holidays*) We break up on Thursday. Empezamos las vacaciones el jueves.

♂ **breakdown** noun

1 (*of a vehicle*) la **avería** fem
We had a breakdown on the motorway. Tuvimos una avería en la autopista.

2 (*in talks, negotiations*) la **ruptura** fem

3 (*nervous collapse*) la **crisis nerviosa**
to have a (nervous) breakdown sufrir [19] una crisis nerviosa

• **breakdown truck** la grúa

♂ **breakfast** noun

el **desayuno** masc
to have breakfast desayunar [17]
We have breakfast at eight. Desayunamos a las ocho.

break-in noun

el **robo** masc

breast noun

1 (*a woman's*) el **pecho** masc

2 (*of chicken, of turkey*) la **pechuga** fem

breaststroke noun

la **braza** fem

breath noun

el **aliento** masc
out of breath sin aliento
to get one's breath recobrar [17] el aliento
to take a deep breath respirar [17] hondo

to **breathe** verb

respirar [17]

breathing noun

la **respiración** fem

breed noun ▷ see **breed** verb

la **raza** fem

to **breed** verb ▷ see **breed** noun

1 (*animals*) **criar** [32]

2 (*to have babies*) **reproducirse** [60]
Rabbits breed fast. Los conejos se reproducen mucho.

breeze noun

la **brisa** fem

brewery noun

la **cervecería** fem

bribe noun ▷ see **bribe** verb

el **soborno** masc

to **bribe** verb ▷ see **bribe** noun

sobornar [17]

brick noun

el **ladrillo** masc
a brick wall una pared de ladrillo

♂ **bride** noun

la **novia** fem
the bride and groom los novios, el novio y la novia

♂ **bridegroom** noun

el **novio** masc

bridesmaid noun

la **dama de honor** fem

♂ **bridge** noun

1 (*over a river*) el **puente** masc
a bridge over the Thames un puente sobre el Támesis

2 (*card game*) el **bridge** masc
to play bridge jugar [27] al bridge

bridle noun

la **brida** fem

brief adjective

breve masc & fem

briefcase noun

el **maletín** masc

briefly adverb

brevemente

briefs plural noun

los **calzoncillos** masc plural

bright adjective

1 (*star, light*) **brillante** masc & fem
bright sunshine un sol radiante

2 (*colour*) **vivo** masc, **viva** fem
bright green socks calcetines de un verde vivo

3 (*clever*) **inteligente** masc & fem
She's not very bright. No es muy inteligente.

to **brighten up** verb

The weather's brightening up. El tiempo está aclarando.

brilliant adjective

1 (*very clever*) **brillante** masc & fem
a brilliant surgeon un brillante cirujano
He's brilliant at maths. Es genial para las matemáticas.

2 (*wonderful*) **fenomenal** masc & fem
The party was brilliant! ¡La fiesta estuvo fenomenal!

a b c d e f g h i j k l m n o p q r s t u v w x y z

a
b
c
d
e
f
g
h
i
j
k
l
m
n
o
p
q
r
s
t
u
v
w
x
y
z

♂ to **bring** *verb*
traer [42]
They brought a present. Trajeron un regalo.
Bring your camera. Trae tu cámara.
It brings good luck. Trae buena suerte.
She's bringing all the children. Trae a todos los niños.
I'll bring the shopping in. Voy a entrar las compras.
• to **bring something back**
devolver [45] **algo**
• to **bring up**
(*children*) **criar** [32]
He was brought up by his aunt. Lo crió su tía.

bristle *noun*
la **cerda** *fem*

Britain *noun*
Gran Bretaña *fem*

♂ **British** *adjective* ▷ see **British** *plural noun*
británico *masc*, **británica** *fem*
the British Isles las islas británicas

♂ **British** *plural noun* ▷ see **British** *adj*
(*the people*) **the British** los británicos *masc plural*

> **WORD TIP** Adjectives and nouns for nationality and regional origin do not have capital letters in Spanish.

broad *adjective*
(*wide*) **ancho** *masc*, **ancha** *fem*
• **broad bean** el haba *fem*

> **WORD TIP** *haba* takes *el* or *un* in the singular even though it is fem.

♂ **broadcast** *noun* ▷ see **broadcast** *verb*
la **emisión** *fem*

♂ to **broadcast** *verb* ▷ see **broadcast** *noun*
(*a programme*) **emitir** [19]

broccoli *noun*
el **brécol** *masc*

♂ **brochure** *noun*
el **folleto** *masc*

broke *adjective*
to be broke no tener [9] un duro (*informal*)

broken *adjective*
roto *masc*, **rota** *fem*
to have a broken leg tener [9] una pierna rota
The window's broken. La ventana está rota.

bronchitis *noun*
la **bronquitis** *fem*

bronze *adjective* ▷ see **bronze** *noun*
de bronce

bronze *noun* ▷ see **bronze** *adj*
el **bronce** *masc*

brooch *noun*
el **broche** *masc*

broom *noun*
(*for sweeping*) la **escoba** *fem*

♂ **brother** *noun*
el **hermano** *masc*
my little brother mi hermanito
My brother's fifteen. Mi hermano tiene quince año.
• **brother-in-law** el cuñado *masc*

♂ **brown** *adjective*
1 (*in colour*) **marrón** *masc & fem*
brown shoes zapatos marrón
2 (*hair, eyes*) **castaño** *masc*, **castaña** *fem*
3 (*tanned in the sun*) **moreno** *masc*, **morena** *fem*
to go brown ponerse [11] moreno, *fem* morena
• **brown bread** el pan integral
• **brown sugar** el azúcar moreno

browser *noun*
el **navegador** *masc*

bruise *noun*
1 (*on a person*) el **moretón** *masc*
2 (*on fruit*) la **magulladura** *fem*

♂ **brush** *noun* ▷ see **brush** *verb*
1 (*for hair, clothes, nails, shoes*) el **cepillo** *masc*
my hair brush mi cepillo del pelo
2 (*for sweeping*) la **escoba** *fem*
3 (*paintbrush*) la **brocha** *fem*

♂ to **brush** *verb* ▷ see **brush** *noun*
1 (*your hair, shoes*) **cepillar** [17]
to brush your hair cepillarse el pelo
She brushed her hair. Se cepilló el pelo.
2 (*your teeth*) to brush your teeth limpiarse [17] los dientes
I'm going to brush my teeth. Voy a limpiarme los dientes.

Brussels *noun*
Bruselas *fem*
• **Brussels sprouts** las coles de Bruselas

bubble *noun*
la **burbuja** *fem*
• **bubble bath** el gel de baño
• **bubblegum** el chicle (de globos)

bucket *noun*
el **cubo** *masc*

English-Spanish

buckle *noun*
  la **hebilla** *fem*

bud *noun*
  el **brote** *masc*

Buddhism *noun*
  el **budismo** *masc*

Buddhist *noun*
  un & una **budista** *masc & fem*

WORD TIP Adjectives and nouns for religion do not have capital letters in Spanish.

budget *noun*
  el **presupuesto** *masc*

budgie *noun*
  el **periquito** *masc*

♂ **buffet** *noun*
1 (*on a train*) el **bar** *masc*
2 (*meal*) el **buffet** *masc*
· **buffet car** el coche restaurante

bug *noun*
1 (*informal: insect*) el **bicho** *masc*
2 (*virus*) el **virus** *masc*
  a stomach bug un virus en el estómago

to **build** *verb*
  construir [54]

builder *noun*
  el & la **albañil** *masc & fem*

♂ **building** *noun*
  el **edificio** *masc*
· **building site** el solar
· **building society** la sociedad de crédito hipotecario

built-in *adjective*
  empotrado *masc*, **empotrada** *fem*

built-up *adjective*
  urbanizado *masc*, **urbanizada** *fem*
  a built-up area una zona urbanizada

bulb *noun*
1 (*for a light*) la **bombilla** *fem*
2 (*in gardening*) el **bulbo** *masc*

bulky *adjective*
  voluminoso *masc*, **voluminosa** *fem*

bull *noun*
  el **toro** *masc*
· **bulldozer** el bulldozer *masc*

♂ **bullet** *noun*
  la **bala** *fem*

bulletin *noun*
  el **boletín** *masc*
  a news bulletin un boletín de noticias

bullfight *noun*
  la **corrida de toros**

 bullfights

This Spanish custom, also popular in some Latin American countries, typically takes place on a Sunday afternoon at 5 o'clock. The season lasts from March to October. A recent law makes it illegal for children under 14 to attend a bullfight.

bullfighter *noun*
  el **torero** *masc*, la **torera** *fem*

bullfighting *noun*
  los **toros**
  Do you like bullfighting? ¿Te gustan los toros?

bullring *noun*
  la **plaza de toros**

bully *noun* ▷ see **bully** *verb*
  el **bravucón** *masc*, la **bravucona** *fem*
  He's a bully. Es un bravucón.

to **bully** *verb* ▷ see **bully** *noun*
  intimidar [17]

bum *noun*
  el **trasero** *masc* (*informal*)

bump *noun* ▷ see **bump** *verb*
1 (*on the head*) el **chichón** *masc*
2 (*in the road*) el **bache** *masc*
3 (*jolt*) la **sacudida** *fem*
4 (*noise*) el **golpe** *masc*

to **bump** *verb* ▷ see **bump** *noun*
1 (*to bang*) **darse** [4] un golpe
  I bumped my head. Me di un golpe en la cabeza.
2 to bump into something chocarse [31] con algo
  I bumped into the table. Me choqué con la mesa.
3 to bump into somebody encontrarse [24] con alguien
  I bumped into Tom. Me encontré con Tom.

bumper *noun*
  el **parachoques** *masc*, pl: los **parachoques**

bumpy *adjective*
1 (*road*) **lleno de baches** *masc*, **llena de baches** *fem*
2 (*ride, plane landing*) **con muchas sacudidas**

bun *noun*
1 (*small cake*) el **bollo** *masc*
2 (*for a burger*) el **panecillo** *masc*

a
b
c
d
e
f
g
h
i
j
k
l
m
n
o
p
q
r
s
t
u
v
w
x
y
z

bunch *noun*
1 (*of flowers*) el **ramo** *masc*
2 (*of carrots, radishes, keys*) el **manojo** *masc*
3 (*of grapes*) a bunch of grapes un racimo de uvas

bundle *noun*
1 (*of clothes*) el **fardo** *masc*
2 (*of papers, letters*) el **paquete** *masc*

bungalow *noun*
   la **casa de una planta**

bunk *noun*
   la **litera** *fem*
• **bunk beds** las literas

ℰ **bureau de change** *noun*
   la **casa de cambio**

burger *noun*
   la **hamburguesa** *fem*

burglar *noun*
   el **ladrón** *masc*, la **ladrona** *fem*
• **burglar alarm** la alarma antirrobo

ℰ **burglary** *noun*
   el **robo** *masc*

ℰ **burn** *noun* ▷ see **burn** *verb*
   la **quemadura** *fem*

ℰ to **burn** *verb* ▷ see **burn** *noun*
1 **quemar** [17]
   I've burned the letters. He quemado las cartas.
   She burnt herself on the grill. Se quemó en la parrilla.
   You'll burn your finger! ¡Te vas a quemar el dedo!
   Mum's burnt her cake. A mamá se le ha quemado el pastel.
2 (*woodland, scrub*) **arder** [18]
   The forest has been burning for two days. El bosque arde desde hace dos días.
3 (*in the sun*) **quemarse**
   I burn easily. Me quemo fácilmente.

burnt *adjective*
   quemado *masc*, **quemada** *fem*

ℰ to **burst** *verb*
1 (*balloons*) **estallar** [17]
2 (*tyres, pipes*) **reventar** [29]
   The tyre burst. Reventó el neumático.
3 to burst out laughing echarse [17] a reír
   to burst into tears echarse [17] a llorar
   to burst into flames empezar [25] a arder

to **bury** *verb*
   enterrar [29]

ℰ **bus** *noun*
1 (*in town*) el **autobús** *masc*, el **bus** *masc*
   by bus en el autobús
   on the bus en el autobús
   a bus ticket un billete de autobús
   to take the bus tomar [17] el autobús
   I go to school by bus. Voy al colegio en el autobús.
   We missed the bus. Perdimos el autobús.
2 (*for long distances*) el **autocar** *masc*
   to go to London by bus ir [8] a Londres en autocar
• **bus driver** el conductor de autobús, la conductora de autobús

bush *noun*
   el **arbusto** *masc*

ℰ **business** *noun*
1 (*commercial dealings*) los **negocios** *masc* plural
   a business letter una carta de negocios
   He's in Leeds on business. Está en Leeds de viaje de negocios.
2 (*firm, company*) la **empresa** *fem*
   small businesses las pequeñas empresas
3 (*concern*) Mind your own business! ¡No te metas en lo que no te importa!
   That's my business! ¡Eso es asunto mío!
• **business class** la clase preferente
• **businessman** el hombre de negocios
• **business trip** el viaje de negocios
• **businesswoman** la mujer de negocios

bus lane *noun*
   el **carril bus**

bus pass *noun*
   el **abono de autobús**

bus route *noun*
   la **línea de autobús**

bus shelter *noun*
   la **marquesina** *fem*

bus station *noun*
   la **estación de autobuses**

ℰ **bus stop** *noun*
   la **parada de autobús**

ℰ **bust** *noun*
   el **busto** *masc*

ℰ **busy** *adjective*
1 (*person*) **ocupado** *masc*, **ocupada** *fem*
   Don't disturb him, he's busy. No lo molestes, está ocupado.
   to be busy doing something estar [2] ocupado, *fem* ocupada haciendo algo
   She's busy painting the kitchen. Está ocupada pintando la cocina.

2 (*day, week*) **ajetreado** *masc*, **ajetreada** *fem*
a very busy day un día muy ajetreado

3 (*station, airport, market, shop*) **muy concurrido** *masc*, **muy concurrida** *fem*
The shops were busy. Las tiendas estaban muy concurridas.

4 (*phones*) **The line's busy.** Está comunicando.

ℰ **but** *conjunction, preposition*
1 (*however*) **pero**
small but strong pequeño pero fuerte
I'll try, but it's difficult. Lo intentaré, pero es difícil.

2 (*to show contradiction*) **not ... but ... no ... sino ...**
not Thursday but Friday no el jueves sino el viernes

3 (*except*) **menos**
anything but that cualquier cosa menos eso
everyone but Leah todos menos Leah
the last but one el penúltimo

ℰ **butcher** *noun*
el **carnicero** *masc*, la **carnicera** *fem*
the butcher's la carnicería

ℰ **butter** *noun* ▷ see **butter** *verb*
la **mantequilla** *fem*
- **buttercup** el botón de oro
- **butterfly** la mariposa

to **butter** *verb* ▷ see **butter** *noun*
untar [17] **con mantequilla**

ℰ **button** *noun*
el **botón** *masc*
the record button el botón de grabar
- **buttonhole** el ojal

ℰ **buy** *noun* ▷ see **buy** *verb*
a good buy una buena compra
a bad buy una mala compra

ℰ to **buy** *verb* ▷ see **buy** *noun*
comprar [17]
I bought the cinema tickets. Compré las entradas para el cine.
to buy something for somebody comprarle algo a alguien
Sarah bought him a sweater. Sarah le compró un jersey.
to buy something from someone comprarle algo a alguien

He bought his bike from Tim. Le compró su bici a Tom .

buyer *noun*
el **comprador** *masc*, la **compradora** *fem*

to **buzz** *verb*
zumbar [17]

buzzer *noun*
el **timbre** *masc*

ℰ **by** *preposition*
1 (*saying how something happens*) **por**
by telephone por teléfono
eaten by a dog comido por un perro
by mistake por equivocación
He got in by the window. Entró por la ventana.

2 (*saying how you do something*) **by bike** en bicicleta
to come by bus venir [15] en autobús
to leave by train salir [63] en tren
to pay by the hour pagar [28] por horas

3 (*saying where something is*) **al lado de**
by the fire al lado del fuego
by the sea al lado del mar
close by cerca

4 (*with time limits*) **para**
It'll be ready by Monday. Estará listo para el lunes.
Kevin was back by four. Kevin estaba de vuelta para las cuatro.
They should have finished by now. Ya deberían haber terminado.

5 (*saying who did something*) **por**
written by Neruda escrito por Neruda
She did it by herself. Lo hizo sola.

6 (*in expressions*)
by the way por cierto
by myself: I was by myself in the house. Estaba solo en la casa. (*boy speaking*)
to take somebody by the hand coger [3] a alguien de la mano
to measure two metres by four medir [57] dos metros por cuatro

bye *exclamation*
adiós
Bye for now! ¡Hasta luego!

bypass *noun*
la **carretera de circunvalación**

a
b
c
d
e
f
g
h
i
j
k
l
m
n
o
p
q
r
s
t
u
v
w
x
y
z

C c

a
b
c
d
e
f
g
h
i
j
k
l
m
n
o
p
q
r
s
t
u
v
w
x
y
z

cab *noun*
1 el **taxi** *masc*
  to call a cab llamar [17] un taxi
2 (*on a lorry*) la **cabina** *fem*

ꞔ **cabbage** *noun*
  el **repollo** *masc*

cabin *noun*
1 (*on a lorry, plane*) la **cabina** *fem*
2 (*on a ship*) el **camarote** *masc*

ꞔ **cable** *noun*
  el **cable** *masc*
• **cable car** el teleférico
• **cable television** la televisión por cable

cactus *noun*
  el **cactus** *masc*

ꞔ **cafe** *noun*
  la **cafetería** *fem*

ꞔ **cafetière** *noun*
  la **cafetera de émbolo**

cage *noun*
  la **jaula** *fem*

cagoule *noun*
  el **canguro** *masc*

ꞔ **cake** *noun*
  el **pastel** *masc*
  Would you like a piece of cake? ¿Quieres un trozo de pastel?
• **cake shop** la pastelería

to **calculate** *verb*
  calcular [17]

calculation *noun*
  el **cálculo** *masc*

calculator *noun*
  la **calculadora** *fem*

calendar *noun*
  el **calendario** *masc*

ꞔ **calf** *noun*
1 (*animal*) el **ternero** *masc*, la **ternera** *fem*
2 (*of your leg*) la **pantorrilla** *fem*

ꞔ to **call** *verb* ▷ see **call** *noun*
1 (*to telephone*) **llamar** [17]
  to call a taxi llamar un taxi
  to call the doctor llamar al médico
  Call this number. Llama a este número.
  Thank you for calling. Gracias por su llamada.
  I'll call you back later. Te llamo más tarde.

2 (*to name*) **llamar**
  They call him Billy. Le llaman Billy.
  They've called the baby Julie. Le han puesto Julie al bebé.
  to be called llamarse [17]
  What's he called? ¿Cómo se llama?
  Her brother is called Dan. Tiene un hermano que se llama Dan.
• to **call in**
  pasar [17]
  I'll call in on my way back. Pasaré por tu casa cuando vuelva.

ꞔ **call** *noun* ▷ see **call** *verb*
  (*on the telephone*) la **llamada** *fem*
  a phone call una llamada telefónica
  to give somebody a call llamar [17] a alguien
  Thank you for your call. Gracias por su llamada.
  I had several calls this morning. Tuve varias llamadas esta mañana.
• **call box** la cabina telefónica

ꞔ **calm** *adjective* ▷ see **calm** *noun, verb*
  tranquilo *masc*, **tranquila** *fem*
  Try to stay calm. Trata de estar tranquilo.

ꞔ **calm** *noun* ▷ see **calm** *adj, verb*
  la **calma** *fem*

ꞔ to **calm** *verb* ▷ see **calm** *adj, noun*
  calmar [17]
• to **calm down**
  calmarse
  He's calmed down a bit. Se ha calmado un poco.
• to **calm somebody down**
  calmar a alguien
  I tried to calm her down. Intenté calmarla.

calmly *adverb*
  con calma

calorie *noun*
  la **caloría** *fem*

camcorder *noun*
  la **videocámara** *fem*

camel *noun*
  el **camello** *masc*

camera *noun*
1 (*for photos*) la **cámara de fotos**
2 (*for films, TV*) la **cámara** *fem*
• **cameraman** el & la cámara *masc & fem*

ᵍ **camp** noun ▷ see **camp** verb
  el **campamento** masc

ᵍ to **camp** verb ▷ see **camp** noun
  acampar [17]

campaign noun
  la **campaña** fem

ᵍ **camper** noun
  el & la **campista** masc & fem
• **camper van** la caravana

ᵍ **camping** noun
  el **camping** masc
  to go camping ir [8] de camping
  **We're going camping in Asturias this
  summer.** Nos vamos de camping a Asturias
  este verano.

ᵍ **campsite** noun
  el **camping** masc

ᵍ **can** noun ▷ see **can** verb
 1 (for food) la **lata** fem
  a can of tomatoes una lata de tomates
 2 (for petrol, oil) el **bidón** masc

ᵍ **can** verb ▷ see **can** noun
 1 (saying you are able to) **poder** [10]
  I can lend you £20. Puedo prestarte veinte
  libras.
  I can't be there before ten. No puedo estar
  allí antes de las diez.
  He cannot come. No puede venir.
  They couldn't come. No pudieron venir.
 2 (with polite questions, polite orders, etc) **You can
  leave your bag here.** Puedes dejar tu bolsa
  aquí.
  Can you open the door, please? ¿Me abres
  la puerta por favor?
  Can I help you? ¿Qué desea? (in a shop)
  You could go tomorrow. Podrías ir
  mañana.
  You could have told me. Me lo podrías
  haber dicho.
 3 (saying you know how to) **saber** [13]
  She can't drive. No sabe conducir.
  Can you play the piano? ¿Sabes tocar el
  piano?
 4 (with words like: see, hear, feel, remember, etc) **I
  can see her well.** La veo bien.
  Can you hear me? ¿Me oyes?
  I can remember that ... Me acuerdo de que
  ...
  I can't see you. No te veo.
  I can't find my keys. No encuentro mis
  llaves.

WORD TIP When you use can with see, hear, feel,
remember, etc, it is not translated into Spanish.
▷ **could**

Canada noun
  Canadá masc

Canadian adjective ▷ see **Canadian** noun
  canadiense masc & fem

Canadian noun ▷ see **Canadian** adj
  un & una **canadiense** masc & fem

WORD TIP Adjectives and nouns for nationality
and regional origin do not have capital letters in
Spanish.

canal noun
  el **canal** masc

canary noun
  el **canario** masc

Canary Islands plural noun
  the Canary Islands las Islas Canarias

to **cancel** verb
  cancelar [17]
  The concert's been cancelled. Han
  cancelado el concierto.

cancer noun ▷ see **Cancer** noun
  el **cáncer** masc
  to have lung cancer tener cáncer de
  pulmón

Cancer noun
 1 (the star sign) el **Cáncer** masc
 2 (person) un & una **cáncer** masc & fem
  I'm Cancer. Soy cáncer.

WORD TIP Use a small letter in Spanish to say I
am ... etc with star signs. Star signs in Spanish are
used without el, un, la, una.

candidate noun
  el **candidato** masc, la **candidata** fem

candle noun
  la **vela** fem
• **candlestick** el candelabro

candyfloss noun
  el **algodón de azúcar**

canned adjective
  en lata
  canned tomatoes tomates en lata

cannon noun
  el **cañón** masc

ᵍ **cannot** verb ▷ **can** verb
  He cannot come. No puede venir.

canoe noun
  la **piragua** fem

canoeing noun
  el **piragüismo** masc
  to go canoeing hacer [7] piragüismo
  I like canoeing. Me gusta hacer
  piragüismo.

a
b
c
d
e
f
g
h
i
j
k
l
m
n
o
p
q
r
s
t
u
v
w
x
y
z

can-opener noun
el **abrelatas** masc, pl: los **abrelatas**

can't short for **cannot** (See: **can**)

canteen noun
la **cantina** fem

canvas noun
1 (fabric) la **lona** fem
2 (painting) el **lienzo** masc

cap noun
1 (hat) el **gorro** masc
a baseball cap un gorro de béisbol
2 (on a bottle, tube) el **tapón** masc

capable adjective
capaz masc & fem
to be capable of doing something ser [1]
capaz de hacer algo
They are capable of winning the cup. Son
capaces de ganar la copa.

capacity noun
la **capacidad** fem

capital adjective ▷ see **capital** noun
1 (city) **capital** masc & fem
2 (letter) **mayúsculo** masc, **mayúscula** fem
It is written with a capital C. Se escribe con
C mayúscula.

capital noun ▷ see **capital** adj
1 (city) la **capital** fem
Madrid is the capital of Spain. Madrid es la
capital de España.
2 (letter) la **mayúscula** fem
in capitals en mayúsculas

capitalism noun
el **capitalismo** masc

capitalist noun
el & la **capitalista** masc & fem

Capricorn noun
1 (the star sign) el **Capricornio** masc
2 (person) un & una **capricornio** masc & fem
Linda's Capricorn. Linda es capricornio.

> **WORD TIP** Use a small letter in Spanish to say I
> am ... etc with star signs. Star signs in Spanish are
> used without el, un, la, una.

captain noun
1 (of a ship, team) el **capitán** masc, la **capitana**
fem
2 (of a plane) el & la **comandante** masc & fem

captivity noun
el **cautiverio** masc
to keep someone in captivity mantener [9]
a alguien en cautiverio

to **capture** verb
capturar [17]

♂ **car** noun
el **coche** masc, (Latin America) el **carro** masc
a car crash un accidente de coche
He parked the car. Aparcó el coche.
We're going by car. Vamos en coche.

♂ **carafe** noun
la **garrafa** fem

caramel noun
el **caramelo** masc

♂ **caravan** noun
la **caravana** fem

♂ **card** noun
1 (for a card game) la **carta** fem
a card game un juego de cartas
to have a game of cards jugar [27] a las
cartas
2 (for phoning, for a cash machine, for Christmas,
etc) la **tarjeta** fem
a birthday card una tarjeta de cumpleaños

cardboard noun
el **cartón** masc

cardigan noun
la **chaqueta (de punto)** fem

cardphone noun
el **teléfono de tarjeta**

care noun ▷ see **care** verb
1 el **cuidado** masc
He took care opening it. Tuvo cuidado al
abrirlo.
to take care of somebody cuidar [17] a
alguien
He takes care of his mother. Cuida a su
madre.
2 (in expressions: be careful) Take care!
¡Cuidado!, (: when saying goodbye) ¡Cuídate!

to **care** verb ▷ see **care** noun
to care about something importarle [17]
algo a alguien
She doesn't care if I come in late. A ella no le
importa si vuelvo tarde.
I couldn't care less! ¡No me importa en
absoluto!
He doesn't care about me. No se preocupa
por mí.

career noun
la **carrera** fem

♂ **careful** adjective
cuidadoso masc, **cuidadosa** fem
Try to be more careful. Procura ser más
cuidadoso.
He's a careful driver. Es un conductor
prudente.
Be careful! ¡Ten cuidado!

carefully *adverb*

1 *(with attention)* **atentamente**
Read the instructions carefully. Lea las instrucciones atentamente.
Listen carefully. Escuchad atentamente.

2 *(to handle)* **con cuidado**
She put the vase down carefully. Colocó el jarrón con cuidado.

3 **Drive carefully!** ¡Conduce con precaución!

careless *adjective*

(person) **descuidado** *masc*, **decuidada** *fem*
He's very careless. Es muy descuidado.
a careless mistake un error por descuido
This is careless work. Este trabajo está hecho sin cuidado.
careless driving la conducción negligente

caretaker *noun*

1 *(in a school)* el & la **conserje** *masc & fem*

2 *(in a block of flats)* el **portero** *masc*, la **portera** *fem*

car ferry *noun*
el **ferry** *masc*

cargo *noun*
la **carga** *fem*

car hire *noun*
el **alquiler de coches**

Caribbean *adjective*
▷ see **Caribbean** *noun*
caribeño *masc*, **caribeña** *fem*

WORD TIP Adjectives and nouns for nationality and regional origin do not have capital letters in Spanish.

Caribbean *noun* ▷ see **Caribbean** *adj*
the Caribbean el Caribe
the Caribbean Sea el mar Caribe

caricature *noun*
la **caricatura** *fem*

carnation *noun*
el **clavel** *masc*

carnival *noun*
el **carnaval** *masc*

ℰ **car park** *noun*
el **aparcamiento** *masc*

ℰ **carpenter** *noun*
el **carpintero** *masc*, la **carpintera** *fem*

carpentry *noun*
la **carpintería** *fem*

carpet *noun*

1 *(fitted)* la **moqueta** *fem*

2 *(rug)* la **alfombra** *fem*

car phone *noun*
el **teléfono de coche**

car radio *noun*
la **radio de coche**

carriage *noun*
el **vagón** *masc*

carrier bag *noun*
la **bolsa** *fem*

ℰ **carrot** *noun*
la **zanahoria** *fem*

ℰ to **carry** *verb*

1 *(a parcel, a school bag, etc)* **llevar** [17]
Can you carry the bag? ¿Puedes llevar la bolsa?

2 *(heavy loads)* **transportar** [17]
The coach was carrying schoolchildren. El autobús transportaba colegiales.

• to **carry on**
seguir [64]
Carry on until the post office. Siga hasta llegar a Correos. *(polite form)*
They carried on talking. Siguieron hablando.

• **carrycot** la cuna portátil

carsick *adjective*
to be carsick marearse [17] al viajar en coche

cart *noun*
el **carro** *masc*

carton *noun*
el **envase** *masc*

ℰ **cartoon** *noun*

1 *(film)* los **dibujos animados**

2 *(comic strip)* la **tira cómica**

3 *(in a newspaper)* la **viñeta** *fem*

cartridge *noun*

1 *(for a pen)* el **recambio** *masc*

2 *(for a gun)* el **cartucho** *masc*

to **carve** *verb*

1 *(wood, stone)* **trinchar** [17]

2 *(meat)* **trinchar** [17]

case *noun*

1 *(suitcase)* la **maleta** *fem*
to pack your case hacer [7] la maleta

2 *(for wine bottles)* la **caja** *fem*

3 *(for glasses)* el **estuche** *masc*

4 *(example)* el **caso** *masc*
a case of flu un caso de gripe
in that case en ese caso ▸▸

That's not the case. No se trata de eso.
in case en caso
in case he's late en caso de que llegue tarde
Check first, just in case. Asegúrate, por si acaso.
in any case de todas formas
In any case, it's too late. De todas formas, es demasiado tarde.

cash *noun*
1 (*money*) el **dinero** *masc*
I've got cash. Yo tengo dinero.
2 (*notes and coins*) el **dinero en efectivo**
to pay in cash pagar [28] en efectivo
£50 in cash cincuenta libras en efectivo
· **cash card** la tarjeta de cajero automático
· **cash desk** la caja
· **cash dispenser** el cajero automático

cashew *noun*
el **anacardo** *masc*

cashier *noun*
el **cajero** *masc*, la **cajera** *fem*

cash point *noun*
el **cajero automático**

♂ **cash register** *noun*
la **caja registradora**

cassette *noun*
la **cinta de cassette**
· **cassette recorder** el cassette

cast *noun*
el **reparto** *masc*
a star-studded cast un reparto estelar

♂ **castle** *noun*
1 (*building*) el **castillo** *masc*
Windsor Castle el castillo de Windsor
2 (*in chess*) la **torre** *fem*

casual *adjective*
informal *masc & fem*

casualty *noun*
1 (*in an accident*) la **víctima** *fem*
2 (*hospital department*) **urgencias** *plural fem*
He's in casualty. Está en urgencias.

WORD TIP *urgencias does not take an article.*

♂ **cat** *noun*
el **gato** *masc*, la **gata** *fem*

Catalan *adjective & noun*
1 **catalán** *masc*, **catalana** *fem*
2 (*person*) un **catalán** *masc*, una **catalana** *fem*
the Catalans los catalanes
3 (*the language*) el **catalán** *masc*

WORD TIP Adjectives and nouns for nationality, regional origin and language do not have capital letters in Spanish.

Catalonia *noun*
Cataluña *fem*

catalogue *noun*
el **catálogo** *masc*

catastrophe *noun*
la **catástrofe** *fem*

catch *noun* ▷ see **catch** *verb*
1 (*on a door*) el **pestillo** *masc*
2 (*drawback*) la **trampa** *fem*
What's the catch? ¿Dónde está la trampa?

to **catch** *verb* ▷ see **catch** *noun*
1 (*a ball, a person*) **coger** [3]
Tom caught the ball. Tom cogió la pelota.
You can't catch me! ¡No me coges!
to catch somebody doing something coger [3] a alguien haciendo algo
He was caught stealing money. Lo cogieron robando dinero.
2 (*in fishing, hunting*) **to catch a fish** pescar [31] un pez
to catch a mouse cazar [22] un ratón
3 (*a bus, a plane*) **coger** [3], **tomar** [17]
Did Jason catch his bus? ¿Cogió Jason el autobús?
4 (*a show, a film*) I want to catch that film. No quiero perderme esa película.
5 (*an illness*) **coger** [3]
I'm catching a cold. Me estoy resfriando.
He's caught chickenpox. Ha cogido la varicela.
6 (*what somebody says*) **entender** [36]
I didn't catch your name. No entendí bien su nombre. (*polite form*)
· to **catch up with somebody**
alcanzar [22] **a alguien**

category *noun*
la **categoría** *fem*

catering *noun*
el **catering** *masc*

caterpillar *noun*
la **oruga** *fem*

♂ **cathedral** *noun*
la **catedral** *fem*
Seville cathedral la catedral de Sevilla

Catholic *adjective* ▷ see **Catholic** *noun*
católico *masc*, **católica** *fem*

Catholic *noun* ▷ see **Catholic** *adj*
  un **católico** *masc*, una **católica** *fem*
  I'm a Catholic. Soy católico.

WORD TIP Adjectives and nouns for religion do not have capital letters in Spanish.

Catholic

Spain is no longer officially a Catholic country but about 43% of the people still go to church regularly. Religious festivals are very popular and most towns and villages have a patron saint.

cattle *plural noun*
  el **ganado** *singular masc*

ᔆ **cauliflower** *noun*
  la **coliflor** *fem*
- **cauliflower cheese**
  la **coliflor con besamel**

cause *noun* ▷ see **cause** *verb*
  la **causa** *fem*
  the cause of the accident la causa del accidente
  It's for a good cause. Es por una buena causa.

to **cause** *verb* ▷ see **cause** *noun*
  causar [17]
  to cause problems causar problemas

caution *noun*
  la **cautela** *fem*

cautious *adjective*
  cauteloso *masc*, **cautelosa** *fem*

cave *noun*
  la **cueva** *fem*

caving *noun*
  la **espeleología** *fem*
  to go caving hacer [7] espeleología

CD *noun*
  el **disco compacto**, el **CD** *masc*
- **CD player** el reproductor de discos compactos

ᔆ **CD-ROM** *noun*
  el **CD-ROM** *masc*

ᔆ **ceiling** *noun*
  el **techo** *masc*
  on the ceiling en el techo

to **celebrate** *verb*
  celebrar [17]
  I'm celebrating my birthday today. Hoy celebro mi cumpleaños.

celebrity *noun*
  el **famoso** *masc*, la **famosa** *fem*
  media celebrities famosos mediáticos

celery *noun*
  el **apio** *masc*

cell *noun*
  la **célula** *fem*
- **cell phone** el teléfono celular

ᔆ **cellar** *noun*
  el **sótano** *masc*

cello *noun*
  el **violonchelo** *masc*
  to play the cello tocar [31] el violonchelo

cement *noun*
  el **cemento** *masc*

cemetery *noun*
  el **cementerio** *masc*

ᔆ **cent** *noun*
  1 (*in the euro system*) el **céntimo** *masc*
  2 (*in the dollar system*) el **centavo** *masc*

centenary *noun*
  el **centenario** *masc*

centigrade *noun*
  el **centígrado** *masc*
  ten degrees centigrade diez grados centígrados

ᔆ **centimetre** *noun*
  el **centímetro** *masc*

central *adjective*
  central *masc & fem*
  central London el centro de Londres
  The office is very central. La oficina es muy céntrica.

Central America *noun*
  América Central *fem*

ᔆ **central heating** *noun*
  la **calefacción central**

ᔆ **centre** *noun*
  el **centro** *masc*
  in the centre of en el centro de
  in the town centre en el centro de la ciudad
  a shopping centre un centro comercial

ᔆ **century** *noun*
  el **siglo** *masc*
  the sixth century el siglo seis
  the twentieth century el siglo veinte
  in the twenty-first century el siglo veintiuno

cereal *noun*
  los **cereales** *masc plural*
  to have cereal for breakfast desayunar [17] cereales

ceremony *noun*
  la **ceremonia** *fem*

ᔆ indicates key words

a b **c** d e f g h i j k l m n o p q r s t u v w x y z

♂ **certain** *adjective*

1 (*sure*) **seguro** *masc*, **segura** *fem*
Are you certain of the address? ¿Estás
seguro de las señas?
I'm certain of it. Estoy seguro.
to be certain that … estar [2] seguro de que
…
Nicky's certain (that) you're wrong. Nicky
está segura de que estás equivocado.
Nobody knows for certain. Nadie lo sabe
con seguridad.

2 (*particular*) **cierto** *masc*, **cierta** *fem*
It's only open on certain days. Está abierto
solamente ciertos días.

certainly *adverb*
Certainly! ¡Por supuesto!
Certainly not! ¡Claro que no!

♂ **certificate** *noun*
el **certificado** *masc*

♂ **chain** *noun*
la **cadena** *fem*

♂ **chair** *noun*
1 (*in general*) la **silla** *fem*
a kitchen chair una silla de cocina
2 (*with arms*) la **butaca** *fem*
· **chair lift** la telesilla

chalet *noun*
1 (*in the mountains*) el **chalet** *masc*
2 (*in a holiday camp*) el **bungalow** *masc*

chalk *noun*
la **tiza** *fem*

challenge *noun*
el **reto** *masc*
The exam was a real challenge. El examen
fue un verdadero reto.

♂ **champion** *noun*
el **campeón** *masc*, la **campeona** *fem*
the world champion el campeón mundial
the world football champions los
campeones mundiales de fútbol

chance *noun*
1 (*opportunity*) la **oportunidad** *fem*
to have the chance to do something tener
[9] ocasión de hacer algo
I had the chance to go to New York. Tuve la
oportunidad de ir a Nueva York.
I haven't had the chance to text him. No he
tenido la oportunidad de mandarle un
mensaje de texto.
2 (*possibility*) la **posibilidad** *fem*
There's a chance that she'll pass. Existe la
posibilidad de que apruebe.
There's little chance of winning. Hay pocas
posibilidades de ganar.

by chance por casualidad
Do you have her address, by any chance?
¿Tienes sus señas por casualidad?

♂ **change** *noun* ▷ see **change** *verb*
1 (*alteration*) el **cambio** *masc*
a change of plan un cambio de planes
They've made some changes to the house.
Han hecho algunos cambios en la casa.
It makes a change from hamburgers. Por lo
menos, es algo distinto a las
hamburguesas.
for a change para variar
Let's eat out for a change. Vamos a comer
fuera, para variar.
2 (*of clothes*) **a change of clothes** una muda de
ropa
3 (*coins*) el **cambio** *masc*
I haven't any change. No tengo cambio.
Keep the change. Quédese con el cambio.

♂ to **change** *verb* ▷ see **change** *noun*
1 (*to make completely different*) **cambiar** [17]
It changed my life. Cambió mi vida.
Liz never changes. Liz no cambia.
2 (*to switch from one thing to another*) **cambiar**
[17] **de**
We changed trains at Crewe. Cambiamos
de tren en Crewe.
She's changed her address. Ha cambiado
de dirección.
to change your mind cambiar de opinión
to change the subject cambiar de tema
to change colour cambiar de color
They changed places. Se cambiaron de
sitio.
3 (*to swap one for another*) **cambiar** [17]
Have you changed the towels? ¿Has
cambiado las toallas?
Can I change it for the larger size? ¿Puedo
cambiarlo por una talla más grande?
4 (*to change into different clothes*) **cambiarse**
[17]
Mike's gone to change. Mike ha ido a
cambiarse.
to change your clothes cambiarse de ropa
I must change my shirt. Tengo que
cambiarme de camisa.

changing room *noun*
1 (*for sports, swimming*) el **vestuario** *masc*
2 (*in a shop*) el **probador** *masc*

♂ **channel** *noun*
1 (*on TV*) el **canal** *masc*
to change channels cambiar [17] de canal
2 (*water course*) el **canal** *masc*
the (English) Channel el Canal de la Mancha
to cross the Channel cruzar [22] el Canal de
la Mancha

Channel Tunnel *noun*
the Channel Tunnel **el Eurotúnel**

chaos *noun*
el **caos** *masc*
It was chaos! ¡Fue un caos!

chapel *noun*
la **capilla** *fem*

chapter *noun*
el **capítulo** *masc*
in Chapter Two en el capítulo número dos

character *noun*
1 (*personality*) el **carácter** *masc*
a house with a lot of character una casa con mucho carácter
2 (*in a book, play, film*) el **personaje** *masc*
the main character el personaje principal

characteristic *noun*
la **característica** *fem*

charcoal *noun*
1 (*for burning*) el **carbón vegetal**
2 (*for drawing*) el **carboncillo** *masc*

ſ **charge** *noun* ▷ see **charge** *verb*
1 (*what you pay*) el **precio** *masc*
an extra charge un suplemento
The admission charge is £5. El precio de admisión es cinco libras.
There's no charge. Es gratis.
2 (*responsible position*) **to be in charge** ser [1] el responsable (*a boy*), ser la responsable (*a girl*)
Who's in charge? ¿Quién es el responsable?
Lucy is in charge. Lucy es la responsable.
to be in charge of something or somebody estar [2] a cargo de algo o alguien
Who's in charge of these children? ¿Quién está a cargo de estos niños?
3 (*for a crime*) la **acusación** *fem*
to be on a charge of theft estar [2] acusado de robo

ſ to **charge** *verb* ▷ see **charge** *noun*
1 (*to get payment*) **cobrar** [17]
They charge ten pounds an hour. Cobran diez libras la hora.
How much do you charge for one day? ¿Cuánto cobran por un día?
We don't charge, it's free. No cobramos, es gratis.
They didn't charge me for the drinks. No me cobraron las bebidas.
2 (*to accuse*) **to charge somebody with something** acusar [17] a alguien de algo

charity *noun*
la **organización benéfica**

charm *noun*
el **encanto** *masc*

ſ **charming** *adjective*
encantador *masc*, **encantadora** *fem*

chart *noun*
1 (*table*) la **tabla** *fem*
2 the weather chart el mapa del tiempo
3 the charts las listas de éxitos
number one in the charts número uno en las listas de éxitos

charter flight *noun*
el **vuelo chárter**

chase *noun* ▷ see **chase** *verb*
la **persecución** *fem*
a car chase una persecución en coche

to **chase** *verb* ▷ see **chase** *noun*
perseguir [64]

ſ **chat** *noun*
la **charla** *fem*
to have a chat with somebody charlar [17] con alguien
• **chatroom** el chat
• **chat show** el programa de entrevistas

to **chatter** *verb*
1 (*to talk*) **cotorrear** [17] (*informal*)
2 (*teeth*) My teeth are chattering. Me castañetean los dientes.

ſ **chauffeur** *noun*
el & la **chófer** *masc & fem*

ſ **cheap** *adjective*
barato *masc*, **barata** *fem*
cheap shoes zapatos baratos
That's very cheap! ¡Eso es muy barato!

cheaply *adverb*
to buy cheaply comprar [17] barato
to sell cheaply vender [18] barato
to eat cheaply comer [18] con poco dinero
to dress cheaply vestir [57] con poco dinero

cheap-rate *adjective*
de tarifa reducida
a cheap-rate phone call una llamada de teléfono de tarifa reducida

cheat *noun* ▷ see **cheat** *verb*
el **tramposo** *masc*, la **tramposa** *fem*

to **cheat** *verb* ▷ see **cheat** *noun*
engañar [17]

♂ to **check** verb ▷ see **check** noun
(to make sure) **comprobar** [24]
He checked the time. Comprobó la hora.
Check they're all back. Comprueba que ya han llegado todos.
Check with your father. Pregunta a tu padre.
• to **check in**
1 (for a flight) **facturar** [17] **el equipaje**
2 (at a hotel) **registrarse** [17]
She checked in at five o'clock. Se registró a las cinco.
• to **check out**
(from a hotel) **irse** [17]

♂ **check** noun ▷ see **check** verb
1 (in a factory, at border controls) el **control** masc
2 (by a doctor) el **examen médico**
3 (in chess) Check! ¡Jaque!
• **check-in** la facturación de equipajes
• **checkout** la caja
at the checkout en caja
• **checkup** el chequeo

cheek noun
1 (of your face) la **mejilla** fem
2 (nerve) What a cheek! ¡Qué cara! (informal)

cheeky adjective
1 (mischievous) **descarado** masc, **descarada** fem
2 (rude) **impertinente** masc & fem

♂ **cheer** noun ▷ see **cheer** verb
1 (applause) Three cheers for Tom! ¡Tres hurras por Tom!
2 (when you have a drink) Cheers! ¡Salud!

♂ to **cheer** verb ▷ see **cheer** noun
(to shout hurray) **vitorear** [17]
• to **cheer on**
animar [17]
• to **cheer somebody up**
animar [17] **a alguien**
Cheer up! ¡Ánimo!

cheerful adjective
alegre masc & fem

♂ **cheese** noun
el **queso** masc
blue cheese queso azul
a cheese sandwich un sándwich de queso
• **cheesecake** la tarta de queso

♂ **chef** noun
el & la **chef** masc & fem

chemical noun
el **producto químico**

♂ **chemist** noun
1 (pharmacist) el **farmacéutico** masc, la **farmacéutica** fem
at the chemist's en la farmacia
2 (scientist) el **químico** masc, la **química** fem

♂ **chemistry** noun
la **química** fem

♂ **cheque** noun
el **cheque** masc
to pay by cheque pagar [28] con cheque
to write a cheque extender [18] un cheque
• **chequebook** el talonario de cheques
• **cheque guarantee card** la tarjeta bancaria

♂ **cherry** noun
la **cereza** fem

♂ **chess** noun
el **ajedrez** masc
to play chess jugar [27] al ajedrez
• **chessboard** el tablero de ajedrez

♂ **chest** noun
1 (part of the body) el **pecho** masc
2 (box) el **arcón** masc

♂ **chestnut** noun
la **castaña** fem
• **chestnut tree** el castaño

♂ **chest of drawers** noun
la **cómoda** fem

to **chew** verb
masticar [31]

chewing gum noun
el **chicle** masc

chick noun
1 (young hen) el **pollito** masc, la **pollita** fem
2 (young bird) el **polluelo** masc, la **polluela** fem

♂ **chicken** noun
el **pollo** masc
roast chicken pollo asado
• **chickenpox** la varicela

chicory noun
la **endivia** fem

chickpea noun
el **garbanzo** masc

♂ **chief** noun
el **jefe** masc, la **jefa** fem
• **chief of police** el jefe de policía, la jefa de policía

♂ **child** noun
(boy) el **niño** masc, (girl) la **niña** fem
Jenny's children los niños de Jenny

childish adjective
infantil masc & fem

childminder *noun*
el **niñero** *masc*, la **niñera** *fem*

Chile *noun*
Chile *masc*

Chilean *adjective* ▷ see **Chilean** *noun*
chileno *masc*, chilena *fem*

Chilean *noun* ▷ see **Chilean** *adj*
un **chileno** *masc*, una **chilena** *fem*

WORD TIP Adjectives and nouns for nationality and regional origin do not have capital letters in Spanish.

chilli *noun*
el **chile** *masc*

chilly *adjective*
(*room, weather*) **frío** *masc*, **fría** *fem*
It's chilly today. Hoy hace fresco.

chimney *noun*
la **chimenea** *fem*

chimpanzee *noun*
el & la **chimpancé** *masc & fem*

ᶴ **chin** *noun*
la **barbilla** *fem*

china *noun*
la **porcelana** *fem*
a china plate un plato de porcelana

China *noun*
China *fem*

Chinese *adjective* ▷ see **Chinese** *noun*
chino *masc*, china *fem*
a Chinese man un chino
a Chinese woman una china
a Chinese meal una comida china

Chinese *noun* ▷ see **Chinese** *adj*
1 (*person*) un **chino** *masc*, una **china** *fem*
2 (*the language*) el **chino** *masc*
the Chinese los chinos

WORD TIP Adjectives and nouns for nationality, regional origin and language do not have capital letters in Spanish.

ᶴ **chip** *noun*
1 (*fried potato*) la **patata frita**
I'd like some chips. Quiero unas patatas fritas.
2 (*microchip*) el **chip** *masc*
3 (*in glass, china*) la **desportilladura** *fem*

chipped *adjective*
desportillado *masc*, desportillada *fem*

chives *noun*
las **cebolletas** *plural fem*

ᶴ **chocolate** *noun*
1 (*the food*) el **chocolate** *masc*
a chocolate ice cream un helado de chocolate
hot chocolate chocolate caliente
milk chocolate chocolate con leche
dark chocolate chocolate sin leche
2 (*item*) a chocolate un bombón
a box of chocolates una caja de bombones

ᶴ **choice** *noun*
la **elección** *fem*
freedom of choice libertad de elección
I had no choice. No tuve más remedio.
It was a good choice. Fue una buena elección.
You have a choice of two flights. Puede elegir entre dos vuelos.

choir *noun*
el **coro** *masc*

choke *noun* ▷ see **choke** *verb*
el **estárter** *masc*

to **choke** *verb* ▷ see **choke** *noun*
atragantarse [17]
She choked on a bone. Se atragantó con un hueso.

ᶴ to **choose** *verb*
elegir [48]
You chose well. Elegiste bien.
Cathy chose the red one. Cathy eligió el rojo.
It's hard to choose from all these colours. Es difícil elegir entre todos estos colores.

to **chop** *verb* ▷ see **chop** *noun*
1 (*wood*) cortar [17]
2 (*vegetables, meat*) cortar [17] en trozos pequeños
3 (*an onion*) picar [31]

chop *noun* ▷ see **chop** *verb*
la **chuleta** *fem*
a lamb chop una chuleta de cordero

• **chopstick** el palillo

chord *noun*
el **acorde** *masc*

chorus *noun*
1 (*of a song*) el **estribillo** *masc*
2 (*a group of singers*) el **coro** *masc*

Christ *noun*
Cristo

christening *noun*
el **bautizo** *masc*

Christian *adjective* ▷ see **Christian** *noun*
cristiano *masc*, cristiana *fem*

a
b
c
d
e
f
g
h
i
j
k
l
m
n
o
p
q
r
s
t
u
v
w
x
y
z

Christian noun ▷ see **Christian** adj
un **cristiano** masc, una **cristiana** fem

Christianity noun
(Religion) el **cristianismo** masc

> **WORD TIP** Adjectives and nouns for religion do not have capital letters in Spanish.

Christian name noun
el **nombre de pila**

ℰ **Christmas** noun
la **Navidad** fem
at Christmas en Navidad
Happy Christmas! ¡Feliz Navidad!
• **Christmas card** la tarjeta de Navidad
• **Christmas carol** el villancico
• **Christmas Day** el día de Navidad
• **Christmas dinner** la cena de Navidad
• **Christmas Eve** la Nochebuena
on Christmas Eve en Nochebuena
• **Christmas present** el regalo de Navidad
• **Christmas tree** el árbol de Navidad

chunk noun
el **trozo** masc

ℰ **church** noun
la **iglesia** fem
to go to church ir [8] a la iglesia
• **churchyard** el cementerio

ℰ **cider** noun
la **sidra** fem

cigar noun
el **puro** masc

ℰ **cigarette** noun
el **cigarrillo** masc

ℰ **cinema** noun
el **cine** masc
to go to the cinema ir [8] al cine

ℰ **circle** noun
el **círculo** masc
to sit in a circle sentarse [17] en círculo
to go round in circles dar [4] vueltas

circuit noun
1 (lap) la **vuelta** fem
2 (racing track) la **pista** fem

circular adjective
circular masc & fem

circumference noun
la **circunferencia** fem

circumstances plural noun
under the circumstances en estas circunstancias

ℰ **circus** noun
el **circo** masc

citizen noun
el **ciudadano** masc, la **ciudadana** fem

city noun
la **ciudad** fem
the city of Seville la ciudad de Sevilla
• **city centre** el centro de la ciudad
in the city centre en el centro de la ciudad

civilian noun
el & la **civil** masc & fem

civilization noun
la **civilización** fem

ℰ **civil servant** noun
el **funcionario** masc, la **funcionaria** fem
She's a civil servant. Es funcionaria.

civil service noun
la **administración pública**

civil war noun
la **guerra civil**

claim noun ▷ see **claim** verb
1 (statement) la **afirmación** fem
2 (on insurance) la **reclamación** fem

to **claim** verb ▷ see **claim** noun
asegurar [17]
He claimed he knew nothing about it.
Aseguró no saber nada de ello.

to **clap** verb
1 aplaudir [19]
Everyone clapped. Todo el mundo aplaudió.
2 to clap your hands dar [4] palmadas

clapping noun
los **aplausos** masc plural

clarinet noun
el **clarinete** masc
to play the clarinet tocar [31] el clarinete

clash noun ▷ see **clash** verb
el **choque** masc

to **clash** verb ▷ see **clash** noun
1 (rival groups) chocar [31]
2 (colours) desentonar [17]
The curtains clash with the wallpaper. Las cortinas desentonan con el papel pintado.

ℰ **class** noun
1 (at school) la **clase** fem
an art class una clase de arte
She's in the same class as me. Está en la misma clase que yo.
2 (social group) la **clase** fem
the middle class la clase media

classic adjective
clásico masc, clásica fem

classical *adjective*
clásico *masc*, **clásica** *fem*
· **classical music** la música clásica

classmate *noun*
el **compañero de clase**, la **compañera de clase**

ſ **classroom** *noun*
la **clase** *fem*

claw *noun*
1 (*of a cat, dog*) la **zarpa** *fem*
2 (*of a crab*) la **pinza** *fem*

clay *noun*
(*for modelling*) la **arcilla** *fem*

ſ **clean** *adjective* ▷ see **clean** *verb*
1 (*not dirty*) **limpio** *masc*, **limpia** *fem*
a clean shirt una camisa limpia
My hands are clean. Tengo las manos limpias.
2 (*air, water*) **puro** *masc*, **pura** *fem*

ſ to **clean** *verb* ▷ see **clean** *adj*
limpiar [17]
I cleaned the whole house. Limpié toda la casa.
to clean your teeth lavarse [17] los dientes
I'm going to clean my teeth. Voy a lavarme los dientes.

cleaner *noun*
1 (*in a public place*) el **limpiador** *masc*, la **limpiadora** *fem*
2 (*cleaning lady*) la **señora de la limpieza**
3 (*cleaning product*) el **producto de limpieza**

ſ **cleaning** *noun*
to do the cleaning hacer [7] la limpieza

cleanser *noun*
1 (*for the house*) el **producto de limpieza**
2 (*for your face*) la **crema limpiadora**

ſ **clear** *adjective* ▷ see **clear** *verb*
1 (*that you can see through*) **transparente** *masc & fem*
clear glass cristal transparente
2 (*cloudless*) **despejado** *masc*, **despejada** *fem*
3 (*easy to understand*) **claro** *masc*, **clara** *fem*
clear instructions instrucciones claras
It's clear that ... Está claro que ...
Is that clear? ¿Está claro?

ſ to **clear** *verb* ▷ see **clear** *adj*
1 (*your papers, rubbish, clothes*) **sacar** [31]
Have you cleared your stuff out of your room? ¿Has sacado todas tus cosas de tu habitación?
2 (*the table*) **recoger** [3]
Can I clear the table? ¿Puedo recoger la mesa?

3 (*a road, a path*) **despejar** [17]
4 (*your throat*) to clear your throat aclararse [17] la voz
5 (*fog, smoke*) **disiparse** [17]
The fog cleared. La niebla se disipó.
· to **clear something up**
recoger [3] algo
I'll just clear up my books. Voy a recoger mis libros.

clearly *adverb*
1 (*to think, to speak, to hear*) **con claridad**
2 (*obviously*) **claramente**
She was clearly worried. Estaba claramente preocupada.

clementine *noun*
la **clementina** *fem*

ſ **clever** *adjective*
1 (*intelligent*) **inteligente** *masc & fem*
Their children are all very clever. Todos sus hijos son muy inteligentes.
2 (*ingenious*) **ingenioso** *masc*, **ingeniosa** *fem*
a clever idea una idea ingeniosa

click *noun* ▷ see **click** *verb*
el **clic** *masc*
a double click un doble clic

to **click** *verb* ▷ see **click** *noun*
hacer [7] **clic en**
Click on the icon. Haz clic en el icono.

ſ **client** *noun*
el & la **cliente** *masc & fem*

cliff *noun*
el **acantilado** *masc*

ſ **climate** *noun*
el **clima** *masc*

to **climb** *verb*
1 (*the stairs*) **subir** [19]
2 (*a hill, a tree*) **escalar** [17]
We climbed Mont Blanc. Escalamos el Mont Blanc.

climber *noun*
el & la **alpinista** *masc & fem*

ſ **climbing** *noun*
el **alpinismo** *masc*
They go climbing in Italy. Practican el alpinismo en Italia.

clinic *noun*
1 (*in a hospital*) el **consultorio** *masc*
2 (*a private hospital*) la **clínica** *fem*

clip *noun* ▷ see **clip** *verb*
1 (*from a film*) el **clip** *masc*
2 (*for your hair*) la **horquilla** *fem*

to **clip** *verb* ▷ see **clip** *noun*
1 **cortar** [17]
2 to **clip together** sujetar [17] con un clip

cloakroom *noun*
1 (*for coats*) el **guardarropa** *masc*
2 (*toilet*) el **lavabo**

clock *noun*
el **reloj** *masc*
to put the clocks forward an hour adelantar [17] los relojes una hora
to put the clocks back atrasar [17] los relojes
• **clock radio** el radiodespertador
• **clockwise** en el sentido de las agujas del reloj

clog *noun*
el **zueco** *masc*

ᵈ **close** *adjective* ▷ see **close** *adv, verb*
1 (*result*) **reñido** *masc*, **reñida** *fem*
2 (*relation*) **cercano** *masc*, **cercana** *fem*
(*friend, relationship*) **She's a close friend of mine.** Es muy amiga mía.
3 (*near*) **cerca** *masc & fem*
not very close no muy cerca

ᵈ **close** *adverb* ▷ see **close** *adj, verb*
1 (*relationship*) **They are very close.** Son muy unidos.
2 (*near*) **cerca**
close to the cinema cerca del cine
The station's very close. La estación está muy cerca.
She lives close by. Vive cerca.

ᵈ to **close** *verb* ▷ see **close** *adj, adv*
cerrar [29]
Close your eyes! ¡Cierra los ojos!
She closed the door. Cerró la puerta.
The post office closes at six. La oficina de correos cierra a las seis.
• to **close down**
(*shops, factories*) **cerrar** [29]

ᵈ **closed** *adjective*
cerrado *masc*, **cerrada** *fem*
'Closed on Mondays' 'Cerrado los lunes'

closely *adverb*
de cerca
to examine something closely examinar [17] algo de cerca

closing date *noun*
la **fecha límite**
the closing date for entries la fecha límite para inscribirse

closing-down sale *noun*
la **liquidación por cierre de negocio**

ᵈ **closing time** *noun*
la **hora de cierre**

cloth *noun*
1 (*for the floor, for wiping surfaces*) la **bayeta** *fem*
2 (*for polishing*) el **trapo del polvo**
3 (*for drying up*) el **paño de cocina**
4 (*fabric by the metre*) la **tela** *fem*

ᵈ **clothes** *plural noun*
la **ropa** *singular fem*
to change your clothes cambiarse [17] de ropa
• **clothes hanger** la percha
• **clothes line** la cuerda de tender
• **clothes peg** la pinza para tender

ᵈ **cloud** *noun*
la **nube** *fem*
• to **cloud over**
nublarse [17]
It clouded over in the afternoon. Se nubló por la tarde.

ᵈ **cloudy** *adjective*
nublado *masc*, **nublada** *fem*

clove *noun*
el **clavo** *masc*
• **clove of garlic** el diente de ajo

clown *noun*
el **payaso** *masc*, la **payasa** *fem*

ᵈ **club** *noun*
1 (*association*) el **club** *masc*
He's in the football club. Está en el club de fútbol.
2 (*in cards*) el **trébol** *masc*
the four of clubs el cuatro de tréboles
3 (*golfing iron*) el **palo de golf**

clue *noun*
1 (*for solving something*) la **pista** *fem*
They have a few clues. Tienen unas cuantas pistas.
I haven't a clue. No tengo ni idea.
2 (*in a crossword*) la **clave** *fem*

clumsy *adjective*
torpe *masc & fem*

clutch *noun* ▷ see **clutch** *verb*
(*in a car*) el **embrague** *masc*

to **clutch** *verb* ▷ see **clutch** *noun*
to clutch something tener [9] algo firmemente agarrado

ᵈ **coach** *noun*
1 (*bus*) el **autobús** *masc*
on the coach en el autobús
by coach en autobús
to travel by coach viajar [17] en autobús

2 (*in sports*) el **entrenador** *masc*, la **entrenadora** *fem*
3 (*railway carriage*) el **vagón** *masc*
· **coach station** la estación de autobuses
· **coach trip** la excursión en autobús

coal *noun*
    el **carbón** *masc*
· **coal mine** la mina de carbón
· **coal miner** el minero, la minera

coarse *adjective*
    basto *masc*, **basta** *fem*

coast *noun*
    la **costa** *fem*
    on the east coast en la costa este

ꞵ **coat** *noun*
1 (*that you wear*) el **abrigo** *masc*
2 (*layer*) **a coat of paint** una capa de pintura
· **coat hanger** la percha

cobweb *noun*
    la **telaraña** *fem*

ꞵ **Coca-Cola**® *noun*
    la **Coca-Cola**® *fem*

cocaine *noun*
    la **cocaína** *fem*

cockerel *noun*
    el **gallo** *masc*

cocoa *noun*
1 (*drink*) el **chocolate** *masc*
2 (*powder*) el **cacao** *masc*

coconut *noun*
    el **coco** *masc*

cod *noun*
    el **bacalao** *masc*

code *noun*
    el **código** *masc*
    the highway code el código de la circulación
    the dialling code for Barcelona el prefijo de Barcelona

ꞵ **coeducational** *adjective*
    mixto *masc*, **mixta** *fem*

coffee *noun*
    el **café** *masc*
    a cup of coffee un café
    a white coffee un café con leche
    A black coffee, please. Un café solo, por favor.
· **coffee break** la pausa para el café
· **coffee cup** la taza de café

coffee machine *noun*
1 (*vending machine*) la **máquina de café**
2 (*electric*) la **cafetera eléctrica**

coffee pot *noun*
    la **cafetera** *fem*

coffee table *noun*
    la **mesa de centro** *fem*

coffin *noun*
    el **ataúd** *masc*

ꞵ **coin** *noun*
    la **moneda** *fem*
    a pound coin una moneda de una libra

coincidence *noun*
    la **coincidencia** *fem*

Coke® *noun*
    la **Coca-Cola**® *fem*
    Two Cokes, please. Dos Coca-Colas, por favor.

colander *noun*
    el **colador** *masc*

ꞵ **cold** *adjective* ▷ see **cold** *noun*
1 (*thing, substance*) **frío** *masc*, **fría** *fem*
    cold milk leche fría
    Your hands are cold. Tienes las manos frías.
2 (*weather, temperature*) **It's cold today.** Hoy hace frío.
    It's cold in the kitchen. Hace frío en la cocina.
3 (*feeling*) **I'm cold.** Tengo frío.
    He was feeling very cold. Tenía mucho frío.

ꞵ **cold** *noun* ▷ see **cold** *adj*
1 (*cold weather*) el **frío** *masc*
    I don't want to go out in this cold. No quiero salir con este frío.
    Come in out of the cold. Entra, que hace frío.
    She was shivering with cold. Estaba temblando de frío.
2 (*illness*) el **resfriado** *masc*
    a bad cold un fuerte resfriado
    to have a cold estar [2] resfriado (*about a boy*), estar resfriada (*about a girl*)
    Carol's got a cold. Carol está resfriada.
· **cold sore** la calentura

to **collapse** *verb*
1 (*roofs, walls, houses*) **derrumbarse** [17]
2 (*people*) **He collapsed in his office.** Sufrió un desmayo en su oficina.

collar *noun*
1 (*on a shirt, etc*) el **cuello** *masc*
2 (*for a dog*) el **collar** *masc*
· **collarbone** la clavícula

colleague *noun*
    el **compañero** *masc*, la **compañera** *fem*

a
b
c
d
e
f
g
h
i
j
k
l
m
n
o
p
q
r
s
t
u
v
w
x
y
z

to **collect** *verb*
1 (*as a hobby*) **coleccionar** [17]
   I collect stamps. Colecciono sellos.
2 (*a person, a thing*) **recoger** [3]
   She collects the children from school. Ella
   recoge a los niños del colegio.
3 (*a fare, money*) **cobrar** [17]
4 (*data, information*) **reunir** [62]
· to **collect in**
  recoger [3]
  Collect in the exercise books, Laura.
  Recoge los cuadernos, Laura.

collection *noun*
1 (*of stamps, CDs, etc*) la **colección** *fem*
2 (*of money*) la **colecta** *fem*
   to hold a collection hacer [7] una colecta

collector *noun*
   el & la **coleccionista** *masc & fem*

college *noun*
1 (*for higher education*) el **colegio**
   universitario
   to go to college ir [8] a la universidad
2 (*for vocational training*) la **escuela de**
   formación profesional
3 (*school*) el **instituto** *masc*

collie *noun*
   el & la **collie** *masc & fem*

collision *noun*
   el **choque** *masc*

Colombia *noun*
   Colombia *fem*

Colombian *adjective & noun*
1 **colombiano** *masc*, **colombiana** *fem*
2 un **colombiano** *masc*, una **colombiana** *fem*
   the Colombians los colombianos

> **WORD TIP** Adjectives and nouns for nationality
> and regional origin do not have capital letters in
> Spanish.

colonel *noun*
   el **coronel** *masc*

♪ to **colour** *verb* ▷ see **colour** *noun*
   colorear [17]
   to colour something red colorear [17] algo
   de rojo

♪ **colour** *noun* ▷ see **colour** *verb*
   el **color** *masc*
   What colour is your car? ¿De qué color es tu
   coche?
   What colour is it? ¿De qué color es?
   Do you have it in a different colour? ¿Lo
   tiene en otros colores?
· **colour blind** daltónico *masc*, daltónica *fem*
· **colour film** (*for a camera*) el carrete de color

colourful *adjective*
   de colores

colouring book *noun*
   el **libro para colorear**

colour supplement *noun*
   el **suplemento a color**

column *noun*
   la **columna** *fem*

♪ **comb** *noun* ▷ see **comb** *verb*
   el **peine** *masc*

♪ to **comb** *verb* ▷ see **comb** *noun*
   to comb your hair peinarse [17]
   I'll just comb my hair. Voy a peinarme.

to **combine** *verb*
   combinar [17]
   They don't combine well. No combinan
   bien.

combination *noun*
   la **combinación** *fem*

♪ to **come** *verb*
   venir [15]
   The bus is coming. Ya viene el autobús.
   Nick came by bike. Nick vino en bici.
   Did Jess come to school yesterday? ¿Vino
   Jess ayer a clase?
   Can you come over for a coffee? ¿Puedes
   venir a tomar un café?
   Come quick! ¡Ven rápido!
   Come on! ¡Venga!
   Come and see! ¡Ven a ver!
   Coming! ¡Ya voy!
· to **come apart**
  deshacerse [7]
  It came apart in my hands. Se deshizo en
  mis manos.
· to **come back**
  volver [45]
  She's coming back to collect us. Volverá
  para recogernos.
· to **come down**
  bajar [17]
  She came down for breakfast. Bajó a
  desayunar.
  I came down the stairs. Bajé la escalera.
· to **come for**
  (*a person*) **venir** [15] **a por**
  My father's coming for me. Mi padre va a
  venir a por mí.
· to **come from**
  ser [1] **de**
  Ian comes from Scotland. Ian es de
  Escocia.
  The wine comes from Spain. El vino es
  español.

- to **come in**
  entrar [17]
  Come in! ¡Adelante!
  She came into the kitchen. Entró en la cocina.
- to **come off**
1 (*buttons*) **desprenderse** [18], (*handles*) **soltarse** [24]
2 (*lids*) **I can't get the lid to come off.** No puedo quitar la tapa.
- to **come out**
  salir [63]
  They came out when I called. Salieron cuando los llamé.
  The CD's coming out soon. El compacto va a salir pronto.
  The sun hasn't come out yet. El sol no ha salido aún.
- to **come to**
1 (*to get to*) **llegar** [28] **a**
  When you come to the church turn right. Gira a la derecha cuando llegues a la iglesia.
2 (*to add up to*) **It comes to 150 euros.** Suma ciento cincuenta euros.
- to **come up**
  subir [19]
  Can you come up a moment? ¿Puedes subir un momento?
- to **come up to somebody**
  acercarse [31] **a alguien**

comedian *noun*
  el **cómico** *masc*, la **cómica** *fem*

comedy *noun*
  la **comedia** *fem*

ℰ **comfortable** *adjective*
1 **cómodo** *masc*, **cómoda** *fem*
  This chair's really comfortable. Esta silla es muy cómoda.
2 **to feel comfortable** estar [2] cómodo
  Are you comfortable there? ¿Estás cómoda ahí?

comfortably *adverb*
  cómodamente

ℰ **comic** *noun*
  (*magazine*) el **cómic** *masc*
- **comic strip** la tira cómica

comma *noun*
  la **coma** *fem*

command *noun*
  la **orden** *fem*

comment *noun*
  (*in a conversation*) el **comentario** *masc*
  He made some rude comments about my

friends. Hizo unos comentarios groseros sobre mis amigos.

commentary *noun*
  la **crónica** *fem*
  the commentary on the match la crónica del partido

commentator *noun*
  el & la **comentarista** *masc & fem*
  a sports commentator un comentarista deportivo

commercial *adjective*
  ▷ see **commercial** *noun*
  comercial *masc & fem*

commercial *noun*
  ▷ see **commercial** *adj*
  el **anuncio de televisión**

to **commit** *verb*
1 (*a crime*) **cometer** [18]
2 **to commit yourself to doing something** comprometerse [18] a hacer algo

committee *noun*
  el **comité** *masc*

common *adjective*
1 **corriente** *masc & fem*
  It's a common problem. Es un problema corriente.
2 **in common** en común
  They have nothing in common. No tienen nada en común.
- **common sense** el sentido común

to **communicate** *verb*
  comunicar [31]

communication *noun*
1 (*message, letter, etc*) la **comunicación** *fem*
2 (*in transport*) **Communications are good.** Las comunicaciones son buenas.

communion *noun*
  la **comunión** *fem*

communism *noun*
  el **comunismo** *masc*

communist *noun*
  un & una **comunista** *masc & fem*

community *noun*
  la **comunidad** *fem*
  the European Community la comunidad europea

to **commute** *verb*
  to commute between Reading and London viajar [17] todos los días de Reading a Londres para ir a trabajar

commuter *noun*
> trains full of commuters trenes llenos de personas que van a trabajar cada día

compact disc *noun*
> el **disco compacto**
- **compact disc player** el compacto

company *noun*
1 (*business*) la **compañía** *fem*
> an insurance company una compañía de seguros
> a theatre company una compañía de teatro
> She's set up a company. Ha montado una compañía.
2 (*companionship*) to keep somebody company hacer [7] compañía a alguien
> The dogs keep me company. Los perros me hacen compañía.

comparatively *adverb*
> **relativamente**

to **compare** *verb*
> **comparar** [17]
> if you compare the Spanish with the English... si comparas el español con el inglés...
> Our house is small compared with yours. Nuestra casa es pequeña comparada con la tuya.

comparison *noun*
> la **comparación** *fem*
> in comparison with something en comparación con algo

 compartment *noun*
> el **compartimento** *masc*

compass *noun*
> la **brújula** *fem*

compatible *adjective*
> **compatible** *masc & fem*

compensation *noun*
> la **indemnización** *fem*

to **compete** *verb*
> to compete in something participar [17] en algo

competent *adjective*
> **competente** *masc & fem*

competition *noun*
1 (*in a magazine, at school*) el **concurso** *masc*
> a poetry competition un concurso de poesía
2 (*in sports*) la **competición** *fem*
> a fishing competition una competición de pesca

3 (*rivalry*) la **competencia** *fem*

competitor *noun*
> (*in sports, business*) el **competidor** *masc*, la **competidora** *fem*

to **complain** *verb*
> **quejarse** [17]
> We complained about the hotel. Nos quejamos del hotel.

complaint *noun*
> la **queja** *fem*
> to make a complaint presentar [17] una queja
> She made a complaint to the manager. Presentó una queja al gerente.

 complete *adjective* ▷ see **complete** *verb*
> **completo** *masc*, **completa** *fem*
> the complete collection la colección completa

 to **complete** *verb* ▷ see **complete** *adj*
1 (*your education, a piece of work*) **terminar** [17]
2 (*a form*) **rellenar** [17]

 completely *adverb*
> **completamente**

complexion *noun*
> el **cutis** *masc*

complicated *adjective*
> **complicado** *masc*, **complicada** *fem*

complication *noun*
> la **complicación** *fem*
> There were complications. Hubo complicaciones.

compliment *noun*
> el **cumplido** *masc*
> to pay somebody a compliment hacer [7] un cumplido a alguien

to **compose** *verb*
> **componer** [11]
> composed of something compuesto de algo

composer *noun*
> el **compositor** *masc*, la **compositora** *fem*

comprehension *noun*
> la **comprensión** *fem*
> a comprehension test un ejercicio de comprensión

 compulsory *adjective*
> **obligatorio** *masc*, **obligatoria** *fem*

 computer *noun*
> el **ordenador** *masc*, (*Latin America*) la **computadora**

to work on a computer trabajar [17] en ordenador

- **computer engineer** el técnico en informática, la técnica en informática
- **computer game** el juego de ordenador
- **computer program** el programa informático
- **computer programmer** el programador, la programadora
- **computer science** la informática

ꝺ **computing** noun
   la **informática** fem

conceited adjective
   engreído masc, **engreída** fem

to concentrate verb
   concentrarse [17]
   I can't concentrate. No puedo concentrarme.
   I was concentrating on the film. Me estaba concentrando en la película.

concentration noun
   la **concentración** fem

concern noun ▷ see **concern** verb
1 (business) **That's no concern of yours.** Eso no es asunto tuyo.
2 (worry) la **preocupación** fem
   There is no cause for concern. No hay razón para preocuparse.

to concern verb ▷ see **concern** noun
   (to affect) **concernir** [14]
   as far as I'm concerned por mi parte
   This doesn't concern you. Esto no te concierne.

ꝺ **concert** noun
   el **concierto** masc
   a concert ticket una entrada para un concierto
   to go to a rock concert ir [8] a un concierto de rock

conclusion noun
   la **conclusión** fem

concrete noun
   el **cemento** masc
   a concrete floor un suelo de cemento

to condemn verb
   condenar [17]

ꝺ **condition** noun
   la **condición** fem
   in good condition en buenas condiciones
   in bad condition en malas condiciones
   weather conditions condiciones meteorológicas
   the conditions of sale las condiciones de venta
   on one condition con una condición
   on condition that you let me pay a condición de que me dejes pagar

conditional noun
   el **condicional** masc

conditioner noun
   el **suavizante** masc

condom noun
   el **condón** masc

conduct noun ▷ see **conduct** verb
   la **conducta** fem

to conduct verb ▷ see **conduct** noun
   (an orchestra, a piece of music) **dirigir** [49]

conductor noun
1 (of an orchestra) el **director de orquesta**, la **directora de orquesta**
2 (on a bus) el **cobrador** masc, la **cobradora** fem

cone noun
1 (for ice cream) el **cucurucho** masc
2 (for traffic) el **cono** masc

confectionery noun
   los **dulces** masc plural
   She works in a confectionery shop. Trabaja en una confitería.

conference noun
   la **conferencia** fem

to confess verb
   confesar [29]

confession noun
   la **confesión** fem

confidence noun
1 (faith in somebody) la **confianza** fem
   to have confidence in somebody tener [9] confianza en alguien
2 (in yourself) la **seguridad en sí mismo**
   He has a lot of confidence. Tiene mucha seguridad en sí mismo.
   You're lacking in confidence. Te falta seguridad en ti mismo.

confident adjective
1 (sure of yourself) **seguro de sí mismo** masc, **segura de sí misma** fem
   You look very confident. Pareces muy seguro de ti mismo.
   She's a confident young woman. Es una joven segura de sí misma.
2 (sure that something will happen) **to be confident that** estar [2] seguro de que
   I'm confident that it will work out all right. Estoy segura de que saldrá bien.

ꝺ indicates key words   **439**

to **confirm** *verb*
confirmar [17]
We'll confirm the date. Confirmaremos la
fecha.

to **confuse** *verb*
confundir [19]
I confuse him with his brother. Lo
confundo con su hermano.

confused *adjective*
1 (*facts, account*) **confuso** *masc*, **confusa** *fem*
He gave us a confused story. Contó una
historia muy confusa.
2 (*person*) **confundido** *masc*, **confundida** *fem*
Now I'm completely confused. Ahora
estoy completamente confundida.
I'm confused about the holiday dates. No
estoy seguro de las fechas de las
vacaciones.
to get confused confundirse [19]
She got confused. Se confundió.

confusing *adjective*
poco claro *masc*, **poco clara** *fem*
The instructions are confusing. Las
instrucciones son poco claras.

confusion *noun*
la **confusión** *fem*

to **congratulate** *verb*
felicitar [17]
I congratulated Tim on his success. Felicité
a Tim por su éxito.
We congratulate you on winning. Te
felicitamos por haber ganado.

♂ **congratulations** *plural noun*
la **enhorabuena** *singular fem*
Congratulations on the baby!
¡Enhorabuena por el bebé!

conjurer *noun*
el **mago** *masc*, la **maga** *fem*

to **connect** *verb*
conectar [17]

connection *noun*
la **conexión** *fem*
a faulty connection una conexión
defectuosa
Sally missed her connection. Sally perdió
su conexión.
There's no connection between his letter
and my decision. No hay relación entre su
carta y mi decisión.

conscience *noun*
la **conciencia** *fem*
to have a guilty conscience no tener [9] la
conciencia tranquila

conscious *adjective*
consciente *masc & fem*

consequence *noun*
la **consecuencia** *fem*

consequently *adverb*
por consiguiente

conservation *noun*
la **protección del medio ambiente**

conservative *adjective*
▷ see **conservative** *noun*
conservador *masc*, **conservadora** *fem*

conservative *noun*
▷ see **conservative** *adj*
un **conservador** *masc*, una **conservadora**
fem

conservatory *noun*
el **jardín de invierno**

to **consider** *verb*
1 (*a suggestion, an idea*) **considerar** [17]
all things considered bien considerado
2 (*to think you might do*) **plantearse** [17]
We're considering buying a flat. Estamos
planteándonos comprar un piso.

considerable *adjective*
considerable *masc & fem*
a considerable number of students un
número considerable de estudiantes

considerate *adjective*
considerado *masc*, **considerada** *fem*

consideration *noun*
la **consideración** *fem*

considering *preposition*
teniendo en cuenta
considering her age teniendo en cuenta su
edad
considering he did it all himself teniendo
en cuenta que lo hizo todo él solo

to **consist** *verb*
to consist of consistir [19] en

consistent *adjective*
constante *masc & fem*

console *noun*
(*Computers*) la **consola** *fem*

consonant *noun*
(*Grammar*) la **consonante** *fem*

constant *adjective*
constante *masc & fem*

constantly *adverb*
constantemente

constipated *adjective*
  estreñido *masc*, **estreñida** *fem*

to **construct** *verb*
  construir [54]

construction *noun*
  la **construcción** *fem*

consulate *noun*
  el **consulado** *masc*

to **consult** *verb*
  consultar [17]

consumer *noun*
  el **consumidor** *masc*, la **consumidora** *fem*

consumption *noun*
  el **consumo** *masc*

to **contact** *verb* ▷ see **contact** *noun*
  ponerse [11] **en contacto con**
  I'll contact you tomorrow. Me pondré en contacto contigo mañana.

contact *noun* ▷ see **contact** *verb*
  el **contacto** *masc*
  We've lost contact. Hemos perdido contacto.
  Rob has contacts in the music business. Rob tiene contactos en el mundo de la música.
  to be in contact with somebody estar [2] en contacto con alguien
• **contact lens** la lentilla

to **contain** *verb*
  contener [9]

container *noun*
  el **recipiente** *masc*

to **contaminate** *verb*
  contaminar [17]

contemporary *adjective*
  contemporáneo *masc*, **contemporánea** *fem*

contents *plural noun*
  el **contenido** *singular masc*
  the contents of my suitcase el contenido de mi maleta

contest *noun*
1 (*competition*) el **concurso** *masc*
2 (*in sport*) la **competición** *fem*

contestant *noun*
  el & la **concursante** *masc & fem*

context *noun*
  el **contexto** *masc*

continent *noun*
  el **continente** *masc*
  on the Continent en Europa continental

continental *adjective*
  a continental holiday unas vacaciones en Europa continental

ℰ to **continue** *verb*
1 **continuar** [20]
  We continued our journey. Continuamos con nuestro viaje.
  'To be continued' 'Continuará'
2 to continue doing something seguir [64] haciendo algo
  Jill continued talking. Jill siguió hablando.

continuous *adjective*
  continuo *masc*, **continua** *fem*
• **continuous assessment** la evaluación continua

contraception *noun*
  la **anticoncepción** *fem*

contraceptive *noun*
  el **anticonceptivo** *masc*

contract *noun*
  el **contrato** *masc*

to **contradict** *verb*
  contradecir [5]

contradiction *noun*
  la **contradicción** *fem*

contrary *noun*
  the contrary lo contrario
  on the contrary al contrario

contrast *noun*
  el **contraste** *masc*

to **contribute** *verb*
  (*money*) **contribuir** [54]

contribution *noun*
  (*to charity, an appeal*) la **contribución** *fem*

control *noun* ▷ see **control** *verb*
  (*of a crowd, animals*) el **control** *masc*
  The police have lost control. La policía ha perdido el control.
  Everything's under control. Todo está bajo control.

to **control** *verb* ▷ see **control** *noun*
  controlar [17]
  to control oneself controlarse [17]

controversial *adjective*
  controvertido *masc*, **controvertida** *fem*
  a controversial decision una decisión controvertida

a
b
c
d
e
f
g
h
i
j
k
l
m
n
o
p
q
r
s
t
u
v
w
x
y
z

ℰ convenient *adjective*

1 (*simple*) **práctico** *masc*, **práctica** *fem*
Frozen vegetables are very convenient. Las verduras congeladas son muy prácticas.

2 (*suitable*) **to be convenient for somebody** venirle [15] bien a alguien o algo
If that's convenient for you. Si te viene bien.

3 (*handy*) **The house is convenient for shops and schools.** La casa está bien situada respecto a tiendas y colegios.

convent *noun*
el **convento** *masc*

conventional *adjective*

1 (*practice*) **convencional** *masc & fem*

2 (*person*) **tradicional** *masc & fem*

conversation *noun*
la **conversación** *fem*

to convert *verb*
convertir [14]
We're going to convert the garage into a workshop. Vamos a convertir el garaje en un taller.

to convince *verb*
convencer [44]
I'm convinced you're wrong. Estoy convencido de que estás equivocado.

convincing *adjective*
convincente *masc & fem*

ℰ cook *noun* ▷ see **cook** *verb*
el **cocinero** *masc*, la **cocinera** *fem*

ℰ to cook *verb* ▷ see **cook** *noun*

1 (*to make food*) **cocinar** [17]
Who's cooking tonight? ¿Quién cocina esta noche?
I like cooking. Me gusta cocinar.

2 (*the vegetables, the pasta, etc*) **cocer** [41]
Cook the carrots for five minutes. Cuece las zanahorias durante cinco minutos.

3 (*to make a meal*) **hacer** [7]
Fran's busy cooking supper. Fran está haciendo la cena.

4 (*food*) **hacerse** [7]
The sausages are cooking. Las salchichas se están haciendo.
Is the chicken cooked? ¿Está hecho el pollo?

cooker *noun*
la **cocina** *fem*
an electric cooker una cocina eléctrica
a gas cooker una cocina de gas

cookery *noun*
la **cocina** *fem*

• **cookery book** el libro de cocina

ℰ cooking *noun*
la **cocina** *fem*
Italian cooking la cocina italiana
home cooking la comida casera
to do the cooking cocinar [27]

ℰ cool *adjective* ▷ see **cool** *noun, verb*

1 (*cold*) **fresco** *masc*, **fresca** *fem*
a cool drink una bebida fresca
It's cool inside. Dentro hace fresco.

2 (*laid-back*) **tranquilo** *masc*, **tranquila** *fem*

3 (*informal: person*) **to be cool** estar [2] en la onda
He's so cool. Está muy en la onda.

4 (*informal: car, jacket*) **molón** *masc*, **molona** *fem*

ℰ cool *noun* ▷ see **cool** *adj, verb*

1 (*coldness*) el **fresco** *masc*
Stay in the cool. Quedarse [17] al fresco.

2 (*calm*) la **calma** *fem*
to lose one's cool perder [36] la calma
He kept his cool. Mantuvo la calma.

ℰ to cool *verb* ▷ see **cool** *adj, noun*
to cool enfriarse [32]

• **to cool down**
enfriarse [32]

to cooperate *verb*
cooperar [17]

ℰ cop *noun*
el & la **poli** *masc & fem* (*informal*)

to cope *verb*
(*to manage*) **defenderse** [36]
She copes well. Se defiende bien.
He can't cope any more. Ya no puede más.

• **to cope with something**

1 (*children, work*) **ocuparse** [17] **de**
I'll cope with the dishes. Yo me ocupo de los platos.

2 (*a problem*) **hacer** [7] **frente a**
She's had a lot to cope with. Ha tenido que hacer frente a muchos problemas.

copper *noun*
el **cobre** *masc*

copy *noun* ▷ see **copy** *verb*

1 (*of a document, picture*) la **copia** *fem*
Make ten copies of this letter. Haz diez copias de esta carta.

2 (*of a book*) el **ejemplar** *masc*

to copy *verb* ▷ see **copy** *noun*
copiar [17]
I copied (down) the address. Copié las señas.

cord *noun*
1 (*string*) la **cuerda** *fem*
2 (*for a blind, etc*) el **cordón** *masc*

ℐ **cordial** *noun*
el **refresco concentrado**

cordless telephone *noun*
el **teléfono inalámbrico**

core *noun*
(*of an apple, pear*) el **corazón** *masc*

cork *noun*
1 (*in a bottle*) el **tapón** *masc*
2 (*the material*) el **corcho** *masc*
• **corkscrew** el sacacorchos

corn *noun*
1 (*wheat*) el **trigo** *masc*
2 (*sweetcorn*) el **maíz** *masc*

ℐ **corner** *noun*
1 (*of a street, page*) la **esquina** *fem*
in the bottom right-hand corner of the
page en la esquina inferior derecha de la
página
on the corner of the street en la esquina de
la calle
It's just round the corner. Está a la vuelta de
la esquina.
2 (*of a room, cupboard*) el **rincón** *masc*
in a corner of the kitchen en un rincón de la
cocina
3 (*of your eye*) out of the corner of your eye por
el rabillo del ojo
4 (*in football*) el **córner** *masc*

cornflakes *noun*
los **copos de maíz**

Cornwall *noun*
Cornualles *masc*

corpse *noun*
el **cadáver** *masc*

correct *adjective* ▷ see **correct** *verb*
correcto *masc*, **correcta** *fem*
the correct sum la cantidad total correcta
the correct answer la respuesta correcta
the correct choice la elección adecuada
Yes, that's correct. Sí, así es.

to **correct** *verb* ▷ see **correct** *adj*
corregir [48]

correction *noun*
la **corrección** *fem*

correctly *adverb*
correctamente
Have you filled in the form correctly? ¿Has
rellenado el formulario correctamente?

to **correspond** *verb*
corresponder [18]

ℐ **correspondence** *noun*
la **correspondencia** *fem*

corridor *noun*
el **pasillo** *masc*

cosmetics *plural noun*
los **cosméticos** *masc plural*

ℐ **cost** *noun* ▷ see **cost** *verb*
el **coste** *masc*
the cost of a new computer el coste de un
nuevo ordenador
the cost of living el coste de la vida

ℐ to **cost** *verb* ▷ see **cost** *noun*
costar [24]
How much does it cost? ¿Cuánto cuesta?
The tickets cost ten pounds. Las entradas
cuestan diez libras.
It costs too much. Cuesta demasiado.

Costa Rica *noun*
Costa Rica *fem*

Costa Rican *adjective & noun*
1 **costarricense** *masc & fem*
2 un & una **costarricense** *masc & fem*
the Costa Ricans los costarricenses

WORD TIP Adjectives and nouns for nationality
and regional origin do not have capital letters in
Spanish.

ℐ **costume** *noun*
1 (*fancy dress*) el **disfraz** *masc*
2 (*for an actor*) el **traje** *masc*

cosy *adjective*
(*room*) **acogedor** *masc*, **acogedora** *fem*
It's cosy by the fire. Se está muy bien al lado
del fuego.

cot *noun*
la **cuna** *fem*

cottage *noun*
la **casita en el campo**

ℐ **cotton** *noun*
1 (*fabric*) el **algodón** *masc*
a cotton shirt una camisa de algodón
2 (*thread*) el **hilo** *masc*
• **cotton wool** el algodón en rama

couch *noun*
el **sofá** *masc*

cough *noun* ▷ see **cough** *verb*
la **tos** *fem*
a nasty cough una tos mala
to have a cough tener [9] tos

to **cough** *verb* ▷ see **cough** *noun*
    toser [18]

could *verb*

1 (*saying you are able to*) **poder** [10]
    I couldn't open it. No podía abrirlo.
    They couldn't smoke there. No podían fumar allí.
    She did all she could. Hizo todo lo que pudo.

2 (*saying you know how to*) **saber** [13]
    He couldn't drive. No sabía conducir.
    I couldn't swim then. Entonces no sabía nadar.

3 (*asking permission, suggesting*) **poder** [10]
    Could I speak to David? ¿Podría hablar con David?
    You could try telephoning. Podrías intentar llamar por teléfono.

4 (*with words like: see, hear, feel, remember, etc*)
    I could see her well. La veía bien.
    She couldn't hear a thing. No oía nada.
    I couldn't find my keys. No encontraba mis llaves.

> **WORD TIP** When you use *could* with *see, hear, feel, remember*, etc, it is not translated into Spanish. ▷ **can**

5 (*for possibilities*) **poder** [10]
    They could be home by now. Puede que ya estén en casa.
    You could be right. Puede que tengas razón.
    I would buy it if I could afford it. Lo compraría si pudiese.
    I could have gone if I'd wanted. Habría podido ir si hubiese querido.

> **WORD TIP** The verb in Spanish, telling you what the possibility is, is in the subjunctive.

couldn't *short for* **could not** (*See:* **could**)

ſ **council** *noun*
    el **consejo** *masc*
    the town council el ayuntamiento
• **council flat** el piso de protección oficial
• **council house** la casa de protección oficial

councillor *noun*
    el **concejal** *masc*, la **concejala** *fem*
    Her uncle is a councillor. Su tío es concejal.

ſ to **count** *verb*

1 (*to reckon up*) **contar** [24]
    I counted my money. Conté mi dinero.
    Thirty-five not counting the children. Treinta y cinco sin contar a los niños.

2 (*to be allowed*) **That doesn't count.** Eso no vale.
• to **count as**

considerarse [17] **como**
Children over twelve count as adults. Los niños mayores de doce años se consideran como adultos.

counter *noun*

1 (*in a shop*) el **mostrador** *masc*
2 (*in a cafe*) la **barra** *fem*
3 (*in a post office, bank*) la **ventanilla** *fem*
4 (*for board games*) la **ficha** *fem*

ſ **country** *noun*

1 (*Spain, Britain, etc*) el **país** *masc*
    a foreign country un país extranjero
    from another country de otro país
2 (*not the town*) el **campo** *masc*
    to live in the country vivir en el campo
• **country dancing** el baile folklórico
• **country road** el camino rural
• **countryside** el campo
• **country walk** el paseo por el campo

county *noun*
    el **condado** *masc*

couple *noun*

1 (*a pair*) la **pareja** *fem*
    a married couple una pareja de casados
2 (*one or two*) **a couple of** un par de
    a couple of times un par de veces
    I've got a couple of things to do. Tengo que hacer un par de cosas.

courage *noun*
    el **valor** *masc*

courgette *noun*
    el **calabacín** *masc*

courier *noun*

1 (*delivery service*) la **mensajería** *fem*
    by courier por mensajería
2 (*on a package holiday*) el & la **guía** *masc & fem*

ſ **course** *noun*

1 (*lessons*) el **curso** *masc*
    a beginners' course un curso para principiantes
    a computer course un curso de informática
    to go on a course asistir [19] a un curso
2 (*part of a meal*) el **plato** *masc*
    the main course el plato principal
3 (*for sport*) **a golf course** un campo de golf
4 (*to show certainty*) **of course** claro
    Yes, of course! ¡Sí, claro!
    He's forgotten, of course. Se ha olvidado, claro.

court *noun*

1 (*for tennis, squash, basketball*) la **cancha** *fem*
2 (*of law*) el **tribunal** *masc*
• **courtyard** el patio

ᵟ cousin *noun*
   el **primo** *masc*, la **prima** *fem*
   my cousin Sonia mi prima Sonia

ᵟ cover *noun* ▷ see **cover** *verb*
1 (*for a book*) la **tapa** *fem*
2 (*for a duvet, cushion*) la **funda** *fem*
   a duvet cover una funda de edredón

ᵟ to cover *verb* ▷ see **cover** *noun*
1 (*to hide*) **cubrir** [46]
   to cover the wound cubrir la herida
   The ground was covered with snow. El
   suelo estaba cubierto de nieve.
   He was covered in mud. Estaba cubierto de
   barro.
2 (*your face, eyes*) **cubrirse** [46]
   She covered her face. Se cubrió la cara.

ᵟ cow *noun*
   la **vaca** *fem*
   mad cow disease la enfermedad de las
   vacas locas

coward *noun*
   el & la **cobarde** *masc & fem*

cowboy *noun*
   el **vaquero** *masc*

crab *noun*
   el **cangrejo** *masc*

crack *noun* ▷ see **crack** *verb*
1 (*in a wall*) la **grieta** *fem*
2 (*in a cup, plate*) la **raja** *fem*
3 (*a cracking noise*) el **crujido** *masc*

to crack *verb* ▷ see **crack** *noun*
1 (*a cup, window, etc*) **hacer** [7] **una raja en**
2 (*a bone*) **fracturar** [17]
3 (*a nut, an egg*) **cascar** [31]
4 (*ice*) **rajarse** [17]
5 (*sticks, etc*) **crujir** [19]

cracker *noun*
   (*biscuit*) la **galleta salada**

to crackle *verb*
   crujir [19]

craft *noun*
   (*at school*) los **trabajos manuales**

crafty *adjective*
   astuto *masc*, **astuta** *fem*
   That was very crafty of her. Eso fue muy
   astuto por su parte.

cramp *noun*
   el **calambre** *masc*
   I've got cramp in my leg. Tengo un
   calambre en la pierna.

crane *noun*
   la **grúa** *fem*

to crash *verb* ▷ see **crash** *noun*
1 (*cars, planes*) **estrellarse** [17]
   The plane crashed. El avión se estrelló.
   to crash into something chocar [31] con
   algo
   The car crashed into a tree. El coche chocó
   con un árbol.
2 (*Computers*) **colgarse** [23]

crash *noun* ▷ see **crash** *verb*
1 (*accident*) el **accidente** *masc*
   a car crash un accidente de coche
2 (*smashing noise*) el **estrépito** *masc*
   a crash of broken glass un estrépito de
   cristales rotos
• **crash course** el curso intensivo
• **crash helmet** el casco

ᵟ crate *noun*
1 (*for china*) el **cajón para embalar**
2 (*for bottles, fruit*) la **caja** *fem*

crawl *noun* ▷ see **crawl** *verb*
   (*in swimming*) el **crol** *masc*

to crawl *verb* ▷ see **crawl** *noun*
1 (*people, babies*) **ir** [8] **a gatas**
2 (*cars in a jam*) **ir** [8] **muy despacio**
   We were crawling along. Íbamos muy
   despacio.

crayon *noun*
1 (*wax*) la **pintura de cera**
2 (*coloured pencil*) el **lápiz de color**

craze *noun*
   la **fiebre** *fem*
   the craze for computer games la fiebre de
   los juegos de ordenador

ᵟ crazy *adjective*
   loco *masc*, **loca** *fem*
   to go crazy volverse [45] loco
   to be crazy about someone, something
   estar [2] loco por alguien, algo
   He's crazy about football. A él le encanta el
   fútbol.
   She's crazy about tennis. A ella le encanta
   el tenis.

to creak *verb*
   (*a hinge*) **chirriar** [32], (*a floorboard*) **crujir**
   [19]

ᵟ cream *noun*
1 (*on milk*) la **nata** *fem*
   strawberries and cream fresas con nata
2 (*for hands, face, etc*) la **crema** *fem*
• **cream cheese** el queso para untar

a
b
c
d
e
f
g
h
i
j
k
l
m
n
o
p
q
r
s
t
u
v
w
x
y
z

crease *noun*
la **arruga** *fem*

creased *adjective*
arrugado *masc*, **arrugada** *fem*

to **create** *verb*
crear [17]

creative *adjective*
creativo *masc*, **creativa** *fem*

creature *noun*
la **criatura** *fem*

creche *noun*
la **guardería** *fem*

credit *noun*
el **crédito** *masc*
to buy something on credit comprar [17]
algo a crédito
• **credit card** la tarjeta de crédito

crew *noun*
1 (*on a ship, plane*) la **tripulación** *fem*
2 (*in rowing, for filming*) el **equipo** *masc*
• **crew cut** el corte de pelo al rape

cricket *noun*
1 (*the game*) el **críquet** *masc*
to play cricket jugar [27] al críquet
2 (*the insect*) el **grillo** *masc*
• **cricket bat** el bate de críquet

crime *noun*
1 (*minor offence*) el **delito** *masc*
Theft is a crime. El robo es un delito.
2 (*murder*) el **crimen** *masc*
3 (*within society*) el **crimen** *masc*
the fight against crime la lucha contra el
crimen

criminal *adjective* ▷ see **criminal** *noun*
criminal *masc & fem*

criminal *noun* ▷ see **criminal** *adj*
el & la **criminal** *masc & fem*

crisis *noun*
la **crisis** *fem*

♂ **crisp** *adjective* ▷ see **crisp** *noun*
crujiente *masc & fem*

♂ **crisp** *noun* ▷ see **crisp** *adj*
la **patata frita**
a packet of (potato) crisps un paquete de
patatas fritas

critical *adjective*
1 (*remark, somebody's condition*) **crítico** *masc*,
crítica *fem*
2 (*moment*) **decisivo** *masc*, **decisiva** *fem*

criticism *noun*
la **crítica** *fem*

to **criticize** *verb*
criticar [31]

Croatia *noun*
Croacia *fem*

crockery *noun*
la **vajilla** *fem*

crocodile *noun*
el **cocodrilo** *masc*

crook *noun*
(*criminal*) el & la **granuja** *masc & fem*

crooked *adjective*
torcido *masc*, **torcida** *fem*
a crooked line una línea torcida

crop *noun*
la **cosecha** *fem*

♂ **cross** *adjective* ▷ see **cross** *noun, verb*
enfadado *masc*, **enfadada** *fem*
She's very cross. Está muy enfadada.
I'm cross with you. Estoy enfadado
contigo.
to get cross enfadarse [17]

♂ **cross** *noun* ▷ see **cross** *adj, verb*
la **cruz** *fem*

♂ to **cross** *verb* ▷ see **cross** *adj, noun*
1 (*to cross over*) **cruzar** [22]
to cross the road cruzar la calle
to cross your legs cruzar las piernas
2 (*to cross each other*) **cruzarse** [22]
The two roads cross here. Las dos
carreteras se cruzan aquí.
• to **cross out**
(*a word, sentence*) **tachar** [17]

cross-Channel *adjective*
a cross-Channel ferry un ferry que cruza el
Canal de la Mancha

cross-country *noun*
el **cross** *masc*
cross-country skiing esquí de fondo

crossing *noun*
la **travesía** *fem*
a Channel crossing una travesía por el
Canal de la Mancha

cross-legged *adjective*
to sit cross-legged sentarse [29] con las
piernas cruzadas

♂ **crossroads** *noun*
el **cruce** *masc*
at the crossroads en el cruce

crossword *noun*
el **crucigrama** *masc*
I'm doing the crossword. Estoy haciendo el crucigrama.

to **crouch** *verb*
ponerse [11] en cuclillas

crow *noun* ▷ see **crow** *verb*
el **cuervo** *masc*

to **crow** *verb* ▷ see **crow** *noun*
(*cockrels*) **cacarear [17]**

crowd *noun*
la **multitud** *fem*
in the crowd en la multitud
a crowd of 5,000 una multitud de cinco mil personas

crowded *adjective*
lleno de gente *masc*, **llena de gente** *fem*

crown *noun*
la **corona** *fem*

crude *adjective*
1 (*rough and ready*) **rudimentario** *masc*, **rudimentaria** *fem*
2 (*vulgar*) **grosero** *masc*, **grosera** *fem*

cruel *adjective*
cruel *masc & fem*

cruelty *noun*
la **crueldad** *fem*
They were treated with great cruelty. Los trataron con gran crueldad.

cruise *noun*
el **crucero** *masc*
to go on a cruise ir [8] de crucero

crumb *noun*
la **miga** *fem*

to **crumple** *verb*
arrugar [28]

crunchy *adjective*
crujiente *masc & fem*

to **crush** *verb*
aplastar [17]

crust *noun*
la **corteza** *fem*

crutch *noun*
la **muleta** *fem*
to be on crutches andar [21] con muletas

♂ **cry** *noun* ▷ see **cry** *verb*
el **grito** *masc*

♂ to **cry** *verb* ▷ see **cry** *noun*
1 (*to weep*) **llorar [17]**
2 (*to call out*) **gritar [17]**

crystal *noun*
el **cristal** *masc*

cub *noun*
1 (*animal*) el **cachorro** *masc*
2 (*scout*) el **lobato** *masc*

Cuba *noun*
Cuba *fem*

Cuban *adjective & noun*
1 **cubano** *masc*, **cubana** *fem*
2 un **cubano** *masc*, una **cubana** *fem*
the Cubans los cubanos

WORD TIP Adjectives and nouns for nationality and regional origin do not have capital letters in Spanish.

cube *noun*
el **cubo** *masc*
an ice cube un cubito de hielo

cubic *adjective*
(*for measurements*) **cúbico** *masc*, **cúbica** *fem*
three cubic metres tres metros cúbicos

cubicle *noun*
1 (*in a changing room*) el **vestuario** *masc*
2 (*in a public lavatory*) el **cubículo** *masc*

cuckoo *noun*
el **cuco** *masc*

cucumber *noun*
el **pepino** *masc*

cuddle *noun* ▷ see **cuddle** *verb*
to give somebody a cuddle dar [4] un abrazo a alguien

to **cuddle** *verb* ▷ see **cuddle** *noun*
abrazar [22]

cue *noun*
(*used in billiards, pool, snooker*) el **taco** *masc*

cuff *noun*
(*on a shirt*) el **puño** *masc*

cul-de-sac *noun*
el **callejón sin salida**

culture *noun*
la **cultura** *fem*

cunning *adjective*
astuto *masc*, **astuta** *fem*

♂ **cup** *noun*
1 (*for drinking*) la **taza** *fem*
a cup of tea una taza de té
2 (*trophy*) la **copa** *fem*

♂ **cupboard** *noun*
el **armario** *masc*
in the kitchen cupboard en el armario de la cocina

cup tie noun
   el **partido de copa**

cure noun ▷ see **cure** verb
   la **cura** fem

to **cure** verb ▷ see **cure** noun
   curar [17]

curiosity noun
   la **curiosidad** fem

curious adjective
   curioso masc, **curiosa** fem

curl noun ▷ see **curl** verb
   el **rizo** masc

to **curl** verb ▷ see **curl** noun
   (hair) **rizar** [22]

curly adjective
   rizado masc, **rizada** fem

currant noun
   la **pasa de Corinto**

ᵟ **currency** noun
   la **moneda** fem
   foreign currency moneda extranjera

current adjective ▷ see **current** noun
   actual masc & fem
 • current affairs los sucesos de actualidad

current noun ▷ see **current** adj
   (of electricity, water) la **corriente** fem

curriculum noun
 1 (national) el **plan de estudios**
 2 (for a single course) el **programa de estudios**

curry noun
   el **curry** masc
   a chicken curry un curry de pollo

ᵟ **cursor** noun
   el **cursor** masc

ᵟ **curtain** noun
   la **cortina** fem

cushion noun
   el **cojín** masc

custard noun
 1 (runny) las **natillas** plural fem
 2 (baked) el **flan** masc

custom noun
   la **costumbre** fem

ᵟ **customer** noun
   el **cliente** masc, la **clienta** fem
 • **customer services** la atención al cliente

ᵟ **customs** plural noun
   la **aduana** singular fem
   to go through customs pasar [17] por la
   aduana
 • customs hall la aduana
 • customs officer el & la agente de aduana

ᵟ **cut** noun ▷ see **cut** verb
   (injury, haircut) el **corte** masc

ᵟ to **cut** verb ▷ see **cut** noun
 1 (with scissors, a knife, a mower, etc) **cortar** [17]
   to cut the grass cortar la hierba
   I've cut the bread. He cortado el pan.
   You'll cut yourself! ¡Te vas a cortar!
   Kevin's cut his finger. Kevin se ha cortado el
   dedo.
   Alicia's had her hair cut. Alicia se ha
   cortado el pelo.
 2 (prices) **recortar** [17]
 • to **cut something down**
   (a tree) **cortar** [17] **algo**
 • to **cut down on something**
   to cut down on fats consumir [19], menos
   grasas
 • to **cut something out**
 1 (a newspaper article) **recortar** [17] **algo**
 2 (sugar, fatty food, etc) **suprimir** [19] **algo**
 • to **cut something up**
   (food) **cortar** [17] **algo en trocitos**

cute adjective
   mono masc, **mona** fem

cutlery noun
   la **cubertería** fem

CV noun
   el **currículum**

to **cycle** verb ▷ see **cycle** noun
   montar [17] **en bicicleta**
   Do you like cycling? ¿Te gusta montar en
   bicicleta?
   We cycle to school. Vamos al colegio en
   bicicleta.

cycle noun ▷ see **cycle** verb
   (bike) la **bicicleta** fem
 • cycle lane el carril de bicicletas
 • cycle race la carrera de ciclismo

ᵟ **cycling** noun
   el **ciclismo** masc
 • cycling holiday las vacaciones en bicicleta

ᵟ **cyclist** noun
   el & la **ciclista** masc & fem

cylinder noun
   el **cilindro** masc
   a gas cylinder una bombona

D d

♂ **dad** noun
1 (father) el **padre** masc
Anna's dad el padre de Ana
My dad works in a bank. Mi padre trabaja en un banco.
2 (daddy) el **papá** masc
Dad's not home yet. Papá no ha llegado a casa aún.

♂ **daddy** noun
el **papá** masc

daffodil noun
el **narciso** masc

daily adjective ▷ see **daily** adv
diario masc, **diaria** fem
his daily visit su visita diaria

daily adverb ▷ see **daily** adj
a **diario**
She visits him daily. Le visita a diario.

dairy products plural noun
los **productos lácteos**

daisy noun
la **margarita** fem

dam noun
la **presa** fem

♂ **damage** noun ▷ see **damage** verb
daño masc
The damage is done. El daño ya está hecho.
There's no damage. No ha habido daños.

to **damage** verb ▷ see **damage** noun
dañar[17]

damn noun ▷ see **damn** excl
(informal) He doesn't give a damn. Le importa un comino.

damn exclamation ▷ see **damn** noun
(informal) Damn! ¡Maldita sea!

damp adjective ▷ see **damp** noun
húmedo masc, **húmeda** fem

damp noun ▷ see **damp** adj
la **humedad** fem
because of the damp a causa de la humedad

♂ **dance** noun ▷ see **dance** verb
el **baile** masc
a folk dance un baile folklórico

♂ to **dance** verb ▷ see **dance** noun
bailar[17]
I like dancing. Me gusta bailar.

dancer noun
el **bailarín** masc, la **bailarina** fem

dancing noun
el **baile** masc
I love dancing. Me encanta bailar.

dancing class noun
la **clase de baile**
to go to dancing classes ir[8] a clase de baile

dandruff noun
la **caspa** fem

Dane noun
un **danés** masc, una **danesa** fem
the Danes los daneses

WORD TIP Adjectives and nouns for nationality and regional origin do not have capital letters in Spanish.

danger noun
el **peligro** masc
to be in danger estar[2] en peligro
to be out of danger estar[2] fuera de peligro

♂ **dangerous** adjective
peligroso masc, **peligrosa** fem
It's dangerous to drive so fast. Es peligroso conducir tan rápido.

Danish adjective & noun
1 **danés** masc, **danesa** fem
2 (the language) el **danés** masc

WORD TIP Adjectives and nouns for nationality, regional origin and language do not have capital letters in Spanish.

to **dare** verb
1 (to be brave enough) **atreverse**[18]
How dare you! ¡Cómo te atreves!
to dare to do something atreverse a hacer algo
I didn't dare to suggest it. No me atreví a sugerirlo.
Don't you dare tell her I'm here! ¡No se te ocurra decirle que estoy aquí!
2 (to challenge someone) I dare you! ¡A que no te atreves! (informal)
I dare you to tell him! ¡A que no te atreves a decírselo! (informal)

daring *adjective*
  osado *masc*, **osada** *fem*
  That was a bit daring! ¡Eso fue un poco osado!

dark *adjective* ▷ see **dark** *noun*
1 (*colour, room*) **oscuro** *masc*, **oscura** *fem*
  a dark blue suit un traje azul oscuro
  She has dark brown hair. Tiene el pelo castaño oscuro.
  The kitchen's a bit dark. La cocina es un poco oscura.
  It's dark in here. Está oscuro aquí.
2 (*night-time*) **to get dark** oscurecer [35]
  It gets dark around five. Oscurece a eso de las cinco.
  It's dark already. Ya es de noche.

dark *noun* ▷ see **dark** *adj*
  in the dark en la oscuridad
  after dark de noche
  to be afraid of the dark tener [9] miedo de la oscuridad

darkness *noun*
  la **oscuridad** *fem*

darling *noun*
  el **querido** *masc*, la **querida** *fem*
  See you later, darling! ¡Te veo luego querido!

dart *noun*
  el **dardo** *masc*
  to play darts jugar [27] a los dardos

data *plural noun*
  los **datos** *masc plural*
• **database** la base de datos

𝄞 **date** *noun*
1 (*on the calendar*) la **fecha** *fem*
  the date of the meeting la fecha de la reunión
  What's the date today? ¿Qué día es hoy?
  to fix a date for something fijar [17] una fecha para algo
2 (*with a boyfriend, girlfriend*) **I have a date with Jerry on Sunday.** He quedado para salir con Jerry el domingo.
3 (*the fruit*) el **dátil** *masc*
• date of birth la fecha de nacimiento

𝄞 **daughter** *noun*
  la **hija** *fem*
  Tina's daughter la hija de Tina
• **daughter-in-law** la nuera

dawn *noun*
  el **amanecer** *masc*

𝄞 **day** *noun*
  el **día** *masc*
  three days later tres días más tarde
  It rained all day. Llovió todo el día.
  It's going to be a nice day tomorrow. Mañana va a hacer buen día.
  the day after al día siguiente
  the day after tomorrow pasado mañana
  the day before el día anterior
  the day before yesterday anteayer
  every day todos los días
• day off el día libre

𝄞 **dead** *adjective* ▷ see **dead** *adv*
  muerto *masc*, **muerta** *fem*
  He's dead. Está muerto.

𝄞 **dead** *adverb* ▷ see **dead** *adj*
  (*informal: really*) **super**
  He's dead nice. Es super majo.
  It's dead easy. Es super fácil.
  It was dead good. Fue genial.
  You're dead right. Tienes toda la razón.
  She arrived dead on time. Llegó justo a la hora.
• dead end el callejón sin salida
• deadline la fecha límite

𝄞 **deaf** *adjective*
  sordo *masc*, **sorda** *fem*
  to go deaf quedarse [17] sordo

deafening *adjective*
  ensordecedor *masc*, **ensordecedora** *fem*

deal *noun* ▷ see **deal** *verb*
1 (*involving money*) el **negocio** *masc*
  It's a good deal. Es un buen negocio.
2 (*pact*) el **trato** *masc*
  I'll make a deal with you. Voy a hacer un trato contigo.
  It's a deal! ¡Trato hecho!
3 (*to describe quantity*) a great deal of energy mucha energía
  I don't have a great deal of time. No tengo mucho tiempo.
  a great deal mucho
  it has improved a great deal ha mejorado mucho

to **deal** *verb* ▷ see **deal** *noun*
  (*in cards*) **repartir** [19]
• to **deal with something** **ocuparse** [17] de algo
  Linda deals with the accounts. Linda se ocupa de las cuentas.
  I'll deal with it as soon as possible. Me ocuparé de ello tan pronto como sea posible.

♂ **dear** *adjective*
1 (*term of affection*) **querido** *masc*, **querida** *fem*
Dear Jo Querida Jo
2 (*expensive*) **caro** *masc*, **cara** *fem*

death *noun*
la **muerte** *fem*
after his father's death después de la muerte de su padre
· **death penalty** la pena de muerte

debate *noun* ▷ see **debate** *verb*
el **debate** *masc*

to **debate** *verb* ▷ see **debate** *noun*
debatir [19]

♂ **debit card** *noun*
la **tarjeta de cobro automático**

debt *noun*
la **deuda** *fem*
to get into debt endeudarse [17]

decade *noun*
década *fem*

decaffeinated *adjective*
descafeinado *masc*, **descafeinada** *fem*

to **deceive** *verb*
engañar [17]

♂ **December** *noun*
diciembre *masc*

WORD TIP Names of months and days start with small letters in Spanish.

decent *adjective*
decente *masc & fem*
a decent salary un sueldo decente
a decent meal una comida decente
He seems a decent enough guy. Parece un tipo decente.

♂ to **decide** *verb*
decidir [19]
to decide to do something decidir hacer algo
She's decided to buy a car. Ha decidido comprarse un coche.
They've decided not to go on holiday. Han decidido no irse de vacaciones.

decimal *adjective*
decimal *masc & fem*
· **decimal point** el punto decimal, la coma
(*Most Spanish-speaking countries use a comma in maths for a decimal point.*)

decision *noun*
la **decisión** *fem*
the right decision la decisión acertada
the wrong decision la decisión errónea
to make a decision tomar [17] una decisión

deck *noun*
(*on a ship*) la **cubierta** *fem*
· **deckchair** la tumbona

to **declare** *verb*
declarar [17]

to **decorate** *verb*
1 (*to put decorations on*) **adornar** [17]
to decorate the Christmas tree adornar el árbol de Navidad
2 (*with paint*) **pintar** [17]
3 (*with wallpaper*) **empapelar** [17]

decoration *noun*
1 (*the act of adornment*) la **decoración** *fem*
2 (*an ornament*) el **adorno** *masc*

decorator *noun*
el **pintor** *masc*, la **pintora** *fem*

decrease *noun* ▷ see **decrease** *verb*
la **disminución** *fem*
a decrease in the number of something una disminución en el número de algo

to **decrease** *verb* ▷ see **decrease** *noun*
disminuir [54]

to **deduct** *verb*
deducir [60]

deep *adjective*
profundo *masc*, **profunda** *fem*
a deep feeling of gratitude un profundo sentimiento de gratitud
a hole two metres deep un agujero de dos metros de profundidad
The river is very deep here. Aquí el río es muy profundo.
How deep is the swimming pool? ¿Qué profundidad tiene la piscina?
· **deep end** (*of a swimming pool*) la parte honda
· **deep freeze** el congelador

deeply *adverb*
profundamente

deer *noun*
el **ciervo** *masc*

defeat *noun* ▷ see **defeat** *verb*
la **derrota** *fem*

to **defeat** *verb* ▷ see **defeat** *noun*
derrotar [17]

defect *noun*
el **defecto** *masc*

defence *noun*
la **defensa** *fem*

to **defend** *verb*
defender [36]

a
b
c
d
e
f
g
h
i
j
k
l
m
n
o
p
q
r
s
t
u
v
w
x
y
z

defender *noun*
1 *(supporter of a cause)* el **defensor** *masc*, la **defensora** *fem*
2 *(in football, etc)* el & la **defensa** *masc & fem*

to **define** *verb*
    definir [19]

definite *adjective*
1 *(clear)* **claro** *masc*, **clara** *fem*
a definite improvement una clara mejora
a definite advantage una clara ventaja
It's a definite possibility. Es claramente una posibilidad.
2 *(certain)* **seguro** *masc*, **segura** *fem*
It's not definite yet. Aún no es seguro.
3 *(exact)* **preciso** *masc*, **precisa** *fem*
a definite answer una respuesta precisa
I don't have a definite idea of what I want. No tengo una idea precisa de lo que quiero.
• **definite article** el artículo definido

definitely *adverb*
1 *(showing your opinion)* **sin ninguna duda**
The blue one is definitely the biggest. El azul es sin ninguna duda el más grande.
Your French is definitely better than mine. Hablas francés mejor que yo sin ninguna duda.
'Are you sure you like this one better?'— 'Definitely.' ¿Estás seguro de que te gusta más éste?'—'Segurísimo.'
2 *(for certain)* She's definitely going to be there. Seguro que va a estar aquí.
Definitely not! ¡En absoluto!
She definitely said she would do it. Dijo que seguro que lo haría.

definition *noun*
    la **definición** *fem*

ℰ **degree** *noun*
1 *(amount, measurement)* el **grado** *masc*
thirty degrees treinta grados
2 *(qualification)* a university degree un título universitario

ℰ **delay** *noun* ▷ see **delay** *verb*
    el **retraso** *masc*
a two-hour delay un retraso de dos horas

to **delay** *verb* ▷ see **delay** *noun*
    retrasar [17]
The flight was delayed by bad weather. El mal tiempo retrasó el vuelo.
The decision has been delayed until Thursday. Retrasaron la decisión hasta el jueves.

deliberate *adjective*
    deliberado *masc*, **deliberada** *fem*

deliberately *adverb*
    a propósito
You did it deliberately. Lo hiciste a propósito.
He left it there deliberately. Lo dejó allí a propósito.

delicate *adjective*
    delicado *masc*, **delicada** *fem*

delicatessen *noun*
    la **charcutería** *fem*

ℰ **delicious** *adjective*
    delicioso *masc*, **deliciosa** *fem*

ℰ **delighted** *adjective*
    encantado *masc*, **encantada** *fem*
They're delighted with their new flat. Están encantados con su nuevo piso.
I'm delighted to hear you can come. Estoy encantado de saber que puedes venir.

to **deliver** *verb*
1 *(goods)* **entregar** [28]
the person who delivered the parcel la persona que entregó el paquete
2 *(mail)* **repartir** [19]

delivery *noun*
    la **entrega** *fem*

demand *noun* ▷ see **demand** *verb*
    la **petición** *fem*

to **demand** *verb* ▷ see **demand** *noun*
    exigir [49]

democracy *noun*
    la **democracia** *fem*

democratic *adjective*
    democrático *masc*, **democrática** *fem*

to **demolish** *verb*
    destruir [54]

to **demonstrate** *verb*
1 *(a theory, a skill)* **demostrar** [24]
2 *(a machine, a product, a technique)* **hacer** [7] **una demostración de**
3 *(to protest)* **manifestarse** [29]
to demonstrate against something manifestarse en contra de algo

demonstration *noun*
1 *(of a machine, product, technique)* la **demostración** *fem*
2 *(protest)* la **manifestación** *fem*

demonstrator *noun*
(in protest) el & la **manifestante** *masc & fem*

denim *noun*
    la **tela vaquera**
a denim jacket una chaqueta vaquera

Denmark *noun*
Dinamarca *fem*

dense *adjective*
denso *masc*, **densa** *fem*

dent *noun* ▷ see **dent** *verb*
la **abolladura** *fem*

to **dent** *verb* ▷ see **dent** *noun*
abollar [17]

dental *adjective*
dental *masc & fem*
- **dental appointment** la cita con el dentista
- **dental floss** el hilo dental
- **dental hygiene** la higiene dental
- **dental surgeon** el cirujano dentista, la cirujana dentista

ʒ **dentist** *noun*
el & la **dentista** *masc & fem*
My mum's a dentist. Mi madre es dentista.

to **deny** *verb*
negar [30]

deodorant *noun*
el **desodorante** *masc*

to **depart** *verb*
salir [63]

ʒ **department** *noun*
1 (*in school, university*) el **departamento** *masc*
the language department el departamento de idiomas
2 (*in a shop*) la **sección** *fem*
the men's department la sección de caballeros
- **department store** los grandes almacenes

ʒ **departure** *noun*
la **salida** *fem*
- **departure gate** la puerta de embarque
- **departure lounge** la sala de embarque

to **depend** *verb*
to depend on something depender [18] de algo
It depends. Depende.
It depends on the price. Depende del precio.
It depends on what you want. Depende de lo que tú quieras

WORD TIP *depende de lo que* is followed by a verb in the subjunctive.

deposit *noun*
1 (*for renting, making bookings, etc*) el **depósito** *masc*
to pay a deposit pagar un depósito
2 (*for buying something*) la **entrada** *fem*

depressed *adjective*
deprimido *masc*, **deprimida** *fem*

depressing *adjective*
deprimente *masc & fem*

depth *noun*
la **profundidad** *fem*

deputy *noun*
el **segundo** *masc*, la **segunda** *fem*
- **deputy head** el subdirector, la subdirectora

to **descend** *verb*
descender [36]

ʒ to **describe** *verb*
describir [52]

ʒ **description** *noun*
la **descripción** *fem*

desert *noun*
el **desierto** *masc*
- **desert island** la isla desierta

 desert

The Atacama desert in northern Chile is the driest place in the world, suffering almost 400 years of drought until 1971.

to **deserve** *verb*
merecer [35]

design *noun* ▷ see **design** *verb*
el **diseño** *masc*
the design of the plane el diseño del avión
a floral design un diseño de flores
fashion design diseño de moda

to **design** *verb* ▷ see **design** *noun*
diseñar [17]

designer *noun*
el **diseñador** *masc*, la **diseñadora** *fem*

desire *noun* ▷ see **desire** *verb*
el **deseo** *masc*

to **desire** *verb* ▷ see **desire** *noun*
desear [17]

ʒ **desk** *noun*
1 (*in an office, at home*) el **escritorio** *masc*
the reception desk la recepción
the information desk Información
2 (*at school*) el **pupitre** *masc*

despair *noun*
la **desesperación** *fem*

desperate *adjective*
1 (*despairing*) **desesperado** *masc*, **desesperada** *fem*
a desperate attempt un intento desesperado ▶▶

a
b
c
d
e
f
g
h
i
j
k
l
m
n
o
p
q
r
s
t
u
v
w
x
y
z

2　(*impatient*) **to be desperate to do something** estar [2] deseando hacer algo
I'm desperate to see you. Estoy deseando verte.

to **despise** *verb*
despreciar [17]

♂ **dessert** *noun*
el **postre** *masc*
What's for dessert? ¿Qué hay de postre?

♂ **destination** *noun*
el **destino** *masc*

to **destroy** *verb*
destruir [54]

destruction *noun*
la **destrucción** *fem*

detached house *noun*
la **casa no adosada**

detail *noun*
el **detalle** *masc*

detailed *adjective*
detallado *masc*, **detallada** *fem*

♂ **detective** *noun*
1　(*police officer*) el & la **agente** *masc & fem*
2　(*for private investigations*) **a private detective**
un detective privado, una detective privada
· **detective novel** la novela policiaca
· **detective story** la novela policiaca

detention *noun*
(*in school*) **to be in detention** estar [2] castigado (*for a boy*), estar castigada (*for a girl*)

detergent *noun*
el **detergente** *masc*

determined *adjective*
decidido *masc*, **decidida** *fem*
to be determined to do something estar [2] determinado a hacer algo
She's determined to leave. Está decidida a irse.

detour *noun*
el **rodeo** *masc*

to **develop** *verb*
1　(*a film*) **revelar** [17]
to get a film developed revelar un carrete de fotos
2　(*people*) **desarrollarse** [17]
how children develop cómo se desarrollan los niños

developing country *noun*
el **país en vías de desarrollo**

development *noun*
el **desarrollo** *masc*

devil *noun*
el **diablo** *masc*

dew *noun*
el **rocío** *masc*

diabetes *noun*
la **diabetes** *fem*

diabetic *adjective* ▷ see **diabetic** *noun*
diabético *masc*, **diabética** *fem*
to be diabetic ser [1] diabético

diabetic *noun* ▷ see **diabetic** *adj*
el **diabético** *masc*, la **diabética** *fem*

diagonal *adjective*
diagonal *masc & fem*

diagnosis *noun*
el **diagnóstico** *masc*

diagram *noun*
el **diagrama** *masc*

to **dial** *verb*
marcar [31]
Dial 00 34 for Spain. Marca 00 34 para España.

dialling tone *noun*
el **tono de marcar**

dialogue *noun*
el **diálogo** *masc*

diameter *noun*
el **diámetro** *masc*

diamond *noun*
1　(*jewel*) el **diamante** *masc*
2　(*in cards*) **diamonds** diamantes
the jack of diamonds la jota de diamantes
3　(*shape*) el **rombo** *masc*

diarrhoea *noun*
la **diarrea** *fem*
to have diarrhoea tener [9] diarrea

diary *noun*
1　(*for dates*) la **agenda** *fem*
I've noted the date of the meeting in my diary. He anotado la fecha de la reunión en mi agenda.
2　(*personal journal*) el **diario íntimo**
to keep a diary tener [9] un diario íntimo

dice *noun*
el **dado** *masc*
to throw the dice tirar [17] los dados

dictation *noun*
el **dictado** *masc*

dictionary *noun*
  el **diccionario** *masc*
  to look up a word in the dictionary buscar
  [31] una palabra en el diccionario

did *verb* ▷ **do**

didn't *short for* **did not** (*See:* **to do**)

to **die** *verb*
1 **morir** [55]
  My grandmother died in January. Mi
  abuela murió en enero.
2 to be dying to do something estar [2]
  deseando hacer algo
  I'm dying to see them! ¡Estoy deseando
  verlos!
• to **die out**
  desaparecer [35]
  The tradition is dying out. La tradición está
  desapareciendo.

diesel *noun*
  el **diesel** *masc*
• **diesel car** el diesel
• **diesel engine** el motor diesel

✎ **diet** *noun*
1 (*what you eat*) la **dieta** *fem*
  to have a healthy diet llevar una dieta
  saludable
2 (*to slim, special requirements*) el **régimen** *masc*
  a salt-free diet un régimen sin sal
  to be on a diet estar [2] a régimen
  to go on a diet ponerse [11] a régimen

✎ **difference** *noun*
1 (*distinction*) la **diferencia** *fem*
  I can't see any difference between the two.
  No puedo ver ninguna diferencia entre los
  dos.
  What's the difference between ...? ¿Qué
  diferencia hay entre ...?
2 (*alteration*) It makes a difference. Eso
  cambia las cosas.
  It makes no difference. Da lo mismo.
  It makes no difference what I say. Da lo
  mismo lo que yo diga.

✎ **different** *adjective*
  distinto *masc*, **distinta** *fem*
  The two sisters are very different. Las dos
  hermanas son muy distintas.
  She's very different from her sister. Es muy
  distinta a su hermana.

✎ **difficult** *adjective*
  difícil *masc & fem*
  It's really difficult. Es muy difícil.
  It's difficult to decide. Es difícil decidir.

difficulty *noun*
  la **dificultad** *fem*
  I had difficulty finding your house. Me
  resultó difícil encontrar tu casa.

to **dig** *verb*
  cavar [17]
  to dig a hole cavar un agujero

digestion *noun*
  la **digestión** *fem*

digital *adjective*
  digital *masc & fem*
  a digital camera una cámara digital
  a digital radio una radio digital

dignity *noun*
  la **dignidad** *fem*

dim *adjective*
1 (*weak*) **tenue** *masc & fem*
  a dim light una luz tenue
2 (*informal: unintelligent*) **tonto** *masc*, **tonta** *fem*
  She's a bit dim. Es un poco tonta.

dimension *noun*
  la **dimensión** *fem*

din *noun*
  el **ruido** *masc*
  They were making a dreadful din. Estaban
  haciendo un ruido enorme.
  Stop making such a din! ¡Deja de hacer
  tanto ruido!

dinghy *noun*
  a sailing dinghy un bote
  a rubber dinghy un bote neumático

✎ **dining room** *noun*
  el **comedor** *masc*

✎ **dinner** *noun*
1 (*evening meal*) la **cena** *fem*
  to have dinner cenar [17]
  to invite somebody to dinner invitar [17] a
  alguien a cenar
2 (*midday meal*) la **comida** *fem*
  to have dinner comer [18]
  to have school dinners comer [18] en el
  colegio

dinner time *noun*
1 (*in the evening*) la **hora de cenar**
2 (*at midday*) la **hora de comer**

dinosaur *noun*
  el **dinosaurio** *masc*

✎ **diploma** *noun*
  el **diploma** *masc*

♂ **direct** *adjective* ▷ see **direct** *adv, verb*
   directo *masc*, **directa** *fem*
   a direct flight un vuelo directo

♂ **direct** *adverb* ▷ see **direct** *adj, verb*
   directo
   The bus goes direct to the airport. El
   autobús va directo al aeropuerto.

♂ to **direct** *verb* ▷ see **direct** *adj, adv*
1 (*a programme, a film, a play, the traffic*) **dirigir**
   [49]
2 (*give directions to*) **to direct someone**
   somewhere indicarle [31] a alguien el
   camino a un lugar
   I directed them to the station. Les indiqué
   el camino a la estación.

♂ **direction** *noun*
1 (*the way to somewhere*) la **dirección** *fem*
   in the other direction en la otra dirección
   in the direction of the church en dirección a
   la iglesia
   in all directions en todas direcciones
   to ask somebody for directions pedir [57] a
   alguien que te indique el camino
2 (*instruction*) **directions for use** instrucciones
   de uso

   directly *adverb*
1 (*to go, fly, deal, ask*) **directamente**
2 (*at once*) **inmediatamente**
   directly afterwards inmediatamente
   después

♂ **director** *noun*
   el **director** *masc*, la **directora** *fem*

♂ **directory** *noun*
   la **guía telefónica**
· **directory enquiries** el servicio de
   información telefónica

   dirt *noun*
   la **suciedad** *fem*

♂ **dirty** *adjective*
   sucio *masc*, **sucia** *fem*
   My hands are dirty. Tengo las manos
   sucias.
   to get dirty ensuciarse [17]
   The curtains get dirty quickly. Las cortinas
   se ensucian rápido.
   to get something dirty ensuciar [17] algo
   I got the floor dirty. Ensucié el suelo.
   You'll get your dress dirty. Te vas a ensuciar
   el vestido.

   disability *noun*
   la **discapacidad** *fem*
   Does he have a disability? ¿Tiene alguna
   discapacidad?

disabled *adjective*
   discapacitado *masc*, **discapacitada** *fem*
   disabled people los discapacitados

disadvantage *noun*
1 la **desventaja** *fem*
2 **to be at a disadvantage** estar [2] en
   desventaja

to **disagree** *verb*
   no estar [2] **de acuerdo**
   I disagree. No estoy de acuerdo.
   I disagree with James. No estoy de acuerdo
   con James.

to **disappear** *verb*
   desaparecer [35]

disappearance *noun*
   la **desaparición** *fem*

♂ **disappointed** *adjective*
   decepcionado *masc*, **decepcionada** *fem*
   I was disappointed with my marks. Mis
   notas me decepcionaron.

disappointment *noun*
   la **decepción** *fem*

disaster *noun*
   el **desastre** *masc*
   It was a complete disaster. Fue un
   completo desastre.

disastrous *adjective*
   desastroso *masc*, **desastrosa** *fem*

disc *noun*
   el **disco** *masc*
   a slipped disc una hernia de disco
   a compact disc un disco compacto

discipline *noun*
   la **disciplina** *fem*

disc jockey *noun*
   el & la **disc-jockey** *masc & fem*

♂ **disco** *noun*
1 (*dance*) el **baile** *masc*
   They're having a disco. Tienen un baile.
2 (*club*) la **disco** *fem*, la **discoteca**

to **disconnect** *verb*
   desconectar [17]
   Have you disconnected the electricity?
   ¿Has desconectado la electricidad?

discount *noun*
   el **descuento** *masc*

to **discourage** *verb*
1 (*to depress*) **desanimar** [17]
2 (*to persuade not to*) **to discourage somebody**
   from doing something convencer [44] a
   alguien de que no haga algo

I discouraged her from buying it. La convencí de que no lo comprara.

WORD TIP *convencer a alguien de que no* is followed by a verb in the subjunctive.

to **discover** *verb*
descubrir [46]

discovery *noun*
el **descubrimiento** *masc*

discreet *adjective*
discreto *masc*, discreta *fem*

discrimination *noun*
la **discriminación** *fem*
racial discrimination discriminación racial

♪ to **discuss** *verb*
1 (*a subject, a topic*) **hablar** [17] **de**
to discuss politics hablar de política
2 (*a problem, a plan*) **discutir** [19]
I'm going to discuss it with Phil. Voy a hablarlo con Phil.

discussion *noun*
la **discusión** *fem*

disease *noun*
la **enfermedad** *fem*

disgraceful *adjective*
vergonzoso *masc*, vergonzosa *fem*

disguise *noun* ▷ see **disguise** *verb*
el **disfraz** *masc*
to be in disguise ir [8] disfrazado (*talking about a man*), ir disfrazada (*talking about a woman*)

to **disguise** *verb* ▷ see **disguise** *noun*
disfrazar [22]
to disguise oneself as something disfrazarse de algo
He was disguised as a woman. Iba disfrazado de mujer.

disgust *noun*
1 (*indignation*) la **indignación** *fem*
2 (*physical revulsion*) el **asco** *masc*

disgusted *adjective*
1 (*indignant*) **indignado** *masc*, **indignada** *fem*
2 (*physically sick*) **asqueado** *masc*, **asqueada** *fem*

♪ **disgusting** *adjective*
asqueroso *masc*, asquerosa *fem*

♪ **dish** *noun*
1 (*plate, item on menu*) el **plato** *masc*
to wash the dishes lavar [17] los platos
The dish of the day is paella. El plato del día es paella.

2 (*serving dish*) la **fuente** *fem*
a large white dish una fuente grande blanca
· **dishcloth** el paño de cocina

dishonest *adjective*
deshonesto *masc*, deshonesta *fem*

dishonesty *noun*
la **falta de honradez**

♪ **dishwasher** *noun*
el **lavaplatos** *masc*

WORD TIP *lavaplatos* does not change in the plural.

to **disinfect** *verb*
desinfectar [17]

disinfectant *noun*
el **desinfectante** *masc*

♪ **disk** *noun*
el **disco** *masc*
a floppy disk un disquete
the hard disk el disco duro
· **disk drive** la disquetera

♪ **diskette** *noun*
el **disquete** *masc*

to **dislike** *verb*
I dislike sport. No me gusta el deporte.
He dislikes my friends. No le gustan mis amigos.

WORD TIP Use *gusta, gustó, gustaba, gustaría*, etc if what you dislike is singular or an infinitive. Use *gustan, gustaron, gustaban, gustarían*, etc if what you dislike is plural.

dismay *noun*
la **consternación** *fem*

to **dismiss** *verb*
(*an employee*) **despedir** [57]

disobedient *adjective*
desobediente *masc & fem*

to **disobey** *verb*
desobedecer [35]
She disobeyed the rules. Desobedeció el reglamento.

display *noun* ▷ see **display** *verb*
la **exposición** *fem*
a handicrafts display una exposición de artesanía
a window display un escaparate
a firework display fuegos artificiales
to be on display estar [2] expuesto

a
b
c
d
e
f
g
h
i
j
k
l
m
n
o
p
q
r
s
t
u
v
w
x
y
z

display

to **display** verb ▷ see **display** noun
exponer [11]

disposable adjective
desechable masc & fem

dispute noun
1 (quarrel) la **disputa** fem
2 (argument) la **polémica** fem

to **disqualify** verb
descalificar [31]

to **dissolve** verb
disolver [45]

ⓢ **distance** noun
la **distancia** fem
from a distance de lejos
in the distance a lo lejos
It's within walking distance. Se puede ir
andando.

distant adjective
distante masc & fem

distinct adjective
claro masc, clara fem

distinctly adverb
1 (to hear, see) claramente
2 (very) It's distinctly odd. Es realmente raro.

to **distract** verb
distraer [42]

to **distribute** verb
distribuir [54]

distribution noun
la **distribución** fem

district noun
1 (in a town) el **barrio** masc
a poor district of Barcelona un barrio pobre
de Barcelona
2 (in the country) la **región** fem

to **disturb** verb
molestar [17]
Sorry to disturb you. Perdona que te
moleste.
'Do not disturb' 'Se ruega no molestar'

ditch noun
la **zanja** fem

dive noun ▷ see **dive** verb
la **zambullida** fem

to **dive** verb ▷ see **dive** noun
tirarse [17]
to dive into the water tirarse al agua

diver noun
(deep-sea) el & la **submarinista** masc & fem

do

ⓢ **diversion** noun
(for traffic) el **desvío** masc

to **divide** verb
dividir [19]

diving noun
1 (from a board) los **saltos de trampolín**
2 (from the surface of the water) el
submarinismo masc
· **diving board** el trampolín

division noun
la **división** fem

divorce noun ▷ see **divorce** verb
el **divorcio** masc

to **divorce** verb ▷ see **divorce** noun
divorciarse [17]
They divorced in Mexico. Se divorciaron en
México.
to get divorced divorciarse

ⓢ **divorced** adjective
divorciado masc, divorciada fem
My parents are divorced. Mis padres están
divorciados.

ⓢ **DIY** noun
el **bricolaje** masc
to do DIY hacer [7] bricolaje
a DIY shop una tienda de bricolaje

dizzy adjective
to feel dizzy estar [2] mareado
I feel dizzy. Estoy mareada.

DJ noun
el & la **disc-jockey** masc & fem

ⓢ to **do** verb
1 (to carry out) hacer [7]
What are you doing? ¿Qué estás haciendo?
I'm doing my homework. Estoy haciendo
mis deberes.
What have you done with the hammer?
¿Qué has hecho con el martillo?
2 (in questions: do is not translated) Did Maria go
to the party? ¿Fue María a la fiesta?
Do you want some strawberries? ¿Quieres
fresas?
When does it start? ¿Cuándo empieza?
How did you open the door? ¿Cómo has
abierto la puerta?
3 (in negative sentences) I don't like this kind of
music. No me gusta este tipo de música.
Rosie doesn't like spinach. A Rosie no le
gustan las espinacas.
You didn't shut the door. No cerraste la
puerta.
It doesn't matter. No importa.

4 (*referring to another verb; do is not translated*) 'Do you live here?' - 'Yes, I do.' ¿Vives aquí?' - 'Sí.'
She has more money than I do. Tiene más dinero que yo.
'I live in Charlton.' - 'So do I.' 'Vivo en Charlton.' - 'Yo también.'
'I didn't phone Gemma.' - 'Neither did I.' 'No llamé a Gemma.' - 'Yo tampoco.'

5 (*in questions*) don't you?, doesn't he?, etc ¿no?
You know Helen, don't you? Conoces a Helen, ¿no?
She left on Thursday, didn't she? Se marchó el jueves , ¿no?

6 (*to be enough*) That'll do. Así basta.
It'll do like that. Así vale.

• to **do something up**
1 (*laces, shoes*) **atar** [17]
I did my shoes up. Me até los zapatos.
2 (*a cardigan, a jacket*) **abrochar** [17]
Do your jacket up. Abróchate la chaqueta.
3 (*a house*) **arreglar** [17]

• to **do with**
1 (*to concern*) **tener** [9] que ver con
It has nothing to do with him. No tiene nada que ver con él.
2 (*to find useful*) I could do with a rest. Me vendría bien un descanso.

• to **do without something**
arreglarse [17] **sin algo**
We can do without mustard. Nos arreglaremos sin mostaza.

ᔑ **doctor** *noun*
médico *masc & fem*
Her mother's a doctor. Su madre es médico.

document *noun*
el **documento** *masc*

documentary *noun*
el **documental** *masc*

dodgems *plural noun*
the dodgems los cochecitos de choque

doesn't *short for* **does not** (*See:* **to do**)

dog *noun*
el **perro** *masc*, la **perra** *fem*

ᔑ **do-it-yourself** *noun*
el **bricolage** *masc*

dole *noun*
el **paro** *masc*
to be on the dole estar [2] en el paro

ᔑ **doll** *noun*
la **muñeca** *fem*

dollar *noun*
el **dólar** *masc*

dolphin *noun*
el **delfín** *masc*

to **dominate** *verb*
dominar [17]

Dominican *adjective & noun*
1 **dominicano** *masc*, **dominicana** *fem*
2 (*person*) un **dominicano** *masc*, una **dominicana** *fem*

> **WORD TIP** Adjectives and nouns for nationality and regional origin do not have capital letters in Spanish.

Dominican Republic *noun*
the Dominican Republic la República Dominicana

domino *noun*
la **ficha de dominó**
to play dominoes jugar [27] al dominó

donation *noun*
la **donación** *fem*

donkey *noun*
el **burro** *masc*

don't *short for* **do not** (*See:* **to do**)

ᔑ **door** *noun*
la **puerta** *fem*
to open the door abrir [46] la puerta
to shut the door cerrar [29] la puerta
to knock on the door llamar [17] a la puerta

doorbell *noun*
el **timbre** *masc*
to ring the doorbell tocar [31] el timbre
There's the doorbell. Llaman a la puerta.

doorstep *noun*
el **umbral de la puerta**

ᔑ **dormitory** *noun*
el **dormitorio** *masc*

dot *noun*
1 (*written*) el **punto** *masc*
2 (*on fabric*) el **lunar** *masc*
3 at ten on the dot a las diez en punto

ᔑ **double** *adjective* ▷ see **double** *adv, verb*
doble *masc & fem*
a double helping una ración doble
a double whisky un whisky doble

ᔑ **double** *adverb* ▷ see **double** *adj, verb*
el **doble**
double the time el doble de tiempo
double the price el doble del precio

ð to **double** *verb* ▷ see **double** *adj, adv*
doblar[17]
Double the first number. Dobla el primer número.
Sales have doubled this month. Las ventas se han doblado este mes.

double bass *noun*
el **contrabajo** *masc*
to play the double bass tocar[31] el contrabajo

double bed *noun*
la **cama de matrimonio**

double-breasted *adjective*
a double-breasted jacket una chaqueta cruzada

to **double-click** *verb*
to double-click on something **hacer**[7] **doble clic** en algo

double-decker bus *noun*
el **autobús de dos pisos**

double glazing *noun*
la **doble ventana** *fem*

double room *noun*
la **habitación doble**

doubles *noun*
(*in tennis, etc*) los **dobles** *masc plural*
to play a game of doubles jugar[27] un partido de dobles

doubt *noun* ▷ see **doubt** *verb*
la **duda** *fem*
There's no doubt about it. No hay ninguna duda al respecto.
I have my doubts. Tengo mis dudas.

to **doubt** *verb* ▷ see **doubt** *noun*
to doubt something dudar[17] algo
I doubt it. Lo dudo.
I doubt that ... dudo que ...
I doubt (that) they'll do it. Dudo que lo hagan.

> **WORD TIP** *dudar que* is followed by a verb in the subjunctive.

doubtful *adjective*
It's doubtful that ... No es seguro que ...
It's doubtful that she'll want to. No es seguro que quiera.

> **WORD TIP** *no es seguro que* is followed by a verb in the subjunctive.

dough *noun*
la **masa** *fem*

doughnut *noun*
el **donut** *masc*

ð **down** *adverb* ▷ see **down** *prep*
abajo
He's down in the cellar. Está abajo, en el sótano.
to come down bajar[17]
She came down from the bedroom. Bajó de la habitación.
to go down bajar[17]
I went down to the kitchen. Bajé a la cocina.
to sit down **sentarse**[29]
She sat down on the sofa. Se sentó en el sofá.

ð **down** *preposition* ▷ see **down** *adv*
(*nearby*) down the road un poco más allá
There's a chemist's just down the road. Hay una farmacia un poco más allá.
to walk down the street bajar[17] la calle
to run down the stairs bajar[17] corriendo la escalera

ð **downstairs** *adverb*
1 (*on the ground floor*) **abajo**
She's downstairs in the sitting-room. Está abajo en el salón.
The dog sleeps downstairs. El perro duerme abajo.
2 (*after a noun*) **de abajo**
the flat downstairs el piso de abajo
the people downstairs la gente de abajo

to **download** *verb*
(*Computers*) **descargar**[28]

to **doze** *verb*
dormitar[17]

dozen *noun*
la **docena** *fem*
a dozen eggs una docena de huevos

drag *noun* ▷ see **drag** *verb*
(*informal*) What a drag! ¡Qué rollo!
(*informal*) She's a bit of a drag. Es un poco pesada.

to **drag** *verb* ▷ see **drag** *noun*
arrastrar[17]

dragon *noun*
el **dragón** *masc*

drain *noun* ▷ see **drain** *verb*
1 (*plughole*) el **desagüe** *masc*
2 (*in a street*) la **alcantarilla** *fem*

to **drain** *verb* ▷ see **drain** *noun*
(*the vegetables*) **escurrir**[19]

drama *noun*
1 (*subject*) el **arte dramático**
2 (*informal: fuss*) He made a big drama about it. Montó una escena por eso.

dramatic *adjective*
dramático *masc*, **dramática** *fem*

draught *noun*
la **corriente de aire**

draughts *noun*
las **damas** *plural fem*
to play draughts jugar[27] a las damas

ᔖto **draw** *verb* ▷ see **draw** *noun*
1　(*with a pencil, pen, etc*) **dibujar**[17]
I can't draw horses. No sé dibujar caballos.
She can draw really well. Dibuja muy bien.
to draw a picture hacer[7] un dibujo
2　(*to close*) to draw the curtains correr[18] las
cortinas
3　(*to attract*) to draw a crowd atraer[42] a una
multitud
4　(*in a match*) **empatar**[17]
We drew three all. Empatamos a tres.
5　(*when choosing*) to draw lots for something
echar[17] algo a suertes

ᔖ**draw** *noun* ▷ see **draw** *verb*
1　(*in a match*) el **empate** *masc*
It was a draw. Fue un empate.
2　(*lottery*) el **sorteo** *masc*
· **drawback** el inconveniente

drawer *noun*
el **cajón** *masc*

ᔖ**drawing** *noun*
el **dibujo** *masc*
· **drawing pin** la chincheta

dreadful *adjective*
terrible *masc & fem*

dreadfully *adverb*
1　(*to sing, act*) **espantosamente**
2　(*very*) I'm dreadfully late. Llego tardísimo.
I'm dreadfully sorry. Lo siento muchísimo.

dream *noun* ▷ see **dream** *verb*
el **sueño** *masc*
to have a dream tener[9] un sueño
I had a horrible dream last night. Tuve un
sueño horrible anoche.

to **dream** *verb* ▷ see **dream** *noun*
soñar[24]
to dream about something soñar con algo

drenched *adjective*
empapado *masc*, **empapada** *fem*
to get drenched empaparse[17]
I got drenched on the way home. Me
empapé yendo a casa.

ᔖ**dress** *noun* ▷ see **dress** *verb*
el **vestido** *masc*

ᔖto **dress** *verb* ▷ see **dress** *noun*
vestir[57]
to dress a child vestir a un niño
·　to **dress up**
disfrazarse[22]
She dressed up as a vampire. Se disfrazó de
vampiro.

ᔖ**dressed** *adjective*
vestido *masc*, **vestida** *fem*
Is Tom dressed? ¿Está Tom vestido?
She was dressed in black trousers and a
yellow shirt. Iba vestida con unos
pantalones negros y una blusa amarilla.
to get dressed vestirse[57]

dresser *noun*
(*for dishes*) el **aparador** *masc*

dressing gown *noun*
la **bata** *fem*

ᔖ**dressing table** *noun*
el **tocador** *masc*

ᔖ**dried** *adjective*
seco *masc*, **seca** *fem*
dried apricots albaricoques secos

dryer *noun* ▷ **drier**

to **drift** *verb*
1　(*boat*) **ir**[8] a la deriva
2　(*snow*) **amontonarse**[17]

drill *noun* ▷ see **drill** *verb*
(*tool*) la **taladradora** *fem*

to **drill** *verb* ▷ see **drill** *noun*
(*a hole*) **hacer**[7] **un agujero en**
He drilled a hole in the wall. Hizo un
agujero en la pared.

ᔖ**drink** *noun* ▷ see **drink** *verb*
1　(*any liquid*) la **bebida** *fem*
a hot drink una bebida caliente
a cold drink un refresco
2　(*alcoholic*) Would you like a drink? ¿Te
apetece beber algo?
to go out for a drink salir[63] a tomar una
copa

ᔖto **drink** *verb* ▷ see **drink** *noun*
beber[18]
He drank a glass of water. Bebió un vaso de
agua.

ᔖ**drive** *noun* ▷ see **drive** *verb*
1　(*outing in a car*) to go for a drive ir[8] a dar
una vuelta en coche
2　(*path leading to a house*) la **entrada para
coches**

a
b
c
.d
e
f
g
h
i
j
k
l
m
n
o
p
q
r
s
t
u
v
w
x
y
z

♂ to **drive** *verb* ▷ see **drive** *noun*

1 (*a car, a taxi, a bus, etc*) **conducir** [60]
to drive a car conducir un coche
She drives very fast. Conduce muy rápido.
I'd like to learn to drive. Me gustaría
aprender a conducir.
Can you drive? ¿Sabes conducir?

2 (*to go somewhere in a car, taxi, bus, etc*) **ir** [8] **en coche**
We drove to Seville. Fuimos en coche a
Sevilla.

3 to drive somebody (to a place) **llevar** [17]
en coche a alguien (a un sitio)
Mum drove me to the station. Mamá me
llevó en coche a la estación.
to drive somebody home **llevar** [17] a
alguien a casa en coche

♂ **driver** *noun*

1 (*of a car, taxi or bus*) el **conductor** *masc*, la
conductora *fem*

2 (*of a racing car*) el & la **piloto** *masc & fem*

driving instructor *noun*
el **instructor de autoescuela**, la
instructora de autoescuela

driving lesson *noun*
la **clase de conducir**

♂ **driving licence** *noun*
el **permiso de conducir**

driving school *noun*
la **autoescuela** *fem*

driving test *noun*
el **examen de conducir**
to take your driving test presentarse [17] al
examen de conducir
Jenny's passed her driving test. Jenny ha
aprobado el examen de conducir.
He's failed his driving test. Ha suspendido
el examen de conducir.

♂ **drizzle** *noun*
la **llovizna** *fem*

♂ **drop** *noun* ▷ see **drop** *verb*
la **gota** *fem*

♂ to **drop** *verb* ▷ see **drop** *noun*

1 (*an object*) I dropped my glasses. Se me
cayeron las gafas.
Careful, don't drop it! ¡Cuidado, que no se
te caiga!

2 (*a course, a subject, a topic*) **dejar** [17]
I'm going to drop history next year. Voy a
dejar la historia el próximo año.

3 (*a person*) **dejar** [17]
Could you drop me at the station? ¿Me
podrías dejar en la estación?

4 (*as a warning*) Drop it! ¡Déjalo ya!

♂ **drought** *noun*
la **sequía** *fem*

♂ to **drown** *verb*
ahogarse [28]
She drowned in the lake. Se ahogó en el
lago.

♂ **drug** *noun*

1 (*medicine*) la **medicina** *fem*

2 (*illegal*) **drugs** las drogas
to be on drugs drogarse [28]

• **drug abuse** el consumo de drogas
• **drug addict** el drogadicto, la drogadicta
• **drug addiction** la drogadicción

drum *noun*
el **tambor** *masc*
(*in a band*) **drums** la batería *fem*
to play (the) drums tocar [31] la batería

• **drum kit** la batería

drummer *noun*
el & la **batería** *masc & fem*

drunk *adjective* ▷ see **drunk** *noun*
borracho *masc*, **borracha** *fem*

drunk *noun* ▷ see **drunk** *adj*
el **borracho** *masc*, la **borracha** *fem*

♂ **dry** *adjective* ▷ see **dry** *verb*
seco *masc*, **seca** *fem*

♂ to **dry** *verb* ▷ see **dry** *adj*

1 (*the plates, the dishes*) **secar** [31]
to dry the dishes secar los platos
to dry your hair secarse el pelo
to dry oneself secarse
I'm going to dry my hair. Me voy a secar el
pelo.
It took ages to dry. Tardó muchísimo en
secarse.

2 (*washing, paint*) to let something dry dejar
[17] que algo se seque

• **dry cleaner's** la tintorería

dryer *noun*

1 (*for hair*) el **secador de pelo** *masc*

2 (*for clothing*) la **secadora** *fem*

dual carriageway *noun*
la **autovía** *fem*

dubbed *adjective*
a dubbed film una película doblada

♂ **duck** *noun*
el **pato** *masc*, la **pata** *fem*

due *adjective*

1 (*expected*) Paul's due back soon. Paul tiene
que volver pronto.
What time is the train due? ¿Cuándo llega
el próximo tren?

to be due to do something tener [9] que
hacer algo
We're due to leave on Thursday. Tenemos
que salir el jueves.
2 (*because of*) **due to** debido a
**The match has been cancelled due to bad
weather.** El partido ha sido cancelado
debido al mal tiempo.

duke *noun*
el **duque** *masc*

dull *adjective*
1 (*boring*) **aburrido** *masc*, **aburrida** *fem*
2 (*not sunny*) **dull weather** tiempo gris
It's a dull day today. Hoy hace un día muy
gris.

dumb *adjective*
1 (*unable to talk*) **mudo** *masc*, **muda** *fem*
to be deaf and dumb ser [1] sordomudo
2 (*stupid*) **tonto** *masc*, **tonta** *fem* (*informal*)
He asked some dumb questions. Hizo unas
preguntas muy tontas.

dummy *noun*
(*for a baby*) el **chupete** *masc*

to **dump** *verb*
1 (*rubbish*) **tirar** [17]
2 (*informal: a person*) **plantar** [17]
She's dumped her boyfriend. Ha plantado
a su novio.

dune *noun*
la **duna** *fem*

dungarees *plural noun*
el **pantalón de peto**

dungeon *noun*
la **mazmorra** *fem*

ᔑ **during** *preposition*
durante
during the night durante la noche
I saw her during the holidays. La vi durante
las vacaciones.

dusk *noun*
el **anochecer** *masc*
at dusk al anochecer

dust *noun* ▷ see **dust** *verb*
el **polvo** *masc*

to **dust** *verb* ▷ see **dust** *noun*
quitar [17] **el polvo a**
to dust the table quitarle el polvo a la mesa

dustbin *noun*
el **cubo** *masc* **de la basura**
to put something in the dustbin tirar [17]
algo al cubo de la basura

dustman *noun*
el **basurero** *masc*

dusty *adjective*
cubierto de polvo *masc*, **cubierta de
polvo** *fem*
The table was very dusty. La mesa estaba
toda cubierta de polvo.

Dutch *adjective & noun*
1 **holandés** *masc*, **holandesa** *fem*
2 (*the people*) **the Dutch** los holandeses
3 (*the language*) **el holandés** *masc*

WORD TIP Adjectives and nouns for nationality
and regional origin do not have capital letters in
Spanish.

duty *noun*
1 el **deber** *masc*
to have a duty to do something tener [9] el
deber de hacer algo
You have a duty to inform us. Tienes el
deber de informarnos.
2 (*nurses, doctors, chemists*) **to be on duty** estar
[2] de guardia
3 (*police*) **to be on duty** estar [2] de servicio
4 **to be on night duty** tener [9] el turno de
noche

duty-free *adjective*
libre de impuestos *masc & fem*
the duty-free shops las tiendas libres de
impuestos
duty-free purchases artículos libres de
impuestos

duvet *noun*
el **edredón** *masc*
· **duvet cover** la funda de edredón

DVD *noun*
el **DVD** *masc*
· **DVD player** el lector de DVD
· **DVD recorder** el grabador de DVD

dwarf *noun*
el **enano** *masc*, la **enana** *fem*

dye *noun* ▷ see **dye** *verb*
el **tinte** *masc*

to **dye** *verb* ▷ see **dye** *noun*
teñir [65]
to dye your hair teñirse el pelo
I'm going to dye my hair pink. Me voy a
teñir el pelo de rosa.

dynamic *adjective*
dinámico *masc*, **dinámica** *fem*

dyslexia *noun*
la **dislexia** *fem*

dyslexic *adjective*
disléxico *masc*, **disléxica** *fem*

E e

a
b
c
d
e
f
g
h
i
j
k
l
m
n
o
p
q
r
s
t
u
v
w
x
y
z

ᵍ each *adjective, pronoun*
1 (*with a noun*) **cada** *masc & fem*
   each time cada vez
   each boy cada chico
2 (*standing for a noun*) **cada uno** *masc*, **cada una** *fem*
   They each have a computer. Cada uno tiene un ordenador.
   She gave us an apple each. Nos dio una manzana a cada uno.
   each of you cada uno de vosotros
   Each of us brought two pounds. Cada uno de nosotros trajo dos libras.
   The tickets cost ten pounds each. Las entradas cuestan diez libras cada una.
3 **each other**
   We know each other. Nos conocemos.
   Do you see each other often? ¿Os veis a menudo?
   They love each other. Se quieren.

   WORD TIP *each other* is usually translated into Spanish using a reflexive verb with: *nos, os, se.*

eagle *noun*
   el **águila** *fem*

   WORD TIP *águila* takes *el* or *un* in the singular even though it is feminine.

ᵍ ear *noun*
1 (*outer ear*) la **oreja** *fem*
2 (*inner ear*) el **oído** *masc*

earache *noun*
   to have earache tener[9] dolor de oídos

ᵍ early *adjective, adverb*
1 (*before the usual time*) **temprano**
   Come early. Ven temprano.
   We should have started earlier. Deberíamos haber empezado más temprano.
   to have an early night acostarse[24] temprano
   We're making an early start. Vamos a salir temprano.
2 (*before a set time*) **pronto**
   Alice likes to arrive early. A Alice le gusta llegar pronto.
   We're early, the train doesn't leave until ten. Hemos llegado pronto, el tren no sale hasta las diez.
3 (*at the beginning of a period*) **primero** *masc*, **primera** *fem*
   in the early months of 2006 en los primeros meses del 2006

in the early afternoon a primera hora de la tarde
in the early hours of the morning de madrugada
4 (*in the morning*) **temprano**
   I get up early. Me levanto temprano.
   It's too early. Es demasiado temprano.
5 (*a while ago*) **earlier** hace un rato
   Your brother phoned earlier. Tu hermano llamó hace un rato.

to earn *verb*
   (*money*) **ganar**[17]
   Richard earns ten pounds an hour. Richard gana diez libras por hora.

earnings *plural noun*
   los **ingresos** *plural masc*

earphones *plural noun*
   los **auriculares** *plural masc*

earring *noun*
   el **pendiente** *masc*, (*Latin America*) el **arete** *masc*

earth *noun*
   la **tierra** *fem*
   life on earth la vida en la tierra
• **earthquake** el terremoto

easily *adverb*
1 (*with no difficulty*) **con facilidad**
2 (*by far*) **con mucho**
   He's easily the best. Es con mucho el mejor.

ᵍ east *adjective, adverb* ▷ see **east** *noun*
   este *invariable masc & fem*
   the east side el lado este
   the east winds los vientos del este
   east of Seville al este de Sevilla
   to travel east viajar[17] hacia el este

   WORD TIP *este* never changes.

ᵍ east *noun* ▷ see **east** *adj, adv*
   el **este** *masc*
   in the east en el este

Easter *noun*
1 (*day*) **Pascua** *fem*
2 (*holiday time*) **Semana Santa** *noun*
   They're coming at Easter. Vienen en Semana Santa.
• **Easter Day** el Domingo de Pascua
• **Easter egg** el huevo de Pascua

ᵹ **eastern** adjective
este invariable masc & fem
Eastern Europe Europa del Este

ᵹ **easy** adjective
fácil masc & fem
It's easy! ¡Es fácil!
It was easy to decide. Fue fácil decidir.

ᵹ to **eat** verb
1 (a fruit, vegetables, bread) **comer** [18]
He was eating a banana. Estaba comiendo un plátano.
We're going to have something to eat. Vamos a comer algo.
2 (a meal) **tomar** [17]
We were eating breakfast. Estábamos tomando el desayuno.
3 to eat out comer [18] fuera

echo noun ▷ see **echo** verb
el **eco** masc

to **echo** verb ▷ see **echo** noun
hacer [7] eco

eclipse noun
el **eclipse** masc

ecological adjective
ecológico masc, **ecológica** fem

ecologist noun
el & la **ecologista** masc & fem

ecology noun
la **ecología** fem

economic adjective
1 (relating to economics) **económico** masc, **económica** fem
2 (profitable) **rentable** masc & fem

economical adjective
económico masc, **económica** fem
It's more economical to buy a big one. Sale más económico comprar uno grande.

economics noun
la **economía** fem

to **economize** verb
economizar [22]
to economize on something economizar algo
We economized on food. Economizamos la comida.

economy noun
la **economía** fem

Ecuador noun
Ecuador masc

Ecuadorian adjective & noun
1 **ecuatoriano** masc, **ecuatoriana** fem
2 un **ecuatoriano** masc, una **ecuatoriana** fem
the Ecuadorians los ecuatorianos

WORD TIP Adjectives and nouns for nationality and regional origin do not have capital letters in Spanish.

eczema noun
el **eczema** masc

ᵹ **edge** noun
1 (of a table, a plate, a cliff) el **borde** masc
the edge of the table el borde de la mesa
2 (of a river, a lake) la **orilla** fem
at the edge of the lake en la orilla del lago
3 (showing nervousness) to be on edge estar [2] nervioso

edible adjective
comestible masc & fem

Edinburgh noun
Edimburgo masc

to **edit** verb
editar [17]

editor noun
1 (of books) el **editor** masc, la **editora** noun
2 (of a newspaper) el **director** masc, la **directora** noun
3 (Computers) el **editor** masc

to **educate** verb
educar [31]

educated adjective
culto masc, **culta** fem

education noun
la **educación** fem

educational adjective
educativo masc, **educativa** fem

effect noun
el **efecto** masc
the effect of the accident el efecto del accidente
The special effects were great. Los efectos especiales eran fenomenales.
to have an effect on something afectar [17] a algo
It had a good effect on the whole family. Afectó positivamente a toda la familia.

effective adjective
eficaz masc & fem

efficient adjective
eficiente masc & fem

a
b
c
d
e
f
g
h
i
j
k
l
m
n
o
p
q
r
s
t
u
v
w
x
y
z

effort *noun*
   el **esfuerzo** *masc*
   to make an effort hacer [7] un esfuerzo
   Jess made an effort to help us. Jess hizo un esfuerzo para ayudarnos.
   He didn't even make the effort to apologize. Ni siquiera se molestó en disculparse.
   It's not worth the effort. No merece la pena.

e.g. *abbreviation*
   p.ej., por ejemplo

♪ **egg** *noun*
   el **huevo** *masc*
   a dozen eggs una docena de huevos
   two boiled eggs dos huevos pasados por agua
- **eggcup** la huevera
- **eggshell** la cáscara de huevo
- **egg white** la clara de huevo
- **egg yolk** la yema de huevo

♪ **eight** *number*
   ocho *invariable number*
   Rosie's eight. Rosie tiene ocho años.
   It's eight o'clock. Son las ocho.

♪ **eighteen** *number*
   dieciocho *invariable number*
   Kate's eighteen. Kate tiene dieciocho años.

♪ **eighth** *adjective* ▷ see **eighth** *noun*
   octavo *masc*, **octava** *fem*
   on the eighth floor en la octava planta

♪ **eighth** *noun* ▷ see **eighth** *adj*
   1 (*fraction*) **an eighth** una octava parte
   2 (*when saying dates*) **the eighth of July** el ocho de julio

♪ **eighties** *plural noun*
   the eighties los años ochenta
   in the eighties en los años ochenta

♪ **eighty** *number*
   ochenta *invariable number*
   eighty-five ochenta y cinco
   She's eighty. Tiene ochenta años.

Eire *noun*
   Eire *masc*, **la República de Irlanda**

♪ **either** *conjunction* ▷ see **either** *pron*
   1 (*to give alternatives*) **either … or** o … o
   You either pay or return it. O pagas o lo devuelves.
   I'll phone either Thursday or Friday. Llamaré o el jueves o el viernes.
   either one or the other o uno u otro

   2 (*when in English you say not … either*) **He doesn't want to go either.** Él tampoco quiere ir.
   I don't know them either. Yo tampoco los conozco.

♪ **either** *pronoun* ▷ see **either** *conj*
   1 (*giving alternatives*) **Choose either (of them).** Elige cualquiera (de los dos).
   2 (*both*) **Either is possible.** Las dos cosas son posibles.
   I don't like either (of them). No me gusta ninguno (de los dos).

elastic *adjective* ▷ see **elastic** *noun*
   elástico *masc*, **elástica** *fem*

elastic *noun* ▷ see **elastic** *adj*
   el **elástico** *masc*
- **elastic band** la goma elástica

♪ **elbow** *noun*
   el **codo** *masc*

♪ **elder** *adjective*
   mayor *masc & fem*
   her elder brother su hermano mayor

elderly *adjective* ▷ see **elderly** *noun*
   an elderly man un anciano
   an elderly woman una anciana
   an elderly couple una pareja de ancianos

elderly *plural noun* ▷ see **elderly** *adj*
   the elderly los ancianos

♪ **eldest** *adjective*
   mayor *masc & fem*
   her eldest brother su hermano mayor

to elect *verb*
   elegir [48]
   She has been elected. Ha sido elegida.

♪ **election** *noun*
   las **elecciones** *plural fem*
   in the election en las elecciones
   to call a general election convocar [31] elecciones generales

electric *adjective*
   eléctrico *masc*, **eléctrica** *fem*

electrical *adjective*
   eléctrico *masc*, **eléctrica** *fem*

electrician *noun*
   el & la **electricista** *masc & fem*

♪ **electricity** *noun*
   la **electricidad** *fem*
   to turn off the electricity desconectar [17] la corriente

a b c d e f g h i j k l m n o p q r s t u v w x y z

electronic *adjective*
  electrónico *masc*, **electrónica** *fem*
· **electronic mail** el correo electrónico

electronics *noun*
  la **electrónica** *fem*

ƒ **elegant** *adjective*
  elegante *masc & fem*

element *noun*
  el **elemento** *masc*

elephant *noun*
  el **elefante** *masc*

ƒ **eleven** *number*
  once *invariable number*
  Josh is eleven. Josh tiene once años.
  It's eleven o'clock. Son las once.

ƒ **eleventh** *adjective* ▷ see **eleventh** *noun*
  onceavo *masc*, **onceava** *fem*
  on the eleventh floor en la onceava planta

ƒ **eleventh** *noun* ▷ see **eleventh** *adj*
  the eleventh of May el once de mayo

to **eliminate** *verb*
  eliminar [17]

else *adverb*
1 (*to ask questions and say no*) **más**
  Who else? ¿Quién más?
  What else? ¿Qué más?
  Would you like something else? ¿Quieres otra cosa?
  nothing else nada más
  I don't want anything else. No quiero nada más.
2 (*in expressions*) **somebody else** otra persona
  Somebody else must have done it. Lo ha debido hacer otra persona.
  something else otra cosa
  everybody else todos los demás
  everything else todo lo demás
  somewhere else en otra parte
  or else si no
  Hurry up, or else we'll be late. Date prisa, que si no vamos a llegar tarde.

ƒ **email** *noun* ▷ see **email** *verb*
1 (*system*) el **correo electrónico**
  to be on email tener [9] una dirección de correo electrónico
2 (*message*) el **email**, el **mail**, el **correo electrónico**
  to send somebody an email mandarle [17] un email a alguien

ƒ to **email** *verb* ▷ see **email** *noun*
1 (*a message*) **enviar** [32] **por correo electrónico**

2 (*a person*) **to email somebody** mandarle [17] un mail a alguien
· **email address** la dirección de correo electrónico

embarrassed *adjective*
  I was terribly embarrassed. Me daba mucha vergüenza.
  She feels a bit embarrassed. Le da un poco de vergüenza.

embarrassing *adjective*
  (*situation, silence*) **violento** *masc*, **violenta** *fem*
  How embarrassing! ¡Qué vergüenza!

embarrassment *noun*
  la **vergüenza** *fem*

embassy *noun*
  la **embajada** *fem*
  the Spanish Embassy la embajada española

to **embroider** *verb*
  bordar [17]

embroidery *noun*
  el **bordado** *masc*

ƒ **emergency** *noun*
1 (*dangerous situation*) la **emergencia** *fem*
  In an emergency, break the glass. En caso de emergencia, rompa el cristal.
  It's an emergency! ¡Es una emergencia!
2 (*medical*) la **urgencia** *fem*
  an emergency operation una operación de urgencia
· **emergency exit** la salida de emergencia
· **emergency landing** el aterrizaje forzoso

emotion *noun*
  la **emoción** *fem*

emotional *adjective*
1 (*person*) **to be emotional** estar [2] emocionado
  to get emotional emocionarse [17]
  She got quite emotional. Se emocionó mucho.
2 (*speech, occasion*) **emotivo** *masc*, **emotiva** *fem*

emperor *noun*
  el **emperador** *masc*

emphasis *noun*
  el **énfasis** *masc*

to **emphasize** *verb*
  recalcar [31]
  He emphasized that it wasn't compulsory. Recalcó que no era obligatorio.

empire *noun*
　el **imperio** *masc*
　the Roman Empire el imperio romano

to **employ** *verb*
　emplear [17]

ℰ **employee** *noun*
　el **empleado** *masc*, la **empleada** *fem*

employer *noun*
　el **patrón** *masc*, la **patrona** *fem*

employment *noun*
　el **empleo** *masc*

empress *noun*
　la **emperatriz** *fem*

ℰ **empty** *adjective* ▷ see **empty** *verb*
　vacío *masc*, **vacía** *fem*
　an empty bottle una botella vacía
　The room was empty. La habitación estaba
　vacía.

to **empty** *verb* ▷ see **empty** *adj*
　vaciar [32]
　I emptied the jug into the sink. Vacié la jarra
　en el fregadero.

enchanting *adjective*
　encantador *masc*, **encantadora** *fem*

to **enclose** *verb*
　(*with a letter*) **adjuntar** [17]
　Please find enclosed a cheque. Se adjunta
　un cheque.

encore *noun*
　el **bis** *masc*
　Encore! ¡Otra!

to **encourage** *verb*
　animar [17]
　to encourage somebody to do something
　animar a alguien a hacer algo
　Mum encouraged me to try again. Mamá
　me animó a intentarlo otra vez.

encouragement *noun*
　el **ánimo** *masc*

encouraging *adjective*
　alentador *masc*, **alentadora** *fem*

encyclopedia *noun*
　la **enciclopedia** *fem*

ℰ **end** *noun* ▷ see **end** *verb*
　1　(*the last part*) el **final** *masc*
　　at the end of the film al final de la película
　　by the end of the day al final del día
　　In the end I went home. Al final me fui a
　　casa.
　　at the end of the year a finales de año

Sally's coming at the end of June. Sally
viene a finales de junio.
　2　(*in a book, film*) 'The End' 'Fin'
　3　(*of a table, garden, stick*) el **extremo** *masc*
　　Hold the other end. Sujeta el otro extremo.
　4　(*of a street, road*) el **final** *masc*
　　at the end of the street al final de la calle
　5　(*of a football pitch*) el **lado** *masc*
　　to change ends cambiar [17] de lado

ℰ to **end** *verb* ▷ see **end** *noun*
　1　(*to make something finish*) **poner** [11] **fin a**
　　They've ended the strike. Han puesto fin a
　　la huelga.
　2　(*to finish*) **terminar** [17]
　　The day ended with a dinner. El día terminó
　　con una cena.
　•　to **end up**
　　terminar [17]
　　We ended up taking a taxi. Terminamos
　　cogiendo un taxi.
　　Ross ended up in Buenos Aires. Ross
　　terminó en Buenos Aires.

endangered *adjective*
　en peligro
　an endangered species una especie en vías
　de extinción

ending *noun*
　el **final** *masc*

endless *adjective*
　interminable *masc & fem*

enemy *noun*
　el **enemigo** *masc*, la **enemiga** *fem*
　to make enemies hacer [7] enemigos

energetic *adjective*
　energético *masc*, **energética** *fem*

energy *noun*
　la **energía** *fem*

ℰ **engaged** *adjective*
　1　(*to be married*) **prometido** *masc*, **prometida**
　　fem
　　They're engaged. Están prometidos.
　　Luisa's engaged. Luisa está prometida.
　　to get engaged prometerse [18]
　2　(*on the telephone*) to be engaged estar [2]
　　comunicando
　　It's engaged, I'll ring later. Está
　　comunicando, llamaré más tarde.
　3　(*toilet*) **ocupado** *masc*, **ocupada** *fem*

engagement *noun*
　el **compromiso** *masc*
　•　**engagement ring** el anillo de compromiso

ℰ **engine** *noun*
　1　(*in a car*) el **motor** *masc*
　2　(*of a train*) la **locomotora** *fem*

ˢ **engineer** *noun*
1 (*repair person*) el & la **técnico** *masc & fem*
2 (*graduate*) el **ingeniero** *masc*, la **ingeniera** *fem*

ˢ **England** *noun*
Inglaterra *fem*
I'm from England. Soy inglés (*boy speaking*)., Soy inglesa (*girl speaking.*)

ˢ **English** *adjective* ▷ see **English** *noun*
inglés *masc*, **inglesa** *fem*
the English team el equipo inglés

ˢ **English** *noun* ▷ see **English** *adj*
1 (*the language*) el **inglés** *masc*
Do you speak English? ¿Hablas inglés?
He answered in English. Contestó en inglés.
my English class mi clase de inglés
our English teacher nuestro profesor de inglés
2 (*the people*) the English los ingleses

WORD TIP Adjectives and nouns for nationality, regional origin, and language do not have capital letters in Spanish.

English Channel *noun*
the English Channel el Canal de la Mancha

Englishman *noun*
un **inglés** *masc*

Englishwoman *noun*
una **inglesa** *fem*

ˢ to **enjoy** *verb*
1 **disfrutar** [17] **de**
Did you enjoy the party? ¿Disfrutaste de la fiesta?
We really enjoyed the concert. Disfrutamos mucho del concierto.
I enjoy swimming. Me gusta nadar.
Do you enjoy living in York? ¿Te gusta vivir en York?
2 to enjoy yourself **divertirse** [14]
We really enjoyed ourselves. Nos divertimos muchísimo.
Did you enjoy yourself? ¿Te divertiste? (*informal*)
Did you enjoy yourselves? ¿Os divertisteis? (*informal*)

enjoyable *adjective*
agradable *masc & fem*

to **enlarge** *verb*
ampliar [32]

enlargement *noun*
(*of a photo*) la **ampliación** *fem*

enormous *adjective*
enorme *masc & fem*

ˢ **enough** *adjective, adverb, pronoun*
1 (*food, money, etc*) **suficiente** *masc & fem*
There's enough for everyone. Hay suficiente para todos.
Is there enough bread? ¿Hay suficiente pan?
There aren't enough ice-creams. No hay suficientes helados.
They don't pay me enough. No me pagan lo suficiente.
2 (*with an adjective, adverb*) **lo suficientemente**
big enough lo suficientemente grande
slowly enough lo suficientemente despacio
3 (*in exclamations*) That's enough! ¡Basta!
I've had enough! ¡Ya estoy harto!

to **enquire** *verb*
informarse [17]
I'm going to enquire about the trains. Voy a informarme sobre los trenes.

enquiry *noun*
to make enquiries about something pedir [57] información sobre algo

to **enrol** *verb*
matricularse [17]
I want to enrol on the course. Quiero matricularme en el curso.

ˢ to **enter** *verb*
1 (*a room, a building*) **entrar** [17] **en**
We all entered the church. Todos entramos en la iglesia.
2 to enter for an exam presentarse [17] a un examen
I'm entering for seven GCSEs. Me voy a presentar a siete asignaturas de GCSE.

to **entertain** *verb*
1 (*to keep amused*) **entretener** [9]
something to entertain the children algo para entretener a los niños
2 (*to have people round*) **invitar** [17] **a gente**
They don't entertain much. No invitan a mucha gente.

entertaining *adjective*
entretenido *masc*, **entretenida** *fem*

entertainment *noun*
(*fun*) el **entretenimiento** *masc*
There wasn't much entertainment in the evenings. Por las noches no había mucho entretenimiento.
There's plenty of entertainment in Tossa. Hay muchas atracciones en Tossa.
· **entertainment guide** la guía del ocio

a
b
c
d
e
f
g
h
i
j
k
l
m
n
o
p
q
r
s
t
u
v
w
x
y
z

enthusiasm *noun*
el **entusiasmo** *masc*

enthusiast *noun*
el **apasionado** *masc*, la **apasionada** *fem*
to be a rugby enthusiast ser [1] un apasionado del rugby

enthusiastic *adjective*
entusiasta *masc & fem*

entire *adjective*
entero *masc*, **entera** *fem*
the entire class la clase entera

entirely *adverb*
completamente

entrance *noun*
la **entrada** *fem*

entry *noun*
la **entrada** *fem*
'No entry' 'Prohibida la entrada'
· **entry phone** el portero automático

envelope *noun*
el **sobre** *masc*

envious *adjective*
envidioso *masc*, **envidiosa** *fem*
to be envious of something tener [9] envidia de algo
He's envious of my exam results. Tiene envidia de las notas de mis exámenes.

environment *noun*
el **medio ambiente**

environmental *adjective*
medioambiental *masc & fem*

environment-friendly *adjective*
ecológico *masc*, **ecológica** *fem*

envy *noun*
la **envidia** *fem*

epidemic *noun*
la **epidemia** *fem*

epilepsy *noun*
la **epilepsia** *fem*
to have epilepsy tener [9] epilepsia

episode *noun*
el **episodio** *masc*

equal *adjective* ▷ see **equal** *verb*
igual *masc & fem*
in equal quantities en cantidades iguales
equal opportunities la igualdad de oportunidades

to **equal** *verb* ▷ see **equal** *adj*
ser [1] **igual a**

equality *noun*
la **igualdad** *fem*

to **equalize** *verb*
empatar [17]
They equalized in the last minute.
Empataron en el último minuto.

equally *adverb*
(*to share*) **en partes iguales**
We divided it equally. Lo dividimos en partes iguales.

equator *noun*
el **ecuador** *masc*

to **equip** *verb*
equipar [17]
well equipped for the walk bien equipado para la marcha

equipment *noun*
1 (*for sport*) los **artículos deportivos**
2 (*in an office, a lab*) el **material** *masc*

equivalent *adjective*
to be equivalent to something ser [1] equivalente a algo

error *noun*
1 (*in spelling, typing*) la **falta** *fem*
a spelling error una falta de ortografía
2 (*in maths, on a computer*) el **error** *masc*

escalator *noun*
la **escalera mecánica**

escape *noun* ▷ see **escape** *verb*
(*from prison*) la **fuga** *fem*

to **escape** *verb* ▷ see **escape** *noun*
1 (*prisoners*) **fugarse** [28]
2 (*dogs, horses*) **escaparse** [17]

escort *noun*
la **escolta** *fem*
a police escort una escolta policial

♂ **especially** *adverb*
especialmente

essay *noun*
la **redacción** *fem*
an essay on pollution una redacción sobre la contaminación

essential *adjective*
esencial *masc & fem*
It's essential to reply quickly. Es esencial responder rápidamente.

estate *noun*
1 (*houses*) la **urbanización** *fem*
2 (*of a landowner*) la **propiedad** *fem*
· **estate agent's** la agencia inmobiliaria
· **estate car** la ranchera

estimate *noun* ▷ see **estimate** *verb*

1 (*quote for work*) el **presupuesto** *masc*
2 (*rough guess*) el **cálculo aproximado**

to **estimate** *verb* ▷ see **estimate** *noun*

1 **calcular** [17]
2 the estimated time of arrival la hora prevista de llegada

etc. *abbreviation*
etcétera, etc

ethnic *adjective*
étnico *masc*, **étnica** *fem*
an ethnic minority una minoría étnica

EU *noun*
(= *European Union*) la **EU** *fem*, la **Unión Europea**

ℰ **euro** *noun*
el **euro** *masc*
The euro is divided into a hundred cents. El euro se divide en cien céntimos.

Europe *noun*
Europa *fem*

ℰ **European** *adjective & noun*
1 **europeo** *masc*, **europea** *fem*
2 (*person*) un **europeo** *masc*, una **europea** *fem*

WORD TIP Adjectives and nouns for nationality and regional origin do not have capital letters in Spanish.

• **European Union** la Unión Europea

eurozone *noun*
la **eurozona** *fem*

to **evaporate** *verb*
evaporarse [17]

ℰ **eve** *noun*
la **víspera**
Christmas Eve la Nochebuena
New Year's Eve la Nochevieja

ℰ **even** *adjective* ▷ see **even** *adv*
1 (*surface, layer*) **plano** *masc*, **plana** *fem*
2 (*number*) **par** *masc & fem*
Six is an even number. Seis es un número par.
3 (*having the same score*) **igualado** *masc*, **igualada** *fem*
Lee and Tony are even. Lee y Tony están igualados.

ℰ **even** *adverb* ▷ see **even** *adj*
1 (*to show something surprising*) **incluso**
Even I could do it. Incluso yo podría hacerlo.
even if incluso si
even if they arrive incluso si llegan
even so aun así

Even so, we had a good time. Aun así lo pasamos bien.
even though aunque
Even though I had a headache, I enjoyed myself. Aunque tenía un dolor de cabeza, me divertí.
2 (*in comparisons*) **aún**
even more difficult aún más difícil
even faster aún más rápido
even more than aún más que
I liked the song even more than their last one. La canción me gustó aún más que la anterior.
3 (*in negative sentences, after without*) **ni siquiera**
Even Lisa didn't like it. Ni siquiera a Lisa le gustó.
without even asking sin ni siquiera preguntar
not even ni siquiera
I don't like animals, not even dogs. No me gustan los animales, ni siquiera los perros.

ℰ **evening** *noun*
1 (*before dark*) la **tarde** *fem*
this evening esta tarde
at six o'clock in the evening a las seis de la tarde
tomorrow evening mañana por la tarde
on Thursday evening el jueves por la tarde
the evening before la tarde anterior
every evening cada tarde
Good evening! ¡Buenas tardes!
the evening meal la cena
2 (*after dark*) la **noche** *fem*
this evening esta noche
at ten in the evening a las diez de la noche
tomorrow evening mañana por la noche
on Thursday evening el jueves por la noche
the evening before la noche anterior
every evening cada noche
Good evening! ¡Buenas noches!
I work in the evening(s). Trabajo por las noches.
3 (*event*) la **velada** *fem*
an evening with Madonna una velada con Madonna
• **evening class** la clase nocturna

ℰ **event** *noun*
1 (*something that happened*) el **acontecimiento** *masc*
2 (*in athletics*) la **prueba** *fem*
the track events las pruebas de atletismo

ℰ indicates key words   471

eventful *adjective*
lleno de incidentes *masc*, **llena de incidentes** *fem*

eventually *adverb*
finalmente

⚡ **ever** *adverb*

1 (*to ask a question*) **alguna vez**
Have you ever been to Spain? ¿Has estado alguna vez en España?
Have you ever noticed that? ¿Lo notaste alguna vez?

2 (*in negative statements*) **nunca**
hardly ever casi nunca
No one ever came. Nunca vino nadie.

3 (*always*) **siempre**
as cheerful as ever tan contento como siempre
the same as ever como siempre
more slowly than ever más despacio que nunca
ever since desde entonces
And it's been raining ever since. Y ha estado lloviendo desde entonces.

⚡ **every** *adjective*

1 (*each*) **todos los** *masc*, **todas las** *fem*
every day todos los días
every Monday todos los lunes
Every house has a garden. Todas las casas tienen jardín.
I've seen every one of his films. He visto todas sus películas.

2 (*showing repetition*) **cada** *masc & fem*
every ten kilometres cada diez kilómetros
every time cada vez
every now and then de vez en cuando
every other day un día sí y otro no

⚡ **everybody** *pronoun*
todo el mundo
everybody knows that ... todo el mundo sabe que ...
everybody else todos los demás

⚡ **everyone** *pronoun* ▷ **everybody**

⚡ **everything** *pronoun*
todo
everything you said todo lo que dijiste
everything else todo lo demás
Everything's ready. Todo está listo.
Everything's fine. Está todo bien.

⚡ **everywhere** *adverb*
por todas partes
There was mud everywhere. Había barro por todas partes.
everywhere she went a todos los sitios a los que fue

Everywhere else is closed. Todos los demás sitios están cerrados.

evidently *adverb*
obviamente

evil *adjective* ▷ **see evil** *noun*
malvado *masc*, **malvada** *fem*

evil *noun* ▷ **see evil** *adj*
el mal *masc*

exact *adjective*
exacto *masc*, **exacta** *fem*
the exact amount la cantidad exacta
It's the exact opposite. Es exactamente lo contrario.

exactly *adverb*
exactamente
They're exactly the same age. Tienen exactamente la misma edad.
Yes, exactly Exacto.

to **exaggerate** *verb*
exagerar[17]

exaggeration *noun*
la exageración *fem*

⚡ **exam** *noun*
el examen *masc*
a history exam un examen de historia
to take an exam presentarse[17] a un examen
I'm taking five exams. Me presento a cinco exámenes.
to pass an exam aprobar[24] un examen
I passed all my exams. Aprobé todos mis exámenes.
to fail an exam suspender[18] un examen
I failed the chemistry exam. Suspendí el examen de química.

exams

Pupils are assessed and graded regularly by their teachers. They are expected to pass all subjects. If they fail they have to retake (*revalidar*). At 16 all students receive a certificate stating the number of years studied and their grades.

examination *noun*
el examen *masc*

to **examine** *verb*
examinar[17]

examiner *noun*
el examinador *masc*, **la examinadora** *fem*

⚡ **example** *noun*
el ejemplo *masc*
for example por ejemplo
to set a good example dar[4] buen ejemplo

ꞩ **excellent** *adjective*
excelente *masc & fem*

ꞩ **except** *preposition*
excepto
except in March excepto en marzo
except Tuesdays excepto los martes
except when it rains excepto cuando llueve

exception *noun*
la **excepción** *fem*
without exception sin excepción
with the exception of con la excepción de

exceptional *masc & fem adjective*
excepcional

ꞩ to **exchange** *verb* ▷ see **exchange** *noun*
cambiar [17]
Can I exchange this shirt for a smaller one?
¿Puedo cambiar esta camisa por una más
pequeña?

ꞩ **exchange** *noun* ▷ see **exchange** *verb*
1 (*of information, students*) el **intercambio** *masc*
an exchange visit un viaje de intercambio
2 (*return*) **in exchange for his help** a cambio
de su ayuda
· **exchange rate** el tipo de cambio

excited *adjective*
1 (*happy*) **entusiasmado** *masc*,
entusiasmada *fem*
to be excited about something estar [2]
entusiasmado con algo
She's really excited about the idea. Está
entusiasmada con la idea.
to get excited entusiasmarse [17]
2 (*noisy, boisterous*) **alborotado** *masc*,
alborotada *fem*
The children were too excited. Los niños
estaban demasiado alborotados.
to get excited alborotarse [17]
**The dogs get excited when they hear the
car.** Los perros se alborotan cuando oyen el
coche.

excitement *noun*
la **emoción** *fem*

ꞩ **exciting** *adjective*
emocionante *masc & fem*
a really exciting film una película
realmente emocionante

exclamation mark *noun*
el **signo de admiración**

to **exclude** *verb*
(*from school*) **to be excluded** ser [1]
expulsado

excursion *noun*
la **excursión** *fem*

ꞩ **excuse** *noun* ▷ see **excuse** *verb*
la **excusa** *fem*
to make excuses poner [11] excusas
Gary has a good excuse. Gary tiene una
buena excusa.
That's no excuse. Eso no es excusa.

ꞩ to **excuse** *verb* ▷ see **excuse** *noun*
(*in apologies*) **Excuse me!** ¡Perdón!

ex-directory *adjective*
to be ex-directory no estar [2] en la guía
telefónica

ꞩ **exercise** *noun*
el **ejercicio** *masc*
a maths exercise un ejercicio de
matemáticas
physical exercise ejercicio físico

ꞩ **exercise book** *noun*
el **cuaderno** *masc*
my Spanish exercise book mi cuaderno de
español

ꞩ **exhausted** *adjective*
agotado *masc*, **agotada** *fem*

exhaust fumes *noun*
los **gases del tubo de escape**

exhaust pipe *noun*
el **tubo de escape**

exhibition *noun*
la **exposición** *fem*
an art exhibition una exposición de obras
de arte

to **exist** *verb*
existir [19]

ꞩ **exit** *noun*
la **salida** *fem*

to **expect** *verb*
1 (*guests, a baby*) **esperar** [17]
We're expecting about thirty people.
Esperamos unas treinta personas.
2 (*an event*) **esperarse** [17]
I didn't expect that. No me esperaba eso.
I didn't expect it at all. No me lo esperaba
en absoluto.
Rain is expected tomorrow. Dicen que va a
llover mañana.
3 (*to suppose*) **suponer** [11]
I expect you're tired. Supongo que estarás
cansado.
I expect she'll bring her boyfriend.
Supongo que traerá a su novio.
I expect so. Supongo que sí.

a
b
c
d
e
f
g
h
i
j
k
l
m
n
o
p
q
r
s
t
u
v
w
x
y
z

expedition *noun*
la **expedición** *fem*

to **expel** *verb*
to be expelled ser[1] expulsado

expenses *noun*
los **gastos** *plural masc*

ꝗ **expensive** *adjective*
caro *masc*, **cara** *fem*
the most expensive hotels los hoteles más caros
Those shoes are too expensive for me.
Esos zapatos son demasiado caros para mí.

experience *noun*
la **experiencia** *fem*
No previous experience required. No se requiere experiencia previa.

experienced *adjective*
con experiencia
You're not experienced enough for this job. No tienes suficiente experiencia para este trabajo.
'Experienced waiter or waitress required'
'Se precisa camarero o camarera con experiencia'

experiment *noun*
el **experimento** *masc*
to do an experiment hacer[7] un experimento

expert *noun*
el **experto** *masc*, la **experta** *fem*
He's a computer expert. Es un experto en informática.

to **expire** *verb*
caducar[31]

expiry date *noun*
la **fecha de caducidad**

ꝗ to **explain** *verb*
explicar[31]

ꝗ **explanation** *noun*
la **explicación** *fem*

to **explode** *verb*
explotar[17]

to **explore** *verb*
explorar[17]

explosion *noun*
la **explosión** *fem*

export *noun* ▷ see **export** *verb*
1 (*item*) el **artículo de exportación**
Cotton is the most important export.

El artículo de exportación más importante es el algodón.
2 (*trade*) la **exportación** *fem*

to **export** *verb* ▷ see **export** *noun*
exportar[17]
Spain exports a lot of wine and olive oil. España exporta mucho vino y aceite de oliva.

exposure *noun*
(*of a film*) la **exposición** *fem*
a twenty-four-exposure film un carrete de veinticuatro fotos

ꝗ **express** *noun* ▷ see **express** *verb*
express train el rápido *masc*

ꝗ to **express** *verb* ▷ see **express** *noun*
expresar[17]
to express yourself expresarse[17]

expression *noun*
la **expresión** *fem*

to **extend** *verb*
(*a building*) **ampliar**[32]

extension *noun*
1 (*extra room for a house*) la **ampliación** *fem*
2 (*telephone*) la **extensión** *fem*
Can I have extension 2347 please? ¿Me puede poner con la extensión veintitrés cuarenta y siete, por favor? (*In Spanish, telephone numbers are usually said in pairs.*)
· **extension lead** el alargador
· **extension number** el número de extensión

extinct *adjective*
1 (*animal, insect*) **extincto** *masc*, **extincta** *fem*
to become extinct extinguirse[50]
2 (*volcano*) **apagado** *masc*, **apagada** *fem*

to **extinguish** *verb*
apagar[28]

extra *adjective, adverb*
They gave us some extra homework. Nos dieron más deberes.
at no extra charge sin coste suplementario
You have to pay extra. Tiene que pagar un suplemento.
Wine is extra. El vino se cobra aparte.
to charge extra for something cobrar[17] un suplemento por algo
extra hot super picante
extra large super grande

extraordinary

extraordinary adjective

extraordinario masc, **extraordinaria** fem

extra-special adjective
super especial masc & fem

extra time noun
(in football, etc) la **prórroga** fem

extravagant adjective
(person) **derrochador** masc, **derrochadora** fem

extreme adjective ▷ see **extreme** noun
extremo masc, **extrema** fem

extreme noun ▷ see **extreme** adj
el **extremo** masc
to go to extremes llevar [17] las cosas al extremo

extremely adverb
extremely difficult dificilísimo
extremely fast rapidísimo

WORD TIP In Spanish, the ending -ísimo, -ísima is often used with adjectives to say *very* or *extremely*.

eye noun
el **ojo** masc
A girl with blue eyes. Una niña con ojos azules.
Shut your eyes! ¡Cierra los ojos!
- **eyebrow** la ceja
- **eyelash** la pestaña
- **eyelid** el párpado
- **eyeliner** el delineador de ojos
- **eye make-up** el maquillaje de ojos
- **eye shadow** la sombra de ojos
- **eyesight** la vista

English-Spanish

a b c d e f g h i j k l m n o p q r s t u v w x y z

♪ indicates key words

F f

fabric noun
la **tela** fem

fabulous adjective
fabuloso masc, **fabulosa** fem

♂ to **face** verb ▷ see **face** noun
1 (to deal with) **enfrentarse** [17] **a**
I face that problem every day. Todos los
días me enfrento a un problema así.
2 (to look in the direction of) **dar** [4] **a**
It faces south. Da al sur.
The hotel faces the sea. El hotel tiene vista
al mar.
3 (to bear the thought of) to be able to face
something soportar algo
I can't face the idea of going back. No
soporto la idea de volver.

♂ **face** noun ▷ see **face** verb
1 (of a person) la **cara** fem
a smiling face una cara risueña
He had a sad face. Tenía una cara triste.
to pull a face hacer [7] muecas
2 (of a clock, watch) la **esfera** fem
· **facecloth** la toalla de cara

facilities plural noun
sports facilities las instalaciones
deportivas
The flat has cooking facilities. El piso tiene
cocina.

fact noun
el **hecho** masc
in fact de hecho
The fact that ... El hecho de que ...
Is that a fact? ¿Es eso cierto?

♂ **factory** noun
la **fábrica** fem

♂ to **fail** verb ▷ see **fail** noun
1 (a test, an exam) **suspender** [18]
I failed my physics exam. He suspendido el
examen de física.
Three students failed. Tres estudiantes
suspendieron.
2 (to not succeed) **fracasar** [1]
He failed in his attempt to beat the record.
Fracasó en su intento de batir el récord.
3 to fail to do something no hacer [7] algo
He failed to contact us. No se puso en
contacto con nosotros.

fail noun ▷ see **fail** verb
1 (in a test, exam) el **suspenso** masc

2 (neglect) **without fail** sin falta
He failed to contact us. No se puso en
contacto con nosotros.

failure noun
1 (lack of success, unsuccessful thing, person) el
fracaso masc
It was a terrible failure. Fue un fracaso
espantoso.
2 (technical fault) a power failure un apagón

♂ **faint** adjective ▷ see **faint** verb
1 (dizzy) to feel faint sentirse [14] mareado
Chloë is feeling faint. Chloë se siente
mareada.
2 (slight) **ligero** masc, **ligera** fem
a faint smell of gas un ligero olor a gas
I haven't the faintest idea. No tengo ni la
más remota idea.
3 (voice, sound) **débil** masc & fem

♂ to **faint** verb ▷ see **faint** adj
desmayarse [17]
Lisa fainted. Lisa se desmayó.

♂ **fair** adjective ▷ see **fair** noun
1 (just, reasonable) **justo** masc, **justa** fem
It's not fair! ¡No es justo!
2 (hair) **rubio** masc, **rubia** fem
She has fair hair. Tiene el pelo rubio.
3 (skin, complexion) **blanco** masc, **blanca** fem
4 (reasonably good) **bastante bueno** masc,
bastante buena fem
His work is fair. Su trabajo es bastante
bueno.

♂ **fair** noun ▷ see **fair** adj
la **feria** fem
· **fairground** el parque de atracciones

♂ **fair-haired** adjective
to be fair-haired tener [9] el pelo rubio

♂ **fairly** adverb
bastante
She's fairly happy. Es bastante feliz.

fairy noun
el **hada** fem

WORD TIP hada takes el or un in the singular even
though it is feminine.

· **fairy tale** el cuento de hadas

faith noun
1 (trust) la **confianza** fem
to have faith in somebody tener [9]
confianza en alguien
2 (in God) la **fe** fem

faithful *adjective*
  fiel *masc & fem*

faithfully *adverb*
  Yours faithfully ... Le saluda atentamente ...

fake *noun*
1 (*thing*) la **falsificación** *fem*
2 (*person*) **impostor** *masc*, **impostora** *fem*

fall *noun* ▷ see **fall** *verb*
  la **caída** *fem*
  to have a fall caerse [34]

♪ to **fall** *verb* ▷ see **fall** *noun*
1 (*to tumble*) **caerse** [34]
  Mind, you'll fall. Cuidado, te vas a caer.
  Tony fell off his bike. Tony se cayó de la bici.
  She fell downstairs. Se cayó por las
  escaleras.
  My jacket fell on the floor. Mi chaqueta se
  cayó al suelo.
2 (*temperatures, prices*) **bajar** [17]
  It fell to minus five last night. La
  temperatura bajó a cinco grados bajo cero
  anoche.

♪ **false** *adjective*
  falso *masc*, **falsa** *fem*
  a false passport un pasaporte falso
• **false alarm** la falsa alarma
• **false teeth** la dentadura postiza

fame *noun*
  la **fama** *fem*

familiar *adjective*
  familiar *masc & fem*
  Your face is familiar. Tu cara me es familiar.

♪ **family** *noun*
  la **familia** *fem*
  a family of six una familia de seis personas
  the Hughes family la familia Hughes
  Ben's one of the family. Ben es uno de la
  familia.
• **family name** el apellido

famine *noun*
  la **hambruna** *fem*

♪ **famous** *adjective*
  famoso *masc*, **famosa** *fem*
  to be famous for something ser [1] famoso
  por algo
  Spain is famous for bullfighting. España es
  famosa por los toros.

fan *noun*
1 (*of a pop group*) el & la **fan** *masc & fem* (*informal*)
  Sarah's an Oasis fan. Sarah es fan de Oasis.
2 (*of a team*) el & la **hincha** *masc & fem*
  Martin's a Chelsea fan. Martin es hincha del
  Chelsea.

3 (*blowing cool air*) el **ventilador** *masc*
4 (*hand-held*) el **abanico** *masc*

fanatic *noun*
  el **fanático** *masc*, la **fanática** *fem*

to **fancy** *verb* ▷ see **fancy** *adj*
1 (*feel like*) Do you fancy a coffee? ¿Te apetece
  un café?
  I fancy the cakes. Me apetecen los pasteles.
  I don't fancy going out. No me apetece
  salir.
2 I really fancy him. Me gusta mucho.
3 (*showing surprise*) (Just) fancy that!
  ¡Imagínate!
  Fancy you being here! ¡Qué casualidad que
  estés aquí!

WORD TIP Use *apetece, etc* or *gusta, etc* if what you
fancy, or don't fancy, is singular or an infinitive in
Spanish. Use *apetecen, etc* or *gustan, etc* if what you
fancy, or don't fancy, is plural.

fancy *adjective* ▷ see **fancy** *verb*
1 (*equipment*) **sofisticado** *masc*, **sofisticada**
  fem
2 (*hotel*) **de lujo**

fancy dress *noun*
  el **disfraz** *masc*
  in fancy dress disfrazado *masc*, disfrazada
  fem
  a fancy-dress party una fiesta de disfraces

♪ **fantastic** *adjective*
  estupendo (*informal*) *masc*, **estupenda** *fem*
  a fantastic holiday unas vacaciones
  estupendas
  Really? That's fantastic! ¿De verdad?¡ Eso
  es estupendo!

♪ **far** *adverb* ▷ see *adj*
1 (*a long way away*) **lejos**
  It's not far. No está lejos.
  Is it far to Cordoba? ¿Está muy lejos
  Córdoba?
  How far is it to Granada? ¿A qué distancia
  está Granada?
  He took us as far as Bilbao. Nos llevó hasta
  Bilbao.
2 (*much*) **mucho**
  far better mucho mejor
  far faster mucho más rápido
  There is far too much noise. Hay
  demasiado ruido.
  There are far too many people. Hay
  demasiada gente.
3 (*to show the extent of something*) as far as I
  know que yo sepa
  by far con mucho
  She is the prettiest by far. Es con mucho la
  más bonita. ▸▸

a
b
c
d
e
f
g
h
i
j
k
l
m
n
o
p
q
r
s
t
u
v
w
x
y
z

so far hasta ahora
So far everything's going well. Hasta ahora todo va bien.

ᔔ **far** *adjective* ▷ see **far** *adv*
(*distant*)
in the far distance a lo lejos
at the far end of the room en el otro extremo de la habitación

ᔔ **fare** *noun*
el **precio del billete**
half fare el medio billete
full fare el billete entero
the return fare to Barcelona el billete de ida y vuelta a Barcelona

Far East *noun*
the Far East el Lejano Oriente

ᔔ **farm** *noun*
la **granja** *fem*

ᔔ **farmer** *noun*
el **agricultor** *masc*, la **agricultora** *fem*

farmhouse *noun*
la **casa de labranza**

farming *noun*
la **agricultura** *fem*

fascinating *adjective*
fascinante *masc & fem*

fashion *noun*
la **moda** *fem*
in fashion de moda
out of fashion pasado de moda

fashionable *adjective*
de moda

fashion model *noun*
el & la **modelo** *masc & fem*

fashion show *noun*
el **desfile de modas**

ᔔ **fast** *adverb* ▷ see **fast** *adj*
1 (*quickly*) **rápido**
She swims very fast. Nada muy rápido.
2 (*soundly*) **to be fast asleep** estar [2] profundamente dormido

ᔔ **fast** *adjective* ▷ see **fast** *adv*
1 (*quick*) **rápido** *masc*, **rápida** *fem*
a fast car un coche rápido
2 (*when you talk about time*) **My watch is fast.** Mi reloj adelanta.
You're ten minutes fast. Vas diez minutos adelantado.
• **fast food** la comida rápida

ᔔ **fasten** *verb*
abrochar
Fasten your seatbelts. Abróchense los cinturones.

ᔔ **fat** *adjective* ▷ see **fat** *noun*
gordo *masc*, **gorda** *fem*
a fat man un hombre gordo
to get fat engordar [17]

ᔔ **fat** *noun* ▷ see **fat** *adj*
la **grasa** *fem*

fatal *adjective*
fatal *masc & fem*

ᔔ **father** *noun*
el **padre** *masc*
my father's office la oficina de mi padre
• **Father Christmas** el Papá Noel
• **father-in-law** el suegro
• **Father's Day** el día del padre

ᔔ **fatty** *adjective*
(*food*) **graso** *masc*, **grasa** *fem*

ᔔ **fault** *noun*
1 (*responsibility*) la **culpa** *fem*
It's Steve's fault. Es culpa de Steve.
It's not my fault. No es culpa mía.
2 (*in tennis*) la **falta** *fem*

ᔔ **favour** *noun*
1 (*kindness*) el **favor** *masc*
to do somebody a favour hacerle [7] un favor a alguien
Can you do me a favour? ¿Me haces un favor?
to ask a favour of somebody pedirle [57] un favor a alguien
2 **to be in favour of something** estar [2] a favor de algo
Estoy a favor de la monarquía. I am in favour of the monarchy.

ᔔ **favourite** *adjective*
favorito *masc*, **favorita** *fem*
my favourite band mi grupo favorito

ᔔ **to fax** *verb* ▷ see **fax** *noun*
1 (*a message*) **enviar** [32] **por fax**
2 (*a person*) **to fax somebody** mandarle [17] un fax a alguien

ᔔ **fax** *noun* ▷ see **fax** *verb*
el **fax** *masc*
• **fax machine** el fax

ᔔ **fear** *noun* ▷ see **fear** *verb*
el **miedo** *masc*

ꝸ to **fear** verb ▷ see **fear** noun
temer [18]

feather noun
la **pluma** fem

feature noun
1 (of your face) el **rasgo** masc
to have delicate features tener [9] rasgos delicados
2 (of a machine, product) la **característica** fem

ꝸ **February** noun
febrero masc
in February en febrero

> **WORD TIP** Names of months and days start with small letters in Spanish.

ꝸ **fed up** adjective
(informal) **to be fed up with something** estar [2] harto de algo (boy speaking), estar harta [2] de algo (girl speaking)
I'm fed up with working every day. Estoy harto de trabajar todos los días (boy speaking)., Estoy harta de trabajar todos los días (girl speaking).

to **feed** verb
dar [4] **de comer a**
Have you fed the dog? ¿Has dado de comer al perro?

to **feel** verb
1 (tired, ill, etc) **sentirse** [14]
I feel tired. Estoy cansada.
I don't feel well. No me siento bien.
2 (cold, hot, thirsty, etc) **to feel cold** tener [9] frío
to feel thirsty tener [9] sed
to feel afraid tener [9] miedo
3 (a sting, a touch, etc) **sentir** [14]
I didn't feel a thing. No sentí nada.
4 **to feel like doing something** tener [9] ganas de hacer algo
I feel like going to the cinema. Tengo ganas de ir al cine.
I feel like some chocolate. Me apetece un poco de chocolate.
Do you feel like a walk? ¿Te apetece dar un paseo?
I don't feel like it. No me apetece.
5 (to touch) **tocar** [3]
Feel my forehead. Tócame la frente.

feeling noun
1 (in your mind) el **sentimiento** masc
a feeling of embarrassment un sentimiento de vergüenza
to show your feelings demostrar [24] los sentimientos
to hurt somebody's feelings herir [14] los sentimientos de alguien

2 (in your body) la **sensación** fem
a dizzy feeling una sensación de mareo
3 (impression) la **impresión** fem
I have the feeling James doesn't like me. Tengo la impresión de que no le caigo bien a James.

felt-tip (pen) noun
el **rotulador** masc

female adjective ▷ see **female** noun
1 (person, population) **femenino** masc, **femenina** fem
2 (animal, insect) **hembra** masc & fem

female noun ▷ see **female** adj
(animal) la **hembra** fem

feminine adjective
femenino masc, **femenina** fem

feminist noun
el & la **feminista** masc & fem

fence noun
la **valla** fem

fern noun
el **helecho** masc

ferry noun
el **ferry** masc, pl: los **ferries**, **ferrys**

to **fetch** verb
ir [8] **a por**
Tom's fetching the children. Tom ha ido a por los niños.
Fetch me the other knife! ¡Vete a por el otro cuchillo!

fever noun
la **fiebre** fem

ꝸ **few** adjective, pronoun
1 (not many) **pocos** masc, **pocas** fem
Few people think that ... Pocas personas piensan que ...
Few believe that ... Pocos creen que ...
2 (some, several) **a few** algunos masc, algunas fem
a few weeks earlier algunas semanas antes
in a few minutes dentro de unos minutos
a few more books unos libros más
Have we any tomatoes? We want a few for the salad. ¿Tenemos tomates? Queremos algunos para la ensalada
quite a few bastantes plural masc & fem
There were quite a few questions. Hubo bastantes preguntas.
Yes, there were quite a few. Sí, hubo bastantes.

♂ **fewer** *adjective*
  menos *masc & fem*
  fewer than six menos de seis
  I have fewer lessons than she does. Tengo
  menos clases que ella.
  There are fewer tourists this year. Hay
  menos turistas este año.

> **WORD TIP** Use *menos de* with numbers.

♂ **fiancé** *noun*
  el **prometido** *masc*

♂ **fiancée** *noun*
  la **prometida** *fem*

  fiction *noun*
  la **ficción** *fem*

♂ **field** *noun*
  el **campo** *masc*
  a field of wheat un campo de trigo
  a football field un campo de fútbol

♂ **fifteen** *number*
  quince *invariable number*
  Lara's fifteen. Lara tiene quince años.

♂ **fifth** *adjective* ▷ see **fifth** *noun*
  quinto *masc*, **quinta** *fem*
  on the fifth floor en la quinta planta

♂ **fifth** *noun* ▷ see **fifth** *adj*
  1 (*fraction*) a fifth una quinta parte
  2 (*in dates*) the fifth of January el cinco de
     enero

♂ **fifties** *plural noun*
  the fifties los años cincuenta
  in the fifties en los años cincuenta

♂ **fifty** *number*
  cincuenta *invariable number*
  She's fifty. Tiene cincuenta años.
  fifty-five cincuenta y cinco

  fig *noun*
  el **higo** *masc*

  fight *noun* ▷ see **fight** *verb*
  1 (*a scuffle, in boxing*) la **pelea** *fem*
  2 (*in war, against illness, poverty*) la **lucha** *fem*

  to **fight** *verb* ▷ see **fight** *noun*
  1 (*in war, against poverty, a disease*) **luchar** [17]
  2 (*to quarrel*) **pelear** [17]
     They're always fighting. Siempre se están
     peleando.

♂ **figure** *noun*
  1 (*number*) la **cifra** *fem*
     a four-figure number un número de cuatro
     cifras

2 (*body shape*) la **figura** *fem*
  She's got a very good figure. Tiene una
  figura estupenda.
3 (*person*) el **personaje** *masc*
  a public figure un personaje público

file *noun* ▷ see **file** *verb*
  1 (*container for records of a person, case*) el
     archivo *masc*
  2 (*Computers*) el **fichero** *masc*
  3 (*folder for documents*) la **carpeta** *fem*

to **file** *verb* ▷ see **file** *noun*
  1 (*documents, records*) **archivar** [17]
  2 (*nails*) to file your nails limarse [17] las uñas

♂ to **fill** *verb*
  llenar [17]
  She filled my glass. Me llenó el vaso.
  • to **fill in**
     (*a form*) **rellenar** [17]
  • to **fill up**
  1 (*rooms, buildings*) **llenarse** [17]
     The church filled up with people. La iglesia
     se llenó de gente.
  2 (*a car tank*) **llenar**
     Fill her up, please! ¡Lleno, por favor!

filling *noun*
  1 (*in cooking*) el **relleno** *masc*
  2 (*in a tooth*) el **empaste** *masc*

♂ **film** *noun*
  1 (*in a cinema*) la **película** *fem*
     Shall we go and see a film? ¿Vamos a ver
     una película?
  2 (*for a camera*) el **carrete de fotos**
     a 24-exposure colour film un carrete de
     color de veinticuatro fotos
  • **film star** la estrella de cine

♂ **filthy** *adjective*
  sucísimo *masc*, **sucísima** *fem*

final *adjective* ▷ see **final** *noun*
  1 (*definite*) **final** *masc & fem*
     the final result el resultado final
  2 (*last*) **último** *masc*, **última** *fem*
     the final instalment el último plazo

final *noun* ▷ see **final** *adj*
  (*Sport*) la **final** *fem*
  the final of the European Cup la final de la
  Copa de Europa

♂ **finally** *adverb*
  finalmente

♂ to **find** *verb*
  encontrar [24]
  Did you find your passport? ¿Has
  encontrado tu pasaporte?

I can't find my keys. No puedo encontrar mis llaves.
- to **find out**
1 (*to enquire*) **informarse** [17]
I don't know, I'll find out. No lo sé, me informaré.
2 (*to discover*) **to find something out** descubrir [46] algo
Lucy found out the truth. Lucy descubrió la verdad.

fine *adjective* ▷ see **fine** *noun*
1 (*to talk about your health*) **bien** *masc & fem*
'How are you?'— 'Fine, thanks.' '¿Cómo estás?'— 'Bien, gracias.'
2 (*to say that something is all right*) **bien** *masc & fem adjective*
'Ten o'clock?'— 'Yes, that's fine.' '¿A las diez?'— 'Sí, está bien.'
Friday will be fine. El viernes está bien.
3 (*very good*) **muy bueno** *masc*, **muy buena** *fem*
She's a fine athlete. Es muy buena atleta.
4 (*weather, day*) **bueno** *masc*, **buena** *fem*
If it's fine. Si hace buen tiempo.
5 (*not coarse, not thick*) **fino** *masc*, **fina** *fem*
fine wool lana fina

fine *noun* ▷ see **fine** *adj*
la **multa** *fem*

ꝑ **finger** *noun*
el **dedo** *masc*
- **fingernail** la uña

ꝑ **finish** *noun* ▷ see **finish** *verb*
1 (*end*) el **final** *masc*
from start to finish del principio al final
2 (*in a race*) la **llegada** *fem*

ꝑ to **finish** *verb* ▷ see **finish** *noun*
terminar [17]
Wait, I haven't finished. Espera, no he terminado.
When does school finish? ¿Cuándo termina el colegio?
Have you finished the book? ¿Has terminado el libro?
to finish doing something terminar [17] de hacer algo
Have you finished telephoning? ¿Has terminado de llamar por teléfono?
- to **finish with**
terminar [17] **con**
Have you finished with the computer? ¿Has terminado con el ordenador?

Finland *noun*
Finlandia *fem*

Finn *noun*
un **finlandés** *masc*, una **finlandesa** *fem*

WORD TIP Adjectives and nouns for nationality and regional origin do not have capital letters in Spanish.

Finnish *adjective & noun*
1 **finlandés** *masc*, **finlandesa** *fem*
2 (*the language*) el **finlandés** *masc*

WORD TIP Adjectives and nouns for nationality, regional origin, and language do not have capital letters in Spanish.

ꝑ to **fire** *verb* ▷ see **fire** *noun*
(*to shoot*) **disparar** [17]
to fire at somebody dispararle a alguien
The police fired at the demonstrators. La policía les disparó a los manifestantes.

ꝑ **fire** *noun* ▷ see **fire** *verb*
1 (*in general, in a grate*) el **fuego** *masc*
to catch fire prenderse [18] fuego
to be on fire estar [2] ardiendo
to light the fire encender [36] el fuego
2 (*accidental*) el **incendio** *masc*
There was a fire at the school. Hubo un incendio en la escuela.
- **fire alarm** la alarma contra incendios
- **fire brigade** el cuerpo de bomberos
- **fire engine** el coche de bomberos
- **fire escape** la escalera de incendios
- **fire extinguisher** el extintor
- **firefighter** el & la bombero
- **fireplace** la chimenea
- **fire station** la estación de bomberos
- **fireworks** los fuegos artificiales

firm *adjective* ▷ see **firm** *noun*
firme *masc & fem*

firm *noun* ▷ see **firm** *adj*
la **empresa** *fem*

ꝑ **first** *noun* ▷ see **first** *adj, adv, pron*
(*in dates*) **the first of May** el primero de mayo

The first submarine was designed and built by Isaac Peral between 1884-1887 and the autogiro, a prototype for the helicopter, was invented by Juan de la Cierva in the early 1920s.

ꝑ **first** *adjective, adverb, pronoun*
▷ see **first** *noun*
1 (*before the others*) **primero** *masc*, **primera** *fem*
for the first time por primera vez
Susan's the first. Susan es la primera.
Christy got here first. Christy llegó aquí primero. ▸▸

Ben came first in the 200 metres. Ben llegó el primero en los doscientos metros.

2 (to begin with) **primero**
First, I'm going to make some tea. Primero voy a hacer té.
first of all en primer lugar
at first al principio
At first he didn't want to. Al principio no quería.

WORD TIP *primer* is used instead of *primero* before a masc singular noun.

• **first aid** los primeros auxilios
• **first aid kit** el botiquín de primeros auxilios

first-class *adjective, adverb*
(ticket, carriage, hotel) **de primera**
a first-class compartment un compartimento de primera
He always travels first-class. Siempre viaja en primera.

first floor *noun*
la **primera planta** *fem*
on the first floor en la primera planta

firstly *adverb*
en primer lugar

♪ **first name** *noun*
el **nombre de pila**

fir tree *noun*
el **abeto** *masc*

♪ to **fish** *verb* ▷ see **fish** *noun*
pescar [31]
Dad was fishing for trout. Papá estaba pescando truchas.

♪ **fish** *noun* ▷ see **fish** *verb*
1 (as a meal) el **pescado** *masc*
Do you like fish? ¿Te gusta el pescado?
2 (in the sea, river) el **pez** *masc*, pl: los **peces**
• **fish and chips** el pescado con patatas fritas

♪ **fisherman** *noun*
el **pescador** *masc*

♪ **fishing** *noun*
la **pesca** *fem*
to go fishing ir [8] a pescar
I love fishing. Me encanta pescar.
Fishing is my favourite sport. La pesca es mi deporte favorito.
• **fishing rod** la caña de pescar
• **fishing tackle** los aparejos de pesca

♪ **fist** *noun*
el **puño** *masc*

♪ **fit** *adjective* ▷ see **fit** *noun, verb*
en forma
to keep fit mantenerse [9] en forma
I feel really fit. Me siento muy en forma.

♪ **fit** *noun* ▷ see **fit** *adj, verb*
el **ataque** *masc noun*
I had a fit. Me dio un ataque.
Your dad'll have a fit when he sees you! ¡A tu padre le va a dar un ataque cuando te vea!

♪ to **fit** *verb* ▷ see **fit** *adj, noun*
1 (garments, shoes) **to fit somebody** estarle [2] bien a alguien
This skirt doesn't fit me. Esta falda no me queda bien.
Does it fit you okay? ¿Te está bien?
2 (to go into) **entrar** [17] **en**
Will my cases all fit in the car? ¿Entrarán todas mis maletas en el coche?
3 (a shelf, a lock, a handle) **poner** [11]
He fitted a lock on the door. Puso una cerradura en la puerta.

fitness *noun*
el **estado físico**
• **fitness training** el entrenamiento

fitted carpet *noun*
la **moqueta** *fem*

♪ **five** *number*
cinco *invariable number*
Oskar's five. Oskar tiene cinco años.
It's five o'clock. Son las cinco.

to **fix** *verb*
1 (to repair) **arreglar** [17]
Mum's fixed the computer. Mamá ha arreglado el ordenador.
2 (to decide on) **fijar** [17]
to fix a date fijar una fecha

fizzy *adjective*
con gas
fizzy water agua con gas

flag *noun*
la **bandera** *fem*

flame *noun*
la **llama** *fem*

flan *noun*
1 (savoury) el **quiche** *masc*
an onion flan un quiche de cebolla
2 (sweet) la **tarta** *fem*

to **flap** *verb*
1 (birds: their wings) **batir** [19]
2 (flags, sails) **agitarse** [17]

flash *noun* ▷ see **flash** *verb*
1 (of light) el **destello** *masc*
a flash of lightning un relámpago
to do something in a flash hacer [7] algo como un relámpago
2 (on a camera) el **flash** *masc*

to **flash** verb ▷ see **flash** noun
1 (lights) **destellar** [17]
    to flash past pasar [17] como un rayo
2 (a light) to flash your headlights hacer [7]
    señas con los faros del coche

flask noun
1 (insulated bottle) el **termo** masc
2 (container) el **frasco** masc

ᵹ **flat** adjective ▷ see **flat** noun
1 (surface) **plano** masc, **plana** fem
2 (countryside, landscape) **llano** masc, **llana** fem
3 (shoes) **de tacón bajo**
4 (deflated) a flat tyre una rueda pinchada

ᵹ **flat** noun ▷ see **flat** adj
    el **piso** masc
    a third-floor flat un piso en la tercera planta
· **flatmate** el compañero de piso, la
    compañera de piso

ᵹ **flavour** noun ▷ see **flavour** verb
    el **sabor** masc
    The sauce had no flavour. La salsa no tenía
    sabor.
    What flavour of ice cream would you like?
    ¿De qué sabor quieres el helado?

ᵹ to **flavour** verb ▷ see **flavour** noun
    sazonar [17]
    vanilla-flavoured con sabor a vainilla

flea noun
    la **pulga** fem

fleet noun
1 (of ships) la **flota** fem
2 (of vehicles) el **parque móvil**

ᵹ **flight** noun
1 (of a plane, bird) el **vuelo** masc
    The flight from Moscow is delayed. El vuelo
    procedente de Moscú lleva retraso.
2 (of stairs) a flight of stairs un tramo de
    escalera
· **flight attendant** el & la auxiliar de vuelo

to **fling** verb
    lanzar [22]

flipper noun
    (for a swimmer) la **aleta** fem

to **flirt** verb
    flirtear [17]

to **float** verb
    flotar [17]

to **flood** verb ▷ see **flood** noun
    inundar [17]

flood noun ▷ see **flood** verb
1 (of water) la **inundación** fem
    the floods in the south las inundaciones del
    sur
    to be in floods of tears estar [2] llorando a
    mares
2 (of letters, complaints) la **avalancha** fem
· **floodlight** el foco

ᵹ **floor** noun
1 (of a room, vehicle) el **suelo** masc
    on the floor en el suelo
2 (storey) la **planta** fem
    the first floor la primera planta
    on the second floor en la segunda planta

flop noun
    el **fracaso** masc

floppy disk noun
    el **disquete** masc

florist noun
    el & la **florista** masc & fem

florist's noun
    la **floristería** fem

flour noun
    la **harina** fem

ᵹ **flower** noun ▷ see **flower** verb
    la **flor** fem

ᵹ to **flower** verb ▷ see **flower** noun
    florecer [35]

ᵹ **flu** noun
    la **gripe** fem
    to have flu tener [9] gripe

fluent adjective
    to be fluent in a language hablar [17] un
    idioma con fluidez
    She speaks fluent Italian. Habla italiano
    con fluidez.

fluently adverb
    con fluidez

fluid noun
    el **fluido** masc

to **flush** verb
1 (to go red) **enrojecer** [35]
2 (the lavatory) to flush the lavatory tirar [17]
    de la cadena

flute noun
    la **flauta** fem
    to play the flute tocar [31] la flauta

fly noun ▷ see **fly** verb
    la **mosca** fem

ᵹ indicates key words　　　　　483

a
b
c
d
e
f
g
h
i
j
k
l
m
n
o
p
q
r
s
t
u
v
w
x
y
z

♂ to **fly** *verb* ▷ see **fly** *noun*

1 *(birds, insects, planes)* **volar** [24]
2 *(time)* **pasar** [17] **volando**
3 *(to travel in a plane)* **ir** [8] **en avión**
We flew to Edinburgh. Fuimos en avión a Edimburgo.
We flew from Gatwick. Salimos desde Gatwick.
4 *(a kite)* **hacer** [7] **volar**

foam *noun*
la **espuma** *fem*
· **foam rubber** la goma espuma

focus *noun* ▷ see **focus** *verb*
to be in focus estar [2] enfocado
to be out of focus estar [2] desenfocado

to **focus** *verb* ▷ see **focus** *noun*
(a camera) **enfocar** [31]

♂ **fog** *noun*
la **niebla** *fem*

foggy *adjective*
a foggy day un día de niebla
It was foggy. Había niebla.

foil *noun*
el **papel de aluminio**

fold *noun* ▷ see **fold** *verb*
el **pliegue** *masc*

to **fold** *verb* ▷ see **fold** *noun*
doblar [17]
· to **fold up**
1 **doblar** [17]
to fold up the sheet doblar la sábana
2 *(by itself)* **doblarse**
The table folds up very easily. La mesa se dobla muy fácilmente.

folder *noun*
la **carpeta** *fem*

to **follow** *verb*
seguir [64]
followed by a dinner seguido de una cena
Follow me! ¡Sígueme!
Do you follow me? ¿Me sigues?

following *adjective*
siguiente *masc & fem*
the following year el año siguiente

fond *adjective*
to be fond of somebody tenerle [9] cariño a alguien
I'm very fond of him. Le tengo mucho cariño.
I'm fond of dogs. Me gustan los perros.

food *noun*
la **comida** *fem*
I like Italian food. Me gusta la comida italiana.
· **food poisoning** la intoxicación alimenticia

fool *noun*
el & la **idiota** *masc & fem*

♂ **foot** *noun*
1 *(of a person)* el **pie** *masc*
He stepped on my foot. Me pisó el pie.
Lucy came on foot. Lucy vino a pie.
2 *(of an animal)* la **pata** *fem*
3 *(the bottom of something)* el **pie** *masc*
at the foot of the stairs al pie de las escaleras
at the foot of the bed a los pies de la cama
4 *(measurement)* el **pie** *masc*
He is six feet tall. Mide seis pies.

♂ **football** *noun*
1 *(the game)* el **fútbol** *masc*
to play football jugar [27] al fútbol
2 *(a ball)* el **balón de fútbol**

footballer *noun*
el & la **futbolista** *masc & fem*

footpath *noun*
el **sendero** *masc*

♂ **for** *preposition*
1 *(saying where something goes, or what it does)* **para**
a present for my mother un regalo para mi madre
petrol for the car gasolina para el coche
sausages for lunch salchichas para comer
It's for cleaning. Es para limpiar.
What's it for? ¿Para qué es?
2 *(giving the reason for something)* **por**
for that reason por esa razón
3 *(giving costs)* **por**
I sold my bike for fifty pounds. Vendí mi bicicleta por cincuenta libras.
4 *(giving a destination)* **para**
the bus for Barcelona el autobús para Barcelona
5 *(asking for a translation)* What's the Spanish for 'bee'? ¿Cómo se dice 'bee' en español?
6 *(in time expressions)* I studied Spanish for four years. Estudié español cuatro años.
I'll be away for four days. Estaré fuera cuatro días.
I've been waiting here for an hour. Llevo esperando aquí una hora.
My brother's been living in London for

three years. Mi hermano lleva tres años viviendo en Londres.

WORD TIP In time expressions in the past or future, *for* is not usually translated

to **forbid** *verb*
prohibir [58]
to forbid somebody to do something prohibir [58] a alguien hacer algo
I forbid you to go out. Te prohíbo salir.

♪ **forbidden** *adjective*
prohibido *masc*, **prohibida** *fem*

force *noun* ▷ see **force** *verb*
la **fuerza** *fem*

to **force** *verb* ▷ see **force** *noun*
forzar [26]
to force somebody to do something forzar a alguien a hacer algo

forecast *noun*
(*for the weather*) el **pronóstico** *masc*

forehead *noun*
la **frente** *fem*

foreign *adjective*
extranjero *masc*, **extranjera** *fem*
in a foreign country en un país extranjero

♪ **foreigner** *noun*
el **extranjero** *masc*, la **extranjera** *fem*

♪ **forest** *noun*
el **bosque** *masc*

forever *adverb*
1 (*for all time*) **para siempre**
I'd like to stay here forever. Me gustaría quedarme aquí para siempre.
2 (*non-stop*) **siempre**
He's forever asking questions. Siempre está preguntando.

forgery *noun*
la **falsificación** *fem*

♪ to **forget** *verb*
olvidarse [17]
I forget his name. Se me ha olvidado su nombre.
We've forgotten the bread! ¡Se nos ha olvidado el pan!
to forget to do something olvidarse [17] de hacer algo
I forgot to phone. Se me olvidó llamar por teléfono.
to forget about something olvidarse [17] de algo
I forgot about the outing. Me olvidé de la excursión.

forgetful *adjective*
olvidadizo *masc*, **olvidadiza** *fem*

to **forgive** *verb*
perdonar [17]
I forgave him. Lo perdoné.
to forgive somebody for doing something perdonar a alguien por algo
I forgave her for losing my ring. La perdoné por perderme el anillo.

♪ **fork** *noun*
el **tenedor** *masc*

♪ **form** *noun* ▷ see **form** *verb*
1 (*document*) el **formulario** *masc*
to fill in a form rellenar [17] un formulario
2 (*shape, kind*) la **forma** *fem*
in the form of something en forma de algo
3 (*fitness*) to be on form estar [2] en forma
4 (*school class*) la **clase** *fem*
5 (*school year*) el **curso** *masc*

♪ to **form** *verb* ▷ see **form** *noun*
formar [17]

formal *adjective*
(*invitation, event, complaint*) **formal** *masc & fem*

♪ **former** *adjective*
antiguo *masc*, **antigua** *fem*
a former pupil un antiguo alumno

WORD TIP *antiguo*, *antigua* meaning *former*, go before the noun.

formula *noun*
la **fórmula** *fem*

fortnight *noun*
quince días *plural masc*
We're going to Spain for a fortnight. Vamos quince días a España.

fortune *noun*
la **fortuna** *fem*
to make a fortune hacer [7] una fortuna

fortunate *adjective*
afortunado *masc*, **afortunada** *fem*

fortunately *adverb*
afortunadamente

♪ **forty** *number*
cuarenta *invariable number*
He's forty. Tiene cuarenta años.
forty-five cuarenta y cinco

forward *adverb* ▷ see **forward** *noun*
hacia adelante
to move forward ir [8] hacia adelante
a seat further forward un asiento de más adelante

a
b
c
d
e
f
g
h
i
j
k
l
m
n
o
p
q
r
s
t
u
v
w
x
y
z

a
b
c
d
e
f
g
h
i
j
k
l
m
n
o
p
q
r
s
t
u
v
w
x
y
z

forward *noun* ▷ see **forward** *adv*
   el & la **delantero** *masc & fem*

foster child *noun*
   el **hijo acogido**, la **hija acogida**

foster family *noun*
   la **familia de acogida**

foul *adjective* ▷ see **foul** *noun*
   espantoso *masc*, **espantosa** *fem*
   The weather's foul. El tiempo está
   horroroso.

foul *noun* ▷ see **foul** *adj*
   (Sport) la **falta** *fem*

ƒ **fountain** *noun*
   la **fuente** *fem*
 • **fountain pen** la pluma

ƒ **four** *number*
   cuatro *invariable number*
   Simon's four. Simon tiene cuatro años.
   It's four o'clock. Son las cuatro.

ƒ **fourteen** *number*
   catorce *invariable number*
   Susie's fourteen. Susie tiene catorce años.

ƒ **fourth** *adjective* ▷ see **fourth** *noun*
   cuarto *masc*, **cuarta** *fem*
   on the fourth floor en la cuarta planta

ƒ **fourth** *noun* ▷ see **fourth** *adj*
  1 (*fraction*) a fourth un cuarto
  2 (*in dates*) the fourth of July el cuatro de julio

fox *noun*
   el **zorro** *masc*

fracture *noun*
   la **fractura** *fem*

ƒ **fragile** *adjective*
   frágil *masc & fem*

frame *noun*
   (*of a picture, photograph*) el **marco** *masc*

France *noun*
   Francia *fem*

frantic *adjective*
   (*effort, search*) **desesperado** *masc*,
   desesperada *fem*
   Mum was frantic with worry. Mamá estaba
   muerta de preocupación.

freckle *noun*
   la **peca** *fem*

ƒ to **free** *verb* ▷ see **free** *adj*
  1 (*a person*) **poner** [11] **en libertad**
  2 (*an animal*) **soltar** [24]

ƒ **free** *adjective* ▷ see **free** *verb*
  1 (*when you don't pay*) **gratis** *masc & fem*
   a free ticket un billete gratis
   The bus is free. El autobús es gratis.
  2 (*at liberty*) **libre** *masc & fem*
   to be free to do something ser [1] libre de
   hacer algo
   You're free to do what you think best. Eres
   libre de hacer lo que te parezca.
   to set somebody free poner [11] a alguien
   en libertad
  3 (*not occupied*) **libre** *masc & fem*
   Are you free on Thursday? ¿Estás libre el
   jueves?
  4 (*not containing*) sugar-free sin azúcar
   lead-free sin plomo

freedom *noun*
   la **libertad** *fem*

free gift *noun*
   el **regalo** *masc*

free kick *noun*
   el **tiro libre**

ƒ to **freeze** *verb*
  1 (*in a freezer*) **congelar** [17]
   frozen peas guisantes congelados
  2 (*in cold weather*) **helarse** [29]

ƒ **freezer** *noun*
   el **congelador** *masc*

freezing *adjective*
  1 (*temperatures*) **bajo cero** *invariable masc &
   fem*
   It's freezing outside! ¡Fuera hace un frío
   que pela! (*informal*)
  2 (*hands, feet*) **helado** *masc*, **helada** *fem*
   I'm freezing! ¡Estoy helado!

French *adjective & noun*
  1 **francés** *masc*, **francesa** *fem*
  2 (*the people*) the French los franceses
  3 (*the language*) el **francés** *masc*
   our French teacher nuestro profesor de
   francés

WORD TIP Adjectives and nouns for nationality,
regional origin, and language do not have capital
letters in Spanish.

 • **French bean** la judía verde
 • **French fries** las patatas fritas, (*Latin America*)
  las papas fritas

Frenchman *noun*
   un **francés** *masc*

French stick *noun*
   la **barra de pan**

French window *noun*
   la **cristalera** *fem*

Frenchwoman *noun*
una **francesa** *fem*

frequently *adverb*
frecuentemente, **a menudo**

ᵟ **fresh** *adjective*
fresco *masc*, **fresca** *fem*
fresh eggs huevos frescos
I'm going out for some fresh air. Voy fuera a tomar un poco el aire.

ᵟ **Friday** *noun*
el **viernes** *masc*
every Friday cada viernes
last Friday el viernes pasado
on Friday el viernes
on Fridays los viernes
The shop is closed on Fridays. La tienda está cerrada los viernes.
I'll phone you on Friday evening. Te llamaré el viernes por la tarde.

WORD TIP Names of months and days start with small letters in Spanish.

ᵟ **fridge** *noun*
la **nevera** *fem*
Put it in the fridge. Ponlo en la nevera.

fried egg *noun*
el **huevo frito**

ᵟ **friend** *noun*
el **amigo** *masc*, la **amiga** *fem*
a friend of mine un amigo mío (*a boy*), una amiga mía (*a girl*)
to make friends with somebody hacerse [7] amigo de alguien
He made friends with Danny. Se hizo amigo de Danny.

friendly *adjective*
1 (*person*) **simpático** *masc*, **simpática** *fem*
2 (*letter, gesture*) **amable** *masc & fem*

friendship *noun*
la **amistad** *fem*

fries *plural noun*
las **patatas fritas**

fright *noun*
el **susto** *masc*
to get a fright asustarse [17]
to give somebody a fright asustar [17] a alguien
You gave me a fright! ¡Me asustaste!

to **frighten** *verb*
asustar [17]

ᵟ **frightened** *adjective*
to be frightened of something tenerle [9] miedo a algo

He was frightened of the dark. Le tenía miedo a la oscuridad.
He was frightened of his father. Le tenía miedo a su padre.
I was frightened to tell him. Tenía miedo de decírselo.
Don't be frightened. No tengas miedo., No te asustes.

frightening *adjective*
espantoso *masc*, **espantosa** *fem*

fringe *noun*
(*of hair*) el **flequillo** *masc*

frog *noun*
la **rana** *fem*

ᵟ **from** *preposition*
1 (*coming from*) **de**
a letter from Tom una carta de Tom
He comes from Dublin. Es de Dublín.
2 (*in distances*) **de**
100 metres from the cinema a cien metros del cine
from seven o'clock onwards de las siete en adelante
3 (*starting from*) **desde**
tickets from ten pounds entradas desde diez libras
from today desde hoy
two years from now dentro de dos años
from then on a partir de entonces
from ... to ... de ... a ...
from Monday to Friday de lunes a viernes
the train from London to Liverpool el tren de Londres a Liverpool
from here to the wall de aquí a la pared
4 (*as a result of*) **de**
She suffers from depression. Sufre de depresión.

ᵟ **front** *adjective* ▷ see **front** *noun*
delantero *masc*, **delantera** *fem*
the front seat el asiento delantero (*of a car*)
in the front row en la fila de delante

ᵟ **front** *noun* ▷ see **front** *adj*
1 (*of an envelope, a car, train, queue*) la **parte de delante**
sitting in the front sentado en la parte de delante
from the front por delante
the front of the class el frente de la clase
The address is on the front. Las señas están en la parte de delante.
2 (*of a building*) la **fachada** *fem*
3 (*of a garment*) la **delantera** *fem*
4 in front of delante de
in front of the TV delante de la televisión
in front of me delante de mí
· front door la puerta de la calle

a
b
c
d
e
f
g
h
i
j
k
l
m
n
o
p
q
r
s
t
u
v
w
x
y
z

frontier *noun*
la **frontera** *fem*

frost *noun*
la **helada** *fem*

frosty *adjective*
1 (*weather, air*) **helado** *masc*, **helada** *fem*
It was frosty this morning. Había helada esta mañana.
2 (*windscreen, grass*) **cubierto de escharcha** *masc*, **cubierta de escarcha** *fem*

to **frown** *verb*
fruncir [66] el ceño

frozen *adjective*
congelado *masc*, **congelada** *fem*
a frozen pizza una pizza congelada

♂ **fruit** *noun*
la **fruta** *fem*
• fruit juice el zumo de fruta
• fruit machine la máquina tragaperras
• fruit salad la macedonia de frutas

frustrating *adjective*
frustrante *masc & fem*

to **fry** *verb*
freír [53]
We fried the fish. Freímos el pescado.

frying pan *noun*
la **sartén** *fem*

fuel *noun*
el **combustible** *masc*

♂ **full** *adjective*
1 (*container*) **lleno** *masc*, **llena** *fem*
This glass is full. Este vaso está lleno.
The train was full of tourists. El tren estaba lleno de turistas.
I'm full. Estoy lleno.
2 (*hotel, flight*) **completo** *masc*, **completa** *fem*
3 (*top*) at full speed a toda velocidad
at full volume a todo volumen
4 (*complete*) **todo** *masc*, **toda** *fem*
the full story toda la historia
to write your name out in full escribir [52] su nombre completo
• full stop el punto

full time *noun* ▷ see **full-time** *adj, adv*
el **final de partido**

full-time *adjective, adverb* ▷ see **full time** *noun*

a tiempo completo
a full-time job un trabajo a tiempo completo
to work full-time trabajar [17] a tiempo completo

fully *adverb*
completamente

fun *noun*
to have fun divertirse [14]
Have fun! ¡Que te diviertas!
We had fun catching the ponies. Nos divertimos atrapando a los poneys.
Skiing is fun. Esquiar es divertido.
I do it for fun. Lo hago para divertirme.
to make fun of somebody reírse [61] de alguien
• funfair el parque de atracciones

funds *noun*
los **fondos** *plural masc*

funeral *noun*
el **funeral** *masc*, los **funerales** *masc pl*

♂ **funny** *adjective*
1 (*amusing*) **gracioso** *masc*, **graciosa** *fem*
a funny story una historia graciosa
How funny you are! ¡Qué gracioso eres!
2 (*strange*) **raro** *masc*, **rara** *fem*
a funny noise un ruido raro
That's funny, I'm sure I paid. Qué raro, estoy seguro de que pagué.

fur *noun*
1 (*on an animal*) el **pelaje** *masc*
2 (*for a coat*) la **piel** *fem*
a fur coat un abrigo de piel

furious *adjective*
furioso *masc*, **furiosa** *fem*
She was furious with Steve. Estaba furiosa con Steve.

♂ **furnished** *adjective*
amueblado *masc*, **amueblada** *fem*
a furnished flat un piso amueblado

♂ **furniture** *noun*
los **muebles** *plural masc*
a piece of furniture un mueble
to buy some furniture comprar [17] muebles

further *adverb*
(*at a greater distance*) **más lejos**
They live even further away. Viven aún más lejos.
further forward más adelante
further back más atrás
further in más adentro
further than the station más allá de la estación
ten kilometres further on diez kilómetros más adelante

fuse *noun*
el **fusible** *masc*

English-Spanish

fuss *noun*
  el **escándalo** *masc*
  to make a fuss montar[17] un escándalo
  He made a fuss about the bill. Montó un escándalo a causa de la factura.

fussy *adjective*
1 (*about how things are done*) **quisquilloso** *masc*, **quisquillosa** *fem*
  to be fussy about something ser[1] muy quisquilloso para algo

2 (*about food*) **maniático** *masc*, **maniática** *fem*
  to be fussy about food ser[1] muy maniático para la comida

future *noun*
  el **futuro** *masc*
  in future en el futuro
  a verb in the future un verbo en el futuro
  In future, ask me first. En el futuro, pregúntame antes.

a
b
c
d
e
f
g
h
i
j
k
l
m
n
o
p
q
r
s
t
u
v
w
x
y
z

G g

gadget noun
el **aparato** masc

to **gain** verb
adquirir [47]
to gain weight aumentar [17] de peso

galaxy noun
la **galaxia** fem

gale noun
el **vendaval** masc

Galicia noun
Galicia fem

Galician adjective & noun
1 **gallego** masc, **gallega** fem
2 (person) un **gallego** masc, una **gallega** fem
the Galicians los gallegos
3 (the language) el **gallego** masc

WORD TIP Adjectives and nouns for nationality, regional origin, and language do not have capital letters in Spanish.

gallery noun
1 (public art museum) el **museo de pintura**
2 (private art shop) la **galería de arte**

gambling noun
el **juego** masc

game noun
1 (with rules) el **juego** masc
a board game un juego de mesa
2 (of cards, etc) la **partida** fem
a game of cards una partida de cartas
3 (match) el **partido** masc
a game of football un partido de fútbol
4 (school sports) **games** los deportes
Jack's very good at games. Jack es muy buen deportista.
• **games console** la consola de juegos

gang noun
1 (one's friends) la **panda** fem
All the gang were there. Toda la panda estaba allí.
2 (of criminals) la **banda** fem

gangster noun
el & la **gángster** masc & fem

gap noun
1 (hole) el **hueco** masc
2 (interval in time) el **intervalo** masc
a two-year gap un intervalo de dos años
an age gap una diferencia de edad
• **gap year** el año libre antes de entrar a la universidad

garage noun
1 (for parking) el **garaje** masc
2 (for fuel) la **estación de servicio**
3 (for repairs) el **taller mecánico**

garden noun
el **jardín** masc

gardener noun
1 (as a job) el **jardinero** masc, la **jardinera** fem
2 (as a hobby) She is a keen gardener. Es una apasionada de la jardinería.

gardening noun
la **jardinería** fem

garlic noun
el **ajo** masc

garment noun
la **prenda** fem

gas noun
el **gas** masc
• **gas cooker** la cocina de gas
• **gas fire** la estufa de gas
• **gas meter** el contador de gas

gate noun
1 (of a garden) la **verja** fem
2 (of a field) el **portillo** masc
3 (at an airport) la **puerta (de embarque)**

to **gather** verb
1 (crowds) **juntarse** [17]
A crowd gathered. Se juntó una multitud.
2 (fruit, vegetables, flowers) **recoger** [3]
3 (to make out) as far as I can gather ... según tengo entendido ...

gay adjective
(homosexual) **gay** masc & fem

GCSEs noun plural
(Son exámenes que se realizan alrededor de los 16 años y abarcan hasta 12 asignaturas. Se califican desde A-star (nota máxima), a N (sin calificar). Muchos alumnos estudian para los A levels después de hacer los GCSEs.)
▷ **A levels**

gear noun
1 (in a car) la **marcha** fem
to change gear cambiar [17] de marcha
in third gear en tercera

2 (*equipment*) el **equipo** *masc*
　camping gear el equipo de acampada
　fishing gear los aparejos de pesca
3 (*things*) las **cosas** *plural fem*
　I've left all my gear at Gary's. He dejado
　todas mis cosas en casa de Gary.
· **gear lever** la palanca de cambio

gel *noun*
　el **gel** *masc*
　hair gel gel para el pelo

Gemini *noun*
1 (*the star sign*) el **Géminis** *masc*
2 (*a person*) un & una **géminis** *masc & fem*
　Steph's Gemini. Steph es géminis.

WORD TIP Use a small letter in Spanish to say *I am ... etc* with star signs. Star signs in Spanish are used without *el, un, la, una*.

gender *noun*
　(*of a word*) el **género** *masc*
　What is the gender of 'casa'? ¿De qué
　género es 'casa'?

ℰ **general** *noun* ▷ see **general** *adj*
　el **general** *masc*
　General O'Donnell el general O'Donnell

ℰ **general** *adjective* ▷ see **general** *noun*
　general *masc & fem*
　in general en general
· **general election** las elecciones generales
· **general knowledge** la cultura general

ℰ **generally** *adverb*
　generalmente

generation *noun*
　la **generación** *fem*

generous *adjective*
　generoso *masc*, **generosa** *fem*

genetics *noun*
　la **genética** *fem*

genius *noun*
　el **genio** *masc*
　Lisa, you're a genius! Lisa, ¡eres un genio!

ℰ **gentle** *adjective*
1 (*person, voice, nature*) **dulce** *masc & fem*
2 (*breeze, murmur, heat*) **suave** *masc & fem*

ℰ **gentleman** *noun*
　el **caballero** *masc*
　ladies and gentlemen señoras y
　caballeros ▷ **gents**

ℰ **gently** *adverb*
1 (*talk*) **dulcemente**
2 (*touch*) **suavemente**
3 (*handle*) **con cuidado**

ℰ **gents** *noun*
1 (*men's toilets*) los **servicios de caballeros**
　Where's the gents? ¿Dónde están los
　servicios de caballeros?
2 (*sign for men's toilets*) **Caballeros**

genuine *adjective*
1 (*real*) **auténtico** *masc*, **auténtica** *fem*
　a genuine diamond un diamante auténtico
2 (*sincere*) **sincero** *masc*, **sincera** *fem*
　She's very genuine. Es muy sincera.

ℰ **geography** *noun*
　la **geografía** *fem*

geology *noun*
　la **geología** *fem*

geometry *noun*
　la **geometría** *fem*

germ *noun*
　el **germen** *masc, pl:* los **gérmenes**

German *adjective & noun*
1 **alemán** *masc*, **alemana** *fem*
　my German class mi clase de alemán
　our German teacher nuestro profesor de
　alemán
2 (*person*) un **alemán** *masc*, una **alemana** *fem*
　the Germans los alemanes
3 (*the language*) el **alemán** *masc*

WORD TIP Adjectives and nouns for nationality, regional origin, and language do not have capital letters in Spanish.

Germany *noun*
　Alemania *fem*

ℰ to **get** *verb*
1 (*to obtain*) **conseguir** [64]
　Fred's got a job. Fred ha conseguido un
　trabajo.
　I got fifteen for my exam. Saqué un quince
　en el examen.
　Where did you get that jacket? ¿De dónde
　has sacado esa chaqueta?
2 (*to receive*) **recibir** [19]
　I got your letter yesterday. Recibí tu carta
　ayer.
　I got a bike for my birthday. Me regalaron
　una bicicleta por mi cumpleaños.
3 (*to fetch*) **ir** [8] **a buscar**
　Go and get some bread. Vete a buscar pan.
　I'll get your bag for you. Voy a buscar tu
　bolso.
4 (*to buy*) **comprar** [17]
　I got a nice shirt in the sales. Compré una
　camisa muy bonita en las rebajas.
5 (*to catch*) **coger** [3]
　She got a cold. Cogió un resfriado.
　I got the train. Cogí el tren. ▸▸

a
b
c
d
e
f
g
h
i
j
k
l
m
n
o
p
q
r
s
t
u
v
w
x
y
z

6 (*informal*) (*to understand*) **entender** [36]
Get it? ¿Entiendes?
7 (*to arrive*) **to get to a place** llegar [28] a un
lugar
When we got to London it was raining.
Cuando llegamos a Londres estaba
lloviendo.
How do I get to the cathedral? ¿Cómo llego
a la catedral?
We got here this morning. Llegamos esta
mañana.
What time did they get there? ¿A qué hora
llegaron?
8 (*to become*) **to get tired** cansarse [17]
She was getting worried. Se estaba
preocupando.
It's getting late. Se está haciendo
tarde.
I'm getting hungry. Me está entrando
hambre.
9 (*to talk about doing a job*) **to get something
done**
I must get some work done. Tengo que
trabajar un poco.
He's going to get that shelf put up. Va a
colocar ese estante.
10 (*to talk about getting a job done by someone
else*) **to get something done**
to get your hair cut cortarse [17] el pelo
My father got the house painted. Mi padre
hizo pintar la casa.
• to **get back**
volver [45]
Mum gets back at six. Mamá vuelve a las
seis.
• to **get something back**
(*to have something returned to you*) **We got
the money back.** Nos devolvieron el
dinero.
Did you get your books back? ¿Te
devolvieron los libros?
• to **get down**
bajar [17]
He got down from the tree. Bajó del
árbol.
• to **get into something**
to get into a vehicle entrar [17] en un
vehículo
He got into the car. Entró en el coche.
• to **get off something**
to get off a vehicle bajarse [17] de un
vehículo
I got off the train at Banbury. Me bajé del
tren en Banbury.
• to **get on**
(*to cope*) **How's Amanda getting on?**
¿Cómo le va a Amanda?

• to **get on something**
to get on a vehicle subir [19] a un vehículo
She got on the train at Reading. Subió al
tren en Reading.
• to **get on with**
to get on with somebody llevarse [17] bien
con alguien
She doesn't get on with her brother. No se
lleva bien con su hermano.
Thomas and Ben get on well. Thomas y Ben
se llevan bien.
• to **get out**
(*to leave*) **to get out of a place** salir [63] de un
lugar
I've got to get out of here. Tengo que salir
de aquí.
Laura got out of the car. Laura salió del
coche.
• to **get something out**
sacar [31] algo
Robert got his guitar out. Robert sacó la
guitarra.
• to **get together**
verse [16]
We must get together soon. Tenemos que
vernos pronto.
• to **get up**
levantarse [17]
I get up at seven. Me levanto a las siete.

ghost *noun*
el **fantasma** *masc*

giant
el **gigante** *masc*

giddy *adjective*
mareado *masc*, **mareada** *fem*
I'm feeling giddy. Me siento mareado.

⌀ **gift** *noun*
1 (*present*) el **regalo** *masc*
a Christmas gift un regalo de Navidad
2 (*talent*) **to have a gift for something** estar
[2] dotado, *fem* dotada para algo
Jo has a real gift for languages. Jo está
realmente dotada para los idiomas.

gig *noun*
el **concierto** *masc*

gigabyte *noun*
el **gigabyte** *masc*
a fifty gigabyte hard disk un disco duro de
cincuenta gigabytes

ginger *noun*
el **jengibre** *masc*
• **ginger-haired** *adj* pelirrojo *masc*,
pelirroja *fem*

Gipsy *noun*
   el **gitano** *masc*, la **gitana** *fem*

giraffe *noun*
   la **jirafa** *fem*

ℰ **girl** *noun*
1 (*child*) la **niña** *fem*
   three boys and four girls tres niños y cuatro niñas
   a little girl una niña pequeña
   when I was a little girl ... cuando yo era pequeña ...
2 (*teenager, young woman*) la **chica** *fem*
   an eighteen-year-old girl una chica de dieciocho años

ℰ **girlfriend** *noun*
1 (*partner in a relationship*) la **novia** *fem*
   Darren's girlfriend la novia de Darren
2 (*female friend*) la **amiga** *fem*
   Lizzie and her girlfriends have gone to the cinema. Lizzie y sus amigas han ido al cine.

ℰ to **give** *verb*
   dar [4]
   to give something to somebody darle [4] algo a alguien
   I gave Sandy the books. Le di los libros a Sandy.
   I'll give you my address. Te daré mis señas.
   Give me the key. Dame la llave.
   Yasmin's dad gave her the money. El padre de Yasmin le dio el dinero.
· to **give something away**
   regalar [17] **algo**
   She's given away all her books. Ha regalado todos sus libros.
· to **give something back to somebody**
   devolverle [45] **algo a alguien**
   I gave her back the keys. Le devolví las llaves.
· to **give in**
   ceder [18]
   She gave in in the end. Al final cedió.
· to **give up**
   rendirse [57]
   I give up! ¡Me rindo!
· to **give up doing something**
   dejar [17] **de hacer algo**
   She's given up smoking. Ha dejado de fumar.

glacier *noun*
   el **glaciar** *masc*

ℰ **glad** *adjective*
   to be glad to do something alegrarse [17] de hacer algo
   I'm glad to hear he's better. Me alegra saber que está mejor.
   I'm glad to be back. Me alegro de haber vuelto.

glamorous *adjective*
1 (*life, job*) **con mucho glamour**
2 (*film star*) **elegante** *masc & fem*

ℰ **glass** *noun*
1 (*for a drink*) el **vaso** *masc*
   a glass of water un vaso de agua
2 (*for windows, etc*) el **cristal** *masc*
   a glass table una mesa de cristal

ℰ **glasses** *plural noun*
   las **gafas** *plural fem*, (*Latin America*) los **anteojos** *masc pl*
   to wear glasses llevar [17] gafas

global *adjective*
   global *masc & fem*
· **global warming** el calentamiento global

globe *noun*
   (*model*) el **globo terráqueo**

gloomy *adjective*
1 (*expression*) **lúgubre** *masc & fem*
2 (*weather*) **gris** *masc & fem*

glory *noun*
   la **gloria** *fem*

glove *noun*
   el **guante** *masc*
   a pair of gloves un par de guantes

glue *noun*
   el **pegamento** *masc*

ℰ **go** *noun* ▷ see **go** *verb*
1 (*turn in a game*) Whose go is it? ¿A quién le toca?
   It's my go. Me toca a mí.
2 (*attempt*) to have a go at doing something intentar [17] hacer algo
   I'll have a go at mending it for you. Intentaré arreglártelo.

ℰ to **go** *verb* ▷ see **go** *noun*
1 (*to travel*) **ir** [8]
   to go to a concert ir [8] a un concierto
   Mark's gone to the dentist's. Mark ha ido al dentista.
   We're going to London tomorrow. Mañana vamos a Londres.
   I have never been abroad. No he estado nunca en el extranjero.
   Have you been to Spain? ¿Has estado en España? ▸▸

a
b
c
d
e
f
g
h
i
j
k
l
m
n
o
p
q
r
s
t
u
v
w
x
y
z

a
b
c
d
e
f
g
h
i
j
k
l
m
n
o
p
q
r
s
t
u
v
w
x
y
z

2 (*to talk about something that you are about to do*) **to be going to do something** ir [8] a hacer algo
I'm going to make some tea. Voy a hacer té.
He was going to phone me. Iba a llamarme.

3 (*person, people*) **irse** [8]
Pauline's already gone. Pauline ya se ha ido.
We're going on holiday tomorrow. Nos vamos de vacaciones mañana.

4 (*trains, planes*) **salir** [63]
The train goes at seven. El tren sale a las siete.

5 (*time*) **pasar** [17]
The time goes quickly. El tiempo pasa rápido.

6 (*to turn out*) **ir** [8]
to go well ir [8] bien
Did the party go well? ¿Qué tal fue la fiesta?
to go badly ir [8] mal
The party went badly. La fiesta no fue buena.

7 (*pain*) **pasarse** [17]
My headache's gone. Se me ha pasado el dolor de cabeza.

8 (*to be used up*) **The money has all gone.** Se ha acabado el dinero.

9 (*to become*) **to go deaf** quedarse [17] sordo
to go pale ponerse [11] pálido
Her face went red. Se puso colorada.

• to **go away**
irse [8]
Go away! ¡Vete!

• to **go back**
volver [45]
I'm going back to Madrid in March. Vuelvo a Madrid en marzo.
I'm not going back there again! ¡No voy a volver nunca!
I went back home. Volví a casa.

• to **go down**
1 (*to descend*) **bajar** [17]
to go down the stairs bajar las escaleras
She's gone down to the kitchen. Ha bajado a la cocina.
2 (*to decrease*) **bajar** [17]
Prices have gone down. Los precios han bajado.
3 (*tyres, balloons, airbeds*) **desinflarse** [17]

• to **go in**
entrar [17]
He went in and shut the door. Entró y cerró la puerta.

• to **go into something**
entrar [17] en algo
Fran went into the kitchen. Fran entró en la cocina.
This file won't go into my bag. Esta carpeta no entra en mi bolsa.

• to **go off**
1 (*bombs*) **estallar** [17]
The bomb went off in the street. **La bomba estalló en la calle.**
2 (*alarm clocks*) **sonar** [24]
My alarm clock went off at six. Mi despertador sonó a las seis.
3 (*fire alarms, burglar alarms*) **dispararse** [17]
The fire alarm went off. La alarma contra incendios se disparó.
4 (*milk, fish, meat*) **echarse** [17] **a perder**
The meat has gone off. La carne se ha echado a perder.

• to **go off something or someone**
I've gone off coffee. Ya no me gusta el café.
I've gone off him. Ya no me gusta.

• to **go on**
1 (*to happen*) **pasar** [17]
What's going on? ¿Qué pasa?
2 (*to continue*) **to go on doing something** seguir [64] haciendo algo
She went on talking. Siguió hablando.
3 (*to talk constantly*) **to go on about something** hablar [17] de algo
He's always going on about his dog. Siempre está hablando de su perro.

• to **go out**
1 (*to make an exit*) **salir** [63]
She went out of the kitchen. Salió de la cocina.
I'm going out tonight. Voy a salir esta noche.
2 (*to have a relationship*) **to be going out with somebody** salir [63] con alguien
She's going out with my brother. Está saliendo con mi hermano.
3 (*lights, fires*) **apagarse** [28]
The light went out. La luz se apagó.

• to **go past something**
pasar [17] por algo
We went past your house. Pasamos por tu casa.

• to **go round** to go round to somebody's house ir [8] a casa de alguien
I went round to Fred's last night. Anoche fui a casa de Fred.

• to **go round something**
1 (*a building, a park, a garden*) **recorrer** [18] algo
2 (*a museum, a monument*) **visitar** [17] algo

- to **go through something**
pasar [17] **por algo**
The train went through York. El tren pasó por York.
You can go through my office. Puedes pasar por mi oficina.
- to **go up**
1 (*to ascend*) **subir** [19]
She's gone up to her room. Ha subido a su habitación.
to go up the stairs subir las escaleras
2 (*to increase*) **subir** [19]
The price of petrol has gone up. El precio de la gasolina ha subido.

goal *noun*
el **gol** *masc*
to score a goal marcar [31] un gol
to win by three goals to two ganar [17] por tres goles a dos
- **goalkeeper** el portero, la portera

goat *noun*
la **cabra** *fem*

god *noun* ▷ see **God** *noun*
el **dios** *masc*

God *noun* ▷ see **god** *noun*
Dios *masc*
to believe in God creer [37] en Dios

godchild *noun*
el **ahijado** *masc*, la **ahijada** *fem*

goddaughter *noun*
la **ahijada** *fem*

goddess *noun*
la **diosa** *fem*

godfather *noun*
el **padrino** *masc*

godmother *noun*
la **madrina** *fem*

godparent *noun*
el **padrino** *masc*, la **madrina** *fem*
my godparents mis padrinos

godson *noun*
el **ahijado** *masc*

goggles *plural noun*
swimming goggles las gafas de natación
skiing goggles las gafas de esquí

go-karting *noun*
el **karting** *masc*
to go go-karting hacer [7] karting

gold *noun*
el **oro** *masc*
a gold bracelet una pulsera de oro

goldfish *noun*
el **pez de colores** *pl:* los **peces de colores**

golf *noun*
el **golf** *masc*
to play golf jugar [27] al golf

golf club *noun*
1 (*place*) el **club de golf**
2 (*stick used to hit a golf ball*) el **palo de golf**

golf course *noun*
el **campo de golf**

golfer *noun*
el & la **golfista** *masc & fem*

♪ **good** *adjective* ▷ see **good** *noun*
1 (*of high quality*) **bueno** *masc*, **buena** *fem*
a good meal una buena comida
She's a good teacher. Es una buena profesora.
His Spanish is very good. Habla español muy bien.
to feel good sentirse [14] bien
2 (*well-behaved*) **bueno** *masc*, **buena** *fem*
Be good! ¡Sé bueno!
3 (*healthy, wholesome*) to be good for you ser [1] bueno para la salud
Tomatoes are good for you. Los tomates son muy buenos para la salud.
4 (*well*) to feel good sentirse [14] bien
I'm not feeling too good. No me siento muy bien.
5 (*skilled*) to be good at something tener [9] facilidad para algo
She's good at languages. Tiene facilidad para las lenguas.
I'm good at cooking. Cocino bien.
6 (*kind*) **amable** *masc & fem*
She's been very good to me. Ha sido muy amable conmigo.
7 (*appealing*) **bien** *masc & fem*
It smelled good. Olía bien.
It tastes good. Sabe bien.
It looks good. Tiene buen aspecto.
8 (*well done*) Good! ¡Muy bien!

WORD TIP *bueno* becomes *buen* before a masculine singular noun.

♪ **good** *noun* ▷ see **good** *adj*
1 (*benefit*) el **bien** *masc*
to do good hacer [7] bien
to do somebody good hacerle [8] bien a alguien
It will do you good. Te hará bien.
2 (*for all time*) for good para siempre
I've stopped smoking for good. He dejado de fumar para siempre.

a
b
c
d
e
f
g
h
i
j
k
l
m
n
o
p
q
r
s
t
u
v
w
x
y
z

♂ goodbye *exclamation*
▷ see **goodbye** *noun*
adiós

♂ goodbye *noun* ▷ see **goodbye** *excl*
to say goodbye **despedirse** [57]
We said goodbye at the airport. Nos despedimos en el aeropuerto.
to say goodbye to somebody **despedirse de alguien**
I must say goodbye to Sam. Tengo que despedirme de Sam.

Good Friday *noun*
el **Viernes Santo**

good-looking *adjective*
guapo *masc*, **guapa** *fem*
Maya's boyfriend's really good-looking. El novio de Maya es muy guapo.

goodness *exclamation*
¡Dios mío!
For goodness' sake! ¡Por Dios!

goods *plural noun*
los **artículos** *plural masc*
· **goods train** el tren de mercancías

goose *noun*
el **ganso** *masc*
· **goose pimples** la carne de gallina

gorgeous *adjective*
precioso *masc*, **preciosa** *fem*
a gorgeous dress un vestido precioso
It's a gorgeous day. Es un día precioso.

gorilla *noun*
el **gorila** *masc*

gosh *exclamation*
¡Dios mío!

gossip *noun* ▷ see **gossip** *verb*
1 (*person*) el & la **cotilla** *masc & fem*
2 (*news*) el **cotilleo** *masc*
What's the latest gossip? ¿Qué hay de nuevo?

to **gossip** *verb* ▷ see **gossip** *noun*
cotillear [17]

government *noun*
el **gobierno** *masc*

mini-info **government**

Spain is a parliamentary democracy and has a written constitution. The central government is responsible for running the country which is divided into 17 autonomous regions (Comunidades Autónomas: CCAA), which control many aspects of regional life.

to **grab** *verb*
1 (*to seize*) **agarrar** [17]
She grabbed my arm. Me agarró el brazo.
2 (*to snatch*) to grab something from somebody **arrebatarle** [17] algo a alguien
He grabbed the book from me. Me arrebató el libro.

graceful *adjective*
elegante *masc & fem*

grade *noun*
(*mark*) la **nota** *fem*
to get good grades **sacar** [31] buenas notas

gradual *adjective*
gradual *masc & fem*

gradually *adverb*
poco a poco
The weather got gradually better. El tiempo mejoró poco a poco.

graduate *noun*
el **licenciado** *masc*, la **licenciada** *fem*

graffiti *plural noun*
los **grafitti** *plural masc*

grain *noun*
el **grano** *masc*

♂ gram *noun*
el **gramo** *masc*

grammar *noun*
la **gramática** *fem*

grammatical *adjective*
gramatical *masc & fem*
a grammatical error un error gramatical

gran *noun*
la **abuelita** *fem*

♂ grandchildren *plural noun*
los **nietos** *plural masc*

granddad *noun*
(*informal*) el **abuelito** *masc*

♂ granddaughter *noun*
la **nieta** *fem*

♂ grandfather *noun*
el **abuelo** *masc*

grandma *noun*
(*informal*) la **abuelita** *fem*

♂ grandmother *noun*
la **abuela** *fem*

grandpa *noun*
(*informal*) el **abuelito** *masc*

♂ grandparents *plural noun*
los **abuelos** *plural masc*

ꝺ **grandson** *noun*
  el **nieto** *masc*

granny *noun*
  (*informal*) la **abuelita** *fem*

ꝺ **grape** *noun*
  la **uva** *fem*
  a bunch of grapes un racimo de uvas
  to buy some grapes comprar[17] uvas

grapefruit *noun*
  el **pomelo** *masc*

graph *noun*
  el **gráfico** *masc*

graphics *noun*
  los **gráficos** *plural masc*

ꝺ **grass** *noun*
1 (*plant*) la **hierba** *fem*
  He was sitting on the grass. Estaba sentado en la hierba.
2 (*lawn*) el **césped** *masc*
  to cut the grass cortar[17] el césped

grasshopper *noun*
  el **saltamontes** *masc, pl:* los **saltamontes**

to **grate** *verb*
  rallar[17]
  grated cheese queso rallado

grateful *adjective*
  agradecido *masc,* **agradecida** *fem*

grater *noun*
  el **rallador** *masc*

grave *noun*
  la **tumba** *fem*

gravel *noun*
  la **grava** *fem*

graveyard *noun*
  el **cementerio** *masc*

gravity *noun*
  la **gravedad** *fem*

gravy *noun*
  la **salsa del asado** *fem*

grease *noun*
  la **grasa** *fem*

ꝺ **greasy** *adjective*
1 (*hands, surface*) **grasiento** *masc,* **grasienta** *fem*
2 (*hair, skin, food*) **graso** *masc,* **grasa** *fem*
  to have greasy skin tener[9] la piel grasa
  I hate greasy food. No soporto la comida grasa.

ꝺ **great** *adjective*
1 (*major, important*) **gran** *masc & fem*
  a great poet un gran poeta
  a great opportunity una gran oportunidad
  great expectations grandes esperanzas
2 (*terrific*) **estupendo** *masc,* **estupenda** *fem*
  It was a great party! ¡Fue una fiesta estupenda!
  Great! ¡Estupendo!
3 a great deal of something muchísimo *masc,* muchísima *fem*
  I've got a great deal of work. Tengo muchísimo trabajo.
  a great many muchos *plural masc,* muchas *plural fem*
  There are a great many things still to be done. Aún quedan muchas cosas por hacer.

Great Britain *noun*
  Gran Bretaña *fem*

Greece *noun*
  Grecia *fem*

greedy *adjective*
  glotón *masc,* **glotona** *fem*

Greek *adjective & noun*
1 **griego** *masc,* **griega** *fem*
2 (*person*) un **griego** *masc,* una **griega** *fem*
  the Greeks los griegos *plural masc*
3 (*the language*) el **griego** *masc*

WORD TIP Adjectives and nouns for nationality, regional origin, and language do not have capital letters in Spanish.

ꝺ **green** *adjective*
1 (*colour*) **verde** *masc & fem*
  a green door una puerta verde
2 (*good for the environment*) **verde** *masc & fem*
  the Green Party el Partido Verde

ꝺ **green** *noun*
1 (*colour*) el **verde** *masc*
  a pale green un verde pálido
2 (*vegetables*) greens las verduras
3 (*ecologists*) the Greens los verdes

greengrocer *noun*
  el **verdulero** *masc,* la **verdulera** *fem*
  the greengrocer's la verdulería

greenhouse *noun*
  el **invernadero** *masc*
• **greenhouse effect** el efecto invernadero

ꝺ **green light** *noun*
  la **luz verde** *fem*

greetings *plural noun*
  Season's Greetings! ¡Feliz Navidad!
• **greetings card** la tarjeta de felicitación

a
b
c
d
e
f
g
h
i
j
k
l
m
n
o
p
q
r
s
t
u
v
w
x
y
z

ᵍ **grey** *adjective*
1 *(colour)* **gris** *masc & fem*
a grey skirt una falda gris
2 *(hair)* **canoso** *masc*, **canosa** *fem*
to have grey hair tener [9] el pelo canoso
· **greyhound** el galgo

grid *noun*
1 *(grating)* la **parrilla** *fem*
2 *(network)* la **red** *fem*

grief *noun*
el **dolor** *masc*

ᵍ **grill** *noun* ▷ see **grill** *verb*
la **parilla** *masc*

ᵍ to **grill** *verb* ▷ see **grill** *noun*
to grill something hacer [7] algo a la parilla
I grilled the sausages. Hice las salchichas a la parilla.
grilled sardines las sardinas a la parilla

grin *noun* ▷ see **grin** *verb*
la **sonrisa** *fem*

to **grin** *verb* ▷ see **grin** *noun*
sonreír [61]

to **grip** *verb*
agarrar [17]

grit *noun*
la **arenilla** *fem*

groan *noun* ▷ see **groan** *verb*
1 *(of pain)* el **gemido** *masc*
2 *(of disgust, boredom)* el **gruñido** *masc*

to **groan** *verb* ▷ see **groan** *noun*
1 *(in pain)* **gemir** [57]
2 *(in disgust, boredom)* **refunfuñar** [17]

ᵍ **grocer** *noun*
el **tendero** *masc*, la **tendera** *fem*
My dad's a grocer. Mi padre es tendero.
the grocer's la tienda de comestibles

ᵍ **groceries** *plural noun*
las **cosas de comer**
to buy some groceries comprar [17] cosas de comer

groom *noun*
el **novio** *masc*

ᵍ **ground** *adjective* ▷ see **ground** *noun*
molido *masc*, **molida** *fem*
· **ground coffee** el café molido

ᵍ **ground** *noun* ▷ see **ground** *adj*
1 *(earth, floor)* el **suelo** *masc*
to sit on the ground sentarse [29] en el suelo
to throw something on the ground tirar [17] algo al suelo

2 *(for sport)* el **campo** *masc*
a football ground un campo de fútbol

ᵍ **ground floor** *noun*
la **planta baja**
We live on the ground floor. Vivimos en la planta baja.

ᵍ **group** *noun*
el **grupo** *masc*

ᵍ to **grow** *verb*
1 *(plants, hair, people)* **crecer** [35]
Your hair's grown. Te ha crecido el pelo.
My little sister's grown a lot this year. Mi hermana pequeña ha crecido mucho este año.
2 *(fruit, vegetables)* **cultivar** [17]
Our neighbour grows strawberries. Nuestro vecino cultiva fresas.
3 to grow a beard dejarse [17] barba
4 *(to become)* to grow old envejecer [35]
to grow tired cansarse [17]
to grow smaller hacerse [7] más pequeño
· to **grow up**
crecer [35]
The children are growing up. Los niños están creciendo.
She grew up in Scotland. Creció en Escocia.

to **growl** *verb*
gruñir [65]

grown-up *noun*
el **adulto** *masc*, la **adulta** *fem*

growth *noun*
el **crecimiento** *masc*

grudge *noun*
to bear a grudge against somebody guardarle [17] rencor a alguien
She bears me a grudge. Me guarda rencor.

gruesome *adjective*
horrible *masc & fem*

to **grumble** *verb*
refunfuñar [17]
She's always grumbling. Siempre está refunfuñando.
to grumble about something refunfuñar por algo

guarantee *noun* ▷ see **guarantee** *verb*
la **garantía** *fem*
a one-year guarantee una garantía de un año

to **guarantee** *verb* ▷ see **guarantee** *noun*
garantizar [22]

to **guard** *verb* ▷ see **guard** *noun*
vigilar [17]

guard *noun* ▷ see **guard** *verb*

1 (*soldier*) el & la **guardia** *masc & fem*
 a prison guard un guardia de prisiones
2 (*on a train*) el **jefe de tren**, la **jefa de tren**
· **guard dog** el perro guardián

guardian *noun*
 el **tutor** *masc*, la **tutora** *fem*

Guatemala *noun*
 Guatemala *fem*

Guatemalan *adjective & noun*

1 **guatemalteco** *masc*, **guatemalteca** *fem*
2 un **guatemalteco** *masc*, una
 guatemalteca *fem*
 the Guatemalans los guatemaltecos

> **WORD TIP** Adjectives and nouns for nationality
> and regional origin do not have capital letters in
> Spanish.

guess *noun* ▷ see **guess** *verb*
 la **adivinanza** *fem*
 Have a guess! ¡Adivina!
 It's a good guess. Lo has adivinado.

to **guess** *verb* ▷ see **guess** *noun*

1 (*to work out*) **adivinar** [17]
 Guess who I saw last night! ¡Adivina a quién
 vi anoche!
 You'll never guess! ¡No lo vas a adivinar
 nunca!
 Guess what? ¿Sabes qué?
2 (*to suppose*) **suponer** [11]
 I guess so. Supongo que sí.
 I guess not. Supongo que no.

guest *noun*

1 (*person coming to your home*) el **invitado** *masc*,
 la **invitada** *fem*
 We've got guests coming tonight.
 Tenemos invitados esta noche.
2 (*person staying at a hotel*) el & la **cliente** *masc &
 fem*

♪ **guide** *noun*

1 (*person who helps tourists*) , el & la **guía** *masc &
 fem*
2 (*guidebook*) la **guía** *fem*
3 (*female member of the scouting
 movement*) Guide la guía *fem*

· **guidebook** la guía
· **guide dog** el perro lazarillo
· **guideline** la pauta

guilty *adjective*
 culpable *masc & fem*
 to feel guilty sentirse [14] culpable

guinea pig *noun*

1 (*pet*) la **cobaya** *fem*
2 (*subject of an experiment*) el **conejillo de
 indias**

guitar *noun*
 la **guitarra** *fem*
 to play the guitar tocar [31] la guitarra
 on the guitar a la guitarra

guitarist *noun*
 el & la **guitarrista** *masc & fem*

gum *noun*

1 (*part of your mouth*) la **encía** *fem*
2 (*chewing gum*) el **chicle** *masc*

gun *noun*

1 (*pistol*) la **pistola** *fem*
2 (*rifle*) el **fusil** *masc*

guy *noun*
 (*informal*) el **tipo** *masc*
 a guy from Newcastle un tipo de Newcastle
 He's a nice guy. Es un tipo muy majo.
· **guy rope** el viento (de una tienda de
 campaña)

♪ **gym** *noun*

1 (*gymnasium*) el **gimnasio** *masc*
 to go to the gym ir [8] al gimnasio
2 (*gymnastics*) la **gimnasia** *fem*

♪ **gymnasium** *noun*
 el **gimnasio** *masc*

gymnast *noun*
 el & la **gimnasta** *masc & fem*

gymnastics *noun*
 la **gimnasia** *fem*
 to do gymnastics hacer [7] gimnasia

H h

⚤ **habit** *noun*
la **costumbre** *fem*
to have a habit of doing something tener
[9] la costumbre de hacer algo
It's a bad habit. Es una mala costumbre.

hacker *noun*
el **pirata informático**, la **pirata
informática**

hadn't *short for* **had not** (*See:* **to have**)

to hail *verb* ▷ see **hail** *noun*
granizar[22]

hail *noun* ▷ see **hail** *verb*
el **granizo** *masc*
· **hailstone** el granizo
· **hailstorm** la granizada

⚤ **hair** *noun*
1 (*on your head*) el **pelo** *masc*
a hair un pelo
to have short hair tener[9] el pelo corto
to brush your hair cepillarse[17] el pelo
to wash your hair lavarse[17] el pelo
to have your hair cut cortarse[17] el pelo
She's had her hair cut. Se ha cortado el
pelo.
2 (*on your body*) el **vello** *masc*
3 (*on an animal, plant*) el **pelo** *masc*
· **hairbrush** el cepillo del pelo

haircut *noun*
el **corte de pelo** *masc*
I like your new haircut. Me gusta tu nuevo
corte de pelo.
to have a haircut cortarse[17] el pelo

⚤ **hairdresser** *noun*
el **peluquero** *masc*, la **peluquera** *fem*
at the hairdresser's en la peluquería
She's a hairdresser. Es peluquera.

hairdryer *noun*
el **secador de pelo** *masc*

hairspray *noun*
la **laca del pelo**

hairstyle *noun*
el **peinado** *masc*

hairy *adjective*
peludo *masc*, **peluda** *fem*

Haiti *noun*
Haití *masc*

Haitian *adjective & noun*
1 **haitiano** *masc*, **haitiana** *fem*
2 un **haitiano** *masc*, una **haitiana** *fem*
the Haitians los haitianos

WORD TIP Adjectives and nouns for nationality
and regional origin do not have capital letters in
Spanish.

⚤ **half** *adjective, adverb* ▷ see **half** *noun, pron*
1 (*divided by two*) **medio** *masc*, **media** *fem*
one and a half hours una hora y media
It's half price. Está a medio precio.
2 (*asleep, drunk, etc*) **medio**
She was half asleep. Estaba medio
dormida.
3 **half a** medio *masc*, media *fem*
half a litre medio litro
half an hour media hora
half an apple media manzana
4 **half the** la mitad de
half the people la mitad de la gente
Half the time he's not here. La mitad del
tiempo no está aquí.

⚤ **half** *noun, pronoun* ▷ see **half** *adj, adv*
1 (*one of two equal parts*) la **mitad** *fem*
half of something la mitad de algo
I gave him half of the money. Le di la mitad
del dinero.
I only want half. Sólo quiero la mitad.
to cut something in half cortar[17] algo por
la mitad
2 (*the fraction*) el **medio** *masc*
three and a half tres y medio
She's five and a half. Tiene seis años y
medio.
3 (*in time expressions*) **an hour and a half** una
hora y media
It's half past three. Son las tres y media.
4 (*Sport*) el **tiempo** *masc*
the first half el primer tiempo
· **half board** la media pensión

half hour *noun*
la **media hora**
every half hour cada media hora

half price *adjective, adverb*
a mitad de precio
half-price CDs compactos a mitad de
precio
I bought it half price. Lo compré a mitad de
precio.

half time *noun*
(*Sport*) el **descanso** *masc*
at half time en el descanso

ℰ **half term** *noun*
las **vacaciones de mitad de trimestre**
What are you doing at half term? ¿Qué vas a hacer durante las vacaciones de mitad de trimestre?

halfway *adverb*
1 (*in distance*) **a mitad de camino**
halfway between Málaga and Granada a mitad de camino entre Málaga y Granada
2 to be halfway through something ir[8] por la mitad de
I'm halfway through my homework. Voy por la mitad de los deberes.

ℰ **hall** *noun*
1 (*in a house*) la **entrada** *fem*
2 (*public building*) el **salón** *masc*
the village hall el salón de actos del pueblo
a concert hall una sala de conciertos

ℰ **hallo** *exclamation* ▷ **hello**

ℰ **ham** *noun*
1 (*cooked*) el **jamón de York**
2 (*cured*) el **jamón serrano**

hamburger *noun*
la **hamburguesa** *fem*

hammer *noun*
el **martillo** *masc*

hammock *noun*
la **hamaca** *fem*

hamster *noun*
el **hámster** *masc*, pl: los **hámsters**

ℰ **hand** *noun* ▷ see **hand** *verb*
1 (*part of your body*) la **mano** *fem*
to have something in your hand tener[9] algo en la mano
to be holding hands (*two people*) ir[8] cogidos de la mano
They were holding hands. Iban cogidos de la mano.
2 (*of a watch, clock*) la **manecilla** *fem*
the hour hand la manecilla de las horas
3 (*help*) to give somebody a hand echar[17] una mano a alguien
Can you give me a hand to move the table? ¿Puedes echarme una mano para mover la mesa?
Do you need a hand? ¿Necesitas que te echen una mano?
4 (*to talk about possible options*) on the one hand ... por un lado ...
on the other hand ... por otro lado ...

ℰ to **hand** *verb* ▷ see **hand** *noun*
to hand something to somebody pasarle [17] algo a alguien
I handed him the keys. Le pasé las llaves.
• to hand something in entregar[17] algo
It must be handed in on Tuesday. Hay que entregarlo el martes.
• **handbag** el bolso
• **handbrake** el freno de mano
• **handcuffs** las esposas

handful *noun*
el **puñado** *masc*
a handful of something un puñado de algo

handicapped *adjective*
disminuido *masc*, **disminuida** *fem*

ℰ **handicrafts** *plural noun*
las **artesanías** *plural fem*
an exhibition of local handicrafts una exposición de artesanías locales

ℰ **handkerchief** *noun*
el **pañuelo** *masc*
a paper handkerchief un pañuelo de papel

ℰ to **handle** *verb* ▷ see **handle** *noun*
1 (*to touch*) **tocar**[31]
Please do not handle the goods. Se ruega no tocar la mercancía.
2 (*to be in charge of*) **encargarse**[28] **de**
Gina handles the accounts. Gina se encarga de la contabilidad.
3 (*people*) **tratar**[17]
She's good at handling people. Es buena para tratar con la gente.
4 (*a situation*) **manejar**[17]
How did they handle the emergency? ¿Cómo manejaron la emergencia?

handle *noun* ▷ see **handle** *verb*
1 (*of a door*) el **picaporte** *masc*
2 (*of a drawer*) el **tirador** *masc*
3 (*of a knife, tool, pan*) el **mango** *masc*
4 (*on a cup, basket*) el **asa** *fem*

WORD TIP *asa* takes el or un in the singular even though it is feminine.

• **handlebars** el manillar

hand luggage *noun*
el **equipaje de mano**

ℰ **handsome** *adjective*
guapo *masc*
He's a very handsome guy. Es un tipo muy guapo.

handwriting *noun*
la **letra** *fem*

a
b
c
d
e
f
g
h
i
j
k
l
m
n
o
p
q
r
s
t
u
v
w
x
y
z

English-Spanish

ℰ **handy** *adjective*
1 (*useful, practical*) **práctico** *masc*, **práctica** *fem*
This knife is very handy . Este cuchillo es muy práctico.
2 (*nearby*) **a mano**
I always keep a notebook handy. Siempre tengo un cuaderno a mano.

ℰ to **hang** *verb*
colgar [23]
We hung the mirror on the wall. Colgamos el espejo en la pared.
There was a mirror hanging on the wall. Había un espejo colgado en la pared.
• to **hang on**
esperar [17]
Hang on a second! ¡Espera un poco!
• to **hang up**
(*on the phone*) **colgar** [23]
She hung up on me. Me colgó.
Don't hang up. No cuelgues. (*informal*)
• to **hang something up**
colgar [23] **algo**
You can hang your coat up in the hall. Puedes colgar el abrigo en la entrada.

hangover *noun*
la **resaca** *fem*
to have a hangover **tener** [9] resaca

to **happen** *verb*
pasar [17]
What's happening? ¿Qué pasa?
What happened to him? ¿Qué le pasó?
It happened in June. Pasó en junio.
What's happened to the can-opener? ¿Dónde se ha metido el abridor?

happily *adverb*
1 (*cheerfully*) **alegremente**
She smiled happily. Sonrió alegremente.
2 (*willingly*) **con mucho gusto**
I'll happily do it for you. Lo haré por ti con mucho gusto.

happiness *noun*
la **felicidad** *fem*

ℰ **happy** *adjective*
1 (*joyful*) **feliz** *masc & fem* (pl: **felices**)
the happy event el feliz acontecimiento
He's a happy person. Es una persona muy feliz.
to make somebody happy **hacer** [7] feliz a alguien
Happy birthday! ¡Feliz cumpleaños!
2 (*pleased*) to be happy **alegrarse** [17]
I'm so happy for you. Me alegro mucho por ti.

She'd be happy to help. Ayudaría con mucho gusto.
3 (*satisfied*) **contento** *masc*, **contenta** *fem*
to be happy with something **estar** [2] contento con algo
She's very happy with her present. Está muy contenta con su regalo.
She's not happy with her work. No está contenta con su trabajo.

ℰ **harbour** *noun*
el **puerto** *masc*

ℰ **hard** *adverb* ▷ see **hard** *adj*
1 (*with force*) **con fuerza**
I pushed it hard. Lo empujé con fuerza.
I hit her hard. Le pegué fuerte.
2 (*a great deal*) **mucho**
to study hard **estudiar** [17] mucho
to try hard **esforzarse** [26] mucho
to work hard **trabajar** [17] duro

ℰ **hard** *adjective* ▷ see **hard** *adv*
1 (*substance*) **duro** *masc*, **dura** *fem*
hard stones piedras duras
The carrots are hard. Las zanahorias están duras.
2 (*question, piece of work*) **difícil** *masc & fem*
a hard question una pregunta difícil
It's hard to know what to do. Es difícil saber qué hacer.
• **hard-boiled egg** el huevo duro
• **hard disk** el disco duro

hardly *adverb*
apenas
I can hardly hear him. Apenas lo oigo.
hardly any casi nada
There's hardly any milk. Casi no hay nada de leche.
hardly ever casi nunca
I hardly ever see them. Casi nunca los veo.

hard up *adjective*
(*informal*) to be hard up **estar** [2] mal de dinero

harm *noun* ▷ see **harm** *verb*
el **daño** *masc*
It won't do you any harm. No te va a hacer daño.

to **harm** *verb* ▷ see **harm** *noun*
to harm somebody **hacerle** [7] daño a alguien
A cup of coffee won't harm you. Una taza de café no te va a hacer daño.

harvest *noun*
la **cosecha** *fem*
to get the harvest in **hacer** [7] la cosecha

hasn't *short for* **has not** (See: **to have**)

♂ **hat** *noun*
  el **sombrero** *masc*

♂ to **hate** *verb*
  odiar [17]
  I hate geography. Odio la geografía.
  I hate ironing. Odio planchar.

hatred *noun*
  el **odio** *masc*

haunted *adjective*
  embrujado *masc*, **embrujada** *fem*

♂ to **have** *verb*
  1 (*to own*) **tener** [9]
  We have a dog and a cat. Tenemos un perro y un gato.
  to have got something tener [9] algo
  What have you got in your hand? ¿Qué tienes en la mano?
  Anna has three brothers. Anna tiene tres hermanos.
  How many sisters have you got? ¿Cuántas hermanas tienes?
  She has a lot of patience. Tiene mucha paciencia.

  2 (*to form past tenses, with have, had + -ed words*) **haber** [6]
  I've finished. He terminado.
  Have you fixed it? ¿Lo has arreglado?
  Rosie hasn't arrived yet. Rosie aún no ha llegado.
  He had lied. Había mentido.
  I have just seen her. Acabo de verla.
  Have you been waiting long? ¿Hace mucho que esperas?

  3 (*in short questions*) **She's done this before, hasn't she?** Ha hecho esto antes, ¿no?
  They have arrived, haven't they? Han llegado ¿no?

  WORD TIP In short questions like *hasn't she*, *haven't you?*, *has, have* are not translated.

  4 **to have to do something** tener [9] que hacer algo
  I have to phone my mum. Tengo que llamar a mi madre.
  Have you got to go? ¿Tienes que ir?
  You don't have to come if you don't want to. No tienes que venir si no quieres.

  5 (*to receive*) **tener** [9]
  We had a letter from him last week. Tuvimos carta de él la semana pasada.
  Have you had any news? ¿Has tenido noticias?

  6 (*food, drink*) **tomar** [17]
  We had a coffee. Tomamos un café.
  What will you have? ¿Qué vais a tomar?
  I'll have an omelette. Voy a tomar una tortilla.

  to have lunch comer [18]
  to have dinner (*in the evening*) cenar [17], (*at midday*) comer [18]

  7 (*to experience, to undergo*) **tener** [9]
  They had an accident. Tuvieron un accidente.
  We had a week in Madrid. Estuvimos una semana en Madrid.
  to have a shower ducharse [17]
  to have a bath bañarse [17]

  8 (*to organize*) **to have a party** dar [4] una fiesta

  9 (*to suffer from*) **tener** [9]
  He has cancer. Tiene cáncer.
  I had flu. Tuve la gripe.
  You've got a cold. Estás resfriado.
  She has stomachache. Le duele el estómago.
  I have a terrible headache. Me duele mucho la cabeza.

  10 (*to give birth to*) **tener** [9]
  She had twins. Tuvo gemelos.

  11 (*to talk about getting a job done by someone else*) **I'm going to have my hair cut.** Voy a cortarme el pelo.
  She's had her TV repaired. Ha arreglado la tele.

  12 **to have just done something** acabar [17] de hacer algo
  Ellie has just arrived. Ellie acaba de llegar
  They've just come in. Acaban de entrar.

  • to **have something on llevar** [17] algo
  What did she have on? ¿Qué llevaba puesto?

haven't *short for* **have not** (*See:* **to have**)

hawk *noun*
  el **halcón** *masc*

hay *noun*
  el **heno** *masc*
  • **hay fever** la fiebre del heno

hazelnut *noun*
  la **avellana** *fem*

♂ **he** *pronoun*
  1 (*'he' is usually part of the verb in Spanish*) **He lives in Newcastle.** Vive en Newcastle.
  He's a student. Es estudiante.
  He's a very good teacher. Es muy buen profesor.
  Here he is! ¡Aquí está!

  2 (*to make clear or emphasize who did something*) **él**
  She went to the theatre, he went to ▸▸

a b c d e f **g h** i j k l m n o p q r s t u v w x y z

♂ indicates key words   503

a
b
c
d
e
f
g
h
i
j
k
l
m
n
o
p
q
r
s
t
u
v
w
x
y
z

the cinema. Ella fue al teatro y él fue al cine.
He did it. Lo hizo él.

WORD TIP *he*, like other subject pronouns *I, you, she*, etc, is generally not translated in Spanish; the form of the verb tells you whether the subject of the verb is *I, we, they*, etc, so *he* is translated only for emphasis or for clarity.

♂ **head** *noun*
1 (*part of the body*) la **cabeza** *fem*
   at the head of the queue a la cabeza de la
   cola
   He had a cap on his head. Tenía un
   sombrero en la cabeza.
2 (*of a school*) el **director** *masc*, la **directora**
   fem
3 (*when tossing a coin*) 'Heads or tails?'—
   'Heads.' '¿Cara o cruz?'— 'Cara.'
• to **head for something**
   dirigirse[49] a algo
   Liz headed for the door. Liz se dirigió a la
   puerta.

♂ **headache** *noun*
   el **dolor de cabeza**
   I've got a headache. Me duele la cabeza.

headlight *noun*
   el **faro** *masc*

headline *noun*
   el **titular** *masc*
   to hit the headlines aparecer[35] en los
   titulares

headmaster *noun*
   el **director** *masc*

headmistress *noun*
   la **directora** *fem*

♂ **head office** *noun*
   la **sede** *fem*

headphones *plural noun*
   los **auriculares** *plural masc*

headquarters *plural noun*
1 (*of an organization*) la **sede** *fem*
2 (*military*) el **cuartel general**

♂ **headteacher** *noun*
   el **director** *masc*, la **directora** *fem*

♂ **health** *noun*
   la **salud** *fem*
   It's bad for your health. Es malo para la
   salud.
• **health centre** el centro médico

healthy *adjective*
1 (*in good health*) **sano** *masc*, **sana** *fem*
   to be healthy estar[2] sano
2 (*good for your health*) **sano** *masc*, **sana** *fem*
   a healthy diet una dieta sana

heap *noun*
   el **montón** *masc*
   I've got heaps of things to do. Tengo
   montones de cosas que hacer.

♂ to **hear** *verb*
   oír[56]
   I can't hear you. No te oigo.
   I can't hear anything. No oigo nada.
   I hear you've bought a dog. He oído que te
   has comprado un perro.
• to **hear about something**
   enterarse[17] de algo
   Have you heard about the concert? ¿Te has
   enterado de lo del concierto?
• to **hear from somebody**
   Have you heard from Amanda? ¿Sabes
   algo de Amanda?
   I haven't heard from them. No sé nada de
   ellos.

hearing aid *noun*
   el **audífono** *masc*

heart *noun*
1 (*part of the body*) el **corazón** *masc*
2 (*in cards*) **hearts** los corazones *masc pl*
   the jack of hearts la jota de corazones
• **heart attack** el ataque al corazón

♂ **heat** *noun* ▷ see **heat** *verb*
   el **calor** *masc*

♂ to **heat** *verb* ▷ see **heat** *noun*
1 (*to become hot*) **calentarse**[29]
   The soup's heating. La sopa se está
   calentando.
2 (*to make hot*) to heat something calentar
   [29] algo
   I'll go and heat the soup. Voy a calentar la
   sopa.

heater *noun*
   la **estufa** *fem*

♂ **heating** *noun*
   la **calefacción** *fem*

heaven *noun*
   el **cielo** *masc*

♂ **heavy** *adjective*
1 (*weighing a lot*) **pesado** *masc*, **pesada** *fem*
   a heavy bag una bolsa pesada
   to be heavy pesar[17] mucho
   My rucksack's really heavy. Mi mochila
   pesa mucho.
   How heavy is it? ¿Cuánto pesa?
2 (*busy*) **ocupado** *masc*, **ocupada** *fem*
   I've got a heavy day tomorrow. Mañana
   tengo un día muy ocupado.
3 (*intense*) heavy rain lluvia fuerte
   to be a heavy drinker beber[18] mucho

hectic *adjective*
    ajetreado *masc*, **ajetreada** *fem*
    a hectic day un día muy ajetreado

hedge *noun*
    el **seto** *masc*

hedgehog *noun*
    el **erizo** *masc*

ᔕ **heel** *noun*
  1 (*of your foot*) el **talón** *masc*
  2 (*of a shoe*) el **tacón** *masc*
    high heels los tacones altos

ᔕ **height** *noun*
  1 (*of a person*) la **estatura** *fem*
    He was of average height. Era de estatura
    mediana.
  2 (*of a building*) la **altura** *fem*
  3 (*of a mountain*) la **altitud** *fem*

heir *noun*
    el **heredero** *masc*, la **heredera** *fem*
    the heir to the throne el príncipe heredero,
    la princesa heredera

helicopter *noun*
    el **helicóptero** *masc*

hell *noun*
    el **infierno** *masc*

ᔕ **hello** *exclamation*
  1 (*greeting*) **hola**
  2 (*on the telephone*) **¿Dígame?**

helmet *noun*
    el **casco** *masc*

ᔕ **help** *noun* ▷ see **help** *verb*
    la **ayuda** *fem*
    to call for help pedir [57] ayuda
    Thanks for your help. Gracias por
    ayudarme.
    Do you need any help? ¿Necesitas ayuda?
    Help! ¡Socorro!

ᔕ to **help** *verb* ▷ see **help** *noun*
  1 (*to assist*) **ayudar** [17]
    to help somebody to do something ayudar
    [17] a alguien a hacer algo
    Can you help me move the table? ¿Me
    ayudas a mover la mesa?
    Can I help you? ¿Qué desea?
  2 (*to serve*) to help yourself to something
    servirse [57] algo
    Help yourself! ¡Sírvete!
    Help yourselves to vegetables. Serviros
    verdura.
  3 (*to avoid*) I can't help it. No lo puedo
    remediar.
    I couldn't help thinking that she was right.

No podía menos que pensar que ella tenía
razón.

helping *noun*
    la **porción** *fem*
    Would you like a second helping? ¿Quieres
    repetir?

hem *noun*
    el **dobladillo** *masc*

ᔕ **hen** *noun*
    la **gallina** *fem*

ᔕ **her** *adjective* ▷ see **her** *pron*
  1 (*before most nouns*) **su** *masc & fem*
    her brother su hermano
    her house su casa
    her children sus niños
  2 (*with parts of the body, clothes*) **ella**, **los**, **las**
    She cut her finger. Se cortó el dedo.
    She's washing her hands. Se está lavando
    las manos.
    She took off her coat. Se quitó el abrigo.

    WORD TIP Spanish uses *el, la, los, las* for *her* with
    parts of the body and clothes.

ᔕ **her** *pronoun* ▷ see **her** *adj*
  1 (*as a direct object*) **la**
    I know her. La conozco.
    I saw her last week. La vi la semana pasada.
    Are you going to see her? ¿Vas a verla?
    Listen to her! ¡Escúchala!
    Don't push her! ¡No la empujes!
  2 (*as an indirect object*) **le**
    I gave her my address. Le di mis señas.
    I lent it to her. Se lo dejó.
  3 (*after a preposition, in comparisons, after the verb*
    to be) **ella**
    with her con ella
    without her sin ella
    He's older than her. Él es mayor que ella.
    It was her. Era ella.

    WORD TIP With an infinitive, or when telling
    someone to do something, *la* joins onto the verb.
    le becomes *se* before the pronouns *lo* or *la*.

ᔕ **herb** *noun*
    la **hierba** *fem*

herd *noun*
  1 (*of cattle*) la **manada** *fem*
  2 (*of goats*) el **rebaño** *masc*

ᔕ **here** *adverb*
  1 (*in this place*) **aquí**
    They live not far from here. Viven no lejos
    de aquí.
    Here they are! ¡Aquí están!
    Tom isn't there at the moment. Tom no está
    aquí en este momento. ▸▸

a
b
c
d
e
f
g
h
i
j
k
l
m
n
o
p
q
r
s
t
u
v
w
x
y
z

2 (*for emphasis*) **Here it is.** Toma.
Here's my address. Toma mis señas.
Here you are. Toma.

hero *noun*
el **héroe** *masc*

heroin *noun* ▷ see **heroine** *noun*
(*the drug*) la **heroína** *fem*

heroine *noun* ▷ see **heroin** *noun*
(*of a story*) la **heroína** *fem*

♪ **hers** *pronoun*
el **suyo** *masc*, la **suya** *fem*
I took my hat and she took hers. Yo cogí mi
sombrero y ella cogió el suyo.
I phoned my mum and Donna phoned hers.
Llamé a mi madre y Donna llamó a la suya.
**I've invited my parents and Karen's invited
hers.** Yo he invitado a mis padres y Karen a
los suyos.
**I showed her my photos and she showed
me hers.** Yo le enseñé mis fotos y ella me
enseñó las suyas.

WORD TIP The form of *suyo* to choose depends
the gender and number of the thing owned.

herself *pronoun*
1 (*reflexive*) **se**
She's hurt herself. Se ha hecho daño.
She washed herself. Se lavó.
2 (*for emphasis*) **ella misma**
She said it herself. Lo dijo ella misma.
3 (*on her own*) **by herself** ella sola
She did it by herself. Lo hizo ella sola.

to **hesitate** *verb*
dudar [17]
to hesitate to do something dudar en hacer
algo

heterosexual *adjective*
heterosexual *masc & fem*

♪ **hi** *exclamation*
hola

hiccups *plural noun*
el **hipo** *masc*
to have hiccups tener [9] hipo

hidden *adjective*
escondido *masc*, **escondida** *fem*

to **hide** *verb*
1 (*person*) **esconderse** [18]
She hid behind the door. Se escondió
detrás de la puerta.
2 (*an object*) **to hide something** esconder [18]
algo
Who's hidden the chocolate? ¿Quién ha
escondido el chocolate?

hide-and-seek *noun*
to play hide-and-seek jugar [27] al
escondite

hi-fi *noun*
el **equipo de alta fidelidad**

♪ **high** *adjective*
1 (*building, wall, mountain*) **alto** *masc*, **alta** *fem*
on a high shelf en una estantería alta
The wall is very high. La pared es muy alta.
How high is the wall? ¿Qué altura tiene la
pared?
The wall is two metres high. La pared tiene
dos metros de altura.
2 (*number, price, temperature, speed*) **alto** *masc*,
alta *fem*
Food prices are very high. El precio de la
comida es muy alto.
at high speed a alta velocidad
high winds vientos fuertes

 high

With five mountain ranges and a high plateau,
Spain is the highest country in Europe after
Switzerland at an average height of 650 metres
above sea level.

Highers *plural noun*
(*Son exámenes que se hacen en Escocia, en hasta
cinco asignaturas, en el penúltimo año de la
educación secundaria.*)

high-heeled *adjective*
de tacón alto
high-heeled shoes los zapatos de tacón
alto

high jump *noun*
el **salto de altura**

♪ **high-speed train** *noun*
el **tren de alta velocidad**

♪ **Highway Code** *noun*
el **Código de la Circulación**

to **hijack** *verb*
secuestrar [17]

hijacking *noun*
el **secuestro** *masc*

hiking *noun*
el **senderismo** *masc*

hilarious *adjective*
divertidísimo *masc*, **divertidísima** *fem*

♪ **hill** *noun*
1 (*low*) la **colina** *fem*
2 (*higher*) la **montaña** *fem*
3 (*sloping street, road*) la **cuesta** *fem*

ⓢ **him** *pronoun*

1 (*as a direct object*) **lo**
I know him. Lo conozco.
I saw him last week. Lo vi la semana pasada.
Are you going to see him? ¿Vas a verlo?
Listen to him! ¡Escúchalo!
Don't push him! ¡No lo empujes!

2 (*as an indirect object*) **le**
I gave him my address. Le di mis señas.
I lent it to him. Se lo dejé.

3 (*after a preposition, in comparisons, after the verb to be*) **él**
with him con él
without him sin él
She's older than him. Ella es mayor que él.
It was him. Era él.

WORD TIP With an infinitive, or when telling someone to do something, *lo* joins onto the verb. *le* becomes *se* before the pronouns *lo* or *la*.

himself *pronoun*

1 (*reflexive*) **se**
He's hurt himself. Se ha hecho daño.
He washed himself. Se lavó.

2 (*for emphasis*) **él mismo**
He said it himself. Lo dijo él mismo.

3 (*on his own*) by himself él solo
He did it by himself. Lo hizo él solo.

ⓢ **Hindu** *adjective & noun*
hindú *masc & fem*
the Hindus los hindúes

WORD TIP Adjectives and nouns for religion do not have capital letters in Spanish.

Hinduism *noun*
(*Religion*) el **hinduismo** *masc*

WORD TIP Adjectives and nouns for religion do not have capital letters in Spanish.

hip *noun*
la **cadera** *fem*

ⓢ **hire** *noun* ▷ see **hire** *verb*
el **alquiler** *masc*
car hire el alquiler de coches
for hire se alquila

to **hire** *verb* ▷ see **hire** *noun*
alquilar [17]
We're going to hire a car. Vamos a alquilar un coche.

his *adjective* ▷ see **his** *pron*

1 (*before most nouns*) **su** *masc & fem*
his brother su hermano
his house su casa
his children sus niños

2 (*with parts of the body, clothes*) **ella**, **los**, **las**
He cut his finger. Se cortó el dedo.
He's washing his hands. Se está lavando las manos.
He took off his gloves. Se quitó los guantes.

WORD TIP Spanish uses *el, la, los, las* for *his* with parts of the body and clothes.

ⓢ **his** *pronoun* ▷ see **his** *adj*
el **suyo** *masc*, la **suya** *fem*
I took my hat and he took his. Yo cogí mi sombrero y él cogió el suyo.
I phoned my mum and Danny phoned his. Llamé a mi madre y Danny llamó a la suya.
I've invited my parents and Steve's invited his. Yo he invitado a mis padres y Steve a los suyos.
I showed him my photos and he showed me his. Yo le enseñé mis fotos y él me enseñó las suyas.

WORD TIP The form of *suyo* to choose depends the gender and number of the thing owned.

historic *adjective*
histórico *masc*, **histórica** *fem*
a historic building un edificio histórico

ⓢ **history** *noun*
la **historia** *fem*

hit *noun* ▷ see **hit** *verb*
(*success*) el **éxito** *masc*
their latest hit su último éxito
The film is a huge hit. La película es un gran éxito.

ⓢ to **hit** *verb* ▷ see **hit** *noun*

1 (*a ball, a door, a table*) **golpear** [17]
He hit the ball. Golpeó la pelota.

2 (*a person*) to hit somebody pegarle [28] a alguien
She hit him with her handbag. Le pegó con el bolso.

3 (*to bang*) to hit your head on something darse [4] un golpe en la cabeza con algo
He hit his head on the table. Se dio un golpe en la cabeza con la mesa.

4 (*to collide with*) to hit chocar [31] con
The car hit a tree. El coche chocó con un árbol.

5 (*to knock over*) She was hit by a car. La atropelló un coche.

hitch *noun* ▷ see **hitch** *verb*
el **problemita** *masc*
There's been a slight hitch. Ha habido un problemita.

to **hitch** *verb* ▷ see **hitch** *noun*
(*informal*) to hitch a lift hacer [7] dedo

ⓢ to **hitchhike** *verb*
hacer [7] **autostop**
We hitchhiked to Valencia. Hicimos autostop hasta Valencia.

♂ **hitchhiker** *noun*
  el & la **autostopista** *masc & fem*

♂ **hitchhiking** *noun*
  el **autostop** *masc*

HIV-negative *adjective*
  seronegativo *masc*, **seronegativa** *fem*

HIV-positive *adjective*
  seropositivo *masc*, **seropositiva** *fem*

♂ **hobby** *noun*
  el **pasatiempo** *masc*

hockey *noun*
  el **hockey** *masc*
  to play hockey jugar[27] al hockey
• **hockey stick** el palo de hockey

to **hold** *verb*
1 (*to have in your hands*) **sostener**[9]
   to hold something in your hand sostener
   algo en la mano
   Can you hold the torch? ¿Puedes sostener
   la linterna?
2 (*to contain*) **contener**[9]
   This jug holds a litre. Esta jarra contiene un
   litro.
3 (*a meeting, a wedding, elections*) **celebrar**[17]
   to hold a meeting celebrar una reunión
• to **hold on**
1 (*to wait*) **esperar**[17]
2 (*on the phone*) Hold on! ¡Un momento!, ¡No
   cuelgue!
• to **hold on to something**
   agarrarse[17] **a algo**
• to **hold somebody up**
   (*to delay*) **entretener**[9] **a alguien**
   I don't want to hold you up. No quiero
   entretenerte.
   I was held up at the dentist's. Me entretuve
   en el dentista.
• to **hold something up**
   (*to raise*) **levantar**[17]
   He held up his glass. Levantó su vaso.

hold-up *noun*
1 (*delay*) el **retraso** *masc*
2 (*traffic jam*) el **atasco** *masc*
3 (*robbery*) el **atraco** *masc*

hole *noun*
  el **agujero** *masc*

♂ **holiday** *noun*
1 (*time away from school, work*) las **vacaciones**
   plural fem
   Where are you going for your holiday?
   ¿Dónde vas de vacaciones?
   Have a good holiday! ¡Que pases unas
   buenas vacaciones!
   to be away on holiday estar[2] de

vacaciones
   to go on holiday irse[8] de vacaciones
   the school holidays las vacaciones
   escolares
2 (*single day*) a public holiday un día de fiesta
   Monday's a holiday. El lunes es fiesta.

Holland *noun*
  Holanda *fem*

hollow *adjective*
  hueco *masc*, **hueca** *fem*

holly *noun*
  el **acebo** *masc*

holy *adjective*
  santo *masc*, **santa** *fem*

♂ **home** *adverb* ▷ see **home** *noun*
  a casa
  Susie's gone home. Susie se ha ido a casa.
  I'll call in and see you on my way home. Te
  iré a visitar de camino a mi casa.
  to get home llegar[28] a casa
  We got home at midnight. Llegamos a casa
  a media noche.

♂ **home** *noun* ▷ see **home** *adv*
1 (*the place where you live*) la **casa** *fem*
   to stay at home quedarse[17] en casa
   I was at home. Estaba en casa.
   to leave home irse[8] de casa
2 (*in sport*) to play at home jugar[27] en casa
3 (*place for group living, institution*) la **residencia**
   fem
   an old people's home una residencia de
   ancianos

♂ **homeless** *adjective*
  sin hogar
  a homeless person una persona sin hogar

home-made *adjective*
  casero *masc*, **casera** *fem*
  home-made cakes pasteles caseros

homeopathy *noun*
  la **homeopatía** *fem*

homesick *adjective*
1 (*when you miss your family*) He is homesick.
   Echa de menos a su familia.
2 (*when you miss your country*) He is homesick.
   Echa de menos a su país.

♂ **homework** *noun*
  los **deberes** *plural masc*
  my Spanish homework mis deberes de
  español
  I did my homework. Hice mis deberes.

homosexual *adjective*
  homosexual *masc & fem*

Honduran *adjective & noun*
1 **hondureño** *masc*, **hondureña** *fem*
2 un **hondureño** *masc*, una **hondureña** *fem*
   the Hondurans los hondureños

WORD TIP Adjectives and nouns for nationality and regional origin do not have capital letters in Spanish.

Honduras *noun*
   Honduras *fem*

ᵹ**honest** *adjective*
1 (*trustworthy*) **honrado** *masc*, **honrada** *fem*
   She seems honest. Parece honrada.
2 (*frank*) **sincero** *masc*, **sincera** *fem*
   to be honest ... para serte sincero ...
   To be honest, I don't like him. Para serte sincero, no me gusta.

honestly *adverb*
   sinceramente

honesty *noun*
   la **honradez** *fem*

honey *noun*
   la **miel** *fem*

honeymoon *noun*
   la **luna de miel** *fem*

honour *noun*
   el **honor** *masc*

hood *noun*
   la **capucha** *fem*

hook *noun*
1 (*for doing up clothes*) el **corchete** *masc*
2 (*for fishing*) el **anzuelo** *masc*
3 (*for hanging pictures, clothes*) el **gancho** *masc*
4 (*on the phone*) to take the phone off the hook descolgar[23] el teléfono

hooligan *noun*
   el **gamberro** *masc*, la **gamberra** *fem*

hooray *exclamation*
   ¡hurra!

Hoover® *noun* ▷ see **hoover** *verb*
   la **aspiradora** *fem*, el **aspirador** *masc*

to **hoover** *verb* ▷ see **Hoover** *noun*
   pasar[17] la aspiradora por
   I hoovered my bedroom. Pasé la aspiradora por mi habitación.

ᵹ**hope** *noun* ▷ see **hope** *verb*
   la **esperanza** *fem*
   to give up hope perder[36] la esperanza

ᵹto **hope** *verb* ▷ see **hope** *noun*
   esperar[17]
   Hoping to see you on Friday. Esperando verte el domingo.

I hope so. Espero que sí.
I hope not. Espero que no.
We hope you'll be able to come. Esperamos que puedas venir.

WORD TIP *esperar que* is followed by a verb in the subjunctive.

hopeless *adjective*
   to be hopeless at something ser[1] un negado para algo
   She's hopeless at geography. Es una negada para la geografía.

horizon *noun*
   el **horizonte** *masc*

horn *noun*
1 (*of an animal*) el **cuerno** *masc*
2 (*of a car*) la **bocina** *fem*
   to sound your horn tocar[31] la bocina
3 (*musical instrument*) la **trompa** *fem*
   to play the horn tocar[31] trompa

horoscope *noun*
   el **horóscopo** *masc*

ᵹ**horrible** *adjective*
   horrible *masc & fem*
   The weather was horrible. El tiempo era horrible.
   She's really horrible! ¡Es realmente horrible!
   He was really horrible to me. Me trató muy mal.

horrific *adjective*
   horroroso *masc*, **horrorosa** *fem*
   a horrific accident un accidente horroroso

horror *noun*
   el **horror** *masc*
· **horror film** la película de terror

ᵹ**horse** *noun*
   el **caballo** *masc*
· **horse racing** las carreras de caballos

hose *noun*
   la **manguera** *fem*

ᵹ**hospital** *noun*
   el **hospital** *masc*
   to be in hospital estar[2] en el hospital
   She's in hospital with appendicitis. Está en el hospital con apendicitis.
   He's going to go into hospital. Lo van a ingresar en el hospital.

hospitality *noun*
   la **hospitalidad** *fem*

a
b
c
d
e
f
g
h
i
j
k
l
m
n
o
p
q
r
s
t
u
v
w
x
y
z

host *noun*
el **anfitrión** *masc*, la **anfitriona** *fem*
My host family is very nice. La familia que me hospeda es muy amable.

hostage *noun*
el **rehén** *masc*, pl: los **rehenes**

hostess *noun*
la **anfitriona** *fem*

ℰ **hot** *adjective*

1 (*drink, meal, object*) **caliente** *masc & fem*
a hot drink una bebida caliente
Be careful, the plates are hot! ¡Cuidado! los platos están calientes.

2 (*person*) **to be hot** tener [9] calor
I'm hot. Tengo calor.
I'm very hot. Tengo mucho calor.
I'm too hot. Tengo demasiado calor.

3 (*weather, temperature in a room*) **to be hot** hacer [7] calor
It's hot. Hace calor.
It's hot today. Hace calor hoy.
It's very hot in the kitchen. Hace mucho calor en la cocina.
a hot day un día caluroso
a hot climate un clima cálido

4 (*spicy*) **picante** *masc & fem*
This curry's too hot for me. Este curry es demasiado picante para mí.

• **hot dog** el perrito caliente

ℰ **hotel** *noun*
el **hotel** *masc*

ℰ **hour** *noun*
la **hora** *fem*
two hours later dos horas más tarde
two hours ago hace dos horas
every hour cada hora
We waited for two hours. Esperamos dos horas.
We've been waiting for hours. Llevamos horas esperando.
to be paid by the hour cobrar [17] por hora
I earn six pounds an hour. Gano seis libras por hora.

hourly *adjective* ▷ see **hourly** *adv*
por hora
There is an hourly bus service. Hay un autobús por hora.
He's paid hourly. Le pagan por hora.

hourly *adverb* ▷ see **hourly** *adj*
cada hora
The trains leave hourly. Los trenes salen cada hora.

ℰ **house** *noun*
la **casa** *fem*
Judy's at my house. Judy está en mi casa.
I'm at Judy's house. Estoy en casa de Judy.
I'm going to Judy's house tonight. Voy a casa de Judy esta noche.
I phoned from Judy's house. Llamé desde casa de Judy.

ℰ **housework** *noun*
las **tareas de la casa**
to do the housework hacer [7] las tareas de la casa

ℰ **housing** *noun*
las **viviendas** *plural fem*
the housing shortage la escasez de viviendas

ℰ **how** *adverb*

1 (*to ask in what way something is done*) **cómo**
How did you do it? ¿Cómo lo hiciste?
I know how to do it. Sé cómo hacerlo.

2 (*to ask about somebody's health*) **cómo**
How are you? ¿Cómo estás?

3 (*to ask what something or someone is like*) **How was the party?** ¿Qué tal fue la fiesta?
How do I look? ¿Cómo or qué tal estoy?

4 (*to talk about quantities and measurements*) **How much is it?** ¿Cuánto cuesta?
How far is it? ¿A qué distancia está?
How long will it take? ¿Cuánto tardará?

5 (*in exclamations*) **qué**
How nice! ¡Qué bonito!

however *adverb*
sin embargo

hug *noun*
el **abrazo** *masc*
to give somebody a hug darle [4] un abrazo a alguien
She gave me a hug. Me dio un abrazo.

huge *adjective*
enorme *masc & fem*

to **hum** *verb*
tararear [17]

human *adjective*
humano *masc*, **humana** *fem*
• **human being** el ser humano

humour *noun*
el **humor** *masc*
to have a sense of humour tener [9] sentido del humor

ℰ **hundred** *number*
cien *invariable*
a hundred cien

about a hundred unos cien
about a hundred people unas cien
personas
hundreds of people cientos de personas
one hundred and six ciento seis
two hundred and ten doscientos diez
two hundred horses doscientos caballos
three hundred boxes trescientas cajas
six hundred seiscientos *masc*, seiscientas
fem

> **WORD TIP** *cien* never changes and translates *hundred* in English. When *hundred* is used in the plural or with other numbers, use *ciento, -cientos, -cientas* as above.

Hungarian *adjective & noun*
1 **húngaro** *masc*, **húngara** *fem*
2 (*person*) un **húngaro** *masc*, una **húngara** *fem*
the Hungarians los húngaros *plural masc*
3 (*the language*) el **húngaro** *masc*

> **WORD TIP** Adjectives and nouns for nationality, regional origin, and language do not have capital letters in Spanish.

Hungary *noun*
Hungría *fem*

hunger *noun*
el **hambre** *fem*

> **WORD TIP** *hambre* takes *el* or *un* in the singular even though it is feminine.

ℰ **hungry** *adjective*
to be hungry tener [9] hambre
I'm hungry. Tengo hambre.

to **hunt** *verb*
(*animals*) **cazar** [22]
· to **hunt for**
1 (*to search for*) **buscar**
2 (*animals*) **ir** [8] **a la caza de**

hurricane *noun*
el **huracán** *masc, pl:* los **huracanes**
a category four hurricane un huracán de
categoría cuatro

ℰ **hurry** *noun* ▷ see **hurry** *verb*
to be in a hurry tener [9] prisa
I'm in a hurry. Tengo prisa.
What's the hurry? ¿Qué prisa hay?

ℰ to **hurry** *verb* ▷ see **hurry** *noun*
darse [4] prisa
I must hurry. Debo darme prisa.
We hurried home. Nos dimos prisa para
llegar a casa.
Hurry up! ¡Date prisa!

ℰ to **hurt** *verb*
1 (*to injure*) to hurt somebody hacer [7] daño
a alguien
You're hurting me! ¡Me estás haciendo
daño!
to hurt yourself hacerse [7] daño
Did you hurt yourself? ¿Te hiciste daño?
to hurt your hand hacerse [7] daño en la
mano
I hurt my arm. Me hice daño en el brazo.
2 (*to give pain*) doler [38]
My back hurts. Me duele la espalda.
My feet hurt. Me duelen los pies.
That hurts! ¡Eso hace daño!

ℰ **husband** *noun*
el **marido** *masc*

ℰ **hut** *noun*
la **cabaña** *fem*

hymn *noun*
el **himno** *masc*

ℰ **hypermarket** *noun*
el **hipermercado** *masc*

hyphen *noun*
el **guión** *masc*

to **hypnotize** *verb*
hipnotizar [25]

a
b
c
d
e
f
g
h
i
j
k
l
m
n
o
p
q
r
s
t
u
v
w
x
y
z

I i

I *pronoun*
1 **yo** (*see Word tip*)
   I am Scottish. Soy escocés.
   I have two sisters. Tengo dos hermanas.
2 (*for emphasis*) **yo**
   I did it. Lo hice yo.
   Tony and I Tony y yo
   I went but Robert didn't. Yo fui pero Robert no.

WORD TIP *I*, like *he, she, they* etc, is generally not translated into Spanish; the ending of the verb tells you if the subject of the verb is *yo, él, ella*, etc, so *I* is translated only for emphasis or for clarity.

Iberia *noun*
   Iberia *fem* (*the name for Spain and Portugal together*)

Iberian *adjective*
   ibérico *masc*, **ibérica** *fem*
   the Iberian Peninsula la Península ibérica

WORD TIP Adjectives and nouns for nationality and regional origin do not have capital letters in Spanish.

ℰ**ice** *noun*
   el **hielo** *masc*
 • iceberg el iceberg, *pl:* los **icebergs**

ℰ**ice cream** *noun*
   el **helado** *masc*
   a chocolate ice cream un helado de chocolate

ice cube *noun*
   el **cubito de hielo**

ice hockey *noun*
   el **hockey sobre hielo**
   to play ice hockey jugar[27] al hockey sobre hielo

ℰ**ice rink** *noun*
   la **pista de hielo**

ice skating *noun*
   el **patinaje sobre hielo**
   to go ice skating ir[8] a patinar sobre hielo

icing *noun*
   el **azúcar glaseado**

icon *noun*
   (*Computers*) el **icono** *masc*

ICT *noun*
   (= *Information and Communications Technology*) la **informática** *fem*

icy *adjective*
1 (*road*) **cubierto de hielo** *masc*, **cubierta de hielo** *fem*
2 (*very cold*) **helado** *masc*, **helada** *fem*
   an icy wind un viento helado

ℰ**ID card** *noun* ▷**identity card**

ℰ**idea** *noun*
   la **idea** *fem*
   What a good idea! ¡Qué buena idea!
   I've no idea. No tengo ni idea.

ideal *adjective*
   ideal *masc & fem*

identical *adjective*
   idéntico *masc*, **idéntica** *fem*

identical twins *plural noun*
   los **gemelos** *plural masc*, las **gemelas** *plural fem*

ℰ**identification** *noun*
   la **identificación** *fem*
   Have you got any other identification?
   ¿Tiene algún otro documento que acredite su identidad?

ℰ**identity card** *noun*
   el **carné de identidad**

ℰ**idiot** *noun*
   el & la **idiota** *masc & fem*

idiotic *adjective*
   idiota *masc & fem*

i.e. *abbreviation*
1 (*in writing*) **i.e.**
2 (*in speech*) **esto es**

ℰ**if** *conjunction*
1 (*in conditionals*) **si**
   if Sue's there ... si Sue está allí ...
   If it rains we'll go to the cinema. Si llueve iremos al cine.
   If I won the lottery ... Si ganase la lotería ...
   If I had it, I would give it to you. Si lo tuviera, te lo daría.
   if only ... ojalá ...
   If only you'd told me. Ojalá me lo hubieses dicho.
   even if incluso si
   We'll go even if it snows Iremos incluso si nieva.
   if I were you ... yo que tú ...
   If I were you, I'd forget it. Yo que tú me olvidaría del asunto.

2 (*whether*) **si**
They asked if he had left. Preguntaron si se
había ido.

WORD TIP When talking about something that
might, or might not, happen, *si* is followed by the
subjunctive.

to **ignore** *verb*
1 (*a person*) **ignorar** [17]
She's been ignoring me all evening. Me ha
estado ignorando toda la noche.
2 (*what somebody says*) **no hacer** [7] **caso de**
Just ignore it. No le hagas caso.

ℰ **ill** *adjective*
enfermo *masc*, **enferma** *fem*
to fall ill enfermar [17]
to be taken ill enfermar [17]
to feel ill sentirse [14] mal

illegal *adjective*
ilegal *masc & fem*

illness *noun*
la **enfermedad** *fem*

illustrated *adjective*
ilustrado *masc*, **ilustrada** *fem*

illustration *noun*
la **ilustración** *fem*

ℰ **image** *noun*
la **imagen** *fem*, *fem pl:* las **imágenes**

imagination *noun*
la **imaginación** *fem*

imaginative *adjective*
imaginativo *masc*, **imaginativa** *fem*

to **imagine** *verb*
imaginarse [17]
You can't imagine how hard it was! ¡No
puedes imaginarte lo difícil que fue!
Imagine that you're very rich. Imagina que
eres muy rico.

to **imitate** *verb*
imitar [17]

imitation *noun*
la **imitación** *fem*

immediate *adjective*
inmediato *masc*, **inmediata** *fem*

ℰ **immediately** *adverb*
inmediatamente
I rang them immediately. Los llamé
inmediatamente.
immediately before justo antes
immediately after justo después

immigrant *noun*
el & la **inmigrante** *masc & fem*

immigration *noun*
la **inmigración** *fem*

impact *noun*
el **impacto** *masc*

impatience *noun*
la **impaciencia** *fem*

impatient *adjective*
impaciente *masc & fem*
to get impatient with somebody
impacientarse [17] con alguien

impatiently *adverb*
con impaciencia

imperfect *noun*
(*Grammar*) el **imperfecto** *masc*

import *noun* ▷ see **import** *verb*
1 (*item*) el **artículo de importación**
Coal is the most important import. El
artículo de importación más importante es
el carbón.
2 (*trade*) la **importación** *fem*

to **import** *verb* ▷ see **import** *noun*
importar [17]

importance *noun*
la **importancia** *fem*

ℰ **important** *adjective*
importante *masc & fem*

ℰ **impossible** *adjective*
imposible *masc & fem*
It's impossible to find a telephone. Es
imposible encontrar un teléfono.

impressed *adjective*
impresionado *masc*, **impresionada** *fem*

impression *noun*
la **impresión** *fem*
to make a good impression on somebody
causar [17] una buena impresión a alguien
I got the impression he was hiding
something. Me dio la impresión de que
estaba ocultando algo.

ℰ to **improve** *verb*
mejorar [17]
to improve something mejorar [17] algo
The weather is improving. El tiempo está
mejorando.

improvement *noun*
1 (*change for the better*) la **mejora** *fem*
2 (*gradual progress*) el **progreso** *masc*

a
b
c
d
e
f
g
h
i
j
k
l
m
n
o
p
q
r
s
t
u
v
w
x
y
z

a
b
c
d
e
f
g
h
i
j
k
l
m
n
o
p
q
r
s
t
u
v
w
x
y
z

ꝸ **in** *adverb* ▷ see **in** *prep*

1   (*at home, around*) **to be in** estar [2]
    Mick's not in at the moment. Mick no está
    en este momento.
    There was nobody in. No había nadie.

2   (*used as part of a verb*) **to come in** entrar [17]
    to go in entrar [17]
    to run in entrar [17] corriendo

ꝸ **in** *preposition* ▷ see **in** *adv*

1   (*to talk about where something or someone is*) **en**
    in Spain en España
    in town en la ciudad
    in my pocket en mi bolsillo
    in the newspaper en el periódico
    to lie in the sun tumbarse [17] al sol
    They live in Barcelona. Viven en Barcelona.
    Paul is in my class. Paul está en mi clase.
    You can't go out in this weather. No
    puedes salir con este tiempo.

2   (*to talk about how something is done*) **en**
    in Spanish en español
    in twos de dos en dos
    They sat in a circle. Se sentaron en un
    círculo.
    He wrote it in pencil. Lo escribió a lápiz.

3   (*wearing*) **de**
    the girl in the pink skirt la chica de la falda
    rosa
    He was in a suit. Llevaba un traje.
    She was dressed in white. Iba vestida de
    blanco.

4   (*during a month, season, year, period of time*) **en**
    in May en mayo
    in 2003 en dos mil tres
    in winter en invierno
    in time con el tiempo
    It will improve with time. Va a mejorar con
    el tiempo.

5   (*during a part of the day*) **por**
    in the morning por la mañana
    in the night por la noche
    at eight in the morning a las ocho de la
    mañana

6   (*at the end of a period of time*) **dentro de**
    I'll phone you in ten minutes. Te llamaré
    dentro de diez minutos.

7   (*to talk about how long it takes to do
    something*) **en**
    She did it in five minutes. Lo hizo en cinco
    minutos.

8   (*after a superlative*) **de**
    the tallest boy in the class el chico más alto
    de la clase
    the biggest city in the world la ciudad más
    grande del mundo

ꝸ **inch** *noun*
    la **pulgada** *masc*

ꝸ to **include** *verb* ▷ see **including** *prep*
    incluir [54]
    Dinner is included in the price. La cena está
    incluida en el precio.
    Service included. Servicio incluido.

ꝸ **including** *preposition* ▷ see **include** *verb*
    incluido *masc*, **incluida** *fem*
    60 pounds including VAT. Sesenta libras
    IVA incluido.
    everyone, including children todo el
    mundo incluidos los niños
    including Sundays incluidos los domingos
    not including Sundays sin incluir los
    domingos

income *noun*
    los **ingresos** *plural masc*
- **income tax** el impuesto sobre la renta

inconvenient *adjective*

1   (*place, arrangement*) **poco conveniente**
    masc & fem

2   (*time*) **inoportuno** *masc*, **inoportuna** *fem*

ꝸ **increase** *noun* ▷ see **increase** *verb*
    el **aumento** *masc*

ꝸ to **increase** *verb* ▷ see **increase** *noun*
    aumentar [17]
    The price has increased by ten pounds. El
    precio ha aumentado diez libras.

incredible *adjective*
    increíble *masc & fem*

incredibly *adverb*
    (*very*) **increíblemente**
    The film's incredibly boring. La película es
    increíblemente aburrida.

indeed *adverb*

1   (*used to emphasize something*) **She's very
    pleased indeed.** Está contentísima.
    I'm very hungry indeed. Tengo muchísima
    hambre.
    Thank you very much indeed. Muchísimas
    gracias.

2   (*certainly*) **'Can you hear his radio?'—
    'Indeed I can!'** ¿Oyes su radio?'— 'Ya lo
    creo.'
    'Do you like it?'— 'I do indeed!' '¿Te
    gusta?'— 'Sí, muchísimo.'

indefinite article *noun*
    (*Grammar*) el **artículo indefinido**

independence *noun*
    la **independencia** *fem*

independent *adjective*
independiente *masc & fem*
· **independent school** la escuela privada

index *noun*
el **índice** *masc*
· **index finger** el dedo índice

India *noun*
la **India** *fem*

Indian *adjective & noun*
1 **indio** *masc*, **india** *fem*
2 un **indio** *masc*, una **india** *fem*
the Indians los indios

> **WORD TIP** Adjectives and nouns for nationality and regional origin do not have capital letters in Spanish.

indigestion *noun*
la **indigestión** *fem*
to have indigestion tener [9] indigestión

indirect *adjective*
indirecto *masc*, **indirecta** *fem*

individual *adjective*
▷ see **individual** *noun*
(for one person: serving, contribution) **individual** *masc & fem*
individual tuition las clases particulares

individual *noun* ▷ see **individual** *adj*
el **individuo** *masc*

indoor *adjective*
1 (*plant*) **de interior**
2 (*swimming pool*) **cubierto** *masc*, **cubierta** *fem*

indoors *adverb*
dentro
to stay indoors quedarse [17] dentro
to go indoors entrar [17]
It's cooler indoors. Hace más fresco dentro.

industrial *adjective*
industrial *masc & fem*
· **industrial estate** la zona industrial

ℰ **industry** *noun*
la **industria** *fem*
the advertising industry la industria de la publicidad

inevitable *adjective*
inevitable *masc & fem*

inevitably *adverb*
inevitablemente

inexperienced *adjective*
inexperto *masc*, **inexperta** *fem*

infected *adjective*
infectado *masc*, **infectada** *fem*

infection *noun*
la **infección** *fem*
an eye infection una infección de ojos
I've got a throat infection. Tengo anginas.

infectious *adjective*
infeccioso *masc*, **infecciosa** *fem*

infinitive *noun*
el **infinitivo** *masc*
in the infinitive en infinitivo

inflation *noun*
la **inflación** *fem*

influence *noun*
la **influencia** *fem*
to be a good influence on somebody ser [1] una buena influencia para alguien

to **inform** *verb*
informar [17]
to inform somebody that ... informar a alguien de que ...
They informed us that there was a problem. Nos informaron de que había un problema.
to inform somebody of something informar a alguien de algo
to keep somebody informed mantener [9] a alguien informado

informal *adjective*
1 (*meal, event*) **informal** *masc & fem*
2 (*language*) **familiar** *masc & fem*
an informal expression una expresión familiar

ℰ **information** *noun*
la **información** *fem*
a piece of information un dato
I need some information about flights to Madrid. Necesito información sobre vuelos a Madrid.
· **information desk** el mostrador de información
· **information office** la oficina de información
· **information technology** la informática

infuriating *adjective*
exasperante *masc & fem*

ingredient *noun*
el **ingrediente** *masc*

initials *plural noun*
las **iniciales** *plural fem*
Put your initials here. Pon tus iniciales aquí.

a
b
c
d
e
f
g
h
i
j
k
l
m
n
o
p
q
r
s
t
u
v
w
x
y
z

injection *noun*
la **inyección** *fem*
to give somebody an injection ponerle [11] una inyección a alguien

⒮ to **injure** *verb* ▷ see **injured** *adj*
herir [14]
She injured herself playing tennis. Se hirió jugando al tenis.
He was slightly injured in the accident. Resultó levemente herido en el accidente.

injured *adjective* ▷ see **injure** *verb*
herido *masc*, **herida** *fem*

injury *noun*
la **herida** *fem*

ink *noun*
la **tinta** *fem*

in-laws *plural noun*
los **suegros** *plural masc*

innocent *adjective*
inocente *masc & fem*

> 🛈 **mini-info**
> **innocents**
>
> The 28 December, *el día de los Inocentes* is Spain's April Fool's Day when students play tricks on each other chanting Mariposa Inocente. It is the day the Church remembers the massacre of innocent children decreed by King Herod in an attempt to kill the baby Jesus.

insane *adjective*
loco *masc*, **loca** *fem*

⒮ **insect** *noun*
el **insecto** *masc*
an insect bite una picadura de insecto

to **insert** *verb*
insertar [17]

⒮ **inside** *adverb* ▷ see **inside** *noun, prep*
dentro
to go inside entrar [17]
She's inside, I think. Creo que está dentro.

⒮ **inside** *noun* ▷ see **inside** *adv, prep*
el **interior** *masc*
the inside of the oven el interior del horno

⒮ **inside** *preposition* ▷ see **inside** *adv, noun*
dentro de
inside the cinema dentro del cine

inside out *adjective, adverb*
del revés
Your jumper's inside out. Llevas el jersey del revés.

to **insist** *verb*
insistir [19]
if you insist si insistes

to insist on doing something insistir en hacer algo
He insisted on paying. Insistió en pagar.
to insist that insistir en que
Ruth insisted that I was wrong. Ruth insistió en que yo estaba equivocada.

inspection *noun*
la **inspección** *fem*

inspector *noun*
el **inspector** *masc*, la **inspectora** *fem*

inspiration *noun*
la **inspiración** *fem*

to **install** *verb*
instalar [17]

instalment *noun*
1 (*of a TV, radio serial*) el **episodio** *masc*
2 (*payment*) el **plazo** *masc*
to pay by instalments pagar [28] a plazos

instance *noun*
1 (*example*) el **ejemplo** *masc*
for instance por ejemplo
2 (*case*) el **caso** *masc*
in this instance en este caso

instant *adjective* ▷ see **instant** *noun*
1 (*coffee, soup*) **instantáneo** *masc*, **instantánea** *fem*
2 (*effect, success*) **inmediato** *masc*, **inmediata** *fem*

instant *noun* ▷ see **instant** *adj*
el **instante** *masc*
Come here this instant! ¡Ven aquí ahora mismo!

⒮ **instead** *adverb*
1 (*as an alternative*) Ted couldn't go, so I went instead. Ted no pudo ir, así que fui yo en su lugar.
We didn't go to the concert, we went to Lucy's instead. No fuimos al concierto, fuimos a casa de Lucy.
2 instead of en vez de
Instead of pudding I had cheese. En vez de dulce tomé queso.
Instead of playing tennis we went swimming. En vez de jugar al tenis nos fuimos a nadar.

instinct *noun*
el **instinto** *masc*

to **instruct** *verb*
to instruct somebody to do something ordenar [17] a alguien que haga algo
The teacher instructed us to stay together.

La profesora nos ordenó que nos quedásemos juntos.

WORD TIP *ordenar que* is followed by the subjunctive.

ᔑ **instructions** *plural noun*
las **instrucciones** *plural fem*
Follow the instructions on the packet. Siga las instrucciones del paquete.
'Instructions for use' 'Modo de empleo'

instructor *noun*
el **profesor** *masc*, la **profesora** *fem*
my driving instructor mi profesor de conducir
a skiing instructor un monitor de esquí

ᔑ **instrument** *noun*
el **instrumento** *masc*
to play an instrument tocar [31] un instrumento

insulin *noun*
la **insulina** *fem*

insult *noun* ▷ see **insult** *verb*
el **insulto** *masc*

to **insult** *verb* ▷ see **insult** *noun*
insultar [17]

insurance *noun*
el **seguro** *masc*
travel insurance seguro de viaje
fire insurance seguro contra incendios
Have you got medical insurance? ¿Tienes seguro médico?

intelligence *noun*
la **inteligencia** *fem*

ᔑ **intelligent** *adjective*
inteligente *masc & fem*

to **intend** *verb*
1 (*to wish*) **querer** [12]
He did it as I intended. Lo hizo como yo quería.
2 (*to plan*) **to intend to do something** tener [9] pensado hacer algo
We intend to spend the night in Rome. Tenemos pensado pasar la noche en Roma.

intensive *adjective*
intensivo *masc*, **intensiva** *fem*
an intensive course un curso intensivo
to be in intensive care estar [2] en cuidados intensivos

intention *noun*
la **intención** *fem*
I have no intention of paying. No tengo ninguna intención de pagar.

ᔑ **interest** *noun* ▷ see **interest** *verb*
1 (*hobby*) la **afición** *fem*
What are your interests? ¿Qué aficiones tienes?
2 (*enthusiasm*) el **interés** *masc*
She showed interest. Mostró interés.
to take (an) interest in something interesarse [17] por algo

ᔑ to **interest** *verb* ▷ see **interest** *noun*
interesar [17]
That doesn't interest me. Eso no me interesa.

interested *adjective*
interesado *masc*, **interesada** *fem*
They seem very interested. Parecen estar muy interesados.
Sean's very interested in cooking. A Sean le interesa mucho la cocina.

ᔑ **interesting** *adjective*
interesante *masc & fem*

to **interfere** *verb*
to interfere in something entrometerse [18] en algo
She always interferes in my affairs. Siempre se entromete en mis asuntos.

ᔑ **interior** *adjective* ▷ see **interior** *noun*
interior *masc & fem*

ᔑ **interior** *noun* ▷ see **interior** *adj*
el **interior** *masc*
• **interior designer** el & la interiorista

ᔑ **international** *adjective*
internacional *masc & fem*

Internet *noun*
Internet *masc or fem*
to be on the Internet estar [2] conectado a Internet
Look for it on the Internet. Búscalo en Internet.

WORD TIP Spanish does not use *el* or *la* with *Internet*.

• **Internet cafe** el cibercafé

interpreter *noun*
el & la **intérprete** *masc & fem*

to **interrupt** *verb*
interrumpir [19]

interruption *noun*
la **interrupción** *fem*

interval *noun*
el **intermedio** *masc*

a b c d e f g h i j k l m n o p q r s t u v w x y z

♪ **interview** *noun* ▷ see **interview** *verb*
la **entrevista** *fem*
a job interview una entrevista de trabajo
a TV interview una entrevista en la tele

♪ to **interview** *verb* ▷ see **interview** *noun*
(*on TV, radio*) **entrevistar** [17]

interviewer *noun*
el **entrevistador** *masc*, la **entrevistadora** *fem*

♪ **into** *preposition*
1 (*showing movement*) to get into bed meterse [18] en la cama
to go into town ir [8] a la ciudad
He's gone into the bank. Ha entrado al banco.
I put the cat into his basket. Puse al gato dentro de su cesta.
We got into the car. Entramos en el coche.
He dived into the pool. Se tiró a la piscina.
She walked into a tree. Se dio contra un árbol.
2 (*showing change, etc*) to translate something into Spanish traducir [60] algo al español
to change pounds into euros cambiar [17] libras a euros
The sorcerer changed her into a stone. El mago la convirtió en una piedra.
3 (*used in division in maths*) Three into fifteen goes five times. Quince dividido por tres es cinco.

to **introduce** *verb*
presentar [17]
She introduced me to her brother. Me presentó a su hermano.
Can I introduce you to my mother? ¿Te puedo presentar a mi madre?

introduction *noun*
1 (*to a person*) la **presentación** *fem*
I'll make the introductions. Yo haré las presentaciones.
2 (*in a book*) la **introducción** *fem*

to **invade** *verb*
invadir [19]

invalid *noun*
el **inválido** *masc*, la **inválida** *fem*

invasion *noun*
la **invasión** *fem*

to **invent** *verb*
inventar [17]

invention *noun*
el **invento** *masc*

inverted commas *plural noun*
las **comillas** *plural fem*
in inverted commas entre comillas

investigation *noun*
la **investigación** *fem*
an investigation into the fire una investigación sobre el fuego

invisible *adjective*
invisible *masc & fem*

invitation *noun*
la **invitación** *fem*
an invitation to dinner una invitación a cenar

♪ to **invite** *verb*
invitar [17]
Kirsty invited me to lunch. Kirsty me invitó a comer.
He's invited me out on Tuesday. Me ha invitado a salir el martes.

invoice *noun*
la **factura** *fem*

to **involve** *verb*
1 (*to entail*) **suponer** [11]
It involves a lot of work. Supone mucho trabajo.
2 (*to consist of*) What does the job involve? ¿En qué consiste el trabajo?
3 (*to participate*) to be involved in something tomar [17] parte en algo
I am involved in the new project. Estoy tomando parte en el nuevo proyecto.

Iran *noun*
Irán *masc*

Iranian *adjective & noun*
1 **iraní** *masc & fem* (*pl:* **iraníes**)
2 un & una **iraní** *masc & fem*
the Iranians los iraníes

> **WORD TIP** Adjectives and nouns for nationality and regional origin do not have capital letters in Spanish.

Iraq *noun*
Irak *masc*

Iraqi *adjective & noun*
1 **iraquí** *masc & fem* (*pl:* **iraquíes**)
2 un & una **iraquí** *masc & fem*
the Iraqis los iraquíes

> **WORD TIP** Adjectives and nouns for nationality and regional origin do not have capital letters in Spanish.

Ireland *noun*
Irlanda *fem*
the Republic of Ireland la República Irlandesa
I'm from Ireland. Soy irlandés (*boy speaking*)., Soy irlandesa (*girl speaking*).

iris *noun*
  el **lirio** *masc*

♪ **Irish** *adjective* ▷ see **Irish** *noun*
  irlandés *masc*, **irlandesa** *fem*

♪ **Irish** *noun* ▷ see **Irish** *adj*
  1   (*the people*) **the Irish** los irlandeses
  2   (*the language*) el **irlandés** *masc*

> **WORD TIP** Adjectives and nouns for nationality, regional origin, and language do not have capital letters in Spanish.

Irishman *noun*
  un **irlandés** *masc*

Irish Republic *noun*
  the Irish Republic la República de Irlanda

Irish Sea *noun*
  the Irish Sea el mar de Irlanda

Irishwoman *noun* ▷ see **Irish** *noun*
  una **irlandesa** *fem*

iron *noun* ▷ see **iron** *verb*
  1   (*for clothes*) la **plancha** *fem*
  2   (*the metal*) el **hierro** *masc*

to **iron** *verb* ▷ see **iron** *noun*
  planchar [17]

ironing *noun*
  to do the ironing planchar [17]
•   **ironing board** la tabla de planchar

irregular *adjective*
  irregular *masc & fem*

irresponsible *adjective*
  irresponsable *masc & fem*

irritating *adjective*
  irritante *masc & fem*

Islam *noun*
  el **Islam** *masc*

Islamic *adjective*
  islámico *masc*, **islámica** *fem*

> **WORD TIP** Adjectives and nouns for religion do not have capital letters in Spanish.

island *noun*
  la **isla** *fem*

♪ **isn't** *short for*
  1   **is not** (See: **to be**)
  2   (*in questions*) **It's beautiful, isn't it?** ¿Es hermoso, verdad?

isolated *adjective*
  aislado *masc*, **aislada** *fem*

Israel *noun*
  Israel *masc*

Israeli *adjective & noun*
  1   **israelí** *masc & fem* (pl: **israelíes**)
  2   un & una **israelí** *masc & fem*
  the Israelis los israelíes

> **WORD TIP** Adjectives and nouns for nationality and regional origin do not have capital letters in Spanish.

issue *noun* ▷ see **issue** *verb*
  1   (*something you discuss*) el **tema** *masc*
  a political issue un tema político
  2   (*edition of a magazine*) el **número** *masc*

to **issue** *verb* ▷ see **issue** *noun*
  distribuir [54]

♪ **it** *pronoun*
  1   (*as the subject*) **él** *masc*, **ella** *fem* (*see Word Tip*)
  'Where's my bag?'— 'It's in the kitchen.'
  '¿Dónde está mi bolso?'— 'Está en la cocina.'
  You should see that film, it's great.
  Deberías ver esa película, es genial.
  'How old is your car?'— 'It's five years old.'
  '¿Cuántos años tiene tu coche?'— 'Cinco.'
  2   (*in impersonal statements*) **Yes, it's true.** Sí, es verdad.
  It doesn't matter. No importa.
  It's a nice day. Hace buen día.
  It's hot. Hace calor.
  It's one o'clock. Es la una.
  It's two o'clock. Son las dos (*Use* son *for two to twelve o'clock*).
  3   (*as the direct object*) **lo** *masc*, **la** *fem*
  My book? I've lost it. ¿Mi libro? Lo he perdido.
  Give me the suitcase, I'll carry it. Dame la maleta, yo la llevo.
  Put it there. Ponlo ahí.
  Don't leave it there. No lo dejes ahí.
  4   (*as the indirect object*) **le**
  I gave it another coat of paint. Le di otra mano de pintura.
  5   (*saying who you are, what something is*) **It was Bill.** Fue Bill.
  It's me. Soy yo.
  Who is it? ¿Quién es?
  What is it? ¿Qué es?
  It was a dress, not a blouse, she bought. Fue un vestido, no una blusa, lo que compró.
  6   (*after prepositions*) **ello**
  I want to talk about it. Quiero hablar de ello.
  Go for it! ¡A por ello!

> **WORD TIP** *it*, like *I, she, he* etc, is generally not translated into Spanish; the ending of the verb tells you if the subject of the verb is *yo, él, ella*, etc, so *it* is translated only for emphasis or for clarity.

a
b
c
d
e
f
g
h
i
j
k
l
m
n
o
p
q
r
s
t
u
v
w
x
y
z

a
b
c
d
e
f
g
h
i
j
k
l
m
n
o
p
q
r
s
t
u
v
w
x
y
z

ℰ IT *noun*
(= *Information Technology*) la **informática** *fem*

Italian *adjective & noun*
1 **italiano** *masc*, **italiana** *fem*
2 (*person*) un **italiano** *masc*, una **italiana** *fem*
the Italians los italianos
3 (*the language*) el **italiano** *masc*
my Italian class mi clase de italiano
our Italian teacher nuestro profesor de
italiano

> **WORD TIP** Adjectives and nouns for nationality,
> regional origin, and language do not have capital
> letters in Spanish.

italics *noun*
la **cursiva** *fem*
in italics en cursiva

Italy *noun*
Italia *fem*

to **itch** *verb*
1 (*clothes*) **picar**[31]
This sweater itches. Este jersey pica.

2 (*part of the body*) My back is itching. Me pica
la espalda.
I'm itching all over. Me pica todo el cuerpo.

item *noun*
el **artículo** *masc*

its *adjective*
1 (*before most nouns*) **su** *masc & fem*
The dog was playing with its toy. El perro
jugaba con su juguete.
It has its problems. Tiene sus problemas.
2 (*with parts of the body*) **el**, **la**, **los**, **las**
The cat was washing its ears. El gato se
lavaba las orejas.

itself *pronoun*
1 (*reflexive*) **se**
The cat is washing itself. El gato se está
lavando.
2 (*on its own*) by itself **solo** *masc*, **sola** *fem*
He left the dog by itself. Dejó al perro solo.

ivory *noun*
el **marfil** *masc*

ivy *noun*
la **hiedra** *fem*

J j

jack *noun*
1 (*in cards*) la **jota** *fem*
the jack of clubs la jota de tréboles
2 (*for a car*) el **gato** *masc*

ᔕ **jacket** *noun*
la **chaqueta** *fem*
· jacket potato la patata asada con la piel

jackpot *noun*
el **premio gordo**
to win the jackpot sacarse [31] el premio gordo

jagged *adjective*
dentado *masc*, dentada *fem*

jail *noun* ▷ see **jail** *verb*
la **cárcel** *fem*

to **jail** *verb* ▷ see **jail** *noun*
encarcelar [17]

ᔕ **jam** *noun*
1 (*for eating*) la **mermelada** *fem*
raspberry jam la mermelada de frambuesas
2 (*in traffic*) el **embotellamiento** *masc*
There was a huge traffic jam. Había un enorme embotellamiento.

Jamaica *noun*
Jamaica *fem*

Jamaican *adjective & noun*
1 jamaicano *masc*, jamaicana *fem*
2 (*person*) un **jamaicano** *masc*, una **jamaicana** *fem*
the Jamaicans los jamaicanos

WORD TIP Adjectives and nouns for nationality and regional origin do not have capital letters in Spanish..

ᔕ **January** *noun*
enero *masc*
in January en enero

WORD TIP Names of months and days start with small letters in Spanish.

jammed *adjective*
atascado *masc*, atascada *fem*

Japan *noun*
Japón *masc*
in Japan en Japón

Japanese *adjective & noun*
1 japonés *masc*, japonesa *fem*
2 (*person*) un **japonés** *masc*, una **japonesa** *fem*
the Japanese los japoneses

3 (*the language*) el **japonés** *masc*

WORD TIP Adjectives and nouns for nationality, regional origin, and language do not have capital letters in Spanish.

jar *noun*
el **tarro** *masc*
a jar of jam un tarro de mermelada

javelin *noun*
la **jabalina** *fem*

jaw *noun*
la **mandíbula** *fem*

jazz *noun*
el **jazz** *masc*

jealous *adjective*
celoso *masc*, celosa *fem*

jealousy *noun*
los **celos** *plural masc*

jeans *noun*
los **vaqueros** *plural masc*
a pair of jeans unos vaqueros
Look at my new jeans. Mira mis vaqueros nuevos.

jelly *noun*
la **gelatina** *fem*

jellyfish *noun*
la **medusa** *fem*

jersey *noun* ▷ see **Jersey** *noun*
1 (*pullover*) el **jersey** *masc*
2 (*for sport*) la **camiseta** *fem*

Jersey *noun* ▷ see **jersey** *noun*
la **isla de Jersey** (*one of the Channel Islands*)

Jesus *noun*
Jesús *masc*
Jesus Christ Jesucristo

jet *noun*
el **avión a reacción**
· jet lag el jet
· jet-ski la moto acuática

jetty *noun*
el **embarcadero** *masc*

Jew *noun*
el **judío** *masc*, la **judía** *fem*

WORD TIP Adjectives and nouns for religion do not have capital letters in Spanish.

jewel *noun*
la **joya** *fem*

English–Spanish

a
b
c
d
e
f
g
h
i
j
k
l
m
n
o
p
q
r
s
t
u
v
w
x
y
z

jeweller noun
  el **joyero** masc, la **joyera** fem
· **jeweller's shop** la joyería

jewellery noun
  las **joyas** plural fem

Jewish adjective
  judío masc, **judía** fem
  He's Jewish. Es judío.

WORD TIP Adjectives and nouns for religion do not have capital letters in Spanish.

jigsaw noun
  el **rompecabezas** invariable masc

⚡ **job** noun
1 (paid work) el **trabajo** masc
  a part-time job un trabajo a tiempo parcial
  a job as a secretary un trabajo como secretaria
  What's your job? ¿En qué trabajas?
  He's got a job at a supermarket. Trabaja en un supermercado.
  I'm out of a job right now. Estoy sin trabajo en este momento.
2 (task) el **trabajo** masc
  It's not an easy job. No es un trabajo fácil.
  She's made a good job of it. Lo ha hecho muy bien.

jobless adjective
  sin trabajo, **en paro**

jockey noun
  el & la **jockey** masc & fem

to **jog** verb
  to go jogging hacer [7] footing
  She goes jogging every day. Hace footing todos los días.

to **join** verb
1 (to become a member of) **hacerse** [7] **socio de**
  He joined the judo club. Se ha hecho socio del club de judo.
2 (to meet up with)
  I'll join you later. Iré más tarde.
· **to join in**
1 (people) **participar** [17]
  Ruth never joins in. Ruth nunca participa.
2 (a discussion, a game) to join in something participar [17] en algo
  Will you join in the game? ¿Quieres participar en el juego?

joiner noun
  el **carpintero** masc, la **carpintera** fem

joint noun
1 (in body) la **articulación** fem
2 (of hash) el **porro** masc
3 (bar, etc) el **antro** masc

joke noun ▷ see **joke** verb
1 (funny story) el **chiste** masc
  to tell a joke contar [24] un chiste
  He's always telling jokes. Siempre está contando chistes.
2 (trick) la **broma** fem
  to play a joke on someone gastarle [17] una broma a alguien
  She played a joke on him. Le gastó una broma.

to **joke** verb ▷ see **joke** noun
  bromear [17]
  She's only joking. Sólo está bromeando.
  You're joking! ¡Qué va!

joker noun
1 (in cards) el **comodín**
2 (in class) el & la **bromista** masc & fem

Jordan noun
  Jordania fem

journalism noun
  el **periodismo** masc

⚡ **journalist** noun
  el & la **periodista** masc & fem
  Sean's dad is a journalist. El padre de Sean es periodista.

⚡ **journey** noun
  el **viaje** masc
  our journey to Seville nuestro viaje a Sevilla
  a bus journey un viaje en autobús
  My journey to school takes half an hour. Me tardo una hora en ir a la escuela en el autobús.

joy noun
  la **alegría** fem

joy-riding noun
  el **delito de robar un coche para dar una vuelta con él a toda velocidad**

joystick noun
  (Computers) el **joystick** masc

Judaism noun
  (Religion) el **judaísmo** masc

WORD TIP Adjectives and nouns for religion do not have capital letters in Spanish.

judge noun ▷ see **judge** verb
  el **juez** masc, la **jueza** fem

to **judge** verb ▷ see **judge** noun
  (a time, distance) **calcular** [17]

judgement noun
1 (sense) el **juicio** fem
  in my judgement a mi juicio
2 (in a court) la **sentencia** fem

judo *noun*
el **judo** *masc*
She does judo. Hace judo.

jug *noun*
la **jarra** *fem*

to **juggle** *verb*
hacer [7] **malabarismos**

juggler *noun*
el & la **malabarista** *masc & fem*

♪ **juice** *noun*
el **zumo** *masc*
Two orange juices, please! ¡Dos zumos de naranja, por favor!

juicy *adjective*
jugoso *masc*, jugosa *fem*

♪ **July** *noun*
julio *masc*
in July en julio

WORD TIP Names of months and days start with small letters in Spanish.

jumble sale *noun*
el **mercadillo de beneficencia**

♪ to **jump** *verb* ▷ see **jump** *noun*
saltar [17]

jump *noun* ▷ see **jump** *verb*
el **salto** *masc*
a parachute jump un salto en paracaídas

♪ **jumper** *noun*
el **jersey** *masc*

junction *noun*
1 (of roads, motorways) el **cruce** *masc*
2 (on a railway) el **empalme** *masc*

♪ **June** *noun*
junio *masc*
in June en junio

WORD TIP Names of months and days start with small letters in Spanish.

♪ **junior** *adjective*
de **primaria**
a junior school una escuela de primaria
the juniors los alumnos de primaria

jungle *noun*
la **selva** *fem*

junk *noun*
la **basura** *masc*
· **junk food** la comida basura
Junk food is bad for you. La comida basura es mala para la salud.
· **junk shop** la tienda de cosas usadas

jury *noun*
el **jurado** *masc*

just *adverb*
1 (shortly) **justo**
just before midday justo antes del mediodía
just after the church justo después de la iglesia
2 (only) **sólo**
just for fun sólo por diversión
It's just for you. Es para ti.
There's just me and Justine. Sólo somos yo y Justine.
3 to be just doing something estar [2] haciendo algo
I'm just finishing my homework. Estoy terminando mis deberes.
I'm just coming! ¡Ya voy!
4 to have just done something acabar [17] de hacer algo
Tom has just arrived. Tom acaba de llegar.
Helen had just called. Helen acababa de llamar.

WORD TIP have just done something is translated by acabo de, etc, i.e. the present tense in Spanish. had just done something is translated by acababa de, etc, i.e. the imperfect tense in Spanish.

justice *noun*
la **justicia** *fem*

to **justify** *verb*
justificar [31]

a
b
c
d
e
f
g
h
i
j
k
l
m
n
o
p
q
r
s
t
u
v
w
x
y
z

K k

kangaroo *noun*
el **canguro** *masc*

karate *noun*
el **kárate** *masc*

kebab *noun*
la **brocheta** *fem*

keen *adjective*
You don't look too keen. No pareces muy
entusiasmado.
He's a keen photographer. Le gusta mucho
la fotografía.
He's not keen on jazz. No le gusta el jazz.
They are keen on the idea. Están
interesados en la idea.

♪ to **keep** *verb*
1 (*to store*) **guardar** [17]
I keep my bike in the garage. Guardo mi
bici en el garaje.
Where do you keep the CDs? ¿Dónde
guardas los CDs?
to keep something for someone guardarle
algo a alguien
Will you keep my seat? ¿Me guardas el
sitio?
to keep somebody waiting hacer [7]
esperar a alguien
He kept us waiting for an hour. Nos hizo
esperar una hora.
2 (*for ever*) **quedarse** [17] **con**
I kept the letter. Me quedé con la carta.
Keep the change! ¡Quédese con el
cambio! (*formal use*)
3 (*secrets, etc*) to keep a secret **guardar** [17] un
secreto
to keep a promise **mantener** [9] una
promesa
4 (*to stay*) Keep calm! ¡Tranquilo! (*boy*),
¡Tranquila! (*girl*)
Keep still! ¡Estate quieto!
Keep out of the sun. No te pongas al sol.
5 to keep on doing something **seguir** [64]
haciendo algo
She kept on talking. Siguió hablando.
Keep straight on. Siga todo recto. (*formal
use*)
6 (*time after time*) to keep on doing something
no **parar** [17] de hacer algo
He keeps on phoning me. No para de
llamarme.

kerb *noun*
el **bordillo de la acera**

ketchup *noun*
el **ketchup** *masc*

kettle *noun*
el **hervidor** *masc*
to put the kettle on poner el agua a hervir

♪ **key** *noun*
1 (*for a lock*) la **llave** *fem*
a bunch of keys un manojo de llaves
2 (*on a keyboard*) la **tecla** *fem*
• **keyboard** el teclado *masc*
• **keyhole** el ojo de la cerradura
• **keyring** el llavero

♪ **kick** *noun* ▷ see **kick** *verb*
1 (*with the foot*) la **patada** *fem*
to give somebody a kick darle [4] una
patada a alguien
2 (*buzz*) She gets a kick out of driving fast. Le
encanta conducir rápido.

to **kick** *verb* ▷ see **kick** *noun*
to kick somebody darle [4] una patada a
alguien
He kicked the referee. Le dio una patada al
árbitro.
to kick the ball darle [4] una patada al balón
• to **kick off**
empezar [25]

kick-off *noun*
el **saque inicial**
The kick-off is at three. El partido empieza a
las tres.

♪ **kid** *noun*
1 (*child*) el **niño** *masc*, la **niña** *fem*
Dad's looking after the kids. Papá está
cuidando a los niños.
2 (*young goat*) el **cabrito** *masc*, la **cabrita** *fem*

to **kidnap** *verb*
secuestrar [17]

kidnapper *noun*
el **secuestrador** *masc*, la **secuestradora**
fem

kidney *noun*
el **riñón** *masc*

♪ to **kill** *verb*
matar [17]
The cat killed the bird. El gato mató al
pájaro.

a
b
c
d
e
f
g
h
i
j
k
l
m
n
o
p
q
r
s
t
u
v
w
x
y
z

The disease kills many people. La enfermedad mata a muchas personas.
She was killed in an accident., She got killed in an accident. Murió en un accidente.

killer *noun*
(*murderer*) el **asesino** *masc*, la **asesina** *fem*
The disease is a killer. La enfermedad es una de las que causa más muertes.

ᔏ **kilo** *noun*
el **kilo** *masc*
a kilo of tomatoes un kilo de tomates
half a kilo of sugar medio kilo de azúcar
five euros a kilo cinco euros el kilo

kilogramme *noun*
el **kilogramo** *masc*

ᔏ **kilometre** *noun*
el **kilómetro** *masc*

kilt *noun*
la **falda escocesa**

ᔏ **kind** *adjective* ▷ see **kind** *noun*
amable *masc & fem*, **bueno** *masc*, **buena** *fem*
Marion was very kind to me. Marion fue muy amable conmigo.
She's very kind. Es muy buena.

ᔏ **kind** *noun* ▷ see **kind** *adj*
el **tipo** *masc*, la **clase** *fem*
all kinds of people toda clase de gente
It's a kind of fruit. Es un tipo de fruta.
They sell souvenirs and that kind of thing. Venden recuerdos y cosas por el estilo.

kindness *noun*
la **amabilidad** *fem*

king *noun*
el **rey** *masc*
King Juan Carlos el rey Juan Carlos
the King and Queen of Spain los reyes de España
the king of hearts el rey de corazones

kingdom *noun*
el **reino** *masc*
the United Kingdom el Reino Unido

ᔏ **kiosk** *noun*
1 (*for newspapers, snacks*) el **quiosco** *masc*
2 (*phonebox*) la **cabina** *fem*

ᔏ **kiss** *noun* ▷ see **kiss** *verb*
el **beso** *masc*
to give somebody a kiss darle [4] un beso a alguien
She gave him a kiss., He gave her a kiss. Le dio un beso

ᔏ to **kiss** *verb* ▷ see **kiss** *noun*
besar [17]
Kiss me! ¡Bésame!
We kissed each other. Nos besamos.
They kiss each other every time they meet. Se dan un beso cada vez que se encuentran.
to kiss somebody goodbye darle [4] un beso de despedida a alguien

kit *noun*
1 (*set*) a tool kit una caja de herramientas
a first-aid kit un botiquín
2 (*clothes, equipment*) el **equipo** *masc*
Where's my gym kit? ¿Dónde está mi equipo de gimnasia?
3 (*for models, furniture*) el **kit** *masc*

ᔏ **kitchen** *noun*
la **cocina** *fem*
the kitchen table la mesa de la cocina
· kitchen roll el papel de cocina

kite *noun*
(*toy*) la **cometa** *fem*
to fly a kite hacer [7] volar una cometa
We fly our kites in the park. Hacemos volar las cometas en el parque.

kitten *noun*
el **gatito** *masc*, la **gatita** *fem*

kiwi fruit *noun*
el **kiwi** *masc*

knack *noun*
el **tranquillo** *masc*
I've got the knack of it now. Ya le he cogido el tranquillo.

ᔏ **knee** *noun*
la **rodilla** *fem*
to be on your knees estar [2] de rodillas

to **kneel** *verb*
1 (*to be kneeling*) **estar** [2] **de rodillas**
2 (*to kneel down*) **arrodillarse** [17]

ᔏ **knickers** *plural noun*
las **bragas** *plural fem*

ᔏ **knife** *noun*
1 (*fixed blade*) el **cuchillo** *masc*
2 (*penknife*) la **navaja** *fem*

knight *noun*
(*in chess*) el **caballo** *masc*

to **knit** *verb*
1 (*a scarf, a sweater*) **tejer** [18]
2 (*as an activity*) **hacer** [7] **punto**

knitting *noun*
el **punto** *masc*

knob *noun*
1 (*on a drawer*) el **tirador** *masc*
2 (*on a door*) el **pomo** *masc*
3 (*of butter*) el **pedacito** *masc*

knock *noun* ▷ see **knock** *verb*
el **golpe** *masc*
a knock on the head un golpe en la cabeza
a knock at the door un golpe en la puerta

to **knock** *verb* ▷ see **knock** *noun*
1 **darse** [4] **un golpe**
I knocked my head. Me di un golpe en la cabeza.
2 (*at the door*) to knock at the door llamar [17] a la puerta
Someone's knocking at the door. Están llamando a la puerta.
• to **knock down**
1 (*a pedestrian, cyclist*) **atropellar** [17]
She was knocked down by a bus. La atropelló un autobús.
2 (*a building*) **derribar** [17]
• to **knock out**
1 (*in competitions*) **eliminar** [17]
United was knocked out in the first round. El United quedó eliminado en la primera vuelta.
2 (*unconscious*) **dejar** [17] **sin sentido**

knocker *noun*
la **aldaba** *fem*

knot *noun*
el **nudo** *masc*
to tie a knot in a string hacer [7] un nudo a la cuerda

ℰ to **know** *verb*
1 (*facts, a language*) **saber** [13]
I know where she is. Sé donde está.
Do you know where their house is? ¿Sabes dónde queda su casa?

I know Spanish and French. Sé español y francés.
He knows it by heart. Se lo sabe de memoria.
Yes, I know. Sí, ya lo sé.
You never know! ¡Nunca se sabe!
2 (*a person, a song, a place*) **conocer** [35]
I know Sharon. Conozco a Sharon.
I don't know her father. No conozco a su padre.
All the people I know. Toda la gente que conozco.
Do you know that song? ¿Conoces esa canción?
Do you know Santiago? ¿Conoces Santiago?
3 to know how to do something saber [13] hacer algo
Steve knows how to make paella. Steve sabe hacer paella.
4 (*a subject, machines*) to know all about someting saber [13] de algo
Lindy knows all about computers. Lindy sabe de ordenadores.

knowledge *noun*
los **conocimientos** *plural masc*
scientific knowledge conocimientos científicos
She did it without the knowledge of her parents. Lo hizo sin que supieran sus padres.

knuckle *noun*
el **nudillo** *masc*

koala *noun*
el **koala** *masc*

Koran *noun*
(*Religion*) el **Corán** *masc*

kosher *adjective*
kosher *invariable adjective*

L l

lab *noun*
 el **laboratorio** *masc*

label *noun*
 la **etiqueta** *fem*

laboratory *noun*
 el **laboratorio** *masc*

Labour *noun*
 los **laboristas** *plural masc*
 to vote Labour votar [17] por los laboristas
 the Labour Party el partido laborista

lace *noun*
 1 (*for a shoe*) el **cordón** *masc*
  to do up your laces atarse [17] los cordones
 2 (*fabric*) el **encaje** *masc*

to **lack** *verb*
 to lack something hacerle [7] falta algo a alguien
 He lacks confidence. Le hace falta confianza.
 We lack funds. Nos hace falta fondos.

lad *noun*
 el **chaval** *masc* (*informal*)

ladder *noun*
 1 (*for climbing*) la **escalera** *fem*
 2 (*in your tights*) la **carrera** *fem*

ladies *noun* ▷ see **lady** *noun*
 1 (*women's toilets*) los **servicios de señoras**
  Where's the ladies? ¿Dónde están los servicios de señoras?
 2 (*sign for women's toilets*) **Señoras**

♂ **lady** *noun* ▷ see **ladies** *noun*
 la **señora** *fem*
 ladies and gentlemen señoras y señores

lager *noun*
 la **cerveza rubia**

laid-back *adjective*
 relajado *masc*, **relajada** *fem*

♂ **lake** *noun*
 el **lago** *masc*

♂ **lamb** *noun*
 1 (*young sheep*) el **cordero** *masc*
 2 (*meat*) el **cordero** *masc*
  a lamb chop una chuleta de cordero

lame *adjective*
 cojo *masc*, **coja** *fem*

♂ **lamp** *noun*
 la **lámpara** *fem*
 • **lamppost** la farola
 • **lampshade** la pantalla

♂ **land** *noun* ▷ see **land** *verb*
 1 (*not the sea*) la **tierra** *fem*
  on dry land en tierra firme
 2 (*property*) a piece of land un terreno
  He has land. Tiene tierras.
 3 (*country*) el **país** *masc*
  a faraway land un país lejano

♂ to **land** *verb* ▷ see **land** *noun*
 1 (*planes, passengers*) **aterrizar** [22]
 2 (*to leave a ship*) **desembarcar** [31]

landing *noun*
 1 (*on the stairs*) el **descansillo** *masc*
 2 (*of a plane*) el **aterrizaje** *masc*
 3 (*from a boat*) el **desembarco** *masc*

landlady *noun*
 1 (*of a rented house*) la **casera** *fem*
 2 (*of a pub*) la **dueña** *fem*

landlord *noun*
 1 (*of a rented house*) el **casero** *masc*
 2 (*of a pub*) el **dueño** *masc*

lane *noun*
 1 (*in the country*) el **camino** *masc*
 2 (*of a motorway, road*) el **carril** *masc*
  a bus lane un carril de autobuses

♂ **language** *noun*
 1 (*Spanish, Italian, etc*) el **idioma** *masc*
  a foreign language un idioma extranjero
 2 (*way of speaking*) el **lenguaje** *masc*
  scientific language lenguaje científico
 3 bad language palabras *plural fem*
  to use bad language decir [5] palabrotas
 • **language lab** el laboratorio de idiomas
 • **language school** la academia de idiomas

lap *noun*
 1 (*your knees*) las **rodillas** *plural fem*
  He sat on his father's lap. Se sentó en las rodillas de su padre.
 2 (*in a race*) la **vuelta** *fem*

laptop *noun*
 el **portátil** *masc*

a
b
c
d
e
f
g
h
i
j
k
l
m
n
o
p
q
r
s
t
u
v
w
x
y
z

♪ large *adjective*
　grande *masc & fem*
　a large house una casa grande
　large cities las ciudades grandes
　a large number of people un gran número
　de gente
　a large quantity of letters una gran
　cantidad de cartas

> **WORD TIP** *grande* becomes *gran* when it comes before a singular noun.

laser *noun*
　el **láser** *masc*
• **laser beam** el rayo láser
• **laser printer** la impresora láser

♪ last *adjective* ▷ see **last** *adv, verb*
　1 (*final in a series*) **último** *masc*, **última** *fem*
　the last time la última vez
　It was the last thing I did. Fue lo último que
　hice.
　to be the last one to do something ser [1] el
　último en hacer algo
　I was the last one to leave. Fui el último en
　salir.
　2 (*previous*) **last week** la semana pasada
　last night anoche
　my last letter mi última carta

♪ last *adverb* ▷ see **last** *adj, verb*
　1 (*after all the others*) **Rob arrived last.** Rob
　llegó el último.
　I came last in the race. Llegué en último
　lugar en la carrera.
　2 (*most recently*) **I last saw him in May.** La
　última vez que lo vi fue en mayo.
　3 (*in expressions*) **and last ...** y por último ...
　At last! ¡Por fin!
　You're here at last! ¡Por fin has llegado!

♪ to last *verb* ▷ see **last** *adj, adv*
　durar [17]
　The film lasted two hours. La película duró
　dos horas.

♪ late *adjective, adverb*
　1 (*after the usual time: people*) **tarde**
　to be late llegar [28] tarde
　We're late. Llegamos tarde.
　They arrived late. Llegaron tarde.
　to be late for something llegar [28] tarde a
　algo
　We were late for the film. Llegamos tarde a
　la película.
　2 (*after the stated time: buses, trains*) **to be late**
　llegar con retraso
　The train was an hour late. El tren llegó con
　una hora de retraso.
　3 (*late in the day*) **tarde**
　We got up late. Nos levantamos tarde.

It's getting late. Se está haciendo tarde.
late last night ayer por la noche ya tarde
Too late! ¡Demasiado tarde!

later *adverb*
　más tarde
　later that same day ese mismo día más
　tarde
　no later than Thursday no más tarde del
　jueves
　I'll explain it to you later. Te lo explicaré
　más tarde.
　See you later! ¡Hasta luego!

latest *adjective* ▷ see **latest** *noun*
　último *masc*, **última** *fem*
　the latest news las últimas noticias

latest *noun* ▷ see **latest** *adj*
　at the latest a más tardar
　the latest in audio equipment lo último en
　equipo de audio

Latin *noun*
　el **latín** *masc*

> **WORD TIP** Adjectives and nouns for languages do not have capital letters in Spanish.

Latin America *noun*
　América Latina *fem*

Latin American *adjective & noun*
　1 **latinoamericano** *masc*, **latinoamericana**
　fem
　2 un **latinoamericano** *masc*, una
　latinoamericana *fem*
　the Latin Americans los latinoamericanos

> **WORD TIP** Adjectives and nouns for nationality and regional origin do not have capital letters in Spanish.

Latvia *noun*
　Letonia *fem*

Latvian *adjective & noun*
　1 **letón** *masc*, **letona** *fem*
　2 un **letón** *masc*, una **letona** *fem*
　the Latvians los letones

> **WORD TIP** Adjectives and nouns for nationality and regional origin do not have capital letters in Spanish.

♪ laugh *noun* ▷ see **laugh** *verb*
　la **risa** *fem*
　She gave a nervous laugh. Soltó una risa
　nerviosa.
　to do something for a laugh hacer [7] algo
　por divertirse

ᵍ to **laugh** *verb* ▷ see **laugh** *noun*
1 **reírse** [61]
　Everybody laughed. Todo el mundo se rió.
2 **to laugh at someone** reírse [61] de alguien
　They laughed at me. Se rieron de mí.

ᵍ **laughter** *noun*
　las **risas** *plural fem*

launch *noun* ▷ see **launch** *verb*
1 (*of a product, a spacecraft*) el **lanzamiento** *masc*
2 (*of a ship*) la **botadura** *fem*

to **launch** *verb* ▷ see **launch** *noun*
1 (*a product, spacecraft*) **lanzar** [22]
2 (*a ship*) **botar** [17]

launderette *noun*
　la **lavandería** *fem*

laundry *noun*
　la **lavandería** *fem*

lavatory *noun*
　el **servicio** *masc*, el **aseo** *masc*

lavender *noun*
　la **lavanda** *fem*

law *noun*
1 (*set of rules*) la **ley** *fem*
　the law la ley
　to pass a law aprobar [24] una ley
　to break the law violar [17] la ley
　It's against the law. Es ilegal.
2 (*subject of study*) el **derecho** *masc*

ᵍ **lawn** *noun*
　el **césped** *masc*
• **lawnmower** el cortacésped

lawyer *noun*
　el **abogado** *masc*, la **abogada** *fem*
　My mother is a lawyer. Mi madre es abogada.

to **lay** *verb*
1 (*to put*) **poner** [11]
　She laid the money on the table. Puso el dinero en la mesa.
2 **to lay the table** poner [11] la mesa
3 (*an egg*) **poner** [11]

lay-by *noun*
　el **área** *fem* **de reposo**
　a lay-by un área de reposo

WORD TIP *área* takes *el* or *un* in the singular even though it is feminine.

layer *noun*
　la **capa** *fem*

laziness *noun*
　la **pereza** *fem*

ᵍ **lazy** *adjective*
　perezoso *masc*, **perezosa** *fem*

to **lead** *verb* ▷ see **lead** *adj, noun*
1 (*to a place*) **llevar** [17]
　He led us to the beach. Nos llevó a la playa.
　The path leads to the sea. El sendero lleva al mar.
2 (*in a match, a race, a competition*) **ir** [8] **ganando**
　They are leading by three goals. Van ganando por tres goles.
3 (*to a result*) **to lead to something** llevar [17] a algo
　One thing leads to another. Una cosa lleva a otra.
　It led to an accident. Causó un accidente.
　This will lead to problems. Esto traerá problemas.
4 (*one's life*) **llevar** [17]
　I lead a quiet life. Llevo una vida tranquila.

lead *adjective* ▷ see **lead** *verb, noun*
　(*role, singer*) **principal**

lead *noun* ▷ see **lead** *adj, verb*
1 (*in races, competitions*) **to be in the lead** llevar [17] la delantera
　Sam's in the lead. Sam lleva la delantera.
　We have a lead of three points. Llevamos una ventaja de tres puntos.
2 (*for electricity*) el **cable** *masc*
3 (*for a dog*) la **correa** *fem*
　Put the dog on a lead. Ponle una correa al perro.
4 (*the metal*) el **plomo** *masc*
5 (*for a pencil*) la **mina** *fem*

ᵍ **leader** *noun*
1 (*of a gang*) el & la **cabecilla** *masc & fem*
2 (*of a political party*) el & la **líder** *masc & fem*
3 (*in a competition*) el **primero** *masc*, la **primera** *fem*

lead-free petrol *noun*
　la **gasolina sin plomo**

lead singer *noun*
　el & la **cantante principal**

leaf *noun*
　la **hoja** *fem*

ᵍ **leaflet** *noun*
　el **folleto** *masc*

league *noun*
　(*in sport*) la **liga** *fem*

lean *adjective* ▷ see **lean** *verb*
　(*meat*) **magro** *masc*, **magra** *fem*

lean | left

to **lean** verb ▷ see **lean** adj

1 (to bend) **echarse** [17]
Lean forward a bit. Échate para delante un poco.
She leaned out of the window. Se asomó por la ventana.

2 (to support yourself) **to lean on something** apoyarse [17] en algo

3 (to prop) **to lean something on something** apoyar [17] algo en algo
Lean the ladder against the tree. Apoya la escalera en el árbol.

leap year noun
el **año bisiesto**

♫ to **learn** verb
aprender [18]
to learn Russian aprender ruso
to learn to drive aprender a conducir

learner driver noun
She's a learner driver. Está aprendiendo a conducir.

♫ **least** adverb, adjective, pronoun

1 (in superlatives) **menos**
the least expensive hotel el hotel menos caro
the least expensive glasses las gafas menos caras
Tony has the least money. Tony es el que menos dinero tiene.
I like the blue shirt least. La camisa azul es la que menos me gusta.
It's the least I can do. Es lo menos que puedo hacer.

2 (slightest) **más mínimo** masc, **más mínima** fem
I haven't the least idea. No tengo ni la más mínima idea.
He didn't show the least interest. No mostró el más mínimo interés.

3 (at a minimum) **at least** por lo menos
There must be at least twenty people. Debe haber por lo menos veinte personas.

4 (at any rate) **at least** al menos
At least, that's what I think. Al menos eso creo.

♫ **leather** noun
el **cuero** masc
a leather jacket una chaqueta de cuero

♫ to **leave** verb

1 (to go away) **irse** [8]
They're leaving tomorrow. Se van mañana.
We left at six. Nos fuimos a las seis.

2 (work, a building, etc) **salir** [63] **de**
I leave school at four. Salgo del colegio a las cuatro.

She left the cinema at ten. Salió del cine a las diez.

3 (in a place) **dejar** [17]
He left his wife at the airport. Dejó a su mujer en el aeropuerto.
You can leave your coats in the hall. Podéis dejar los abrigos en la entrada.

4 (to abandon) **dejar** [17] **a**
He left his wife. Dejó a su mujer.

5 (to forget) **dejarse** [17]
He left his umbrella on the train. Se dejó el paraguas en el tren.

6 **to leave school** dejar [17] los estudios
Guy left school at sixteen. Guy dejó los estudios a los dieciséis años.

7 **to be left** quedar [17]
There are two cakes left. Quedan dos pasteles.
We have ten minutes left. Nos quedan diez minutos.
I've got no money left. No me queda dinero.

· **to leave out**

1 (to omit) **omitir** [19]
I left out the most important part. Omití lo más importante.

2 (to exclude) **excluir** [54]
She feels left out. Se siente excluida.

lecture noun

1 (at university) la **clase** fem
2 (public) la **conferencia** fem

lecturer noun
el **profesor** masc, la **profesora** fem

ledge noun

1 (of a window) la **repisa** fem
2 (on a cliff) el **saliente** masc

leek noun
el **puerro** masc

♫ **left** adjective ▷ see **left** adv, noun
izquierdo masc, **izquierda** fem
his left foot el pie izquierdo
on the left hand side a mano izquierda

♫ **left** adverb ▷ see **left** adj, noun
(to turn, look) **a la izquierda**
Turn left at the church. Gira a la izquierda en la iglesia.

♫ **left** noun ▷ see **left** adj, adv

1 (direction) la **izquierda** fem
the second street on the left la segunda calle a la izquierda
on my left a mi izquierda
It's on the left. Está a la izquierda.
to drive on the left conducir [60] por la izquierda

2 (in politics) **the left** la izquierda

left-click noun ▷ see **left-click** verb
el **clic con el botón izquierdo**

to **left-click** verb ▷ see **left-click** noun
hacer [7] **clic con el botón izquierdo**
Left-click the icon. Haz clic en el icono con
el botón izquierdo.

left-hand noun
the left-hand side la parte izquierda

left-handed adjective
zurdo masc, **zurda** fem

ℰ **left-luggage locker** noun
la **consigna automática**

ℰ **left-luggage office** noun
la **consigna** fem

leftovers plural noun
las **sobras** plural fem

ℰ **leg** noun
1 (person's) la **pierna** fem
my left leg mi pierna izquierda
to break your leg romperse [40] una pierna
to pull somebody's leg tomarle el pelo a
alguien
They're pulling your leg. Te están tomando
el pelo.
2 (of a table, chair, animal) la **pata** fem
3 (in cooking) a leg of chicken un muslo de
pollo
a leg of lamb una pierna de cordero

legal adjective
legal masc & fem

legend noun
la **leyenda** fem

leggings plural noun
los **leggings** plural masc

ℰ **leisure** noun
el **tiempo libre**
in my leisure time en mi tiempo libre
• leisure centre el polideportivo

ℰ **lemon** noun
el **limón** masc
a lemon yoghurt un yogur de limón

ℰ **lemonade** noun
1 (made with real lemons) la **limonada** fem
2 (fizzy drink) la **gaseosa** fem

lemon juice noun
el **zumo de limón**

ℰ to **lend** verb
dejar [17]
to lend something to somebody dejarle
algo a alguien

I lent Judy my bike. Le dejé mi bici a Judy.
Will you lend it to me? ¿Me lo dejas?

length noun
1 (of fabric, board, etc) el **largo** masc
2 (of a film, play) la **duración** fem
3 (of a book, list) la **extensión** fem

ℰ **lens** noun
1 (in a camera) la **lente** fem
2 (in glasses) el **cristal** masc
3 (contact lens) la **lentilla** fem

Lent noun
la **Cuaresma** fem

lentil noun
la **lenteja** fem

Leo noun
1 (the star sign) el **Leo** masc
2 (a person) un & una **leo** masc & fem
Mary's Leo. Mary es leo.

> **WORD TIP** Use a small letter in Spanish to say I
> am ... etc with star signs. Star signs in Spanish are
> used without el, un, la, una.

leotard noun
la **malla** fem

lesbian noun
la **lesbiana** fem

ℰ **less** pronoun, adjective, adverb
1 (not so much) **menos**
Richard eats less. Richard come menos.
less time menos tiempo
It's less interesting. Es menos interesante.
less quickly than us menos rápido que
nosotros
2 (with amounts, numbers) less than menos de
less than a kilo menos de un kilo
less than three hours menos de tres horas
3 (in comparisons) less than menos que
You spend less than me. Gastas menos que
yo.

lesson noun
la **clase** fem
the history lesson la clase de historia
a driving lesson una clase de conducir
to take tennis lessons tomar [17] clases de
tenis

to **let** verb
1 (to allow) **dejar** [17]
Let her speak. Déjala hablar.
Will you let me go alone? ¿Me dejas ir sola?
The police let us through. La policía nos
dejó pasar.
She lets me use her bike. Me deja usar su
bici.
Let me help you. Déjame que te ayude. ▸▸

ℰ indicates key words   531

2 **to let go of something** soltar [24] algo
　Let go of my hand. Suéltame la mano.
　Let go of me! ¡Suéltame!

3 (*in suggestions, orders*) **Let's go!** ¡Vámonos!
　Let's not talk about it. No hablemos de ello.
　Let's see if Tuesday is ok. Vamos a ver si el
　martes conviene.
　Let's eat out. Vamos a comer fuera.

4 (*to rent out*) **alquilar** [17]
　'Flat to let' 'Se alquila apartamento'

• **to let in**
　(*to allow to enter*) **dejar** [17] **entrar**
　Don't let the cat in! ¡No dejes entrar al gato!

• **to let off**

1 (*fireworks*) **tirar** [17]

2 (*a bomb*) **hacer** [7] **estallar**

3 (*to excuse from*) **perdonar** [17]
　She let me off returning the money. Me
　perdonó que devolviera el dinero.

• **to let out**
　(*to allow to leave*) **dejar** [17] **salir**
　Let me out of here! ¡Déjame salir de aquí!

lethal *adjective*
　mortal *masc & fem*

ʃ **letter** *noun*

1 (*written message*) la **carta** *fem*
　a letter for you from Delia una carta de
　Delia para ti

2 (*of the alphabet*) la **letra** *fem*
　M is the letter after L. M es la letra que viene
　depués de L.

• **letterbox** el **buzón**

lettuce *noun*
　la **lechuga** *fem*

leukaemia *noun*
　la **leucemia** *fem*

level *adjective* ▷ see **level** *noun*

1 (*street, floor*) **plano** *masc*, **plana** *fem*

2 (*ground*) **llano** *masc*, **llana** *fem*

level *noun* ▷ see **level** *adj*
　el **nivel** *masc*
　at street level a nivel de la calle

• **level crossing** el **paso a nivel**

lever *noun*
　la **palanca** *fem*

liar *noun*
　el **mentiroso** *masc*, la **mentirosa** *fem*

liberal *adjective*
　liberal *masc & fem*
　the Liberal Democrats los demócratas
　liberales

liberty *noun*
　la **libertad** *fem*

Libra *noun*

1 (*the star sign*) el **Libra** *masc*

2 (*a person*) un & una **libra** *masc & fem*
　John's Libra. John es libra.

WORD TIP Use a small letter in Spanish to say *I
am … etc* with star signs. Star signs in Spanish are
used without *el, un, la, una*.

librarian *noun*
　el **bibliotecario** *masc*, la **bibliotecaria** *fem*
　Mark's a librarian. Mark es bibliotecario.

ʃ **library** *noun*
　la **biblioteca** *fem*
　a public library una biblioteca pública

ʃ **licence** *noun*

1 (*for driving, fishing*) el **permiso** *masc*
　a driving licence un permiso de conducir

2 (*for a TV*) la **licencia** *fem*

to lick *verb*
　lamer [18]

lid *noun*
　la **tapa** *fem*
　She took the lid off. Quitó la tapa.

lie *noun* ▷ see **lie** *verb*
　la **mentira** *fem*
　to tell lies decir [5] mentiras

ʃ **to lie** *verb* ▷ see **lie** *noun*

1 (*to be stretched out*) **estar** [2] **tumbado** (*boy*),
　estar [2] **tumbada** (*girl*)
　Jimmy was lying on the bed. Jimmy estaba
　tumbado en la cama.

2 (*for a little while*) **to lie down** tumbarse [17]
　Come and lie down in the sun. Ven a
　echarte al sol

3 (*object*) **estar** [2]
　Her coat lay on the bed. Su abrigo estaba
　sobre la cama.

4 (*not to tell the truth*) **mentir** [14]
　He's lying. Está mintiendo.

lieutenant *noun*
　el & la **teniente** *masc & fem*

ʃ **life** *noun*
　la **vida** *fem*
　all my life toda mi vida
　She's full of life Está llena de vida.
　That's life! ¡Así es la vida!

lifebelt *noun*
　el **salvavidas** *masc, pl*: los **salvavidas**

lifeboat *noun*
　el **bote salvavidas**

lifeguard *noun*
　el & la **socorrista** *masc & fem*

life jacket *noun*
el **chaleco salvavidas**

lifestyle *noun*
el **estilo de vida**

ſ to **lift** *verb* ▷ see **lift** *noun*
levantar [17]

ſ **lift** *noun* ▷ see **lift** *verb*
1 (*in a building*) el **ascensor** *masc*
Let's take the lift. Vamos a coger el ascensor.
2 (*a ride*) **to give somebody a lift somewhere** llevar [17] a alguien a un lugar
Tom gave me a lift to the station. Tom me llevó a la estación.
Can you give me a lift? ¿Me puedes llevar?

ſ to **light** *verb* ▷ see **light** *adj, noun*
1 **encender** [36]
We lit a fire. Encendimos un fuego.

ſ **light** *adjective* ▷ see **light** *verb, noun*
1 (*not heavy*) **ligero** *masc*, **ligera** *fem*
a light meal una comida ligera
light clothes ropa ligera
2 (*not dark*) a light room una habitación con mucha luz
It gets light at six. Se hace de día a las seis.
3 (*in colours*) **claro** *masc*, **clara** *fem*
light green verde claro
He has light blue eyes. Tiene ojos azul claro.

ſ **light** *noun* ▷ see **light** *verb, adj*
1 (*as opposed to darkness*) la **luz** *fem*
a ray of light un rayo de luz
Bring it into the light. Tráelo a la luz.
2 (*electric*) la **luz** *fem, fem pl:* las **luces**
to turn the light on encender [36] la luz
to turn off the light apagar [28] la luz
Are your lights on? ¿Tienes las luces encendidas?
3 (*streetlight*) la **farola** *fem*
4 (*for traffic*) **the lights** el semáforo
The lights were green. El semáforo estaba en verde.
5 (*for a cigarette*) **Have you got a light?** ¿Tienes fuego?
• **light bulb** la bombilla

lighter *noun*
el **encendedor** *masc*

ſ **lightning** *noun*
el **relámpago** *masc*
a flash of lightning un relámpago
The tree was struck by lightning. Cayó un rayo en el árbol.

light switch *noun*
el **interruptor de la luz**

ſ **like** *preposition, conjunction*
1 (*similar to*) **como**
like this como esto
someone like me alguien como yo
sports like badminton deportes como el badminton
He talks like an old man. Habla como un viejo.
I want a hat like this one. Quiero un sombrero como este.
What's it like? ¿Cómo es?
What was the weather like? ¿Qué tiempo hizo?
2 **to look like someone** parecerse [35] a alguien
Cindy looks like her father. Cindy se parece a su padre.
3 (*to indicate how something should be done*) **like this** así
You do it like this. Se hace así.
like that así
Don't talk to me like that! ¡No me hables así!
4 (*as*) **como**
like I said como dije (yo)
5 (*as if*) It sounds like they've already arrived. Por lo que se ve, parece que ya han llegado.

ſ to **like** *verb*
1 (*see Word Tip*) I like fish. Me gusta el pescado (*pescado* is singular, so *gusta*).
I like it. Me gusta.
I don't like spicy food. No me gusta la comida picante.
Did you like the film? ¿Te gustó la película?
She likes my brother. Le gusta mi hermano.
I like dogs. Me gustan los perros (*perros* is plural, so *gustan*).
I don't like cats. No me gustan los gatos.
She likes bike riding. Le gusta montar a bici (*montar* is an infinitive, so *gusta*).
Dad likes going fishing. A papá le gusta ir a pescar (*Use a when a person is mentioned.*).
2 (*to say which you like most or least*)
I like pistachio best. El que más me gusta es el pistacho.
I like vanilla least. La que menos me gusta es la vainilla.
I like those the best. Los que más me gustan son aquellos.
3 (*to ask or say what you, or someone else, wants*)
I'd like to buy it. Quiero comprarlo.
Would you like a coffee? ¿Quieres un café?
What would you like to eat? ¿Qué quieres comer?
Would you like to go to the beach? ¿Quieres ir a la playa? ▸▸

a
b
c
d
e
f
g
h
i
j
k
l
m
n
o
p
q
r
s
t
u
v
w
x
y
z

I would like to use the phone. Quisiera hacer una llamada.

4 (*to say what you wish you could do*)
Me gustaría ser astronauta. I'd like to be an astronaut.
Le gustaría ir a la India. She'd like to go to India.

WORD TIP Use *gusta, gustó, gustaba, gustaría, etc* if what you like, or don't like, is singular or an infinitive in Spanish. Use *gustan, gustaron, gustaban, gustarían, etc* if what you like, or don't like, is plural.

likely *adjective*
probable *masc & fem*
It's not very likely. No es muy probable.
She's likely to phone. Es probable que llame.

WORD TIP *ser probable que* is followed by the subjunctive.

lime *noun*
(*the fruit*) la **lima** *fem*

limit *noun*
el **límite** *masc*
the speed limit el límite de velocidad

♪ **line** *noun*
1 (*on paper*) la **línea** *fem*
a straight line una línea recta
to draw a line trazar [**22**] una línea
2 (*queue*) la **cola** *fem*
to stand in line hacer [**7**] cola
The children were standing in line. Los niños hacían cola.
3 (*for a phone*) la **línea** *fem*
The line's bad. No se oye bien.
Hold the line, please. No cuelgue, por favor. (*formal use*)

♪ **linen** *noun*
el **lino** *masc*

to **link** *verb* ▷ see **link** *noun*
(*two places*) **conectar** [**17**]
The terminals are linked by a shuttle service. Las terminales están conectadas por un servicio de enlace.

link *noun* ▷ see **link** *verb*
la **conexión** *fem*
What's the link between the two? ¿Qué conexión hay entre los dos?

lion *noun*
el **león** *masc*

lip *noun*
el **labio** *masc*
• **lip-read** leer [**37**] los labios
• **lipstick** el lápiz de labios

liquid *adjective* ▷ see **liquid** *noun*
líquido *masc*, **líquida** *fem*

liquid *noun* ▷ see **liquid** *adj*
el **líquido** *masc*

liquidizer *noun*
la **licuadora** *fem*

list *noun*
la **lista** *fem*

♪ to **listen** *verb*
escuchar [**17**]
I wasn't listening. No estaba escuchando.
to listen to something escuchar [**17**] algo
Listen to the music. Escucha la música.
You're not listening to me. No me estás escuchando.

literature *noun*
la **literatura** *fem*

Lithuania *noun*
Lituania *fem*

Lithuanian *adjective & noun*
1 **lituano** *masc*, **lituana** *fem*
2 un **lituano** *masc*, una **lituana** *fem*
the Lithuanians los lituanos

WORD TIP Adjectives and nouns for nationality, regional origin, and language do not have capital letters in Spanish.

♪ **litre** *noun*
el **litro** *masc*
a litre of milk un litro de leche

litter *noun*
(*rubbish*) la **basura** *fem*
• **litter bin** papelera *fem*

♪ **little** *adjective, pronoun*
1 (*small*) **pequeño** *masc*, **pequeña** *fem*
a little boy un niño pequeño
a little break una pequeña pausa
2 (*not much*) **poco** *masc*, **poca** *fem*
We have very little time. Tenemos muy poco tiempo.
3 a little un poco
We have a little money. Tenemos un poco de dinero.
Just a little, please. Sólo un poco, por favor.
It's a little late. Es un poco tarde.
a little more un poco más
a little less un poco menos
4 little by little poco a poco

♪ to **live** *verb* ▷ see **live** *adj*
1 (*to be alive*) **vivir** [**19**]
(*for*) as long as I live mientras viva
2 (*to reside*) **vivir** [**19**]
Susan lives in York. Susan vive en York.
They live at number 57. Viven en el número cincuenta y siete.
They live together. Viven juntos.

♂ **live** *adjective* ▷ see **live** *verb*

1 (*broadcast*) **en directo** *masc & fem*
a live concert un concierto en directo

2 (*alive*) **vivo** *masc*, **viva** *fem*

liver *noun*
el **hígado** *masc*

♂ **living** *noun*
to earn a living ganarse [17] la vida
· **living room** el salón

to **load** *verb* ▷ see **load** *noun*
cargar [28]
He loaded the crates onto the van. Cargó las cajas en la camioneta.
to load a program (into a computer) cargar [28] un programa (en un ordenador)

load *noun* ▷ see **load** *verb*

1 (*on a lorry*) el **cargamento** *masc*

2 a bus-load of tourists un autobús lleno de turistas

3 (*informal: lots of*) **loads of** un montón de
loads of people un montón de gente
They've got loads of money. Tienen un montón de dinero.

loaf *noun*
a loaf of bread un pan
a loaf of wholemeal bread un pan integral

to **loan** *verb* ▷ see **loan** *noun*
prestar [17]

loan *noun* ▷ see **loan** *verb*
el **préstamo** *masc*

♂ **lobby** *noun*
el **vestíbulo** *masc*

lobster *noun*
la **langosta** *fem*

local *adjective*
the local library la biblioteca del barrio
the local newspaper el periódico local

local *noun*

1 (*pub*) our local el bar de nuestro barrio

2 (*people*) the locals la gente del lugar

locally *adverb*
en la zona

to **lock** *verb* ▷ see **lock** *noun*
to lock the door cerrar [29] la puerta con llave
The door was locked. La puerta estaba cerrada con llave.

lock *noun* ▷ see **lock** *verb*

1 (*with a key*) la **cerradura** *fem*

2 (*on a canal*) la **esclusa** *fem*

locker *noun*
el **armario** *masc*
· **locker room** el vestuario

lodger *noun*
el **inquilino** *masc*, la **inquilina** *fem*

loft *noun*
el **desván** *masc*

log *noun* ▷ see **log** *verb*

1 (*of tree*) el **tronco** *masc*

2 (*record*) el **diario** *masc*

to **log** *verb* ▷ see **log** *noun*
registrar [17]
· **to log on entrar** [17] **al sistema**
· **to log out salir** [63] **del sistema**

logical *adjective*
lógico *masc*, **lógica** *fem*

lollipop *noun*
la **piruleta** *fem*

London *noun*
Londres *masc*
We went to London. Fuimos a Londres.
the London streets las calles de Londres

Londoner *noun*
el & la **londinense** *masc & fem*

WORD TIP Adjectives and nouns for regional origin do not have capital letters in Spanish.

loneliness *noun*
la **soledad** *fem*

♂ **lonely** *adjective*
solitario *masc*, **solitaria** *fem*
She has a lonely life. Tiene una vida solitaria.
to feel lonely sentirse [14] solo (*a boy*), sentirse [14] sola (*a girl*)

♂ **long** *adjective, adverb* ▷ see **long** *verb*

1 (*to talk about distance, extent*) **largo** *masc*, **larga** *fem*
a long journey un viaje largo
a very long book un libro muy largo
She's got long hair. Tiene el pelo largo.
It's five metres long. Mide cinco metros de largo.
How long is the corridor? ¿Cuánto mide el pasillo de largo?
a long way muy lejos
We're a long way from the cinema. Estamos muy lejos del cine.

2 (*to talk about time*) **largo** *masc*, **larga** *fem*
a long film una película larga ▸▸

a long illness una enfermedad larga
It's been a long day. Ha sido un día muy largo.
How long is the film? ¿Cuánto dura la película?
It's an hour long. Dura una hora.
a long time mucho tiempo
a long time ago hace mucho tiempo
I've been here for a long time. He pasado mucho tiempo aquí.
He stayed for a long time. Se quedó mucho tiempo.
not long afterwards no mucho después
Have you been waiting long? ¿Llevas mucho rato esperando?
This won't take long. Esto no llevará mucho tiempo.
I won't be long. No tardo mucho.

3 (*to talk about how long it takes to do something*) **how long?** ¿cuánto tiempo?
How long have you been here? ¿Cuánto tiempo llevas aquí?
How long did it take you to get there? ¿Cuánto tardaste en llegar?

4 (*for the period of time*) **as long as** mientras
as long as she was alive mientras vivió ella
I'll remember it as long as I live. Lo recordaré mientras viva.

5 (*on condition that*) **as long as** siempre que
You can go as long as you're back by 12 Puedes ir siempre que vuelvas antes de las 12.

WORD TIP *siempre que* is followed by a verb in the subjunctive.

to **long** *verb* ▷ see **long** *adj, adv*
to long to do something tener [9] muchas ganas de hacer algo
I'm longing to see you. Tengo muchas ganas de verte.

longer *adverb*
no longer ya no
He doesn't work here any longer. Ya no trabaja aquí.
I no longer know. Ya no lo sé.
They no longer live here. Ya no viven aquí.

long jump *noun*
el **salto de longitud**

long-life milk *noun*
la **leche uperizada**

loo *noun*
el **váter** *masc* (*informal*)

♪ to **look** *verb* ▷ see **look** *noun*

1 (*to see, glance*) **mirar** [17]
I wasn't looking. No estaba mirando.
Look! A squirrel! ¡Mira! ¡Una ardilla!

He looked away. Miró hacia un lado.
He walked away without looking back. Se alejó sin mirar atrás.
She looked down the street. Miró calle abajo.
I looked out of the window. Miré por la ventana
Look where you're going! ¡Mira por dónde vas!
He looked me straight in the eye. Me miró a los ojos.

2 (*to search*) **mirar** [17]
Look under the bed. Mira debajo de la cama.

3 (*to seem*) **parecer** [35]
Melanie looked pleased. Melanie parecía contenta.
You look well. Tienes buen aspecto.
He looks ill. Tiene mal aspecto.
The salad looks delicious. La ensalada tiene un aspecto delicioso.

4 to look like someone parecerse [35] a alguien
Sally looks like her aunt. Sally se parece a su tía.
They look like each other. Se parecen.
It looks like rain. Parece que va a llover.
What does the house look like? ¿Cómo es la casa?

• **to look after cuidar** [17]
Dad's looking after the baby. Papá está cuidando al niño.
I'll look after your luggage. Yo te cuido el equipaje.

• **to look at mirar** [17]
Andy was looking at the photos. Andy estaba mirando las fotos.

• **to look for buscar** [31]
I'm looking for the keys. Estoy buscando las llaves.
I've been looking for you everywhere. Te he estado buscando por todas partes

• **to look forward to something:** I'm looking forward to the holidays. Estoy deseando que lleguen las vacaciones.
She's looking forward to the trip. Está deseando ir de viaje.

• **to look out** (*to be careful*) **tener** [9] **cuidado**
Look out, it's hot! ¡Cuidado, quema!

• **to look something up buscar** [17] **algo**
You can look it up in the dictionary. Puedes buscarlo en el diccionario.

♪ **look** *noun* ▷ see **look** *verb*

1 (*glance*) la **mirada** *fem*
to have a look at something mirar [17] algo

to have a look round the town visitar[17] la ciudad
to have a look round the shops ver[16] tiendas

2 (*search*) **to have a look for something** buscar[31] algo

loose *adjective*
1 (*screw, knot*) **flojo** *masc*, **floja** *fem*
2 (*garment*) **amplio** *masc*, **amplia** *fem*
• **loose change** el cambio

♂ **lorry** *noun*
 el **camión** *masc*
• **lorry driver** el camionero, la camionera

♂ to **lose** *verb*
 perder[36]
 We lost. Perdimos.
 We lost the match. Perdimos el partido.
 Sam's lost his watch. Sam ha perdido su reloj.

loss *noun*
 la **pérdida** *fem*

♂ **lost** *adjective*
 perdido *masc*, **perdida** *fem*
 I'm lost. Estoy perdido (*boy speaking*)., Estoy perdida (*girl speaking*).
 Are you lost? ¿Te has perdido? (*informal use*), ¿Se ha perdido? (*formal use*)
 to get lost perderse[36]
 We got lost in the woods. Nos perdimos en el bosque.
• **lost property** los objetos perdidos
• **lost property office** la oficina de objetos perdidos

♂ **lot** *noun*
1 **a lot** mucho
 Jason eats a lot. Jason come mucho.
 I spent a lot. Gasté mucho.
 I've got a lot to do. Tengo mucho que hacer.
 I like her a lot. Me gusta mucho.
 Your house is a lot bigger than ours. Tu casa es mucho más grande que la nuestra.
 'What are you doing tonight?'— 'Not a lot.' ¿Qué haces esta noche?— 'No mucho.'
2 **a lot of** mucho *masc*, mucha *fem*
 a lot of coffee mucho café
 a lot of people mucha gente
 a lot of books muchos libros
 What a lot of books you've got! ¡Cuántos libros tienes!
3 **lots** mucho *masc*, mucha *fem*
 I've got lots to do. Tengo mucho que hacer.
 'How many seats are there left?'— 'Lots.' '¿Cuántos asientos quedan?'— 'Muchos.'

4 **the lot** todos *plural masc*, todas *plural fem*
 'How many did she eat?'— 'The lot.' '¿Cuántos comió?'— 'Todos.'
 I bought him some chips and he ate the lot. Le compré unas patatas fritas y se las comió todas.

lottery *noun*
 la **lotería** *fem*
 to win the lottery tocarle [31] la lotería a alguien
 She won the lottery. Le tocó la lotería.

ℹ️ lotteries

The Spanish *Lotería Nacional* is one of the biggest in the world. Each year at Christmas *El Gordo* (The Fat One) is drawn. This marks the start of the Christmas celebrations.

---

loud *adverb* ▷ see **loud** *adj*
 (*when speaking*) **alto**
 to say something out loud decir[5] algo en voz alta

loud *adjective* ▷ see **loud** *adv*
 (*noise, scream, applause*) **fuerte** *masc & fem*
 a loud banging unos golpes fuertes
 a loud shout un grito fuerte
 The radio is very loud. La radio está muy fuerte.
 to speak in a loud voice hablar[17] en voz alta
• **loudspeaker** el altavoz *masc* (*pl*: altavoces)

lounge *noun*
 (*in a house, hotel*) el **salón** *masc*

♂ to **love** *verb* ▷ see **love** *noun*
1 (*a person*) **querer**[12]
 I love you. Te quiero.
 They love each other. Se quieren.
2 (*a thing, a place, an activity*) **She loves London.** Le encanta Londres.
 I'd love to come. Me encantaría venir.
 I love dancing. Me encanta bailar.
 Wayne loves burgers. A Wayne le encantan las hamburguesas.

WORD TIP The subject of *encantar* is what you love, so if what you love is singular, use *encanta* etc, if it is plural, use *encantan* etc.

♂ **love** *noun* ▷ see **love** *verb*
1 (*in general*) el **amor** *masc*
 his love for his country su amor a su patria
 her love of animals su amor a los animales
 to be in love with somebody estar[2] enamorado, enamorada de alguien
 She's in love with Jake. Está enamorada de Jake.
 He's in love with Kylie. Está enamorado de Kylie. ▸▸

2 (*in messages, letters*) **Gina sends her love.**
Gina manda recuerdos.
With love from Charlie con cariño de
Charlie
Lots of love, Ann. Con mucho cariño, Ann
3 (*in tennis, etc*) **nada** *fem*
15-love 15-nada

ᔓ **lovely** *adjective*
1 (*beautiful to look at*) **precioso** *masc*, **preciosa**
fem
a lovely house una casa preciosa
2 **It's a lovely day.** Hace un día muy bueno.
We had lovely weather. Tuvimos un
tiempo muy bueno.
3 (*enjoyable*) **I had a lovely time at their house.**
Lo pasé muy bien en su casa.
It's lovely to see you! ¡Qué alegría verte!
4 (*food, meal*) **riquísimo** *masc*, **riquísima** *fem*

lover *noun*
1 (*romantic partner*) **el & la amante** *masc & fem*
2 (*fan*) **a music lover** un amante de la
música (*boy*), una amante de la música (*girl*)

ᔓ **low** *adjective*
bajo *masc*, **baja** *fem*
a low table una mesa baja
at a low price a un precio bajo
in a low voice en voz baja

lower *adjective*
(*lip, jaw, status*) **inferior** *masc & fem*

loyal *adjective*
leal *masc & fem*

loyalty *noun*
la lealtad *fem*
• **loyalty card** la tarjeta de fidelidad

ᔓ **luck** *noun*
la suerte *fem*
Good luck! ¡Buena suerte!, ¡Suerte!

Bad luck! ¡Qué mala suerte!
with a bit of luck con un poco de suerte

 luck

Black cats and Tuesday the 13th bring bad luck in
Spain and Latin America.

luckily *adverb*
afortunadamente
luckily for them afortunadamente para
ellos

ᔓ **lucky** *adjective*
1 (*to have good luck*) **to be lucky** tener [**9**]
suerte
We were lucky. Tuvimos suerte.
2 (*to bring good luck*) **to be lucky** traer [**42**]
suerte
It's supposed to be lucky. Se supone que
trae suerte.
• **lucky number** el número de la suerte

ᔓ **luggage** *noun*
el equipaje *masc*

lump *noun*
1 (*on the body*) **el bulto** *masc*
2 (*of sugar*) **el terrón** *masc*
3 (*of cheese*) **trozo** *masc*

lung *noun*
el pulmón *masc*

Luxembourg *noun*
Luxemburgo *masc*

luxurious *adjective*
lujoso *masc*, **lujosa** *fem*

luxury *noun*
el lujo *masc*
a luxury hotel un hotel de lujo

lyrics *plural noun*
la letra *fem*

M m

mac *noun*
el **impermeable** *masc*

macaroni *noun*
los **macarrones** *plural masc*

machine *noun*
la **máquina** *fem*

machinery *noun*
la **maquinaria** *fem*

♪ **mad** *adjective*
1 (*crazy*) **loco** *masc*, **loca** *fem*
She's completely mad! ¡Está completamente loca!
2 (*angry*) **enfadado** *masc*, **enfadada** *fem*
to be mad with somebody estar [2] enfadado con alguien
My mum will be mad! ¡Mamá se pondrá hecha una furia! (*informal*)
3 (*enthusiastic*) She's mad about horses. Le encantan los caballos.
to be mad about somebody estar [2] loco por alguien

♪ **madam** *noun*
la **señora** *fem*
Yes, madam. Sí, señora.

madness *noun*
la **locura** *fem*

♪ **magazine** *noun*
la **revista** *fem*
a music magazine una revista de música

magazine

Hola magazine was started in 1944 by the Sánchez Junco family. They launched *Hello*, the English edition, in 1988.

maggot *noun*
el **gusano** *masc*

magic *adjective* ▷ see **magic** *noun*
1 (*casting spells*) **mágico** *masc*, **mágica** *fem*
a magic wand una varita mágica
2 (*great*) **fantástico** *masc*, **fantástica** *fem*

magic *noun* ▷ see **magic** *adj*
la **magia** *fem*

magician *noun*
el **mago** *masc*, la **maga** *fem*

magnet *noun*
el **imán** *masc*

magnifying glass *noun*
la **lupa** *fem*

maid *noun*
la **criada** *fem*

maiden name *noun*
el **apellido de soltera**

♪ **mail** *noun*
el **correo** *masc*
to send something by mail mandar [17] algo por correo
I put it in the mail. Lo eché al correo.

mail order *noun*
la **venta por correo**
a mail order catalogue un catálogo de venta por correo
to buy something by mail order comprar [17] algo por correo

♪ **main** *adjective*
principal *masc & fem*
the main entrance la entrada principal
• **main course** el plato principal, el plato fuerte

mainly *adverb*
principalmente

main road *noun*
la **carretera principal**

majesty *noun*
1 (*of a view, etc*) la **majestuosidad** *fem*
2 (*king, queen*) la **majestad** *fem*
su majestad your majesty

major *adjective* ▷ see **major** *noun*
muy importante *masc & fem*
a major problem un problema muy importante

major *noun* ▷ see **major** *adj*
el & la **comandante** *masc & fem*

Majorca *noun*
Mallorca *fem*

majority *noun*
la **mayoría** *fem*

♪ **make** *noun* ▷ see **make** *verb*
la **marca** *fem*
What make is your bike? ¿De qué marca es tu bici?

♪ to **make** verb ▷ see **make** noun

1 (a sandwich, dress, noise) **hacer** [7]
   I made an omelette. Hice una tortilla.
   to make a meal preparar [17] una comida
   She made her bed. Hizo su cama.
   Don't make a noise. No hagas ruido.

2 (to manufacture) **fabricar** [31]
   They make computers. Fabrican
   ordenadores.
   'Made in Spain' 'Fabricado en España'
   It's made of plastic. Es de plástico.

3 (money) **ganar** [17]
   He makes eighty pounds a day. Gana
   ochenta libras al día.

4 (payments, changes, phone calls) **hacer** [7]
   They have made a lot of changes. Han
   hecho muchos cambios.
   I have to make a phone call. Tengo que
   hacer una llamada de teléfono.

5 (a comment, joke) **hacer** [7]
   May I make a suggestion? ¿Puedo hacer
   una sugerencia?

6 (sad, happy, hungry, rich, etc) to make
   somebody sad poner [11] triste a alguien
   It made me sad. Me puso triste.
   They make me very happy. Me hacen muy
   feliz.
   I'll make you rich. Te haré rico.
   It made him really annoyed. Le dio mucha
   rabia.
   It makes me so angry. Me da tanta
   rabia.
   That makes me hungry. Eso me da
   hambre.
   It made me sleepy. Me dio sueño.

7 (to force) to make somebody do something
   obligar [28] a alguien a hacer algo
   She made him give the money back. Le
   obligó a devolver el dinero.
   You can't make me go. No puedes
   obligarme a ir.

8 (to cause) to make somebody do something
   hacer [7] a alguien hacer algo
   He made me wait. Me hizo esperar.
   She makes me laugh. Me hace reír.
   Look what you've made me do! ¡Mira lo
   que me has hecho hacer!

9 (to add up to) **sumar** [17]
   Two and three make five. Dos y tres suman
   cinco.

10 (to turn up) I can't make it tonight. No
    puedo venir esta noche.

11 (to cope) to make do arreglárselas [17]
    to make do with something arreglárselas
    con algo
    We'll have to make do with that.
    Tendremos que arreglárnoslas con eso.

• **to make up**

1 (to invent) **inventarse** [17]
   She made up an excuse. Se inventó una
   excusa.

2 (after a quarrel) hacer [7] las paces
   They've made up now. Han hecho las paces
   ahora.
   to make up with someone hacer [7] las
   paces con alguien

♪ **make-up** noun
   el **maquillaje** masc
   I don't wear make-up. Yo no uso
   maquillaje.
   to put on your make-up ponerse [11] el
   maquillaje
   Jo's putting on her make-up. Jo se está
   poniendo el maquillaje.

male adjective

1 (person, population) **masculino** masc,
   masculina fem
   a male voice una voz masculina

2 (animal, insect) **macho** masc & fem
   a male rat una rata macho

3 (sex: on a form) **varón** masc & fem

mall noun
   el **centro comercial**

mammal noun
   el **mamífero** masc

♪ **man** noun

1 (person) el **hombre** masc
   four men and five women cuatro hombres
   y cinco mujeres

2 (mankind) el **hombre** masc
   Modern man is taller than his ancestors. El
   hombre moderno es más alto que sus
   antepasados.

to **manage** verb

1 (a business, team) **dirigir** [49]
   She manages a travel agency. Ella dirige
   una agencia de viajes.

2 (to cope) **arreglárselas** [17]
   I can manage. Puedo arreglármelas.

3 (to achieve) to manage to do something
   conseguir [64] hacer algo
   I didn't manage to get in touch with her.
   No conseguí ponerme en contacto con
   ella.

management noun

1 (running, administration) la **dirección** fem
   the management of the company la
   dirección de la empresa

2 (management staff) los **directivos** plural masc

ₔ **manager** noun
1 (of a company, bank) el **director** masc, la **directora** fem
2 (of a shop, restaurant) el **encargado** masc, la **encargada** fem
3 (in sport, entertainment) el & la **manager** masc & fem

manageress noun
la **encargada** fem

managing director noun
el **consejero delegado**, la **consejera delegada**

mango noun
el **mango** masc

maniac noun
el **loco** masc, la **loca** fem
She drives like a maniac. Conduce como una loca.

mankind noun
la **humanidad** fem

manner noun
1 (way, fashion) la **forma** fem
He was behaving in a ridiculous manner. Se estaba comportando de forma ridícula.
in a manner of speaking por así decirlo
2 (politeness) manners **modales** plural masc
Have you forgotten your manners? ¿Dónde están tus modales?
to have good manners tener [9] buena educación
It's bad manners to talk like that. No es de buena educación hablar así.

mansion noun
la **mansión** fem

mantelpiece noun
la **repisa de la chimenea**

manual noun
el **manual** masc

to **manufacture** verb
fabricar [31]

manufacturer noun
el & la **fabricante** masc & fem

ₔ **many** adjective, pronoun
1 (a lot) **muchos** masc, **muchas** fem
many people mucha gente
She has got many friends. Tiene muchos amigos.
There aren't many onions left. No quedan muchas cebollas.
Many of them came. Muchos de ellos vinieron.
very many muchos masc, muchas fem

There aren't very many glasses. No hay muchos vasos.
2 not many no muchos masc, no muchas fem
'Have we got any potatoes?' — 'Not many?' ¿Tenemos patatas? — 'No muchas.'
3 so many tantos masc, tantas fem
I have so many things to do! ¡Tengo tantas cosas que hacer!
We've never scored so many goals. Nunca hemos marcado tantos goles.
4 too many demasiados masc, demasiadas fem
That's too many! ¡Esos son demasiados!
I've got too many things to do. Tengo demasiadas cosas que hacer.
There were too many people. Había demasiada gente.
5 How many? ¿cuántos? masc, ¿cuántas? fem
How many are there? ¿Cuántos hay?
How many sisters have you got? ¿Cuántas hermanas tienes?
I don't know how many there are. No sé cuántos hay.
6 (in comparisons) as many as tantos como masc pl, tantas como fem pl
She has as many as I have. Tiene tantos como yo.
There aren't as many sheep as before. No hay tantas ovejas como antes.
7 (to say all that) as many as todos los que plural masc, todas las que plural fem
Take as many as you like. Lleva todos los que quieras.

ₔ **map** noun
1 (of a country, region) el **mapa** masc
a road map un mapa de carreteras
2 (of a town) el **plano** masc

marathon noun
el or la **maratón** masc or fem

marble noun
1 (the stone) el **mármol** masc
a marble fireplace una chimenea de mármol
2 (toy) la **canica** fem
to play marbles jugar [27] a las canicas

march noun ▷ see **march** verb
la **marcha** fem

to **march** verb ▷ see **march** noun
marchar [17]

ₔ **March** noun
el **marzo** masc
in March en marzo

WORD TIP Names of months and days start with small letters in Spanish.

a b c d e f g h i j k l m n o p q r s t u v w x y z

mare *noun*
la **yegua** *fem*

margarine *noun*
la **margarina** *fem*

margin *noun*
el **margen** *masc* (*pl:* **márgenes**)

marijuana *noun*
la **marihuana** *fem*

♂ **mark** *noun* ▷ see **mark** *verb*
1 (*at school*) la **nota** *fem*
I got a good mark for my Spanish homework. Saqué una buena nota en los deberes de español.
What mark did you get for Spanish? ¿Qué nota sacaste en español?
2 (*sign, symbol*) la **marca** *fem*
He made a mark on the wall. Hizo una marca en la pared.
3 (*stain*) la **mancha** *fem*
a dirty mark una mancha de suciedad

♂ to **mark** *verb* ▷ see **mark** *noun*
1 (*to correct*) **corregir** [48]
He marked the exams. Corrigió los exámenes.
2 (*to write*) **marcar** [31]
I've marked the price on the lid. He marcado el precio en la tapa.
3 (*to stain*) **manchar** [17]
The coffee marked the carpet. El café manchó la alfombra.

♂ **market** *noun*
el **mercado** *masc*

marketing *noun*
el **marketing** *masc*

marmalade *noun*
la **mermelada de naranja**

♂ **marriage** *noun*
1 (*relationship*) el **matrimonio** *masc*
2 (*ceremony*) el **casamiento** *masc*

♂ **married** *adjective*
casado *masc*, **casada** *fem*
to be married estar [2] casado
She's married. Está casada.
They've been married for twenty years. Llevan casados veinte años.
a married couple un matrimonio

to **marry** *verb*
to marry somebody casarse [17] con alguien
She married a Spaniard. Se casó con un español.
to get married casarse [17]
They got married in July. Se casaron en julio.

♂ **marvellous** *adjective*
maravilloso *masc*, **maravillosa** *fem*
The weather's marvellous. El tiempo es maravilloso.
How marvellous! ¡Qué maravilla!

marzipan *noun*
el **mazapán** *masc*

mascara *noun*
el **rímel** *masc*

masculine *adjective*
▷ see **masculine** *noun*
masculino *masc*, **masculina** *fem*

masculine *noun* ▷ see **masculine** *adj*
(*in Spanish and other grammars*) el **masculino** *masc*
in the masculine en masculino

to **mash** *verb*
(*potatoes, vegetables*) **triturar** [17]

mashed potatoes *plural noun*
el **puré de patatas**

mask *noun*
la **máscara** *fem*

mass *noun*
1 (*large amount*) **masses of something** un montón de algo
They've got masses of money. Tienen un montón de dinero.
There's masses left over. Queda un montón.
2 (*Religion*) la **misa** *fem*
to go to mass ir [8] a misa

massacre *noun*
la **matanza** *fem*

massage *noun*
el **masaje** *masc*

massive *adjective*
enorme *masc & fem*

mat *noun*
1 (*doormat*) el **felpudo** *masc*
2 (*bathmat*) la **alfombrilla** *fem*
3 (*for a hot dish*) el **salvamanteles** *masc* (*pl:* **salvamanteles**)

♂ **match** *noun* ▷ see **match** *verb*
1 (*for lighting a fire*) la **cerilla** *fem*
a box of matches una caja de cerillas
2 (*in sports*) el **partido** *masc*
a football match un partido de fútbol
We watched the match. Vimos el partido.
Who won the match? ¿Quién ganó el partido?
They lost the match. Perdieron el partido.

ɗ to **match** verb ▷ see **match** noun
  hacer [7] **juego con**
  The jacket matches the skirt. La chaqueta
  hace juego con la falda.

ɗ **mate** noun
  el **amigo** masc, la **amiga** fem
  I'm going out with my mates tonight. Voy a
  salir esta noche con mis amigos.

material noun
1 (fabric) la **tela** fem
2 (information) el **material** masc
  teaching materials material educativo
3 (substance) la **materia** fem
  raw materials materias primas

ɗ **mathematics** noun
  las **matemáticas** plural fem

ɗ **maths** noun
  las **matemáticas** plural fem
  I like maths. Me gustan las matemáticas.
  Anna's good at maths. A Anna se le dan
  bien las matemáticas.

ɗ **matter** noun ▷ see **matter** verb
1 (question, issue) el **asunto** masc
  Let's say no more about the matter No
  digamos más sobre el asunto.
2 (problem) What's the matter? ¿Qué pasa?
  What's the matter with Lucy? ¿Qué le pasa
  a Lucy?
  There's something the matter with her.
  Algo le pasa.
3 (in expressions) As a matter of fact, I've never
  been to Spain. La verdad es que nunca he
  estado en España.
  no matter how cheap it is ... por barato que
  sea ...
  No matter how hard I try, you're never
  happy. Por mucho que me esfuerce, nunca
  estás contento.

ɗ to **matter** verb ▷ see **matter** noun
  (to be important) **importar** [17]
  the things that matter lo que importa
  It matters a lot to me. Me importa mucho.
  It doesn't matter. No importa.
  It doesn't matter if it rains. No importa que
  llueva.
  You can write it in Spanish or French, it
  doesn't matter. Puedes escribirlo en
  español o en francés, da lo mismo.

mattress noun
  el **colchón** masc

maximum adjective
  ▷ see **maximum** noun
  máximo masc, **máxima** fem

maximum noun ▷ see **maximum** adj
  el **máximo** masc

may verb
1 (to ask permission) May I close the door?
  ¿Puedo cerrar la puerta?
2 (to talk about a possibility) She may be ill.
  Puede que esté enferma.
  We may go to Spain. Puede que vayamos a
  España.

> **WORD TIP** puede que is followed by a verb in the
> subjunctive.

ɗ **May** noun
  el **mayo** masc
  in May en mayo

> **WORD TIP** Names of months and days start with
> small letters in Spanish.

maybe adverb
  quizás
  maybe not quizás no
  Maybe he's forgotten. Quizás se ha
  olvidado.
  Maybe they've got lost. Quizás se han
  perdido.

mayonnaise noun
  la **mayonesa** fem

mayor noun ▷ see **mayoress** noun
  el **alcalde** masc, la **alcaldesa** fem

mayoress noun ▷ see **mayor** noun
  la **alcaldesa** fem

ɗ **me** pronoun
1 (as a direct or indirect object) **me**
  She knows me. Me conoce.
  She gave me the documents. Me dio los
  documentos.
  Can you help me, please? ¿Puedes
  ayudarme por favor?
  Listen to me! ¡Escúchame!
  Wait for me! ¡Espérame!
  Don't push me! ¡No me empujes!

> **WORD TIP** With an infinitive, or when telling
> someone to do something, me joins onto the verb.

2 (after prepositions) **mí**
  behind me detrás de mí
  They left without me. Se fueron sin mí.
  with me conmigo
  I took her with me. La traje conmigo.
3 (in comparisons and with 'to be') **yo**
  She's older than me. Es mayor que yo.
  It's me. Soy yo.
  Me too! ¡Yo también!

meadow noun
  el **prado** masc

a
b
c
d
e
f
g
h
i
j
k
l
m
n
o
p
q
r
s
t
u
v
w
x
y
z

♂ **meal** *noun*
la **comida** *fem*
They have three meals a day. Hacen tres comidas al día.
Enjoy your meal! ¡Que aproveche!

♂ **mean** *adjective* ▷ see **mean** *verb*
1 (*with money*) **tacaño** *masc*, **tacaña** *fem*
2 (*nasty*) She's really mean to her brother. Trata muy mal a su hermano.
What a mean thing to do! ¡Qué maldad!

♂ to **mean** *verb* ▷ see **mean** *adj*
1 (*to signify*) **querer** [12] **decir**
What do you mean? ¿Qué quieres decir?
What does that mean? ¿Qué quiere decir eso?
That's not what I meant. Eso no es lo que quería decir.
2 (*to imply*) **suponer** [11]
That means that I'll have to do it again. Eso supone que voy a tener que hacerlo otra vez.
3 (*to intend*) **to mean to do something** tener [9] la intención de algo
I meant to phone my mother. Tenía la intención de llamar a mi madre.
4 (*to be supposed to*) She was meant to be here at six. Se supone que ella tenía que estar aquí a las seis.
This is meant to be easy. Se supone que esto es fácil.

meaning *noun*
el **significado** *masc*

♂ **means** *noun*
el **medio** *masc*
a means of transport un medio de transporte
by means of something por medio de algo
a means of doing something una forma de hacer algo
We have no means of contacting him. No tenemos forma de contactar con él.
by all means por supuesto

meantime *adverb*
for the meantime por ahora
in the meantime mientras tanto

meanwhile *adverb*
mientras tanto
Meanwhile she was waiting at the station. Mientras tanto ella estaba esperando en la estación.

measles *noun*
el **sarampión** *masc*

to **measure** *verb*
medir [57]

measurements *plural noun*
1 (*of a room, an object*) las **medidas** *plural fem*
the measurements of the room las medidas de la habitación
2 (*of a person*) la **medida** *fem*
to take somebody's measurements tomarle [17] las medidas a alguien
my waist measurement mi medida de cintura

♂ **meat** *noun*
la **carne** *fem*

Mecca *noun*
La Meca *fem*
Fueron a la Meca. They went to Mecca.

♂ **mechanic** *noun*
el **mecánico** *masc*, la **mecánica** *fem*
He's a mechanic. Es mecánico.

medal *noun*
la **medalla** *fem*
the gold medal la medalla de oro

media *plural noun*
the media los medios de comunicación

medical *adjective* ▷ see **medical** *noun*
médico *masc*, **médica** *fem*

medical *noun* ▷ see **medical** *adj*
la **revisión médica**
to have a medical someterse [18] a una revisión médica

♂ **medicine** *noun*
1 (*drug*) el **medicamento** *masc*
¿Te has tomado el medicamento? Have you taken your medicine?
2 (*science*) la **medicina** *fem*
alternative medicine medicina alternativa
She's studying medicine. Está estudiando medicina.

medieval *adjective*
medieval *masc & fem*

Mediterranean *noun*
the Mediterranean el Mediterráneo

♂ **medium** *adjective*
mediano *masc*, **mediana** *fem*
Small, medium or large? ¿Pequeño, mediano o grande?

medium-sized *adjective*
de tamaño mediano *masc & fem*
a medium-sized house una casa de tamaño medio

♂ to **meet** *verb*
1 (*by chance*) **encontrarse**[24] **con**
I met Rosie outside the baker's. Me encontré con Rosie en la puerta de la panadería.
2 (*by appointment*) **haber**[6] **quedado (con)**
We're meeting at six. Hemos quedado a las seis.
I'm meeting him at the museum. He quedado con él en el museo.
Shall we meet after work? ¿Quedamos después del trabajo?
3 (*to get to know*) **conocer**[35] **a**
I met a Spanish girl last week. Conocí a una chica española la semana pasada.
Have you met Oskar? ¿Conoces a Oskar?
4 (*in introductions*) **Tom, meet Ann.** Tom, te presento a Ann.
Pleased to meet you! ¡Encantado! (*man speaking*), ¡Encantada! (*woman speaking*)
5 (*off a train, bus, plane*) **recoger**[3]
My dad's meeting me at the station. Mi padre va a ir a recogerme a la estación.

♂ **meeting** *noun*
la **reunión** *fem*
There's a meeting at ten o'clock. Hay una reunión a las diez.
She's in a meeting. Está en una reunión.

megabyte *noun*
el **megabyte** *masc*

♂ **melon** *noun*
el **melón** *masc*

to **melt** *verb*
1 (*snow, butter, ice cream*) **derretirse**[57]
It melts in your mouth. Se derrite en la boca.
2 to melt something **derretir**[57] algo
Melt the butter in a saucepan. Derretir la mantequilla en una sartén.

member *noun*
1 (*of a party, committee*) el & la **miembro** *masc & fem*
She's a member of the Labour Party. Es miembro del partido laborista.
2 (*of a club*) el **socio** *masc*, la **socia** *fem*

Member of Parliament *noun*
el **diputado** *masc*, la **diputada** *fem*

memorial *noun*
el **monumento** *masc*
a war memorial un monumento a los caídos

to **memorize** *verb*
to memorize something **aprender**[18] algo de memoria

memory *noun*
1 (*of a person, computer*) la **memoria** *fem*
You have a good memory! ¡Tienes buena memoria!
I have a bad memory. Tengo mala memoria.
2 (*of the past*) el **recuerdo** *masc*
I have good memories of my stay in Spain. Tengo buenos recuerdos de mi estancia en España.

to **mend** *verb*
1 (*a watch*) **arreglar**[17]
2 (*a road*) **reparar**[17]
3 (*clothes*) **coser**[18]

mental *adjective*
mental *masc & fem*
• **mental arithmetic** los cálculos mentales

to **mention** *verb*
mencionar[17]
Your name was mentioned. Se mencionó tu nombre.
'Thank you.'— 'Don't mention it.' 'Gracias.'— 'De nada.'

♂ **menu** *noun*
1 (*in a restaurant*) la **carta** *fem*, el **menú** *masc*
What's on on the menu? ¿Qué hay en la carta?
Have you got a set menu? ¿Tienen un menú del día?
I'll take the 20 euro menu. Tomaré el menú de €20.
2 (*Computers*) el **menú** *masc*

WORD TIP *el menú* is usually a set menu with limited choice.

MEP *noun*
(= *Member of the European Parliament*) el **eurodiputado** *masc*, la **eurodiputada** *fem*
She's an MEP. Es eurodiputada.

to **merge** *verb*
1 (*documents, companies*) **fusionar**[17]
2 (*roads*) **confluir**[54]

meringue *noun*
el **merengue** *masc*

merit *noun*
el **mérito** *masc*

merry *adjective*
1 (*happy*) **alegre** *masc & fem*
Merry Christmas! ¡Feliz Navidad!
2 (*informal: mildly drunk*) **achispado** *masc*, **achispada** *fem*

merry-go-round *noun*
el **tiovivo** *masc*

a
b
c
d
e
f
g
h
i
j
k
l
m
n
o
p
q
r
s
t
u
v
w
x
y
z

mess *noun*
> el **desorden** *masc*
> What a mess! ¡Qué desorden!
> My papers are in a mess. Mis papeles están desordenados.
> Don't make a mess! ¡No desordenes nada!
- **to mess about**
  hacer [7] **el tonto**
  Stop messing about! ¡Deja de hacer el tonto!
- **to mess about with something**
  jugar [27] **con algo**
  It's dangerous to mess about with matches. Es peligroso jugar con cerillas.
- **to mess something up**
  desordenar [17] **algo**
  You've messed up all my papers. ¡Me has desordenado todos mis papeles!

message *noun*
> el **mensaje** *masc*
> a telephone message un recado

messenger *noun*
> el **mensajero** *masc*, la **mensajera** *fem*

messy *adjective*
1. (*dirty*) It's a messy job. Es un trabajo sucio.
2. (*untidy*) He's a messy eater. Se ensucia mucho comiendo.
   Her writing's really messy. Escribe sin poner cuidado.

metal *noun*
> el **metal** *masc*

meter *noun*
1. (*electricity, gas, taxi*) el **contador** *masc*
   to read the meter leer [37] el contador
2. (*for parking*) a parking meter un parquímetro

method *noun*
> el **método** *masc*

Methodist *noun*
> el & la **metodista** *masc & fem*
> I'm a Methodist. Soy metodista.

> **WORD TIP** Adjectives and nouns for religion do not have capital letters in Spanish.

♂ **metre** *noun*
> el **metro** *masc*
> It's five metres long. Mide cinco metros de largo.

metric *adjective*
> **métrico** *masc*, **métrica** *fem*

Mexican *adjective* ▷ see **Mexican** *noun*
> **mexicano** *masc*, **mexicana** *fem*

Mexican *noun* ▷ see **Mexican** *adj*
> un **mexicano** *masc*, una **mexicana** *fem*

> **WORD TIP** Adjectives and nouns for nationality and regional origin do not have capital letters in Spanish.

Mexico *noun*
> **México** *masc*

microchip *noun*
> el **microchip** *masc* (*pl*: **microchips**)

♂ **microcomputer** *noun*
> el **microordenador** *masc*, (*Latin America*) la **microcomputadora** *fem*

microphone *noun*
> el **micrófono** *masc*

microscope *noun*
> el **microscopio** *masc*

microwave oven *noun*
> el **microondas** *masc* (*pl*: **microondas**)

♂ **midday** *noun*
> el **mediodía** *masc*
> at midday al mediodía

♂ **middle** *noun*
1. (*of a place*) el **medio** *masc*
   in the middle of the room en medio de la habitación
2. (*of a period of time*) in the middle of the night en mitad de la noche
   in the middle of the day alrededor del mediodía
   in the middle of the year a mediados de año
3. (*of an activity*) to be in the middle of doing something estar [2] haciendo algo
   When she phoned I was in the middle of washing my hair. Cuando llamó estaba lavándome el pelo.

middle-aged *adjective*
> de mediana edad *masc & fem*
> a middle-aged woman una mujer de mediana edad
> some middle-aged couples unas parejas de mediana edad

middle-class *adjective*
> de clase media *masc & fem*
> a middle-class family una familia de clase media
> some middle-class students unos estudiantes de clase media

Middle East *noun*
> the Middle East el Oriente Medio

middle finger *noun*
> el **dedo corazón**

midge *noun*
el **mosquito pequeño**

♂ **midnight** *noun*
la **medianoche** *fem*
at midnight a medianoche

Midsummer's Day *noun*
la **noche de San Juan**

midwife *noun*
la **comadrona** *fem*

might *verb*
I might invite Jo. Puede que invite a Jo.
Amanda might know. Puede que Amanda
lo sepa.
He might have forgotten. Puede que se
haya olvidado.
'Are you going to phone him?'— 'I might.'
'¿Vas a llamarlo?'— 'Quizás.'

migraine *noun*
la **jaqueca** *fem*

mike *noun*
(*informal*) el **micro** *masc*

mild *adjective*
1 (*soap, cheese*) **suave** *masc & fem*
2 (*climate*) **templado** *masc*, **templada** *fem*
It's quite mild today. Hoy no hace frío.

mile *noun*
la **milla** *fem* (*in Spain distances are measured in
kilometres; to convert miles roughly to kilometres,
multiply by 8 and divide by 5*)
The village is ten miles from Chester. El
pueblo está a dieciseis kilómetros de
Chester.
It's miles better! ¡Es mil veces mejor!

mileage *noun*
la **distancia en millas**
What's the mileage on your car? ¿Cuántas
millas ha hecho tu coche?

♂ to **milk** *verb* ▷ see **milk** *noun*
ordeñar [17]

♂ **milk** *noun* ▷ see **milk** *verb*
la **leche** *fem*
full-cream milk leche entera
skimmed milk leche desnatada
semi-skimmed milk leche semidesnatada
• **milk chocolate** el chocolate con leche
• **milkman** el lechero
• **milkshake** el batido

millennium *noun*
el **milenio** *masc*

millimetre *noun*
el **milímetro** *masc*

million *noun*
el **millón** *masc*
a million people un millón de personas
two million people dos millones de
personas

millionaire *noun*
el **millonario** *masc*, la **millonaria** *fem*

mince *noun*
la **carne picada**

♂ to **mind** *verb* ▷ see **mind** *noun*
1 (*to look after*) **cuidar** [17]
Can you mind my bag for me? ¿Me cuidas el
bolso?
Could you mind the baby for ten minutes?
¿Puedes cuidar del niño diez minutos?
2 (*to be bothered*) do you mind if ...? ¿te
importa que ...?
Do you mind if I close the door? ¿Te
importa que cierre la puerta?
I don't mind the heat. No me molesta el
calor.
I don't mind. No me importa.
Never mind! ¡No importa!
3 (*to be careful*) Mind the step! ¡Cuidado con el
escalón!

♂ **mind** *noun* ▷ see **mind** *verb*
1 (*brain*) la **mente** *fem*
a logical mind una mente lógica
It crossed my mind that ... Se me pasó por
la cabeza que ...
2 (*opinion*) to change your mind cambiar [17]
de opinión
I've changed my mind. He cambiado de
opinión.
to make up your mind decidirse [19]
I can't make up my mind. No puedo
decidirme.

♂ **mine** *noun* ▷ see **mine** *pron*
la **mina** *fem*
a coal mine una mina de carbón

♂ **mine** *pronoun* ▷ see **mine** *noun*
el **mío** *masc*, la **mía** *fem*
She took my hat and I took mine. Ella cogió
su sombrero y yo cogí el mío.
Tessa phoned her mum and I phoned mine.
Tessa llamó a su madre y yo llamé a la mía.
Karen's invited her parents and I've invited
mine. Karen ha invitado a sus padres y yo a
los míos.
She showed me her photos and I showed
her mine. Ella me enseñó sus fotos y yo le
enseñé las mías.

miner *noun*
> el **minero** *masc*, la **minera** *fem*
> Her father was a miner. Su padre era
> minero.

♂ **mineral water** *noun*
> el **agua mineral**

> **WORD TIP** *agua* takes *el* or *un* in the singular even
> though it is fem.

minibus *noun*
> el **microbús** *masc*

minimum *adjective*
> ▷ see **minimum** *noun*
> **mínimo** *masc*, **mínima** *fem*
> the minimum age la edad mínima

minimum *noun* ▷ see **minimum** *adj*
> el **mínimo** *masc*

miniskirt *noun*
> la **minifalda** *fem*

minister *noun*
> 1 (*in government*) el **ministro** *masc*, la **ministra**
>   *fem*
> 2 (*of a church*) el **pastor** *masc*, la **pastora** *fem*

minor *adjective*
> **menor** *masc & fem*
> a minor problem

minority *noun*
> la **minoría** *fem*

mint *noun*
> 1 (*herb*) la **menta** *fem*
> 2 (*sweet*) el **caramelo de menta**

minus *preposition*
> 1 (*in sums*) **menos**
>   Seven minus three is four. Siete menos tres
>   es cuatro.
> 2 (*to talk about temperature*) It was minus ten
>   this morning. Esta mañana hacía diez
>   grados bajo cero.

♂ **minute** *noun*
> el **minuto** *masc*
> It's five minutes' walk from here. Está a
> cinco minutos andando de aquí.
> I'll be ready in two minutes. En dos minutos
> estoy lista.
> Just a minute! ¡Un momento!

miracle *noun*
> el **milagro** *masc*

♂ **mirror** *noun*
> 1 (*looking-glass*) el **espejo** *masc*
>   I looked at myself in the mirror. Me miré al
>   espejo.
> 2 (*rear-view mirror in a car*) el **retrovisor** *masc*

to **misbehave** *verb*
> portarse[17] **mal**

mischief *noun*
> to get up to mischief hacer[7] travesuras

mischievous *adjective*
> **travieso** *masc*, **traviesa** *fem*

miser *noun*
> el **avaro** *masc*, la **avara** *fem*

miserable *adjective*
> 1 (*person*) **triste** *masc & fem*
>   He was miserable without her. Estaba
>   triste sin ella.
>   I feel really miserable today. Hoy tengo el
>   ánimo por los suelos.
> 2 (*weather*) It's miserable weather. Un
>   tiempo deprimente.

misery *noun*
> la **miseria** *fem*
> He was in misery. Estaba muy triste.

♂ to **miss** *verb*
> 1 (*to fail to catch, see, etc*) **perder**[36]
>   She missed her train. Perdió el tren.
>   I missed the film. Me perdí la película.
>   to miss an opportunity perder una
>   oportunidad
> 2 (*a target, goal*) The ball missed the goal. La
>   pelota no entró en la portería.
>   You missed! ¡Fallaste!
> 3 (*to be absent from*) **faltar**[17] a
>   He's missed several classes. Ha faltado a
>   varias clases.
> 4 (*to long to see*) I miss you. Te echo de menos.
>   She's missing her sister. Echa de menos a
>   su hermana.
>   I miss Madrid. Echo de menos Madrid.

♂ **Miss** *noun*
> la **señorita** *fem* (*usually abbreviated to Srta.*)
> Miss Jones la Srta. Jones
> Good afternoon, Miss Jones. Buenas
> tardes, señorita Jones.

missile *noun*
> el **misil** *masc*

missing *adjective*
> the missing piece la pieza que falta
> the missing documents los documentos
> que faltan
> the missing link el eslabón perdido
> There's a plate missing. Falta un plato.
> There are three forks missing. Faltan tres
> tenedores.
> Is there anybody missing? ¿Falta alguien?
> to go missing desaparecer[35]
> Several things have gone missing lately.

Han desaparecido varias cosas
últimamente.
Three people have gone missing. Han
desaparecido tres personas.

mist *noun*
la **neblina** *fem*

to **mistake** *verb* ▷ see **mistake** *noun*
confundir[19]
I mistook you for your brother. Te confundí
con tu hermano.

ʃ **mistake** *noun* ▷ see **mistake** *verb*
el **error** *masc*
by mistake por error
a spelling mistake una falta de ortografía
to make a mistake cometer[18] un error
Sorry, I made a mistake. Perdona, cometí
un error.
It was my mistake. Fue un error mío.

mistaken *adjective*
to be mistaken estar[2] equivocado
She's mistaken. Está equivocada.

mistletoe *noun*
el **muérdago** *masc*

to **misunderstand** *verb*
entender[36] **mal**
I misunderstood. Lo entendí mal.

misunderstanding *noun*
el **malentendido** *masc*
There's been a misunderstanding. Ha
habido un malentendido.

to **mix** *verb* ▷ see **mix** *noun*
1 (*to combine*) **mezclar**[17]
Mix all the ingredients together. Mezclar
todos los ingredientes.
2 (*to socialize*) **to mix with** tratarse[17] con
She mixes with lots of interesting people.
Se trata con mucha gente interesante.
• **to mix up**
1 (*to mess up*) **desordenar**[17]
You've mixed up all my papers. Has
desordenado todos mis papeles.
2 (*to confuse*) **confundir**[19]
I get him mixed up with his brother. Lo
confundo con su hermano.
You've got it all mixed up! ¡Te has
confundido!

mix *noun* ▷ see **mix** *verb*
1 (*mixture*) la **mezcla** *fem*
a good mix of people una buena mezcla de
gente
2 (*set of ingredients*) **cake mix** preparado para
hacer un pastel

ʃ **mixed** *adjective*
variado *masc*, **variada** *fem*
a mixed programme un programa variado
• **mixed salad** la ensalada mixta

mixer *noun*
la **batidora** *fem*

mixture *noun*
la **mezcla** *fem*
a mixture of jazz and rock una mezcla de
jazz y rock

to **moan** *verb*
1 (*in pain*) **gemir**[57]
2 (*to complain*) **quejarse**[17]
Stop moaning! ¡Deja de quejarte!

mobile home *noun*
la **caravana fija**

mobile phone *noun*
el **móvil** *masc noun*, el **teléfono móvil**
to call somebody on their mobile llamar
[17] a alguien al móvil

mock *noun* ▷ see **mock** *verb*
(*mock exam*) el **examen de práctica**

to **mock** *verb* ▷ see **mock** *noun*
burlarse[17] **de**
Stop mocking me! ¡Deja de burlarte de mí!

model *noun*
1 (*type*) el **modelo** *masc*
the latest model el último modelo
2 (*fashion model*) el & la **modelo** *masc & fem*
She's a model. Es modelo.
3 (*of a plane, car, etc*) la **maqueta** *fem*
a model of Westminster Abbey una
maqueta de la abadía de Westminster
He makes models. Construye maquetas.
• **model aeroplane** el aeromodelo
• **model railway** el ferrocarril de juguete

ʃ **modem** *noun*
el **módem** *masc, pl:* **módems**

moderate *adjective*
moderado *masc*, **moderada** *fem*

modern *adjective*
moderno *masc*, **moderna** *fem*
• **modern languages** las lenguas modernas

to **modernize** *verb*
modernizar[22]

moisturizer *noun*
1 (*lotion*) la **loción hidratante**
2 (*cream*) la **crema hidratante**

mole *noun*
1 (*the animal*) el **topo** *masc*
2 (*mark on skin*) el **lunar** *masc*

a
b
c
d
e
f
g
h
i
j
k
l
m
n
o
p
q
r
s
t
u
v
w
x
y
z

♂ moment noun
  el **momento** masc
  at the moment en este momento
  at the right moment en el momento
  preciso
  at any moment en cualquier momento
  for the moment de momento
  He'll be here in a moment. Llegará en
  cualquier momento.

♂ monarchy noun
  la **monarquía** fem

♂ Monday noun
  el **lunes** masc
  every Monday cada lunes
  last Monday el lunes pasado
  on Monday el lunes
  on Mondays los lunes
  The museum is closed on Mondays. El
  museo cierra los lunes.
  I'll phone you on Monday evening Te
  llamaré el lunes por la tarde.

  WORD TIP Months of the year and days of the
  week start with small letters in Spanish.

♂ money noun
  el **dinero** masc
  I haven't got enough money. No tengo
  suficiente dinero.
  to make money hacer [7] dinero
  They gave me my money back (in a
  shop.) Me devolvieron el dinero.
  • **money box** la hucha

mongrel noun
  el **chucho** masc (informal)

monitor noun
  (Computers) el **monitor** masc

monkey noun
  1 (animal) el **mono** masc
  2 (informal: child) **You little monkey!** ¡Diablillo!

monster noun
  el **monstruo** masc

♂ month noun
  el **mes** masc
  in the month of May en el mes de mayo
  this month este mes
  next month el próximo mes
  We're leaving next month. Nos vamos el
  próximo mes.
  last month el mes pasado
  every month todos los meses
  in two months' time dentro de dos meses
  at the end of the month a final de mes

monthly adjective
  mensual masc & fem
  a monthly payment una mensualidad

♂ monument noun
  el **monumento** masc
  a monument to the king un monumento al
  rey

mood noun
  el **humor** masc
  to be in a good mood estar [2] de buen
  humor
  to be in a bad mood estar [2] de mal humor
  **'Do you want to go out?'— 'I'm not in the
  mood.'** ¿Quieres salir?'— 'No me
  apetece.'

moody adjective
  temperamental masc & fem

moon noun
  la **luna** fem
  by the light of the moon a la luz de la luna

moonlight noun
  la **luz de la luna**
  by moonlight a la luz de la luna

moor noun
  el **páramo**

moped noun
  el **ciclomotor** masc

moral adjective ▷ see **moral** noun
  moral masc & fem

moral noun ▷ see **moral** adj
  la **moraleja** fem
  the moral of the story la moraleja de la
  historia

morals plural noun
  la **moralidad** fem

♂ more adverb, adjective, pronoun
  1 (extra) **más**
  Julie eats more. Julie come más.
  more cake más pastel
  a few more glasses unos cuantos vasos más
  We need three more. Necesitamos tres
  más.
  more easily más fácilmente
  This one is more interesting. Este es más
  interesante.
  2 (with numbers, amounts) **more than** más de
  more than a kilo más de un kilo
  more than two hours más de dos horas
  3 (in comparisons) **more than** más que
  The book's more interesting than the film.
  El libro es más interesante que la película.
  He eats more than me. Come más que yo.

4 (*in expressions*) **more and more** cada vez más
Books are getting more and more expensive. Los libros están cada vez más caros.
more or less más o menos
It's more or less finished. Está más o menos terminado.
any more más
I don't want any more. No quiero más.
I don't like it any more. Ya no me gusta.

♂ **morning** *noun*
la **mañana** *fem*
this morning esta mañana
tomorrow morning mañana por la mañana
yesterday morning ayer por la mañana
in the morning por la mañana
She doesn't work in the morning. No trabaja por las mañanas.
on Friday morning el viernes por la mañana
on Friday mornings los viernes por la mañana
at six o'clock in the morning a las seis de la mañana
every morning todas las mañanas
Good morning! ¡Buenos días!

Morocco *noun*
Marruecos *masc*

mortgage *noun*
la **hipoteca** *fem*

Moscow *noun*
Moscú *masc*

mosque *noun*
la **mezquita** *fem*

mosquito *noun*
el **mosquito** *masc*, (*Latin America*) el **zancudo** *masc*
a mosquito bite una picadura de mosquito

♂ **most** *adjective, adverb, pronoun*
1 (*in superlatives*) **más**
the most interesting film la película más interesante
the most exciting story la historia más emocionante
the most boring books los libros más aburridos
I've got the most time. Soy el que más tiempo tiene.
What I hate most is the noise. Lo que más odio es el ruido.
She ate the most. Fue la que más comió.
2 (*nearly all: with a plural noun*) **la mayoría de**
most of my friends la mayoría de mis amigos

Most children like chocolate. A la mayoría de los niños les gusta el chocolate.
3 (*nearly all: with a singular noun*) **most of** la mayor parte de
most of the time la mayor parte del tiempo
Most of it is clear. La mayor parte está claro.
They've eaten most of the chocolate. Se han comido casi todo el chocolate.
4 (*in expressions*) **at most** como máximo
two days, at most como máximo dos días

♂ **mother** *noun*
la **madre** *fem*
my mother mi madre
Kate's mother la madre de Kate
• **mother-in-law** la suegra
• **Mother's Day** el día de la Madre (*in Spain, the first Sunday in May*)

motivated *adjective*
motivado *masc*, **motivada** *fem*

motivation *noun*
el **motivo** *masc*

motor *noun*
el **motor** *masc*

♂ **motorbike** *noun*
la **motocicleta** *fem*

motorboat *noun*
la **motora** *fem*

motorcycle *noun*
la **motocicleta** *fem*

motorcyclist *noun*
el & la **motociclista** *masc & fem*

motorist *noun*
el & la **automovilista** *masc & fem*

motor racing *noun*
las **carreras de coches**

♂ **motorway** *noun*
la **autopista** *fem*

mouldy *adjective*
mohoso *masc*, **mohosa** *fem*

♂ **mountain** *noun*
la **montaña** *fem*
in the mountains en las montañas
• **mountain bike** la bicicleta de montaña

mountaineer *noun*
el **montañero** *masc*, la **montañera** *fem*

mountaineering *noun*
el **montañismo** *masc*
to go mountaineering hacer [7] montañismo

mountainous *adjective*
montañoso *masc*, **montañosa** *fem*

a
b
c
d
e
f
g
h
i
j
k
l
m
n
o
p
q
r
s
t
u
v
w
x
y
z

♂ **mouse** *noun* ▷ see **mousse** *noun*
(*animal, on a computer*) el **ratón** *masc*

mousse *noun* ▷ see **mouse** *noun*
(*pudding, hair product*) la **mousse** *fem*
chocolate mousse mousse de chocolate

moustache *noun*
el **bigote** *masc*

♂ **mouth** *noun*
la **boca** *fem*
Open your mouth wide. Abra bien la boca.
Shut your mouth! ¡Cállate la boca!

mouthful *noun*
1 (*of food*) el **bocado** *masc*
2 (*of drink*) el **trago** *masc*

mouth organ *noun*
la **armónica** *fem*
to play the mouth organ tocar[31] la
armónica

♂ **move** *noun* ▷ see **move** *verb*
1 (*to a different house*) la **mudanza** *fem*
2 (*in a game*) Your move! ¡Tu turno!

♂ to **move** *verb* ▷ see **move** *noun*
1 (*to change your position, place*) **moverse**[38]
She didn't move. No se movió.
Move up a bit. Córrete un poco.
We moved to another table. Nos
cambiamos de mesa.
She moved to a new school. Cambió de
colegio.
2 (*to change the position of an object*) **cambiar**
[17] **de sitio**
You've moved the picture. Has cambiado
el cuadro de sitio.
Can you move your bag, please? ¿Puedes
correr tu bolsa, por favor?
3 (*an object, a part of the body*) **mover**[38]
She moved her hand. Movió la mano.
4 (*car, traffic*) **avanzar**[22]
The traffic was moving slowly. El tráfico
avanzaba lentamente.
5 to move forward avanzar[22]
He moved forward a step. Avanzó un paso.
6 (*to move house*) **mudarse**[17]
We're moving on Tuesday. Nos mudamos
el martes.
They've moved house. Se han mudado de
casa.
They've moved to Spain. Se han ido a vivir
en España.
7 (*emotionally*) **conmover**[38]
It really moved me. Me conmovió de
verdad.
to be moved estar[2] conmovido, *fem*
conmovida

• to **move in**
mudarse[17]
When are you moving in? ¿Cuándo se
mudan?
• to **move out**
mudarse[17]
I'm moving out at the end of the month.
Me mudo a finales del mes.

movie *noun*
la **película** *fem*
to go to the movies ir[8] al cine

moving *adjective*
1 (*in motion*) **en marcha** *masc & fem*
a moving vehicle un vehículo en marcha
2 (*emotionally*) **conmovedor** *masc*,
conmovedora *fem*
It's a very moving film. Es una película muy
conmovedora.

MP *noun*
(= *Member of Parliament*) el **diputado** *masc*, la
diputada *fem*
She's an MP. Es diputada.

MP3 *noun*
el **MP3** *masc*
• **MP3 player** el reproductor de MP3

♂ **Mr** *noun*
el **señor** *masc* (*usually abbreviated to* Sr.)
Mr Angus Brown el Sr. Angus Brown
Good afternoon, Mr Brown. Buenas tardes,
señor Brown.

♂ **Mrs** *noun*
la **señora** *fem* (*usually abbreviated to* Sra.)
Mrs Mary Hendry la Sra. Mary Hendry
Good afternoon, Mrs Hendry. Buenas
tardes, señora Hendry.

♂ **Ms** *noun*
la **señora** *fem* (*usually abbreviated to* 'Sra.')
Ms Jane Brown la Sra. Jane Brown
Good afternoon, Ms Brown. Buenas tardes,
señora Brown.

WORD TIP There is no direct equivalent to Ms in
Spanish, but *señora* may be used whether a
woman is married or not.

♂ **much** *adverb, pronoun, adjective*
1 (*with a verb*) **mucho**
not much no mucho
Do you go out much? ¿Sales mucho?
We don't go out much. No salimos mucho.
She doesn't eat much. No come mucho.
very much mucho
I don't watch television very much. No veo
mucho la tele.
2 (*with a comparative*) **mucho**
much more mucho más

much bigger mucho más grande
Your house is much older than mine. Tu casa es mucho más vieja que la mía
He won't stay much longer. No se va a quedar mucho más.

3 (with a noun) **mucho** masc, **mucha** fem
We don't have much time. No tenemos mucho tiempo.
There isn't much butter left. No queda mucha mantequilla.
very much mucho masc, mucha fem
There isn't very much milk. No queda mucha leche.

4 **not much** no mucho masc, no mucha fem
'Did you add salt?'— 'Not much.' '¿Has puesto sal?'— 'No mucha.'

5 **so much** tanto masc, tanto fem
You shouldn't have given me so much coffee. No deberías haberme dado tanto café.
I have so much to do! ¡Tengo tanto que hacer!
We liked it so much! ¡Nos gustó tanto!

6 **too much** demasiado masc, demasiada fem
too much ink demasiada tinta
I drank too much wine. Bebí demasiado vino.
That's far too much! ¡Eso es demasiado!

7 **how much?** ¿cuánto? masc, ¿cuánta? fem
How much is it? ¿Cuánto cuesta?
How much do you want? ¿Cuánto quieres?
How much milk do you want? ¿Cuánta leche quieres?

8 **as much as** tanto como masc, tanta como fem
She drank as much milk as I did. Bebió tanta leche como yo.
There isn't as much as before. No hay tanto como antes.

9 **as much as** tanto como
You can take as much as you like. Puedes coger tanto como quieras.

mud noun
el **barro** masc

muddle noun
el **desorden** masc
to be in a muddle estar[2] todo desordenado

muddy adjective
lleno de barro masc, **llena de barro** fem
a muddy road una carretera llena de barro
Your boots are all muddy. Tus botas están llenas de barro.

♪ **muffled** adjective
sordo masc, **sorda** fem
a muffled shout un grito sordo

mug noun ▷ see **mug** verb
la **taza alta**
a mug of coffee una taza alta de café

to **mug** verb ▷ see **mug** noun
to mug somebody atracar[31] a alguien
My brother was mugged in the park. Atracaron a mi hermano en el parque.

mugging noun
el **atraco** masc

multiplication noun
la **multiplicación** fem

to **multiply** verb
multiplicar[31]
to multiply six by four multiplicar seis por cuatro

♪ **mum** noun
1 (mother) la **madre** fem
Tom's mum la madre de Tom
I'll ask my mum. Preguntaré a mi madre.
2 (within the family) **mamá** fem
Mum's not back yet. Mamá no ha vuelto todavía.

♪ **mummy** noun
1 (mother) la **mamá** fem
Susan's mummy is a teacher. La mamá de Susan es profesora.
2 (within the family) **mamá** fem
Mummy's not back yet. Mamá no ha vuelto todavía.
3 (preserved body) la **momia** fem

mumps noun
las **paperas** plural fem

murder noun ▷ see **murder** verb
el **asesinato** masc

to **murder** verb ▷ see **murder** noun
asesinar[17]

murderer noun
el **asesino** masc, la **asesina** fem

muscle noun
el **músculo** masc

♪ **museum** noun
el **museo** masc
to go to the museum ir[8] al museo

♪ **mushroom** noun
el **champiñón** masc

♪ **music** noun
la **música** fem
pop music música pop
classical music música clásica

a
b
c
d
e
f
g
h
i
j
k
l
m
n
o
p
q
r
s
t
u
v
w
x
y
z

musical *adjective* ▷ see **musical** *noun*

1 (*instrument, evening, ability*) **musical** *masc & fem*
   a musical **instrument** un instrumento musical

2 (*musically gifted*) They're a very musical family. Toda la familia tiene dotes para la música.

musical *noun* ▷ see **musical** *adj*
   el **musical** *masc*

musician *noun*
   el **músico** *masc*, la **música** *fem*
   He is a musician. Es músico.

Muslim *adjective* ▷ see **Muslim** *noun*
   musulmán *masc*, musulmana *fem*

Muslim *noun* ▷ see **Muslim** *adj*
   el **musulmán** *masc*, la **musulmana** *fem*

> **WORD TIP** Adjectives and nouns for religion do not have capital letters in Spanish.

ⓘ Muslim Spain

The Moors (an Islamic people from North Africa) invaded Spain in 711 AD and stayed until 1492. They left behind many common words, place names, surnames, and buildings.

♪ **mussel** *noun*
   la **mejillón** *masc*

♪ **must** *verb*

1 (*to say you have to*) **tener** [9] **que**, **deber** [18]
   You must be there at eight. Tienes que estar allí a las ocho., Debes estar allí a las ocho (*speaking to one person*).
   You must bring sun block. Debéis llevar filtro solar., Tenéis que llevar filtro solar (*speaking to more than one person*).
   I must lock the door. Tengo que cerrar la puerta con llave.

2 (*to say something is probable*) **deber**, **deber de**
   You must be tired. Debes estar cansado (*to a boy*)., Debes estar cansada (*to a girl*).

It must be five o'clock. Deben ser las cinco.
He must have forgotten. Debe haberse olvidado.

> **WORD TIP** You can also use *debes de*, *deben de*, *debe de* in these examples.

♪ **mustard** *noun*
   la **mostaza** *fem*

mustn't *short for* **must not** (*See:* **must**)

♪ **mutton** *noun*
   la **carne de ovino** *fem*

♪ **my** *adjective*

1 (*before most nouns*) **mi** *masc & fem*
   my book mi libro
   my sister mi hermana
   my children mis hijos

2 (*with parts of the body, clothes*) **el**, **la**, **los**, **las**
   I cut my finger. Me corté el dedo.
   I'm washing my hands. Me estoy lavando las manos.
   My feet hurt. Me duelen los pies.
   I took off my hat. Me quité el sombrero.

> **WORD TIP** Spanish uses *el*, *la*, *los*, *las* for *my* with parts of the body and clothes.

myself *pronoun*

1 (*reflexive*) **me**
   I've hurt myself. Me he hecho daño.
   I washed myself. Me lavé.

2 (*for emphasis*) **yo mismo** *masc*, **yo misma** *fem*
   I said it myself. Lo dije yo mismo.

3 (*on your own*) **by myself** yo solo *masc*, yo sola *fem*
   I did it by myself. Lo hice yo solo (*boy speaking*)., Lo hice yo sola (*girl speaking*).

♪ **mysterious** *adjective*
   misterioso *masc*, misteriosa *fem*

mystery *noun*

1 (*enigma*) el **misterio** *masc*

2 (*book*) la **novela de misterio**

N n

Ñ, ñ

ñ is a separate letter in the Spanish alphabet, which has 27 letters. Very few Spanish words start with *k*, *w* and *ñ*.

nail *noun*
1 *(on a finger, toe)* la **uña** *fem*
   to bite your nails morderse **[38]** las uñas
2 *(used for hanging, joining things)* el **clavo** *masc*
· **nailbrush** el cepillo de uñas
· **nail file** la lima de uñas
· **nail scissors** las tijeras de uñas
· **nail varnish** el esmalte de uñas
· **nail varnish remover** el quitaesmalte

♂ **name** *noun*
1 *(of a person)* el **nombre** *masc*
   I've forgotten her name. Se me ha olvidado su nombre.
   What's your name? ¿Cómo te llamas?
   My name is Lily. Me llamo Lily.
2 *(of a book, film)* el **título** *masc*

 names

Traditionally Spaniards have two surnames, using one from their father's side and one from their mother's side. They also use many nicknames, e.g. Francisco, Paco; José, Pepe; Juana, Pacha; María Teresa, Maité.

nanny *noun*
   la **niñera** *fem*

♂ **napkin** *noun*
   la **servilleta** *fem*

nappy *noun*
   el **pañal** *masc*

narrow *adjective*
   estrecho *masc*, **estrecha** *fem*
   a narrow street una calle estrecha

♂ **nasty** *adjective*
1 *(spiteful)* **malo** *masc*, **mala** *fem*
   They are really nasty to her. Son realmente malos con ella.
   That was a nasty thing to do. Eso fue una crueldad.
   to have a nasty temper tener **[9]** mal carácter
2 *(unpleasant: job, habit)* **desagradable** *masc & fem*
   That's a nasty job. Ese es un trabajo desagradable.

3 *(taste, smell)* **repugnante** *masc & fem*
   It smells nasty. Tiene un olor repugnante.
4 *(situation)* **feo** *masc*, **fea** *fem*
   The situation turned nasty. La cosa se puso fea.

WORD TIP *malo* becomes *mal* before a masc singular noun.

nation *noun*
   la **nación** *fem*

national *adjective*
   nacional *masc & fem*
· **national anthem** el himno nacional

nationality *noun*
   la **nacionalidad** *fem*

national park *noun*
   el **parque nacional**

Nativity scene *noun*
   el **belén** *masc*

♂ **natural** *adjective*
1 *(found in nature, not manufactured)* **natural** *masc & fem*
   natural resources recursos naturales
   I'm a natural blonde. Soy rubia natural.
2 *(born)* **nato** *masc*, **nata** *fem*
   He is a natural leader. Es un líder nato.
3 *(normal, expected)* **natural** *masc & fem*
   It's natural that he should do that. Es natural que haga eso.

WORD TIP *ser natural que* is followed by a verb in the subjunctive.

naturally *adverb*
   naturalmente

♂ **nature** *noun*
1 *(the natural world)* la **naturaleza** *fem*
   the laws of nature las leyes de la naturaleza
2 *(temperament)* la **naturaleza** *fem*
   by nature por naturaleza
· **nature reserve** la reserva natural

♂ **naughty** *adjective*
   travieso *masc*, **traviesa** *fem*
   Don't be so naughty. No seas tan travieso.
   You naughty girl! ¡Mala!

nausea *noun*
   las **náuseas** *plural fem*

navel *noun*
   el **ombligo** *masc*

to **navigate** *verb*
navegar[28]

navy *noun*
la **marina** *fem*
My uncle's in the navy. Mi tío está en la marina.

navy-blue *adjective*
azul marino *invariable adj*
navy-blue gloves guantes azul marino

ᵟ **near** *adjective* ▷ see **near** *adv, prep*
cercano *masc*, **cercana** *fem*
the nearest shop la tienda más cercana

ᵟ **near** *adverb, preposition* ▷ see **near** *adj*
1 (*nearby*) **cerca**
They live quite near. Viven bastante cerca.
to go near to something acercarse[31] a algo
Don't go any nearer to the edge. No te acerques más al borde.
2 (*close to*) **cerca de**
I live near the station. Vivo cerca de la estación.
Don't go too near the fire. No te acerques demasiado al fuego.
3 (*in time*) Your birthday's getting nearer. Se acerca tu cumpleaños.

ᵟ **nearby** *adverb* ▷ see **nearby** *adj*
cerca
There's a park nearby. Hay un parque cerca.

nearby *adjective* ▷ see **nearby** *adv*
cercano *masc*, **cercana** *fem*
a nearby park un parque cercano

ᵟ **nearly** *adverb*
casi
nearly empty casi vacío
We're nearly there. Ya casi hemos llegado.

neat *adjective*
1 (*well-organized*) **ordenado** *masc*, **ordenada** *fem*
a neat desk un pupitre ordenado
2 (*your clothes, the way you look*) **arreglado** *masc*, **arreglada** *fem*
She always looks very neat. Siempre va muy arreglada.
3 (*garden*) **muy cuidado** *masc*, **muy cuidada** *fem*

necessarily *adverb*
not necessarily no necesariamente

ᵟ **necessary** *adjective*
necesario *masc*, **necesaria** *fem*
if necessary si es necesario

ᵟ **neck** *noun*
(*of a person, garment, bottle*) el **cuello** *masc*

necklace *noun*
el **collar** *masc*

nectarine *noun*
la **nectarina** *fem*

ᵟ **need** *noun* ▷ see **need** *verb*
la **necesidad** *fem*
There's no need, I've done it already. No hay necesidad, ya lo he hecho.
There's no need to wait. No hay necesidad de esperar.

ᵟ to **need** *verb* ▷ see **need** *noun*
1 (*to require*) **necesitar**[17]
We need bread. Necesitamos pan.
They need help. Necesitan ayuda.
Do you need the hammer? ¿Necesitas el martillo?
Everything you need. Todo lo que necesites.
2 (*to have to*) to need to do something tener [9] que hacer algo
I need to drop in at the bank. Tengo que pasarme por el banco.
She'll need to check. Tendrá que comprobarlo.
3 (*to be obliged to*) You needn't decide today. No hace falta que decidas hoy.
You needn't wait. No hace falta que esperes.

needle *noun*
la **aguja** *fem*

negative *noun*
(*of a photo*) el **negativo** *masc*

neglected *adjective*
descuidado *masc*, **descuidada** *fem*

ᵟ **neighbour** *noun*
el **vecino** *masc*, la **vecina** *fem*
We're going round to the neighbours'. Vamos a casa de los vecinos.

neighbourhood *noun*
el **barrio** *masc*
a nice neighbourhood un barrio agradable

neither *conjunction*
1 (*used in sentences with nor*)
neither... nor ni ... ni
I have neither the time nor the money. No tengo ni tiempo ni dinero.
2 (*nor*) **tampoco**
Neither do I. Yo tampoco.
'I didn't go.'— 'Neither did I.' 'No fui.'— 'Yo tampoco.'

3 (*with gustar*) **'I don't like fish.'**— **'Neither do I.'** 'No me gusta el pescado.'— 'Ni a mí tampoco.'
'I didn't like the film.'— **'Neither did Kirsty.'** 'No me gustó la película.'— 'Ni a Kirsty tampoco.'
'Which do you like?'— **'Neither.'** ¿Cuál te gusta?'— 'Ninguno.'

ᵟ **nephew** *noun*
el **sobrino** *masc*

nerve *noun*
1 (*in the body*) el **nervio** *masc*
2 (*courage*) el **valor** *masc*
  to lose one's nerve perder[36] el valor
3 (*cheek*) la **cara** *fem*
  You've got a nerve! ¡Vaya cara que tienes!
  (*informal*)

nervous *adjective*
  nervioso *masc*, **nerviosa** *fem*
  to feel nervous estar[2] nervioso
• **nervous breakdown** la crisis nerviosa

nest *noun*
  el **nido** *masc*

net *noun*
  la **red** *fem*
  (*Computers*) **the Net** la Red

Netherlands *noun*
  the Netherlands los Países Bajos

nettle *noun*
  la **ortiga** *fem*

network *noun*
  la **red** *fem*

neutral *adjective* ▷ see **neutral** *noun*
1 (*not taking sides*) **neutral** *masc & fem*
2 (*colour*) **neutro** *masc & fem*

neutral *noun* ▷ see **neutral** *adj*
  (*in a gearbox*) el **punto muerto**
  to be in neutral estar[2] en punto muerto

ᵟ **never** *adverb*
  nunca
  He never helps. Nunca ayuda.
  Ben never smokes. Ben no fuma nunca.
  I've never seen the film. No he visto nunca la película.
  'Have you ever been to Spain?'— **'No, never.'** ¿Has estado alguna vez en España?'— 'No, nunca.'
  Never again! ¡Nunca más!

nevertheless *adverb*
  sin embargo

ᵟ **new** *adjective*
1 (*unused, recently acquired*) **nuevo** *masc*, **nueva** *fem*
  a new car un coche nuevo
  Have you seen their new house? ¿Has visto su casa nueva?
2 (*different*) **nuevo** *masc*, **nueva** *fem*
  to start a new job empezar[25] una nueva vida
  Debbie's new boyfriend el nuevo novio de Debbie

ᵟ **news** *plural noun*
1 (*everyday gossip*) la **noticia** *fem*
  a piece of good news una buena noticia
  Have you heard the news? ¿Te has enterado de la noticia?
  Any news? ¿Hay alguna noticia?
2 (*on TV, radio*) las **noticias** *plural fem*
  the midday news las noticias del mediodía

newsagent *noun*
  el **vendedor de periódicos**, la **vendedora de periódicos**
  at the newsagent's en la tienda de periódicos

ᵟ **newspaper** *noun*
  el **periódico** *masc*

newsreader *noun*
  el **presentador** *masc*, la **presentadora** *fem*

ᵟ **New Year** *noun*
  el **Año Nuevo**
  Happy New Year! ¡Feliz Año Nuevo!

New Year's Day *noun*
  el **día de Año Nuevo**

New Year's Eve *noun*
  la **Nochevieja** *fem*

New Zealand *noun*
  Nueva Zelanda *fem*

New Zealander *noun*
  el **neozelandés** *masc*, la **neozelandesa** *fem*

WORD TIP Adjectives and nouns for nationality and regional origin do not have capital letters in Spanish.

ᵟ **next** *adjective* ▷ see **next** *adv*
1 (*to talk about the future*) **próximo** *masc*, **próxima** *fem*
  next week la próxima semana
  next Thursday el próximo jueves
  next year el próximo año
  the next time I see you la próxima vez que te vea
  The next train is at ten. El próximo tren sale a las diez. ▸▸

a
b
c
d
e
f
g
h
i
j
k
l
m
n
o
p
q
r
s
t
u
v
w
x
y
z

I'll see you next Thursday. Te veré el próximo jueves.
the week after next la semana que viene no, la otra

2 (*to talk about the past*) **siguiente** *masc & fem*
the next day al día siguiente
The next day we went to Valencia. Al día siguiente fuimos a Valencia.

3 (*following*) **siguiente** *masc & fem*
I'm getting off at the next stop. Me bajo en la siguiente parada.

4 (*neighbouring*) **in the next room** en la habitación de al lado

⚹ **next** *adverb* ▷ see **next** *adj*
1 (*afterwards*) **luego**
What did he say next? ¿Qué dijo luego?

2 (*now*) **ahora**
What shall we do next? ¿Qué hacemos ahora?

3 (*beside*) **next to someone, something** al lado de alguien, algo
the girl next to Pat la chica que está al lado de Pat
It's next to the baker's. Está al lado de la panadería.

4 (*virtually*) **It's next to impossible.** Es casi imposible.
I bought it for next to nothing. Lo compré por poquísimo dinero.

next door *adverb* ▷ see **next-door** *adj*
al lado
the girl next door la chica de al lado
They live next door. Viven al lado.

next-door *adjective* ▷ see **next door** *adv*
de al lado *masc & fem*
our next-door neighbours nuestros vecinos de al lado

NGO *noun*
(= *Non-Governmental Organization*) **ONG** *fem*
(*Organización No-Gubernamental*)

Nicaragua *noun*
Nicaragua *fem*

Nicaraguan *adjective & noun*
1 **nicaragüense** *masc & fem*
2 un & una **nicaragüense** *masc & fem*
the Nicaraguans los nicaragüenses

> **WORD TIP** Adjectives and nouns for nationality and regional origin do not have capital letters in Spanish.

⚹ **nice** *adjective*
1 (*pleasant, enjoyable*) **agradable** *masc & fem*
We had a very nice evening. Pasamos una tarde muy agradable.
Brighton's a very nice town. Brighton es

una ciudad muy agradable.
Have a nice time! ¡Que lo pases bien!

2 (*attractive: object, place*) **bonito** *masc*, **bonita** *fem*
That's a nice dress. Ese vestido es bonito.

3 (*attractive: person*) **guapo** *masc*, **guapa** *fem*
You look nice in that dress. Estás muy guapa con ese vestido.

4 (*kind, friendly*) **bueno** *masc*, **buena** *fem*
to be nice to somebody ser [1] bueno con alguien
She's been very nice to me. Ha sido muy buena conmigo.
He's a really nice person. Es muy buena persona.

5 (*food*) **rico** *masc*, **rica** *fem*
The food was really nice. La comida estaba muy rica.

6 (*weather*) **bueno** *masc*, **buena** *masc*
It's a nice day. Hace buen día.
We had nice weather. Tuvimos buen tiempo.

> **WORD TIP** bueno becomes buen before a masc singular noun.

to **nick** *verb*
(*to steal*) **mangar** [28] (*informal*)

nickname *noun*
el **apodo** *masc*

⚹ **niece** *noun*
la **sobrina** *fem*

⚹ **night** *noun*
la **noche** *fem*
tomorrow night mañana por la noche
last night anoche
I saw Greg last night. Anoche vi a Greg.
at night por la noche
It's cold at night. Hace frío por la noche.
on Friday night el viernes por la noche
on Friday nights los viernes por la noche
all night long toda la noche
every night todas las noches
to stay the night with somebody pasar [17] la noche con alguien
Good night! ¡Buenas noches!
· **night club** el club nocturno

nightdress *noun*
el **camisón** *masc*

nightie *noun*
el **camisón** *masc*

nightmare *noun*
la **pesadilla** *fem*
to have a nightmare tener [9] una pesadilla

night time *noun*
la **noche** *fem*

nil *noun*
  cero *masc*
  They won four-nil. Ganaron cuatro a cero.

ꝺ **nine** *number*
  nueve *invariable number*
  Jake's nine. Jake tiene nueve años.
  It's nine o'clock. Son las nueve.

ꝺ **nineteen** *number*
  diecinueve *invariable number*
  Jonny's nineteen. Jonny tiene diecinueve
  años.

nineties *plural noun* ▷ see **ninety** *number*
  the nineties los años noventa
  in the nineties en los años noventa

ꝺ **ninety** *number* ▷ see **nineties** *plural noun*
  noventa *invariable number*
  He's ninety. Tiene noventa años.
  ninety-five noventa y cinco

ninth *adjective* ▷ see **ninth** *noun*
  noveno *masc*, **novena** *fem*
  on the ninth floor en la novena planta

ninth *noun* ▷ see **ninth** *adj*
1 (*fraction*) a ninth una novena parte
2 (*when saying dates*) the ninth of June el nueve
  de junio

nitrogen *noun*
  el **nitrógeno** *masc*

ꝺ **no** *adjective* ▷ see **no** *adv*
1 (*not any*) We've got no bread. No tenemos
  pan.
  No problem! ¡Sin problema!
  They've got no children. No tienen hijos.
  The room has no windows. La habitación
  no tiene ninguna ventana.
2 (*on a notice*) 'No smoking' 'Prohibido fumar'
  'No parking' 'Prohibido aparcar'

ꝺ **no** *adverb* ▷ see **no** *adj*
  no
  I said no. He dicho que no.
  No thank you. No, gracias.
  'Have you seen John?'— 'No, I haven't.'
  'Has visto a John?'— 'No.'

ꝺ **nobody** *pronoun*
  nadie
  'Who's there?'— 'Nobody.' ¿Quién está
  ahí?'— 'Nadie.'
  There's nobody there. No hay nadie.
  Nobody knows me. Nadie me conoce.
  Nobody answered. No contestó nadie.

to **nod** *verb*
  (*to say yes*) **asentir** [14] **con la cabeza**
  He nodded. Asintió con la cabeza.

ꝺ **noise** *noun*
  el **ruido** *masc*
  to make a noise hacer [7] ruido

noisy *adjective*
  ruidoso *masc*, **ruidosa** *fem*

none *pronoun*
  ninguno *masc*, **ninguna** *fem*
  'How many students failed the exam?'—
  'None.' ¿Cuántos estudiantes
  suspendieron?'— 'Ninguno.'
  None of the girls knows him. Ninguna de
  las chicas lo conoce.
  There's none left. No queda nada.
  There are none left. No queda ninguno.

nonsense *noun*
  las **tonterías** *plural fem*
  to talk nonsense decir [5] tonterías
  Nonsense! She's at least thirty. ¡Tonterías!
  Tiene por lo menos treinta años.

ꝺ **non-smoker** *noun*
  el **no fumador** *masc*, la **no fumadora** *fem*

non-stop *adjective* ▷ see **non-stop** *adv*
  (*train, flight*) **directo** *masc*, **directa** *fem*

non-stop *adverb* ▷ see **non-stop** *adj*
  sin parar
  She talks non-stop. Habla sin parar.

noodles *plural noun*
  los **fideos** *plural masc*

ꝺ **noon** *noun*
  el **mediodía** *masc*
  at (twelve) noon a mediodía

ꝺ **no one** *pronoun*
  nadie
  'Who's there?'— 'No one.' ¿Quién está
  ahí?'— 'Nadie.'
  There's no one there. No hay nadie.
  No one knows me. Nadie me conoce.
  No one answered. Nadie contestó.

nor *conjunction*
1 (*used in sentences with neither*) **neither ... nor** ni
  ... ni
  I have neither the time nor the money. No
  tengo ni tiempo ni dinero.
2 (*neither*) **tampoco**
  Nor do I. Yo tampoco.
  'I didn't go.'— 'Nor did I.' 'No fui.'— 'Yo
  tampoco.'
3 (*with gustar*) 'I don't like fish.'— 'Nor do I.'
  'No me gusta el pescado.'— 'Ni a mí
  tampoco.'
  'I didn't like the film.'— 'Nor did Kirsty.'
  'No me gustó la película.'— 'Ni a Kirsty
  tampoco.'

a
b
c
d
e
f
g
h
i
j
k
l
m
n
o
p
q
r
s
t
u
v
w
x
y
z

♂ **normal** *adjective*

normal *masc & fem* **That's absolutely normal.** Eso es absolutamente normal.
to get back to normal volver[45] a la normalidad

normally *adverb*
normalmente

♂ **north** *adjective, adverb* ▷ see **north** *noun*

norte *masc & fem*
the north side la parte norte
a north wind un viento del norte
north of Madrid al norte de Madrid
to travel north viajar[17] hacia el norte

WORD TIP *norte* never changes.

♂ **north** *noun* ▷ see **north** *adj, adv*

el norte *masc*
in the north of England en el norte de Inglaterra

North America *noun*
Norteamérica *fem*

North American *adjective & noun*
1 **norteamericano** *masc*, **norteamericana** *fem*
2 (*person*) un **norteamericano** *masc*, una **norteamericana** *fem*
the North Americans los norteamericanos

WORD TIP Adjectives and nouns for nationality and regional origin do not have capital letters in Spanish.

northeast *adjective & adverb*
▷ see **northeast** *noun*

noreste *masc & fem*
in northeast England en el noreste de Inglaterra

WORD TIP *noreste* never changes.

northeast *noun* ▷ see **northeast** *adj, adv*
el noreste *masc*

♂ **Northern Ireland** *noun*
Irlanda del Norte

♂ **Northern Irish** *adjective*
de Irlanda del norte
He's Northern Irish. Es de Irlanda del norte.

North Pole *noun*
the North Pole el Polo Norte

North Sea *noun*
the North Sea el mar del Norte

northwest *adjective & adverb*
▷ see **northwest** *noun*

noroeste *masc & fem*
in northwest Scotland en el noroeste de Escocia

WORD TIP *noroeste* never changes.

northwest *noun* ▷ see **northwest** *adj, adv*
el noroeste *masc*

Norway *noun*
Noruega *fem*

Norwegian *adjective & noun*
1 **noruego** *masc*, **noruega** *fem*
2 (*person*) un **noruego** *masc*, una **noruega** *fem*
the Norwegians los noruegos
3 (*the language*) el **noruego** *masc*

WORD TIP Adjectives and nouns for nationality, regional origin and language do not have capital letters in Spanish.

♂ **nose** *noun*
la nariz *fem*
to blow your nose sonarse[24] la nariz

nosebleed *noun*
la hemorragia nasal
to have a nosebleed tener[9] una hemorragia nasal

nostril *noun*
la fosa nasal

♂ **not** *adverb*
1 (*with adjectives and adverbs*) **no**
not on Saturdays los sábados no
Not all alone! ¡Completamente solo no!
It's not bad. No está mal.
2 (*with verbs*) **no**
It's not my car. No es mi coche.
I don't know. No sé.
Sam didn't phone. Sam no llamó.
We decided not to wait. Decidimos no esperar.
She told me not to cry. Me dijo que no llorara.
3 (*in no way*) **not at all** en absoluto
I'm not at all worried No estoy preocupada en absoluto.
4 (*when somebody says thank you*) **not at all** de nada
'Thanks very much.'—'Not at all.' 'Muchas gracias.'— 'De nada.'

♂ **note** *noun*
1 (*short letter*) la **nota** *fem*
She left me a note. Me dejó una nota.
2 (*reminder*) el **apunte** *masc*
to take notes tomar[17] apuntes

3 (*banknote*) el **billete** *masc*
  a ten-pound note un billete de diez libras
4 (*in music*) la **nota** *fem*
• **notebook** el cuaderno *masc*
• **notepad** el bloc *masc*

ℰ **nothing** *pronoun*
1 (*in general*) **nada**
  nothing new nada nuevo
  nothing special nada especial
  'What did you say?'— 'Nothing.' '¿Qué
  dijiste?'— 'Nada.'
2 (*with verbs*) **no ... nada**
  She knows nothing. No sabe nada.
  There was nothing there. No había nada
  allí.
  I saw nothing. No vi nada.
  There's nothing happening. No está
  pasando nada.
  There's nothing new. No hay nada nuevo.
  They do nothing but fight. No hacen más
  que pelearse.

ℰ to **notice** *verb* ▷ see **notice** *noun*
  notar [17]
  I didn't notice anything. No noté nada.

ℰ **notice** *noun* ▷ see **notice** *verb*
1 (*sign*) el **letrero** *masc*
2 (*to pay attention*) **to take notice of somebody**
  hacerle [7] caso a alguien
  Don't take any notice of her! ¡No le hagas
  caso!
3 (*advance warning*) **to do something at
  short notice** hacer [7] algo con poca
  antelación
  They cancelled the match at short notice.
  Cancelaron el partido con poca
  antelación.
• **notice board** el tablón de anuncios

ℰ **nought** *noun*
  el **cero** *masc*

ℰ **noun** *noun*
  el **nombre** *masc*

ℰ **novel** *noun*
  la **novela** *fem*

novelist *noun*
  el & la **novelista** *masc & fem*

ℰ **November** *noun*
  el **noviembre** *masc*
  in November en noviembre

WORD TIP Names of months and days start with
small letters in Spanish.

ℰ **now** *adverb*
1 (*at the present time*) **ahora**
  Where is he now? ¿Dónde está ahora?

They live in the country now. Ahora viven
en el campo.
Now's your chance Esta es tu oportunidad.
2 He's busy just now. Está ocupado en este
  momento.
  I saw her just now in the corridor. Acabo de
  verla en el pasillo.
3 (*to talk about the past*) **ya**
  They've all gone home now. Ya se han ido
  todos a casa.
  It was too late to change now. Ya era
  demasiado tarde para cambiar.
4 (*nowadays*) **hoy en día**
  Divorce is easier now. Hoy en día es más
  fácil divorciarse.
5 (*to emphasize a statement, question*)
  Now, look here! ¡Espera un momento!
  Now, who's next? ¿Bueno ¿ahora a quién le
  toca?
6 (*in expressions*) Now, now. ¡Vamos, vamos!
  Now, now, don't cry. Vamos, vamos, no
  llores.
  now and then de vez en cuando
  We see each other now and then. Nos
  vemos de vez en cuando.
  now then vamos a ver
  Now then, what's going on here? Vamos a
  ver ¿qué es lo que pasa aquí?
  from now on de ahora en adelante
  She will work hard from now on. Trabajará
  duro de ahora en adelante.
  just now en este momento
  He's busy just now. Está ocupado en este
  momento.
  I saw her just now in the corridor. Acabo de
  verla en el pasillo.
  right now ahora mismo
  Do it right now! ¡Hazlo ahora mismo!

ℰ **nowadays** *adverb*
  hoy en día
  Nowadays they are quite common. Hoy en
  día son bastante comunes.

ℰ **nowhere** *adverb, pronoun*
1 (*no place*) **ninguna parte**
  There's nowhere to park. No hay sitio
  donde aparcar.
  Nowhere was open yet. Todavía no había
  nada abierto.
  The car just appeared out of nowhere. El
  coche apareció de la nada.
2 (*in no place*) **en ninguna parte**
  nowhere in Spain en ninguna parte de
  España
  She was nowhere to be found. No se la
  encontraba por ningún lado. ▶

a
b
c
d
e
f
g
h
i
j
k
l
m
n
o
p
q
r
s
t
u
v
w
x
y
z

ℰ indicates key words   561

3 (*to no place*) **a ninguna parte**
'Where did she go after work?'—
'Nowhere.' '¿Dónde fue después del
trabajo?'— 'A ninguna parte.'

4 **nowhere near**, **Warsaw is nowhere near
Moscow.** Varsovia está lejísimos de Moscú.
His answer was nowhere near right. Se
equivocó por mucho.

nuclear *adjective*
nuclear *masc & fem*
a nuclear power station una central
nuclear

nude *noun*
el **desnudo** *masc*
in the nude desnudo *masc*, desnuda *fem*

nuisance *noun*
1 (*person*) el **pesado** *masc*, la **pesada** *fem*
He's a real nuisance. Es un verdadero
pesado.
2 **It's a nuisance.** Es un fastidio.

numb *adjective*
entumecido *masc*, **entumecida** *fem*
My fingers are numb with cold. Tengo los
dedos entumecidos del frío.

♂ **number** *noun*
el **número** *masc*
my new phone number mi nuevo número
de teléfono

a large number of visitors un gran número
de visitantes
I live at number thirty-one. Vivo en el
número treinta y uno.
The third number is a 7. El tercer número es
un siete.
• **number plate** la matrícula

nun *noun*
la **monja** *fem*

♂ **nurse** *noun*
el **enfermero** *masc*, la **enfermera** *fem*
Janet's a nurse. Janet es enfermera.

nursery *noun*
1 (*for children*) la **guardería** *fem*
2 (*for plants*) el **vivero** *masc*
• **nursery school** el jardín de infancia

nursing *noun*
la **enfermería** *fem*

nut *noun*
1 (*walnut*) la **nuez** *fem*
2 (*almond*) la **almendra** *fem*
3 (*peanut*) el **cacahuete** *masc*
4 (*hazelnut*) la **avellana** *masc*
5 (*for a bolt*) la **tuerca** *fem*

♂ **nylon** *noun*
el **nylon** *masc*

a
b
c
d
e
f
g
h
i
j
k
l
m
n
o
p
q
r
s
t
u
v
w
x
y
z

O o

oak *noun*
el **roble** *masc*

oar *noun*
el **remo** *masc*

oasis *noun*
el **oasis** *masc* (pl: **oasis**)

obedient *adjective*
obediente *masc & fem*

to **obey** *verb*
(*a person*) **obedecer** [35]
to obey the rules respetar [17] las reglas

object *noun* ▷ see **object** *verb*
el **objeto** *masc*

to **object** *verb* ▷ see **object** *noun*
oponerse [11]
If you don't object ... Si no te opones ...
She objected to my suggestion. Se opuso a
mi sugerencia.

objection *noun*
la **objeción** *fem*, el **inconveniente** *masc*

oboe *noun*
el **oboe** *masc*
to play the oboe tocar [31] el oboe

obsessed *adjective*
obsesionado *masc*, **obsesionada** *fem*
She's obsessed with her diet. Está
obsesionada con su dieta.

obsession *noun*
la **obsesión** *fem*
He has an obsession with cleanliness. Tiene
obsesión con la limpieza.

obvious *adjective*
obvio *masc*, **obvia** *fem*

obviously *adverb*
evidentemente
The house is obviously empty.
Evidentemente la casa está vacía.
'Do you want to come too?'— 'Obviously,
but it's a bit difficult.' '¿Tú quieres venir
también?'— 'Evidentemente, pero es un
poco difícil.'

occasion *noun*
la **ocasión** *fem*
a special occasion una ocasión especial
on various occasions en varias ocasiones

occasional *adjective*
He sends us the occasional letter. De vez en
cuando nos manda una carta.

occasionally *adverb*
de vez en cuando

occupation *noun*
la **ocupación** *fem*

occupied *adjective*
ocupado *masc*, **ocupada** *fem*

to **occur** *verb*
1 **ocurrir** [19]
The accident occurred on Monday. El
accidente ocurrió el lunes.
2 **ocurrir**
It occurred to me that we might lose
them. Se me ocurrió que podríamos
perderlos.
It had never occurred to her. Nunca se le
había ocurrido.

ocean *noun*
el **océano** *masc*
the Atlantic Ocean el océano Atlántico
the Pacific Ocean el océano Pacífico

o'clock *adverb*
at ten o'clock a las diez
exactly five o'clock las cinco en punto
It's one o'clock. Es la una.
It's three o'clock. Son las tres.

♪ **October** *noun*
el **octubre** *masc*
in October en octubre

WORD TIP Names of months and days start with
small letters in Spanish.

♪ **odd** *adjective*
1 (*strange*) **raro** *masc*, **rara** *fem*
That's odd, I'm sure I heard the phone.
Qué raro, estoy seguro de que oí el
teléfono.
2 (*number*) **impar** *masc & fem*
Three is an odd number. El tres es un
número impar.
3 (*sock, shoe*) **desparejado** *masc*,
desparejada *fem*
an odd sock un calcetín desparejado

odds and ends *plural noun*
los **cachivaches** *plural masc*

a
b
c
d
e
f
g
h
i
j
k
l
m
n
o
p
q
r
s
t
u
v
w
x
y
z

of preposition

1   (belonging to) **de**
the name of the flower el nombre de la flor
the end of my work el final de mi trabajo
the beginning of the concert el principio del concierto
the sixth of June el seis de junio

WORD TIP de + el becomes del.

2   (with quantities) **a kilo of tomatoes** un kilo de tomates
some of them algunos masc, algunas fem
a lot of them muchos masc, muchas fem
We ate a lot of it. Comimos mucho.
Ray has two bikes but he's selling one of them. Ray tiene dos bicicletas, pero va a vender una.

3   (about people) **a friend of mine** un amigo mío, una amiga mía
two of us dos de nosotros
There are two of us. Somos dos.

4   (saying what something is made of) **de**
a bracelet made of silver una pulsera de plata
a cup of tea una taza de té

5   (with tastes, smells) **a taste of lemons** un sabor a limones
a strong smell of fish un fuerte olor a pescado

off adjective, adverb, preposition

1   (electricity, lights) **apagado** masc, **apagada** fem
Is the telly off? ¿Está apagada la tele?
to turn off the lights apagar [28] la luz
Switch the engine off. Apaga el motor.

2   (tap, water, gas) **cerrado,** masc, **cerrada** fem
to turn off the tap cerrar [29] el grifo

3   (not at work, school) **a day off** un día libre
Caro took three days off work. Caro se tomó tres días libres en el trabajo.
Maya's off school today. Maya no ha venido al colegio hoy.
He's off sick. No ha venido al trabajo porque está enfermo.

4   (to show movement) **I'm off.** Me voy.
to take something off (to remove) quitar [17] algo
Take your books off the table. Quita los libros de la mesa.
He took his shirt off. Se quitó la camisa.

5   (down from) **It fell off the chair.** Se cayó de la silla.
He got off the train. Bajó del tren.
Don't jump off the wall! ¡No saltes del muro!

6   (cancelled) **suspendido,** fem **suspendida**
The match is off. El partido se ha suspendido.

7   (food, drink) **to be off** estar malo, fem mala
The milk's off. La leche está cortada.

offence noun

1   (crime) el **delito** masc

2   (hurt feelings) **to take offence** ofenderse [18]
He takes offence easily. Se ofende fácilmente.

offer noun ▷ see **offer** verb

1   (of help, a job) la **oferta** fem
a job offer una oferta de trabajo

2   (in a shop) **'On special offer'** 'De oferta especial'

to **offer** verb ▷ see **offer** noun

1   (a present, reward, job) **ofrecer** [35]
He offered her a coffee. Le ofreció una café.

2   **to offer to do something** ofrecerse [35] a hacer algo
Mike offered to drive me to the station. Mike se ofreció a llevarme a la estación.

office noun
la **oficina** fem
He's still in the office. Todavía está en la oficina.
He works in an office. Trabaja de oficinista.
•   **office block** el bloque de oficinas
•   **office worker** el & la oficinista

officer noun
el & la **oficial** masc & fem

official adjective
oficial masc & fem
the official version la versión oficial

off-licence noun
la **tienda de vinos y licores**

offside adverb
fuera de juego

often adverb
a menudo
He's often late. A menudo llega tarde.
I'd like to see Eric more often. Me gustaría ver a Eric más a menudo.
Do you go often? ¿Vas a menudo?
How often? ¿Con qué frecuencia?
How often do you see Rosie? ¿Con qué frecuencia ves a Rosie?

oil noun
el **aceite** masc
olive oil aceite de oliva
suntan oil aceite bronceador
Check the oil before starting the engine.

Revisa el aceite antes de encender el motor.
- **oil painting** el óleo

ointment *noun*
la **pomada** *fem*

ᵹ OK, **okay** *adjective, adverb*

1 (*showing agreement*) **vale**
OK, tomorrow at ten. Vale, mañana a las diez.

2 (*to ask or give permission*) **Is it OK to use the phone?** ¿Puedo usar el teléfono?
Is it OK with you if I come on Friday? ¿Te va bien si vengo el viernes?
It's OK if you don't want to do it. No pasa nada si no quieres hacerlo.

3 (*person*) **majo** (*informal*) *masc*, **maja** *fem*
Daisy's OK. Daisy es maja.

4 (*nothing special*) **The film was OK.** La película no estuvo mal.

5 (*not ill*) **Are you OK?** ¿Estás bien?
I'm OK now. Ahora estoy bien.

ᵹ old *adjective*

1 (*not young, not new*) **viejo** *masc*, **vieja** *fem*
an old man un hombre viejo
an old lady una señora vieja
an old friend of mine un viejo amigo mío
old people los ancianos
Bring some old clothes. Trae ropa vieja.
the oldest restaurant in town el restaurante más antiguo de la ciudad

2 (*previous*) **antiguo** *masc*, **antigua** *fem*
my old school mi antiguo colegio
their old address su antigua dirección
Her old car was a Fiat. Su antiguo coche era un Fiat.
in the old days antiguamente

3 (*to talk about age*) **How old are you?** ¿Cuántos años tienes?
James is ten years old. James tiene diez años.
a three-year-old child un niño de tres años
my older sister mi hermana mayor
She's older than me. Es mayor que yo.
He's a year older than me. Es un año mayor que yo.
- **old age** la vejez
- **old-age pensioner** el & la pensionista

old-fashioned *adjective*

1 (*clothes, music, style*) **pasado de moda** *masc*, **pasada de moda** *fem*

2 (*person*) **anticuado** *masc*, **anticuada** *fem*
My parents are so old-fashioned. Mis padres son tan anticuados.

olive *noun*
la **aceituna** *fem*
- **olive oil** el aceite de oliva
- **olive tree** el olivo

ᵢ olives

Spain is the world's leading olive producer and the average Spaniard consumes 10 litres of olive oil a year.

Olympic Games, **Olympics** *plural noun*
los **Juegos Olímpicos**

ombudsman *noun*
the ombudsman el defensor del pueblo *masc*, la defensora del pueblo *fem*

omelette *noun*
la **tortilla** *fem*
a cheese omelette una tortilla de queso

to **omit** *verb*
omitir [19]

ᵹ on *adjective* ▷ see **on** *prep*

1 (*TV, light, oven, radio*) **to be on** estar [2] encendido, *fem* encendida
All the lights were on. Todas las luces estaban encendidas.
Is the radio on? ¿Está encendida la radio?
I've put the microwave on. He encendido el microondas.
You left the tap on! ¡Dejaste abierto el grifo!

2 (*machine*) **estar en marcha**
The dishwasher's on. El lavaplatos está en marcha.

3 (*clothes*) **I put my best jeans on.** Me puse los mejores vaqueros.
What did she have on? ¿Qué llevaba puesto?
He had nothing on. Estaba desnudo.

4 (*happening*) **What's on TV?** ¿Qué ponen en la tele?
What's on this week at the cinema? ¿Qué ponen en el cine esta semana?
Is the party still on? ¿No se ha suspendido la fiesta?

5 (*continuing*) **Is the programme still on?** ¿Sigue en pie el programa?
He keeps on about his accident. No para de hablar de su accidente.

ᵹ on *preposition* ▷ see **on** *adj*

1 (*showing position*) **en**
on the desk en la mesa
on the road en la carretera
on the beach en la playa
on the left (hand side) a la izquierda
the first turn on the right la primera calle a la derecha ▸▸

2   (*in expressions of time*) **on March 21st** el 21 de marzo
on rainy days los días de lluvia
He's arriving on Tuesday. Llega el martes.
It's shut on Saturdays. Cierra los sábados.
on Monday morning el lunes por la mañana
on Thursday afternoons los jueves por la tarde
on her birthday el día de su cumpleaños

3   (*for buses, trains, etc*) **She arrived on the bus.** Llegó en autobús.
I met Jackie on the train. Me encontré con Jackie en el tren.
I slept on the plane. Dormí en el avión.
Let's go on our bikes! ¡Vayamos en las bicis!

4   (*happening*) **on TV** en la tele
on the radio en la radio
It's come out on DVD. Ha salido en DVD.

5   (*showing an activity*) **to be on holiday** estar de vacacciones
to be on strike estar [2] de huelga
I'm on the phone. Estoy hablando por teléfono.
Are you on the computer? ¿Estás usando el ordenador?

⚹ **once** *adverb*
1   (*one time*) **una vez**
once a day una vez al día
more than once más de una vez
once upon a time érase una vez
Try once more. Inténtalo una vez más.
I've tried once already. Ya lo he intentado una vez.
We've seen her once or twice. La hemos visto un par de veces.

2   (*in expressions: immediately*) **at once** inmediatamente, enseguida
The doctor came at once. El médico vino inmediatamente.
  (: *at the same time*) **at once** a la vez
I can't do two things at once. No puedo hacer dos cosas a la vez.

⚹ **one** *number* ▷ **see one** *pron*
1   (*the number*) **uno** *masc*, **una** *fem*
one apple una manzana
one son un hijo
It's one o'clock. Es la una.

2   (*only*) **único** *masc*, **única** *fem*
Sunday is my one free day. El domingo es mi único día libre.

WORD TIP *uno* becomes *un* before a masc singular noun.

⚹ **one** *pronoun* ▷ **see one** *number*
1   **uno** *masc*, **una** *fem*
one of us uno de nosotros, una de nosotras

one of my friends uno de mis amigos, una de mis amigas
One never knows. Uno nunca sabe., Una nunca sabe.
If you want a pen I've got one. Si quieres un boli yo tengo uno.

2   **this one** este *masc*, esta *fem*
I like that jumper, but this one's cheaper. Me gusta ese jersey, pero este es más barato.
Do you want this shirt or this one? ¿Quieres esta camisa o esta otra?

3   **that one** ese *masc*, esa *fem*
'Which video?'— 'That one.' '¿Qué vídeo?'— 'Ese.'

4   **that one (there)** aquel *masc*, **aquella** *fem*
'Which CD?'— 'That one.' '¿Qué CD?'— 'Aquel.'

5   **which one?** ¿cuál?
'My foot's hurting.'— 'Which one?' 'Me duele el pie.'— '¿Cuál?'
'I was talking to those boys.'— 'Which ones?' 'Estaba hablando con esos chicos.'— '¿Cuáles?'

6   **another one** otro *masc*, otra *fem*
I've already had a coffee, but I'll have another one. Ya he tomado un café pero voy a tomar otro.
I liked the tee-shirt so much that I bought another one. Me gustó tanto la camiseta que compré otra.

one's *adjective*
to wash one's hands lavarse [17] las manos
One must pay one's debts. Uno debe pagar sus deudas.

oneself *pronoun*
1   (*reflexive*) **se**
to wash oneself lavarse [17]
to hurt oneself hacerse [7] daño

2   (*for emphasis*) **uno mismo,** *fem* **una misma**
One has to do everything oneself. Hay que hacerlo todo uno mismo., Hay que hacerlo todo una misma.

⚹ **one-way street** *noun*
la **calle de sentido único**

⚹ **onion** *noun*
la **cebolla** *fem*

online, on-line *adjective, adverb*
en línea
You have to be online to download it. Tienes que estar en línea para bajarlo.
What do I have to do to go online? ¿Qué debo hacer para conectarme con Internet?

ꝺ **only** *adjective* ▷ see **only** *adv, conj*
único *masc,* **única** *fem*
the only free seat el único asiento libre
the only thing to do lo único que se puede hacer
I am an only child. Soy hijo único.

ꝺ **only** *adverb, conjunction* ▷ see **only** *adj*
1 (*with a verb*) **sólo**
They've only got two bedrooms. Sólo tienen dos habitaciones.
Anne's only free on Fridays. Anne sólo tiene libres los viernes.
There are only three left. Sólo quedan tres.
'How long did they stay?'— 'Only two days.' ¿Cuánto tiempo se quedaron?'— 'Sólo dos días.'
2 (*but*) **pero**
I'd walk, only it's raining. Iría andando, pero está lloviendo.
3 (*for emphasis*) only just: I've only just seen it. Acabo de verlo.

onto *preposition*
sobre
It fell onto the tablecloth. Cayó sobre el mantel.
She climbed onto the wall. Se subió al muro.
The band came out onto the stage. El grupo salió al escenario.

ꝺ **open** *adjective* ▷ see **open** *noun, verb*
abierto *masc,* **abierta** *fem*
The door's open. La puerta está abierta.
The baker's is open. La panadería está abierta.

ꝺ **open** *noun* ▷ see **open** *adj, verb*
in the open al aire libre

ꝺ to **open** *verb* ▷ see **open** *adj, noun*
1 (*a door, etc*) **abrir** [46]
Can you open the door for me? ¿Me puedes abrir la puerta?
Sam opened his eyes. Sam abrió los ojos.
The banks open at nine. Los bancos abren a las nueve.
2 (*by itself*) **abrirse** [46]
The door opened. La puerta se abrió.

open-air *adjective*
al aire libre
an open-air swimming pool una piscina al aire libre

opener *noun*
el **abridor** *masc*

ꝺ **opening** *noun*
1 (*space*) la **abertura** *fem*
2 (*opportunity*) la **oportunidad** *fem*

opera *noun*
la **ópera** *fem*

to **operate** *verb*
1 (*a machine*) **manejar** [17]
Can you operate a crane? ¿Sabes manejar una grúa?
This button operates the wipers. Este botón hace funcionar los limpiabrisas.
2 (*on a patient*) **operar** [17]
Will they have to operate on him? ¿Tendrán que operarlo?

operation *noun*
la **operación** *fem*
She's had an operation. La han operado.

ꝺ **opinion** *noun*
la **opinión** *fem*
in my opinion en mi opinión
• **opinion poll** la encuesta de opinión

opponent *noun*
el & la **oponente** *masc & fem*

opportunity *noun*
la **oportunidad** *fem*
to have the opportunity of doing something tener [9] la oportunidad de hacer algo
I took the opportunity to see her. Aproveché la oportunidad para verla.

opposed *adjective*
to be opposed to something oponerse [11] a algo
They are opposed to any change in the rules. Se oponen a cualquier cambio de las reglas.

ꝺ **opposite** *adjective* ▷ see **opposite** *adv, noun, prep*
1 (*direction, side, view*) **opuesto** *masc,* **opuesta** *fem*
She went off in the opposite direction. Se fue en la dirección opuesta.
2 (*facing*) **de enfrente**
in the house opposite en la casa de enfrente

ꝺ **opposite** *adverb* ▷ see **opposite** *adj, noun, prep*
enfrente
They live opposite. Viven enfrente.

ꝺ **opposite** *noun* ▷ see **opposite** *adj, adv, prep*
the opposite lo contrario
The opposite of narrow is wide. Lo contrario de estrecho es ancho.
No, quite the opposite. No, todo lo contrario.

a
b
c
d
e
f
g
h
i
j
k
l
m
n
o
p
q
r
s
t
u
v
w
x
y
z

ᵟ opposite *preposition* ▷ **see opposite** *adj,*
adv, noun
enfrente de
opposite the station enfrente de la
estación

opposition *noun*
la **oposición** *fem*

ᵟ optician *noun*
el & la **oculista** *masc & fem*
I have to go the optician's. Tengo que ir a la
óptica.

optimist *noun*
el & la **optmista** *masc & fem*
I'm an optimist. Soy optimista.

optimistic *adjective*
optimista *masc & fem*

ᵟ or *conjunction*
1 (*to show alternatives*) **o, u**
English or Spanish? ¿Inglés o español?
silver or gold plata u oro
Yesterday or today? ¿Ayer u hoy?

WORD TIP *o* is the usual translation for *or*, but
u must be used before a word starting with *o-*
or *ho-*.

2 (*when in English you say not ... or ...*) **ni ... ni ...**
not in June or July ni en junio ni en julio
I don't have a cat or a dog. No tengo ni un
gato ni un perro.
3 (*otherwise*) **si no**
Phone Mum, or she'll worry. Llama a
mamá, si no se va a preocupar.

oral *noun*
(*exam*) el **oral** *masc*
the Spanish oral el oral de español

ᵟ orange *adjective* ▷ **see orange** *noun*
naranja
my orange socks mis calcetines naranja

WORD TIP *naranja* does not change in the plural.

ᵟ orange *noun* ▷ **see orange** *adj*
1 (*the fruit*) la **naranja** *fem*
an orange juice un zumo de naranja
an orange tree un naranjo
2 (*the colour*) el **naranja** *masc*
Orange suits you. El naranja te queda bien.

orchard *noun*
el **huerto** *fem*

orchestra *noun*
la **orquesta** *fem*
a symphony orchestra una orquesta
sinfónica

ᵟ order *noun* ▷ **see order** *verb*
1 (*arrangement*) el **orden** *masc*
in the right order ordenado, *fem* ordenada
The books are in the right order. Los libros
están ordenados.
Put them in order. Ponlos en orden.
in the wrong order desordenado, *fem*
desordenada
in alphabetical order en orden alfabético
2 (*command*) la **orden** *fem*
That's an order. Es una orden.
3 (*in a restaurant, cafe*) **Can I take your orders?**
¿Les tomo la nota?
4 (*not functioning*) **'Out of order'** 'No funciona'
5 (*to show purpose*) **in order to do something**
para hacer algo
We hurried in order to be on time. Nos
dimos prisa para llegar a tiempo.

ᵟ to order *verb* ▷ **see order** *noun*
1 (*in a restaurant*) **pedir**[57]
We ordered steaks. Pedimos filetes.
2 (*in a shop*) **encargar**[23]
I ordered her new album. Encargué su
nuevo álbum.
3 (*a taxi*) **llamar**[17]
4 (*to command*) **ordenar**[17]
I order you to get out. Os ordeno que
salgáis.

ᵟ ordinary *adjective*
normal *masc & fem*
an ordinary day un día normal
I wore my ordinary clothes. Me puse la ropa
de todos los días.

organ *noun*
1 (*Music*) el **órgano** *masc*
to play the organ tocar[31] el órgano
2 (*of the body*) el **órgano** *masc*
an organ transplant un trasplante de
órgano

organic *adjective*
1 (*food*) **biológico** *masc*, **biológica** *fem*
2 (*farming*) **ecológico** *masc*, **ecológica** *fem*

organization *noun*
la **organización** *fem*

to organize *verb*
organizar[22]

ᵟ original *adjective*
original *masc & fem*
The original version was better. La versión
original era mejor.
It's a really original novel. Es una novela
realmente original.

originally *adverb*
al principio
Originally we wanted to take the car. Al
principio queríamos llevar el coche.
He's from Ireland originally. Es de origen
irlandés.

Orkneys *plural noun*
the Orkneys las Órcadas *plural fem*

ornament *noun*
el **adorno** *masc*

orphan *noun*
el **huérfano** *masc*, la **huérfana** *fem*

ℰ **other** *adjective, pronoun*
1 (*with a singular noun*) **otro** *masc*, **otra** *fem*
the other day el otro día
We took the other road. Cogimos la otra
carretera.
the other one el otro, *fem* la otra
I don't like this book, give me the other
one. No me gusta este libro, dame el otro.
As well as this book he bought one other.
Además de este libro compró otro más.
2 (*with a plural noun*) **otros** *masc*, **otras** *fem*
the other two cars los otros dos coches
He has two other brothers. Tiene otros dos
hermanos.
He has two other sisters. Tiene otras dos
hermanas.
3 (*the remainder*) the others los otros, *fem* las
otras, los demás, *fem* las demás
Where are the others? ¿Dónde están los
otros?
All the others have left. Todos los demás se
han ido.
4 (*in expressions*) somebody or other alguien
something or other algo
somewhere or other en algún sitio
every other week una semana sí y otra no

otherwise *adverb* ▷ see **otherwise** *conj*
(*in other ways*) **aparte de eso**
The flat's a bit small but otherwise it's
lovely. El piso es pequeño, pero aparte de
eso es precioso.

otherwise *conjunction* ▷ see
otherwise *adv*
(*or else*) **si no**
I'll phone home, otherwise they'll worry.
Voy a llamar a casa, si no van a
preocuparse.

ℰ **ought** *verb*
deber [18]
I ought to go now. Debería irme ahora.
They ought to know the address. Deberían
saber las señas.

You oughtn't to have any problems. No
deberías tener ningún problema.

WORD TIP *ought* is translated by the conditional
tense of *deber: debería, deberías,* etc.

ℰ **our** *adjective*
1 **nuestro** *masc*, **nuestra** *fem*
our brother nuestro hermano
our house nuestra casa
our friends nuestros amigos
our houses nuestras casas
2 (*with parts of the body, clothes*) **el, la, los, las**
We changed our clothes before going out.
Nos cambiamos de ropa antes de salir.
We got our shoes dirty. Nos ensuciamos
los zapatos.
We should wash our hands. Deberíamos
lavarnos las manos.

WORD TIP Spanish uses *el, la, los, las* for *our* with
parts of the body and clothes.

ours *pronoun*
1 (*for a singular noun*) **el nuestro** *masc*, **la
nuestra** *fem*
Their team's stronger than ours. Su equipo
es más fuerte que el nuestro.
The class next door is noisier than ours. La
clase de al lado es más ruidosa que la
nuestra.
2 (*for a plural noun*) **los nuestros** *masc*, **las
nuestras** *fem*
They brought their parents, so we had to
bring ours. Trajeron a sus padres, así que
tuvimos que traer a los nuestros.
She showed us her photos and we showed
her ours. Ella nos enseñó sus fotos y
nosotros le enseñamos las nuestras.

ourselves *pronoun*
1 (*reflexive*) **nos**
We introduced ourselves. Nos
presentamos.
We wore ourselves out playing tennis. Nos
agotamos jugando al tenis.
2 (*for emphasis*) **nosotros solos** *masc*,
nosotras solas *fem*
In the end we did it ourselves. Al final lo
hicimos nosotros solos.

ℰ **out** *adverb*
1 (*outside*) **fuera**
out in the rain bajo la lluvia
It's cold out there. Hace frío ahí fuera.
They're out in the garden. Están en el
jardín.
2 (*of a room, for the evening or day, as a couple*) to
go out salir [63]
He went out of the room. Salió de la
habitación. ▸▸

Are you going out this evening? ¿Vas a salir esta noche?

Alison's going out with Danny at the moment. Alison está saliendo ahora con Danny.

He's asked me out. Me ha pedido que salga con él.

3 (*absent*) **to be out** no estar [2]
when they were out cuando ellos no estaban
My mum's out. Mi madre no está.

4 (*light, fire*) **apagado**, *fem* **apagada**
Are all the lights out? ¿Están apagadas todas las luces?
The fire was out. El fuego estaba apagado.

5 (*to show movement*) **to drink out of a glass** beber [18] de un vaso
He threw it out of the window. Lo tiró por la ventana.
She took the photo out of her bag. Sacó la foto del bolso.
He got out of the car. Bajó del coche.

6 (*in statistics*) **out of: Four out of ten people have tried it.** Cuatro de cada diez personas lo han probado.

outing *noun*
la **excursión** *fem*
to go on an outing ir [8] de excursión

outline *noun*
(*of an object*) el **contorno** *masc*

out-of-date *adjective*
1 (*no longer valid*) **caducado** *masc*, **caducada** *fem*
My passport's out of date. Mi pasaporte está caducado.

2 (*old-fashioned*) **pasado de moda** *masc*, **pasada de moda** *fem*
He always wears such out-of-date clothes. Siempre lleva ropa tan pasada de moda.

♪ **outside** *adjective* ▷ see **outside** *adv, noun, prep*
exterior *masc & fem*

♪ **outside** *adverb* ▷ see **outside** *adj, noun, prep*
fuera
It's cold outside. Hace frío fuera.

♪ **outside** *noun* ▷ see **outside** *adj, adv, prep*
la **parte de fuera**
It's blue on the outside. La parte de fuera es azul.

♪ **outside** *preposition* ▷ see **outside** *adj, adv, noun*
fuera de
I'll meet you outside the cinema. Te veo fuera del cine.

outskirts *plural noun*
las **afueras** *plural fem*
on the outskirts of York en las afueras de York

outstanding *adjective*
excepcional *masc & fem*

oven *noun*
el **horno** *masc*
I've put it in the oven. Lo he puesto en el horno.

♪ **over** *adverb, preposition*
1 (*above*) **encima de**
There's a mirror over the sideboard. Hay un espejo encima del aparador.

2 (*to show movement*) **por encima de**
She jumped over the fence. Saltó por encima de la valla.
He threw the ball over the wall. Tiró la pelota por encima del muro.

3 (*more than*) **más de**
It will cost over a hundred pounds. Costará más de cien libras.
He's over sixty. Tiene más de sesenta años.

4 (*during*) **durante**
over the weekend durante el fin de semana
over Christmas durante las Navidades

5 (*finished*) **when the meeting's over** cuando la reunión haya acabado
It's all over now. Ahora todo ha acabado.

6 (*in expressions*) **over here** aquí
The drinks are over here. Las bebidas están aquí.
over there allí
She's over there talking to Julian. Está allí, hablando con Julián.
over the phone por teléfono
to ask someone over invitar [17] a alguien
Can you come over on Saturday? ¿Puedes venir el sábado?
all over the place por todas partes
all over the house por toda la casa

♪ **overcast** *adjective*
nublado *masc*, **nublada** *fem*

overcrowded *adjective*
abarrotado *masc*, **abarrotada** *fem*

overdose *noun*
la **sobredosis** *fem*

overdraft *noun*
el **descubierto** *masc*

a
b
c
d
e
f
g
h
i
j
k
l
m
n
o
p
q
r
s
t
u
v
w
x
y
z

to **overflow** *verb*
1 (*water*) **derramarse** [17]
2 (*river*) **desbordarse** [17]

overseas *adverb*
    en el extranjero
    Dave works overseas. Dave trabaja en el extranjero.

ᔆ to **overtake** *verb*
    (*another car*) **adelantar** [17]

ᔆ **overtime** *noun*
    las **horas extras**
    to work overtime trabajar [17] horas extras

ᔆ to **owe** *verb*
    deber [18]
    I owe Rick ten pounds. Le debo diez libras a Rick.

owing *adjective*
1 (*still to pay*) **a pagar**
    There's five pounds owing. Quedan cinco libras a pagar.
2 owing to (*because of*) **debido a**
    owing to the snow debido a la nieve

ᔆ **owl** *noun*
    el **búho** *masc*

ᔆ **own** *adjective* ▷ see **own** *verb*
1 (*to show possession*) **propio** *masc*, **propia** *fem*
    my own computer mi propio ordenador
    I've got my own room. Tengo mi propia habitación.
2 (*by yourself*) on your own solo, *fem* sola
    Annie did it on her own. Annie lo hizo sola.

WORD TIP *propio* and *propia* go before the noun.

ᔆ to **own** *verb* ▷ see **own** *adj*
    tener [9]

owner *noun*
    el **dueño** *masc*, la **dueña** *fem*

oxygen *noun*
    el **oxígeno** *masc*

oyster *noun*
    la **ostra** *fem*

ozone layer *noun*
    la **capa de ozono**

a
b
c
d
e
f
g
h
i
j
k
l
m
n
o
p
q
r
s
t
u
v
w
x
y
z

P p

Pacific *noun*
the Pacific Ocean el océano Pacífico

pack *noun* ▷ see **pack** *verb*
1 (*packet*) el **paquete** *masc*
2 (*of cards*) a pack of cards una baraja

to **pack** *verb* ▷ see **pack** *noun*
1 (*before a journey*) **hacer** [7] **las maletas**
He's already packed. Ya ha hecho la
maleta.
I'll pack my case tonight. Voy a hacer la
maleta esta noche.
2 (*breakables*) **embalar** [1]
These plates must be packed carefully. Hay
que embalar estos platos con cuidado.

package *noun*
el **paquete** *masc*
• **package holiday** el viaje organizado
• **package tour** el viaje organizado

packed lunch *noun*
la **comida preparada desde casa**

ℰ **packet** *noun*
1 (*pack*) el **paquete** *masc*
a packet of biscuits un paquete de galletas
2 (*bag*) la **bolsa** *fem*
a packet of crisps una bolsa de patatas
fritas

packing *noun*
to do your packing hacer [7] las maletas

pad *noun*
(*of paper*) el **bloc** *masc*

paddle *noun* ▷ see **paddle** *verb*
1 (*for a canoe*) **pala** *fem*
2 (*in the sea, etc*) **chapoteo** *masc*

to **paddle** *verb* ▷ see **paddle** *noun*
1 (*a canoe*) **remar** [17]
2 (*in the sea, etc*) **chapotear** [17]

padlock *noun*
el **candado** *masc*

ℰ **page** *noun*
la **página** *fem*
on page seven en la página siete

ℰ **pain** *noun*
el **dolor** *masc*
to have a pain dolerle [38] a alguien
I've got a pain in my leg. Me duele la pierna.
Where's the pain? ¿Dónde te duele?
to be a pain in the neck ser [1] un

pesado (*boy*), ser [1] una pesada (*girl*)
Kirsty's a real pain in the neck. Kirsty es una
verdadera pesada.
• **painkiller** el analgésico

paint *noun* ▷ see **paint** *verb*
la **pintura** *fem*
'Wet paint' 'Recién pintado'

to **paint** *verb* ▷ see **paint** *noun*
pintar [17]
to paint something pink pintar algo de rosa

paintbrush *noun*
1 (*artist's*) el **pincel** *masc*
2 (*for decorating*) la **brocha** *fem*

painter *noun*
el **pintor** *masc*, la **pintora** *fem*

ℰ **painting** *noun*
1 (*picture*) el **cuadro** *masc*
a painting by Monet un cuadro de Monet
2 (*activity*) la **pintura** *fem*
I prefer painting to drawing. Prefiero la
pintura al dibujo.

pair *noun*
1 (*of items, clothes*) el **par** *masc*
a pair of socks un par de calcetines
a pair of shoes un par de zapatos
a pair of jeans unos vaqueros
a pair of trousers unos pantalones
a pair of knickers unas bragas
a pair of scissors unas tijeras
2 (*of people*) la **pareja** *fem*
to work in pairs trabajar [17] en parejas

Pakistan *noun*
el **Paquistán** *masc*

Pakistani *adjective & noun*
1 **paquistaní** *masc & fem*
My grandparents are Pakistani. Mis
abuelos son paquistaníes.
2 (*person*) el & la **paquistaní** *masc & fem*
the Pakistanis los paquistaníes
My brother's married to a Pakistani. Mi
hermano está casado con una paquistaní.

WORD TIP Adjectives and nouns for nationality
and regional origin do not have capital letters in
Spanish.

palace *noun*
el **palacio** *masc*

♂ **pale** *adjective*
1 *(complexion)* **pálido** *masc*, **pálida** *fem*
   to turn pale palidecer [35]
   You look pale! ¡Estás pálida!
2 *(with colours)* **pale green** verde pálido
   pale green curtains cortinas verde pálido

> **WORD TIP** *verde pálido* and other combinations do
> not change in the plural.

palm *noun*
1 *(of your hand)* la **palma** *fem*
2 *(the tree)* la **palmera** *fem*

♂ **pamphlet** *noun*
   el **folleto** *masc*

♂ **pan** *noun*
1 *(saucepan)* la **cacerola** *fem*
   a pan of water una cacerola de agua
2 *(frying-pan)* la **sartén** *fem*

♂ **pancake** *noun*
   el **crepe** *masc*

panel *noun*
1 *(for a discussion)* el **panel** *masc*, *(for a quiz
   show)* el **equipo** *masc*
2 *(for a wall, bath)* el **panel** *masc*
· **panel game** el concurso por equipos

panic *noun* ▷ see **panic** *verb*
   el **pánico** *masc*

to **panic** *verb* ▷ see **panic** *noun*
   dejarse [17] llevar por el pánico
   Don't panic! ¡No pierdas la calma!

panties *plural noun*
   las **bragas** *plural fem*

pantomime *noun*
   la **pantomima** *fem*

pants *plural noun*
   los **calzoncillos** *plural masc*

♂ **paper** *noun*
1 *(for writing, drawing, wrapping)* el **papel** *masc*
   a sheet of paper una hoja de papel
   a paper hanky un pañuelo de papel
2 *(newspaper)* el **periódico** *masc*
   It was in the paper. Salió en el periódico.
   to do a paper round repartir [19] los
   periódicos
· **paperback** el libro de bolsillo
· **paper boy** el repartidor de periódicos
· **paperclip** el clip
· **paper girl** la repartidora de periódicos
· **paper towel** la toalla de papel

parachute *noun*
   el **paracaídas** *masc (pl: **paracaídas**)*

parade *noun*
   el **desfile** *masc*

paradise *noun*
   el **paraíso** *masc*

paragraph *noun*
   el **párrafo** *masc*
   New paragraph Punto y aparte

Paraguayan *adjective & noun*
1 **paraguayo** *masc*, **paraguaya** *fem*
2 *(person)* el **paraguayo** *masc*, la **paraguaya**
   fem
   the Paraguayans los paraguayos

> **WORD TIP** Adjectives and nouns for nationality
> and regional origin do not have capital letters in
> Spanish.

parallel *adjective*
   paralelo *masc*, **paralela** *fem*
   Our road is parallel to the High Street.
   Nuestra calle es paralela a la Calle Mayor.

Paralympics, **Paralympic Games**
   plural noun
   los **Juegos Paralímpicos**

paralysed *adjective*
   paralizado *masc*, **paralizada** *fem*

♂ **parcel** *noun*
   el **paquete** *masc*
   He's left his parcel of books behind. Se ha
   dejado el paquete de libros.

♂ **pardon** *noun*
   I beg your pardon. Perdón *(familiar form).*,
   Perdone *(polite form)*.
   Pardon? ¿Cómo dices? *(familiar form)*,
   ¿Cómo dice? *(polite form)*

♂ **parents** *plural noun*
   my parents mis padres
   a parents' evening una reunión de padres

♂ **park** *noun* ▷ see **park** *verb*
   el **parque** *masc*

♂ to **park** *verb* ▷ see **park** *noun*
1 *(person)* aparcar [31]
   You can park outside the house. Puedes
   aparcar fuera de la casa.
2 *(a car)* to park a car aparcar [31] un coche
   Where did you park the car? ¿Dónde has
   aparcado el coche?

♂ **parking** *noun*
   el **aparcamiento** *masc*
   'No parking' 'No aparcar'
· **parking meter** el parquímetro
· **parking space** el sitio para aparcar
· **parking ticket** la multa

parliament *noun*
   el **parlamento** *masc*
   the Spanish parliament las Cortes

parrot *noun*
el **loro** *masc*

parsley *noun*
el **perejil** *masc*

part *noun*
1 la **parte** *fem*
a part of the garden una parte del jardín
the last part of the concert la última parte del concierto
That's part of your job. Eso es parte de tu trabajo.
2 to take part in something participar [17] en algo
3 (*in a play*) el **papel** *masc*
4 (*for a car, machine*) la **pieza** *fem*
spare parts piezas de repuesto

particular *adjective*
particular *masc & fem*
nothing in particular nada en particular

particularly *adverb*
especialmente
not particularly interesting no especialmente interesante

partly *adverb*
en parte

partner *noun*
1 (*in a game*) la **pareja** (man or woman)
2 (*the person you live with*) el **compañero**, la **compañera**
3 (*in business*) el **socio**, la **socia**

partridge *noun*
la **perdiz** *fem*

part-time *adjective, adverb*
a tiempo parcial
part-time work trabajo a tiempo parcial
to work part-time trabajar [17] a tiempo parcial

♪ **party** *noun*
1 (*celebration*) la **fiesta** *fem*
a Christmas party una fiesta de Navidad
to have a birthday party celebrar [17] una fiesta de cumpleaños
We've been invited to a party at the Smiths' house. Estamos invitados a una fiesta en casa de los Smith.
2 (*group*) el **grupo** *masc*
a party of schoolchildren un grupo de colegiales
a rescue party un equipo de rescate
3 (*in politics*) el **partido** *masc*
the Labour Party el Partido laborista

♪ **pass** *noun* ▷ see **pass** *verb*
1 (*to let you in*) el **pase** *masc*

2 (*for bus, train travel*) el **abono** *masc*
3 (*in mountains*) el **puerto de montaña**
4 (*in an exam*) el **aprobado** *masc*
to get a pass in history sacar [31] un aprobado en historia

♪ to **pass** *verb* ▷ see **pass** *noun*
1 (*a place, building*) pasar [17] **por**
We passed your house. Pasamos por tu casa.
2 (*to overtake*) adelantar [17] **a**
We passed a bus. Adelantamos a un autobús.
3 (*to give*) pasar [17]
Could you pass me the salt please? ¿Me pasas la sal, por favor?
4 (*time*) pasar [17]
The time passed slowly. El tiempo pasaba lentamente.
5 (*in an exam*) aprobar [24]
Did you pass? ¿Aprobaste?
to pass an exam aprobar un examen

passenger *noun*
el **pasajero** *masc*, la **pasajera** *fem*

passion *noun*
la **pasión** *fem*

passionate *adjective*
apasionado *masc*, **apasionada** *fem*

passive *adjective* ▷ see **passive** *noun*
pasivo *masc*, **pasiva** *fem*

passive *noun* ▷ see **passive** *adj*
(*Grammar*) la **voz pasiva**

Passover *noun*
la **Pascua judía**

♪ **passport** *noun*
el **pasaporte** *masc*
an EU passport un pasaporte de la Unión Europea
I have to get a passport. Tengo que sacar el pasaporte.

password *noun*
la **contraseña** *fem*

♪ **past** *adjective* ▷ see **past** *adv, noun, prep*
1 (*recent*) último *masc*, última *fem*
in the past few weeks en las últimas semanas
2 (*over*) Winter is past. Ya ha pasado el invierno.

WORD TIP *último* always goes before the noun.

♪ **past** *noun* ▷ see **past** *adj, adv, prep*
(*Grammar*) el **pasado** *masc*
in the past en el pasado

♪ **past** adverb, preposition ▷ see **past** adj, noun

1 (alongside) **to go past something** pasar [17] por delante de algo
We went past the school. Pasamos por delante del colegio.
Go past the station and turn left. Pasa la estación y gira a la izquierda.
Ahmed went past in his new car. Ahmed pasó en su coche nuevo.

2 (the other side of) **más allá de**
It's just past the post office. Está un poquito más allá de la oficina de correos.

3 (to talk about the time) **ten past six** las seis y diez
half past four las cuatro y media
It's a quarter past two. Son las dos y cuarto.

♪ **pasta** noun
la **pasta** fem
I like pasta. Me gusta la pasta.

pasteurized adjective
pasteurizado masc, **pasteurizada** fem

pastry noun
la **masa** fem

patch noun
1 (of colour) la **mancha** fem
2 (for repairs) el **parche** masc

♪ **path** noun
(track) el **camino** masc, (very narrow) el **sendero** masc

patience noun
1 (calm) la **paciencia** fem
2 (card game) el **solitario** masc
to play patience hacer [7] solitarios

♪ **patient** adjective ▷ see **patient** noun
paciente masc & fem
to be patient tener [9] paciencia

♪ **patient** noun ▷ see **patient** adj
el & la **paciente** masc & fem
heart patients los enfermos del corazón

patiently adverb
pacientemente

patio noun
el **patio** masc

patrol noun
la **patrulla** fem
• **patrol car** el coche patrulla

pattern noun
1 (on wallpaper, fabric) el **diseño** masc
2 (for dressmaking) el **patrón** masc
3 (for knittting) el **modelo** masc

♪ **pavement** noun
la **acera** fem
on the pavement en la acera
a pavement cafe un café con terraza

paw noun
la **pata** fem

pawn noun
el **peón** masc

♪ **pay** noun ▷ see **pay** verb
el **sueldo** masc

♪ to **pay** verb ▷ see **pay** noun
1 **pagar** [28]
to pay cash pagar al contado
to pay by cheque pagar con cheque
to pay by credit card pagar con tarjeta de crédito
I'm paying. Pago yo.

2 **to pay for something** pagar [28] algo
Tony paid for the drinks. Tony pagó las bebidas.
It's all paid for. Todo está pagado.

3 **to pay somebody back** (money) devolverle [45] dinero a alguien

4 (attention) **to pay attention** prestar [17] atención

5 **to pay a visit to somebody** hacer [7] una visita a alguien

payment noun
el **pago** masc

pay phone noun
el **teléfono público**

PC noun
(Computers) el **PC** masc

♪ **pea** noun
el **guisante** masc
pea soup crema de guisantes

♪ **peace** noun
la **paz** fem
We went into the garden for some peace and quiet. Salimos al jardín para poder estar tranquilos.
Just leave her in peace. Déjala tranquila.

peaceful adjective
tranquilo masc, **tranquila** fem

♪ **peach** noun
el **melocotón** masc
a peach tree un melocotonero

peacock noun
el **pavo real**

a
b
c
d
e
f
g
h
i
j
k
l
m
n
o
p
q
r
s
t
u
v
w
x
y
z

peak *noun*
(*of a mountain*) el **pico** *masc*
- **peak period** la temporada alta
- **peak rate** la tarifa máxima
- **peak time** la hora punta

♪ **peanut** *noun*
el **cacahuete** *masc*
- **peanut butter** la mantequilla de cacahuete

♪ **pear** *noun*
la **pera** *fem*
a pear tree un peral

pearl *noun*
la **perla** *fem*

peasant *noun*
el **campesino** *masc*, la **campesina** *fem*

pebble *noun*
el **guijarro** *masc*

pedal *noun* ▷ see **pedal** *verb*
el **pedal** *masc*

to **pedal** *verb* ▷ see **pedal** *noun*
pedalear [17]

♪ **pedestrian** *noun*
el **peatón** *masc*, la **peatona** *fem*
- **pedestrian crossing** el paso peatonal
- **pedestrian precinct** la zona peatonal

pee *noun*
to have a pee hacer [7] pis (*informal*)

♪ **peel** *noun* ▷ see **peel** *verb*
1 (*of an apple*) la **piel** *fem*
2 (*of an orange*) la **cáscara** *fem*

♪ to **peel** *verb* ▷ see **peel** *noun*
(*fruit, vegetables*) pelar [17]

peg *noun*
(*hook*) el **gancho** *masc*
a clothes peg una pinza de la ropa
a tent peg una piqueta

pen *noun*
1 (*ballpoint*) el **bolígrafo** *masc*, el **boli** *masc* (*informal*)
2 (*fountain pen*) la **pluma** *fem*

penalty *noun*
1 (*fine*) la **multa** *fem*
2 (*in football, rugby*) el **penalty** *masc*
- **penalty area** el área de castigo

WORD TIP *área* takes *el* and *un* in the singular even though it is fem.

pence *plural noun*
los **peniques** *plural masc*

♪ **pencil** *noun*
el **lápiz** *masc*
to write in pencil escribir [52] a lápiz
You have to write in pencil. Hay que escribir a lápiz.
- **pencil case** el estuche para lápices
- **pencil sharpener** el sacapuntas

WORD TIP *sacapuntas* does not change in the plural.

pendant *noun*
el **colgante** *masc*

♪ **penfriend** *noun*
el **amigo por correspondencia**, la **amiga por correspondencia**
My Spanish penfriend is called Cristina. Mi amiga por correspondencia española se llama Cristina.

penis *noun*
el **pene** *masc*

penknife *noun*
la **navaja** *fem*

penny *noun*
el **penique** *masc*

♪ **pension** *noun*
la **pensión** *fem*
a retirement pension una pensión de jubilación

pensioner *noun*
el & la **pensionista** *masc & fem*

♪ **people** *plural noun*
1 (*when you count them*) la **persona** *fem*
ten people diez personas
several people varias personas
How many people are coming? ¿Cuántas personas van a venir?
2 (*giving a general idea*) la **gente** *fem*
The people round here are very nice. La gente de por aquí es muy simpática.
There are some bad people in the village. Hay gente mala en el pueblo.
People say he's very rich. La gente dice que es muy rico.

WORD TIP *gente* takes a singular verb.

♪ **pepper** *noun*
1 (*the spice*) la **pimienta** *fem*
2 (*the vegetable*) el **pimiento** *masc*
a green pepper un pimiento verde
- **peppermill** el molinillo de pimienta
- **pepperpot** el pimentero

peppermint *noun*
la **menta** *fem*
a peppermint tea una infusión de menta

per *preposition*
> **por**
> ten pounds per person diez libras por persona

per cent *adverb*
> **por ciento**
> sixty per cent of the students un sesenta por ciento de los estudiantes
> a hundred per cent of the applicants el cien por cien de los solicitantes

WORD TIP Spanish always has *el* or *un* before percentages.

percentage *noun*
> el **porcentaje** *masc*

percussion *noun*
> la **percusión** *fem*
> to play percussion tocar [31] la percusión

perfect *adjective*
1 (*faultless*) **perfecto** *masc*, **perfecta** *fem*
> She speaks perfect English. Habla un inglés perfecto.
2 (*ideal*) **ideal** *masc & fem*
> the perfect place for a picnic el sitio ideal para un picnic
• **perfect tense** (*Grammar*) el perfecto, el pretérito perfecto

perfectly *adverb*
> **perfectamente**

to **perform** *verb*
1 (*a piece of music, role*) **interpretar** [17]
2 (*a play*) **representar** [17]
3 (*a song*) **cantar** [17]

performance *noun*
1 (*playing, acting*) la **interpretación** *fem*
> a wonderful performance of Macbeth una maravillosa interpretación de Macbeth
2 (*a show*) el **espectáculo** *masc*
> The performance starts at eight. El espectáculo empieza a las ocho.
3 (*how well someone does*) la **actuación** *fem*

performer *noun*
> el & la **artista** *masc & fem*

ℰ **perfume** *noun*
> el **perfume** *masc*
> a bottle of perfume un frasco de perfume

ℰ **perhaps** *adverb*
> **quizás**
> Perhaps he's missed the train. Quizás ha perdido el tren.
> Perhaps it's in the drawer? ¿A lo mejor está en el cajón?

period *noun*
1 (*of time*) el **periodo** *masc*
> a two-year period un periodo de dos años
2 (*in school*) la **clase** *fem*
> a forty-five-minute period una clase de cuarenta y cinco minutos
3 (*menstruation*) la **regla** *fem*, el **periodo** *masc*
> to have your period tener [9] la regla

perm *noun*
> la **permanente** *fem*

permanent *adjective*
> **permanente** *masc & fem*

permanently *adverb*
> **permanentemente**

permission *noun*
> el **permiso** *masc*
> to get permission to do something conseguir [64] permiso para hacer algo

permit *noun* ▷ see **permit** *verb*
> el **permiso** *masc*

to **permit** *verb* ▷ see **permit** *noun*
> **permitir** [19]
> to permit somebody to do something permitir a alguien hacer algo
> Smoking is not permitted. Está prohibido fumar.
> weather permitting ... si el tiempo lo permite ...

ℰ **person** *noun*
> la **persona** *fem*
> He's a very unpleasant person. Es una persona muy antipática.
> There's room for one more person. Hay sitio para una persona más.
> She's appearing in person. Aparecerá en persona.

WORD TIP *persona* is fem, but it is used for males or females.

personal *adjective*
> **personal** *masc & fem*

personality *noun*
> la **personalidad** *fem*

personally *adverb*
> **personalmente**
> Personally, I'm against it. Personalmente, estoy en contra.

personal stereo *noun*
> el **walkman**® *masc*

perspiration *noun*
> el **sudor** *masc*

to **persuade** *verb*
convencer [44]
to persuade somebody to do something
convencer a alguien para que haga algo
Try to persuade her to come with us. Trata
de convencerla para que nos acompañe.
We persuaded Tim to wait a bit.
Convencimos a Tim para que esperara un
poco.

WORD TIP *para que* is followed by a verb in the
subjunctive.

peseta *noun*
la **peseta** *fem* (*Former Spanish currency replaced
by the euro; 500 pesetas = 3.00 euros.*)

pessimistic *adjective*
pesimista *masc & fem*

pest *noun*
1 (*insect, rodent, etc*) la **plaga** *fem*
2 (*annoying person*) el **pesado** *masc*, la **pesada**
fem

to **pester** *verb*
fastidiar [17]

pet *noun*
1 (*animal*) la **mascota**, el **animal doméstico**
a pet dog un perro de compañía
Do you have a pet? ¿Tienes mascota?
2 (*favourite person*) el **favorito** *masc*, la
favorita *fem*
Julie is teacher's pet. Julie es la favorita de la
maestra.

petal *noun*
el **pétalo** *masc*

pet name *noun*
el **apodo cariñoso**

ᔰ **petrol** *noun*
la **gasolina** *fem*
lead-free petrol gasolina sin plomo
to fill up with petrol llenar [17] el depósito
de gasolina
to run out of petrol quedarse [17] sin
gasolina
· **petrol pump** el surtidor
· **petrol station** la gasolinera
· **petrol tank** el depósito de gasolina

petticoat *noun*
la **enagua** *fem*

pharmacist *noun*
el **farmacéutico** *masc*, la **farmacéutica** *fem*

pharmacy *noun*
la **farmacia** *fem*

pheasant *noun*
el **faisán** *masc*

philosophy *noun*
la **filosofía** *fem*

ᔰ to **phone** *verb* ▷ see **phone** *noun*
1 (*person*) **llamar** [17] **por teléfono**
He arrived while I was phoning. Llegó
mientras llamaba por teléfono.
2 (*a person*) to phone somebody llamar [17] a
alguien
I'll phone you tonight. Te llamaré esta
noche.

ᔰ **phone** *noun* ▷ see **phone** *verb*
el **teléfono** *masc*
She's on the phone. Está hablando por
teléfono.
I was on the phone to Sophie. Estaba
hablando por teléfono con Sophie.
You can book by phone. Puedes reservar
por teléfono.
· **phone book** la guía telefónica
· **phone box** la cabina telefónica

phone call *noun*
la **llamada telefónica**
Phone calls are free. Las llamadas
telefónicas son gratis.
to make a phone call hacer [7] una llamada
(telefónica)

phone card *noun*
la **tarjeta telefónica**

phone number *noun*
el **número de teléfono**

photo *noun*
la **foto** *fem*
to take a photo hacer [7] una foto
I took a photo of their house. Hice una foto
de su casa.
to take a photo of somebody hacerle [7]
una foto a alguien
He took three photos of me. Me hizo tres
fotos.

photocopier *noun*
la **fotocopiadora** *fem*

photocopy *noun* ▷ see **photocopy** *verb*
la **fotocopia** *fem*

to **photocopy** *verb*
▷ see **photocopy** *noun*
fotocopiar [17]

photograph *noun*
▷ see **photograph** *verb*
la **fotografía** *fem*
to take a photograph hacer [7] una
fotografía
to take a photograph of somebody hacerle
una fotografía a alguien

I took a photograph of her. Le hice una fotografía.

to **photograph** verb
▷ see **photograph** noun
fotografiar [32]

photographer noun
el **fotógrafo** masc, la **fotógrafa** fem

photography noun
la **fotografía** fem

phrase noun
la **frase** fem
· phrase-book el manual de conversación

physical adjective
físico masc, física fem

physicist noun
el **físico** masc, la **física** fem

ℰ **physics** noun
la **física** fem
nuclear physics la física nuclear

physiotherapist noun
el & la **fisioterapeuta** masc & fem

physiotherapy noun
la **fisioterapia** fem

pianist noun
el & la **pianista** masc & fem

piano noun
el **piano** masc
a piano lesson una clase de piano
to play the piano tocar [31] el piano
Steve played it on the piano. Steve lo tocó al piano.

ℰ **pick** noun ▷ see **pick** verb
Take your pick! ¡Escoge!

ℰ to **pick** verb ▷ see **pick** noun
1 (to choose) **escoger** [3]
Pick a card. Escoge una carta.
2 (for a team) **seleccionar** [17]
I've been picked for Saturday. Me han seleccionado para el sábado.
3 (fruit) **recoger** [3]
4 (flowers) **coger** [3]
· to pick up
1 (to lift) **coger** [3]
to pick up the phone coger el teléfono
He picked up the papers and went out. Cogió los papeles y salió.
2 (from the floor) **recoger** [3]
Pick up that piece of paper. Recoge ese papel.
3 (to collect together) **recoger** [3]
I'll pick up the toys. Voy a recoger los juguetes.

4 (a person, an item) **recoger** [3]
I'll pick you up at six. Te recogeré a las seis.
He picked her up from the airport. Fue a buscarla al aeropuerto.
I'll pick up the keys tomorrow. Recogeré las llaves mañana.
5 (to learn) **aprender** [18]
You'll soon pick it up. Lo aprenderás pronto.

picnic noun
el **picnic** masc
to have a picnic hacer [7] un picnic

pickpocket noun
el & la **carterista** masc & fem

ℰ **picture** noun
1 (painting) el **cuadro** masc
a picture by Picasso un cuadro de Picasso
He painted a picture of a horse. Pintó un caballo.
2 (drawing) el **dibujo** masc
Draw me a picture of your house. Hazme un dibujo de tu casa.
3 (in a book) la **ilustración** fem
a book with lots of pictures un libro con muchas ilustraciones
4 (cinema) the pictures el cine
to go to the pictures ir [8] al cine

pie noun
1 (sweet) el **pastel** masc
an apple pie un pastel de manzana
2 (savoury) la **empanada** fem
a meat pie una empanada de carne

ℰ **piece** noun
1 (bit) el **trozo** masc
a big piece of cheese un trozo grande de queso
a piece of furniture un mueble
four pieces of luggage cuatro maletas
a piece of information un dato
That's a piece of luck! ¡Qué suerte!
2 (that you fit together) la **pieza** fem
the pieces of a jigsaw las piezas de un rompecabezas
to take something to pieces desmontar [17] algo
3 (coin) la **moneda** fem
a 50p piece una moneda de cincuenta peniques

pierced adjective
to have pierced ears tener [9] agujeros en las orejas

ℰ **pig** noun
el **cerdo** masc, la **cerda** fem

a
b
c
d
e
f
g
h
i
j
k
l
m
n
o
p
q
r
s
t
u
v
w
x
y
z

a
b
c
d
e
f
g
h
i
j
k
l
m
n
o
p
q
r
s
t
u
v
w
x
y
z

pigeon noun
  la **paloma** fem

piggy bank noun
  la **hucha** fem

pigsty noun
  la **pocilga** fem
  Your room is a pigsty. Tu habitación está hecha una pocilga.

pigtail noun
  la **trenza** fem

pile noun
1 (neat stack) la **pila** fem
  a pile of plates una pila de platos
2 (heap) el **montón** masc
  a pile of dirty shirts un montón de camisas sucias
  • to pile something up
1 (neatly) **apilar** [17] **algo**
2 (in a heap) **amontonar** [17] **algo**

pilgrimage noun
  la **peregrinación** fem
  to go on a pilgrimage irse [8] de pereginación

♪ **pill** noun
  la **pastilla** fem
  the pill (contraceptive) la píldora
  to be on the pill tomar [17] la píldora

pillow noun
  la **almohada** fem
  • pillow case el almohadón

pilot noun
  el & la **piloto** masc & fem

pimple noun
  el **grano** masc

pin noun
1 (for sewing) el **alfiler** masc
2 (on a plug) a three-pin plug un enchufe de tres clavijas
  • to pin up
1 (a hem) **prender** [18] **con alfileres**
2 (a notice) **poner** [11]

PIN noun
  (= Personal Identification Number) el **PIN** masc

pinball noun
  el **flipper** masc
  a pinball machine un flipper
  to play pinball jugar [27] al flipper

pinch noun ▷ see **pinch** verb
  el **pellizco** masc

to **pinch** verb ▷ see **pinch** noun
1 (with your fingers) to pinch somebody pellizcar [31] a alguien
2 (to steal) **mangar** [28] (informal)
  Somebody's pinched my bike. Alguien me ha robado la bici.

pine noun
  el **pino** masc
  a pine table una mesa de pino
  pine trees pinos

♪ **pineapple** noun
  la **piña** fem

pine cone noun
  la **piña** fem

ping-pong noun
  el **ping-pong** masc
  to play ping-pong jugar [27] al ping-pong

♪ **pink** adjective
  rosa
  my pink dress mi vestido rosa
  pink socks calcetines rosa

  WORD TIP rosa adj does not change in the plural.

pint noun
  la **pinta** fem

pip noun
  la **pepita** fem

pipe noun
1 (for gas, water) la **tubería** fem
2 (for smoking) la **pipa** fem
  He smokes a pipe. Fuma en pipa.

Pisces noun
1 (the star sign) el **Piscis** masc
2 (person) un & una **piscis** masc & fem
  Kirsty's Pisces. Kirsty es pisces.

  WORD TIP Use a small letter in Spanish to say I am ... etc with star signs. Star signs in Spanish are used without el, un, la, una.

pistachio noun
  el **pistacho** masc

pit noun
  el **foso** masc

♪ **pitch** noun ▷ see **pitch** verb
  el **campo** masc
  a football pitch un campo de fútbol

♪ to **pitch** verb ▷ see **pitch** noun
  to pitch a tent montar [17] una tienda

♪ **pity** noun ▷ see **pity** verb
1 (shame) la **lástima** fem
  What a pity! ¡Qué lástima!
  It would be a pity to miss the beginning. Sería una lástima perderse el principio.

2 (for a person) la **piedad** fem
to have pity on somebody tener [9] piedad de alguien
Have pity on us! ¡Ten piedad de nosotros!

♂ to **pity** verb ▷ see **pity** noun
to pity somebody compadecer [35] a alguien

♂ **pizza** noun
la **pizza** fem

♂ **place** noun ▷ see **place** verb
1 (spot, seat, destination) el **sitio** masc
in a warm place en un sitio caliente
all over the place por todos sitios
a place for the car un sitio para el coche
to change places cambiarse [17] de sitio
Will you keep my place? ¿Me guardas el sitio?
Rome is a wonderful place. Roma es un lugar maravilloso.
2 (in a race) el **lugar** masc
in first place en primer lugar
3 (home) at your place en tu casa
We'll go round to Zafir's place. Iremos a casa de Zafir.
4 (event) to take place tener [9] lugar
The competition will take place at four. La competición tendrá lugar a las cuatro.
5 (position) If I was in your place ... Si yo estuviese en tu lugar ...
• **place mat** el individual
• **place setting** el cubierto

♂ to **place** verb ▷ see **place** noun
poner [11]
He placed his cup on the table. Puso su taza en la mesa.

♂ **plain** adjective
1 (simple) **sencillo** masc, **sencilla** fem
plain cooking la cocina sencilla
2 (unflavoured) **natural** masc & fem
a plain yoghurt un yogur natural
3 (chocolate) **plain chocolate** chocolate sin leche
4 (not patterned) **liso** masc, **lisa** fem
plain curtains cortinas lisas
5 (unattractive) **poco atractivo** masc, **poco atractiva** fem

plait noun
la **trenza** fem

♂ **plan** noun ▷ see **plan** verb
1 (arrangement in advance) el **plan** masc
What are your plans for this summer? ¿Qué planes tienes para este verano?
to go according to plan salir [63] según el plan

Everything went according to plan. Todo salió según el plan.
2 (map) el **plano** masc

♂ to **plan** verb ▷ see **plan** noun
1 (to intend) **planear** [17]
Ricky's planning a trip to Italy. Ricky está planeando un viaje a Italia.
to plan to do something planear [17] hacer algo
We're planning to leave at eight. Planeamos salir a las ocho.
2 (to organize) **organizar** [22]
I'm planning my day. Estoy organizándome el día.
3 (a house, garden) **diseñar** [17]
a well-planned kitchen una cocina bien diseñada

plane noun
el **avión** masc
We went by plane. Fuimos en avión.

planet noun
el **planeta** masc

♂ **plant** noun ▷ see **plant** verb
la **planta** fem
a house plant una planta de interior
I have to water the plants. Tengo que regar las plantas.

♂ to **plant** verb ▷ see **plant** noun
plantar [17]
I've planted daffodils in these pots. He plantado narcisos en estas macetas.
They planted the fields with wheat. Plantaron los campos de trigo.

♂ **plaster** noun
1 (sticking plaster) la **tirita** fem
2 (for walls) el **yeso** masc
3 (for a broken limb) to have your leg in plaster tener [9] una pierna escayolada

plastic noun
el **plástico** masc
a plastic bag una bolsa de plástico

♂ **plate** noun
el **plato** masc
a plate of chips un plato de patatas fritas

♂ **platform** noun
1 (in a station) el **andén** masc, la **vía**
the train arriving at platform six el tren que llega al andén número seis
2 (for lecturing, performing) el **estrado** masc

a b c d e f g h i j k l m n o p q r s t u v w x y z

♂ indicates key words   581

♪ **play** *noun* ▷ see **play** *verb*

1 (*drama*) la **obra** *fem*
a play by Shakespeare una obra de Shakespeare
Our school is putting on a play. Nuestro colegio está preparando una obra.

2 (*in sports*) el **juego** *masc*
out of play fuera de juego
Play was interrupted three times. Se interrumpió el juego tres veces.

♪ to **play** *verb* ▷ see **play** *noun*

1 (*a game, sport*) **jugar** [27]
to play tennis jugar al tenis
The children were playing with a ball. Los niños estaban jugando con una pelota.
Wales play Scotland tomorrow. Gales juega mañana contra Escocia.
They were playing cards. Estaban jugando a las cartas.

2 (*music, an instrument*) **tocar** [31]
Omar plays the drums. Omar toca la batería.
They play all kinds of music. Tocan todo tipo de música.

3 (*a tape, a CD, a record*) **poner** [11]
Play me your new CD. Ponme tu nuevo compacto.

4 (*a role*) Who's playing Hamlet? ¿Quién hace el papel de Hamlet?
I'm playing the baddy. Yo represento el malo.

♪ **player** *noun*

1 (*in sport*) el **jugador** *masc*, la **jugadora** *fem*
a football player un jugador de fútbol

2 (*musician*) el **músico** *masc*, la **música** *fem*
a guitar player un guitarrista
She's a trumpet player. Es trompetista.

playground *noun*
el **patio de recreo**

♪ **playing card** *noun*
el **naipe** *masc*

playing field *noun*
el **campo de juego**

playroom *noun*
el **cuarto de los juguetes**

♪ **pleasant** *adjective*
agradable *masc & fem*
a very pleasant smell un olor muy agradable
She's not very pleasant. Es poco agradable.
Have a pleasant time! ¡Que lo pasen bien!

♪ **please** *adverb*
por favor
Two coffees, please. Dos cafés, por favor.

Could you turn the TV off, please? ¿Puedes apagar la tele, por favor?
Please may I have a clean fork? ¿Me trae un tenedor limpio, por favor?

♪ **pleased** *adjective*
contento *masc*, **contenta** *fem*
I'm very pleased. Estoy muy contento.
I was really pleased! ¡Me puse muy contento!
She was pleased with her present. Se puso muy contenta con su regalo.
Pleased to meet you! ¡Encantado de conocerte! (*boy speaking*), Encantada de conocerte! (*girl speaking*)

♪ **pleasure** *noun*

1 (*pleasant thing*) el **placer** *masc*
It's a pleasure to hear him play. Es un placer oírlo tocar.

2 (*as a polite reply*) with pleasure con mucho gusto
'Thank you very much.'— 'It's a pleasure.'
'Muchas gracias.'— 'De nada.'

plenty *pronoun*

1 (*lots*) **bastante**
He's got plenty of experience. Tiene bastante experiencia.
There's plenty of bread. Hay bastante pan.
There are plenty of cases. Hay bastantes casos.
She's got plenty of ideas. Tiene bastantes ideas.
There were plenty of them. Había bastantes.

2 (*quite enough*) **de sobra**
We've got plenty of time for a coffee. Tenemos tiempo de sobra para tomar un café.
Thank you, that's plenty! Gracias, eso es suficiente.

pliers *plural noun*
los **alicates** *plural masc*

plug *noun*

1 (*electrical*) el **enchufe** *masc*

2 (*in a bath, sink*) el **tapón** *masc*
to pull out the plug quitar [17] el tapón

• to plug something in
enchufar [17] algo

♪ **plum** *noun*
(*la*) **ciruela** *fem*
a plum tart una tarta de ciruelas
a plum tree un ciruelo

plumber *noun*
el **fontanero** *masc*, la **fontanera** *fem*
He's a plumber. Es fontanero.

plump *adjective*
regordete *masc*, **regordeta** *fem*

plural *noun*
(*Grammar*) el **plural** *masc*
in the plural en plural

plus *preposition*
más
three children plus the baby tres niños más el bebé
Two plus three equals five. Dos más tres es igual a cinco.

p.m. *adverb*
at two p.m. a las dos de la tarde
at nine p.m. a las nueve de la noche

WORD TIP Use *de la tarde* for times up to 8 p.m., and *de la noche* for times after that.

poached egg *noun*
el **huevo escalfado**

ˢ**pocket** *noun*
el **bolsillo** *masc*
She had her hands in her pockets. Tenía las manos en los bolsillos.

ˢ**pocket money** *noun*
1 (*for children*) la **paga** *fem*
2 (*for minor purchases*) el **dinero para gastos personales**

poem *noun*
el **poema** *masc*

poet *noun*
el & la **poeta** *masc & fem*

poetry *noun*
la **poesía** *fem*

ˢ**point** *noun* ▷ see **point** *verb*
1 (*in time*) el **momento** *masc*
at this point in time en este momento
At that point the police arrived. En ese momento llegó la policía.
to be on the point of doing something estar [2] a punto de hacer algo
He was on the point of leaving. Estaba a punto de marcharse.
2 (*in space*) el **punto** *masc*
the highest point on the island el punto más alto de la isla
3 (*tip*) la **punta** *fem*
the point of a nail la punta de un clavo
4 (*in games, contests, exams*) el **punto** *masc*
fifteen points to eleven quince puntos a once
5 (*subject*) el **punto** *masc*
We discussed various points. Tratamos diversos puntos.

6 (*meaning, main issue*) I don't see the point of that. No lo entiendo.
That's not the point. No se trata de eso.
7 (*purpose*) el **sentido** *masc*
What's the point of waiting? ¿Qué sentido tiene esperar?
There's no point in phoning, he's out. No tiene sentido llamar, ha salido.
8 (*argument*) That's a good point! ¡Es verdad!
She made the point that ... Observó que ...
9 (*feature*) her strong point su punto fuerte
She doesn't see his bad points. No le ve los defectos.
10 (*in decimal numbers*) **6 point 4** seis coma cuatro (*Use a comma for the decimal point, so 6.4 = 6,4*)

ˢ**to point** *verb* ▷ see **point** *noun*
señalar [17]
a notice pointing to the station un cartel señalando hacia la estación
It's rude to point. Es de mala educación señalar con el dedo.
to point at somebody señalar [17] a alguien
He pointed at one of the children. Señaló a uno de los niños.
He pointed his finger at me. Me señaló con el dedo.
• **to point out**
señalar [17]
I'll point her out to you. Te la señalaré.
James pointed out the cathedral. James señaló la catedral.
He pointed out to them that he was ill. Les señaló que estaba enfermo.

ˢ**pointless** *adjective*
(*attempt*) **vano** *masc*, **vana** *fem*
It's pointless arguing with him. No tiene sentido discutir con él.

ˢ**point of view** *noun*
el **punto de vista**
from my point of view desde mi punto de vista

poison *noun* ▷ see **poison** *verb*
el **veneno** *masc*

to poison *verb* ▷ see **poison** *noun*
envenenar [17]

poisonous *adjective*
venenoso *masc*, **venenosa** *fem*

poker *noun*
1 (*for a fire*) el **atizador** *masc*
2 (*the card game*) el **póker** *masc*

Poland *noun*
Polonia *fem*

polar bear *noun*
el **oso polar**

pole *noun*
1 *(for a tent)* el **mástil** *masc*
2 *(point of the globe)* el **polo** *masc*
the North Pole el Polo Norte

Pole *noun*
(person) un **polaco** *masc*, una **polaca** *fem*

> **WORD TIP** Adjectives and nouns for nationality and regional origin do not have capital letters in Spanish.

ꟁ **police** *plural noun*
the police la policía
The police are coming. Ya viene la policía.

> **WORD TIP** *policía* takes a singular verb.

· **police car** el coche de policía
· **policeman** el policía
· **police officer** el & la agente
· **police station** la comisaría
· **policewoman** la mujer policía

 police

Spain has three police forces; a local force for towns over 5000 inhabitants; the national force for towns over 20 000 inhabitants. The Civil Guard controls rural areas, roads, coasts and airports.

policy *noun*
1 *(plan)* la **política** *fem*
2 *(document)* la **póliza** *fem*

polish *noun* ▷ see **polish** *verb*
1 *(for furniture)* la **cera** *fem*
2 *(for shoes)* el **betún** *masc*

to **polish** *verb* ▷ see **polish** *noun*
(shoes, furniture) **sacar** [31] **brillo a**

Polish *adjective & noun*
1 **polaco** *masc*, **polaca** *fem*
2 *(the people)* the Polish los polacos
3 *(the language)* el **polaco** *masc*

> **WORD TIP** Adjectives and nouns for nationality, regional origin and language do not have capital letters in Spanish.

ꟁ **polite** *adjective*
educado *masc*, **educada** *fem*
to be polite to somebody ser [1] educado, *fem* educada con alguien
You should be more polite to your teacher. Deberías ser más educado con tu profesora.

political *adjective*
político *masc*, **política** *fem*

politician *noun*
el **político** *masc*, la **política** *fem*

politics *plural noun*
la **política** *fem*

ꟁ **polluted** *adjective*
contaminado *masc*, **contaminada** *fem*
The river is very polluted. El río está muy contaminado.

ꟁ **pollution** *noun*
la **contaminación** *fem*

polo-necked *adjective*
de cuello alto
a polo-necked sweater un jersey de cuello alto

polythene bag *noun*
la **bolsa de plástico**

ꟁ **pond** *noun*
1 *(natural)* la **laguna** *fem*
2 *(man-made)* el **estanque** *masc*

pony *noun*
el **poni** *masc*
· **ponytail** la cola de caballo

poodle *noun*
el **caniche** *masc*

pool *noun*
1 *(swimming pool)* la **piscina** *fem*
2 *(of water, blood)* el **charco** *masc*
3 *(the game)* el **billar americano**
to have a game of pool jugar [27] al billar americano
4 *(competition)* the football pools las quinielas
to do the pools hacer [7] las quinielas

ꟁ **poor** *adjective*
1 *(having little money)* **pobre** *masc & fem*
a poor area una zona pobre
a poor family una familia pobre
2 *(unfortunate)* **pobre** *masc & fem*
Poor Tanya failed her exam. La pobre Tanya suspendió el examen.
3 *(bad)* **malo** *masc*, **mala** *fem*
This is poor quality. Esto es de mala calidad.
The weather was pretty poor. El tiempo fue bastante malo.

pop *noun*
el **pop** *masc*
a pop concert un concierto de pop
a pop star una estrella del pop
a pop song una canción de pop
· **to pop into**
entrar [17] **un momento**
I'll just pop into the bank. Voy a entrar un momento en el banco.

popcorn *noun*
las **palomitas de maíz**

pope *noun*
(*Religion*) el **papa** *masc*

poppy *noun*
la **amapola** *fem*

popular *adjective*
popular *masc & fem*

population *noun*
la **población** *fem*

population

Mexico City with more than 20 million inhabitants, and growing, is the largest city in the world; its population is larger than the entire population of Australia.

porch *noun*
el **porche** *masc*

ᔑ **pork** *noun*
el **cerdo** *masc*
a pork chop una chuleta de cerdo

porridge *noun*
las **gachas** *plural fem*

ᔑ **port** *noun*
1 (*for ships*) el **puerto** *masc*
2 (*the drink*) el **oporto** *masc*

portable *adjective*
portátil *masc & fem*
a portable computer un **portátil**

porter *noun*
1 (*at a station, airport*) el **mozo de las maletas**
2 (*in a hotel*) el **portero** *masc*

portion *noun*
(*of food*) la **ración** *fem*

portrait *noun*
el **retrato** *masc*

Portugal *noun*
Portugal *masc*

Portuguese *adjective & noun*
1 **portugués** *masc*, **portuguesa** *fem*
2 (*person*) el **portugués** *masc*, la **portuguesa** *fem*
the Portuguese los portugueses
3 (*the language*) el **portugués** *masc*

WORD TIP Adjectives and nouns for nationality, regional origin and language do not have capital letters in Spanish.

posh *adjective*
elegante *masc & fem*
a posh house una casa elegante

position *noun*
la **posición** *fem*

positive *adjective*
1 (*sure*) **seguro** *masc*, **segura** *fem*
I'm positive he's left. Estoy seguro de que se ha ido.
2 (*enthusiastic*) **positivo** *masc*, **positiva** *fem*
a positive reaction una reacción muy positiva
Try to be more positive. Intenta tener una actitud más positiva.

ᔑ **possession** *noun*
1 (*ownership*) la **posesión** *fem*
She took possession of the house. Tomó posesión de la casa.
2 **possessions** (*belongings*) las pertenencias
All my possessions are in the flat. Todas mis pertenencias están en el piso.

possibility *noun*
la **posibilidad** *fem*

ᔑ **possible** *adjective*
posible *masc & fem*
if possible si es posible
It's possible. Es posible.
as quickly as possible tan rápidamente como sea posible

possibly *adverb*
1 (*maybe*) **posiblemente**
'Will you be at home at midday?'—'Possibly.' ¿Estarás en casa a mediodía?'—'Posiblemente.'
2 (*for emphasis*) How can you possibly believe that? Pero, ¿cómo puedes creerte eso?
I can't possibly arrive before Thursday. No puedo llegar antes del jueves de ninguna manera.

ᔑ to **post** *verb* ▷ see **post** *noun*
to post a letter echar [17] una carta al correo
to post something to somebody mandarle [17] algo a alguien
I'll post the books to you. Te mandaré los libros por correo.

ᔑ **post** *noun* ▷ see **post** *verb*
1 (*postal system*) el **correo** *masc*
to send something by post mandar [17] algo por correo
2 (*letters*) Is there any post for me? ¿Hay alguna carta para mí?
3 (*pole*) el **poste** *masc*
4 (*job*) el **puesto** *masc*
the post advertised in the paper el puesto anunciado en el periódico
· **postbox** el buzón
· **postcard** la postal
· **postcode** el código postal

a b c d e f g h i j k l m n o **p** q r s t u v w x y z

♂ **poster** *noun*
1 (*for decoration*) el **póster** *masc* (*pl*: **pósters**)
I've bought a Coldplay poster. He comprado un póster de Coldplay.
2 (*for advertising*) el **cartel** *masc*
I saw the poster for the concert. Vi el cartel del concierto.

♂ **postman** *noun*
el **cartero** *masc*
Pat is a postman. Pat es cartero.
Has the postman been? ¿Ha pasado el cartero?

♂ **post office** *noun*
la **oficina de correos**
He went to the post office. Fue a la oficina de correos.

to **postpone** *verb*
posponer [11]

postwoman *noun*
la **cartera** *fem*
My mother is a postwoman. Mi madre es cartera.

♂ **pot** *noun*
1 (*jar*) el **tarro** *masc*
a pot of honey un tarro de miel
2 (*teapot*) la **tetera** *fem*
I'll make a pot of tea. Voy a hacer té.
3 (*for a plant*) la **maceta** *fem*
4 (*for cooking*) the pots and pans los cacharros

♂ **potato** *noun*
la **patata** *fem*, (*Latin America*) la **papa**
fried potatoes patatas fritas
• **potato crisps** las patatas fritas de bolsa

pottery *noun*
la **cerámica** *fem*

♂ **pound** *noun*
(*money, weight*) la **libra** *fem*
fourteen pounds catorce libras
a pound of apples una libra de manzanas
How much is that in pounds? ¿Cuánto es eso en libras?

to **pour** *verb*
1 (*a liquid*) **echar** [17]
He poured the milk into the pan. Echó la leche en la cacerola.
2 (*a drink*) **servir** [57]
to pour the tea servir el té
I poured him a drink. Le serví una bebida.
3 (*to rain heavily*) **llover** [38] **a cántaros**
It's pouring with rain. Está lloviendo a cántaros.

♂ **poverty** *noun*
la **pobreza** *fem*

powder *noun*
el **polvo** *masc*

power *noun*
1 (*electricity*) la **corriente eléctrica**
2 (*energy*) la **energía** *fem*
nuclear power energía nuclear
3 (*over people*) el **poder** *masc*
to be in power estar [2] en el poder
• **power cut** el apagón

powerful *adjective*
poderoso *masc*, **poderosa** *fem*

power point *noun*
el **enchufe** *masc*

power station *noun*
la **central eléctrica**

practical *adjective*
práctico *masc*, **práctica** *fem*
• **practical joke** la broma pesada

♂ **practice** *noun*
1 (*in general*) la **práctica** *fem*
in practice en la práctica
theory and practice la teoría y la práctica
2 (*training: for sport*) el **entrenamiento** *masc*
hockey practice el entrenamiento de hockey
to be out of practice estar [2] desentrenado
3 (*training: for an instrument*) to do your piano practice hacer [7] los ejercicios de piano
Musicians must keep in practice. Los músicos tienen que practicar continuamente.
He's out of practice. Le falta práctica.

♂ to **practise** *verb*
1 (*in general*) **practicar** [31]
I went to Granada to practise my Spanish. Fui a Granada para practicar mi español.
2 (*for sport*) **entrenar** [17]
The team practises on Wednesdays. El equipo entrena los miércoles.

♂ to **praise** *verb*
elogiar [17]
to praise somebody for something elogiar [17] a alguien por algo
We praised them for their efforts. Los elogiamos por sus esfuerzos.

pram *noun*
el **cochecito de bebé**

♂ **prawn** *noun*
la **gamba** *fem*

to **pray** *verb*
rezar [22]

prayer *noun*
la **oración** *fem*

precious *adjective*
precioso *masc*, **preciosa** *fem*

precise *adjective*
preciso *masc*, **precisa** *fem*

to **predict** *verb*
predecir [5]

♂ to **prefer** *verb*
preferir [14]
I prefer coffee to tea. Prefiero el café al té.
I'd prefer to go to Paris. Preferiría ir a París.

pregnant *adjective*
embarazada *fem*

pregnancy *noun*
el **embarazo** *masc*

prejudice *noun*
el **prejuicio** *masc*
a prejudice un prejuicio
racial prejudice los prejuicios raciales

prejudiced *adjective*
to be prejudiced tener [9] prejuicios

premiere *noun*
el **estreno** *masc*

preparation *noun*
1 (*act of preparing*) la **preparación** *fem*
2 (*arrangements in advance*) los **preparativos**
the Christmas preparations los
preparativos para Navidad

♂ to **prepare** *verb*
1 (*to make ready*) **preparar** [17]
to prepare somebody for something
preparar [17] a alguien para algo
Our teacher is preparing us for the exam.
La profesora nos está preparando para el
examen.
Prepare yourself for a shock! ¡Prepárate!
2 (*food*) **preparar** [17]
She prepared a paella. Preparó una paella.
3 to prepare for something prepararse para
algo
I've got to prepare for the exam. Tengo
que prepararme para el examen.

prepared *adjective*
1 (*ready*) **preparado** *masc*, **preparado** *fem*
to be prepared for something estar [2]
preparado para algo
I wasn't prepared for the news. No estaba
preparada para la noticia.
2 (*willing*) **dispuesto** *masc*, **dispuesta** *fem*
I'm prepared to pay half. Estoy dispuesta a
pagar la mitad.

preposition *noun*
(*Grammar*) la **preposición** *fem*

♂ **pre-recorded** *adjective*
pregrabado *masc*, **pregrabada** *fem*

to **prescribe** *verb*
recetar [17]

prescription *noun*
la **receta** *fem*
on prescription con receta

♂ **present** *adjective* ▷ see **present** *verb, noun*
1 (*attending*) **presente** *masc & fem*
Is Tracy present? ¿Está presente Tracy?
to be present at something asistir [19] a
algo
Fifty people were present at the funeral.
Cincuenta personas asistieron al funeral.
2 (*current*) **actual** *masc & fem*
the present situation la situación actual
at the present time en este momento

♂ **present** *noun* ▷ see **present** *adj, verb*
1 (*gift*) el **regalo** *masc*
to give somebody a present hacerle [17] un
regalo a alguien
He gave Laura a present. A Laura le hizo un
regalo.
2 (*the current time*) el **presente** *masc*
That's all for the present. Eso es todo por
ahora.
3 (*Grammar*) el **presente** *masc*
in the present (tense) en presente

♂ to **present** *verb* ▷ see **present** *adj, noun*
1 (*to hand over*) **entregar** [28]
to present something to somebody
entregarle algo a alguien
The headteacher will present the prize to
her. El director le entregará el premio.
2 (*a TV programme*) **presentar** [17]

presenter *noun*
(*on TV*) el **presentador** *masc*, la
presentadora *fem*

♂ **president** *noun*
el **presidente** *masc*, la **presidenta** *fem*

to **press** *verb* ▷ see **press** *noun*
1 (*a button, doorbell*) **pulsar** [1]
She pressed the button. Pulsó el botón.
2 (*to push*) **empujar** [17]
Press here to open. Para abrir, empuje aquí.

press *noun* ▷ see **press** *verb*
the press la prensa
• **press conference** la rueda de prensa

a
b
c
d
e
f
g
h
i
j
k
l
m
n
o
p
q
r
s
t
u
v
w
x
y
z

pressure noun
la **presión** fem
- **pressure gauge** el manómetro
- **pressure group** el grupo de presión

to **pretend** verb
fingir [49]
to pretend to do something fingir hacer algo
He's pretending not to hear. Está fingiendo no oír.

ƒ **pretty** adjective ▷ see **pretty** adv
bonito masc, **bonita** fem
a pretty dress un vestido bonito

ƒ **pretty** adverb ▷ see **pretty** adj
bastante masc & fem
It was pretty embarrassing. Fue bastante vergonzoso.

to **prevent** verb
1 (a crime, an accident) **prevenir** [15]
2 (a war, disaster) **evitar** [17]
3 to prevent somebody from doing something impedir [57] a alguien hacer algo
There's nothing to prevent you from leaving. No hay nada que te impida irte.

previous adjective
anterior masc & fem
the previous day el día anterior

previously adverb
antes

ƒ **price** noun
el **precio** masc
the price per kilo el precio por kilo
CDs have gone up in price. Los compactos han subido de precio.
- **price list** la lista de precios
- **price ticket** la etiqueta del precio

pride noun
el **orgullo** masc

priest, noun
el **sacerdote** masc

ƒ **primary school** noun
la **escuela primaria**
- **primary school teacher** el maestro, la maestra

ƒ **prime minister** noun
el **primer ministro** masc, la **primera ministra** fem

prince noun
el **príncipe** masc
Prince Charles el príncipe Carlos

princess noun
la **princesa** fem
Princess Anne la Princesa Ana

ƒ **principal** adjective ▷ see **principal** noun
principal masc & fem

ƒ **principal** noun ▷ see **principal** adj
el **director** masc, la **directora** fem

print noun
1 (on a page) la **letra** fem
in small print en letra pequeña
2 (photo) la **copia** fem
a colour print una copia a color

ƒ **printer** noun
(machine) la **impresora** fem

print-out noun
la **copia en papel**

prison noun
la **cárcel** fem
in prison en la cárcel

prisoner noun
el **preso** masc, la **presa** fem

ƒ **private** adjective
1 (not public) **privado** masc, **privada** fem
in private en privado
a private school una escuela privada
'Private property' 'Propiedad privada'
2 (lesson) **particular** masc & fem
to have private lessons tener [9] clases particulares

privilege noun
el **privilegio** masc

ƒ **prize** noun
el **premio** masc
the prize for the best athlete el premio al mejor atleta
to win a prize ganar [17] un premio
- **prize-giving** la entrega de premios
- **prizewinner** el ganador, la ganadora

ƒ **probable** adjective
probable masc & fem
the most probable explanation la explicación más probable
It's probable that it will rain. Es probable que llueva.

probably adverb
probablemente

ƒ **problem** noun
el **problema** masc
It's a serious problem. Es un problema grave.
She has a weight problem. Tiene problemas con el peso.
No problem! ¡No hay problema!

procession noun
1 (parade) el **desfile** masc
2 (at a religious festival) la **procesión** fem

produce noun ▷ see **produce** verb
  los **productos** plural masc

to **produce** verb ▷ see **produce** noun
1 (to give out) **producir** [60]
  It produces a lot of heat. Produce mucho calor.
2 (to show) **presentar** [17]
  I produced my passport. Presenté mi pasaporte.

producer noun
  el **productor** masc, la **productora** fem

♂ **product** noun
  el **producto** masc
  dairy products productos lácteos

production noun
1 (of a film) la **producción** fem
2 (of a play, an opera) la **puesta en escena**
  a new production of Hamlet una nueva puesta en escena de Hamlet
3 (by a factory) la **producción** fem

profession noun
  la **profesión** fem

professional adjective
  ▷ see **professional** noun
  profesional masc & fem
  She's a professional singer. Es cantante profesional.

professional noun
  ▷ see **professional** adj
  el & la **profesional** masc & fem
  He's a professional. Es un profesional.

professor noun
  el **catedrático** masc, la **catedrática** fem

profit noun
  los **beneficios** plural masc

profitable adjective
  rentable masc & fem

♂ **program** noun ▷ see **programme** noun
  (Computers) el **programa**
  a computer program un programa de ordenador
  You can download the program from the website. Puedes bajar el programa del sitio web.

♂ **programme** noun ▷ see **program** noun
  el **programa** masc
  What's your programme for tomorrow? ¿Qué programa tienes para mañana?

programmer noun
  el **programador** masc, la **programadora** fem

progress noun
1 el **progreso** masc
  to make progress (in your work) hacer [7] progresos
2 to be in progress estar [2] en curso

project noun
1 (at school) el **trabajo** masc
2 (plan) el **proyecto** masc
  a project to build a bridge un proyecto para construir un puente

projector noun
  el **proyector** masc

promise noun ▷ see **promise** verb
  la **promesa** fem
  to make a promise hacer [7] una promesa
  to break a promise no cumplir [19] con una promesa
  It's a promise! ¡Lo prometo!

to **promise** verb ▷ see **promise** noun
  to promise to do something prometer [18] hacer algo
  I've promised to be home by ten. He prometido estar en casa a las diez.

to **promote** verb
  ascender [36]
  She's been promoted. La han ascendido.

♂ **promotion** noun
1 (at work) el **ascenso** masc
2 (special offer) la **promoción** fem

prompt adjective
  pronto masc, **pronta** fem
  a prompt reply una pronta respuesta

pronoun noun
  (Grammar) el **pronombre** masc

♂ to **pronounce** verb
  pronunciar [17]
  It's hard to pronounce. Es difícil de pronunciar.
  How do you pronounce it? ¿Cómo se pronuncia?

pronunciation noun
  la **pronunciación** fem

proof noun
  las **pruebas** plural fem
  They've got proof. Tienen pruebas.
  There's no proof. No hay pruebas.

a
b
c
d
e
f
g
h
i
j
k
l
m
n
o
p
q
r
s
t
u
v
w
x
y
z

propaganda noun
la **propaganda** fem

propeller noun
la **hélice** fem

proper adjective
1 (real, genuine) **de verdad**
a proper doctor un médico titulado
I need a proper meal. Necesito una comida de verdad.
2 (correct) **adecuado** masc, **adecuada** fem
the proper tool la herramienta adecuada
Leave it in its proper place. Déjalo en su sitio.

properly adverb
bien
Hold it properly. Sujétalo bien.
Is it properly wrapped? ¿Está bien envuelto?

property noun
la **propiedad** fem
'Private property' 'Propiedad privada'

to **propose** verb
1 (to suggest) **proponer** [11]
2 (in engagements) He proposed to her. Le pidió que se casara con él.

prostitute noun
la **prostituta** fem

to **protect** verb
proteger [3]

protection noun
la **protección** fem

protein noun
la **proteína** fem

protest noun ▷ see **protest** verb
la **protesta** fem
in spite of their protests a pesar de sus protestas

to **protest** verb ▷ see **protest** noun
1 (to grumble) **protestar** [17]
He protested about the noise. Protestó por el ruido.
2 (to demonstrate) **manifestarse** [29]

Protestant adjective & noun
1 **protestante** masc & fem
2 el & la **protestante** masc & fem

WORD TIP Adjectives and nouns for religion do not have capital letters in Spanish.

protester noun
el & la **manifestante** masc & fem

protest march noun
la **manifestación** fem

proud adjective
orgulloso masc, **orgullosa** fem
I'm very proud of you. Estoy muy orgullosa de vosotros.

to **prove** verb
probar [24]

proverb noun
el **refrán** masc

to **provide** verb
proveer [37]
They've provided us with food. Nos han provisto de comida.

provided conjunction
siempre que
provided you do it siempre que tú lo hagas

WORD TIP siempre que is followed by a verb in the subjunctive.

province noun
la **provincia** fem

♂ **prune** noun
la **ciruela pasa**

PS abbreviation
(at the end of a letter) **PD**

psychiatrist noun
el & la **psiquiatra** masc & fem
He's a psychiatrist. Es psiquiatra.

psychological adjective
psicológico masc, **psicológica** fem

psychologist noun
el **psicólogo** masc, la **psicóloga** fem
She's a psychologist. Es psicóloga.

psychology noun
la **psicología** fem

PTO abbreviation
(= Please Turn Over) **sigue al dorso**

pub noun
el **bar** masc

♂ **public** adjective ▷ see **public** noun
público masc, **pública** fem
the public library la biblioteca pública
• **public address system** el sistema de megafonía

ꟼ **public** *noun* ▷ see **public** *adj*
   the public el público
   in public en público
   It's open to the public at weekends. Está abierto al público los fines de semana.

ꟼ **public holiday** *noun*
   el **día de fiesta**
   The first of January is a public holiday. El uno de enero es fiesta.

publicity *noun*
   la **publicidad** *fem*

public school *noun*
   el **colegio privado**

public transport *noun*
   el **transporte público**

to **publish** *verb*
   publicar [31]

publisher *noun*
1 (*person*) el **editor** *masc*, la **editora** *fem*
2 (*company*) la **editorial** *fem*

ꟼ **pudding** *noun*
   (*dessert*) el **postre** *masc*
   For pudding we've got strawberries. De postre tenemos fresas.

puddle *noun*
   el **charco** *masc*

Puerto Rican *adjective & noun*
1 **puertorriqueño** *masc*, **puertorriqueña** *fem*
2 (*person*) el **puertorriqueño** *masc*, la **puertorriqueña** *fem*
   the Puerto Ricans los puertorriqueños

WORD TIP Adjectives, and nouns for nationality and regional origin do not have capital letters in Spanish.

puff pastry *noun*
   el **hojaldre** *masc*

to **pull** *verb*
   tirar [17]
   to pull a rope tirar de una cuerda
   Pull hard! ¡Tira fuerte!
• **to pull down**
   (*a blind*) **bajar** [17]
• **to pull in**
   (*at the roadside*) **parar** [17]
• **to pull something out**
   sacar [31] **algo**
   He pulled a letter out of his pocket. Sacó una carta del bolsillo.

ꟼ **pullover** *noun*
   el **jersey** *masc*
   a wool pullover un jersey de lana

pulse *noun*
   el **pulso** *masc*
   The doctor took my pulse. El médico me tomó el pulso.

pump *noun* ▷ see **pump** *verb*
   la **bomba** *fem*
   a bicycle pump una bomba de bicicleta

to **pump** *verb* ▷ see **pump** *noun*
   (*oil, water*) **bombear** [17]
   They were pumping the water out of the cellar. Estaban bombeando el agua del sótano.
• **to pump up**
   (*a tyre*) **inflar** [17]

punch *noun* ▷ see **punch** *verb*
1 (*in boxing*) el **puñetazo** *masc*
2 (*the drink*) el **ponche** *masc*

to **punch** *verb* ▷ see **punch** *noun*
1 (*a person*) to punch somebody darle [4] un puñetazo a alguien
   He punched me. Me dio un puñetazo.
2 (*a ticket*) **picar** [31]

punctual *adjective*
   puntual *masc & fem*

punctuation *noun*
   la **puntuación** *fem*
• **punctuation mark** el signo de puntuación

puncture *noun*
   el **pinchazo** *masc*
   We had a puncture. Tuvimos un pinchazo.

to **punish** *verb*
   castigar [28]

punishment *noun*
   el **castigo** *masc*

ꟼ **pupil** *noun*
1 (*in a school*) el **alumno** *masc*, la **alumna** *fem*
2 (*of your eye*) la **pupila** *fem*

puppet *noun*
   el **títere** *masc*

puppy *noun*
   el **cachorro** *masc*, la **cachorra** *fem*
   a labrador puppy un cachorro de labrador

ꟼ to **purchase** *verb*
   comprar [17]
   to purchase something from somebody comprarle algo a alguien

a
b
c
d
e
f
g
h
i
j
k
l
m
n
o
p
q
r
s
t
u
v
w
x
y
z

pure *adjective*
   puro *masc*, **pura** *fem*

ᔰ **purple** *adjective*
   morado *masc*, **morada** *fem*
   a purple tee-shirt una camiseta morada

purpose *noun*
1 (*reason*) el **propósito** *masc*
   What was the purpose of her call? ¿Qué
   propósito tenía su llamada?
2 on purpose a propósito
   She did it on purpose. Lo hizo a propósito.

to **purr** *verb*
   ronronear [17]

ᔰ **purse** *noun*
   el **monedero** *masc*
   I'm always forgetting my purse. Siempre
   me olvido del monedero.

ᔰ **push** *noun* ▷ see **push** *verb*
   el **empujón** *masc*
   to give something a push dar [4] un
   empujón a algo
• **pushchair** la sillita de niño

ᔰ to **push** *verb* ▷ see **push** *noun*
1 (*to shove*) **empujar** [17]
   He pushed me. Me empujó.
   Stop pushing! ¡Deja de empujar!
2 (*a bell, button*) **apretar** [29]
• **to push something away**
   apartar [17] **algo**
   She pushed her plate away. Apartó su
   plato.

ᔰ to **put** *verb*
1 (*to place*) **poner** [11]
   You can put it in the fridge. Puedes ponerlo
   en la nevera.
   Where did you put my bag? ¿Dónde has
   puesto mi bolso?
   Put your suitcase here. Pon tu maleta
   aquí.
   Put your address here. Pon tus señas
   aquí.
2 (*to put inside*) **meter** [18]
   I put it in the drawer. Lo metí en el cajón.
• **to put away**
   guardar [17]
   I'll put the shopping away. Voy a guardar la
   compra.
• **to put back**
   volver [45] **a poner**
   He put it back in the wardrobe. Lo volvió a
   poner en el armario.
• **to put down**
   poner [11]
   She put the vase down on the table. Puso el
   jarrón en la mesa.

• **to put off**
1 (*to postpone*) **aplazar** [22]
   He put off my lesson till Thursday. Aplazó
   mi clase hasta el jueves.
2 (*to turn you against*) It put me off Chinese
   food! ¡Hizo que se me quitaran las ganas de
   tomar comida china!
   Don't be put off! ¡No te desanimes!
• **to put on**
1 (*clothing, make-up*) **ponerse** [11]
   I'll just put my shoes on. Voy a ponerme los
   zapatos.
2 (*lights, heating*) **encender** [36]
   Could you put the lamp on? ¿Puedes
   encender la lámpara?
3 (*the TV, radio*) **poner** [11]
   Shall we put on the telly? ¿Ponemos la tele?
   Don't put on Oasis again. No vuelvas a
   poner a Oasis.
4 (*a play*) **montar** [17]
   We're putting on a Spanish play. Estamos
   montando una obra española.
• **to put out**
1 (*to put outside*) **sacar** [31]
   Put the rubbish out. Saca la basura.
2 (*a light, a fire, a cigarette*) **apagar** [28]
   She put the lights out. Apagó las luces.
3 (*part of your body*) to put out your hand
   extender [36] la mano
• **to put through**
   pasar [17] **con**
   I'll put you through to the manager. Le
   paso con el gerente.
• **to put up**
1 (*your hand*) **levantar** [17]
   He put up his hand. Levantó la mano.
2 (*a picture*) **poner** [11]
   I've put up some photos in my room. He
   puesto algunas fotos en mi habitacion.
3 (*a notice*) **colgar** [23]
4 (*the price*) **subir** [19]
   They've put up the price of the tickets. Han
   subido el precio de las entradas.
5 (*for the night*) Can you put me up on Friday?
   ¿Puedo quedarme a dormir en tu casa el
   viernes?
• **to put up with something**
   aguantar [17] **algo**
   I don't know how she puts up with it. No sé
   cómo lo aguanta.

a b c d e f g h i j k l m n o **p** q r s t u v w x y z

puzzle *noun*
el **rompecabezas** *masc*, el **puzzle** *masc*

WORD TIP *rompecabezas* does not change in the plural.

puzzled *adjective*
confuso *masc*, **confusa** *fem*

♂ **pyjamas** *plural noun*
el **pijama** *masc*
a pair of pyjamas un pijama

Where are my pyjamas? ¿Dónde está mi pijama?

pylon *noun*
la **torre de alta tensión**

pyramid *noun*
la **pirámide**

Pyrenees *noun*
the Pyrenees los Pirineos (*The mountains between Spain and France.*)

Q q

quail *noun*
la **codorniz** *fem*

qualification *noun*
1 (*certificate, degree, etc*) el **título** *masc*
2 **qualifications** la titulación *fem*
vocational qualifications la titulación profesional

qualified *adjective*
1 (*as a teacher*) **cualificado** *masc*, **cualificada** *fem*
She's a qualified ski instructor. Es una monitora de esquí cualificada.
2 (*having a degree, diploma*) **titulado** *masc*, **titulada** *fem*
a qualified architect un arquitecto titulado

to **qualify** *verb*
1 (*in sport*) **clasificarse** [31]
They've qualified for the quarter finals. Se han clasificado para los cuartos de final.
2 **to qualify for a benefit** tener [9] derecho a un beneficio
We qualify for a reduction. Tenemos derecho a una reducción.

quality *noun*
la **calidad** *fem*
good quality jeans vaqueros de buena calidad
a poor quality recording una grabación de calidad inferior

quantity *noun*
la **cantidad** *fem*

quarantine *noun*
la **cuarentena** *fem*

quarrel *noun* ▷ see **quarrel** *verb*
la **pelea** *fem*
to have a quarrel tener [9] una pelea

to **quarrel** *verb* ▷ see **quarrel** *noun*
pelearse [17]
They're always quarrelling. Siempre se están peleando.

quarry *noun*
la **cantera** *fem*

♪ **quarter** *noun*
1 (*fraction*) la **cuarta parte** *fem*
a quarter of the class una cuarta parte de la clase
three quarters of the class las tres cuartas partes de la clase

2 (*when telling the time*) el **cuarto** *masc*
a quarter past ten las diez y cuarto
a quarter to ten las diez menos cuarto
at a quarter to one a la una menos cuarto
a quarter of an hour un cuarto de hora
three quarters of an hour tres cuartos de hora
an hour and a quarter una hora y cuarto
3 (*with weights, measures*) **a quarter of a kilo** un cuarto de kilo
three quarters of a litre tres cuartos de litro
• **quarter finals** los cuartos de final

quartet *noun*
el **cuarteto** *masc*
a jazz quartet un cuarteto de jazz

quay *noun*
el **muelle** *masc*

♪ **queen** *noun*
la **reina** *fem*
Queen Elizabeth la reina Isabel
the Queen of Spain la reina de España

query *noun*
la **pregunta** *fem*
Do you have any queries? ¿Hay alguna duda?

♪ to **question** *verb* ▷ see **question** *noun*
interrogar [28]
She was questioned about her business interests. La interrogaron acerca de sus negocios.

♪ **question** *noun* ▷ see **question** *verb*
1 (*when you ask*) la **pregunta** *fem*
to ask a question hacer [7] una pregunta
I asked her a question. Le hice una pregunta.
He didn't answer my question. No contestó a mi pregunta.
2 (*problem*) la **cuestión** *fem*
the question of his frequent absences la cuestión de sus frecuentes faltas de asistencia
It's a question of time. Es cuestión de tiempo.
It's out of the question! ¡Bajo ningún concepto!
• **question mark** el signo de interrogación

questionnaire *noun*
el **cuestionario** *masc*
to fill in a questionnaire rellenar [17] un cuestionario

queue *noun* ▷ see **queue** *verb*
1 (*of people*) la **cola** *fem*
  to stand in a queue estar [2] en la cola
2 (*of cars*) la **fila** *fem*

to **queue** *verb* ▷ see **queue** *noun*
  hacer [7] **cola**
  We were queueing for hours. Estábamos
  haciendo cola durante horas.

ᵹ **quick** *adjective*
  rápido *masc*, **rápida** *fem*
  a quick lunch una comida rápida
  It's quicker by motorway. Es más rápido
  por la autopista.
  to have a quick look at something echarle
  [17] un vistazo rápido a algo
  Quick! there's the bus! ¡De prisa, que viene
  el autobús!
  Be quick! ¡Date prisa!

quickly *adverb*
  rápidamente
  I'll just quickly phone my mother. Voy a
  llamar rápidamente a mi madre.

ᵹ **quiet** *adjective*
1 (*person, machine*) **silencioso** *masc*,
  silenciosa *fem*
  a quiet engine un motor silencioso
  The children are very quiet. Los niños están
  muy silenciosos.
  to keep quiet no hablar [17]
  Please keep quiet. Por favor, no hablen.
2 (*music, voice*) **suave**
  some quiet music una música suave
  in a quiet voice en voz baja
3 (*neighbourhood*) **tranquilo** *masc*, **tranquila**
  fem
  a quiet street una calle tranquila
  We had a quiet day at home. Pasamos un
  día tranquilo en casa.

quietly *adverb*
1 (*to move*) **sin hacer ruido**
  He got up quietly. Se levantó sin hacer
  ruido.

2 (*to speak*) **en voz baja**
3 (*to read, play*) **en silencio**

quilt *noun*
  el **edredón** *masc*
  a continental quilt un edredón nórdico

ᵹ **quite** *adverb*
1 **bastante**
  quite often bastante a menudo
  It's quite cold outside. Hace bastante frío
  fuera.
  That's quite a good idea. Es una idea
  bastante buena.
  He sings quite well. Canta bastante bien.
2 **not quite** no … todavía
  The meat's not quite cooked. La carne no
  está hecha todavía.
  'Was it like this?'—'Not quite.' '¿Era así?'—
  'No exactamente.'
3 **quite a …** bastante
  quite a lot of money bastante dinero
  quite a few people bastante gente
  I have quite a lot of friends here. Tengo
  bastantes amigos aquí.

quiz *noun*
  el **concurso** *masc*

quotation *noun*
  la **cita** *fem*

quotation marks *plural noun*
  (*Grammar*) las **comillas** *plural fem*
  in quotation marks entre comillas

quote *noun* ▷ see **quote** *verb*
1 (*from a book, speech*) la **cita** *fem*
2 (*for work*) el **presupuesto** *masc*
  We asked the builder for a quote. Le
  pedimos un presupuesto al contratista.
3 (*in text*) **in quotes** entre comillas

to **quote** *verb* ▷ see **quote** *noun*
  citar [17]

a
b
c
d
e
f
g
h
i
j
k
l
m
n
o
p
q
r
s
t
u
v
w
x
y
z

R r

rabbi *noun*
  el **rabino** *masc*, la **rabina** *fem*

♂ **rabbit** *noun*
  el **conejo** *masc*

race *noun*
  1 (*sports event*) la **carrera** *fem*
  a cycle race una carrera de bicicletas
  to have a race echar[17] una carrera
  2 (*ethnic group*) la **raza** *fem*

racer *noun*
  (*bike*) la **bicicleta de carreras**

racetrack *noun*
  1 (*for horses*) la **pista de carreras**
  2 (*for cars*) el **circuito** *masc*
  3 (*for cycles*) el **velódromo** *masc*

racing *noun*
  las **carreras** *plural fem*
  · **racing car** el coche de carreras
  · **racing driver** el & la piloto de carreras

racial *adjective*
  racial *masc & fem*
  racial discrimination discriminación racial

racism *noun*
  el **racismo** *masc*

racist *adjective* ▷ see **racist** *noun*
  racista *masc & fem*

racist *noun* ▷ see **racist** *adj*
  el & la **racista** *masc & fem*

racket *noun*
  1 (*for tennis*) la **raqueta** *fem*
  2 (*noise*) el **jaleo** *masc*
  What a racket! ¡Qué jaleo!

radar *noun*
  el **radar** *masc*

radiator *noun*
  el **radiador** *masc*

♂ **radio** *noun*
  la **radio** *fem*
  to listen to the radio escuchar[17] la radio
  to hear something on the radio oír[56] algo en la radio
  · **radio station** la emisora de radio

radish *noun*
  el **rabanito** *masc*

radius *noun*
  el **radio** *masc*

raffle *noun*
  la **rifa** *fem*

raft *noun*
  la **balsa** *fem*

rag *noun*
  el **trapo** *masc*

rage *noun*
  la **furia** *fem*
  He went red with rage. Se puso rojo de furia.
  She's in a rage. Está furiosa.

rail *noun*
  1 (*railway*) **to go by rail** ir[8] en tren
  2 (*on a balcony, bridge*) la **baranda** *fem*
  3 (*on stairs*) el **pasamanos** *masc, pl:* los pasamanos
  4 (*for a train*) el **raíl** *masc*

railings *plural noun*
  la **verja** *fem*

♂ **railway** *noun*
  1 (*transport system*) el **ferrocarril** *masc*
  the railways los ferrocarriles
  2 (*track*) la **vía férrea**
  They were playing on the railway. Estaban jugando en la vía férrea.
  · **railway carriage** el vagón de tren

railway line *noun*
  1 (*track*) la **vía férrea**
  2 (*route*) la **línea de ferrocarril**

railway station *noun*
  la **estación de trenes**
  opposite the railway station enfrente de la estación de trenes

♂ **rain** *noun* ▷ see **rain** *verb*
  la **lluvia** *fem*
  I went out in the rain. Salí cuando llovía.
  We were caught in the rain Nos cogió la lluvia.
  It looks like rain. Parece que va a llover.

♂ **to rain** *verb* ▷ see **rain** *noun*
  llover[38]
  It's raining. Está lloviendo.
  It's going to rain. Va a llover.
  · **rainbow** el arco iris
  · **raincoat** el impermeable
  · **rainfall** las precipitaciones

♂ **rainy** *adjective*
  lluvioso *masc*, **lluviosa** *fem*

to raise *verb*

1 (*to lift up*) **levantar**[17]
  She raised her head. Levantó la cabeza.

2 (*prices, salaries*) **subir**[19]

3 (*some money*) **recaudar**[17]
  to raise money for something recaudar dinero para algo

4 (*the standards*) **mejorar**[17]

5 (*a child, family*) **criar**[17]

raisin *noun*
  la **pasa** *fem*

rally *noun*

1 (*meeting*) la **concentración** *fem*

2 (*sports event*) el **rally** *masc, pl:* los **rallys**

3 (*in tennis*) el **peloteo** *masc*

rambler *noun*
  el & la **excursionista** *masc & fem*

rambling *noun*
  to go rambling **ir**[8] de excursión

ramp *noun*
  (*for a wheelchair*) la **rampa** *fem*

range *noun*

1 (*choice*) la **gama** *fem*
  a wide range of colours una amplia gama de colores

2 (*of mountains*) la **cordillera** *fem*

rap *noun*

1 (*knock on a door*) el **golpe** *masc*

2 (*music*) el **rap** *masc*

rape *noun* ▷ see **rape** *verb*
  la **violación** *fem*

to rape *verb* ▷ see **rape** *noun*
  violar[17]

♂ **rare** *adjective*

1 (*not common*) **poco común** *masc & fem*
  a rare bird un pájaro poco común

2 (*steak*) **poco hecho** *masc,* **poco hecha** *fem*
  a rare steak un filete poco hecho

♂ **raspberry** *noun*
  la **frambuesa** *fem*
  raspberry jam mermelada de frambuesa
  a raspberry tart una tarta de frambuesas

rat *noun*
  la **rata** *fem*

♂ **rate** *noun*

1 (*speed*) el **ritmo** *masc*
  I read at a rate of 100 pages a day. Leo a un ritmo de cien páginas por día.
  at this rate a este paso
  at any rate en todo caso

2 (*level*) el **índice** *masc*
  the birth rate el índice de natalidad
  rate of interest tipo de interés

3 (*charge*) la **tarifa** *fem*
  reduced rates tarifas reducidas
  What are the rates for children? ¿Cuáles son las tarifas para niños?

rather *adverb*

1 (*somewhat*) **bastante**
  I'm rather busy. Estoy bastante ocupado.
  rather a lot of bastante
  I've got rather a lot of work. Tengo bastante trabajo.
  There are rather a lot of mistakes. Hay bastantes errores.

2 (*showing a preference*) **I'd rather wait.** Preferiría esperar.
  I'd rather walk than go by bus. Prefiero andar a ir en autobús.
  I'd rather not think about that. Prefiero no pensar en eso.

3 (*in expressions*) **rather than** en vez de
  We went to Spain rather than France. Fuimos a España en vez de Francia.
  in summer rather than winter en verano más que en invierno

raw *adjective*
  crudo *masc,* **cruda** *fem*

ray *noun*
  el **rayo** *masc*

razor *noun*
  (*safety razor*) la **máquina de afeitar**
  • **razor blade** la cuchilla

RE *noun*
  (= *Religious Education*) la **religión** *fem*

reach *noun* ▷ see **reach** *verb*
  el **alcance** *masc*
  to be out of somebody's reach **estar**[2] fuera del alcance de alguien
  The book was out of my reach. El libro estaba fuera de mi alcance.
  to be within somebody's reach **estar**[2] al alcance de alguien
  The cup was within my reach. La taza estaba a mi alcance.
  The hotel is within easy reach of the sea. El hotel está muy cerca del mar.

to reach *verb* ▷ see **reach** *noun*

1 (*your destination*) **llegar**[28] **a**
  We reached the church. Llegamos a la iglesia.
  The team reached the final. El equipo llegó a la final. ▸▸

a
b
c
d
e
f
g
h
i
j
k
l
m
n
o
p
q
r
s
t
u
v
w
x
y
z

2 *(to stretch far enough)* **alcanzar** [22]
I stood on a box to reach it. Me subí a una caja para alcanzarlo.
I can't reach! ¡No alcanzo!

♂ to **read** *verb* ▷ see **reading** *noun*
leer [37]
What are you reading at the moment? ¿Qué estás leyendo en este momento?
I'm reading a detective novel. Estoy leyendo una novela policiaca.
I read about it in the paper. Lo leí en el periódico.
He read out the list. Leyó la lista.

♂ **reading** *noun* ▷ see **read** *verb*
la **lectura** *fem*
I don't like reading. No me gusta la lectura.
Some easy reading for the beach. Lectura fácil para la playa.

reading

One of the first novels ever written was the *Don Quijote* by Miguel de Cervantes; part one came out in 1605 and part two in 1615. The novel has continued to be very influential ever since.

♂ **ready** *adjective*
1 *(food)* **preparado** *masc*, **preparada** *fem*
Supper's not ready yet. La cena aún no está preparada.
to get something ready *(a meal, things)* preparar [17] algo
He got the meal ready. Preparó la comida.
I'll get your room ready. Voy a preparar tu habitación.
2 *(person)* **listo** *masc*, **lista** *fem*
Are you ready to leave? ¿Estás listo para salir?
to get ready prepararse [17]
I'm getting ready to go out. Me estoy preparando para salir.
I was getting ready for bed. Estaba preparándome para irme a la cama.

♂ **ready-cooked meal** *noun*
la **comida precocinada**

real *adjective*
verdadero *masc*, **verdadera** *fem*
Is that his real name? ¿Es ése su verdadero nombre?
Her real father is dead. Su verdadero padre está muerto.
He's a real bore. Es un verdadero pesado.
It's a real diamond. Es un diamante de verdad.

to **realize** *verb*
darse [4] **cuenta**
I hadn't realized. No me había dado

cuenta.
to realize (that) ... darse cuenta de que ...
I didn't realize (that) he was French. No me di cuenta de que era francés.
Do you realize what time it is? ¿Te das cuenta de la hora que es?

really *adverb*
1 *(in fact)* The tomato is really a fruit. El tomate en realidad es una fruta.
Is it really midnight? ¿De verdad son las doce de la noche?
'Do you like it?' 'Not really.' '¿Te gusta?'— 'No mucho.'
2 *(for emphasis)* The film was really good. La película fue buenísima.
It was really hot. Hacía mucho calor.
I really don't know. Realmente no lo sé.
really and truly de verdad
3 *(to show surprise)* Really? ¿De verdad?
'She is very famous.'— 'Really?' 'Es muy famosa.'— '¿De verdad?'

♂ **reason** *noun*
la **razón** *fem*
the reason for something la razón de algo
the reason for the delay la razón del retraso
the reason why I phoned la razón por la que llamé

reasonable *adjective*
razonable *masc & fem*

rebel *noun*
el & la **rebelde** *masc & fem*

rebellion *noun*
la **rebelión** *fem*

♂ **receipt** *noun*
el **recibo** *masc*
Could I have a receipt please? ¿Me podría dar un recibo, por favor?
She received a blow to the head. Recibió un golpe en la cabeza.
to receive treatment ser [1] tratado
He received an honorary doctorate. Le confirieron un doctorado honoris causa.

♂ to **receive** *verb*
recibir [19]
I received your letter. Recibí tu carta.
She received a blow to the head. Recibió un golpe en la cabeza.

♂ **receiver** *noun*
el **auricular** *masc*
to pick up the receiver descolgar [23] el auricular
to put down the receiver colgar [23] el auricular

♂ **recent** *adjective*
reciente *masc & fem*
a recent change un cambio reciente

recently *adverb*
recientemente

♂ **reception** *noun*
1 (*in a hotel, office, etc*) la **recepción** *fem*
He's waiting at reception. Está esperando
en recepción.
2 (*social event*) la **recepción** *fem*
a big wedding reception un gran banquete
de bodas
3 (*on TV, radio*) la **recepción** *fem*
4 (*response, reaction*) la **acogida** *fem*
to get a good reception tener [9] buena
acogida

receptionist *noun*
el & la **recepcionista** *masc & fem*
My sister works as a receptionist. Mi
hermana trabaja como recepcionista.

♂ **recipe** *noun*
la **receta** *fem*
Can I have the recipe for your salad? ¿Me
puedes dar tu receta de la ensalada?

to **reckon** *verb*
creer [37]
I reckon it's a good idea. Creo que es una
buena idea.

to **recognize** *verb*
reconocer [35]

♂ to **recommend** *verb*
recomendar [29]
Can you recommend a dentist? ¿Puedes
recomendarme un dentista?
I recommend the fish soup. Recomiendo la
sopa de pescado.

recommendation *noun*
la **recomendación** *fem*

♂ to **record** *verb* ▷ see **record** *noun*
(*onto a tape, CD*) **grabar** [17]
They're recording a new album. Están
grabando un nuevo álbum.

♂ **record** *noun* ▷ see **record** *verb*
1 (*in sport, etc*) el **récord** *masc, pl:* los **récords**
to hold the world record tener [9] el récord
mundial.
It's a world record. Es un récord mundial.
record sales récord de ventas
2 (*document*) el **documento** *masc*
official records documentos oficiales
3 (*of events*) **to keep a record of something**
llevar [17] un registro de algo

the hottest summer on record el verano
más caluroso del que se tienen datos
4 (*personal details*) **medical records** historial
médico
to have a (criminal) record tener [9]
antecedentes penales
I'll just check your records. Voy a mirar tu
ficha.
5 (*of attendance*) el **registro** *masc*
**He keeps a record of attendance at
meetings.** Lleva un registro de asistencia a
las reuniones.
6 (*of music*) el **disco** *masc*
a Robbie Williams record un disco de
Robbie Williams

recorder *noun*
1 (*musical instrument*) la **flauta dulce**
to play the recorder tocar [31] la flauta
dulce
2 (*electrical device*) **a cassette recorder** un
cassette
a video recorder una cámara de vídeo

♂ **recording** *noun*
la **grabación** *fem*

♂ **record player** *noun*
el **tocadiscos** *masc, pl:* los **tocadiscos**

to **recover** *verb*
(*from an illness*) **recuperarse** [17]
She's recovered now. Ya se ha recuperado.

recovery *noun*
(*from an illness*) la **recuperación** *fem*
• **recovery vehicle** la grúa

rectangle *noun*
el **rectángulo** *masc*

rectangular *adjective*
rectangular *masc & fem*

to **recycle** *verb*
reciclar [17]

recycling *noun*
el **reciclaje** *masc*

♂ **red** *adjective*
1 (*in general*) **rojo** *masc*, **roja** *fem*
a red shirt una camisa roja
a bright red car un coche rojo vivo
2 (*in the face*) **to go red** ponerse [11] colorado (
boy), ponerse [11] colorada (*girl*)
3 (*hair*) **to have red hair** ser [1] pelirrojo
4 (*wine*) **tinto** *masc*, **tinta** *fem*

Red Cross *noun*
the Red Cross la Cruz Roja

redcurrant *noun*
la **grosella** *fem*
redcurrant jelly jalea de grosellas

♂ **red-haired** *adjective*
pelirrojo *masc*, **pelirroja** *fem*

♂ **red light** *noun*
la **luz roja**

♂ to **reduce** *verb*
reducir[60]
They've reduced the price. Han reducido el precio.

♂ **reduced** *adjective*
(*price, weight, numbers*) **reducido** *masc*,
reducida *fem*
reduced-price tickets entradas a precios reducidos

♂ **reduction** *noun*
1 (*in numbers, size, spending*) la **reducción** *fem*
a reduction in costs una reducción de gastos
2 (*in price*) la **rebaja** *fem*
a 5% reduction una rebaja del cinco por ciento

redundant *adjective*
(*from a job*) He was made redundant. Lo despidieron por reducción de plantilla.

to **refer to** *verb*
referirse[14] a
She's referring to you. Se refiere a ti.

referee *noun*
(*in sport*) el & la **árbitro** *masc & fem*

reference *noun*
1 (*allusion*) la **referencia** *fem*
to make reference to something hacer[7] referencia a algo
2 (*for a job*) la **referencia** *fem*
She gave me a good reference. Me dio una buena referencia.

referendum *noun*
el **referéndum** *masc*, pl: los **referéndums**

refill *noun*
1 (*for a pen*) el **recambio** *masc*
2 (*for a lighter*) la **carga** *fem*

to **reflect** *verb*
reflejar[17]

reflection *noun*
1 (*in a mirror*) el **reflejo** *masc*
2 (*thought*) la **reflexión** *fem*
on reflection pensándolo bien

reflexive *adjective*
reflexivo *masc*, **reflexiva** *fem*
a reflexive verb un verbo reflexivo

refreshing *adjective*
refrescante *masc & fem*

refreshment *noun*
el **refresco** *masc*

refrigerator *noun*
la **nevera** *fem*

refuge *noun*
el **refugio** *masc*
a mountain refuge un refugio (de montaña)
to take refuge refugiarse[17]
He took refuge in the ruins. Se refugió en las ruinas.

refugee *noun*
el **refugiado** *masc*, la **refugiada** *fem*

refund *noun* ▷ see **refund** *verb*
el **reembolso** *masc*

to **refund** *verb* ▷ see **refund** *noun*
reembolsar[17]

refuse *noun* ▷ see **refuse** *verb*
(*rubbish*) los **desperdicios** *plural masc*

to **refuse** *verb* ▷ see **refuse** *noun*
negarse[30]
I refused. Me negué.
to refuse to do something negarse a hacer algo
He refuses to help. Se niega a ayudar.

regards *plural noun*
los **recuerdos** *plural masc*
Regards to your parents. Recuerdos a tus padres.
Nat sends his regards. Nat manda recuerdos.

reggae *noun*
el **reggae** *masc*

♂ **region** *noun*
la **región** *fem*
an industrial region una región industrial

regional *adjective*
regional *masc & fem*

♂ **register** *noun* ▷ see **register** *verb*
(*in a school*) la **lista** *fem*

♂ to **register** *verb* ▷ see **register** *noun*
inscribirse[52]
He registered for a German course. Se inscribió en un curso de alemán.

registered letter *noun*
la **carta certificada**

registration number *noun*
(*of a vehicle*) el **número de matrícula**

to **regret** *verb*
to regret something arrepentirse [14] de algo

regular *adjective*
1 (*shape, pulse, verb*) **regular** *masc & fem*
2 (*frequent*) **regular visits** visitas frecuentes
3 (*customer*) **habitual** *masc & fem*

regularly *adverb*
regularmente

ſ **regulation** *noun*
la **norma** *fem*
safety regulations normas de seguridad
It's against the regulations. Va contra el reglamento.

rehearsal *noun*
el **ensayo** *masc*

to **rehearse** *verb*
ensayar [17]

reign *noun* ▷ see **reign** *verb*
el **reinado** *masc*

to **reign** *verb* ▷ see **reign** *noun*
reinar [17]

rein *noun*
la **rienda** *fem*

to **reject** *verb*
rechazar [22]

related *adjective*
1 (*subject, ideas*) **relacionado** *masc*, **relacionada** *fem*
2 (*people*) **We're not related.** No somos parientes.

relation *noun*
el & la **pariente** *masc & fem*
my relations mis parientes

relationship *noun*
la **relación** *fem*
We have a good relationship. Tenemos una buena relación.

relative *noun*
el & la **pariente** *masc & fem*
all my relatives todos mis parientes

to **relax** *verb*
relajarse [17]
I'm going to relax and watch telly tonight. Esta noche voy a relajarme y ver la tele.

relaxation *noun*
el **esparcimiento** *masc*
Tennis is her relaxation. El tenis es su esparcimiento.

relaxed *adjective*
relajado *masc*, **relajada** *fem*

relaxing *adjective*
relajante *masc & fem*

relay race *noun*
la **carrera de relevos**

release *noun* ▷ see **release** *verb*
1 (*of a film*) el **estreno** *masc*
this week's new releases los estrenos de esta semana
2 (*of a prisoner, hostage*) la **puesta en libertad**

to **release** *verb* ▷ see **release** *noun*
1 (*a film*) **estrenar** [17]
2 (*a record, video*) **sacar** [31]
3 (*a person*) **poner** [11] **en libertad**

reliable *adjective*
1 (*person*) **responsable** *masc & fem*
2 (*information*) **fidedigno** *masc*, **fidedigna** *fem*

relief *noun*
el **alivio** *masc*
What a relief! ¡Qué alivio!

relieved *adjective*
aliviado *masc*, **aliviada** *fem*
I was relieved to hear you'd arrived. Fue un alivio oír que habías llegado.

religion *noun*
la **religión** *fem*

religious *adjective*
religioso *masc*, **religiosa** *fem*
Jane's not religious. Jane no es religiosa.

reluctant *adjective*
reacio *masc*, **reacia** *fem*
He's reluctant to go. Se muestra reacio a ir.

to **rely** *verb*
to rely on somebody contar [24] con alguien
I'm relying on you for Saturday. Cuento contigo para el sábado.

ſ to **remain** *verb*
1 (*to stay*) **quedarse** [17]
The best thing is to remain silent. Lo mejor es quedarse callado.
How long do you intend to remain in the country? ¿Cuánto tiempo piensa quedarse en el país?
2 (*to be left*) **quedar** [17]
This is all that remains of the city. Esto es todo lo que queda de la ciudad.
There are less than five minutes remaining. Quedan menos de cinco minutos.

remark *noun*
　el **comentario** *masc*
　to make remarks about something hacer
　[7] comentarios sobre algo

♂ to **remember** *verb*
　acordarse [24]
　I don't remember. No me acuerdo.
　to remember something acordarse de algo
　I can't remember the number. No me
　acuerdo del número.
　to remember to do something acordarse
　de hacer algo
　Remember to shut the door! ¡Acuérdate de
　cerrar la puerta!
　I remembered to bring the CDs. Me acordé
　de traer los compactos.

♂ to **remind** *verb*
　recordar [24]
　to remind somebody of something
　recordarle a alguien a algo
　It reminds me of Paris. Me recuerda París.
　to remind somebody of somebody
　recordarle a alguien a alguien
　He reminds me of Frank. Me recuerda a
　Frank.
　to remind somebody to do something
　recordarle a alguien que haga algo
　Remind your mother to pick me up.
　Recuérdale a tu madre que me recoja.
　Oh, that reminds me ... ¡Ah!, por cierto ...

　WORD TIP *recordarle a alguien que* is followed by
　the subjunctive.

remote control *noun*
　el **mando a distancia**

to **remove** *verb*
　quitar [17]
　He removed his jacket. Se quitó la
　chaqueta.
　The chairs had all been removed. Habían
　quitado todas las sillas.

to **renew** *verb*
　(*a licence, etc*) **renovar** [24]

♂ to **rent** *verb* ▷ see **rent** *noun*
　alquilar [17]
　Simon's rented a flat. Simon ha alquilado
　un piso.

♂ **rent** *noun* ▷ see **rent** *verb*
　el **alquiler** *masc*

♂ **rental** *noun*
　el **alquiler** *masc*

to **repair** *verb* ▷ see **repair** *noun*
　arreglar [17]
　to get something repaired arreglar algo

We've had the television repaired. Hemos
arreglado la televisión.

repair *noun* ▷ see **repair** *verb*
　la **reparación** *fem*

to **repay** *verb*
　devolver [45]
　He repaid me the money he owed me. Me
　devolvió el dinero que me debía.

♂ **repeat** *noun* ▷ see **repeat** *verb*
　(*of a programme*) la **repetición** *fem*

♂ to **repeat** *verb* ▷ see **repeat** *noun*
　repetir [57]
　Could you repeat the question? ¿Podría
　repetir la pregunta?

replacement *noun*
1　(*person*) el **sustituto** *masc*, la **sustituta** *fem*
2　(*thing*) **When can you find me a**
　replacement? ¿Para cuándo me puedes
　encontrar otro?

♂ to **reply** *verb* ▷ see **reply** *noun*
　contestar [17]
　He replied that he hadn't seen me.
　Contestó que no me había visto.
　to reply to something contestar a algo
　I still haven't replied to the letter. Aún no
　he contestado a la carta.

reply *noun* ▷ see **reply** *verb*
　la **contestación** *fem*
　I didn't get a reply to my letter. No recibí
　contestación a mi carta.
　I phoned her but there was no reply. La
　llamé pero nadie cogió el teléfono.

♂ to **report** *verb* ▷ see **report** *noun*
1　(*a problem, accident*) **informar** [17] **sobre**
2　(*a crime*) **denunciar** [17]
　We've reported the theft. Hemos
　denunciado el robo.
3　(*to present yourself*) **presentarse** [17]
　I had to report to reception. Tuve que
　presentarme en recepción.

♂ **report** *noun* ▷ see **report** *verb*
1　(*piece of news*) la **noticia** *fem*
　Reports are coming in of an accident. Están
　llegando noticias de un accidente.
2　(*newspaper article*) el **reportaje** *masc*
3　(*account of an event*) el **informe** *masc*
　an official report un informe oficial
4　(*school report*) el **boletín de notas**

reporter *noun*
　el & la **periodista** *masc & fem*

representative *noun*
　el & la **representante** *masc & fem*

republic *noun*
  la **república** *fem*

reputation *noun*
  la **reputación** *fem*
  a good reputation una buena reputación
  to have a reputation for something tener [9] fama de algo
  She has a reputation for honesty. Tiene fama de honesta.

to **request** *verb* ▷ see **request** *noun*
  pedir [57]

request *noun* ▷ see **request** *verb*
  la **petición** *fem*
  on request a solicitud

to **rescue** *verb* ▷ see **rescue** *noun*
  rescatar [17]
  They rescued the dog. Rescataron al perro.

rescue *noun* ▷ see **rescue** *verb*
  el **rescate** *masc*
  to come to somebody's rescue acudir [19] en auxilio de alguien
  • **rescue party** el equipo de rescate
  • **rescue worker** el & la socorrista

to **research** *verb* ▷ see **research** *noun*
  (*the causes, a problem*) **investigar** [28]
  to research into something investigar sobre algo
  a well-researched programme un programa bien documentado

research *noun* ▷ see **research** *verb*
  la **investigación** *fem*
  research into Aids la investigación sobre el sida
  to do research investigar [28]

to **resemble** *verb*
  parecerse [35] a
  She resembles her aunt. Se parece a su tía.

♪ **reservation** *noun*
  (*booking*) la **reserva** *fem*
  to make a reservation hacer [7] una reserva

♪ to **reserve** *verb* ▷ see **reserve** *noun*
  reservar [17]
  This table is reserved. Esta mesa está reservada.

reserve *noun* ▷ see **reserve** *verb*
  1 (*stock*) la **reserva** *fem*
  We have some in reserve. Tenemos algo de reserva.
  2 (*special area*) **a nature reserve** una reserva natural
  3 (*substitute player*) el & la **reserva** *masc & fem*

resident *noun*
  el & la **residente** *masc & fem*

residential *adjective*
  residencial *masc & fem*
  a residential area un área residencial

to **resign** *verb*
  dimitir [19]
  to resign from something dimitir algo
  She resigned from the committee. Dimitió su cargo en la comisión.

resignation *noun*
  (*from a post*) la **dimisión** *fem*

to **resist** *verb*
  (*an offer, temptation*) **resistir** [19]
  I can't resist! ¡No puedo resistirlo!

to **resit** *verb*
  to resit an exam volver [45] a presentarse a un examen

♪ **resort** *noun*
  1 (*for holidays*) **a holiday resort** un centro turístico
  a ski resort una estación de esquí
  a seaside resort un centro turístico costero
  2 (*recourse*) **as a last resort** como último recurso

to **respect** *verb* ▷ see **respect** *noun*
  respetar [17]

respect *noun* ▷ see **respect** *verb*
  el **respeto** *masc*

respectable *adjective*
  respetable *masc & fem*

respectful *adjective*
  respetuoso *masc*, **respetuosa** *fem*

responsibility *noun*
  la **responsabilidad** *fem*

responsible *adjective*
  responsable *masc & fem*
  He's not very responsible. No es muy responsable.
  to be responsible for something ser [1] responsable de algo
  I'm responsible for booking the rooms. Soy responsable de reservar las habitaciones.
  He's responsible for the delay. Él es el responsable del retraso.

♪ to **rest** *verb* ▷ see **rest** *noun*
  (*to relax*) **descansar** [17]
  Don't disturb him, he's resting. No lo molestes, que está descansando.

a
b
c
d
e
f
g
h
i
j
k
l
m
n
o
p
q
r
s
t
u
v
w
x
y
z

♂ **rest** *noun* ▷ see **rest** *verb*

1 (*relaxation*) el **descanso** *masc*
   ten days' complete rest diez días de
   completo descanso

2 (*short break*) **to have a rest** descansar[17]
   to stop for a rest parar[17] para descansar

3 (*remainder*) **the rest** el resto
   the rest of the day el resto del día
   the rest of the world el resto del mundo
   The rest of the money is mine. El resto del
   dinero es mío.

4 (*others*) **the rest** los otros
   The rest have gone home. Los otros se han
   ido a casa.

♂ **restaurant** *noun*
   el **restaurante** *masc*
  • **restaurant car** el coche-comedor

to **restore** *verb*
   restaurar[17]

♂ **result** *noun*
   el **resultado** *masc*
   the exam results los resultados del examen
   as a result como consecuencia de ello
   As a result we missed the ferry. Como
   consecuencia de ello perdimos el ferry.

to **retire** *verb* ▷ see **retired** *adj*
   (*from work*) **jubilarse**[17]
   She retires in June. Se jubila en junio.

retired *adjective* ▷ see **retire** *verb*
   (*from work*) **jubilado** *masc*, **jubilada** *fem*
   a retired couple una pareja de jubilados

retirement *noun*
   la **jubilación** *fem*

♂ to **return** *verb* ▷ see **return** *noun*

1 (*to come back, get home*) **volver**[45]
   to return from holiday volver de
   vacaciones
   He returned ten minutes later. Volvió diez
   minutos más tarde.
   I'll ask her to phone as soon as she returns.
   Le diré que te llame en cuanto vuelva.

2 (*to give back*) **devolver**[45]
   Gemma never returned the video. Gemma
   no devolvió nunca el vídeo.

♂ **return** *noun* ▷ see **return** *verb*

1 (*to a place*) la **vuelta** *fem*
   on his return a su vuelta
   the return journey el viaje de vuelta

2 (*ticket*) el **billete de ida y vuelta**

3 (*birthday greeting*) **Many happy returns of
   the day!** ¡Feliz cumpleaños!

4 (*in expressions*) **by return of post** a vuelta de
   correo

in return a cambio
in return for his help a cambio de su ayuda
  • **return fare** el precio del billete de ida y
   vuelta
  • **return ticket** el billete de ida y vuelta

reunion *noun*
   la **reunión** *fem*
   a class reunion una reunión de ex
   compañeros de clase

revenge *noun*
   la **venganza** *fem*
   to get one's revenge on someone vengarse
   [28] de alguien

to **reverse** *verb* ▷ see **reverse** *noun*

1 (*in a car*) **dar**[4] **marcha atrás**
   She reversed her car into the garage. Entró
   en el garaje dando marcha atrás.

2 (*when making a phone call*) **to reverse the
   charges** llamar[17] a cobro revertido

reverse *noun* ▷ see **reverse** *verb*

1 (*of a coin*) el **reverso** *masc*

2 (*gear*) la **marcha atrás**

3 (*of a page*) el **dorso** *masc*

4 (*opposite*) **The reverse is true.** Es al
   contrario.

to **review** *verb* ▷ see **review** *noun*
   escribir[52] **la crítica de**
   The film was well reviewed. La película
   recibió buenas críticas.

review *noun* ▷ see **review** *verb*
   (*of a book, play, film*) la **crítica** *fem*

to **revise** *verb*
   repasar[17]
   Tessa's busy revising for her exams. Tessa
   está muy ocupada repasando para los
   exámenes.

revision *noun*
   el **repaso** *masc*

revolting *adjective*
   asqueroso *masc*, **asquerosa** *fem*
   The sausages are revolting. Las salchichas
   están asquerosas.

revolution *noun*
   la **revolución** *fem*
   the French Revolution la Revolución
   Francesa

♂ to **reward** *verb* ▷ see **reward** *noun*
   recompensar[17]
   He was rewarded for handing it in. Lo
   recompensaron por haberlo entregado.

♪ **reward** *noun* ▷ **see reward** *verb*
　la **recompensa** *fem*
　a **£100 reward** una recompensa de cien
　libras

rewarding *adjective*
　gratificante *masc & fem*

to **rewind** *verb*
　rebobinar[17]

rhubarb *noun*
　el **ruibarbo** *masc*

rhyme *noun*
　la **rima** *fem*

rhythm *noun*
　el **ritmo** *masc*

rib *noun*
　la **costilla** *fem*

ribbon *noun*
　la **cinta** *fem*

♪ **rice** *noun*
　el **arroz** *masc*
　chicken and rice pollo y arroz
　• **rice pudding** el arroz con leche

♪ **rich** *adjective*
　1　(*person, country*) **rico** *masc*, **rica** *fem*
　　the rich and the poor los ricos y los pobres
　　We're not very rich. No somos muy ricos.
　2　(*food*) **con alto contenido de grasas,**
　　huevos, azúcar, etc
　　Avoid rich foods Evite las comidas pesadas.

rid *adjective*
　to get rid of something deshacerse[7] de
　algo
　We got rid of the car. Nos deshicimos del
　coche.

riddle *noun*
　la **adivinanza** *fem*

♪ to **ride** *verb* ▷ **see ride** *noun*
　1　(*a bicycle*) **He learned to ride a bike.**
　　Aprendió a montar en bicicleta.
　　Can you ride a bike? ¿Sabes montar en
　　bicicleta?
　2　(*a horse*) **I am learning to ride.** Estoy
　　aprendiendo a montar a caballo.
　　I've never ridden a horse. Nunca he
　　montado a caballo.

♪ **ride** *noun* ▷ **see ride** *verb*
　1　(*on a bicycle*) **to go for a ride** ir[8] a montar en
　　bicicleta
　2　(*on a horse*) **to go for a ride** ir[8] a montar a
　　caballo

rider *noun*
　1　(*of a horse*) el & la **jinete** *masc & fem*
　2　(*of a bicycle*) el & la **ciclista** *masc & fem*
　3　(*of a motorbike*) el & la **motorista** *masc & fem*

ridiculous *adjective*
　ridículo *masc*, **ridícula** *fem*

♪ **riding** *noun*
　la **equitación** *fem*
　to go riding hacer[7] equitación
　• **riding school** la escuela de equitación

rifle *noun*
　el **rifle** *masc*

♪ **right** *adjective* ▷ **see right** *adv, noun*
　1　(*not left*) **derecho** *masc*, **derecha** *fem*
　　my right hand mi mano derecha
　2　(*correct*) **correcto** *masc*, **correcta** *fem*
　　the right answer la respuesta correcta
　　the right telephone number el teléfono
　　correcto
　　Is this the right address? ¿Son éstas las
　　señas?
　3　(*person*) **to be right** tener[9] razón
　　You see, I was right. ¿Ves? tenía yo razón.
　4　**You were right to stay at home.** Hiciste
　　bien en quedarte en casa.
　　He was right not to say anything. Hizo bien
　　en no decir nada.
　5　(*just, morally correct*) **to be right** ser[1] justo
　　What they did wasn't right Lo que hicieron
　　no fue justo.
　　It's not right to talk like that. No está bien
　　hablar así.

right *adverb* ▷ **see right** *adj, noun*
　1　(*to turn, look*) **a la derecha**
　　Turn right at the lights. Gira a la derecha en
　　el semáforo.
　2　(*correctly*) **bien**
　　You're not doing it right. No lo estás
　　haciendo bien.
　3　(*completely*) **right at the bottom** al fondo del
　　todo
　　right now ahora mismo
　　right at the beginning justo al principio
　　right in the middle justo en medio
　4　(*okay*) **vale**
　　Right, let's go. Vale, vamos.

♪ **right** *noun* ▷ **see right** *adj, adv*
　1　(*direction*) la **derecha** *fem*
　　the second street on the right la segunda
　　calle a la derecha
　　on my right a mi derecha
　　It's on the right. Está a la derecha.
　　to drive on the right conducir[60] por la
　　derecha ▸▸

a
b
c
d
e
f
g
h
i
j
k
l
m
n
o
p
q
r
s
t
u
v
w
x
y
z

2 (*entitlement*) el **derecho** *masc*
the right to strike el derecho a hacer huelga
You have no right to say that. No tienes derecho a decir eso.

right-click *noun* ▷ see **right-click** *verb*
el **clic con el botón derecho**

to **right-click** *verb* ▷ see **right-click** *noun*
hacer [7] **clic con el botón derecho**
Right-click the icon. Haz clic en el icono con el botón derecho.

right-hand *adjective*
on the right-hand side a mano derecha

right-handed *adjective*
diestro *masc*, **diestra** *fem*

to **ring** *verb* ▷ see **ring** *noun*

1 (*bells, phones*) **sonar** [24]
The phone rang. Sonó el teléfono.

2 (*somebody*) **llamar** [17]
I'll ring you tomorrow. Te llamaré mañana.
Could you ring for a taxi? ¿Podrías llamar un taxi?

• **to ring back**
volver [45] **a llamar**
I'll ring you back later. Te volveré a llamar más tarde.

• **to ring off**
colgar [23]

ring *noun* ▷ see **ring** *verb*

1 (*on the phone*) **to give somebody a ring**
llamar [17] a alguien

2 (*for your finger*) el **anillo** *masc*

3 (*circle*) el **círculo** *masc*

4 (*on a doorbell*) There was a ring at the door.
Llamaron a la puerta.

• **ring tone** el tono de llamada

to **rinse** *verb*
enjuagar [28]

ripe *adjective*
maduro *masc*, **madura** *fem*
Are the tomatoes ripe? ¿Están maduros los tomates?

rip-off *noun*
It's a rip-off! ¡Es una estafa!

♪ to **rise** *verb* ▷ see **rise** *noun*

1 (*sun*) **salir** [63]
when the sun rose cuando salió el sol

2 (*prices*) **subir** [19]
The price has risen by $200. El precio ha subido dos cientos dólares.

♪ **rise** *noun* ▷ see **rise** *verb*
la **subida** *fem*
a rise in price una subida de precio
a pay rise un aumento de sueldo

to **risk** *verb* ▷ see **risk** *noun*
(*your life, reputation*) **arriesgar** [28]
She risked her life. Arriesgó su vida.

risk *noun* ▷ see **risk** *verb*
el **riesgo** *masc*
to take risks arriesgarse [28]

rival *noun*
el & la **rival** *masc & fem*

♪ **river** *noun*
el **río** *masc*
the River Plate el Río de la Plata

♪ **road** *noun*

1 (*out of a town*) la **carretera** *fem*
the road to London la carretera de Londres

2 (*in a town*) la **calle** *fem*
on the other side of the road al otro lado de la calle

3 (*in expressions*) **across the road** enfrente
They live across the road from us. Viven enfrente de nosotros.

• **road accident** el accidente de carretera

• **road map** el mapa de carreteras

 roads

The world's longest road, the Pan-American Highway (25,750 km), runs from Alaska to Argentina with less than 100 km between Panama and Colombia still to be completed.

roadside *noun*
el **borde de la carretera**
by the roadside al borde de la carretera

road sign *noun*
la **señal de tráfico**

roadworks *plural noun*
las **obras** *plural fem*

♪ to **roast** *verb* ▷ see **roast** *noun, adj*
asar [17]
I've roasted the potatoes. He asado las patatas.

♪ **roast** *noun* ▷ see **roast** *adj*
el **asado** *masc*

♪ **roast** *adjective* ▷ see **roast** *noun*
asado *masc*, **asada** *fem*

• **roast beef** el rosbif

• **roast potatoes** las patatas asadas

to **rob** *verb*

1 (*person*) **robar** [17]

2 (*a bank*) **atracar** [31]

robber noun
el **ladrón** masc, la **ladrona** fem
a bank robber un atracador

robbery noun
el **robo** masc
a bank robbery un atraco a un banco

rock noun
1 (big stone) la **roca** fem
She was sitting on a rock. Estaba sentada en una roca.
2 (the material) la **piedra** fem
3 (music) el **rock** masc
a rock band un grupo de rock
to dance rock and roll bailar [17] rock and roll

rock climbing noun
la **escalada en roca**
to go rock climbing hacer [7] escalada

rock star noun
la **estrella de rock**

rocket noun
el **cohete** masc

rocking horse noun
el **caballito de balancín**

rocky adjective
rocoso masc, **rocosa** fem

rod noun
1 (bar) la **varilla** fem
2 (fishing rod) la **caña de pescar**

role noun
el **papel** masc
He played the role of the king. Interpretó el papel del rey.

ᵭ **roll** noun
1 (of material) el **rollo** masc
a roll of fabric un rollo de tela
a toilet roll un rollo de papel higiénico
2 (of bread) a bread roll un panecillo
• to roll something up
(a carpet) **enrollar** [17] **algo**
He rolled up his sleeves. Se remangó las mangas.

rollerblades plural noun
los **patines en línea**

rollercoaster noun
la **montaña rusa**

roller skates plural noun
los **patines de ruedas**

Roman Catholic adjective & noun
1 **católico** masc, **católica** fem

2 el **católico** masc, la **católica** fem

WORD TIP Adjectives and nouns for religion do not have capital letters in Spanish.

ᵭ **romantic** adjective
romántico masc, **romántica** fem

roof noun
el **tejado** masc
• roof rack la baca

rook noun
1 (in chess) la **torre** fem
2 (the bird) el **grajo** masc

ᵭ **room** noun
1 (part of a building) la **habitación** fem
a three-room flat un piso de tres habitaciones
She's in the other room. Está en la otra habitación.
It's the biggest room in the house. Es la habitación más grande de la casa.
2 (bedroom) la **habitación** fem
Lola's in her room. Lola está en su habitación.
3 (space) el **sitio** masc
There is enough room for two. Hay sitio suficiente para dos.
There was very little room. Había muy poco espacio.

root noun
la **raíz** fem

rope noun
la **cuerda** fem

ᵭ **rose** noun
la **rosa** fem
• rosebush el rosal

ᵭ **rosé wine** noun
el **vino rosado**

to **rot** verb
pudrirse [59]

rota noun
la **lista de turnos**

rotten adjective
podrido masc, **podrida** fem

rough adjective ▷ see **rough** adv
1 (scratchy) **áspero** masc, **áspera** fem
2 (vague) **aproximado** masc, **aproximada** fem
a rough idea una idea aproximada
3 (stormy) a rough sea un mar agitado
4 (difficult) to have a rough time pasarlo [17] mal
5 (ill) He feels a bit rough today. Hoy no está muy bien.

rough *adverb* ▷ see **rough** *adj*
  to sleep rough dormir[51] a la intemperie

roughly *adverb*
  (*approximately*) **aproximadamente**
  roughly ten per cent aproximadamente el diez por ciento
  It takes roughly three hours. Lleva aproximadamente tres horas.

ɗ **round** *adjective* ▷ see **round** *adv, prep, noun*
  redondo *masc*, **redonda** *fem*
  a round table una mesa redonda

round *adverb* ▷ see **round** *adj, prep, noun*
1 (*in a circle*) **all the year round** todo el año
  They ran round and round. Dieron vueltas y vueltas corriendo.
2 (*to a place*) **to go round to somebody's house** ir[8] a casa de alguien
  We invited Sally round for lunch. Invitamos a Sally a comer.

round *preposition* ▷ see **round** *adj, adv, noun*
1 (*encircling*) **alrededor de**
  round the city alrededor de la ciudad
  round my arm alrededor de mi brazo
  They were sitting round the table. Estaban sentados alrededor de la mesa.
  It's just round the corner. Está a la vuelta de la esquina.
2 (*through*) **to go round the shops** ir[8] de tiendas
  to go round a museum visitar[17] un museo

round *noun* ▷ see **round** *adj, adv, prep*
1 (*in a competition*) la **vuelta** *fem*
2 (*of cards*) la **partida** *fem*
3 (*of drinks*) la **ronda** *fem*
  It's my round. Esta ronda la pago yo.

ɗ **roundabout** *noun*
1 (*for traffic*) la **rotonda** *fem*
2 (*in a fairground*) el **tiovivo** *masc*

ɗ **route** *noun*
  la **ruta** *fem*
  The best route is via Leeds. La mejor ruta es pasando por Leeds.
  a bus route el recorrido de un autobús

to **row** *verb* ▷ see **row** *noun*
1 (*in a boat*) **remar**[17]
  It's your turn to row. Te toca remar.
  We rowed across the lake. Cruzamos el lago remando.
2 (*to argue*) **reñir**[65]

row *noun* ▷ see **row** *verb*
1 (*of seats*) la **fila** *fem*
  in the front row en la primera fila
  in the back row en la última fila
2 (*line*) la **hilera** *fem*
  a row of huts una hilera de cabañas
3 (*succession*) **four times in a row** cuatro veces seguidas
4 (*quarrel*) la **pelea** *fem*
  to have a row pelearse[17]
  They've had a row. Se han peleado.
  I had a row with my parents. Me peleé con mis padres.
5 (*noise*) el **ruido** *masc*
  They are making a terrible row! ¡Están haciendo un ruido terrible!

rowing *noun*
  el **remo** *masc*
  to go rowing practicar[31] el remo
• **rowing boat** el bote de remos

royal *adjective*
  real *masc & fem*
  the royal family la familia real

to **rub** *verb*
  frotar[17]
  to rub your eyes frotarse los ojos
• **to rub something out** **borrar**[17] algo

rubber *noun*
1 (*eraser*) la **goma de borrar**
2 (*the material*) la **goma** *fem*
  rubber soles suelas de goma
• **rubber band** la goma elástica

rubbish *adjective* ▷ see **rubbish** *noun*
  The film was rubbish. La película fue una porquería.
  They're a rubbish band. Es una porquería de grupo.

rubbish *noun* ▷ see **rubbish** *adj*
1 (*for the bin*) la **basura** *fem*
2 (*nonsense*) las **estupideces** *plural fem*
  You're talking rubbish! ¡Estás diciendo estupideces!
• **rubbish bin** el cubo de la basura

ɗ **rucksack** *noun*
  la **mochila** *fem*

rude *adjective*
1 (*person*) **maleducado** *masc*, **maleducada** *fem*
2 (*words, behaviour*) That's rude. Eso es de mala educación.
3 a rude joke una broma grosera
  a rude word una palabrota

rug *noun*
1 (*on the floor*) la **alfombra** *fem*
2 (*to keep someone warm*) la **manta de viaje**

rugby *noun*
  el **rugby** *masc*
  to play rugby jugar [27] al rugby
  a rugby match un partido de rugby

to **ruin** *verb* ▷ see **ruin** *noun*
1 (*an outfit, a toy, a carpet*) **estropear** [17]
  You'll ruin your jacket. Vas a estropear tu chaqueta.
2 (*a day, holiday*) **fastidiar** [17] (*informal*)
  It ruined my holiday. Me fastidió las vacaciones.

ruin *noun* ▷ see **ruin** *verb*
  la **ruina** *fem*
  in ruins en ruinas

rule *noun*
  la **regla** *fem*
  the rules of the game las reglas del juego
  the school rules el reglamento del colegio
  as a rule como norma

ruler *noun*
  la **regla** *fem*
  I've lost my ruler. He perdido mi regla.

rumour *noun*
  el **rumor** *masc*

⚡ **run** *noun* ▷ see **run** *verb*
1 (*jog*) to go for a run ir [8] a correr
2 (*in cricket*) la **carrera** *fem*
3 (*period of time*) in the long run a la larga

⚡ to **run** *verb* ▷ see **run** *noun*
1 (*to move quickly*) **correr** [18]
  I ran ten kilometres. Corrí diez kilómetros.
  Kitty ran for the bus. Kitty corrió para coger el autobús.
  He ran across the pitch. Cruzó el campo corriendo.
2 (*to organize*) **organizar** [22]
  Who's running this concert? ¿Quién organiza el concierto?
3 (*a business*) **dirigir** [49]
  He ran the firm for forty years. Dirigió la compañía durante cuarenta años.
4 (*trains, buses*) **circular** [17]
  The buses don't run on Sundays. Los autobuses no circulan los domingos.
  The trains run every half hour. Hay trenes cada media hora.
  They run extra trains on Saturdays. Los sábados ponen más trenes.
5 (*an engine*) **hacer** [7] **funcionar**, (*a computer program*) **pasar** [17]
  (*a bath*) to run a bath preparar [17] un baño

6 (*to flow*) **correr** [18]
  Drops of sweat ran down his face. Le corrían gotas de sudor por la cara.
  The water ran cold. Empezó a salir agua fría.
  The river runs through the town. El río pasa por la ciudad.
• to run away
  huir [54]
• to run into
  chocar [31] **con**
  The car ran into a tree. El coche chocó con un árbol.
• to run out of something
  I'm running out of money. Se me está acabando el dinero.
• to run somebody over
  atropellar [17] **a alguien**
  You'll get run over! ¡Te van a atropellar!

runner-up *noun*
  el **segundo** *masc*, la **segunda** *fem*

running *noun*
  Running is good exercise. Correr es un buen ejercicio.

runway *noun*
  la **pista** *fem*

to **rush** *verb* ▷ see **rush** *noun*
1 (*to hurry*) **darse** [4] **prisa**
  I must rush! ¡Tengo que darme prisa!
  Louise was rushed to hospital. Llevaron a Louise corriendo al hospital.
2 (*to run*) She rushed into the street. Salió corriendo a la calle.
  I rushed into the room. Entré corriendo en la habitación.

rush *noun* ▷ see **rush** *verb*
  to be in a rush tener [9] prisa
  Sorry, I'm in a rush. Perdona, tengo prisa.

rush hour *noun*
  la **hora punta**
  in the rush hour a la hora punta

Russia *noun*
  Rusia *fem*

Russian *adjective & noun*
1 **ruso** *masc*, **rusa** *fem*
2 (*person*) un **ruso** *masc*, una **rusa** *fem*
  the Russians los rusos
3 (*the language*) el **ruso** *masc*

WORD TIP Adjectives and nouns for nationality, regional origin, and language do not have capital letters in Spanish.

rusty *adjective*
  oxidado *masc*, **oxidada** *fem*

rye *noun*
  el **centeno** *masc*

a
b
c
d
e
f
g
h
i
j
k
l
m
n
o
p
q
r
s
t
u
v
w
x
y
z

S s

a
b
c
d
e
f
g
h
i
j
k
l
m
n
o
p
q
r
s
t
u
v
w
x
y
z

Sabbath *noun*
1 *(Jewish)* el **sábado** *masc*
2 *(Christian)* el **domingo** *masc*

WORD TIP Months of the year and days of the week start with small letters in Spanish.

sack *noun* ▷ see **sack** *verb*
1 *(container)* el **saco** *masc*
2 *(for dismissal)* **to give somebody the sack** despedir [57] a alguien
He got the sack. Le despidieron.

to **sack** *verb* ▷ see **sack** *noun*
to sack somebody despedir [57] a alguien

sacred *adjective*
sagrado *masc*, **sagrada** *fem*

sacrifice *noun*
el **sacrificio** *masc*

♂ **sad** *adjective*
triste *masc & fem*
to feel sad sentirse [14] triste

saddle *noun*
1 *(for a horse)* la **silla de montar**
2 *(for a bike)* el **sillín**
• **saddlebag** la alforja

♂ **safe** *adjective*
1 *(out of danger)* **seguro** *masc*, **segura** *fem*
to feel safe sentirse [14] seguro, *fem* segura
2 **to be safe from something** estar [2] a salvo de algo
We'll be safe from the storm in here. Aquí dentro estaremos a salvo de la tormenta.
3 *(not dangerous)* **seguro** *masc*, **segura** *fem*
The path is safe. El camino es seguro.
This ladder's not safe. Esta escalera no es segura.
4 **to be safe and sound** estar [2] sano y salvo
The girls were safe and sound. La niñas estaban sanas y salvas.

safety *noun*
la **seguridad** *fem*
• **safety belt** el cinturón de seguridad
• **safety pin** el imperdible

Sagittarius *noun*
el **Sagitario** *masc*
Kylie's Sagittarius. Kylie es sagitario.

WORD TIP Use a small letter in Spanish to say *I am …* etc with star signs. Star signs in Spanish are used without *el, un, la, una*

sail *noun*
la **vela** *fem*

sailing *noun*
la **vela** *fem*
to go sailing ir [8] a hacer vela
She does a lot of sailing. Practica mucho la vela.
• **sailing boat** el bote de vela
• **sailing ship** el barco de velero

sailor *noun*
el **marinero** *masc*

saint *noun*
el **santo** *masc*, la **santa** *fem*

sake *noun*
for your mother's sake por tu madre
For heaven's sake! ¡Por el amor de Dios!

♂ **salad** *noun*
la **ensalada** *fem*
a tomato salad una ensalada de tomate
• **salad dressing** el aliño para la ensalada

♂ **salami** *noun*
el **salchichón** *masc*

salary *noun*
el **sueldo** *masc*

♂ **sale** *noun*
1 *(selling)* la **venta** *fem*
the sale of the house la venta de la casa
These items are for sale. Estos artículos están en venta.
'For sale' 'Se vende'
2 **the sales** las rebajas
I bought it in the sales. Lo compré en las rebajas.

♂ **sales assistant** *noun*
el **dependiente** *masc*, la **dependienta** *fem*

♂ **salesman** *noun*
el **representante** *masc*
He's a salesman. Es representante.

♂ **saleswoman** *noun*
la **representante** *fem*

saliva *noun*
la **saliva** *fem*

salmon *noun*
el **salmón** *masc*
smoked salmon salmón ahumado

ꝺ **salt** *noun*
  la **sal** *fem*
  Le has echado demasiada sal. You've put
  too much salt on it.
• **salt cellar** el salero

ꝺ **salty** *adjective*
  salado *masc*, **salada** *fem*

to **salute** *verb*
  saludar [17]

Salvadorean *adjective & noun*
1 **salvadoreño** *masc*, **salvadoreña** *fem*
2 el **salvadoreño** *masc*, la **salvadoreña** *fem*
  the Salvadoreans los salvadoreños

> **WORD TIP** Adjectives and nouns for nationality
> and regional origin do not have capital letters in
> Spanish.

Salvation Army *noun*
  el **Ejército de Salvación**

ꝺ **same** *adjective* ▷ see **same** *pron*
1 (*with a singular noun*) **mismo** *masc*, **misma**
  fem
  at the same time al mismo tiempo
  She said the same thing. Ella dijo lo mismo.
  It's the same girl as yesterday. Es la misma
  chica que ayer.
  Their car's the same as ours. Su coche es el
  mismo que el nuestro.
  Her birthday's the same day as mine. Su
  cumpleaños es el mismo día que el mío.
2 (*with a plural noun*) **mismos** *plural masc*,
  mismas *plural fem*
  They were wearing the same shoes.
  Llevaban los mismos zapatos.
  She always sings the same songs. Siempre
  canta las mismas canciones.
3 **to look the same** parecer [35] iguales
  They all look the same to me. Todos me
  parecen iguales.

ꝺ **same** *pronoun* ▷ see **same** *adj*
1 **the same** lo mismo
  It's not the same. No es lo mismo.
  It's always the same. Es lo mismo que
  siempre.
  He said the same as yesterday. Dijo lo
  mismo que ayer.
2 (*replying to greetings*) **The same to you!**
  ¡Igualmente!
  'Happy New Year!'— 'The same to you!'
  'Feliz Año Nuevo!'— ¡Igualmente!'

sample *noun*
  la **muestra** *fem*
  a free sample una muestra gratuita

sand *noun*
  la **arena** *fem*

sandal *noun*
  la **sandalia** *fem*
  a pair of sandals un par de sandalias

sand castle *noun*
  el **castillo de arena**

sandpaper *noun*
  el **papel de lija**

ꝺ **sandwich** *noun*
  el **sándwich** *masc*
  a ham sandwich un sándwich de jamón
  a toasted cheese sandwich un tostado de
  queso

sanitary towel *noun*
  la **compresa** *fem*

Santa Claus *noun*
  Papá Noel *masc*

sarcasm *noun*
  el **sarcasmo** *masc*

sarcastic *adjective*
  sarcástico *masc*, **sarcástica** *fem*

sardine *noun*
  la **sardina** *fem*

satchel *noun*
  la **cartera** *fem*

ꝺ **satellite** *noun*
  el **satélite** *masc*
• **satellite dish** la antena parabólica
• **satellite television** la televisión por vía
  satélite

satisfactory *adjective*
  satisfactorio *masc*, **satisfactoria** *fem*

ꝺ **satisfied** *adjective*
  satisfecho *masc*, **satisfecha** *fem*
  to be satisfied with something estar [2]
  satisfecho con algo
  He's very satisfied with the results. Está
  muy satisfecho con el resultado.

to **satisfy** *verb*
  satisfacer [7]

satisfying *adjective*
1 (*pleasing*) **satisfactorio** *masc*, **satisfactoria**
  fem
2 (*filling*) **a satisfying meal** una comida que
  llena

ꝺ **Saturday** *noun*
  el **sábado** *masc*
  on Saturday el sábado
  every Saturday todos los sábados
  next Saturday el próximo sábado
  last Saturday el sábado pasado
  on Saturdays los sábados ▶▶

Spanish

I'm going out on Saturday. Voy a salir el sábado.
See you on Saturday! ¡Te veo el sábado!
The museum is closed on Saturdays. El museo cierra los sábados.
to have a Saturday job trabajar [17] los sábados

WORD TIP Months of the year and days of the week start with small letters in Spanish.

sauce noun
la **salsa** fem
tomato sauce salsa de tomate

♂ **saucepan** noun
el **cazo** masc
to wash the saucepans lavar [17] los cazos

♂ **saucer** noun
el **platillo** masc
flying saucers platillos volantes

♂ **sausage** noun
1 la **salchicha** fem
pork sausages salchichas de cerdo
2 (salami) el **salchichón** masc

savage noun
el & la **salvaje** masc & fem

to **save** verb
1 (to rescue) **salvar** [17]
to save somebody's life salvarle la vida a alguien
The doctors saved his life. Los médicos le salvaron la vida.
2 (money, energy, time, etc) **ahorrar** [17]
I've saved £60. He ahorrado sesenta libras.
Try to save electricity. Intenta ahorrar electricidad.
We took a taxi to save time. Tomamos un taxi para ahorrar tiempo.
I walk to school to save money. Voy al colegio a pie para ahorrar dinero.
3 (to put aside) **guardar** [17]
Save the cake for later. Guarda el pastel para luego.
4 (Computers) **guardar** [17]
You must save your files. Hay que guardar tus ficheros.
5 (a goal) **parar** [17]
• to **save up**
ahorrar [17]
I'm saving up to go to Spain. Estoy ahorrando para ir a España.

savings plural noun
los **ahorros** plural masc
to spend your savings gastar [1] los ahorros

♂ **savoury** adjective
salado masc, **salada** fem
a savoury pancake un crepe salado
I prefer savoury things to sweet things. Prefiero lo salado a lo dulce.

saw noun
la **sierra** fem

saxophone noun
el **saxofón** masc
to play the saxophone tocar [31] el saxofón

♂ to **say** verb ▷ see **saying** noun
1 (in general) **decir** [5]
She says she's tired. Dice que está cansada.
What did you say to him? ¿Qué le has dicho?
The letter doesn't say how much I have to pay. La carta no dice cuánto hay que pagar.
He said to wait for him here. Dijo que lo esperásemos aquí.
2 (to repeat) to say something again repetir [57] algo
3 (in expressions) ... as they say ... como dicen
He hasn't arrived. That is to say, he won't make it. No ha llegado. Es decir, no va a llegar a tiempo.
That goes without saying. Eso no hace falta ni decirlo.

saying noun ▷ see **say** verb
el **dicho** masc
as the saying goes ... como dice el dicho ...

scab noun
la **costra** fem

scale noun
1 (size) la **escala** fem
on a large scale en gran escala
the scale of the disaster la escala del desastre
2 (in music) la **escala** fem
3 (of a fish) la **escama** fem

scales plural noun
la **balanza** fem
kitchen scales una balanza de cocina
bathroom scales una báscula de baño

scalp noun
el **cuero cabelludo**

scandal noun
1 (disgraceful event) el **escándalo** masc
2 (gossip) el **chismorreo** masc

Scandinavia noun
Escandinavia fem

Scandinavian *adjective & noun*

1 **escandinavo** *masc*, **escandinava** *fem*
2 el **escandinavo** *masc*, la **escandinava** *fem*
the Scandinavian los escandinavos

> **WORD TIP** Adjectives and nouns for nationality
> and regional origin do not have capital letters in
> Spanish.

scanner *noun*
el **escáner** *masc*

scar *noun*
la **cicatriz** *fem*

scarce *adjective*
escaso *masc*, **escasa** *fem*

scarcely *adverb*
apenas
I could scarcely see it. Apenas lo veía.

scare *noun* ▷ see **scare** *verb*

1 el **susto** *masc*
to give somebody a scare darle [4] un susto
a alguien
2 a bomb scare una amenaza de bomba
• **scarecrow** el espantapájaros

> **WORD TIP** *espantapájaros* does not change in the
> plural.

to **scare** *verb* ▷ see **scare** *noun*
to scare somebody asustar [17] a alguien
You scared me! ¡Me has asustado!

scared *adjective* ▷ see **scare** *noun, verb*
asustado *masc*, **asustada** *fem*
to be scared estar [2] asustado *masc*,
asustada *fem*
I'm scared! ¡Estoy asustado!
to be scared of something tenerle [9]
miedo a algo
He's scared of dogs. Les tiene miedo a los
perros.

scarf *noun*

1 (*for warmth*) la **bufanda** *fem*
2 (*of silk, etc*) el **foulard** *masc*

scary *adjective*
de miedo
a scary film una película de miedo

scene *noun*

1 (*of an accident, a crime*) la **escena** *fem*
the scene of the crime la escena del crimen
2 (*world*) el **mundo** *masc*
the music scene el mundo de la música
3 (*sight*) scenes of violence escenas violentas
4 (*fuss*) to make a scene montar [17] un
número (*informal*)

scenery *noun*

1 (*landscape*) el **paisaje** *masc*
2 (*in a theatre*) el **decorado** *masc*

♂ **schedule** *noun*
el **programa** *masc*
We have a very busy schedule. Tenemos un
programa muy apretado.
The repairs are behind schedule. Las
reparaciones van atrasadas.

scheduled flight *noun*
el **vuelo regular**

scheme *noun*
el **plan** *masc*

scholarship *noun*
la **beca** *fem*

♂ **school** *noun*

1 (*primary*) la **escuela**
2 (*secondary*) el **colegio** *masc*
to go to school ir [8] al colegio
She's still at school. Todavía va al colegio.
When I leave school, I'll go to ... Cuando
termino el colegio, iré a ...
• **schoolbook** el libro de texto
• **schoolboy** el colegial
• **schoolchildren** los colegiales
• **schoolfriend** el compañero del colegio, la
compañera del colegio
• **schoolgirl** la colegiala
• **school uniform** el uniforme escolar
• **school year** el año escolar

♂ **science** *noun*
la **ciencia** *fem*
a science teacher un profesor de ciencias
I like science. Me gustan las ciencias.
• **science fiction** la ciencia ficción

scientific *adjective*
científico *masc*, **científica** *fem*

scientist *noun*
el **científico** *masc*, la **científica** *fem*

scissors *plural noun*
las **tijeras** *plural fem*
a pair of scissors unas tijeras

scoop *noun*

1 (*of ice-cream*) la **bola** *fem*
How many scoops would you like?
¿Cuántas bolas quieres?
2 (*in a newspaper*) la **primicia** *fem*

score *noun* ▷ see **score** *verb*

1 (*Sport*) el **resultado** *masc*
The score was three two. El resultado fue
tres a dos.
What's the score? ¿A cómo van?
2 (*in a test, card game*) la **puntuación** *fem*

a
b
c
d
e
f
g
h
i
j
k
l
m
n
o
p
q
r
s
t
u
v
w
x
y
z

to **score** verb ▷ see **score** noun
1 (a goal) **marcar** [31]
Lenny scored a goal. Lenny marcó un gol.
2 (points) **conseguir** [64]
I scored three points. Conseguí tres
puntos.
3 (to keep score) **llevar** [17] **la puntuación**

Scorpio noun
1 (the star sign) el **Scorpio** masc
2 (person) un & una **scorpio** masc & fem
Jess is Scorpio. Jess es escorpio.

> **WORD TIP** Use a small letter in Spanish to say I
> am ... etc with star signs. Star signs in Spanish are
> used without el, un, la, una.

♂**Scot** noun
el **escocés** masc, la **escocesa** fem
the Scots los escoceses

> **WORD TIP** Adjectives and nouns for nationality
> and regional origin do not have capital letters in
> Spanish.

♂**Scotland** noun
Escocia fem
in Scotland en Escocia
We're from Scotland. Somos de Escocia.

Scots adjective
escocés masc, escocesa fem
a Scots accent un acento escocés

Scotsman noun
un escocés masc

Scotswoman noun
una escocesa fem

♂**Scottish** adjective
escocés masc, escocesa fem
a Scottish accent un acento escocés

> **WORD TIP** Adjectives and nouns for nationality
> and regional origin do not have capital letters in
> Spanish.

scout noun
el **explorador** masc

scrambled eggs noun
los **huevos revueltos**

scrap noun
a scrap of paper un trocito de papel

to **scrape** verb
rayar [17]

scratch noun ▷ see **scratch** verb
1 (on your skin) el **arañazo** masc
2 (in paint, wood) el **rayón** masc

to **scratch** verb ▷ see **scratch** noun
(with nails, claws) **arañar** [1]
to scratch yourself rascarse [31]
to scratch your head rascarse [31] la cabeza

♂**scream** noun ▷ see **scream** verb
el **grito** masc
a scream of terror un grito de terror

♂to **scream** verb ▷ see **scream** noun
gritar [17]
He screamed with pain. Gritó de dolor.
They screamed for help. Gritaron pidiendo
ayuda.

♂**screen** noun
la **pantalla** fem
on the screen en la pantalla
a flat screen TV un televisor de pantalla
plana

screw noun ▷ see **screw** verb
el **tornillo** masc

to **screw** verb ▷ see **screw** noun
to screw something down ajustar [17] algo
con tornillos
to screw a lid on enroscar [30] una tapa
• **screwdriver** el destornillador

to **scribble** verb
garabatear [17]

to **scrub** verb
cepillar [17]
to scrub your nails cepillarse las uñas

scuba diving noun
el **submarinismo** masc

sculpture noun
la **escultura** fem

sculptor noun
el **escultor** masc, la **escultora** fem
She's a sculptor. Es escultora.

♂**sea** noun
el **mar** masc
a village by the sea un pueblo a orillas del
mar
• **seafood** el marisco
• **seagull** la gaviota

seal noun ▷ see **seal** verb
(the animal) la **foca** fem

to **seal** verb ▷ see **seal** noun
(an envelope) **cerrar** [29]

seaman noun
el **marinero** masc

search noun ▷ see **search** verb
la **búsqueda** fem
the search for the treasure la búsqueda del
tesoro
• **search engine** el buscador

to **search** *verb* ▷ see **search** *noun*

1 (*to look for*) **buscar** [31]
I've searched my desk but I can't find the letter. He buscado en mi escritorio pero no encuentro la carta.
to search for something buscar [31] algo
I've been searching everywhere for the scissors. He buscado las tijeras por todas partes.
I searched the room for the money. Revisé la habitación buscando el dinero.

2 (*a building, person*) **registrar** [17]
The police searched the house. La policía registró la casa.

seashell *noun*
la **concha de mar**

seasick *adjective*
to be seasick estar [2] mareado, *fem* mareada
to get seasick marearse [17]

seaside *noun*
la **costa** *fem*
at the seaside en la costa

ℰ **season** *noun*

1 (*for sport, fruit*) la **temporada** *fem*
the rugby season la temporada de rugby
the high season la temporada alta
the low season la temporada baja
Strawberries are not in season at the moment. Ahora no es temporada de fresas.

2 (*time of year*) the four seasons of the year las cuatro estaciones del año
• **season ticket** el abono de temporada

ℰ **seat** *noun*

1 (*in general*) el **asiento** *masc*
Take a seat. Toma asiento.
the front seat el asiento delantero
the back seat el asiento trasero
Can you keep my seat? ¿Puedes guardarme el sitio?

2 (*in a cinema, theatre*) la **localidad** *fem*
to book seats reservar [17] localidades
• **seatbelt** el cinturón de seguridad

ℰ **second** *adjective* ▷ see **second** *noun*
segundo *masc*, **segunda** *fem*
for the second time por segunda vez
on the second floor en la segunda planta
He comes every second Friday. Viene cada dos viernes.

ℰ **second** *noun* ▷ see **second** *adj*

1 (*unit of time*) el **segundo** *masc*
Just a second. Un segundo, por favor.

2 (*to talk about the date*) **the second of July** el dos de julio
We leave on the second. Nos vamos el día dos.

second class *adjective*
(*ticket, hotel*) **de segunda clase**
a second class team un equipo de segunda clase

ℰ **secondary school** *noun*
el **colegio de enseñanza secundaria**

ℰ **second-hand** *adjective, adverb*
de segunda mano
a second-hand bike una bicicleta de segunda mano
I bought it second hand. Lo compré de segunda mano.

secondly *adverb*
en segundo lugar

secret *adjective* ▷ see **secret** *noun*
secreto *masc*, **secreta** *fem*
a secret plan un plan secreto

secret *noun* ▷ see **secret** *adj*
el **secreto** *masc*
in secret en secreto
to keep a secret guardar [17] un secreto

secretarial college *noun*
la **escuela de secretariado**

ℰ **secretary** *noun*
el **secretario** *masc*, la **secretaria** *fem*
the secretary's office la secretaría
She's a secretary. Es secretaria.

secretly *adverb*
en secreto

sect *noun*
la **secta** *fem*

ℰ **section** *noun*
la **sección** *fem*

security *noun*
la **seguridad** *fem*

security guard *noun*
el **guarda jurado**, la **guarda jurada**
He's a security guard. Es guarda jurado.

ℰ to **see** *verb*

1 (*in general*) **ver** [16]
I saw Lindy yesterday. Vi a Lindy ayer.
Have you seen the film? ¿Has visto la película?
We saw him leave ten minutes ago. Lo vimos salir hace diez minutos.
They see each other every day. Se ven todos los días. ▸▸

a
b
c
d
e
f
g
h
i
j
k
l
m
n
o
p
q
r
s
t
u
v
w
x
y
z

You must see a doctor. Tienes que ver al médico.
Let's see. A ver.

2   (*to make out*) **to be able to see something** ver[16] algo
I can't see anything. No veo nada.

3   (*to say good-bye*) **See you!** ¡Hasta luego!
See you on Saturday! ¡Hasta el sábado!
See you soon! ¡Hasta pronto!
See you tomorrow! ¡Hasta mañana!

4   (*to accompany*) **to see somebody home** acompañar[17] a alguien a casa

• **to see to something**
ocuparse[17] **de algo**
Joe's seeing to the drinks. Joe se ocupa de las bebidas.

seed *noun*
la **semilla** *fem*
to plant seeds plantar[17] semillas

ᵟ to **seem** *verb*
parecer[35]
It seems she's left. Parece que se ha ido.
He seems quite shy. Parece bastante tímido.
It seems odd to me. Me parece raro.
They seem to be out. Parece que no están.
The museum seemed to be closed. Parecía que el museo estaba cerrado.

seesaw *noun*
el **balancín** *masc*

to **select** *verb*
seleccionar[17]

selection *noun*
la **selección** *fem*

self-confidence *noun*
la **confianza en sí mismo**
She has a lot of self-confidence. Tiene mucha confianza en sí misma.

self-confident *adjective*
seguro de sí mismo *masc*, **segura de sí misma** *fem*

self-conscious *adjective*
cohibido *masc*, **cohibida** *fem*

self-employed *adjective*
autónomo *masc*, **autónoma** *fem*
My father's self-employed. Mi padre es autónomo.
the self-employed los autónomos

selfish *adjective*
egoísta *masc & fem*

ᵟ **self-service** *adjective*
de auto servicio
a self-service restaurant un autoservicio

ᵟ to **sell** *verb*
vender[18]
to sell something to somebody venderle algo a alguien
I sold him my bike. Le vendí mi bici.
They don't sell bread. No venden pan.
The house has been sold. La casa se ha vendido.
The concert's sold out. No quedan localidades para el concierto.

sell-by date *noun*
la **fecha límite de venta**

seller *noun*
el **vendedor** *masc*, la **vendedora** *fem*

Sellotape® *noun*
el **celo** *masc*

ᵟ **semi** *noun*
la **casa adosada**
We live in a semi. Vivimos en una casa adosada.

• **semicircle** el semicírculo
• **semicolon** el punto y coma
• **semi-detached house** la casa adosada
• **semi-final** la semifinal
• **semi-skimmed milk** la leche semidesnatada

ᵟ to **send** *verb*
mandar[17]
to send something to somebody mandarle algo a alguien
I sent her a text on her birthday. Le mandé un SMS el día de su cumpleaños.

• **to send somebody back**
hacer[7] **volver a alguien**
• **to send something back**
devolver[45] **algo**
• **to send for somebody**
hacer[7] **llamar a alguien**
The headmistress sent for us. La directora nos hizo llamar.
Send for the doctor! ¡Llama al médico!
• **to send for something**
pedir[57] **algo**
I sent for a brochure. Les escribí para pedir un folleto.

senior citizen *noun*
la **persona de la tercera edad**

sensation *noun*

1   (*feeling*) la **sensibilidad** *fem*
She had no sensation in her fingers. No tenía sensibilidad en los dedos.

2   (*impact*) la **sensación** *fem*
She caused a sensation. Causó sensación.

a
b
c
d
e
f
g
h
i
j
k
l
m
n
o
p
q
r
s
t
u
v
w
x
y
z

sensational *adjective*
sensacional *masc & fem*
a sensational goal un gol sensacional

sense *noun*
1 (*being sensible*) el **sentido** *masc*
common sense sentido común
It makes a lot of sense. Tiene mucho sentido.
It doesn't make much sense to buy it. No tiene mucho sentido comprarlo.
2 to have a sense of humour tener [9] sentido del humor
She has no sense of humour. No tiene sentido del humor.
3 (*meaning*) el **significado**
4 (*ability*) the sense of smell el olfato
the sense of touch el tacto

ᔔ**sensible** *adjective*
sensato *masc*, **sensata** *fem*
She's very sensible. Es muy sensata.
It's a sensible decision. Es una decisión sensata.
Tell him to be sensible and come home. Dile que sea razonable y vuelva a casa.

sensitive *adjective*
sensible *masc & fem*
for sensitive skin para pieles sensibles

ᔔ**sentence** *noun* ▷ see **sentence** *verb*
1 (*Grammar*) la **oración** *fem*
Write two sentences in Spanish. Escribe dos oraciones en español.
2 (*in law*) la **sentencia** *fem*

ᔔ to **sentence** *verb* ▷ see **sentence** *noun*
condenar [17]
to sentence somebody to something condenar a alguien a algo
She was sentenced to five years' imprisonment. Fue condenada a cinco años de prisión.

sentimental *adjective*
sentimental *masc & fem*

separate *adjective* ▷ see **separate** *verb*
1 (*holidays, accounts*) **separado** *masc*, **separada** *fem*
They have separate rooms. Tienen habitaciones separadas.
2 (*away from each other*) **aparte** *masc & fem*
in a separate pile en un montón aparte
on a separate sheet of paper en una hoja de papel aparte
3 (*meaning, problem*) **distinto** *masc*, **distinta** *fem*
That's a separate issue. Ése es un asunto distinto.

to **separate** *verb* ▷ see **separate** *adj*
1 **separar** [17]
to separate the good from the bad separar lo bueno de lo malo
2 (*couples, partners*) **separarse** [17]
Her parents have separated. Sus padres se han separado.

separately *adverb*
por separado

separation *noun*
la **separación** *fem*

ᔔ**September** *noun*
el **septiembre** *masc*
in September en septiembre
Term starts on the fifth of September. El trimestre empieza el cinco de septiembre.

WORD TIP Names of months and days start with small letters in Spanish.

sequel *noun*
la **continuación** *fem*

ᔔ**serial** *noun*
la **serie** *fem*
the last episode of the serial el último episodio de la serie

series *noun*
la **serie** *fem*
a television series una serie de televisión

ᔔ**serious** *adjective*
1 (*not funny*) **serio** *masc*, **seria** *fem*
I'm serious about it. Estoy hablando en serio.
She's not serious about it. No se lo toma en serio.
2 (*injury, mistake, condition, etc*) **grave** *masc & fem*
We have a serious problem. Tenemos un problema grave.
His condition is serious. Está grave.

seriously *adverb*
1 (*not joking*) **en serio**
Seriously, I have to go now. En serio, tengo que irme.
Seriously? ¿En serio?
2 to take somebody seriously tomarse [17] en serio a alguien
3 (*ill, injured*) **gravemente**
She's seriously injured. Está gravemente herida.

servant *noun*
el **criado** *masc*, la **criada** *fem*

a
b
c
d
e
f
g
h
i
j
k
l
m
n
o
p
q
r
s
t
u
v
w
x
y
z

serve noun ▷ see **serve** verb
(in tennis) el **saque** masc
It's your serve. Te toca sacar.

to **serve** verb ▷ see **serve** noun
1 (in general) **servir** [57]
to serve the soup servir la sopa
2 (in a shop) **atender** [36]
Are you being served? ¿Le atienden?
3 (in tennis) **sacar** [31]

ℰ **service** noun ▷ see **service** verb
1 (in restaurants, shops, etc) el **servicio** masc
The service is very slow. El servicio es muy lento.
Service is included. El servicio está incluido.
the emergency services los servicios de emergencia
2 (in a church) el **oficio religioso**
3 (of a car, machine) la **revisión** fem

ℰ to **service** verb ▷ see **service** noun
(a car, machine) **revisar** [1]

service charge noun
el **servicio** masc
What's the service charge? ¿Cuánto se cobra por el servicio?

ℰ **service station** noun
la **estación de servicio**

serviette noun
la **servilleta** fem

ℰ **session** noun
la **sesión** fem
a recording session una sesión de grabación

ℰ **set** adjective ▷ see **set** noun, verb
at a set time a una hora determinada
a set menu un menú del día
a set price un precio fijo

ℰ **set** noun ▷ see **set** adj, verb
1 (for games) el **juego** masc
a chess set un juego de ajedrez
a train set un tren de juguete
2 (of keys, tools) el **juego** masc
a set of spanners un juego de llaves inglesas
3 (in tennis) el **set** masc

ℰ to **set** verb ▷ see **set** adj, noun
1 (a date, time) **fijar** [17]
2 (a record) **establecer** [35]
3 (the table) to set the table poner [11] la mesa
4 (a watch, alarm clock, etc) **poner** [11]
to set a watch poner [11] el reloj en hora
I've set my alarm for seven. He puesto el despertador para las siete.

5 (a film, play) **ambientar** [1]
The novel is set in Majorca. La novela está ambientada en Mallorca.
6 (sun) **ponerse** [11]
· to set off
salir [63]
We're setting off at ten. Salimos a las diez.
They set off for Barcelona tomorrow. Salen para Barcelona mañana.
· to set off something
1 (fireworks) **tirar** [17]
2 (an alarm) **hacer** [7] **sonar**
· to set out
salir [63]
They set out for Seville yesterday. Salieron ayer para Sevilla.

settee noun
el **sofá** masc

to **settle** verb
1 (a bill) **pagar** [28]
2 (a problem) **solucionar** [17]

ℰ **seven** number
siete invariable number
Khalil's seven. Khalil tiene siete años.
It's seven o'clock. Son las siete.

ℰ **seventeen** number
diecisiete invariable number
Jason's seventeen. Jason tiene diecisiete años.

ℰ **seventh** adjective ▷ see **seventh** noun
séptimo masc, **séptima** fem
on the seventh floor en la séptima planta

ℰ **seventh** noun ▷ see **seventh** adj
1 (fraction) a seventh una séptima parte
2 (in dates) the seventh of April el siete de abril
She came on the seventh. Vino el día siete.

seventies plural noun
the seventies los años setenta
in the seventies en los años setenta

ℰ **seventy** number
setenta invariable number
seventy-five setenta y cinco
He's seventy. Tiene setenta años.

ℰ **several** adjective, pronoun
varios plural masc, **varias** plural fem
He took several. Tomó varios.
I've seen her several times. La he visto varias veces.
I've seen several of his films. He visto varias películas suyas.

severe *adjective*
1 (*person*) **severo** *masc*, **severa** *fem*
2 (*weather*) **malo** *masc*, **mala** *fem*
3 (*injury*) **grave** *masc & fem*

Seville *noun*
   Sevilla *fem*

to **sew** *verb*
   coser [18]

sewer *noun*
   la **alcantarilla** *fem*

sewing *noun*
   la **costura** *fem*
   I like sewing. Me gusta la costura.
  • **sewing machine** la máquina de coser

sex *noun*
1 (*gender*) el **sexo** *masc*
   the opposite sex el sexo opuesto
2 (*intercourse*) las **relaciones sexuales**
   to have sex with someone tener [9]
   relaciones sexuales con alguien
  • **sex education** la educación sexual

sexism *noun*
   el **sexismo** *masc*

sexist *adjective*
   sexista *masc & fem*
   sexist remarks comentarios sexistas

sexual *adjective*
   sexual *masc & fem*
  • **sexual harassment** el acoso sexual

sexuality *noun*
   la **sexualidad** *fem*

sexy *adjective*
   sexy *invariable adjective*

shabby *adjective*
   gastado *masc*, **gastada** *fem*

shade *noun*
1 (*from the sun*) la **sombra**
   in the shade en la sombra
2 (*of a colour*) el **tono** *masc*
   a shade of green un tono verde

shadow *noun*
   la **sombra** *fem*

to **shake** *verb*
1 (*to tremble*) **temblar** [29]
   Her hands are shaking. Le tiemblan las
   manos.
   The ground was shaking. Temblaba la
   tierra.
2 (*a bottle, medicine*) **agitar** [17]
   Shake before use. Agitar antes de abrir.

3 (*a cloth, building*) **sacudir** [19]
   The explosion shook the building. La
   explosión sacudió el edificio.
4 (*someone's hand*) to shake hands with
   somebody darle [17] la mano a alguien
   She shook hands with me. Me dio la mano.
   We shook hands. Nos estrechamos la
   mano.
5 (*meaning no*) to shake your head negar [30]
   con la cabeza

shall *verb*
   Shall I come with you? ¿Voy contigo?
   Shall we stop now? ¿Paramos ya?

shallow *adjective*
   (*water, river*) **poco profundo** *masc*, **poco**
   profunda *fem*
   the shallow end of the pool la parte poco
   profunda de la piscina
   The water's very shallow here. El agua es
   muy poco profunda aquí.

shambles *noun*
   el **caos** *masc*
   It was a total shambles! ¡Fue un caos total!

shame *noun*
1 (*feeling*) la **vergüenza** *fem*
   Shame on you! ¡Debería darte vergüenza!
2 (*pity*) What a shame! ¡Qué pena!
   It's a shame she can't come. Qué pena que
   no pueda venir.

♪ **shampoo** *noun*
   el **champú** *masc*
   I bought a herbal shampoo. Compré un
   champú de hierbas.

shamrock *noun*
   el **trébol** *masc*

shandy *noun*
   la **clara** *fem*
   a shandy una clara

shape *noun*
   la **forma** *fem*
   What shape is it? ¿Qué forma tiene?
   to be in good shape estar [2] en buena
   forma

share *noun* ▷ see **share** *verb*
1 (*portion*) la **parte** *fem*
   your share of the money tu parte del dinero
   my share of the bill lo que me corresponde
   de la cuenta
2 (*in a company*) la **acción** *fem*

to **share** *verb* ▷ see **share** *noun*
   compartir [19]
   to share the costs compartir los costes
   I'm sharing a room with Emma. Comparto una habitación con Emma.
- to **share out**
   repartir [19]

shark *noun*
   el **tiburón** *masc*

sharp *adjective*
1 (*knife, blade*) **afilado** *masc*, **afilada** *fem*
   a sharp pencil un lápiz con mucha punta
   a sharp bend una curva cerrada
   This knife isn't very sharp. Este cuchillo no está muy afilado.
2 (*clever*) **listo** *masc*, **lista** *fem*

to **sharpen** *verb*
1 (*a knife, blade*) **afilar** [17]
2 (*a pencil*) **sacarle** [31] **punta a**

sharpener *noun*
   el **sacapuntas** *masc, pl:* los **sacapuntas**

to **shave** *verb*
   afeitarse [17]
   He's shaving. Se está afeitando.
   to shave off your beard afeitarse [17] la barba
   to shave your legs afeitarse [17] las piernas
- **shaving cream** la crema de afeitar
- **shaving foam** la espuma de afeitar

♪ **she** *pronoun*
1 **ella** (*see Word Tip*)
   She's in her room. Está en su cuarto.
   She's a student. Es estudiante.
   She's a very good teacher. Es muy buena profesora.
   Here she is! ¡Aquí está!
2 (*for emphasis*) **ella**
   She did it. Lo hizo ella.

> **WORD TIP** *she*, like other subject pronouns *he*, *you*, *we* etc, is generally not translated in Spanish; the form of the verb tells you whether the subject of the verb is *I*, *we*, *they*, etc, so *she* is translated only for emphasis or for clarity.

shed *noun*
1 (*in a garden*) el **cobertizo** *masc*
2 (*industrial*) la **nave** *fem*

♪ **sheep** *noun*
   la **oveja** *fem*
   a flock of sheep un rebaño de ovejas
- **sheepdog** el perro pastor

♪ **sheet** *noun*
1 (*for a bed*) la **sábana** *fem*
2 (*of paper*) la **hoja de papel**
   a blank sheet una hoja en blanco

3 (*of glass, metal*) la **plancha** *fem*

♪ **shelf** *noun*
1 (*at home*) el **estante** *masc*
   a set of shelves una estantería
2 (*in a shop, fridge*) la **balda** *fem*

shell *noun*
1 (*of an egg, a nut*) la **cáscara** *fem*
2 (*seashell*) la **concha** *fem*
3 (*explosive*) el **proyectil** *masc*
- **shellfish** el marisco

shelter *noun*
   el **refugio** *masc*
   in the shelter of the tree al abrigo del árbol
   to take shelter from the rain refugiarse [17] de la lluvia

sherry *noun*
   el **jerez** *masc*

Shetland Islands *noun*
   las **islas Shetland**

shield *noun*
   el **escudo** *masc*

shift *noun* ▷ see **shift** *verb*
   el **turno** *masc*
   the day shift el turno de día
   to be on night shift hacer [7] el turno de noche

to **shift** *verb* ▷ see **shift** *noun*
   to shift something mover [38] algo

shin *noun*
   la **espinilla** *fem*

♪ to **shine** *verb*
   brillar [17]
   The sun's shining. Brilla el sol.

shiny *adjective*
   brillante *masc & fem*

ship *noun*
   el **barco** *masc*
   a passenger ship un barco de pasajeros

♪ **shirt** *noun*
   la **camisa** *fem*

to **shiver** *verb*
   temblar [29]

shock *noun* ▷ see **shock** *verb*
1 (*mental*) el **shock** *masc*
   in a state of shock en estado de shock
   It was a shock. Fue un shock.
   It gave me a shock. Me llevé un shock.
2 (*electric*) la **descarga eléctrica**
   I got an electric shock. Me dio una descarga eléctrica.

to **shock** verb ▷ see **shock** noun
horrorizar [22]

shocked adjective
horrorizado masc, **horrorizada** fem
We were shocked. Nos quedamos
horrorizados.

shocking adjective
1 (news) **horroroso** masc, **horrorosa** fem
2 (behaviour) **vergonzoso** masc, **vergonzosa** fem

ꝗ **shoe** noun
el **zapato** masc
a pair of shoes un par de zapatos
What size shoes do you wear? ¿Qué
numero calzas?
· **shoelace** el cordón de zapato
· **shoe polish** el betún
· **shoe shop** la zapatería

to **shoot** verb
1 (to fire) **disparar** [17]
to shoot at somebody disparar a alguien
She shot him in the leg. Le disparó en la
pierna.
He was shot in the arm. Le dispararon en el
brazo.
2 (to kill) **matar** [17] **a tiros**
He was shot by terrorists. Los terroristas lo
mataron a tiros.
3 (to execute) **fusilar** [17]
4 (in football, hockey) **chutar** [1]
5 (a film) **rodar** [24]

shooting noun
1 (shots) el **tiroteo** masc
2 (hunting) la **caza** fem
target shooting tiro al blanco
3 (murder) el **asesinato** masc

ꝗ **shop** noun ▷ see **shop** verb
la **tienda** fem
a record shop una tienda de discos
a shoe shop una zapatería
to go round the shops ir [8] de tiendas

to **shop** verb ▷ see **shop** noun
1 **hacer** [7] **compras**
She spent the whole day shopping. Pasó el
día entero haciendo compras.
I always shop at the market. Compro
siempre en el mercado.
2 to go shopping ir [8] de compras
On Saturdays I always go shopping. Los
sábados siempre voy de compas.

ꝗ **shop assistant** noun
el **dependiente** masc, la **dependienta** fem
Brad's a shop assistant. Brad trabaja de
dependiente.

ꝗ **shopkeeper** noun
el **tendero** masc, la **tendera** fem

shoplifter noun
el **ladrón** masc, la **ladrona** fem

shoplifting noun
el **hurto en las tiendas**

ꝗ **shopping** noun
las **compras** plural fem
Can you put the shopping away? ¿Puedes
guardar las compras?
I've got a lot of shopping to do. Tengo
muchas cosas que comprar.
· **shopping centre**, **shopping mall** el centro
comercial
· **shopping trolley** el carrito

ꝗ **shop window** noun
el **escaparate** masc

shore noun
la **orilla del mar**

ꝗ **short** adjective
1 (in general) **corto** masc, **corta** fem
a short dress un vestido corto
a short break un descanso corto
a short visit una visita corta
a short time ago hace poco tiempo
She has short hair. Tiene el pelo corto.
It's a short walk from the station. Queda
bastante cerca de la estación.
2 (person) **bajo** masc, **baja** fem
He's quite short. Es bastante bajo.
3 to be short of something andar [21] escaso
de algo
We're a bit short of money at the moment.
De momento andamos escasos de dinero.
We're getting short of time. Se nos está
acabando el tiempo.

shortage noun
la **escasez** fem

shortbread noun
la **galleta de mantequilla**

shortcrust pastry noun
la **pasta quebrada**

short cut noun
el **atajo** masc
to take a short cut tomar [1] un atajo

to **shorten** verb
acortar [17]

shortly adverb
dentro de poco

a
b
c
d
e
f
g
h
i
j
k
l
m
n
o
p
q
r
s
t
u
v
w
x
y
z

shorts plural noun
los **shorts** plural masc
a pair of shorts unos shorts
my red shorts mis shorts rojos

short-sighted adjective
miope masc & fem
I'm short-sighted. Soy miope.

short-sleeved adjective
de manga corta
a short-sleeved shirt una camisa de manga
corta

shotgun noun
la **escopeta** fem

should verb
1 (should + verb) You should ask Simon.
Deberías preguntárselo a Simon.
The potatoes should be cooked now. Las
patatas deberían estar hechas ya.
2 (should + have) You should have told me.
Deberías habérmelo dicho.
You shouldn't have stayed. No deberías
haberte quedado.

WORD TIP should is translated by debería, etc.
should have is translated by debería, etc + haber.

3 (in expressions) I should forget it if I were you.
Yo en tu lugar me olvidaría del asunto.
I should think he's forgotten. Yo diría que
se ha olvidado.

shoulder noun
el **hombro** masc
• **shoulder bag** el bolso

shout noun ▷ see **shout** verb
el **grito** masc
to give a shout dar [4] un grito
He gave a a shout of pain. Dio un grito de
dolor.

to shout verb ▷ see **shout** noun
gritar [17]
Stop shouting! ¡Deja de gritar!
They shouted at us to come back. Nos
gritaron que volviésemos.

shovel noun
la **pala** fem

show noun ▷ see **show** verb
1 (on stage) el **espectáculo** masc
We went to see a show. Fuimos a ver un
espectáculo.
2 (on TV) el **programa** masc
He has a TV show. Tiene un programa en la
tele.
3 (exhibition) el **salón** masc
the motor show el salón del automóvil

to show verb ▷ see **show** noun
1 (in general) **enseñar** [17]
to show something to somebody enseñar
algo a alguien
I'll show you my photos. Te enseño mis
fotos.
to show somebody how to do something
enseñarle a alguien cómo hacer algo
He showed me how to make paella. Me
enseñó cómo hacer paella.
2 (to demonstrate) **demostrar** [1]
You must show that you understand how it
works. Tienes que demostrar que
entiendes cómo funciona.
• **to show off**
presumir [19]
She's always showing off. Siempre está
presumiendo.

shower noun
1 (in a bathroom) la **ducha** fem
I have a shower every day. Me ducho todos
los días.
2 (of rain) el **chaparrón** masc

showing noun
(of a film) la **proyección** fem

show-off noun
el **fanfarrón** masc, la **fanfarrona** fem

to shriek verb
gritar [17]
He shrieked with pain. Gritó de dolor.

shrimp noun
el **camarón** masc

shrine noun
el **santuario** masc

to shrink verb
encoger [3]

Shrove Tuesday noun
el **martes de Carnaval**

to shrug verb
to shrug your shoulders encogerse [3] de
hombros

to shuffle verb
to shuffle the cards barajar [17] las cartas

shut adjective ▷ see **shut** verb
cerrado masc, **cerrada** fem
The doors are shut. Las puertas están
cerradas.

to shut verb ▷ see **shut** adj
cerrar [29]
Shut the door, please. Cierra la puerta, por
favor.

a
b
c
d
e
f
g
h
i
j
k
l
m
n
o
p
q
r
s
t
u
v
w
x
y
z

The shops shut at six. Las tiendas cierran a las seis.

• **to shut up**
callarse [17]
Shut up! ¡Cállate! (*to one person*), ¡Cállad! (*to more than one person*)

shuttlecock *noun*
el **volante** *masc*

♂ **shy** *adjective*
tímido *masc*, **tímida** *fem*

shyness *noun*
la **timidez** *fem*

Sicily *noun*
Sicilia *fem*

♂ **sick** *adjective*
1 (*ill*) **enfermo** *masc*, **enferma** *fem*
Amy's off sick today. Amy está enferma hoy y no ha venido.
2 (*when you vomit*) **to be sick** devolver [45]
I was sick several times. Devolví varias veces.
to feel sick tener [9] ganas de devolver
3 (*bored*) **to be sick of something** estar [2] harto, *fem* harta de algo
I'm sick of that song. Estoy harto de esa canción.
4 **a sick joke** una broma de mal gusto

sickness *noun*
la **enfermedad** *fem*

♂ **side** *noun*
1 (*of the street, room, etc*) el **lado** *masc*
on the other side of the street al otro lado de la calle
on the wrong side en el lado equivocado
They were sitting side by side. Estaban sentados juntos.
2 (*edge*) el **borde** *masc*
by the side of the pool al borde de la piscina
at the side of the road al borde de la carretera
by the side of the river a la orilla del río
3 (*team*) el **equipo** *masc*
She plays on our side. Juega en nuestro equipo.
4 (*in an argument*) **to take sides** tomar [17] partido
I'm on your side. (*I agree with you*) Estoy de tu lado.

♂ **sideboard** *noun*
el **aparador** *masc*

siege *noun*
el **sitio** *masc*

sieve *noun*
el **tamiz** *masc*

sigh *noun* ▷ see **sigh** *verb*
el **suspiro** *masc*

to **sigh** *verb* ▷ see **sigh** *noun*
suspirar [17]

♂ **sight** *noun*
1 (*something seen*) el **espectáculo** *masc*
It was a marvellous sight. Era un espectáculo maravilloso.
2 (*eyesight*) la **vista** *fem*
to have poor sight tener [9] mala vista
to know somebody by sight conocer [35] a alguien de vista
I know her by sight. La conozco de vista.
I'd lost sight of them. Los había perdido de vista.
3 (*when you see*) She faints at the sight of blood. Se desmaya a la vista de sangre.
It was love at first sight. Fue amor a primera vista.
4 (*place worth seeing*) **the sights** los lugares de interés
to see the sights of Barcelona visitar [17] los lugares de interés de Barcelona

sightseeing *noun*
to do some sightseeing hacer [7] turismo

sign *noun* ▷ see **sign** *verb*
1 (*notice*) el **letrero** *masc*
There's a sign on the door. Hay un letrero en la puerta.
2 (*of improvement, life, etc*) la **señal** *fem*
3 (*of the Zodiac*) el **signo** *masc*
What sign are you? ¿De qué signo eres?

to **sign** *verb* ▷ see **sign** *noun*
1 (*a document, etc*) **firmar** [17]
to sign a cheque firmar un cheque
2 (*using sign language*) **comunicarse** [31] por señas
• **to sign on**
(*as unemployed*) **inscribirse** [17] al paro

signal *noun*
la **señal** *fem*

signature *noun*
la **firma** *fem*

significance *noun*
la **importancia** *fem*

significant *adjective*
importante *masc & fem*

sign language *noun*
el **lenguaje de gestos**

signpost *noun*
　la **señal** *fem*

♪ **silence** *noun*
　el **silencio** *masc*

silent *adjective*
　silencioso *masc*, **silenciosa** *fem*

silk *adjective* ▷ see **silk** *noun*
　de seda
　a silk shirt una camisa de seda

silk *noun* ▷ see **silk** *adj*
　la **seda** *fem*

silky *adjective*
　sedoso *masc*, **sedosa** *fem*

silly *adjective*
　tonto *masc*, **tonta** *fem*
　It was a silly thing to do. Hacer eso fue una
　tontería.

silver *adjective* ▷ see **silver** *noun*
　de plata
　a silver spoon una cuchara de plata

silver *noun* ▷ see **silver** *adj*
　la **plata** *fem*

SIM card *noun*
　la **tarjeta SIM**

similar *adjective*
　parecido *masc*, **parecida** *fem*
　Their essays are very similar. Sus trabajos
　son muy parecidos.

similarity *noun*
　el **parecido** *masc*

♪ **simple** *adjective*
　sencillo *masc*, **sencilla** *fem*

to **simplify** *verb*
　simplificar [31]

simply *adverb*
　sencillamente

sin *noun*
　el **pecado** *masc*

♪ **since** *adverb, conjunction, preposition*
　1 **desde**
　I've been in Madrid since Saturday. Estoy
　en Madrid desde el sábado.
　I've been learning Spanish since last year.
　Estoy aprendiendo español desde el año
　pasado.
　I haven't seen her since. No la he visto
　desde entonces.
　I haven't seen her since Monday. No la he
　visto desde el lunes.
　Since when? ¿Desde cuándo?

2 **desde que**
　since I have known her desde que la
　conozco
　since I've been learning Spanish desde que
　aprendo español

3 (*because*) **como**
　Since it was raining, the match was
　cancelled. Como estaba lloviendo,
　cancelaron el partido.

> **WORD TIP** Spanish uses the present tense where
> English uses *have done* or *have been doing*.

sincere *adjective*
　sincero *masc*, **sincera** *fem*

sincerely *adverb*
　Yours sincerely, ... Atentamente, ...

to **sing** *verb*
　cantar [17]

singer *noun*
　el & la **cantante** *masc & fem*

singing *noun*
　el **canto** *masc*
　a singing lesson una lección de canto
　I like singing. Me gusta cantar.

♪ **single** *adjective* ▷ see **single** *noun*
　1 (*not married*) **soltero** *masc*, **soltera** *fem*
　a single man un soltero
　a group of single women un grupo de
　solteras
　2 (*only one*) a single room una habitación
　individual
　a single bed una cama individual
　3 (*in expressions*) **not a single ...** ni un solo ...,
　fem ni una sola ...
　I haven't had a single reply. No he tenido ni
　una sola respuesta.
　every single ... todos los, *fem* todas las ...
　every single day todos los días
　every single girl todas las chicas

♪ **single** *noun* ▷ see **single** *adj*
　(*ticket*) el **billete de ida**
　a single to Valencia un billete de ida para
　Valencia

single parent *noun*
　a single-parent family una familia
　monoparental
　She's a single parent. Es madre soltera.

singular *noun*
　(*Grammar*) el **singular** *masc*
　in the singular en singular

♪ **sink** *noun* ▷ see **sink** *verb*
　1 (*in a kitchen*) el **fregadero** *masc*
　2 (*in a bathroom*) el **lavabo** *masc*

ᶚ to **sink** _verb_ ▷ see **sink** _noun_
   hundirse [19]

ᶚ **sir** _noun_
   el **señor** _masc_
   Yes, sir. Sí, señor.

ᶚ **sister** _noun_
   la **hermana** _fem_
   my little siser mi hermanita
   My sister's ten. Mi hermana tiene diez
   años.
   · **sister-in-law** la cuñada

ᶚ to **sit** _verb_
   1 **sentarse** [29]
      You can sit on the sofa. Puedes sentarte en
      el sofá.
      I can sit on the floor. Me puedo sentar en el
      suelo.
   2 to be sitting **estar** [2] sentado
      Leila was sitting on the sofa. Leila estaba
      sentada en el sofá.
   3 to sit an exam **presentarse** [17] a un
      examen
      She's sitting her driving test on Thursday.
      Se presenta al examen de conducir el
      jueves.
   · **to sit down**
      sentarse [29]
      He sat down on a chair. Se sentó en una
      silla.
      Do sit down. Siéntate (_informal form_).,
      Siéntese (_polite form_).

ᶚ **site** _noun_
   a building site una obra
   1 a camp site un camping

ᶚ **sitting room** _noun_
   el **salón** _masc_, la **sala de estar**

   situation _noun_
   la **situación** _fem_

ᶚ **six** _number_
   seis _invariable number_
   Tom's six. Tom tiene seis años.
   It's six o'clock. Son las seis.

ᶚ **sixteen** _number_
   dieciséis _invariable number_
   Hannah's sixteen. Hannah tiene dieciséis
   años.

ᶚ **sixth** _adjective_ ▷ see **sixth** _noun_
   sexto _masc_, **sexta** _fem_
   on the sixth floor en el sexto piso

ᶚ **sixth** _noun_ ▷ see **sixth** _adj_
   1 (_fraction_) a sixth una sexta parte
   2 (_in dates_) the sixth of June el seis de junio
      He called me on the sixth. Me llamó el día
      seis.

sixties _plural noun_
   the sixties los años sesenta
   in the sixties en los años sesenta

ᶚ **sixty** _number_
   sesenta _invariable number_
   sixty-five sesenta y cinco
   She's sixty. Tiene sesenta años.

ᶚ **size** _noun_
   1 el **tamaño** _masc_
      the size of the house el tamaño de la casa
      What size is it? ¿De qué tamaño es?
   2 (_of clothes_) la **talla** _fem_
      What size do you take? ¿Qué talla usas?
   3 (_of shoes_) el **número** _masc_
      I take a size thirty-eight. Calzo el número
      treinta y ocho.
   4 (_in measurements_) las **medidas** _plural fem_
      What size is the window? ¿Qué medidas
      tiene la ventana?

skate _noun_ ▷ see **skate** _verb_
   el **patín** _masc_
   an ice skate un patín de hielo
   a roller skate un patín de ruedas

to **skate** _verb_ ▷ see **skate** _noun_
   1 (_on ice_) **hacer** [7] patinaje sobre hielo
   2 (_on the ground_) **hacer** [7] patinaje sobre
      ruedas

skateboard _noun_
   el **monopatín** _masc_

skateboarding _noun_
   to go skateboarding patinar [17] con el
   monopatín

skater _noun_
   el **patinador** _masc_, la **patinadora** _fem_

skating _noun_
   el **patinaje**
   to go skating (_on the ground_) ir [8] a patinar,
   (_on ice_) ir a patinar sobre hielo
   · **skating rink** la pista de patinaje

skeleton _noun_
   el **esqueleto** _masc_

sketch _noun_
   1 (_drawing_) el **boceto** _masc_
   2 (_in comedy_) el **sketch** _masc_

to **ski** _verb_ ▷ see **ski** _noun_
   esquiar [32]

a
b
c
d
e
f
g
h
i
j
k
l
m
n
o
p
q
r
s
t
u
v
w
x
y
z

♂ **ski** *noun* ▷ see **ski** *verb*
  el **esquí** *masc*
  · **ski boot** la bota de esquí
  · **ski lift** el telesquí
  · **ski pants** los pantalones de esquí
  · **ski resort** la estación de esquí
  · **ski suit** el traje de esquí

to **skid** *verb*
1 (*car*) **patinar** [8]
  The car skidded. El coche patinó.
2 (*person*) **resbalarse** [17]
  I skidded. Me resbalé.

skier *noun*
  el **esquiador** *masc*, la **esquiadora** *fem*

♂ **skiing** *noun*
  el **esquí** *masc*
  to go skiing ir [8] a esquiar

skilful *adjective*
  habilidoso *masc*, **habilidosa** *fem*

skill *noun*
  la **habilidad** *fem*
  It's not one of my skills. No es una de mis habilidades.

skimmed milk *noun*
  la **leche desnatada**

♂ **skin** *noun*
  la **piel** *fem*
  · **skinhead** el & la cabeza rapada

skinny *adjective*
  flaco *masc*, **flaca** *fem*

skip *noun* ▷ see **skip** *verb*
  el **contenedor** *masc*

to **skip** *verb* ▷ see **skip** *noun*
1 (*a meal, chapter*) **saltarse** [17]
  I skipped the third chapter. Me salté el tercer capítulo.
2 **to skip a lesson** faltar [17] a clase

skipping rope *noun*
  la **comba** *fem*

♂ **skirt** *noun*
  la **falda** *fem*
  a long skirt una falda larga
  a straight skirt una falda de tubo
  a mini-skirt una minifalda

♂ **sky** *noun*
  el **cielo** *masc*

skyscraper *noun*
  el **rascacielos** *invariable masc*
  a fifty-storey skyscraper un rascacielos de cincuenta pisos

---
WORD TIP *rascacielos* never changes.
---

to **slam** *verb*
  cerrar [29] **de un portazo**
  She slammed the door. Cerró la puerta de un portazo.

slang *noun*
  el **argot** *masc*

slap *noun* ▷ see **slap** *verb*
1 (*on the face*) la **bofetada** *fem*
2 (*on the bottom*) el **azote** *masc*

to **slap** *verb* ▷ see **slap** *noun*
  to slap somebody (*in the face*) dar [4] una bofetada a alguien, (*on the bottom*) dar [4] un azote a alguien

slate *noun*
  la **pizarra** *fem*

slave *noun*
  el **esclavo** *masc*, la **esclava** *fem*

sledge *noun*
  el **trineo** *masc*

sledging *noun*
  to go sledging ir [8] en trineo

♂ **sleep** *noun* ▷ see **sleep** *verb*
  el **sueño** *masc*
  six hours' sleep seis horas de sueño
  I had a good sleep. Dormí bien.
  She couldn't get to sleep. No pudo conciliar el sueño.
  The film sent me to sleep. La película me hizo dormir.
  to go to sleep dormirse [51]

♂ to **sleep** *verb* ▷ see **sleep** *noun*
  dormir [51]
  She's sleeping. Está durmiendo.
  Sleep well. Que duermas bien.

♂ **sleeping bag** *noun*
  el **saco de dormir**

sleeping pill *noun*
  el **somnífero** *masc*

sleepy *adjective*
  to be sleepy tener [9] sueño
  I feel sleepy. Tengo sueño.
  I was getting sleepy. Me estaba entrando sueño.

sleeve *noun*
  la **manga** *fem*
  to roll up your sleeves arremangarse [28]

♂ **slice** *noun* ▷ see **slice** *verb*
1 (*of bread, cheese*) la **rebanada** *fem*
  a slice of bread and butter una rebanada de pan con mantequilla

6 (*therefore*) **así que**
He woke up late so he missed his bus. Se
despertó tarde así que perdió el bus.

7 (*for emphasis*) **So what's your name?** ¿Y
cómo te llamas?
So what shall we do? ¿Y entonces qué
hacemos?
So what? ¿Y qué?

8 **so do I, so did I, so am I, so was I** yo también
'I work in Truro.'— 'So do I.' 'Trabajo en
Truro.'— 'Yo también.'
'I have a headache.'— 'So do I.' 'Me duele la
cabeza.'— 'A mí también.'
'I like Green Day.'— 'So do I.' 'Me gusta
Green Day.'— 'A mí tambien.'
'I used to live in Leeds.'— 'So did I.' 'Vivía
antes en Leeds.'— 'Yo también.'
'We're Irish.'— 'So are we.' 'Somos
irlandeses.'— 'Nosotros tambien.'

9 **so do we, so did we** nosotros también

10 (*with 'think', 'hope', 'expect', etc*) **I think so.**
Creo que sí.
I hope so. Espero que sí.

soaked *adjective*
empapado *masc*, **empapada** *fem*
to be soaked to the skin estar [2]
empapado hasta los huesos

♪ **soap** *noun*

1 (*for washing*) **el jabón** *masc*
a bar of soap una pastilla de jabón

2 (*on TV*) **la telenovela** *fem*
• **soap powder** el jabón en polvo

sober *adjective*
to be sober estar [2] sobrio, *fem* sobria

soccer *noun*
el fútbol *masc*
to play soccer jugar [27] al fútbol

social *adjective*
social *masc & fem*

socialism *noun*
el socialismo *masc*

socialist *adjective* ▷ see **socialist** *noun*
socialista *masc & fem*

socialist *noun* ▷ see **socialist** *adj*
el & la socialista *masc & fem*

social security *noun*

1 (*benefit*) **la asistencia social**
to be on social security recibir [19]
asistencia social

2 (*the system*) **social security** la seguridad
social

social worker *noun*
el & la asistente social
She's a social worker. Es asistente social.

society *noun*
la sociedad *fem*

sociology *noun*
la sociología *fem*

♪ **sock** *noun*
el calcetín *masc*
a pair of socks un par de calcetines

socket *noun*
el enchufe *masc*

sofa *noun*
el sofá *masc*
• **sofa bed** el sofá-cama

♪ **soft** *adjective*
suave *masc & fem*
• **soft drink** el refresco
• **soft toy** el muñeco de peluche
• **software** el software

♪ **softly** *adverb*

1 (*to touch*) **suavemente**
I softly touched her arm. Le toqué
suavemente el brazo.

2 (*to speak*) **bajito**

soil *noun*
la tierra *fem*

solar energy *noun*
la energía solar

soldier *noun*
el & la soldado *masc & fem*

solicitor *noun*
el abogado *masc*, **la abogada** *fem*
She's a solicitor. Es abogada.

solid *adjective*

1 (*pure*) **macizo** *masc*, **maciza** *fem*
a table made of solid pine una mesa de pino
macizo
a solid gold ring un anillo de oro macizo
solid silver plata maciza

2 (*not flimsy*) **sólido** *masc*, **sólida** *fem*
a solid house una casa sólida

solo *adjective, adverb* ▷ see **solo** *noun*
en solitario
a solo album un álbum en solitario
to play solo tocar [31] en solitario

solo *noun* ▷ see **solo** *adj, adv*
el solo *masc*
a guitar solo un solo de guitarra

soloist *noun*
el & la solista *masc & fem*

♪ indicates key words

a
b
c
d
e
f
g
h
i
j
k
l
m
n
o
p
q
r
s
t
u
v
w
x
y
z

♂ **some** *adjective, adverb*

1 (*with a singular noun*) **algún,** *fem* **alguna**
in some way de alguna manera
Some day he'll come. Algún día vendrá.

2 (*with a plural noun*) **unos,** *fem* **unas**
I've bought some eggs. He comprado unos huevos., He comprado huevos.
We picked some flowers. Cogimos unas flores., Cogimos flores.

3 (*certain*) **algunos,** *fem* **algunas**
Some people think he's wrong. Algunas personas piensan que no tiene razón.

4 (*with a mass noun*) **algo de**
some sugar algo de azúcar
We need bread. Necesitamos pan.
Would you like some butter? ¿Quieres mantequilla?'
Can you lend me some money? ¿Puedes prestarme dinero?
He's eaten some of it. Ya ha comido un poco.

WORD TIP With words like *sugar, bread, butter,* and plural nouns, *some* is often not translated.

♂ **somebody, someone** *pronoun*
alguien
There's somebody at the door. Hay alguien en la puerta.

WORD TIP *alguien* never changes.

somehow *adverb*

1 **de alguna manera**
I've got to finish it somehow. Tengo que terminarlo de alguna manera.

2 I somehow think they will come. No sé por qué, pero creo que vendrán.

somersault *noun*
la **voltereta** *fem*

♂ **something** *pronoun*
algo (*invariable*)
something pretty algo bonito
something interesting algo interesante
There's something wrong. Algo va mal.
I've got something to tell you. Tengo algo que decirte.
This CD is really something! ¡Este CD sí que es genial!
a guy called Pete something or other un tipo llamado Pete no sé cuánto.

sometime *adverb*
un día de estos
Give me a ring sometime. Llámame un día de estos.
I'll ring you sometime next week. Te llamaré un día de la semana que viene.

♂ **sometimes** *adverb*
a veces
I sometimes go by train. A veces voy en tren.

♂ **somewhere** *adverb*
to go somewhere ir [8] a algún sitio
I've left my bag somewhere. He dejado mi bolso en algún sitio.
I've met you somewhere before. Te he conocido antes en algún sitio.

♂ **son** *noun*
el **hijo** *masc*
her youngest son su hijo menor

♂ **song** *noun*
la **canción** *fem*
They sang my favourite song. Cantaron mi canción favorita.

son-in-law *noun*
el **yerno** *masc*

♂ **soon** *adverb*

1 **pronto**
It will soon be the holidays. Pronto llegarán las vacaciones.
See you soon! ¡Hasta pronto!, ¡Hasta ahora!
It's too soon. Es demasiado pronto.
How soon will they be here? ¿Cuándo llegarán?

2 as soon as ... tan pronto como ...
as soon as possible tan pronto como sea posible
As soon as she arrives. Tan pronto como llegue.

WORD TIP *tan pronto que* is followed by the subjunctive.

sooner *adverb*

1 (*earlier*) **antes**
She arrived sooner than us. Llegó antes que nosotros.

2 (*showing preference*) I would sooner ... preferiría ...
I'd sooner wait. Preferiría esperar.

soprano *noun*
el & la **soprano** *masc & fem*

sore *adjective* ▷ see **sore** *noun*
He has a sore throat. Le duele la garganta.
My legs are sore. Me duelen las piernas.

sore *noun* ▷ see **sore** *adj*
la **llaga** *fem*

♂ **sorry** *adjective*

1 (*showing regret*) **to be sorry** sentirlo [14]
I'm really sorry. Lo siento mucho.
to be sorry about something sentir [14] algo

I'm sorry I forgot your birthday. Siento haberme olvidado de tu cumpleaños.

WORD TIP *sentir + lo* is used to say you're sorry, but when you say *what* you are sorry about, don't use *lo*.

2 (*when interrupting*) **Sorry to disturb you.** Perdona que te moleste (*informal form*)., Perdone que le moleste (*polite form*).

3 (*to get past*) **Sorry!** ¡Perdón!

4 (*asking someone to repeat*) **Sorry?** ¿Perdón?

5 (*showing sympathy*) **to feel sorry for somebody** compadecer [35] a alguien **I feel sorry for her.** La compadezco.

6 (*when apologizing*) **to say you're sorry** pedir [57] perdón **He said he was sorry for what he had done.** Pidió perdón por lo que había hecho.

sort *noun*
   el **tipo** *masc*
   What sort of music do you like? ¿Qué tipo de música te gusta?
   all sorts of ... todo tipo de ...
   for all sorts of reasons por todo tipo de razones
 • **to sort something out**

1 (*a room, papers, etc*) **ordenar** [17] **algo** **I must sort out my things.** Tengo que ordenar mi cosas.

2 (*a problem, etc*) **solucionar** [17] **Liz is sorting it out.** Liz lo está solucionando.

soul *noun*

1 (*spirit*) el **alma** *fem* **the soul** el alma

2 (*music*) el **soul** *masc*

WORD TIP *alma* takes *el* and *un* in the singular even though it is fem.

ᶿ **to sound** *verb* ▷ see **sound** *noun*
   sonar
   Her name sounds Italian. Su nombre suena italiano.
   You sound surprised. Suenas sorprendida.
   He sounded tired. Sonó cansado.
   It sounds easy. Parece fácil.
   It sounds great! ¡Parece buena idea!

ᶿ **sound** *noun* ▷ see **sound** *verb*

1 (*noise*) el **ruido** *masc* **the sound of voices** el ruido de voces

2 (*volume*) el **volumen** *masc* **to turn down the sound** bajar [17] el volumen
 • **sound asleep** profundamente dormido *masc*, profundamente dormida *fem*
 • **sound card** la tarjeta de sonido
 • **sound effect** el efecto sonoro
 • **sound system** el equipo de sonido
 • **soundtrack** la banda sonora

ᶿ **soup** *noun*

1 (*clear*) el **consomé** *masc*

2 (*thick*) la **sopa** *fem*

3 (*puréed*) la **crema** *fem* **mushroom soup** la crema de champiñones
 • **soup plate** el plato de sopa
 • **soup spoon** la cuchara sopera

sour *adjective*
   (*taste*) **agrio** *masc*, **agria** *fem*
   sour cream nata agria
   a sweet and sour sauce una salsa agridulce
   to go sour cortarse [1]
   The milk's gone sour. La leche se ha cortado.

ᶿ **south** *adjective, adverb* ▷ see **south** *noun*
   sur *invariable adj*
   the south side la parte sur
   a south wind un viento del sur
   south of Burgos al sur de Burgos
   to travel south viajar [17] hacia el sur

WORD TIP *sur* never changes.

ᶿ **south** *noun* ▷ see **south** *adj, adv*
   el **sur** *masc*
   in the south of Scotland en el sur de Escocia

South Africa *noun*
   Sudáfrica *fem*

South African *adjective & noun*

1 **sudafricano** *masc*, **sudafricana** *fem*

2 el **sudafricano** *masc*, la **sudafricana** *fem* **the South Africans** los sudafricanos

WORD TIP Adjectives and nouns for nationality and regional origin do not have capital letters in Spanish.

ᶿ **South America** *noun*
   Sudamérica *fem*

ᶿ **South American** *adjective & noun*

1 **suramericano** *masc*, **suramericana** *fem*

2 (*person*) el **suramericano** *masc*, la **suramericana** *fem* **the South Americans** los suramericanos

WORD TIP Adjectives and nouns for nationality and regional origin do not have capital letters in Spanish.

southeast *adjective, adverb* ▷ see **southeast** *noun*
   sureste *invariable adj*
   in southeast England en el sureste de Inglaterra

WORD TIP *sureste* never changes.

southeast *noun* ▷ see **southeast** *adj, adv*
   el **sureste** *masc*

South Pole *noun*
   el **Polo Sur**

ᶿ indicates key words   631

southwest *adjective, adverb*
▷ see **southwest** *noun*
suroeste *invariable adj*
in southwest Scotland en el suroeste de
Escocia

WORD TIP *suroeste never changes.*

southwest *noun* ▷ see **southwest** *adj,*
adv
el **suroeste** *masc*

souvenir *noun*
el **recuerdo** *masc*

soya *noun*
la **soja** *fem*
soya milk leche de soja

♂ **space** *noun*
1 *(room)* el **sitio** *masc*
Is there enough space? ¿Hay suficiente
sitio?
There's enough space for two. Hay
suficiente sitio para dos.
2 *(gap)* el **espacio** *masc*
Leave a space. Deja un espacio.
3 *(Astronomy)* el **espacio** *masc*
in space en el espacio
• **spacecraft** la nave espacial
• **space shuttle** el transbordador espacial

spade *noun*
1 *(tool)* la **pala** *fem*
2 *(in cards)* la **pica** *fem*
the queen of spades la reina de picas

spaghetti *noun*
los **espaguetis** *plural masc*

♂ **Spain** *noun*
España *fem*
He's from Spain. Es español.
She's from Spain. Es española.

♂ **Spaniard** *noun*
el **español** *masc*, la **española** *fem*
the Spaniards los españoles *plural masc*

WORD TIP Adjectives and nouns for nationality
and regional origin do not have capital letters in
Spanish.

spaniel *noun*
el **spaniel** *masc*

♂ **Spanish** *adjective* ▷ see **Spanish** *noun*
1 **español** *masc*, **española** *fem*
Pedro's Spanish. Pedro es español.
Lola's Spanish. Lola es española.
2 *(teacher, lesson)* **de español**
the Spanish class la clase de español

♂ **Spanish** *noun* ▷ see **Spanish** *adj*
1 *(the language)* el **español** *masc*
our Spanish teacher nuestro profesor de
español
to speak Spanish hablar [17] español
I'm learning Spanish. Estoy aprendiendo
español.
Say it in Spanish. Dilo en español.
2 *(the people)* the Spanish los españoles

WORD TIP Adjectives and nouns for nationality,
regional origin and language do not have capital
letters in Spanish.

spanner *noun*
la **llave inglesa**

♂ to **spare** *verb* ▷ see **spare** *adj*
Can you spare a moment? ¿Tienes un
momento libre?
I can't spare the time. No tengo tiempo
para eso.
We have eggs to spare. Nos sobran huevos.

♂ **spare** *adjective* ▷ see **spare** *verb*
1 *(part, battery)* **de repuesto**
a spare battery una batería de repuesto
2 *(extra)* **de más**
We have a spare ticket. Tenemos una
entrada de más.
• **spare room** la habitación de invitados
• **spare wheel** la rueda de repuesto

♂ **spare time** *noun*
el **tiempo libre**
in my spare time en mi tiempo libre

sparrow *noun*
el **gorrión** *masc*

♂ to **speak** *verb*
1 **hablar** [17]
She speaks two languages. Habla dos
idiomas.
Do you speak Spanish? ¿Hablas español?
'Spanish spoken here' 'Se habla español'
spoken Spanish el español hablado
2 to speak to somebody hablar [17] con
alguien
She's speaking to Rashid. Está hablando
con Rashid.
We've never spoken to her. Nunca hemos
hablado con ella.
I'll speak to him about it. Hablaré sobre ello
con él.
3 *(on the phone)* Who's speaking? ¿Quién es?
Jane speaking. Soy Jane.

speaker *noun*
1 *(of a language)* a Spanish speaker un
hablante de español
an English speaker un hablante de inglés
2 *(on a music system)* el **altavoz** *masc*

3 (*giving a speech, etc*) el & la **conferenciante** *masc & fem*

spear *noun*
la **lanza** *fem*

ᵹ **special** *adjective*
especial *masc & fem*
a special offer una oferta especial
today's special la especialidad del día

specialist *noun*
el & la **especialista** *masc & fem*

ᵹ **speciality** *noun*
la **especialidad** *fem*
the chef's speciality la especialidad del día
the house speciality la especialidad de la casa

to **specialize** *verb*
to specialize in something especializarse [22] en algo

specially *adverb*
especialmente
I came specially in order to see you. Vine especialmente para verte.
They are specially for you. Son especialmente para ti.
not specially no especialmente

spectacles *noun*
las **gafas** *plural fem*

spectacular *adjective*
espectacular *masc & fem*

ᵹ **spectator** *noun*
el **espectador** *masc*, la **espectadora** *fem*

speech *noun*
el **discurso** *masc*
to make a speech dar [4] un discurso

speechless *adjective*
1 **sin habla**
I was speechless. Me quedé sin habla.
2 to be speechless with rage quedarse [17] mudo de cólera

speed *noun*
la **velocidad** *fem*
What speed was he doing? ¿A qué velocidad iba?
a twelve-speed bike una bici de doce marchas
• to speed up
acelerar [17]

speed camera *noun*
el **radar (de control de velocidad)**

speeding *noun*
He was fined for speeding. Le multaron por exceso de velocidad.

speed limit *noun*
el **límite de velocidad**

ᵹ **spell** *noun* ▷ see **spell** *verb*
1 (*of time*) el **periodo** *masc*
a busy spell un periodo de mucho trabajo
2 (*of weather*) a cold spell una ola de frío
sunny spells intervalos de sol

ᵹ to **spell** *verb* ▷ see **spell** *noun*
1 (*in writing*) **escribirse** [52]
How do you spell it? ¿Cómo se escribe?
How do you spell your surname? ¿Cómo se escribe tu apellido?
2 (*out loud*) **deletrear** [17]
Shall I spell it for you? ¿Te lo deletreo?
• **spell checker** el corrector ortográfico

spelling *noun*
la **ortografía** *fem*
a spelling mistake una falta de ortografía
• **spelling checker** el corrector ortográfico

ᵹ to **spend** *verb*
1 (*money*) **gastar** [17]
I've spent all my money. Me he gastado todo el dinero.
2 (*time*) **pasar** [17]
We spent three days in Barcelona. Pasamos tres días en Barcelona.
She spends her time surfing the web. Pasa el tiempo navegando la web.

spice *noun*
la **especia** *fem*

spicy *adjective*
picante *masc & fem*
I don't like spicy food. No me gustan los platos picantes.

spider *noun*
la **araña** *fem*

to **spill** *verb*
derramar [17]
I've spilled beer on the table. He derramado cerveza en la mesa.

spinach *noun*
las **espinacas** *plural fem*
Do you like spinach? ¿Te gustan las espinacas?

spire *noun*
la **aguja** *fem*

spirit *noun*
to get into the spirit of the occasion entrar [17] en el ambiente

a b c d e f g h i j k l m n o p q r s t u v w x y z

spirits *plural noun*
1 (*alcohol*) las **bebidas alcohólicas**
2 (*showing mood*) **to be in good spirits** estar [2] de buen humor

to **spit** *verb*
escupir [19]
to spit something out escupir algo

spite *noun*
1 **in spite of something** (*despite*) a pesar de algo
In spite of everything, we went. A pesar de todo, fuimos.
2 (*nastiness*) la **maldad** *fem*
to do something out of spite hacer [7] algo por maldad

spiteful *adjective*
1 (*person*) **malo** *masc*, **mala** *fem*
2 (*comment*) **malicioso** *masc*, **maliciosa** *fem*

splash *noun* ▷ see **splash** *verb*
1 (*in the water*) **He fell in the water with a splash.** Hizo plaf al caer al agua.
2 (*of colour*) **a splash of colour** un toque de color

to **splash** *verb* ▷ see **splash** *noun*
salpicar [31]

♪ **splendid** *adjective*
espléndido *masc*, **espléndida** *fem*
They made us a splendid meal. Nos prepararon una comida espléndida.

splinter *noun*
la **astilla** *fem*

to **split** *verb*
1 (*with an axe, a knife*) **partir** [19]
to split a piece of wood partir un trozo de madera
2 (*to come apart*) **rajarse** [17]
The lining has split. El forro se ha rajado.
3 (*to divide up*) **dividirse** [19]
They split the money between them. Se dividieron el dinero entre ellos.
• **to split up**
1 (*married couple, group*) **separarse** [17]
2 **She's split up with her boyfriend.** Ha roto con su novio.

to **spoil** *verb*
1 **arruinar** [17]
It completely spoiled the evening. Arruinó la tarde completamente.
to spoil the surprise arruinar la sorpresa
2 (*food*) **estropear** [17]
3 (*a child*) **malcriar** [32]

spoiled *adjective*
malcriado *masc*, **malcriada** *fem*
a spoiled child un niño malcriado

spoilsport *noun*
el & la **aguafiestas** *masc & fem* (pl: **aguafiestas**)

spokesperson *noun*
el & la **portavoz** *masc & fem* (pl: **portavoces**)

sponge *noun*
la **esponja** *fem*
• **sponge cake** el bizcocho

sponsor *noun* ▷ see **sponsor** *verb*
el **patrocinador** *masc*, la **patrocinadora** *fem*

to **sponsor** *verb* ▷ see **sponsor** *noun*
patrocinar [17]

spooky *adjective*
espeluznante *masc & fem*

♪ **spoon** *noun*
la **cuchara** *fem*
a soup spoon una cuchara sopera
a teaspoon una cucharilla

spoonful *noun*
1 (*large*) la **cucharada** *fem*
2 (*small*) la **cucharadita** *fem*

♪ **sport** *noun*
el **deporte** *masc*
my favourite sport mi deporte favorito
to be good at sport tener [9] facilidad para los deportes
Do you do any sports? ¿Practicas algún deporte?

sports bag *noun*
la **bolsa de deportes**

sports car *noun*
el **coche deportivo**

sports centre *noun*
el **polideportivo** *masc*

sports club *noun*
el **club deportivo**

♪ **sportsman** *noun*
el **deportista** *masc*
amateur sportsmen deportistas amateurs

sportswear *noun*
la **ropa de deporte**

♪ **sportswoman** *noun*
la **deportista** *fem*
She's a professional sportswoman. Es deportista profesional.

spot *noun* ▷ see **spot** *verb*

1 (*in fabric*) el **lunar** *masc*
a red tie with black spots una corbata roja con lunares negros

2 (*on your skin*) el **grano** *masc*
I've got spots. Tengo granos.
to be covered in spots estar [2] cubierto de granos

3 (*stain*) la **mancha** *fem*

4 (*place*) el **sitio** *masc*
a beautiful spot un sitio precioso

5 (*spotlight*) el **foco** *masc*, (*in the home*) la **luz direccional**

to spot *verb* ▷ see **spot** *noun*

1 (*a person, an object*) **divisar** [17]
I spotted her in the crowd. La divisé entre la multitud.

2 (*an error*) **encontrar** [24]

spotlight *noun*

1 (*in a theatre, etc*) el **foco** *masc*

2 (*in the home*) la **luz direccional**

spotty *adjective*
(*pimply*) **lleno de granos** *masc*, **llena de granos** *fem*

sprain *noun* ▷ see **sprain** *verb*
el **esguince** *masc*

to sprain *verb* ▷ see **sprain** *noun*
to sprain your ankle hacerse [7] un esguince en el tobillo

spray *noun*

1 (*of seawater*) la **espuma** *fem*

2 (*spray can*) el **espray** *masc*

to spread *verb*

1 (*news, diseases*) **propagarse** [28]

2 (*jam, cement, glue*) **extender** [36]

spring *noun*

1 (*the season*) la **primavera** *fem*
in the spring en primavera
spring flowers flores de primavera

2 (*in a chair, etc*) el **muelle** *masc*

3 (*giving water*) el **manantial** *masc*

springtime *noun*
la **primavera** *fem*
in springtime en primavera

spring water *noun*
el **agua de manantial**

> **WORD TIP** *agua* takes *el* or *un* in the singular even though it is fem.

sprint *noun* ▷ see **sprint** *verb*
el **esprint** *masc*

to sprint *verb* ▷ see **sprint** *noun*
correr [18] **a toda velocidad**
She sprinted after the thief. Salió corriendo a toda velocidad tras el ladrón.

sprout *noun*
(*Brussels sprout*) el **col de Bruselas**

spy *noun* ▷ see **spy** *verb*
el & la **espía** *masc & fem*

to spy *verb* ▷ see **spy** *noun*
to spy on somebody espiar [32] a alguien

spying *noun*
el **espionaje** *masc*

♪ **square** *adjective* ▷ see **square** *noun*
cuadrado *masc*, **cuadrada** *fem*
a square box una caja cuadrada
three square metres tres metros cuadrados
The room is five metres square. La habitación tiene cinco metros cuadrados.

♪ **square** *noun* ▷ see **square** *adj*

1 (*shape*) el **cuadrado** *masc*

2 (*in a town*) la **plaza** *fem*
the main square la plaza mayor
in the village square en la plaza del pueblo

squash *noun*

1 (*drink*) lemon squash la limonada
orange squash la naranjada

2 (*sport*) el **squash** *masc*
to play squash jugar [27] al squash

to squeak *verb*

1 (*doors, hinges*) **chirriar** [32]

2 (*people, animals*) **chillar** [17]

to squeeze *verb*

1 (*someone's hand, a tube*) **apretar** [29]

2 (*a lemon, an orange*) **exprimir** [19]

squid *noun*
el **calamar** *masc*

squirrel *noun*
la **ardilla** *fem*

to stab *verb*
apuñalar [17]

stable *adjective* ▷ see **stable** *noun*
estable *masc & fem*

stable *noun* ▷ see **stable** *adj*
la **cuadra** *fem*

stack *noun*
(*pile*) el **montón** *masc*
stacks of something montones de algo
She's got stacks of CDs. Tiene montones de compactos.

a b c d e f g h i j k l m n o p q r s t u v w x y z

stadium *noun*
el **estadio** *masc*
a football stadium un estadio de fútbol

staff *noun*
1 (*of a company*) el **personal** *masc*
2 (*in a school*) el **profesorado** *masc*

stage *noun*
1 (*in a theatre, etc*) el **escenario** *masc*
to come on stage salir [63] al escenario
2 (*phase*) la **etapa** *fem*
the first stage of the project la primera etapa del proyecto
3 At this stage it's hard to know. A estas alturas es difícil saberlo.

stain *noun* ▷ see **stain** *verb*
la **mancha** *fem*

to **stain** *verb* ▷ see **stain** *noun*
manchar [17]

stainless steel *noun*
el **acero inoxidable**
a stainless steel knife un cuchillo de acero inoxidable

stair *noun*
1 (*step*) el **escalón** *masc*
2 **stairs** las escaleras
I met her on the stairs. Me la encontré en las escaleras.

staircase *noun*
las **escaleras** *plural fem*
a spiral staircase una escalera de caracol

stale *adjective*
1 (*bread*) **duro** *masc*, **dura** *fem*
2 (*news*) **añejo** *masc*, **añeja** *fem*

stalemate *noun*
(*in chess*) las **tablas** *plural fem*

stall *noun*
1 (*at markets, fairs*) el **puesto** *masc*
2 (*in a theatre*) the stalls el patio de butacas

to **stamp** *verb* ▷ see **stamp** *noun*
1 (*a letter*) **poner** [11] sello(s) a
2 (*a ticket, passport*) **sellar** [17]
3 to stamp your foot dar [4] una patada en el suelo

stamp *noun* ▷ see **stamp** *verb*
el **sello** *masc*
• **stamp album** el álbum de sellos
• **stamp collection** la colección de sellos

to **stand** *verb*
1 **estar** [2] **de pie**
They were standing. Estaban de pie.
We were standing outside the cinema. Estábamos delante del cine.

I'm standing here waiting for you. Estoy aquí esperándote.
2 to stand on something pisar [17] algo
You're standing on my foot. Me estás pisando.
3 (*to bear*) **soportar** [17]
I can't stand her. No la soporto.
I can't stand waiting. No soporto esperar.
• to stand for something
significar [31]
What does 'plc' stand for? ¿Qué significa 'plc'?
• stand up
ponerse [11] **de pie**
Everybody stood up. Todo el mundo se puso de pie.

standard *adjective* ▷ see **standard** *noun*
estándar *masc & fem*
the standard price el precio estándar

standard *noun* ▷ see **standard** *adj*
el **nivel** *masc*
the standard of living el nivel de vida

Standard grades *plural noun*
(*Exámenes escoceses que se realizan alrededor de los 16 años y que pueden abarcar hasta 7 asignaturas. Se califican desde 1 (nota máxima) hasta 7 (por haber terminado el curso). Muchos alumnos continúan estudiando para los Highers y Advanced Highers después de hacer los Standard grades.*)
▷ **Highers**

stands *noun*
(*in stadiums*) la **tribuna** *fem*

staple *noun* ▷ see **staple** *verb*
la **grapa** *fem*

to **staple** *verb* ▷ see **staple** *noun*
grapar [17]
to staple the pages together grapar las hojas

stapler *noun*
la **grapadora** *fem*

star *noun* ▷ see **star** *verb*
la **estrella** *fem*
She's our star pupil. Es nuestra alumna estrella.
a star performance una actuación estelar
He's a film star. Es una estrella de cine.

to **star** *verb* ▷ see **star** *noun*
to star in a film protagonizar [22] una película

to **stare** *verb*
mirar [17] **fijamente**
He was staring at me. Me estaba mirando fijamente.
What are you staring at? ¿Qué miras?

star sign *noun*
el **signo del zodíaco**
What star sign are you? ¿De qué signo eres?

ʃ **start** *noun* ▷ see **start** *verb*
1 (*in general*) el **principio** *masc*
at the start al principio
at the start of the film al principio de la película
from the start desde el principio
We knew from the start that it was going to be difficult. Sabíamos desde el principio que iba a ser difícil.
2 **to make a start on something** empezar [25] algo
I've made a start on my essay. He empezado mi trabajo.
3 (*of a race*) la **salida** *fem*

ʃ **to start** *verb* ▷ see **start** *noun*
1 (*in general*) **empezar** [25]
The film starts at eight. La película empieza a las ocho.
I've started the book. He empezado el libro.
2 **to start doing something** empezar [25] a hacer algo
I've started learning Spanish. He empezado a aprender español.
3 **to start a business** montar [17] un negocio
4 (*cars*) **arrancar** [31]
She started the car. Arrancó el coche.
The car wouldn't start. El coche no arrancaba.

ʃ **starter** *noun*
(*for a meal*) el **entrante** *masc*
What would you like as a starter? ¿Qué quieres de entrante?

to starve *verb*
morirse [55] **de hambre**
Thousands are starving. Miles de personas se están muriendo de hambre!
I'm starving! ¡Me muero de hambre!

ʃ **state** *noun* ▷ see **state** *verb*
1 (*condition*) el **estado** *masc*
The house is in a very bad state. La casa está en muy mal estado.
2 (*administrative*) el **estado** *masc*
the state el estado
3 (*USA*) **the States** (los) Estados Unidos
They live in the States. Viven en Estados Unidos.

ʃ **to state** *verb* ▷ see **state** *noun*
1 (*your intention, an opinion*) **declarar** [17]
2 (*your address, income, occupation, a reason*) **indicar** [31]

statement *noun*
la **declaración** *fem*

ʃ **station** *noun*
1 (*for buses, trains*) la **estación** *fem*
the railway station la estación de trenes
the bus station la estación de autobuses
2 **the police station** la comisaría
3 **a radio station** una emisora de radio
a TV station un canal de televisión

stationary *adjective*
estacionario *masc*, **estacionaria** *fem*

stationer's *noun*
la **papelería** *fem*

stationery *noun*
los **artículos de papelería**

statistics *noun*
1 (*subject*) la **estadística** *fem*
2 (*figures*) **the statistics** las estadísticas

statue *noun*
la **estatua** *fem*

status *noun*
el **estatus** *masc*

ʃ **stay** *noun* ▷ see **stay** *verb*
la **estancia** *fem*
our stay in Alicante nuestra estancia en Alicante
Enjoy your stay! ¡Que disfruten de su estancia!

ʃ **to stay** *verb* ▷ see **stay** *noun*
1 **quedarse** [17]
I'll stay here. Me quedaré aquí.
How long are you staying? ¿Cuánto tiempo te quedas?
to stay with somebody quedarse [17] con alguien
I'm going to stay with my sister this weekend. Me voy a quedar con mi hermana este fin de semana.
Can you stay the night? ¿Podéis quedaros a dormir?
2 (*to spend time*) **We're going to stay in Málaga for three days.** Vamos a pasar tres días en Málaga.
3 (*temporarily*) **hospedarse** [17]
Where are you staying? ¿Dónde te hospedas?

• **to stay in**
no salir [63]
I'm staying in tonight. Esta noche no salgo.

steady *adjective*
1 **estable** *masc & fem*
   a steady job un trabajo estable
2 **constante**
   a steady increase un incremento constante
3 (*hand, voice*) **firme** *masc & fem*
4 **to hold something steady** sostener [9] algo
   firmemente

♪ **steak** *noun*
   el **filete** *masc*, el **bistec** *masc*
   steak and chips bistec con patatas fritas

♪ to **steal** *verb*
   robar [17]
   He stole them from me. Me los robó.

♪ **steam** *noun*
   el **vapor** *masc*
   • **steam engine** la locomotora de vapor
   • **steam iron** la plancha a vapor

steel *noun*
   el **acero** *masc*

steep *adjective*
   empinado *masc*, **empinada** *fem*
   a steep slope una cuesta empinada

steeple *noun*
1 (*spire*) la **aguja** *fem*
2 (*tower*) el **campanario** *masc*

steering wheel *noun*
   el **volante** *masc*

step *noun*
1 (*footstep*) el **paso** *masc*
   to take a step forwards dar [4] un paso
   hacia adelante
2 (*stair*) el **escalón** *masc*
   'Mind the step.' 'Cuidado con el escalón.'
• **to step back**
   retroceder [18]
• **to step forward**
   avanzar [22]
• **to step into**
   (*a lift*) **entrar** [17] **en**

stepbrother *noun*
   el **hermanastro** *masc*

stepdaughter *noun*
   la **hijastra** *fem*

♪ **stepfather** *noun*
   el **padrastro** *masc*

stepladder *noun*
   la **escalera de mano**

♪ **stepmother** *noun*
   la **madrastra** *fem*

stepsister *noun*
   la **hermanastra** *fem*

stepson *noun*
   el **hijastro** *masc*

♪ **stereo** *noun*
   el **estéreo** *masc*
   • **stereo system** el equipo de música

sterling *noun*
   la **libra esterlina**
   We paid in sterling. Pagamos en libras
   esterlinas.

stew *noun*
   el **estofado** *masc*

steward *noun*
   el **camarero** *masc*

stewardess *noun*
   la **camarera** *fem*

stick *noun* ▷ see **stick** *verb*
   el **palo** *masc*
   a walking stick un bastón

to **stick** *verb* ▷ see **stick** *noun*
1 (*with glue*) **pegar** [28]
   I stuck it in my note book. Lo pegué en mi
   cuaderno.
2 (*to put*) **poner** [11]
   Stick them on my desk. Ponlos en mi mesa.

sticker *noun*
   la **pegatina** *fem*

sticky *adjective*
1 (*covered with glue*) **pegajoso** *masc*, **pegajosa**
   fem
   My hands are sticky. Tengo las manos
   pegajosas.
2 (*adhesive*) **adhesivo** *masc*, **adhesiva** *fem*
   sticky paper papel adhesivo
   • **sticky tape** la cinta adhesiva

stiff *adjective*
   to feel stiff estar [2] entumecido
   to have stiff legs tener [9] las piernas
   entumecidas
   to have a stiff neck tener [9] tortícolis

♪ **still** *adjective* ▷ see **still** *adv*
1 **quieto** *masc*, **quieta** *fem*
   Sit still! ¡Siéntate quieto!
   Keep still! ¡Estate quieto!
   Keep it still. No lo muevas.
2 (*mineral water*) sin gas

♪ **still** *adverb* ▷ see **still** *adj*
   todavía, **aún**
   He's still sleeping. Todavía está
   durmiendo.
   There's still a lot of beer left. Todavía queda

mucha cerveza.
Do you still live in London? ¿Vives todavía en Londres?, ¿Vives aún en Londres?
I've still not finished. Todavía no he terminado, Aún no he terminado.

sting noun ▷ see **sting** verb
la **picadura** fem
wasp stings picaduras de avispa

to **sting** verb ▷ see **sting** noun
picar [31]
I was stung by a bee. Me picó una abeja.

stink noun ▷ see **stink** verb
la **peste** fem
What a stink! ¡Qué peste!

to **stink** verb ▷ see **stink** noun
apestar [17]
It stinks of cigarette smoke in here. Aquí apesta a tabaco.

to **stir** verb
remover [38]

stitch noun
1 (in sewing) la **puntada** fem
2 (in knitting) el **punto** masc
3 (surgical) el **punto de sutura**

to **stock** verb ▷ see **stock** noun
(in a shop) **vender** [18]
They don't stock dictionaries. No venden diccionarios.

stock noun ▷ see **stock** verb
1 (in a shop) el **estock** masc
to have something in stock tener [9] algo en estock
2 (supply) la **reserva** fem
I always have a stock of pencils. Siempre tengo una reserva de lápices.
3 (for cooking) el **caldo** masc
chicken stock caldo de pollo
· **stock cube** la pastilla de caldo
· **stock exchange** la bolsa de valores

stocking noun
la **media (de liguero)**

ᵟ **stomach** noun
el **estómago** masc
The fish upset my stomach. El pescado me sentó mal al estómago.

ᵟ **stomachache** noun
el **dolor de estómago**
to have stomachache tener [9] dolor de estómago
Dominic had stomachache. Dominic tenía dolor de estómago.

stone noun
1 la **piedra** fem
a stone wall una pared de piedra
to throw a stone tirar [17] una piedra
2 (in fruit) el **hueso** masc

stool noun
el **taburete** masc

ᵟ **stop** noun ▷ see **stop** verb
la **parada** fem
the bus stop la parada de autobús
He gets off at the next stop. Se baja en la próxima parada.

ᵟ to **stop** verb ▷ see **stop** noun
1 (people, vehicles) **parar** [17]
He stopped in front of the shop. Paró enfrente de la tienda.
Does the train stop in Cordoba? ¿Para el tren en Córdoba?
The music stopped. La música paró.
2 (to stop working) **pararse** [17]
The engine stopped. El motor se paró.
3 **to stop something, somebody** parar [17] algo, a alguien
Stop the engine. Para el motor.
She stopped me in the street. Me paró en la calle.
4 **to stop doing something** dejar [17] de hacer algo
He's stopped smoking. Ha dejado de fumar.
She never stops asking questions. Nunca deja de hacer preguntas.
5 **to stop somebody doing something** impedir [57] a alguien hacer algo
There's nothing to stop you going on your own. Nada te impide ir solo.

stopwatch noun
el **cronómetro** masc

store noun ▷ see **store** verb
(shop) la **tienda** fem

to **store** verb ▷ see **store** noun
1 (to keep) **guardar** [17]
2 (on a computer) **almacenar** [17]

storey noun
el **piso** masc
a three-storey house una casa de tres pisos

stork noun
la **cigüeña** fem

ᵟ **storm** noun
la **tormenta** fem
a snowstorm una tormenta de nieve
a rainstorm una tormenta de lluvia

stormy *adjective*
tormentoso *masc*, tormentosa *fem*

ʃ **story** *noun*
1 la **historia** *fem*
to tell a story contar [24] una historia
the story of her life la historia de su vida
2 (*tale*) el **cuento** *masc*

stove *noun*
1 (*cooker*) la **cocina** *fem*
2 (*heater*) la **estufa** *fem*

ʃ **straight** *adjective* ▷ see **straight** *adv*
1 **recto** *masc*, **recta** *fem*
a straight line una línea recta
2 to have straight hair tener [9] el pelo liso
3 (*not crooked*) **derecho** *masc*, **derecha** *fem*
Put it straight. Ponlo derecho.

ʃ **straight** *adverb* ▷ see **straight** *adj*
1 (*in direction*) **recto**
Go straight ahead. Sigue todo recto.
2 (*in time*) **directamente**
He went straight to the doctor's. Fue
directamente al médico.
Come straight home after the film. Vuelve
enseguida a casa cuando termine la
película.
straight away en seguida

strain *noun* ▷ see **strain** *verb*
la **tensión** *fem*

to **strain** *verb* ▷ see **strain** *noun*
1 (*the vegetables, rice*) **colar** [17]
2 (*a muscle*) **hacerse** [7] **un esguince en**

strange *adjective*
extraño *masc*, extraña *fem*
a strange situation una situación extraña

ʃ **stranger** *noun*
el **desconocido** *masc*, la **desconocida** *fem*
Don't speak to strangers. No hables con
desconocidos.

to **strangle** *verb*
estrangular [17]

strap *noun*
1 (*on a handbag, a watch*) la **correa** *fem*
a watchstrap una correa de reloj
2 (*on a shoe*) la **tira** *fem*
3 (*for clothing*) el **tirante** *masc*

straw *noun*
1 la **paja** *fem*
a straw hat un sombrero de paja
2 a drinking straw una pajita

ʃ **strawberry** *noun*
la **fresa** *fem*
strawberry jam mermelada de fresa
a strawberry milkshake un batido de fresa

stream *noun*
el **arroyo** *masc*

ʃ **street** *noun*
la **calle** *fem*
I met Simon in the street. Me encontré con
Simon en la calle.
• **streetlamp** el farol
• **street map** el plano de la ciudad
• **streetwise** avispado *masc*, avispada *fem*

strength *noun*
la **fuerza** *fem*

stress *noun* ▷ see **stress** *verb*
1 (*in general*) la **tensión** *fem*
2 (*Grammar*) el **acento** *masc*

to **stress** *verb* ▷ see **stress** *noun*
recalcar [31]
to stress the importance of something
recalcar la importancia de algo

to **stretch** *verb*
(*clothes, shoes*) **dar** [4] **de sí**
This jumper has stretched. Este jersey ha
dado de sí.

stretcher *noun*
la **camilla**

strict *adjective*
estricto *masc*, estricta *fem*

strike *noun* ▷ see **strike** *verb*
la **huelga** *fem*
to go on strike ponerse [11] en huelga
to be on strike estar [2] en huelga

to **strike** *verb* ▷ see **strike** *noun*
1 (*to hit*) **golpear** [17]
2 (*clocks*) **dar** [4]
The clock struck six. El reloj dio las seis.
3 (*to go on strike*) **ponerse** [11] **en huelga**

striker *noun*
1 (*in football*) el **delantero** *masc*, la **delantera**
fem
2 (*striking worker*) el & la **huelguista** *masc & fem*

string *noun*
1 (*for parcels, etc*) el **cordel** *masc*
2 (*for a musical instrument*) la **cuerda** *fem*

to **strip** *verb* ▷ see **strip** *noun*
(*to undress*) **desnudarse** [17]

strip *noun* ▷ see **strip** *verb*
la **tira** *fem*
• **strip cartoon** la tira cómica

stripe *noun*
  la **raya** *fem*

striped *adjective*
  de rayas
  a striped shirt una camisa de rayas

stroke *noun* ▷ see **stroke** *verb*
1 (*in swimming*) la **brazada** *fem*
2 (*Medicine*) el **derrame cerebral**
  to have a stroke sufrir[19] un derrame
  cerebral

to stroke *verb* ▷ see **stroke** *noun*
  acariciar[17]

ᶴ **strong** *adjective*
1 (*in general*) **fuerte** *masc & fem*
2 (*material*) **resistente** *masc & fem*
3 (*accent*) **marcado** *masc*, **marcada** *fem*
  a strong Welsh accent un marcado acento
  galés

struggle *noun* ▷ see **struggle** *verb*
1 (*fight*) la **lucha** *fem*
  a power struggle una lucha por el poder
  the struggle for independence la lucha por
  la independencia
2 (*difficult time*) It's been a struggle. Ha sido
  muy difícil.

to struggle *verb* ▷ see **struggle** *noun*
1 (*violently*) **forcejear**[17]
  She struggled with the two robbers.
  Forcejeó con los dos ladrones.
2 (*to do something*) **luchar**[17]
  They have struggled to survive. Han
  luchado para sobrevivir.
3 (*to find it difficult*) I'm struggling to finish my
  homework. Me cuesta terminar mis
  deberes.

stubborn *adjective*
  terco *masc*, **terca** *fem*

stuck *adjective*
  (*jammed*) **atascado** *masc*, **atascada** *fem*
  The drawer's stuck. El cajón está atascado.

stud *noun*
1 (*on a belt, jacket*) la **tachuela** *fem*
2 (*on a boot*) el **taco** *masc*
3 (*earring*) el **pendiente de bolita**

ᶴ **student** *noun*
  el & la **estudiante** *masc & fem*
  She's a medical student. Es estudiante de
  medicina.

studio *noun*
  el **estudio** *masc*
• **studio flat** el estudio

ᶴ **to study** *verb*
  estudiar[17]
  He's studying for his exams. Está
  estudiando para los exámenes.
  She's studying medicine. Estudia medicina.

stuff *noun* ▷ see **stuff** *verb*
1 (*things*) las **cosas** *plural fem*
  We can put all this stuff in the attic.
  Podemos poner todas estas cosas en el
  desván.
  You can leave your stuff at my house.
  Puedes dejar tus cosas en mi casa.
2 (*substance*) la **cosa** *fem*

to stuff *verb* ▷ see **stuff** *noun*
1 (*to shove*) **meter**[18]
  She stuffed her things into her backpack.
  Metió sus cosas en su mochila.
2 (*Cooking*) **rellenar**[17]
  stuffed aubergines berenjenas rellenas

stuffing *noun*
  (*Cooking*) el **relleno** *masc*

stuffy *adjective*
  (*atmosphere*) **viciado** *masc*, **viciada** *fem*
  It's very stuffy in here. Aquí dentro falta
  aire.

stunned *adjective*
1 (*dazed*) **aturdido** *masc*, **aturdida** *fem*
2 (*amazed*) **atónito** *masc*, **atónita** *fem*

stunning *adjective*
  sensacional *masc & fem*

stunt *noun*
  (*in films*) la **escena peligrosa**

ᶴ **stupid** *adjective*
  estúpido *masc*, **estúpida** *fem*
  a stupid man un hombre estúpido
  That was really stupid. Eso fue una
  verdadera estupidez.
  to do something stupid hacer[7] una
  estupidez
  He did something stupid and deleted it.
  Hizo una estupidez y lo borró.
  Stop acting stupid. Deja de hacerte el tonto.
  Don't be stupid! ¡No seas tonto!

stutter *noun* ▷ see **stutter** *verb*
  to have a stutter tartamudear[17]

to stutter *verb* ▷ see **stutter** *noun*
  tartamudear[17]

style *noun*
1 (*way*) el **estilo** *masc*
  a style of living un estilo de vida
  He has his own style. Tiene su propio estilo.
2 (*fashion*) la **moda** *fem*
  It's the latest style. Es la última moda.

ᵍsubject *noun*
1 (*of a conversation, etc*) el **tema** *masc*
the subject of my talk el tema de mi charla
2 (*at school*) la **asignatura** *fem*
My favourite subject is biology. Mi asignatura favorita es la biología.

submarine *noun*
el **submarino** *masc*

subscription *noun*
la **suscripción** *fem*
to take out a subscription to something suscribirse [52] a algo

subsidy *noun*
la **subvención** *fem*

substance *noun*
la **sustancia** *fem*

substitute *noun* ▷ see **substitute** *verb*
1 (*person*) el **sustituto** *masc*, la **sustituta** *fem*
2 (*ingredient*) el **sucedáneo** *masc*

to **substitute** *verb* ▷ see **substitute** *noun*
sustituir [54]

ᵍsubtitled *adjective*
(*film*) **subtitulado** *masc*, **subtitulada** *fem*

ᵍsubtitles *plural noun*
los **subtítulos** *plural masc*

to **subtract** *verb*
restar [17]

ᵍsuburb *noun*
el **barrio residencial de las afueras**
a suburb of Edinburgh un barrio residencial de las afueras de Edimburgo
in the suburbs of London en los barrios residenciales de las afueras de Londres

subway *noun*
1 (*underpass*) el **paso subterráneo**
2 (*underground railway*) el **métro**

to **succeed** *verb*
1 (*to manage*) **lograr** [17]
to succeed in doing something lograr hacer algo
We've succeeded in contacting her. Hemos logrado contactar con ella.
2 (*to be successful*) **tener** [9] **éxito**
to succeed in life tener éxito en la vida

success *noun*
el **éxito** *masc*
a great success un gran éxito

successful *adjective*
1 **de éxito**
He's a successful singer. Es un cantante de mucho éxito.

2 to be successful in doing something lograr [17] hacer algo

successfully *adverb*
satisfactoriamente

such *adjective, adverb*
1 **tan**
I've had such a busy day! ¡He tenido un día tan ocupado!
It's such a long way. Queda tan lejos.
It's such a pity. Es una verdadera lástima.
They're such nice people! ¡Son gente tan simpática!
How could he say such a thing? ¿Cómo pudo decir tal cosa?
There's no such thing. No hay tal cosa.
2 such a lot of tantos, *fem* tantas
I've got such a lot of things to tell you! ¡Tengo tantas cosas que contarte!
3 such as como
in big cities such as Glasgow en grandes ciudades como Glasgow

to **suck** *verb*
chupar [17]

ᵍsudden *adjective*
repentino *masc*, **repentina** *fem*
a sudden death una muerte repentina
all of a sudden de repente

ᵍsuddenly *adverb*
de repente
to die suddenly morir [55] de repente
He suddenly started to laugh. De repente empezó a reír.
Suddenly the light went out. De repente se apagó la luz.

suede *noun*
el **ante** *masc*
a suede jacket una chaqueta de ante

to **suffer** *verb*
sufrir [19]

ᵍsugar *noun*
el & la **azúcar** *masc or fem*
brown sugar azúcar morena
Would you like sugar? ¿Quieres azúcar?

to **suggest** *verb*
sugerir [14]
I suggest you go. Sugiero que vayas tú.

suggestion *noun*
la **sugerencia** *fem*
to make a suggestion hacer [7] una sugerencia

suicide *noun*
el **suicidio** *masc*
to commit suicide suicidarse [17]

♂ **suit** *noun*
1 (man's) el **traje** *masc*
2 (woman's) el **traje de chaqueta**

♂ **suitable** *adjective*
1 **adecuado** *masc*, **adecuada** *fem*
a suitable hotel un hotel adecuado
to be suitable for someone, something ser
[1] adecuado para alguien, algo
It's not suitable for minors. No es
adecuado para los menores de edad.
It's suitable for dry-cleaning. Es adecuado
para el lavado en seco.
2 (clothing) **apropiado** *masc*, **apropiada** *fem*
I don't have any suitable shoes. No tengo
zapatos apropiados.

♂ **suitcase** *noun*
la **maleta** *fem*

to **sulk** *verb*
enfurruñarse [17]

sum *noun*
la **suma** *fem*
a large sum of money una suma
importante de dinero
• **to sum up**
resumir [19]

to **summarize** *verb*
resumir [19]

summary *noun*
el **resumen** *masc*

♂ **summer** *noun*
el **verano** *masc*
in summer en verano
summer clothes la ropa de verano
the summer holidays las vacaciones de
verano
We spent the summer holidays in
Mallorca. Pasamos las vacaciones de
verano en Mallorca.

summertime *noun*
el **verano** *masc*
in summertime en verano

summit *noun*
la **cumbre** *fem*

♂ **sun** *noun*
el **sol** *masc*
to sit in the sun sentarse [29] al sol
The sun's in my eyes. Me da el sol en los
ojos.
• **sunbathe** tomar [17] el sol
• **sunblock** el filtro solar
• **sunburn** la quemadura solar

sunburned *adjective*
1 (tanned) **moreno** *masc*, **morena** *fem*
2 (Medicine) to get sunburned quemarse [17]

♂ **Sunday** *noun*
el **domingo** *masc*
on Sunday el domingo
I'm going out on Sunday. Voy a salir el
domingo.
See you on Sunday! ¡Hasta el domingo!
on Sundays los domingos
The museum is closed on Sundays. El
museo cierra los domingos.
every Sunday todos los domingos
last Sunday el domingo pasado
next Sunday el próximo domingo

WORD TIP Months of the year and days of the
week start with small letters in Spanish.

sunflower *noun*
el **girasol** *masc*
sunflower oil el aceite de girasol

sunglasses *plural noun*
las **gafas de sol**

sunlight *noun*
la **luz del sol**

♂ **sunny** *adjective*
1 (day) a sunny day un día de sol
It's going to be sunny. Va a hacer sol.
2 (place) **soleado** *masc*, **soleada** *fem*
in a sunny room en una habitación soleada
There will be sunny intervals and scattered
showers. Habrá intervalos soleados y
chubascos aislados.

sunrise *noun*
la **salida del sol**
at sunrise al amanecer

sunroof *noun*
el **techo solar**

sunset *noun*
la **puesta de sol**
at sunset al atardecer

sunshine *noun*
el **sol** *masc*
in the sunshine al sol

sunstroke *noun*
la **insolación** *fem*
to get sunstroke coger [3] una insolación

♂ **suntan** *noun*
el **bronceado** *masc*
to get a suntan broncearse [17]
• **suntan lotion** la loción bronceadora
• **suntan oil** el aceite bronceador

super *adjective*
genial *masc & fem*
We had a super time! ¡Lo pasamos genial!

§ **supermarket** *noun*
el **supermercado** *masc*
an all-night supermarket un supermercado que está abierto toda la noche

supernatural *adjective*
supernatural *masc & fem*

superstitious *adjective*
supersticioso *masc*, **supersticiosa** *fem*

to **supervise** *verb*
supervisar[17]

supervisor *noun*
el **supervisor** *masc*, la **supervisora** *fem*

§ **supper** *noun*
la **cena** *fem*
I had supper at Sandy's. Cené en casa de Sandy.
We had eggs and bacon for supper. Cenamos huevos y tocino.

supplement *noun*
el **suplemento** *masc*

supplies *plural noun*
(of food) las **provisiones** *plural fem*

§ to **supply** *verb*
suministrar[17]
The school supplies the books. El colegio suministra los libros.
to supply somebody with something suministrar algo a alguien
The farm supplies us with eggs and milk. La granja nos suministra huevos y leche.

§ **supply** *noun* ▷ see **supply** *verb*
1 las **reservas** *plural fem*
We have a good supply of coal. Tenemos reservas abundantes de carbón.
2 to be in short supply escasear[17]
Oil is in short supply. Escasea el petróleo.
• supply teacher el profesor suplente, la profesora suplente

support *noun* ▷ see **support** *verb*
el **apoyo** *masc*
He has a lot of support. Tiene mucho apoyo.

to **support** *verb* ▷ see **support** *noun*
1 (to back up) **apoyar**[17]
Her parents have really supported her. Sus padres la han apoyado mucho.
2 (a team) **ser**[1] **hincha de**
Graeme supports Manchester. Graeme es hincha del Manchester.
3 (with money) to support a family mantener[9] una familia

supporter *noun*
el & la **hincha** *masc & fem*
a Chelsea supporter un hincha del Chelsea

to **suppose** *verb*
suponer[11]
I suppose she is coming. Supongo que sí viene.

supposed *adjective*
to be supposed to do something tener[9] que hacer algo
You're supposed to wear a helmet. Tienes que usar casco.
He was supposed to be here at six. Tenía que estar aquí a las seis.

§ **sure** *adjective*
1 **seguro** *masc*, **segura** *fem*
I'm sure she'll come soon. Estoy seguro de que vendrá pronto.
Are you sure? ¿Estás seguro?
Are you sure you have enough money? ¿Seguro que tienes suficiente dinero?
Are you sure you saw her? ¿Estás seguro de que la viste?
2 Sure! ¡Claro!
'Can you shut the door?'—'Sure!' '¿Puedes cerrar la puerta?'—'¡Por supuesto!'

surely *adverb*
Surely she couldn't have forgotten! ¡No es posible que se haya olvidado!

WORD TIP *no es posible que* is followed by a verb in the subjunctive.

§ **surf** *noun* ▷ see **surf** *verb*
la **espuma** *fem*

§ to **surf** *verb* ▷ see **surf** *noun*
1 (in the sea) **hacer**[7] **surfing**
2 (on the Net) **navegar**[28]

surface *noun*
la **superficie** *fem*

surfboard *noun*
la **tabla de surf**

surfer *noun*
1 (in the sea) el & la **surfista** *masc & fem*
2 (on the Net) el & la **internauta** *masc & fem*

surfing *noun*
  el **surfing** *masc*
  to go surfing hacer[7] surfing

surgeon *noun*
  el **cirujano** *masc*, la **cirujana** *fem*
  She's a surgeon. Es cirujana.

surgery *noun*
1 (*treatment*) la **cirugía** *fem*
  laser surgery cirugía láser
  to have surgery operarse[17]
2 (*doctors' offices*) el **consultorio** *masc*
  the dentist's surgery la consulta del dentista

♪ **surname** *noun*
  el **apellido** *masc*
  Her second surname is López. Su segundo apellido es López.

surprise *noun*
  la **sorpresa** *fem*
  What a surprise! ¡Qué sorpresa!

surprised *adjective*
  sorprendido *masc*, **sorprendida** *fem*
  We were surprised to see her. Nos sorprendió verla.
  I'm surprised they arrived so early. Me sorprende que hayan llegado tan temprano.

♪ **surprising** *adjective*
  sorprendente *masc & fem*

surrender *noun* ▷ see **surrender** *verb*
  la **rendición** *fem*

to **surrender** *verb* ▷ see **surrender** *noun*
1 to surrender to somebody entregarse[28] a alguien
  They surrendered to the police. Se entregaron a la policía.
2 (*a castle, town*) **entregar**[28]

♪ to **surround** *verb*
1 **rodear**[17]
2 to be surrounded by something estar[2] rodeado de algo
  The town is surrounded by hills. La ciudad está rodeada de colinas.

♪ **survey** *noun*
1 (*of opinion*) la **encuesta** *fem*
2 (*of a house, building site, etc*) la **inspección** *fem*

to **survive** *verb*
  sobrevivir[19]

survivor *noun*
  el & la **superviviente** *masc & fem*

suspect *adjective* ▷ see **suspect** *noun, verb*
  sospechoso *masc*, **sospechosa** *fem*
  a suspect package un paquete sospechoso

suspect *noun* ▷ see **suspect** *adj, verb*
  el **sospechoso** *masc*, la **sospechosa** *fem*

to **suspect** *verb* ▷ see **suspect** *adj, noun*
  sospechar[17]

to **suspend** *verb*
  to be suspended ser[1] expulsado

suspense *noun*
  el **suspense** *masc*

suspicious *adjective*
  sospechoso *masc*, **sospechosa** *fem*
  to be suspicious of someone, something sospechar[17] de alguien, algo
  a suspicious parcel un paquete sospechoso
  a suspicious-looking individual un individuo de apariencia sospechosa

swallow *noun* ▷ see **swallow** *verb*
  (*bird*) la **golondrina** *fem*

to **swallow** *verb* ▷ see **swallow** *noun*
  tragar[28]

swamp *noun*
  el **pantano** *masc*

swan *noun*
  el **cisne** *masc*

to **swap** *verb*
  cambiar[17]
  Do you want to swap? ¿Quieres que cambiemos?
  He's swapped his bike for a computer. Ha cambiado su bici por un ordenador.
  to swap seats with somebody cambiarse [17] de sitio con alguien

to **swear** *verb*
  decir[5] palabrotas
  He swears a lot. Dice muchas palabrotas.

swearword *noun*
  la **palabrota** *fem*

sweat *noun* ▷ see **sweat** *verb*
  el **sudor** *masc*

to **sweat** *verb* ▷ see **sweat** *noun*
  sudar[17]

sweater *noun*
  el **suéter** *masc*

sweatshirt *noun*
  la **sudadera** *fem*

Swede noun
un **sueco** masc, una **sueca** fem

> **WORD TIP** Adjectives and nouns for nationality and regional origin do not have capital letters in Spanish.

Sweden noun
Suecia fem

Swedish adjective & noun
1 **sueco** masc, **sueca** fem
2 (the language) el **sueco** masc

> **WORD TIP** Adjectives and nouns for nationality, regional origin and language do not have capital letters in Spanish.

to **sweep** verb
barrer [18]

ꝗ **sweet** adjective ▷ see **sweet** noun
1 (food, smile) **dulce** masc & fem
I try not to eat sweet things. Intento no comer cosas dulces.
2 (kind) **encantador** masc, **encantadora** fem
She's a sweet person. Es realmente encantadora.
It was really sweet of him. Ha sido un detalle encantador.
3 (cute) **rico** masc, **rica** fem
He looks really sweet in that hat! ¡Está muy rico con ese sombrero!
• **sweetcorn** el maíz tierno

ꝗ **sweet** noun ▷ see **sweet** adj
1 (wrapped) el **caramelo** masc
She loves sweets. Le encantan los caramelos.
2 (dessert) el **postre** masc
For sweet there's caramel custard. De postre hay flan.
• **sweetshop** la tienda de golosinas

swelling noun
la **hinchazón** fem

to **swerve** verb
virar [17] **bruscamente**
The car swerved to avoid the cyclist. El coche viró para esquivar al ciclista.

ꝗ **swim** noun ▷ see **swim** verb
to go for a swim ir [8] a nadar

ꝗ to **swim** verb ▷ see **swim** noun
nadar [17]
I swam ten lengths today. Hoy nadé diez largos.
She swam to the boat. Nadó hasta la barca.
Can you swim? ¿Sabes nadar?
to swim across the river cruzar [22] el río a nado

swimmer noun
el **nadador** masc, la **nadadora** fem
She's a strong swimmer. Es muy buena nadadora.

ꝗ **swimming** noun
la **natación** fem
to go swimming ir [8] a nadar
• **swimming cap** el gorro de baño
• **swimming pool** la piscina
• **swimming trunks** el bañador

ꝗ **swimsuit** noun
el **traje de baño**

swindle noun
la **estafa** fem
What a swindle! ¡Qué estafa!

swing noun
el **columpio** masc

Swiss adjective & noun
1 **suizo** masc, **suiza** fem
2 (person) el **suizo** masc, la **suiza** fem
the Swiss los suizos

> **WORD TIP** Adjectives and nouns for nationality and regional origin do not have capital letters in Spanish.

ꝗ **switch** noun ▷ see **switch** verb
el **interruptor** masc
I can't find the light switch. No encuentro el interruptor de la luz.

ꝗ to **switch** verb ▷ see **switch** noun
(to change) **cambiar** [17]
to switch places cambiar de sitio
• **to switch something off**
apagar [28] **algo**
Switch it off! ¡Apágalo!
• **to switch something on**
encender [36] **algo**
He switched the light on. Encendió la luz.

Switzerland noun
Suiza fem

swollen adjective
hinchado masc, **hinchada** fem

to **swop** verb ▷ **swap**

sword noun
la **espada** fem
• **swordfish** el pez espada

ꝗ **syllabus** noun
el **programa** masc
to be on the syllabus estar [2] en el programa

sympathetic *adjective*
comprensivo *masc*, **comprensiva** *fem*

to **sympathize** *verb*
to sympathize with somebody
compadecer [35] a alguien
I sympathize with you. Te compadezco.

sympathy *noun*
la **compasión** *fem*

symphony *noun*
la **sinfonía** *fem*
• **symphony orchestra** la orquesta
sinfónica

symptom *noun*
el **síntoma** *masc*

synagogue *noun*
(Religion) la **sinagoga** *fem*

synthesizer *noun*
el **sintetizador** *masc*

synthetic *adjective*
sintético *masc*, **sintética** *fem*

syringe *noun*
la **jeringa** *fem*

syrup *noun*
el **jarabe** *fem*
cough syrup el jarabe para la tos

system *noun*
el **sistema** *masc*

a
b
c
d
e
f
g
h
i
j
k
l
m
n
o
p
q
r
s
t
u
v
w
x
y
z

a
b
c
d
e
f
g
h
i
j
k
l
m
n
o
p
q
r
s
t
u
v
w
x
y
z

T t

♂ **table** *noun*
1 (*piece of furniture*) la **mesa** *fem*
on the table en la mesa
to be sitting at the table estar[2] sentado a
la mesa
2 (*list*) la **tabla** *fem*
the ten-times table la tabla del cuatro
multiplication tables las tablas de
multiplicar
• **tablecloth** el mantel
• **table football** el futbolín
• **table mat** el salvamanteles, *pl*: los
salvamanteles

tablespoon *noun*
la **cuchara de servir**
a tablespoon of flour una cucharada
grande de harina

♂ **tablet** *noun*
la **pastilla** *fem*
Take the tablets twice a day. Tómese las
pastillas dos veces al día.

table tennis *noun*
el **ping-pong** *masc*
to play table tennis jugar[27] al ping-pong

tackle *noun* ▷ see **tackle** *verb*
1 (*in football*) la **entrada** *fem*
2 (*in rugby*) el **placaje** *masc*
3 (*equipment*) **fishing tackle** aparejos de pesca

to **tackle** *verb* ▷ see **tackle** *noun*
1 (*in football*) **entrarle**[17] **a**
2 (*in rugby*) **placar**[31]
3 (*a job, problem*) **abordar**[17]

tact *noun*
el **tacto** *masc*

tactful *adjective*
diplomático *masc*, **diplomática** *fem*
That wasn't very tactful. Eso no fue muy
diplomático.

tactic *noun*
la **táctica** *fem*

tadpole *noun*
el **renacuajo** *masc*

tail *noun*
1 (*dog's, cat's*) el **rabo** *masc*
2 (*horse's, fish's, bird's*) la **cola** *fem*
3 (*when tossing a coin*) **'Heads or tails?'**—
"Tails.' '¿Cara o cruz?'—"Cruz.'

tailor *noun*
el **sastre** *masc*

♂ to **take** *verb*
1 (*to carry*) **llevar**[17]
Take this to your mother. Lleva esto a tu
madre.
I'll take my camera with me. Me llevaré la
cámara.
2 (*to drive, transport*) **llevar**[17]
to take somebody somewhere llevar a
alguien a un lugar
We took him to the station. Lo llevamos a la
estación.
This bus takes you into the centre. Este
autobús te lleva al centro.
I'll take you in the car. Te llevo en el coche.
I must take the car to the garage. Tengo
que llevar el coche al garaje.
3 (*to lead*) **llevar**[17]
He took them upstairs Los llevó arriba.
This path takes you to the main road. Este
camino te lleva a la carretera.
4 (*a train, plane, bus*) **coger**[3], **tomar**[17]
I took the bus. Cogí el autobús.
We had to take a taxi. Tuvimos que coger
un taxi.
5 (*to hold*) **coger**[3], **tomar**[17]
Take my hand. Cógeme la mano.
6 (*to remove, steal*) **llevarse**[17]
Somebody's taken my purse! ¡Alguien se
me ha llevado el monedero!
7 (*talking about time*) **llevar**[17]
It takes two hours. Lleva dos horas.
How long does it take to make? ¿Cuánto
tiempo lleva hacerlo?
Don't take too long! ¡No tardes
demasiado!
8 **tomar**[17], (*a sweet, food, medicine*) **tomar**
[17]
He took a chocolate. Tomó un bombón.
Do you take sugar? ¿Tomas azúcar?
Have you taken your tablets? ¿Te has
tomado las pastillas?
9 (*to accept*) **aceptar**[17]
Do you take cheques? ¿Aceptan cheques?
He wouldn't take the money. No quiso
aceptar el dinero.
Take his advice. Sigue sus consejos.
10 (*an exam, a test, a course*) **hacer**[7]
She's taking her driving test. Va a hacer el
examen de conducir.

I'm taking a Russian course. Estoy
haciendo un curso de ruso.

11 (*with clothes, shoes*) **What size do you take?**
¿Qué talla usas?
What size shoes do you take? ¿Qué
número calzas?

12 (*notes, etc*) **tomar** [17]
He took my name and address. Me tomó el
nombre y la dirección.
He took my temperature. Me tomó la
temperatura.

13 (*to need*) Going there takes courage. Hay
que tener valor para ir allí.
It took four men to lift it. Se necesitaron
cuatro hombres para levantarlo.

14 (*to tolerate*) **aguantar** [17]
I won't take any more nonsense from you.
No pienso aguantarte más tonterías.
I can't take it any longer! ¡No puedo más!

15 (*to interpret*) **tomarse** [17]
I don't know how to take that remark. Ese
comentario no sé cómo tomármelo.
She took it the wrong way. Se lo tomó a
mal.

WORD TIP See the **Word Tip** at *coger* in the
Spanish-English section about the differences in
regional use between *coger* and *tomar*.

• **to take something apart**
  desmontar [17] **algo**
• **to take something away**
  llevarse [17] **algo**
  He took the dirty dishes away. Se llevó los
  platos sucios.
• **to take something back**
  devolver [45] **algo**
  I took the book back to the library. Devolví
  el libro a la biblioteca.
• **to take down**
1 **bajar** [17]
  Cheryl's taken the cups down. Cheryl ha
  bajado las tazas.
2 (*curtains, decorations, etc*) **quitar** [17]
3 (*notes*) **apuntar** [17]
• **to take off**
1 (*clothes, shoes*) **quitarse** [17]
  He took off his shirt. Se quitó la camisa.
  Take your feet off the sofa. Quita los pies
  del sofá.
2 (*from a price*) **rebajar** [17]
  He took five pounds off the price. Rebajó
  cinco libras del precio.
3 (*planes*) **despegar** [28]
• **to take out**
1 (*a pen, wallet*) **sacar** [31]
  Eric took out his wallet. Eric sacó su cartera.
  I took the toy out of the box. Saqué el
  juguete de la caja.

2 (*a friend*) He's taking me out to lunch.
Me ha invitado a comer fuera.
She took me out to the theatre. Me invitó a
ir al teatro.
• **to take up**
1 (*to carry*) **subir** [19]
Could you take these towels up? ¿Puedes
subir estas toallas?
2 (*a hobby*) He's taken up badminton. Ha
empezado a jugar al badminton.
3 (*time*) **llevar** [17]
My homework took up most of the
afternoon. Hacer los deberes me llevó la
mayor parte de la tarde.

takeaway *noun*
1 (*meal*) la **comida para llevar**
an Indian takeaway una comida india para
llevar
2 (*the outlet*) el **restaurante que hace
comida para llevar**

tale *noun*
la **historia** *fem*

talent *noun*
el **talento** *masc*
to have a talent for something estar [2]
dotado *masc*, dotada *fem* para algo

talented *adjective*
He's really talented. Tiene mucho talento.

♪ **talk** *noun* ▷ see **talk** *verb*
1 (*conversation*) la **conversación** *fem*
after our talk después de nuestra
conversación
I had a talk with Rob about it. Hablé con
Rob acerca de ello.
2 (*lecture*) la **charla** *fem*
She's giving a talk on Hungary. Va a dar una
charla sobre Hungría.

♪ to **talk** *verb* ▷ see **talk** *noun*
hablar [17]
I was talking to Jason about football.
Estuve hablando con Jason sobre fútbol.
What's he talking about? ¿De qué está
hablando?
We'll talk about it later. Hablaremos de
ello más tarde.

talkative *adjective*
hablador *masc*, **habladora** *fem*
He's very talkative! ¡Es muy hablador!

♪ **tall** *adjective*
alto *masc*, **alta** *fem*
the tallest buildings in the city los edificios
más altos de la ciudad
She's very tall. Es muy alta.
I'm 1.7 metres tall. Mido un metro setenta.
How tall are you? ¿Cuánto mides?

a
b
c
d
e
f
g
h
i
j
k
l
m
n
o
p
q
r
s
t
u
v
w
x
y
z

English-Spanish

tambourine *noun*
la **pandereta** *fem*

tame *adjective*
(*animal*) **domesticado** *masc*, **domesticada** *fem*

tampon *noun*
el **tampón** *masc*

♂ to **tan** *verb* ▷ see **tan** *noun*
broncearse [17]
I tan easily. Me bronceo fácilmente.

♂ **tan** *noun* ▷ see **tan** *verb*
el **bronceado** *masc*
to get a tan broncearse [17]

tangerine *noun*
la **mandarina** *fem*

tank *noun*
1 (*for petrol, water*) el **depósito** *masc*
a fish tank una pecera
2 (*military vehicle*) el **tanque** *masc*

tanker *noun*
1 (*ship*) el **petrolero** *masc*
2 (*truck*) el **camión cisterna**

tanned *adjective*
bronceado *masc*, **bronceada** *fem*

♂ to **tap** *verb* ▷ see **tap** *noun*
dar [4] **un golpecito en**
He tapped her on the shoulder. Le dio un golpecito en el hombro.

♂ **tap** *noun* ▷ see **tap** *verb*
1 (*for water*) el **grifo** *masc*
the hot tap el grifo del agua caliente
the cold tap el grifo del agua fría
to leave the taps running dejar [17] los grifos abiertos
2 (*light blow*) el **golpecito** *masc*
She gave me a tap on the shoulder. Me dio un golpecito en el hombro.

tap-dancing *noun*
el **claqué** *masc*
to do tap-dancing hacer [7] claqué

to **tape** *verb* ▷ see **tape** *noun*
grabar [17]
I want to tape the film. Quiero grabar la película.

tape *noun* ▷ see **tape** *verb*
1 (*for recording*) la **cinta** *fem*
a blank tape una cinta virgen
my tape of the Stones mi cinta de los Stones
I've got it on tape. Lo tengo en cinta.
2 (*adhesive*) la **cinta** *fem*
sticky tape la cinta adhesiva

· **tape measure** la cinta métrica
· **tape recorder** el magnetofón

tar *noun*
el **alquitrán** *masc*

target *noun*
el **objetivo** *masc*

♂ **tart** *noun*
la **tarta** *fem*
a raspberry tart una tarta de frambuesas

tartan *adjective*
de tela escocesa
a tartan skirt una falda de tela escocesa

task *noun*
la **tarea** *fem*

♂ to **taste** *verb* ▷ see **taste** *noun*
1 (*foods*) **saber** [13]
The soup tastes horrible. La sopa sabe fatal.
to taste of something saber a algo
It tastes of strawberries. Sabe a fresas.
2 (*to try*) **probar** [24]
Taste this. Prueba esto.
Do you want to taste it? ¿Quieres probarlo?

♂ **taste** *noun* ▷ see **taste** *verb*
1 (*flavour*) el **sabor** *masc*
the taste of onions el sabor a cebolla
2 (*for clothes, decor, etc*) el **gusto** *masc*
in bad taste de mal gusto
She has good taste. Tiene buen gusto.

tasty *adjective*
sabroso *masc*, **sabrosa** *fem*

tattoo *noun*
el **tatuaje** *masc*
He's got a tattoo on his arm. Tiene un tatuaje en el brazo.

Taurus *noun*
1 (*the star sign*) el **Tauro** *masc*
2 (*person*) un & una **tauro** *masc & fem*
Jo's Taurus. Jo es tauro.

WORD TIP Use a small letter in Spanish to say *I am ...* etc with star signs. Star signs in Spanish are used without *el, un, la, una.*

tax *noun*
el **impuesto** *masc*

taxi *noun*
el **taxi** *masc*
by taxi en taxi
to take a taxi tomar [17] un taxi
· **taxi driver** el & la taxista
· **taxi rank** la parada de taxis

TB *noun*
la **tuberculosis** *fem*

♪ **tea** *noun*
1 (*the drink*) el **té** *masc*
a cup of tea una taza de té
a herbal tea una infusión
to have a cup of tea tomar [17] una taza de té
Two teas, please. Dos tés, por favor.
2 (*afternoon snack*) la **merienda** *fem*
to have tea merendar [29]
3 (*evening meal*) la **cena** *fem*
to have tea cenar [17]
• **teabag** la bolsita de té

to **teach** *verb*
1 (*a subject*) **enseñar** [17]
She's teaching me Italian. Me está enseñando italiano.
to teach yourself something aprender [18] algo por su cuenta
Anne taught herself Italian. Anne ha aprendido italiano por su cuenta.
2 (*to work as a teacher*) **dar** [4] **clases de**
Her mum teaches maths. Su madre da clases de matemáticas.
She's been teaching for five years. Es profesora desde hace cinco años.

♪ **teacher** *noun*
1 (*in a secondary school*) el **profesor** *masc*, la **profesora** *fem*
our biology teacher nuestra profesora de biología
My father's a teacher. Mi padre es profesor.
2 (*in a primary school*) el **maestro** *masc*, la **maestra** *fem*
She's a primary school teacher. Es maestra.

teaching *noun*
la **enseñanza** *fem*

♪ **team** *noun*
el **equipo** *masc*
a football team un equipo de fútbol
Our team won. Nuestro equipo ganó.

teapot *noun*
la **tetera** *fem*

to **tear** *verb* ▷ see **tear** *noun*
1 (*clothes*) **romper** [40]
You've torn your shirt. Te has roto la camisa.
2 (*by itself*) **romperse** [40]
It tears easily. Se rompe fácilmente.
• **to tear off**
1 (*carefully*) **recortar** [17]
2 (*roughly*) **arrancar** [31]
• **to tear open**
1 (*carefully*) **abrir** [46]
2 (*roughly*) **rasgar** [28]
• **to tear up**

romper [40]
She tore up the letter. Rompió la carta.

tear *noun* ▷ see **tear** *verb*
1 (*when you cry*) la **lágrima** *fem*
to be in tears estar [2] llorando
2 (*in clothing*) el **roto** *masc*
I've got a tear in my jeans. Tengo un roto en los vaqueros.

teaspoon *noun*
la **cucharita** *fem*
a teaspoonful of ... una cucharadita de ...

♪ **teatime** *noun*
la **hora de merendar**

tea towel *noun*
el **paño de cocina**

technical *adjective*
técnico *masc*, **técnica** *fem*
• **technical college** la escuela politécnica

technician *noun*
el **técnico** *masc*, la **técnica** *fem*

technological *adjective*
tecnológico *masc*, **tecnológica** *fem*

technology *noun*
la **tecnología** *fem*
information technology la informática *fem*

teddy bear *noun*
el **osito de peluche**

♪ **teenage** *adjective*
1 (*girl, boy*) **adolescente** *masc & fem*
They have a teenage son. Tienen un hijo adolescente.
2 (*films, magazines*) **para adolescentes**
a teenage magazine una revista para adolescentes

♪ **teenager** *noun*
el & la **adolescente** *masc & fem*
a group of teenagers un grupo de adolescentes

teens *plural noun*
to be in your teens ser [1] un, una adolescente
He's in his teens. Es un adolescente.

♪ **tee-shirt** *noun*
la **camiseta** *fem*

♪ **telegram** *noun*
el **telegrama** *masc*

a b c d e f g h i j k l m n o p q r s **t** u v w x y z

telegraph pole noun
  el **poste telegráfico**

♪ to **telephone** verb ▷ see **telephone** noun
  llamar [17] **por teléfono**
  I'll telephone the doctor. Llamaré al médico.

♪ **telephone** noun ▷ see **telephone** verb
  el **teléfono** masc
  She's on the telephone. Está hablando por teléfono.
- **telephone box** la cabina telefónica
- **telephone call** la llamada telefónica
- **telephone card** la carta telefónica
- **telephone directory** la guía telefónica
- **telephone kiosk** la cabina telefónica
- **telephone number** el número de teléfono

♪ **television** noun
1 (the medium) la **televisión** fem
  She's watching television. Está viendo la televisión.
  I saw it on television. Lo vi en televisión.
2 (TV set) el **televisor** masc
  to turn the television on poner [11] el televisor
- **television news** las telenoticias, el telediario
- **television programme** el programa de televisión
- **television set** el televisor

♪ to **tell** verb
1 (to inform) **decir** [5]
  I told her straight away. Le dije enseguida.
  Have you told Jack? ¿Se lo has dicho a Jack?
  I didn't tell anyone. No se lo dije a nadie.
  as I was telling you como te decía
  to tell somebody something decirle [5] algo a alguien
  I told him it was true. Le dije que era verdad.
  That's what she told me. Eso es lo que me dijo.
  I told myself that it wasn't true. Me dije a mi mismo que no era verdad.
2 (to instruct) to tell somebody to do something decirle [5] a alguien que haga algo
  Do as you're told. Haz lo que se te dice.
  He told me to do it myself. Me dijo que lo hiciera yo mismo.
  She told me not to wait. Me dijo que no esperara.

  WORD TIP decirle a alguien que is followed by the subjunctive when it means to tell somebody to do something.

3 (to explain) **decir**
  Tell me how to do it. Dime cómo hacerlo.

4 (a story) **contar** [24]
  She told me about Frank. Me contó lo de Frank.
  Tell me about your holiday. Cuéntame qué tal tus vacaciones.
5 (the difference, etc) **notar** [17]
  to tell the difference notar la diferencia
  you can tell ... se nota ...
  You can tell it's old. Se nota que es viejo.
  You can tell she's cross. Se nota que está enfadada.
  I can't tell them apart. No puedo distinguirlos.
- **to tell off**
  regañar [17]

telly noun
  (informal) la **tele** fem
  to watch telly ver [16] la tele
  I like watching telly. Me gusta ver la tele.

temper noun
  el **humor** masc
  to be in a bad temper estar [2] de mal humor
  to be in a good temper estar [2] de buen humor
  to lose your temper perder [36] los estribos

♪ **temperature** noun
  la **temperatura** fem
  the water temperature la temperatura del agua
  to have a temperature tener [9] fiebre

temporary adjective
1 (in general) **temporal** masc & fem
2 (worker) **eventual** masc & fem

temptation noun
  la **tentación** fem

tempted adjective
  tentado masc, **tentada** fem
  I'm tempted to go. Estoy tentado de ir.

tempting adjective
  tentador masc, **tentadora** fem

♪ **ten** number
  diez invariable number
  Harry's ten. Harry tiene diez años.
  It's ten o'clock. Son las diez.

to **tend** verb
  to tend to do something tender [36] a hacer algo
  He tends to talk a lot. Tiende a hablar mucho.

tendency noun
  la **tendencia** fem

tennis *noun*
  el **tenis** *masc*
  to play tennis jugar [27] al tenis
- **tennis ball** la pelota de tenis
- **tennis court** la cancha de tenis
- **tennis player** el jugador de tenis, la jugadora de tenis
- **tennis racket** la raqueta de tenis

tenor *noun*
  el **tenor** *masc*

tenpin bowling *noun*
  los **bolos** *plural masc*
  to go tenpin bowling jugar [27] a los bolos

tense *adjective* ▷ see **tense** *noun*
  tenso *masc*, **tensa** *fem*

tense *noun* ▷ see **tense** *adj*
  (Grammar) el **tiempo** *masc*
  the present tense el presente
  in the future tense en futuro

ᔓ **tent** *noun*
  la **tienda** *fem*

ᔓ **tenth** *adjective* ▷ see **tenth** *noun*
  décimo *masc*, **décima** *fem*
  on the tenth floor en la décima planta

ᔓ **tenth** *noun* ▷ see **tenth** *adj*
1 (fraction) a tenth una décima parte
2 (in dates) the tenth of April el diez de abril

ᔓ **term** *noun*
1 (in school) el **trimestre** *masc*
2 (word) el **término** *masc*
  technical terms términos técnicos
3 (period) el **periodo** *masc*
  a five-year term un periodo de cinco años
  in the short term a corto plazo
  in the long term a largo plazo
4 (relations) to be on good terms with somebody llevarse [17] bien con alguien
  to be on bad terms with somebody llevarse [17] mal con alguien
  We're on bad terms. No nos llevamos bien.

terminal *noun*
  la **terminal** *fem*
  terminal two la terminal dos
  a computer terminal una terminal de ordenador

terrace *noun*
1 (of a cafe) la **terraza** *fem*
2 (row of houses) la **hilera de casas adosadas**
3 (in a stadium) the terraces las gradas

ᔓ **terrible** *adjective*
  espantoso *masc*, **espantosa** *fem*
  The weather was terrible. El tiempo fue espantoso.

terribly *adverb*
1 (very) **muy**
  not terribly clean no muy limpio que digamos
2 (badly) **fatal**
  I played terribly. Jugué fatal.

terrific *adjective*
1 **increíble** *masc & fem*
  at a terrific speed a una velocidad increíble
  a terrific amount una cantidad increíble
2 Terrific! ¡Fenomenal!

terrified *adjective*
  aterrorizado *masc*, **aterrorizada** *fem*

to **terrify** *verb*
  aterrar [17]

territory *noun*
  el **territorio** *masc*

terrorism *noun*
  el **terrorismo** *masc*

terrorist *noun*
  el & la **terrorista** *masc & fem*

ᔓ to **test** *verb* ▷ see **test** *noun*
1 (a student) **examinar** [17]
  to test somebody on something examinar a alguien sobre algo
  What are we going to be tested on? ¿Sobre qué nos van a examinar?
2 (knowledge, skills) **evaluar** [20]
3 (a product) **probar** [24] **algo**
  He tested the recipe on me. Probó la receta conmigo.
  These cosmetics have not been tested on animals. No se han utilizado animales en las pruebas de laboratorio de estos cosméticos.
4 (blood, urine) **analizar** [22]
5 (vision, hearing) **examinar** [17]
  You need your eyes tested. Tienes que hacerte examinar la vista.

ᔓ **test** *noun* ▷ see **test** *verb*
1 (of knowledge, skills, etc) la **prueba** *fem*
  a maths test una prueba de matemáticas
  to put something to the test poner [11] algo a prueba
2 (of a product, bomb) la **prueba** *fem*
  nuclear tests pruebas nucleares
3 (Medicine) el **análisis** *masc*
  a blood test un análisis de sangre
  an eye test un examen de la vista

to **text** *verb* ▷ see **text** *noun*
  mandar [17] un mensaje de texto a
  I'll text you tomorrow. Te mandaré un mensaje (de texto) mañana.

a
b
c
d
e
f
g
h
i
j
k
l
m
n
o
p
q
r
s
t
u
v
w
x
y
z

text noun ▷ see **text** verb
el **texto** masc
- **textbook** el libro de texto
- **text message** el mensaje de texto, el SMS

Thames noun
the Thames el Támesis

than preposition, conjunction
1 (in comparisons) **que**
His house is bigger than mine. Su casa es más grande que la mía.
She can swim better than me. Sabe nadar mejor que yo.
They have less money than we do. Tienen menos dinero que nosotros.
2 (in comparisons with numbers) **de**
more than forty más de cuarenta
less than thirty years menos de treinta años
more than once más de una vez

to **thank** verb
dar [4] **las gracias a**

thanks plural noun
las **gracias** plural fem
No thanks. No gracias.
Thanks a lot. Muchas gracias.
Thanks for your letter. Gracias por tu carta.
thanks to gracias a
It was thanks to Micky. Fue gracias a Micky.

thank you exclamation
gracias
Thank you very much for the cheque. Muchas gracias por el cheque.
No thank you. No, gracias.
a thank-you letter una carta de agradecimiento

that conjunction ▷ see **that** adv, adj, pron
que
I knew that he was wrong. Sabía que no tenía razón.

WORD TIP that can be omitted in English, but que must always be used in Spanish.

that adverb ▷ see **that** conj, adj, pron
tan
It's not that funny. No es tan divertido.
Their house isn't that big. Su casa no es tan grande.

that adjective ▷ see **that** conj, adv, pron
1 (in general) **ese** masc, **esa** fem
that dog ese perro
that blue car ese coche azul
that woman esa mujer
that one ese masc, esa fem
'Which cake would you like?'— 'That one, please.' '¿Qué pastel quieres?'—'Ese, por favor.'
2 (for something further away) **aquel** masc, **aquella** fem
from that day on desde aquel día
Of all the skirts I like that one best. De todas las faldas me gusta má aquella.

that pronoun ▷ see **that** adj, adv, conj
1 (in general) **ese** masc, **esa** fem, **eso** no gender (see Word Tip)
That's not his car. Ese no es su coche.
That's my bedroom. Esa es mi habitación.
That's not what you told me. Eso no es lo que tú me dijiste.
That's not true. Eso no es cierto.
Did you see that? ¿Has visto eso?
What's that? ¿Qué es eso?
Who's that? ¿Quién es?
Where's that? ¿Dónde está?
2 (for something further away) **aquel** masc, **aquella** fem, **aquello** no gender
Not this one, that one. Este no, aquel.
What's that? ¿Qué es aquello?
3 (as a relative pronoun) **que**
the book that's on the table el libro que está en la mesa
the girl that I saw la chica que vi
4 (with a verb + preposition) **el que** masc, **la que** fem
the drawer that I put it in el cajón en el que lo metí
5 (in expressions) **that is** es decir
We all go, all the students, that is. Vamos todos, es decir, todos los estudiantes.

WORD TIP eso and aquello are used for things that are not obviously either masc or fem.

to **thaw** verb ▷ see **thaw** noun
1 (snow, ice) **derretirse** [57]
2 (frozen food) **descongelarse** [17]

thaw noun ▷ see **thaw** verb
el **deshielo** masc

the determiner
1 (before a masc noun) **el**
the cat el gato
the boy el chico
the branches of the tree las ramas del árbol
We went to the park. Fuimos al parque.
2 (before a fem noun) **la**
the table la mesa
the girl la chica
3 (before masc plural nouns) **los**
the plates los platos
the men los hombres

4 (*before fem plural nouns*) **las**
the windows las ventanas
the women las mujeres

WORD TIP *de + el* becomes *del*; *a + el* become *al*.

♪ theatre *noun*
el **teatro** *masc*
to go to the theatre ir [8] al teatro

theft *noun*
el **robo** *masc*
He was charged with theft. Lo acusaron de
robo.

♪ their *adjective*
1 (*before nouns*) **su** *masc & fem*, **sus** *plural masc
& fem*
their flat su piso
their mother su madre
their presents sus regalos
2 (*with parts of the body, clothes*) **el, la, los, las**
She has an injured hand. Tiene la mano
herida.
They're washing their hands. Se están
lavando las manos.
They got their shoes dirty. Se ensuciaron
los zapatos.

WORD TIP Spanish uses *el, la, los, las* for *their* with
parts of the body and clothes.

theirs *pronoun*
el **suyo** *masc*, la **suya** *fem*
Our garden's smaller than theirs. Nuestro
jardín es más pequeño que el suyo.
Our house is bigger than theirs. Nuestra
casa es más grande que la suya.
Our shoes were newer than theirs.
Nuestros zapatos eran más nuevos que los
suyos.
Our photos were better than theirs.
Nuestras fotos eran mejores que las suyas.

♪ them *pronoun*
1 (*as a direct object*) **los** *masc*, **las** *fem* (*see Word
Tip*)
I like your shoes. Where did you buy them?
Me gustan tus zapatos. ¿Dónde los
compraste?
She has two brothers, but I don't know
them. Tiene dos hermanos, pero no los
conozco.
Remember Ann and Lisa? I saw them last
week. ¿Te acuerdas de Ann y Lisa? Las vi la
semana pasada.
He has a son and a daughter, do you know
them? Tiene un hijo y una hija ¿los
conoces?
I don't want to see them. No quiero verlos.
Listen to them! ¡Escúchalos!
Don't push them! ¡No los empujes!

2 (*as an indirect object*) **les**
I gave them my address. Les di mis señas.
I lent it to them. Se lo dejé.
Give it back to them! ¡Devuélveselo!
3 (*after prepositions, in comparisons, after the verb
to be*) **ellos** *masc*, **ellas** *fem*
I'll go with them. Iré con ellos (*two boys; a boy
and a girl, etc*)., Iré con ellas (*only girls*).
She's older than them. Es mayor que
ellos (*two boys; a boy and a girl, etc*)., Es mayor
que ellas (*only girls*).
without them sin ellos (*two boys; a boy and a
girl, etc*), sin ellas (*only girls*)
It's them! ¡Son ellos (*two boys; a boy and a girl,
etc*)!, ¡Son ellas (*only girls*)!

WORD TIP With a mixed masc and fem group,
Spanish uses the masc form. *le* and *les + lo* or *la*
become *se*.

theme park *noun*
el **parque temático**

themselves *pronoun*
1 (*reflexive*) **se**
They've hurt themselves. Se han hecho
daño.
They helped themselves. Se sirvieron.
2 (*for emphasis*) **ellos mismos** *plural masc*,
ellas mismas *plural fem*
The boys can do it themselves. Los chicos
pueden hacerlo ellos mismos.
The girls will tell you themselves. Las chicas
te lo dirán ellas mismas.
3 (*on their own*) **ellos solos**
plural masc, ellas solas *plural fem*
They did it by themselves. Lo hicieron ellos
solos (*talking about some boys, or boys and girls*).
They did it by themselves. Lo hicieron ellas
solas (*talking about some girls*).

WORD TIP With a mixed masc and fem group,
Spanish uses the masc form *ellos*.

♪ then *adverb*
1 (*next*) **luego**
Have a shower and then make your bed.
Dúchate y luego haz la cama.
I went to the post office and then the bank.
Fui a Correos y luego al banco.
2 (*at that time*) **entonces**
We were living in York then. Entonces
vivíamos en York.
3 (*in that case*) **entonces**
Then why worry? Entonces ¿para qué
preocuparse?
That's all right then. Entonces vale.
4 (*in expressions*) by then para entonces
By then it was too late. Para entonces era
demasiado tarde.

a
b
c
d
e
f
g
h
i
j
k
l
m
n
o
p
q
r
s
t
u
v
w
x
y
z

theory noun
la **teoría** fem
in theory en teoría

♂ **there** adverb

1 (in general) **ahí**
Put it there. Ponlo ahí.
Stand there. Ponte ahí.
They're in there. Están ahí dentro.
over there ahí
She's over there talking to Mark. Está ahí
hablando con Mark.
down there ahí abajo
up there ahí arriba
Look up there! ¡Mira ahí arriba!

2 (for somewhere further away) **allí**
Put it there. Ponlo allí.
Stand there. Ponte allí.
over there allí
She's over there talking to Mark. Está allí
hablando con Mark.
down there allí abajo
up there ahí arriba, (further away) allí arriba

3 (for somewhere even further away) **allá**
over there, across the river allá, al otro lado
del río
'Do you mean here?' - 'No, further over
there.' ¿Dices aquí?' - 'No, más allá.'

4 (standing for something already mentioned)
I've seen photos of London but I've never
been there. He visto fotos de Londres, pero
nunca he estado.
Yes, I'm going there on Tuesday. Sí, voy a ir
el martes.
Lots of his friends were there. Estaban
muchos de sus amigos.

5 (to indicate something) **there is** hay
there are hay
There's a cat in the garden. Hay un gato en
el jardín.
There was no bread. No había pan.
Yes, there's enough. Sí, hay suficiente.
There are three seats. Hay tres asientos.

6 (in exclamations) **ahí**
There they are! ¡Ahí están!
There she is! ¡Ahí está!
There's the bus coming! ¡Ahí viene el
autobús!

therefore adverb
por lo tanto
He had lived in Madrid and therefore spoke
Spanish well. Había vivido en Madrid y por
lo tanto hablaba español bien.

thermometer noun
el **termómetro** masc

these adjective, pronoun
estos masc, **estas** fem
these envelopes estos sobres
these postcards estas postales
one of these days un día de estos
These are the best. Estos son los
mejores. ▷ **this**

♂ **they** pronoun

1 **ellos** masc, **ellas** fem (see Word Tip)
'The knives?'— 'They're in the drawer.'
'¿Los cuchillos?'— 'Están en el cajón.'
I bought some apples but they're not very
nice. Compré unas manzanas pero no
están muy buenas.
They are teachers. Son profesores.
Here they are! ¡Aquí están!

2 (for emphasis) **ellos** masc, **ellas** fem
They did it. Lo hicieron ellos (two boys;
a boy and a girl, etc)., Lo hicieron ellas (only
girls).

WORD TIP they, like other subject pronouns, is
generally not translated in Spanish; the form of
the verb tells you whether the subject of the verb
is I, we, they, etc, so they is translated only for
emphasis or for clarity. With a mixed group,
Spanish uses the masc form ellos.

♂ **thick** adjective

1 (in general) **grueso** masc, **gruesa** fem
a thick layer of stones una capa gruesa de
piedras

2 (fog, fumes) **denso** masc, **densa** fem

3 (stupid) **burro** masc, **burra** fem

thickness noun

1 (of a wall, paper) el **espesor** masc

2 (of fog) la **densidad** fem

♂ **thief** noun
el **ladrón** masc, la **ladrona** fem

thigh noun
el **muslo** masc

♂ **thin** adjective

1 (in general) **delgado** masc, **delgada** fem
to get thin adelgazar [22]

2 (skinny) **flaco** masc, **flaca** fem
She's very thin. Es muy flaca.

3 (slice) **fino** masc, **fina** fem

4 (soup, sauce) **poco espeso** masc, **poco
espesa** fem

♂ **thing** noun

1 (object) la **cosa** fem
shops full of pretty things tiendas llenas de
cosas preciosas
There's no such thing. No hay tal cosa.

2 (situation, event, act) la **cosa** fem
A very strange thing happened. Pasó algo
muy raro..

How could you do such a thing? ¿Cómo pudiste hacer una cosa así?
The things you say! ¡Qué cosas dices!
The best thing to do is ... Lo mejor que se puede hacer es ...
I want to do the right thing. Quiero hacerlo correcto.
The same thing happened to me. Me pasó lo mismo

3 (*thingamajig, gadget*) el **chisme** *masc* (*informal*)
Use that thing to open it. Usa ese chisme para abrirlo.

4 (*matter*) el **asunto** *masc*
I'm fed up with the whole thing. Estoy harto del asunto.

5 **things** (*belongings, equipment*) las cosas
You can put your things in my room. Puedes poner tus cosas en mi habitación.
He washed the breakfast things. Lavó las cosas del desayuno.
Bring your swimming things. Traigan traje de baño y toalla, etcétera.

6 (*important point*) The thing is, I've lost her address. Lo que pasa es que he perdido sus señas.

7 (*unfortunate person*) You poor thing! ¡Pobrecito!
He didn't know what to do, poor thing! El pobre no sabía qué hacer.

♪ to **think** *verb*

1 (*to go over in your mind*) **pensar** [29]
He thought for a moment. Pensó un momento.
to think about somebody, something pensar en alguien, algo.
I'm thinking about you. Estoy pensando en ti.
He's always thinking about money. Siempre piensa en dinero.
She's thinking of studying medicine. Está pensando estudiar medicina.

2 (*to have an opinion*) **pensar** [29]
Tony thinks it's silly. Tony piensa que es una tontería.
What do you think of my new jacket? ¿Qué piensas de mi chaqueta nueva?
What do you think of that? ¿Qué piensas de eso?
What do you think of it? ¿Qué te parece?

3 (*to believe*) **creer** [37]
Do you think they'll come? ¿Crees que vendrán?
No, I don't think so. No, creo que no.
I think he's already left. Creo que ya se ha ido.

4 (*to imagine*) **imaginar** [17]
I never thought it would be like this! ¡Nunca me imaginé que sería así!
Just think! We'll soon be in Spain! ¡Imagínate! ¡Pronto estaremos en España!

♪ **third** *adjective* ▷ see **third** *noun*
tercero *masc*, **tercera** *fem*
on the third floor en la tercera planta

♪ **third** *noun* ▷ see **third** *adj*
1 (*fraction*) a third un tercio
2 (*in dates*) the third of March el tres de marzo

thirdly *adverb*
en tercer lugar

♪ **Third World** *noun*
the Third World el Tercer Mundo

thirst *noun*
la **sed** *fem*

♪ **thirsty** *adjective*
to be thirsty tener [9] sed
I'm thirsty. Tengo sed.
We were all thirsty. Todos teníamos sed.

♪ **thirteen** *number*
trece *invariable number*
Ahmed's thirteen. Ahmed tiene trece años.

♪ **thirty** *number*
treinta *invariable number*
thirty-five treinta y cinco
She's thirty. Tiene treinta años.

♪ **this** *adjective* ▷ see **this** *pron*
1 (*with a masc noun*) **este**
this paintbrush este pincel
this tree este árbol
2 (*with a fem noun*) **esta**
this cup esta taza
this morning esta mañana
3 this one este (*for a masc noun*), esta (*for a fem noun*)
If you need a pen, use this one. Si necesitas un boli, usa este.
If you want a lamp, take this one. Si quieres una lámpara, toma esta. ▷ these

♪ **this** *pronoun* ▷ see **this** *adj*
1 (*for a masc noun*) **este**
This is my car. Este es mi coche.
Who is this? ¿Quién es este?
2 (*for a fem noun*) **esta**
This is the best photo. Esta es la mejor foto.
Who is this? ¿Quién es esta?
3 (*without gender*) **esto**
Can you hold this for a moment? ¿Puedes sostener esto un momento?
What's this? ¿Qué es esto? ▶▶

a
b
c
d
e
f
g
h
i
j
k
l
m
n
o
p
q
r
s
t
u
v
w
x
y
z

4 (*on the phone*) **This is Tracy.** Soy Tracy.
5 (*in introductions*) **This is my sister Carla.**
Te presento a mi hermana Carla.
▷ **these**

thistle *noun*
el **cardo** *masc*

thorough *adjective*
1 (*search*) **a fondo**
2 (*person*) **concienzudo** *masc*, **concienzuda**
fem

♂**those** *adjective* ▷ see **those** *pron*
1 (*with a masc pl noun*) **esos**, (*with a fem pl*
noun) **esas**
those books esos libros
those cups esas tazas
2 (*for things further away*) **aquellos** *plural masc*,
aquellas *plural fem*
those trees aquellos árboles
those houses aquellas casas

♂**those** *pronoun* ▷ see **those** *adj*
1 (*for a masc pl noun*) **esos**, (*for a fem pl*
noun) **esas**
Knives? Take those. ¿Cuchillos? Toma
esos.
If you need cups, take those. Si necesitas
tazas, toma esas.
2 (*for things further away*) **aquellos** *pl masc*,
aquellas *pl fem*
Not these ones, those ones. Estos no,
aquellos.
What are those? ¿Qué son aquellos?

though *conjunction*
1 (*although*) **aunque**
though it's cold aunque hace calor
though he's older than she is aunque es
mayor que ella
2 (*however*) **It was a good idea, though.** Aun
así era una buena idea.

thought *noun*
el **pensamiento** *masc*

thoughtful *adjective*
1 (*considerate*) **amable**
It was really thoughtful of you. Fue muy
amable de tu parte.
2 (*deep in thought*) **pensativo** *masc*, **pensativa**
fem

thoughtless *adjective*
desconsiderado *masc*, **desconsiderada**
fem

♂**thousand** *number*
mil *masc & fem*
a thousand mil
about a thousand people unas mil
personas

a thousand euros mil euros
three thousand tres mil
two thousand and seven dos mil siete
Thousands of tourists come every year.
Miles de turistas vienen cada año.

thread *noun* ▷ see **thread** *verb*
el **hilo** *masc*

to **thread** *verb* ▷ see **thread** *noun*
(*a needle*) **enhebrar** [17]

threat *noun*
la **amenaza** *fem*

to **threaten** *verb*
amenazar [22]
to threaten to do something amenazar con
hacer algo

♂**three** *number*
tres *invariable number*
Lily's three. Lily tiene tres años.

♂**three-quarters** *plural noun*
tres cuartos *plural masc*

thrilled *adjective*
encantado *masc*, **encantada** *fem*
I was thrilled to hear from you. Me encantó
tener noticias tuyas.

thriller *noun*
1 (*book*) la **novela de suspense**
2 (*film*) la **película de suspense**

thrilling *adjective*
emocionante *masc & fem*

♂**throat** *noun*
la **garganta** *fem*
to have a sore throat tener [9] dolor de
garganta

through *preposition, adjective*
1 (*across*) **a través de**
a path through the forest un camino a
través del bosque
to go through something atravesar [29]
algo
We went through the park. Atravesamos el
parque.
2 (*by way of*) **por**
through the window por la ventana
a through train un tren directo
The train went through Leeds. El tren fue
por Leeds.
to go through customs pasar [17] la aduana

throughout *preposition*
throughout the match durante todo el
partido
throughout the world por todo el mundo

ꝰ to **throw** *verb*
  tirar [17]
  Throw me the ball! ¡Tírame la pelota!
  I threw the letter into the bin. Tiré la carta a la basura.
  He threw the book on the floor. Tiró el libro al suelo.
  We were throwing snowballs. Estábamos tirando bolas de nieve.
  • **to throw something away**
  tirar [17] **algo**
  I've thrown away the old newspapers. He tirado los periódicos viejos.
  • **to throw somebody out**
  echar [17] **a alguien**
  • **to throw something out**
  tirar [17] **algo a la basura**
  • **to throw up**
  devolver [45]

thumb *noun*
  el **pulgar** *masc*

thunder *noun*
  los **truenos** *plural masc*
  a peal of thunder un trueno
  • **thunderstorm** la tormenta eléctrica

ꝰ **Thursday** *noun*
  el **jueves** *masc*
  on Thursday el jueves
  I'm going out on Thursday. Voy a salir el jueves.
  See you on Thursday! ¡Hasta el jueves!
  on Thursdays los jueves
  The museum is closed on Thursdays. El museo cierra los jueves.
  every Thursday todos los jueves
  last Thursday el jueves pasado
  next Thursday el próximo jueves

> **WORD TIP** Months of the year and days of the week start with small letters in Spanish.

to **tick** *verb*
1 (*clocks*) **hacer** [7] **tictac**
2 (*on paper*) **marcar** [31]

ꝰ **ticket** *noun*
1 (*for a film, an exhibition, etc*) la **entrada** *fem*
  two tickets for the concert dos entradas para el concierto
2 (*for a plane, a train, etc*) el **billete** *masc*
  a bus ticket un billete de autobús
3 (*from a machine*) el **ticket** *masc*
4 (*fine*) a parking ticket una multa
• **ticket inspector** el revisor, la revisora

ꝰ **ticket office** *noun*
1 (*at a station*) el **mostrador de venta de billetes**
2 (*at a cinema, etc*) la **taquilla** *fem*

to **tickle** *verb*
  hacerle [7] **cosquillas a**

ꝰ **tide** *noun*
  la **marea** *fem*
  at high tide cuando la marea está alta
  The tide is out. La marea está baja.

ꝰ **tidy** *adjective* ▷ see **tidy** *verb*
1 (*room, person*) **ordenado** *masc*, **ordenada** *fem*
  My flat mate is very tidy. Mi compañero de piso es muy ordenado.
2 (*homework*) **bien presentado** *masc*, **bien presentada** *fem*
3 (*in appearance*) **bien arreglado** *masc*, **bien arreglada** *fem*
  She always looks tidy. Siempre va bien arreglada.

ꝰ to **tidy** *verb* ▷ see **tidy** *adj*
  ordenar [17]

ꝰ **tie** *noun* ▷ see **tie** *verb*
1 (*that you wear*) la **corbata** *fem*
  a red tie una corbata roja
2 (*in a match*) el **empate** *masc*

ꝰ to **tie** *verb* ▷ see **tie** *noun*
1 (*a knot, a bow*) **atar** [17]
  to tie your shoelaces atarse los zapatos
2 to tie a knot in something hacer [7] un nudo en algo
3 (*in a match*) **empatar** [17]
  We tied two all. Empatamos a dos.

tiger *noun*
  el **tigre** *masc*

tight *adjective*
1 (*too small*) **to be tight** apretar [29]
  The skirt's a bit tight. La falda me aprieta un poco.
  These shoes are too tight. Estos zapatos me aprietan mucho.
2 (*close-fitting*) **ceñido** *masc*, **ceñida** *fem*
  She was wearing a tight dress. Llevaba un vestido ceñido.

to **tighten** *verb*
  apretar [29]

tightly *adverb*
  fuerte
  Hold it tightly. Agárralo fuerte.

ꝰ **tights** *plural noun*
  las **medias** *plural fem*
  a pair of tights un par de medias

tile *noun*
1 (*for floors, walls*) el **azulejo** *masc*
2 (*for roofs*) la **teja** *fem*

a
b
c
d
e
f
g
h
i
j
k
l
m
n
o
p
q
r
s
t
u
v
w
x
y
z

till *noun* ▷ see **till** *prep*
la **caja** *fem*
Pay at the till. Pase a pagar por caja.

till *preposition* ▷ see **till** *noun*
hasta
till then hasta entonces
till now hasta ahora
They're here till Sunday. Están aquí hasta el domingo.
She won't be back till ten. No volveré hasta las diez.

time *noun*
1 (*on the clock*) la **hora** *fem*
ten o'clock Spanish time las diez hora española
on time a la hora
What time is it? ¿Qué hora es?
It's time for lunch. Es hora de comer.
2 (*an amount of time*) el **tiempo** *masc*
We've got lots of time. Tenemos mucho tiempo.
I don't have the time to drink coffee. No tengo tiempo para tomar café.
He talked for a long time. Habló durante mucho tiempo.
She hasn't called me for a long time. Hace mucho que no me llama.
3 (*moment*) el **momento** *masc*
at any time en cualquier momento
Is this a good time to phone? ¿Es buen momento para llamar?
4 (*in expressions*) from time to time de vez en cuando
at times a veces
for the time being por ahora
in time a tiempo
I arrived just in time. Llegué justo a tiempo.
5 (*in a series*) la **vez** *fem, fem pl:* las **veces**
the first time la primera vez
six times seis veces
the first time I saw you la primera vez que te vi
three times a year tres veces al año
6 to have a good time pasarlo [17] bien
We had a really good time. Lo pasamos muy bien.
Have a good time! ¡Que lo pases bien!
7 (*Maths*) Three times two is six. Tres por dos son seis.

time off *noun*
1 (*free time*) el **tiempo libre**
2 (*leave*) los **días libres**

timetable *noun*
el **horario** *masc*
the bus timetable el horario de los autobuses
the school timetable el horario de clases

tin *noun*
la **lata** *fem*
a tin of tomatoes una lata de tomates
• tin foil el papel aluminio

tinned *adjective*
en lata
tinned peas guisantes en lata

tin opener *noun*
el **abrelatas** *masc, pl:* los **abrelatas**

tiny *adjective*
diminuto *masc,* **diminuta** *fem*

tip *noun* ▷ see **tip** *verb*
1 (*the end*) la **punta** *fem*
the tip of my finger la punta de mi dedo
2 (*money*) la **propina** *fem*
Give the waiter a tip. Dale una propina al camarero.
3 (*useful hint*) el **consejo** *masc*

to **tip** *verb* ▷ see **tip** *noun*
(*a waiter, etc*) darle [4] una propina a

tiptoe *noun*
on tiptoe de puntillas

tired *adjective*
1 cansado *masc,* cansada *fem*
I'm tired. Estoy cansado.
You look tired. Pareces cansado.
2 to be tired of something estar [2] harto *masc,* harta *fem* de algo
He's tired of London. Está harto de Londres.
I'm tired of watching TV. Estoy harta de ver la tele.

tiring *adjective*
cansado *masc,* cansada *fem*

tissue *noun*
el **pañuelo de papel**
Do you have a tissue? ¿Tienes un pañuelo de papel?

title *noun*
el **título** *masc*

to *preposition*
1 (*showing movement*) a
to London a Londres
to Spain a España
to Paul's house a casa de Paul
the road to London la carretera de Londres.
She's gone to the office. Se ha ido a la oficina.
I'm going to school. Voy al colegio.

I'm going to the dentist's tomorrow. Voy al dentista mañana.

2 (*until*) **hasta**
from beginning to end desde el principio hasta el final
from Monday to Friday de lunes a viernes

3 (*to a person*) **a**
Give the book to Leila. Dale el libro a Leila.
Who did you give it to? ¿A quién se lo diste?
to talk to somebody hablar [17] con alguien
He didn't talk to me. No habló conmigo.
I was nice to them. Fui amable con ellos.

4 (*in order to*) **para**
I went out to help her. Salí para ayudarla.

5 (*in time expressions*) It's ten to nine. Son las nueve menos diez.
It's twenty to. Son menos veinte.

6 (*in infinitives*) We're ready to go. Estamos listos para irnos.
It's easy to do. Es fácil de hacer.
I have nothing to do. No tengo nada que hacer.
I have a lot of homework to do. Tengo muchos deberes que hacer.

ℰ **toast** *noun*
1 (*made from bread*) **el pan tostado**
a piece of toast una tostada
two slices of toast dos tostadas
2 (*to your health*) **el brindis** *masc*
to drink a toast to the future brindar [17] por el futuro

toaster *noun*
el tostador *masc*

ℰ **tobacco** *noun*
el tabaco *masc*

ℰ **tobacconist's** *noun*
el estanco *masc*

ℰ **today** *adverb, noun*
hoy
She arrives today. Llega hoy.
Today's her birthday. Hoy es su cumpleaños.

ℰ **toe** *noun*
el dedo del pie
my big toe el dedo gordo del pie
• **toenail** la uña de un dedo del pie

toffee *noun*
el toffee *masc*

together *adverb*
juntos *plural masc*, **juntas** *plural fem*
Kate and Lindy arrived together. Kate y Lindy llegaron juntas.
They all left together. Se fueron todos juntos.

ℰ **toilet** *noun*
1 (*in a house*) **el baño** *masc*
She's gone to the toilet. Ha ido al baño.
2 (*in a public place*) **el servicio** *masc*
Where's the toilet? ¿Dónde está el servicio?
Where are the toilets? ¿Dónde están los servicios
• **toilet paper** el papel higiénico
• **toilet roll** el rollo de papel higiénico

token *noun*
1 (*for a machine, game*) **la ficha** *fem*
2 (*as a present*) **el cheque regalo**
a CD token un cheque regalo para un CD

ℰ **toll** *noun*
1 (*on a motorway*) **el peaje** *masc*
2 (*number*) **el número** *masc*
The death toll is 25. El número de víctimas mortales asciende a 25.

ℰ **tomato** *noun*
el tomate *masc*
a tomato salad una ensalada de tomate
tomato sauce salsa de tomate

ℰ **tomorrow** *adverb*
mañana
tomorrow afternoon mañana por la tarde
tomorrow morning mañana por la mañana
tomorrow night mañana por la noche
the day after tomorrow pasado mañana
I'll do it tomorrow. Lo haré mañana.

ton *noun*
la tonelada *fem*
She gets tons of letters. Recibe montones de cartas.

ℰ **tongue** *noun*
la lengua *fem*
to stick your tongue out sacar [31] la lengua

tonic *noun*
la tónica *fem*
a gin and tonic un gin tonic

ℰ **tonight** *adverb*
esta noche
I'm going out tonight. Voy a salir esta noche.

tonsillitis *noun*
las anginas *plural fem*

ℰ **too** *adverb*
1 demasiado
too often demasiado a menudo
It's too expensive. Es demasiado caro.
The tickets are too expensive. Las entradas son demasiado caras. ▸▸

2 **too much** demasiado
He eats too much. Come demasiado.

3 *(before nouns)* **too much** demasiado *masc*, demasiada *fem*
It takes too much time. Lleva demasiado tiempo.
I watch too much TV veo demasiada televisión

4 **too many** demasiados *masc pl*, demasiadas *fem pl*
too many beers demasiadas cervezas
There are too many accidents. Hay demasiados accidentes.

5 *(as well)* **también**
Karen's coming too. Karen también viene.
Me too! ¡Yo también!

6 *(very)* **muy**
I'm not too convinced. No estoy muy convencida.

WORD TIP Only when *demasiado* comes before a noun, can it become *demasiada, demasiados, demasiadas.*

tool *noun*
la **herramienta** *fem*
• **tool kit** el juego de herramientas

ʃ **tooth** *noun*
1 el **diente** *masc*
to brush your teeth cepillarse [17] los dientes
2 *(back tooth)* la **muela** *fem*

toothache *noun*
el **dolor de muelas**
to have toothache tener [9] dolor de muelas

ʃ **toothbrush** *noun*
el **cepillo de dientes**

ʃ **toothpaste** *noun*
la **pasta de dientes**

ʃ **top** *adjective* ▷ see **top** *noun*
1 *(step, floor)* **último** *masc*, **última** *fem*
It's on the top floor. Está en el último piso.
2 *(bunk, drawer, shelf)* **de arriba**
3 in the top left-hand corner en la esquina superior izquierda

ʃ **top** *noun* ▷ see **top** *adj*
1 *(of a ladder, stairs)* lo **alto** *masc*
the top of ... lo alto de ...
at the top of the stairs en lo alto de las escaleras
to be at the top of the list encabezar [22] una lista
2 *(of a page, container, box)* la **parte superior**
The top of the box is red. La parte superior de la caja es roja.

3 on top of something *(a table, wardrobe)* encima de algo
It's on top of the chest-of-drawers. Está encima de la cómoda.
4 *(of a mountain)* la **cima** *fem*
5 *(of a bottle)* el **tapón** *masc*
6 *(of a pen)* el **capuchón** *masc*
7 *(of a jar)* la **tapa** *fem*

topic *noun*
el **tema** *masc*

topping *noun*
la **guarnición** *fem*
Which topping do you want? ¿Qué guarnición quieres?

torch *noun*
la **linterna** *fem*

torn *adjective*
roto *masc*, **rota** *fem*

tornado *noun*
el **tornado** *masc*

tortoise *noun*
la **tortuga** *fem*

torture *noun* ▷ see **torture** *verb*
la **tortura** *fem*

to **torture** *verb* ▷ see **torture** *noun*
torturar [17]

Tory *noun*
el **conservador** *masc*, la **conservadora** *fem*

ʃ **total** *adjective* ▷ see **total** *noun*
total *masc & fem*

ʃ **total** *noun* ▷ see **total** *adj*
el **total** *masc*

totally *adverb*
totalmente

ʃ **touch** *noun* ▷ see **touch** *verb*
1 *(contact)* to be in touch estar [2] en contacto
to get in touch with somebody contactarse [17] con alguien
to stay in touch with somebody mantenerse [9] en contacto con alguien
We've lost touch. Hemos perdido el contacto.
We ought to get in touch. Deberíamos ponernos en contacto.
He's out of touch with fashion. No está al corriente de la moda.
2 *(a little bit)* un **poco** *masc*
a touch of vanilla un poco de vainilla
It was a touch embarrassing. Fue un poco embarazoso.

a b c d e f g h i j k l m n o p q r s t u v w x y z

♂ to **touch** verb ▷ see **touch** noun

1 tocar [31]
He touched her hand. Le tocó la mano.
Don't touch! ¡No toques!

2 (emotionally) **conmover** [38]
I was touched. Me conmoví.

tough adjective

1 (meat, climate, person) **duro** masc, **dura** fem
a tough guy un tipo duro
The meat's tough. La carne está dura.
Fortunately, she's tough.
Afortunadamente, es fuerte.

2 (measure, discipline, teacher) **severo** masc,
severa fem

3 (fabric) **resistente** masc & fem

4 (question, decision, job) **difícil** masc & fem
Things are tough at the moment. Las cosas
están difíciles en este momento.
Tough luck! ¡Mala suerte!

tour noun

1 la **visita** fem
a tour of the city una visita a la ciudad
a package tour un viaje organizado
We did the tour of the castle. Hicimos la
visita al castillo.

2 (by a band, group) la **gira** fem
to go on tour ir [8] de gira

tourism noun
el **turismo** masc

♂ **tourist** noun
el & la **turista** masc & fem
• **tourist information office** la oficina de
información y turismo

♂ **towards** adverb
hacia
towards the door hacia la puerta
towards the end of the concert casi al final
del concierto

♂ **towel** noun
la **toalla** fem

tower noun
la **torre** fem
the Tower of London la Torre de Londres
• **tower block** el bloque de apartamentos

♂ **town** noun
la **ciudad** fem
to go into town ir [8] a la ciudad
• **town centre** el centro de la ciudad
• **town hall** el ayuntamiento

toxic adjective
tóxico masc, **tóxica** fem

♂ **toy** noun
el **juguete** masc

trace noun ▷ see **trace** verb
el **rastro** masc
There is no trace of it. No hay rastro de ello.

to **trace** verb ▷ see **trace** noun

1 (a missing person) **localizar** [22]

2 (with tracing paper) **calcar** [31]

tracing paper noun
el **papel de calco**

♂ **track** noun

1 (for sport) la **pista** fem
a track event una prueba de atletismo

2 (path) el **sendero** masc

3 (song) el **tema** masc
This is my favourite track. Es mi tema
favorito.

4 (for cars) a racing track un circuito
• **track suit** el chandal

tractor noun
el **tractor** masc

trade noun
(profession) el **oficio** masc

trade mark noun
la **marca comercial**
a registered trade mark una marca
registrada

trade union noun
el **sindicato** masc

tradition noun
la **tradición** fem

traditional adjective
tradicional masc & fem

♂ **traffic** noun
el **tráfico** masc
• **traffic jam** el embotellamiento
• **traffic lights** el semáforo
• **traffic warden** el & la guardia municipal

tragedy noun
la **tragedia** fem

tragic adjective
trágico masc, **trágica** fem

trail noun
(path) el **sendero** masc
a nature trail un sendero ecológico

trailer noun

1 (on a car) el **remolque** masc

2 (of a film) el **trailer** masc

a
b
c
d
e
f
g
h
i
j
k
l
m
n
o
p
q
r
s
t
u
v
w
x
y
z

to train *verb* ▷ see **train** *noun*

1 (*for a profession*) **estudiar** [17]
He's training to be a nurse. Está estudiando para ser enfermero.

2 (*professionals*) **formar** [17]
They train people to use computers. Enseñan informática.

3 (*in sport*) **entrenar** [17]
The team trains on Saturdays. El equipo entrena los sábados.

♪ **train** *noun* ▷ see **train** *verb*
el **tren** *masc*
the train to York el tren para York
He's coming by train. Viene en tren.
• **train ticket** el billete de tren
• **train timetable** el horario de trenes

♪ **trainer** *noun*
1 (*of an athlete, a horse*) el **entrenador** *masc*, la **entrenadora** *fem*
2 (*shoe*) la **zapatilla de deporte**
my new trainers mis zapatillas de deporte nuevas

♪ **training** *noun*
1 (*for a career*) la **formación** *fem*
2 (*for sport*) el **entrenamiento** *masc*

tram *noun*
el **tranvía** *masc*

trampoline *noun*
la **cama elástica**

transfer *noun*
1 (*of money*) la **transferencia** *fem*
2 (*to a new post*) el **traslado** *masc*
3 (*sticker*) la **calcomanía** *fem*

to translate *verb*
traducir [60]
to translate something into Spanish traducir algo al español

translation *noun*
la **traducción** *fem*

translator *noun*
el **traductor** *masc*, la **traductora** *fem*
I'd like to be a translator. Me gustaría ser traductora.

transparent *adjective*
transparente *masc & fem*

transplant *noun*
el **trasplante** *masc*

♪ **transport** *noun*
el **transporte** *masc*
air transport el transporte aéreo
public transport transporte público

trap *noun*
la **trampa** *fem*

♪ **to travel** *verb* ▷ see **travel** *noun*
viajar [17]
to travel by train viajar en tren
I want to travel. Quiero viajar.

♪ **travel** *noun* ▷ see **travel** *verb*
los **viajes** *plural masc*
foreign travel los viajes al extranjero
a travel brochure un folleto de viajes
• **travel agency** la agencia de viajes
• **travel agent** el & la agente de viajes

♪ **traveller** *noun*
1 (*for business, pleasure*) el **viajero** *masc*, la **viajera** *fem*
2 (*as a lifestyle*) to be a traveller llevar [17] una vida nómada
• **traveller's cheque** el cheque de viaje

travelling *noun*
el **viajar**
I like travelling. Me gusta viajar.

travel-sick *adj*
to be travel-sick, to get travel-sick marearse [17] en los viajes

tray *noun*
la **bandeja** *fem*

to tread *verb*
to tread on something pisar [17] algo

treasure *noun*
el **tesoro** *masc*

treat *noun* ▷ see **treat** *verb*
el **capricho** *masc*
to give yourself a treat darse [4] un capricho
It's a little treat. Es un caprichito.
I took them to the pool as a treat. Les llevé a la piscina como algo especial.

to treat *verb* ▷ see **treat** *noun*
1 **tratar** [17]
the doctor who treated me el médico que me trató
He treats his dog well. Trata bien a su perro.
2 to treat somebody to something invitar [17] a alguien a algo
I'll treat you to an ice cream. Te invito a un helado.
3 to treat yourself darse [4] un capricho
I treated myself to a new dress. Me compré un vestido para darme un capricho.

treatment *noun*
1 (*medical*) el **tratamiento** *masc*
2 (*of a person, an object, etc*) el **trato** *masc*

treaty noun
el **tratado** masc

ℰ **tree** noun
el **árbol** masc
• **tree trunk** el tronco

tremendous adjective
tremendo masc, **tremenda** fem
a **tremendous victory** una tremenda victoria
a **tremendous athlete** un atleta formidable

trend noun
1 (fashion) la **moda** fem
2 (tendency) la **tendencia** fem

trendy adjective
de moda

trial noun
(legal) el **juicio** masc

triangle noun
el **triángulo** masc

tribe noun
la **tribu** fem

tribute noun
el **homenaje** masc

trick noun ▷ see **trick** verb
1 (in cards, etc) el **truco** masc
a **card trick** un truco con las cartas
It doesn't work, there must be a trick to it. No funciona, debe tener truco.
2 (a joke) la **broma** fem
to **play a trick on somebody** gastarle [17] una broma a alguien

to **trick** verb ▷ see **trick** noun
engañar [17]
He tricked me! ¡Me engañó!

tricky adjective
1 (sensitive) **delicado** masc, **delicada** fem
a **tricky situation** una situación delicada
2 (difficult) **difícil** masc & fem

tricycle noun
el **triciclo** masc

Trinidad noun
Trinidad fem

Trinidadian adjective & noun
1 **trinitense** masc & fem
2 un & una **trinitense** masc & fem
the **Trinidadians** los trinitenses

WORD TIP Adjectives and nouns for nationality and regional origin do not have capital letters in Spanish.

ℰ **trip** noun ▷ see **trip** verb
el **viaje** masc
a **trip to Florida** un viaje a Florida
a **day trip to Bristol** un viaje de un día a Bristol
to **go on a trip** hacer [7] un viaje
He's on a business trip. Está en viaje de negocios.

ℰ to **trip** verb ▷ see **trip** noun
tropezar [25]
Nicky tripped over a stone. Nicky tropezó con una piedra.

to **triple** verb
triplicar [31]
The price has tripled. El precio se ha triplicado.

ℰ **trolley** noun
el **carro** masc

trombone noun
el **trombón** masc
to **play the trombone** tocar [31] el trombón

trophy noun
el **trofeo** masc

trouble noun
1 los **problemas** plural masc
We had trouble with the car. Tuvimos problemas con el coche.
Steve's in trouble. Steve tiene problemas.
What's the trouble? ¿Cuál es el problema?
to **get into trouble** meterse [18] en problemas
2 (difficulty) I had trouble finding a seat. Me costó encontrar un sitio.
It's not worth the trouble. No vale la pena.
The trouble is, I've forgotten the number. El problema es que he olvidado el número.
It's no trouble! ¡No es ningún problema!

ℰ **trousers** plural noun
los **pantalones** plural masc
a **pair of trousers** unos pantalones, un par de pantalones

ℰ **trout** noun
la **trucha** fem

truant noun
to **play truant** hacer [7] novillos.
She's playing truant. Está haciendo novillos.

ℰ **truck** noun
el **camión** masc

ℰ **true** adjective
a **true story** una historia verídica
to **be true** ser [1] verdad
Is that true? ¿Es eso verdad?
It's true she's absent-minded. Es verdad que es despistada.

a b c d e f g h i j k l m n o p q r s **t** u v w x y z

‑ly *adverb*
de veras

rump *noun*
el **triunfo** *masc*
Spades are trumps. Las picas son triunfo.

trumpet *noun*
la **trompeta** *fem*
to play the trumpet tocar [31] la trompeta

trunk *noun*
1 (*of a tree*) el **tronco** *masc*
2 (*of an elephant*) la **trompa** *fem*
3 (*for clothes*) el **baúl** *masc*

trunks *plural noun*
swimming trunks el bañador *masc*

trust *noun* ▷ see **trust** *verb*
la **confianza** *fem*

to **trust** *verb* ▷ see **trust** *noun*
confiar [32]
I trust her. Confío en ella.

truth *noun*
la **verdad** *fem*
To tell the truth, I'd completely forgottten.
Si quieres que te diga la verdad, me había
olvidado completamente.

♂ **try** *noun* ▷ see **try** *verb*
el **intento** *masc*
It's my first try. Es mi primer intento.
You should have a try. Deberías intentarlo.
to have a try intentarlo [17]

♂ to **try** *verb* ▷ see **try** *noun*
1 **intentar** [17]
to try to do something intentar hacer algo
I'm trying to open it. Estoy intentando
abrirlo.
to try hard to do something esforzarse [26]
por hacer algo
She's trying hard to learn Arabic. Se está
esforzando por aprender árabe.
2 (*to taste*) **probar** [24]
Try this sauce. Prueba esta salsa.
• to try something on
(*clothes*) **probarse** [26] **algo**
Can I try it on? ¿Me lo puedo probar?

♂ **T-shirt** *noun*
la **camiseta** *fem*

tub *noun*
1 (*for food*) la **tarrina** *fem*
2 (*bath*) la **bañera** *fem*

tube *noun*
1 el **tubo** *masc*
2 (*London underground*) **the tube** el metro

tuberculosis *noun*
la **tuberculosis** *fem*

♂ **Tuesday** *noun*
el **martes** *masc*
on Tuesday el martes
I'm going out on Tuesday. Voy a salir el
martes.
See you on Tuesday! ¡Hasta el martes!
on Tuesdays los martes
The museum is closed on Tuesdays. El
museo cierra los martes.
every Tuesday todos los martes
last Tuesday el martes pasado
next Tuesday el próximo martes

WORD TIP Months of the year and days of the
week start with small letters in Spanish.

tuition *noun*
las **clases** *plural fem*
piano tuition clases de piano
private tuition clases particulares

tulip *noun*
el **tulipán** *masc*

tumble-drier *noun*
la **secadora** *fem*

tummy *noun*
la **barriga** *fem*

♂ **tuna** *noun*
el **atún** *masc*

tune *noun*
la **melodía** *fem*

♂ **tunnel** *noun*
el **túnel** *masc*
the Channel Tunnel el Eurotúnel

turban *noun*
el **turbante** *masc*

Turk *noun*
un **turco** *masc*, una **turca** *fem*
the Turks los turcos

WORD TIP Adjectives and nouns for nationality
and regional origin do not have capital letters in
Spanish.

turkey *noun*
el **pavo** *masc*

Turkey *noun*
Turquía *fem*

Turkish *adjective & noun*
1 **turco** *masc*, **turca** *fem*
2 (*the language*) el **turco** *masc*

WORD TIP Adjectives and nouns for nationality,
regional origin and language do not have capital
letters in Spanish.

a b c d e f g h i j k l m n o p q r s t u v w x y z

ℰ **turn** *noun* ▷ see **turn** *verb*

1 (*in a game*) el **turno** *masc*
It's your turn. Es tu turno.
Whose turn is it? ¿A quién le toca?
It's Jane's turn to play. Es el turno de Jane.
to take turns driving turnarse [17] para conducir

2 (*in a road*) la **curva** *fem*

ℰ to **turn** *verb* ▷ see **turn** *noun*

1 **girar** [17]
Turn your chair round. Gira la silla.
Turn left at the next set of lights. Gira a la izquierda en el próximo semáforo.

2 (*a page, mattress*) **dar** [4] **la vuelta a**

3 (*to become*) **ponerse** [11]
She turned red. Se puso roja.

• **to turn back**
volverse [45]
We turned back. Nos volvimos.

• **to turn off**

1 (*road*) **girar** [17]

2 (*a light, TV, etc*) **apagar** [28]

3 (*the gas, a tap, etc*) **cerrar** [29]

• **to turn on**

1 (*a light, TV, etc*) **encender** [36]

2 (*a tap*) **abrir** [46]

• **to turn out**

1 to turn out well salir [63] bien
to turn out badly salir [63] mal
It all turned out well in the end. Todo salió bien al final.
The holiday turned out badly. Las vacaciones salieron mal.

2 It turned out that I was wrong. Resultó que estaba equivocado.

• **to turn over**

1 (*in bed*) **darse** [4] **la vuelta**

2 (*a page*) **dar** [4] **la vuelta a**

• **to turn up**

1 (*to arrive*) **presentarse** [17]
They turned up an hour late. Se presentaron con una hora de retraso.

2 (*the gas*) **abrir** [46] **más**

3 (*the heating, volume*) **subir** [19]
Can you turn up the volume? ¿Puedes subir el volumen?

turning *noun*
la **bocacalle** *fem*
Take the first turning on the right. Toma la primera bocacalle a la derecha.
Take the first turning on the left. Toma la primera bocacalle a la izquierda.

turnip *noun*
el **nabo** *masc*

turquoise *adjective*
turquesa *masc & fem*

turtle *noun*
la **tortuga** *fem*

TV *noun*
la **tele** *fem*
I saw her on TV. La vi en la tele.

tweezers *plural noun*
las **pinzas** *plural fem*

ℰ **twelfth** *adjective* ▷ see **twelfth** *noun*
doceavo *masc*, **doceava** *fem*
on the twelfth floor en la duodécima planta

ℰ **twelfth** *noun* ▷ see **twelfth** *adj*
(*in dates*) the twelfth of May el doce de mayo

ℰ **twelve** *number*
doce *invariable number*
Tara's twelve. Tara tiene doce años.
It's twelve o'clock. Son las doce de la mañana (*midday*)., Son las doce de la noche (*midnight*).

ℰ **twenty** *number*
veinte *invariable number*
twenty-one veintiuno
twenty-five veinticinco
Marie's twenty. Marie tiene veinte años.

twice *adverb*

1 (*two times*) **dos veces**
I've asked him twice. Le he preguntado dos veces.

2 (*double the amount, number*) **twice as much** sugar el doble de azúcar
twice as many tourists dos veces más turistas

twig *noun*
la **ramita** *fem*

twilight *noun*
el **anochecer** *masc*

ℰ **twin** *noun* ▷ see **twin** *verb*
el **gemelo** *masc*, la **gemela** *fem*
her twin sister su hermana gemela
Helen and Tim are twins. Helen y Tim son gemelos.

ℰ to **twin** *verb* ▷ see **twin** *noun*
Oxford is twinned with León. Oxford está hermanado con León.

to **twist** *verb*
girar [17]

a
b
c
d
e
f
g
h
i
j
k
l
m
n
o
p
q
r
s
t
u
v
w
x
y
z

o *number*
dos *invariable number*
two by two dos por dos
Ben's two. Ben tiene dos años.

type *noun* ▷ see **type** *verb*
el tipo *masc*
What type of computer is it? ¿Qué tipo de ordenador es?

to **type** *verb* ▷ see **type** *noun*
(*on a typewriter*) **escribir** [52] **a máquina**
I'm learning to type. Estoy aprendiendo a escribir a máquina.
I was busy typing some letters. Estaba ocupada escribiendo unas cartas a máquina.

typewriter *noun*
la máquina de escribir

typical *adjective*
típico *masc*, **típica** *fem*

typing *noun*
la mecanografía *fem*
Her typing is awful. Escribe muy mal a máquina.

typist *noun*
el mecanógrafo *masc*, **la mecanógrafa** *fem*

tyre *noun*
el neumático *masc*

U u

UFO *noun*
(= *Unidentified Flying Object*) el **ovni** *masc* (=
Objeto Volador No Identificado)

ᶘ **ugly** *adjective*
feo *masc*, **fea** *fem*
What an ugly dog! ¡Qué perro más feo!

UK *noun*
el **Reino Unido**

Ulster *noun*
el **Ulster**

ulcer *noun*
la **úlcera** *fem*

ᶘ **umbrella** *noun*
el **paraguas** *invariable masc*
She forgot her umbrella. Se le olvidó el
paraguas.

WORD TIP *paraguas never changes.*

umpire *noun*
el **árbitro** *masc*, la **árbitra** *fem*

UN *noun*
(= *United Nations*) la **ONU** *fem* (= *Organización
de las Naciones Unidas*)

unable *adjective*
to be unable to do something no poder [10]
hacer algo
He's unable to come. No puede venir.

unavoidable *adjective*
inevitable *masc & fem*

unbearable *adjective*
insoportable *masc & fem*

unbelievable *adjective*
increíble *masc & fem*

uncertain *adjective*
incierto *masc*, **incierta** *fem*
I'm uncertain whether they are coming.
No estoy seguro si vienen o no.

ᶘ **uncle** *noun*
el **tío** *masc*
my Uncle Tom mi tío Tom
our uncle and aunt from Dublin nuestros
tíos de Dublín

ᶘ **uncomfortable** *adjective*
incómodo *masc*, **incómoda** *fem*
This bed's very uncomfortable. Esta cama
es muy incómoda.
Are you uncomfortable? ¿Estás incómodo?

unconscious *adjective*
inconsciente
Tessa's unconscious. Tessa está
inconsciente.

ᶘ **under** *preposition*
1 (*underneath*) **debajo de**
under the bed debajo de la cama
It's under there. Está ahí debajo.
to go under something pasar [17] por
debajo de algo
2 (*less than*) **menos de**
under £20 menos de veinte libras
children under five niños menores de cinco
años

under-age *adjective*
to be under-age ser [1] menor de edad

ᶘ **underground** *adjective*
▷ see **underground** *noun*
subterráneo *masc*, **subterránea** *fem*
an underground car park un parking
subterráneo

ᶘ **underground** *noun*
▷ see **underground** *adj*
(*railway*) el **metro** *masc*
We went on the underground. Fuimos en
metro.

to **underline** *verb*
subrayar [17]

ᶘ **underneath** *adverb, preposition*
1 **debajo**
Look underneath. Mira debajo.
It's painted green underneath. Está
pintado de verde por debajo.
2 (+ *noun, pronoun*) **debajo de**
It's underneath these papers. Está debajo
de esos papeles.

ᶘ **underpants** *plural noun*
los **calzoncillos** *plural masc*
my underpants mis calzoncillos
a pair of underpants unos calzoncillos

underpass *noun*
1 (*for pedestrians*) el **paso subterráneo**
2 (*for traffic*) el **paso inferior**

ᶘ to **understand** *verb*
entender [36]
Do you understand? ¿Entiendes?
I don't understand. No entiendo.
They understand Portuguese. Entienden
portugués.
I can't understand what he's saying. No
entiendo lo que dice.

a
b
c
d
e
f
g
h
i
j
k
l
m
n
o
p
q
r
s
t
u
v
w
x
y
z

ᶘ indicates key words   669

rstandable adjective
comprensible masc & fem
That's understandable. Eso se entiende.

nderwear noun
la **ropa interior**

to **undo** verb
1 (a button, garment) **desabrochar** [17]
2 (your shoelaces) **desatar** [17]
3 (a parcel, knot) **deshacer** [7]

undone adjective
1 (buttons) **to come undone** desabrocharse [17]
2 (shoelaces) **to come undone** desatarse [17]

♂ to **undress** verb
to get undressed desvestirse [57]
I got undressed. Me desvestí.

♂ **unemployed** adjective
▷ see **unemployed** noun
parado masc, **parada** fem
She's unemployed. Está parada.

♂ **unemployed** noun
▷ see **unemployed** adj
the unemployed los parados
There are two million unemployed. Hay dos millones de parados.

♂ **unemployment** noun
el **paro** masc

uneven adjective
irregular masc & fem

unexpected adjective
inesperado masc, **inesperada** fem

unexpectedly adverb
de improviso

unfair adjective
injusto masc, **injusta** fem
It's unfair to young people. Es injusto para la gente joven.

to **unfasten** verb
desabrochar [17]

to **unfold** verb
desdoblar [17]

unforgettable adjective
inolvidable masc & fem

♂ **unfortunate** adjective
desgraciado masc, **desgraciada** fem
They were unfortunate enough to miss the plane. Tuvieron la desgracia de perder el avión.

♂ **unfortunately** adverb
desgraciadamente
Unfortunately I've forgotten his address.

Desgraciadamente he perdido su dirección.

unfriendly adjective
antipático masc, **antipática** fem

ungrateful adjective
desagradecido masc, **desagradecida** fem

♂ **unhappy** adjective
1 (miserable) **infeliz** masc & fem
an unhappy childhood una infancia infeliz
2 (discontented) **to be unhappy** no estar [2] contento

unhurt adjective
ileso masc, **ilesa** fem
They were unhurt in the crash. Salieron ilesos del accidente.

♂ **uniform** noun
el **uniforme** masc
in school uniform con el uniforme del colegio

uninhabited adjective
desierto masc, **desierta** fem

union noun
1 (in general) la **unión** fem
2 (trade union) el **sindicato** masc
• **Union Jack** la bandera del Reino Unido

♂ **unique** adjective
único masc, **única** fem

unit noun
1 (of measurement) la **unidad** fem
2 (in a kitchen) el **módulo** masc
3 (in hospitals, etc) el **servicio** masc

United Kingdom noun
el **Reino Unido**

United Nations noun
las **Naciones Unidas**

United States plural noun
los **Estados Unidos**
the United States of America los Estados Unidos de América

WORD TIP Often referred to only as Estados Unidos without los.

universe noun
el **universo** masc

♂ **university** noun
la **universidad** fem
university life la vida universitaria
He's a university lecturer. Es profesor universitario.
I want to go to university. Quiero ir a la universidad.

a
b
c
d
e
f
g
h
i
j
k
l
m
n
o
p
q
r
s
t
u
v
w
x
y
z

unjust *adjective*
injusto *masc*, **injusta** *fem*

unkind *adjective*
poco amable *masc & fem*

unknown *adjective*
desconocido *masc*, **desconocida** *fem*

♪ **unleaded petrol** *noun*
la gasolina sin plomo

♪ **unless** *conjunction*
a no ser que
… unless he does it … a no ser que lo haga
… unless you tell her … a no ser que se lo digas

> **WORD TIP** *a no ser que* is followed by a verb in the subjunctive.

unlikely *adjective*
poco probable *masc & fem*
It's unlikely. Es poco probable.
It's unlikely they'll come. Es poco probable que vengan.

to **unload** *verb*
descargar [28]

to **unlock** *verb*
to unlock a door abrir [46] una puerta
The car's unlocked. El coche está abierto.
The door was unlocked. La puerta no estaba cerrada con llave.

unlucky *adjective*
(person) **de poca suerte**
to be unlucky no tener [9] suerte
I was unlucky, she'd gone. No tuve suerte, ya se había ido.
Thirteen is an unlucky number. El trece trae mala suerte.

unmarried *adjective*
soltero *masc*, **soltera** *fem*

unnatural *adjective*
poco natural *masc & fem*

unnecessary *adjective*
no necesario *masc*, **no necesaria** *fem*
It's unnecessary to book. No es necesario reservar.

to **unpack** *verb*
(a suitcase, etc) **deshacer** [7]
I unpacked my rucksack. Saqué las cosas de mi mochila.
We'll unpack and then come down. Deshacemos las maletas y bajamos.

unpaid *adjective*
1 (bill) **sin pagar**
2 (work) **no remunerado**

unpleasant *adjective*
desagradable *masc & fem*

unpopular *adjective*
poco popular *masc & fem*

unrealistic *adjective*
poco realista *masc & fem*

unreasonable *adjective*
poco razonable *masc & fem*
He's being unreasonable. No está siendo nada razonable.

unreliable *adjective*
poco fidedigno *masc*, **poco fidedigna** *fem*
unreliable data datos poco fidedignos
This computer is unreliable. No te puedes fiar de este ordenador.
He's unreliable. Es muy informal.

to **unroll** *verb*
desenrollar [17]

unsafe *adjective*
peligroso *masc*, **peligrosa** *fem*

unsatisfactory *adjective*
insatisfactorio *masc*, **insatisfactoria** *fem*

to **unscrew** *verb*
1 (a screw) **destornillar** [17]
2 (a lid) **desenroscar** [31]

unsuccessful *adjective*
fallido *masc*, **fallida** *fem*
to be unsuccessful fracasar [17]
I tried, but I was unsuccessful. Lo intenté pero fracasé.

untidy *adjective*
desordenado *masc*, **desordenada** *fem*
The house is always untidy. La casa siempre está desordenada.

to **untie** *verb*
desatar [17]

♪ **until** *preposition*
1 **hasta**
until now hasta ahora
until then hasta entonces
until the tenth hasta el diez
until Monday hasta el lunes
2 not until … no hasta …
not until September no hasta septiembre
It won't be finished until Friday. No estará terminado hasta el viernes.

unusual *adjective*
poco corriente *masc & fem*
an unusual beetle un escarabajo poco corriente
Storms are unusual in June. Las tormentas son poco corrientes en junio.

a b c d e f g h i j k l m n o p q r s t **u** v w x y z

unwell *adjective*
to feel unwell sentirse [14] mal
She's feeling unwell. Se siente mal.
You look unwell. Tienes mala cara.

unwilling *adjective*
to be unwilling to do something no querer
[12] hacer algo
She's unwilling to wait. No quiere esperar.

to **unwrap** *verb*
desenvolver [45]

ᶴ **up** *adverb, preposition*
1 (*in a higher place*) **arriba**
up here aquí arriba
up there ahí arriba
up on the roof en el tejado
up in Glasgow en Glasgow
Hands up! ¡Manos arriba!

2 (*showing movement*) **to go up** subir [19]
We went up the street. Subimos la calle.
I ran up the stairs. Subí la escalera
corriendo.
I'll go up to Bristol this weekend. Iré a
Bristol este fin de semana.
It's just up the road. Está en esta calle un
poco más arriba.
She came up to me. Se acercó a mí.

3 (*not in bed*) **to be up** estar [2] levantado
Liz isn't up yet. Liz aún no está levantada.
to get up levantarse [17]
We got up at six. Nos levantamos a las seis.
I was up late last night. Me acosté tarde
anoche.
She was up all night. No se acostó en toda
la noche.

4 **up to ...** hasta ...
up to here hasta aquí
up to fifty people hasta cincuenta personas

5 (*in expressions*) What's up? ¿Qué pasa?
What's up with him? ¿Qué le pasa?
What's she up to? ¿Qué está haciendo?
It's up to you to decide. Tú tienes que
decidir.

uphill *adverb*
cuesta arriba

upright *adjective*
derecho *masc*, **derecha** *fem*
to stand upright estar [2] derecho, *fem*
derecha
Put it upright. Ponlo derecho.

upset *adjective* ▷ see **upset** *noun, verb*
disgustado *masc*, **disgustada** *fem*
He's upset. Está disgustado.

upset *noun* ▷ see **upset** *adj, verb*
1 (*in sport, etc*) la **sorpresa**
2 **to have a stomach upset** estar [2] mal del
estómago

to **upset** *verb* ▷ see **upset** *adj, noun*
to upset somebody disgustar [17] a alguien

upside down *adjective*
boca abajo
I turned them upside down. Los puse boca
abajo.

ᶴ **upstairs** *adverb*
arriba
Mum's upstairs. Mamá está arriba.
to go upstairs subir [19]
Don't go upstairs, he's asleep. No subas,
está dormido.

up-to-date *adjective*
1 (*in fashion*) **moderno** *masc*, **moderna** *fem*
2 (*data*) **actualizado** *masc*, **actualizada** *fem*

ᶴ **urgent** *adjective*
urgente *masc & fem*
She's in urgent need of help. Necesita
ayuda urgentemente.

urgently *adverb*
urgentemente
She wants to see you urgently. Quiere
verte urgentemente.

us *pronoun*
1 (*as direct and indirect object*) **nos**
She knows us. Nos conoce.
They saw us. Nos vieron.
He gave us a cheque. Nos dio un cheque.
They lent it to us. Nos lo dejaron.
Can you help us, please? ¿Puedes
ayudarnos por favor?
Listen to us! ¡Escúchanos!
Wait for us! ¡Espéranos!
Don't push us! ¡No nos empujes!

2 (*in comparisons*) **nosotros** *masc*, **nosotras**
fem
She's older than us. Es mayor que nosotros.

3 (*with prepositions*) **nosotros** *masc*, **nosotras**
fem
behind us detrás de nosotros
They left without us. Se fueron sin nosotros
with us con nosotros, *fem* nosotras

4 (*with to be*) It's us! ¡Somos nosotros! (*all boys;
boys and girls*), ¡Somos nosotras! (*all girls*)

US, USA *noun*
(= *United States, United States of America*) los
EE.UU. *plural masc* (*Estados Unidos*)

use noun ▷ see **use** verb
1 el **uso** masc
It has many uses. Tiene muchas aplicaciones
to make use of something hacer [7] uso de algo
'Instructions for use' 'Instrucciones de uso'
2 to be no use: It's no use. Es inútil.
It's no use phoning. Es inútil llamar.

to use verb ▷ see **use** noun
usar [17]
We use nails. Usamos clavos.
It's easy to use. Es fácil de usar .
I used scissors to open the parcel. Usé tijeras para abrir el paquete.

• **to use up**
1 (food) **consumir** [19] **todo**
2 (money, petrol) **gastar** [17] **todo**

used adjective, verb
1 to be used to something estar [2] acostumbrado a algo
I'm used to getting up early. Estoy acostumbrado a levantarme temprano.
She's not used to it. No está acostumbrada.
We're not used to eating in restaurants. No estamos acostumbrados a comer en restaurantes.
2 to get used to something acostumbrarse [17] a algo
I've got used to living here. Me he acostumbrado a vivir aquí.
I'm not used to it yet. Todavía no me he acostumbrado.
3 (about a past activity) She used to smoke. Antes fumaba.
They used to live in the country. Vivían en el campo.

used verb ▷ see **used** adj
She used to smoke. Antes fumaba.
They used to live in the country. Vivían en el campo.

useful adjective
útil masc & fem
It's very useful to me. Me es muy útil.
She finds the mixer very useful. La batidora le parece muy útil.

useless adjective
inútil masc & fem
You're useless! ¡Eres un inútil!
I'm useless at football. Soy negado para el fútbol.
This knife is useless. Este cuchillo no sirve para nada.

user noun
el **usuario** masc, la **usuaria** fem
• **user-friendly** fácil de usar

usual adjective, adverb
1 (time, place, problem) **de siempre**
It's the usual problem. Es el problema de siempre.
2 (method) **habitual** masc & fem
3 (in expressions) as usual como siempre
It's colder than usual. Hace más frío de lo normal.

usually adverb
normalmente
I usually leave at eight. Normalmente salgo a las ocho.

utensil noun
el **utensilio** masc

U-turn noun
el **cambio de sentido**
to do a U-turn cambiar [17] de sentido

a
b
c
d
e
f
g
h
i
j
k
l
m
n
o
p
q
r
s
t
u
v
w
x
y
z

vacancy noun
(in a small hotel) **'Vacancies'** 'Habitaciones libres'
'No vacancies' 'Completo'
2 (for a job) la **vacante**
a job vacancy una oferta de trabajo

vacant adjective
(room, seat) **libre** masc & fem

to **vaccinate** verb
vacunar [17]
to vaccinate somebody against something vacunar a alguien contra algo

vaccination noun
la **vacuna** fem
to have a vaccination vacunarse [17]

vacuum noun ▷ see **vacuum** verb
el **vacío** masc
• **vacuum cleaner** la aspiradora

to **vacuum** verb ▷ see **vacuum** noun
pasar [17] **la aspiradora**
I'm going to vacuum the living room. Voy a pasar la aspiradora por el salón.

vagina noun
la **vagina** fem

vague adjective
poco preciso masc, **poco precisa** fem

vaguely adverb
vagamente

vain adjective
1 (attempt) **vano** masc, **vana** fem
in vain en vano
2 (person) **vanidoso** masc, **vanidosa** fem

valentine card noun
la **tarjeta del día de San Valentín**

Valentine's Day noun
el **día de San Valentín**

valid adjective
válido masc, **válida** fem

valley noun
el **valle** masc

valuable adjective
valioso masc, **valiosa** fem
to be valuable ser [1] valioso
That watch is very valuable. Este reloj es muy valioso.
He gave us some valuable information. Nos dio información muy valiosa.

to **value** verb ▷ see **value** noun
valorar [17]

value noun ▷ see **value** verb
el **valor** masc

van noun
la **furgoneta** fem

vandal noun
el **vándalo** masc, la **vándala** fem

vandalism noun
el **vandalismo** masc

to **vandalize** verb
destrozar [22]

♂ **vanilla** noun
la **vainilla** fem
a vanilla ice cream un helado de vainilla

to **vanish** verb
desaparecer [35]

♂ **varied** adjective
variado masc, **variada** fem
She has had a varied career. Ha tenido una carrera variada.

variety noun
la **variedad** fem

♂ **various** adjective
varios plural masc, **varias** plural fem
There are various ways of doing it. Hay varias formas de hacerlo.

WORD TIP varios always goes before the noun.

to **vary** verb
variar [32]
It varies a lot. Varía mucho.

vase noun
el **jarrón** masc

vast adjective
enorme masc & fem

VAT noun
(= Value Added Tax) el **IVA** masc (Impuesto al Valor Añadido)

VCR noun
(= Videocassette Recorder) la **cámara de vídeo**

VDU noun
(= Visual Display Unit) el **monitor** masc

♂ **veal** noun
la **ternera** fem

a
b
c
d
e
f
g
h
i
j
k
l
m
n
o
p
q
r
s
t
u
v
w
x
y
z

ᔕ vegetable noun
la **verdura** fem
vegetable soup sopa de verduras
We grow our own vegetables. Cultivamos nuestras propias verduras.

ᔕ vegetarian adjective
▷ see **vegetarian** noun
vegetariano masc, **vegetariana** fem
vegetarian food comida vegetariana
He's vegetarian. Es vegetariano.

ᔕ vegetarian noun ▷ see **vegetarian** adj
el **vegetariano** masc, la **vegetariana** fem

ᔕ vehicle noun
el **vehículo** masc

vein noun
la **vena** fem

velvet noun
el **terciopelo** masc

vending machine noun
la **máquina expendedora**

Venezuela noun
Venezuela fem

Venezuelan adjective & noun
1 **venezolano** masc, **venezolana** fem
2 un **venezolano** masc, una **venezolana** fem
the Venezuelans los venezolanos

WORD TIP Adjectives and nouns for nationality and regional origin do not have capital letters in Spanish.

ventilation noun
la **ventilación** fem

verb noun
el **verbo** masc

verdict noun
el **veredicto** masc

verge noun
1 (roadside) el **arcén** masc
2 to be on the verge of doing something
estar [2] a punto de hacer algo
I was on the verge of leaving. Estaba a punto de irme.

ᔕ version noun
la **versión** fem
There are several versions of what happened. Hay varias versiones de lo que pasó.

versus preposition
contra
Arsenal versus Chelsea Arsenal contra Chelsea

vertical adjective
vertical masc & fem

vertigo noun
el **vértigo** masc

ᔕ very adjective ▷ see **very** adv
1 (just) It was the very thing he was looking for. Era justo lo que buscaba.
The very person I need! ¡Justo la persona que necesito!
2 (in expressions) in the very middle justo en medio
at the very end justo al final
at the very front justo delante

ᔕ very adverb ▷ see **very** adj
muy
very well muy bien
It's very difficult. Es muy difícil.
very much mucho
I like it very much. Me gusta mucho.

vest noun
la **camiseta** fem

vet noun
el **veterinario** masc, la **veterinaria** fem
She's a vet. Es veterinaria.

via preposition
por
to go via somewhere ir [8] por un lugar
We're going via Dover. Vamos por Dover.
We'll go via the bank. Pasaremos por el banco.

vicar noun
el **párroco** masc

vicious adjective
1 (dog) **fiero** masc, **fiera** fem
2 (attack) **feroz** masc & fem

victim noun
la **víctima** fem

victory noun
la **victoria** fem

ᔕ to video verb ▷ see **video** noun
grabar [17]
I'll video it for you. Yo te lo grabo.

ᔕ video noun ▷ see **video** verb
1 (film) el **vídeo** masc
to watch a video ver [16] un vídeo
I've got it on video. Lo tengo en vídeo.
2 (cassette) la **cinta de vídeo**
I bought a video. He comprado una cinta de vídeo.
3 (video recorder) el **vídeo** masc
• **video camera** la cámara vídeo
• **video game** el videojuego
• **video recorder** el vídeo
• **video shop** la tienda de vídeos

a
b
c
d
e
f
g
h
i
j
k
l
m
n
o
p
q
r
s
t
u
v
w
x
y
z

noun

(~tlook) la **vista** *fem*
~oom with a view of the lake una
~abitación con vista al lago
(sight) la **vista** *fem*
to disappear from view perderse [36] de
vista
The hotel came into view. El hotel apareció
ante nuestra vista.

3 *(opinion)* la **opinión** *fem*
in my view en mi opinión
her views on the plan su opinión sobre el
plan

♂ **viewer** noun
(Television) el & la **televidente** *masc & fem*

viewpoint noun
el **punto de vista**

vile adjective
horrible *masc & fem*

villa noun
el **chalet** *masc*

♂ **village** noun
el **pueblo** *masc*

villager noun
el & la **habitante de un pueblo**

vine noun
la **vid** *fem*

♂ **vinegar** noun
el **vinagre** *masc*

vineyard noun
el **viñedo** *masc*

violence noun
la **violencia** *fem*

violent adjective
violento *masc*, **violenta** *fem*

violin noun
el **violín** *masc*
to play the violin tocar [31] el violín

violinist noun
el & la **violinista** *masc & fem*

virgin noun
la **virgen** *fem*

Virgo noun
1 *(the star sign)* el **Virgo** *masc*
2 *(a person)* un & una **virgo** *masc & fem*
Robert's Virgo. Robert es virgo.

WORD TIP Use a small letter in Spanish to say *I
am* ... etc with star signs. Star signs in Spanish are
used without *el, un, la, una*.

---

virtual reality noun
la **realidad virtual**

virus noun
(Computers, Medicine) el **virus** *masc*, pl: los
virus
anti-virus software software anti virus

visa noun
el **visado** *masc*

visible adjective
visible *masc & fem*

♂ to **visit** verb ▷ see **visit** noun
visitar [17]
We visited Auntie Pat at Christmas.
Visitamos a la tía Pat en Navidad.
We visited the castle. Visitamos el castillo.

♂ **visit** noun ▷ see **visit** verb
la **visita** *fem*
This is my first visit to Vigo. Esta es la
primera vez que visito Vigo.
to pay a visit to somebody hacerle [7] una
visita a alguien
My father paid us a visit. Mi padre nos hizo
una visita.

visitor noun
1 *(guest)* la **visita** *fem*
We've got visitors this evening. Esta tarde
tenemos visita.
2 *(tourist)* el & la **visitante** *masc & fem*

visual adjective
visual *masc & fem*

vital adjective
importantísimo *masc*, **importantísima**
fem
It's vital to book. Es importantísimo
reservar.

vitamin noun
la **vitamina** *fem*

vivid adjective
1 *(colour, imagination)* **vivo** *masc*, **viva** *fem*
to have a vivid imagination tener [9] una
imaginación muy viva
2 *(memory, dream)* **vívido** *masc*, **vívida** *fem*

vocabulary noun
el **vocabulario** *masc*

vocational adjective
vocacional *masc & fem*

vodka noun
el **vodka** *masc*

⚡ **voice** *noun*
la **voz** *fem, fem pl:* las **voces**
to raise your voice levantar [17] la voz
to lower your voice bajar [17] la voz
Keep your voice down! ¡No levantes la voz!
She spoke in a low voice. Habló en voz baja
• **voice mail** el buzón de voz

volcano *noun*
el **volcán** *masc*

volleyball *noun*
el **vóleibol** *masc*
to play volleyball jugar [27] al vóleibol

volume *noun*
el **volumen** *masc*
the volume of letters el volumen de cartas
to turn down the volume bajar el volumen
What is the volume of this bottle? ¿Qué capacidad tiene esta botella?

voluntary *adjective*
voluntario *masc,* **voluntaria** *fem*
to do voluntary work trabajar [17] de voluntario *masc,* voluntaria *fem*

to **volunteer** *verb* ▷ see **volunteer** *noun*
to volunteer to do something ofrecerse [35] a hacer algo

She volunteered to cook dinner a hacer la cena.

volunteer *noun* ▷ see **volunteer**
el **voluntario** *masc,* la **voluntaria** *fem*
• **volunteer aid worker** el & la coopera

⚡ to **vomit** *verb*
vomitar [17]

⚡ **vote** *noun* ▷ see **vote** *verb*
el **voto** *masc*
We won by two votes. Ganamos por dos votos.

⚡ to **vote** *verb* ▷ see **vote** *noun*
votar [17]
to vote for somebody votar a alguien
She always votes for the Greens. Siempre vota a los verdes.

voucher *noun*
el **vale** *masc*

vowel *noun*
(*Grammar*) la **vocal** *fem*

voyage *noun*
el **viaje** *masc*

vulgar *adjective*
grosero *masc,* **grosera** *fem*

b
c
d
e
f
g
h
i
j
k
l
m
n
o
p
q
r
s
t
u
v
w
x
y
z

...e noun
...r eating) el **gofre** masc

...age noun, **wages** plural noun
el **sueldo** masc

wagon noun
el **vagón** masc

♂ **waist** noun
la **cintura** fem
- **waistband** la pretina
- **waistcoat** el chaleco
- **waist measurement** la medida de cintura

♂ **wait** noun ▷ see **wait** verb
la **espera** fem
an hour's wait una espera de una hora
You're going to have a long wait. Tendrás
que esperar un buen rato.

♂ to **wait** verb ▷ see **wait** noun
1 **esperar** [17]
They're waiting in the car. Están esperando
en el coche.
She kept me waiting. Me tuvo esperando.
I'm waiting to see the nurse. Estoy
esperando para ver a la enfermera.
2 to wait for something esperar algo
Wait for the signal. Espera la señal.
Wait for me! ¡Espérame!
1 (in excitement) I can't wait to open it! ¡Estoy
deseando abrirlo!

♂ **waiter** noun
el **camarero** masc
I'm a waiter. Soy camarero.
We left the waiter a tip. Le dejamos una
propina al camarero.

waiting list noun
la **lista de espera**

♂ **waiting room** noun
la **sala de espera**

♂ **waitress** noun
la **camarera** fem
I work as a waitress. Trabajo de camarera.

♂ to **wake** verb
1 (somebody else) **despertar** [29]
Jess woke me at six. Jess me despertó a las
seis.
Don't wake the baby. No despiertes al
bebé.

2 (yourself) **despertarse** [29]
I woke up at six. Me desperté a las seis.
Wake up! ¡Despiértate!

♂ **Wales** noun
el **País de Gales**
I'm from Wales. Soy galés (boy speaking).,
Soy galesa (girl speaking.)

WORD TIP Adjectives and nouns for nationality
and regional origin do not have capital letters in
Spanish.

♂ **walk** noun ▷ see **walk** verb
el **paseo** masc
to go for a walk ir [8] a dar un paseo
We went for a walk in the woods. Fuimos a
dar un paseo por el bosque.
We'll go for a little walk round the village.
Daremos un paseo por el pueblo.
It's about five minutes' walk from here.
Está a unos cinco minutos de aquí a pie.
to take the dog for a walk sacar [31] a
pasear al perro

♂ to **walk** verb ▷ see **walk** noun
1 **andar** [21]
I like walking on sand. Me gusta andar
sobre la arena.
2 (on foot) **ir** [8] **andando**
It's not far, we can walk. No está lejos,
podemos ir andando.
- to walk around
dar [4] **una vuelta por**
We walked around the old town. Dimos
una vuelta por la parte vieja de la ciudad.
- to walk with somebody
acompañar a alguien
I'll walk to the bus stop with you. Te
acompaño hasta la parada del autobús.

walking noun
1 **hacer** [7] **senderismo**
We're going walking in Scotland. Vamos a
hacer senderismo en Escocia.
2 It's within walking distance of the sea. Se
puede ir andando hasta la playa.

walking stick noun
el **bastón** masc

walkman® noun
el **walkman**® masc

♂ **wall** noun
1 (of a house) la **pared** fem
2 (of a garden) el **muro** masc
She jumped off the wall. Saltó del muro.

3 (*of a city*) la **muralla** *fem*
the Great Wall of China la Gran Muralla de China

ſ **wallet** *noun*
la **cartera** *fem*

wallpaper *noun*
el **papel pintado**

walnut *noun*
la **nuez** *fem, fem pl*: las **nueces**

to **wander** *verb*
to wander around town pasear [17] por la ciudad
to wander off alejarse [17]

ſ **want** *noun* ▷ see **want** *verb*
all our wants todo lo que necesitamos

to **want** *verb* ▷ see **want** *noun*
1 querer [12]
Do you want some coffee? ¿Quieres café?
What do you want to do? ¿Qué quieres hacer?
I want to go to the beach. Quiero ir a la playa.
He wants to be a pilot. Quiere ser piloto.
We don't want to go with them. No queremos ir con ellos.
2 to want someone to do something querer que alguien haga algo
What do you want me to do? ¿Qué quieres que haga?
I want them to help me. Quiero que me ayuden.

WORD TIP *querer que* is followed by the subjunctive.

war *noun*
la **guerra** *fem*

ward *noun*
(*Medicine*) la **sala** *fem*

ſ **wardrobe** *noun*
el **armario** *masc*
Why don't you hang your shirts in the wardrobe? ¿Por qué no cuelgas las camisas en el armario?

warehouse *noun*
el **almacén** *masc*

warm *adjective* ▷ see **warm** *verb*
1 (*climate, water*) **templado** *masc*, **templada** *fem*
2 (*breeze, voice*) **cálido** *masc*, **cálida** *fem*
3 (*food, drink, bath*) **caliente** *masc & fem*
I'll keep your dinner warm. Te tendré la comida caliente.
4 (*day, person*) It's warm today. Hoy hace calor.

I'm warm. Tengo calor.
Are you warm enough? ¿Tienes frío?
5 (*friendly*) **caluroso** *masc*, **calurosa** *fem*
a warm welcome una bienvenida calur

to **warm** *verb* ▷ see **warm** *adj*
calentar [29]
to warm the plates calentar los platos
• to warm up
1 (*weather*) It's warming up. Está empezando a hacer más calor.
2 (*athlete*) entrar [17] en calor
3 calentar [29]
I'll warm up some soup for you. Te calentaré un poco de sopa.

warmth *noun*
el **calor** *masc*

to **warn** *verb*
advertir [14]
I warn you, it's expensive. Te lo advierto, es caro.
to warn somebody to do something advertir a alguien que haga algo
He warned me to lock the car. Me advirtió que cerrase el coche.

warning *noun*
la **advertencia** *fem*

wart *noun*
la **verruga** *fem*

ſ to **wash** *verb* ▷ see **wash** *noun*
lavar [17]
to wash the dishes lavar los platos
I've washed your jeans. He lavado tus vaqueros.
to wash your hands lavarse las manos
I've washed my hands. Me he lavado las manos.
to wash your hair lavarse la cabeza
You have to wash your hair. Tienes que lavarte la cabeza.
to get washed lavarse [17]
• to wash up
lavar los platos

ſ **wash** *noun* ▷ see **wash** *verb*
to give something a wash lavar [17] algo
to have a wash lavarse [17]
• **washbasin** el lavabo

ſ **washing** *noun*
1 (*dirty*) la **ropa sucia**
2 (*clean*) la **ropa limpia**
• **washing machine** la lavadora
• **washing powder** el detergente

...g-up noun
...atos sucios
...o the washing-up lavar [17] los platos
...ashing-up liquid el lavavajillas

...sn't short for **was not**▷ **to be**

asp noun
la **avispa** fem

waste noun ▷ see **waste** verb
1 (of food, money, paper) el **desperdicio** masc
2 (of time) It's a waste of time. Es una pérdida de tiempo.

to **waste** verb ▷ see **waste** noun
1 (food, money, paper) **desperdiciar** [17]
2 (time) **perder** [36]
You're wasting your time. Estás perdiendo el tiempo.

waste-bin noun
el **cubo de la basura**

wastepaper-basket noun
la **papelera** fem

watch noun ▷ see **watch** verb
el **reloj** masc
My watch is fast. Mi reloj está adelantado.
Your watch is slow. Tu reloj está atrasado.

to **watch** verb ▷ see **watch** noun
1 (to look at) **mirar** [17]
I'm watching a blackbird in the garden. Estoy mirando un mirlo en el jardín.
2 (films, TV) **ver** [16]
He was watching TV. Estaba viendo la televisión.
3 (to keep a check on) Watch the time. Estate atento al reloj.
Could you watch the baby for a while? ¿Puedes cuidar al niño un rato?
4 (suspicious person) **vigilar** [17]
5 (to be careful) Watch you don't spill it. Ten cuidado de no tirarlo.
• to watch out
Watch out! ¡Cuidado!
Watch out for wasps. Cuidado con las avispas.

water noun ▷ see **water** verb
el **agua** fem
drinking water el agua potable
a glass of water un vaso de agua

WORD TIP agua takes el and un in the singular even though it is fem.

to **water** verb ▷ see **water** noun
regar [30]
to water the plants regar las plantas

watercolours plural noun
las **acuarelas** plural fem

waterfall noun
la **cascada** fem

watering can noun
la **regadera** fem

watermelon noun
la **sandía** fem

waterproof adjective
impermeable masc & fem

water-skiing noun
el **esquí acuático**
to go water-skiing hacer [7] esquí acuático

water sports plural noun
los **deportes naúticos**

wave noun ▷ see **wave** verb
1 (in the sea) la **ola** fem
2 (saying hello) el **saludo** masc
3 (saying goodbye) el **adiós** masc
She gave him a wave from the bus. (to say hello) Le saludó con la mano desde el autobús., (to say goodbye) Le dijo adiós con la mano desde el autobús.

to **wave** verb ▷ see **wave** noun
1 (to say hello) **saludar** [17], (to say goodbye) **decir** [5] adiós
2 (a flag, newspaper) **agitar** [17]

wax noun
la **cera** fem

way noun
1 (road, route) el **camino** masc
on the way en camino
the way to town el camino a la ciudad
We asked the way to the station. Preguntamos el camino a la estación.
Do you know the way to Caernarfon? ¿Sabes cómo se llega a Caernarfon?
on the way back en el camino de vuelta
'Give Way' 'Ceda el Paso'
2 (direction) la **dirección** fem
Which way did he go? ¿En qué dirección se fue?
Come this way. Ven por aquí.
to be in the way estorbar [17]
3 (position) Put it the right way up. Ponlo bien.
the wrong way up boca abajo
Your jumper is the wrong way round. Tu jersey está al revés.
4 (distance) It's a long way. Está muy lejos.
Terry went all the way to York. Terry fue hasta York.
5 (manner) la **manera** fem
a way of talking una manera de hablar
Do it this way. Hazlo de esta manera.
He does it his way. Lo hace a su manera.

I did it the wrong way. Lo hice mal.
That's not the way to do it. No se hace así.
Either way, she's wrong. Sea como sea,
está equivocada.

6 (in expressions) **No way!** ¡Ni hablar!
by the way por cierto

• **way in** la entrada
• **way out** la salida

we pronoun

1 **nosotros** masc, **nosotras** fem (see Word Tip)
We live in Carlisle. Vivimos en Carlisle.
We're going to the cinema tonight. Vamos
a ir al cine esta noche.

2 (for emphasis) **nosotros** masc, **nosotras** fem
We did it. Lo hicimos nosotros.

> **WORD TIP** we, like other subject pronouns he, you,
> they, is generally not translated in Spanish; the
> form of the verb tells you whether the subject of
> the verb is I, she, it, etc, so we is translated only for
> emphasis or for clarity.

ᵟ **weak** adjective

1 (feeble) **débil** masc & fem
Her voice was weak. Su voz era débil.

2 (coffee, tea) **poco cargado** masc, **poco
cargada** fem

wealth noun
la **riqueza** fem

wealthy adjective
rico masc, **rica** fem

weapon noun
el **arma** fem

> **WORD TIP** arma takes el and un in the singular
> even though it is feminine.

ᵟ **wear** noun ▷ see **wear** verb

1 (clothing) **children's wear** ropa de niños
sports wear ropa de deporte

2 (use) I bought some shoes for everyday
wear. Compré unos zapatos para todos los
días.

ᵟ **to wear** verb ▷ see **wear** noun
llevar [17]
to wear make-up llevar maquillaje
Tamsin's wearing her trainers. Tamsin
lleva sus zapatillas de deporte.
He was wearing black trousers. Llevaba
pantalones negros.
She often wears red. A menudo viste de
rojo.
Wear your new dress. Ponte el vestido
nuevo.
What are you going to wear? ¿Qué te vas a
poner?

ᵟ **weather** noun
el **tiempo** masc
in bad weather cuando hace mal tiempo

The weather was hot Hacía calor
What's the weather like? ¿Qué tie
hace?
The weather is fine. Aquí hace buen
tiempo.

ᵟ **weather forecast** noun
el **pronóstico del tiempo**
The weather forecast is rain. El pronóstico
del tiempo dice que va a llover.

ᵟ **web** noun

1 (of a spider) la **telaraña** fem

2 (Internet) the **Web** la Web

• **website** el sitio web

ᵟ **wedding** noun
la **boda** fem
The wedding was held in Wigan. Se celebró
la boda en Wigan.

ᵟ **Wednesday** noun
el **miércoles** masc
on Wednesday el miércoles
I'm going out on Wednesday. Voy a salir el
miércoles.
See you on Wednesday! ¡Hasta el
miércoles!
on Wednesdays los miércoles
The museum is closed on Wednesdays. El
museo cierra los miércoles.
every Wednesday cada miércoles
last Wednesday el miércoles pasado
next Wednesday el próximo miércoles

> **WORD TIP** Months of the year and days of the
> week start with small letters in Spanish.

weed noun
la **mala hierba**

ᵟ **week** noun
la **semana** fem
last week la semana pasada
next week la próxima semana
this week esta semana
for weeks durante semanas
a week today una semana a partir de hoy

weekday noun
on weekdays entre semana

weekend noun
el **fin de semana**
last weekend el fin de semana pasado
next weekend el próximo fin de semana
every weekend cada fin de semana
They're coming for the weekend. Vienen a
pasar el fin de semana.
I'll do it at the weekend. Lo haré durante el
fin de semana.
Have a nice weekend! ¡Que pases un buen
fin de semana!

...jective, adverb

...*agazine)* **semanal** *masc & fem*
...y **magazine** una revista semanal
..., *to deliver)* **semanalmente, cada**
...ana
...e her weekly. La veo cada semana.

...**veigh** *verb*
pesar [17]
to weigh something pesar algo
How much do you weigh? ¿Cuánto pesas?
I weigh 50 kilos. Peso cincuenta kilos.
to weigh yourself pesarse [17]

weight *noun*
el **peso** *masc*
to put on weight engordar [17]
to lose weight adelgazar [22]

weird *adjective*
estrafalario *masc*, **estrafalaria** *fem*

♂ **welcome** *adjective* ▷ see **welcome** *noun*, *verb*
1 *(to a place)* **bienvenido** *masc*, **bienvenida** *fem*
You're welcome any time. Siempre eres bienvenido.
Welcome to Leeds! ¡Bienvenidos a Leeds! *(to several people)*
2 *(as an answer)* 'Thank you!'— 'You're welcome!' 'Gracias.'—'De nada.'

♂ **welcome** *noun* ▷ see **welcome** *adj, verb*
la **bienvenida** *fem*
They gave us a warm welcome. Nos dieron una calurosa bienvenida.

♂ to **welcome** *verb* ▷ see **welcome** *adj, noun*
dar [4] **la bienvenida a**
We welcomed our Italian guests. Dimos la bienvenida a nuestros invitados italianos.

♂ **well** *adverb* ▷ see **well** *noun*
1 **bien**
to feel well sentirse [14] bien
Terry played well. Terry jugó bien.
The operation went well. La operación salió bien.
I'm very well, thank you. Estoy muy bien, gracias.
Well done! ¡Bien hecho!
2 *(in expressions)* as well también
Kevin's coming as well. Kevin también viene.
as well as además de
He has a broken arm as well as flu. Además de una gripe, tiene un brazo roto.
3 *(in questions, statements)* Well, what's the problem? Entonces, ¿cuál es el problema?

Well, well! Look who it is! ¡Anda! Mira quién es!
Very well then, you can go. Muy bien, entonces ya puedes irte.

♂ **well** *noun* ▷ see **well** *adv*
(for water) el **pozo** *masc*

♂ **well-behaved** *adjective*
a well-behaved child un niño que se porta bien
Be well behaved. Pórtate bien.

♂ **well-done** *adjective*
(Cooking) **muy hecho** *masc*, **muy hecha** *fem*

♂ **well-dressed** *adjective*
bien vestido *masc*, **bien vestida** *fem*
a well-dressed old lady una anciana bien vestida

wellington (boot) *noun*
la **bota de goma**

well-known *adjective*
conocido *masc*, **conocida** *fem*
a well-known singer un conocido cantante

♂ **well-off** *adjective*
acomodado *masc*, **acomodada** *fem*
the well-off residents of Knightsbridge los vecinos acomodados de Knightsbridge

♂ **Welsh** *adjective* ▷ see **Welsh** *noun*
galés *masc*, **galesa** *fem*
a Welsh recipe una receta galesa
My grandparents are Welsh. Mis abuelos son galeses.

♂ **Welsh** *noun* ▷ see **Welsh** *adj*
1 *(the people)* the Welsh los galeses
2 *(the language)* el **galés** *masc*
Everybody here speaks Welsh. Aquí todo el mundo habla galés.

WORD TIP Adjectives and nouns for nationality, regional origin and language do not have capital letters in Spanish.

♂ **Welshman** *noun*
un **galés** *masc*

♂ **Welshwoman** *noun*
una **galesa** *fem*

♂ **weren't** *short for* **were not** ▷ **to be**

♂ **west** *adjective, adverb* ▷ see **west** *noun*
oeste
the west side la parte oeste
a west wind un viento del oeste
west of Toledo al oeste de Toledo
to travel west viajar [17] hacia el oeste
West Africa África Occidental

WORD TIP *oeste* never changes.

Left margin letters: c d e f g h i j k l m n o p q r s t u v **w** x y z

west *noun* ▷ see **west** *adj, adv*
el **oeste** *masc*
in the west of Ireland en el oeste de Irlanda

western *adjective* ▷ see **western** *noun*
oeste *masc & fem invariable*, **occidental**
masc & fem
Western Europe Europa Occidental

western *noun* ▷ see **western** *adj*
(*film*) la **película de vaqueros**

West Indian *adjective & noun*
1 **afroantillano** *masc*, **afroantillana** *fem*
2 (*person*) un **afroantillano** *masc*, una
afroantillana *fem*
the West Indians los afroantillanos

WORD TIP Adjectives and nouns for nationality
and regional origin do not have capital letters in
Spanish.

West Indies *plural noun*
las **Antillas** *fem*
in the West Indies en las Antillas

wet *adjective*
1 (*in general*) **mojado** *masc*, **mojada** *fem*
The grass is wet. La hierba está mojada.
My shirt is wet. Tengo la camisa mojada.
to get wet mojarse [17]
We got wet. Nos mojamos.
2 (*weather*) **lluvioso** *masc*, **lluviosa** *fem*
a wet day un día lluvioso

whale *noun*
la **ballena** *fem*

what *adjective, pronoun*
1 (*asking questions: in general*) **qué** (*see Word tip*)
What is it? ¿Qué es?
What's the matter? ¿Qué pasa?
What did you say? ¿Qué has dicho?
What's she doing? ¿Qué está haciendo?
What did you buy? ¿Qué has comprado?
What's happening? ¿Qué pasa?
What time is it? ¿Qué hora es?
2 (*asking for precise information*) **¿cuál?**
What's your address? ¿Cuál es su
dirección?
What's the problem? ¿Cuál es el
problema?
3 (*in surprise*) What? ¿Cómo?
4 (*asking for a description*) What's it like?
¿Cómo es?
What's her name? ¿Cómo se llama?
5 (*after Spanish prepositions*) What for? ¿Para
qué?
What colour is it? ¿De qué color es?
What make is it? ¿De qué marca es?
What's it for? ¿Para qué sirve?
What did you buy it for? ¿Para qué lo has
comprado?
What country is it in? ¿En qué país está?

6 (*without a question*) **lo que**
Tell me what you bought. Dime lo qu[e]
comprado.
She told me what had happened. Me dij[o]
que había pasado.
What I want is a car. Lo que quiero es un
coche.

WORD TIP When *qué*, *cuál* and *cómo* are used in
questions, they always have an accent.

wheat *noun*
el **trigo** *masc*

wheel *noun*
la **rueda** *fem*
the spare wheel la rueda de repuesto
the steering wheel el volante
· **wheelbarrow** la carretilla
· **wheelchair** la silla de ruedas

when *adverb, conjunction*
1 (*in questions*) **cuándo**
When's she arriving? ¿Cuándo llega?
When's your birthday? ¿Cuándo es tu
cumpleaños?
Ask when the next train is leaving.
Pregunta cuándo sale el próximo tren.
2 (*in statements*) **cuando**
It was raining when I went out. Estaba
lloviendo cuando salí.
Call me when he arrives. Llámame cuando
llegue.

WORD TIP When *cuándo* is used in a question, it
always has an accent.

whenever *adverb*
1 (*any time*) **cuando**
Come whenever you like. Ven cuando
quieras.
2 (*each time*) **siempre que**
Whenever we go out, we lock the door.
Siempre que salimos, cerramos la puerta
con llave.

where *adverb, conjunction, pronoun*
1 (*in questions*) **dónde**
Where are the plates? ¿Dónde están los
platos?
Where do you live? ¿Dónde vives?
Where are you going? ¿Dónde vas?
I don't know where they live. No sé dónde
viven.
2 (*in statements*) **donde**
the place where I live el lugar donde vivo
This is where I left it. Ahí es donde lo dejé.

WORD TIP When *dónde* is used in a question, it
always has an accent.

a
b
c
d
e
f
g
h
i
j
k
l
m
n
o
p
q
r
s
t
u
v
w
x
y
z

...er *conjunction*

...n't know **whether** he's back or not. No si ha vuelto o no.

...ich *adjective, pronoun*

1 *(in questions)* **qué**
Which CD did you buy? ¿Qué compacto compraste?
Which drawer did she put it in? ¿En qué cajón lo metió?

2 **which one** cuál
Which one do you prefer? ¿Cuál de ellos prefieres?
'I saw your sister.'— 'Which one?' 'Vi a tu hermana.'— '¿A cuál?'

3 *(relative pronoun)* **que**
the lamp which is on the table la lámpara que está en la mesa
the book which you chose el libro que escogiste
the DVD which I told you about el DVD del que te hablé
the office in which she works la oficina en la que trabaja

WORD TIP When *qué, cuál* are used in a question, they always have an accent.

♪ **which** *pronoun* ▷ see **which** *adj*

1 *(in questions)* **cuál**
Which of these jackets is yours? ¿Cuál de estas chaquetas es la tuya?

2 *(relative pronoun)* **que**
the lamp which is on the table la lámpara que está en la mesa
the book which you chose el libro que escogiste
the DVD which I told you about el DVD del que te hablé
the office in which she works la oficina en la que trabaja

♪ **while** *noun, conjunction*

1 *(long time)* **for a while** durante un tiempo
She worked here for a while. Trabajó aquí durante un tiempo.
after a while después de un tiempo
every once in a while cada de vez en cuando

2 *(short time)* **for a while** durante un rato
I read for a while. Leí durante un rato.
after a while después de un rato
in a little while dentro de un ratito

3 *(at the same time as)* **mientras**
Make some coffee while I finish my homework. Haz un café mientras termino los deberes.

♪ **while** *conjunction* ▷ see **while** *noun*
You can make some tea while I'm finishing my homework. Puedes hacer un té mientras termino los deberes.

whip *noun* ▷ see **whip** *verb*
el **látigo** *masc*

to **whip** *verb* ▷ see **whip** *noun*
(cream) **montar** [17]
whipped cream la nata montada

whirlpool *noun*
el **remolino** *masc*

whiskers *plural noun*
los **bigotes** *plural masc*

whisky *noun*
el **whisky** *masc*

whisper *noun* ▷ see **whisper** *verb*
el **susurro** *masc*
to speak in a whisper hablar [17] en susurros

to **whisper** *verb* ▷ see **whisper** *noun*
susurrar [17]

whistle *noun* ▷ see **whistle** *verb*
1 *(sound)* el **silbido** *masc*
2 *(instrument)* el **silbato** *masc*

to **whistle** *verb* ▷ see **whistle** *noun*
silbar [17]

♪ **white** *adjective* ▷ see **white** *noun*
blanco *masc*, **blanca** *fem*
white wine vino blanco
a white shirt una camisa blanca

♪ **white** *noun* ▷ see **white** *adj*
1 *(colour)* el **blanco** *masc*
2 *(of an egg)* **an egg white** una clara de huevo
• **white coffee** el café con leche

Whitsun *noun*
el **Pentecostés** *masc*

who *pronoun*
1 *(in questions)* **quién** *masc & fem*
Who wants a sweet? ¿Quién quiere un caramelo?
Who are they? ¿Quiénes son?

2 *(relative, as the subject)* **que** *masc & fem*
my friend who lives in Madrid mi amigo que vive en Madrid
the girl who lives next door la chica que vive al lado

3 *(relative, as the object: for one person)* **el que** *masc*, **la que** *fem*
the girl who I sent it to la chica a la que se lo envié

4 *(relative, as the object: more than one person)* **los que** *plural masc*, **las que** *plural fem*

the friends who we've invited los amigos a los que hemos invitado
the girls who we've invited las chicas a las que hemos invitado

WORD TIP When *quién* is used in a question, it always has an accent.

whole *adjective, noun*
todo *masc*, **toda** *fem*
the whole time todo el tiempo
the whole morning toda la mañana
the whole world todo el mundo
our whole family toda la familia
the whole of the class toda la clase
on the whole en general

whole *noun* ▷ see **whole** *adj*
the whole of the class toda la clase

ℰ **wholemeal bread** *noun*
el **pan integral**

whom *pronoun*
1 (*in questions*) **quién** *masc & fem*
Whom did you see? ¿A quién viste?
2 (*as a relative pronoun*) **que**
the person whom I saw la persona que vi
the teacher whom I saw el profesor que vi
the people whom I saw las personas que vi
3 (*after a preposition: for one person*) **el que** *masc*, **la que** *fem*
the person to whom I wrote la persona a la que escribí
the manager to whom I wrote el gerente al que escribí
4 (*after a preposition: for more than one person*) **los que** *plural masc*, **las que** *plural fem*
the people to whom I wrote las personas a las que escribí
the teachers to whom we wrote los profesores a los que escribimos

WORD TIP When *quién* is used in a question, it always has an accent.

whose *pronoun, adjective*
1 (*in questions*) **de quién**
Whose is it? ¿De quién es?
Whose is this jacket? ¿De quién es esta chaqueta?
Whose shoes are they? ¿De quién son estos zapatos?
I know whose it is. Sé de quién es.
2 (*as a relative: before a singular noun*) **cuyo** *masc*, **cuya** *fem*
the man whose wallet has disappeared el hombre cuya cartera ha desaparecido
the woman whose car has disappeared la mujer cuyo coche ha desaparecido
3 (*as a relative; before a plural noun*) **cuyos** *pl masc*, **cuyas** *pl fem*

the people whose names are on personas cuyos nombres están e◼
a friend whose daughters I give les◼
un amigo a cuyas hijas doy clases

WORD TIP *cuyo* and *cuya* agree with the nou◼ follows, not the person who 'owns.'

why *adverb*
por qué
Why did she phone? ¿Por qué llamó?
Nobody knows why he did it. Nadie sabe por qué lo hizo.

wicked *adjective*
1 (*bad*) **malvado** *masc*, **malvada** *fem*
2 (*brilliant*) **genial** *masc & fem*

ℰ **wide** *adjective* ▷ see **wide** *adv*
ancho *masc*, **ancha** *fem*
a piece of paper 20 cm wide un trozo de papel de veinte centímetros de ancho
a wide range una amplia gama
The river is very wide here. El río es muy ancho aquí.
How wide is it? ¿Cuánto mide de ancho?

ℰ **wide** *adverb* ▷ see **wide** *adj*
to be wide awake estar completamente despierto
to be wide open estar [2] abierto de par en par

ℰ **wide-screen television** *noun*
el **televisor de pantalla grande**

to **widen** *verb*
ensanchar [17]

ℰ **widow** *noun*
la **viuda** *fem*
war widows viudas de guerra

ℰ **widower** *noun*
el **viudo** *masc*
a widower who lived on his own un viudo que vivía solo

width *noun*
el **ancho** *masc*

ℰ **wife** *noun*
la **mujer** *fem*
This is my wife. Te presento a mi mujer.

wig *noun*
la **peluca** *fem*

wild *adjective*
1 (*animal*) **salvaje** *masc & fem*
2 (*plant*) **silvestre** *masc & fem*
3 (*party*) **desenfrenado** *masc*, **desenfrenada** *fem*
4 (*idea*) **disparatado** *masc*, **disparatada** *fem*
5 (*person*) to be wild about something estar [2] loco por algo

b
c
d
e
f
g
h
i
j
k
l
m
n
o
p
q
r
s
t
u
v
w
x
y
z

ℰ indicates key words   685

...un

...mme on wildlife in Africa un
...ma sobre la flora y la fauna de África
...ife park la reserva natural

...verb

...using future tenses in Spanish) **I will see you**
soon., **I'll see you soon.** Te veré pronto.
He'll be pleased to see you. Estará
contento de verte.
Will he come today? ¿Vendrá hoy?
It won't rain. No lloverá.
He'll be pleased to see you. Estará
contento de verte.
There won't be a problem. No habrá
problemas.
You won't forget it, will you? No lo
olvidarás ¿verdad?

2 (*using the present tense in Spanish*) **I'll call them**
right now. Los llamo ahora mismo.
Will you give me a lift to the station? ¿Me
llevas a la estación?
Will you have a drink? ¿Quieres beber
algo?
Will you help me? ¿Me ayudas?
The car won't start. El coche no arranca.
He won't open the door. No quiere abrir la
puerta.

3 (*for future plans*) **ir** [8] **a hacer**
I'll see them this evening. Voy a verlos esta
tarde.
What will they do? ¿Qué van a hacer?

willing *adjective*
to be willing to do something estar [2]
dispuesto *masc*, dispuesta *fem* a hacer algo
I'm willing to pay for it. Estoy dispuesto a
pagarlo.

willingly *adverb*
de buena gana

willow *noun*
el **sauce** *masc*
a weeping willow un sauce llorón

ᔔ **win** *noun* ▷ see **win** *verb*
la **victoria** *fem*
our win over Everton nuestra victoria sobre
Everton

ᔔ to **win** *verb* ▷ see **win** *noun*
ganar [17]
We won! ¡Hemos ganado!
Granada won by two goals. El Granada
ganó por dos goles.
I've won the lottery! ¡Me ha tocado la
lotería!

ᔔ to **wind** *verb* ▷ see **wind** *noun*
1 (*a wire, rope*) **enrollar** [17]
2 (*a clock*) **dar** [4] **cuerda a**

ᔔ **wind** *noun* ▷ see **wind** *verb*
el **viento** *masc*
the North wind el viento del norte
• **wind farm** el parque eólico
• **wind instrument** el instrumento de
viento

mini-info *wind power*

Spain is the second largest producer of wind-
powered electricity in the world after Germany.

ᔔ **window** *noun*
1 (*in a building*) la **ventana** *fem*
to look out of the window mirar [17] por la
ventana
2 (*in a car, bus, train*) la **ventanilla** *fem*

ᔔ **windscreen** *noun*
el **parabrisas** *masc, pl:* los **parabrisas**
• **windscreen wipers** los limpiaparabrisas

ᔔ **windsurfing** *noun*
el **windsurf** *masc*
to go windsurfing hacer [7] windsurf
• **windsurfing board** la tabla de windsurf

windy *adjective*
1 (*place*) **con mucho viento**
2 (*day*) **de viento**
It's windy today. Hoy hace viento.

ᔔ **wine** *noun*
el **vino** *masc*
a glass of white wine una copa de vino
blanco
a bottle of red wine una botella de vino
tinto

wing *noun*
1 (*of a bird*) el **ala** *fem*
the wing el ala
2 (*in sport*) el & la **alero** *masc & fem*

WORD TIP *ala* takes *el* and *un* in the singular even
though it is fem.

to **wink** *verb*
to wink at somebody guiñar [17] el ojo a
alguien

winner *noun*
el **ganador** *masc*, la **ganadora** *fem*

winning *adjective*
(*team*) **ganador** *masc*, **ganadora** *fem*

winnings *plural noun*
las **ganancias** *plural fem*

ꝺ **winter** noun
  el **invierno** masc
  in winter en invierno
  winter sports los deportes de invierno

ꝺ to **wipe** verb
  limpiar [17]
  I'll just wipe the table. Voy a limpiar la mesa.
  to wipe your nose limpiarse [17] la nariz
- **to wipe up**
  (dishes) **secar** [17]

wire noun
  el **alambre** masc
  an electric wire un cable
- **wire netting** la red de alambre

ꝺ **wireless** adjective
  inalámbrico masc, **inalámbrica** fem

ꝺ **wise** adjective
  sabio masc, **sabia** fem
  a wise man un sabio

wish noun ▷ see **wish** verb
1 (something hoped for) el **deseo** masc
  Make a wish! ¡Piensa un deseo!
2 (in letters) Best wishes, Ann Saludos de Ann.

to **wish** verb ▷ see **wish** noun
1 (in greetings) I wished him a happy birthday.
  Le deseé un feliz cumpleaños.
2 (saying what you want) I wish you were here.
  Ojalá estuvieses aquí.

> **WORD TIP** ojalá is followed by a verb in the subjunctive.

wit noun
  el **ingenio** masc

witch noun
  la **bruja** fem

ꝺ **with** preposition
1 **con**
  with James con James
  with me conmigo
  with you contigo
  with them con ellos
  with pleasure con gusto
  Beat the eggs with a fork. Bate los huevos con un tenedor.
  He took his umbrella with him. Se llevó el paraguas.
2 (in descriptions) a girl with blue eyes una chica de ojos azules
  the man with the red shirt el hombre de la camisa roja
  the boy with the broken arm el chico con el brazo roto

3 (at the house of) We're staying the n...
  Frank. Nos quedamos a dormir en c...
  Frank.
4 (after past participles) **de**
  filled with water lleno de agua
  covered with mud cubierto de barro
  red with rage rojo de ira

ꝺ **without** preposition
  sin
  without you sin ti
  without sugar sin azúcar
  without a sweater sin un jersey
  without looking sin mirar

witness noun
  el & la **testigo** masc & fem

witty adjective
  ingenioso masc, **ingeniosa** fem

wizard noun
  el **brujo** masc

wolf noun
  el **lobo** masc

ꝺ **woman** noun
  la **mujer** fem
  a woman friend una amiga
  a woman lawyer una abogada
  a young woman una joven

wonder noun ▷ see **wonder** verb
  la **maravilla** fem
  No wonder you're tired. No es extraño que estés cansado.

to **wonder** verb ▷ see **wonder** noun
  preguntarse [17]
  I wonder why he did it. Me pregunto por qué lo hizo.
  I wonder where Jack is. Me pregunto dónde está Jack.

wonderful adjective
  maravilloso masc, **maravillosa** fem

ꝺ **won't** short for **will not** ▷ **will**

ꝺ **wood** noun
1 (material) la **madera** fem
  The lamp is made of wood. La lámpara está hecha de madera.
2 (trees) el **bosque** masc
  a walk through the wood un paseo por el bosque

wooden adjective
  de madera

woodwork noun
  la **carpintería** fem

a
b
c
d
e
f
g
h
i
j
k
l
m
n
o
p
q
r
s
t
u
v
w
x
y
z

...n
...fem

...en *adjective*
...ana
...ollen gloves guantes de lana.

...ord *noun*
la **palabra** *fem*
a long word una palabra larga
in other words en otras palabras
What's the French word for 'window'?
¿Cómo se dice 'ventana' en francés?
to have a word with somebody hablar [17]
con alguien

2 to give somebody your word prometer [18]
algo a alguien
He broke his word. Rompió su promesa.

3 (*lyrics*) the words of a song la letra de una
canción

• **word processing** el tratamiento de textos
• **word processor** el procesador de textos

♂ **work** *noun* ▷ see **work** *verb*

1 (*your job*) el **trabajo** *masc*
She's at work. Está en el trabajo.
He's out of work. Está sin trabajo.
I've got some work to do. Tengo trabajo
que hacer.
Ben's off work. Ben no ha ido a trabajar
porque está enfermo.

2 to be hard work ser [1] difícil
It's hard work to understand it. Es difícil
entenderlo.

♂ to **work** *verb* ▷ see **work** *noun*

1 (*at your job*) **trabajar** [17]
She works in an office. Trabaja en una
oficina.
Dad works at home. Papá trabaja en la
casa.
Ruth works in accounts. Ruth trabaja en
contabilidad.
He works nights. Trabaja por las noches.
I've worked hard for the exam. He
estudiado mucho para el examen.

2 (*to operate*) **hacer** [7] **funcionar**
Can you work the DVD recorder? ¿Sabes
hacer funcionar la grabadora de DVD?

3 (*to function*) **funcionar** [17]
The dishwasher's not working. El
lavavajillas no funciona.
That worked really well! ¡Eso ha
funcionado muy bien!

• to **work out**

1 **entender** [36]
I can't work it out. No lo entiendo.

2 (*to calculate*) **calcular** [17]
I'll work out how much it would cost.
Calcularé cuánto puede costar.

3 (*to exercise*) **hacer** [7] **ejercicio**

4 (*to go well*) **salir** [63] **bien**

worked up *adjective*
to get worked up ponerse [11] nervioso,
fem nerviosa

worker *noun*

1 (*in a factory*) el **trabajador** *masc*, la
trabajadora *fem*

2 (*in an office, a bank*) el **empleado** *masc*, la
empleada *fem*

♂ **work experience** *noun*
las **prácticas de trabajo**
to do work experience hacer [7] prácticas
I did work experience in a hospital.
Hice prácticas en un hospital.
to be on work experience estar [2]
haciendo prácticas

working-class *adjective*
de **clase obrera**
a working-class background un ambiente
de clase obrera
a working-class district un barrio
obrero

work of art *noun*
la **obra de arte**

workshop *noun*
el **taller** *masc*

workstation *noun*
(*Computers*) el **terminal de trabajo**

world *noun*
el **mundo** *masc*
the longest river in the world el río más
largo del mundo
the western world el mundo occidental

World Cup *noun*
the World Cup la Copa del Mundo

world war *noun*
la **guerra mundial**
the Second World War la segunda Guerra
Mundial

worm *noun*
el **gusano** *masc*

worn out *adjective*

1 (*person*) **agotado** *masc*, **agotada** *fem*

2 (*clothes, shoes*) **gastado** *masc*, **gastada** *fem*

♂ **worried** *adjective*
preocupado *masc*, **preocupada** *fem*
They're worried. Están preocupados.
I'm worried I'll fail the exam. Tengo miedo
de suspender.
to be worried about someone estar [2]
preocupado por alguien

We're worried about Susan. Estamos preocupados por Susan.
I'm worried about the delay. Me preocupa el retraso.

ᔓ **worry** *noun* ▷ see **worry** *verb*
la **preocupación** *fem*
My biggest worry is the cost. Mi mayor preocupación es el coste.

ᔓ to **worry** *verb* ▷ see **worry** *noun*
preocuparse [17]
She worries about the slightest thing. Se preocupa por la menor tontería.
Don't worry! ¡No te preocupes!
There's nothing to worry about. No hay razón para preocuparse.

worrying *adjective*
preocupante *masc & fem*

worse *adjective*
peor *masc & fem*
It was even worse this time. Fue aún peor esta vez.
to get worse empeorar [17]
The weather's getting worse. El tiempo está empeorando.
Things are getting worse and worse. Las cosas van cada vez peor.

worst *adjective*
the worst el peor
It was the worst day of my life. Fue el peor día de mi vida.
if the worst comes to the worst en el peor de los casos

worth *adjective*
1 to be worth valer [43]
How much is it worth? ¿Cuánto vale?
2 to be worth doing something valer la pena hacer algo
It's worth trying. Vale la pena intentarlo.
It's not worth it. No vale la pena.

to **would** *verb*
1 (using the Spanish conditional tense) That would be a good idea. Eso sería una buena idea.
If we asked her she would help us. Si le preguntásemos, nos ayudaría.
2 (expressing wishes) I would like to go to the cinema. Me gustaría ir al cine.
We would like to do that. Nos gustaría hacer eso.
3 (in polite requests) Would you mind ...? ¿Te importa ...?
Would you mind closing the window? ¿Te importa cerrar la ventana?

I would like an omelette. Quisier[a] tortilla.
I would like four tickets. Quería cua[tro] entradas.
4 (offering things) Would you like ...? ¿Quieres ...?
Would you like something to eat? ¿Quiere[s] comer algo?
Would you like a lift to the station? ¿Quieres que te lleve a la estación?
5 (in refusals) He wouldn't answer. No contestaba.
The car wouldn't start. El coche no arrancaba.

ᔓ **wouldn't** *short for* **would not** (See: **would**)

wound *noun* ▷ see **wound** *verb*
la **herida** *fem*

to **wound** *verb* ▷ see **wound** *noun*
herir [14]

to **wrap** *verb*
envolver [45]
I'm going to wrap (up) my presents. Voy a envolver mis regalos.
Could you wrap it for me please? ¿Me lo envuelve, por favor?
Shall I gift-wrap it for you? ¿Se lo envuelvo para regalo?

wrapping paper *noun*
el **papel de envolver**

wreck *noun* ▷ see **wreck** *verb*
(of a train, car, etc) los **restos**
I feel a wreck! ¡Estoy hecho polvo!

to **wreck** *verb* ▷ see **wreck** *noun*
1 (an object, a car) **destrozar** [22]
2 (a plan, an occasion) **arruinar** [17]
It's wrecked my evening! ¡Me ha arruinado la tarde!

wrestler *noun*
el **luchador** *masc*, la **luchadora** *fem*

wrestling *noun*
la **lucha** *fem*

wrinkle *noun*
la **arruga** *fem*

wrinkled *adjective*
arrugado *masc*, **arrugada** *fem*

wrist *noun*
la **muñeca** *fem*

b
c
d
e
f
g
h
i
j
k
l
m
n
o
p
q
r
s
t
u
v
w
x
y
z

…erb

…story) **escribir** [52]

…te her a letter. Le escribiré una carta.

…rite to somebody escribirle a alguien

…ote to Jean yesterday. Ayer le escribí a …an.

We write to each other a lot. Nos escribimos mucho.

to write an essay redactar [17] un ensayo

2 to write somebody a cheque extenderle [36] un cheque a alguien

• to write down

anotar [17]

I wrote down her telephone number. Anoté su número.

writer *noun*

el **escritor** *masc*, la **escritora** *fem*

writing *noun*

la **escritura** *fem*

♂ **wrong** *adjective*

1 *(factually)* the wrong answer la respuesta equivocada

I've brought the wrong CD. He traído el CD equivocado.

It's the wrong address. No son las señas correctas.

The information was wrong. La información era incorrecta.

2 *(mistaken)* to be wrong equivocarse [31]

I was wrong. Me equivoqué.

You're wrong. Te has equivocado

3 *(not as it should be)* Something's wrong. Pasa algo.

What's wrong? ¿Qué pasa?

What's wrong with her? ¿Qué le pasa?

b
c
d
e
f
g
h
i
j
k
l
m
n
o
p
q
r
s
t
u
v
w
x
y
z

X x

xerox *noun* ▷ see **xerox** *verb*
  la **fotocopia** *fem*

to **xerox** *verb* ▷ see **xerox** *noun*
  fotocopiar [17]

♪ **X-ray** *noun* ▷ see **X-ray** *verb*
  la **radiografía** *fem*

She had an X-ray. Le hicieron una
radiografía.
I saw the X-rays. Vi las radiografías.

♪ to **X-ray** *verb* ▷ see **X-ray** *noun*
  hacer [7] **una radiografía de**
They X-rayed his knee. Le hicieron una
radiografía de la rodilla.

...t *noun*
(*sailing boat*) el **velero** *masc*
(*luxury boat*) el **yate** *masc*

to **yawn** *verb*
bostezar [22]

year *noun*
1 el **año** *masc*
last year el año pasado
six years ago hace seis años
the whole year todo el año
year after year año tras año
Happy New Year! ¡Feliz Año Nuevo!
They lived in Murcia for years. Vivieron en Murcia durante años.
He's seventeen years old. Tiene diecisiete años.
2 (*at school*) el **año scolar**
I'm in year eleven. Estoy en quinto de ESO (*the equivalent in the Spanish system.*)

yearly *adjective, adverb*
anual *masc & fem*, **cada año**
a yearly event un acontecimiento anual

to **yell** *verb*
gritar [17]

yellow *adjective*
amarillo *masc*, **amarilla** *fem*

yes *adverb*
sí
Yes, I know. Sí, ya lo sé.
'Is Tom there?'— 'Yes, he is.' '¿Está Tom ahí?'— 'Sí.'

yesterday *adverb*
ayer
yesterday afternoon ayer por la tarde
yesterday morning ayer por la mañana
the day before yesterday anteayer
I saw her yesterday. La vi ayer.

yet *adverb*
1 (*with a negative*) **aún**
not yet aún no
It's not ready yet. No está listo aún.
2 (*in a question*) **ya**
Have you finished yet? ¿Has terminado ya?

yoga *noun*
la **yoga** *fem*

yoghurt *noun*
el **yogur** *masc*
a banana yoghurt un yogur de plátano
a plain yoghurt un yogur natural

yolk *noun*
la **yema** *fem*

you *pronoun*
1 (*as the subject: informal*) **tú**, (*pl*) **vosotros, vosotras**; (*polite*) **usted**, (*pl*) **ustedes** (*see Word Tip*)
Do you want to go to the cinema? ¿Quieres ir al cine? (*one person*)., ¿Queréis ir al cine? (*more than one person*).
2 (*for emphasis: to one person*) **tú**, (*pl*) **vosotros** *plural masc*, **vosotras** *plural fem*
You said it! ¡Tú lo dijiste!
But you all saw it! ¡Pero todos vosotros lo visteis!
3 (*polite form: to one person*) **usted**, (*pl*) **ustedes**
Are you our new teacher? ¿Es usted nuestro nuevo profesor?
Are you Mr and Mrs Atkins? ¿Son ustedes los señores Atkins?
4 (*as direct and indirect object: to one person*) **te**, (*to one more than one person*) **os**
I'll write to you. Te escribiré.
I'll write to you. Os escribiré.
5 (*as direct and indirect object polite form: to one person*) **le**, (*pl*) **les**
I saw you. Le vi.
I saw you. Les vi (*more than one*).
I shall send you the document. Le mandaré el documento.
Dear Mr and Mrs Jones, I am sending you the information ... Estimados señor y señora Jones: Les mando la información ...
I shall send it to you on Monday. Se lo mandaré el lunes.

WORD TIP When used with another pronoun, *le* and *les* become *se*.

6 (*in comparisons*) **tú**, (*pl*) **vosotros** *masc*, **vosotras** *fem*
He's older than you. Es mayor que tú., Es mayor que vosotros.
7 (*with prepositions*) for you para ti, (*pl*) para vosotros *masc* vosotras *fem*
in front of you delante de ti, delante de vosotros
with you contigo, con vosotros
8 (*polite form: with prepositions and in comparisons*) **usted**, (*pl*) **ustedes**
for you para usted, para ustedes

She's older than you. Es mayor que usted., Es mayor que ustedes.

WORD TIP *you*, like *I*, *he*, *they* etc, is generally not translated into Spanish; the ending of the verb tells you if the subject of the verb is *tú*, *vosotros*, *usted*, etc, so *you* is translated only for emphasis or clarity.

ɟ **young** *adjective*
joven *masc & fem*
a young woman una joven
a couple of young men un par de jóvenes
young people la gente joven
He's younger than me. Es más joven que yo.
Tessa's two years younger than me. Tessa tiene dos años menos que yo.
I'm the youngest in the team. Soy el más joven del equipo.

ɟ **your** *adjective*
1 (*to one person*) **tu**
I like your skirt. Me gusta tu falda.
You've forgotten your CDs! ¡Te has olvidado tus compactos!
2 (*to more than one person*) **vuestro** *masc*, **vuestra** *fem*
Your Spanish exam is on Friday. Vuestro examen de español es el viernes.
Your rucksacks are in the car. Vuestras mochilas están en el coche.
3 (*formal form*) **su**
Thank you for your hospitality. Gracias por su hospitalidad.
Your letters have arrived. Han llegado sus cartas.
4 (*with parts of the body, clothes*) **el**, **la**, **los**, **las**
Show me your hand. Muéstrame la mano.
Take your shoes off. Quítate los zapatos.
You've cut your hand. Se ha cortado la mano (*polite form*).
Do you want to take your coat off? ¿Quiere quitarse el abrigo? (*polite form*)

WORD TIP Spanish uses *el*, *la*, *los*, *las* for *your* with parts of the body and clothes.

yours *pronoun*
1 (*to one person*) **el tuyo** *masc*, **la tuya** *fem*
a friend of yours un amigo tuyo, una amiga tuya
My brother's younger than yours. Mi hermano es más joven que el tuyo.
These aren't my glasses, are they yours? Estas gafas no son mías, ¿son tuyas?
Yours are better. Los tuyos son mejores.
2 (*to more than one person*) **el vuestro** *masc*, **la vuestra** *fem*
a friend of yours un amigo vuestro, una amiga vuestra
Our house is smaller than yours. Nuestra

casa es más pequeña que la vuestra.
Our car is smaller than yours. Nuestro coche es más pequeño que el vuestro.
Our children are older than yours. Nuestros hijos son mayores que los vuestros.
3 (*formal form*) **el suyo** *masc*, **la suya** *fem*
Excuse me, is this book yours? ¿Perdone, es suyo este libro?
Excuse me, are these books yours? ¿Perdone, son suyos estos libros?

WORD TIP The form of *tuyo*, *vuestro* or *suyo* to choose depends on whether the thing owned is *masc*, *fem*, *singular* or *plural*.

ɟ **yourself** *pronoun*
1 (*reflexive*) **te**
You'll hurt yourself. Vas a hacerte daño.
2 (*for emphasis*) **tú mismo** *masc*, **tú misma** *fem*
Did you do it yourself? ¿Lo hiciste tú mismo?, ¿Lo hiciste tú misma?
by yourself solo *masc*, sola *fem*
3 (*polite form: reflexive*) **se** *masc & fem*
You've hurt yourself. Se ha hecho daño.
4 (*polite form: for emphasis*) **usted mismo** *masc*, **usted misma** *fem*
as you yourself will understand como usted mismo comprenderá

yourselves *pronoun*
1 (*reflexive*) **os**
when you have washed yourselves cuando os hayáis lavado
Help yourselves. Servidos.
by yourselves solos *masc*, solas *fem*
2 (*for emphasis*) **vosotros mismos** *plural masc*, **vosotras mismas** *plural fem*
Did you do it yourselves? ¿Lo hicisteis vosotros mismos?, ¿Lo hicisteis vosotras mismas?
3 (*polite form: reflexive*) **se**
Please, help yourselves. Sírvanse, por favor.
4 (*polite form: for emphasis*) **ustedes mismos** *plural masc*, **ustedes mismas** *plural fem*
Did you do it yourselves? ¿Lo hicieron ustedes mismos?, ¿Lo hicieron ustedes mismas?

ɟ **youth** *noun*
1 (*stage of life*) la **juventud** *fem*
2 (*young people*) la **juventud** *fem*
today's youth la juventud de hoy, los jóvenes de hoy
3 (*young male*) el **joven** *masc*
about ten youths unos diez jóvenes
• **youth club** el club juvenil
• **youth hostel** el albergue juvenil

a b c d e f g h i j k l m n o p q r s t u v w x y z

ɟ indicates key words

Z

zany *adjective*
  chiflado *masc*, **chiflada** *fem*

zebra *noun*
  la **cebra** *fem*
- **zebra crossing** el paso de cebra

zero *noun*
  el **cero** *masc*

to **zigzag** *verb*
  zigzaguear [17]

zip *noun*
  la **cremallera** *fem*

zodiac *noun*
  el **zodiaco** *masc*
  the signs of the zodiac los signos del zodiaco

zone *noun*
  la **zona** *fem*

zoo *noun*
  el **zoo** *masc*

zoom lens *noun*
  la **lente de zoom**

a
b
c
d
e
f
g
h
i
j
k
l
m
n
o
p
q
r
s
t
u
v
w
x
y
z